INTRODUCTION TO
COMPARATIVE LAW

INTRODUCTION
TO
COMPARATIVE LAW

BY

KONRAD ZWEIGERT
(1911–1996)

AND

HEIN KÖTZ
M.C.L. (Mich.), F.B.A., Professor, University of Hamburg
Director, Max Planck Institute for Foreign and International Private Law

Third Revised Edition

translated from the German by
TONY WEIR
Fellow of Trinity College, Cambridge

CLARENDON PRESS · OXFORD

Oxford University Press, Great Clarendon Street, Oxford OX2 6DP

Oxford New York

Athens Auckland Bangkok Bogotay Buenos Aires
Calcutta Cape Town Chennai Dar es Salaam Delhi Florence Hong Kong
Istanbul Karachi Kuala Lumpur Madrid Melbourne Mexico City Mumbai
Nairobi Paris Singapore Taipei Tokyo Toronto Warsaw

and associated companies in
Berlin Ibadan

Oxford is a registered trade mark of Oxford University Press

Published in the United States
by Oxford University Press Inc., New York

First edition published 1977 © North-Holland Pub. Co.
Second edition published 1987 © Oxford University Press and J. C. B. Mohr (Paul Siebeck)
Third edition published 1998 © Oxford University Press and J. C. B. Mohr (Paul Siebeck)
The moral rights of the author have been asserted

British Library Cataloguing in Publication Data
Data available

Library of Congress Cataloging in Publication Data
Data available
ISBN 0–19–826860–2
ISBN 0–19–826859–9(Pbk)

7 9 10 8 6

Printed in Great Britain on acid-free paper by
Biddles Ltd., Guildford and King's Lynn

Preface to the Third Edition

Auf Vergleichen lässt sich wohl alles Erkennen, Wissen zurückführen.

*Novalis**

A generous and elevated mind is distinguished by nothing more certainly than an eminent degree of curiosity; nor is that curiosity ever more agreeably or usefully employed, than in examining the laws and customs of foreign nations.

Samuel Johnson**

* Works III (ed. Minor, Jena 1907) 45, fragment 229.
** Boswell's Life of Johnson I (ed. Hill and Powell, Oxford 1934) 89.

While this work may well prove of use to any lawyer with an interest in discovering how comparative law can broaden his horizons, it is primarily designed for the younger generation. They seem more interested in broad horizons than their elders, and in their career they will need to know more law than is provided by most legal education, which is still unduly national. This book is designed to help them in that respect, as well as to counteract the provincialism, bemoaned by Jhering, which vitiates legal scholarship when it is confined within political frontiers and its practitioners retreat into the shell of their own national systems.

The years which have passed since the publication of the second edition have been very eventful. The 'socialist legal family' is dead and buried, and although it will take a long time to erase the traces of more than forty years of total subjection to political ideology, it seemed right to discard the chapters on socialist law. On the other hand, the 'Europeanization' of private law is now very much in the air, and people have begun to see that it is only by means of comparative law that it will be possible to elicit structures of private law common to Europe as a whole. Axel Flessner and I decided to make a start on this many years ago, and the first volume of our *European Contract Law* is now in print:[1] parts of it have found their way into the present volume.

The *Introduction to Comparative Law* now has more readers outside Germany than inside it: it has been translated into Italian (by Barbara Pozzo and Estella Cigna), Japanese (Masao Oki), Russian (Jurij Jumaschev) and Chinese (Pan Handian, Mi Jian, Gad Hongjun and He Weifang), and

[1] Hein Kötz, *European Contract Law*: vol. I, Formation, Validity, and Content of Contracts; Contract and Third Parties (trans. Tony Weir, Clarendon Press, Oxford 1997).

further translations are in preparation. The need to make the text translatable and comprehensible to readers abroad has affected the way it was written. Heine once referred to 'the clarity and ease with which the French order their thoughts' but attributed it 'to a barren single-mindedness and restrictive formalism much worse than the florid disorder and inelegant excesses of German journalists'.[2] He was not speaking of legal writing in particular, but in any case I have done my best to imitate the former and avoid the latter.

This edition would never have seen the light of day had I not been wafted in 1994 to what may well be called an academic lawyer's paradise. The Arthur Goodhart Professorship of Legal Science in Cambridge University enabled me to devote myself almost entirely to writing for a whole year, during which the Master and Fellows of Trinity College received me in their midst with great warmth and showed me how to combine ironical respect for academic tradition with undeviating concern for scholarship of the highest quality.

Finally, a work about Tony Weir's translation. Thanks to its pith, poise and precision there are places where it may be thought to read better than the text in German. Indeed, the late John Fleming, a master comparatist fluent in both languages, was heard to observe that for once the translation was an improvement on the original—though he was kind enough to add that in this instance the original, too, was quite acceptable.

Cambridge, September 1995   Hein Kötz

---

[2] H. Heine, *Lutetia* (Report of 3 June 1840, Part I), in IX *Werke* (10 vols., Insel, 1910) 65 f.

Contents

PART I

vii

PART II

Abbreviations

I. WORKS CITED BY AUTHOR'S NAME ONLY

CHESHIRE/FIFOOT/FURMSTON	*The Law of Contract* (12th edn. 1991)
CORBIN	*On Contracts, A Comprehensive Treatise on the Working Rules of Contract Law* (1950 ff.)
GHESTIN	*Traité de droit civil, Les Obligations: Le Contrat: formation* (2nd edn. 1988)
MAZEAUD/CHABAS	HENRI, LÉON and JEAN MAZEAUD, *Leçons de droit civil*, vol. ii(1): Obligations, Théorie générale (8th edn. 1991, by CHABAS)
MAZEAUD/TUNC	HENRI MAZEAUD, LÉON MAZEAUD and ANDRÉ TUNC, *Traité théorique et pratique de la responsabilité civile délictuelle et contractuelle*, vol. I (6th edn. 1965), vol. II (5th edn. 1958), vol. III (5th edn. 1960)
PLANIOL/RIPERT	*Traité pratique de droit civil français*, vol. VI (2nd edn. by ESMEIN, 1952), vol. VII (2nd edn. by ESMEIN, RADOUANT, and GABOLDE, 1954)
POLLOCK/WINFIELD	POLLOCK's *Principles of the Law of Contract* (13th edn. by WINFIELD, 1950)
PROSSER/KEETON	PROSSER and KEETON, *On the Law of Torts* (5th edn. 1984)
RIPERT/BOULANGER	*Traité de droit civil d'après le Traité de* PLANIOL, vol. I (1956), vol. II (1957)
TREITEL	*Law of Contract* (7th edn. 1987)
VINEY	*La responsabilité: Conditions* (1982) = *Traité de droit civil* (ed. GHESTIN) vol. IV (1982)
WILLISTON	*A Treatise on the Law of Contracts* (3rd edn. by JAEGER, 1957 ff.)

2. OTHER ABBREVIATIONS*

A.(2d)	Atlantic Reporter (Second Series)
ABGB	Austrian General Civil Code
AC	Law Reports, Appeal Cases (from 1891)
AcP	*Archiv für die civilistische Praxis*
ALJR	Australian Law Journal Reports (from 1958)
All ER	All England Law Reports (from 1936)
ALR	General Land Law for the Prussian States

* For decisions from Common Law jurisdictions two citations are sometimes given in the text: the second of such citations is generally easier to follow up, and it is the only one here explained.

ALR (2d)	American Law Reports Annotated (Second Series)
Am. J. Comp. L.	*American Journal of Comparative Law*
Am. Jurist	*American Jurist and Law Magazine* (1829–43)
Ann. Dir. Comp.	*Annuario di Diritto Comparato*
Ann. Fac. Istanb.	*Annales de la Faculté de droit d'Istanbul* (from 1951)
Ann. Fac. Liège	*Annales de la Faculté de droit, d'économie et de sciences sociales de Liège* (from 1976)
App. Cas.	Law Reports, Appeal Cases (1875–90)
Archbürg R	*Archiv für bürgerliches Recht*
Ark. L. Rev.	*Arkansas Law Review* (from 1946)
ARSP	*Archiv für Rechts-und Sozialphilosophie*
Austr. LJ	*Australian Law Journal* (from 1927)
AWD	*Aussenwirtschaftsdienst des Betriebs Beraters*
BAG	Bundesarbeitsgericht
BAGE	Decisions of the German Federal Labour Court (Bundesarbeitsgericht)
Bank Arch.	*Bankarchiv*
Basler jur. Mitt.	*Basler juristiche Mitteilungen* (from 1954)
BB	*Der Betriebsberater* (from 1946)
BBl.	*Bundesblatt der Schweizerischen Eidgenossenschaft*
BGB	German Civil Code
BGBl.	*Bundesgesetzblatt*
BGE	Decisions of the Swiss Federal Court (Bundesgericht)
BGHZ	Decisions of the German Federal Supreme Court (Bundesgerichtshof) in civil matters
BlZüRspr.	*Blätter für Zürcherische Rechtsprechung*
Bol. Inst. Méx.	*Boletin del Instituto de derecho comparado de México*
Bol. Mex. der. comp. NS	*Boletin Mexicano de derecho comparado* (from 1968)
Bost. Ind. Com. L. Rev.	*Boston College Industrial and Commercial Law Review*
Brit. YB Int. L.	*British Year Book of International Law*
Bull. civ.	Bulletin des arrêts de la Cour de cassation, chambres civiles
Bull. Soc. lég. comp.	*Bulletin de la Société de législation comparée* (1873–1948, then *Revue internationale de droit comparé*)
BUL Rev.	*Boston University Law Review* (from 1921)
BVerfG	Bundesverfassungsgericht
BVerfGG	Statute of the German Constitutional Court (Bundesverfassungsgerichtsgesetz)
BVerwGE	Decisions of the German Federal Administrative Court (Bundesverwaltungsgericht)

BW	Dutch Civil Code (Burgerlijk Wetboek)
Calif. L. Rev.	*California Law Review*
Camb. LJ	*Cambridge Law Journal*
can.	canon
Can. Bar Rev.	*Canadian Bar Review*
Cass.	Supreme Court of Cassation (Italy)
Ch.	Law Reports, Chancery Division (from 1891)
Ch. D.	Law Reports, Chancery Division (1875–90)
Ch. réun.	Cour de Cassation, Chambres réunies
cif	cost, insurance, freight
CISG	United Nations Convention on the International Sale of Goods (Vienna, 1980)
Civ.	Cour de Cassation, Chambre civile
CLR	Commonwealth Law Reports (Australia)
Clunet	*Journal du droit international*, founded by Clunet
Cmd., Cmnd., Cm.	Command Paper
Cod. Iur. Can.	Codex Iuris Canonici
Colum. J. Transnat'l L.	*Columbia Journal of Transnational Law* (from 1962)
Colum. L. Rev.	*Columbia Law Review*
Com.	Cour de Cassation, Chambre commerciale et financière
Comp. Int. LJS Afr.	*Comparative and International Law Journal of South Africa*
Comp. L. Yb.	*Comparative Law Yearbook* (from 1977)
Cornell L. Rev.	*Cornell Law Review* (from 1915, called *Cornell Law Quarterly* till 1967)
Crim.	Cour de Cassation, Chambre criminelle
Curr. Leg. Prob.	*Current Legal Problems* (from 1948)
D.	*Recueil Dalloz de doctrine, de jurisprudence et de législation* (1945–64); *Recueil Dalloz et Sirey de doctrine, de jurisprudence et de législation* (from 1965)
DA	Dalloz, *Recueil analytique de jurisprudence et de législation* (1941–44)
DC	Dalloz, *Recueil critique de jurisprudence et de législation* (1941–44)
DH	Dalloz, *Recueil hebdomadaire de jurisprudence* (1924–40)
DJZ	*Deutsche Juristenzeitung* (1896–1936)
DLR 2d	Dominion Law Reports, Second Series (Canada)
DNotZ	*Deutsche Notar-Zeitschrift*
DP	Dalloz, *Recueil périodique et critique de jurisprudence, de législation et de doctrine* (1825–1940)
DPCI	*Droit et pratique du commerce international* (from 1975)

DR	*Deutsches Recht*
Duke LJ	*Duke Law Journal*
ECE	Economic Commission for Europe
EEC	European Economic Community
Eng. Rep.	English Reports (1307–1865)
EU	European Union
Ev. Bl.	*Evidenzblatt der Rechtsmittelentscheidungen* (Austria, 1934–46)
Ex. D.	Law Reports, Exchequer Division (1875–80)
F.(2d)	Federal Reporter (Second Series)
FamRZ	*Ehe und Familie im privaten und öffentlichen Recht* (from 1954); *Zeitschrift für das gesamte Familienrecht* (from 1962)
FGO	Ordinance of the Financial Court in Germany (Finanzgerichtsordnung)
fob	free on board
Foro it.	*Il Foro Italiano*
Foro pad.	*Il Foro padano*
F. Supp.	Federal Supplement
Gaz. Pal.	*Gazette du Palais*
Gaz. Trib.	*Gazette des Tribunaux*
Geo. Wash. L. Rev.	*George Washington Law Review* (from 1932)
GG	German Basic Law (Grundgesetz)
Giust. civ.	*Giustizia civile*
GIU (NF)	Decisions of the Austrian Supreme Court (Oberster Gerichtshof), collection founded by GLASER and UNGER (new series from 1900)
GVG	Gerichtsverfassungsgesetz
Harv. L. Rev.	*Harvard Law Review*
HGB	German Commercial Code (Handelsgesetzbuch)
HR	Dutch Supreme Court (Hoge Raad)
ICLQ	*International and Comparative Law Quarterly*
Incoterms	International Commercial Terms
Ind. LJ	*Indiana Law Journal* (from 1925)
Int. Enc. Comp. L.	*International Encyclopedia of Comparative Law*
Inter-Am. L. Rev.	*Inter-American Law Review*
Int. Leg. Mat.	International Legal Materials
Iowa L. Rev.	*Iowa Law Review*
IPrax	*Praxis des Internationalen Privat- und Verfahrensrechts*
JBl.	*Juristische Blätter*
J. Bus. L.	*Journal of Business Law*
J. Comp. Leg.	*Journal of Comparative Legislation and International Law*
JCP	*Juris-Classeur périodique, La Semaine juridique*

Jher. Jb.	*Jherings Jahrbücher für die Dogmatik des bürgerlichen Rechts*
J. Int. Jur. Komm.	*Journal der Internationalen Juristenkommission* (1957–68)
JL & Econ.	*Journal of Law and Economics* (from 1958)
J. Leg. Ed.	*Journal of Legal Education*
J. Leg. Stud.	*Journal of Legal Studies* (from 1972)
JR	*Juristische Rundschau*
J. Soc. Comp. Leg.	*Journées de la Société de législation comparée* (from 1979)
JSPTL	*Journal of the Society of Public Teachers of Law* (1924–38, from 1947), then, from 1981, *LS*
JT	*Journal des Tribunaux* (from 1881)
Jur Jb.	*Juristen-Jahrbuch*
Jur. Rev.	*Juridical Review* (from 1889)
JuS	*Juristische Schulung*
JW	*Juristische Wochenschrift*
JZ	*Juristenzeitung*
KB	Law Reports, King's Bench (1901–52)
KO	Konkursordnung
La. L. Rev.	*Louisiana Law Review*
L. and Soc. Rev.	*Law and Society Review*
L. Contemp. Probl.	*Law and Contemporary Problems*
LJ Ch.	Law Journal Reports, Chancery (1831–1949)
LM	LINDENMAIER, MÖHRING, *et al.*, Reference Work to the Decisions of the German Supreme Court (Bundesgerichtshof)
LQ Rev.	*The Law Quarterly Review*
LR Ch. App.	Law Reports, Chancery Appeal Cases (1865–75)
LRCP	Law Reports, Common Pleas Cases (1865–75)
LR Ex.	Law Reports, Exchequer Cases (1865–75)
LRHL	Law Reports, English and Irish Appeals (1866–75)
LRPC	Law Reports, Privy Council Appeals (1865–75)
LRQB	Law Reports, Queen's Bench (1865–75)
LS	*Legal Studies* (from 1981, previously *JSPTL*)
LT	Law Times Reports (1859–1947)
LuftVG	German Air Traffic Act (Luftverkehrsgesetz)
LZ	*Leipziger Zeitschrift*
McGill LJ	*McGill Law Journal* (from 1952)
Mass.	*Massimario*
MDR	*Monatsschrift für deutsches Recht*
Mich. L. Rev.	*Michigan Law Review*
Minn. L. Rev.	*Minnesota Law Review*
mn.	marginal note
Mod. L. Rev.	*Modern Law Review*
Mont.	Montagu, Reports of Cases in Bankrupty (1832)

Mot.	*Motive zu dem Entwurfe eines Bürgerlichen Gesetzbuches für das Deutsche Reich* (1896)
no.	number
NBW	Nieuw Burgerlijk Wetboek
NE (2d)	North Eastern Reporter (Second Series)
Ned. Jur.	*Nederlandse Jurisprudentie*
NJW	*Neue Juristische Wochenschrift*
NW (2d)	North Western Reporter (Second Series)
NWUL Rev.	*Northwestern University Law Review*
NY	Reports of Cases Decided in the Court of Appeals of the State of New York (1877–1921)
NYS (2d)	New York Supplement (Second Series)
NYL Forum	*New York Law Forum*
NYUL Rev.	*New York University Law Review*
NZULR	*New Zealand Universities Law Review*
ObTr.	Decisions of the Prussian Supreme Court (Obertribunal)
OER	*Osteuropa-Recht* (from 1955)
OGH	Austrian Supreme Court (Oberster Gerichtshof)
OGHZ	Decisions in civil matters of the Supreme Court for the British Zone of Germany
ÖJZ	*Österreichische Juristen-Zeitung*
OLGE	Decisions in civil matters of the Oberlandesgerichte in Germany
OR	Swiss Code of Obligations
Oxf. J. Leg. Stud.	*Oxford Journal of Legal Studies* (from 1981)
P.	Law Reports, Probate Division (from 1891)
P. (2d)	Pacific Reporter (Second Series)
Prot.	Protokolle der Kommission für die 2. Lesung des Entwurfs des BGB
QB	Law Reports, Queen's Bench (1891–1900, from 1952)
QBD	Law Reports, Queen's Bench Division (1875–90)
Qd.R.	Queensland Reports (from 1958)
RabelsZ	*Rabels Zeitschrift für ausländisches und internationales Privatrecht*
Rec. des Cours	Recueil des Cours (from 1923)
Req.	Cour de Cassation, Chambre de requêtes
Rev. Contemp. L.	*Review of Contemporary Law*
Rev. dr. int. dr. comp.	*Revue de droit international et de droit comparé*
Rev. dr. unif.	*Revue de droit uniforme*
Rev. hell. dr. int.	*Revue hellénique de droit international* (from 1948)
Rev. int. dr. comp.	*Revue internationale de droit comparé*
Rev. jur. Univ. Puerto Rico	*Revista jurídica de la Universidad de Puerto Rico* (from 1932)

Rev. trim. dr. civ.	*Revue trimestrielle de droit civil*
RGZ	Decisions in civil matters of the German Imperial Court (Reichsgericht)
RheinZ	*Rheinische Zeitschrift für Zivil-und Prozeßrecht des In- und Auslandes*
Riv. dir. com.	*Rivista del diritto commerciale e del diritto generale delle obbligazioni*
Riv. it. sci. giur.	*Rivista italiana per le scienze giuridiche*
RIW	*Recht der internationalen Wirtschaft* (1954/55–1957 and from 1975)
ROHG	Decisions of the German Imperial Commercial Court (Reichsoberhandelsgericht)
ROW	*Recht in Ost und West*
RSFSR	Russian Socialist Federated Soviet Republic
RVO	German Imperial Insurance Ordinance (Reichsversicherungsordnung)
s.	section
S.	*Recueil Sirey* (1791–1954, 1957–64)
S. Afr. LJ	*South African Law Journal*
SavZ/Germ.	*Zeitschrift der Savigny-Stiftung für Rechtsgeschichte, Germanistische Abteilung*
SavZ/Rom.	*Zeitschrift der Savigny-Stiftung für Rechtsgeschichte, Romanistische Abteilung*
Scand. Stud. L.	*Scandinavian Studies in Law*
Schw ZBGR	*Schweizerische Zeitschrift für Beurkundungs- und Grundbuchrecht*
SE (2d)	South Eastern Reporter (Second Series)
Seuff A	*Seuffert's Archiv*
SJZ	*Schweizerische Juristen-Zeitung*
SLT	*Scots Law Times*
So.	Southern Reporter
Soc.	Cour de Cassation, Chambre sociale
Som.	Sommaire
Stan. L. Rev.	*Stanford Law Review*
StGB	German Penal Code (Strafgesetzbuch)
StVG	German Road Traffic Act (Strassenverkehrsgesetz)
Süddt. JZ	*Süddeutsche Juristenzeitung*
SW (2d)	South Western Reporter (Second Series)
Sydney L. Rev.	*Sydney Law Review*
SZ	Decisions of the Austrian Supreme Court (Oberster Gerichtshof) in civil and judiciary matters
Tex. L. Rev.	*Texas Law Review*
TLR	Times Law Reports
Trib. civ.	Tribunal civil

Trib. com.	Tribunal de commerce
Trib. gr. inst.	Tribunal de grande instance
Trib. paix	Tribunal de paix
Tul. L. Rev.	*Tulane Law Review*
U. Chi. L. Rev.	*University of Chicago Law Review*
UCC	Uniform Commercial Code
U. Ill. L. Forum	*University of Illinois Law Forum* (from 1949)
ULFIS	Uniform Law on the Formation of Contracts for the International Sale of Goods
ULIS	Uniform Law on the International Sale of Goods
UNCITRAL	United Nations Commission of International Trade Law
UNIDROIT	L'Unification du droit
U. Pa. L. Rev.	*University of Pennsylvania Law Review*
US	United States Supreme Court Reports
U. Tor. LJ	*University of Toronto Law Journal* (from 1935)
UWG	German Law of Unfair Competition (Gesetz gegen den unlauteren Wettbewerb)
Va. L. Rev.	*Virginia Law Review*
Vand. L. Rev.	*Vanderbilt Law Review*
Verh. DJT	*Verhandlungen des Deutschen Juristentages*
Vers R	*Versicherungsrecht*
VLR	Victorian Law Reports (1875–1956, Australia)
VRS	Verkehrsrechts-Sammlung
VVG	German Law of the Insurance Contract (*Versicherungsvertragsgesetz*)
Wash. L. Rev.	*Washington Law Review*
Wis. L. Rev.	*Wisconsin Law Review* (from 1920)
WLR	Weekly Law Reports
WM	*Wertpapier-Mitteilungen*, Part IV
Yale LJ	*Yale Law Journal*
ZaöRV	*Zeitschrift für ausländisches öffentliches Recht und Völkerrecht* (1929–44; from 1950)
ZBernJV	*Zeitschrift des Bernischen Juristenvereins*
ZBl.	*Zentralblatt für die juristische Praxis* (Austria)
ZfRV	*(Austrian) Zeitschrift für Rechtsvergleichung* (from 1960)
ZGB	Civil Code (Switzerland, East Germany)
ZgesHR	*Zeitschrift für das gesamte Handelsrecht und Wirtschaftsrecht* (1858–1944, from 1948)
ZgesStW	*Zeitschrift für die gesamte Staatswissenschaft*
ZPO	German Code of Civil Procedure (Zivilprozessordnung)
ZSR	*Zeitschrift für schweizerisches Recht*
ZStW	*Zeitschrift für die gesamte Strafrechtswissenschaft*

ZvglRW	*Zeitschrift für vergleichende Rechtswissenschaft* (1878–1942, 1953 ff.)
ZVR	*Zeitschrift für Verkehrsrecht* (Austria)
ZZP	*Zeitschrift für Zivilprozeß*

Table of Cases in English

PART I

A. GENERAL CONSIDERATIONS

I

The Concept of Comparative Law

ADAM, 'Ethnologische Rechtsforschung', in: Adam/Trimborn, *Lehrbuch der Völkerkunde* (3rd edn. 1958) 189.

BANAKAS, 'Some Thoughts on the Method of Comparative Law: The Concept of Law Revisited', *Rev. hell. dr. int.* 33 (1980) 155.

v. BENDA-BECKMANN, 'Einige Bemerkungen über die Beziehung zwischen Rechtssoziologie und Rechtsvergleichung', *ZvglRW*78 (1979)51.

——, 'Ethnologie und Rechtsvergleichung', *ARSP* (1981) 310.

CARBONNIER, 'L'Apport du droit comparé à la sociologie juridique', in: *Livre du centenaire de la Société de législation comparée* I (1969) 75.

COING, 'Die Bedeutung der europäischen Rechtsgeschichte für die Rechtsvergleichung', *RabelsZ* 32 (1968) 1.

DE CRUZ, *A Modern Approach to Comparative Law* (1993).

DROBNIG, 'Methods of Sociological Research in Comparative Law', *RabelsZ* 35 (1971) 496.

DROBNIG/REHBINDER (eds.), *Rechtssoziologie und Rechtsvergleichung* (1977, with important contributions from Drobnig, Gessner, Heldrich, Rehbinder, Terré, Zweigert, and others).

GENZMER, 'Zum Verhältnis von Rechtsgeschichte und Rechtsvergleichung', *ARSP* 41 (1954/55) 326.

——, 'A Civil Lawyer's Critical Views on Comparative Legal History', 15 *Am. J. Comp. L.* 87 (1966).

HAILBRONNER, 'Ziele und Methoden völkerrechtlich relevanter Rechtsvergleichung', *ZaöRV* 36 (1976) 190.

LAMBERT, 'Conception générale et définition de la science du droit comparé', Procèsverbaux des séances et documents, Congrès international de droit comparé I (1905) 26, printed in: Zweigert/Puttfarken (eds.), *Rechtsvergleichung* (1978) 30.

LEGRAND, Book Review, 58 *Mod. L. Rev.* 262 (1995).

MARTINY, 'Rechtsvergleichung und vergleichende Rechtssoziologie', *Zeitschrift für Rechtssoziologie* 1 (1980) 65.

POSPISIL, *The Ethnology of Law* (2nd edn., 1978).

POUND, 'Some Thoughts About Comparative Law', in: *Festschrift Ernst Rabel* 1 (1954) 7.

——, 'Comparative Law in Space and Time', 4 *Am. J. Comp. L.* 70 (1955).

RABEL, *Aufgabe und Notwendigkeit der Rechtsvergleichung* (1925), reprinted in: Rabel, *Gesammelte Aufsätze* III (ed. Leser, 1967) 1.

RHEINSTEIN, 'Legal Systems: Comparative Law and Legal Systems', in: *International Encyclopedia of the Social Sciences* IX (ed. Sills, 1968) 204.

——, *Einführung in die Rechtsvergleichung* (2nd edn., 1987).

SACCO, *Introduzione al diritto comparato* (5th edn., 1992).

SCHWARZ-LIEBERMANN V. WAHLENDORF, *Droit comparé, Théorie générale et principes* (1978).

STONE, 'The End to Be Served by Comparative Law', 25 *Tul. L. Rev.* 325 (1951).

TALLON, 'Comparative Law: Expanding Horizons', 10 *JSPTL* 265 (1968).

WENGER, 'Rechtsgeschichte und Rechtsvergleichung', in: *Mémoires de l'Académie internationale de droit comparé* III 1 (1953) 149.

YNTEMA, 'Roman Law as the Basis of Comparative Law', in *Law—A Century of Progress* 1835–1935 II (1937) 346.

ZWEIGERT, 'Das soziologische Dimension in der Rechtsvergleichung', *RabelsZ* 38 (1974) 299.

——/PUTTFARKEN (eds.), *Rechtsvergleichung* (1978).

I

BEFORE we try to discover the essence, function, and aims of comparative law, let us first say what 'comparative law' means. The words suggest an intellectual activity with law as its object and comparison as its process. Now comparisons can be made between different rules in a single legal system, as, for example, between different paragraphs of the German Civil Code. If this were all that was meant by comparative law, it would be hard to see how it differed from what lawyers normally do: lawyers constantly have to juxtapose and harmonize the rules of their own system, that is, compare them, before they can reach any practical decision or theoretical conclusion. Since this is characteristic of every national system of law, 'comparative law' must mean more than appears on the surface. The extra dimension is that of internationalism. Thus 'comparative law' is the comparison of the different legal systems of the world.

Comparative law as we know it started in Paris in 1900, the year of the World Exhibition. At this brilliant panorama of human achievement there were naturally innumerable congresses, and the great French scholars ÉDOUARD LAMBERT and RAYMOND SALEILLES took the opportunity to found an International Congress for Comparative Law. The science of comparative law, or at any rate its method, was greatly advanced by the occurrence of this Congress, and the views expressed at it have led to a wealth of productive research in this branch of legal study, young though it is.

The temper of the Congress was in tune with the times, whose increasing wealth and splendour had given everyone, scholars included, an imperturbable faith in progress. Sure of his existence, certain of its point and convinced of its success, man was trying to break out of his local confines and peaceably to master the world and all that was in it. Naturally enough, lawyers were affected by this spirit; merely to interpret and elaborate their own system no longer satisfied them. This outgoing spirit permeates all the Congress papers; the whole Congress was dominated by a disarming belief in progress. What LAMBERT and SALEILLES had in mind was the development of nothing less than a common law of mankind (*droit commun de l'humanite*). A world law must be created—not today, perhaps not even tomorrow—but created it must be, and comparative law must create it. As LAMBERT put it (above p. 1, pp. 26 ff.), comparative law must resolve the accidental and divisive differences in the laws of peoples at similar stages of cultural and economic development, and reduce the number of divergencies in law, attributable not to the political, moral, or social qualities of the different nations but to historical accident or to temporary or contingent circumstances.

Comparative law has developed continuously since then, despite great changes in man's attitude towards existence. The belief in progress, so characteristic of 1900, has died. World wars have weakened, if not destroyed, faith in world law. Yet despite a more sceptical way of looking at the world, the development and enrichment of comparative law has been steady. Comparative lawyers have come to know their field better, they have refined their methods and set their sights a little lower, but they remain convinced that comparative law is both useful and necessary. Scholars are more resistant to fashionable pessimism than people in other walks of life; they have no immediate aim, only the ultimate goal of discovering the truth. This is true also of research in comparative law; it has no immediate aim. But if one did want to adduce arguments of utility, comparative law must be at least as useful as it was, especially as technological developments since 1900 have made the world ever smaller and, to all appearances, national isolationism is on the wane. Furthermore, by the international exchanges which it requires, comparative law procures the gradual approximation of viewpoints, the abandonment of deadly complacency, and the relaxation of fixed dogma. It affords us a glimpse into the form and formation of legal institutions which develop in parallel, possibly in accordance with laws yet to be determined, and permits us to catch sight, through the differences in detail, of the grand similarities and so to deepen our belief in the existence of a unitary sense of justice.

Despite all this, comparative law still occupies a rather modest position in academic curricula (see further Ch. 2 IV below). Though LAMBERT's great claims in this respect, as developed in his report of 1900 (above p. 1, pp. 53 ff.) were much more realistic than his dream of a 'droit commun de l'humanité', they have not yet been realized anywhere in the world. He thought that it would be greatly to the good of society if pride of place in academic studies were accorded to comparative private law, the heartland of all comparative law. For if clear and consistent general principles of law were established, this would promote international trade and advance the general standard of living, and if lawyers were induced to look beyond their borders, international exchanges would increase. Future lawyers would have to be exposed to 'comparative common legislation' and comparative law while still at university. This would refresh and enrich the study of their native law, which was increasingly confining itself to interpreting the actual texts and neglecting principle for doctrinal detail.

It may indeed be that the mere interpretation of positive rules of law in the way traditionally practised by lawyers does not deserve to be called a science at all, whether intellectual or social. Perhaps legal studies only become truly scientific when they rise above the actual rules of any national system, as happens in legal philosophy, legal history, the sociology of law, and comparative law.

Now it is precisely the broad principles which comparative law lets one see; it can help the economist by discovering the social preconditions of particular rules of law, and by the comparisons it makes across time it can assist the legal historian. Students today are often put off by textual disputes, arid logomachies, and logical demonstrations, which prevent their seeing the living problems which lurk behind these technical facades. For this reason LAMBERT claimed for comparative law a place in the curriculum equal to that of the home system: four lectures a week should be given in comparative law for each of three semesters. Everything he said is as valid today as when he said it in 1900, but though much has improved in many countries in the ensuing century, the radical restructuring of the curriculum which he showed to be necessary has yet to take place.

II

Comparative lawyers compare the legal systems of different nations. This can be done on a large scale or on a smaller scale. To compare the spirit and style of different legal systems, the methods of thought and procedures they use, is sometimes called *macrocomparison*. Here, instead of concentrating on individual concrete problems and their solutions, research is done into methods of handling legal materials, procedures for resolving and deciding disputes, or the roles of those engaged in the law. For example, one can compare different techniques of legislation, styles of codification, and methods of statutory interpretation, and discuss the authority of precedents, the contribution made by academics to the development of law, and the diverse styles of judicial opinion. Here too one could study the different ways of resolving conflicts adopted by different legal systems, and ask how effective they actually are. Attention may be focused on the official state courts: how is the business of proving the facts and establishing the law divided between attorneys and judges? What role do lay judges have in civil or criminal proceedings? What special arrangements, if any, are made for small claims? But one should not confine one's study to the state courts and judges: one should take account of all actual methods of settling disputes. Studying the various *people* engaged in the life of the law, asking what they do, how, and why, is a very promising field of work for comparative lawyers. First of all one would look at the judges and the lawyers, the people, whatever they are called, who apply or advise on the law in any system. But it can also be profitable to compare other persons involved in the law, such as the lawyers in Ministries and Parliaments who work on forthcoming legislation, notaries, the experts who appear in court, the claims adjusters of insurance companies and, last but not least, those who teach law in universities.

Microcomparison, by contrast, has to do with specific legal institutions or problems, that is, with the rules used to solve actual problems or particular conflicts of interests. When is a manufacturer liable for the harm caused to a consumer by defective goods? What rules determine the allocation of loss in the case of traffic accidents? What factors are relevant for determining the custody of children in divorce cases? If an illegitimate child is disinherited by his father or mother, what rights does he have? The list of possible examples is endless.

The dividing line between macrocomparison and microcomparison is admittedly flexible. Indeed, one must often do both at the same time, for often one has to study the *procedures* by which the rules are in fact applied in order to understand why a foreign system solves a particular problem in the way it does.

For example, no picture of the rules which apply when a patient is suing a doctor for damages can be complete or accurate unless it describes how malpractice is established in court and tells us whether the experts are appointed by the court or are chosen by the parties themselves to battle it out in the courtroom, as happens in Common Law countries.—Nor could one give a true picture of the American law regarding the strict liability of the manufacturer just by listing the elements of a successful claim at law. One must also say that the claim will be decided in a trial by jury and show what roles the judge, lawyers, and jury play in such proceedings and how this influences the substantive law, by noting, for example, that in such a claim the plaintiff's attorney normally stipulates for a fee of 30–50 per cent of the damages awarded and that the jury takes account of this fact when fixing the damages. Indeed, one must cast one's net wider still. Tort liability is just one of the ways of improving the quality of products and reducing the risks to the public: administrative and criminal law may have a contribution to make, and if product liability law seems to play a different and more important role in the United States than in Europe (see below Ch. 42 V), this may perhaps be because Americans take a less sanguine view than Europeans of the efficacy or cost of administrative controls and criminal sanctions. These examples must suffice to show that 'microcomparison' may not work at all unless one takes into account the general institutional contexts in which the rules under comparison have evolved and are actually applied.

III

In order to understand what comparative law really is, it is as well to distinguish it from related areas of legal science, that is, to show what comparative law is *not*.

Since comparative law necessarily has to deal with foreign law, it must be distinguished from those other branches of legal science which have to do mainly or occasionally with other legal systems. As has often been observed, the mere study of foreign law falls short of being comparative law. For example, in 1937 the League of Nations produced a study of The Status of Women in the World, consisting merely of reports from different countries on their own solution of the problem. There was no real comparison of the solutions presented, and so at most one could call it descriptive comparative law. One can speak of comparative law only if there are specific comparative reflections on the problem to which the work is devoted. Experience shows that this is best done if the author first lays out the essentials of the relevant foreign law, country by country, and then uses this material as a basis for critical comparison, ending up with conclusions about the proper policy for the law to adopt, which may involve a reinterpretation of his own system.

The neighbouring areas of legal science which also deal with foreign law, and from which comparative law must be distinguished, are private international law, public international law, legal history, legal ethnology, and finally sociology of law.

1. *Comparative Law and Private International Law*

These two areas are, on the face of it, entirely distinct, but they interact. Private international law, or conflict of laws, is a part of the positive national law, while comparative law seems to present itself as a *science pure*. Private international law tells us which of several possible systems of law should be applied in a particular case which has foreign connections; it contains rules of competence which determine which specific national law is to be applied and which lead to its application. One could therefore say that private international law is basically more selective than comparative. Comparative law, on the other hand, deals with several legal orders at the same time, and does so without having any practical aim in view.

Yet comparative law is enormously valuable for private international law, indeed so indispensable for its development that the methods of private international law today are essentially those of comparative law.

The most striking example is the well-known theory of *qualification* or *characterization*, which tells us how to understand those concepts, such as marriage, contract, and tort, which figure as connecting factors in the national rules of private international law. On one view (qualification according to the *lex fori*) these concepts are to be given the same meaning as they have in the substantive national law; according to the theory of qualification developed by ERNST RABEL (see RABEL, 'Das Problem der Qualifikation', *RabelsZ* 5 (1931) 241), they are to be understood in the light of comparative law, independently of the *lex fori*. Comparative law also has to be used in the *application of the foreign law* indicated by the conflict rules of the home system. Suppose that in a will which is governed by English law the widow is made 'lifetenant' or a third party is appointed 'trustee'. These terms must somehow be converted into the language of the legal system which is controlling the disposal of the estate. The only way of doing this is to compare the English institutions with the nearest thing in the legal system involved: the German lawyer would therefore consider *Vorerbschaft*, *Nießbrauch*, and *Testamentsvollstrecker*. Now in English law the estate does not vest directly in the 'heirs', but goes to a 'personal representative', that is, a person who must administer the estate on behalf of those entitled to it, and divide the estate between them after paying off its debts. In Germany, these English rules cause difficulties in drafting the certificate of entitlement (*Erbschein*) which persons with rights of succession may demand, and these difficulties can only be resolved by intensive researches of comparative law. 'For example, if a person dies intestate, leaving a widow and several adult children, the certificate must indicate that the moveables in the estate pass under English law to the administrator appointed by the English probate court, who must manage the property in trust (*zu treuen Händen*) for the beneficiaries and use the net proceeds of the estate, after payment of its debts, to provide the widow with the personal chattels and the sum of [£125,000] after which one half of the rest is divided between the children in equal portions, and the other half is administered in trust (*zu treuen Händen*) for the widow, the children being entitled to equal parts of it on her death' (see the instructive treatment of this question by GOTTHEINER, 'Zur Anwendung englischen Erbrechts auf Nachlässe in Deutschland', *RabelsZ* 21 (1956) 33 ff., 71). Comparative law is also essential for the proper treatment of the concept of *ordre public* in private international law. Sometimes a foreign rule which is indicated by the conflict rules of the forum is so shocking to the *ordre public* of the forum that it cannot be applied, but in order to discover whether this is so one must make a comparison between the foreign rule and the closest analogue in the home system. Finally, there is the question of *renvoi*, whether consistency of decision—the principal aim of private international law—is best advanced by applying or not applying the conflicts rule of a foreign system which remits the matter back to the forum. This also can only be solved by the comparative method, and it was ERNST RABEL'S comparative work on 'Conflict of Laws' which conclusively showed how absurd it was to carry on applying national tests in an area like conflicts law which is devoted to international intercourse (see especially vol. I (2nd edn., 1958), 3 ff., 103 f.).

2. Comparative Law and Public International Law

At first sight there is little in common between comparative law and *public international law*, for public international law, or the law of nations, is essentially a supranational and global system of law. Yet comparative law is essential to the understanding of 'the general principles of law recognized by civilized nations' which are laid down as being one of the sources of public international law by art. 38 (1) (c) of the Statute of the International Court of Justice—whether this means principles of law accepted by all nations without exception, which would include only a few trivial truisms, or rather the principles of law accepted by a large majority of nations. The recognition of such general principles is rendered more difficult by the basic differences of attitude between the developed industrial nations and those in process of development. Now one of the aims of comparative law is to discover which solution of a problem is the best, and perhaps one could include as a 'general principle of law' the solution of a particular problem which emerges from a proper evaluation of the material under comparison as being the best. To do this would avoid reducing the valuable notion of 'general principles of law' to a mere minimum standard, and could gradually lead us to accept progressive solutions as being examples of such general principles.

The methods of comparative law can also be extremely useful in interpreting treaties, and in helping to understand some of the concepts and institutions of customary international law. The rule *pacta sunt servanda*, the idea behind the *clausula rebus sic stantibus*, and the theory of *abus de droit* in international law all have their roots in institutions of municipal private law, and it is only through comparative law that they can be made to yield their full potential.

3. *Comparative Law, Legal History, and Legal Ethnology*

The relationship between comparative law and legal history is surprisingly complex. At first sight one is tempted to say that while comparative law studies legal systems coexistent in space, legal history studies systems consecutive in time. But there is more to it than that. For one thing, all legal history involves a comparative element: the legal historian cannot help bringing to the study of his chosen system, say Roman law, the various preconceptions of the modern system he is familiar with; thus he is bound to make comparisons, consciously if he is alert, unconsciously if he is not. Again, unless the comparatist is content merely to record the actual state of play, he really has to take account of the historical circumstances in which the legal institutions and procedures under comparison evolved. How does historical research differ from comparative work? Where does one end and the other begin? At what point must the comparatist yield the floor to the legal historian? The questions admit of no rational answer. Legal history and comparative law are much of a muchness; views may differ on which of these twin sisters is the more comely, but there is no doubt that the legal historian must often use the comparative method and that if the comparatist is to make sense of the rules and the problems they are intended to solve he must often investigate their history.

The founders of comparative legal ethnology, J. J. BACHOFEN (*Das Mut-*

terrecht (1861)) and Sir HENRY MAINE, had an aim rather different from that of true comparatists, namely to produce a general world history of law as part of a general history of civilization. At its outset legal ethnology rested on a specific belief, stemming from the teachings of AUGUSTE COMTE, the historical dialectic of HEGEL, and BASTIAN's theories of elementary and folk ideas. This belief, now regarded as invalid, was that mankind, with its common psyche, follows the same path of development in everything regardless of location or race. This belief led scholars to focus on the so-called primitive systems of law, if systems they can be called, still to be found among backward peoples. From the legal practices of these peoples they drew conclusions about the condition many ages ago, at a period from which we have no legal muniments or even evidence of any kind, of the legal systems which are now highly developed. Foremost among such scholars were H. H. POST in his *Einleitung in das Studium der ethnologischen Jurisprudenz* (1886) and JOSEPH KOHLER in his *Zeitschrift für vergleichende Rechtswissenschaft*. The basic tenet of ethnological legal studies, namely that all peoples develop as it were in parallel from a common original condition, was controverted principally by the so-called theory of cultural groups (*Kulturkreislehre*) according to which every cultural development of any group anywhere was, as a historical event, unique. The adherents of this theory could not deny the surprising similarities between the legal institutions of different peoples at the same stage of development, but sought to explain them as being the result of adoption or migration. Certainly such events did take place, but they cannot explain all the instances of parallel development. The more modern view, represented by KOSCHAKER, is that the development of a legal system is the product of factors, some of which are typical and occur everywhere, and some of which are atypical. According to KOSCHAKER the typical factors are not natural and inevitable, like BASTIAN's elementary ideas, but historical: a group of people in a particular geographical social and economic situation develops in a particular way with regard to law as well as other things. Such a typical development may be influenced by atypical factors, such as race, special aptitudes, or historical accident. The principal aim of legal ethnology, therefore, must be to distinguish the typical factors from the atypical aberrancies, for otherwise no safe conclusions could be drawn for our original law from the legal practices of surviving primitive peoples.

Nowadays we see legal ethnology not so much as a constituent of a general history but more as a branch of ethnology and comparative law which concentrates on the legal aspects of surviving societies, unhappily called 'primitive' because they are not yet equipped with all the apparatus of civilization. Its discipline is historical only in seeking to discover 'the origins and early stages of law in relation to particular cultural phenomena' (ADAM (above p. 1), 192). But the few older societies hitherto untouched are being increasingly exposed to the modernizing influence of the expanding industrial revolution and being drawn into the community of mankind. Accordingly the task of modern legal ethnology is to study the changes suffered by societies already observed in adjusting to the intrusion of a higher civilization. Thus to a large extent legal ethnology has become a branch of modern comparative law, one of whose most pressing tasks it is to assist the legal systems of developing societies by giving them the benefits of its comparative researches. To this aim legal ethnology has its special contribution to make.

4. *Comparative Law and Sociology*

After the discussion in recent years of the relation between *sociology of law* and comparative law, it now seems to be generally agreed that the two disciplines not only have a great deal to learn from each other but also use much the same methods.

Sociology of law aims to discover the causal relationships between law and society. It seeks to discover patterns from which one can infer whether and under what circumstances law affects human behaviour and conversely how law is affected by social change, whether of a political, economic, psychological, or demographic nature. This is an area where it is very difficult to construct theories, but if one can support one's theory with comparative data from other nations and cultures, it will be much more persuasive.

Legal sociologists use a technique quite like the 'control group' of experimental natural scientists: if in a given sector of experience two systems have different rules and one can show that the relevant social facts in those countries are also different, this may point towards the hypothesis that the social facts and the rules are causally connected (see examples given below pp. 37 ff.). Likewise if one brings in the time dimension, one may be able to show that as the social development in different countries converges (or diverges) the rules in force there also converge (or diverge). If people behave the same way in similar situations despite a difference in the rules which purport to control their conduct, one may infer that the rules are ineffectual, and the same inference may be drawn when the rules are the same but people behave differently. On all this see MARTINY (above p. 1): he shows how the sociology of law can use the discoveries of comparative law, while making it clear that the practice of international and intercultural legal sociology is a very difficult matter indeed.

If comparative sociology of law can make use of the experience and discoveries of comparative law, comparative lawyers undoubtedly have a great deal to learn from legal sociologists. This is important, first, for what one can call the *definition of the problem*. Comparative lawyers have long known that only rules which perform the same function and address the same real problem or conflict of interests can profitably be compared. They also know that they must cut themselves loose from their own doctrinal and juridical preconceptions and liberate themselves from their own cultural context in order to discover 'neutral' concepts with which to describe such problems or conflicts of interests (on this see further Ch. 3 II). Legal sociologists not only accept this but apply it with a rigour which the comparative lawyer finds stimulating, if also a bit worrying, for legal sociologists can sometimes show that concepts and features which the comparative lawyer regards as 'neutral' and therefore suitable for the definition of the problem are in fact nationally or culturally conditioned, or that they implicitly presuppose the existence of a particular social context which in reality exists in only one of the places under comparison and not in the other. Once the problem has been defined and it comes to the question of the *statement of the rules* which the systems under review use to resolve it, the situation is similar. Here too comparative lawyers agree that one must take account not only of legislative rules, judicial decisions, the 'law in the books', and also of general conditions of business, customs, and practices, but in fact of everything whatever which helps to mould human conduct in the situation under consideration (on this see below Ch. 3 II and III). Sociologists of law take this for granted, since they start out from the assumption that human behaviour is controlled by many factors other than law, but lawyers find it more difficult—and comparative lawyers are generally lawyers of some kind. They have to force themselves to be sufficiently receptive to the non-legal forces which control conduct, and here they have much to learn from the more open-minded sociologists of law. So also when the comparative lawyer comes to *explain his findings*, that is, to describe the causes of the legal similarities or differences which he has discovered. He knows, of course, that causal factors may exist anywhere throughout the fabric of social life, but often he will have to go to the sociology of law to learn just how far he must cast his net, so as to include, for example, the distribution of political power, the economic system, religious and ethical values, family structure, the basis of agriculture and the degree of industrialization, the organization of authorities and groups, and much else besides.

One must not forget that comparative law has several different goals. In its *theoretical-descriptive* form the principal aim is to say how and why certain legal systems are different or alike. In this respect it must, as we have shown, work on and profit from the theoretical models and empirical data produced by the sociology of law. But comparative law can also aim to provide advice on legal policy. In its *applied* version, comparative law suggests how a specific problem can most appropriately be solved under the given social and economic circumstances. In such cases the comparative lawyer often acts under considerable pressure: he may be pressed to say how the positive law should be altered on a particular point, how a perceived gap should be filled, or exactly what rules should be adopted in an international uniform law, and he may have to come up with detailed proposals in a very short time. In such circumstances he has to operate with assumptions which, plausible as they may be, would rightly be derided by the sociologist of law as simple working hypotheses. But this does not mean that they are necessarily false. Without

in the least suggesting that the comparative lawyer can ignore the insights
and discoveries of the legal sociologist, he often cannot avoid adopting, however tentatively and provisionally, theses which the sociologist of law would
regard as unproven, but which are nevertheless cogent enough to carry
weight in discussions or decisions about changing the law.

2

The Functions and Aims of Comparative Law

AUBIN, 'Die rechtsvergleichende Interpretation autonom-internen Rechts in der deutschen Rechtsprechung', *RabelsZ* 34 (1970) 458.

BLANC-JOUVAN,'Réflexions sur l'enseignement du droit comparé', *Rev. int. dr. comp.* 40 (1988) 751.

BLECKMANN, 'Die Rolle der Rechtsvergleichung in den Europäischen Gemeinschaften', *ZvglRW* 75 (1976) 106.

COING, 'Rechtsvergleichung als Grundlage von Gesetzgebung im 19. Jahrhundert', *Ius commune* VII (1978) 160.

DAIG, 'Zur Rechtsvergleichung und Methodenlehre im Europäischen Gemeinschaftsrecht', *Festschrift Zweigert* (1981) 395.

R. DAVID, 'The International Unification of Private Law', in: *International Encyclopedia of Comparative Law* II (1971) Ch. 5.

DÖLLE, 'Der Beitrag der Rechtsvergleichung zum deutschen Recht', in: *Hundert Jahre deutsches Rechtsleben, Festschrift zum 100jährigen Bestehen des deutschen Juristentages 1860–1960* II (1960) 19.

DROBNIG, 'The Use of Foreign Law by German Courts', in *German National Reports in Civil Law Matters for the XIVth Congress of Comparative Law* (ed. Jayme, 1994).

DROBNIG/DOPPFFEL, 'Die Nutzung der Rechtsvergleichung durch den deutschen Gesetzgeber', *RabelsZ* 46 (1982) 253.

DUTOIT, 'L'Importance du droit comparé dans l'enseignement juridique', in: *Recueil des travaux suisses présentés au IXe Congrès international de droit comparé* (1976) 21.

EVERLING, 'Rechtsvereinheitlichung durch Richterrecht in der Europäischen Gemeinschaft', *RabelsZ* 50 (1986) 193.

FERID, 'Die derzeitige Lage von Rechtsvergleichung und IPR in der Bundesrepublik Deutschland', *ZfRV* 22 (1981) 86.

FRANKENBERG, 'Critical Comparisons: Re-Thinking Comparative Law', 26 *Harv. Int. L. J.* 411 (1975).

GROSSFELD, *The Strength and Weakness of Comparative Law* (1990).

——, 'Vom Beitrag der Rechtsvergleichung zum deutschen Recht', *AcP* 184 (1984) 289.

HILL, 'Comparative Law, Law Reform and Legal Theory', 9 *Oxf. J. Leg. Stud.* 111 (1989).

HIRSCH, *Rezeption als sozialer Prozess* (1981).

JACOBS, 'The Uses of Comparative Law in the Law of the European Communities, Legal History and Comparative Law', in *Essays in Honour of A. Kiralfy* (ed. Plender, 1990) 99.

JUNKER, 'Rechtsvergleichung als Grundlagenfach', *JZ* 1994, 921.

KAHN-FREUND, 'On Uses and Misuses of Comparative Law', 37 *Mod. L. Rev.* 1 (1974).

KÖTZ, 'Gemeineuropäisches Zivilrecht', *Festschrift Zweigert* (1981) 481.

——, 'Rechtsvergleichung und Rechtsdogmatik', *RabelsZ* 54 (1990) 203.

——, 'Europäische Juristenausbildung', *ZEuP* 1993, 268.

——, 'Rechtsvergleichung und gemeineuropäisches Privatrecht', in *Gemeinsames Privatrecht in der Europäischen Gemeinschaft* (ed. Müller-Graff, 1993).

KOZYRIS, 'Comparative Law for the 21st Century, New Horizons and New Technologies', 69 *Tul. L. Rev.* 165 (1994).

KROPHOLLER, *Internationales Einheitsrecht, Allgemeine Lehren* (1975).

KÜBLER, 'Rechtsvergleichung als Grundlagendisziplin der Rechtswissenschaft', *JZ* 1977, 113.

LAWSON, 'Comparative Law as an Instrument of Legal Culture', in LAWSON, *The Comparison, Selected Essays* II 68 (1977).

LEGEAIS, 'L'utilisation de droit comparé par les tribunaux', *Rev. int. dr. comp.* 46 (1994) 347.

LUTTER, 'Die Auslegung angeglichenen Rechts', *JZ* 1992, 593.

MANSEL, 'Rechtsvergleichung und europäische Rechtseinheit', *JZ* 1991, 529.

MARKESINIS, 'Comparative Law: A Subject in Search of an Audience', 53 *Mod. L. Rev.* 1 (1990).

MARTINY, 'Autonome und einheitliche Auslegung im europäischen internationalen Zivilprozessrecht', *RabelsZ* 45 (1981) 427.

VON MEHREN, 'The Role of Comparative Law in the Practice of International Law', *Festschrift Neumayer* 479 (1985).

NEUHAUS/KROPHOLLER, 'Rechtsvereinheitlichung—Rechtsverbesserung?' *RabelsZ* 45 (1981) 73.

NEUMAYER, 'Fremdes Recht aus Büchern, fremde Rechtswirklichkeit und die funktionelle Dimension in den Methoden der Rechtsvergleichung', *RabelsZ* 34 (1970) 411.

——, 'Rechtsvergleichung als Unterrichtsfach an deutschen Universitäten', *Festschrift Zweigert* (1981) 501.

PESCATORE, 'Le Recours dans la jurisprudence de la Cour de justice des Communautés Européennes à des normes déduites de la comparaison des droits des États membres', *Rev. int. dr. comp.* 32 (1980) 337.

POUND, 'The Place of Comparative Law in the American Law School Curriculum', 8 *Tul. L. Rev.* 161 (1934).

SACCO, 'Legal Formants, A Dynamic Approach to Comparative Law', 39 *Am. J. Comp. L.* 343 (1991).

——, *La comparaison juridique au service de la connaissance du droit* (1991).

——, *Introduzione al diritto comparato* (5th edn. 1992).

SCHERMERS, 'Legal Education in Europe', 30 *Cmn. Mkt. L. Rev.* 9 (1993).

SCHLESINGER, 'The Role of the "Basic Course" in the Teaching of Foreign and Comparative Law', 19 *Am. J. Comp. L.* 616 (1971).

E. STEIN, 'Uses, Misuses—and Nonuses of Comparative Law', 72 *NWUL Rev.* 198 (1977).

TALLON, 'Les Perspectives de l'enseignement universitaire de droit comparé', *Festschrift Zajtay* (1982) 479.

UYTERHOVEN, *Richterliche Rechtsfindung und Rechtsvergleichung* (1959).

WATSON, 'Legal Transplants and Law Reform', 92 *LQ Rev.* 79 (1976).
ZWEIGERT, 'Rechtsvergleichung als universale Interpretationsmethode', *RabelsZ* 15 (1949/50) 5.

I

IT is beyond dispute today that the scholarly pursuit of comparative law has several significant functions. This emerges from a very simple consideration, that no study deserves the name of a science if it limits itself to phenomena arising within its national boundaries. For a long time lawyers were content to be insular in this sense, and to some extent they are so still. But such a position is untenable, and comparative law offers the only way by which law can become international and consequently a science.

In the natural and medical sciences, and in sociology and economics as well, discoveries and opinions are exchanged internationally. This is so familiar a fact that it is easy to forget its significance. There is no such thing as 'German' physics or 'British' microbiology or 'Canadian' geology. These branches of science are international, and the most one can say is that the contributions of the various nations to the different departments of world knowledge have been outstanding, average, or modest. But the position in legal science is astonishingly different. So long as Roman law was the essential source of all law on the Continent of Europe, an international unity of law and legal science did exist, and a similar unity, the unity of the Common Law, can still be found, up to a point, in the English-speaking world. On the European continent, however, legal unity began to disappear in the eighteenth century as national codes were put in the place of traditional Roman law. The consequence was that lawyers concentrated exclusively on their own legislation, and stopped looking over the border. At a time of growing nationalism, this legal narcissism led to pride in the national system. Germans thought German law was the ark of the covenant, and the French thought the same of French law: national pride became the hallmark of juristic thought. Comparative law has started to put an end to such narrowmindedness.

The primary aim of comparative law, as of all sciences, is knowledge. If one accepts that legal science includes not only the techniques of interpreting the texts, principles, rules, and standards of a national system, but also the discovery of models for preventing or resolving social conflicts, then it is clear that the method of comparative law can provide a much richer range of model solutions than a legal science devoted to a single nation, simply because the different systems of the world can offer a greater variety of solutions than could be thought up in a lifetime by even the most imaginative jurist who was corralled in his own system. Comparative law is an 'école de vérité' which extends and enriches the 'supply of solutions' (ZITELMANN) and offers the scholar of critical capacity the opportunity of finding the 'better solution' for his time and place.

Like the lively international exchange on legal topics to which it gives rise, comparative law has other functions which can only be mentioned here in the briefest way. It dissolves unconsidered national prejudices, and helps us to fathom the different societies and cultures of the world and to further international understanding; it is extremely useful for law reform in developing countries; and for the development of one's own system the critical attitude it engenders does more than local doctrinal disputes.

But four particular practical benefits of comparative law call for closer attention: comparative law as an aid to the legislator (II); comparative law as a tool of construction (III); comparative law as a component of the curriculum of the universities (IV); and comparative law as a contribution to the systematic unification of law (V), and the development of a private law common to the whole of Europe (VI).

II

Legislators all over the world have found that on many matters good laws cannot be produced without the assistance of comparative law, whether in the form of general studies or of reports specially prepared on the topic in question.

Ever since the second half of the nineteenth century legislation in *Germany* has been preceded by extensive comparative legal research. This was true when commercial law was unified, first in Prussia and then in the German Empire, and also, after the Empire had acquired the necessary legislative powers, of the unification of private law, law of civil procedure, law of bankruptcy, law of judicature (courts system), and criminal law. Account was taken not only of the different laws then in force in Germany, including the French law in force in the Rhineland, but also of Dutch, Swiss, and Austrian law (see COING and DÖLLE (above p. 13 and below)). As to the present, it can be said that no major legislation since the Second World War has been undertaken without more or less extensive research in comparative law. This is true not only of reforms in German and family law (see DROBNIG/DOPFFEL (above p. 13)), but also of numerous other laws, such as the law of commercial agents, company law, anti-trust law, the introduction of the dissenting opinion in the Federal Constitutional Court, the draft law of privacy (admittedly never enacted), the law for the compensation for victims of violent crime, the law regarding changes of sex, the law on legal advice for the indigent, and much more. Comparative legal studies also underlay the recent proposals of the Commission for the Reform of the Law of Obligations set up by the Federal Ministry of Just-ice: see, for instance, the submission of the Max Planck Institute for Foreign and International Law on 'Modern Development of Contract Law in Europe', published in *Gutachten und Vorschläge zur Überarbeitung des Schuldrechts* I (ed. Ministry of Justice, 1981) 1. Here one of the motive forces was a concern to bring German law closer to that of other European countries by importing the rules of the Vienna Convention on

International Sales (CISG), itself based on comparative research.—In *Great Britain*, too, legislative proposals are grounded on comparative work. One example is the Pearson *Report on Civil Liability and Compensation for Personal Injury and Death* (see below p. 669), and though England has not yet felt able to follow the United States, France, and Germany in adopting a 'right of privacy', a 'droit au respect de la vie privée' or an 'allgemeines Persönlichkeitsrecht' (see below p. 704), foreign law has been consulted on the question of its introduction. The English Law Commission likewise refers to foreign law whenever appropriate, as it did when the question was whether to confer contractual rights on third parties (see below p. 469).

Comparative law has been proving extremely useful in the countries of Central and Eastern Europe where legislators face the need to reconstruct their legal systems after the collapse of the Soviet system. The experience of other European countries helps them choose the solution which best suits their own legal traditions, overshadowed for much of the century though they have been. Even outside Europe states which used to be 'Soviet republics' are finding that foreign laws can be of assistance in framing domestic legislation, as have the Republic of China and many of the developing nations in Africa.

Of course one must proceed with intelligence and caution. If comparative analysis suggests the adoption of a particular solution to a problem arrived at in another system one cannot reject the proposal simply because the solution is foreign and *ipso facto* unacceptable. To those who object to the 'foreignness' of importations, RUDOLPH V. JHERING has given the conclusive answer:

'The reception of foreign legal institutions is not a matter of nationality, but of usefulness and need. No one bothers to fetch a thing from afar when he has one as good or better at home, but only a fool would refuse quinine just because it didn't grow in his back garden.' (*Geist des römischen Rechts*, Part I (9th edn., 1955) 8 f.)

Whenever it is proposed to adopt a foreign solution which is said to be superior, two questions must be asked: first, whether it has proved satisfactory in its country of origin, and secondly, whether it will work in the country where it is proposed to adopt it. It may well prove impossible to adopt, at any rate without modification, a solution tried and tested abroad because of differences in court procedures, the powers of the various authorities, the working of the economy, or the general social context into which it would have to fit.

The 'reception' of foreign law and the question whether and under what circumstances it can succeed has provoked an interesting controversy between KAHN-FREUND and WATSON (above p. 14–15). (See also STEIN and HIRSCH (above p. 13–14), all with further references.)

III

Another practical use of comparative law lies in the interpretation of national rules of law. On this matter the standard textbooks say nothing, dealing only with the old question whether a law should be given the meaning attributed to it by the legislator at the time of enactment, or whether the statute, treated as leading a kind of independent life of its own, may not be interpreted in the light of changing social conditions. Our present question is whether the interpreter of national rules is able or entitled to invoke a superior foreign solution. It is clear that such foreign material cannot be used in order to bypass unequivocal national rules: the principle of respect for an unambiguous enactment must not be infringed in any legal system. But the question may be raised when the construction of a rule is doubtful, or where there is a lacuna in the system which the judge must fill. The purely logical techniques at our disposal are insufficient, and it is unconvincing to play with analogy or the *argumentum e contrario*. The rule applied all over the Continent which determines how a judge must find the law when all else fails is formulated in the Swiss Civil Code, art. 1 pars. 2 and 3, as follows:

'If no statutory provisions can be found, the judge must apply customary law, failing which he must decide according to the rule he would, were he a legislator, decide to adopt. In so doing the judge must follow accepted doctrine and tradition.'

The principal thought underlying this provision is that gaps in the Swiss Civil Code are to be filled in the spirit of the national, that is, the Swiss, law. But will this do? If the judge is to decide in the way he would have decided had he been a legislator, must we not ask: how does a modern legislator reach his decisions? Now we have already seen that, to a great degree, the modern legislator takes his solutions from comparative law. Thus, thanks to the greater breadth of vision which we obtain from comparative law, we must include the comparative method among the criteria traditionally applied to the interpretation of national rules. There may still be questions about how far this can and should be done. For example, should one, in using the comparative law method of interpretation, consult only related systems like those of Switzerland and France, or also systems that are quite different in style, such as the Common Law? Can the judge choose whichever of the foreign solutions seems to him the best, or can he choose only a solution which is common to a number of other systems? May we, with the help of comparative law, reach an interpretation of our legal rules which is independent of, perhaps even at odds with, the conceptual structure of our own system? These questions, with the possible exception of the last one, should receive a bold rather than a timid answer (see further in ZWEIGERT (above p. 15)).

As may be seen from the law reports, comparative law has often helped the courts to clarify and amplify *German* law, though it is true that comparative law arguments are usually deployed in conjunction with normal methods of interpretation, and thus serve to confirm and support a result reached by a traditional route. One excellent example is the development by the Bundesgerichtshof of the principle that the victim of an invasion of the 'general right of personality' may claim damages at large (see Ch. 43 below), a principle which the Bundesgerichtshof sought to defend against criticism by saying that

'In almost all the legal systems which, like ours, put a prime value on the individual, damages for pain and suffering are regarded as the proper private law sanction for invasions of the personality. The availability of such damages does not adversely affect the freedom of the press, which those systems also treat as of fundamental importance, so the objection that the award of such damages in cases of invasions of personality improperly invades or unduly imperils the constitutionally guaranteed freedom of the press is clearly without substance' (BGHZ 39, 124, 132). In another decision the Bundesgerichtshof held that the claim for such damages was limited to cases where the invasion of the right of personality had been particularly serious; the Court observed that such a limitation 'is also to be found in Swiss law, which is more concerned with legal protection of the personality than the BGB (see art. 49 I OR)' (BGHZ 35, 363, 369). In another case a seriously disabled child who would never have been born at all but for the negligence of its mother's doctor in failing to detect its probable condition sued the doctor for 'wrongful life'. In dismissing the child's claim the Bundesgerichtshof referred to *McKay* v. *EssexHA* [1982] QB 1166 and comparable American decisions (BGHZ 86, 240, 250 f.). Further examples from German courts are analysed by DROBNIG (above p. 13).

In general it must be said that comparative law has a much greater role to play in the application and development of law than the German courts yet allow. The situation is rather better in other European countries such as Greece and Portugal, and above all in Switzerland, where the decisions of the Bundesgericht are replete with comparative law (see BGE 114 II 131 and UYTERHOVEN, above p. 14). The French Cour de Cassation is certainly deaf to any such arguments, but this is because it has adopted a style of judgment which precludes any reference to considerations of sociology, legal history, policy or comparative law (see below p. 123). It is different in the Common Law countries. Courts in England, Australia, Canada, and other commonwealth countries have long made reciprocal reference to each other's decisions and are now invoking continental law to a remarkable degree.

In *White* v. *Jones* [1995] 2 AC 207 the question was whether a lawyer had to pay for the harm suffered by a third party as a result of his incompetence in following the instructions of his client. The opinion of LORD GOFF contains a marvellous comparative treatment of the problem, with reference to the German doctrine of contracts with protective effect for third parties. (See, too, the opinion of STEYN LJ in the Court of Appeal ibid. at 236). In the event the House of Lords, like the Bundesgerichtshof (see BGH *JZ* 1966, 141, noted by LORENZ and BGH *NJW* 1977, 2073), granted the claim of the third party, but in tort rather than contract (see below p. 614). See also LORD GOFF in *Woolwich Building Soc'y* v. *Inland Revenue Comm'rs* [1993] AC 70, 174 (claim for restitution of taxes illegally exacted, see below p. 574); BINGHAM MR in *Interfoto Picture Library* v. *Stiletto Visual Programmes* [1988] 1 All ER 348, 352 ff. (good faith in negotiations); LORD GOFF in *Henderson* v. *Merrett Syndicates* [1994] 3 All ER 506, 523 ff. (concurrence of claims in contract and tort, see below p. 618); BINGHAM MR in *Kaye* v. *Robertson* [1991] FSR 62 (invasion of privacy, see below p. 704). See also the decision of the Supreme Court of Canada in *Norsk Pacific Steamship Co.* v. *Canadian National Ry.* [1992] 1 SCR 1021, which referred to numerous foreign decisions on the question of liability in tort for pure economic loss. In a note on this decision MARKESINIS makes a telling plea for courts to make more use of arguments from comparative law (109 *LQ Rev.* 5 (1993)). So, too, von BAR says: 'What a step forward it would be if the supreme courts of the states of the European Union accepted the idea of *persuasive authority*, if they felt bound to inquire whether the case before them had not already been decided somewhere else in the Union, and if, supposing there were a sort of "dominant European view" on the matter, they had to say why they were prevented from adopting it by the present state of their own law! If our courts were imbued with a European spirit, their reasoning would be greatly enlivened, and if the law, like other disciplines worthy of the name, were open to the world, its prospect of recapturing the intellectual elite of the country would be much enhanced.' ('Vereinheitlichung und Angleichung von Deliktsrecht in der Europäischen Union', *ZfRV* 35 (1994) 221, 231.)

When judges of a superior court are faced with a difficult problem of principle it is surely wrong for them to disregard solutions and arguments which have been proposed or adopted elsewhere just because they happen to emanate from foreign courts and writers. President ODERSKY of the Bundesgerichtshof was quite right to say:

'in giving his opinion the national judge is not only entitled to engage with the views of other courts and legal systems; he is also entitled, when applying his own law and naturally giving full weight to its proper construction and development, to take note of the fact that a particular solution conduces to the harmonisation of European law. In appropriate cases this argument enables him at the end of the day to adopt the solutions of other legal systems, and it is an argument he should use with increasing frequency as the integration of Europe proceeds.' ('Harmonisierende Auslegung und europäische Rechtskultur', *ZEuP* 1994, 1, 2.)

Taking comparative arguments into account certainly means more work for the judge, but nowadays, thanks to the researches of comparatists, there are many areas in which foreign material is much more accessible; in any case, even on the continent where the principle *iura novit curia* obtains, the court can look to the parties to proffer such material and if necessary insist that they do so.

The situation is different when *uniform laws* are being interpreted. Such laws normally result from international conventions, governmental co-operation, or supranational or international legislation, and since the underlying aim is to unify the law, their construction and development must be geared to this goal. This means that when a national judge is faced with a uniform law, he must not simply deploy his trusty old national rules of construction but modify them so as to arrive at an internationally acceptable result which promotes legal uniformity. This often calls for a *comparative law interpretation*: the judge must look to the foreign rules which formed the basis of the provision to be applied, he must take account of how courts and writers abroad interpret it, and he must make good any gaps in it with general principles of law which he has educed from the relevant national legal systems.

For details see LUTTER (above p. 14), especially at p. 604, and KROPHOLLER (above p. 14) 258 ff., 278 ff., 298 ff.—This is undoubtedly a hard and demanding task, and it may be beyond the powers of national judges who have to apply uniform law only very seldom. The only sure way to avoid national divergences in the construction and development of a uniform law is to grant jurisdiction to an international court. For the member states of the Common Market the Court of Justice of the European Communities is the leading example: it has already used the method of comparative legal interpretation in a large number of decisions with great success. On this see BLECKMANN, DAIG, PESCATORE, and MARTINY (above pp. 13–14).

IV

1. Comparative law also has an important function in legal education. In legal education as in legal science generally it is too limiting smugly to study only one's national law, and for universities and law schools so to act at a time when world society is becoming increasingly mobile is appallingly unprogressive. Comparative law offers the law student a whole new dimension; from it he can learn to respect the special legal cultures of other peoples, he will understand his own law better, he can develop the critical standards which might lead to its improvement, and he will learn how rules of law are conditioned by social facts and what different forms they can take. What he learns in this science, as in others, will prove useful in practice too. Here we need only mention how useful comparative law is in conflict of laws, for the interpretation of treaties, for those who are involved in international adjudication, arbitration, or administration, or concerned with the unification of law. The younger generation of lawyers, and probably their successors as well, will be faced with an unparalleled 'internationalization' of legal life. But it is the general educational value of comparative law which is most important: it shows that the rule currently operative is only one of

several possible solutions; it provides an effective antidote to uncritical faith
in legal doctrine; it teaches us that what is often presented as pure natural
law proves to be nothing of the sort as soon as one crosses a frontier, and
it keeps reminding us that while doctrine and categories are essential in
any system, they can sometimes become irrelevant to the functioning and
efficacy of the law in action and degenerate into futile professorial games.

2. Despite all this, and notwithstanding the considerable improvement in
the last few decades, the place occupied by comparative law in the university
curriculum is still rather modest.

In *Germany* the teaching of comparative law varies quite widely from university to
university. For the moment almost all universities offer a general 'Introduction to
Comparative Law' which, in addition to giving an overview of the legal systems of
the world, covers the aims and methods of the discipline and its relationship with
other specialties with an international legal flavour. Rather less common are
lecture-courses on a particular legal system, such as French law, or a group of related
legal systems, such as the Common Law; even where such courses are on offer, it is
noticeable that universities tend to specialize in, say, English law, or French law.
Even less common is the 'comparison of institutions' in which one tries to see what
all the relevant legal systems, or several of them, do in a particular area of law, such
as contract or company law, and treats it comparatively from beginning to end, with
each national rule being seen in conjunction with its functional counterpart in the
other legal systems. But if the teaching of comparative law is perhaps just acceptable,
the picture is wretched indeed when one comes to the vital question of the place of
comparative law in *examinations*. Comparative law has never been a compulsory
examination subject, although relevant questions are occasionally set as a test of
the candidate's 'general juridical culture'. A student will admittedly be examined in
the subjects which fall within his chosen 'group of elective subjects', though not much
weight may be given to it, but in many of the *Länder* comparative law is regrettably
yoked to family law or the law of succession in a single option. It is small comfort to
learn that elsewhere in Europe complaints are raised about the provincialism of legal
education; see the reports on the situation in Belgium (Meulders-Klein), France
(Mouly), Greece (Yokaris), Great Britain (Jolowicz), Italy (Sacco), and Switzerland
(Stoffel), published in *Rev. int. dr. comp.* 40 (1988) 703.

Although the need to open legal education up to comparative law is an
urgent one everywhere, Germany faces a unique obstacle. In other European
countries individual law faculties are fairly free to decide what subjects to
teach and examine and to adapt them, if necessary, to the changing world.
Law faculties in Germany do not have this freedom, and will never have it
as long as they remain under the curse which deprives them of all initiative
in this area, namely the system whereby future lawyers are examined by the
state. Germany is the only country in Europe, almost in the whole world,
where the state acts as 'external' examiner at the end of a candidate's legal
studies in an examination whose content is prescribed in detail by statute.
Under this system it makes no difference how good, wide-ranging or im-

aginative the teaching in the faculty is, or how well the student performs during his time at university, especially if he studies abroad. If this is ever to change in Germany legal education must be 'deregulated', so that, like everywhere else in the world, examinations are conducted by the university and not by the state, and law faculties finally acquire some freedom of action and a chance to compete with each other.

The prospect of any such deregulation is still poor: with a few honourable exceptions the ministries of justice in the Länder are in thrall to the practice of examination by the state, and most faculties have no interest in getting the system changed. For relief one may have to look, as in many other cases, to the European Union. Under the Rome Treaty foreign lawyers wishing to render legal services or establish a law practice in Germany must be treated basically on the same footing as German lawyers, and if a large number of young foreigners with a good legal education came to Germany, it might become politically possible to overcome the opposition of the state examination bodies and the even more regrettable indifference of many law faculties.

3. In order to see how the teaching of comparative law will and should develop, we must look at law teaching as a whole.

The critical feature of the academic teaching of law today is the constant increase in the bulk of the material to be learnt. Students in the past could learn to think like lawyers by concentrating on private law, but nowadays it is necessary to master not only criminal law, which has not increased so much in volume, but also the vast bulk of constitutional and administrative law, business law, labour law, and social security law. It is no longer possible to cram comparative law and legal sociology into a law course which already has to contain so much material.

From this it follows that we must *integrate comparative law into the teaching of national law*. That means that the problem being studied must be set in the context of the solutions obtaining in the most significant legal systems; then one must make a critical appraisal in order to determine which solution is best suited here and now to the national society as it is. Only in this way can one highlight the characteristics of the solution which is accepted in the positive law, and at the same time encourage the reforming spirit and develop a sense of how the law can be improved. Only in this way can it be shown that in certain areas—such as contract law, tort, and company law—a *ius commune* for all Europe is beginning to develop or already exists.

It follows from this that a textbook of comparative law should not try to stuff the student full of further foreign legal data; it should rather lay out the different approaches to a problem, state the critical arguments which illuminate and enliven it, and then indicate which is the best solution here and now. This involves that 'national' textbooks should be rewritten in the light of comparative law, and that in the long run all teachers of law should master the comparative method so as to obtain the necessary information for themselves.

As early as 1934 ROSCOE POUND expressed, more precisely and tersely, the view here put forward:

'What is aimed at by such a course [sc. in comparative law] may be done more effectively by a group of teachers who are conscious of the possibilities of comparative law in their daily teaching and know how to realise those possibilities. Hence I suggest that the law teacher of the future should ground himself in comparative law and should bring out continually other modes of treatment of the questions he takes up from the standpoint of our law, as shown by the civil law and the modern codes, just as he canvasses the modes of treatment in different English-speaking jurisdictions. I suggest that he continually seek to lead the student by concrete examples to appreciate that there is no one doctrine or rule or institution or conception for every case in every land in every time. In other words, I believe comparative law will best be taught, for the purposes of our professional instruction, in the course of teaching the law of the land, except as graduate students are able, after due training in the civil law, to go deeply into some of its particular problems' (above p. 14, p. 168). Such 'integrated' law teaching has been opposed by SCHLESINGER and NEU-MAYER (*Festschrift Zweigert* 507 f.) and defended afresh by KÖTZ (*RabelsZ* 36 (1972) 570 ff.).

V

1. *Unification of Law—Concept and Function*

The final function of comparative law to be dealt with here is its significant role in the preparation of projects for the international unification of law. The political aim behind such unification is to reduce or eliminate, so far as desirable and possible, the discrepancies between the national legal systems by inducing them to adopt common principles of law. The method used in the past and still often practised today is to draw up a uniform law on the basis of work by experts in comparative law and to incorporate it in a multi-partite treaty which obliges the signatories, as a matter of international law, to adopt and apply the uniform law as their municipal law. For states which are members of the European Union, the harmonization of law by supra-national means (Community guidelines and directives) is of ever-increasing significance.

Unification cannot be achieved by simply conjuring up an ideal law on any topic and hoping to have it adopted. One must first find what is common to the jurisdictions concerned and incorporate that in the uniform law. Where there are areas of difference, one must reconcile them either by adopting the best existing variant or by finding, through comparative methods, a new solution which is better and more easily applied than any of the existing ones. Preparatory studies in comparative law are absolutely essential here;

without them one cannot discover the points of agreement or disagreement in the different legal systems of the world, let alone decide which solution is the best. A model of such a preparatory study is ERNST RABEL, *Das Recht des Warenkaufs* I (1936: reprinted 1957); II (1958), which was of vital importance for the unification of international sales law.

The advantage of unified law is that it makes international legal business easier. In the area they cover, unified laws avoid the hazards of applying private international law and foreign substantive law. Unified law thus reduces the legal risks of international business, and thereby gives relief both to the businessman who plans the venture and to the judge who has to resolve the disputes to which it gives rise. Thus unified law promotes greater legal predictability and security. International treaties for the unification of law often try to obtain the accession of all the states in the world, but none has yet succeeded. All unification of law so far has been limited in its geographical area of application, by force of circumstance rather than by design. Sometimes, however, schemes for the unification of law are designed to apply only within a limited area (regional unification of law, for example, in Scandinavia or the Benelux countries; here one can include also the *rapprochement* or harmonization of laws envisaged by the Treaty of the European Economic Community).

Multilateral treaties are very difficult to achieve and rather clumsy in operation; furthermore, their results in the field of unification of law are not very satisfactory (see 3 below). Accordingly, one must think of alternative means of achieving the goal. One way would be to produce model laws, a method which has been used for the internal unification of law within the British Commonwealth and especially in the United States. This method is less heavy-handed since the adoption of such laws by the different countries is a matter of recommendation rather than of obligation.

Other methods have been proposed by RENÉ DAVID in his encyclopedia article: for example, the creation of a new and universal *ius commune*, applicable to international relationships to which national systems of law may be insufficiently adapted.—DAVID also urges a more widespread and international use of the device of *Restatements of the Law*, as practised in the United States. Every several state in the United States has its own private and commercial law, and the legislative competence of the Congress in Washington is rather limited. Nevertheless the laws of the several states have a great deal in common, thanks to the Common Law tradition. This common law in each principal area of law is set out in a series of books, called *Restatements*, with additional volumes which give the deviations in each state (see below pp. 251 f.).

Welcome though any idea is which tends to the greater harmonization of laws, overall the most suitable method for the immediate future seems to be that of *model laws*, provided that they are carefully drafted on the foundations of comparative law.

Running parallel with uniform enacted laws there may arise a kind of universal contract law, since in certain spheres of activity (such as wholesale trade in primary commodities, banking, insurance, and transport) there are general conditions or customs of business which are the same or similar in many countries. Here one might instance the Conditions of Business of the London Corn Trade Association, the General Conditions for the Supply of Plant and Machinery for Export, produced by the UN Economic Commission for Europe, and the so-called Incoterms (such as fob and cif clauses) and the Uniform Customs and Practices on Documentary Credits drawn up by the International Chamber of Commerce in Paris. Many observers think of these rules as forming a nascent, perhaps actual, *lex mercatoria* of a new and autonomous variety (on the whole question see SPICKHOFF, *RabelsZ* 56 (1992) 116 and KROPHOLLER, *Internationales Privatrecht* (2nd edn. 1994) §11 I 3, both with references to the extensive literature).

2. *Areas and Agencies*

Since the end of the nineteenth century the unification of law has produced its main results in private law, commercial law, trade and labour law, in copyright and industrial property law, and in the law of transport by rail, sea, and air, as well as in parts of procedural law, especially in connection with the recognition of foreign judgments and awards. Even where the substantive private law should not, or cannot, be unified, it may be possible to achieve a harmony of outcome by unifying the rules of conflicts of law, and thereby avoid differences attributable to the accident of the forum.

It is in private law in the widest sense that the world forces tending towards the integration of law are at their strongest.

The results already achieved by way of unification of law are too numerous to be listed here (compare ZWEIGERT/KROPHOLLER, *Quellen des Internationalen Einheitsrechts*, 3 vols. (1971 ff.)). The League of Nations and the United Nations Organization have done much for the law of negotiable instruments and of arbitration, the Rome Institute for the Unification of Private Law (UNIDROIT, founded in 1926) has worked on the law of sale of goods, the Hague Conferences have helped in private international law, and various international organizations have advanced the unification of the law of transport, copyright, and labour. In 1966 the United Nations Organization resolved to set up a Commission for International and Commercial Law (UNCITRAL) charged with promoting the harmonization and unification of international trade law. Its greatest achievement so far is the Convention on Contracts for the International Sale of Goods (CISG) concluded in Vienna in April 1980 (see VON CAEMMERER/SCHLECHTRIEM, *Kommentar zum Einheitlichen UN-Kaufrecht* (2nd edn. 1995)).

3. *Experience*

In the past, enthusiasts have planned to unify the law of the whole world; people now realize that only the specific needs of international legal business can justify the vast amount of energy which is required to carry through any project for the unification of law. These needs are most pressing in the fields of law mentioned above (less, for example, in land law, family law, and the law of inheritance), and even there only for particular topics or specific institutions.

One must not underestimate the difficulties involved in the preparation and adoption of uniform laws. Some of these have psychological causes, such as dislike of novelty or pride in the national law, others are technical (differences in legal concepts or presuppositions, which only intensive preparatory studies in comparative law can overcome) or political: national parliaments are reluctant to adopt in their entirety the agreed drafts of international conferences. These difficulties are lessened somewhat if the uniform law is made applicable only to international transactions. Then each state has two concurrent sets of rules in the same area. This is what happens in the sale of goods, for example: internal transactions are covered by municipal law, while CISG, if adopted in the state whose courts are seised of the matter, applies to 'international' sales, that is, contracts of sale between parties with places of business in different states.

When uniform laws are applied by national courts, there is always the risk that the uniformity of law apparently achieved in that area will be eroded by its being differently construed and applied in the different member states. This risk cannot be wholly excluded by even the most careful drafting. Just as in any country a Supreme Court of Cassation or Appeal is needed to procure that the law is uniformly applied, so in the long run an international court is necessary to ensure the uniform application of uniform laws. The uniform construction of the law of the European Economic Union is guaranteed by the Court of the European Communities (arts. 164 ff., Treaty of Rome), and it is to be welcomed that the member states have also entrusted to this court the power to interpret legal concepts used in certain treaties made pursuant to art. 220, Treaty of Rome. But apart from a few minor exceptions, this is the only court so far with power to give a uniform construction to uniform law. Until an international court is set up, the best that can be done is to procure that at least the highest courts of the member nations know what their opposite numbers have decided (see above p. 20). If a uniform law is being differently construed in the different member states, it is impermissible to have recourse to the rules of conflicts law in order to determine whether in a particular case it is the law as applied, for example, in France or as applied in Germany which is to control (*aliter* the French Court of Cassation in *Hocke*, Rev. crit. 53 (1964) 264, and the Federal German Supreme Court,

IPRspr. 1962–1963 no. 44). If the substantive law has been unified, it is the substantive law which must control, and not the rules of conflicts law. In brief: unification of substantive law excludes the application of private international law. Until we have an international court for the construction of uniform laws, the highest municipal courts should adopt as their own whichever construction, proposed or actually adopted elsewhere, seems to them the best and proper one.

VI

If barriers to trade within the European Union are to be overcome, legislation in the form of ratification of international treaties or Regulations and Directives is clearly indispensable in certain areas. Even so, it is increasingly being questioned whether legislation is really the best way to unify the whole of European law. Unification hitherto has been sporadic, impinging on specific points only, so that in some areas the result is a patchwork of overlapping scraps of national and unified law with ill-defined areas of operation and different animating principles; far from simplifying the application of the law, unification of this kind has made it much more difficult. It is now clear that unified legislation can deprive member states and their courts of the freedom to alter and develop their law and introduce a barrier to change which thwarts the adoption of much needed adjustments at the national level. True, a state can always seek to have the unified law changed, but it would take years of negotiation to obtain the agreement of all the other states involved even if it were possible at all.

The point is developed in Kötz, 'Rechtsvereinheitlichung—Nutzen, Kosten, Methoden, Ziele', *RabelsZ* 50 (1986) 1; Behrens, 'Voraussetzungen und Grenzen der Rechtsfortbildung durch Rechtsvereinheitlichung', *RabelsZ* 50 (1986) 19.

Accordingly people are now beginning to see that legislation is not necessarily the ideal way to unify the law; it has costs as well as gains, and they must be soberly calculated and weighed against each other. The law of Europe cannot be unified by sporadic texts. What we need is to 'Europeanize' the way lawyers think, write, and learn. Legal history and comparative law teach us as much, and people are now readier to accept it. The idea that legislation is the only possible source of law is an error from the Age of Enlightenment which should have had its quietus long ago. German and French law today do not turn exclusively on the wording of legislative texts, and European law cannot turn exclusively on European unifying legislation. Years ago Coing was quite right to say that

'unification of law cannot come about simply by laying down uniform rules, as was sometimes thought in the nineteenth century. In many cases it may be necessary, but it is also essential that it be accompanied by progressive legal scholarship on which the courts in different countries can rely. . . . Our mission must be to reinduce in our jurists an attitude of mind and a common way of thought which will enable them to do justice to the unified rules and apply them in a consistent manner' ('Jus commune, nationale Kodifikation und internationale Abkommen, drei historische Formen der Rechtsvereinheitlichung', in *Le nuove frontiere del diritto* (Atti del Congreso di Bari) I, 171, 192 (1979)).

It is significant that the herald of this mission was a *legal historian*. COING was not writing on a *tabula rasa* or proposing anything novel when he referred to a common European outlook on law: he was reminding us of something we have tended to forget, namely that right up to the eighteenth century, when the idea of codification took root, Europe actually did enjoy a unity of legal outlook under the *ius commune*. Codification then made its triumphal progress through the nascent nation states with the deplorable result that lawyers stopped looking beyond their national borders. But two centuries of legal nationalism have not destroyed the fundamental unity of European private law, as research in legal history has demonstrated; it has also shown us that even the Common Law of England was affected by its contacts with continental legal culture.

See ZIMMERMANN, 'Das römisch-kanonische ius commune als Grundlage europäischer Rechtseinheit', *JZ* 1992, 8; SCHMIDLIN, 'Gibt es ein gemeineuropäisches System des Privatrechts?' in SCHMIDLIN (ed.), *Vers un droit européen commun/Skizzen zum gemeineuropäischen Privatrecht* (1994) 33; SCHULZE, 'Allgemeine Rechtsgrundsätze und europäisches Privatrecht', *ZEuP* 1993, 442; KNÜTEL, 'Rechtseinheit in Europa und römisches Recht', *ZEuP* 1994, 244; ZIMMERMANN, 'Der europäische Charakter des englischen Rechts, Historische Verbindungen zwischen civil law und common law', *ZEuP* 1993, 4; GORLA/MOCCIA, 'A "Revisiting" of the Comparison between Continental Law and English Law (16th–19th Century)', 2 *J Leg. Hist.* 143 (1981); MOCCIA, 'English Law Attitudes to the Civil Law', 2 *J Leg. Hist.* 157 (1981); HELMHOLZ, 'Continental Law and Common Law: Historical Strangers or Companions?' [1990] *Duke LJ* 1207; NÖRR, 'The European Side of the English Law, A Few Comments from a Continental Historian', in COING/NÖRR (eds.), *Englische und kontinentale Rechtsgeschichte: Eine Forschungsprojekt* (1985) 15; GORDLEY, 'Common Law and Civil Law: Eine überholte Unterscheidung', *ZEuP* 1993, 498; GLENN, 'La civilisation de la common law', *Rev. int. dr. comp.* 45 (1993) 559.

This presents comparative law with a challenge. No longer can it confine itself to making proposals for the reform of national law, valuable though that is, for as long as it does so, it will inevitably be tainted with nationalism, regarding national legal systems as given and fixed, and looking to divergences and convergences only to see what can be of use to them. Comparative law must now go beyond national systems and provide a comparative basis on which to develop a system of law for all Europe; it can do this by taking particular areas of law such as contract, tort, credit arrangements, company law, and family law and showing what rules are generally accepted throughout Europe and whether they are developing on convergent or divergent lines. What is needed is a body of legal literature which presents the different areas of law from a European perspective, not focusing on any particular legal system or its systematics and not addressed to readers of any particular nation. Of course such works must take account of rules of French, German, and English law, but they should treat them as local variations on a theme, a theme common to all Europe. They must take account of the powerful social policies which have influenced private law throughout Europe, such as the protection of the consumer and the environment, and social security provision in the event of accident, illness, and unemployment. They must not confine themselves to the substance of the law, they must also portray the way it is created and applied, and study the legislative processes in the different countries, their method of applying the law, the style of their judgments, and the training and professional activities of their legal practitioners. The principal aim of the enterprise is not to ascertain the rules, or even compare them with a view to improving the national law: it is to make people conscious of European private law as a subject for research and teaching, common to all the countries of Europe.

These issues have been much discussed in recent years. See, for example, the articles by COING, DAVID, and SACCO in CAPPELLETTI (ed.), *New Perspectives for a Common Law of Europe* (1978); KÖTZ, 'Gemeineuropäisches Zivilrecht', *Festschrift Zweigert* (1981) 481; KRAMER, 'Europäische Privatrechtsvereinheitlichung', *JBl.* 1988, 477; COING, 'Europäisierung der Rechtswissenschaft', *NJW* 1990, 937; HONDIUS, 'Naar een Europese rechtenstudie', *Ned. Jur. (Speciaal)* 1991, 517; FLESSNER, 'Rechtsvereinheitlichung durch Rechtswissenschaft und Juristenausbildung', *RabelsZ* 56 (1992) 243; REMIEN, 'Illusion und Realität eines europäischen Privatrechts', *JZ* 1992, 277; REMIEN, 'Ansätze für ein Europäisches Privatrecht?', *ZVglRWiss* (1988) 105; ULMER, 'Vom deutschen zum europäischen Privatrecht?', *JZ* 1992, 1; MÜLLER-GRAFF, 'Europäisches Gemeinschaftsrecht und Privatrecht', *NJW* 1993, 13; MÜLLER-GRAFF, *Privatrecht und europäisches Gemeinschaftsrecht* (2nd edn. 1991); see also KÖTZ, 'A Common Private Law for Europe', in DE WITTE/FORDER (eds.), *The Common Law of Europe and the Future of Legal Education* (1992) 31; KOOPMANS, 'Toward a New "Ius Commune"', ibid.; KRAMER, 'Vielfalt und Einheit der Wertungen im Europäischen Privatrecht', *Festschrift Koller* (1993) 729; GOODE, 'The European Law School', 13 *LS* 1 (1994).—Two periodicals started in 1993 proclaim on their masthead their devotion to the development of European private law (*Zeitschrift für europäisches Privatrecht* and *European Review of Private Law*).—A 'Commission of European Contract Law' under the presidency of OLE LANDO has been occupied since 1980 with the production of 'Principles of European Contract Law'; see LANDO, 'Principles of European Contract Law, An Alternative or a Precursor of European Legislation', *RabelsZ* 56 (1992) 261; DROBNIG, 'Ein Vertragsrecht für Europa', *Festschrift Steindorff* (1990) 1149. The first volume of the Commission's conclusions has been published:

LANDO/BEALE (ed.), *The Principles of European Contract Law, Part I: Performance, Non-performance and Remedies* (1995).

In 1989 the European Parliament in Strasbourg passed a resolution (OJ EC No. C 158/400) requesting 'that a start be made on the necessary preparatory work on drawing up a common European Code of Private Law', but it is very far from certain that the necessary political will exists at present; nor is it clear that any actual need for it has been demonstrated or that it falls within the competence of the European Union.

On this see TILMANN, 'Zur Entwicklung eines europäischen Zivilrechts', *Festschrift Oppenhoff* (1985) 495; TILMANN, *ZEuP* 1995, 534; GANDOLFI, 'Pour un code européen des contrats', *Rev. int. dr. comp.* 91 (1992) 70; LANDO, 'Is Codification Needed in Europe?', *Eur. Rev. P. L.* 1 (1993) 157; MENGONI, *L'Europa dei codici o un codice per l'Europa* (1993); see also the articles in HARTKAMP and others (eds.), *Towards a European Civil Code* (1994).

One thing is certain, however. One cannot even begin to contemplate a European Civil Code until the way has been prepared by thoroughgoing research. History tells us as much. For example, the law in pre-revolutionary France used to be very diverse, with customary laws in the North and received Roman Law in the South, until in the sixteenth and seventeenth centuries a series of famous writers, including DUMOULIN, COQUILLE, and DOMAT, gradually elicited out of them a 'droit commun français'. It never actually existed as strict law anywhere, but was so successful in providing a doctrinal basis for the unification of French law that the eventual Code civil could be finalized in four months (see below p. 82). Again, when EUGEN HUBER published his work on *System und Geschichte des Schweizer-ischen Privatrechts* in 1893 there was really no such thing as Swiss private law, only a great diversity of private laws in the cantons. Greatly to his credit, HUBER based his presentation of the cantonal laws on the concept of a Swiss private law, more ideal than real, and when the Confederation finally opted for the unification of Swiss private law it was his research that provided the basis that was needed. Legal scholars today are faced with a similar challenge. They too must use the comparative method, though their material is not just the customary laws of France or the cantonal laws of Switzerland but the positive private law of all the countries in Europe. This is some task! But if we succeed in it, we will have produced the indispensable intellectual groundwork for a European Civil Code against the day when political and practical considerations enable it to be put on the agenda.

3

The Method of Comparative Law

ANCEL, *Utilité et méthodes de droit comparé* (1971).
CONSTANTINESCO, *Rechtsvergleichung* II: *Die rechtsvergleichende Methode* (1972).
DÖLLE, 'Rechtsdogmatik und Rechtsvergleichung', *RabelsZ* 34 (1970) 403.
DROBNIG, 'Methodenfragen der Rechtsvergleichung im Lichte der "International Encyclopedia of Comparative Law"', in: *Ius privatum gentium, Festschrift Max Rheinstein* I (1969) 221.
EÖRSI, *Comparative Civil (Private) Law* (1979).
ESSER, *Grundsatz und Norm in der richterlichen Fortbildung des Privatrechts* (2nd edn. 1964).
FIKENTSCHER, *Methoden des Rechts in vergleichender Darstellung*, 4 vols. (1975–7).
FRANKENBERG, 'Critical Comparisons: Re-Thinking Comparative Law', 26 *Harv. Int. LJ* 457 (1985).
JESCHECK, *Entwicklung, Aufgaben und Methoden der Strafrechtsvergleichung* (1955).
KAHN-FREUND, 'Comparative Law as an Academic Subject', 82 *LQ Rev.* 40 (1966).
KÖTZ, 'Rechtsvergleichung und Rechtsdogmatik', *RabelsZ* 54 (1990) 203.
NEUMAYER, 'Ziele und Methoden der Rechtsvergleichung', in: *Recueil des travaux suisses présentés au Congrès international de droit comparé* 9 (1976) 45.
RABEL, *Aufgabe und Notwendigkeit der Rechtsvergleichung* (1925), reprinted in: Rabel, *Gesammelte Aufsätze* III (ed. Leser, 1967) 1.
——, 'Die Fachgebiete des Kaiser-Wilhelm-Instituts für ausländisches und internationales Privatrecht', in: *25 Jahre Kaiser Wilhelm-Gesellschaft zur Förderung der Wissenschaften* III (1937) 77, reprinted in: Rabel, *Gesammelte Aufsätze* III (ed. Leser, 1967) 180.
RHEINSTEIN, 'Comparative Law—Its Functions, Methods and Usages', 22 *Ark. L. Rev.* 415, printed in: RHEINSTEIN, *Gesammelte Schriften* I (1979) 251.
——, *Einführung in die Rechtsvergleichung* (2nd edn. 1987).
SANDROCK, *Über Sinn und Methode der zivilistischen Rechtsvergleichung* (1966).
SCHLESINGER, 'The Common Core of Legal Systems, An Emerging Subject of Comparative Study', in: *Twentieth Century Comparative and Conflicts Law, Legal Essays in Honor of Hessel E. Yntema* (1961) 65.
ZACHER (ed.), *Methodische Probleme des Sozialrechtsvergleichs* (1977).
ZWEIGERT, 'Rechtsvergleichung, System und Dogmatik', *Festschrift Bötticher* (1969) 443.
——, 'Die kritische Wertung in der Rechtsvergleichung, *Festschrift Schmitthoff* (1973) 403.

I

ACCORDING to GUSTAV RADBRUCH, 'sciences which have to busy themselves with their own methodology are sick sciences' (*Einführung in die
Rechtswissenschaft* (12th edn., 1969) 253). Though generally true, this is not
a diagnosis which fits modern comparative law. For one thing, comparatists
all over the world are perfectly unembarrassed about their methodology, and
see themselves as being still at the experimental stage. For another, there has
been very little systematic writing about the methods of comparative law.
There are thus no signs of the disease in question. The same is true of comparative law as practised by legislators for a long time. Since the great codifications of Western Europe, national enactments and international
regulations of all kinds have been preceded by critical and comparative sur-
veys. This has been very successful and, because of its success, has given rise
to no methodological worries. The same is true of modern comparative law
as a critical method of legal *science*, as described and practised by RABEL,
though the reasons for this are different: so recent a discipline could not
be expected to have an established set of methodological principles. Even
today the right method must largely be discovered by gradual trial and error.
Experienced comparatists have learnt that a detailed method cannot be laid
down in advance; all one can do is to take a method as a hypothesis and test
its usefulness and practicability against the results of actually working with
it. Earlier theories, some examples of which have been given in the previous
chapter, committed the error of supposing that the basis, goals, and methods
of comparative law could be determined a priori from a philosophy or
scheme of law. Even today it is extremely doubtful whether one could draw
up a logical and self-contained methodology of comparative law which had
any claim to work perfectly. Most probably there will always remain in comparative law, as in legal science generally, let alone in the practical application of law, an area where only sound judgment, common sense, or even
intuition can be of any help. For when it comes to evaluation, to determining
which of the various solutions is the best, the only ultimate criterion is often
the practical evidence and the immediate sense of appropriateness.

If there is a 'sick science' in RADBRUCH's sense today it is not comparative
law but rather legal science as a whole. Though the hollowness of the traditional attitudes—unreflecting, self-assured, and doctrinaire—has increasingly been demonstrated, they are astonishingly vital. New and more realistic
methods, especially those of empirical sociology, have been developed, but it
is mere wishful thinking to suppose that they characterize our legal thought.
One of these new methods is comparative law and it is preeminently adapted
to putting legal science on a sure and realistic basis. Comparative law not
only shows up the emptiness of legal dogmatism and systematics but,

because it is forced to abandon national doctrines and come directly to grips with the demands of life for suitable rules, it develops a new and particular system, related to those demands in life and therefore functional and appropriate. Comparative law does not simply criticize what it finds, but can claim to show the way to a better mastery of the legal material, to deeper insights into it, and thus, in the end, to better law. It therefore makes good sense to pay quite close attention to the method of comparative law—not because comparative law is sick, but because legal science in general is sick, and comparative law can cure it.

We are concerned not only with a method of *thinking*—the principles whose application gives the right results—but also a method of *working*: How does one actually set about a task in comparative law? This at least the beginner can expect from an introductory work, to be told the lessons of experience so that he does not set to work without any guidance at all, and waste his time in unprofitable detours.

II

As in all intellectual activity, every investigation in comparative law begins with the posing of a question or the setting of a working hypothesis—in brief, an idea. Often it is the feeling of dissatisfaction with the solution in one's own system which drives one to inquire whether perhaps other legal systems may not have produced something better. Contrariwise, it may be the pure and disinterested investigation of foreign legal systems which sharpens one's criticism of one's own law and so produces the idea or working hypothesis.

The basic methodological principle of all comparative law is that of *functionality*. From this basic principle stem all the other rules which determine the choice of laws to compare, the scope of the undertaking, the creation of a system of comparative law, and so on. Incomparables cannot usefully be compared, and in law the only things which are comparable are those which fulfil the same function. This proposition may seem self-evident, but many of its applications, though familiar to the experienced comparatist, are not obvious to the beginner. The proposition rests on what every comparatist learns, namely that the legal system of every society faces essentially the same problems, and solves these problems by quite different means though very often with similar results. The question to which any comparative study is devoted must be posed in purely functional terms; the problem must be stated without any reference to the concepts of one's own legal system. Thus instead of asking, 'What formal requirements are there for sales contracts in foreign law?' it is better to ask, 'How does foreign law protect parties from surprise, or from being held to an agreement not seriously intended?' Instead of asking, 'How does foreign law regulate *Vorerbschaft* and *Nacherbschaft*?'

one should try to find out how the foreign law sets about satisfying the wish of a testator to control his estate long after his death. To take another example: only in Germany does one meet with the concept of 'disappearance of enrichment' (*Wegfall der Bereicherung*, §818 par. 3 BGB), yet all systems must resolve the conflict which arises when a person who is bound to restore a thing received under an invalid contract no longer has the thing to restore. One must never allow one's vision to be clouded by the concepts of one's own national system; always in comparative law one must focus on the concrete problem.

The beginner often jumps to the conclusion that a foreign system has 'nothing to report' on a particular problem. The principle of functionality applies here. Even experienced comparatists sometimes look for the rule they want only in the particular place in the foreign system where their experience of their own system leads them to expect it: they are unconsciously looking at the problem with the eyes of their own system. If one's comparative researches seem to be leading to the conclusion that the foreign system has 'nothing to report' one must rethink the original question and purge it of all the dogmatic accretions of one's own system. The German legal system in particular is conceptually so highly developed that its practitioners think of it as being almost a product of natural law and have great difficulty in disentangling themselves from its concepts. It is only when one has roamed through the entire foreign legal system without avail, asking a local lawyer as a last resort, that one can safely conclude that it really does not have a solution to the problem. This hardly ever happens, but even if it does, that is no reason to terminate one's comparative study. To ask *why* a foreign system has not felt the need to produce a legal solution for a particular problem may lead to interesting conclusions about it, or about one's own law. Sometimes the solution in one's own system is quite superfluous, thought up in the interests of theoretical completeness by the academics who drafted the Code (compare the 'joke transaction' (*Scherzgeschäft*) of §118 BGB). Often a solution is provided by custom or social practice, and has never become specifically legal in form. The same is true if there is something about the structure of the foreign society which makes the adoption of a legal solution unnecessary. Again an inquiry into the source of so different a sense of justice may produce interesting conclusions.

This, then, is the negative aspect of the principle of functionality, that the comparatist must eradicate the preconceptions of his native legal system; the positive aspect tells us which areas of the foreign legal system to investigate in order to find the analogue to the solution which interests him.

The basic principle for the student of foreign legal systems is to avoid all limitations and restraints. This applies particularly to the question of 'sources of law'; the comparatist must treat as a source of law whatever moulds or affects the living law in his chosen system, whatever the lawyers there would treat as a source of law, and he must accord those sources the same relative weight and value as they do. He must attend, just as they do, to statutory and customary law, to case-law and legal writing, to standard-form contracts and general conditions of business, to trade usage and custom. This is quite essential for the comparative method. But it is not enough. To prepare us for his view of the full requirements of the comparative method, RABEL says: 'Our task is as hard as scientific ideals demand . . .' and then he proceeds:

'The student of the problems of law must encompass the law of the whole world, past and present, and everything that affects the law, such as geography, climate and race, developments and events shaping the course of a country's history—war, revolution, colonisation, subjugation—religion and ethics, the ambition and creativity of individuals, the needs of production and consumption, the interests of groups, parties and classes. Ideas of every kind have their effect, for it is not just feudalism, liberalism and socialism which produce different types of law; legal institutions once adopted may have logical consequences; and not least important is the striving for a political or legal ideal. Everything in the social, economic and legal fields interacts. The law of every developed people is in constant motion, and the whole kaleidoscopic picture is one which no one has ever clearly seen' (above p. 32, at pp. 3 ff.).

But one must be realistic. It is too much to say that one must systematically master all this knowledge and then keep it in mind before one is allowed to embark on any kind of comparative work. But RABEL's demands are justified if they are understood to mean that the comparatist must make every effort to learn and remember as much as he can about foreign civilizations, especially those whose law has engendered the great families of legal systems.

Writers often stress the number of traps, snares, and delusions which can hinder the student of comparative law or lead him quite astray. It is impossible to enumerate them all or wholly to avoid them, even by the device of enlisting multinational teams for comparative endeavours. The best advice one can give the novice is EICHENDORFF's: 'Hüte dich, sei wach und munter' (Watch out, be brave, and keep alert). Even so, the cleverest comparatists sometimes fall into error; when this happens the good custom among workers in the field is not to hound the forgivable miscreant with contumely from the profession, but kindly to put him right.

RABEL once said that in their explorations on foreign territory comparatists may come upon 'natives lying in wait with spears' (*RabelsZ* 16 (1951) 341); but let his wit not frighten us out of ours.

III

The comparatist who wants to find in a foreign system the rules which are functionally equivalent to those which interest him in his native law requires both imagination and discipline. Many instances could be given, some of which are treated *in extenso* below. Suppose that the question is how to enable persons incapable of acting for themselves (minors, lunatics, persons under interdict) to participate in legal affairs. For the European lawyer the notion of 'statutory representative' provides the ideal, if not the only imaginable answer. The idea is so self-evident that he thinks nothing of it: every child from the day he is born is provided with a person—the local youth authority if all else fails—who is comprehensively empowered by statute to represent him. Yet the Common Law has got by quite satisfactorily without any such legal institution. There the parents of a child are not automatically entitled or bound to represent him in legal affairs generally or in litigation in particular. When an infant is making a claim, he does so through a person appointed by the court for this purpose, called his 'next friend'. When an infant is being sued, the court similarly appoints a 'guardian *ad litem*'. Should a minor become entitled to an estate, the court in certain circumstances appoints an 'administrator *duranteminoreaetate*'. Furthermore a child may under certain circumstances be declared a 'ward of court', whereupon the court itself assumes powers of representation which in the normal case it later transfers to others. In the Common Law 'trustees' have the duties in relation to a child's property which on the Continent are performed by the statutory representative, for it has long been the rule in Anglo-American law to transfer property not to the child himself but to a trustee to manage on the child's behalf. This example shows that what the Continental lawyer sees as being a single problem and solves with a single institution is seen by the common lawyer as being a bundle of more specific problems which he solves with a plurality of legal institutions, most of them of ancient pedigree. (See further Ch. 32 III.) One should be frank enough to say, however, that though the English system has a certain antiquarian charm about it, it is so extremely complex and difficult to understand that no one else would dream of adopting it.

But we must not too readily infer that it is only the Continental systems, with their tendency to abstraction and generalization, which develop the grand comprehensive concepts, while the Common Law, with its inductive and makeshift habits, produces low-level legal institutions specially adapted to solve particular concrete problems. Things may be the other way round. A counterexample demonstrates once again that even if the legal institutions in different systems are historically and conceptually quite different, they may still perform the same function in the same way. The counterexample is the Anglo-American *trust*. The trust stems from a brilliantly simple notion: interests in a piece of property are split between a 'trustee', who has powers of administration and disposition, and others, often successive in time, who have a defined right to part of the proceeds of the property. This unitary conception is used by common lawyers in family law, in the law of succession, in the law of charities and companies, and even in the law of unjust enrichment; the trust thus satisfies a great many needs well known to European lawyers who deal with them with the aid of a whole panoply of extremely heterogeneous legal institutions.

Many more examples could easily be given. One system may meet a need by the *rei vindicatio* or the *actio negatoria* while another satisfies it by a claim in tort; claims for support in one country may be replaced in another by public relief of poverty; and claims for the division of property in one place may be paralleled by devices of inheritance law in another, or vice versa. All these examples are instances of the replacement of one legal rule by another *legal* rule, albeit of a different conceptual stamp. But often the comparatist must go beyond the purely legal devices, for he finds that the function performed in his own system by a rule of law is performed in a foreign system not by a legal rule at all, but by an extralegal phenomenon. One can only discern this by investigating the facts behind the law. Thus there may be general conditions of business which have not found their way into the books, but which in practice supersede or bypass rules of law fixed by the legislature or the judiciary. There may also be unwritten rules of commercial practice, matters of implicit agreement, which inhibit a party from using a right which the legal system accords to him. It may even be the case that a particular social problem, regulated in one system by rules of law, is wholly unregulated somewhere else, being controlled by mechanisms which operate outside the legal system altogether. Of course such a situation must be investigated, and the results brought into the comparison, for where a problem is solved by extralegal means one cannot simply assert that the foreign *law* does not deal with the problem without giving a false and misleading picture even of that legal system.

An example of this is provided by the question, when are offers binding? In German law the offeror is bound by his offer, in the sense that he cannot effectively withdraw it, either during a period set by himself or during a reasonable period (§145 BGB). In the Common Law, barring legislative intervention, the offeror may withdraw his offer at any time until it has been accepted, even when he has said that it will remain open for a stated time. The *reality* in both systems is quite different from what one would infer from these legal rules. It is well known that German merchants often insert terms like 'freibleibend', 'ohne Obligo', and 'Lieferungsmöglichkeit vorbehalten', which often appear also in general conditions of business; such clauses not only prevent the offer from being binding, they may prevent its being an offer at all, and have the effect of turning it into an invitation to submit offers, an *invitatio offerendi*. Contrariwise, the Common Law has developed several devices which weaken the practical effect of the rule that offers are freely revocable. What is especially interesting for us is that there are extralegal inhibitions which limit capricious revocation: such a revocation is legally effective but it is regarded as unfair and therefore not done (see below Ch. 26 V).

Another example shows how the comparatist must sometimes look outside the law. All developed legal systems, one might think, must have legal rules which protect the purchaser of an interest in land from the harm which could result from any outstanding and unknown property rights of third parties. But the German system with its land register and its concept of 'public reliance' (*öffentlicher Glaube*) was and is nearly unique. It has been imitated recently by other countries, especially France, and even the Anglo-American systems have for some time been experimenting, though their register system operates successfully only in a few densely populated areas. But by and large England and the United States have stuck to the old 'conveyancing' system, whereby the purchaser's attorney has to search through the deeds provided by the vendor in order to see that there is an unbroken chain of title. This system is so tiresome and expensive that 'Title Insurance Companies' have sprung up in the United States. These are private insurance companies which guarantee the insured against any loss he may suffer should a third person's rights diminish the value of his property. Companies will enter such an insurance contract only when they have checked their own sources and have established that the risk of the emergence of any conflicting interest is slight. These companies often have a monopoly in their locality and they have often been in business since the turn of the century, so the evidence they possess is virtually complete. In fact the function performed by the German land register is performed in the United States by the files and books of Title Insurance Companies. For details of 'conveyancing' and 'Title Insurance Companies', see the comparative study of v. HOFFMANN, *Das Recht des Grundstückskaufs* (1982).

The examples we have given point to a conclusion which the comparatist so often reaches that one can almost speak of a basic rule of comparative law: different legal systems give the same or very similar solutions, even as to detail, to the same problems of life, despite the great differences in their historical development, conceptual structure, and style of operation. It is true that there are many areas of social life which are impressed by especially strong moral and ethical feelings, rooted in the particularities of the prevailing religion, in historical tradition, in cultural development, or in the character of the people. These factors differ so much from one people to another that one cannot expect the rules which govern such areas of life to be congruent. Should freedom of testation be curtailed in the interests of a decedent's widow and family? Under what conditions should divorce be possible? Should same-sex marriages be permitted, or some comparable legal regime be on offer? Should unmarried persons be allowed to adopt? Different legal systems answer these questions quite differently, and the answers they give are sometimes maintained with such fervour that when

courts have occasion, thanks to a rule of conflicts law, to apply the rule of a
foreign country, they tend to ask whether that different rule is consistent
with the *ordre public* of their own jurisdiction. So there are areas in comparative law where judgment must be suspended, where the student simply cannot say which solution is better.

Thus for more than a decade the European Union has been trying to create a European company ('societas Europea') which would operate under the same conditions
in all member states. It has not succeeded. The principal obstacle has been that states
have quite different views on how, if at all, workers should participate in decision-
making within the company.—Again, while one should not exaggerate the differences
between England and the continent in matters of civil procedure, many of them do
reflect old-established ideas ingrained in their legal culture; for example, English lawyers are convinced that the only way to reach a decision is by 'trial', by a single continuous concentrated oral proceeding in which all the parties produce their whole
case at one sitting—factual assertions, evidence, legal argument—before a judge
who renders his decision on the spot (see below p. 271 f.).

But if we leave aside the topics which are heavily impressed by moral views
or values, mainly to be found in family law and in the law of succession, and
concentrate on those parts of private law which are relatively 'unpolitical',
we find that as a general rule developed nations answer the needs of legal
business in the same or in a very similar way. Indeed it almost amounts
to a *'praesumptio similitudinis'*, a presumption that the practical results are
similar. As a working rule this is very useful, and useful in two ways. At
the outset of a comparative study it serves as a heuristic principle—it tells
us where to look in the law and legal life of the foreign system in order to
discover similarities and substitutes. And at the end of the study the same
presumption acts as a means of checking our results: the comparatist can rest
content if his researches through all the relevant material lead to the conclusion that the systems he has compared reach the same or similar practical
results, but if he finds that there are great differences or indeed diametrically
opposite results, he should be warned and go back to check again whether
the terms in which he posed his original question were indeed purely functional, and whether he has spread the net of his researches quite wide
enough.

IV

The question how the comparatist should set out and how far he should go
in his search for material is intimately related to the meaning and purpose of
comparative law, to its very methods of thought. That is why we have
already dealt with it, concluding that he should go as deep as possible into
his chosen systems. But there is an anterior question, namely which legal sys-

tems he should choose to compare in the first place. Here sober self-restraint is in order, not so much because it is hard to take account of everything as because experience shows that as soon as one tries to cover a wide range of legal systems the law of diminishing returns operates. There are good reasons for this. Mature legal systems are often adopted or extensively imitated by others; as long as these other so-called 'affiliated' legal systems maintain the style of the parent system, they usually do not possess to the same degree that blend of originality and balanced maturity in solving problems which characterizes the 'significant' legal system. While they are at this stage of development, the comparatist may ignore the affiliate and concentrate on the parent system. This proposition, however, is more of a working rule than a firm conclusion of comparative methodology, since in fact the matter is rather subtle and complex.

To show what delicacy is required, take the case of the scholar in private law who wants to include the Romanistic systems in his comparative study. In addition to France, the parent system, he must also consider Italy where, behind a façade prevailing in the early stages, one finds an impressive wealth of ideas on private law matters, stimulated, perhaps, by the codification of 1942. The legal systems of Spain and Portugal, on the other hand, do not often call for or justify very intensive investigation.

Much the same can be said of the Common Law family. The eighteenth-century comparatist could safely have concentrated on the law of England and ignored North America. Today the situation is quite different, if not the other way round. Though England is unquestionably the parent system, the law of the United States, while staying in the family, has developed so distinctive a style (see below Ch. 17) that a comparatist would fall into error if he drew only on English, to the exclusion of American, law.

It is difficult to speak generally of how the comparatist should limit his field of inquiry, since it all depends on the precise topic of his research. If he is comparing the style of different families of law, rather than particular institutions or solutions of particular problems, then he can generally limit himself to the parent systems of the great legal families. If, on the other hand, he is dealing with particular questions, the following rule of thumb may be suggested. Some problems of private law, especially in the law of contract, tort, and property, are 'classical'. For these it will normally be sufficient to study English and American law in the Anglo-Saxon family, French and Italian law in the Romanistic family, and, in the Germanic systems, Germany and Switzerland (though here perhaps the native lawyer stands too close to see properly). It is worth while to bring in the law of Denmark and Sweden of the Nordic systems, despite the language difficulties, because of their refreshing lack of dogma. For questions of a more specific nature, outside the heartlands of private law already mentioned, a different principle of selection applies, but even here it is rarely safe to ignore the parent systems. To give just a few examples: questions of anti-trust law will find more answers in the United States than in France; the limitation of liability of trading concerns is distinctively, though perhaps not best, treated in Liechtenstein; fairness of trial has received more attention in England than elsewhere. Finally there may be quite topical legal problems with which legislators and judges all over the world are currently grappling. Here the comparatist may often have to consider the solutions offered by quite small jurisdictions. Thus *England* has had many more cases involving carriage by sea than any other country; *Sweden* has found quite original ways to protect consumers who take out insurance or rent dwellings; the Canadian Province of *Quebec* has replaced tort law by accident insurance to compensate victims of highway accidents, and *New Zealand* has extended this to *all* accidents (see Ch. 42 VI below). In family law there is much to be learnt from the legislation of the *Scandinavian* countries. It is clear, therefore, that the rule proposed is simply a rule of thumb, and no substitute for the experience and flair which a comparatist urgently needs if he is to make a proper choice of legal systems to study.

DROBNIG (above p. 32) has doubted whether in principle the comparatist need study only the great 'parent' systems. He points out that these systems have no monopoly of legal inventiveness and that therefore the comparatist should invoke all the legal systems of the world which might make any contribution to the problem being studied. After such a world-wide investigation the comparatist should present, in the form it takes in a representative system, each of the different types of solution which are to be found. DROBNIG developed this view in the context of the *International Encyclopedia of Comparative Law*—an undertaking backed by enormous financial resources, in which hundreds of comparatists from all over the world participate. In the case of wholesale research like this (see ZWEIGERT, *RabelsZ* 31 (1967) 539), it is possible and justifiable to accede to DROBNIG's exacting demands, since provision was made for each of the participating scholars to visit libraries and question expert colleagues in almost every country, in order to obtain a complete picture of the world's legal systems. In such a situation there was no need to exclude a priori and without detailed investigation any legal system at all, even if it had no great legal experience and had not therefore been able to test by case-law and try by scholarly criticism the solutions adopted. But most comparative research is not done by international teams with world-wide coverage, and it might not be desirable if it were. Comparative law is still useful and necessary when undertaken by an individual, and the comparison of individual systems, as opposed to those of the whole world, is important, indeed indispensable. So although making a selection may be painful, it is unavoidable on practical grounds. If a selection must be made, a criterion of selection must be adopted, and for this purpose the rules of thumb outlined above—for they are no more than that—still seem to offer a useful point of departure.

V

As one researches the chosen legal systems one makes comparisons the whole time, often quite unconsciously: comparison, indeed, stimulates the enterprise and determines the choice of materials. But as a creative activity going beyond the mere actual absorption of the data, the process of comparison proper starts only when the reports on the different legal systems have been completed. To present such reports before the comparison proper begins is an established method of research and a proven way of constructing works on comparative law. Separate reports should be offered for each legal system or family of legal systems, and they should be objective, that is, free from any critical evaluation, though containing all significant qualifications or modifications. Whoever reads or uses a work on comparative law must be made familiar with the basic material, or he will be in no position to make the necessary comparisons, but in any case it is useful to give jurists access to legal systems hitherto unfamiliar to them. Occasionally an unusual topic will demand a different method of treatment, for example, where the problem under scrutiny involves several different sub-questions or crops up in cases of different types: then it may be desirable to devote separate treatment to each sub-question or type of case, and provide a country report on each.

But merely to juxtapose without comment the law of the various jurisdictions is not comparative law: it is just a preliminary step. The actual comparison which then begins is the most difficult part of any work in comparative law, and the process is so much affected by the peculiarities of the particular problem and of its solutions in the different systems that it is impossible to lay down any firm rules about it. One can only tentatively state some basic generalities.

It goes without saying that a comparative analysis will bring out the differences between the actual solutions. It is, indeed, the feeling of surprise that such differences exist which first prompts us to undertake comparative researches. But one does not gain much by simply listing the similarities and differences one discovers: this is really just to repeat in a clearer form what is already contained in the reports on each jurisdiction. This may be sufficient where each of the jurisdictions gives a clear and easily comprehensible solution to the problem in question, but things are not often as easy as this, as our examples have shown. Furthermore, it is precisely the more taxing legal questions which justify comparative treatment. The process of comparison at this stage involves adopting a new point of view from which to consider all the different solutions. The objective report which sets out the law of a particular jurisdiction will give a comprehensive portrayal of its legal solution to a practical problem, but it does so 'on its own terms', with its particular statutory rules or decisions, its characteristic conceptual form, and in its systematic context: the significance of this has been brought out above. But when the process of comparison begins, each of the solutions must be freed from the context of its own system and, before evaluation can take place, set in the context of all the solutions from the other jurisdictions under investigation. Here too we must follow the principle of functionality: the solutions we find in the different jurisdictions must be cut loose from their conceptual context and stripped of their national doctrinal overtones so that they may be seen purely in the light of their function, as an attempt to satisfy a particular legal need. If we find that different countries meet the same need in different ways, we must ask why. This is a particularly demanding task, since the reasons may lie anywhere in the whole realm of social life, and one may have to venture into the domains of other social sciences, such as economics, sociology or political science (see above p. 10 f.).

VI

The next step in the process of comparison is to build a system. For this one needs to develop a special syntax and vocabulary, which are also in fact necessary for comparative researches on particular topics. The system must be very flexible, and have concepts large enough to embrace the quite heterogeneous legal institutions which are functionally comparable. To give an example: all legal systems have somehow to distinguish those expressions of a person's will which have a binding effect from those which do not, but the legal techniques they use for this purpose are very different. One way is to insist on purely objective requirements (formality, typicality of object, quid pro quo), while at a more developed stage it may be left to the judge as a matter of pure interpretation. Thus a system of comparative law must have a category which includes 'form', 'causa' (in one of its protean meanings) and 'consideration', and which also suggests that it is concerned with distinguishing the legally binding expression of will from the merely social utterance: perhaps 'indicia of earnestness' would do.

To take another example. It has been said that the principle that an unjust enrichment must be restored is 'ubiquitous' (ESSER, above p. 32, p. 367). So it is, but it appears in various guises and serves very various functions. What in one system is seen as a claim for restitution appears in another as a claim in tort and in a third as a claim for rescission of contract. A system of comparative law must here find a higher concept related to the function common to all these claims, or several different higher concepts, one for each of the different functions of restitutionary claims and capable of including claims of a different cast but similar practical object: perhaps one might have 'restitution of payments gone wrong', 'restitution for appropriating the property of others', 'restitution for unjustifiably using another's thing', and so on (see V. CAEMMERER, 'Bereicherung und unerlaubte Handlung', *Festschrift Rabel* I (1954) 333). There are simpler examples: we should talk of 'breach of contract' rather than '*Unmöglichkeit*' [impossibility], 'liability for others' is a better expression than 'liability for assistants', 'liability for servants' or 'respondeat superior'; 'strict liability' is more comprehensive than '*Gefährdungshaftung*' or '*théorie du risque*', and so on.

A system of comparative law will thus seem to be rather a loose structure. The component concepts cast a wider net than those of national systems: this is because the functional approach of comparative law concentrates on the real live problem which often lurks unseen behind the concepts of the national systems. The system produced by comparative law is, however, functionally coherent: its concepts identify the demands that a particular slice of life poses for the law in all systems where the social and economic conditions are similar and provide a realistic context within which to compare and contrast the various solutions, however much they may differ technically or substantially. DROBNIG has shown that the wider the international coverage of a comparative work is, the more necessary, though the more problematical, the development of such structural concepts is (above p. 32, at pp. 228 ff.). The task is not, however, different in nature from that of the librarian who needs a supranational system of concepts if he is to arrange his foreign materials in topical categories rather than simply in national groupings.

It now becomes unmistakably clear that an international legal science is possible. After a period of national legal developments, producing academically and doctrinally sophisticated structures, each apparently peculiar and incomparable, private law can once again become, as it was in the era of natural law, a proper object for international research, without losing its claim to scientific exactitude and objectivity. To this recognition of the fact that law, and especially private law, may properly be studied outside national boundaries, comparative law has greatly contributed, though other legal disciplines also have long been pointing the way. The jurisprudence of interests, the *Freirechtsschule*, the sociology of law, legal realism—all these have played a part by criticizing purely national conceptualism, deprecating scholarship which is territorially limited, and emphasizing that legal science should study the actual problems of life rather than the conceptual constructs which seek to solve them. Law is 'social engineering' and legal science is a social science. Comparative lawyers recognize this: it is, indeed, the intellectual and methodological starting-point of their discipline. Comparative law is thus closely in tune with current trends in legal science when it asks what the function of legal institutions in different countries may be, rather than what their doctrinal structure is, and when it orders the solutions of the various systems upon a realistic basis by testing them for their responsiveness to the social needs they seek to fill. It adds the international dimension and generates a supply of material beyond the imagination of even the cleverest stay-at-home lawyer. The vision of a universal comparative legal science is already sketched in the preface to JHERING's *Geist des römischen Rechts*:

'... legal science has degenerated into the jurisprudence of states, limited like them by political boundaries—a discouraging and unseemly posture for a science! But it is up to legal science itself to cast away these chains and to rediscover for all time that quality of universality which it long enjoyed: this it will do in the different form of comparative law. It will have a distinct method, a wider vision, a riper judgment, a less constrained manner of treating its material: the apparent loss [of the formal community of Roman law] will in reality prove a great gain, by raising law to a higher level of scientific activity.' (JHERING, *Geist des römischen Rechts auf den verschiedenen Stufen seiner Entwicklung*, Part I (7th/8th edn., 1924) p. 15.)

JHERING's vision is on the point of becoming reality, and comparative law has greatly helped to bring this about. If law is seen functionally as a regulator of social facts, the legal problems of all countries are similar. Every legal system in the world is open to the same questions and subject to the same standards, even countries of different social structures or different stages of development. Our universal legal science must have a structure and all the conceptual apparatus for ordering, organizing, and transmitting its material; we have shown above what form these must take. These cannot be laid down a priori, but only achieved inductively through continuing experiments in comparative law. In doing this comparative law will itself begin to be truly international. Though great progress has been made, most German work in comparative law even today still starts from a particular question or legal institution in German law, proceeds to treat it comparatively, and ends, after evaluating the discoveries made, by drawing conclusions—proposals for reform, new interpretations—for German law alone. The same is doubtless true of comparative studies in other countries. This activity could be called national comparative law. What we must aim for is a truly international comparative law which could form the basis for a universal legal science. This new legal science could provide the scholar with new methods of thought, new systematic concepts, new methods of posing questions, new material discoveries, and new standards of criticism: his scientific scope would be increased to include the experience of all the legal science in the world, and he would be provided with the means to deal with them. It would facilitate the mutual comprehension of jurists of different nationalities and allay the misunderstandings which come from the prejudices, constraints, and diverse vocabularies of the different systems.

VII

After doing his research the comparatist must proceed to a critical evaluation of what he has discovered. Sometimes one of the solutions will appear 'better' or 'worse' for the reasons given above (see p. 39). Often, however, he will find that the different solutions are equally valid, or that, as RABEL said, 'a reasoned choice is hard to make' (*RabelsZ* 16 (1951) 357). Often he will find that one solution is clearly superior. Finally, he may be able to fashion a new solution, superior to all others, out of parts of the different national solutions. The comparatist must consider all this, and be explicit about it. It is true that RABEL wanted to distinguish such evaluation on policy grounds from comparative law properly so-called, as being a 'distinct activity . . . because, though neither task is free from subjectivity, the pure comparison of laws can in general claim for its conclusions and theoretical pronouncements a greater degree of general validity than can value-judgements and conclusions directed to practical matters like legislative policy . . .' ('Fachgebiete', above p. 32, at p. 186). Much could be said on the question whether the critical evaluation of law is a legitimate scientific activity; it raises the famous dispute over KELSEN's pure theory of law, and this is not the place to give a final answer. The fact is, as RABEL said: 'Lawyers who are used to criticism and are animated by the desire to improve the law can hardly prevent themselves from seeing and commenting upon the better practical rule.'

In fact the comparatist is in the best position to follow his comparative researches with a critical evaluation. If he does not, no one else will do it, and if no one does it, comparative law will deserve BINDER's sour description of 'piling up blocks of stone that no one will build with'. The comparatist uses just the same criteria as any other lawyer who has to decide which of the possible solutions is most suitable and just. The comparatist is no more adept at this than the lawyer who remains rooted in the law of his homeland, but he does have more material at his disposal, he is aware of solutions which would not occur to the homespun lawyer, however imaginative, and he is not blinded by faith in the superiority of his own system. If it is objected that evaluation is inevitably subjective, we can turn again to RABEL for rebuttal: 'If the picture presented by a scholar is coloured by his background or education, international collaboration will correct it' (*RabelsZ* 16 (1951) 359).

4

The History of Comparative Law

ANCEL, 'Les grandes étapes de la recherche comparative au XXe siècle', in: *Studi in memoria di Andrea Torrente* (1968) 21.

——, 'Cent ans de droit comparé en France', in: *Livre du centenaire de la Société de législation comparée* (1969) 3.

BROWN, 'A Century of Comparative Law in England: 1869–1969', 19 *Am. J. Comp. L.* 232 (1971).

CONSTANTINESCO, *Rechtsvergleichung* I (1971), Part 2.

——, 'Les Débuts du droit comparé en Allemagne', in: *Miscellanea W. J. Ganshof van der Meersch* II (1972) 737.

DAVID, *Droit civil comparé* (1950) 397–429.

DÖLLE, 'Der Beitrag der Rechtsvergleichung zum deutschen Recht', in: *Hundert Jahre deutsches Rechtsleben, Festschrift zum 100jährigen Bestehen des Deutschen Juristentages* II (1960) 19.

GORLA, 'Prolegomeni ad una storia de diritto comparato europeo', *Foro it.* 103 (1980) V 11.

HUG, 'The History of Comparative Law', 45 *Harv. L. Rev.* 1027 (1932).

JESCHECK, *Entwicklung, Aufgaben und Methoden der Strafrechtsvergleichung* (1955).

KADEN, 'Rechtsvergleichung', in: *Rechtsvergleichendes Handwörterbuch* VI (ed. Schlegelberger, 1938) 9.

v. MEHREN, 'An Academic Tradition for Comparative Law?', 19 *Am. J. Comp. L.* 624 (1971).

MOLINA PASQUEL, 'Veinticinco años de evolución del derecho comparado: 1940–1965', *Bol. Mex. der. comp. NS* 2 (1969) 57.

POLLOCK, 'The History of Comparative Jurisprudence', 5 *J. Soc. Comp. Leg.* (2nd ser.) 74 (1903).

POUND, 'Comparative Law in the Formation of American Common Law', in: *Acta academiae universalis iurisprudentiae comparativae* I (1928) 183.

——, 'The Revival of Comparative Law', 5 *Tul. L. Rev.* 1 (1930).

RABEL, *Aufgabe und Notwendigkeit der Rechtsvergleichung* (1925), reprinted in: Rabel, *Gesammelte Aufsätze* III (ed. Leser, 1967) 1.

——, 'Die Fachgebiete des Kaiser Wilhelm-Instituts für ausländisches und internationales Privatrecht', in: *25 Jahre Kaiser Wilhelm-Gesellschaft zur Förderung der Wissenschaften* III (1937) 77, reprinted in: Rabel, *Gesammelte Aufsätze* III (ed. Leser, 1967) 180.

RHEINSTEIN, *Einführung in die Rechtsvergleichung* (2nd edn. 1987) Chs. 5–7.

SARFATTI, 'Les premiers pas du droit comparé', in: *Mélanges Maury* II (1960) 237.

STURM, 'Geschichte, Methode und Ziel der Rechtsvergleichung', *JR* (1975) 231.

ZAJTAY, 'Réflexions sur l'évolution du droit comparé', *Festschrift Zweigert* (1981) 595.

ZWEIGERT, 'Die Gestalt Joseph Storys', *ZgesStW* 105 (1949) 590.

——, 'Jherings Bedeutung für die Entwicklung der rechtsvergleichenden Methode', in: *Jherings Erbe, Göttinger Symposion zur 150. Wiederkehr des Geburtstags von Rudolph von Jhering* (1970) 240. Extended version in English: ZWEIGERT/SIEHR, 'Jhering's Influence on the Development of Comparative Legal Method', 19 *Am. J. Comp. L.* 215 (1971).

I

IT is in *Greece*, owing to the characteristic interest of Greek thinkers in political structures, that we find the earliest comparative researches. In his *Laws*, PLATO makes a comparison of the laws of the Greek city-states; he not only describes them, but also tests them against the ideal constitution he constructs out of them. Prior to writing his *Politics*, ARISTOTLE also examined the constitutions of no less than 153 city-states, though only the portion devoted to Athens has come down to us. This work can be described as philosophical speculation on the basis of comparative law. The only trace of comparative private law is in a fragment of THEOPHRASTUS's 'On Laws': so far as we can tell, THEOPHRASTUS's approach is quite modern, for he tries to discover the general principles in the various Greek legal systems, and then, in another chapter, to set against these principles the deviant particular rules— the very method used more recently by OTTO VON GIERKE in his presentation of German private law, and most spectacularly by EUGEN HUBER in his portrayal of the private laws of the Swiss cantons.

The *Roman Empire* offers no examples of efforts in comparative law. The Roman jurists, like those of England in later times, were too convinced of the superiority of their legal and political system to pay much attention to foreign laws. CICERO described all non-Roman law as 'confused and quite absurd'. The occasional references to foreign rules of law are just historical footnotes or theoretical amusements. But an interesting work of comparative law comes from the post-classical era, say from the third or fourth century AD. This is the *Collatio legum Mosaicarum et Romanarum*, in which excerpts from the classical Roman jurists are set against the laws of Moses, presumably with the aim of furthering Christian belief by showing that Roman and biblical law were similar.

At the beginning of the *Middle Ages* legal skill was at a low ebb, and thereafter canon and Roman law acquired such authority that no other kind of law had any interest for scholars. Furthermore the warrior chiefs believed that the conqueror could impose his law on the peoples he conquered—a coarse idea inimical to comparative law. But if writings on comparative

law are not to be found on the Continent, there are two works by FORTES-
CUE (died 1485) in England, *De Laudibus legum Angliae* and *The Governance
of England*. In these we have comparison of English and French law; it is
not, however, an objective analysis, but is obviously designed to demonstrate
the superiority of English law.

In the *Age of Humanism*, when lawyers were interested in *elegantia juris*,
there were more serious attempts at comparative legal analysis. Special mention should be made of STRUVE and STRYCK in the late seventeenth century,
for their comparisons of Roman and German private law. The first representatives of the *Age of Enlightenment and Natural Law*, scholars like WOLF and
NETTELBLADT, were very little likely to help comparative law on its way.
For them, natural law was an intellectual construct to be produced by speculation a priori without reference to any empirically discovered material,
though one is entitled to wonder whether behind their supposedly a priori
system there does not lurk some 'concealed comparative law'. Yet two leading spirits of the age, BACON and LEIBNIZ, emphatically advanced the cause
of comparative law without actually practising it. In his essay *De dignitate et
augmentis scientiarum* (1623) BACON stated that the lawyer must free himself
from the 'vincula' of his national system before he can estimate its true
worth: the object of judgment (the national law) cannot be the standard of
judgment. This perception, as valid now as ever, justifies all comparative
researches. For his part, LEIBNIZ endorses comparative law from the standpoint of universal history: his plan for a 'Theatrum legale' involved a comparative portrayal of the laws of all peoples, places, and times. Nothing
immediately came of these writings, but we find that subsequent natural lawyers such as GROTIUS, PUFENDORF, and MONTESQUIEU expressly used the
method of comparative law to give empirical support to the teachings of natural law. The contribution of this age, therefore, is less the systematic practice of comparative law than the recognition of the theoretical value of its
methods. Mention must also be made of SAVIGNY's predecessor at Göttin-
gen, HUGO (died 1844), who aimed to produce an empirical natural law by
making a comparison of all existing positive laws.

SAVIGNY's *historical school of jurisprudence*, on the other hand, had a particularly repressive effect on the development of comparative law. At first
sight this is not easy to understand, since comparative law might (though
it also might not) have produced some support for their view that all law
is a product of the *Volksgeist*. But SAVIGNY and his followers rejected the
study of any but Roman and German law: 'It is the history of our own
laws—the Germanic laws, Roman law and canon law—which is and will
remain the most important' ('Stimmen für und wider neue Gesetzbücher',
SavZ 3 (1816) 5 f.).

II

Comparative law, as it is practised today, has two quite distinct roots: 'legislative comparative law', when foreign laws are invoked in the process of drafting new national laws, and 'scientific or theoretical comparative law', when the comparison of different legal systems is undertaken simply in order to improve our legal knowledge.

Legislative comparative law has the longer and more continuous history—though still not a very long one—and its methods raise fewer problems. In Germany it starts in the mid-nineteenth century. The older codes—the Prussian General Land Law of 1794 and the Austrian General Civil Code of 1811—are based more on natural law thinking than on extended comparative studies of foreign law. The same is true of the most influential code of the eighteenth century, the French Civil Code of 1804. This elegant practitioners' work, beautifully drafted, was produced in an astonishingly short time, with the principal aim—so far as it was comparative at all—of amalgamating the Roman *droit écrit* of Southern France with the principally Germanic *coutumes* of the North (compare below pp. 77 f.).

Legislative comparative law in Germany grew with the movement for the codification and unification of law within Germany. It started in that area of law where unification is most urgently called for—commercial law. The General German Negotiable Instruments Law of 1848 and the General German Commercial Code of 1861 were both based on comparative studies, not only of the laws of the different regions of Germany, which included in the Rhineland the French Commercial Code, but also of other European commercial codes, especially the Dutch Commercial Code (*Wetboek van Koophandel*) of 1838. Proof of this is to be found in the Prussian 'Entwurf eines Handelsgesetzbuches für die Preussischen Staaten nebst Motiven' (Berlin 1857) which laid the basis for the German Commercial Code of 1861 and the 'Protokolle der Kommission zur Beratung eines allgemeinen Deutschen Handelsgesetzbuches' (1857 ff.). The company law reforms contained in the Novellen of 1870 and 1884 were also based on extensive comparative researches which are preserved in the Parliamentary papers and contain a veritable treasurehouse of material for the comparative history of European company law. All subsequent reforms of company law, up to the reforms of the law relating to corporate securities of the 1930s and the great reform of 1965, have also been based on wide-ranging comparative studies and affected at critical points by discussion of the foreign solutions.

But legislative comparative law was used elsewhere than in commercial law. Comparative studies preceded almost all the most important pieces of legislation, which this is not the place to list or itemize. Mention must, however, be made of the prolonged reforms of criminal law, for one of the early monuments of German comparative law is the fifteen volumes of the *Verglei-chende Darstellung des deutschen und des ausländischen Strafrechts* (1905–09); on this and subsequent developments in comparative criminal law, see JESCHECK, above p. 48, pp. 13 ff.).

Mention must be made of one final instance of the successful use of comparative law in legislation, for it culminated in the German Civil Code, which unified the private law of Germany as from 1 January 1900. In the preparation of this Code, careful consideration was given to the solutions accepted in all the systems then in force in the various parts of Germany. These included the *Gemeines Recht*, the Prussian Law, and the French Civil Code which was in force in the Rhineland and also, in a modified form, in Baden. Furthermore, on nearly all the more important questions, the comparative research was extended to include Austrian and Swiss law. Now one might have expected that, in the theoretical and scientific task of expounding the Code, German legal scholars would have used this comparative method which had proved so useful in creating it. Nothing of the sort occurred. They focused exclusively on the wording of the new texts, and if these seemed to need construction, they had recourse to the conceptual apparatus of the *ius commune*. Once the work of legislation was over, comparative law faded into the background and ceased to have any effect.

III

Scholarly comparative law has had a very different development from legislative comparative law: while the latter has developed continuously, the history of the former is marked by hesitations and rejections followed by periods of exaggerated optimism.

1. It took comparative law a very long time to obtain recognition in Germany where lawyers had long been attacked for their parochialism. FEUER-BACH was one of the first to reproach German legal scholars when he said in 1810 that 'all their scholarship was devoted exclusively to what was native or naturalised'.

'Anatomists have their comparative anatomy, so why do jurists not have comparative law? There is no more fertile source of discoveries in any practical science than comparison and combination. A thing has to be contrasted with many other things before it can become really clear, and its particularity and essential nature can be revealed only by showing how it is similar and how it is different. Just as the science of linguistics comes from comparing languages, so if universal jurisprudence (indeed, legal scholarship *tout court*) is to vitalise and vindicate particular forms of legal scholarship it needs to compare the laws and legal practices of other nations at all times and places, the most like and the most different.' One must 'look to other peoples and scrutinise their laws and practices in order to sharpen one's perception of one's own law and see it in a new light, or even enrich it with new matter' (ANSELM VON FEUERBACH, 'Blick auf die teutsche Rechtswissenschaft', in Feuerbach, *Kleine Schriften vermischten Inhalts* (1833) 152, 162 f.). For more detail see MOHNHAUPT, 'Universalgeschichte, Universal-Jurisprudenz und rechtsvergleichende Methode im Werk P. J. A. Feuerbachs', in Mohnhaupt (ed.), *Rechtsgeschichte in den beiden deutschen Staaten* (1988–1990) (1991) 97.

FEUERBACH's demand for comprehensive comparative law as the basis of universal legal science set him on a collision course with SAVIGNY and the Historical School. He rejected as too narrow SAVIGNY's view that one should focus only on German (= Roman) law. He sided with THIBAUT in his famous quarrel with SAVIGNY over whether codification were possible and desirable, and agreed with him that

'ten lively lectures on the Persian or Chinese conception of law would do more to stimulate true juristic intelligence than a hundred addresses on the pitiful bunglings of the law of intestate succession between Augustus and Justinian' (THIBAUT, 'Über die Nothwendigkeit eines allgemeinen bürgerlichen Rechts für Deutschland', in Thibaut, *Civilistische Abhandlungen* (1814) 433).

FEUERBACH's charges were echoed a few decades later when JHERING lamented how legal science had degenerated into the law of political states—'a discouraging and unseemly posture for a science!' (see the full quotation above, p. 46). JHERING was no more a comparatist than FEUERBACH, though there are a number of references to foreign laws scattered through his works, but had it not been for his successful struggle on behalf of a teleological approach to law in the context of real life comparative law could not have developed in the way it has. (For details, see ZWEIGERT, 'Jherings Bedeutung' (above p. 49) *passim*).

Neither the historical school of jurisprudence, with its equation—more dogmatic than historical—of the *Volksgeist* with Roman Law, nor the conceptual jurisprudence of the pandectists, nor yet the legal positivism of the turn of the century provided conditions in which comparative law could flourish: indeed, it had no recognized place in legal science. BIERLING may be taken as typical of the positivists: comparative law is 'of little or no use for learning the principles of law' (*Juristische Prinzipienlehre* I (1894) 33). Even when, in the early twentieth century, positivism yielded to the neo-Kantian search for 'just law', the attitude adopted towards comparative law remained ambiguous. STAMMLER unequivocally discountenanced comparative law as a means of discovering the just law: the comparison of laws which were factually conditioned could never lead to the perception of those unconditionally valid modes of thought which were needed for any scientific study of law (*Lehrbuch der Rechtsphilosophie* (1922) 11 f.). Even RADBRUCH, in an essay 'On Comparative Legal Method' (*Monatschrift für Kriminalpsychologie und Strafrechtsreform* 2 (1902/1906) 422), denied that comparative law had any significance for the underlying idea of law, though he powerfully defended its value for the legislator as 'a useful means of obtaining the widest possible view of actual law'. No amount of study of actual systems could teach us anything about just law, for the notion of just law is arrived at not empirically, but a priori (id., 423). In a later work he denied comparative law any place in the 'proper dogmatic and systematic' science of law, and classed it along with legal history and sociology of law as 'the social theory of law' (*Rechtsphilosophie* (4th edn. Wolf, 1950) 210).

It will be clear even from this brief sketch of the prevailing attitudes among German legal scholars how much opposition comparative law had to overcome in order to establish itself as a legal discipline. Its history may seem to show a steady development, but it was long regarded by most legal scholars all over the world as simply an esoteric game for a handful of outsiders. This attitude may be attributed to the fact that in their everyday activities lawyers have to deal mainly with the law of their own country, but it has been greatly reinforced during this period by the prejudices of positivism and of national legal cultures, and we cannot in good conscience say that this attitude has wholly disappeared. Even now comparative law is not yet regarded as an indispensable international component of a *culture juridique*.

2. Even if conscious antipathy to comparative law was not expressed so strongly and dogmatically elsewhere as it was in Germany, the picture was not very different; scholars were not much readier to busy themselves with other peoples' law; national prejudices were very widespread. In the same breath in which he attacked the introversion of German lawyers, RABEL felt bound to inveigh against the equally poor standing of comparative law in other countries (*Aufgabe* (above p. 48) at 12 ff.). It is against this background that we must see the successful development of comparative law.

3. There is an astonishing similarity in the way different countries in the early nineteenth century embarked on the purposive and systematic comparison of different legal systems, that is, modern comparative law. Its intellectual origins are also similar. The purposes are practical, namely reform and improvement of the law at home, rather than theoretical, philosophical, or speculative; but a part was played also by natural curiosity about other peoples' law and by the impartial feeling that perhaps those others had something to offer—a contrast with the haughty concentration of legal scholars on their own newly codified systems. ZACHARIÄ used quite characteristic language in the first issue of the world's first periodical devoted to comparative law—the *Kritische Zeitschrift für Rechtswissenschaft und Gesetzgebung des Auslandes* (no. 1 (1829) 25 f.):

'If, after this survey of the present extent of exchange between European peoples in literary matters, and of the previous situation with regard to law, we may conclude that legislative or jurisprudential developments in any European country will be of some

interest in other European countries, the idea behind this periodical, namely to famil-
iarize the German public with foreign laws and legal writings, requires no justification.'

In Germany special mention must be made of ZACHARIÄ's co-founder and
co-editor, MITTERMAIER. He was professor at Heidelberg and the leader of a
group of jurists, mainly from Southern Germany, who were interested in the
practical uses of foreign and comparative law, probably, as HUG says (above
p. 48, at p. 1056) under the stimulus of the recent introduction of the Code
Napoléon in the Rhineland and in Baden. This did not limit the interests of
the group, however, which extended to all modern legal systems, and it is
especially noteworthy that this was the first time that European jurists
demonstrated a deep understanding of the Common Law of England and
the United States. The 28 volumes of the *Kritische Zeitschrift*, as WARNKÖNIG
was to say (*KritZ* 28 (1856) 391), offer a nearly complete view of three decades of legislation and legal science abroad. It is true that the mere discovery
and portrayal of foreign law is not comparative law, but the contributors
almost always drew comparisons with their own legal systems.

MITTERMAIER was the first to practise comparative law by systematically
juxtaposing, comparing, and evaluating the law of various systems, and he
did it on the grand scale. It is true that his aim was primarily practical—
the reform of criminal procedure in the *Gemeines Recht*—but that does not
in the least diminish his achievement in producing a series of scientific works
which withstand all criticism. MITTERMAIER's comparisons of particular
areas of law or of legal institutions were both comprehensive and detailed.
He did not stop at the statutory texts, but went into the reality of law
as practised in the courts, and even into its factual, political, and social
background.

It was clearly MITTERMAIER's example which led FOELIX to found the
Revue étrangère de législation in *France* in 1834. His avowed aim was to help
French jurists improve their knowledge of foreign laws, as well as to promote the improvement of French law. This must have seemed a most unpro-
mising undertaking at a time when French jurists regarded their Civil Code
with an awe bordering on superstition, and after a few issues the journal,
which kept changing its name, had to devote more and more space to purely
French law. The portion devoted to foreign law, to which FOELIX as editor
was restricted, kept shrinking, and in 1850 the *Revue* ceased to appear. Even
so, FOELIX seems to have had more success in establishing comparative law
as an independent discipline in France than MITTERMAIER and his group had
in Germany, for the collapse of comparative law studies in France in the face
of positivism was much less marked. A chair of comparative legal history
was founded at the Collège de France in 1831, and after holding courses in
comparative criminal law from 1838, the Faculty of Law at Paris founded
a chair in that subject in 1846. Although FOELIX did not see the fulfilment

of his wish to have courses given in comparative private law, it is fair to say that it was his initiative, and in particular his starting the *Revue*, which gave the first impetus to the development of comparative legal studies in France.

In England the Privy Council, as the highest court of the Empire, had to apply the law of several different foreign systems; this led to a need for 'a more ready access to the sources from whence an acquaintance might be derived with those systems of foreign jurisprudence' (BURGE, *Commentaries on Colonial and Foreign Laws* (1838) p. v). It was the aim of BURGE to satisfy this need with his *Commentaries on Colonial and Foreign Laws, generally, and in their conflict with each other, and with the Law of England* (1838). According to BURGE himself (id., vi) these included: the 'civil law' (as the English used to call Roman law); the law of Holland before the introduction of the French Civil Code; Spanish law; the *coutumes* of Paris and Normandy; the French law then in force; Scots law; English law; the local laws of the colonies in the West Indies and North America; the laws of the United States of America. BURGE's work had three aims: first, to give a comprehensive survey of the sources and rules of law in all the systems in force in the British Empire, secondly, to compare their family law, their law of persons, property, and succession, and thirdly, to show the principles of conflict of laws in the various topics. The book was highly regarded both on the Continent and in the United States as a basic work of comparative law (see HUG (above p. 48) at 1065), and in 1924 the exigent RABEL himself stated that though the work was designed for the use of the Privy Council, 'the range of material and quality of treatment make it useful as a substitute for a primer of comparative private law' (*Aufgabe* (above p. 48) at p. 12, no. 12).

A similarly practical aim, namely to satisfy the need of English tradesmen for information about the commercial law of other peoples, underlay the other notable first-fruit of English comparative law. This is LEONE LEVI's *Commercial Law of the World; or, the Mercantile Law of the United Kingdom, compared with the Codes and Laws of Commerce of the following Mercantile Countries* [58 are listed], *and the Institutes of Justinian* (1854). LEVI compared English commercial law with the trade laws of almost every country in the world. Each of his topical subdivisions begins with a short description of the relevant English law; then follows a statement of the foreign rules of law—concentrating on statutory texts and dealing rather superficially with judicial practice—and finally an 'analysis of the law' in which he indicates the similarities and differences between the various legal systems. It is worth noting that LEVI was so impressed by the success of the German General Ordinance on Bills of Exchange of 1848 that he put forward the idea of an international unified code of commercial law: this was to be achieved by international conferences, and his work was to be a basic document (see LEVI, id., vol. I, p. xv). Thus LEVI was the first to propose the international unification of a whole area of law on the basis of comprehensive comparative law.

The period 1800–50 saw an early flowering of comparative law in the United States of America as well. American law at this stage was far from being merely the child of English law, whose traditionalism ill suited the economic, social, and political conditions of a new land only just occupied and not yet developed. Furthermore the War of Independence and the later war of 1812 had left a distaste for England and everything English. It was therefore with full consciousness that, whenever new and more suitable rules had to be developed, the most famous and influential American jurists of this period reached for Roman and European law, especially for French doctrine. This was true of both JOSEPH STORY and JAMES KENT, of the former, perhaps, to an even more marked degree. Nor was this recourse to foreign legal sources just a matter of theory. The works of KENT and STORY had a great effect on the practice of the courts as well as on legal teaching; indeed KENT's *Commentaries* formed the essential basis of American law at this time. Furthermore, both writers were themselves judges and so, as never before to such an extent in any country in the Anglo-American legal family, we find a series of judicial decisions, many of them well known, which are openly and explicitly based on the Civil Law. (See, for details, POUND (above p. 48; POUND, 'The Influence of French Law in America', 3 *Ill. L. Rev.* 354 (1909).) This open interest in foreign law was not, as in other countries, the prerogative of a few scholars; it was part of the contemporary American legal scene. In 1829, the anonymous reviewer of two books on Roman law said that 'in the liberal course of professional studies general or comparative jurisprudence must be a constituent part' (2 *Am. Jurist* 60 (1829)). The syllabus and reading-list of the Harvard Law School contained a section on Civil Law which recommended JUSTINIAN's *Institutes*, POTHIER's *Law of Obligations*, and DOMAT's *Loix civiles* among others (4 *Am. Jurist* 217, 220 (1830)). There was also at this time a great demand for a Chair of Civil Law at Harvard (see, in general, HUG (above p. 48), 1068 n. 176). This interest in Civil Law is attributable in great part to the natural law thinking of the American Independence movement; by the middle of the century it had greatly diminished, and by the time of the Civil War it had quite disappeared.

A similar, though less dramatic, decline in comparative law is observable in other countries, and we must agree with HUG (above p. 48, at pp. 1069 f.) that after the middle of the nineteenth century people lost almost all interest in comparative law as a method of discovering law and of putting the discoveries to practical use.

4. The idea of 'comparative law' remained alive, however, though it came gradually to refer to a pursuit which we have earlier (above pp. 9 f.) distinguished from modern comparative law, namely 'legal ethnology' or 'universal legal history'. This species of 'comparative legal science' as it was known in Germany, became the practice of a veritable school, often influenced by

significant trends of philosophical thought. In Germany the idea of development contained in HEGEL's philosophy of history, though not his dialectic, was the admitted source of the works of GANS (*Das Erbrecht in weltgeschichtlicher Entwicklung* I (1824), especially the Preface at p. xxxix), of UNGER (*Die Ehe in ihrer welthistorischen Entwicklung* (1850)), of POST (for example, *Bausteine für eine allgemeine Rechtswissenschaft auf vergleichendethnologischer Grundlage* I (1880)), of KOHLER (especially *Einleitung in die vergleichende Rechtswissenschaft* (1885)), and many others. In France LERMINIER's *Introduction générale à l'histoire du droit* (1829) was clearly influenced by GANS, and in Italy AMARI's *Critica di una scienza delle legislazione comparate* (1857) was written under the influence of VICO's philosophy (see in detail ROTONDI, above p. 48). The leading work of the English school is HENRY MAINE's *Ancient Law* (1861).

5. This school of (historical) comparative legal science played a great part in the revitalization of modern comparative law towards the end of the nineteenth century, marked by a sudden growth of institutions, such as learned societies, periodicals, and professorial chairs. This occurred first and most strongly in France. POLLOCK (above p. 48) points to 1869 as the year in which comparative law gained full recognition as a new branch of legal science. That year saw the founding of the 'Société de législation comparée' which, along with its periodical, now called the *Revue internationale de droit comparé*, is still in existence today. In 1876 an 'Office de législation étrangère et de droit international' was set up in the French Ministry of Justice. But it is its acceptance into the university curriculum which marks the final recognition of comparative law as a new scholarly discipline. The founding in Paris in 1846—in the first flowering of comparative law—of a Chair in comparative criminal law has already been mentioned. In 1892 a Chair of comparative maritime and commercial law was established, a Chair of comparative constitutional law in 1895, and finally, in 1902, a Chair of comparative private law, held by SALEILLES and LÉVY-ULLMANN among others (see DAVID (above p. 48) at 408 f.).

Almost nothing similar was happening in Germany at this time. The *Zeitschrift für vergleichende Rechtswissenschaft*, founded by BERNHÖFT and COHN in 1878, was primarily devoted to comparative legal history. Germany had to wait until the foundation of the Internationale Vereinigung für vergleichende Rechtswissenschaft und Volkswirtschaftslehre in 1894 in order to obtain a society analogous to the Société de législation comparée in France. The Vereinigung was the brainchild of FELIX MEYER, *Kammergerichtsrat* in Berlin, and although it had very considerable fame and success, and survives to this day as the Gesellschaft für Rechtsvergleichung, full recognition of comparative law as a scholarly discipline was not achieved, as it was in France, by incorporation into the university syllabus before the Great War.

England at this time was also still heavily influenced by the historical school. Even in 1903 FREDERICK POLLOCK could still say, 'It makes no great difference whether we speak of historical jurisprudence or of comparative jurisprudence, or, as the Germans seem inclined to do, of the general history of law' (above p. 48, at p. 76). The early institutions in England must be considered in the light of this observation. HENRY MAINE became the first Professor of 'Historical and Comparative Jurisprudence' at Oxford in 1869, and in 1894 a Chair of 'History of Law and Comparative Law' was founded at University College in London, thanks to a bequest of £10,000 by the High Court judge SIR RICHARD QUAIN. But 1894 also saw the foundation of the 'Society of Comparative Legislation' on the French model, which gave modern comparative law a home in England. The Society has remained in existence up to the present day, as has its journal, now entitled the *International and Comparative Law Quarterly*.

It is a matter for speculation to what causes we should attribute this rebirth of interest in comparing the rules of foreign systems actually in force. No doubt the most important cause was the increase in economic and commercial contacts which called for a better knowledge of foreign rules or even for unified rules. The re-emergence of comparative law coincides with the first great efforts of international co-operation and unification of law, such as the treaties on copyright and trade-marks, the Universal Postal Union, and the first Hague Convention on Private Law. But the characteristic high-point of this stage of comparative law was the Paris Congress of Comparative Law of 1900. The aim set for comparative law by this Congress, so far as one can formulate it in view of the large number of contributors, was to discover the 'droit commun législatif' (SALEILLES) or the common 'stock of solutions' (ZITELMANN), and thus to bring the different systems of law closer together. The Paris Congress not only identified the aims of comparative law, as it then was; it also stamped its character with its optimistic and progressive pursuit of world unity, yet limited its scope, for its assumption that only similar things could be compared led to rather a narrow concentration on statutory law and on the legal systems of Continental Europe. MARC ANCEL's summing-up is quite accurate:

'At this stage in methodology, the principal aim and object of comparison is to create a rational science of law which could permit the formulation of norms appropriate to nineteenth century society in Continental Europe' ('Les grandes étapes' (above p. 48) at p. 26).

6. After the First World War the picture changes somewhat. German jurists were forced out of their 'remarkable introversion' (RABEL, *Aufgabe* (above p. 48) at 17) by Article X of the Treaty of Versailles which sought to regulate the pre-war legal relationships between nationals of combatant states. At first 'they naively supposed with their pre-war assumptions that

German concepts and methods would largely suffice to interpret and apply the Treaty of Versailles' (H. ISAY, quoted by RABEL, *Aufgabe* (above p. 48) at 19). But 'the Treaty was drafted in foreign languages, the German translation not being authentic, and it was the legal systems and perspectives of the victor nations, namely England and France, which provided the mode of drafting, the conceptual apparatus, the rules of interpretation, and the style. In such a situation there was no alternative but to investigate those systems . . .' (DÖLLE (above p. 48) at 20, citing references to works on the Treaty of Versailles). The comparative law thus required was admittedly a tool of advocacy designed to promote particular interests in litigation rather than objective scholarship, but the practical necessity of investigating so many cases produced results of value for science. It fell to RABEL, who himself had to interpret the Treaty as a member of the mixed Italian–German court of Arbitration, to free comparative law from this merely ancillary role. He saw comparative law as an independent juristic discipline whose practical usefulness to those applying the Treaty of Versailles was, scientifically speaking, contingent and collateral, even if it produced interesting data. Indeed, when, in his first basic book, *Aufgabe und Notwendigkeit der Rechtsvergleichung* (1925), he states the arguments for comparative law, the Treaty of Versailles and the other consequences of the war are given only a passing mention (*Aufgabe* (above p. 48) at 18 ff.).

The fact that other countries also experienced it shows that this upsurge of interest in comparative law in Germany is not wholly attributable to the confrontation with other systems necessitated by the Treaty of Versailles. According to ANCEL ('Les Grandes Étapes' (above p. 48) at 26), the second phase of twentieth-century comparative law begins at the end of the First World War. In this phase the institutions are consolidated, individual research is devoted to concrete and realistic problems, and the limitation to Continental Europe is overcome. The foundation of the 'major' institutes for comparative law was not simply an advantage for technicians, but was of deep and substantial importance: the kind of work in comparative law which was just beginning urgently needed research institutes which united teams of experts and specialized libraries; the development of comparative law from that period up to the present day would have been impossible without them. Even during the War, in 1916, an Institute for Comparative Law was founded in the University of Munich, at RABEL's instigation, and several other German universities followed suit after the War was over. Then in 1926 the Kaiser-Wilhelm-Gesellschaft founded in Berlin the Kaiser-Wilhelm Institute of Foreign and International Private Law, under RABEL, at the same time as it founded the companion Institute for Public Law, Foreign and International, under VIKTOR BRUNS. The Institute very quickly became the centre of comparative legal studies in Germany and one of the most important research institutes in the world. It is now in Hamburg, under the name of the Max-Planck-Institut für ausländisches und internationales Privatrecht.

In France the Institut de droit comparé was founded in 1920 by ÉDOUARD LAMBERT in Lyons. This was followed in 1932 by the Institut de droit comparé of Paris University, founded by LÉVY-ULLMANN who was also its first director. At the international level, the Académie internationale de droit comparé emerged in 1924, and has since held periodic International Congresses of Comparative Law which have proved very useful. Nor must one underestimate the significance for comparative law of the founding in 1926, by the League of Nations at SCIALOJA's instigation, of the Institut international pour l'unification du droit privé (UNIDROIT) in Rome, although its aims are not purely comparative.

Gradually the accent shifted from the discussion of fundamental questions—what are the aims and uses of comparative law, and what is its place in legal science generally?—which had obsessed the Paris Congress of 1900 to individual studies of particular factual problems, so-called 'recherche concrète' (ANCEL, 'Les grandes étapes' (above p. 48) at 27). As RABEL said in 1924 (*Aufgabe* (above p. 48) at 22) 'the principal task for scholars is to work on the detailed questions with all the care and exactitude at our command'. Eleven years later he could report as a fact what he had proposed as a plan: people had realized that there was so much juristic material to be studied, so many insights to be won, that it would unduly limit comparative law to determine in advance what its goals should be or what place in the system it should adopt. 'In fact comparative law has as many different aims as legal science itself; it would be impossible to enumerate them, and we need not attempt it' (RABEL, 'Fachgebiete' (above p. 48) at 79).

As research became concrete its scope expanded. The Paris Congress sought to find its 'droit commun législatif' in the positive legislation of Continental Europe; it compared codes and texts. At the 'second stage' of comparative law in the twentieth century this limitation was definitively overcome: comparative law moved on to the comparison of the legal solutions which 'are given to the same actual problems by the legal systems of different countries seen as a complete whole' (RABEL, 'Fachgebiete' (above p. 48) at 82). So far as method is concerned, this second stage is still with us: the method taught and practised today comes from the research which RABEL evolved and perfected.

There is a clear connection between the shift of focus from purely statutory law and the 'discovery' of the Common Law. RABEL and LAMBERT both recommended an intensive investigation of the Common Law when particular problems were being dealt with. The exclusive concentration of comparative law on the Romanistic and Germanic systems had already met with some opposition on the ground of the national and doctrinal constraints this imposed, but the extension to the Common Law was a step into the unknown. A handful of experts had some familiarity with a few special areas of law with an international flavour (for example, maritime law) but, apart from this, the Common Law was quite unknown to the jurists of Continental Europe. Admittedly work had started before the First World War on a project to produce a German commentary on English private law, undertaken by FELIX MEYER's Internationale Vereinigung für vergleichende Rechtswissenschaft, with financial support from the Berlin Chamber of Commerce and the Senates of Hamburg and Bremen, but the War had put an end to it. The gap between the Common Law and the Continental systems in history, structure, and method must have seemed unbridgeable; to cross it was a challenge to comparative law, but it was a challenge which let scholars see that if one poses one's questions properly, that is, in terms of function, and if one investigates a legal system in its entirety, such differences are really immaterial. At the turn of the century the axiom 'only comparables can be compared' was taken to mean that comparison was possible only between systems whose structures and concepts were comparable. This construction of the theoretical axiom was belied by the success of the practical 'Experiment' of RABEL's and LAMBERT's institutes, for in the 1920s and 1930s they produced a stream of first-rate works. This extension of comparative legal studies to include the Common Law along with Romanistic and Continental European systems definitively broke the bounds set by the Paris Congress of 1900; after the necessary abandonment of the view that only systems with comparable systematic structures offered a basis for comparison, it was shown to be profitable and useful to compare systems which were entirely different, and that the true basis for comparison was *similarity of function and of social need,* the means of satisfying which may be conceptually very different. This provided comparative law with a methodologically sound starting-point and also, to a large extent, a tool for the investigation of extremely different legal systems.

Many causes have contributed to the modern form of comparative law—the extension of scope from European statutory law to areas not bounded by nationality, the adoption of a method which investigates a legal system in all its aspects but always with an eye to particular function, the establishment of special institutes, fully equipped with the personnel and plant needed for sustained work, and finally the representation of comparatists from all countries in the Association internationale des sciences juridiques. The methods of RABEL and his contemporaries at home and abroad have won through. The problems they identified and the programmes they established constitute the tasks of comparative law today.

B. THE LEGAL FAMILIES OF THE WORLD

5

The Style of Legal Families

ARMINJON/ NOLDE/WOLFF, *Traité de droit comparé* I (1950) 42–53.

CLARK, 'The Idea of the Civil Law Tradition', in *Comparative and Private International Law, Essays in Honor of John H. Merryman* (1990) 11.

CONSTANTINESCO, 'Ideologie als determinierendes Element zur Bildung der Rechtskreise', *ZfRV* 19 (1978) 161.

——, 'Über den Stil der "Stiltheorie" in der Rechtsvergleichung', *ZvglRW* 78 (1979) 154.

R. DAVID, *Traité élémentaire de droit civil comparé* (1950) 222–6.

——, *Les grands systèmes de droit contemporains* (9th edn. by Jauffret-Spinosi, 1988).

EÖRSI, *Comparative Civil (Private) Law* (1979).

A. ESMEIN, 'Le Droit comparé et l'enseignement du Droit', in: *Congrès international de droit comparé , Procès-verbaux des séances et documents* I (1905) 445.

FRIEDMAN, 'Some Thoughts on Comparative Legal Culture', in *Comparative and Private International Law, Essays in Honor of John H. Merryman* (1990) 49.

LAWSON, 'The Family Affinities of Common-law and Civil-law Legal Systems', 6 *Hastings Int. Comp. L. Rev.* 85 (1982).

LÉVY-ULLMANN, 'Observations générales sur les communications relatives au droit privé dans les pays étrangers', in: *Les Transformations du droit dans les principaux pays depuis cinquante ans* I (1922) 81.

MALMSTRÖM, 'The System of Legal Systems, Notes on a Problem of Classification in Comparable Law', *Scand. Stud. L.* 13 (1969) 127.

MARTINEZ-PAZ, *Introducción al estudio del derecho civil comparado* (1934, reprinted 1960) 149–60.

MERRYMAN, *The Civil Law Tradition, An Introduction to the Legal Systems of Western Europe and Latin America* (2nd edn., 1985).

SAUSER-HALL, *Fonction et méthode du droit comparé* (1913).

SCHNITZER, *Vergleichende Rechtslehre* I (2nd edn., 1961) 133–42.

WIEACKER, *Privatrechtsgeschichte der Neuzeit* (2nd edn., 1967) 496–513.

I

THE theory of 'legal families' seeks to provide the answer to several distinct questions in comparative law. Can we divide the vast number of legal systems into just a few large groups (legal families)? How do we decide what these groups should be? And, supposing we know what the groups should be, how do we decide whether a particular legal system belongs to one group rather than another? We make these groupings primarily for taxonomic purposes, so as to arrange the mass of legal systems in a comprehensible order. But there is another way in which this may make the comparatist's task easier. If one or two legal systems prove representative of each of these large groups, then the comparatist can, under certain conditions, concentrate on those systems, at any rate at the present stage of comparative law (see above Ch. 3 IV).

Of the many attempts to devise such groupings, that of ARMINJON/ NOLDE/WOLFF is the most penetrating. ESMEIN had earlier divided the legal world into the Romanistic, Germanic, Anglo-Saxon, Slav, and Islamic families, but ARMINJON/NOLDE/WOLFF objected to this on the ground that the criterion of division was not evident. This objection is arguably unfair; ESMEIN's grouping was particularly good for his time, and he did state what principles of distinction he had in mind: 'For this purpose we must classify the laws of different countries, enacted or customary, by dividing them into a small number of families or groups, each of which constitutes an original system of law; and the teaching of comparative law, if it is to be scientific, must start with a survey of the historical sources, the general structure, and particular characteristics of each of these systems' (above p. 63 at p. 451).

Other criteria of division have been adopted. LÉVY-ULLMANN (above p. 63) started out by treating the *sources of law* as critical; SAUSER-HALL saw *race* as the crucial test, on the ground that 'ce n'est qu'à l'intérieur de chaque race que nous pouvons constater une évolution juridique particulière (above p. 63, at 102). SCHNITZER (above p. 63), MALMSTRÖM (above p. 63), and EÖRSI (above p. 63) have made other proposals, the last from the viewpoint of Marxist legal theory.

ARMINJON/NOLDE/WOLFF were of the view that modern systems of law should be grouped in accordance with their *substance* 'paying due heed to originality, derivation, and common elements', and without any reference to extrinsic factors such as geography or race. This produced an attractive division into seven legal families: the French, German, Scandinavian, English, Russian, Islamic, and Hindu (above p. 63 at pp. 47 f.).

RENÉ DAVID, whose treatise was published in 1950, also criticized earlier writers for failing to produce convincing criteria of distinction, and himself concluded that only two such criteria were satisfactory: the criterion of *ideology* (the product of religion, philosophy, or political, economic, or social structure) and the criterion of legal technique: differences of legal technique being of secondary importance, the principal ground of distinction is philosophical basis or conception of justice. On this principle he distinguishes five legal families: Western systems, socialist systems, Islamic law,

Hindu law, and Chinese law (Traité (above p. 63) at pp. 222 ff.). DAVID subsequently modified his position: he now has three legal families—the Romanistic–German family, the Common Law family, and the socialist family—along with a further loosely knit group of 'other systems', consisting of Jewish law, Hindu law, and the law of the Far East, along with a new group of African and Malagasy law (see *Les Grands Systèmes* (above p. 63) 19 ff.).

II

ARMINJON/NOLDE/WOLFF's division of legal systems into seven families is the most convincing of the groupings so far put forward, especially in its rejection of external criteria: 'Any rational classification of modern legal systems must be based on a study of their substance' (above p. 63 at p. 47). The authors are, however, reticent about the standpoint to be adopted for such study. We are told that, as with languages in comparative linguistics, legal systems are to be put into families on the basis of similarities and relationship, but it is never made really clear which common qualities are the crucial ones. It is often obvious enough that one system is a parent system (like the Common Law of England), but we need more help with the difficult question whether a system is affiliated to one parent or to another, especially as legal systems have been known to adopt new parents.

Whenever one is concerned with the identification of legal families or the classification of a particular system, two matters in particular must be borne in mind.

1. The theory of legal families has so far proceeded as if the only law worth taking into account were what European lawyers call private law. This is partly because comparatists have hitherto concentrated on private law, and partly because it is only private lawyers, so far as one can see, who have been interested in the theory. ARMINJON/NOLDE/WOLFF alone make it clear that their division is based on, and therefore valid only for, private law (above p. 63 at p. 47). Such groupings, therefore, may be highly relative. For example, it is quite possible that a system is to be put in one family for private law purposes, and in another for purposes of constitutional law. Thus German private law unquestionably belongs in the German legal family, but one might well put German constitutional law in a group which included the United States and Italy and excluded England and France, depending on the weight one attributes to the presence or absence of judicial review of constitutionality as being the hallmark of a constitutional system. But even if one concentrates on private law, a similar difficulty may arise. Thus the Arabian countries belong to Islamic law as far as family and inheritance law is concerned, just as India belongs to Hindu law, but the economic law of these countries (including commercial law and the law of contract and tort) is heavily impressed by the legal thinking of the colonial

and mandatary powers—the Common Law in the case of India, French law in the case of most of the Arab states. So in the theory of legal families much depends on the area of law one has in mind.

2. Much also depends on the period of which one is speaking. Usually comparatists may largely ignore sudden legislative changes, since the meat of comparative law is not positive law but critical comparison. But the division of the world's legal systems into families, especially the attribution of a system to a particular family, is susceptible to alteration as a result of legislation or other events, and can therefore be *only temporary*. For example, current developments in Japan make it seem increasingly difficult to class it along with the People's Republic of China in a 'Far-Eastern' legal family, as was done in the previous edition. It is true that for a long time the many codes on the European model which were enacted in Japan had very little influence on the realities of legal life there, but it now appears that the traditional distaste for written rules of law and litigation is so much on the wane that it can no longer be put in a family of oriental systems. (See Ch. 20 I, 21 I.)

It is possible for a quite *new* legal family to emerge as time goes by, and we may at the moment be approaching the time when the systems of sub-Saharan Africa should be classed together as an *African legal family*. These African legal systems have long been an object of fascination to comparative lawyers, legal ethnologists, and legal sociologists, despite the appalling difficulties of doing research on them (see the instructive and comprehensive piece by BRYDE, 'Afrikanische Rechtssysteme', *JuS* 1982, 8). *Legal ethnologists* find Africa extremely important for research because in relation to family and land law and questions of dispute resolution the mass of Africans still live under indigenous customary law. The rules of such law vary enormously, partly because of the great differences in race, language, culture, and lifestyle between the various tribes and peoples on this vast continent, and partly because the existing 'traditional' law has been very variously influenced by Islamic law and the law of the ex-colonial powers. *Sociologists of law* love discussing African law, for it is a concrete instance of their central problem, namely the relationship between law and social change and, in special relation to African conditions, the question what contribution law, especially 'modern' law, has made and can or will make to the desired political, social, and economic 'development' in African countries, a question relevant to all developing countries (see, for example, TRUBEK/ GALANTER, 'Scholars in Self-Estrangement: Some Reflections on the Crisis in Law and Development Studies in the United States', 1974 *Wis. L. Rev.* 1062; MERRYMAN, 'Comparative Law and Social Change: On the Origins, Style, Decline and Revival of the Law and Development Movement', 25 *Am. J. Comp. L.* 457 (1977); BRYDE, *The Politics and Sociology of African Legal Development* (1976); FUCHS, 'Recht und Entwicklungsländer', *ZvglRW* 80 (1981) 355). The African legal systems also provide a rich field of material for the study of the *reception of foreign law*, for all African legal systems are still influenced to a considerable extent by the laws of the earlier colonial powers, partly because European law has served as a model, especially in the area of the law of obligations, commercial law, criminal law, and administrative law, and partly because, by studying in Europe or at an African university founded on a European model, African lawyers have absorbed European legal traditions which have stayed with them in their subsequent careers as officials, judges, and lawyers. As a result there is still a deep divide between the previous French and Belgian colonies on the one hand, and those that were British on the other. This is why it is much easier for a lawyer from Ghana to understand a lawyer from Kenya, Uganda, or even from England, which are far away, than a lawyer from the Ivory Coast next door (see below pp. 112 ff.). Even so, the problems facing all African legal systems are basically similar, and with a little co-operation could be studied at a general level. Those for whom this is the main consideration may therefore speak of an African legal family, notwithstanding the differences we have mentioned (see in this sense M'BAYE, 'The African Conception of Law', II *Int. Enc. Comp. L.* Ch. 1 (1975) 138). See also ALLOTT, 'Towards the Unification of Laws in Africa', 14 *ICLQ* 366 (1965); ALLOTT, 'The Unification of Laws in Africa', 16 *Am. J. Comp. L.* 51 (1968); BAMODU, 'Transnational Law, Unification and Harmonization of International Commercial Law in Africa', 38 *J. Afr. L.* 125 (1994).

It will be clear from these examples that one's division of the world into legal families and the inclusion of systems in a particular family is vulnerable to alteration by historical development and change. So in the theory of legal families much depends on the period of time of which one is speaking.

3. Objection has been raised to all the different connecting factors which have been used to put the legal systems of the world into groups. It is argued that instead of basing categorizations so much on historical development, legal content or the observable techniques of the rules of law, one should inquire whether countries have the same legal culture, that is, whether its citizens have similar attitudes to law and similar expectations of it (see especially FRIEDMAN (above p. 63) and LEGRAND (58 *Mod. L. Rev.* 262 (1995)), with further references). The objection must be taken seriously: comparative sociology, ethnology or political science may indeed come up with different criteria and groupings. So far, however, as FRIEDMAN himself admits, nothing worthwhile has emerged. Accordingly, even if the path here proposed is only second-best, we shall proceed along it until a better one is on offer.

III

The unsatisfactory feature of most previous attempts to distinguish the legal families and to attribute individual systems to them is that they are one-dimensional, that is, they seek to make everything turn on a *single* criterion.

In our view the critical thing about legal systems is their *style*, for the styles of individual legal systems and groups of legal systems are each quite distinctive. The comparatist must strive to grasp these *legal styles*, and to use distinctive stylistic traits as a basis for putting legal systems into groups.

The concept of style which originated in the literary and fine arts has long been used in other fields. Style in the arts signifies the distinctive element of a work or its unity of form, but many other disciplines use this fertile concept to indicate a congeries of particular features which the most diverse objects of study may possess. In law we find the concept used in the Codex Iuris Canonici; canon 20 lays down that if there is no clear and express rule, the rule to be applied is to be found by analogy or inferred from the general principles of law consistent with canonical equity, from constant leading doctrine, and from the *style* and practice of the Roman Curia. Another social science, economics, uses the notion of the 'style of an economy' in one of its branches. ARTHUR SPIETHOFF defines it thus: the 'style of an economy' is the totality of features which flesh out a distinctive form of economic life; his subsequent discussion of methodological questions and of the 'determination of the characteristics of economic styles' is not relevant for us in view of the differences between the two disciplines. (See SPIETHOFF, 'Die Allgemeine Volkswirtschaftslehre als geschichtliche Theorie', in *Festgabe Sombart* (1933) 56, 75 ff.)

We must therefore ask which are the factors which contribute to the juristic style of whole groups of legal systems; for this purpose, experience, inadequate though it doubtless is, must be our guide. It is not every trivial difference between legal systems which can rank as an element in their style. Only 'important' or 'essential' differentiating qualities are hallmarks. As SPIETHOFF says: 'there can never be any final proof of what is "important" or "essential". How many styles a scholar identifies and how he identifies them are largely matters for his judgment. The aim, however, is quite clear: to see the differences in reality, past and present, contained in distinctive forms of economic life' (ibid., 57). One indication of the 'importance' of a feature in a legal system is if the comparatist from another system finds it very surprising. In consequence it is easier to discover the stylistically distinctive elements in a foreign system than in one's own. From this it follows that in the long run international co-operation will be needed to determine the different styles of law.

The following factors seem to us to be those which are crucial for the style of a legal system or legal family: (1) its historical background and development, (2) its predominant and characteristic mode of thought in legal matters, (3) especially distinctive institutions, (4) the kind of legal sources it acknowledges and the way it handles them, and (5) its ideology.

1. It is self-evident that *historical development* is one of the factors which determines the style of modern legal systems. The Common Law is perhaps the clearest example of this, but it is not so easy to group the systems of the European Continent. They stem from Roman and Germanic law, but should they all (with the admitted exception of Nordic law, which stands by itself) be put in one legal family, as DAVID and MALMSTRÖM do, or should there be a Germanic family (Germany, Austria, Switzerland, and a few affiliated systems) and a Romanistic family (France and all the systems which adopted

the French Civil Code, along with Spain, Portugal, and South America)? ARMINJON/NOLDE/WOLFF seems to us to be right in opting for the latter alternative (above p. 63 at p. 50). Subsequent events may obliterate the stylistic significance of common origins, and here there are two subsequent events. First, the great movement of reception to which the French Civil Code gave rise and in which Germany, Austria, and Switzerland took no part. Secondly, the development in German-speaking countries in the nineteenth century, under pandectist influence, of a formal legal technique with extremely clear-cut concepts which, far from forming the basis of a thorough codification in France, whose traditions look more to the political and forensic spheres, had hardly any effect there at all. If one puts into a single 'Romanistic–Germanic legal family' the Romanistic systems, the laws of Germany, Austria, and Switzerland, and even the Nordic systems, one may be misled into concentrating on the relatively abstract common features which distinguish them as a group from, say, the Common Law; one may too easily overlook the fact that in the concert of European law the three groups mentioned have each their own very distinctive voice. It is true, of course, that the Romanistic, Germanic, and Nordic systems each have a closer relationship with each other than with the Common Law; but given their recent development and the presence of the other stylistically distinctive features to be mentioned shortly, clarity requires us to put them into different legal families.

2. Another hallmark of a legal system or family is a *distinctive mode of legal thinking*. Thus the Germanic and Romanistic families are marked by a tendency to use abstract legal norms, to have a well-articulated system containing well-defined areas of law, and to think up and to think in juristic constructions. When one looks at the very different situation in the Common Law one realizes just how distinctive these stylistic elements are.

The tradition of the English Common Law has been one of gradual development from decision to decision; historically speaking, it is case-law, not enacted law. On the Continent the development since the reception of Roman law has been quite different, from the interpretation of JUSTINIAN's Corpus Iuris to the codification, nation by nation, of abstract rules. So Common Law comes from the court, Continental law from the study; the great jurists of England were judges, on the Continent professors. On the Continent lawyers, faced with a problem, even a new and unforeseen one, ask what solution the rule provides; in England and the United States they predict how the judge would deal with the problem, given existing decisions. These differences in style run through the whole legal system. On the Continent lawyers think abstractly, in terms of institutions; in England concretely, in terms of cases, the relationship of the parties, 'rights and duties'. On the Continent, the system is conceived as being complete and free from gaps, in England lawyers feel their way gradually from case to case. On the Continent lawyers delight in systematics, in England they are sceptical of every generalization. On the Continent lawyers operate with ideas, which often, dangerously enough, take on a life of their own; in England they think in pictures; and so one could continue.

These differences in style correspond with the differences in the Continental and English mentalities, attributable to different historical developments, especially those of an intellectual order. If we may generalize, the European is given to making plans, to regulating things in advance, and therefore, in terms of law, to drawing up rules and systematizing them. He approaches life with fixed ideas, and operates deductively. The Englishman improvises, never making a decision until he has to: 'we'll cross that bridge when we come to it'. As MAITLAND said, he is an empiricist. Only experience counts for him; theorizing has little appeal; and so he is not given to abstract rules of law. Convinced, perhaps from living by the sea, that life will controvert the best-laid plans, the Englishman is more at home with case-law proceeding cautiously step-by-step than with legislation which purports to lay down rules for the solution of all future cases.

One must avoid putting undue stress on this difference. We shall see (see below Ch. 18) that in many areas of law on the continent legislated rules are either non-existent or inconclusive, and that in actual practice there is as much judge-made law as in England. Conversely, too, the idea that enactments are simply islets in an ocean of case-law is no more than a nostalgic anachronism even in England, let alone the United States.

There is another stylistic element in legal thinking which is found in several legal families, indeed in all Western law. It is what RUDOLPH V. JHERING called the 'struggle for law'. The principle is that though the goal of law is peace, one must struggle to achieve it. In other words, it is the duty of a person, owed both to himself and to the idea of law itself, to fight for his rights. Our Western laws of procedure are bottomed on this view. JHERING thought it was invariable and many people today regard it as a truism, but the comparatist who turns his eyes to the Far East finds that this is not so of the legal systems there, as they were at any rate until recently.

In those systems law is a secondary and subordinate means of achieving social order, and it is used only as a last resort. The harmony of society is seen as reflecting the general harmony of the world as evidenced in nature and the cosmos. The arid logic and external compulsion inherent in law make it a very rudimentary means of achieving order, though no doubt it is suitable for uncivilized peoples. Among civilized peoples, principles of behaviour should be obeyed voluntarily, and then they will prove effective in the community life of family, clan, and village; they come not from the law, but from a mass of unwritten rules of behaviour harmoniously integrated by tradition. These rules are not directed to procuring that everyone obtains his due, but to preserving social harmony. In consequence it is no solution to a dispute to have a winner and a loser; instead the claimant must take great care to let his opponent 'save face'. Thus in the Far East law does not lead to a judicial decision in favour of one party, but to a peaceable settlement or amicable composition (see further below p. 286 f.). There is much of the wisdom of the Orient here, and there are some echoes of it in the West. Thus a bad settlement, we say, is better than a good lawsuit, and a legal adviser may pride himself on never having had to go to court. Despite this, there is still this critical difference in style, that in the West man naturally fights for his rights and seeks a clear decision, treating a compromise as a thing perhaps to be settled for, and in the East the face-saving compromise is the ideal and a firm decision only a necessary evil.

In this area comparative law has a particular need for the assistance of legal sociology, given that in certain legal systems statutes and codes which in form and substance are quite like those in Europe may prove to be quite peripheral features, surprisingly remote from the real forces which mould legal life there. It is not only the student of oriental systems who may have to inquire into this. The information we have about the operation of the legal systems of Latin America suggests that there also written law is not very significant in practice, and that as a means of resolving social conflicts formal proceedings before an independent state judge have nothing like the importance they do in Europe or North America. (See, for example, GESSNER, *Recht und Konflikt, Eine soziologische Untersuchung privatrechtlicher Konflikte in Mexico* (1976).) Much work remains to be done: comparative sociological research in law has only just started.

3. Certain *legal institutions* are so distinctive that they lend a characteristic style to a legal system. One might instance the doctrine of consideration in the Common Law (Ch. 29), or the trust, or the concept of agency (Ch. 32 I), or the amazing proliferation of different torts (Ch. 40 II), or the many peculiarities of the law of property such as the 'various degrees of property', or the way a decedent's estate passes to an administrator or executor, not to mention the remarkable features of the law of evidence. In the Romanistic family one could mention the concept of *cause*, the *action directe*, the action *in rem verso* (Ch. 38 II), and the institution of *negotiorum gestio*, common to continental systems but so foreign to the Common Law. In the Germanic family perhaps one could instance the general clauses which open the door to judge-made law, the doctrine of the abstract real contract, liability for *culpa in contrahendo*, the doctrine of the collapse of the foundation of the transaction (Ch. 37 II), the entrenched position of the institution of unjustified enrichment, and the land register.

4. The style of legal systems is obviously also marked by the choice of *sources of law* which they recognize and by the methods of interpreting and handling them in connection with the court machinery and rules of procedure. Since LÉVY-ULLMANN many introductions to comparative law, books and articles have been devoted to these topics, especially and repeatedly to the supposed opposition between statutory and case-law systems, with all the refinements of the doctrine of precedent and the niceties of statutory construction (see below Ch. 18). No one can deny that differences exist on this matter, but they have generally been exaggerated. For comparative law as a whole and for the theory of legal families in particular, the question of sources of law is of minor importance.

5. Finally, the style of a legal system may be marked by an *ideology*, that is, a religious or political conception of how social or economic life should be organized. Islamic and Hindu law offer examples of this and until recently this was the ground on which 'socialist legal systems' were treated as a special legal family (see Chs. 23–27 of the second edition). This is not a factor which helps us distinguish between the various 'Western' legal systems; here other criteria must be sought.

IV

These are the stylistic factors which enable us to identify the families of legal systems and to attribute individual systems to them, but the weight to be given to each of these factors varies according to the circumstances. As was said above, ideology is an effective ground for distinguishing the religious systems, but does not help us to separate the legal families of the West. There it is history, mode of thought and distinctive institutions which distinguish the legal families. Sources of law are a distinguishing feature of Islamic and Hindu law and also help us to divide the Common Law from the Continental legal families, but we cannot use them as a basis for distinguishing between the Germanic, Nordic, and Romanistic families.

There are some 'hybrid' systems of law which it is not easy to put in the right family—Greece, for example (Ch. 11 IV), Louisiana (Ch. 8 VII), the Province of Quebec (Ch. 8 VII), Scotland (Ch. 14 VI), South Africa (Ch. 16 VI), Israel (Ch. 16 VII), the Philippines, Puerto Rico, the People's Republic of China, and some others. With them the question must be which family they are closest to in style. This calls for delicacy. Often one finds that some areas of law in a system bear the marks of one 'parent', others of another. In such a case an exclusive attribution to one or other is impossible, except with regard to particular areas of law such as family law or inheritance law or commercial law. Sometimes a legal system is in the process of moving towards a particular legal family; in such a case it is often extremely doubtful at which point of time the change of family is complete, and it may not be possible to fix upon an exact moment. In any case, as the example of 'hybrid' systems shows, any division of the legal world into families or groups is a rough and ready device. It can be quite useful for the novice, by putting the confusing variety of legal systems into some kind of loose order, but the experienced comparatist will have developed a 'nose' for the distinctive style of national legal systems and will either not use the device of legal families at all, or will use it with all the circumspection called for by any attempt to force into a schematic order social phenomena as highly complex as living legal systems.

One must therefore keep calm when new proposals for divisions of legal systems are aired, and the view here put forward is subjected to criticism on various different assumptions (see, for example, BENDA-BECKMANN and CONSTANTINESCO, *ZvglRWiss* 78 [1979] 5 and 154; EÖRSI (above p. 63) 45 f.; ZAJTAY (above p. 63)). It should be borne in mind that since every writer has a special purpose in mind or a particular thesis to prove, he must be allowed to decide what systems to deal with and how to group them in the way that best suits his purpose or thesis. Thus in *The Civil Law Tradition* (2nd edn. 1985) MERRYMAN treats as very much alike all the legal systems in Western Europe and Latin America which are more or less influenced by Roman law. There is nothing wrong with that, though not everyone will agree that the systems of Southern Europe and Latin America are really 'typical' of the 'civil law tradition', while those of France and Germany are 'untypical' (on this see CLARK (above p. 63), at 18 ff.).—We differ from both MERRYMAN and DAVID in electing to divide continental systems into the Romanesque, the German, and the Scandinavian legal families. This is because we want to emphasize the special tonalities which these three legal families bring to the concert of European law. Those with other aims will draw other distinctions. Thus for ATIYAH/SUMMERS the character of a legal system depends very much on whether 'form' or 'substance' predominates in its judicial reasoning, its interpretation of statutes or its court procedures. After analysing and comparing the case-law, the legislative techniques, the role of judge and advocate, and the nature of legal training in England and the United States, they conclude that the two legal systems are really very different, so different indeed that many a reader will think that English law, with its tendency to more formal argument, is closer to the continental systems than to that of the United States (*Form and Substance in Anglo-American Law, A Comparative Study of Legal Reasoning, LegalTheory, and Legal Institutions* (1987)). We rather agree with DAVID, who concluded his treatment of the controversies of classification by saying: 'Much ink has been spilt on the subject, but to little purpose. "Legal families" do not exist like human families: the idea is used purely for explanatory purposes, to indicate the extent of difference and similarity in the various legal systems. It follows that all classifications have their utility: it all depends on the point of view adopted by the writer in question and the aspects of the matter which interest him most.' (*Les Grands Systèmes*, 22.)

It was not the aim of this excursus to offer a new grouping of legal systems but rather to use the concept of style in the context of law to elucidate better than has hitherto been done the criteria which should be employed in grouping the legal systems together and deciding which group a particular system belongs to. The grouping to which we are led and which will serve as our basis for the introduction to the great legal systems of the world is only slightly different from that of ARMINJON/NOLDE/WOLFF: (1) Romanistic family; (2) Germanic family; (3) Nordic family; (4) Common Law family. Other sections will be devoted to the law of the People's Republic of China, Japanese law, Islamic law, and Hindu law.

I. THE ROMANISTIC LEGAL FAMILY

6

The History of French Law

ARMINJON/NOLDE/WOLFF, *Traité de droit comparé* I (1950) 120 ff.

BRISSAUD, *Manuel d'histoire du droit privé* (1935).

DAWSON, 'The Codification of the French Customs', 38 *Mich. L. Rev.* 765 (1940).

——, *The Oracles of the Law* (1968).

A. ESMEIN, *Précis élémentaire de l'histoire du droit français de 1789 à 1814* (1908).

——, *Cours élémentaire d'histoire du droit français* (15th edn., 1925).

FENET, *Recueil complet de travaux préparatoires du Code civil* (1836).

HEINSHEIMER, *Die Zivilgesetze der Gegenwart* I (1932): *Frankreich, Code civil*, Introduction V ff.

HEYMANN, 'Romanische Rechtsordnungen', in: *Handwörterbuch der Rechtswissenschaft* V (1928) 151.

KOSCHAKER, *Europa und das römische Recht* (2nd edn., 1953).

LE CODE CIVIL, LIVRE DU CENTENAIRE, 2 vols. (1904), with essays by SOREL, ESMEIN, VIGIÉ, SALEILLES and others.

MITTEIS, 'Die germanischen Grundlagen des französischen Rechtes', *SavZ/Germ.* 63 (1943) 137.

OLIVIER MARTIN, *La Coutume de Paris—Trait d'union entre le droit romain et les législations modernes* (1925).

RABEL, 'Private Laws of Western Civilization—The French Civil Code', 10 *La. L. Rev.* 107 (1950).

SAVATIER, *L'art de faire les lois—Bonaparte et le Code civil* (1927).

WILHELM, 'Gesetzgebung und Kodifikation in Frankreich im 17. und 18. Jahrhundert', *Ius commune* 1 (1967) 241.

——, 'Portalis und Savigny', in: *Aspekte europäischer Rechtsgeschichte, Festgabe für Coing* (1982) 445.

I

THE Code civil of 1804 is not only the heart of private law in France but also the great model for the codes of private law of the whole Romanistic legal family. The Code was generated by the spirit of the French Revolution which sought to eradicate the feudal institutions of the past and to implant in their place the natural law values of property, freedom of contract, family, and family inheritance. The revolutionary events of the years after 1789 were very important for the Code, but there is more to it than that. For all the impetus of revolution, the Code carefully absorbs the results of a long historical development, and most of it is a felicitous blend of traditional legal institutions from the *droit écrit* of the South, influenced by Roman law, and the *droit coutumier* of the North, influenced by the Germanic–Frankish customary law. Though in many respects the Code civil makes a revolutionary takeoff, it bears throughout the marks of its heritage of the pre-revolutionary law, the *ancien droit*. Accordingly we shall first trace the development of French law up to the Revolution, so far as this is necessary in order to understand the achievement of those who drafted the Code civil. Then we shall deal briefly with the *droit intermédiaire* of the revolutionary period and with the legislative history of the Code, before turning to the Code itself.

II

The Romans established their law in Gaul as they did in all the provinces they conquered, but when the Western Roman Empire collapsed in 476, Roman law did not lose its validity in the Germanic states which succeeded it; it survived, especially in the kingdoms of the Visigoths and the Burgundians, as the law for the subject peoples of non-German origin. In 506 Alaric II, King of the Visigoths, passed a statute—the Breviarium Alaricianum or Lex Romana Wisigothorum—containing a résumé of and commentary on the Codex Theodosianus and some other Roman sources; this contributed to the survival of some knowledge of Roman law in the southern part of France despite the great migrations of the fifth and sixth centuries. In the North of France, on the other hand, the incursion of the Franks and the founding of the Frankish state did largely oust Roman law, since the Franks brought with them their own developed customary laws of Germanic origin, and later crystallized them in several statutes of which the most important is the Lex Salica. The renaissance of Roman law studies in North Italy in the eleventh and twelfth centuries was immediately taken up in the South of France; the study of the Corpus Iuris was well established in the Universities of Montpellier and Toulouse in the twelfth century. Acquaintance with Roman law gradually filtered northwards, without of course displacing the traditional customary laws of the Franks. Thus the territory of France became divided for legal purposes into the area of *droit écrit* in the South influenced by Roman law, and the area of *droit coutumier* in the North, based on Germanic customs (*coutumes*). The dividing line ran parallel with the Loire from the mouth of the Gironde to the Lake of Geneva, so that the northern three-fifths of France as it is today were controlled by the *droit coutumier*, the southern two-fifths by the *droit écrit*.

One must not overestimate the sharpness of the division between the *droit écrit* and the *droit coutumier*. In the South, for example in the urban regions of Bordeaux and Toulouse, there were written *coutumes* influenced by Roman law but containing strong Germanic elements. Nor was Roman law entirely rejected by the *droit coutumier* in the North. Some parts of the law, for example contract law, were inadequately regulated by the *coutumes* and therefore lawyers readily had recourse to the better developed and more refined Roman law; and the view was accepted in the North that Roman law as *ratio scripta* could be called upon to supplement and explain the *coutumes* when they gave no answer to particular questions. But it must be noticed that, unlike the later situation in Germany when Roman law was received, Roman law was not regarded as authoritative or valuable on the ground that it was the law of the Roman Empire. On the contrary, the French Kings were especially interested in protecting their sovereignty against the Empire and the Emperor, and the royalist lawyers emphasized that if Roman law was accepted in France, this was not because it had been laid down by Rome, but on the ground that it had been accepted by custom or by reason of its inherent quality: *non ratione imperii sed imperio rationis*. Thus in France, unlike Germany later, there was never any serious discussion of a complete reception of Roman law into France; it was effective only in so far as this was the local custom, as in the South, or, as in the North, on the grounds of its inherent merit.

In the tenth and eleventh centuries, as the Carolingians gave way to the Capetians, Frankish law broke up into many different systems, according to the territories, some extremely small, won by princes and prelates (compare MITTEIS, above p. 74, at pp. 152 ff.). A number of law-books were written in the thirteenth century, mainly by famous practitioners, recording the custom of a particular region. Among the most important are the *Livre de Jostice et de Plet* which portrayed the *Coutume* of Orleans, strongly impressed by Roman and canon law, the *Coutumes de Beauvaisis* by PHILIPPE DE BEAUMANOIR, and the great collection of Norman customary law (*Grand Coutumier de la Normandie*) which to this day provides the basis for the private law of the Channel Islands. It remained true, however, that the customary laws of Northern France depended principally on oral tradition; the judge who did not know the appropriate rule of the relevant *coutume* had to discover it by means of an 'enquête par turbe', in which a number of local inhabitants had to say what they remembered the substance of the *coutume* to be. The proliferation of *coutumes* and the difficulty of discovering their content naturally gave rise to great legal uncertainty. This called the French King on to the scene in the fifteenth century. By the Ordonnance of Montils-les-Tours of 1454, Charles VII ordained that the customs of the various territories should be written down and that those which were already recorded should be drafted anew, with the co-operation of a royal commission of experts. The task of recording the *coutumes* took longer than expected. Charles VII's instruction had to be repeated several times by his successors, and they also had to overcome the opposition of some of the territories, especially Normandy (see the detailed description in DAWSON, above p. 74). But the intervention of the King greatly strengthened the power of the traditional customary laws to withstand Roman law. As the French historian of law OLIVIER MARTIN wrote, 'That France was saved from the massive reception of Roman law which took place in Germany is clearly attributable to the King's success in having the customs recorded in the sixteenth century' (above p. 74, p. 13). It is also clear that the recording of the *coutumes* was necessary for the gradual development of a common customary law of France (*droit coutumier commun*), and finally for the amalgamation of *droit coutumier* and *droit écrit,* without which the Code civil of 1804 could never have unified the law in France.

By the end of the eighteenth century all the important customs of more than purely local significance had been recorded in accordance with the royal mandate. Yet on the eve of the French Revolution, on one estimate, there were no fewer than 60 customary laws of extensive significance (*coutumes générales*), some of which were interrelated, and as many as 300 *coutumes* of limited territorial application (*coutumes locales*).

The juxtaposition of different *coutumes* led to legal problems whenever a case had connections with more than one region, as where a Breton drew up his will in Paris, where the *coutume* laid down different rules regarding testamentary capacity or form. Thus in the sixteenth century French lawyers were especially active in the area of law which today we call private international law; the names of DUMOULIN (1500–66) and, even more, D'ARGENTRÉ (1519–90) stand out; see the fundamental work of GAMILLSCHEG, *Der Einfluss Dumoulins auf die Entwicklung des Kollisionsrechts* (1955).

While the writing down of the more important *coutumes* could reduce the uncertainty of the law, it could not diminish the substantial differences between them, much less the great legal division between the *pays du droit écrit* and the *pays du droit coutumier*. As the French Kings consolidated their power, the multiplicity of legal systems became more and more unsatisfactory, and the creation of a unitary private law common to the whole of France was increasingly felt to be necessary.

The assimilation of the particular customary laws was considerably promoted by the *Coutume de Paris*. It became increasingly important after its publication in 1510. This was mainly attributable to the influential decisions of the Parlement de Paris, whose very wide jurisdiction included almost the whole of the area of *droit coutumier* with the exception of Brittany and Normandy. Its judges therefore had to apply a very broad range of different *coutumes*, and, as one would expect, when they had to solve disputed questions or fill gaps in the law, they tended to develop unitary rules. Consistently enough, the new and extended edition of the *Coutume de Paris* in 1580 contained a digest (abrégé) of the decisions of the Parlement on *questions générales*. Gradually it came to be accepted that the *Coutume de Paris* could be applied everywhere, even in preference to Roman law, so as to supplement any gaps in the regional laws.

A series of important jurists played a most conspicuous role in the gradual development of a common private law for the whole of France. They were not professors, but practitioners, attorneys, legal advisers, royal administrators, and judges. Of these, DUMOULIN is pre-eminent. He was the first to state the view that there was such a thing as a common law of France; it consisted of the totality of the ideas of law which found expression in the different *coutumes*. His works, especially his famous and influential commentary on the First Book of the *Coutume de Paris*, were mainly directed to discovering these general legal principles; to this end he constantly made critical comparisons of the different *coutumes*, and applied the principle that 'deficiente consuetudine . . . non est recurrendum ad ius Romanum, sed ad vicinas et generales et promiscuas consuetudines Galliae' (see GAMILLSCHEG (above p. 74) at 88 ff.). COQUILLE (1523–1603) wrote a commentary on the *Coutume* of the County of Nevers, and an *Institution au droit français*, both of which expressly used the methods of comparative law in the interest of harmonizing and assimilating the various customs—the very task which comparative law still has to perform today, with the difference that it is no longer the customs of localities but the legal systems of nations which have to be assimilated and harmonized.

DUMOULIN, COQUILLE, and other like-minded authors of the sixteenth century could not by themselves have had such a determinative effect on the development of a common customary law had there not been, especially in Paris, a well-regarded and powerful body of professional lawyers pledged to achieve the same goals. As KOSCHAKER has emphasized, the careful and moderate acceptance of Roman law in France, like its rejection in England, of which we shall shortly be speaking, is attributable to the fact that in both countries there developed early a well-organized and therefore powerful group of practising lawyers, allied with the King, interested in the centralization of justice in the royal courts, and devoted to the national law.

By the fourteenth century professional judges, trained in the law and of bourgeois background, had replaced the clergymen, barons, and noble courtiers in the Court of Paris; before long they were appointed by the King, not just for particular cases or particular sessions, but for an indeterminate period ('à tant qu'il nous plaira') and were normally chosen from the group of practising lawyers and legal advisers on the proposal of the Parlement. We may find it very shocking today that in the fifteenth and sixteenth centuries the King allowed judicial positions to be sold and inherited, but it contributed to the consolidation of the legal profession in France.

'The fact that he could sell his office made the judge in practice irremovable, and the fact that the office could be inherited led to the development of a large number of families with a strong juristic tradition. . . . In consequence there arose a sort of hereditary nobility of lawyers, une noblesse de robe, of families proud of their status, with education and style of living to match, which prevented the bureaucratisation of the judiciary which occurred in Germany. . . . It was men like these, in practice as lawyers with the Parlement of Paris, whether as judges or as attorneys or as legal authors, who created the common private law of France. This law was largely the old law of France, partly because the coutume de Paris, though not strictly speaking common law, was much more important than the other customs, but it did not lose its connection with Roman law, from which it took some mature concepts and also some substantive rules of law. Just as in England it was the jurists who rejected the reception of Roman law, so here it was the jurists who, if they did not reject the reception, at least tempered its influence and so were able to maintain a large part of the national law' (KOSCHAKER (above p. 74) 169, 223).

In the seventeenth and eighteenth centuries we find the first jurists whose works provided the draftsmen of the Code with material and model. First there is BOURJON, a Parisian lawyer expert in the Custom of his native city; his influential work had the significant title *Le Droit commun de la France et la coutume de Paris réduit en principes* (1720). DOMAT (1625–96) was less a practitioner than a philosopher like his influential friend PASCAL; he was a great systematizer and his work *Les Loix civiles dans leur ordre naturel* (1689), in which he put into an order suggested by the new ideas of natural law the rules of Roman law adapted to the needs of the time, greatly contributed to the scientific basis of the Code civil. The jurist with the greatest influence on the draftsmen of the Code civil was POTHIER (1699–1772). He was not a great organizer of a vast mass of material nor a very original thinker; indeed, according to the historian A. DUMAS, 'he sometimes did no more than repeat in good French what DUMOULIN had already said in bad Latin'. Yet POTHIER knew both Roman and customary law inside out, though he took from them both rather eclectically, and his numerous small writings on the law of obligations, sale, hire, gift, and so on are characterized by great elegance of style, extreme lucidity, and conceptual accuracy.

Royal ordinances also had a certain effect on the eventual unification of French law. Until the sixteenth century these ordinances dealt with questions of feudalism, procedural law, and court organization. Only later did they regulate areas of substantive private law as well. The Ordonnance de Moulins (1566) dealt with a subject close to procedure. It laid down that oral testimony should be inadmissible in lawsuits worth more than 100 pounds. This formalistic rule is preserved in the Code civil (art. 1341; see below pp. 366 ff.) though of course the monetary limit has been altered. From the seventeenth century we have the Ordonnance du Commerce (1673) and the Code de la Marine (1681) which contained special rules for commercial law and maritime law, and thereby laid the basis for that division between private law in the narrow sense and commercial law which the Romanistic and Germanic legal families (except Switzerland and Italy) still recognize by having different codes, much to the surprise of Anglo-American lawyers. Louis XIV's Chancellor DAGUESSEAU was responsible for three ordinances of particular importance; one concerned the law of gift (1731), the second the law of wills (1735), with the remarkable feature of laying down different rules for the *pays du droit écrit* and the *pays du droit coutumier*, and the third the law of *fideicommissa* (1747). The Civil Code incorporated significant parts of the first two ordinances, but there was not much scope for the third since the *fideicommissum* was regarded by the Code civil as an institution of a feudal system which had been rendered obsolete. On the whole matter see WILHELM, 'Gesetzgebung und Kodifikation' (above p. 74).

Despite all these efforts France on the eve of the Revolution was still very far indeed from having a unified private law. The chasm between *droit écrit* and *droit coutumier* was as wide as ever. It is true that all the important *coutumes* of more than local significance had been codified, but this only made it easier to see the differences between them. VOLTAIRE's mockery was justified:

'Is it not an absurd and terrible thing that what is true in one village is false in another? What kind of barbarism is it that citizens must live under different laws? . . . When you travel in this kingdom you change legal systems as often as you change horses' (*Œuvres de Voltaire* VII (1838) Dialogues p. 5).

The idea of a 'droit coutumier commun' or, as people were coming to say more often, a 'droit français' had been clearly formulated for a century and a half. It had become the leading theme of French jurisprudence and this had laid the intellectual basis for the great work of unification of law in theory and practice. But before this idea of a unified French private law could become reality, two things were needed: first the powerful political impetus of the French Revolution, secondly the authority and decisiveness of NAPOLEON.

III

The 'droit intermédiaire', the law of the revolutionary period between the first session of the Assemblée Constituante of 1789 and the coming to power of NAPOLEON BONAPARTE in 1799, altered the traditional social order with almost unparalleled speed and thoroughness. All the institutions of the *ancien régime* were rooted out in very short order—the absolute monarchy, the interlocking powers of King, nobility, clergy, and judiciary (*noblesse de robe*), the old territorial division of the country into provinces, the feudal regime of land, the courts system, and the tax system. In its place was put the vision of the Enlightened Society, as sketched by DIDEROT, VOLTAIRE, and ROUSSEAU: according to this, man is a rational and responsible creature who acquires at birth an inalienable right to freedom of conscience, belief, and economic activity. No longer does man have to deal with the intermediary status groups of the *ancien régime*, but only with the state itself, which is bound through its legislation to free its citizens from the traditional authority of feudal, church, family, guild, and status groups, and to equip all its citizens with equal rights.

In pursuit of these aims the hectic legislation of the early years of the Revolution was sometimes too radically individualistic in the area of private law, and many of the extreme positions it adopted had to be abandoned by the more composed draftsmen of the Code civil. In 1791, decrees of the Assemblée Constituante abolished without compensation all feudal servitudes and cancelled all the privileges of primogeniture along with all the other differences based on age and sex which existed in the laws of succession. Estates both moveable and immoveable were to be divided completely and equally between the descendants or other heirs in intestacy: 'All heirs of equal degree succeed in equal parts to the property which vests in them by law.' This still left the possibility that the decedent might by *will* seek to prefer some persons over others, or to attempt to bind the inheritance for a long period of time. This possibility the Revolution also did away with; fideicommissary substitutions, which performed the same function as the *Nacherbfolge* of German law, were forbidden, and they even went so far, in the interests of dividing up landed property, as to abolish freedom of testation and donation. The National Convention in 1793 decreed that 'the power of disposing of one's goods whether on death, or inter vivos, or by contractual donation in direct line, is abolished: in consequence all descendants will have an equal part of the property of ascendants'. The testator with children could dispose by will of only one-tenth of his estate, the testator with collaterals of only one-sixth, and this only in favour of third parties unrelated to him, for otherwise the 'sainte égalité' of relatives entitled to succeed would have been infringed.

The changes in family law were equally far-reaching. *Patria potestas*, which in the *pays du droit écrit* had allowed the father to exercise some paternal power even over adults, was abolished as being inconsistent with the rights of man. Restraints on marriage laid down by canon law were severely curtailed, and the requirements of marriage, particularly the requirement of parental consent, reduced to a minimum. Marriage itself was regarded as a civil contract (*contrat civil*), with the consequence, amazing for its time, that either spouse could announce a wish to terminate the contract and then obtain a divorce; it was sufficient to assert that there was 'incompatibility of temperament or character' between the spouses. The justification for this principle was made clear: 'individual freedom entails the freedom to divorce, since it would be lost if the engagement of marriage were irrevocable'. Only civil marriages were lawful, and the central register of civil status was introduced. Illegitimate children recognized by their parents were equated with legitimate children, save that 'adulterine' children, that is, children at the time of whose conception either parent was married to a third party, could not have more than one-third of the inheritance of a legitimate child.

One of the most important aims of the Revolution from the very beginning was to unify the private law. The Assemblée Constituante itself had decreed: 'A code of civil law common to the whole kingdom will be drawn up.' In 1793 CAMBACÉRÈS tendered a first draft which was immediately rejected on the ground of being too comprehensive and complicated, although it had only 697 articles: what was wanted were 'simpler and more philosophical conceptions' (see FENET (above p. 74) I, p. XLVIII). The next year CAMBACÉRÈS offered a second draft with only 297 articles, but this time the National Convention found it too sparse and terse. The indefatigable CAMBACÉRÈS produced a third draft in 1796 and laid it before the Council of Five Hundred, the Directorate's legislative organ, but its protracted consideration of the draft was rudely interrupted by NAPOLEON's taking power at the end of 1799.

Things now began to move more briskly. Under the constitution introduced by NAPOLEON the executive power and the power of initiating legislation was vested in three Consuls; NAPOLEON was the First Consul, and the two others had only advisory roles. Draft legislation was to be prepared by the Conseil d'État on the proposal of the Consuls, and was then to be referred by the Consuls to the Tribunat, who could adopt or reject the draft, but not alter it. Then the draft had to be laid before the Corps Législatif, which was just a caricature of a Parliament, since it also had no power to discuss the draft, but only to hear the views of the representatives of the government and the Tribunat and then to adopt it as a law or to reject it. After this constitution was adopted, NAPOLEON devoted himself with energy and circumspection to the creation of a Code civil. He appointed a Commission of only four persons to draft it; these were no revolutionary hotspurs, but experienced practitioners. The representatives of the *droit coutumier* were TRONCHET, President of the Court of Cassation, and BIGOT DE PRÉAMENEU; both had previously been advocates at the Parliament of Paris; the representatives of the *droit écrit* were PORTALIS, a high administrative official and a brilliant speaker and writer, and MALEVILLE, judge of the Court of Cassation. In the astonishingly short period of four months this Commission produced a draft. It was shown to the Court of Cassation and the Courts of Appeal and then, along with their views on it, laid before the Conseil d'État for discussion under the chairmanship of a Consul, normally NAPOLEON himself. There the decision was taken to divide the Code into large sections and to submit these sections separately to the legislative process. But the very first section met with opposition in the Tribunat. Some of its members were very suspicious of the abolition of the Directorate and the rise to power of the young General NAPOLEON. One of these was BENJAMIN CONSTANT, who expressed strong opposition to the First Consul in the salon of his close friend MADAME DE STAËL, and was later to gain fame for the polemics he wrote in exile. Suspicion and envy rather than reasons of substance led the

Tribunat to reject the first portions of the Code, and the Corps Législatif to follow suit. NAPOLEON's reaction must have surprised them. He withdrew the whole legislative project, saying that the calmness and unanimity required for so important a project had not yet been achieved. He then purged the Tribunat of all the members hostile to him, including CONSTANT, and procured that in future the Tribunat should be asked unofficially what position it would take before the draft law was laid before it and the Corps Législatif. After the lapse of only a year, NAPOLEON set the legislative process in motion again, and in 1803 and 1804 thirty-six separate statutes were passed without opposition; they were finally consolidated by the law of 31 March 1804 and brought into force under the title of 'Code civil des Français'.

What part did NAPOLEON himself take in the creation of the Code civil? As we have seen, his energy and determination were needed to force the Code through the legislative process, but we are now interested in his influence on its form and substance. NAPOLEON, as chairman, took a very lively part in no less than 57 of the 102 meetings at which the Conseil d'État considered the text of the drafting committee. Of course, NAPOLEON had no legal training; he was a soldier, and indeed was heavily preoccupied at the time in question by military adventures against the English. He was absent when some important matters, such as, for example, the law of obligations and the law of matrimonial property, were being discussed by the Conseil d'État, and he took very little part in purely legal debates. Yet his contribution to the formation of the Code civil was quite substantial. Then a man of 34 and head of state, NAPOLEON had, according to all contemporary evidence, a most powerful and fascinating personality. At the meetings of the Conseil d'État he constantly focused attention on the realities of life rather than the technicalities of law; he immediately saw the practical relevance of abstract rules; he put an abrupt end to any hair-splitting discussions, and by clear and simple questions kept bringing the discussion back to the practical and concrete; above all, he insisted on a style of drafting which was transparently clear and comprehensible to a non-lawyer like himself. It has been said that the Code civil owes the clarity and comprehensibility of its language to the fact that its draftsman had constantly to ask himself whether the words he had chosen would withstand the criticisms of a highly intelligent layman like NAPOLEON, unfamiliar with the jargon of the law. THIBEAUDEAU, who took part in the discussions as a member of the Conseil d'État, is probably not exaggerating in the following passage from his memoirs where he describes NAPOLEON's participation:

'He started, maintained and guided [the discussion], and when it flagged he revived it. . . . He spoke quite simply and naturally, without affectation, but with the freedom and tone one finds in a conversation whose natural flow depends on the subject-matter, the diversity of opinions and the stage of the discussion. At this no member of the Council was better than he; in his capacity to go straight to the heart of a question, in the appropriateness of his ideas and the strength of his arguments he was as good as any: in originality of expression and apt turn of phrase he was often the best.' (Quoted in SOREL, *Livre du Centenaire* I, pp. XXV f.)

NAPOLEON left many marks on the actual substance of the Code, too. His support for the idea of a strong patriarchally organized family was constant and eloquent; here his central idea was, in SAVATIER's words (above p. 74, at p. 25), 'A strong family in an omnipotent state with a Napoleon at the top'. His strong support for divorce by mutual consent and for adoption may be explained on personal grounds. At the time NAPOLEON planned to found a dynasty, having obtained by referendum in 1802 the consulship for life as well as the right to nominate his successor, and since he knew that his marriage to JOSEPHINE BEAUHARNAIS would remain childless, remarriage and adoption seemed to be ways to procure a family and thus a successor. NAPOLEON himself was very proud of his part in creating the Code civil, as is shown by his famous observation, made years later in exile on St. Helena: 'It is not in winning 40 battles that my real glory lies, for all those victories will be eclipsed by Waterloo. But my Code civil will not be forgotten, it will live forever.'

7

The Spirit and Essential Features
of the Code Civil

In addition to the literature cited above p. 74:
AUDIT, 'Recent Revisions of the French Civil Code', 38 *La. L. Rev.* 747 (1978).
BOEHMER, 'Der Einfluß des Code Civil auf die Rechtsentwicklung in Deutschland',
    AcP 151 (1950/1951) 289.
——, 'Grundlagen des französischen Privatrechts im 20. Jahrhundert, *RabelsZ* 18
    (1953) 480.
BÜRGE, *Das französische Privatrecht im 19. Jahrhundert zwischen Tradition und Pandekten-
    wissenschaft, Liberalismus und Etatismus* (1991).
DAVID, *English Law and French Law* (1980).
——, *French Law, Its Structure, Sources and Methodology* (1972).
FERID/SONNENBERGER, *Das Französische Zivilrecht* Chs. 1 and 2.
FIKENTSCHER, *Methoden des Rechts in vergleichender Darstellung*, vol. I (1975) Ch. 6.
FRIEDRICH, 'The Ideological and Philosophical Background', in: *The Code Napoleon
    and the Common Law World* (ed. B. Schwartz, 1956) 1.
GÉNY, *Méthode d'interprétation et sources en droit privé positif*, 2 vols. (2nd edn., 1954).
GORDLEY, 'Myths of the French Civil Code', 42 *Am. J. Comp. L.* 459 (1994).
KAHN-FREUND/LÉVY/RUDDEN, *A Source-Book on French Law* (3rd edn. 1991).
LAWSON, 'The Approach to French Law', 34 *Ind. LJ* 531 (1959).
——, 'Réflexions d'un juriste anglais sur le cent-cinquantenaire du Code civil', *Rev.
    int. dr. comp.* 6 (1954) 665.
MURDOCK, 'Le Code civil vu par un Américain', *Rev. int. dr. comp.* 6 (1954) 678.
PORTALIS, *Discours, rapports et travaux inédits sur le Code civil* (ed. F. Portalis, 1844).
RIPERT, *Le Régime démocratique et le droit civil moderne* (2nd edn., 1948).
SAVATIER, *Les Métamorphoses économiques et sociales du droit privé d'aujourd'hui*, 3 vols.
    (3rd edn., 1959–64).
——, 'Destin du Code civil français', *Rev. int. dr. comp.* 6 (1954) 637.
THIEME, *Das Naturrecht und die europäische Privatrechtsgeschichte* (1947).
TUNC, 'The Grand Outlines of the Code', in: *The Code Napoleon and the Common Law
    World* (ed. B. Schwartz, 1956) 19.
——, 'Methodology of the Civil Law in France', 50 *Tul. L. Rev.* 459 (1976).
WIEACKER, *Das Sozialmodell der klassischen Privatrechtsgesetzbücher* (1953).
——, *A History of Private Law in Europe* (trans. Weir, 1995) 257 ff.

I

OTHER great codes came into force in Central and Western Europe at the
end of the eighteenth and the beginning of the nineteenth centuries, but

beyond doubt the French Code civil is intellectually the most significant and historically the most fertile. Like the General Land Law for the Prussian States (1794) and the General Civil Code of Austria (1811), the Code civil is founded on the creed of the Enlightenment and the law of reason that social life can be put into a rational order if only the rules of law are restructured according to a comprehensive plan. The means by which these codes sought to achieve this goal and the historical situations in which they tried to do so were very different. Despite the recurrent influence of the spirit of the Enlightenment, the Prussian Land Law remains essentially rooted in the class structure of Frederick's state: its paternalistic authoritarianism did not leave the subject much room for play, and judges and scholars were inhibited from creative development by its rigid specificity of detail. The Austrian General Civil Code, in contrast, is much more strongly pervaded with the idealism and rationalism of the Enlightenment, and differs from the Prussian Land Law in being brief, general, lucid, and easily comprehended: but it was in advance of social reality, for in the early nineteenth century Austria under METTERNICH was the great champion, at home and abroad, of the restoration of absolute monarchy, and those were not propitious conditions for a powerful development of the liberal ideas of the Code. In France the situation was different; the Prussian and Austrian codes were decreed by an enlightened despot; in France it was the *bourgeoisie* which by revolutionary means had brought down the socially obsolete institutions of the *ancien régime*, had founded the new state on the principle of the equality of citizens, and had then, *out of this very situation*, created a code which vindicated the demands of the Revolution for liberty and equality. Only in France was the Code the product of a revolutionary movement, only in France was there complete congruence between social reality and the idea of society on which the Code was based.

Of course one must distinguish ideology and reality. Contemporaries saw the Code civil as a product of revolution, but closer investigation shows that it rests also on a large number of traditional legal institutions tenaciously conserved. Several provisions of the Code civil can certainly be read as declarations of faith in the freedom of ownership and contract.

Thus art. 544 states that 'ownership is the right to enjoy and dispose of property in the most absolute manner, provided that one does not use it in a manner prohibited by law or regulation', and according to art. 1134(1) 'Contracts formed in the statutory manner have the force of law for the parties who made them.'

But it is not clear that in adopting these provisions the fathers of the Code civil really meant to ring in a new era of individualism and liberalism. Recent research has shown that the formulae of arts. 544 and 1134 had been common coin in European legal circles for centuries, that they were almost unconsciously taken over by the draftsmen of the Code civil (see GORDLEY (above p. 85)) and that it was only later, in the mid-nineteenth century, that they were converted into liberal manifestos (see in particular BÜRGE (above p. 85)). It is true, however, that the Code civil held fast to the important achievements of the Revolution—the principle of equal division of estates, the complete secularization of marriage, the total abolition of feudal servitudes, and the prohibition of fideicommissary substitutions, to take a few examples. But the Code did abandon or qualify many rules of the *droit intermédiaire* which seemed to have gone too far. Thus divorce is retained, but the ground of mutual consent is severely restricted by many complex rules of procedure. The freedom to dispose of one's property on death or in life had been largely abolished in the aim of parcelling out landed estates; it was reintroduced by the Code, though only up to the 'quotité disponible', that is, to a much lesser degree than in the German or Anglo-American legal systems.

To the *droit intermédiaire*, it was inconsistent with the rights of man that an adult's freedom to marry be dependent on his parents' consent. The conflict between the individual's interest in free self-determination and the social interest in maintaining patriarchally organized family groups was resolved by the Code in favour of the latter: a man under the age of 25 and a woman under the age of 21 could not marry at all without the permission of their parents or, if the parents were dead, their grandparents. At 25, a man could marry without his parents' consent but only if he had sought their consent three times by issuing at monthly intervals a 'respectful request' (*sommation respectueuse*) served by a *huissier*. For a man of 30, a single sommation was sufficient. A similar step, which some would see as retrogressive, was taken in matrimonial law in relation to the equality of husband and wife. To begin with, the revolutionary principle of the equality of citizens had been quite simply applied between spouses; thus CAMBACÉRÈS in his First Draft had proposed that 'the rights of spouses in the administration of their property are equal. Every legal act which sells, binds, burdens or pledges the property of either spouse requires the consent of both.' (FENET (above p. 74) I. 20.) But in his Third Draft CAMBACÉRÈS abandoned this position and, as the Code civil was later to do, gave the right to administer the property to the husband alone: it was true that all social relationships should be controlled by the principle of equality, but in the matrimonial sphere the precedence of the husband was part of the 'natural order' and to deny it would lead to 'quarrels which would destroy the pleasures of domestic life'. (FENET (above p. 74) I. 156.) It was much the same in the law of divorce. The Code civil did not hesitate to lay down that the husband could demand a divorce simply by proving his wife's adultery, whereas the wife could seek divorce on the ground of the husband's adultery only 'when he has kept his mistress in the matrimonial home'. PORTALIS seemed to regard this rule as self-evident: 'The infidelity of a wife bespeaks greater vice and has more dangerous consequences than that of a husband.'

In the difficult problem of making an accommodation between the *droit coutumier* and the *droit écrit*, the draftsmen of the Code civil showed a sure and skilful touch. Their main aim here was to produce a reasonable and balanced compromise. In his *Discours Préliminaire* PORTALIS wrote:

'We have made a compromise, if such an expression may be used, between the droit écrit and the customs, whenever we have been able to reconcile their provisions or to modify each in the light of the other, without infringing the unity of the system or causing widespread dissatisfaction.' (FENET (above p. 74) I. 481.)

The *droit écrit*, which was nearly pure Roman Law, provided almost the whole of contract law, the draftsmen having relied extensively on the classical treatment by POTHIER, as well as the law of neighbours, the law of wills, and the system of dowry as a contractual property regime. The *coutumes*, especially the Custom of Paris, won through principally in family law and in the law of inheritance, with their strong emphasis on the unity of the family and on the domestic power of husband and parents, in the forced heirship of relatives, in the statutory property regime of community of moveables, and in the administration of wills. Acquisitive prescription in good faith (see art. 2279 Code civil) is also in line with Germanic legal thinking; but the principle of publicity in German land law is found in the Code civil only in the shadow form of a system of transcription and inscription. By and large one must accept the paradoxical conclusion that the French Code civil, the leading code of the Romanistic family, contains more Germanic legal ideas than the German Civil Code a century later which, owing to the influence of the Historical School of Law and the pandectists, belongs much more to the Roman tradition.

It is often asked how much the Code civil was influenced by *natural law* thinking. As a matter of intellectual history it is clear that the Code as a whole would never have existed but for the idea of codification which comes from natural law. Furthermore the Code civil is based on the tenet of natural law that there are autonomous principles of nature, quite independent of religious belief, from which one can infer a system of legal rules which, if given intelligible form according to a plan, can act as the basis for an orderly, reasonable, and moral life in society. The early versions of the Code civil, more strongly and directly influenced by the Revolution, are largely dominated by this idea; but its hold diminished as work on the Code progressed.

On this matter see THIEME (above p. 85) 25 ff., 38 ff.; HEINSHEIMER (above p. 74) at 7; WIEACKER, *History of Private Law* (1995) 269 f.—The Draft of the Commission originally contained an introductory section, clearly taken from DOMAT's introduction to his *Loix civiles*. Art. 1 was as follows: 'There is a universal and unchanging law which is the source of all positive laws: it is none other than natural reason, which governs all mankind.' Elsewhere the judge who finds the applicable statute unclear is instructed to decide as a 'ministre d'équité'; by 'équité' is understood 'the return to natural law, or to practices accepted in the absence of positive law' (FENET (above p. 74, II. 3,7). The Conseil d'État deleted almost the whole of this introductory section on the practitioners' argument that *omnis definitio in iure periculosa*: 'Laws are acts of will. Definition, teaching and scholarship are the matter of science. The matter of legislation is command and disposition properly so-called' (PORTALIS (above p. 85) at p. 100).—The weakening of the influence of natural law thinking can also be seen in the changing attitude to the value of traditional legal institutions: CAMBACÉRÈS believed that nothing but obstacles to thorough legal reform could be found 'in our institutions, our customs and our habits' (FENET (above p. 74) I. 140).—This antihistorical attitude, quite typical of the reformist zeal of natural lawyers, was not shared at all by the Drafting Committee: 'It is useful to maintain everything which it is not necessary to destroy: laws should respect social practices unless they are vicious. We too often act as if at every moment the human race came to a complete stop and made a fresh start, without any kind of communication between one generation and the next. . . . We have recently been too fond of change and reform; where institutions and laws are concerned, if centuries of ignorance have made for abuse, centuries of enlightened philosophy have too often made for excess.' (FENET (above p. 74) I. 481 f.)

Thus although the idea and conception of the Code civil are the product of the natural law of the eighteenth-century Enlightenment, the value of historical continuity was increasingly recognized as it took practical shape. The Code seemed to many contemporaries to be a 'reaction against the Revolution', but succeeding generations who have seen its extraordinary influence have acclaimed it on the ground of its 'spirit of moderation and wisdom'.

II

The draftsmen of all the natural law codes were much exercised by the question of the proper position of the judge in relation to statute. Doctrinaire adherents of the principle of separation of powers often held the exaggerated view that the judge should have no power at all to develop the law and that statutes should be so detailed that the judge could apply them quite mechanically.

Thus in the decree which introduced the Land Law of Prussia, FRIEDRICH WIL-HELM II expressly forbade the judges 'to indulge in any arbitrary deviation, however slight, from the clear and express terms of the laws, whether on the ground of some allegedly logical reasoning or under the pretext of an interpretation based on the supposed aim and purpose of the statute'; otherwise 'Our very great displeasure and severe sanctions will be incurred'; in cases of doubt the judges were to submit the problem to the statutory commission. The Land Law with its 17,000-odd paragraphs often amuses us today by the detail into which it descends, but its intention was to give the judge a precise answer to every question and thus to render interpretation, so far as possible, wholly unnecessary.

Here also the draftsmen of the Code civil adopted a more sensible course. It is true that during the period of the *droit intermédiaire* the principle of division of powers was still taken very seriously; thus in 1790 a statute ordained that the courts 'must apply to the Corps législatif whenever they believe it necessary either to interpret a law or to make a new one'. The Tribunal de Cassation—later the Cour de Cassation—was set up about the same time to quash judicial decisions which by these standards had misconstrued the written law. The new system, based on the teaching of MONTESQUIEU, had no place for the sort of judicial development of law which had occurred in the Parlements under the *ancien régime*. Of course the principle that the courts must submit questions of interpretation to the Corps Législatif for a decision was never really taken seriously. The drafting committee were emphatic in their opposition to any such proceeding: the function of the legislator was to set up *general* rules; interference with the resolution of questions of interpretation affecting the affairs of private individuals would be time-consuming and undignified, the quality of legislation would suffer and lawsuits would be prolonged. Consequently art. 4 Code civil provides without any qualification that if a judge refuses to make a decision 'on the ground that the law is silent or obscure or inadequate' he may be held responsible.

The Code civil also avoids the danger of being too detailed. The draftsmen clearly realized that even the most ingenious legislator could not foresee and determine all the possible problems which might arise and that therefore room must be left for judicial decisions to make the law applicable to unforeseen individual cases and suited to the changing circumstances of society. PORTALIS's observations on this matter are among the most impressive in his *Discours Préliminaire*: they show clearly that the dichotomy between statute-law of the Continental variety and the case-law of the Common Law is by no means so fundamental as theorists of the sources of law keep trying to tell us:

'The task of legislation is to determine the general maxims of law, taking a large view of the matter. It must establish principles rich in implications rather than descend into the details of every question which might possibly arise. The application of the law belongs to the magistrate and the lawyer, steeped in the general spirit of the legislation. . . . There is a legislative skill as well as a judicial skill, and the two are quite distinct. The skill of the legislator is to discover the principles in each area which most conduce to the common weal; the skill of the judge is to put these principles into action, and to extend them to particular circumstances by wise and reasoned application. . . . To the courts may be left those unusual and extraordinary cases which no reasonable legislation could deal with, the varied and contested trivia with which the legislator had no time to deal, and all those matters which it would be futile to try to foresee, and which could not be safely defined even if one did cursorily foresee them. We shall leave some gaps, and they will be filled in due course by experience. National codes are created in time; indeed, people do not really create them at all.' (FENET (above p. 74) I. 470, 475 f.)

The best-known example of the compressed legislative style of the Code civil is found in arts. 1382–6. These five laconic paragraphs cover the entire French law of delict, a subject-matter to which the General Civil Code of Austria, otherwise so terse, having only half as many paragraphs as the Code civil, devotes about 40, and the German Civil Code 31. These rules of the

Code civil, now 190 years old, are still in force, almost unaltered despite all the economic and technological changes which have taken place, and it is therefore no surprise to find that today they are barely recognizable under a heavy gloss of case-law to which new layers are added every year. Perhaps the draftsmen of the Code civil went too far in compression here (see Ch. 40 IV); yet in 1804, when the Industrial Revolution had hardly started, the social problem of compensating the victims of accidents had nothing like the importance it has today.

The way the Code civil is drafted gives the courts room for interpretation, for its terms are often inexact, incomplete, or ambiguous, far from having the terminological exactitude which the German Civil Code inherited from the pandectists. Thus according to art. 778 of the Code civil, an inheritance may be accepted either 'dans un acte authentique ou privé' or by means of an 'acte qui suppose nécessairement son intention d'accepter': here in the same sentence the word 'acte' is used in the sense of 'deed' and in the sense of 'action', a lapse of which the fathers of the German Code would certainly not have been guilty. In arts. 544 ff. Code civil, the notion of 'propriété' is used in the sense of ownership of things (moveable or immoveable), while in the Title of the Third Book ('des différentes manières dont on acquiert la propriété') it is used in the sense of wealth of all types. According to art. 1147 Code civil, a person has to pay damages for breach of contract, unless he proves that a 'cause étrangère qui ne peut lui être imputée' was the reason for non-performance; according to art. 1148 the duty to make compensation ceases in the event of 'force majeure' or 'cas fortuit'. The relationship between 'cause étrangère', 'force majeure', and 'cas fortuit' is never made clear. The list of technical inaccuracies of this kind could easily be prolonged.

On the other hand, the Code civil is a masterpiece from the point of view of style and language. It has often been praised for its clear and memorable phrases, and for the absence of cross-references and jargon, all of which has significantly contributed to the popularity of the Code in France. STENDHAL is said to have read part of the Code every day in order to refine his feeling for the language ('pour prendre le ton'), and PAUL VALÉRY described the Code civil as 'the greatest book of French literature' (cited by THIEME (above p. 85) at 38 f.). The dry and dogmatic language of the *German* Code is very unattractive in comparison. For example, compare art. 212 Code civil with §1353 BGB. The French provision is concrete: 'Spouses owe each other the duty of fidelity, succour and companionship'. The German text offers the rather pale technical term of 'matrimonial community'. Art. 312 Code civil is almost an epigram: 'The child conceived in marriage takes the husband for its father'; in §1591 BGB the legislator goes straight into the technical details of the requirements for legitimacy. The idea *pacta sunt servanda* is given in art. 1134 Code civil a striking and almost moving formula: 'Agreements made according to law have the force of law for the parties to them'. §241 BGB on the other hand instructs us, somewhat didactically, that 'by reason of the creditor-debtor relationship . . . the creditor is entitled to demand performance from the debtor'—a textbook formulation which admittedly makes it perfectly clear, to the lawyer at any rate, what meanings are going to be attributed in the succeeding paragraphs to the ideas of 'creditor-debtor relationship' and 'performance'. Yet the elegant sheen of the wording in the Code civil is often paid for by a lack of substance, as closer investigation shows. WIND-SCHEID made the criticism 'that the famed precision of its expressions is quite often only superficial, not that true inner precision which comes from complete clarity of thought' (*Zur Lehre des Code Napoleon von der Ungültigkeit der Rechtsgeschäfte* (1847) V). An example can immediately be given: the famous formula 'en fait de meubles la possession vaut titre' (art. 2279). This provision could hardly be bettered for dramatic tautness, but one must realize that it gives only the shadowiest indication of the underlying thought: it was left to the courts of France to resolve the following questions: Under what conditions is possession a ground of defence to a *rei vindicatio*? What is meant by 'possession'? Is good faith required? If so, what constitutes good faith, and at what moment of time must it be established? §932 BGB may lack the urbanity of art. 2279 of the Code civil, but it certainly contains more precise information.

The subject-matter of the Code civil is set out as follows. A brief introductory title contains only six articles, all that remains of the much fuller *Livre préliminaire* originally planned. The *First Book* is entitled 'Des Personnes' (arts. 7–515). It opens with provisions concerning the enjoyment of civil rights; these rights, according to art. 8, attach to every Frenchman. Rules about the acquisition and loss of French nationality followed, well demonstrating the national character of the Code, but in 1927 these rules were greatly expanded and promulgated in the form of a special statute. The following few articles about the legal status of foreigners have formed the basis on which the French courts have created an impressive structure of private international law and procedure, and of law relating to foreigners. The next section contains an extensive treatment of the register of civil status; this is a matter which a German lawyer could hardly imagine as forming part of his Civil Code but it seemed especially important to the draftsmen of the Code for whom the secularization of family relationships was one of the achievements of the Revolution. The following sections deal with domicile, disappearance, marriage, divorce, children born inside and outside marriage, adoption, parental power, and guardianship. *Book Two* ('Des biens et des différentes modifications de la propriété'; arts. 516–710) starts with general provisions about things, distinguishing moveables and immoveables and dealing with components and accessories. The ownership of things, their fruits and profits, is then covered, followed by rules about usufruct and the rights of use and habitation, as well as servitudes. The acquisition of ownership by means of contract is not dealt with here, because French law adheres to the principle that a contractual act automatically operates as a conveyance of ownership (gift, sale, exchange: see arts. 938, 1138, 1583); thus there is no separate conveyance contract or delivery, actual or constructive, to be regulated by the law of property (contrast §§873, 925, 929 ff. BGB).

All the rest of the Code civil—twice as many articles as in the first two books together—falls in *Book Three*, under the title 'Des différentes manières dont on acquiert la propriété' (arts. 711–2281). First there are the rules of succession, which is seen as a special form of the *acquisition of ownership*, like gift, with which it is closely associated. There follows a section on the general law of contract, with articles concerning capacity, construction, joint debtors, contractual penalties, set-off, formal requirements, and rules of evidence; next there is a section on 'obligations formed without agreement', consisting of eleven provisions on the law of unjustified enrichment ('quasi-contracts'; see Ch. 38 III); and then the five articles on the law of delict. Next comes matrimonial property law, and then the special contracts—sale, exchange, lease, the contract of services and of service (employment being treated, on the Roman model, as a 'contrat de louage'), then partnership, loan, deposit, agency, suretyship, and compromise. Book Three ends with security rights (pledge, hypothec, and lien) and prescription.

The structure of the Code civil is plainly unsatisfactory. Matrimonial property law would be much better placed next to the law of husband and wife in the First Book, and the law of succession, instead of being placed with the property law in Book Three, might have been better grouped with family law or put in a separate book of its own. To say that a claim for compensation based on tort is a special 'mode of acquiring ownership' seems to miss the point. Planiol is justified in saying that Book Three is a rag-bag of heterogeneous matters:

'It is not very logical to put all these various topics in a single book' (*Traité élémentaire de droit civil* I (5th edn., 1950) 33). It is true that Planiol does not regard the absence of scientific order in the Code civil as very serious: 'A scientific order, although very suitable in a lecture-course or a textbook, is neither necessary nor even useful in a code. Teaching requires a special method because it is a kind of initiation. Codes are made for people who have completed their studies, practitioners who are familiar with the law. In consequence, it is enough that the topics be set out in a clear and convenient manner' (id., 36).

III

The original Code civil was the law-book of the third estate, the bourgeoisie which in the French Revolution had worsted the feudal groups dominant in the *ancien régime* and subsequently, in the Restoration after the fall of Napoleon, had consolidated its position with growing self-confidence and political influence. The ideal man in the mind of the draftsmen is therefore not the little man, the artisan or the day-labourer, but the man of property, the responsible man of judgment and reason, knowledgeable about affairs and familiar with the law, and it is this ideal which gives the Code its particular flavour. In this view, the existence of the bourgeoisie depended on guaranteed personal freedom, especially the freedom to engage in economic activities, and on property, especially landed property. Freedom of contract is therefore the principle which dominates the law of obligations in the Code civil, restricted as little as possible by mandatory rules of law, called in France 'lois d'ordre public' (see art. 6). Consonant with this view of the citizen's responsibility is the conclusion evinced by the general formula of art. 1382 Code civil, that if a person causes harm by behaviour which is reprehensibly careless ('faute') he must pay for it; this accommodated both the freedom of activity and the individual's desire for responsibility which *stricter* forms of liability might have narrowed and constrained. The great problem of how to regulate the position of the dependent worker was not recognized by the legislator, but unlike the draftsmen of the German Civil Code of 1896, he is not really to be blamed for this, since in 1804 industrial mass production had hardly started. The rules of family law in the Code civil reflect the patriarchal family typical of the successful bourgeoisie of the early nineteenth century; the husband and father is head of the family, and it is he alone who has paternal power over the children, including the power, by refusing his permission, to prevent the marriage of his son until 25 and his daughter until 21. As for the relationship of the spouses, the original art. 213 Code civil speaks for itself: 'The husband must protect the wife, the wife obey her husband.' The wife was supposed to be running the household and educating the children, and to be unexperienced in business affairs; without her husband's permission therefore she could neither enter contracts nor conclude dispositions, even when the spouses had chosen by antenuptial contract to retain their separate property. Interference by the state in the closed family circle was regarded as intolerable; the supervision of guardians and juveniles now performed by officials was given to a 'conseil de famille', including more distant relatives such as uncles, aunts, cousins, and in-laws, who were then part of the family in a way which is not usual today. The great protection afforded to the family circle is a leading characteristic of French family law, and its concern to preserve the family property has had an effect on the law of succession as well. There are severe restrictions on the freedom to dispose on one's assets by gift or will as one chooses: even today in France a person can dispose only of a *part* of his property—the so-called 'quotité disponible'; as to the rest, called the 'réserve', members of the family have more than just a right to monetary payment of their statutory part, they are actually forced heirs.

When one considers what economic and social changes have occurred since the time of NAPOLEON, and how differently the family is now regarded, one may well ask how the Code civil can have remained in force in France until this day. How can a Code which came into force nearly 200 years ago have withstood the tremendous political, economic, and social storms which have raged over France in the nineteenth and twentieth centuries?

In many areas, especially in family and inheritance law, it is the *legislator* who has kept the Code in line with changing social reality by altering its text. *Patria potestas* has been gradually eroded, the business capacity of the married woman admitted, her position on the death of her husband improved, and the right of illegitimate children to be maintained or recognized by the father accepted. In the law of contract also, wherever it was clear that the free play of contractual autonomy led to consequences which seemed unacceptable to new social value-judgments, the legislator has expanded or modified the rules of the Code civil, mainly by special statutes. Thus in the contracts of lease, carriage, employment, and insurance so many mandatory provisions are imposed by law that almost nothing is left of the unrestrained freedom to conclude and determine the content of contracts which so appealed to the draftsmen of the Code civil.

But the *courts* (*jurisprudence*) as well as the legislator have played a leading part in adjusting the rules of the Code civil to modern requirements; they have continually been construing these rules so as to develop, extend, or limit them and have brought new legal ideas into play as well as developing old ones. The task of the courts in this has been made easier because, as we have already seen, the principles of the Code civil are often unclear and deliberately designed to require completion, the concepts used are frequently indefinite and ambiguous, many individual rules are incomplete, and the systematic interplay of different provisions is often faulty. It is easy to give examples of the creative legal activity of the French courts. For instance, out of the rule of art. 1384 of the Code civil they have developed a law of *accident compensation* which is much better adapted to the special dangers of the modern world with its advanced technology than the system of compensation which the draftsmen of the Code had in mind (see Ch. 42 III). In labour law the courts, strongly supported by the legislature, have developed rules for the social protection of workmen and employees which go far beyond the inadequate provisions of arts. 1780 f., and indeed this whole important area of law now really falls outside the Code civil and, as in Germany, is widely regarded as being an independent area of law. The courts developed the doctrine of abuse of rights which has proved useful in limiting the right of the owner of property to deal with it exactly as he chooses (see art. 544 Code civil), the right to dismiss an employee, the right to strike, the right to take steps in legal procedure and other rights, for if the exercise of a right seems to a court to constitute an abuse of right (*abus d'un droit*), an injunction may be issued or liability in damages imposed (see Ch. 40 IV). Art. 1121 Code civil permits some contracts for the benefit of third parties and invalidates others, all in rather obscure language; here the courts developed rules relating to the *insurance contract*, which the legislature took over into the statute of 1930. The courts also developed a general claim based on *unjustified enrichment*, which had received an extremely patchy treatment in arts. 1376 ff. Code civil in relation to the payment of a thing not due (see Ch. 38 III). There was no statutory regulation at all of the 'astreinte', a legal device for enforcing judicial orders for performance, and this the courts themselves developed. The practice of the courts has also played a significant part in family and inheritance law. Thus, to give a few examples, the courts have so qualified the strict prohibition of successive heirship in art. 896 Code civil than one can now create successive entitlements to an inheritance simply by having one's will skilfully drafted. Many years before the enactment of the basic reform statutes, the courts had accepted claims for maintenance by an illegitimate child, although this was hard to reconcile with the original meaning of art. 340 Code civil, according to which *any* 'recherche de la paternité' was excluded.

'Thus quite large areas of French private law have ceased to be *droit écrit* and have become common law, almost without our noticing it. The famous and striking opposition between the sources of law recognized by Anglo-Saxon and French law respectively has been very materially reduced.' (RIPERT (above p. 85) II. 15, no. 9.) There have frequently been lively disputes in France on the question whether or not judicial decisions are strictly speaking a source of law. The dominant view is still that they are not; but great scholars like PLANIOL, JOSSERAND, LAMBERT, and HÉBRAUD have accepted that they are. Fortunately people are becoming tired of this question, for it is now clear that one's answer depends entirely on one's definition of 'source of law'. If the test of a rule is its validity in social reality and its viability in fact, then there can really be no doubt at all that the rules which have been created by the courts and confirmed by repeated decision have all the qualities of rules of law.

As the Code aged, *legal writing* (*doctrine*) became increasingly significant in the development of French private law. In the years immediately following the enactment of the Code legal writing went through an unfruitful and positivistic stage, merely expounding the text of the Code, grammatically and logically, and ignoring judicial decision entirely (*école de l'exégèse*). The picture changed, however, towards the end of the nineteenth century. Under the influence of GÉNY and SALEILLES, scholars realized that the school of exegesis was not giving any help to judges in the task of applying the Code civil to changed circumstances; GÉNY's new school, called the 'école de la libre recherche scientifique', allowed the judge a greater freedom with the text of the Code and encouraged him to construe the Code not simply logically and systematically, but in the light of the requirements of society as it developed, the actual usages and practices in the relevant areas of commerce, and also the results of the researches of sociologists and comparative lawyers.

In this dispute between the schools the multi-volume treatises of French private law, of which the three most important and comprehensive are those of BAUDRY/ LACANTINERIE, BEUDANT, and PLANIOL/RIPERT, took an intermediate position. These treatises all have their own refined systematic structure, often quite different from the statutory structure of the Code civil, but, thanks to the practical and sober good sense of French jurists, never lose themselves in exalted subtleties of doctrine. They all deal carefully with judicial decisions, which are sometimes criticized quite severely, though never with that dogmatic tone of dismissal occasionally to be found in German textbooks. In language and style these treatises are often of splendid eloquence and perfect lucidity, even if one sometimes has the feeling that the text could be compressed somewhat without any loss of substance. This is less true of the more recent textbooks, of which those of COLIN/CAPITANT, CARBONNIER, MARTY/RAYNAUD, and MAZEAUD call for especial mention. Often enough the development of French law has been spurred on not by textbooks or articles, but by case-notes; those by THALLER and LABBÉ, the best-known 'arrêtistes' of the nineteenth century, are especially important for the basis of modern French private and commercial law.

With the help of legislation, judicial decision, and legal writing, the Code civil has been able to adapt itself to modern developments; this can be seen from the fact that though there have frequently been demands for a thorough overhaul of the Code, all attempts have so far proved abortive. In the centenary year of the Code civil, 1904, a committee was set up to reform it, consisting of 100 persons, many of whom were not lawyers; their labours soon ground to a halt. Another committee charged with the reform of the Code civil was set up in 1945, in the first flush of post-war feeling; it had only 12 members, under the chairmanship of JULLIOT DE LA MORANDIÈRE, Professor of the Paris Faculty of Law. In 1954 this committee produced the draft of an Introductory Book and of Book One, on the law of persons and the family, and in 1961 it produced a draft of Book Two, on the law of inheritance and gift, but neither of these drafts led to actual legislation. Recently the work of the committee of reform has come to a complete stop, and instead the French legislator has undertaken partial reforms of the Code civil, of which the most important concern matrimonial property law, the law of adoption, the legal position of illegitimate children, and the rules of incapacity.

Although the proposals for total reform led to nothing, the discussion and documents of the committee of reform (Travaux de la commission de réforme du Code civil (1974 ff.)) are full of interest to those concerned with questions of comparative law and unification of law. On this, see JULLIOT DE LA MORANDIÈRE, 'The Reform of the French Civil Code', 97 *U. Pa. L. Rev.* 1 (1948); HOUIN, 'Les travaux de la commission de réforme du Code civil', *Rev. trim. dr. civ.* 49 (1951) 34; PASCAL, 'A Report on the French Civil Code Revision Project', 25 *Tul. L. Rev.* 205 (1951); ANCEL, 'The Revision of the French Civil Code', 25 *Tul. L. Rev.* 435 (1951).

8

The Reception of the Code Civil

ADOMEIT/FRÜHBECK, *Einführung in das spanische Recht* (1993).

AMOS, 'The Code Napoleon and the Modern World', 10 *J. Comp. Leg.* 222 (1928).

ARMINJON/NOLDE/WOLFF, *Traité de droit comparé* I (1950) 136 ff.

BARHAM, 'A Renaissance of the Civilian Tradition in Louisiana', 33 *La. L. Rev.* 357 (1973).

——, 'Methodology of the Civil Law in Louisiana', 50 *Tul. L. Rev.* 474 (1976).

BATIZA, 'Origins of Modern Codification of the Civil Law: The French Experience and its Implications for Louisiana Law', 56 *Tul. L. Rev.* 477 (1982).

BAUDOUIN, 'The Impact of the Common Law on the Civilian Systems of Louisiana and Quebec', in: Dainow (ed.), *The Role of Judicial Decisions and Doctrine in Civil Law and Mixed Jurisdictions* (1974) 1.

BOEHMER, 'Der Einfluß des Code civil auf die Rechtsentwicklung in Deutschland, *AcP* 151 (1950/1951) 289.

CAPPELLETTI/MERRYMAN/PERILLO, *The Italian Legal System, An Introduction* (1967).

CASTÁN VÁZQUEZ, 'El sistema del derecho privado iberoamericano', *Estudios de derecho* 28 (1969) 5.

CHABANNE, 'Napoléon, son code et les Allemands', *Études Lambert* (1975) 397.

CHABAS, 'Réflexions sur l'évolution du droit sénégalais', in: *Études juridiques offertes à Julliot de la Morandière* (1964) 127.

CHORUS/GERVER/HONDIUS/KOEKKOEK (eds.), *Introduction to Dutch Law for Foreign Lawyers* (1993).

CIAN, 'Fünfzig Jahre italienischer Codice civile', *ZEuP* 1993, 120.

GERLACH, 'Die moderne Entwicklung der Privatrechtsordnung in Spanien', *ZvglRWiss* 85 (1986) 247.

DAINOW, 'Le Droit civil de la Louisiane', *Rev. int. dr. comp.* 6 (1954) 19.

ISHIMOTO, 'L'influence du Code civil français sur le droit civil japonais', *Rev. int. dr. comp.* 6 (1954) 744.

JOBIN, 'L'influence de la doctrine française sur le droit civil québecois', *Rev. int. dr. comp.* 44 (1992) 381.

KINDLER, *Einführung in das italienische Recht* (1993).

KOSCHAKER, *Europa und das römische Recht* (2nd edn., 1953).

LE CODE CIVIL, LIVRE DU CENTENAIRE II (1904), with articles on the effects of the Code civil in Germany, Belgium, Canada, Egypt, Italy, the Netherlands, Romania, and Switzerland.

LIMPENS, 'Territorial Expansion of the Code', in: *The Code Napoleon and the Common Law World* (ed. B. Schwartz, 1956) 92.

MACDONALD, 'Understanding Civil Law Scholarship in Quebec', 23 *Osgoode Hall L. J.* 573 (1985).

Mousseron, 'La réception au Proche-Orient du droit français des obligations', *Rev. int. dr. comp.* 20 (1968) 37.

Neumayer, 'Deutsche und französische Zivilrechtswissenschaft—Besinnliches zu einem Nachbarschafts- und Partnerschaftsverhältnis unter Verwandten', in: *Ius privatum gentium, Festschrift Max Rheinstein* I (1969) 165.

Noda, 'La réception du droit français au Japon', *Rev. int. dr. comp.* 15 (1963) 543.

Ortun, 'L'Unification du droit civil espagnol', *Rev. int. dr. comp.* 18 (1966) 413.

Piret, 'Le Code Napoléon en Belgique', *Rev. int. dr. comp.* 6 (1954) 753.

Salacuse, *An Introduction to Law in French-Speaking Africa* I: *Africa South of the Sahara* (1969).

Schnitzer, *Vergleichende Rechtslehre* I (2nd edn., 1961) 200 ff.

Solus, 'Die französischen Besitzungen und Kolonien', in: *Rechtsvergleichendes Handwörterbuch* I (ed. Schlegelberger, 1929) 535.

Travaux de la Semaine Internationale de Droit 1950 (1954), with essays on the effects of the Code civil in Europe, America, and the Near East.

Tyan, 'Les Rapports entre droit musulman et droit européen occidental, en matière de droit civil', *ZvglRW* 65 (1963) 18.

Valladao, *Le Droit latino-américain* (1954).

Yiannopoulos, 'Louisiana Civil Law: A Lost Cause?', 54 *Tul. L. Rev.* 830 (1980).

Zajtay, 'Les Destinées du Code civil', *Rev. int. dr. comp.* 6 (1954) 792.

——, 'La Réception des droits étrangers et le droit comparé', *Rev. int. dr. comp.* 9 (1957) 686.

Zekoll, 'Zwischen den Welten—Das Privatrecht von Louisiana als europäisch-amerikanische Mischrechtsordnung', in Zimmermann (ed.), *Amerikanische Rechtskultur und europäisches Privatrecht* (1995) 11.

I

In order to understand the extraordinary influence of the Code civil in the nineteenth and twentieth centuries, it is useful to recall the very favourable circumstances attending its birth. On the one hand, the Code was still inspired by the enlightened enthusiasm of the French Revolution, appealing to all the forces of progress; it was the first codification in the world to loosen all the bonds of feudalism and shed the shackles of the past, and it implemented those demands of the Revolution which were most to influence the future: it gave equality to all citizens, it secularized family law, it emancipated landed property, it granted freedom to engage in economic activities, and it protected the family. On the other hand, when the Code was drafted the fanaticism of the Revolution had cooled off considerably, and in the relatively stable political situation under Napoleon people could have second thoughts without seeming reactionary. Thus the draftsmen of the Code could make good use of the principles of law which had been slowly developed by the courts of the *ancien régime* and which had been carefully elaborated and refined by the writers of the seventeenth and eighteenth centuries. In this way, a happy compromise was struck between the powerful appeal of revolutionary ideas and the solid craftsmanship of traditional legal institutions.

Furthermore, NAPOLEON's part in the Code civil seemed to the world to lend it some of his charisma, and its language was forceful and thrilling, free from heavy logic and detailed digression. The Code civil answered the needs and interests of the nineteenth-century bourgeoisie but still offered great scope for variant progressive interpretation, since many of its outline principles called for amplification and it had many technical faults, omissions, and imprecisions, all of which were creatively used by French judges and writers to great effect as the Code grew older. This may help to explain why the Code civil spread not only to the Latin peoples of Europe, but also to Eastern Europe, the Near East, to Central and South America, and even to some parts of North America, and why it had a prolonged influence on the development of law in other European countries, especially Germany.

One must not suppose, however, that the Code civil was received in these countries as the result of a careful evaluation of its merits, in the way that a customer in a shop might choose the goods which best suited him. PAUL KOSCHAKER has shown that the reception of foreign law is not so much a 'question of quality' as a 'question of power': 'reception occurs when the law being received is in a position of power, at least intellectually and culturally, as being the law of a country which still enjoys political power or did so until so recently that its strength and culture are still clearly remembered' (above p. 98, p. 138). KOSCHAKER used this idea primarily to explain the reception of Roman law in Central Europe, which in his view was attributable not to any qualitative superiority of Roman law, but to the fact that as the law of the Imperium Romanum, and consequently the law of the Holy Roman Empire of the Germans, its authority and claim to validity could rest on the idea of Roman civilization. But KOSCHAKER has also applied his idea to the reception of the Code civil: it had such a wide influence 'because it was the Code of the French Empire, whose military prowess, backed by a brilliantly integrated civilization, made such a deep impression on people not only during its brief life but many years after it was over' (above p. 98, p. 136). This is certainly right, especially if we remember that the reception is attributable not only to the political power of the *French Empire*, or to the spiritual influence of *French civilization*, but also in a great measure to the merits of the *Code civil* itself; for in the nineteenth century the Code enjoyed intellectual authority and an almost supernatural appeal as the Code of the Great Revolution, which had abolished the *ancien régime* and produced for the first time legal unity and equality for the citizens of a centrally organized national state. Nor must one forget that the spread of the Code civil throughout the world was greatly helped by its admirable language and the easy flexibility of its expression, in brief, by its very *quality*.

II

Between 1804 and 1812 the Code civil came into force in many regions as the result of French military expansion eastwards under the revolutionary regimes and later under NAPOLEON; they were later to win or win back their sovereignty, but their private law retained the impress of the ideas of the French Code. We shall look first at Belgium, Luxembourg, and the Netherlands.

(*a*) The territory we now know as *Belgium* was ruled by Austria from 1713 until its cession to France by the Peace of Campo Formio of 1797. The territory was incorporated into France, and the Code civil came into force there automatically in 1804, and remained in force despite the fall of NAPOLEON and the unification of Holland and Belgium by the Congress of Vienna under WILLIAM I of Orange. When Belgium became independent in the revolution of 1830, its new Constitution contained a provision that the French codes, the Code civil and the Code de Commerce of 1807, should be fundamentally revised 'dans le plus court délai possible'. So far as the Code civil is concerned, this provision has remained unimplemented to the present day. Instead, the Belgian legislature has, as time went by, passed a large number of special laws in order to modernize the Code civil; often the legislature has followed in the wake of new French legislation, but frequently enough it has gone its own way and on occasion has anticipated reforms in France—for example, in the field of mortgage the unsatisfactory rules of the Code civil were replaced in Belgium in 1851, four years earlier than in France. Although the Belgian courts apply nearly the same statutory text as the French courts, they have sometimes reached divergent results (much the same thing happens in the European sphere where different national courts apply the identical texts of unified laws, such as the law of negotiable instruments, and reach divergent interpretations which cannot be resolved until the foundation of a European court with jurisdiction to watch over the unity of law). In general, however, legal thought and judicial decision in Belgium are very close to those in France:

'Despite the important independent work of Belgian courts and scholars, it is obvious that they have never made a systematic break with their counterparts in France. For us . . . Dalloz, the Revue trimestrielle, Colin et Capitant, Planiol et Ripert are used almost as frequently as our own periodicals and treatises' (DE HER-VEN, *Travaux* (above p. 99) 610).—The same is true, *mutatis mutandis*, for Luxembourg, which came to France in 1795 also from the Habsburgs; the Code civil remained in force during the Union of the Crown with the Netherlands and on its independence in 1890. Indeed, the version of the Code civil which is in force in Luxembourg today is closer to the original text than are the current versions in France and Belgium. On this, see BERNECKER, *RabelsZ* 27 (1962/1963) 263.

(*b*) For a time after the outbreak of war between the French revolutionary government and the coalition of the Kings of Europe, the *Netherlands* maintained an uneasy neutrality, but as the French were militarily successful came more and more under their sway. In 1806 NAPOLEON forced the Dutch to accept his brother LOUIS as King, and saw to it that in 1809 a version of the Code civil was enacted with marginal adaptations to Dutch legal practices. After the abdication of LOUIS in 1810, NAPOLEON brusquely annexed the territory of the Netherlands, as a mere 'alluvium from French rivers', and brought the Code civil in its original form into effect. The Code civil remained in force after the liberation of the country and the creation of a kingdom of the Netherlands which included the territory of Belgium. Work on a new civil code came to a halt with the separation of Belgium in 1830, and the 'Burgerlijk Wetboek' was not promulgated until 1838. Apart from family law it was substantially a translation of the French Code civil, though it is different in structure. In Holland the law was criticized in the nineteenth century, more openly than in Belgium. Although the criticism increased in the twentieth century, it was rather a surprise in 1947 when a royal decree tasked Professor MEIJERS of Leyden to draft a new civil code. MEIJERS sent Parliament a series of thorny questions, and had frequent consultations with businessmen and attorneys. The first four books of the draft are essentially his. On his death in 1954 a three-man commission was set up with a permanent staff and continued work on the 'Nieuw Burgerlijk Wetboek' or NBW. Despite delays and occasional doubts about the enterprise, it was possible to produce Book One on the law of persons and the family in 1970, followed six years later by Book Two on the law of legal persons, including companies, corporations, and foundations. Books Three, Five, Six, and Seven, dealing with contract, tort, and property came into force on 1 January 1992.

A review of the law in force since 1 January 1992 can be found in articles by HON-DIUS, HARTKAMP, and FRANKEN in *AcP* 91 (1991) 378–432. See also DROBNIG, 'Das neue niederländische bürgerliche Gesetzbuch aus vergleichender und deutscher Sicht' (1993) 1 *Eur. Rev. PL* 171. There is a partial translation into French and English by HAANAPPEL and MACKAAY, *New Netherlands Civil Code, Patrimonial Law (Property, Obligations and Special Contracts)* (1990).—It is noteworthy that the NBW, like the Swiss and Italian models, abandons the obsolete distinction between civil and commercial law. It incorporates the law on the protection of consumers, including not only the provisions about judicial control of general conditions of business (art. 6:231 ff.) but also, in the sections on sale and suretyship, the special rules which protect consumers in those areas. It is also worth mentioning that the general rules on legal acts in the economic sphere have been 'factored out' in Book Three, which is where one finds the rules on the invalidity of acts-in-law on grounds of illegality or immorality, and on avoidance for error, deceit, and 'improper exploitation of circumstances', as well as on agency and trust ('bewind'). Book Six contains rules on 'Obligations in General' (for example, liability for non-performance, assignment, tort, and unjust enrichment) as well as 'Contracts in general' (for example, formation by offer and acceptance, contracts for the benefit of third parties, modification of contracts in the light of changed circumstances). Finally in Book Seven there are provisions on the special types of contract, such as sale. The complexity of the structure is rather reminiscent of the German BGB, and not all lawyers in the Netherlands are thrilled by it. Then, too, the frequent use of 'general clauses', for example, that the decision must accord with 'fairness and equity' recalls §242 BGB (see art. 6:2, 248, 258 NBW). Given also its concern with precise and technical expression and detail the NBW can be said to belong, like the BGB but unlike the Code civil and the Swiss Civil Code, to the 'learned' codes. Even so one cannot allocate it either to the German or the Romanistic legal family. Founded on intensive comparative law, it is akin on many points to the Common Law (as on avoidance of contracts for error or 'improper exploitation of circumstances'), and on others follows the Vienna Convention on International Sales (as on liability for breach of contract). One can only conclude that it has hit upon a style of its own, founded on the European *ius commune*.

III

In large parts of Germany and Switzerland also the Code civil had a prolonged influence.

(*a*) In *Germany*, the Code civil automatically came into force in 1804 in those territories West of the Rhine which had already passed to France by the Treaty of Lunéville so as to form part of French territory. In addition, after the creation of the Rheinbund and especially after NAPOLEON's successful Prussian campaign of 1806–07, the Code civil crossed the Rhine and penetrated far to the east: it came into force in the Kingdom of Westphalia, in the Grand Duchies of Baden and Frankfurt, in Danzig, and even in Hamburg and Bremen, as parts of the 'Hanseatic Departments'. It was also to be introduced in the other principalities of the Rheinbund. This development came to an end with the War of Liberation, but the Code civil kept its hold in all the territories west of the Rhine and in a few other parts of the Rhenish province of Prussia. In the Grand Duchy of Baden it remained in force in a translation called the 'Badisches Landrecht', which contained a number of judicious additions by BRAUER to fit it to German circumstances.

One result of the fact that the Code civil was in force in the Rhineland and in Baden for almost a century until the enactment of the BGB and was applied by the courts there, with appeal, after 1879, to the Imperial Court (Second (Rhenish) Civil Chamber), was that great German scholars applied to French law the methods which German legal science had developed in the nineteenth century, and produced work which had a strong effect in France itself. The *Handbuch des französischen Civilrechts* (1808) by ZACHARIÄ VON LINGENTHAL has pride of place here. This was the first methodical and systematic treatment of French private law anywhere which broke away from the unsatisfactory structure of the Code civil. It was soon translated into French by AUBRY and RAU, professors at Strasbourg, and as edition followed edition the work developed in independence and strength; the latest is the seventh edition, produced by ESMEIN and PONSARD. Earlier editions contributed much to the overthrow of the École de l'Exégèse in France, and the work had a steady influence on the courts; even today it is regarded by French writers as the most significant textbook of private law of the nineteenth century. The names of CROME, KOHLER, HEINSHEIMER, and SALEILLES are particularly associated with the manifold cross-fertilizations between German and French legal scholarship; on this, see BOEHMER, above p. 98, NEUMAYER, above p. 98, and ANDREAS B. SCHWARTZ, 'Einflüsse deutscher Zivilistik im Auslande', in: *Symbolae friburgenses in honorem Ottonis Lenel* (1935) 425, 435 ff., also BÜRGE (above p. 85) and WITZ, *Droit privé allemand—Actes juridiques, Droits subjectifs* (1992) 1 ff.: 'Le dialogue juridique franco-allemand'.

(b) In *Switzerland*, the Code civil applied in the Canton of Geneva and in the Bernese Jura as from 1804, for both of these territories belonged to the French Republic. Both territories joined the confederation in 1815 after the fall of NAPOLEON, but the Code remained in force. During the nineteenth century, the Swiss cantons produced their own codes; throughout western Switzerland, in the Cantons of Vaud (1819), Fribourg (1834/1850), Ticino (1837), Valais (1855), and Neuchâtel (1854/1855), the French Code served as the model; it was often only in family and inheritance law that local legal customs survived. In 1912 these cantonal laws were replaced by the Swiss Civil Code in which, as we shall see (below Ch. 13), French legal institutions still play a part, though not so significant a one as native and German elements.

IV

Although the enactment of the BGB and the ZGB greatly diminished the influence of French law in Germany and Switzerland, the legal systems of *Italy, Spain*, and *Portugal* must still be reckoned as belonging to the Romanistic legal family.

(a) In *Italy*, as elsewhere, the Code civil entered in the train of NAPOLEON's armies. Sicily and Sardinia escaped French occupation thanks to the help of the English fleet, but in the rest of Italy the Code civil came into force, if only for a short time. In the enthusiasm of liberation from the dominance of NAPOLEON, the Code was repealed almost everywhere in 1814, but it soon became clear that the traditional law of canon and Roman origins was inadequate for the needs of the time, and so the individual Italian territories gradually produced new civil codes all of which were based on the Code civil; it was only in the territories ruled by Austria, especially Lombardy and the Veneto, that the Austrian ABGB of 1811 controlled. Although there were many different civil codes in Italy their common reliance on the Code civil formed a basis for a unified private law, and it was not long after the Kingdom of Italy was called into being in 1861 by the great national movement for unification called the 'Risorgimento' that the enactment of the Codice civile of 1865 unified the law of Italy. This Code was substantially based on the French codification, but differed from it, for example, by having an introductory portion 'disposizioni preliminari', in which for the first time private international law, at the instance of the great Italian lawyer and statesman MANCINI, was accorded detailed regulation.

It is not surprising that the Italian lawyers of the nineteenth century looked exclusively to France. The works at their disposal consisted almost exclusively of translations of French authors of the École de l'Exégèse, with several Italian translations of the work of AUBRY and RAU. But a change was felt towards the end of the nineteenth century, as Italian legal scholars came more and more under the influence of the historical and dogmatic methods of the *German* school of pandectists. There was an enormous upsurge of research into legal history, especially Roman legal history, but in private law also Italian authors seized on and developed ideas from German legal scholarship, as SCIALOJA did in his famous work on *Negozi giuridici* (1893). Even today as one goes through the incredibly copious Italian legal literature, one finds late echoes of German pandectist methods—in particular a tendency to think in purely theoretical and unrealistic terms and a striking absence of any critical evaluation of judicial decisions (on this, see the apt observations of CAPPELLETTI/MERRYMAN/PERILLO (above p. 98, at pp. 170 ff.)). Only recently has a change gradually set in, thanks to the beneficial influence of comparative law.

In the social changes which followed the First World War, a plan for a complete reform of civil and commercial law was mooted. A reform commission set up in 1923 reported in 1930–6 with the drafts of four books of a new Codice civile; the first three dealt with the law of persons and family, the law of succession, and the law of property. Book Four, which dealt with the law of obligations and contracts, was a faithful translation of a draft produced in 1928 by a joint commission of French and Italian representatives under the chairmanship of SCIALOJA and LARNAUDE with the aim of unifying the law of obligations in France and Italy.

In 1939 however a decision was suddenly taken to expand the Civil Code substantially: it was to deal not only with private law in the traditional sense, but with all the possible personal and professional relationships of the citizen. One particular consequence of this was a demand to include commercial law. The existing draft of Book Four was withdrawn, and in its place a new Book Four was produced which in addition to sale, lease, and services dealt with the more sophisticated transactions of modern economic life, such as carriage, agency, forwarding, insurance, and bank credits. There was also a new Book Five, entitled 'Del lavoro', which dealt not only with the law of collective and individual labour, but also with the law of partnerships and companies, with the names of firms and trade marks, patents, unfair competition, and the law of monopolies. The concluding Book Six deals with the protection of rights; in the tradition of the Code civil it contains rules relating to evidence, hypothec and pledge, enforcement of judgments, and prescription. The Codice civile came into force on 21 April 1942, and contains 2969 articles.

Apart from including nearly the whole of commercial and economic law (on this, see ROTONDI, 'Entstehung und Niedergang des autonomen Handelsrechts in Italien', *AcP* 167 (1967) 29), the Codice civile makes no radical break with the French tradition: 'the main lines of the Code Napoleon can still be found today in the Italian civil code which, indeed, is not easily understood without some familiarity with the great French work . . .' (BERRI, *Travaux* (above p. 99) 631). The Codice shows its modernity, however, by dealing with many fact situations unknown at the time of the older codifications in France and even Germany. Thus, for example, arts. 1341 f. of the Codice civile contain provisions relating to '*general conditions of business*', and transactions formed by signing sets of *standard terms* or printed *contractual forms* ('moduli o formulari'). The *assumption of contracts* is dealt with in arts. 1406 ff. The rules relating to *contracts for the benefit of third parties* stem from French judicial decisions based on art. 1121 Code civil, with some contribution from §§ 328 ff. BGB (compare arts. 1411 ff.). The Codice accepts the French principle relating to breach of contract that an unperformed contract can be rescinded only on judicial complaint made by the innocent party; he is, however, afforded the possibility of making a written demand for performance within a set period, on the expiry of which the contract is rescinded by force of statute (art. 1454). The Codice civile did not adopt all the abstract conceptual refinements of the German BGB and in particular not the General Part. The notion of 'legal act' was also found uncongenial; instead arts. 1321 ff. deal with 'contracts in general' by saying that their rules are also to be applied, if possible, to 'unilateral *inter vivos* acts affecting property or obligations' (art. 1324). As in France, the law of unjustified enrichment distinguishes between the payment of a thing not due (arts. 2033 ff.) and the 'general claim for enrichment' (arts. 2041 f.) which was developed by the French courts without statutory basis. In the law of delict the Codice is also generally in line with French judicial decision, but there is the noteworthy limitation that damages for pain and suffering can be awarded only when the harmful behaviour is also criminal (art. 2059 Codice civile, 185 Codice penale).

If the basic principles of the law of obligations are clearly similar in the Italian and French codes, there are fundamental differences in the area of matrimonial law. In post-revolutionary *France* the principle of separation of church and state has been strictly observed, while in *Italy* the so-called Lateran Treaty of 11 Feb. 1929 brought the state and the Catholic church into very close association: according to art. 1 of the Treaty the Catholic religion is 'la sola religione dello stato'. The old Codice civile of 1865 regarded marriage as a secular affair in the tradition of the Enlightenment, and therefore accepted the principle that marriage must be entered into before the civil authorities. But by art. 34 of the Concordat the Italian state 'accords private law effects to the sacrament of marriage regulated by canon law'. It follows from this that marriage may be concluded not only before state officials but also before Catholic priests; in the latter case the state official is bound forthwith to enter the marriage in the state register, whereupon the same effects follow, as from the date of the ceremony, as attach to a marriage made before the state officials. Almost all marriages made in Italy today take this 'canonical' form, also called the 'concordat form'. In addition to the official and the canon forms of marriage, the Codice civile offers a third form for non-Catholic citizens: if the general preconditions set out in arts. 84 ff. are satisfied, they may be married before the minister of any religious community recognized by the state; such a marriage must also be entered in the state register.

The Codice civile used not to recognize the possibility of divorce at all. Under art. 151 Codice civile a court could grant a request for separation from a spouse who was in gross breach of his matrimonial obligations, by desertion, maltreatment, or threatening or insulting behaviour, but the bond of matrimony remained intact and neither of the separated spouses could remarry. After many years of bitter public disputes, a law was brought into force in December 1970 which makes civil law divorce possible. Efforts were made to topple this law by means of a referendum and recourse to the Italian Constitutional Court, but they were fruitless.

The law of divorce in Italy today is based essentially on the principle of the breakdown of the marriage. The court will decree a divorce when the affective harmony and communal life of the spouses can no longer be maintained or restored. This is presumed by law after three years of separation. Such separation must be based on an agreement of the spouses confirmed by the court or, in the absence of such an agreement, on a separation order by the court if life together is found to be intolerable.

(*b*) The most striking thing about the development of the law in *Spain* is the continuing vitality of the *fueros*, or laws particular to different localities, which developed in the course of the Middle Ages in individual provinces, counties and boroughs. *Las Siete Partidas*, a thirteenth-century law-book heavily influenced by Roman sources, also had particular importance, for in Castile it obtained the force of statute, and in other parts of the country it gradually obtained subsidiary force, after the local *fueros*. Thus until the nineteenth century the law of the Spanish kingdom was the so-called 'fuero system': the 'compilaciones' of royal laws and ordinances had force everywhere, then there were the *fueros* or local customary laws, and finally *Las Siete Partidas*. In the nineteenth century there was a plan to create a unified Spanish private law, stimulated by the impressiveness of the French Code, but the resistance of the several provinces was too great. Only the most urgent reforms, of land law and the law of mortgage, could be carried through by special statutes. Commercial law was codified in 1829, after the French model, and was greatly modernized in 1885, but the Código civil had to wait until 1889. This code, which is still in force, relies heavily on the Code civil, especially in the area of the law of obligations, where most of the provisions are a simple translation of the French text. In family and inheritance law, on the other hand, the Código contains many institutions indigenous to Spain, especially those from prior Castilian law.

But even the Código civil has not produced complete legal unity in Spain. Only the rules of matrimonial law and the general provisions in the introductory section concerning the effect of statutes and of private international law are valid throughout the country. The other parts of the Código civil have only subsidiary force in those regions which previously had the *fuero* system (see art. 12). These regions cover about a quarter of the Spanish territory and include parts of Northern Spain which are extremely important economically and culturally, and where there is a continuing or renewed movement for autonomy, for example Catalonia (with Barcelona), the Basque provinces of Álava, Vizcaya, and Navarra (with Bilbao and Pamplona), and Galicia (including Corunna). The fueral laws of these regions are often contained in materials of very varied historical provenance and an attempt is being made to codify them: the fueral law of Aragón was collected in 1925 and brought into force as an appendix to the Código civil; it is only recently that the fueral laws of most of the other regions have been identified and enacted in statutes. These fueral laws are being codified not only in the interest of legal certainty, but also so as to provide a basis for the future creation of a private law common to the whole of Spain. This aim is also being advanced by the Supreme Court of Spain, which applies common legal ideas when the applicable fueral law is uncertain or inadequate; in doing this the Court may rely on art. 6 Código civil, which instructs the judge, in the absence of statutory provisions, to apply the local customs and then 'los principios generales del derecho'. On this matter see HIERNEIS, *Das besondere Erbrecht der sogenannten Foralrechtsgebiete Spaniens* (1966).

(*c*) In *Portugal* the law has been fairly well unified since the fifteenth century, consisting of the ordinances of King ALFONSO V, as edited and expanded by his successors, especially PHILIP III in 1603; the room left for the operation of local customs and canon law was relatively slight. The modern codification movement started in Portugal at the beginning of the nineteenth century, but came to nothing by reason of the stressful political conflict between the liberals and the restorationists. Commercial law, because of its wider implications, was codified in 1833 on the basis of the private work of FERREIRA BORGES, who relied on French law; this was replaced in 1888 by a sleeker and more modern version which took account of the Commercial Codes of Italy and Spain which had followed on the Code de Commerce. Professor SEABRA of the University of Coimbra was entrusted with the preparation of a Civil Code, and his draft came into effect in 1867, after the approval of King and Parliament, as the Código Civil. This code has since been replaced by the Código Civil of 1966, which is remarkable for the intelligent attention it pays to foreign legislation—especially German, Swiss, and Italian—to the point where one may wonder whether Portuguese private law ought still to be included in the Romanistic legal family. At the same time, when one compares it with the modern Italian and the forthcoming Dutch codifications, it seems a rather retrogressive and conservative product. On the one hand, labour law and commercial law have been rigorously excluded, and it deals only with what remains of 'classical' private law; on the other hand, much to the surprise of the German comparatist, it adopts the pandectist divisions of the BGB and much of its conceptual apparatus. Family and inheritance law disclose conservative features characteristic of Mediterranean Europe.

Apart from its inclusion of private international law, the 'General Part' of the Código Civil deals with essentially the same materials as the BGB: first, the law of natural persons (with admirably far-reaching protection of the individual's personality against invasions of his privacy and publication of his picture or private letters) and of juristic persons (corporations and foundations), followed by the law of property, under the influence of §§90 ff. BGB, and finally the rules relating to acts in law (*factos juridicos*), using the concepts of 'negocio juridico' with which the German reader is quite familiar, and 'declaração negocial'; it contains rules on error, deceit, duress, form, agency, conditions, legality and immorality, usury, and so on; in the case of usury, the code in art. 283 offers the exploited party the interesting possibility of demanding that the other party *modify* the contract 'segundo juizos de equidade'. The section on the exercise and protection of rights follows the romanistic tradition in including the law of proof. Book Two of the Código Civil, the law of obligations, is divided into two parts; the first part deals with creditor-debtor relationships 'in general', and the second deals with the special types of contract. The first section follows the Italian Codice civile in many points (for example, in the rules of assumption of contracts and the collapse of the foundation of a transaction) and deals also with the law of delict and, according to the German pattern, *negotiorum gestio* and the law of unjustified enrichment. It is noteworthy that all security rights such as suretyship, the transfer of securities, pledge, mortgage, rights of priority, and also the oblique action of a creditor, are dealt with in the general law of obligations. Book Three contains the law of property (possession, ownership, and real rights), while Books Four and Five, as in the German BGB, deal with family law and the law of succession.

V

In the nineteenth century France was one of the greatest colonial powers in the world, with particular spheres of influence in the Near East, in Africa, in Indochina, and in Oceania. Almost all these territories are now fully independent, but in all of them, though to varying degrees, the French legal tradition is still influential. This will be illustrated very briefly for the Near East, the states of the Maghreb, and francophone Africa.

(*a*) Halfway through last century, nearly the whole of the Near East was under the control of the Turks, though that control was shortly to collapse. In this vast area private law was codified only in part. The Ottoman rulers had introduced a Code of Commerce (1850), an Ordinance regulating procedure in commercial cases (1861), and a few other special statutes relating to commercial law, all based on French models. But Islamic law controlled the heartland of private law; there was a rather incomplete and casuistic code called the Majalla, promulgated between 1869 and 1876, which covered the law of property and obligations (see also below p. 309), but family and inheritance law were not codified, the special courts for the different religious communities each using relevant sources.

In the 1870s Egypt became largely independent, as to both home and foreign affairs, within the Ottoman Empire. It had become strategically very important after the completion of the Suez Canal and was heavily in debt, so it was the great European powers, especially the principal creditors, England and France, who had most influence in the country rather than the Egyptians themselves. In 1876 Egypt signed a treaty with the European countries which treated the so-called 'Mixed Tribunals'. The judges in these tribunals were mostly European and had competence, by and large, for all civil and commercial suits in which either party was a foreigner. They applied the so-called 'Codes Mixtes', which, agreeably to the European powers, were principally French in origin, being indeed no more than hastily compiled epitomes of the Code civil (apart from the law of family and inheritance), the Code de Commerce, and other French codes. The so-called Mixed Tribunals had no jurisdiction in suits concerning family and inheritance law; if foreigners were involved, special consular courts had jurisdiction, while if Egyptians were involved the relevant courts of the different religious communities stepped in. Native courts were set up in 1883 for litigation between Egyptians concerning property and obligations, and 'Codes Mixtes', with a few concessions to the relevant Islamic law, were brought into force for them also. There thus arose in Egypt a sharp division between cases involving family relations or inheritance, for which there were *religious* courts applying *religious* law, mainly Islamic, and disputes on economic matters, for which there were *state* courts applying law principally of *French* origin.

A few years after the First World War, Egypt became an independent kingdom but had to concede extensive privileges to England in relation to the Canal Zone and other installations. Not until 1937 could Egypt arrange by treaty that the jurisdiction of the consular courts should pass to the 'Mixed Tribunals' which would cease to operate after a transitional period of twelve years. It was determined at the same time to proceed with the preparation of a new Egyptian Civil Code.

This Civil Code came into force in 1949, and rests largely on the work of the Egyptian legal scholar As-SANHŪRĪ. Although As-SANHŪRĪ and the Egyptian legislator emphasized that Islamic law was considered throughout in the preparation of the Code, the Code appears on closer investigation to be principally orientated towards *French* law, and to contain only a few rules of Islamic origin, such as those relating to gift and pre-emption. The code draws on the French-Italian draft Code of Obligations of 1928 (see above p. 105), the Italian Civil Code of 1942, and also on many legal ideas developed by the French courts. Thus, for example, we find in codified form the French doctrine of liability in damages for abuse of rights (see p. 619 f.); here too we find the doctrine of the collapse of the basis of a transaction, not accepted by France but adopted by the Codice civile (see Ch. 37 III). The Egyptian Civil Code did not adopt the obsolete rules of the Code Civil concerning the avoidance of a contract on the ground of material disproportion between performance and counter-performance (see below pp. 329 ff.); instead it adopts a rule similar to that in §138.2 BGB which it has been proposed to enact in France. On this, see MOUSSERON (above p. 99) 74 ff., and MAURY, *Travaux* (above p. 99) 840 ff., who concludes his study of the Egyptian Code as follows: 'It is always clear that the Civil Code of Egypt is closely related to the Code civil of France and, even more so, to French private law as a whole; taking everything into account, they are members of the same family; but the more recent code does not simply follow or imitate its predecessor; the Egyptian legislator thought afresh and made corrections and additions; the work he produced is in many respects original' (above p. 99, p. 842). The Egyptian Civil Code is silent on family and inheritance law: on these matters religious law still applies. Nevertheless the special jurisdictions of the religious courts were abolished in 1955 and family and inheritance cases transferred to the state courts. Work has been going on for many years on the codification of family and inheritance law—a political hot potato—but so far only a few special laws have been passed.

After the collapse of the Ottoman Empire, *Syria* and the *Lebanon* were put under French mandate in 1922 by the League of Nations. Turkey itself replaced its traditional private law by the Swiss Code in 1926 (see below Ch. 13 III), but in Syria and the Lebanon Islamic law remained in force. In economic matters in Majalla was gradually replaced by modern codes. Thus in 1932 the Lebanon enacted a Code des Obligations et des Contrats, drafted by French lawyers, led by Professor JOSSERAND. The Lebanese Code of Procedure of 1933 and Code of Commerce of 1942 are also largely based on French law. In Syria French influence was relatively slight, but a series of codes came into force there after the Second World War closely following the Egyptian texts and thus indirectly influenced by the Romanistic legal tradition. This is especially true of the Civil Code which they borrowed from Egypt in 1949.

Since 1949 the Egyptian Civil Code has been received by almost all states in the Arab League: Iraq (1951), Libya (1953), Qatar (1971), Sudan (1971), Somalia (1973), Algeria (1975), Jordan (1976), and Kuwait (1980). In effecting the reception, some countries, especially Iraq and Jordan, have given more weight to Islamic law than others, but it cannot yet be said to what extent private law will be affected by the Islamic revival which is taking place virtually everywhere in the Near East. On this see below p. 311.

(*b*) In *Algeria, Tunisia*, and *Morocco*, the states of the Maghreb, the main political influence since the beginning of the nineteenth century has been French. In consequence their law of obligations and commercial law has been virtually identical with the French equivalent. Thus in Algeria the Code civil and the Code de commerce were introduced *in toto* in 1834, while Tunisia and Morocco acquired a Code des obligations et des contrats in 1906 and 1913 respectively, which was a version of the relevant sections of the Code civil adapted to local circumstances. All these colonial statutes remained in force when French domination came to an end except in so far as they were inconsistent with independence. The reforms of recent years such as the new Tunisian Commercial Law of 1959 and Export Trade Law of 1962 leave French influence as unmistakable as ever. By contrast, the family and inheritance law applicable to all Muslim citizens of these countries is Islamic law, which was codified in Tunisia in 1956 and in Morocco in 1958.

(c) The most extensive French colonies, all of which have now obtained national independence, were in sub-Saharan Africa. There are still many economic and cultural links between the new African states and France, but French attempts to forge a closer legal liaison, like the Commonwealth, by means of the 'Union française' and later the 'Communauté française' have not been a lasting success.

One of the great units of the French empire was French West Africa; despite efforts to maintain its unity as a state, since 1960 this territory has broken into no less than eight independent states: *Senegal, Mauretania, Mali, Niger, Guinée, Burkina Faso, Ivory Coast,* and *Benin.* Much the same is true of French Equatorial Africa which in 1960 produced *Gabon, Congo (Brazzaville), Chad,* and the *Central African Republic.* We must add *Togo* and *Cameroon,* previously German but administered by France after the First World War, and also *Madagascar* which was under French control from 1885 until independence in 1960. If one takes into account the previous Belgian colonies—*Ruanda* and *Burundi* (which were earlier part of German East Africa) as well as *Zaïre*—it will be clear how significant a part of Africa is French-speaking and influenced by French and Belgian legal ideas.

The French introduced their codes, especially the Code civil and the Code de commerce, sometimes with modifications in the light of particular circumstances, into all their colonial territories shortly after taking possession of them. Any alterations made in these laws at home were regularly followed in the colonies. It is true that the French laws did not apply to everyone. They applied to all French citizens who had left France to reside in the colonies, their offspring (who were French citizens by blood), and naturalized citizens, but in principle no one else was subject to the French statutes, especially not the natives of African origin. It is true that these people obtained French citizenship by art. 80 of the French Constitution of 27 Oct. 1946, but they remained 'citoyens français de statut local', subject not to the rules of the Code civil but to the rules of African customary law, or, should they be Muslims, the rules of Islamic law. This division of substantive law was reflected in a division of jurisdictions. The French had their own courts system, closely allied to that of France and even divided between private law courts and administrative courts, from which there might be a final appeal to the Court of Cassation or the Conseil d'État in Paris; the natives had their own native courts, staffed by tribal dignitaries, Islamic judges (cadis), French colonial officials, and, in the upper courts, some French career judges.

French colonial policy always sought in the long run to assimilate the native populations. English policy was different: true to the principle of 'Indirect Rule' (see below p. 220), English colonial administrators relied as much as possible on existing native rulers, kept the local courts decentralized, and left mature native law almost intact. The French, on the other hand, inspired by the egalitarian ideals of the Great Revolution and a belief in the superiority of 'civilisation française', constantly strove to lead the native population step by step to the higher level of metropolitan culture. In consequence French colonial legislation always offered the African population the possibility of opting for French law. Thus in all the colonies Africans could conclude individual legal acts, such as marriage or a will, under French law, or submit a particular dispute to French law, whether by agreement or implicitly by calling on a French court for adjudication. Furthermore it was made relatively easier for natives in the colonies to become naturalized French citizens, and in this way opt for French private law. But all these attempts to procure a legal assimilation were unsuccessful, except in Senegal, the most developed of the colonies; French law never really displaced the personal law of the African populations, whether African customary law or Islamic law.

On obtaining independence the new African states undertook a fundamental reconstruction of their law. In particular they abolished the system of divided courts; all courts now apply French law, which still, in principle, regulates constitutional, administrative, commercial, labour, and social law, as well as the African customary law and Islamic law which control family and inheritance. New codes are in process of preparation everywhere, using French legal terminology and French techniques of codification. Thus in 1964 Senegal enacted a Code des obligations, a thoroughly modern and original version of the rules of contract and delict of the Code civil. The codification of family and inheritance law has also been undertaken, but here there are very great practical difficulties, stemming principally from the differences between the African customary laws and Islamic law.

VI

After long and bloody struggles in the early nineteenth century *South* and *Central America* wrested their independence from the colonial power of Spain. The newly founded states of Latin America needed national and unifying civil codes; the only available model was the French Code civil. Spanish law was out of the question as being the law of the previous colonial power; in any case it was neither codified nor uniform even in Spain where local customary laws survived. In contrast, the French Code civil was a product of the Great Revolution, rooted in a world of ideas on which the Latin Americans had frequently drawn to justify their own struggles for independence. In its compactness and terseness of phrase the Code civil was far ahead of any other model, and furthermore it was so full of traditional concepts and ideas, especially from Roman law, that its reception represented no breach with the legal institutions familiar to the Spanish and Portuguese settlers. The civil codes of the Latin American states are consequently heavily influenced by the Code civil, though to different degrees. It is true that French influence has declined in the twentieth century, rather more in commercial than in private law, since legislators have increasingly drawn on other sources, especially Italian, German, and Swiss law, and even, in some cases, the Common Law, as by introducing the Anglo-American trust. Even so, there can be no doubt today that as regards private law the states of Central and South America belong to the Romanistic legal family.

Within the systems of Latin America, we can first distinguish a group whose codes are especially close to the Code civil, as being more or less translations of it: in this group fall the codes of Haiti (1825), Bolivia (1830), and the Dominican Republic (1845/1884). A second and more significant group is headed by the Civil Code of Chile (1855), which despite its reliance on French law is, along with the Civil Code of Argentina, the most independent and original product of Latin American legislation.

The draftsman chosen by the government of Chile was the Venezuelan ANDRÉS BELLO. He spent twenty years on the task, drawing on the Roman legal tradition as well as on French sources, and paying particular attention to *Las Siete Partidas* and to SAVIGNY's thinking. But the Code also contains ideas which in view of its date— before the middle of last century—are remarkably novel and original. This Code was the first to devote a special title in Book One on the Law of Persons to *juristic* persons, it is generous in its recognition of contracts for the benefit of third parties, and contains detailed rules on fiduciary ownership, which the Code civil did not recognize. In its structure it is superior to the Code civil, and in its language it is equally clear and forceful. The Code was later adopted by Ecuador (1860) and Colombia (1873) as well as by several of the Central American states; it also had a great influence on other Latin American legal systems, especially on the Civil Codes of Venezuela (1862) and Uruguay (1868). On the Civil Code of Chile see ARNOLD, *JZ* 1956, 773, and on the importance of ANDRÉS BELLO, see SAMTLEBEN, *RabelsZ* 46 (1982) 421.

The Argentinian Civil Code of 1869 is the work of DALMACIO VÉLEZ SARSFIELD, professor at the University of Córdoba in Argentina; he was also largely responsible for the Commercial Code of Argentina which had come into force in 1859. The Code civil was his principal model, but he also relied on French and other legal writers, as is shown by his frequent footnotes, which are still reproduced in modern editions of the Code; for example, he took several provisions directly from the textbook of AUBRY and RAU, and his private international law mainly from teachings of SAVIGNY and

STORY. But VÉLEZ SARSFIELD also used the Civil Code of Chile, statutes of Spain, the preparatory materials for the Brazilian Code, and other sources, in a brilliantly eclectic manner. The Code he produced was later introduced, almost word for word, in Paraguay (1876).

Brazil had no civil code until 1916, though there were numerous drafts, especially from TEIXEIRA DE FREITAS and BEVILAQUA. In addition to the Code civil it was able to draw on the Portuguese and Italian codes, as well as those of Germany and Switzerland. The structure of the Code, especially its 'General Part', is largely traceable to German influence.

VII

In *North America* there are two areas where the French legal tradition is still vital: *Louisiana* and *Quebec*. The survival of Romanistic law in these two territories is of the greatest interest to comparative lawyers, for Louisiana and Quebec are both members of federal states otherwise entirely dominated by the Common Law; at a time of constantly increasing interfusion on an economic and cultural plane it is clear that the Common Law must exercise a strong influence on these 'islands' of the Romanistic legal tradition, to the point, indeed, that the question has been raised whether in these regions the traditional Civil Law can for long resist its effects. Not only are important areas of private law in Louisiana and Quebec covered by statutes of federal force throughout the United States or Canada which are drafted in the language and spirit of the Common Law, but there are also covert influences of Anglo-American legal thought since, for example, many lawyers in Louisiana are educated in law schools orientated towards the Common Law, and the Supreme Court of Canada, which as a final court of appeal also applies the law of Quebec, is mainly staffed by judges who feel more at home in the Common Law. In Louisiana the consciousness of linguistic and cultural separateness is less marked than it is in Quebec, and the danger, if danger it be, of gradual erosion of the characteristic differences in its style of legal thinking must be taken seriously, though it is sought to resist it by insisting on the particular methods of 'civilian' legal thought. Louisiana and Quebec offer the comparatist a rare chance to observe, as it actually occurs, the interaction of different styles of law, and it is therefore natural that both places should have flourishing and world-famous centres of comparative legal studies.

On the precarious situation of the 'outposts' of 'civilian' jurisprudence in the legal territories of the Common Law, which include Scotland and South Africa as well as Louisiana and Quebec (below Ch. 14 VI, 16 VI), see SMITH, 'The Preservation of the Civilian Tradition in "Mixed Jurisdictions"', in: *Civil Law in the Modern World* (ed. Yiannopoulos, 1965) 3.

(a) *Louisiana*, named after LOUIS XIV, became a French colony at the end of the seventeenth century; at that time it included the whole of the Mississippi valley and marched in the north with the Canadian possessions of the French king. French law obtained, primarily the royal ordinances, followed by the Coutume de Paris. In consequence of her difficulties with England, the other great colonial power in North America, France ceded to Spain in 1762 the city of New Orleans and all of Louisiana west of the Mississippi. The Spanish governors immediately introduced the law of Spain, though they did not succeed in obliterating the French law of the settlers. In 1800, under the threat of NAPOLEON's new military power, Spain had to cede Louisiana back to France; NAPOLEON's attention was fixed on the European scene, so in 1803 he sold this immense territory at a bargain price to the United States, which administered the southern part, the Louisiana of today, as a federal 'Territory of Orleans'; in 1812 it was admitted to the Union as an independent state.

A few years after its accession to the United States, Louisiana's House of Representatives commissioned the drawing up of a Civil Code, which was to codify the law in force—that is, the Spanish law. Nevertheless the draftsmen of the Code turned mainly to *French* law, not only because it was familiar and had proved satisfactory during the period of Spanish rule, but principally because any lawyer then entrusted with the task of producing a code was bound to be drawn first and foremost to the model of the Code civil which had just come into force. It is disputed whether the draftsmen had at their disposal the final version of the Code civil, or only the draft produced by NAPOLEON's commission, or even just the final draft of CAMBACÉRÈS. In any case the Code which came into force in 1808, apart from some infiltrations from Spanish sources, especially from *Las Siete Partidas*, is firmly based on French law, and the new edition and expansion of the Code in 1825 and 1870 did not alter that situation to any great extent.

In many important areas of law the connection between the law of Louisiana and the law of its neighbouring states is extremely close. This is true not only in areas which are governed by federal laws in the United States, such as bankruptcy, patent, and trade mark law, but also in areas where the individual states have legislative power, as in the law of bills and notes, the law of securities and banking, insurance and company law, for here Louisiana has followed the style and content of the legislation in neighbouring states, and it may well be that the *construction* of these statutes by its courts is also in line with the practice of American law in general. Louisiana has also adopted (with the exception of §2 on Sales) the Uniform Commercial Code, that great work of unification of law in the United States (see below p. 252). Strong influences of the Common Law are to be found even outside trade and economic law. Thus, for example, the legal institution of the trust, a typical creation of the Common Law, has been taken over in modified form by a special statute in Louisiana. So far as the law of delict is concerned, though the rules in the Civil Code are an almost literal translation of the articles of the Code civil (see arts. 2315 ff. Civil Code of Louisiana), the courts have surreptitiously brought in many of the ideas and forms of action of Anglo-American negligence law. In the law of contract also the concealed influence of Anglo-American legal ideas is very considerable, since Louisiana provides a very narrow base for the development of an independent civil legal doctrine, and contact with modern French legal science is made very difficult by the language barrier. It is true that recently parts of the Civil Law textbooks of AUBRY and RAU and of PLANIOL have been translated into English and that the universities of the state lay great store by the scientific practice of Civil Law, but only the future will show what effect this will have on the law in action. Today Louisiana belongs neither entirely to the Civil Law nor yet to the Common Law; it is in an intermediate position and seems to be a 'système juridique sui generis' (DAINOW (above p. 98) 32).

(*b*) The territory which is now the Canadian province of *Quebec* was originally part of the huge French colony of 'New France', which stretched from the mouth of the St. Lawrence far into the Middle West of what is now the United States. Here too French domination came to an end with their defeat in the war with England: by the Peace of Paris France had to cede its Canadian possessions to England. The English accorded the French Canadians full religious freedom by the Quebec Act, 1774, and recognized French law, especially the Coutume de Paris, as the basic private law of the province. We shall not dwell on the disputes between the French and English populations of Canada which have lasted with fluctuating intensity until the present day, save to say that the legal separateness of the Province of Quebec, whose population amounts to nearly one-third of that of the whole of Canada, has never been lost.

Until recently the Province of Quebec stood out in the law of Canada, otherwise dominated by the Common Law, by dint of having the *Code civil du Bas Canada* of 1866. This code was based on the French Code civil but went its own way on several matters, as by including the law on commercial transactions. In time the Code of 1866 came to seem obsolete, so in 1955 the Parliament of Quebec resolved on the preparation of a new code, one based on civilian traditions, which would confirm Quebec's desire for independence in legal matters. After many years of work led by Professor CRÉPEAU family law (Book Two) was enacted in 1981, and in 1987 the law of persons, succession, and property (Books One, Three, and Four). The whole 'Code civil du Québec' came into force on 1 January 1994.

The code is a significant piece of legislation, substantially French but based throughout on comparative studies. On many points it connects with the Common Law (for example in the law of security and trusts), in others on the law of the European Community (product liability), and in others on the UN Convention on

International Sales (transfer of risk). See CRÉPEAU, 'La réforme du code civil du Québec', *Rev. int. dr. comp.* 31 (1979) 269; CABRILLAC, 'Le nouveau code civil du Québec', D.S. 1993 Chron. 267; PINEAU, 'La philosophie générale du nouveau code civil du Québec', (1992) 71 *Can. Bar Rev.* 423; LEGRAND, 'Civil Law Codification in Quebec: A Case of Decivilianization', *ZEuP* 1993, 574.

Civil Law has a better chance of maintaining itself against the emanations of the Common Law in Quebec than in Louisiana. For in Quebec the French tradition exists outside the legal system as a decisive factor in the whole cultural life of French Canadians. Furthermore the Province of Quebec, with its large population and significant economic power, has a much larger influence in the federation of Canada than Louisiana has in the United States. It is also important that in the legal life of Quebec the French language is still more current than English. Of course French Canadian lawyers sometimes complain that French legal language has been ruined by the adoption of Anglicisms, and that judges of Anglo-Canadian background often surreptitiously introduce legal ideas of the Common Law by using English expressions. Nevertheless most of the important books on the private law of Quebec which are used in the universities and in practice are written in French, and access to recent French legal literature is certainly much easier in Quebec than in Louisiana. In any case the legal systems of Louisiana and Quebec offer the comparatist fascinating models of a symbiosis of Civil Law and Common Law, and show that a political unit may comprise states of different legal traditions, even when those legal traditions are as different as those of Rome and Westminster.

9

Courts and Lawyers in France

BELLET, 'Grandeur et servitudes de la Cour de cassation', *Rev. int. dr. comp.* 32 (1980) 293.

——, 'France: La Cour de cassation', *Rev. int. dr. comp.* 30 (1978) 193.

BÉNABENT, 'Avocats: Premières vues sur la "nouvelle profession"', *JCP* 1991. I. 3499.

BORÉ, *La Cassation en matière civile* (1980).

BRETON, 'L'Arrêt de la Cour de cassation', *Ann. Université des Sciences Sociales de Toulouse* 23 (1975) 5.

CAPPELLETTI, 'Der italienische Zivilprozeß, Ein rechtsvergleichender Überblick', *RabelsZ* 30 (1966) 254.

——, MERRYMAN/PERILLO, *The Italian Legal System* (1967).

——, PERILLO, *Civil Procedure in Italy* (1965).

CORVES, 'Zur Praxis der Kassation in Frankreich', *DRiZ* (1966) 139.

R. DAVID, *Le Droit français* I: *Les Données fondamentales du droit français* (1960).

DAVID/DE VRIES, *The French Legal System* (1958).

HAMELIN/DAMIEN, *Les Règles de la nouvelle profession d'avocat* (3rd edn., 1977).

HERZOG, *Civil Procedure in France* (1967).

LEMAIRE, *Les Règles de la profession d'avocat et les usages du barreau de Paris* (3rd edn., 1975).

LINDON, 'La motivation des arrêts de la Cour de cassation', *JCP* 1975. I. 2681.

MIMIN, *Le style des jugements* (4th edn., 1978).

OLIVER, 'The Future of the Legal Profession in France', 53 *Aust. LJ* 502 (1979).

PÉDAMON, Anwaltsberuf im Wandel (no. III of *Arbeiten zur Rechtsvergleichung*, 1982) 37.

PERDRIAU, 'La chambre mixte et l'assemblée plénière de la Cour de cassation', *JCP* 1994.I.3798.

TOUFFAIT/TUNC, 'Pour une motivation plus explicite des décisions de justice, notamment de celles de la Cour de cassation', *Rev. trim. dr. civ.* 72 (1974) 487.

WEST, 'Reforming the French Legal Profession: Towards Increased Competitiveness in the Single Market', 11 *J. Leg. Stud.* 189 (1991).

ZWEIGERT, 'Der Jurist in Frankreich und Deutschland, Versuch einer vergleichenden Typologie', in: *Festschrift Hans G. Ficker* (1967) 498.

I

JUST as the French Code civil has served as a model for the private law of many countries of the Romanistic legal family, so has the French *system of courts*. We shall concentrate here on the *Court of Cassation*, the highest French court in civil and criminal matters, which deserves special attention, since it differs in characteristic respects from the comparable supreme courts of the Anglo-American and German legal families.

The Court of Cassation was created by the legislation of the French Revolution. Under its original title 'Tribunal de Cassation', its first function was to assist the legislature rather than to act as a court: its task was to see that the courts did not deviate from the text of the laws and so encroach on the powers of the legislature. In those days even the *construction* of a statute ranked as a 'deviation' from its text, as did the judicial completion of an incomplete law. This was because the provincial courts of the *ancien régime*—the 'Parlements'—had often used the device of construction to evade or restrict the reforming laws of the king. Furthermore it seemed to conflict with the principle of separation of powers for the judges to be empowered to construe statutes; so courts were allowed to refer doubtful questions of construction to the legislature—the 'référé facultatif'. The fact that the Tribunal de Cassation was originally outside the courts system proper had two consequences: first, it could only quash ('casser') the decisions of the courts, not substitute its own decision on the merits; secondly, the courts were not bound by the decisions of the Tribunal de Cassation, but could decide the matter on remand exactly as they had done the first time; if this second decision was questioned, the Tribunal de Cassation was bound to lay the question in dispute before the legislature for final solution—the 'référé obligatoire.'

The revolutionary distrust of judicial legal development in all its forms evaporated fairly quickly; the courts never used the 'référé facultatif', and the text of the Civil Code itself recognizes the need for judicial interpretation (see above Ch. 7 II), so the Tribunal de Cassation, which NAPOLEON renamed the 'Cour de Cassation', itself gradually took over the task of construing the statute and of quashing the judgments of lower courts which had misconstrued it. The principle still remains, however, that the Court of Cassation cannot itself render a decision on the merits, but can only quash the decision under attack and remit the matter for rehearing to another court of the same level. Even today that court is not bound to follow the view of the Court of Cassation: if it refuses to do so and this second judgment is brought to the Court of Cassation, the combined chambers of the court of Cassation decide the matter. If the second decision is quashed, the matter is remitted to a third court, which is then bound to follow the view of the law laid down by the Court of Cassation.

In *Italy* this rather cumbrous procedure is simplified. There also the Corte di Cassazione may only quash the decision under attack, but the court to which the matter is remanded is thereupon bound to follow the view of the law laid down by the Court of Cassation; see art. 384, par. 1 Codice di procedura civile.

It should be noticed that in principle every decision of a French court is liable to attack before the Court of Cassation, provided that other remedies are unavailable or have been exhausted. Thus decisions which are unappealable, because of their low monetary value, for example, may be taken to the Court of Cassation which may therefore have to review the decision of a *tribunal d'instance*. If the preconditions are satisfied the Cour de Cassation is *obliged* to render a decision: it has no power to select cases of special significance. In consequence the Court is grossly overworked, delivering about 18,000 decisions on applications for review every year in civil matters alone.

In *Italy* the right to have judicial decisions reviewed by the Court of Cassation is laid down in the *Constitution* of 1948: see art. III. It is true that the Codice di procedura civile of 1942 denies review to judgments of *juges de paix* which are not subject to appeal (art. 360), but art III of the Constitution, as construed by the courts, permits review by the Court of Cassation even in these cases; see Cass. 9 Feb. 1962, n. 271, Giust. Civ. Rep. 1962, s.v. 'Cassazione civile' n. 163.

In principle the Court of Cassation only answers *questions of law; questions of fact* are left to the 'uncontrolled judgement of the judges of fact' (*appréciation souveraine des juges de fait*). Of course the distinction between questions of law and questions of fact is notoriously difficult, so the Court of Cassation can very often determine the extent of its activities. The principal factor it considers is whether any decision it makes will be of general significance and so help to maintain uniformity in the courts. Contrariwise, the Court of Cassation adopts a position of restraint when it appears that a legal development is still in full flood; in such a case it often leaves the issue unresolved, saying that it is (ostensibly) a question of fact on which the trial judge has the final say.

For the French Court of Cassation, foreign law is in principle a question of fact; it therefore refuses to quash a judgment on the ground that foreign law has been wrongly applied, but it reserves the right to intervene in a case where the court below has wholly failed to apply foreign law as required by a rule of French conflicts law, or where a very gross error has been made in applying foreign law, or where it is a question of general significance (compare ZAJTAY, *Zur Stellung des ausländischen Rechts im französischen internationalen Privatrecht* (1963)).—The construction of *contracts* is also in principle a matter for the trial courts, but the Court of Cassation may intervene when general conditions of business or standard form contracts are being construed, or when the trial judge has 'denatured' the contract by his construction, or has attributed to it a meaning inconsistent with the words of a 'clause claire et précise (See Ch. 30 II).—Art. 360 par. 5 Codice di procedura civile puts the Italian Court of Cassation in a similar position to indulge in covert appreciation of questions of fact.

The French Court of Cassation has six chambers. Three chambers deal with litigation arising out of the general private law, a fourth deals with trade and economic law, the fifth with labour and social security matters, and the sixth with criminal law. Each civil chamber has at least fifteen judges, so that in the Court of Cassation as a whole there are about a hundred judges, in addition to about thirty-five 'conseillers référendaires', junior judges who do preparatory work on the cases for decision and take part in the decision-making process, though usually without a vote. A quorum of five judges is required in the civil and criminal chambers, in simple cases three. With such a large number of judges there is a risk that different benches may adopt different methods of judging cases, so when there may be contradictory decisions or when there is a 'question de principe' to solve the President of the Court or the individual chambers can remit a decision to a 'Chambre Mixte'. The 'Chambre Mixte' is made up of judges from the chambers concerned in the matter in question, each chamber sending its President, its senior judge, and two other judges. Judges chosen in this way from *all* the chambers constitute the 'Assemblée Plénière' (formerly the Chambres Réunies). Apart from ceremonial occasions, the Assemblée Plénière meets only when a decision is up for review a second time, because of the refusal of the lower court to which the matter was remanded after being quashed on the first occasion to adopt the view of the law enunciated by the Court of Cassation (see PERDRIAU, above p. 119). The Court of Cassation also has a special team of state attorneys, led by the Procureur Général, who co-operate not only in criminal matters, but in all civil matters as well; the French view is that at the level of the Court of Cassation the public, whom the state attorney represents, has an interest in the maintenance of law even in *civil* matters. In lower courts the participation of a state attorney in civil suits is necessary only in questions involving status and guardianship, though there is a right of intervention in all cases.

The content, structure, and phraseology of the decisions of the Court of Cassation, and to a lesser extent those of lower courts, are extremely characteristic of the particular style of French legal thought. From the external point of view every decision of a French court consists of a single sentence, which in the case of the Court of Cassation reads either 'The court . . . dismisses [the demand for cassation]' or 'The Court . . . quashes [the judgment under attack] and remits the matter to the Court of . . .'. All the reasons for the judgment are to be found between the subject and predicate of this sentence, in the form of a string of subordinate clauses, all beginning with the formula 'attendu que . . .' ('whereas . . .'). There is no particular section devoted to the facts of the case or the history of the litigation; indeed, the facts are referred to only so far as may be necessary to clarify the particular grounds on which cassation is urged ('moyens'), the reasoning of the lower court or the particular view of the Court of Cassation, and even then the reference may be very allusive. Furthermore, especially in the Court of Cassation, every effort is made to make the text of the judgment as dense and compact as possible. Subsidiary considerations are eschewed; and when the decision must be quashed on one ground, other grounds are not even considered. Asides, divagations, and efflorescences are never to be found in the Court of Cassation, and hardly ever below; nor are there references to the background of the case, legal history, legal policy, or comparative law. In a widely used guide to the style of judgments MIMIN wrote:

'Extrajuridical arguments which do not assist in the solution of a case are among those which lend a merely sophistical appearance to a decision. To invoke consider-ations of economics, sociology or diplomacy is to confuse different types of arguments and to conceal the correctness of sound reasoning' (above p. 119, pp. 255 f.).

Judgments of the Court of Cassation never contain references to previous decisions made by itself or any other court, or even references to legal writ-ing; such references occasionally appear in the judgments of lower courts, but MIMIN regards them as objectionable even there (above p. 119, pp. 273 ff.). In consequence, decisions of the Court of Cassation are very rarely longer than 4–5 pages of typescript, and are often no more than a few lines long. They are generally marked by polished elegance, formal clarity, and stylistic refinement; often, however, they seem to be frozen in a pedantic ritual of empty formalism, inappropriate to the uniqueness of the concrete facts of life behind the case, which indeed can often only be guessed at. It is difficult to believe that these decisions are the work of judges of flesh and blood who ever indulged in the luxury of doubt; it seems to be required by the 'majesté de la loi' that a judgement should appear in perfect purity as the act of an anonymous body.

The style of judgments in the Cour de Cassation has been criticized by French writers as well as by foreigners (see DAWSON, *The Oracles of the Law* (1968) 375, 410 f.; KÖTZ, *Über den Stil höchstrichterlicher Entscheidungen* (1973)). TOUFFAIT/TUNC (above p. 119) have shown that because the judgments generally give only the deci-sion and not the real reasons behind it, no dialogue between the Cour de Cassation and the legal public is possible and they make clear with a wealth of examples how trying it is for a French lawyer to have to venture a view on the possible scope of a terse and cryptic judgment without any expectation that the court will ever respond to what he says. They therefore propose that the Procrustean method of giving decisions in the form of 'attendus' be abandoned and that the judges should be required 'to give their reasoning, with an explanation why they decided in the way they did, and without concealing any of the relevant considerations'. To similar effect is WITZ, *Rev. trim. dr. civ.* 91 (1992) 737. Needless to say, these proposals have had no effect so far; indeed, they have been roundly dismissed (see BRETON (above p. 119)).

Since the reforms of 1958 the French courts system below the level of the Court of Cassation is of the two-tier model familiar elsewhere in Continental Europe. Civil matters are decided at first instance by a single judge in the *tribunaux d'instance*, of which there are 471 in the whole of France, an aver-age of 5 for each of the 90 departments. They can hear cases whose monetary value does not exceed 30,000 francs; their decision in litigation involving up to 13,000 francs is unappealable, though recourse to cassation is always possible. All other civil suits go first of all to one of the 180 *tribunaux de grande instance*, where three judges sit. Commercial cases, whatever their value, are first heard by *tribunaux de commerce* set up by governmental decree as required in the centres of commerce. At the moment there are about 230 of them. Three judges also sit on a *tribunal de commerce*, but instead of being career judges they are indirectly elected by the tradesmen of the jurisdictional area. Many of them, of course, have a basic knowledge of law, since in France legal education is nothing like as specialized as it is in Germany, and many educated laymen know some law. Labour disputes go first of all to the *conseil de prud'hommes*, which are also staffed by honorary lay judges. A bench is normally constituted by equal numbers of employers and workmen, but in the event of disagreement a judge with a casting vote is called from the *tribunal d'instance*. Special first instance tribunals exist for litigation arising out of tenancies, social security, and eminent domain.

Although, as we have seen, there are several special tribunals at first instance, alongside the general civil courts, on appeal the principle of unified jurisdiction is observed; since the reforms of 1958 all appeals to go to the *cours d'appel*, no matter whether the judgment in question was rendered by a *tribunal d'instance*, a *tribunal de grande instance*, or one of the special tribunals; the only exception is for some social security cases. If the sum in issue is less than 13, 000 francs no appeal is possible, even in commercial or labour disputes. As there are only 35 courts of appeal this makes justice in France very centralized. Most of them serve two to four departments, though the court of appeal of Bastia hears appeals only from the department of Corsica. The Court of Appeal of Paris is especially important, for its catchment area includes nearly a fifth of the whole population of France; it has nearly 200 judges whose prestige, position, and pay are greater than those of the judges in the provinces. Courts of Appeal sit in chambers with three judges, which may specialize in particular areas of law, especially in the larger courts.

II

Judges in France, like those in Italy and Germany, are *career judges*; they opt for a judicial career early in life, they are appointed by the state after passing the necessary examinations, and they are generally promoted to more important positions in higher courts on the basis of their performance and years of service. Here is RENÉ DAVID's picture of the career of the judge and the state attorney, both of whom in France are called 'magistrats':

'In France it is often family tradition or personal inclination which attracts people to the career of magistrat. In addition, it also appeals to some people who are not very ambitious, who prefer the security of a modest but assured salary to the risks of competition or the uncertainties of a life in business. A person who chooses to be a magistrat can count on a quiet life whose early years at any rate will be spent in a provincial town, and this life will not be troubled by undue responsibility: a judge in France sits alone only in very small cases, private or public; matters of any importance come before a tribunal with several members, whose decisions, in accordance with a principle of French law, are anonymous' (above p. 119, pp. 49 f.).

In France lawyers of different branches follow different systems of training. Certainly future advocates, notaries, judges, and state attorneys must all follow the same four-year law course in a university, which leads to the 'maîtrise en droit' once the university examination is passed. But then the paths diverge. The future 'magistrat' has to pass a further, rather difficult examination conducted by the state, success in which gives him the right to attend the 'École Nationale de la Magistrature' in Bordeaux. This school was founded in 1958 on the model of the famous 'École Nationale d'Administration', and it admits about 200 young lawyers a year. They are sworn in as 'auditeurs de justice' and are paid by the state during their period of training which lasts two and a half years. They spend time at different courts and state attorney's offices, and receive intensive instruction to develop their specialist legal knowledge, including disciplines like forensic medicine, criminology, and business accounting. This period of training culminates in a further examination, and then the successful candidates, of whom for many years about 60 per cent have been women, take up posts as judges and state attorneys; the range of choice available to them depends on their performance in the final examination.

French judges are guaranteed complete independence: they cannot be removed or even promoted against their will. The promotion of judges depends principally on the decision of a central committee on promotion, which contains prominent judges as well as officials of the Ministry of Justice and has before it the annual reports submitted by Presidents of Courts on the performance of the judges set under them. When judges are to be named to the Court of Cassation the Conseil supérieur de la Magistrature plays an important part; this is a committee of eminent judges whose members are chosen by the President of the Republic from a list prepared by the superior courts. This procedure more or less ensures that the political views of judges play no part in their promotion; if, on the other hand, men of a very independent cast of mind are not very likely to be promoted, this is not a fault of the French system in particular, but one which exists whenever the bridge between 'inferior' and 'superior' judges has to be crossed on the basis of a superior's evaluation of an inferior's performance in office.

In contrast to the judge in the Anglo-American legal system, the judge in France can hardly ever make a name for himself during his professional career. Only on trivial cases in the lowest courts does he sit alone; if he is one of a bench of judges, he is not permitted to deliver a dissenting opinion, and even if he writes the decision of the court the rigorous style of judgments in France requires him to repress all his personal characteristics. Yet this obviously reflects the internal attitude of French judges.

'Judges in France do not like to put themselves forward as creating rules of law. In practice, of course, they have to do so; it is not, and could not be, the function of a judge mechanically to apply well-known and predetermined rules. But judges in France make every effort to give the impression that this is how it is: in their decisions they keep claiming to be applying a statute; only rarely, if ever, do they put forward unwritten general principles or maxims of equity which might suggest to observers that judges were being creative or subjective' (DAVID, above p. 119, p. 50). In fact judges all over the world like to be seen as 'applying' the law rather than as forming it, even interstitially, in a creative manner. MAX WEBER concluded that 'the very judges who, objectively speaking, are the most "creative" have felt themselves to be just the mouthpiece of legal rules, as merely interpreting and applying them, latent though they may be, rather than as creating them.' (*Wirtschaft und Gesellschaft* II (4th edn., 1956) 512).

III

Until recently the business of advising and representing parties in legal affairs, which has long been done in Germany by the unified profession of the *Rechtsanwalt*, was in France divided between *avocat*, *avoué*, and *conseil juridique*. Although the sole profession to survive the reforms of 1971 and 1990 is that of *avocat* we shall give a brief description of the different types of lawyer that used to exist, partly because traces of the distinctions remain and partly because the present rules would otherwise be incomprehensible.

1. *Avocat* and *avoué*.—For a long time a major distinction was drawn in France between the preparation of a case, essentially regarded as a minister-ial matter, and the presentation of the facts and questions of law to the court, which was thought to be a task calling for special eloquence, grasp of doctrine, liberal education, and mental and professional distance from the minutiae of the proceedings. The former task fell to the *avoué*, the latter to the *avocat*.

The old-style *avocat* did all the oral pleading; the rest of the trial, the written part, fell to the *avoué*. The *avoué* did what was needed to get the court proceedings started, he drafted the statement of claim or the defence and any other documents, he saw to the distribution of the judgment, entered the appeal, supervised the execution, and so on. The task of the *avocat* was said to be *la plaidoirie*, while that of the *avoué* was *la procédure, l'écriture et la postulation*. The functions of *avocat* and *avoué* were mutually exclusive: neither could trespass on the prerogatives of the other. The *avocat* was a member of a liberal profession, the *avoué* an *officer ministériel*, holder of an office, as was evident from the fact that his fees, unlike those of the *avocat*, were fixed by an official tariff, not by negotiation with the client, and that the number of *avoués* admitted to any court was strictly limited.

The distinction between the functions of *postulation* and *plaidoirie* came under increasingly heavy criticism. The litigant could not see why he had to engage two professionals in even the simplest case. The duplication delayed the proceedings and rendered it more costly, since both were doing much the same work. The division of roles in the trial itself was also problematical, since assembling and presenting the facts in writing is not rationally separable from oral argument on the applicable legal rules. Indeed it often happened, especially in big cities, that the documents handed in to court were drafted by the *avocat* and simply signed by the *avoué* on his headed paper. For all these reasons the two professions were combined in 1971 in the '*nouvelle profession d'avocat*'. Now it is only before the appellate courts that the prior division of labour obtains. In other courts all procedural steps are taken by the 'nouvel avocat'. Indeed it is only in the *tribunal de grande instance* and the higher courts that an attorney is required at all, for in other courts the parties may be represented by other persons. But in one respect the old distinction between *avocat* and *avoué* is retained in the *tribunal de grande instance*: although the *avocat* may plead before any *tribunal de grande instance* in France, he is like the *avoué* before him in being unable to take the purely procedural steps in a lawsuit except in the court in whose area he has his chambers. Thus a person who wants a Paris attorney to represent him in litigation in Bordeaux has to retain an attorney with chambers in Bordeaux as well, so that he may do what was previously done by the *avoué*. It is different in the *tribunaux d'instance* and the commercial and labour courts, where the *avocat* may conduct the entire lawsuit irrespective of geographical considerations. The *avocat* may not appear before the Cour de Cassation or the Conseil d'État, where the representation of litigants is still entrusted to a special group of lawyers, who, like the former *avoués*, are *officers ministériels* rather than independent professionals. So far as remuneration goes, the old distinction between 'postulation' and 'plaidoirie' has been maintained. For purely procedural steps the *avocat* receives payment in accordance with a fixed tariff (just like the former *avoué*), but he can negotiate the honorarium for advice and pleading with his client without reference to any tariff.

2. *Avocat* and *conseil juridique*.—Only an *avocat* may address a state court on behalf of a litigant, but until recently it was open to others to give legal advice. These other legal advisers, called 'conseils juridiques', were in brisk competition with the *avocats* and won a good deal of work away from them; they concentrated on giving advice to businesses and were readier to meet the increasing demand for expertise in specialist areas of law as well as business management, tax matters, and international affairs. The *conseil juridique* had to be registered, just like the *avocat*, but all that was needed for this

was a degree in law or business management. Foreigners thus qualified were automatically admitted to practise as *conseils juridiques*, though only to give advice on foreign and international law. This liberal attitude made Paris a veritable Mecca for foreign lawyers and law firms for twenty years or so, but the distinction between *avocat* and *conseil juridique* was at odds with the position elsewhere in Europe where only one kind of legal adviser was known, and decisions of the European Court of Justice on freedom of establishment and the provision of legal services made legislative intervention imperative. The Law of 31 December 1990 accordingly merged the professions of *avocat* and *conseil juridique* (for details see BÉNABENT (above p. 119)) and added to the twenty thousand or so *avocats* in France in 1990 approximately five thousand *conseils juridiques*. All these are members of one of the 180 chambers of advocates (*barreaux*) and practise as *avocats*, so that now for the first time in France no one may give legal advice for reward unless he has first been admitted as *avocat*.

3. The two reforms have also made major changes in the professional life of lawyers. Traditionally the French *avocat* was a sole practitioner, a generalist able to deal with business of all kinds. Nowadays, however, thanks to economic and social developments in France as elsewhere, a client can only get proper advice from someone with specialist knowledge and expertise, which no attorney can possess in all areas of law at the same time. Furthermore, a modern attorney's office requires staff and equipment such as no sole practitioner could afford. There was thus an increasing need for new forms of co-operation between attorneys. Laws of 1971 and 1990 therefore opened up a whole range of other forms of co-operation between lawyers. Various forms of office-sharing are possible, as well as legal partnerships of the kind known in Germany, and one can even incorporate a company of attorneys (*société civile professionnelle*). Such a company has independent legal personality, its own firm name, and its own capital, but the personal liability of the attorneys who are members of it remains unlimited.

Whereas Germany still clings to the ideal of the all-purpose lawyer (*Einheitsjurist*) and insists that all lawyers undergo the same training, whatever branch of the profession they propose to enter—a training far too prolonged, geared to training judges, and heavily regulated by the state—the system in France is like that in the rest of Europe. After spending four years studying law at University and gaining the *maîtrise*, a youngster planning to be an attorney or commercial lawyer will, if well advised, spend a further year acquiring specialist knowledge and taking the 'Diplome d'études supérieures' (DESS). If he still wants to become an attorney he must gain admittance to a 'Centre national de formation professionnelle', where he spends a year doing practical exercises and following courses given by professors, attorneys, and judges. On passing the final examination he will be awarded the 'Certificate d'aptitude pour la profession d'avocat' (CAPA), and must then spend two years in the office of an *avocat* as an *avocat stagiaire*. During this period he is permitted to give legal advice and appear in court, and at the end of it he is qualified, without any further examination, to appear as *avocat* before any court in France other than the Conseil d'État and the Cour de Cassation.

IV

One may often throw some light on the characteristic style of a legal system by asking which *type of lawyer* it regards as representative. France and Germany are alike in not having developed the type of the wise judge which other people find so remarkable in the Anglo-American systems. But France and Germany differ, if we are right, in that in France the representative type of lawyer is the *avocat*, the lawyer who pleads before the courts, while the ideal German lawyer is the learned Doctor Iuris, the trained scholar who is to be found in all legal careers, especially among professors, but among judges and barristers as well.

In France the lawyer most often in the public eye is the *avocat* with his brilliant oratory and his special prestige. Although the traditional view that the *avocat* has no monetary contractual relationship with his client is virtually without significance today, the social prestige of the *avocat* still rests on the belief that when he appears in court he comes not so much as the agent of a particular party as in the exercise of a kind of public office. There are historical reasons for the high reputation of the *avocat*, for he is the representative of the self-confident French bourgeoisie which emerged triumphant from the Revolution of 1789. From that Revolution, like the July Revolution of 1830, the French lawyer learnt that one has to fight for the rights of the individual not in the study, but in the forum, on the floor of Parliament, and in the halls of justice. This explains the public standing of the French *avocat* and his importance in French politics. For a long time one could justly say that the Parliament of France consisted half of mayors and half of advocates. Thus the revolutionary spirit of the French bourgeoisie has lived on in the advocate for two hundred years. It is true that like the French bourgeoisie, these advocates are by our standards today rather conservative, but theirs is a conservatism rooted in the belief that one should act with energy and commitment for the protection of freedom once won, for the maintenance of rights which have been earned, of 'droits acquis'. The German lawyer, on the other hand, is typical of a bourgeoisie which is the product of revolutions which failed to succeed or failed to occur. While the impression of the French Revolution and the War of Liberation was fresh the German lawyer was still ready enough to leap on the barricades— consider the dispute between THIBAUT and SAVIGNY—but after 1848 he withdrew from public life like the rest of the bourgeois intelligentsia. At the time, towards the beginning of the nineteenth century, when the lawyers in France were constructing the noble edifice of administrative law—especially through the jurisprudence of the Conseil d'État—to protect the freedoms of the citizens against high-handed intervention by the state, the German lawyer was turning to the meditative cultivation of private law, supposed to be 'unpolitical'. At the turn of the century in Germany lawyers who had theretofore abstained from public life and politics and had shut themselves up in the ivory tower of legal learning began to co-operate with the established powers; but this was the very time in France when the conscience of the nation was shocked by the Dreyfus affair. It is significant that ÉMILE ZOLA's famous article in *L'Aurore* of 13 Jan. 1898 started with the words: 'J'accuse . . .' and continued in the style of a prosecutor's speech in court; this is a further indication of how the methods of thought and speech characteristic of the *avocat* are consciously used in France in the interests of maintaining the standards of law and morality in the public life of the nation.

One can also see marked differences when one asks which *legal virtues* are regarded as specially important in Germany and France. The ideal qualities of a German lawyer are expressed by ideas such as thoroughness, exactitude, learnedness, a strong tendency to tolerate academic disputes and the ability to construct concepts of law with which to master the variety of legal life. The French lawyer, especially the *avocat*, but also the judge, aims at clarity and brevity of expression, eloquence, style, effect, and form. This form is not something purely external, but structural in legal thought itself: 'La forme donne l'être à la chose.' French lawyers have no time for pedantry, for the 'querelles d'Allemand', for the urge to be right in trivia irrelevant to the solution of actual problems. The German lawyer, on the other hand, willingly dons the cloak of learning and is eager to widen his knowledge. This is immediately obvious when one compares the style of judgments of German and French courts. The superior German court gives reasons which are wide-ranging and loaded with citations like a textbook, while the French Court of Cassation goes in for lapidary 'whereas'-clauses. But the same conclusion follows from the characteristics of the legal language in the two countries. STENDHAL may, according to tradition, have read the Code civil frequently in order to improve his style, but one could hardly advise a German novelist to attend to the Prussian General Land Law or the BGB. Indeed, one has the impression that in France there is very little room for a special legal language and that the French legal writer is the equal of the great masters of the French novel in writing in a manner which is clear and unpretentious and often brilliantly elegant. Germany, on the other hand, has developed a specialist legal language in which obscurity too often rates as profundity and which, even when it is not pure jargon, still makes it more difficult for the intelligent citizen to know what is going on in the law than is really desirable for public faith in its activities.

This also helps to explain why in France, unlike Germany, legal studies are part of a *general education*, why the Frenchman regards a basic legal knowledge—as RENÉ DAVID writes (above p. 119, p. 46)—as an 'élément presque normal de la culture générale'. Many young people at French universities study law without having any intention of taking up a legal career: laws is not just the object of a special training but an area in which one can learn to think clearly, to express oneself lucidly, and to practise oratorical skills. The other side of the coin is that the teaching of law in France is often a matter of rarefied principle, of not being occupied with the practical question of finding the right legal solution for the problems of social reality. But to study law in this general, unpractical, and rather 'literary' manner is a way of furthering the education of young people who are not going to be lawyers. Therefore among educated Frenchmen one often meets with a certain familiarity with basic legal ideas. It may or may not be true, as one says, that the French peasant keeps a copy of the Code civil next to his Bible. But it does seem as if SOREL was right to say: 'There is, so far as I know, no other country where the private law has entered so deeply into the customs of the country, and forms so intimate a part of its intellectual, emotional and literary life' (*Livre du Centenaire du Code Civil* I (1904) p. xxxv).

II. THE GERMANIC LEGAL FAMILY

IO

The History of German Law

BOEHMER, *Grundlagen der bürgerlichen Rechtsordnung*, Book 2, Part 1: *Dogmen-geschichtliche Grundlagen des bürgerlichen Rechts* (1951).
COING, *Epochen der Rechtsgeschichte in Deutschland* (1967).
HATTENHAUER, *Europäische Rechtsgeschichte* (2nd edn. 1994).
KOSCHAKER, *Europa und das römische Recht* (2nd edn., 1953).
HANS SCHLOSSER, *Grundzüge der neueren Privatrechtsgeschichte* (4th edn., 1982).
THIEME, *Das Naturrecht und die europäische Privatrechtsgeschichte* (1947).
WESENBERG, *Neuere deutsche Privatrechtsgeschichte im Rahmen der europäischen Rechtsentwicklung* (2nd edn., rev. Wesener, 1969).
WIEACKER, *A History of Private Law in Europe* (trans. Weir, 1995).

NOT everyone would agree that among the legal systems of Continental Europe a distinction should be drawn between a *Romanistic* and a *German* legal family. It is certainly true that the Romanistic and German legal families are much more closely related to each other than either of them is to the Common Law, but in our view this consideration does not by itself justify us in ignoring the important differences of style to be found in the Continental European systems. We have mentioned some of the differences already in Ch. 9, when we were comparing Germany and France, the representative systems of the German and Romanistic legal families, with regard to the style of their statutory language, the form of their judgments, and the type of jurist they see as characteristic. But the point and purpose of distinguishing these two legal families becomes much clearer if we also take historical development into account. It is for this reason that we shall say something about the history of German private law. What follows is in no way intended as an integral sketch of German legal history; for this purpose the reader should rely on authors of repute and consult, for example, the basic works of WIEACKER, KOSCHAKER, and HATTENHAUER. In line with the aim of this book, we shall here try briefly to tell the *foreign* reader in what characteristic points German legal history has diverged from that of the French—Romanistic systems and the English system. Since a different historical development may have a decisive influence on the modern character of a legal system, such a historical sketch can surely help us to understand the particular style which distinguishes the German from the Romanistic legal families today, and both of them from the systems based on the Common Law.

II

During the Middle Ages the whole of Europe came into contact with ancient civilization; the influence of Roman law as a part of ancient civilization was therefore felt throughout medieval Europe, England included. Certainly Roman law had a different impact at different times in different countries. When Germany came in contact with Roman law it was relatively late— not before the middle of the fifteenth century to any great extent, but its effects, which we call the 'reception of Roman law', were much greater in Germany than in France and enormously greater than in England. This contact meant not only a widespread acceptance of legal institutions and concepts of Roman law but also a much more extensive scientific system- atization of legal thought than occurred elsewhere.

The reasons which gave the reception in Germany this particular character are to be found in the political situation after the Hohenstaufens. Central imperial power was weakened and the power of the territorial rulers and bor- oughs was correspondingly increasing. Though this decentralization of power had many consequences for German history, we cannot here inquire whether it was attributable to the Emperors' having overextended themselves in Italy to the neglect of the inner Empire, or because the defects in the Ger- man feudal system, as compared with France and England, made it incap- able of producing a tight centralization of power. In any case it is certain that the reduction of imperial power in favour of the principalities was very conducive to the reception of Roman law, since because of it there was no common German private law, no common German courts system, and no common German fraternity of lawyers which could, as the examples of France and England show, have opposed and delayed the introduction of Roman law.

In the Germany of the Middle Ages there were no central political and judicial organs to lay the foundations of common German private law by pruning, rationalizing, and elaborating the traditional and very diverse laws of the various peoples and cities. In particular there were no strong central courts endowed with imperial authority nor any group of imperial lawyers to make the effort to produce a unified private law for the Empire, a German common law. England had the royal courts in London, attended by an organ- ized corporation of lawyers with great political influence; Paris was not only the seat of the French King and the royal organs and offices, but also the seat of the most important court in the land, so it was also the residence of the best judges, lawyers, and legal writers, who were eager to increase the King's influence since his interests coincided with their own; but in Germany the imperial power grew weaker and weaker while the power of the territorial rulers grew. The German Kaiser had no fixed abode and did his business on the move; there were no central administrative bodies, no staff of royal officials, no effective royal jurisdiction. It is true that there was the Reichshofgericht, which as the highest court of the Empire could in theory call up from the lower courts any case which had not been finally decided, and which acted as a court of appeal for all the regular courts of the Empire. But its influence was not very great since it was not wholly independent of the Emperor, it judges did not have tenure, and it did not even stay in the same place. Furthermore, the landed rulers had enough political power to exact privileges *de non evocando* and *de non appellando* which gravely reduced the jurisdiction of the Reichshofgericht. The Reichskammergericht with career judges and a fixed abode (originally in Frankfurt) was set up in 1495; but for the development of a common German private law 1495 was too late (see KOSCHAKER (above p. 132) 212 ff.).

The weakness of imperial power in Germany, the absence of a strong system of imperial justice, and the non-existence of an influential class of imperial jurists made it easier for the reception of Roman law to make its way in Germany, but this does not explain why Roman law came into Germany in the first place, why its entry was so triumphant, and why the local laws, variegated though they might be, seemed to be so unsatisfactory. The fact is that the legal methods developed by Germanic law became increasingly unsuited to the needs of the time. In the accepted view, the judge made his decisions on the basis of traditional legal knowledge, practical wisdom, experience, and practicality, and from an intuitive perception of what best answered the objective and concrete facts of the case. But such an irrational method of finding law, unreasoningly based on tradition, seemed increasingly incongruous as the social and economic circumstances of the later Middle Ages became more complex, variegated, and developed. There was thus a legal vacuum and Roman law flowed in, not because its rules were substantially better or juster than those of the traditional German law but because it offered a whole range of concepts and methods of thinking which enabled lawyers to grasp difficult factual problems, to place them in a rational framework, to see their implications, and to make them the object of reasoned argument. Had the indigenous law been collected, ordered, and rationalized by an organized group of judges and jurists, the categories of Roman law could have been used, as the French experience shows, to enrich it and make it suitable to the altered circumstances of the times, but in Germany the necessary social and political conditions just did not exist; the traditional law was still in a 'pre-scientific' stage, diverse and disorderly, so that instead of being harmoniously integrated into the local legal culture under the supervision of an organized class of lawyers, Roman legal ideas and institutions were adopted wholesale in many parts of the country and for many areas of law. A further factor was that Roman law was not just another foreign law, but was the law of the *imperium romanum*, which could claim authority on the ground that the Holy Roman Empire of the Germans, as its name suggests, was the successor of the Roman Empire, and that the German Kaiser saw himself as the heir of the Roman Caesar (see the extensive development in KOSCHAKER (above p. 132) 70 ff., 113 ff.).

Jurists trained in Roman law were first employed in ecclesiastical institutions, the principalities, and the boroughs, but by the end of the fifteenth century they had increasingly taken the practice of law from the untrained practitioners and had themselves moved into judicial positions. At first, these jurists all obtained their legal education in the famous Law Faculties of North Italy, but later the German universities began to give regular courses in Roman law, at the instance of rulers eager to maintain their cadre of lawyers. In the course of the sixteenth and seventeenth centuries these lawyers, in their roles as law teachers in universities, as clerks to courts and cities, as writers of legal opinions, as legal advisers of rulers and boroughs, as draftsmen of the legal documents of principalities and towns, created the 'usus modernus pandectarum' out of the Roman law which had been received and the indigenous legal ideas which continued in force everywhere. Admittedly no unified German common private law was developed: the political impotence of the Empire and the manifold particularism of small and tiny principalities and cities made this impossible. While France under an energetic monarchy and a growing centralization could set about creating a 'droit français commun', in Germany it was only in a few large jurisdictions that any synthesis of the Roman and native laws was achieved, for example Saxony (CARPZOV, 1595–1666), the Baltic States (MEVIUS, 1609–70), and Württemberg (LAUTERBACH, 1618–78).

III

A decisive change occurred in the intellectual climate of Europe in the seventeenth century: that powerful march of mind called '*The Enlightenment*' sought to free the individual from his medieval shackles by subjecting the traditional authorities in religion, politics, law, and culture to rational criticism, and to make it possible for him to create a new view of the world on the basis of reason. The effects of this intellectual movement on the law were immense. It gave the lawyer a standpoint from which he could see his way through the *usus modernus pandectarum* with its variety of historically conditioned detail, purge it of obsolete legal institutions, and put it in a new systematic order. One particular product of the Enlightenment is the idea of *codification*, the idea that the diverse and unmanageable traditional law could be replaced by comprehensive legislation, consciously planned in a rational and transparent order. These new intellectual movements had quite different effects in different parts of Europe. *English* law was the least influenced, since it had been so stamped by historical experience and contemporary empiricism that it was very unreceptive to the ideal of a theoretical and unhistorical law of reason, such as was to be developed on the Continent. It is true that the codification of English law on a rational basis found a redoubtable champion in JEREMY BENTHAM (1748–1832), but the conceptual methods of legal thinking of the Enlightenment and the law of reason could never make headway against the sober, practised, and traditionalistic conservatism of the English lawyers, especially of the tightly organized class of judges and attorneys in the Inns of Court. In *France* it was different: here DOMAT and POTHIER had reviewed the traditional legal materials from the standpoint of the law of reason and had presented them in systematic form in influential books, with the result that in many areas of law the future draftsmen of the Code civil found fully fashioned rules ready for them to adopt. More important, however, and crucial for the French experience, was the fact that in France the ideas of the Enlightenment and the law of reason took the form of *direct political action* and led to the Revolution of 1789, to the overthrow of the *ancien régime*, to the constitution of a unitary state resting on the ideal of the equality of all citizens, and finally to the creation of a Civil Code, not *laid down* by an enlightened despot but, leaving aside the midwifery of NAPOLEON, *forced through* by a triumphant third estate.

In *Germany* it was different again: here the law of reason gradually broke loose from its roots in general philosophy and became a system of principles of private law to be taught and learnt. The great systematizers were PUFENDORF, THOMASIUS and CHRISTIAN WOLFF; by rigorous logical–mathematical deduction they inferred rules of increasing particularity from the most general principles of the law of reason and made the law appear as an artful and articulated system, orderly and comprehensible. A rational and abstract method of thought gradually came to predominate in the universities, often more concerned with the refinement of learned definitions and the construction of consistent systems than to keep in touch with social reality, of whose value the *usus modernus pandectarum*, for all that it was difficult, opaque, and obsolete, had had a greater sense. It was in this period that 'the German professor, with all his good and bad points, theoretical, unworldly and doctrinaire, entered the German faculties of law and . . . stamped them with the characteristics they have basically retained to this day' (KOSCHAKER (above p. 132) 249).

The ethereal intellectual constructions of the professors of the law of reason had no direct influence on German legal practice, but the German princes and their high officials, brought up in the spirit of the Enlightenment, found these new ideas very appealing; they became the intellectual stimulus for the many movements for reform in the eighteenth century which sought to humanize the practice of law in the German principalities and to free their legislation from the grip of Roman authorities. These attempts were not, as in France, the product of a passion for freedom and a tempestuous demand for reform by a large class of citizens, but came from the altruistic paternalism of enlightened authorities eager to perform their duty. The first of the codes of this period was the Codex Maximilianeus Bavaricus Civilis of 1756, written by the Bavarian Chancellor v. KREITTMAYR—a code which essentially contains the Bavarian variants of the *usus modernus pandectarum* but nevertheless clearly shows the contemporary legislator's belief in reason, for it solves long-contested questions in a reasonable manner and it is drafted in clear and pointed German. But, apart from the General Civil Code of Austria of which we shall speak in Ch. 12, the most important of the great codifications of the Age of Reason is the *General Land Law for the Prussian States*, which prevailed in the old Prussian territories of Germany from 1794 until the BGB came into force.

The first steps towards this Code took place early in the eighteenth century, but work on the project only began in earnest on the initiative of FREDERICK II, who in this venture was very much the pupil of the French *philosophes*. His men v. CARMER and SUAREZ impressed it with the spirit of the law of reason and the atmosphere of FREDERICK's special brand of enlightened absolutism. Its structure reflects the system of PUFENDORF who saw man as having a 'double nature', as an individual on the one hand, and on the other as a part of larger groups in society; thus the first part deals with the rules relating to the individual's property, and the second part with the individual's legal position in the various communities of which he was a part; here the Land Law deals with the legal position of the individual as member of a family, as member of a household (including the domestic staff), as member of associations or companies, as member of one of the various classes (burghers, farmers, nobility), and finally as a citizen of the state. The contrast with the radical egalitarianism of the Code civil will be immediately apparent, for the Land Law remains rooted in the class structure of FREDERICK's Prussia; this Code was not designed to alter society but to portray it faithfully, completely, and objectively so that everyone could be told in comprehensible if condescending language just where he stood in the state complex. There is no suggestion in the Code that the citizen in society should ever be free from the tutelage of the state or given the opportunity to create his own social world in a responsible manner: 'the real driving force [in the General Land Law] is the claim of an omnipotent administration to look into and regulate permanently and completely every detail of the life of its subjects' (KUNKEL, *SavZ/Rom.* 71 (1954) 534).

On the General Land Law see also LUIG, *AcP* 194 (1994) 521 and DILCHER, *ZEuP* 1994, 446.—The legislator's passion for completeness and comprehensiveness and the enlightened wish to make the Code comprehensible, popular, and educational, led him to abandon juristic and conceptual consistency and to adopt a style of language which was discursive and pedagogic; with so many individual rules the Code has about 17,000 paragraphs, and though practical and realistic in substance, and in style often quite striking and objective, the Code as a whole is extremely hard going, almost impossible for either professor or practitioner to master: KUNKEL (above p. 132) described it as a 'monstrous anti-intellectual undertaking', not only because of its mass of special cases but also because it kept the judges and the subjects of law in leading strings. We have already said that judges were threatened with punishment if they went in for any 'independent' construction and development of the statute, and that if they were in any doubt about the meaning of a provision they were to call on the Law Commission or the Minister of Justice (see above p. 89); it was consistent, then, to lay down in §6 of the Introduction that in judicial decisions thenceforth 'the opinions of legal writers or previous decisions of the courts will be ignored. . . .' The consequence was that the Land Law never attracted independent judicial or scholarly elaboration; must less was it capable of acting as a model for the unification of private law within Germany.

IV

As the eighteenth century gave way to the nineteenth and the codes of Prussia and Austria came into force, the star of the law of reason was already sinking. KANT's critique of perception had put paid to the optimistic hypothesis that human reason could discover generally valid ethical postulates. The law of reason had also forfeited its enlightening spirit of reform by compounding with the enlightened absolutism of Central Europe, often in statutory form; to the ambitious bourgeoisie of the nineteenth century it came to seem more and more the tool of territorial authoritarianism, a device for regulating the citizen's existence without allowing him any room for play. Rationalism was ousted by the new intellectual movements which now started. HERDER had made people see that cultural manifestations like poetry and language are not produced by abstract reason but evolve historically, as he thought, from the people who keep them in a process of constant change. The Romantic movement uncovered the elemental irrational powers in human life and dealt in concepts like 'people', 'development', 'soul', 'feeling', and 'sensibility'. At such a time it is not surprising that the optimistic rationalism of the Enlightenment should seem a dull placebo.

It was in this intellectual situation that the German *Historical School of Law* arose with FRIEDRICH CARL V. SAVIGNY, one of the great figures of German law, as its unquestioned head (1779–1861). In contrast to the Enlightenment view that the legal order is a deliberately planned and purposive creation of an official legislator guided by reason, SAVIGNY and the Historical School of Law saw law as a historically determined product of civilization, having its roots deep in the spirit of the people and maturing

there in long processes. Like language, poetry, and religion, law is the product not of the formative reason of a particular legislator, but an organic
growth, rather like a plant, of the 'inner secret powers' of the 'spirit of the
people' working through history. For the adherents of the Historical School
of Law all true law is customary law, developed, handed down, and captured
in usage and manners; the law-bearers are the people and, as the people's
representatives, the lawyers.

This root idea of the Historical School of Law emerged very clearly in the
famous confrontation in 1814 between SAVIGNY and THIBAUT, a professor at
Heidelberg, on the desirability of a unified German civil code. In the wave of
patriotism which swept Germany after the Wars of Liberation THIBAUT had
written a piece entitled 'Über die Nothwendigkeit eines allgemeinen bürgerlichen Rechts für Deutschland' in which he proposed to replace the intolerable diversity of the German territorial laws by a general German civil code,
on the pattern of the Code civil, and thus to lay the basis for the political
unification of Germany. At the time this proposal had no chance of bearing
fruit, since the fall of NAPOLEON was followed immediately in Central
Europe by the Restoration, and the dynasticism of the various German
rulers rendered democratic integration of the whole of Germany and so
the unification of German law very unlikely. But SAVIGNY's opposition,
added to these unpropitious political circumstances, finally killed THIBAUT's
proposals. In a polemical piece entitled 'Vom Beruf unsrer Zeit für
Gesetzgebung und Rechtswissenschaft' SAVIGNY maintained that the time
was not yet ripe for the production of a unified German civil code. He did
not accept the Code civil and the Austrian Code as precedents; as a conservative, traditionalistic, and class-conscious aristocrat he found their egalitarian tendency and antihistorical rationalism quite repellent, and he criticized
their faults of structure and substance very sharply, if somewhat superficially.
SAVIGNY's basic view was that legislation, being inorganic and unscientific,
was not the right way to create a common German law and would do
violence to the traditions it opposed; what was needed in his view was a
thorough absorption and cultivation of the legal material which was to hand,
as it had grown through time, a task he would entrust to an 'organically
progressive legal science which would be common to the whole nation'.

Since for SAVIGNY all law was the product of history, he and his followers
concentrated on the historical development of law. In this, SAVIGNY realized
that the *Germanic* sources of law had played a great part, and consequently
he insisted on the study of *this* aspect of legal historical development and
thereby greatly stimulated the study of Germanic law in Germany. But he
and his followers turned exclusively to *Roman* law, not in the form it had
taken in the Middle Ages or in the *usus modernus pandectarum* but in the
form of *ancient* Roman law as it appeared in the Corpus Iuris. It was rather
inconsistent of them to give this preference to Roman law in its original form

since in the programme of the Historical School of Law *all* the forces which had had effects on German legal history must be equally entitled to attention. The real reason was that SAVIGNY accepted the educational principles of contemporary humanism and adopted the aesthetic ideas of classicism, just as WINCKELMANN had done for the plastic arts and GOETHE for poetry; for him, therefore, the highest educational value resided in a return to the purity and truth of ancient law. This idealization of Roman law led SAVIGNY and, to an even greater extent, his followers to the thoroughly unhistorical view that the legal forms and institutions created by the Romans belonged to a higher and purer conceptual world and possessed a sort of eternal validity. They did not recognize or did not admit the fact that even in Roman times law was simply a means to the end of a rational ordering of communal life and thus must be seen as dependent on the changing social, economic, and cultural conditions of Roman society. Instead they thought that the Corpus Iuris placed at their disposal a store of legal institutions of eternal validity which could be put to direct use as valid law, if only they were set in the right order. Accordingly SAVIGNY and his followers, from PUCHTA to WINDSCHEID, addressed themselves to schematizing, ordering, and integrating the concepts of Roman law; so it was that the Historical School of Law produced the *Pandectist School* whose only aim was the dogmatic and systematic study of Roman material. Their method of treatment was once again marked by that exaggerated dogmatism which we noted in the period of the law of reason, save that it was directed to rules of Roman law rather than particular postulates supposedly grounded in reason. For them the legal system was a closed order of institutions, ideas, and principles developed from Roman law: one only had to apply logical or 'scientific' methods in order to reach the solution of any legal problem. In this way the application of law became a merely 'technical' process, a sort of mathematics obeying only the 'logical necessity' of abstract concepts and having nothing to do with practical reason, with social value judgments, or with ethical, religious, economic, or policy considerations. No matter how urgently commerce might demand that a claim should be assignable without the co-operation of the debtor, that a debt should be capable of being taken over by a third party, or that a contract should be enforceable by a third party, if such a legal construction could not be arrived at with the devices present in the legal system, then it was 'logically impossible' and the devil might take the hindmost. A method of legal thinking which put 'conceptual calculus' before the careful observation of social reality could only arise in a legal culture which was dominated by remote and theorizing professors and which lacked an organized and powerful class of practising lawyers such as had contributed in France to the development of a unified code whose merits were everywhere recognized, or such as had helped to maintain in England the traditional stock of juristic techniques. But in Germany at the time there was neither a unified private law nor a centralized judiciary, there was no class of practising lawyers bound together by professional solidarity, and the integration of legal life on the *political* and *practical* levels was delayed by the unbroken influence of powerful territorial rulers until late in the nineteenth century. In such a situation the Pandectist School could at least claim for itself that by producing a method of studying law which was common to the whole of Germany it had brought about integration at the *theoretical* level. The pandectists created a set of clear and clearly distinguished concepts which contributed much to the technical sophistication of the BGB, and which had a considerable effect abroad as well, because of the Roman legal materials on which it was grounded. But they did not bother to seek out the real forces in legal life, and they did not ask what ethical, practical, or social justification for their principles there might be; consequently much of what they wrote is hairsplitting pedantry and legal spillikins. This has admittedly been recognized for some time, yet these methods of conceptual jurisprudence are still at work behind the scenes in Germany. As is especially evident to comparative lawyers, trained by their ecumenical experience to be sceptical of the dogmatisms of particular nations, the situation today is that while no one has a good word to say for conceptual jurisprudence lawyers in Germany are still a very long way from adopting in their everyday activity a method of solving problems which is related to their factual content.

V

The first moves towards the codification of unified German private law occurred about the middle of the nineteenth century. The pacemakers were the internationally significant topics of commercial law and the law of negotiable instruments. The law of negotiable instruments was unified in 1848 by the Wechselordnung, and commercial law by the General German Commercial Code of 1861; both enactments were gradually adopted word for word by all the states of the Deutscher Bund. Work also began with the unification of general private law. In 1865 a draft of the law of obligations (Dresdner Entwurf) was produced by a team of famous professors and judges; this pure pandectist production was later to serve as a model for the law of obligations in the BGB. After BISMARCK's efforts had led to the creation of the Empire in 1871, the first priorities were unification of the courts system, civil procedure, and bankruptcy; the ensuing 'Reichsjustizgesetze' which came into force in 1879 are still law in Germany today, though they have been altered in many particulars. Under the Imperial Constitution central legislative competence in private law was limited to the law of obligations, commerce, and negotiable instruments, but in 1873 on the proposal of the National Liberal members LASKER and MIQUEL this was extended to the whole of private law; this was the signal for work to start on the codification of German private law, work which was to last for more than twenty years.

In 1874 a *First Commission* was appointed and charged with producing a draft. It had eleven members, including six judges, three officials from the Ministry, and two professors (though no practising lawyer); the leading fig-ures were probably GOTTLIEB PLANCK, a prominent judge also famous as a liberal politician, and BERNHARD WINDSCHEID, the most outstanding pan-dectist professor of his day. The Commission did its work in seclusion, with-out any contact with representatives of commerce or other social groups, and thirteen years later, in 1887, published a First Draft with supporting 'Motive'. A storm of criticism broke out. In addition to a host of suggestions for improvements on points of detail, there were attacks of principle. There was general objection to its unduly scholastic structure, largely attributable to the abstract conceptualism of the Pandectist School, as well as to the legal jargon in which it was drafted, accurate and precise at the cost of clarity and comprehensibility, and finally to its unduly complicated system of cross-referencing. The criticism of OTTO v. GIERKE made a great impression; in a very spirited attack he took exception to the Draft for bypassing many legal traditions of Germanic origin which were still vital among the German people, and for ousting the traditional ethical obligations and relationships of trust in family and society in favour of an extreme and impersonal indi-vidualism. The objections of ANTON MENGER, a Viennese academic socialist, were even more pointed, though not much notice was taken at the time; his book on *Das bürgerliche Recht und die besitzlosen Volksklassen* (1891) showed how the principle of freedom of contract could lead to the suppression of the socially weaker classes because the socially stronger could dictate the terms of contracts, and how the institutions of private property and succes-sion guaranteed to the propertied classes, who alone benefited from them, the perpetuation of their power of controlling the means of production. These criticisms had no great practical effect. It is true that the *Second Com-mission* which was called into being in 1890 included a few laymen (one bank director, one chief forester, a professor of national economy, and no less than three of the landed gentry!), and that their labours were more public than those of the First Commission. But the alterations made by the Second Commission, necessary and insufficient though they were, were mainly to the *language* of the draft; in substance they added only a few 'drops of socialist oil' to the soulless individualism of the First Draft. The Second Draft with its 'Protokolle' was published in 1895, passed through the legislative process with a few relatively insubstantial alterations, and was adopted in the sum-mer of 1896 by the Reichstag, only the Social Democrats voting against. At the Emperor's personal request, the date of entry into force was set for 1 Jan. 1900; the new century was to have a brilliant start.

II

The German Civil Code

BOEHMER, *Einführung in das bürgerliche Recht* (2nd edn., 1965) 65 ff.
COING, 'Erfahrungen mit einer bürgerlich-rechtlichen Kodifikation in Deutschland', *Zvgl RW* 81 (1982) 1.
DIEDERICHSEN, 'Die Industriegesellschaft als Herausforderung an das bürgerliche Recht', *NJW* 1975, 1801.
DÖLLE, *Vom Stil der Rechtssprache* (1949).
——, 'Das Bürgerliche Gesetzbuch in der Gegenwart', in: *Fünfzigjahrfeier des deutschen Bürgerlichen Gesetzbuches* (ed. Nipperdey, 1950) 14 ff.
ESSER, 'Gesetzesrationalität im Kodifikationszeitalter und heute', in: Vogel, *100 Jahre oberste deutsche Justizbehörde, Vom Reichsjustizamt zum Bundesministerium der Justiz* (1977) 13.
R. GMÜR, *Das schweizerische Zivilgesetzbuch verglichen mit dem deutschen Bürgerlichen Gesetzbuch* (1965).
HEDEMANN, 'Fünfzig Jahre Bürgerliches Gesetzbuch', *JR* 1950, 1.
ISELE, 'Ein halbes Jahrhundert deutsches Bürgerliches Gesetzbuch', *AcP* 150 (1949) 1.
LAUFS, 'Beständigkeit und Wandel—80 Jahre deutsches BGB', *JuS* 1981, 853.
RABEL, 'Zum 25. Geburtstag des Bürgerlichen Gesetzbuchs', *DJZ* 26 (1921) 515, reprinted in: Rabel, *Gesammelte Aufsätze* I (ed. Leser, 1965) 389.
——, 'The German and the Swiss Civil Codes', 10 *La. L. Rev.* 265 (1950).
F. SCHMIDT, 'The German Abstract Approach to Law, Comments on the System of the Bürgerliches Gesetzbuch', 1965 *Scand. Stud. L.* 131.
ANDREAS B. SCHWARZ, *Das schweizerische Zivilgesetzbuch in der ausländischen Rechtsentwicklung* (1950).
——, 'Einflüsse deutscher Zivilistik im Auslande', in: *Symbolae friburgenses in honorem Ottonis Lenel* (1935) 425 ff.
WIEACKER, *History of Private Law* (tr. Weir, 1995) 385 ff.

I

CODES of private law are stamped by the particular historical situation in which they are produced. Many codes consolidate the results of a recent reconstruction of society; their advantage is that the idea of man and the model of society which inspired them may be expected to remain valid for a considerable period. Other codes, by contrast, are created at a time of relative social and political stability; their spirit is often retrospective and reflective, seeking to maintain a situation favourable to the establishment. The German BGB is one of these rather conservative codes: RADBRUCH said that

143

it is more 'the cadence of the nineteenth than the upbeat to the twentieth century', and ZITELMANN observed (*DJZ* 1900, 3) that 'rather than boldly anticipating the future it prudently sums up the past'. The Code does indeed accurately reflect the society of BISMARCK's Empire. The chief role in the state at that time was played by a liberal *grande bourgeoisie* which had produced the imperial German nationstate by co-operating with the conservative powers of authoritarian Prussia. It was the day of a marked liberalism in economics, of the belief that the general good would spontaneously ensue from the interplay of economic forces provided that the state did not interfere. In the 1870s and 1880s, admittedly, some movements towards social justice, paternalistic though they were, led to the enactment of provisions to protect workmen and to the impressive statutory construction of a social insurance system. But in private law these progressive tendencies made no headway; private lawyers were so concerned with positivistic exegesis that they either did not see or deliberately blinded themselves to the great social challenges of the time which any onlooker with insight could easily see. For example, the draftsmen of the BGB seem to have taken no notice of the great social change which was occurring in Germany in the final decades of the nineteenth century; commerce and industry were becoming much more important economically than farming, and urban populations were expanding rapidly, especially with industrial workers. Yet for the BGB the typical citizen is not the small artisan or the factory worker but rather the moneyed entrepreneur, the landed proprietor, and the official, people who can be expected to have business experience and sound judgment, capable of succeeding in a bourgeois society with freedom of contract, freedom of establishment, and freedom of competition, and able to take steps to protect themselves from harm.

II

In language, method, structure, and concepts the BGB is the child of the deep, exact, and abstract learning of the German Pandectist School with all the advantages and disadvantages which that entails. Not for the BGB the simple common sense of the Austrian General Civil Code, the clear and popular style of the Swiss Code, or the sprung diction of the Code civil, instinct with the ideal of equality and freedom among citizens. The BGB is not addressed to the citizen at all, but rather to the professional lawyer; it deliberately eschews easy comprehensibility and waives all claims to educate its reader; instead of dealing with particular cases in a clear and concrete manner it adopts throughout an abstract conceptual language which the layman, and often enough the foreign lawyer as well, finds largely incomprehensible, but which the trained expert, after many years of familiarity, cannot help admiring for its precision and rigour of thought. The concepts used by the draftsmen—'Verfügung', 'Vollmacht', 'Einwilligung', 'unverzüglich', 'in gutem Glauben', and many others—are always used in exactly the same sense. Sentence construction indicates where burden of proof lies, and repetitions are avoided by means of cross-references to amplifying sections. But the BGB has none of the elegance and rich compactness of the Code civil, none of its epigrammatical pith and suppressed passion; instead, in deference to accuracy, clarity, and completeness it often goes in for a prim Chancery style, complex syntax, and rather Gothic cumbrousness, even where it would have been easy enough to hit upon more lively and clearer words. The BGB, then, is no work of literature, but 'the legal calculating machine par excellence' (A. B. SCHWARZ, *Das schweiz. ZGB* (above p. 143) 8), 'legal filigree work of extraordinary precision' (ISELE (above p. 143) 6), 'perhaps the code of private law with the most precise and logical legal language of all time' (GMÜR (above p. 143) 28). In France, Austria, and Switzerland ordinary citizens may have a feeling of warm affection, of closeness to their Code; in Germany not even the lawyer does; instead, the undeniable technical merits of the BGB exact a cool, even grudging, admiration.

Following the divisions arrived at the Pandectist School, the BGB has five books, each devoted to a different subject matter. Two of these areas deal with questions related at the factual level: *Family Law* (Book IV) and the *Law of Succession* (Book V). The *Law of Property* (Book III) and the *Law of Obligations* (Book II) concern 'iura in rem' and 'iura in personam' respectively, a conceptual division derived from Roman law. Thus the *law of property* deals with 'real rights' which a person enjoys *in respect of a particular thing* and can assert against *all the world*, such as ownership, mortgage, usufruct, and pledge. In the *law of obligations*, on the other hand, we are concerned with 'personal' rights, which give one person a claim against another *particular person* on the basis of contract, unjustified enrichment, or tort. This division makes for clarity of thought but it has the consequence that rules governing a single transaction may be placed in widely separated parts of the Code, while provisions closer together may concern quite distinct factual problems. For example, it is obvious to the Anglo-American lawyer that the 'law of sale' should deal not only with the question whether and when the purchaser can demand delivery of the goods he has agreed to buy, but also with the question whether and when the ownership in those goods passes to him. In contrast, the BGB deals with the first of these questions in the law of obligations (§§ 433 ff.) and with the second a long way away in the law of property (§§ 929 ff.). The Anglo-American follows the view that all aspects of a unitary transaction should be dealt with in the same place in the system, while the German lawyer recognises that since ownership in things may pass not only by a reason of a sale but also by *gift* or *exchange*, it conduces to the orderly and rational disposition of the law to give unitary treatment to the passing of ownership as a whole.

Contrariwise, a common lawyer cannot see much affinity between the law of sale and the law of tort; even in the lecture-room he treats them as quite independent areas of law. For the BGB, a common characteristic of sale and tort is that they both afford one person a right 'to claim something' from another, so that both matters are dealt with in the law of obligations and still form part of the same course of instruction.

These four books on Obligations, Property, Family Law, and Succession are preceded by a book with the title 'General Part' (*Allgemeiner Teil*)—a legacy of the Pandectist School whose value to the BGB has been gravely doubted. The General Part does not contain general rules about the exercise of rights in society (see art. 2 ZGB) or basic principles of the construction of statutes, customary law, the powers of the judge, or burden of proof (see art. 1 ZGB, 1 ff. Codice civile), which would have been perfectly sensible and indeed desirable. Instead, the General Part sets out to expound certain basic institutions common to the whole of private law which the lawyer meets with in the law of obligations as well as the law of property, family law, and the law of succession. As GUSTAV BOEHMER said, these matters are 'factored out'. It was thought that this would make for greater logical compactness and internal economy in the Code and would avoid tiresome repetitions. The legal institutions which appear in the General Part were not invented by the draftsmen of the BGB; they were taken over from the learned pandectists of the nineteenth century who distilled them from particular cases by means of a long and wearisome process of increasing generalization. Here are to be found general provisions concerning 'natural persons' (capacity, majority, interdiction, domicile) and 'legal persons', ending with a detailed regulation of the law of juristic entities and foundations, not really suitable for a 'General' Part, followed by some definitions appertaining to the law of property, and finally general rules about 'legal acts' and prescription. Much of this material is in the General Part only because of an exaggerated passion for abstraction: the provisions on 'natural persons' (§§1 ff.) and on 'things' (§§90 ff.) could simply have been included in family law and property law respectively. The idea of 'legal act' is also far too abstract a notion. For the German scholar, 'legal act' includes not only the normal type of contract such as sale or lease and also the so-called 'real contract', namely that special agreement needed in German law to transfer a real right or create a real right over another's property, but it also includes the contract of family law, such as the contract of adoption or the agreement made by bride and bridegroom before the registrar at the marriage ceremony, and even includes the making of a will, the giving of notice to terminate or to rescind a contract, as well as, for example, the resolution to increase a company's capital made by a formal meeting of its shareholders. Although legal declarations of such diverse sources and significance fall within the concept of 'legal act', the BGB enacts rules about voidability on the grounds of error, deceit, or duress, about agency, conditions, and so on, which it solemnly asserts to be applicable to *all* legal acts of whatever type. This extreme position has proved an inexhaustible source of controversy about the range of application of these general rules. In fact it was only the normal contracts which the draftsmen of §§116 ff. BGB had in mind, and so the provisions we have mentioned apply only to *this* type of legal act; it would therefore be preferable to have the rules on voidability on the ground of error, deceit, and duress, rules about agency and so on, contained in the *law of contract* and to direct the judge to apply these rules, if really applicable, to other kinds of legal declarations, deeds or relationships as well (as in art. 7 ZGB, 1324 Codice civile, §876 ABGB). Of course it makes no difference for the practical operation of law where in the Code the concept of domicile is defined, where agency is regulated, or where one finds the rules which determine when a contract may be rescinded for fraud: the judge or lawyer who knows his way around the Code will find the applicable paragraphs (and also, through the commentaries, the relevant judicial decisions) regardless of the internal 'correctness' of their location in the system. But the abstract conceptual calculus of the General Part may still mislead the novice, and sometimes the practising lawyer as well, by suggesting that the correct solution of a living problem depends more on being able to classify it correctly than on seeing and understanding all its factual aspects.

For German discussions of the merits and demerits of the General Part, see WIEACKER (above p. 143) 486 ff.; A. B. SCHWARZ, *Das schweiz. ZGB* (above p. 143) 25 ff.; BOEHMER (above p. 143) 68 ff.; KOSCHAKER, *Europa und das römische Recht* (2nd edn., 1953) 279 ff.; all these contain further references. For the criticisms of a Swedish lawyer, see FOLKE SCHMIDT (above p. 143).

More than anything else, the general theories elaborated by the German pandectists and the General Part of the BGB which rests on their achievements have exercised a particular fascination on foreigners. We have already seen the effect of these doctrines on *Italian* law (see above Ch. 8 IV) and will shortly see their importance for *Austrian* and *Swiss* law. In *France* also the General Part has had a strong influence, principally through the mediation of RAYMOND SALEILLES, a pioneer of comparative law; his two influential works on the general law of obligations in the BGB and on the theory of the declaration of will induced the authors of French textbooks on private law to break away from the structure of the Code civil and present 'general theories' such as we find in equivalent German books. In England the teaching of the pandectists had very little effect. This is hardly surprising since only in a few areas did England grant admission to Roman institutions and methods of thought: English lawyers, if only to secure their professional monopoly by keeping the law obscure, blocked any attempts to rationalize the concepts and structure of their law as a whole. German teaching did have a great influence on a few professors of law, especially JOHN AUSTIN (1790–1859), the acknowledged founder of 'jurisprudence', the legal discipline known in Germany as 'Allgemeine Rechtslehre'. After profound study of the Civil Law and its theoretical foundations he declared that an English jurist who can get to the Continent to study law 'escape[s] from the empire of chaos and darkness to a world that seems by comparison the region of order and light' (*Lectures on Jurisprudence* (5th edn., 1885) 58). Other famous Anglo-American jurists such as HOLLAND, SALMOND, ANSON, POLLOCK, and MAITLAND were also familiar with German pandectist teaching and used their knowledge of those methods in their textbooks on 'jurisprudence' and the 'law of contract'. MAITLAND's observation when the BGB came into force shows that these English lawyers recognized the intellectual merits of German pandectism; he said that it was 'the best code that the world has yet seen'; 'never, I should think, has so much first-rate brain power been put into an act of legislation'.

On the influences of German private legal scholarship abroad, see ANDREAS B. SCHWARZ, 'Einflüsse deutscher Zivilistik im Auslande' (above p. 143) 471, from which the citations from MAITLAND are taken.—The Civil Codes of *Brazil* and *Portugal* have followed the BGB in having a General Part, though with many deviations (see above p. 109, 115); the same is true of the *Greek* and *Japanese* Codes (see below Ch. 11 IV, Ch. 21 III), and the new Civil Code of the *Netherlands* also follows the German model to a limited extent (see above Ch. 8 II). During the work on the reform of the Code civil in France which started after the Second World War but has since been abandoned there was much discussion of the question whether the new code should have a 'Livre préliminaire' containing at least the rules concerning the 'acte juridique'; see *Travaux de la Commission de réforme du Code civil* (1945/1946) 97 ff. and (1946/1947) 229 ff.; also *Travaux de l'Association Henri Capitant* I (1945) 73 ff. The outcome was an agreement to have a 'livre préliminaire' containing only the rules of conflicts of law in time and space; the doctrine of legal acts was to be contained in a special Book IV ('des actes et des faits juridiques'), to follow the first three books on Persons, Succession, and Property. See JULLIOT DE LA MORANDIÈRE in: *Avant-project du Code civil* (ed. Ministère de la Justice, 1955) 25 ff.—The General Part was *not* adopted in *Switzerland* or *Italy*.—On the whole question see IONESCU, 'Le Problème de la partie introductive du Code civil', *Rev. int. dr. comp.* 19 (1967) 579.

III

Given that the BGB is impregnated with the legal values of bourgeois liberalism and is thus, to use an expression of RADBRUCH, 'more cadence of the nineteenth century than the upbeat of the twentieth', how has it been able, without fundamental revision, to survive the political, economic, and social crises and catastrophes of recent German history, including the period of total perversion of law under Hitler? Here we can make only a few observations about the development of the law of contract and delict, and of family law.

The *law of contract* in the BGB is unequivocally dominated by the bourgeois idea that contracting parties are formally free and equal. This idea expresses itself in the legal principles of freedom of contract and the duty to respect contracts: on the one hand, everyone—servant as well as master, consumer as well as manufacturer—is entitled to decide, freely and on his own responsibility, what contracts to enter and on what terms; on the other hand, contracts so formed must be adhered to in all cases, precisely because they arose from the free decision of reasonable contracting parties of sound judgment. Only a few marginal rules seek to protect those for whom the freedom of contract is nugatory, as being economically inferior to the other contracting party or dependent on him in some other way: thus contracts are void under §138 BGB if they are *contra bonos mores* or if one party has exploited the plight, inexperience, or lack of judgment of the other. In addition, contractual penalties may be modified by the court if they are unduly high (§343 BGB). Yet the tenant receives virtually no special protection, and the section on the contract of employment contains only a few rules requiring the 'person entitled to the services' to see to the safety of the place of work and to provide sick-pay within limits.

These few 'drops of oil' have proved to be quite inadequate. As the bourgeois state of the nineteenth century gave way to the social democracy of our own time, legislator and judge alike have had to qualify and limit the liberal principles of the law of contract wherever they gave one party power to threaten those basic conditions of decent life which the social state of today must guarantee to its citizens. Where, as often happened, the interlocking rules of the BGB afforded no sufficient basis on which the legal power of the individual might be modified in the interests of social morality, development had to take the form of creating important areas of law *outside* the Code. This happened in the law of competition and monopolies, in the law of housing, landlord and tenant, and agricultural holdings, but most of all in the law of employment. The draftsmen of the BGB simply did not see the great problem of how to regulate the situation of dependent labourers; indeed they adopted an anti-labour, almost a police-state position, since they deliberately gave trade unions the legal form of the 'corporation without legal personality' with the quite unsatisfactory consequence that trade unions could not even sue in their own name. (But see now BGHZ 42, 210; 50, 325.) Here the *legislator* stepped in and produced a fundamental change by means of provisions concerning security of employment, worker participation, minimum rates of pay, and so on, but the *courts* also without much statutory basis imposed on the employee a general duty of fidelity and on the employer a general duty of care for the safety and welfare of his employees and a duty to treat them equally, principles which are used today to solve the very great variety of concrete problems which may arise out of the contract of employment. Thus developed the great mass of *labour law*, largely independent of the provisions of the BGB which were inadequate, incomplete, and old-fashioned even in 1900.

But this tendency to emphasize the mutuality of social responsibility has led to extremely significant legal developments even in the area of private contractual law. This 'moralization' of contractual relations was made possible by the famous 'general clause' of §242 BGB, which is still much relied on today. That clause simply says in quite general terms that everyone must perform his contract in the manner required by good faith (*Treu und Glauben*) in view of the general practice in commerce, yet the courts, left more or less in the lurch by the draftsmen, have had to rely on it in order to solve the extremely important economic and social problems which arose after the First World War with the collapse of the economy, inflation, and revaluation, and after the Second World War from the loss of East Germany and the change of currency. The rigorous individualism of the original contract law of the BGB has been qualified by means of devices developed by the courts, with names such as 'clausula rebus sic stantibus', 'collapse of the basis of the transaction' (see Ch. 37), 'improper exercise of rights', 'venire contra factum proprium' and 'Verwirkung' (forfeiture of right, especially by laches). The courts long used §242 BGB in order to control the content of General Conditions of Business: standard terms excluding or limiting one party's liability were invalidated as inconsistent with good faith if 'they are inequitable on a balancing of the interests of those who typically enter such transactions' (BGH NJW 1963, 99, 100; for the actual position today see Ch. 24 IV). Thus the general clause of §242 BGB has proved a splendid device for adapting the law of contract to the changed social and moral attitudes of society. HEDEMANN has called this 'the flight into the general clauses' and though the development was inevitable, it is true that it runs the risk of producing judicial decisions which are undirected, exuberant, and variable. Legal writers here have an important and responsible task, to put some order into the variety of cases so that they may be surveyed, learnt, and mastered, to reveal and criticize the value-judgments of the courts, and so to produce some degree of certainty in the law even where the general clauses and legal institutions they engender are being applied.

The *tort* law of BGB still rests on the principle of liability for fault. So far as compensation for *accidents* is concerned, this principle has been greatly weakened both by statute and by judicial decision. There are special statutes for important types of accidents which grant the victim compensation for his loss without his having to prove any fault in the defendant. These cover industrial accidents, railway accidents, traffic accidents, aircraft accidents, and accidents in electricity, gas, and nuclear power stations, as well as many others. But the general principle of liability for fault has also been altered in response to the growing need to protect large sections of the community from the distress and impoverishment which an accident may cause: here the courts have greatly improved the victim's position in many ways—by vastly extending the duty of care, by treating the mere facts as evidence of fault, or even by openly reversing the burden of proof and sabotaging §831 BGB (see Ch. 41 IV)—to such a degree indeed that it is not easy in practice to distinguish between liability for fault and strict liability. This development was made very much easier because *insurance*, now much more widely used by the public and often required by law, provides a device for spreading individual losses among the community at large and so diminishes the chance that a defendant held liable in damages will be personally ruined. Apart from the case of accidents, the principle of fault still applies in full force to compensation for material and immaterial harms. The courts have gradually extended protection against intentional and negligent invasions to some interests which the draftsmen of the BGB did not see fit to protect: here one may mention interests of personality and the so-called 'right in an established and active trade or business' (see the full treatment in Ch. 40 II, 43 II).

In *family law* also the BGB originally bore the marks of the conservative and patriarchal age of the bourgeoisie. It was for the husband to make decisions during the marriage and it was the husband who exercised parental power. The rules of matrimonial property were devised on the basis of the prevailing practice among the classes of officers and officials that the spouses brought to the marriage an interest-bearing capital sum which was to be administered by the husband. The rules of divorce and illegitimacy were influenced by Christian morality. Accordingly, the BGB used to permit divorce only when the breakdown of the marriage was attributable to the fault or insanity of the defendant spouse. In comparison with legitimate children illegitimate children were deliberately disfavoured, for fear that extra-marital adventures, which the law discountenanced, might otherwise be legalized and that immorality and undesirable concubinage might be encouraged. An illegitimate child was treated in law as unrelated to his father; instead he was fobbed off with a claim for maintenance whose amount depended on his *mother*'s social position and which came to an end when he was 16.

Most of the work of bringing family law into line with altered social and economic circumstances has been done by the legislature, through the only really deep incisions which have been made in the text of the Code. The work of reform after the Second World War received a striking impetus from the Basic Law which provides that men and women should have equal rights and that all rules of private law inconsistent with this principle should cease to have effect on 31 March 1953 (see art. 3 par. 2, 117 GG). The legislature, however, allowed this date to go by without taking any action, so there was a lacuna in the law which had to be filled by the courts. Four years elapsed before the Law of Equal Rights of Man and Woman came into force in 1957; it made important alterations in private law, some of which had been anticipated by judicial decision. Thus in *matrimonial property* law the statutory régime is to be one of separate property, with the modification that acquisitions by the spouses during the marriage are to be divided between them; on *divorce* the proceeds are to be divided equally between the spouses, while if the marriage is dissolved by *death*, the surviving spouse's statutory right of succession is proportionately increased (the so-called property regime of 'community of acquisition'). The draftsmen of the Law of Equal Rights decided to maintain the husband's priority in regard to the exercise of *parental power* (called *parental care* since 1979) and especially the right to be the *statutory representative* of his children, only to be told by the Federal Constitutional Court that such a provision was void as being inconsistent with Art. 3 GG (BVerfG NJW 1959, 1483). The legal position of *illegitimate children* has been decisively improved by a law which came into force in 1970, also pursuant to express constitutional mandate (see art. 6 par. 5 GG). The preconditions and consequences of *divorce* are now determined by a Law of 1976. This Law abandons the principle of fault and adopts the principle of breakdown of the marriage, for it declares that a marriage may be dissolved 'when it has collapsed' (§1565 BGB). The fault of the parties is in general equally irrelevant for the *consequences* of divorce, especially with regard to the validity and extent of a claim for maintenance. An important innovation deals with the adjustment of pension rights and rights to other benefits (*Versorgung*): if during the marriage one spouse has acquired greater rights of this sort than the other, the latter is to receive one half of the difference. This is done by creating new entitlements in the disadvantaged party (and proportionally diminishing those of the partner) carrying an independent personal claim against the body liable to provide the benefit or pension in the future. Furthermore, the law of adoption was reconstructed by an enactment in 1976, and the law of parental care by a Law of 1979. Indeed, there is hardly a paragraph in family law that is recognizably the same as in 1900.

Despite this, the structure of the BGB, taken by and large, looks very much the same as it did a century ago, for all the intervening changes in economic and social conditions since then. In part this is explained by the fact that areas of law which were developing very rapidly have assumed an independent existence outside the BGB but many areas of law, especially family law, have been greatly altered and modernized by intervening *legislation*. Still, the maintenance of the general structure of the BGB is really the work of the *courts*, whose performance in fitting the original text of the code to modern demands and keeping it socially vital has been as significant as it has often been misunderstood. In the result, whole parts of the BGB, just as of the Code civil, are covered by a heavy gloss of judicial decision, often to the point where a mere reading of the text will not disclose the law as it actually is. But while in France it was the gaps and technical imperfections of the Code civil which gave the judges their opportunity to develop the law, the courts in Germany have relied above all on the general clauses of §§138, 157, 242, and 826 BGB. These general clauses have operated as a kind of safety valve, without which the rigid and precise terms of the BGB might have exploded under the pressure of social change.

But now we must ask whether this increasing divergence between the provisions of the Code and the rules of the actual law is still acceptable. Certain types of contract and heads of liability which are vital for the citizen receive no mention at all in the BGB; contracts of other types are hived off in special laws which can fall outside the purview of commentators and scholars; in many areas judge-made law has become so predominant that the foundation of codal texts could be withdrawn without any risk of having the edifice collapse. This is why the Ministry of Justice is considering redrafting the law of obligations in the BGB with a view to bringing it back into touch with modern legal practice. On this see the *Reports and Proposals for the Remoulding of the Law of Obligations* (three volumes ed. Federal Ministry of Justice, 1981–83). Meanwhile a Commission set up by the Ministry has made proposals to update the provisions in the BGB regarding liability for breach of contract, the rules relating to contracts of sale and services, and prescription. See the Final Report of the Commission for the Reform of the Law of Obligations (ed. Ministry of Justice, 1992).

After the collapse of the Soviet Union and the peaceful revolution in East Germany the internal border in Germany disappeared. The two legal systems clearly had to be harmonized. At the outset it was thought that this would take some time, but in order to facilitate the flow of capital from the West certain laws had to be introduced quite quickly, so many of the West German laws on the currency, the economy, and labour matters were brought into force in East Germany by the Treaty of 18 May 1990. Political developments occurred apace, however, and that very summer while the negotiations over accession were proceeding, the idea gained acceptance that West German law as a whole should be brought into force in the East. This was no foregone conclusion, for the East already had a modern code, the *Zivilgesetzbuch* of 1976. Despite its pieties about raising socialist morality and the need for the citizen to develop into a 'rounded socialist person', the ZGB contained many sensible rules couched in simple realistic language, especially in family law, but it soon emerged that it had one critical defect: because it dealt only with the relations between individuals on the one hand, and between individuals and state-owned enterprises on the other, it was not at all adapted to relations between organizations in a market economy. It was suggested that family and inheritance law could at least be retained for the time being, pending subsequent unification, but that would have meant having internal rules of conflict of laws to determine which law was to apply, so on 3 October 1990 the whole of West German law, including the BGB, was brought into force throughout the country by the treaty of unification of 31 August 1990. Many a citizen in the East felt that this was rather brutal, and one can sympathize with the feeling, but there was really no practical or reasonable alternative.

IV

In the course of the nineteenth century the Historical School of Law and the Pandectist School exerted an influence which reached far beyond the boundaries of Germany and gave new life to legal theory in many European countries, especially Italy, France, and Austria, but even England as well. Thus when the BGB came into force in 1900 it could count on lively interest abroad because it expressly sought to give legislative form to the pandectist achievements in method and concept. The Code, indeed, was much admired on all sides, more perhaps abroad than in Germany at the time, but it really only influenced legal *theory* and legal *doctrine*; there was very little *practical* reception of the BGB, at any rate very much less than of the Code civil a century earlier. One reason for this was that its sophisticated structure and abstract conceptualist language was seen abroad as a typical product of German scholarship which, despite its technical merits, was not likely to take root very easily in alien legal soil, but the critical fact was that the more developed states of the world outside the Common Law family had already equipped themselves with civil codes during the nineteenth century and there was therefore no widespread need to import foreign models.

Even so, in the years following its enactment, the BGB had a great influence in quite widespread regions of the world, though political changes since then have diminished or extinguished it. As to the *Far East*, *Siam* and *China* introduced civil codes between 1925 and 1935 which, apart from family and inheritance law, were largely based on German law (see ARMINJON/NOLDE/WOLFF, *Traité de droit comparé* II 427 ff. (1950)), *Japan* having already adopted most of the BGB and the Code of Civil Procedure at the turn of the century (see below Ch. 21).—*Eastern and Southeastern Europe* used to be another area of influence. After gaining a degree of independence in the Austro-Hungarian Empire *Hungary* repealed the Austrian General Civil Code in 1861, and its courts began to rely increasingly on German law in addition to old Hungarian customary law and principles of Austrian law: German law also provided a series of statutes on commercial law and civil procedure. Several drafts for a Hungarian Civil Code were based on German law, and though they never actually became law, the courts treated them rather as if they had (see HEYMANN, *Das ungarische Privatrecht und der Rechtsausgleich mit Ungarn* (1917); EÖRSI, 'Richterrecht und Gesetzesrecht in Ungarn', *RabelsZ* 30 (1966) 117). The *Baltic* states were also clearly influenced by German law. *Czechoslovakia* and *Yugoslavia* came into existence in 1918; the principal influence was originally Austrian law, but subsequent legislation and drafts of private law statutes paid considerable attention to German law (see KORKISCH, 'Das Privatrecht Ost-Mitteleuropas in rechtsvergleichender Sicht', *RabelsZ* 23 (1958) 201). *Poland* and *Romania*, in contrast, then belonged to the Romanistic legal family (see CONSTANTINESCU, *Travaux de la Semaine internationale de droit* 1950

(1954) 664). In deference to the changed political climate after the Second World War almost all these countries introduced new civil codes (see Ch. 24 IV of the second edition). Nowadays their legal systems need to be thoroughly overhauled. It would perhaps have been best if the countries of Eastern Europe could have agreed on a common plan and enacted at least a common law of obligations modelled on that of Western Europe, but that was never a real possibility. There has been a resurgence of national pride, and each country must go its own way. Sometimes they look to German and Swiss law, sometimes to the new Civil Code of the Netherlands, sometimes to the Vienna Convention on International Sales, and occasionally, in commercial and economic matters, to the Common Law.

The Pandectist School and the BGB had a particular influence on the Civil Code of *Greece*. Plans for a Greek civil code go back to the War of Liberation of 1821–27 in which the Greek people won their independence from Turkish domination. For a long time it remained doubtful what the model for such a code should be. Since the Greek Liberation Movement was essentially based on the ideas which led to the French Revolution, many voices were raised in favour of a reception of the Code civil but others wanted to codify the law of Roman Byzantium which, primarily in the form of a private collection of statutes of HARMENOPOULOS from 1345, had been the law of Greece during the nearly four centuries of Turkish domination. This was the view which won through in the course of the nineteenth century. During this period Greek lawyers increasingly ignored the alterations and additions which Byzantine Emperors had made to the Corpus Iuris of JUSTINIAN and concentrated instead on the Roman law of the Corpus Iuris as elaborated by the German pandectists. Contact with Germany was established in 1835 when the Wittelsbachs came to the Greek throne in the person of Prince OTTO, for he brought with him a group of legal advisers, including, V. MAURER, a professor from Munich, whose contribution to procedural and penal legislation constituted a valuable form of 'legal aid to developing countries'. As a result of these contacts with Germany, the second half of the nineteenth century saw *German* professors teaching pandectist law at Athens University and writing textbooks alongside *Greek* professors trained in Germany; this meant that the Roman law familiar to the Greeks by reason of their history came in practice to take the form it had received at the hands of the pandectists. After many abortive attempts, preparatory work on a Civil Code for Greece entered a decisive phase in 1930, by which time all were agreed to look first to the *German* Code as being in closest contact with Roman law. The Greek Civil code was promulgated in 1940 but involvement in the Second World War and German occupation of the country delayed its entry into force until 23 February 1946.

In its structure the Greek Civil Code reflects the BGB. The General Part precedes books on the Law of Obligations, the Law of Property, Family Law, and the Law of Succession. In content also the Greek Civil Code relies predominantly on the German Code, but it always takes account of subsequent German legal practice which filled gaps in the BGB or developed its rules. At the same time there are many echoes of Swiss law, and to a lesser extent rules have also been taken from the French Code civil and the Italian Code. In linguistic and conceptual style the Code steers a middle course between the German and the Swiss Codes, avoiding the sophisticated interfusion and the abstract conceptualist language of the BGB without aiming for the simple and popular tone characteristic of the Swiss Code.

On the origins and content of the Greek Civil Code, see MACRIS, 'Die Grundgedanken für die Ausarbeitung des Entwurfs eines griechischen Zivilgesetzbuchs', *RabelsZ* 9 (1935) 586; GOGOS, 'Das griechische Bürgerliche Gesetzbuch vom 15.3.1940', *AcP* 149 (1944) 78; ZEPOS, 'The New Greek Civil Code of 1946', 28 *J. Comp. Leg.* 56 (1946); ZEPOS, 'Der Einfluß des schweizerischen Privatrechts auf das griechishe Zivilgesetzbuch', *SJZ* 1960, 358; MARIDAKIS, 'La Tradition européenne et le Code civil hellénique', in: *L'Europa e il diritto romano, Studi in memoria di Paolo Koschaker* II (1954) 157; PLAGIANAKOS, *Die Entstehung des griechischen Zivilgesetzbuches* (1963); SONTIS, 'Das griechische Zivilgesetzbuch im Rahmen der Privatrechtsgeschichte der Neuzeit', *SavZ/Rom.* 78 (1961) 355.

12

The General Civil Code of Austria

EBERT, 'Gesetzgebung und Rechtswissenschaft, Ein Beitrag zur Zeit des späten Natur-rechts in Österreich', *SavZ/Germ*. 85 (1968) 104.

ARMIN EHRENZWEIG, *System des österreichischen allgemeinen Privatrechts* I, 1 (2nd edn., 1951) 17 ff.

GSCHNITZER, 'Hundertfünfzig Jahre Allgemeines Bürgerliches Gesetzbuch', *JBl*. 1962, 405.

VON HARRASOWSKY, *Der Codex Theresianus und seine Umarbeitungen* I (1883).

KLANG, 'Der Oberste Gerichtshof und die Entwicklung des bürgerlichen Rechts', in: *Festschrift zur Hundertjahrfeier des österreichischen Obersten Gerichtshofes* (1950) 80.

——/GSCHNITZER, *Kommentar zum Allgemeinen bürgerlichen Gesetzbuch* I, 1 (2nd edn., 1964).

FRANZ KLEIN, 'Die Lebenskraft des Allgemeinen Bürgerlichen Gesetzbuches', in: *Festschrift zur Jahrhundertfeier des Allgemeinen Bürgerlichen Gesetzbuches* I (1911) 1.

KLEIN-BRUCKSCHWAIGER, '150 Jahre österreichisches ABGB', *JZ* 1963, 739.

KORKISCH, 'Die Entstehung des österreichischen Allgemeinen Bürgerlichen Gesetzbuches', *RabelsZ* 18 (1953) 263.

VON MAYR, 'Das Bürgerliche Gesetzbuch als Rechtsquelle, Einst und jetzt, in: *Festschrift zur Jahrhundertfeier des Allgemeinen Bürgerlichen Gesetzbuchs* I (1911) 379.

OGRIS, *Der Entwicklungsgang der österreichischen Privatrechtswissenschaft im 19. Jahrhundert* (1968).

——, 'Zur Geschichte und Bedeutung des österreichischen ABGB', *Liber memorialis François Laurent* (1989) 373.

PFAFF/HOFMANN, *Excurse über österreichisches allgemeines bürgerliches Recht* I (2nd edn., 1878).

VON SCHEY, *Das österreichische Allgemeine Bürgerliche Gesetzbuch, Vortrag aus Anlaß der Jahrhundertfeier* (1911).

STEINWENTER, 'Der Einfluß des römischen Rechts auf die Kodifikation des bürgerlichen Rechts in Österreich', in: *L'Europa e il diritto romano, Studi in memoria di Paolo Koschaker* I (1954) 403.

UNGER, *System des österreichischen allgemeinen Privatrechts* I (5th edn., 1892).

WEISS, 'Hundertvierzig Jahre Allgemeines Bürgerliches Gesetzbuch', *JBl*. 1951, 249.

WELLSPACHER, 'Das Naturrecht und das ABGB', in: *Festschrift zur Jahrhundertfeier des Allgemeinen Bürgerlichen Gesetzbuches* I (1911) 173.

VON ZEILLER, *Commentar über das Allgemeine Bürgerliche Gesetzbuch für die gesammten deutschen Erbländer der oesterreichischen Monarchie* I–VI (1811–13).

I

THE third of the great codes which came into force in Europe at the end of the eighteenth and the beginning of the nineteenth century is the Austrian *General Civil Code* of 1811. Like the Prussian Land Law and the Code civil, this Code is founded on the ideal of codification characteristic of the Age of Enlightenment, on the belief, later so fiercely contested by SAVIGNY, that comprehensive legislation, deliberately planned, rationally and lucidly constructed, and backed by the authority of the state, should replace the unwieldy and old-fashioned traditional law, often cumbrous and uneven. Among these three great codes of natural law the Austrian Code has its own flavour and distinctive characteristics.

Preparatory work on the code started in the middle of the eighteenth century when the Empress MARIA THERESIA was embarking on the fundamental administrative reforms which were to turn the Austrian hereditary territory into a state in the modern sense. One of the great obstacles was the variety and complexity of the laws in the various parts of the royal Austrian territory, so in 1753 the Empress charged a Commission with the task of preparing a code; her instruction was

'that in drafting the code the Commission should limit itself to *private law*, leaving the present law in force so far as may be, and bringing the various laws of the provinces into agreement so far as conditions permit, using the *Gemeines Recht* and its best exponents as well as the laws of other countries and always referring back to the common law of reason whenever correction or completion is called for' (cited by ZEILLER (above p. 157) I. 7 f.).

The Empress's instructions make it clear that the Code which was envisaged was, unlike the Prussian Land Law, to be limited to *general* private law, leaving aside not only the particular laws of special groups or classes of persons but also the whole of public law as well as any other 'political' law. The bodies of law which were to be incorporated in the Code were also specified: the laws of the various territories, the Roman *Gemeines Recht* (in the form of the *Usus modernus pandectarum*), and finally the 'common law of reason'.

In 1766 the Commission produced a draft, called the *Codex Theresianus*. It was immediately considered in the Austrian Imperial Council but the reception was predominantly critical: the draft was far too comprehensive, it was too like a textbook, and it was incomprehensible without a knowledge of Roman law, in which it was too firmly rooted. The Empress agreed with the view of her Council and called for a reworking of the Code on the basis of the following principles:

'1. Statute and textbook should not be confused; definitions and divisions and such other matters as smack more of the lecture-room than the legislative chamber should be left out of the Code. 2. Everything should be stated as briefly as possible, consistently with clarity . . . Unusual cases should either be omitted or brought under general principles. 3. Ambiguity and vagueness must be carefully avoided. But even in respect of clarity moderation must be observed; clarity must not be used as a pretext for introducing unnecessary repetitions nor for explaining cases where a reasonable man would have no doubts. 4. The Code should not be tied to Roman law but should be founded throughout on natural equity . . .' (cited by v. HARRASOWSKY (above p. 157) 11 f.).

FREDERICK II is said to have made a similar criticism of the size of the draft of the Prussian Land Law when it was put before him: 'But it is very big; laws must be short and to the point.' In Austria, however, the draftsmen paid heed to such criticisms. They first attacked the law of persons and reduced it from 1,500 paragraphs to a bare 300; this was brought into force in 1787 under the Emperor JOSEPH II as the *Josephinisches Gesetzbuch*. Reworking of the other parts of the Codex Theresianus started under LEO-POLD II: in 1790 he appointed a new Commission under the chairmanship of MARTINI, an eminent exponent of the law of nature at Vienna University and head of the Imperial Ministry of Justice. In 1796 MARTINI produced a 'Draft of a General Civil Code' (*Entwurf eines Allgemeinen Bürgerlichen Gesetzbuches*) which broke free from the Codex Theresianus and from Roman law, and for the first time gave weight to the doctrines and postulates of the law of reason. This draft was put before the administration of the Austrian territory for their views, and in 1801 was referred to a new Commission for final polishing, along with the reservations ('Monita') which had been entered. The leading spirit of the Commission was FRANZ V. ZEILLER, who ranks along with MARTINI as the real creator of the Austrian code. ZEILLER was also an adherent of natural law which he had learnt from MAR-TINI at Vienna University and taught there after him but, perhaps under the influence of KANT's theory of knowledge, he had broken away from the dry and doctrinal formalism of the law of reason; he sought to make a compromise between the claims of natural reason and the empirical realities of Austrian life. ZEILLER formulated the supporting considerations which accompanied the final version of the draft of the Commission, submitted to the Emperor FRANZ I in 1808:

'Laws rest on the general and unchanging principles of reason and justice . . . This is why the civil codes of civilized nations agree in most of their provisions and why the states of Europe have been able to use old Roman law as a principal source of rules for deciding disputes. At the same time every state needs its indigenous and peculiar statutes suited to its own particular circumstances . . . The climate, resources, commerce, traditional forms of intercourse, and the candid or devious character of the inhabitants, all these have a definite effect on the rules concerning the legal form and various types of legal transaction, wills, contracts, securities, and the right to compensation for harm' (quoted by PFAFF/HOFMANN (above p. 157) 62 f.).

As a convinced supporter of the philosophy of the Enlightenment, ZEIL-LER took the ultimate source of all law to be reason, but his sound practical sense led him to keep out of the Code those dogmas of the law of reason which were unduly theoretical and remote from life. Thus the law of reason afforded the draftsmen a firm standpoint amid the unmanageable and largely obsolete chaos of the old *Gemeines Recht* and it also influenced the structure and phrasing of the Code, giving it at many points its unmistakable natural law flavour (see §§7 and 12 ABGB). On the other hand the Code is quite free from exaggerated and unrealistic dogmatism and it retains many institutions of the *Gemeines Recht* and provincial laws which seemed to the draftsmen to be reasonable and appropriate. Thus, rather like the Code civil, the Austrian Code of 1811 strikes a happy balance between the critical ration-ality demanded by the times and a sound sense of the value of tradition.

II

The General Civil Code was founded on enlightened principles—equality of citizens, freedom of private legal relationships from state control, freedom of economic activity—but this was in striking contrast with the actual social conditions in Austria in 1811 when the Code came into force. Thus although §16 ABGB laid down that 'every human being is entitled to be treated as a person by reason of his intrinsic rights, made manifest by reason', the peasantry in large parts of the Austrian kingdom at the time was in a state of feudal dependence barely distinguishable from serfdom; indeed §1146 ABGB laid down that the 'rights and obligations . . . between the owners of land and the local peasantry are to be found in the constitution of the rele-vant province and in political provisions'. So while the Code is based on the aim of easing legal commerce between citizens, it makes no attempt to curtail the numerous rights and privileges of feudal classes, which were controlled by 'political' provisions relating to 'hunting, forests, commerce, the servant classes, or the relationship between landed proprietors and the local peas-antry'. §7 ABGB is forward-looking in giving the judges freedom, under certain conditions, to fill gaps in the law by calling upon 'principles and natural law', but in the decades after the Code came force the Imperial administration kept issuing petty decrees dealing with the most insignificant legal questions, almost as if Austria had had the 'reference to the statutory commission' of Prussian law or the 'référé' of the *droit intermédiaire* of France. In spirit the General Code was far ahead of actual social conditions in the authoritarian and absolutist Austrian state, and FRANZ KLEIN is right to say that the Austrian code was really 'an anachronism' at the date of its enactment (above p. 157, p. 17).

A turning-point came in 1848, the year of revolutions. The only specific-ally legal change was the abolition of the status of rural subservience but the new ideas of the liberty of the press, freedom of occupation, and the right to participate in politics and matters of state spread gradually from the bourgeoisie throughout society. In the period of restoration after 1848 there were admittedly many retrogressive steps. Thus imperial legislation pursuant to the Concordat of 1855 subjected to canon law the marriage of Catholics which had been regulated in the ABGB, gave jurisdiction in matrimonial matters to ecclesiastical courts, and put almost all education under the supervision of the church. The Concordat was replaced only twelve years later after the constitutional reforms of 1867 had brought a liberal majority into the Austrian Reichstag; recognition was accorded only to civil marriage, matrimonial litigation was returned to the secular courts, and the supervision of schools was taken away from the church. In the 1870s and 1880s as rural conditions gradually changed, as industry caught on, as the country was opened up to commerce, and as the economic institutions of capitalism came to the fore, the ABGB with its libertarian and individualist outlook came increasingly to be congruent with social and economic reality in Austrian life (see KLEIN (above p. 157) 16 ff.).

The decisions of the Austrian courts show a similar development. Just as in Prussia after 1794 and in France after 1804, the enactment of the Code was followed by a period of pure exposition, the judges hewing to the letter of the statute with neither wish nor taste for the historical or comparative varieties of legal study. Here too the situation did not change until after 1848. Then Austria came into contact once again with German scholarship, which in the juristic field meant contact with the Historical School of Law and with the Pandectist School which grew out of it. The leader of this pro-German school of thought was JOSEF UNGER, professor at Vienna University since 1855. In his writings he sharply attacked the 'literalism' of the exegetical school, their 'reasoning on the surface of the law', their 'logical petit-point'. One can almost hear the voice of SAVIGNY in UNGER's statement that in lieu of the exegetical method one must adopt 'the historical-philosophical method, which consists in learning to understand the peculiar phenomena of the present by means of a deep and loving study of the past'. UNGER said 'that the only hope for law in Austria is to be found in the School of Historical Law founded by SAVIGNY and PUCHTA . . .'; he was therefore emphatic in urging his colleagues to 'water the fallow fields of Austrian legal study with the abundant stream of German scholarship' (UNGER (above p. 157) pp. iii–v, 640 f., 647; see also OGRIS (above p. 157) 11 ff.).

UNGER's own work greatly helped to forge the links between Austrian law and German pandectist doctrines. Although his *System des österreichischen allgemeinen Privatrechts* (1856 ff.) was never finished, it absorbed all the scholarship of German pandectist literature and dealt lovingly and in detail with the General Part of private law without which, as he said (above p. 157, p. 641), the lawyer is at sea in the law 'like a pilot without a compass'.

UNGER and his followers had to erect the structures of pandectist theory on a statutory text based on natural law, a task which clearly presented grave difficulties (see examples in OGRIS, above p. 157, pp. 16 ff.). UNGER had very little time for the 'principles of natural law' occasionally referred to in the ABGB. In §7, where the judge is directed to use these principles as a standard of construction, UNGER saw 'no more than the satisfaction of a purely theoretical bias of the draftsmen'. He found that §§16 and 17, where a human being is described as the titulary of intrinsic natural rights which entitle him to legal personality, were 'wholly otiose paragraphs without any practical significance' (above p. 157, p. 71). Since the time of UNGER, Austrian and German legal scholars have worked closely and fruitfully together; his *System* had an effect on Austrian legal writing comparable to that of ZACHARIÄ's Handbook on the French (see above pp. 103); since then, unlike the Code on which they are grounded, textbooks of private law in Austria all include a generous 'General Part' containing general theories, as developed by the German pandectists, on the sources of law, persons, property, and legal acts.

III

In its formal and technical construction the ABGB is much clearer, more comprehensible, and more 'modern' than the Prussian Land Law, much criticized by ZEILLER for its 'artificial structure which even the most indefatigable legal expert can barely master' (quoted in PFAFF/HOFMANN (above p. 157) 48). Instead of the streamlined phrasing of the French Code civil the ABGB has many explanatory and theoretical provisions of a rather fatherly tone, and though these are strictly unnecessary they somehow make the Code clearer and easier to understand. (On this compare v. MAYR (above p. 157) 385 ff.) §14 ABGB specifies the parts into which the Code is divided, a matter which was already clear from the Table of Contents. Countless provisions kindly inform the reader that a particular question is dealt with elsewhere (see, for example, §§450, 603). The Code contains many purely explanatory or instructive definitions without juristic content. Thus §44 ABGB explains the marriage contract by saying that thereby 'two persons of different sexes [declare] their will in legal form to live together in indissoluble community, to have children, to educate them, and to give each other mutual support'. The Code is often drafted with a wealth of specific detail; while it seldom reaches the tiresome prolixity of the Prussian Land Law (but see the nearly laughable casuistry of §§487–503, 556–683), it is very far from the glacial phraseology of the *German* Code 85 years later. Compare, for example, the provision in §45 ABGB on the law relating to premarital engagements: 'Regardless of the circumstances in which it is made or the conditions to which it is subject, the contract of affiancement or preliminary promise of marriage creates no legal obligation either to proceed to the marriage itself or to do what was promised in the event of withdrawal.' §1297 BGB, in contrast, reads: 'No claim for the fulfilment of a promise to marry will lie. The promise of a penalty in the event of failure to marry is null.'

With only 1,502 paragraphs the ABGB is strikingly shorter than the Code civil or the BGB. The draftsmen were able to achieve this brevity only by leaving significant gaps which have caused considerable difficulties for the Austrian courts.

In view of the gaps in the Code as well as the many defects which had come to light in comparison with the German Code, the Austrian government accepted UNGER's proposal to set up a 'Commission to Revise the ABGB'. This Commission and its successors worked for ten years and it was not until 1914–16 that three *Teilnovellen* were enacted, of which the third in particular made considerable alterations in the text of the Code. About 180 provisions in the ABGB were redrafted, completed, or repealed; these emendations, all based on the model of the German BGB, affected nearly all the areas of law dealt with in the ABGB, especially the general law of contract, tenancy, and lease, and the contract of employment and services. The Teilnovellen excited considerable criticism, but in EHRENZWEIG's judgment they have proved generally satisfactory: 'Laws get better year by year as the magic wand of practice makes their defects disappear' (above p. 157, p. 35).

The structure of the ABGB is much like the system of the Institutes of GAIUS: there is a short introduction followed by three sections devoted to the Law of Persons, the Law of Property and 'Provisions Common to the Law of Persons and the Law of Property'.

The Introduction includes general provisions about entry into force, area of application, retroactive effect, and statutory construction. We have already mentioned §7 ABGB, a remarkable provision, very progressive in comparison with the Prussian Land Law, which instructs the judge how to act when faced with a gap in the law: when a case cannot be decided on the basis of the words or the natural meaning of a statute, the judge must look to the solutions laid down by the statute for comparable cases and to the reasons underlying other allied statutes: if the matter is still in doubt, it must be decided by the judge 'by applying the principles of natural law to the particular facts of the case, carefully sifted and maturely evaluated'. In practice this provision has not been used very much, because the judges preferred to make law behind a smokescreen of traditional techniques of construction rather than be openly creative (see KLANG (above p. 157) 84 ff.).

The *First Part* of the ABGB 'On the Rights of Persons' contains in its first principal division a great variety of rules concerning the 'Rights attaching to personal qualities or relationships'. Here there are rules about legal capacity, the protection of mental defectives, the position of the 'moral person', and finally some rules relating to foreigners and private international law, which was the subject of a totally new Law of 1978. The second principal division deals with *matrimonial law*. This was fundamentally altered by several reform laws of the 1970s, and now reflects the principle of equality of treatment in art. 7 of the Austrian Constitution. The same applies to the Law of Children and Guardianship in the third and fourth principal divisions.

The *Second Part* is devoted to the Law of Property and is by far the longest in the ABGB. Its first section deals with *Real Rights in Things*—possession, ownership, pledge, servitudes, and, astonishingly enough, the law of succession, regarded as the right to succeed to a decedent's estate or part of it (see §§308, 532)—and the second section deals with *Personal Rights in Property*, 'by dint of which one person is bound to perform something for another' (§§ 307, 859); it is at this point we find the whole of the law of contract and delict.

First we have the *general* rules of contract law: they deal with offer and acceptance, capacity, and invalidity of contacts on the ground of error, deceit, or duress—rules which strike us today as rather progressive (see Ch. 31 II)—followed by rules relating to illegality and immorality and formal requirements. All these provisions are found in Germany in the General Part of the BGB where they are laid down as applicable not only to contracts but generally to all 'legal acts'. In the ABGB, on the other hand, §876—which was brought into the Code by the Third Teilnovelle—provides that the rules on error, deceit, and duress are to be applied 'to other expressions of will requiring communication'.—The general rules on breach of contract (§§918–21 ABGB) likewise stem from the Third Teilnovelle and indirectly from the BGB.

These general provisions are followed by rules for the *special types of contract*: here we find the treatment of, for example, gift, deposit, loan of both kinds, sale, and also marriage settlements between spouses. Of historical interest is the section on 'Powers of Attorney and Other Forms of Agency'. The legislator does not make the distinction between the power to act for another and the underlying contract which confers that power—the distinction was 'discovered' by LABAND in Germany only seventy years later—and treats the two as a unitary transaction, the 'Contract creating a power of agency' (*Bevollmächtigungsvertrag*) (§ 1002 ABGB). The general rules relating to lease, for both types of which (*Miete, Pacht*) the Code uses an old-fashioned expression (*Bestandsvertrag*), have been largely replaced or greatly restricted by the numerous special statutes provoked by the housing shortage. Much the same is true of the provisions relating to the contract of employment, thoroughly overhauled though they were in the Third Teilnovelle: they are almost completely overshadowed by the mass of modern statues on industrial matters.

The *tort law* of the ABGB clearly shows the influence of natural law thinking; deliberately rejecting the multiplicity of Roman forms of action in delict, §1295 adopts a general clause, valid for liability in contract and delict alike: 'everyone who has suffered harm is entitled to claim compensation from the person who was at fault in causing it'.

The ABGB recognises no cases of liability *without* fault. Even where the harm is caused by an animal or by the collapse of a building or structure, or by the fall of parts of it, the custodian of the animal or the possessor of the building can avoid liability if he proves that he had taken all necessary precautions (see §§1319 f.). In the rules relating to *vicarious liability* the Third Teilnovelle reintroduced the distinction between contractual and tortious liability: if the contractor uses the assistance of another person in the performance of a *contractual* obligation, he is liable to his contractor for the faults of that person without more ado (§1313*a* ABGB), but a person against whom a *delictal* claim is brought, though liable without proof of *culpa in eligendo*, is liable only if his assistant, in the eyes of the court, was 'incompetent' (*untüchtig*) (§1315 ABGB).—Modern developments in the area of accident law have taken place outside the ABGB, just as in Germany they have taken place outside the BGB; if a person is accidentally injured at work, on the highway, or by means of a train or airplane, his claim is controlled by special statutes which do not require any fault on the part of the defendant. There is one point, however, on which the Austrian courts have been more courageous than their German neighbours: they have recognized that even in the absence of a special statutes liability may be strict when the harm has been caused by the 'dangerous activity' of the defendant entrepreneur; it is for the judge to decide when an activity is 'dangerous' (see Ch. 42 II).

The *Third Part* of the ABGB deals with 'Regulations common to the law of persons and the law of property'. In addition to extinctive and acquisitive prescription, we here find *suretyship* and the *pledge contract* under the title 'Reinforcement of Rights', and under the title 'Alteration of Rights' a special treatment of *assignment* and the *taking over of a debt*. In the section on 'Termination of Rights' are the rules concerning the various ways of extinguishing a debt, for example, *set-off*, *release*, and *payment*; it is in an appendix to the provisions on payment that we find the rules on unjustified enrichment, under the rubric 'Payment of a Thing Not Due'. In comparison with the orderly structure of the *German* BGB this may seem very capricious, but erroneous though the location of this legal institution may be, no one has shown that it has in the least affected its *functional operation*. By and large the brevity and theoretical inadequacies of the ABGB have made it possible to adopt a flexible construction: 'It has been possible to exploit its poverty and turn its need into a virtue' (GSCHNITZER, JBl 1957, 371).

IV

The ABGB has not had anything like the effect abroad of the Code civil. This is not so much because Austria after 1811 did not conquer any lands on which to confer its Code as NAPOLEON did in Holland, Italy, and Germany. More important for the lack of external effect is the fact that the ABGB was the Code of a restoration-minded monarchy in thrall to the powers of the past during the decades under METTERNICH and soon to be faced with the constant danger of that inner collapse which threatens polyethnic states. The Code civil, on the other hand, was the law-book of a powerful unitary state, born of a successful revolution and politically outward-looking throughout the nineteenth century. Furthermore, no famous statesman and charismatic leader like NAPOLEON stood over the cradle of the ABGB, only the enlightened officials of an absolute and authoritarian state. In consequence it is not surprising that the ABGB has relatively little effect on the outside world. Yet as the nineteenth century proceeded, the Code had an effect in many of the non-German speaking parts of the Austro-Hungarian Empire: in Hungary it was in force for only a few years, but it was accepted in Croatia and Slavonia and in Bosnia and Hercegovina, as well as, somewhat abbreviated, in the adjacent territories of Serbia and Montenegro. The ABGB was in force in Lombardy and the Veneto until the Risorgimento. Even after the break-up of the Austro-Hungarian monarchy in 1918 the ABGB maintained a tenacious hold in the parts of Poland, Yugoslavia, and Czechoslovakia which had theretofore been Austrian, for it was only after the Second World War that it was replaced there by the new civil codes of the socialist states.

Although since 1719 *Liechtenstein* had been an Imperial Principate and consequently not part of the Austro-Hungarian Kingdom, it received large parts of Austrian law including the ABGB. After the First World War Liechtenstein separated from Austria and turned to Switzerland, since when its legislation has largely followed the Swiss model, the only parts of the ABGB left with practical effect being those relating to succession, marriage, and children. See, in detail, GSCHNITZER, *Gedächtnisschrift Ludwig Marxer* (1963) 19.

13

The Swiss Civil Code

DESCHENAUX, 'Der Einleitungstitel [des schweizerischen Zivilgesetzbuchs]', in: *Schweizerisches Privatrecht* II: *Einleitung und Personenrecht* (ed. Gutzwiller, 1967) 1.

EGGER, 'Einleitung und Personenrecht,' in: *Zürcher Kommentar zum Schweizerischen Zivilgesetzbuch* I (2nd edn., 1930).

——, 'Das schweizerische Zivil- und Handelsrecht,' in: Egger, *Ausgewählte Schriften und Abhandlungen* I (ed. Hug, 1957) 145.

ELSENER, 'Geschichtliche Grundlegung, Rechtsschulen und kantonale Kodifikationen bis zum Schweizerischen Zivilgesetzbuch', in: *Schweizerisches Privatrecht* I: *Geschitchte und Geltungsbereich* (ed. Gutzwiller, 1969) 1.

GAUYE, 'Eugen Huber und das deutsche Bürgerliche Gesetzbuch' [with a hitherto unpublished essay by Eugen Huber of 1910 entitled "Das Verhältnis des schweizerischen Zivilgesetzbuches zum deutschen Bürgerlichen Gesetzbuche"], *ZSR* 80 (1961) 63.

RUDOLF GMÜR, *Das schweizerische Zivilgesetzbuch verglichen mit dem deutschen Bürgerlichen Gesetzbuch* (1965).

GUTZWILLER, 'Der Standort des schweizerischen Rechts', *ZSR* 80 (1961) 243.

HIRSCH, 'Die Einflüsse und Wirkungen ausländischen Rechts auf das heutige türkische Recht', *ZgesHR* 116 (1954) 201.

HIRSCH, *Rezeption als sozialer Prozess, Erläutert am Beispiel der Türkei* (1981).

EUGEN HUBER, *Schweizerisches Civilgesetzbuch, Erläuterungen zum Vorentwurf* (1902).

KOHLER, 'Eugen Huber und das schweizer Zivilgesetzbuch', *RheinZ* 5 (1913) 1.

KRAMER, 'Die Lebenskraft des schweizerischen Obligationenrechts', *ZSR* 102 (1983) 241.

LIVER, 'Das schweizerische Zivilgesetzbuch, Kodifikation und Rechtswissenschaft', *ZSR* 80 (1961) 193.

——, 'Einleitung', in: *[Berner] Kommentar zum schweizerischen Zivilrecht* I (1966).

——/MERZ, 'Das schweizerische Zivilgesetzbuch, Entstehung und Bewährung', *ZSR* 81 (1962) 9, 30.

MERZ, 'Fünfzig Jahre schweizerisches Zivilgesetzbuch', *JZ* 1962, 585.

——, 'Die Quellen des schweizerischen Obligationenrechts von 1881, Ein Beispiel interner Rechtsvereinheitlichung', *Festschrift Zweigert* (1981) 667.

——, 'Das schweizerische Obligationenrecht von 1881, Übernommenes und Eigenständiges', in: *Hundert Jahre schweizerisches Obligationenrecht* (Peter/Stark/Tercier ed., 1982) 3.

VON OVERBECK, 'Some Observations on the Role of the Judge under the Swiss Civil Code', 37 *La. L. Rev.* 681 (1977).

PRITSCH, 'Die Rezeption des Schweizerischen Zivilrechts in der Türkei', *SJZ* 23 (1926/27) 273.

PRITSCH, 'Das Schweizerische Zivilgesetzbuch in der Türkei', *ZvglRW* 59 (1957) 123.

RABEL, 'Bürgerliches Gesetzbuch und schweizerisches Zivilgesetzbuch', *DJZ* 15 (1910) 26, reprinted in Rabel, *Gesammelte Aufsätze* III (ed. Leser, 1967) 144.

——, 'Streifgänge im schweizerischen Zivilgesetzbuch', *RheinZ* 2 (1910) 308, 4 (1912) 135, reprinted in Rabel, *Gesammelte Aufsätze* I (ed. Leser, 1965) 179, 210.

——, 'Einige bemerkenswerte Neuheiten im schweizerischen Zivilgesetzbuch', *GZ* 62 (1911) 161, reprinted in Rabel, *Gesammelte Aufsätze* I (ed. Leser, 1965) 268.

——, 'The German and the Swiss Civil Codes', 10 *La. L. Rev.* 265 (1950).

SAUSER-HALL, 'La réception des droits européens en Turquie', in: *Recueil de travaux publié par la Faculté de Droit de l'Université de Genève* (1938) 323.

ANDREAS B. SCHWARZ, *Das schweizerische Zivilgesetzbuch in der ausländischen Rechtsentwicklung* (1950).

SIEHR, 'Die Zeitschrift für schweizerisches Recht und das schweizerische Privatrecht in der deutschen Rechtspraxis', *ZSR* 100 (1981) 51.

SIMONIUS, 'Zur Erinnerung an die Entstehung des Zivilgesetzbuchs', *ZSR* 76 (1957) 293.

STARR/POOL, 'The Impact of a Legal Revolution in Rural Turkey', 8 *L. and Soc. Rev.* 534 (1974).

TUOR, *Das schweizerische Zivilgesetzbuch* (8th edn., rev. Schnyder, ed. Jäggi, 1968).

VELIDEDEOGLU, 'Erfahrungen mit dem schweizerischen Zivilgesetzbuch in der Türkei', *ZSR* 81 (1962) 51.

YUNG, 'Le Code civil suisse et nous,' *ZSR* 80 (1961) 323.

I

UNLIKE the Holy Roman Empire, the German-speaking part of Switzerland did not experience a comprehensive reception of Roman law. It is true that in many areas, such as Basle and Schaffhausen, Roman law had a certain validity and that the Swiss were ready enough to take over individual institutions of Roman law in order to make good the gaps in indigenous legal practices, but the self-determination and independence of the community of the confederacy was such that there was never any question of the reception of Roman law as a whole. After defending their independence against the German Emperor almost continually throughout the fifteenth century, the Swiss felt themselves to be no part of the Empire and so never tasted the quality of Roman law as *imperial* law. Furthermore, in Switzerland, unlike the German Territories, there were no princely administrations and no staffs of educated lawyers with an interest in the extension of Roman law. Thus until the end of the eighteenth century the law in the compact territory of the confederation of German-speaking Switzerland was a popular law based on indigenous legal practices and applied by elected lay judges (see LIVER, *Berner Kommentar* (above p. 167) nn. 14 ff.; ELSENER (above p. 167) 26 ff.).

After the French Revolution the Enlightenment idea of codification also took root in Switzerland. The territory of the confederacy was occupied by the French army in 1798 and with French aid a unitary state of Switzerland, the 'Eine und Unteilbare Helvetische Republik', was set up, but it lasted only a very short time. Meanwhile a decision to create a unified private law was immediately taken. When NAPOLEON fell, Switzerland quickly reverted to being a loose union of relatively independent cantons but the Enlightenment idea of collecting the private law into a code remained, though now at the level of the canton, and led to the adoption by almost all cantons of their own civil codes in the course of the nineteenth century.

In the west and south of Switzerland, cantons such as Geneva, Vaud, Valais, and Ticino (see above p. 104) had long been close to legal developments in France and it was natural that their codes should be substantially founded on the Code civil. The first of the German-speaking cantons to adopt a code was Berne in 1826/1831, which gave a lead to a second group of cantons. The Bernese Code, founded on old Bernese law, took its structure and much else from the Austrian ABGB which seemed to the conservative cantonal government at that time of restoration to be a more acceptable model than the Code civil. The cantons of Lucerne, Solothurn, and Aargau followed the Bernese model. The important private law code of the canton of Zurich (1853/1855) led the third group. It was the first code to contain reflections of the new German theories of the Historical School of Law and the Pandectist School, which KELLER, professor at the Political Institute in Zurich and pupil of SAVIGNY, had made known. The creator of the Code was BLUNTSCHLI who, like KELLER, had absorbed the teachings of the pandectists by prolonged study in Germany; at the same time he had an intimate knowledge of the private law of Zurich and thus was particularly well suited for the work of codification. This Code had a much greater effect than any other cantonal code on the Civil Code of Switzerland; it maintains strong links with the native legal traditions which it incorporates with remarkable originality into the system of the *Gemeines Recht* and in addition it is drafted in an especially clear and popular style. The codes of many cantons in Northern and Eastern Switzerland followed the Zurich model.

Throughout the second half of the nineteenth century the need for unification of law in Switzerland gradually made itself felt. Commerce was increasingly crossing cantonal borders, and with the growing movement of population inside Switzerland citizens were often adopting as their domicile a canton other than the one where they were born. In consequence intercantonal conflict of laws became disproportionately significant: 'A legal system is bound to suffer when preliminary questions regarding the area of validity of laws and rules regarding their application bulk much larger than substantive law' (EGGER, *Zürcher Kommentar* (above p. 167) General Introduction, n. 19). A lively discussion now took place on the constitutional question whether the federal legislature should be given competence to legislate on matters of private law. The old arguments from the dispute between

SAVIGNY and THIBAUT were heard once again but the principal fear expressed was that any extension of federal competence might lead to a sad levelling of the vital variety of cantonal laws. The constitutional reforms of 1874 gave the federal legislature competence in some areas of private law, especially for the law of obligations and commercial law; this made it possible for a unified Swiss law of obligations to come into force in 1881, based primarily on the General German Commercial Code of 1861 and the 'Dresdner Entwurf' of 1865 (see above Ch. 10 V). It now fell to the Schweizerische Juristenverein to take a decisive initiative on the question of general codification: in 1884 it resolved that a comprehensive and comparative portrayal of the private law of all the Swiss cantons should be made so as to clear the path for the unification of law. Professor EUGEN HUBER, who was then teaching in Basle, was prevailed upon to accept this task and thus came on the scene the man whose splendid talents were largely responsible for giving Switzerland its Civil Code.

Within a few years HUBER had written his 'System und Geschichte des schweizerischen Privatrechts' (1886/1893), a work whose first three volumes took stock of the existing legal systems in the cantons and whose fourth volume contained a history of Swiss law. Even before the last volume appeared RUCHONNET, who as head of the department of police and justice in the confederacy performed the functions of a Swiss Minister of Justice, had charged HUBER with the preparation of a draft code. The Swiss Civil Code is thus really the work of a single man. The first version of HUBER's draft was already complete when, in 1898, an alteration of the Constitution of the confederacy gave the federal legislature competence for the whole of private law. In 1900 the draft was laid before the public for discussion, considered by a commission of experts, and finally brought before the Swiss Parliament. From the very beginning right through to the successful outcome, HUBER was closely involved in all stages of legislation; not only did he draft the Code but he also piloted it with great deftness through all the procedures of Parliament, of which he was himself to become a member. His experience as a journalist, for after his doctoral dissertation he became for a while the Chief Editor of the *Neue Zürcher Zeitung*, also helped him to win public support for the Code by means of newspaper articles and public lectures.

Biographical studies of EUGEN HUBER are numerous; in particular see MAX RÜMELIN, *Eugen Huber* (1923); GUHL, 'Eugen Huber', in: *Schweizer Juristen der letzten hundert Jahre* (1945) 323; EGGER, 'Eugen Huber und das schweizerische Zivilgesetzbuch', in: Egger, *Ausgewählte Schriften und Abhandlungen* I (ed. Hug, 1975) 105.

The Civil Code was adopted by the Swiss Parliament on 10 December 1907. According to the Swiss Constitution any federal statute is subject to referendum if 30,000 citizens or eight cantons so demand, but no referendum was called for. The interval before the coming into force of the Code on

1 January 1912 was used to amplify the code of obligations of 1881 and to fit it to the Civil Code. Time was too short to do more than update the general provisions of the law of obligations (including the general law of contract and the law of delict and unjust enrichment) and the law of the special types of contract. This revised part of the law of obligations came into force at the same time as the Civil Code. It is in the form of a special federal statute with separately numbered articles but it is clear from the title of the law that the Law of Obligations is substantially the fifth part of the Civil Code of which the first four parts deal with the law of persons, family law, the law of succession, and the law of property. The rest of the law of obligations, dealing with the whole of the law of associations (including the law of companies and partnerships) as well as, *inter alia*, the law of business associations and negotiable instruments, was not revised until 1936 when it was attached to the law of obligations. In 1971 the section dealing with the contract of service (*Dienstvertrag*) was recodified under the more modern heading of contract of employment (*Arbeitsvertrag*) (arts. 319–62 OR).

It follows from this that Switzerland has no special commercial code. In principle the same rules apply to commercial and civil transactions, as they did in the Zurich code of private law. Nevertheless there are some special provisions which apply only to *commercial* transactions: thus, for example, by arts. 191, 205 OR, in the case of a contract of sale, buyer and seller may calculate their damages *in abstracto* only if the transaction is one 'in line of commerce'.

It should be noted that in Switzerland the rules enacted since the Second World War in order to protect the weaker contracting party have not been sidetracked into special laws, as has happened in most of the European systems, but have been incorporated into the OR. So, too, with labour law, including the law of industrial relations, to be found since 1971 in arts. 319–62 OR; sales contracts involving payment by instalments have been integrated into the sales law of the OR (arts. 226a–228).

II

With the coming into force of the Swiss Civil Code the concert of European private law codes was enriched with a powerful new voice representing the particular style of Swiss legal thinking. Most lawyers abroad admired the Code and many expressed themselves in ecstatic tones; in Germany, indeed, voices were raised in favour of the immediate repeal of the BGB and its replacement by the Swiss Civil Code. In fact, the admirers of the ZGB necessarily included all those who found the language and technique of the German code too complex, its structure too sophisticated, and its conceptualism too extreme. In Switzerland all these defects had been avoided. The new Code was drafted in a popular and clear *language*, had an easily comprehended, relatively open *structure*, and instead of the 'abstract casuistry' which the BGB carried even into detail, made its statutory rules *deliberately incomplete* so that often it only sketched in an area within which the judge had to operate, using the standards of what was appropriate and reasonable and equitable.

So far as the *linguistic style* of the code is concerned, the primary aim of EUGEN HUBER was to produce a code which was readable and easily understood:

> 'the code must speak in popular ideas. The man of reason who has thought about his times and their needs should have the feeling, as he reads it, that the statute speaks to him from the heart . . . The injunctions of the legislator must therefore, so far as the material permits, be comprehensible to everyone, or at least to those who are involved in the activities regulated by the statute. Its provisions must mean something to educated laymen, even if they will always mean more to the specialist' (HUBER (above p. 167) 2, 12).

The code therefore avoids technical jargon and internal cross-references. Nor does it try surreptitiously to allocate the burden of proof by peculiarities of sentence construction. Instead we find clear and striking expressions and terms: 'Spouses are jointly responsible for the support of the family, according to their respective abilities' (art. 163(1)); 'A spouse may claim fair and regular payment for managing the household, looking after the children or helping the other in his profession or business' (art. 164(1)); land may be burdened by a servitude 'for a person's special use, such as for target practice or for passage on foot or by vehicle' (art. 781); 'marriage emancipates' (art. 14.2); 'everyone has capacity . . .' (art. 1.1), and so on. Simple sentences are always preferred to complex sentences, even if juristic elegance is sometimes lost; short codal articles are preferred to long ones; German words are preferred to foreign ones; picturesque expressions are preferred to blander words, even at the expense of precision (see, in general, HUBER (above p. 167) 14 ff.).

The *structure* of the ZGB, with its five sections on the law of persons, family law, law of succession, law of property, and law of obligations, by and large reflects the divisions developed by the pandectists (HUBER (above p. 167) 20 ff.). There are historical reasons for the location of the law of obligations at the end, but it can also be justified on the principle that the law of persons and the law of the family should precede the law of economic intercourse, and on the aesthetic ground that the relatively short sections on the law of property and the law of inheritance could not well be placed after the law of obligations which, with the inclusion of the whole of commercial law and the law of companies, extends to more than 1,100 articles. But there is another and more important respect in which the ZGB abandons the system of the pandectists: it has no General Part. One explanation is that the codes of the cantons never had a General Part and no unfortunate consequences had ensued; again, the old law of obligations of 1881 had general rules about *contracts* so that any attempt to make general rules about *legal acts* would have involved a crucial alteration of the law of obligations which was generally satisfactory. But most of all, the good practical sense of the Swiss led them to realise that these general rules are applied principally in the *law of obligations* and that it is essentially doctrinaire to insist that rules for the *whole* Code be contained in a separate General Part (*Botschaft des Bundesrates zum schweizerischen ZGB* (1904) 9). Thus the general rules on persons and things which appear at the outset of the German Code are placed in the Swiss Civil Code in the context in which they have their practical application, that is, in the law of persons and property; instead of having general rules on legal acts, art. 7 ZGB contains a provision according to which 'the general provisions of the law of obligations regarding the creation, performance and termination of contracts . . . are applicable to other relationships of private law'. RABEL was one of the most severe critics of this rule. In 1912 he predicted that it would lead to grave practical difficulties since the writers and the courts—especially the lay judges of Switzerland—would not be equal to the task posed by art. 7 ZGB: apart from these practical advantages, there was an aesthetic need to 'put the roof on the structure of legal principles' by having a General Part; otherwise the rest of the code would lie about 'like disordered heaps of rubble' (*RheinZ* 4 (1912) 14 f.). RABEL's prediction does not seem to have been fulfilled. At any rate after half a century of experience with the Code neither the practising lawyers nor the scholars in Switzerland have found the absence of a General Part to be a serious defect: 'It may be said with assurance that the fears that the courts might not be adequate to the task of sensibly applying the provisions of the Code of Obligations by analogy to other relationships have shown themselves to be unfounded' (FRIEDRICH, in: *Berner Kommentar zum ZGB* I 1 (1962) art. 7, n. 28; see also GMÜR (above p. 157, p. 53).

Another characteristic of the Swiss ZGB is the *deliberate incompleteness* of its statutory rules. The draftsmen of the BGB felt bound to make the Code complete, and therefore qualified their abstract principles with exceptions and limitations which are often carried down with scrupulous care to the last detail; the ZGB, on the other hand, is content to give merely an outline of the legal institution in question which is then for the judge to fill in on the basis of the way he sees the particular case in front of him: 'At the point where the greatest difficulties begin, the BGB settles down to the task with particular satisfaction and the ZGB gives up completely' (RABEL *RheinZ* 2 (1910) 320). In consequence the length at which topics are treated in the two codes varies greatly. Thus to the question of future interests under a will the ZGB devotes 5 articles, the BGB 47. Contracts for the benefit of third parties get two articles in the OR, eight in the BGB. For adoption there are 18 Swiss articles as against 32 articles in the BGB, in matrimonial property law 74 as against 144, in the law of succession 192 as against 464; in total the ZGB (including the first two parts of the Code of Obligations, which correspond to the law of obligations in the BGB) disposes in roughly 1,600 articles of the material which occupies 2,385 articles, normally longer, in the BGB.

Another characteristic of the ZGB is that it makes very extensive use of general clauses which the judge must particularize by constructing rules, maxims, and standards, by differentiating distinct types of cases and by specifying the relevant viewpoints. The BGB, on the other hand, in its concern for certainty in the law and predictability of judicial decision, makes much more use of precisely determined sets of facts so as to reduce judicial discretion to the minimum. Of course many general clauses are common to the two codes. Art. 2 ZGB reads: 'Everyone . . . in exercising his rights and in performing his duties [must] act in good faith' (*nach Treu und Glauben*); and the BGB in §§157, 242 has similar provisions which perform the same function although their more modest location in the Code makes their moral significance less striking. But often the ZGB is content with a general clause or a concept of rather vague reference where the BGB prefers exactitude and precision, even if it is often, as time has shown, much more ungenerous and rigid. It is easy to give examples.

According to art. 28 par. 1 ZGB and 49 OR a person who has been injured 'in his personality' may seek an injunction and under certain circumstances a sum of money as *solatium*. Since it was deliberately left to the judges to decide what were injuries to the 'personality', the Swiss courts were in a position to afford legal protection to outraged honour and invaded privacy. The draftsmen of the BGB, on the other hand, with equal deliberation, refused to include 'honour' or 'personality' in the list of protected rights in §823 par. 1 BGB, doubtless because they were extremely difficult to define. It took the Bundesgerichtshof to bring about a change here with its cases on the 'right to personality'. These cases also raise the question of damages for *immaterial harm*: here too the courts in Germany had to break loose from the unduly narrow rule of §253 BGB; now damages for pain and suffering (Schmerzensgeld) are allowed in Germany, as they are by art. 49 OR, where the injury to personality is especially severe (see Ch. 43 II). To take another example: if a person has caused damage by a tort, in Switzerland it is the task of the judge according to art. 43 par. 1 OR to determine in what form and in what amount compensation must take place; here the judge must 'take account of the circumstances as well as the seriousness of the fault'. If the tortfeasor caused the harm unintentionally and without gross negligence, the judge can reduce the amount of damages if the payment of *full* compensation would reduce the tortfeasor to a state of want (*Notlage*) (art. 44 par. 2 OR). By art. 99 par. 3 OR these rules also apply where liability is based on *breach of contract*; here the judge has further room for manoeuvre since the extent of liability is to be determined 'according to the special nature of the transaction' and in particular is to be moderated 'if the transaction was one which offered no advantage for the debtor'. German law, on the other hand, is committed in these cases to the 'all-or-nothing' principle, whereby the defendant either has to pay full compensation or none at all. For a long time there have been suggestions that the law should be changed so as effectively to introduce into Germany the more flexible Swiss system (compare LANGE, WILBURG, and HAUSS in *Verh. DJT* 43 (1960)).—Or take art. 45 par. 3 OR. By this provision a tortfeasor who has killed a person is bound to compensate all those who by the death have lost 'the person who supported them' (Versorger). §844 par. 2 BGB is differently drafted: a person can claim damages for wrongful death only if the decedent 'was actually or potentially bound by law to support him'. No doubt this rule is clearer; but a girl whose fiancé or a child whose stepfather is killed can have no claim in Germany since the stepfather is never 'bound by law to support' the child and the fiancé becomes bound to support the girl only on marriage. The Swiss Bundesgericht came to a different conclusion in BGE 66 II 219, 72 II 165. Of course it may on occasion be difficult to determine whether the affiancement was seriously intended or whether the stepfather was in fact supporting the child; this difficulty Swiss law is prepared to accept but German law, more concerned with certainty in the law, is not.—It is consistent, therefore, that the Swiss law of delict should start with a general clause (see art. 41 OR) while the BGB specifies the several combinations of factual circumstances which give rise to a remedy. In the view of the draftsmen of the BGB, a general clause would not have answered 'the dominant conception among German people regarding the position of the judge'; therefore it seemed better 'that the statute should provide the judge with a certain objective standard on which to base his decision' (Protokolle II p. 571). As things have turned out, the rigid system of the BGB has long since been exploded by the courts and to all intents and purposes replaced by a general clause (see the basic article of v. CAEMMERER in: *Hundert Jahre deutsches Rechtsleben, Festschrift zum 100jährigen Bestehen des Deutschen Juristentages* II (1960) 49).

The deliberate reliance of the Swiss Civil Code on judicial amplification can be explained in large part by the peculiar nature of Swiss legal practice even today. As we have said, Switzerland never really had a reception of Roman law and this meant in particular that the legal system never got into the hands of 'learned' jurists and was not turned into an esoteric science as happened in the German Empire. Law has always had an open and popular quality in the exposed community life of the Swiss cantons and the citizen who goes to law does not expect the judge to justify his decision by linking it in a completely logical manner with some leading principle. It is the personal qualities of the judge which lend authority to his judgment; he is not *appointed* by a higher authority on the ground of his specialist knowledge but normally *elected* as a leading citizen by the inhabitants of the immediate area. This tradition is still vital in Switzerland today. Below the Bundesgericht it is the law of the cantons which determines the courts structure and the law of civil procedure; even today judges of first instance in some cantons are laymen with the assistance of a specialist 'clerk of court' (*Gerichtsschreiber*) especially for the drafting of the decision. It is natural in these circumstances that the Civil Code should use more open rules, that it should on many points be deliberately incomplete, and be drafted in an easily comprehensible style; an unduly specialist or 'learned' code might well have provoked a referendum.

It must also be borne in mind that the Civil Code had the difficult task of creating legal unity in a federal state whose member cantons had always been especially proud of their independence and which had almost all equipped themselves with their own codes towards the end of the previous century. The Civil Code therefore had to leave room for cantonal rules at many points, for example, where the topic was intimately connected with the locality (as in neighbour law) or with the authorities of the canton (for example, in the law of guardianship). Some questions are openly left to local usage or 'the form normal in the locality' (see, for example, art. 642, 644 ZGB). Often also the ZGB permits the choice of several local versions of a particular legal institution: security in land may be created in any one of three ways (*Schuldbrief, Gült, Grundpfandverschreibung*). Doubtless the especial problems of unifying Swiss law led the legislator to avoid too detailed a regulation of individual questions and instead to leave a certain room for play to the discretion of the judges. Had he not done so, the susceptibilities of the cantons might have been aroused and the risk of a referendum increased.

In view of what has been said, it will be clear why the Swiss Civil Code, in its famous art. 1, openly admits the gaps in the law, entrusts the judge with the task of filling these gaps and gives him standards with which to proceed to the task. In art. 1 par. 2 and 3 we read:

'If no relevant provision can be found in a statute, the judge must decide in accordance with the customary law and, in its absence, in accordance with the rule which he would, were he the legislator, adopt. In so doing he must pay attention to accepted doctrine and tradition.'

There is really nothing fundamentally new in this provision, because ever since the decline of conceptualist positivism everyone has recognized that a legal order will still have gaps, even after all the possibilities of reasonable interpretation and analogy have been exhausted, and that they have to be filled by creative judicial activity. But the ZGB has won admiration and applause for putting this idea in such a fine verbal form and in a place where it cannot be overlooked. 'This is probably the first time that a modern legislator has given official recognition in a great formula to the fact that the judge is his indispensable auxiliary' (GÉNY, *Méthode d'interprétation et sources en droit privé positif* II (2nd edn., 1954) 328). Note, however, that art. 1 ZGB does not allow the judge to fill the gap in the law on the basis merely of his subjective feeling of what would be just in the particular case before him. He is bound to decide the particular case on the basis of a general *rule* and in order to find this rule he must pay attention to 'accepted doctrine and tradition'. HUBER has well dealt with the objection that this makes the judge too free and independent:

'[The judge] will certainly be freer than he is today when he is expected to be able to find everything in the statute, using if necessary the most suspicious artifices of interpretation, but he will perform his function in a much worthier manner if such artifices are not expected of him. He will have to recognize that the law as enacted has its gaps which cannot be filled by construction. Once he has recognized this, he will give his judgment not on the basis that the statute has no gaps but on the ground that the legal system as a whole has none; he will state the rule of law which he would, as legislator, choose as being congruent with the other rules in the system.' (HUBER (above p. 167) 37.)

In conclusion, then, we see that the characteristic traits of the ZGB are largely attributable to the particular circumstances in Switzerland and the traditions of its legal life. This is a fact one must always bear in mind when comparing the ZGB and the BGB. In particular one must not apply to these codes criteria which their draftsmen did not see as relevant in the historical, political, and social circumstances attending their work. All the German lawyers at the end of the nineteenth century had passed through the School of the Pandectists and so were equipped to deal with a technically splendid code that promised legal certainty; to such persons legislation like the Swiss code which leaves the solution of important questions entirely to the judges would have seemed a return to the 'pre-scientific' stage. Contrariwise, the practice of law in the cantons of Switzerland was far too localized and personal and the Swiss judges were too little specialist for the adoption of a code like the BGB with its demanding, difficult, and pedantic techniques, its precise, disciplined, and artificial language. But perhaps we may make one prediction; the day may not be too far distant when the project of a *European Civil Code* will be undertaken; if so, the style of legislation to be aimed at will be that of the ZGB and not of the BGB. This is not because *popularity* is an ideal for which such a code should aim; such an ideal may make sense in the intimate confines of Switzerland but to suppose that it is apt for modern life all over Europe seems to be sheer romanticism. The open texture of the Swiss model with its style of draftsmanship which calls for judicial amplification seems preferable on two other grounds: first because the legal unification of Europe would be impossible unless judges were left with a defined area of play, and secondly because we have come to understand and approve of the procedure by which a judge can gradually develop the scope of legislative provisions which have been openly drafted, and we no longer see in this, as the draftsmen of the BGB with their positivistic outlook did, any great risk for the certainty of law.

EUGEN HUBER himself, when the draft of the ZGB was being debated in the Swiss Parliament, expressed the hope that after its unification Swiss law would 'as international law develops, gain respect of a quite different order from that which could be expected of cantonal laws, a law which, if it should ever come to the creation of a *European Code*, might have a not insignificant influence of the outcome' (quoted by EGGER, in: 'Vom Krieg und vom Frieden', *Festschrift für Max Huber* (1944) 44). On the same theme see also A. B. SCHWARZ (above, p. 168) 55 ff., RUDOLF GMÜR (above p. 167) 195 ff., and especially HANS MERZ (above p. 167) 589.

III

The Swiss ZGB won great admiration abroad because of its intrinsic merits. Almost every legislator in countries whose private law is codified has learnt something from the Swiss experience which he has used in drafting a new civil code—as in Italy and Greece—or in reforming existing laws. But there has been only one *total reception* of the Swiss ZGB, namely in *Turkey*. After KEMAL ATATÜRK created the Republic of Turkey in 1922 the Swiss Code, including the Code of Obligations, was brought into force almost word for word as the new Turkish Civil Code of 1926.

It is not entirely clear precisely why the Turkish legislature opted for the Swiss ZGB. HIRSCH, who spent many years in Turkey as Professor of Law and legal adviser to the Turkish government, attributes it to the 'chance' that the then Minister of Justice had studied law in Switzerland and had been convinced by his teachers there that the Swiss laws were the best and most modern in the world: 'If the Minister of Justice had studied in Germany, [he would] have recommended the adoption of the German BGB with equal enthusiasm . . ., perhaps not the most modern of Codes, but . . . much better suited to Turkish jurists who have a long tradition of purely scholarly legal education than the Swiss laws with their numerous gaps which call for a free and unliteral method of interpretation' (above p. 167, p. 206). But in the view of SAUSER-HALL the decision of the Turkish legislature was based also on the formal merits of the Swiss ZGB, especially its brevity, lucidity and comprehensibility, as well as on the fact that it would be much easier to translate the French version of the ZGB and use commentaries in French because French is much more commonly understood in Turkey than German (above p. 168, p. 345 f.).

This instance of reception is especially interesting because it is so remarkable. In order to effect a radical modernisation of Turkish life, the legislator, at a stroke, abolished the Islamic legal practices which had been valid for centuries, having hardly been affected at all by the reform legislation of the last Sultans of the Ottoman Empire; in their place was introduced a code which was adapted to the needs of a society entirely different in its social, religious and economic structure. Nowhere else in the world can one so well study how in the reception of a foreign law there is a mutual interaction between the interpretation of the foreign text and the actual traditions and usages of the country which adopted it, with the consequent gradual development of a new law of an independent nature.

The adoption of Swiss family law has led to very grave difficulties, which have not yet been overcome. Under the old law, for instance, a marriage was validly constituted if the future spouses or their parents made the relevant contractual declaration in front of witnesses; it was normal, though not necessary to the validity of the marriage, for an Islamic priest to be involved in the ceremony. The new code of 1926 recognized only civil marriages, but the Turks in the country and small towns held fast to their old usages, the more so since the new form of marriage was not dissolved by repudiation; the result was that the number of children who were illegitimate by statute but legitimate in the eyes of the people became so large that a series of special statutes had to be passed so as to legitimate them. On this and kindred problems arising from the reception of Swiss law in Turkey, see the essays of HIRSCH, PRITSCH, STARR/POOL and VELIDEDEOGLU (above pp. 167–68), as well as the various contributions to Annal. Fac. Istanb. 5 (1956).

III. THE ANGLO-AMERICAN LEGAL FAMILY

14
The Development of the English Common Law

BAKER, *An Introduction to English Legal History* (3rd edn. 1990).

BRUNNER, *Geschichte der englischen Rechtsquellen im Grundriß* (1909).

van CAENEGEM, *The Birth of the English Common Law* (2nd edn. 1988).

R. DAVID, *Introduction à l'étude du droit privé de l'Angleterre* (1948).

——, *English Law and French Law* (1980).

DONAHUE, 'Ius commune, Canon law, and Common Law in England', 66 *Tul. L. Rev.* 1745 (1992).

EMSLIE, 'The Law of Scotland, Its Interest for the Comparative Lawyer', 1982 *Curr. Leg. Prob.* 25.

FIKENTSCHER, *Methoden des Rechts in vergleichender Darstellung* II (1977).

HANBURY, *English Courts of Law* (5th edn., rev. Yardley, 1979).

HOLDSWORTH, *A History of English Law*, 16 vols. (1903 ff.).

——, *Some Makers of English Law* (1938).

MAITLAND, *The Forms of Action at Common Law* (1936).

MANCHESTER, *Modern Legal History of England and Wales 1750–1950* (1980).

MILSOM, *Historical Foundations of the Common Law* (2nd edn. 1981).

PETER, *Actio und Writ, Eine vergleichende Darstellung römischer und englischer Rechtsbehelfe* (1957).

——, 'Englisches Recht', in: *Handwörterbuch zur deutschen Rechtsgeschichte* I (ed. Erler and E. Kaufmann, 1967) 922.

——, *Römisches Recht und englisches Recht* (1969).

PLUCKNETT, *A Concise History of the Common Law* (5th edn., 1956).

POLLOCK/MAITLAND, *The History of English Law Before the Time of Edward I*, 2 vols. (1898, reprinted 1952).

T. B. SMITH, *British Justice: The Scottish Contribution* (1961).

——, *Scotland, The Development of Its Laws and Constitution* (1962).

——, *Studies Critical and Comparative* (1962).

STEIN, 'The Influence of Roman Law on the Law of Scotland', 1963 *Jur. Rev.* 205.

——, *Roman Law and English Jurisprudence Yesterday and Today* (1969).

——, 'Logic and Experience in Roman and Common Law', 59 *Boston UL Rev.* 433 (1979).

——, 'Roman Law, Common Law, and Civil Law', 66 *Tul. L. Rev.* 1591 (1992).

WALKER, *The Scottish Legal System* (4th edn. 1976).

——, 'Some Characteristics of Scots Law', 18 *Mod. L. Rev.* 321 (1955).

WILLOCK, 'The Scottish Legal Heritage Revisited', in: Grant (ed.), *Independence and Devolution, The Legal Implications for Scotland* (1976) 1.

I

To the lawyer from the Continent of Europe English law has always been something rich and strange. At every step he comes across legal institutions, procedures, and traditions which have no counterpart in the Continental legal world with which he is familiar. Contrariwise, he scans the English legal scene in vain for much that seemed to him to be an absolute necessity in any functioning system, such as a civil code, a commercial code, a code of civil procedure, and an integrated structure of legal concepts rationally ordered. He finds that legal technique, instead of being directed primarily to interpreting statutory texts or analysing concrete problems so as to 'fit them into the system' conceptually, is principally interested in precedents and types of case; it is devoted to the careful and realistic discussion of live problems and readier to deal in concrete and historical terms than think systematically or in the abstract.

More than any other legal system now in force, English law demands a study of its historical origins. Of course modern Continental systems too can only be fully understood in the light of their history; the well-known dictum of HOLMES: 'The life of the law has not been logic: it has been experience' (*The Common Law* (1881) 1) is true of other systems though it was coined for the Anglo-American one. Yet some legal systems are more consciously tied to their past than others, more attached to traditional forms of legal thinking despite social and economic change, and none more than England. In fact no country has clung as firmly as England to its own style of law throughout the centuries or been so free from major convulsions in its legal life. Many areas in Germany accepted Roman law in its entirety and Roman law had an essential influence on the principles of the law in France, although traditional law was not entirely ousted, but the influence of Roman law on the Common Law of England has never been more than peripheral. Nor was England affected in practice by the idea of *codification*, the idea, born of the law of nature and the Enlightenment, that the disorderly and patchy historical growth of law could be pruned and planed into a generally comprehensible form as a result of deliberate and planned legislation based on a rational system. And, finally, England never had an explosive *political upheaval* such as occurred in France in 1789, where one of the principal effects of the Revolution was to overturn the legal system of the *ancien régime* and replace it by a radically new system which, for all that it kept the old institutions, as we have seen, nevertheless represented a decisive new start; such a thing has never happened to English law.

In view of this, we must start our brief introduction to Anglo-American law with a sketch of the principal threads of English legal history. This will help to explain why England never experienced a reception of Roman law or a movement for codification and consequently why English law has had that unbroken development which so fascinates the Continental observer, and the legal historian above all. But even if the reader has no interest in the past, he will find it useful to take this trip into legal history; without it he would have difficulty in understanding the special style, the technical expressions, and the conceptual divisions of the Common Law as it is today.

II

English legal history begins in 1066 when the Normans under WILLIAM I dealt a crushing defeat to the Anglo-Saxons in the Battle of Hastings and thereby made possible the gradual domination of nearly the whole of the British Isles in the following years. It is true that in the previous centuries England had had its own legal practices, some of which were in written form, when it was a loosely organized state under the Anglo-Saxon kings, especially ALFRED THE GREAT (871–900). WILLIAM I did not abrogate these traditional laws or make any sudden change in English law in 1066, but the subsequent effect of the Norman kings and their officials on the administration of law was so profound that we can confidently ignore any earlier influences.

One of the great achievements of WILLIAM I and his successors was the construction of a tight, integrated, and rather simply organized *feudal system*, with the King as the supreme feudal overlord. WILLIAM regarded himself as the lawful heir to the Anglo-Saxon throne and treated his opponents as rebels; he therefore took all their land and divided it in fee among some 1,500 of his most important followers; as a condition of holding the land granted to them or letting others hold it from them as inferiors they had to take an oath of fealty and perform specified services or pay sums of money. Thus the view that all title to land was traceable directly or indirectly to the Crown was accepted in England very early, and ever since the thirteenth century the expression 'fee' ('feodum' or 'feudum'), which on the Continent was mainly restricted to military knight-service, has been used in England to describe *any* heritable right to hold land. Even modern English land law rests on the supposition, which is admittedly insignificant in practice, that all land in England is in the ownership of the Crown and that the citizen cannot have more than a limited right to use a particular plot of land (see the extensive treatment in MEGARRY/WADE, *The Law of Real Property* (4th edn. 1975) 13 ff.; GRAY, *Elements of Land Law* (2nd edn. 1993) 51 ff.).

WILLIAM I and his successors saw to it that the land of their magnates was geographically dispersed; great feudal estates were allowed only on the marches of the country, where they served to protect the borders against the hostile Scots and Welsh without presenting any real threat to the central power. The barons of England therefore never obtained the position of power achieved by the possessors of the great crown fiefs in France and Germany, whose political influence often greatly exceeded that of the central authority of King or Kaiser, to whom they submitted in France only in the fourteenth century and in medieval Germany not at all.

Given the strict construction of the feudal pyramid and the consequent centralization of power in the King, the Normans, with the talent for organization which they had demonstrated in founding other states elsewhere, were able to develop an effective central royal authority. The tax system was put on a new basis by WILLIAM I himself who had all property holdings inscribed in the Domesday Book in 1086. The taxes paid by feudal inferiors were thoroughly checked by the Curia Regis, a council consisting of the King and his advisers; gradually, under HENRY I (1110–35) there developed out of the Curia Regis a supreme Treasury—the Exchequer (Scaccarium Regis)—which was not simply an investigative body but gradually took on the character of a court as it decided all legal questions connected with taxes.

Fiscal reasons also underlay the increasing intervention by the central royal administration in civil and criminal law (see HOLDSWORTH (above p. 180) II. 173 f.). The most important taxpayers were the biggest landowners. The Curia Regis therefore had an interest in private legal disputes over large estates, especially when their holders were 'tenants in chief' whose right to the land depended directly on the King. If the taxes were regularly to come in there must be peace in the land. Thus the King took exclusive jurisdiction over all serious crimes; the fines and confiscations proved a significant new source of income. In this way royal justice developed in the twelfth and thirteenth centuries from a special jurisdiction for affairs of state into a general jurisdiction of wide coverage; in consequence there gradually developed out of the Curia Regis three permanent central courts, staffed by professional judges, capable of acting in the absence of the King, and fixed at Westminster; their jurisdiction was established by 1300 and lasted unaltered into the seventeenth century.

In addition to the Court of Exchequer, these were the Court of Common Pleas, with jurisdiction over normal lawsuits between private individuals and power to supervise and review the traditional lower courts, which had been run since 1066 by royal officials called sheriffs, and the Court of King's Bench which dealt mainly with matters of particular political importance. In addition, the King sent 'travelling justices' (*justiciarii itinerantes*) into the provinces with increasing frequency from the twelfth century onwards, where they replaced the sheriffs and held court in the name of the King—an institution which still exists in England today.

Thus started a development in England which in the following centuries led to the centralization of justice and to the unification of English law. The jurisdictions of local borough and feudal courts diminished in importance, not only because of the prestige and authority of the royal judges but also because the *procedure* of the royal courts was more modern and progressive, as were the *forms of action* made available by the royal administration.

At the same time the local rules of law which had come down from Anglo-Saxon times gradually lost their importance; they were never formally abrogated but they gradually faded into insignificance beside the law applied by the royal judges. Thus England very early enjoyed a unified law, called for this reason the 'common law', whereas the 'droit commun français' did not develop in France until the sixteenth century, or the '*Gemeines Recht*' in Germany until the nineteenth century and even then only in the theory of the pandectists. Thus there never existed in England one of the essential motor powers behind the idea of codification, which even on the Continent rested on the practical need to unify the law as well as on the philosophy of the Enlightenment and the thinking of natural lawyers.

Litigation in the middle ages was founded on 'writs'. In those days a writ (Latin: *breve*) was a letter from a superior, ecclesiastical or secular, containing a message to the addressee, normally a request or an instruction. In law, 'writ' meant a command of the King directed to the relevant official, judge, or magistrate, containing a brief indication of a matter under dispute and instructing the addressee to call the defendant into his court and to resolve the dispute in the presence of the parties. Such writs were issued in the name of the King by the highest royal officials—the Capitalis Justiciarius, later the Chancellor—on payment of a fee by the plaintiff, without hearing the defendant. Since many of the complaints in respect of which the plaintiff sought a writ were substantially similar, the text of the individual writs very soon became standardized with only the name and address of the parties having to be filled in, and they became known to practitioners by short titles ('forms of action'). Towards the end of the twelfth century the Chancellor was issuing about 75 established types of writ, a number which grew considerably in the thirteenth and fourteenth centuries. They were collected together in semi-official collections, the 'Registers of Writs', which had a wide circulation among practising lawyers.

In the early days most writs were designed to implement claims arising out of feudal law. Thus, for example, the *writ of right* enabled a vassal to demand that the defendant refrain from interfering with his right to possess and use a plot of land. By the *writ of customs and services* the feudal superior could come before the royal courts to demand that the vassal perform his services, and the latter could use the *writ of replevin* to make good his claim that the superior release the chattels on which he had distrained in order to exact the feudal services (see the extensive treatment by PETER, *Actio und Writ* (above p. 180) 21 ff., 105 ff.). Two royal judicial officials, GLANVILL (died 1190) and BRACTON (died 1268), wrote books which show how 'procedural thinking' dominated English law at the time. These books, the oldest works recognized as a source of law by English legal writers ('books of authority'), present the law in force in the form of a list of the writs current in practice, with comments and, in the case of BRACTON, notes on decisions of the royal courts.

The plaintiff embarking on litigation had to give very careful consideration to the question which writ suited the substance of his complaint and would best help him to pursue it. It was important to make the correct choice, since the complaint would be dismissed if the wrong writ were chosen, and it was difficult, because each set of facts had its own writ and the distinction between the different sets of facts became increasingly complex as the number of writs increased. In addition, each writ had its own special rules of procedure. This allowed the Chancellor and the judges to attach more up-to-date methods of proof to particular writs and thus to make royal justice more attractive to the public. In certain types of complaint the royal officials were able to abandon the methods of proof by ordeal (as by battle) and by oath, which gradually came to seem antiquated, and to replace them by using a 'jury' of twelve sworn men to find the facts.

But the Chancellor was never free to invent new writs simply because he thought this would help the proper and orderly development of the law. The royal judges would sometimes treat new writs to which they were unaccustomed as void, and the barons were constantly irritated because the uncontrolled issuance of writs amounted to legislation in which they had no part. An attempt was made to curb the powers of the Chancellor and his office in the Statute of Westminster II in 1285. The statute allowed the Chancellor or his officials to issue a new writ if the facts were 'in consimili casu' with a situation for which a writ already existed, but in cases of dispute or doubt the matter should be submitted to the next session of Parliament.

On this basis the Common Law had a remarkably continuous period of growth from the fourteenth to the seventeenth century; many forms of action gradually died away and were forgotten, but others had offshoots which became independent in the course of time and led in their turn to new developments. We cannot go into this process in greater detail here but we must give at least a brief indication of the striking history of the writ of trespass (for a lengthy treatment, see MAITLAND, *Forms of Action* (above p. 180) 53 ff., 65 ff.). Originally a writ of trespass could be issued only where a person had caused bodily injury to another or had interfered with his possession of tangible property forcibly or by breach of the peace—*vi et armis contra pacem domini regis*. But soon cases appeared in which there was no direct physical attack or where the harm to the plaintiff was only an indirect result of a particular act or omission on the part of the defendant. From about 1350, ostensibly relying on the formula in the Statute of Westminster, 'in consimili casu', the Chancellor allowed an 'action of trespass sur le case' or 'action on the case' which not only developed in time into the different sets of fact which now afford a remedy in the law of *tort* (see Ch. 40 III), but also became the basis of the subsequent law of *contract*. In a famous case in 1348 the claim was that the defendant ferryman had overloaded his ship and caused it to founder, thereby causing the loss of the plaintiff's horse which had been entrusted to him for carriage. At that time there was no general claim for damages based on breach of contract. Certainly some claims of a contractual nature could be brought under the writs of *covenant* and *debt*, but *covenant* could not be used here since there was no document under seal and *debt* applied only to claims for a sum fixed in advance, such as a claim for the amount of a loan or agreed rent. Nor could a claim be based on *trespass*, for the loss of the horse was not directly attributable to any act of the ferryman. In this case the Chancellor allowed an 'action on the case', basing himself on the fact that the ferryman in performing a public service undertook ('assumpsit') the duty to bring his customer's property unharmed to the other bank. Thus gradually 'assumpsit' became a special variant of the 'action on the case', available at first only where a person had misperformed in some public calling, such as ferryman, farrier, or physician, but later extended to other cases of misperformance, and not long afterwards to cases of nonperformance of contractual promises.

It will already have struck the careful reader of the last few pages that the development of the Common Law in the Middle Ages is very similar to the development of *Roman law* in many points. Rome, like England, gave judicial protection to rights only if the plaintiff could obtain a particular document of claim (formula, writ) from a non-judicial official (Praetor, Chancellor). In both systems the number of such documents of claim was normally limited, they were collected together in registers (*Edictum perpetuum*, Register of Writs), and they increased in number as new claims were developed in course of time (*actiones utiles*, writs 'in consimili casu'). The very similar ways in which litigation was initiated led legal practitioners in Rome and England to think not so much in terms of rights as in terms of types of action, and to interest themselves more in the concrete *facts* which fell within the various actions or writs rather than in elaborating the substantive law into a *system* based on some rational method. Thus Roman law and medieval Common Law were both dominated by 'procedural thinking'; in both systems the rules of *substantive law* emerged later, 'secreted in the interstices of procedural law' (MAINE, *Early Law and Custom* (1889) 389). In many other respects also the historical development of the two legal systems ran parallel, despite the intervening millennium. POLLOCK and MAITLAND were right to say that at the very time when the Glossators and Commentators of Western Europe were trying 'to adopt as their own the ultimate results of Roman legal history, England was unconsciously reproducing that history' (above p. 180, II. 558).

Compare the detailed studies of PETER, above p. 180, especially *Actio und Writ*, which successfully combine research in legal history and comparative law.—If we remember the unconscious parallelism of legal development in Rome and England we will find it easier to understand the really astonishing fact that in point of legal techniques the English lawyers have much more in common with the Roman lawyers than do the nineteenth century pandectists who expressly followed the Roman tradition: 'It may be a paradox, but it seems to be the truth that there is more affinity between the Roman jurist and the common lawyer than there is between the Roman jurist and his modern civilian successor. Both the common lawyer and the Roman jurist avoid generalisations and, so far as possible, definitions. Their method is intensely casuistic. They proceed from case to case, being more anxious to establish a good working set of rules, even at the risk of some logical incoherence which may, sooner or later, create a difficulty, than to set up anything like a logical system. That is not the method of the Pandectist. For him the law is a set of rules to be deduced from a group of primary principles, the statement of which constitutes the 'Allgemeiner Teil' of his structure. It is true that he has to make concessions to popular needs and that the superstructure is not quite so securely based on these fundamental principles as might have been expected. But the point of interest is that his method is not that of the Roman or of the common lawyer. (BUCKLAND/MCNAIR, *Roman Law and Common Law* (2nd edn., 1952) p. xiv.)

III

Towards the end of the fourteenth century the legal creativity of the royal courts gradually began to wane. It became clear that the procedure of these courts was in many respects too crude and formalistic and that the applicable law was too rigid and incomplete; suits were being lost because of technical errors, because witnesses had been bribed, because of tricks of procedure, or because of the opponent's political influence. Thus as early as the fourteenth century parties who had lost a lawsuit in the King's courts on one of these grounds or who could not obtain an appropriate writ petitioned the King for an order compelling his adversary to do as morality and good conscience, if not the strict rules of the Common Law, required. The King used to transmit such petitions to his highest administrative official, the Chancellor. The Chancellor had an intimate knowledge of the Common Law and its remedies since it was he who issued the writs, and as the 'keeper of the King's conscience' and a prominent churchman he was best fitted to judge whether in the particular case the petitioner ought to receive the favour he sought 'for the love of God and in the way of charity'. In time these petitions were addressed directly to the Chancellor and the decisions he made developed into a complex of special rules of law which are still referred to in England, as they have been ever since the fifteenth century, as '*equity*'.

The Chancellor's special procedure for dealing with these petitions was fundamentally different from that of the royal courts. Unless the substance of the petitioner's claim was obviously hopeless, the Chancellor called the person named in the petition to a hearing which took place before himself rather than before a royal court. The defendant was called by a special writ carrying the threat of a steep penalty—*subpoena centum librarum*—and therefore called a 'writ of subpoena'. Since the purpose of the hearing before the Chancellor was to discover whether, as the petitioner complained, the defendant had behaved in a way which was contrary to morals and good conscience, the formal rules of proof used in the royal courts did not apply: the petitioner's opponent had to make a sworn statement to the Chancellor about the whole affair and give answers under oath to his questions. The Chancellor decided all matters of fact and law by himself without a jury, and the decision he eventually reached was executed by a process involving heavy penalties.

Throughout the fifteenth century the Chancellor decided more or less as he thought fit; decisions were consequently much coloured by the individual preferences of the churchman then in office. But after 1529 when the first secular Lord Chancellor, THOMAS MORE, was appointed, equity jurisdiction began to follow the model of the Common Law and developed rules and doctrines, originally in a very fluid and uncertain form, to which the Chancellor had recourse when similar fact-situations arose. Regular publication of the Chancellor's decisions began towards the end of the sixteenth century and before long he felt almost as bound by precedent as the judges of the Common Law courts. His activity came to be seen as being more and more *judicial*, and his office became the separate Court of Chancery; at the outset the Chancellor was the sole judge, but from 1730 onwards he was helped by his immediate subordinate, the Master of the Rolls. In the eighteenth century it was beyond doubt that 'equity', the rules of law applied by the Court of Chancery, was as much fixed by decisions and as much formed into technical legal rules as the rules of the Common Law.

It will be clear by now that the expression 'Common Law' has several meanings. Often 'Common Law' denotes the totality of the law of the Anglo-American legal family, as opposed to 'Civil Law' which denotes the law of the Continental legal systems and their followers, heavily influenced by law from Roman sources. In a *narrower sense* 'Common Law' refers only to that part of the law which was created by the King's courts in England, as opposed to 'statute law', on the one hand, which comprises the enactments of Parliament, and the rules and practice of 'equity' on the other. By 'equity' is meant not a group of maxims of fairness, but a part of substantive law distinguished from the rest by the fact that it was developed by the decisions of a particular court, the Court of Chancery.

In practice the most important group of rules developed by equity are the rules of 'trusts' (earlier called 'uses'). As early as the twelfth and thirteenth centuries it had become normal for a vassal who wanted to avoid the feudal burdens attaching to land to transfer to a 'trustee' the land he held of his superior; to the outside world the 'trustee' would appear to own the land, but he was bound to let the settlor have possession and profits during his lifetime and then, either on his death or when his heirs reached manhood, to deal with the property in a prescribed way in favour of another ('cestui que trust' or 'beneficiary'). If a trustee refused to deal with the property in the way he had undertaken, performance of the trust could not be enforced by complaining to the royal courts, because there was no writ to vindicate such claims and the procedure of the Common Law courts was then too rigid and formalistic to permit the trust agreement to be fully established. Here the Chancellor came to the assistance of the settlor and the beneficiaries; he saw the trustee's behaviour in breach of the trust agreement as being contrary to morality, as an offence against 'good conscience', and held that while the property in question doubtless belonged to the trustee 'at law', that is, in accordance with the rules of the Common Law, nevertheless he was obliged 'in equity' to deal with the property in the way he had promised by the trust agreement. In his decisions the Chancellor gradually refined this principle into very detailed rules; after the feudal system had disappeared they were utilized in the most varied areas of law, with the result that the trust can now be described as an institution typical of the style of Anglo-American law.

Equity also developed a number of *remedies* which greatly supplemented the rather crude system of pleas in the Common Law. Thus the old Common Law with its archaic formalism clung to the view that a person could not protect himself *in advance* against the illegal behaviour of another, but had to wait until the harm had already been caused and then bring a claim for damages. This was unacceptable to the Chancellor with his more sensitive conscience. Under certain circumstances he would grant an '*injunction*' to prevent a future legal wrong which would be unconscionable. The Chancellor had eventually to decide many ancillary questions: under what conditions might an 'injunction' be issued, given the various cases which might occur? Could the injunction be used to prevent a threatened *breach of contract*? Could it be used as a temporary device pending the final judicial determination of a disputed question? and so on. In making such decisions, the Chancellor never operated *deductively* by developing a general principle recognized as sound, but *inductively* by dealing with each concrete problem as is came before him.

While the rules of Equity and Common Law were applied in different courts, as they were in England until 1873, the Chancellor was sometimes ready to issue an 'injunction' to prevent a party from instituting or continuing a lawsuit before the Common Law courts, or from executing a judgment he had obtained there. In the seventeenth century this practice led to a violent confrontation between Lord Chancellor ELLESMERE and Chief Justice COKE: COKE was of the view that the Chancellor had no right to sit in judgement over the Common Law courts by brusquely forbidding the continuation of active lawsuits or forbidding the execution of judgments lawfully obtained. ELLESMERE calmly answered that 'when a judgment [of the Common Law Courts] is obtained by oppression, wrong and a hard conscience, the Chancellor will frustrate and set it aside, not for any error or defect in the judgment, but for the hard conscience of the party'; *Earl of Oxford's Case* (1615) 1 W. & T. 615, 21 Eng. Rep. 485, 487. The dispute was submitted to King JAMES I, who decided it in favour of his Chancellor. Since that time it has been clear that in cases of conflict the rules of equity should prevail, but no other open confrontation between equity and Common Law has arisen.

'Specific performance' is another legal remedy which developed in equity jurisprudence. The remedies offered by the Common Law to victims of breach of contract were insufficient because, having developed out of the writ of trespass, they only sounded in damages. Cases were therefore brought before the Chancellor, and if he felt that it was unfair to restrict the innocent party to a claim for damages, he would allow, under conditions which gradually became fixed and clear, a claim for *performance of the contract in specie*.

On this, see the detailed treatment in Ch. 35 IV.—Another of the Chancellor's inventions is the '*equitable doctrine of part performance*', now the doctrine of *proprietary estoppel*: if parties have concluded a contract for the sale of landed property which is invalid for want of form, the purchaser who in reliance on the contract 'has materially changed his position' may demand 'specific performance' from the Chancellor although 'at law' the contract is void. See below p. 376.—Here is a further example: like Roman law, the Common Law long held to the view that claims could not be transferred and that the transferee of a claim could enforce it only with the agreement of the transferor. Here also the Chancellor's intervention was helpful: claims which he himself had developed by his decisions, such as the claim of a beneficiary under a trust, he held to be assignable without more ado, but he could not simply decree the transferability of claims which were enforceable 'at law', such as a claim for damages in tort, for that would have been an open alteration of the Common Law. Instead, he could issue a judgment ordering the assignor to agree to the assignee's enforcing the claim; the assignee, equipped with this judgment, was then in a position to sue the debtor, admittedly in the Common Law court which had jurisdiction (see Ch. 33 IV). A survey of the important rules and doctrines of Equity, including those mentioned here, may be found in SCHWARZ, 'Equity' (above p. 180, pp. 122 ff.) and WEIR, 'The Common Law System', II *Int. Enc. Comp. L.* Ch. 2 (1974) 77; see also, apart from treatises devoted to the law of trusts, PETTIT, *Equity and the Law of Trusts* (7th edn. 1993); HANBURY/MARTIN, *Modern Equity* (14th edn. 1993).

These examples will have made it clear that the rules of Equity did not openly contradict those of the Common Law and did not seek to oust or replace them. Instead, equity added marginalia, glosses, and supplements to the Common Law; they are often extremely important and sometimes go so far, to speak frankly, as effectively to neutralize the Common Law rules. To the outward eye, however, the Chancellor always professed reverence for the Common Law, and announced that his decisions simply created *supplementary* rules. Thus it is possible, though it is not easy, to imagine English law without *equity*, but it is impossible to conceive of English law without the *Common Law* in the narrow sense. MAITLAND wrote on this:

'We ought to think of the relation between common law and equity not as that between two conflicting systems, but as that between code and supplement, that between text and gloss. And we should further remember this, that equity was not a self-sufficient system—it was hardly a system at all—but rather a collection of additional rules. Common law was, we may say, a complete system—if the equitable jurisdiction of the Chancery had been destroyed there would still have been law for every case, somewhat rude law it may be, and law imperfectly adapted to the needs of our time, but still law for every case. On the other hand, if the common law had been abolished, equity must have disappeared also, for at every point it presupposed a great body of common law' (*Equity* (above p. 180) 153).

IV

The nature of English law and the course of its development were fundamentally affected by the fact that very early in its history there arose a class of *jurists* who organized themselves in a kind of guild and so exercised very great political influence. Because the King's entourage and the royal courts which gradually emerged from it were all located in London in the early Middle Ages they attracted a large number of persons skilled in law; these were mainly churchmen to begin with, but later included laymen as the knowledge of law spread outside the church. Then, as today, a distinction was drawn between attorneys (*attornati*), experienced men of business who advised the parties on the law, and pleaders (*advocati*), who specialized in the oral presentation of cases before the courts. Around the beginning of the fourteenth century these legal practitioners organized themselves in several independent guilds (Inns of Court) of which four still exist today: Lincoln's Inn, Gray's Inn, Inner Temple, and Middle Temple. These lawyers' guilds were controlled by 'benchers', a group of successful senior practitioners with power to co-opt new members. They represented the guild in its external affairs, strove to prevent 'unfair competition' by lesser breeds who knew the law, kept careful watch over the maintenance of professional etiquette, and possessed extensive disciplinary powers. Whereas on the Continent legal education has always been the province of *universities* and consequently rather theoretical and remote from practice, in England it was the monopoly of the Inns of Court throughout the whole Middle Ages and until the nineteenth century. It is obvious that in these circumstances legal education would tend to be primarily practical and empirical, more the development of a professional skill than a scholarly science. The acolyte learnt his law by taking part in court proceedings, by appearing in moots (hypothetical lawsuits) in which the benchers acted as judges, by attending regular lectures delivered by practitioners of experience, and above all by constant association with his seniors, who advanced their own education by daily discussions of practical problems. At the end of this training there was the solemn 'call to the Bar', conducted by the benchers of each Inn, as it still is today, in the four Inns already mentioned; the state had and has no part in it at all. But these guilds of lawyers were interested not only in teaching their young members law but also in forming their character, giving them a general education, and creating professional solidarity. For this purpose lawyers and aspirants lived cheek by jowl in the buildings of the guild, took their meals together, attended divine service together, made common use of the library which each Inn possessed, and joined in making music and organizing solemn feasts and dramatic entertainments. SHAKESPEARE's *As You Like It* is said to have had its world première in the Hall of the Middle Temple in 1601.

As early as the time of HENRY III (1216–72) there had been a tendency to choose the judges of the royal courts from the ranks of lawyers; from the beginning of the fourteenth century this became a fixed practice which is still adhered to today although not required by statute. Indeed, the judges in the early days were chosen from a particularly small élite of lawyers, the 'serjeants-at-law' (*servientes ad legem*). Only the most competent and well-regarded lawyers were promoted to the rank of serjeant by the Chancellor on the nomination of the judges in the Court of Common Pleas. On nomination they left their own Inn of Court and joined the *Serjeants Inn* where they stayed even if later appointed to the judiciary. The relations between the judges and this élite group of lawyers were therefore particularly close and friendly, for not only did they meet in court but they also had frequent social intercourse as members of the same Inn where they could talk shop. A serjeant was publicly referred to as 'brother' by the judges and could, by taking part in any lawsuit as 'amicus curiae', lend assistance to his 'brother' on the bench.

In the sixteenth century the opposition between barristers, who appeared in court, and attorneys, the other legal advisers, became more marked. Until that time members of both professions had lived together in the same Inns. Now the barristers began to claim that they appeared in court not as the representative of either party but pursuant to the *nobile officium* of independent counsel; they consequently declined to involve themselves with the ministerial tasks attaching to the institution of lawsuits, they regarded direct contact with the client, unless introduced by an attorney, as undesirable, and they treated it as unprofessional to make a formal legal claim for the payment of fees. Towards the end of the sixteenth century the attorneys, who were in direct contact with the parties and who were concerned with the preparation of lawsuits, especially the collection of evidence and procedural steps, were excluded from membership of the Inns of Court. Solidarity among those who remained, barristers specializing in oral presentation of cases and in giving legal opinions, became consequently even closer.

The attorneys were concerned with procedural steps before the Common Law courts; the same functions were performed before the Court of Chancery by the newer profession of *solicitors*. In 1739 the 'Society of Gentlemen Practisers in the Courts of

Law and Equity' was founded to include both attorneys and solicitors. This was the predecessor of the 'Law Society' which is today the professional body of business lawyers, now given the common denomination of 'solicitors' (see below Ch. 15 III).

MAX WEBER has pointed out how great an influence on the style of law in a society is exercised by the professional training, activity, organization, and interests of its most prestigious lawyers, whom WEBER calls 'lawyers of rank' (*Rechtshonoratioren*). This idea is especially illuminating when applied to the English legal scene. The character of English law has unquestionably been deeply marked by the fact that the leading lawyers have never been professors or officials but always legal practitioners, that they lived, judges and barristers alike, in the closest social and professional contact at the central seat of the major courts, that they were strictly organized in powerful professional bodies, and that the Inns of Court not only saw to the recruitment of new lawyers and admitted them to the profession but also had a monopoly of their legal education. This has never been better described than by MAX WEBER who, after a sketch of the training programme in the Inns of Court in the Middle Ages, wrote:

Legal teaching of this kind naturally led to a rather formalistic treatment of law, dominated by precedent and analogy . . . Legal practitioners did not aim . . . to produce reasoned structures but rather lists of contracts and actions which would be useful in practice because they suited the typical and recurrent particular needs of litigants. This produced what in civilian countries is called 'cautelary jurisprudence' . . . No system of rational law, nor even a rational systematization of law, can emerge from the forces inherent in cautelary jurisprudence. Such ideas as it produced were linked to fact situations which were formal in the sense of being concrete, recognizable, current, and quotidian, and the principle of distinction between them turned on external factors; if these ideas needed extending, this was done by the methods already indicated. They were not general concepts, which are formed by means of abstraction from the particular and by the logical processes of generalization and subsumption, and then applied syllogistically in the form of norms. When legal practice and teaching are purely empirical, legal thinking always moves from the particular to the particular and never tries to rise from the particular case to the general principles from which the decision in the particular case can then be deduced. Instead, it is trapped in words which it applies, construes, and stretches in all directions as the need of the moment dictates; should this prove inadequate, it has recourse to 'analogies' or technical fictions. Nevertheless, if the lists of contracts and actions required by the practical needs of litigants are sufficiently elastic, it is possible for the positive law to retain an extremely archaic character and remain formally unaltered despite great changes in the economic sphere . . . But no rational legal education or legal theory can develop from such a situation. For when legal practitioners, and barristers in particular, are in control of legal education and have a guild-like monopoly of admission to legal practice, economic factors, namely an interest in fees, become very important and help to stabilize the positive law; this ensures that it will continue to be applied in a purely empirical manner and that its rationalization by legislation or scholarship will be obstructed. Any assault on traditional legal procedure threatens the material interests of the practitioners, for it is they who control the relations of the lists of contracts and actions to the formal norms on the one hand and to the needs of litigants on the other.' MAX WEBER, *Wirtschaft und Gesellschaft* (4th edn., 1956) 457 f.; see also the apt observations of KOSCHAKER, *Europa und das römische Recht* (2nd edn., 1953) 170 ff.

This sociological view of the professional background of English legal life helps us to understand why England never had a comprehensive reception of *Roman law*. Of course, from its earliest days the Common Law had manifold contacts with Civil Law. Thus in the middle of the twelfth century, a time when Roman law was hardly known at all in Germany, it was being taught in Oxford or Canterbury by Magister VACARIUS from Bologna. Roman-canon law was applied by the ecclesiastical courts which obtained jurisdiction over matrimonial affairs and succession to moveables under the first Norman kings. BRACTON himself as a churchman was familiar with Roman law, but he used its concepts and methods of thought only so far as was necessary to put some articulation and order into the indigenous English legal material. Finally, one can find some influences of Roman law in the equity practice of the Chancellor, himself a churchman until the sixteenth century, for he used canon law as a model for the *inquisitorial procedure* which he introduced in his court.

In mercantile and maritime law Roman influences were rather stronger. Trade in the Middle Ages was mainly in the hands of commercial men of different nationalities who travelled from country to country and from fair to fair and had special 'international' legal customs which were strongly coloured by Roman law. The normal procedure of the Common Law courts was ill adapted to dealing with the legal transactions of commercial men; instead, special courts grew up at the most important fairs and places of trade, and they applied an 'international' *lex mercatoria* rather than the Common Law. Much the same was true for maritime law; special courts of shipping arose in the major ports and the King later set up several courts of Admiralty which mainly applied Civil Law. Until the nineteenth century these special commercial courts had to fight for their jurisdiction with the Common Law courts, a struggle which terminated in favour of the Common Law courts. One result of this was that the 'law merchant' has long since ceased to be a separate body of law and has been completely incorporated into the Common Law, especially through the decisions of the famous judge LORD MANSFIELD. Nevertheless, the influence of Roman law in the areas of mercantile and maritime law was relatively strong and can be detected even today: 'This branch of English Law has undoubtedly drunk deep out of the well of old Roman Law, as well as the living waters of mercantile custom' (POTTER (above p. 180) 204).

At only one period in English legal history did the Common Law face the threat of being entirely ousted or at least pushed into the wings by Roman law: this was the period of the Tudors and Stuarts in the sixteenth and seventeenth centuries, the time of the great conflict between Parliament and the English kings who wanted an absolute monarchy. In this dispute Roman law had a great appeal for the royalists for it alone could support the political claim that whatever pleased the king had the force of law. Common Law was somewhat weakened at this time because, beside the courts which had existed time out of mind, a series of new royal courts and quasi-judicial bodies were created, especially the 'Star Chamber', a superior court which dealt with crimes of political significance; these courts were set up directly to implement the royal will and used a procedure based on the Roman-canon model. The lawyers who worked in these courts as judges and advocates, like those in the Courts of Admiralty, had been educated in Civil Law at the English universities, and had formed a special guild in Doctor's Commons since 1511. The intellectual climate of the period was also quite favourable for the reception of Roman law. Churchmen and educated laymen, though admittedly not practising lawyers, had such a passion for the ideas of the Renaissance and humanism that they often complained of the 'barbaric' and formalistic nature of the Common Law and were in favour of adopting the Civil Law which seemed to them to be clearer and more comprehensible (see the extensive treatment in HOLDSWORTH (above p. 180) IV. 217 ff.).

Despite all this, England never did have a comprehensive reception of Roman law. We have already seen one reason—the closed organization, the professional solidarity, and the political influence which the class of English lawyers, who were devoted to the maintenance of the Common Law on grounds of principle and profit alike, had built up over three centuries. But it is equally important that these lawyers consciously threw all their weight behind Parliament, the eventual victor in the political battles of the time. The Common Law became a mighty weapon in the hands of the Parliamentary party in the struggle against the absolutist prerogatives of the King, for in its long history it had developed a certain tenacity, its very cumbrous and formalistic technique serving to make it less vulnerable to direct attack from above. Ever since then, Englishmen have thought of the Common Law as being the essential *guarantee of freedom*, serving to protect the citizen against the arbitrary inroads of absolute authority, a function which on the Continent is performed by the *Constitution*.

The leader of the movement against absolute monarchy was one of the most famous of English lawyers, EDWARD COKE (1552–1634). As Chief Justice of the Court of Common Pleas and later of the Court of King's Bench, COKE was the most famous lawyer of his day and a passionate admirer of the Common Law. We have already seen how he fought for the precedence of Common Law over equity, and how he was false-footed in this question only by the fiat of the King. Shortly after this dispute COKE fell into disfavour with the King and was dismissed from judicial office. He then devoted himself to leading the Parliamentary opposition in the struggle against the royalists. He was also a splendid writer whose best-known book is a commentary on a work on land law by LITTLETON, published in 1481. 'Coke upon Littleton', a 'book of authority', greatly helped to preserve in the English land law of today many concepts and ideas which can be traced through COKE's book right back to the early Middle Ages.

After bitter struggles in the course of the seventeenth century the absolutist claims of the Stuarts were defeated and brought under firm Parliamentary control; thereupon all threats to the survival of the Common Law as the 'supreme law of the land' disappeared and a long period of internal peace began ('Age of Settlement'). In this period the English Bar produced a whole series of eminent judges, under whom Common Law and equity developed peacefully, adapting themselves to the needs of a country where industry and trade, internal and external, increasingly vied in importance with agriculture. Here we can only mention LORD MANSFIELD (1705–93) who was Chief Justice of the Court of King's Bench for more than thirty years, an expert in Civil Law, and the founder of English commercial law.

All the great English lawyers hitherto, from GLANVILL and BRACTON to COKE and MANSFIELD, were practitioners and almost always important judges, but in the eighteenth century we first find in WILLIAM BLACKSTONE (1723–80) a lawyer who, after a merely moderate career as a barrister, became Professor in Oxford and—one might almost say, nevertheless—had a lasting influence on English law. BLACKSTONE's fame rests on his *Commentaries on the Laws of England*, a four-volume systematic portrayal, based on his lectures, of the whole of English law, not only private law and the law of procedure but also constitutional law and criminal law. On its first appearance, the *Commentaries* had an amazing success, and since then it has been reproduced in countless editions not only in England but also in other Common Law countries. The book was praised for the pleasant clarity of its style, the sure accuracy of its legal propositions, and its intelligent concentration on what was vital and central. The *Commentaries* certainly do not reach that level of systematical and theoretical mastery of the legal material which was being achieved on the Continent at the time, but BLACKSTONE did not have a centuries-old tradition of university-taught doctrine on which to build. BLACKSTONE's significance lies in his being the first to order and control the *rudis indigestaque moles* of amorphous English case-law which the occasional irruption of statute rendered even more confused, and to present it in a clear and comprehensible manner and in a form which from the literary and didactic point of view was extremely successful; he made English law seem comprehensible to the educated layman as well as to the professional lawyer.

For an evaluation of BLACKSTONE, see ANDREAS B. SCHWARZ, *Das englische Recht* (above p. 180) 67 f.; ANDREAS B. SCHWARZ, 'Der Einfluß der Professoren auf die

Rechtsentwicklung im Laufe der Jahrhunderte', printed in: SCHWARZ, *Rechts-geschichte und Gegenwart* (1960) 181, 193; HOLDSWORTH, *Some Makers* (above p. 180) 238 ff.; THIEME, *Das Naturrecht und die europäische Privatrechtsgeschichte* (1947) 32 ff.

V

After the defeat of NAPOLEON England's external position was one of the unprecedented strength but internally the nineteenth century started with a period of serious political and social crisis. The centre of economic activity had moved to trade and industry and workers had increasingly migrated to the cities, but both Houses of Parliament were still composed of extremely conservative aristocrats, bishops, and landed gentry. The Continent of Europe, impoverished by NAPOLEON's wars, offered a very poor market outlet for English industry, so that the number of unemployed grew alarmingly and wages dropped. The landed proprietors nevertheless introduced tariffs on corn which prevented the import of cheap grain and thus increased the misery of the people. As starvation, strikes, and Luddism spread, the forces of progress in England began to realise that political and social reforms were inevitable if a revolution was to be avoided. The electoral legislation of 1831/2, over the opposition of the House of Lords, gave the middle classes a share of political power for the first time; this meant that important reforms could be carried through in other areas as well. The poor law was fundamentally reconstructed, the employment of children was limited, and the great change was made from protective tariffs to free trade; finally, through legislative intervention, the legal scene was given the modernization it badly needed.

The intellectual voice of the age, often called the 'Age of Reform' in England, was JEREMY BENTHAM (1748–1832), a social reformer and lawyer. He was the leader of the Utilitarian School which scrutinized the traditional institutions of society in order to determine whether they were appropriate and useful to the central aim of any social order, namely 'the greatest good of the greatest number'. Such a school, unhistorical in its method and concerned only with considerations of expediency, was bound to find a perfect butt in the traditional institutions of the Common Law. Indeed, for BENTHAM, the rules of Common Law, often based on historical accident rather than rational design, were simply obstacles in the way of major social reform, and the same was true of the traditionalism of the conservative practitioners typified by the English barrister whom BENTHAM savagely criticized. His particular wrath was reserved for BLACKSTONE whose classical and conservative presentation of the results of history BENTHAM rightly found to be wholly uncritical. Thus BENTHAM became a passionate propagandist for thorough reform of English legal life, a reform he thought could be achieved only by comprehensive codification.

BENTHAM's views had an enormous influence on English law in the nineteenth century but his call for complete codification of the Common Law found little response. Given their practical sense and their collective interests, English lawyers could not tolerate the thought of replacing the Common Law with a code worked out at a table on the basis of a particular social philosophy. But credit must be given to the reformist proposals of BENTHAM and his school for the many special enactments, especially in the latter half of the nineteenth century, which altered the courts structure and the law of civil procedure in England and, to a lesser degree, the substantive law.

At the time, indeed, the English law of procedure presented a picture which any uncommitted observer must have found in many respects grotesque. There was a baroque profusion of courts whose jurisdictions sometimes overlapped and sometimes differed in a manner so complex as to be comprehensible only to adepts. There were special rules of procedure for every court, indeed for every form of action brought before a particular court, often with technical peculiarities which had long since lost all meaning. The courts of Common Law and the Court of Equity controlled separate parts of the substantive law with the result that the victim of a simple occurrence who wanted both an injunction and damages had the bother of going to two different courts. Attempts were made to overcome these inconveniences step by step by a series of special statutes until finally the courage was summoned up for a great reform of the courts structure and the law of procedure, by the enactment of the Judicature Act, 1873; it came into force in 1875 and still constitutes the basis of the present situation in England.

The main thrust of the reform was to transform the *courts system.* The numerous independent courts were brought within a single *Supreme Court of Judicature*, consisting of the High Court of Justice and the Court of Appeal. The High Court contains several divisions of which each specializes in types of litigation which were formerly within the exclusive jurisdiction of an independent court or courts. Claims which previously had to be *rejected* because the court had no jurisdiction can now be simply *transferred* to the relevant division within the same court. To begin with, the three divisions of Queen's Bench Division, Exchequer Division, and Common Pleas Division reflected the business of the prior independent courts of those names, but since 1881 these three divisions have been amalgamated in the *Queen's Bench Division.* Legal matters which were previously heard by the Court of Chancery were now transferred to the *Chancery Division.* Finally, questions of the validity of wills and marriages, and questions of admiralty law, for which there had previously been three separate courts, were referred to a single division, namely the *Probate, Divorce, and Admiralty Division.* These areas of law, familiarly referred to as 'wills, wives, and wrecks', seem rather heterogeneous, but the explanation is that the rules of succession, matrimonial law, and admiralty law which this division was to apply were all rather strongly coloured by Roman law. Sitting over the High Court with its three divisions is the *Court of Appeal*, an amalgamation of the several different courts which before the reform operated independently as courts of appeal. A third instance, not forming part of the Court of Judicature, was provided by a statute of 1876, in the special Judicial Committee of the House of Lords; it is composed of the Lord Chancellor and other judges raised to life peerages for this purpose.

The second important effect of the reform was to *consolidate* the areas of Common Law (in the narrow sense) and equity. This means that all divisions of the High Court as well as the Court of Appeal must apply all the rules and principles of English law, regardless of whether they were developed 'at law' or 'in equity'. Previously, for example, the Court of the Queen's Bench could not give effect to a defence which was recognized only 'in equity'; the litigant had to go to the Court of Chancery so that in a *second* suit the plaintiff in the *first* suit might be enjoined from continuing it. Today, the Queen's Bench Division *itself* can and must test the 'equitable defence' and, if it is established, reject the plaintiff's claim. The conflict between 'law' and 'equity', which is theoretically possible, is resolved by Judicature Act, s. 25 (11), which lays down that the rules of equity shall prevail. Now one must not conclude from the 'fusion' of these two bodies of law that the difference between them has become without meaning. Within the High Court the division of business is such that even today the matters which must be determined by the rules of equity, however diverse they may be, are dealt with by the Chancery Division. This means that there are some barristers who specialise in 'chancery work' and it is from these specialists that the judges of the Chancery Division are chosen. Thus despite the 'fusion' of the bodies of 'law' and 'equity', the distinction is still vital today in the mind of the English lawyer, and the division is maintained in legal education and in legal writing, the two areas still being covered in different lecture courses and different books.

The final achievement of the reform of 1873 was to abolish the technical procedural consequences of the *writ-system*. In BLACKSTONE's time the plaintiff still had to announce at the outset of the litigation which of the 70–80 different forms of action his demand was based on. His choice was final and it conclusively determined which precedents could be invoked to decide the case, how the defendant was to be summoned, how evidence was to be adduced, and how the judgment should be executed. It often happened in such a system that the plaintiff in a difficult case chose the wrong form of action and thus lost his claim on purely technical grounds. The Judicature Act, by abolishing the 'forms of action', put the finishing touch to a development carried forward by a series of special statutes from 1832 to 1860. Today all trials in the High Court are started by the same 'writ of summons', that is, a formal demand in which the plaintiff describes the basis and substance of his claim in untechnical language; he no longer has to specify a particular type of claim. At the same time the Judicature Act went far to unify the rules of procedure. It is true that many details of procedure still depend on whether the plaintiff is seeking a divorce, probate of a will, or a judgment in damages, but these differences are now seen to be variations in what is in principle a unitary form of procedure before the High Court rather than fundamentally different types of process depending on the particular 'form of action'. This is not to say that the Judicature Act has in any way weeded out the traditional 'procedural type of legal thinking'. Modern presentations of the law of contact, tort, unjustified enrichment, and property still often divide up the material in terms of the traditional forms of action so that the 'forms of action', while they may have lost their procedural significance, have maintained their function as a method of ordering and developing the substantive law: 'The forms of action we have buried, but they still rule us from their graves' (MAITLAND, *Forms of Action* (above p. 180) 2).

Substantive law also was more altered by legislation in the nineteenth century than theretofore. It is true that in all periods of English legal history, including the earliest, there had been statutes affecting private law, but such statutes did not aim at any complete or comprehensive regulation of a particular area of law; they were generally simply *ad hoc* enactments, designed to change individual rules developed by the case-law whose practical effects seemed to the King and his advisers, and subsequently to Parliament, to be inconvenient. BENTHAM and his school would have accorded a much more important role to legislation, since they believed that legislation was the only way to achieve legal certainty and to bring the law into a simpler and generally comprehensible form. On this last point BENTHAM's demands coincided with the interests of English commerce, and so towards the end of the nineteenth century several comprehensive laws were enacted which covered specific areas of commercial law: the Bills of Exchange Act, 1882, the Partnership Act, 1890, the Sale of Goods Act, 1893, and the Marine Insurance Act, 1906. But these statutes did not deliberately represent any legal breakthrough: they were simply 'codifying statutes', that is, orderly presentations of existing rules which had been developed by the courts of Common Law. It follows that if there is any doubt about the purpose of a provision, it is permissible to go back to judicial decisions rendered *before* the statutes came into force. Apart from commercial law, such statutes as regulate important areas of private law are almost all products of the twentieth century. As yet there is no comprehensive codification of family law or the law of succession or the law of contract or the law of tort. For this purpose England still prefers special statutes which deal with particular questions, such as the law of matrimonial property, intestate succession, adoption, illegitimacy, administration of estates, or credit transactions, and even these statutes can be understood only against the background of the unwritten Common

Law, for they use the concepts and categories and invariably presuppose the rights and doctrines which have been developed by the courts.

The Law of Property Act, 1925, is a very good example of this. This statute constituted a fundamental reform and simplification of English land law among other matters, but at every stage it uses the traditional basic concepts of the Common Law which in this area are especially old-fashioned. The foreign lawyer will therefore find this statute a perfectly closed book until he masters the basic concepts of English land law; the statute itself does nothing to explain them.

In the area of modern social legislation the English practitioner is overwhelmed by new enactments just as much as his German and French colleagues. For some time now, just as on the Continent, the English legal practitioner has barely been able to wade through the proliferating comprehensive enactments regarding housing, the protection of tenants, industrial law, social security, traffic and insurance law, the law of unfair competition and monopolies, and many other matters.

It follows from all this that the dichotomy, once so familiar, between the Common Law as a creation of the judiciary and the Civil Law as a creation of the legislature has lost much of the plausibility it enjoyed even at the beginning of this century. It is beyond dispute that the English courts have lost their leading role as creators of law to Parliament and to ministers with power to issue statutory instruments, especially in modern social law, while on the Continent the courts base themselves on the actual words of the ageing codes only in the most technical sense and the legislator in enacting *new* provisions is perfectly willing to adopt general formulae which throw the burden of legal creativity on to the courts. Today the old question whether statute or judicial decision is the primary source of law gives us very little help towards understanding the basic difference between Common Law and Civil Law. The more important question, in our view, is whether in deciding individual cases judges on the Continent and in England use *methods of finding and applying law* which are different in character. To this matter we shall shortly return.

VI

If our survey of English legal history has given the impression that the Common Law of England covers the whole of the British Isles, this false impression should be allayed. Great Britain is not legally unified at all; Scotland, in particular, with which we shall now briefly deal, has a legal system quite different from the Common Law.

But the *Channel Islands*, including Jersey and Guernsey, have their own legal system, too, as fairly independent dominions of the British Crown. At the time when England was conquered by the Normans, these islands were part of the Duchy of

Normandy, a fact which leads Channel Islanders to joke that England is their oldest colony; this explains why the law of these islands still rests today on Norman customary law as contained in the Grand Coutumier de la Normandie (see above p. 76) and in later collections.

Until the beginning of the eighteenth century Scotland and England were independent kingdoms on British soil. Their relations had their ups and downs. In 1292 EDWARD I, King of England, defeated the Scots and brought the whole island under the control of the English Crown, but only a few years later the Scots conducted a great war of liberation and won their independence back again. These events taught the Scots that the only way to fend off their powerful neighbour to the South was to make an alliance with some power hostile to England: that power was France. For more than 200 years the Auld Alliance with France was the corner-stone of Scottish policy in opposing English aggression. Thanks to this alliance Scotland was opened to cultural influence from Continental Europe and for centuries Scots law developed in close contact with European legal scholarship. In the fourteenth and fifteenth centuries Scots lawyers went to the Universities of Orleans, Avignon, and Louvain for their education and to Leyden, Utrecht, and Groningen after Scotland turned to Calvinism. Thus Scotland had a true reception of Roman law; at the same time, in contrast to the Common Law which developed in insular self-sufficiency, Scots law acquired a cosmopolitan and 'international' character, with a very distinctive combination of indigenous customary law (especially the feudal land law), Scots statutes, Roman law, and the teachings of natural law. *The Institutions of the Law of Scotland* (1681) by LORD STAIR, statesman and judge, is a work designed on the Romanistic model and still a classical portrayal of Scots law.

From the beginning of the seventeenth century the same monarch wore the crowns of Scotland and England, and in 1707 the two countries combined from the point of view of constitutional and international law also. Both Parliaments ratified a treaty by which both Scotland and England ceased to exist as independent states and which instead created the 'United Kingdom of Great Britain'. Thereafter it has been a solecism, albeit a very common one, to refer to the 'English' Parliament, the 'English' Constitution, or the 'English' Crown.

The Treaty of 1707 laid down that the traditional courts system of Scotland should remain unimpaired; it further provided

that the Laws which concern public Right, Policy and Civil Government may be made the same throughout the whole United Kingdom; but that no alteration be made in Laws which concern private Right, except for evident utility of the subjects within Scotland.

The union of the two kingdoms thus left Scots law essentially as it was. It is true that towards the end of the eighteenth century the contacts with

European legal scholarship were broken: traffic with the Continent became impossible in the Napoleonic Wars and when peace returned to Europe the position had been decisively changed, for the Code civil had been introduced in France and Holland and was monopolizing attention everywhere.

In the period starting with the nineteenth century Scots law came very strongly under the influence of English Common Law. Enactments of the British Parliament, both numerous and important, in the areas of private law, commercial law, economic law, administrative law, and social law apply in England and Scotland identically or alike. Decisions of the House of Lords have introduced into Scots law many unwritten rules of the Common Law. Until 1876 there were no Scots lawyers in the House of Lords in its judicial capacity and even today they constitute a minority of the judges who hear appeals from Scottish decisions, so it has quite often happened, as Scots lawyers never tire of saying, that the purity of Scots law has been sullied by the introduction of English legal ideas. English influence also comes from the fact that even where rules of Scots law should really be applied Scots lawyers and judges often have recourse to English decisions and textbooks, which are naturally more numerous. Scotland has also adopted the English doctrine of the binding force of precedent, though with some limitations. But the Scottish courts also pay great attention to the so-called 'institutional writers'; these are a dozen or so Scots writers, especially STAIR, MACKENZIE, ERSKINE, and BELL, who between 1680 and 1820 wrote basic works on Scots law and enjoy in Scotland a reputation analogous to that formerly enjoyed on the Continent by DOMAT, POTHIER, or GROTIUS.

Despite these overt or covert effects of English Common Law, Scots law has so far managed to maintain its independence in the heartland of private law, not least because that independence has been powerfully asserted since the Second World War by brilliant scholars in the Scottish Law Faculties such as T. B. SMITH and WALKER (above p. 180).

See, however, the criticism of WILLOCK (above p. 180).—The law of contract, for example, as on the Continent, rests on the principle that every agreement intended to be contractually binding by the parties, according to the judge's finding, is valid and actionable; Scots law does not have the additional requirement of consideration (see Ch. 29 II). Scotland, unlike England, accepts contracts for the benefit of third parties; the claim for specific implement of a contract is in principle *always* admissible, not just exceptionally as in England (see Ch. 35 IV). Since the time of the 'institutional writers', Scotland has accepted the view that all claims for the return of an indebitum rest on a unitary basis, while English Common Law has only recently reached that position (see Ch. 38 IV). In Scotland almost the whole of the law of delict is covered by general liability for culpa (which developed from the *actio legis Aquiliae*) and the *actio iniuriarum*; here, in contrast to English law with its great profusion of separate torts (see Ch. 40 III), the law of Scotland operates with only a few high-level principles and concepts, thereby demonstrating that inner economy which 'civilian' legal thought regards as a virtue.

It is an open question whether Scots law will be able in the long run to resist the influence of Common Law and whether in the future the area within which it can develop its own solutions may not become more and more restricted. One must realize that Scots law is not reinforced by codification, as the law of Louisiana is, nor by using a separate language, like the law of Quebec; nor is Scotland in the position of South Africa (see below Ch. 16 VI) of being its own legislator, for Scotland must often trim its legal sails to the winds blowing from Westminster. However this may be, it is clear that Scots law deserves particular attention from comparative lawyers as a special instance of the symbiosis of the English and Continental legal traditions; this may be of some assistance to those who embark on the great project of the future, namely to procure a gradual approximation of Civil Law and Common Law.

15

Courts and Lawyers in England

ABEL, 'Between Market and State: The Legal Profession in Turmoil', 52 *Mod. L. Rev.* 285 (1989).

ABEL-SMITH/STEVENS, *In Search of Justice—Society and the Legal System* (1968).

BENSON REPORT, The Royal Commission on Legal Services (Chairman: Sir Henry Benson) Cmnd. 6748 (1979).

DE BOOR, *Die Methode des englischen Rechts und die deutsche Rechtsreform* (1934).

BUNGE, *Zivilprozess und Zwangsvollstreckung in England* (1995).

GOLDSCHMIDT, *English Law from the Foreign Standpoint* (1937).

GRIFFITHS, *The Politics of the Judiciary* (1976).

HAZELL (ed.), *The Bar on Trial* (1978).

JACKSON/SPENCER, *The Machinery of Justice in England* (7th edn. 1989).

JOLOWICZ, 'Les décisions de la Chambre des Lords', *Rev. int. dr. comp.* 31 (1979) 521.

JONES, 'Should Judges be Politicians?: The English Experience', 57 *Ind. LJ* 211 (1982).

MANN, 'Fusion of the Legal Professions?', 93 *Law Q. Rev.* 367 (1977).

MEGARRY, *Lawyer and Litigant in England* (1962).

MILTON, *The English Magistracy* (1967).

REID, 'The Judge as Lawmaker', 12 *JSPTL* 22 (1972).

SCARMAN, 'The English Judge', 30 *Mod. L. Rev.* 1 (1967).

SHETREET, *Judges on Trial, A Study of the Appointment and Accountability of the English Judiciary* (1976).

STEVENS, *Law and Politics, The House of Lords as a Judicial Body 1800–1976* (1978).

ZANDER, *Lawyers and the Public Interest, A Study in Restrictive Practices* (1968).

——, *Legal Services for the Community* (1978).

——, *A Matter of Justice, The Legal System in Ferment* (1989).

——, *The Law-Making Process* (4th edn. 1994).

——, 'Promoting Change in the Legal System', 42 *Mod. L. Rev.* 489 (1979).

——, 'The English Legal Profession,' in: *Anwaltsberuf im Wandel* (Arbeiten zur Rechtsvergleichung no. III, 1982) 59.

I

LAWYERS from other countries have long been fascinated by the institutions of English legal life and by the men who run them. This fascination has not always conduced to objectivity of judgment about English justice. The European who addresses himself to this theme often has in his mind's eye the romantic picture of a judge, robed in scarlet and heavily bewigged, holding court in a splendidly panelled hall and making law with wise authority from fat volumes of reports. People are especially surprised to be told that an industrial state like England with nearly 50 million inhabitants can get by with only a few dozen judges. One sometimes hears the view that this tiny number of judges is explained by the fact that lawyers' fees and court fees are so exorbitant in England that law is only open to plutocrats, or the view that Bench and Bar conspire to preserve a legal system which has lots of old world charm but is seriously in need of reform, or the view that young English lawyers are trained exclusively in offices, on the theory that a university education in law is not only unnecessary but actually harmful. There may or may not be a grain of truth in these views but they certainly give a one-sided and false impression of English justice; in the following section we shall try to present a picture, necessarily only in outline, which is rather nearer the truth.

II

The English citizen who is involved in civil litigation normally comes into contact not with the High Court in London, much less the Court of Appeal or the House of Lords, but with the Magistrates' Courts or the County Courts which are spread throughout the land.

1. *Magistrates' courts* are staffed by 'Justices of the Peace', magistrates without any legal training, three of whom constitute a bench under a chairman chosen by themselves. Only in the larger towns are there professional paid 'stipendiary magistrates' who have legal training and who sit alone. Justices of the Peace, of whom at the moment there are about 30,000 in England, divided between about 1,000 courts, are nominally appointed by the Queen but really chosen by the Lord Chancellor from lists provided by local commissions. The choice is normally made from people who have shown some interest in public affairs by being active in local government, trades unions, professional organizations, chambers of commerce, or in some other way; but party political considerations also play some part in the selection of magistrates. To be a Justice of the Peace is not a full-time job and many of them are retired; it is an honorary position which attracts only a small payment for expenses. But the social prestige attaching to the position is considerable: persons of rank in provincial towns and even tycoons see it as an honour to be a Justice of the Peace and to be able to put the initials JP after their names.

The jurisdiction of Magistrates' Courts is mainly in *criminal law*, where they deal with all minor offences, especially the vast number of traffic offences. Their procedure is summary, without a jury, and is very swift, especially since the defendant in trivial cases often pleads guilty and no evidence need be called.

For more serious crimes where a jury is called for, there is a special court, the Crown Court. Depending on the gravity of the charge, cases in the Crown Court are tried either before a full-time judge or before a 'Recorder', an experienced barrister or solicitor in professional practice who is commissioned to serve as judge from time to time. The Crown Court may also contain up to four Justices of the Peace.

So far as *private law* is concerned, the jurisdiction of Magistrates' Courts is principally in matters of family law: they hear claims for maintenance between spouses and between parents and children, legitimate or illegitimate, issue separation orders, apply the laws about the care of children, agree to adoptions, supervise guardians, and have extensive competence in matters concerning the protection of children.

Although for some time Justices of the Peace have been required on nomination to follow courses which introduce them to the most important legal questions likely to arise, it is nevertheless necessary to have a skilled lawyer constantly at their side to advise them. In the Magistrates' courts this function is performed by the so-called 'clerk to the justices', a solicitor whose task it is, part-time or, in the larger towns, full-time, to supervise the administration of the court, to see to the procedure in court, and above all to advise the Justices when problems arise during a sitting. For this purpose the clerk may, should the justices so wish, take part in the deliberations prior to judgment.

2. *County Courts* were introduced in England by statute 'only' in 1846. The aim was to provide within easy reach of the parties courts which could determine private law disputes involving relatively low sums at rather small cost.

There are about 270 County Courts in England, so situated in the country that everyone is within easy distance of one. The courts are manned by a single judge, called 'Circuit Judges'. There are also 'District Judges' in the County Courts who hear cases involving £5,000 or less in simple and informal proceedings. To these Circuit and District Judges, approximately 770 in number at present, must be added the 'Recorders' who sometimes sit in the County Court; these are usually practising barristers charged by the Lord Chancellor to take on occasional judicial functions.

County Courts deal with civil matters involving £25,000 or less, and may hear cases involving larger sums, for cases of up to £50,000 are only heard by the High Court if they are particularly difficult or raise questions of special importance. In equity cases the County Courts' jurisdiction rises to £30,000. Furthermore, modern social legislation has reserved for the County Courts a whole series of very important matters, notably those arising from housing law and legislation protecting tenants. The practical importance of the County Courts is shown by the fact that about 85 per cent of all civil actions are first heard in these courts: 'If we consider that from a social point of view the importance of a court is the number of *persons* whose affairs it deals with, there can be no doubt that County Courts are the most important civil courts in the country. (JACKSON/SPENCER (above p. 205) 33.)

3. When people abroad or even in England speak of English justice, they think in the first place of the *High Court of Justice* in London. This court consists today of three divisions: the Queen's Bench Division, the Chancery Division, and the Family Division. The number of High Court judges has risen from only 25 in 1925 to 97 at the present time, and it will probably increase still more. Each judge is attached to one of the three divisions mentioned. Today there are 63 in the Queen's Bench Division, presided over by the Lord Chief Justice, 15 in the Chancery Division under the Vice-Chancellor, and a further 19 in the Family Division under the President. Except for appeals from judgments of lower courts and for some proceedings of an administrative nature, all cases in the High Court are decided by a single judge.

The division of business in the High Court allocates to the Queen's Bench Division the cases which before 1873 fell within the jurisdiction of the old Common Law courts. These include claims for damages for tort (mainly traffic or industrial accidents) and for breach of contract. The Queen's Bench Division has several specialized subdivisions, the 'Commercial Court' which hears disputes between businessmen and enterprises in commercial matters, the 'Admiralty Court', concerned with maritime collisions, maritime creditors' rights, cargo claims, and arrest of vessels, and the 'Divisional Court', which applies administrative law. Judges in the *Chancery Division* hear cases affecting the administration of estates, bankruptcy, and the property of incapable persons, and resolve questions of trust law, company law, and intellectual property; accordingly that division has a strong equity flavour. Family matters are dealt with in the *Family Division*.

A number of important judicial tasks in the High Court are performed by the many 'masters' and 'registrars', who are chosen from barristers or solicitors with a certain professional experience. They perform many varied tasks (see DIAMOND, 76 *LQ Rev.* 504 (1960)) of which the main one is to work closely with parties and their legal advisers in the preliminary steps of procedure so that when the matter comes before the judge, it can be decided without delay in a single oral hearing. The master also decides, with appeal to a judge, whether the trial should be referred to a County Court, what security, if any, should be given, and questions regarding expert opinions and methods of proof. Furthermore, on proper motion of the parties, he sees to it that before the oral trial begins the parties provide their opponent with full information about the facts they propose to prove and the relevant documents in their possession. The master also tries to get the parties to agree as many facts as possible so as to reduce the amount that must be proved and thereby lighten the task of the judge. Because the trial is so carefully prepared and because the parties must fully disclose what positions they propose to adopt, many suits are terminated by compromise, admission or withdrawal of claim before the oral trial ever starts.

4. The *Court of Appeal* hears appeals from judgments of the High Court, and, with some limitations, appeals from the County Courts as well. In theory the Lord Chancellor presides but in practice his role is performed by another judge, called the 'Master of the Rolls'—a title borne since the seventeenth century by the Chancellor's senior subordinate in Chancery. In addition to the Master of the Rolls the Court of Appeal consists of 29 'Lord Justices of Appeal', who sit in divisions of three or occasionally two. The Court of Appeal reviews every point of law on which the judgment below was based but often feels itself bound by trial judge's findings of fact, even if they have legal consequences. Thus the Court of Appeal does not hear again the evidence presented at the trial and new evidence is admitted only within very strict limits.

5. The *House of Lords* is the highest court, not only for England, but also for Scotland (except for criminal cases) and Northern Ireland, which in other respects have their own system of courts. Decisions are made by a special judicial committee which contains, apart from the present Lord Chancellor and predecessors who have demitted office on a change of government, ten judges who bear the title 'Lord of Appeal in Ordinary', called 'Law Lords' for short. The committee is normally composed of five judges and hears appeals from judgments of the Court of Appeal provided that, in view of the importance of the case, leave to appeal has been granted either by the Court of Appeal or by the House of Lords itself.

Brief mention must finally be made of the *Judicial Committee of the Privy Council*. The Privy Council is an advisory body which developed out of the old Curia Regis and the task of its judicial committee is to give the Queen advice, which is invariably followed, on petition made to her as the fount of justice by parties who have unsuccessfully exhausted the legal procedures in the national courts of Commonwealth countries. Appeal to the Privy Council has been abolished by many important members of the Commonwealth: Canada, India, Pakistan, and, in 1982, Australia have all declared that the decisions of their own highest courts are final. But even today it is not uncommon for the Privy Council to hear cases from countries as diverse as New Zealand, Sierra Leone, Bermuda, Gibraltar, and Mauritius, an impressive indication of the world-wide spread of the Common Law tradition.

6. High Court judges are nominated by the Queen on the proposal of the Lord Chancellor who selects them from among barristers with at least ten years practical experience (the same pool as provides most Circuit and District judges); on appointment they receive the accolade of a knighthood. As a member of the government, the Lord Chancellor is a politician who has often spent many years in the House of Commons but it must be said that for the last fifty years at least political considerations have played next to no part in the nomination of judges. In the narrow and familiar circle of

barristers a *communis opinio* readily determines which of their number are fit for judicial office and a Lord Chancellor would quickly incur public reproach or, worse still, public ridicule if he proposed for a judgeship a barrister who was politically committed but professionally incapable. Once appointed, judges are wholly independent. Under the formula of the Act of Settlement 1701, which is still in force today, a judge holds his office only 'during good behaviour subject to a power of removal by His Majesty on an address presented to His Majesty by both Houses of Parliament', but no English judge has ever been removed from office since that date and no one in England is quite sure how exactly one would set about it (see JACK-SON/SPENCER, above p. 205, pp. 368 ff.). Even desire for promotion, which can temper the independence of judges on the Continent, plays no great role in England. High Court judges have already reached a peak position and for many of them a further move up to the Court of Appeal or the House of Lords would not be very attractive.

All judges, even Circuit Judges, are chosen from among the group of successful and well-regarded barristers (see p. 213). This ensures that the higher courts are manned by judges who are extremely competent and very experienced in practice, able to command the respect of the whole legal profession. But in the view of many people, this restricted principle of choice has the disadvantage that the English judges tend to be of an extremely conservative temperament: a person who has enjoyed a brilliant professional career will hardly be disposed to criticize and reform the very circumstances which made it possible. This tendency to stability may also be reinforced by the fact that a judge is never appointed before he is 40, and usually not until he is past 50; he retires at age 70. To be more specific, the charge has occasionally been made that the marked individualism of English judges led them, especially until the marked individualism of English judges led them, especially until the Second World War, to adopt a perverse attitude to modern social legislation and give an unduly restrictive construction to many of their provisions contrary to the clearly discernible will of Parliament (see JACKSON/SPENCER (above p. 205) 377 ff., and ABEL-SMITH/STEVENS (above p. 205) 166 ff.).

Parliament itself has reacted to this. According to many writers, it was in a deliberate attempt to render modern statutes on social security, tax, agricultural holdings, and landlord and tenant 'judge-proof' that Parliament referred disputes in these areas not to the ordinary courts but to special 'tribunals', of which there are now an enormous number; their procedure is relatively simple and cheap, they are often staffed by laymen, and they are often closely linked with relevant government departments. The number of appeals to the Court of Appeal in these areas is small and diminishing. This very fact helps us to understand how England gets by with so relatively small a number of judges, especially when one considers that Germany, for instance, has three levels of separate courts for administrative and social matters.

Whatever one may think of the conservatism of the English judges, it seems clear that England has never been readier for reform or more energetically critical of the existing system than today. Some radicals have demanded the 'nationalization' of all professional lawyers, much as doctors were nationalized in the National Health Service, and would leave no part of the courts system untouched. In present circumstances these proposals may seem unrealistic but it must be granted that an increasing number of leading and influential jurists see the law of procedure and the courts system as in need of drastic reform (see JACOB, *The Fabric of English Justice* (1987) 246 ff., and in particular ZANDER, *A Matter of Justice, The Legal System in Ferment* (1989)). The process was started off by the Courts and Legal Services Act 1990, and further reforms are awaited. So far as the reform of substantive law is concerned, England and Scotland have each had a five-member 'Law Commission' since 1965. They have a well-equipped staff to help them in their demanding task

'to take and keep under review all the law . . . with a view to its systematic development and reform, including in particular the codification of such law, the elimination of anomalies, the repeal of obsolete and unnecessary enactments, the reduction of the number of separate enactments and generally the simplification and modernisation of the law' (Law Commissions Act 1965 s. 3). Many of the Law Commission's proposals have resulted in legislation which has modernized and improved English law on important topics. The Law Commission's programme of work originally contained a plan to codify the whole law of contract. This project has been abandoned. The advantages and disadvantages of the codification of English law are discussed in many recent articles of great interest to anyone from a Civil Law jurisdiction: see, for example, SCARMAN, *A Code of English Law?* (1966); HAHLO, 'Here lies the Common Law: Rest in Peace', 30 *Mod. L. Rev.* 241 (1967): DIAMOND, 'Codification of the Law of Contract, 31 *Mod. L. Rev.* 361 (1968); DONALD, 'Codification in Common Law Systems', 47 *Austr. LJ* 160 (1973); KERR, 'Law and Reform in Changing Times', 96 *LQ Rev.* 515 (1980); NORTH, 'Problems of Codification in a Common Law Country,' *RabelsZ* 46 (1982) 94; ANTON, 'Obstacles to Codification', 1982 *Jur. Rev.* 15. Also, from the point of view of a continental observer, KÖTZ, 'Taking Civil Codes Less Seriously', 50 *Mod. L. Rev.* 1 (1987).

In recent years various aspects of the English legal system have repeatedly come under investigation by Committee and criticism by writers. It may be that London's importance as a legal centre will diminish as the limits on the financial jurisdiction of the County Courts are raised and more criminal cases are heard by the Crown Courts. Noteworthy, too, are the English experiments with novel forms of 'informal' resolution of minor disputes in private law. In non-litigious matters advice to the relatively deprived has been provided not only by solicitors but also, most successfully, by 'Citizens Advice Bureaux'. Such fascination as the English system of justice still exercises on the Continental observer depends now not so much on the admittedly astonishing position of the English judge as on the interesting question how in the years to come England will manage to effect a compromise between its tendency to cling tenaciously to traditional legal institutions and the need which exists in all modern societies to provide effective justice for every citizen.

III

Professional lawyers in England are divided into *solicitors* and *barristers*. This distinction, which has cropped up several times in the preceding pages, is a further peculiar characteristic of English legal life which must now be briefly considered.

1. The typical English *solicitor* is an independent lawyer who gives legal advice to a client on personal and business affairs. In practice on his own or in partnership with other solicitors, he carries through transactions involving land, drafts contracts and wills, undertakes the administration of estates, and advises his client on tax, commercial, insurance, and company law matters. Solicitors alone are empowered to take the necessary steps prior to trial. They may also act in the name of their client in the procedure which precedes the oral hearing before the judge. In the trial itself they have a right of audience only in the Magistrates' Courts and the County Courts. Although solicitors have for years been campaigning against this restriction, which they regard as unjustified, the bitter resistance of the Bar saw to it that the door was opened only very slightly by the Courts and Legal Services Act 1990: the conditions attached to a solicitor's 'right of audience' are so stringent that no significant change in practice is likely in the foreseeable future.

Most solicitors' offices are naturally not so much concerned in the preparation, initiation, or conduct of trials as with transactions concerning land. Registers of land exist in most areas of the country, but they are not as sophisticated as in Germany. If the title is not registered, the title of a vendor or mortgagor must be investigated carefully by any purchaser or mortgagee. Even if it is registered, most people who are buying and selling houses wish their interests to be protected from the contractual stage to the completion of the transaction. This business, called 'conveyancing', falls mainly to solicitors (who had, indeed, a legal monopoly of it until very recently), and the fees for the conveyancing of houses constitute nearly half of the profession's income.

In 1989 there were about 60,000 registered solicitors in England. About 13,000 of these were employed by local authorities or in business. Of the 9,100 solicitors' firms about 80 per cent have four partners or less, 14 per cent have between five and ten, and the rest more than ten. There is normally one salaried assistant solicitor to every three partners, in large firms one to every two. In 1991 there were 6 firms with more than 500 solicitors.

The professional organization of solicitors is the *Law Society*, of which as many as 85 per cent of all practising solicitors are members. There is no legal requirement for a solicitor to be a member but the Law Society has statutory power to lay down rules, with the agreement of the Lord Chancellor and other leading judges, regarding the training and admission of solicitors. The Law Society also finances the Solicitors' Complaints Bureau which can bring disciplinary proceedings before the Solicitors' Disciplinary Tribunal, an independent judicial body. Solicitors' fees in private matters are normally a matter for agreement between solicitor and client. The courts, however, retain the power to review a solicitor's charges in any case involving court proceedings, and in other cases the Law Society will do so if a client complains.

2. *Barristers* specialize in advocacy before the higher courts, essentially the preparation of written documents and the oral presentation before the court. Here barristers have a monopoly which rests not on the provisions of any statute but on a long-established practice of the judges according to which a party who does not appear *personally* can have no legal adviser in court other than a barrister. Barristers also give oral legal advice or written opinions and draft complicated wills, land contracts, or trust deeds; indeed, some barristers do nothing else. In these areas there is a certain competition between barristers and large firms of solicitors, but it is quite normal for a solicitor in a case of particular difficulty to seek the opinion of a barrister, many of whom specialize in particular topics and therefore have an extremely detailed knowledge of the relevant judicial precedents. One very striking fact is that the etiquette of the Bar forbids any direct contact with the client. Thus a person who wishes to institute a suit in the High Court or to obtain a barrister's opinion must always do so through a solicitor. If a conference becomes necessary between the barrister and the client who is thus brought into contact with him, the barrister is bound by professional etiquette to hold his conference in the presence of the solicitor and in his own chambers, so far as possible. The choice of barrister normally falls to the solicitor since only a few litigants have any preferences, so it follows that a barrister's success depends very much on his links with the large firms of solicitors.

Even today barristers are not entitled to form partnerships. Instead, barristers occupy 'sets of chambers' in loose groups of about twelve to fifteen, often specializing in particular areas of law. In London all these chambers are situated in the Inns of Court, in buildings possessed for centuries and steeped in tradition, not far from the High Court. The chief of staff in these sets of chambers is the *clerk*. The clerk makes the contact between solicitors and the barristers in his chambers, fixes appointments, gives information about the individual barrister's programme of work, and agrees with the solicitor on the fee payable to the barrister by the client. The amount of these fees is not fixed by statute but depends on the difficulty and importance of the case as well as the reputation and standing of the barrister in question. Since the clerk receives a fixed percentage of the fees paid to the barristers in his chambers, he is naturally interested in fixing the fee as high as possible, without losing the business to another set of chambers. Until recently it was regarded as unprofessional for barristers and solicitors to have *direct* transactions regarding fees without the clerk as intermediary, and this is still extremely unusual.

The method of fixing fees and the prohibition of partnership make it difficult for young barristers to make a living at the outset of their career, but the more they succeed in obtaining a certain reputation and in maintaining good contacts with firms of solicitors, the more sought-after they become and the higher the fees they can, through their clerk, prescribe. For barristers who are greatly in demand the burden of work can be very heavy, since advocacy can only be performed in person and the barrister is in principle obliged to accept every brief which is offered provided that the stipulated fee is paid. At a certain moment in a very successful career barristers will face the question whether they should not lighten their work-load by petitioning the Lord Chancellor to submit their name to the Queen for nomination as *Queen's Counsel* (abbreviated QC). Queen's Counsel form the élite of the Bar from whom High Court and Circuit judges are normally chosen. They stand in high regard in court and in the Inns, and are entitled to wear a robe of silk. For this reason, when a person has recently been promoted to the rank of Queen's Counsel, one says that 'he has taken silk'. Queen's Counsel can demand particularly high fees and normally appear in court in company with a 'junior' barrister, for whom of course the party must pay an additional fee; in consequence of this great expense, Queen's Counsel are briefed only for important and interesting suits. No barrister may *claim* to be appointed Queen's Counsel; whether the Lord Chancellor accepts such a petition and proposes nomination to the Queen depends on whether the petitioner has, in practice at the Bar for at least ten years, achieved the requisite degree of success in his profession and renown among his peers. About one in ten of the 6,500 odd active barristers in 1990 were Queen's Counsel, and of these over 90 per cent had chambers in London.

The professional organizations for barristers are the four *Inns of Court*, all of equal standing, known as 'The Honourable Society of Lincoln's Inn', 'of the Inner Temple', 'of the Middle Temple' and 'of Gray's Inn'. The business of these four Inns is conducted by the so-called 'benchers', not elected by the members of their Inn but co-opted for life by the other benchers. Most of them are now practising barristers, mainly Queen's Counsel, but some are judges, for judges remain members of their Inn even after appointment.

In addition to running the business of their Inn of Court and administering its property, benchers admit students, who must become members of an

Inn before their training, and call them to the Bar once they have completed it. Other institutions are of general importance for barristers. The most important of these is the *General Council of the Bar*. With members elected from the whole Bar, it represents the Bar's interests in public when threatened by legislation, the Law Society, and other organizations. It also lays down guidelines for professional conduct at the Bar. The training of future barristers is organized by the *Council of Legal Education* under the general direction of the Bar Council.

For details on the profession of the barrister and his position in the whole context of English legal life, reference may be made to the works of MEGARRY and ABEL-SMITH/STEVENS (above p. 205). The former is written from the point of view of a successful Queen's Counsel and gives a clear and flowing account of the activities of English barristers and judges; it conveys the impression that everything is really all for the best in the state of justice in England, and that drastic reforms are unnecessary if not actually harmful. ABEL-SMITH/STEVENS, on the other hand, have done some empirical sociological research and raise the question whether the practice of law in England today is responsive to the demand of a modern society that it should be a 'social service'. The authors give a distinctly negative answer to this question and they do so with details which will give the foreign lawyer pause for thought, especially if he is unduly in love with English law. ZANDER (*Lawyers and the Public Interest*, above p. 212) sees the principal aim of the monopolies and professional duties of English barristers and solicitors, whether fixed by statute or tradition, as being to limit free competition in the production and distribution of legal services. The crucial question is whether these restrictive practices are justified as being in the public interest; the author thinks that by and large they are not. See also the critical analysis in HAZELL (above p. 205). Copious data are to be found in the BENSON REPORT (above p. 205) on which see also ZANDER, 1980 *Curr. Leg. Prob.* 33.

3. The *training of lawyers* in England also has many features which will surprise the observer from abroad. The training is directed to the profession of *lawyer*, rather than of *judge* as in Germany. This is only natural because there is no such thing as a 'judicial career' in England: one only becomes a judge after many years of successful practice as a barrister. Again, the bifurcation of the legal profession means that there are different methods of training and examination for solicitors and barristers. As one would expect from the historical development of the legal professions in England, these methods of training and examination are the responsibility of the respective professional organizations, the Law Society and the Bar Councils, not of the state or the universities. Of course it is possible to study law in almost all of the British universities and to emerge, normally after three years, as a Bachelor of Laws (Bachelor of Arts in Oxford and Cambridge). It is true that most of those admitted as barristers and solicitors possess a university degree in law, but this is not required, and indeed one can become a solicitor without being a graduate at all. The Inns of Court do require

budding barristers to have a degree, but it need not be a degree in law. Many distinguished English judges took a degree in some other subject: LORD DIP-LOCK read chemistry, LORD DENNING mathematics, and LORD WILBER-FORCE classics before training to be a barrister—*after* leaving the university!

Today a distinction is drawn between the 'academic' and 'professional' stages of legal training. For most people the 'academic' stage consists of three years study of law in a university. Those who graduate in some other discipline before opting for the Bar satisfy the academic stage by taking a one-year course prescribed and overseen by the professional bodies, leading to the Common Professional Examination.

At the 'professional' stage the paths of future solicitors and barristers diverge. The future barrister spends a year at the Inns of Court Law School in London, and the future solicitor takes a comparable course elsewhere in London or in the provinces, the teaching and examining being done largely by judges and practitioners.

The examination passed, the future solicitor must spend two years under a 'training contract' in a solicitors' office. He is then admitted as a solicitor, but must still serve for three years as an assistant solicitor before he can prac-tise on his own or as a partner in a firm of solicitors: in this way the public can be protected from lawyers of undue youth and inexperience.

The further training of a *barrister* is much the same. He must be entered as a 'bar student' in one of the four Inns of Court and spend a year in barris-ters' chambers as a 'pupil' gaining practical experience under the supervision of a pupil-master.

The bar student must also keep a specified number of 'dining tems'. 'Dining terms', of which there are four per year, are periods of about three weeks during which bar students may take an evening meal in the Dining Hall of their Inn. One 'keeps a din-ing term' by dining at least three times during it, and one must keep eight terms in this manner, that is, have dined on twenty-four occasions, before one may be admitted as a barrister. The explanation of this institution is that in the old days the communal dinner was an occasion for contact between barristers and youngsters, for conversa-tions on legal matters and for moots. In our times this practice has largely lost its point, especially in view of the large numbers of students: 'Today it is difficult to find any student who can see any value or utility in the ritual of dining in hall. The food, it is said, is poor or scanty or both, and the conversation does no more than pass the time; but the Inn requires it, and so one must go through the pointless ceremony' (MEGARRY (above p. 205) p. 114; see also the criticisms contained in the BENSON REPORT (above p. 205) 641 ff).

After passing his exams the candidate is 'called to the Bar' in a formal ceremony, and thereby becomes a barrister.

4. Whether the division of the legal profession into two branches should be maintained is the subject of recurrent and lively debate in England. *In favour* of the split, it is said that to have barristers who specialize in advocacy

is a great advantage for the parties and for the court: for the *parties* because the barrister is more detached from the case, can see it with fresh eyes, and has special experience in pleading, gained by constant practice; for the *court* because co-operation with lawyers can be made easier, more trusting, and free from fiction if judges have to deal with only a small circle of experienced specialists. *Against* the division of the legal professions one often hears the objection that it greatly increases the expense and duration of legal proceedings, since the same case is being worked on by two lawyers one after the other, and sometimes both together. One thing is sure, that it makes sense to have specialized competences within the legal profession, as, for example, for conveyancing or for the conduct of cases in court. What is in issue is only whether the kind and extent of such specialization should be fixed by compulsory rules as in England, or whether it should not be left, as on the continent and in the United States, to the free play of the forces of the market (see JACKSON/SPENCER (above p. 205) 353 ff., ABEL-SMITH/ STEVENS (above p. 205) 304 ff.), with a reply by F. A. MANN (above p. 205).

16

The Spread of the Common Law
Throughout the World

ALLOTT (ed.), *The Future of African Law* (1960).
——, *New Essays in African Law* (1970).
——, *Judicial and Legal Systems in Africa* (2nd edn., 1970).
BAKER, *The Legal Systems of Israel* (1968).
BENTWICH, 'The Migration of the Common Law: Israel', 76 *LQ Rev.* 64 (1960).
BIN-NUN, *The Law of the State of Israel* (1990).
BOSE, 'The Migration of the Common Law: India', 76 *LQ Rev.* 59 (1960).
COTRAN, 'The Place and Future of Customary Law in East Africa', in: *East African Law Today* (ed. British Institute of International and Comparative Law, 1966) 72.
DANIELS, *The Common Law in West Africa* (1964).
DANNENBRING, 'Heutiges römisch-holländisches Recht, Vom Privatrecht der Republik Südafrika', *ZfRV* 6 (1965) 56.
DERRETT, 'The Role of Roman Law and Continental Laws in India', *RabelsZ* 24 (1959) 657.
——, 'Justice, Equity and Good Conscience', in: *Changing Law in Developing Countries* (ed. Anderson, 1963) 114.
DHAVAN, 'Borrowed Ideas: On the Impact of American Scholarship on Indian Law', 33 *Am. J. Comp. L.* 505 (1985).
ELIAS, *British Colonial Law, A Comparative Study of the Interaction between English and Local Laws in British Dependencies* (1962).
FRIEDMANN, *The Effect of Foreign Law on the Law of Israel* (1975).
GALANTER, *Law and Society in Modern India* (1989).
GLEDHILL, *Pakistan, The Development of Its Laws and Constitution* (2nd edn., 1967).
——, *The Republic of India, The Development of Its Laws and Constitution* (2nd edn., 1964).
GUTTMANN, 'The Reception of the Common Law in the Sudan', 6 *ICLQ* 401 (1957).
HAHLO/KAHN, *The Union of South Africa, The Development of Its Laws and Constitution* (1960).
——, *The South African Legal System and Its Background* (1968).
HOSTEN, 'The Permanence of Roman Law Concepts in South African Law', 2 *Comp. Int. LJS Afr.* 192 (1969).
——, 'Legal Sources and the Codification Movement in South Africa', *Liber Memorialis François Laurent* (1989) 301.
JAIN, *Outlines of Indian Legal History* (4th edn., 1981).
JENNINGS/TAMBIAH, *The Dominion of Ceylon, The Development of Its Laws and Constitution* (1952).

KASER, 'Das römische Recht in Südafrika', *SavZ/Rom.* 81 (1964) 1.

LASKIN, *The British Tradition in Canadian Law* (1969).

LATHAM, 'The Migration of the Common Law: Australia', 76 *LQ Rev.* 54 (1960).

MATSON, 'The Common Law Abroad: English and Indigenous Laws in the British Commonwealth', 42 *ICLQ* 753 (1993).

VON MEHREN, 'Law and Legal Education in India: Some Observations', 78 *Harv. L. Rev.* 1180 (1965).

MORAN, 'The Migration of the Common Law: The Republic of Ireland', 76 *LQ Rev.* 69 (1960).

NICHOLLS, 'The Migration of the Common Law: Canada', 76 *LQ Rev.* 74 (1960).

PATON (ed.), *The Commonwealth of Australia, The Development of Its Laws and Constitutions* (1952).

RABELLO (ed.), *European Legal Traditions and Israel* (1994).

RAJANAYAGAM, 'The Reception and Restriction of English Commercial Law in Ceylon', 18 *ICLQ* 378 (1969).

SCHREINER, *The Contribution of English Law to South African Law; and the Rule of Law in South Africa* (1967).

SETALVAD, *The Common Law in India* (1960).

——, *The Role of English Law in India* (1966).

ZELTNER, 'Das Vertragsrecht des Staates Israel', *RabelsZ* 39 (1975) 56.

——, 'Einführung in das israelische Privatrecht', in: *Beiträge zum deutschen und israelischen Privatrecht* (Neue Kölner rechtswissenschaftliche Abhandlungen no. 81, 1977) 9.

ZIMMERMANN, *Dar römisch-holländische Recht in Südafrika* (1983).

——, 'Das südafrikanische Privatrecht im Schnittpunkt zwischen Common law und Civil law', *ZfRV* 26 (1985) 111.

I

NEARLY a third of all the people alive today live in regions where the law has been more or less strongly marked by the Common Law. This is the legacy of the fact that Great Britain was once the greatest colonial power in the world. By centuries of tenacious effort the Britons succeeded in establishing themselves on every continent and gradually brought vast overseas territories under the control of the British Crown; they created and maintained an enormous colonial empire, by peaceful colonization, through the establishment and furtherance of trade links, and by military exploits against indigenous rulers or competing European colonial powers, especially France. In the train of this colonial expansion English settlers, merchants, and administrators took the Common Law to North America, India, Australia, New Zealand, and to large parts of Africa and South-east Asia. Almost all the overseas possessions of the British Crown are now independent. As early as 1776 the United States declared its independence and broke away from the British state. Canada, Australia, New Zealand, India, Pakistan, the Republic of South Africa, and a large number of important states in East and West Africa, including Ghana, Nigeria, Kenya, Uganda, and Tanzania, are all now completely independent in internal and external affairs, although most of them remain within the Commonwealth and thus have close political and economic links with the United Kingdom. Nevertheless the whole law of these countries—not just the substantive law, but also the law of procedure, the courts system, the structure of legal professions, the whole style of legal thought and debate—is still strongly influenced by the legal ideas, institutions, and methods of the Common Law.

From the historical standpoint one can distinguish two groups of British colonies. One group comprises those territories which at the time of their first settlement were either unoccupied or occupied only by natives at a very early stage of civilization and not yet politically organized; in these colonies, called 'settled colonies', such as Australia, New Zealand, and North America, the Common Law of the incomers applied automatically, except in so far as particular social, economic, geographical, or climatic circumstances might render any of its rules inappropriate. The second group of colonies comprised lands already controlled by native princes or other European colonial powers which came under British control by conquest or cession ('conquered' or 'ceded colonies'): here it was a firm principle of English colonial policy to leave intact the law already in force in these territories, and often the existing courts system as well. Thus when they took over the French possessions in North America, the English recognized, in the Quebec Act, 1774, that the French-Canadians should retain their private law, then based on the Coutume de Paris (see above Ch. 8 VII b). By the same principle of English colonial policy, the Roman-Dutch law which had been introduced by the Dutch in the middle of the seventeenth century into their territories in Southern Africa was left in force there when those territories were incorporated into the British colonial empire (see the full development below Ch. 16 VI). The English followed this principle even when the law they found in the new territories was not, like French or Roman-Dutch law, a variant of the Civil Law: in India and in the colonies of Africa the British administration did not try to replace the Islamic, Hindu, or unwritten African customary law then in force with the rules of the Common Law. After incorporation into the British Empire, these territories retained the family law, marriage law, and law of succession of the native populations. Of course if the local law had no appropriate rules or the rules they had were undesirable in the eyes of the English the colonial legislature filled the gaps by following the model of the Common Law. Hence many areas of law which are not codified or are only partially codified in Great Britain even today are regulated in the colonies by comprehensive statutes; one instance is the law of contract.

In the following pages we shall attempt to show how the Common Law spread throughout the world by taking a few chosen countries as examples.

II

Dutch sailors had set foot in *Australia* several times in the course of the seventeenth century, but their descriptions of the country made it seem so inhospitable that for more than a hundred years no one made any attempt at settlement. Only after JAMES COOK landed on the East Coast of Australia in 1770 and took the country in the name of the British Crown did England embark on a process of settlement, for which at first they used transported convicts as labourers. The law in force was the English Common Law, and a statute of the British Parliament in 1828 laid down that the law of the existing Australian colonies should be the Common Law with the addition of such English statutes as were in force in England on 25 July 1828. In the first half of the nineteenth century all the Australian colonies, starting with New South Wales, were gradually given the right to elect a local legislature. Soon after gold was discovered and the economy started to prosper the transportation of convicts ceased to be necessary, for tens of thousands of settlers, mainly of English, Scottish, and Irish descent, flooded into the land; between 1830 and 1860 the population grew from 70,000 to 1,100,000. Towards the end of the century it became necessary to federate the several Australian colonies. There were considerable difficulties but finally a draft Constitution was agreed, adopted by referendum in the several colonies, and brought into force by the British Parliament as the Commonwealth of Australia Constitution Act, 1900. Under the Constitution Australia is a federal state with six members (New South Wales, Victoria, Queensland, Tasmania, South Australia, and Western Australia), each of which has its own constitution, its own government, and its own Parliament. The federal legislature has competence only in the areas specified by the Constitution, such as external relations, defence, currency and coins, customs, as well as insurance and banking, negotiable instruments and bankruptcy, the protection of trade, and matrimonial law. All the rest of private and commercial law, as well as criminal law, is reserved to the competence of the several states. In consequence, although Australia has only 14 million inhabitants, it contains six different legal systems, one of which, that of Tasmania, applies to a bare 400,000 inhabitants. To these one must add the territories which are federally administered, where federal law applies. But when one looks more closely, one finds that in the principal areas of private law, commercial law, and procedural law all these legal systems are nearly identical, or at least very similar. This is because throughout Australia the law has come from the English Common Law without any serious deviation either in judicial decisions or legislation. It is true that the courts of Australia are not bound by English precedents, but English decisions, especially those of the Court of Appeal and House of Lords, are treated with great respect and normally followed, even if this means that Australian courts have to abandon a previous decision of their own. Thus Dixon J., in a judgment of the highest court in Australia, said:

'I think that if this Court is convinced that a particular view of the law has been taken in England from which there is unlikely to be any departure, wisdom is on the side of the Court's applying that view to Australian conditions, notwithstanding that the Court has already decided the question in the opposite sense . . . Where a general proposition is involved the Court should be careful to avoid introducing into Australian law a principle inconsistent with that which has been accepted in England. The common law is administered in many jurisdictions, and unless each of them guards against needless divergences of decision its uniform development is imperilled.' *Waghorn* v. *Waghorn* (1941–2) 65 CLR 289, 297.

In their legislation also, the member states have often limited themselves to adopting English models or relying heavily on them. Thus all states except New South Wales adopted the English court reforms of 1873; they have also adopted, word for word, numerous statutes on commercial matters, such as the English Sale of Goods Act, 1893. Their general law of contract and land law are very similar. Yet on occasion Australia has developed original solutions of its own: thus in *family law* there is the modern Family Law Act of 1975, and in *land law* a land registration system, not unlike the German one, was introduced in the middle of the nineteenth century, at the instance of TORRENS, who was not a lawyer, and over the bitter opposition of those who were; it now operates with great success in the whole of Australia and is beginning to attract adherents in other countries of the Anglo-American legal family.

With regard to the system of courts, one must distinguish between the courts of the several states and the Commonwealth courts. The *states* have lower courts rather like the English Magistrates' Courts and County Courts to deal with minor disputes. The highest court of each state, the Supreme Court, acts both as a court of appeal and as a court of first instance in important civil and criminal matters. Hearings are normally before a single judge, from whom an appeal lies to a bench of three judges in the same court. The *Commonwealth* courts, apart from those in the commonwealth territories, do not act as full courts of first instance but as superior courts; by far the most important is the *High Court of Australia*. It hears appeals from the judgments of the Supreme Courts of the several states, whether federal law or state law is involved. Furthermore the High Court also deals with constitutional disputes, such as suits between the Commonwealth and a state or between states, and cases where a Commonwealth statute is alleged to be void as being outside the legislative competence of the Commonwealth. On the other hand, the High Court has no power to strike down a statute on the ground that it infringes a constitutionally protected right of the citizen: unlike the American Constitution, the Australian Constitution contains no catalogue of 'basic rights'.

By no means all the states in Australia have adopted the English distinction between barristers and solicitors, though the most densely populated states have done so, namely New South Wales, Queensland, and Victoria. In the other three states every lawyer is admitted as both barrister and solicitor though it is possible, and in the larger cities even normal, for a lawyer to specialize as a barrister or as a solicitor in the course of his professional career.

All in all, one can conclude that Australian law and English law are still very similar in their method and procedure, in their basic legal ideas, in the way their law is applied, and in their techniques of drafting and construing statutes. Even where differences exist, English and Australian lawyers have no difficulty at all in understanding each other. It seems that of all the great countries outside Europe which belong to the Anglo-American legal family, Australia is the one whose law is still closest to that of England.

III

Canada, like Australia, is a federal state composed of previous British colonies but, unlike Australia, much of it was not originally settled by colonists from England, Scotland, and Ireland; the region of the St. Lawrence River was already heavily settled by French citizens when it was ceded to Britain along with all the other French possessions in North America by the Treaty of Paris in 1763. At first there was a distinct preponderance of French in the population of the Canadian colonies but during the American War of Independence many thousands of loyalists left what is now the United States and moved North of the Great Lakes, and the Anglo-Saxon population of 'Upper Canada' gradually approximated to the French settlement in 'Lower Canada'. In 1791 an Act was passed by the British Parliament which divided Canada into two parts, one predominantly French and one predominantly English, both under the sovereignty of the British Crown but each having its own Parliament and its own government. There then ensued in both parts repeated movements for independence and much unrest and revolt, so in 1840 the British Colonial Office tried another system under which the regions were united and each was given an equal number of seats in the common Parliament. This system also proved unstable by reason of the constant rivalry between the two almost equal populations, and a lasting solution was only reached with a plan to found a federation containing not only Upper Canada and Lower Canada but also the other colonial regions subject to the British Crown in North America. In 1867, Parliament in London enacted the *British North America Act* on the basis of proposals originating in Canada. This statute created the federal state 'Dominion of Canada' of which originally there were four member provinces: Quebec, Ontario, New Brunswick, and Nova Scotia. Two years later with the agreement of the British

Parliament Canada paid £300,000 and obtained all the sovereign rights which the Hudson's Bay Company had enjoyed since 1670 over the huge area of the North West Territories, on the basis of an English royal patent. In 1871 British Columbia joined the Canadian union, and independent provinces were carved out of the North West Territories and admitted to the federation—Manitoba in 1870 and Saskatchewan and Alberta in 1905. Finally, in 1949, Newfoundland became a province of Canada; since that date the entire North American continent has been divided between the United States and Canada.

The system of courts in Canada is much like that in Australia: in addition to the provincial courts with a Court of Appeal at the head of each, there are federal courts—the Federal Court which has jurisdiction essentially over acts of the federal administration, and above all the *Supreme Court of Canada* whose principal task is to hear appeals from the highest provincial courts.

The law in Canada, apart from Quebec, was quite unequivocally modelled on law in England until recently. Canadian courts regarded decisions of the House of Lords and the Privy Council as binding and treated decisions of the other English courts as having 'persuasive authority'. English methods of legal education prevailed; law teachers in Canada usually had a degree in law from an English university. But since the end of the Second World War and especially since the abolition of appeals to the Privy Council in 1949, though its effect was primarily psychological, there seems to have been an increasing independence in Canadian legal thought; instead of being guided solely by the methods and institutions of English law, more attention is being paid to promptings from the United States.

IV

In the sixteenth and seventeenth centuries *India* was a country with a large population and a high level of cultural development which had long been ruled by powerful Grand Moguls of the Islamic faith. There was thus no question of the Portuguese and Dutch, or later the French and English, being able to colonize the country on their arrival in India. Their aim was rather to forge as strong trade links as possible while fully respecting the sovereignty of the native princes. This explains why it was not the governments of the European colonial powers which had dealings with India but special trading companies acting under royal patent, of which the most famous and successful was the English 'East India Company' which came into being in 1600 with the blessing of ELIZABETH I. In 1612 the Grand Mogul of India allowed this company to establish its first settlement in Surat, north of Bombay, and in the following decades it set itself up in many other places on the east and west coasts and gradually ousted the competition of other European colonial powers. In the eighteenth century the Grand

Mogul's empire gradually fell to pieces and the country was rent by frequent wars; the English occasionally had to resort to arms in self-defence and British influence was maintained by winning over the local Indian potentates by persuasion, bribery, or threats, or by making deft use of their disputes. So alongside the original desire of the English to engage in profitable trade with the Indians there gradually developed a stronger interest in open political control of the country and finally in the extension of the British colonial empire. We cannot here give the details of this development, but at the beginning of the twentieth century the whole of the Indian subcontinent, including Burma, was under English control. About 60 per cent of this immense land mass was British territory directly administered by British officials; the rest comprised a very large number of native states whose princes had recognized the sovereignty of the British crown and who administered their states under the eye of the British.

Under the original patent issued to it, the East India Company was given power to make regulations for the administration of its overseas settlements and their senior officials could punish on the spot those who broke these rules or committed criminal acts. This naturally applied only to Englishmen in the Company's service, but in the course of time as the number of Company outposts increased and trade prospered, numerous Indians entered the service of the Company and centres of administrative activity and trade developed. Of these, the so-called 'Presidency towns', the ports of Madras, Bombay, and Calcutta, were especially important. In 1726 an ordinance of the British Crown gave these three towns special royal courts—the 'Mayor's Courts'—to resolve disputes between parties in those towns, whether English or Indian, and to give judgment 'according to justice and right'; 'justice and right' meant the English Common Law with the addition of such English statutes as were in force in 1726, in so far as these rules were not inapplicable because of local conditions. It soon became apparent that the Common Law was inappropriate to disputes between Indians on family or succession matters and towards the end of the eighteenth century the Mayor's Courts in the three cities mentioned were abolished and replaced by Supreme Courts, staffed by professional English judges; these courts were mainly to apply the Common Law, but Islamic or Hindu law was to control in litigation between Muhammadans or Hindus concerning family or succession law. Judges were to supplement their familiarity with these legal systems by obtaining information from named experts in the two religions.

In the course of time very large territories came under the administration of the East India Company as a result of treaties with Indian princes and the occasional military exploit. Here the situation was much the same. The provincial courts, introduced by the English towards the end of the eighteenth century and staffed by English administrators, were instructed to apply Islamic or Hindu law depending on the faith of the parties whenever the case involved 'inheritance, marriage, caste and other religious usages and institutions'. In all other matters without religious connotations and in every case where the parties were neither Muhammadan nor Hindu the court was instructed to decide 'according to justice, equity and good conscience'.

Under these circumstances the Common Law, apart from family and succession law, naturally became the 'common law' of India in the course of the nineteenth century. In the 'Presidency towns' this followed from the fact that the courts were bound to apply the Common Law, except in religious cases. It is true that in the provinces the principle of decision was to be 'justice, equity and good conscience' but even there the administrative officials were soon replaced as judges by barristers trained in England who tended to suppose, conveniently enough, that 'justice, equity and good conscience' meant simply the rules of the Common Law with which they were familiar, so far as they were appropriate to Indian conditions. As the Privy Council, the final court of appeal from Indian courts after 1833, once observed in a judgment:

'the matter must be decided by equity and good conscience, generally interpreted to mean the rules of English law if found applicable to Indian society and circumstances' (*Waghela Rajsanji* v. *Shekh Masludin* [1887] LR 14 IA 89, 96; see the further decisions mentioned by JAIN (above p. 218) 576 ff.).

Other judges took the wider view that one could only find out what 'justice, equity and good conscience' implied in particular cases by making a critical comparative survey of the developed legal systems of the world; in many judgments one finds well-educated and open-minded judges taking the Civil Law, especially Roman law, into account in addition to the Common Law (see the extensive treatment by DERRETT (above p. 218) I). But by and large it may certainly be said that the whole of the Common Law, except family law and the law of succession, established itself in India and took up residence there, though often in a very modified form.

Admittedly the law at that time was in an extremely confused, even chaotic condition. In addition to English statutes prior to 1726, of which it was often not clear whether they should be treated as received into India, there were English statutes subsequent to that date so far as they professed to apply in India, and finally there were regulations from the provincial governments in Bombay, Madras, and Calcutta which often differed since they were produced quite independently. Furthermore the courts in the 'Presidency towns' applied the Common Law to a greater extent than the provincial courts to whom the formula 'justice, equity and good conscience' offered considerable room for play. In this situation the unification and codification of Indian law struck many people as a matter of urgency; there was agreement and support in England, where many Members of Parliament were swayed by the ideas of BENTHAM. A British statute in 1833 therefore provided that a 'Law Commission in India' be set up; it was to collect together the rules of positive law in

India, to put them into some order, and then codify them in a manageable way. The first President of this Commission was MACAULAY, the famous English historian, essayist, and politician. In a very short time he succeeded in producing a draft of an Indian Penal Code; it was mainly based on English criminal law, itself largely uncodified, but it also paid some attention to European models, especially the French Code pénal. These efforts at reform had no practical consequences before 1857, the year of the great mutiny in northern India, in consequence of which the British Crown itself took over responsibility for the administration of India from the East India Company. In 1859 a Code of Civil Procedure, in 1860 the Criminal Code drafted by MACAULAY, and in 1861 an Ordinance relating to Criminal Procedure were enacted. Further statutes followed in quick succession.

The Indian Succession Act came into force in 1865. It unified the law of succession for all Indians, such as Christians and Jews, who were not subject to either Islamic or Hindu law. Though this statute too was based on the Common Law, it deliberately abandoned many archaic formalities of English succession law.—The Indian Contract Act of 1872 is especially interesting. It codified rules from the sanctum of classical judge-made law in England, such as the rules concerning the formation of contracts by offer and acceptance, consideration, mistake, deceit, duress and misrepresentation, illegality and immorality, breach of contract, unjust enrichment (under the unhelpful heading 'Of certain relations resembling those created by contract'), as well as suretyship and agency. The portions of the Indian Contract Act concerning sale of goods and partnership were later replaced by the Sale of Goods Act, 1930, and the Partnership Act, 1932, both of which are nearly congruent with the English prototypes. Other statutes in this area are the Specific Relief Act, 1877, the Transfer of Property Act, 1882, and the Indian Trusts Act, 1882. All these statutes are still in force today both in India and Pakistan, though they have been redrafted or much modified.

The striking fact about political development in India in the twentieth century is the long drawn out process by which the Indian people obtained the right to legislate for and administer their country from an unwilling and unyielding British government, first internally in the provinces and then centrally for external affairs as well. It became clear that the Muslims and the Hindus would prefer not to live together in a single Indian state after independence, and so when the British Parliament granted complete independence by means of the India Independence Act, 1947, *two* new states immediately came into being: India and Pakistan. The Indian princes, more than 500 of them, who had theretofore lived under the sovereignty of the British Crown also obtained full freedom; they were entitled to attach themselves to either of the two states as they wished, and in the following years all of them did so.

The Constitution of India came into force in 1950. Constitutionally India is a federal state with 15 member states, including Kashmir, and a number of federal territories. The central Parliament is given exclusive jurisdiction in some areas, such as large industry and big business, external trade, banking and insurance, company law, and the law of negotiable instruments. The member states have exclusive jurisdiction in matters of local importance such as local administration, police, and land management. Private law, criminal law, and procedural law fall within the concurrent legislative competence of the federation and the member states. Important areas of Hindu family and succession law, about 85 per cent of the total population of India today being Hindu, have since been unified by federal statutes; as all the statutes from the colonial period which were in force on the day of independence have in principle remained in force, the private law of India today is mainly codified law.

Unlike the Constitutions of Australia and Canada, the Constitution of India contains a list of basic rights; any statute which infringes these basic rights can be held void by the High Courts, the highest courts of the member states, or by the *Supreme Court of India*, the highest court in the land. The Supreme Court is not only a constitutional court, however; it also decides appeals against judgments of the High Courts in cases involving more than a certain value, or if leave has been given in a matter of important principle by the High Court or the Supreme Court itself.

Court procedure in civil and criminal matters basically follows the Common Law. Thus the binding force of precedent, the position of the judge, free to deliver concurring or dissenting judgments, the importance of procedure in legal remedies, the role of lawyers in matters of procedure, and much else remind us clearly of the Common Law model. Given the diversity of language, race, religion, and civilization among the people of India, with the grave risks this presents for its political unity, the relative homogeneity of the legal system throughout India, resting as it does on the Common Law, must rank as one of the most important contributions of the departed colonial masters to the integration of the country.

V

The Common Law also had a great influence on the legal systems of those states which formed part of the British empire in Africa. In West Africa these countries are *Sierra Leone, Gambia, Nigeria*, and *Ghana; Liberia*, founded in 1821 as a settlement for emancipated slaves from the United States and an independent republic since 1847, has a legal system which bears the marks more of American than of English Common Law. In East Africa the countries which belonged to the British zone of influence were principally *Kenya* and *Uganda*, and, since 1920, Tanganyika; Tanganyika had previously been German East Africa, and united with Zanzibar to form the *Republic of Tanzania* in 1964.

In 1814 the *Seychelles*, an archipelago in the Indian Ocean about 950 miles off the coast of Africa, was ceded by France to Britain and incorporated into the British Empire. The French Code civil and Code de Commerce which were in force at that time remained in force, but numerous English ordinances were introduced during the next 150 years. The results were inconvenient until the enactment in 1976, the year of independence, of a Code civil thoroughly reworked and modernized by the comparatist CHLOROS. This is an interesting 'experiment in Franco-British codification'. See CHLOROS, The Projected Reform of the Civil Law of the Seychelles: An Experiment in Franco-British Codification', 48 *Tul. L. Rev.* 815 (1974); CHLOROS, *Codification in a Mixed Jurisdiction, the Civil and Commercial Law of Seychelles* (1977).

The student of legal development in these countries of East and West Africa will see that the reception of the Common Law took a similar form everywhere: it was provided, either by order in council issued by the monarch or by ordinance of the colonial legislature, that the law of the colony in question should be

'the common law, the doctrines of equity and the statutes of general application which were in force in England on the 24th day of July, 1874'—to take the rule in the Gold Coast, now Ghana. The formulas by which the reception was made in Sierra Leone in 1862, in Kenya in 1897, in Uganda in 1902, and in Tanganyika in 1920 were very similar. These formulas raised numerous questions in practice. For example, it might be a matter of doubt whether an English statute was designed for a specifically 'English' problem or whether the law was a statute 'of general application' so as to have validity in the colonies also. The judges enjoyed a certain room for play as a result of the widespread proviso which laid down that English law was to be applied by the colonial courts 'so far only as local circumstances permit and subject to such qualifications as local circumstances may render necessary'. Again, it might be a question of doubt whether or in what cases colonial judges should regard decisions of English courts subsequent to the date of reception as being binding precedents, as having 'persuasive authority', or as being simply negligible. On this, see ALLOTT, *Systems* (above p. 218) 9 ff.

The special legislation of the British colonies and their independent successors are also based on British models.

Thus the English Sale of Goods Act, 1893, applies in all four states of West Africa, some of which enacted it before and some after independence, often with alterations; the Sales Act, 1962 of Ghana is particularly interesting as an attempt to modernize the English law of sales (see MERTENS, 'Das Kaufgesetz Ghanas von 1962', *RabelsZ* 27 (1962/1963) 519). The courts of these countries had previously applied the English Sale of Goods Act on one of two grounds: either it was a 'statute of general application' which automatically became law in the colony because it was in force in England at the time of the reception of the Common Law in that colony, or it was simply a codification of judge-made law and therefore in substance 'common law' (in the narrow sense) and applicable as such in the colonies by reason of the general formula of reception. East Africa generally followed the Indian legislation and consequently adopted the Indian Contract Act, 1872, and later, still following the Indian example, the English Sale of Goods Act as well. The Indian Contract Act has since been repealed in the East African states; Kenya and Uganda adopted English contract law by general reference in 1960, and in 1961 Tanganyika replaced it by a new Contract Act which admittedly greatly resembles that of India. The numerous statutes which these African states have passed since independence in order to regulate the economy and its administration are also patterned in form and substance on English enactments.

All this might lead one to the conclusion that in the areas of Africa which were previously under British rule most legal relations today are governed by the rules of English Common Law. This conclusion would be wholly erroneous. The fact is that to much the largest part of the African population the Common Law is of almost no practical significance; the legal relations of Africans, in contract and land matters as well as family and succession matters, are principally governed by the rules of customary African law, and in many regions also by the rules of Islamic law. This is a consequence of the principle of English colonial policy which we have already mentioned, namely that the population of a region which had been annexed or ceded or conquered should generally retain its existing law and that the administration of the territory should so far as possible be left in the hands of the traditional executive and judicial bodies (the principle of 'Indirect Rule'). This principle had two particular consequences for the African parts of the British Empire: unwritten African customary laws, which often varied from tribe to tribe, remained in force for the native population, as did the Islamic law prevalent in many regions, provided that in the view of the colonial masters they were not 'repugnant to natural justice and morality'. Secondly, the existing African courts, where the tribal chief or other notables applied the customary law, were basically left unaffected; the colonial administrators were only interested in seeing that certain elementary principles of procedure, mainly in criminal cases, were adhered to, and that there was a possibility of appeal to higher courts, eventually to a final court staffed by English judges. In this way the imported English law, the African customary laws, and, where applicable, Islamic law coexisted in the African territories of the British Empire.

Obviously enough, this quite often gave rise to doubts whether English law or customary law should be applied in a particular case. Thus, for example, it might be a question whether the English law of succession should apply when an African died in a city where he had lived for a long time in the European style with his close family. Should African customary law apply to a contract between Africans concluded in writing in the English language? Which law of divorce was to apply when the marriage was valid by African customary law because the bride's father had entered the contract and paid the price, and also by English law as being in the *statutory* form, which Africans could always use, of celebration before state officials, with or without a church ceremony? The rules by which one decides which of the competing legal systems is to be applied are usually called 'interpersonal private law', on the analogy of 'international private law'.

During the colonial period the English showed very little interest in African customary laws; in the main they regarded them simply as an object for anthropological study, perhaps secretly expecting that in the long run they would die out and be gradually replaced by English law. Today the attitude has changed, and it seems that the African states are eager to maintain all the indigenous institutions and values which their peoples have in common. Thus many of them have started on the task, normally with the help of English specialists, of recording the various customary laws and making an orderly 'Restatement' of them; many states regard such a 'Restatement' simply as a means of finding one's way about, while others want to give it statutory force and thus replace unwritten law by written law. At the same time these countries must try so far as possible to approximate the different customary laws which are in force in their territory or even to unify them, though such a task will be horribly difficult wherever there is a great diversity of race, language, and life-styles among the tribes and peoples which constitute a state. In any case the dual system of courts from the colonial period, some applying only customary law and others applying the Common Law, has been abolished everywhere and decisions in the lower courts are being given more and more not by tribal elders and other such people but by professional African judges who have often been educated at the newly founded universities in Africa, most of which still have English and American lawyers on their staffs. The great task in the future for these African states will be to unify their internal legal system, so far as possible, and to codify their law, using the legal terminology and statutory techniques of the Common Law and incorporating the basic values and institutions of African customary law, especially in the field of family and inheritance law. At the same time the legislators should try to keep in mind the goal of unifying the commercial law of Africa as a whole, and for this purpose they should do their best to avoid closing off their national law or giving its development any special twist.

VI

The law of the *Republic of South Africa* merits the particular attention of comparatists, first because Roman law has shown a greater vitality in South Africa than anywhere else in the world by surviving to the present day, and secondly because in the course of its history this Roman law has interacted quite remarkably with English Common Law.

It is really a historical accident that Roman law still survives in South Africa. In 1652, on the orders of the Dutch East India Company, the

Dutchman JAN VAN RIEBEECK established a settlement at the Cape of Good Hope; its principal purpose was to provide water and victuals for Dutch ships which were making the long journey to the Dutch East Indies. Very soon this victualling station developed into a flourishing colony which increased its population by attracting Dutch, French, and German settlers and enlarged its land area by gradually extending its borders to east and north. The law of the Cape Colony was the law of the metropolis, specifically the law of the Province of Holland, the most influential province of the Republic of the Netherlands and the seat of the Dutch East India Company at the time. The law then in force in the Province of Holland was Roman law. It had been received into Holland in the form given to it by the Glossators and Commentators, and in the seventeenth and eighteenth centuries Dutch legal scholars, after historical research, had adapted it to the practical needs of the time with an admixture of a good deal of old Dutch customary law; of these we may mention HUGO GROTIUS (1583–1645), ARNOLDUS VINNIUS (1588–1657), JOHANNES VOET (1647–1713), CORNELIS VAN BYNKERSHOEK (1673–1743), and DIONYSIUS VAN DER KEESSEL (1738–1816). In 1795, during the Napoleonic Wars, the English seized the Cape in order to secure their sea links with India and finally took it into possession in 1806 as a British colony; the 'Roman–Dutch law' which then obtained in the Cape Colony remained in force. In the Dutch homeland, however, Roman–Dutch law was abolished by the decree of NAPOLEON and replaced in 1809 by the Code civil; the Burgerlijk Wetboek of 1838 which was based on it was later introduced into the Dutch East Indies. Thus Roman–Dutch law survived only in those areas which had come under British rule and had left the Dutch Empire before it adopted a Civil Code on the French model. The only countries of which this is true apart from South Africa are *Sri Lanka*, previously *Ceylon* (since 1799) and parts of *Guyana* (since 1803).

But Roman–Dutch law has not been able to hold on as well in Sri Lanka as in South Africa, mainly because Dutch and Afrikaans are no longer spoken in Sri Lanka and so there is no longer access to the Dutch or even the Roman sources. English Common Law clearly dominates in Sri Lanka, especially in the law of contract and in commercial law; on this, see JENNINGS/TAMBIAH (above p. 219) and RAJA-NAYAGAM (above p. 219). In Guyana the tenure of Roman–Dutch law was precarious from the very beginning and in 1916 it was replaced by the English Common Law (see DALTON, 'The Passing of Roman–Dutch Law in British Guiana,' 36 *S. Afr. LJ* 4 (1919)).

The influence of English Common Law made itself felt in the Cape Colony as soon as it was incorporated into the British Empire. The first interest of the British was to organize and modernize the constitution, administration, and courts system of the new colony. The law of evidence and procedure in both civil and criminal matters were immediately reconstructed on the pattern of the Common Law, and English was introduced as the sole language of the courts. Since very close economic connections developed between South Africa and Great Britain, and Roman–Dutch law had no rules suited to modern commercial practice, it was only natural that many English statutes were adopted almost word for word in South Africa in the fields of negotiable instruments, bankruptcy, maritime law, insurance, and partnership law. But English law also seeped into South Africa surreptitiously. Whenever Roman–Dutch law seemed to be unclear, inadequate, or obsolete, the courts had a tendency to rely on English case-law with which the lawyers and judges, most of whom had been trained in London, were certainly more familiar than with the old texts of GROTIUS and VOET. The strength of the influence of English legal ideas can be partially explained by the fact that in the second half of the nineteenth century Great Britain stood at the peak of its political and economic power in the world. Furthermore at the time there was very little independent legal scholarship in South Africa to keep Roman–Dutch traditions alive. Nor must it be overlooked that in the course of the nineteenth century many thousands of Boers, disenchanted with the English for abolishing slavery and afraid that their life-style would be anglicized, quit the Cape Colony and trekked to the North where they founded three independent Boer republics, Natal, the Orange Free State, and Transvaal. In the course of time all three of these republics were incorporated into the British Empire, the Orange Free State and Transvaal only after the English won the Boer War in 1902. Shortly after the end of the Boer War the white population of the colonies in Southern Africa came to realize that on economic grounds at least they must become more closely linked. In 1910 the Cape Colony and the three previous Boer republics joined together to form the 'Union of South Africa', whose constitution was laid down by the British Parliament in the South Africa Act, 1909.

Some parts of Southern Africa remained for the time being under British administration and did not join the Union. Today they are independent (*Lesotho, Botswana, Swaziland, Zimbabwe*). In all these states Roman–Dutch law of the South African stamp applies, at least to the white population. But Britain had other territories lying further to the north, which are independent today under the names of *Zambia* and *Malawi*; apart from the African customary law their law is basically English Common Law.

After the creation of the Union of South Africa in 1910 the progressive anglicization of the law came to a stop. Several factors contributed to this, such as the sense of political independence from Britain, the recognition of English and Afrikaans as equal languages, and the blossoming of South African universities which not only took over the training of native jurists but also worked on the sources of Roman–Dutch law and made it accessible to the public. Since then the courts of South Africa have clearly been paying great attention to the texts of the old Dutch writers and to the rules which have developed from them; they evaluate them with care and adapt them to modern circumstances. The Common Law still dominates in constitutional and administrative law, and in commercial and procedural law; and the traditions of English law are still strong in the courts structure, the position of the judge, the doctrine of binding precedent, and the activities of the legal professions. On the other hand, Common Law has had negligible influence in family and succession law and in the law of property, all of which are unequivocally dominated by Roman methods of thinking. Thus, for example, South Africa has held to a unitary concept of ownership, sharply distinguished from limited real rights and from possession in a way quite foreign to the Common Law. A clear distinction is also made between the *contract* which involves the passing of property and the *conveyance transaction*, which is effective only if in addition to delivery or constructive delivery there is the necessary consent of the parties. South African judges and lawyers make constant use in appropriate cases of such legal figures as *occupatio, accessio, specificatio, traditio* and *constitutum possessorium*. Nor has South Africa received the Anglo-American legal institution of the trust, although the courts have succeeded in producing most of the desired legal effects by using Roman concepts: thus *fidei commissum* performs the function of the testamentary trust, the *stipulatio alteri* performs that of the trust declared *inter vivos* and the *donatio ad pias causas* performs the functions of a charitable trust for the public benefit.

On this see the extensive treatment by HAHLO, 'The Trust in South African Law', 78 *S. Afr. LJ* 195 (1961).—Common Law influences are rather stronger in the general law of contract and in the law of tort. Thus the South African courts have taken over the 'mail-box' theory and the concept of innocent misrepresentation (see Ch. 26 II, 31 IV); towards the end of the nineteenth century there was an intensive flirtation with the doctrine of consideration, which was subsequently and conclusively jilted. The foundations of the law of tort today are certainly the *actio legis Aquiliae* and the *actio iniuriarum* but there are clear echoes of English law in the doctrine of causation and contributory negligence; vicarious liability and the action of defamation, indeed, are pure Common Law. But by and large even in the law of contract and tort the basic conceptual structure of the Roman law has been maintained and in the solution of particular questions citations from the texts of the Digest and the old Dutch writers are fruitfully and unselfconsciously made. See, by way of example, *Essa* v. *Divaris*, 1947 (1) SA 753 (AD), where the court was faced with the question whether the strict liability of the *stabularius* for the loss of a horse he had lodged, as laid down in the Praetor's Edict (D. 4.9.1 pr.), could be applied to the proprietor of a parking lot for the loss of a truck which had been parked there. Here and in other cases the continental reader is surprised, not so much that the problem is raised in the terms of Roman categories of thought, for this is often true today in Germany and France as well, as by the fact that in the decisions of the South African courts the development of the law, from the classical Roman jurists through JUSTINIAN and the Gloss and VOET and VINNIUS up to modern times, stands out as being so continuous. European lawyers today are not generally so conscious of the continuity of legal development because the civil codes give the impression of having interrupted it, even if this is not the case.

No simple answer can be given to the question whether the law of South Africa should be put in the Anglo-American legal family or whether it should be classed with those legal systems which have developed on the basis of Roman law. The latter view will be adopted by those who think the critical factor is the nature of the basic concepts and structures of the legal order in question; in South Africa, these are unquestionably Roman, at any rate if one concentrates on the uncodified law. But those who pay more attention to the techniques of applying the law in the courts today will have a different opinion; the way the trial is conducted, the methods of proof, the treatment of precedents, as well as the courts structure and the activities and position of judges and lawyers are all clearly based on English models; and the same is true of the law in very important areas such as trade and partnership law, which is codified. Thus South African law appears as a 'hybrid' law in which, as it seems to us, the elements of Roman–Dutch and English law are so intermixed that it cannot without distortion be put in one or other pigeonhole:

'Like a jewel in a brooch, the Roman-Dutch law in South Africa today glitters in a setting that was made in England. Even if it were true (which it is not) that the whole of South African private law and criminal law had remained pure Roman–Dutch law, the South African legal system as a whole would still be a hybrid one, in which civil- and common-law elements jostle each other' (HAHLO/KAHN, *The South African Legal System* (above p. 218, p. 585 f.).

VII

It is no easier to decide to which legal family the law of *Israel* should be allocated. This is principally because the present law in Israel comes from different historical strata: some from the Ottoman period, some from legislation influenced by the Common Law during the British Mandate (1922–48), and some from enactments of the Israeli legislature since 1948, as further developed by the courts.

After Great Britain received Palestine from the League of Nations as a Mandated Territory in 1922, the British Palestine Order in Council of 10 August 1922 came into force. This provided in art. 46 that the courts were to apply the Ottoman law in force on 1 November 1914 and subsequent Ottoman laws, plus rules brought into force by the mandatary authority. In line with normal British colonial administration (see above p. 220) it was further provided that where no legislative rule was applicable the courts were to decide 'according to the substance of the common law, and the doctrines of equity', always 'subject to such qualifications as local circumstances render necessary'.

Even the Ottoman law in force in Palestine in 1922 had very various origins. The law of property was laid down in the Majalla (a collection of rules of Islamic law of the Hanafi brand (see pp. 307 f.), made between 1869 and 1876 by the Turkish administration); in the area of family and succession law, uncodified Islamic law applied, while enactments lifted verbatim by the Turkish sultans from French sources controlled much of commercial law. The law in Palestine was extensively Anglicized during the British Mandate, though it lasted barely thirty years. This was done in part by replacing the Ottoman laws of French provenance by provisions of English origin, in part by introducing laws already in force in Great Britain, for example as regards bills of exchange, partnership, companies, and intangible property. In tort and criminal law, for instance, statutes were introduced which reproduced the rules of English case-law in the form of paragraphs, case-law being easier to export to the colonies in this form. The Anglicization of the law was facilitated because the courts applied the Common Law not only where there was no positive law on the particular issue (or indeed in the whole area, such as restitution or conflicts of law), but also where existing provisions were unclear and required interpretation, a not uncommon occurrence with the Ottoman laws.

After the foundation of the State of Israel on 14 May 1948 one of the first acts of the legislature was to enact the Law and Administration Ordinance of 1948, §11 of which provided that the law in force at the time should remain in force except in so far as it was altered or repealed by ordinances of the new legislature. Much alteration and repeal has taken place. But one must distinguish: the Common-Law-based ordinances from the time of the Mandate are still very much in force, so that commercial and company law remain largely English, notwithstanding that since 1972 decisions of English courts construing these enactments are only of persuasive authority and no longer binding. By contrast, the rules of Ottoman origin are much less significant, since the Majalla has been largely ousted by numerous statutes enacted by the Israeli legislature since 1965 to reform parts of the law of obligations and property. Many of these enactments touch the law of contract, agency and assignment, and contracts of sale and gift, as well as the law of real property and succession. These laws, which will eventually be brought together in a civil code, are Continental in *form*, laying down only essential principles, often using indefinite terms whose specification is left to the courts, sometimes deploying general clauses, and consciously avoiding the baroque detail characteristic of English lawmaking (see below Ch. 18 III). As to *content*, the Israeli legislature has learnt much from comparative law, using, in addition to the Common Law, the law of Continental European systems and the Uniform Sales Law of The Hague. It inheres in the comparative law background of these statutes—and indeed it is expressly provided in some of them—that their terms should be construed, any lacuna filled, and their application developed 'autonomously' and 'self-referentially' rather than by recourse to English law. There is no doubt that the influence of the Common Law on the *content* of Israeli positive private law is on the wane, but it remains true that the style and methods of legal development are in the traditions of the Common Law:

'Israeli case-law remains typical of that in countries following the common law tradition. The manner of discussion, the mode of reasoning and the general approach are all characteristic of the common law systems. This is also true of the attitude of judges, jurists and attorneys to precedent, to the role of the courts and to their contribution to the development of law' (FRIEDMANN (above p. 218) 22).

17

The Law of the United States of America

ATIYAH/SUMMERS, *Form and Substance in Anglo-American Law, A Comparative Study of Legal Reasoning, Legal Theory, and Legal Institutions* (1987).

CALABRESI, *A Common Law for the Age of Statutes* (1982).

CLARK/ANSAY, *Introduction to the Law of the United States* (1992).

COING, 'Neue Strömungen in der nordamerikanischen Rechtsphilosophie,' *ARSP* 38 (1949) 536.

FARNSWORTH, *An Introduction to the Legal System of the United States* (2nd edn., 1987).

FIKENTSCHER, *Methoden des Rechts* II (1975).

FRIEDMAN, *A History of American Law* (1973).

——, *American Law* (1984).

GILMORE, *The Ages of American Law* (1977).

GRISWOLD, *Law and Lawyers in the United States, The Common Law Under Stress* (1964).

HAY, *An Introduction to United States Law* (1976).

——, *Einführung in das amerikanische Recht* (4th edn., 1995).

HONNOLD (ed.), *The Life of the Law, Readings on the Growth of Legal Institutions* (1964).

HURST, *The Growth of American Law* (1950).

KAHN-FREUND, 'English Law and American Law—Some Comparative Reflections,' in: *Essays in Jurisprudence in Honor of Roscoe Pound* (1962) 362.

KARLEN, *Appellate Courts in the United States and England* (1963).

——, *Judicial Administration—The American Experience* (1970).

POSNER, *The Federal Courts, Crisis and Reform* (1985).

POUND, *The Formative Era of American Law* (1938).

——, 'The Development of American Law and Its Deviation from English Law,' 67 *LQ Rev.* 49 (1951).

RABEL, 'Deutsches und amerikanisches Recht,' *RabelsZ* 16 (1951) 340.

REIMANN, 'Amerikanisches Privatrecht und europäische Rechtseinheit—Können die USA als Vorbild dienen?', in ZIMMERMANN (ed.), *Amerikanische Rechtskultur und europäisches Privatrecht* (1995) 132.

RHEINSTEIN, 'Die Rechtshonoratioren und ihr Einfluß auf Charakter und Funktion der Rechtsordnungen,' *RabelsZ* 34 (1970) 1.

RUESCHEMEYER, *Juristen in Deutschland und in den USA, Eine vergleichende Unter-suchung von Anwaltschaft und Gesellschaft* (1976).

RUMBLE, *American Legal Realism* (1968).

SCHLESINGER, *Die Rolle des Supreme Court im Privat-und Prozeßrecht der Vereinigten Staaten* (1965).

STEIN, 'The Attraction of the Civil Law in Post-Revolutionary America,' 52 *Va. L. Rev.* 403 (1966).

Weiss, *Die Theorie der richterlichen Entscheidungstätigkeit in den Vereinigten Staaten von Amerika* (1971).

Wengler, 'Die Anpassung des englischen Rechts durch die Judikatur in den Vereinigten Staaten,' in: *Festschrift Rabel* I (1954) 39.

Yntema, 'American Legal Realism in Retrospect,' 14 *Vand. L. Rev.* 317 (1960).

I

THE United States of America occupies an especially important place in the Common Law family, and thus calls for a more detailed treatment even in an introductory work such as this. This is not only because the United States is one of the mightiest countries in the world in terms of political influence and economic and military power, but mainly because in the two hundred years since the Declaration of Independence its law has gone through a quite distinctive development and has in many ways left its English model far behind. Unlike England, the United States has a written Constitution which gives the country a federal structure and contains a list of basic rights which may not be infringed by the legislature, the judiciary, or the executive. But other factors, the particular political ideals of the Founding Fathers, the diversity of the population in terms of race, religion and culture, the vast extent of its territory, and above all the astonishing vigour of its social and economic development, all these have helped American law to devise methods and solutions which make its study much more interesting and challenging for the Continental observer than English law, which is often too absorbed in cherishing its traditions.

Settlement of the North American continent began in the first half of the seventeenth century. Small colonies were set up first in Virginia and later elsewhere on the East Coast; they had little contact with each other and their links even with England were rather loose. In the early days when the main task facing the settlers was to secure their own survival against the elements and the Red Indians, there was hardly any need for courts and lawyers. Furthermore many of the colonies such as Massachusetts and Pennsylvania had a religious regime in which any disputes which arose were settled by ministers with the Bible rather than by lawyers with the Common Law. At the beginning of the eighteenth century this picture began to change; there was an increase in trade between the colonies and abroad, especially with England, and theocracy lost its hold in the various settlements. A class of lawyers gradually arose, many of whom had received their training in the Inns of Court in London, often before emigration. Gradually, too, lawbooks from England became widespread, especially BLACKSTONE's *Commentaries on the Laws of England*, almost as many copies of which were sold in the relatively unpopulated colonies of America as in England. Reaction to English imperialism in the mid-eighteenth century gave rise to the movement for American independence; on both sides the principal spokesmen were lawyers, and there were no less than 25 lawyers among the 56 signatories of the Declaration of Independence of 1776. Throughout the war with England until its end in 1781 the representatives of the newly independent American states strove for closer political links with each other, but it was not until 1787 that the Constitutional Convention of Philadelphia, where again more than half of the participants were lawyers, was able to thrash out a Federal Constitution which came into force in 1789 for its 13 member states and which is still, with the addition of a few amendments, in force today. The continuity of the Constitution is amazing; the United States has spread across the whole North American continent, it has developed from a prairie on the edge of civilization into the greatest industrial nation in the world, and it has survived a Civil War and two World Wars, yet still the Constitution has remained virtually unchanged.

Prior to independence those who settled in America agreed that the law of the several colonies should in principle be the English Common Law plus any statutes passed specially for them. There were some qualifications. At the beginning of the nineteenth century judges quite often quoted and applied rules of civil law or civilian authors. This was so, for example, where there was no clear rule in the Common Law, where the case involved an area of law in which even in England the Civil Law was recognized as a source (admiralty law, negotiable instruments, commercial law), and where there was need for a rule of law whose authority was universally recognized.

On this see HELMHOLZ, 'Use of the Civil Law in Post-Revolutionary American Jurisprudence' (1992) 66 *Tul. L. Rev.* 1649; STEIN, 'The Attraction of the Civil Law in Post-Revolutionary America' (1966) 52 *Va. L. Rev.* 403; more generally on the influence of Roman and continental European law in America, see HOEFLICH, 'Roman Law in American Legal Culture' (1992) 66 *Tul. L. Rev.* 1723; HOEFLICH, 'Transatlantic Friendships in the First Half of the Nineteenth Century' (1987) 35 *Am. J. Comp. L.* 599.—English Common law was also held inapplicable if conditions in America made it inappropriate. For example, the English rule was that the occupier of land was responsible for the harm which his cattle had caused on the land of a neighbour, regardless of any fault on his part; such a rule might work satisfactorily in a heavily populated land in which one may expect farmers to fence in their beasts so as to prevent harm to their neighbours. But in America, with huge areas almost devoid of people and fit only to be used as pasturage, it was different. Here the principle evolved that it was not for the farmer to fence in his beasts but rather for the occupier of buildings, woods, or agricultural land to protect his property by fencing the beasts out. The rules of the English Common Law regarding the use of water were also unsuited for the dry areas of the American West, where water is extremely scarce and must therefore be available not just to the riparian but also to other landowners for irrigation. The English rules of mining law were also inappropriate: quite different rules for the delimitation of mineral rights were naturally called for in a 'gold-rush' situation when tens of thousands of prospectors simultaneously rushed into unoccupied areas in search of the precious metal. These and other examples from American legal history decisively demonstrate how much the content of law is determined by the climatic, geographical, economic, and social conditions obtaining at the time, and how they change together. On the way the American courts applied English law, see WENGLER (above p. 239) and KIMBALL (above p. 238) 205 ff., 267 ff., which contains very remarkable documentary sources.

The rules of English Common Law were also much altered by *legislation* in the various states. Many of the American settlers had left their European homes precisely because they were politically, spiritually, or economically oppressed by the rulers there, so the political ideals of an extremely egalitarian and radically democratic society dominated the Houses of Representatives of the American states at the beginning of the nineteenth century and found their strongest expression during the presidency of ANDREW JACKSON (1829–37). Accordingly, the several states passed a great number of statutes which purged land law, family law, and law of succession of its feudal English elements, and also simplified court procedure, abolished professional monopolies, protected needy debtors, especially small manual labourers, against recourse by creditors, and rendered criminal law rather more humane. The actual practice of law was also affected by this development. The view that one could not be a lawyer or a judge without special training or special knowledge struck many people as smacking of medieval privilege, and many of the states enacted provisions whereby every citizen, without more, could practise as a lawyer, unless he were actually in trouble with the criminal law. Provisions of this kind survived in Massachusetts until 1935 and in Indiana until 1933. ROSCOE POUND has described this as a 'deprofessionalisation' of the practice of law; one consequence is that the behaviour of lawyers in court and their standards of professional conduct still strike the foreign observer as being in many respects distinctly informal. In those days it also seemed undemocratic that judges should be nominated by the executive and left in office for long terms or even for life. Consequently almost all states enacted laws providing that judges should be elected by the House of Representatives or directly by the people and that they should stand for re-election after relatively short periods in office. Even today in a clear majority of American states judges are chosen directly by the people in public elections in which candidates mostly appear quite openly on the 'Democratic' or 'Republican' ticket and have their electoral campaigns supported by the relevant party organization. The judges in the rest of the states and the judges in the federal courts are nominated by the executive (the Governor in the states, and the President for federal office), though the agreement of the legislature is often called for. Even in these cases the choice of judge does not simply depend on their professional qualifications, but is affected to an astonishing degree by considerations of party loyalty, of patronage, and of political bargaining. This is clearly true for the judges of the lower state courts but even the federal judges nominated by the President are normally members of his party.

For many years the Bar Associations, the professional organizations of lawyers in America, have been trying with some success to procure that professional competence plays a larger part in the selection of judges. In consequence of their efforts many states have abolished popular election for judicial office and have adopted a system whereby the Governor chooses a judge for each vacant seat from a list of three qualified candidates proposed by an independent committee; the judge who is nominated in this way must put himself up for popular election when his period in office expires, but as no candidate is opposed to him he can normally count on confirmation. The Bar Associations also try to influence the choice of judges by the chief executive. Names of candidates being considered for federal judgeships are normally submitted to a special committee of the American Bar Association, and it is very rare for a President to nominate a candidate whom this committee, after close investigation, has found unsuitable, for in such a case there would be unfavourable publicity.

Another great question of legal policy in the nineteenth century was whether the Common Law in its American form should be comprehensively codified. In 1811 JEREMY BENTHAM wrote a letter to President MADISON, in which he persuasively laid out the advantages of such a step and offered to undertake the task of preparing a code himself. He received a polite but firm refusal. Nevertheless the ideas of BENTHAM and his school were so influential, the example of the French Code so impressive, and the discontent over the unmanageable condition of the Common Law so widespread that the idea of codification took root, first of all in Massachusetts and then in New York, where it found a splendid protagonist in DAVID DUDLEY FIELD, a New York lawyer; from there the idea of codification spread to the other states of the Union and provoked serious discussion everywhere, rather reminiscent of the dispute between THIBAUT and SAVIGNY taking place in Germany about the same time (see p. 139). First of all, FIELD drafted a Code of Civil Procedure whose principal feature was the abolition of the traditional distinction between actions 'at law' and 'in equity', a reform which greatly simplified court procedure in civil matters. New York adopted this code in 1848, and in the following years it became the model for similar codes of procedure in many other states. But with the Civil Code, in which he also had the principal hand, FIELD had less success. The movement for codification had already lost much of its impetus in 1865 when he published his draft. The recent diffusion of the commentaries and treatises of KENT and STORY had helped American law to seem more manageable and orderly but, even more important, the idea of codification ran into strong opposition from the legal profession, which had become organized on the East Coast in the mid-nineteenth century and had become a very influential part of the bourgeois establishment; lawyers had very little interest in seeing their familiar techniques of legal research rendered valueless by means of a code such as

FIELD proposed. But the situation was different in many states of the American *West* where the simpler social circumstances of the 'frontier society' still obtained; here belief in the value of a code whose rational structure made it comprehensible to a simple layman greatly outweighed the interest of lawyers in maintaining received legal traditions. Towards the end of the century the 'Field Code' came into force in North Dakota, South Dakota, Idaho, Montana, and California, and it is still in force in those states today, though with many alterations; one must, however, recognize that its practical significance as a source of law is quite different from what a civil lawyer would expect of a civil code in his own country (see below Ch. 18 III).

On the history of the idea of codification in the United States see HERMAN, 'Schicksal und Zukunft der Kodifikationsidee in Amerika', in ZIMMERMANN (ed.), *Amerikanische Rechtskultur und europäisches Privatrecht* (1995) 45; REIMANN, 'The Historical School Against Codification: Savigny, Carter, and the Defeat of the New York Civil Code' (1989) 37 *Am. J. Comp. L.* 95.

In the course of the nineteenth century there was increasing tension between the industrialized and commercial North, with its concern for protective tariffs, and the planter aristocracy of the agrarian South. This tension came to breaking point over the question of slavery. In a notorious decision of 1857, *Dred Scott* v. *Sandford* (19 How. 393), the Supreme Court decided that a negro slave could not be a citizen of the United States even if he had lived for a time in a state where slavery was not accepted. This decision provoked enormous anger in the North; after ABRAHAM LINCOLN was elected President in 1860 as the candidate of the Republican party which had been founded only a few years previously, the Southern states seceded from the Union and civil war became inevitable. The victory of the North saved the unity of the federation, reinforced federal power, especially by developing the emergency powers of the President, and made the abolition of slavery possible.

II

After the end of the Civil War headlong economic expansion took place in the United States. Enormous progress was made in a few decades: the American West was opened by the construction of railroads, new industries were built up, and the mineral resources of the country were exploited. This called for legal creativity in the fields of company law, the law of insurance and carriage, and in credit, banking, and stock exchange law. These legal creations naturally reflected the prevalent ideas of the time concerning the proper way to order the economy and society as they had been set down, for example, in the works of the English philosopher HERBERT SPENCER, especially in his book *Social Statics* (1850): in this view the only way to ensure the progress of civilization and the maximization of the general good was to give entrepreneurs the greatest possible scope for their freedom of activity, their enterprise, and their individualism. Governmental intervention in the economic process in the interests of protecting the weak was seen as wrong; sacrifices had to be borne by the individual in the name of progress and economic growth. It was not only the substance of the law but also the manner of its presentation and application which answered the needs of the entrepreneurs: financiers, industrialists, and investors were interested in the predictability and stability of judicial decision, and so a situation arose towards the end of the century similar to that in Germany at the height of conceptual jurisprudence when the economic and social policies were very similar: the law took more fixed forms and the judges saw their primary task as being to put the existing stock of rules in dogmatic order; they had a tendency to draw legal consequences from the place in the system where the applicable legal rule had previously been put; this allowed the judges to enjoy the illusion that they could thus insulate themselves from the political and social conflicts of the time and serve as the mere ministers of a timeless sense of justice.

The powerful upsurge of economic activity after the Civil War and the opening up of new and complex areas of law led to major changes in the way American lawyers were trained. Theretofore it had been normal for youngsters to obtain the necessary skills either in the English Inns of Court or by apprenticing themselves to an American lawyer so as to learn trial procedure and the drawing up of deeds, to acquire the tricks of their master's trade and perhaps even to read a little in the *Commentaries* of BLACKSTONE or KENT. Already by the end of the eighteenth century there were some universities where professors were charged with delivering lectures on law. That the study of law should be regarded as a practical preparation for the legal profession and not, as at the English universities, a means of furthering a general education was a view which was accepted under the influence of STORY, a professor at the Harvard Law School from 1829 and a judge of the Supreme Court as well (see KEGEL, *RabelsZ* 43 (1979) 609). The level of legal education, which normally lasted no longer than a year, was admittedly fairly low. Students were admitted to study law without any preparation and normally there were no examinations at all. But a fundamental change set in after 1870. The pacemakers of this development were the Law School of Harvard University and its Dean LANGDELL. Thanks to his efforts the Faculty was greatly increased, the length of the period of instruction was extended to three years, a strict control of performance was established by examinations, and gradually a college education was demanded as a precondition to admission to the Law School. LANGDELL also invented the so-called 'case method', a style of teaching which is still prevalent in American legal education today, though with many variations. The basic idea of this method is that the rules of law should be presented to the student in the context of actual decided cases and should be explained, set in relation to other rules, and subjected to critical discussion only in the context of such cases. The American Bar Association, which had a professional interest in the improvement of legal education, helped to procure the adoption of the demanding Harvard model by the law schools of other universities. The habit of learning practical legal skills in an attorney's office as an apprentice gradually died away and in the United States now, unlike England, law schools have an unchallenged monopoly of legal education.

As the law schools began to flourish, a group of lawyers came on the scene who were to be of great significance for American law in the course of the twentieth century: these were the *professors*. Their influence is connected with a fundamental alteration in legal methods of thinking, coinciding with a change in the view of American society about its ethical and social obligations. This change is best seen in the gradual weakening of the extreme individualistic ideas of the 'social Darwinism' of the period of expansion, and in the growing tendency of the state from the beginning of the twentieth century to subject economic life to supervision and control and deliberately to limit the freedom of activity of the entrepreneur whenever it might cause unacceptable hardship to individual citizens. Even before the turn of the century Congress had moved to repress really gross abuses of contractual freedom; for example, it subjected railroad companies to state supervision and created for this purpose the Interstate Commerce Commission in 1887, the first of the great federal authorities which supervise economic affairs. The Sherman Act of 1890 and the Clayton Act of 1914, with the construction given to them by the courts, afford the federal authorities very extensive powers to repress agreements and practices which are in restraint of trade. Electricity, water, and gas utilities, the news industry, broadcasting, road transport, shipping, and air traffic, all of which are still conducted in the United States, unlike Europe, by private undertakers, were all gradually subjected to state control which soon moved from merely restraining abuses to taking positive action to procure that consumers should receive a proper service at a reasonable price. Numerous statutes were also enacted to protect workmen: federal or state legislation brought in social accident insurance, fixed minimum wages, limited child labour, and set maximum daily hours of work. In this the United States was reproducing a situation which had been brought about in Germany many decades earlier by the social legislation of Bismarck's Empire, patriarchal and paternalistic in tone.

These measures of economic and social policy met with determined opposition from the entrepreneurs of America, in which they could often count on the support of the judges until the 1930s. Thus in 1905 the Supreme Court struck down as unconstitutional a New York statute which forbade the employment of bakers for more than ten hours per day and sixty hours per week: according to the majority such a statute deprived the workers as well as the entrepreneurs of the freedom to conclude contracts of employment 'without due process of law', that is, in breach of the Four-teenth Amendment. But Justice HOLMES delivered a passionate dissenting opinion, whose high-point was the lapidary observation 'The Fourteenth Amendment does not enact Mr. Herbert Spencer's Social Statics' (see *Lochner* v. *State of New York*, 198 US 45 (1905)). As late as 1918 the Supreme Court struck down a federal statute which under certain conditions prohibited the transport of goods whose production involved the employment of children under 14 years of age (see *Hammer* v. *Dagen-hart*, 247 US 251 (1918)). Indeed the first of the New Deal legislation with which Presi-dent ROOSEVELT aimed to bring the country out of the great economic crisis of the 1930s was frustrated by a bare majority of the Supreme Court on constitutional grounds. Here, however, the Court went too far. With ROOSEVELT's enormous elect-oral majority in the autumn of 1936 it became clear that the greater part of the people approved of his legislative plans and he put before Congress the drafts of a statute which would have given him the power to nominate an additional judge to the Supreme Court whenever one of the existing judges, nominated for life, reached the age of 70 without retiring; no less than six of the nine judges were over that age at the time. The President vigorously defended his 'court-packing plan' in public: 'We have reached the point as a nation where we must take action to save the Con-stitution from the court and the court from itself' (*New York Times*, 10 March 1937, p. 1). Whether Congress would at the end of the day have approved the plan is uncer-tain; the question never had to be answered, as one of the judges altered his position and thus converted the minority into the majority—an event not unfairly described by the witticism 'A switch in time saved nine'.

As one can imagine, the analytical and conceptual methods current at the beginning of the century gradually came to seem very implausible in the face of the development of a reformist economic and social policy relying increas-ingly on purposive legislative intervention such as we have outlined; a con-tributory factor may well have been the general acceptance in the United States between 1910 and 1930 of the pragmatic philosophy of WILLIAM JAMES and JOHN DEWEY which opposed all kinds of formalistic, deductive and abstract reasoning; even lawyers must have felt its impact. As early as his publication in 1881 of 'The Common Law' HOLMES in a famous passage attacked the view that the Common Law was an eternally valid manifest-ation of higher reason hovering over the troubled waters of the present, which could be concretized for the individual case by an act of perception on the part of an intellectually detached judge operating on logical and deductive principles:

'The life of the law has not been logic: it has been experience. The felt necessities of the time, the prevalent moral and political theories, intuitions of public policy, avowed or unconscious, even the prejudices which judges share with their fellow-men, have had a good deal more to do than the syllogism in determining the rules by which men should be governed' (id., 1).

In many other places as well, including many of his judgments in court, HOLMES brilliantly critized traditional modes of thought. But ROSCOE

POUND, who ranks in America as the founder of 'sociological jurisprudence' was the first to turn these criticisms into a complete new programme. POUND and his school saw a legal system as being a phenomenon which intimately interacts with the prevalent political, economic, and social circumstances in a given society and which constantly alters with them in a living process of development. They are not interested in the abstract content of 'black letter rules' nor in the logical and analytical connections which may exist between them in a particular system. What they want to discover about legal rules is what concrete effects in social reality they aim to produce as soon as they become 'law in action' by the behaviour of judges or administrative authorities. Thus for POUND law is in the first place a means for the ordering of social interests, and the judge in balancing out these interests should be a 'social engineer' who can only perform his task properly if he has an accurate knowledge of the actual circumstances on which his decision will have an effect. POUND also insisted that teachers of law should have this knowledge:

'The modern teacher of law should be a student of sociology, economics and politics as well. He should know not only what the courts decide and the principles by
which they decide, but quite as much the circumstances and conditions, social and
economic, to which these principles are to be applied . . . [and] the state of popular
thought and feeling which makes the environment in which the principles must operate in practice. Legal monks who pass their lives in an atmosphere of pure law, from
which every worldly and human element is excluded, cannot shape practical principles to be applied to a restless world of flesh and blood. The most logical and skill-
fully reasoned rules may defeat the end of the law in their practical administration
because not adapted to the environment in which they are to be enforced' (POUND,
'The Need for a Sociological Jurisprudence,' 19 *Green Bag* 611–12 (1907), cited by
RUMBLE (above p. 238) 13).

The theories of sociological jurisprudence were further developed in the 1930s by a group of American lawyers representing the school of 'legal real-ism' and carried by them, in the view of many, to extremes. The best-known members of this group were KARL N. LLEWELLYN and JEROME N. FRANK, who are much more sceptical than POUND in their view of the value of abstractly formulated rules of law as descriptions or predictions of the actual behaviour of judges. For them law cannot be learnt from the 'paper rules' of textbooks but only from keen observation of 'judicial behaviour', that is, *what the courts actually do*. In this they adopt the standpoint of HOLMES, who said in a phrase which has become proverbial, that by law he under-stood 'the prophecies of what the courts will do in fact, and nothing more pretentious' ('The Path of the Law,' 10 *Harv. L. Rev.* 457, 460 f. (1897)). So LLEWELLYN: he describes judges, judicial officials and lawyers as 'officials of the law' and then defines as follows: 'What these officers do about dis-putes is, to my mind, the law itself' (*The Bramble Bush* (1951) 12). Pursuant to this idea, the 'realists' saw their principal task as being the discovery and analysis of the factors which lead the 'law official', especially the judge, to decide the concrete case in the way he does and not otherwise. They started from the conviction that the traditional doctrines of law were relatively insignificant for the actual decision on the merits in many cases and simply offered a means whereby the judge could *ex post facto* 'rationalize' a decision which he had arrived at by another path. Even the principle of the binding force of precedents seemed to the 'realists' to be very far indeed from guaranteeing that certainty of law and predictability of future decisions claimed for it by orthodoxy: for, as LLEWELLYN tried to show, the judge had at his disposal dozens of techniques by which he could cull exactly what he wanted out of previous decisions. What really determined the disposal of a case—and that was what legal scholarship and research should look to—was rather the particular social and economic context of the particular case, a matter wholly ignored by the traditional rules of law which are generally far too widely framed. Another determinant is the judge's personal predilections and antipathies, as well as his moral values and his political beliefs; a further critical factor is the degree to which the judge at first instance got the facts of the case wrong or failed to understand them.

Many of the ideas developed by 'sociological jurisprudence' and 'legal realism' obviously underlie the 'École de la libre recherche scientifique' in France (see above p. 96) and the 'Freirechtsschule' in Germany, as well as the frequent demands that we should investigate the facts behind the law and have greater co-operation between the sciences of law and sociology. But in Germany and France these ideas did not have the enormous response in all areas of legal life which the ideas of POUND and the realists had in the United States: 'the attitude towards legal problems, characterised as realistic jurisprudence . . . has dominated legal thinking in the United States during the past generation, even to the point of becoming commonplace' (YNTEMA (above p. 239) 325). For example, in the area of *legal education*, a glance at a recent American casebook shows that law courses nowadays cover much more than court decisions and the rules of law formulated in them; they also cover economic facts, medical, psychiatric, and criminological information, the usages of business life, and the standard forms of contract. Consistently enough, the faculties of the large law schools today often include political scientists, doctors, and sociologists who co-operate closely with the lawyers in both teaching and research. Even in the practice of the courts there are many alterations which can be traced back to this new way of thinking. Thus already in 1907, in the case of *Muller* v. *Oregon*, 208 US 412 (1908), LOUIS BRANDEIS put before the Supreme Court, of which he was later to become a famous judge, a brief containing a wide range of factual data and comparative legal material germane to the question of law in dispute; the 'Brandeis brief' caused a sensation at the time but it has since become a fixed concept in America and has established itself in constitutional disputes and also in other matters. Then there are many judges in the United States whose judgments demonstrate the influence of 'sociological jurisprudence' by displaying a scepticism about doctrine, a sense of reality, and an open weighing of the social interests at stake. And finally *legal writing* shows how firmly established in the United States these new ideas are. For while in Germany, with few exceptions, these questions are discussed only at the level of principle and philosophy in a rudimentary manner, in the United States for some decades past writers have addressed themselves to the much more difficult task of testing the value of sociological research methods by applying them to practical problems of law.

Rules of law have thus been analysed in the light of sociology and political science. Recently they have also been analysed in terms of *economics*. POSNER's *Economic Analysis of Law* (2nd edn., 1977) is the leading work. Its hypothesis is that in order to maximize the general welfare the limited resources available in any society should be made available to those individuals who can use them to best advantage. This is normally achieved through exchange transactions whereby a person gives up certain assets, such as property or services, in order to obtain from his partner other assets which have a greater value for him than those he gives up. Under certain conditions the situation produced by such operations is 'efficient', since all scarce resources have been channelled by market operations to the place where their use is of the greatest value, and the general good cannot be increased by any further exchange operations. This hypothesis can be used to test legal rules in order to see whether they contribute to an 'efficient' distribution of scarce resources or, to put the point in another way, whether they promote a situation in which the acts of individuals directed to their own private gain also conduce to the advantage of society. To take an example from the law of tort, one can show that the courts habitually classify conduct as 'negligent' and therefore impose liability if the steps which the person causing the harm could have taken to avoid it would have cost less than the expense due to the occurrence of the damage. Or in contract law one could say that whether or not the courts should hold an exculpatory clause invalid as being 'contrary to good faith', 'unconscionable', or 'unfair' should depend on whether or not it places the relevant risk on the party who can more cheaply avoid it or, in the case of a risk which it is impossible or uneconomic to avoid, insure against it. This 'economic analysis' is applied to all aspects of law by professorial votaries in the leading law schools in the United States, and there are special periodicals for its practitioners and critics. Of course there are limits to the utility of this approach but there is no doubt that it can help one to recognize the conflicts of aim which lurk in problems of legal policy, to determine the necessary priorities, and to discuss them rationally after a sober evaluation of means and ends, cost, and utility.

III

The United States has been said to possess 'perhaps the most complicated legal structure that has ever been devised and made effective in man's effort to govern himself' (GRISWOLD (above p. 238) 3). The point of this observation becomes clear when one sees the problems which have arisen in the United States from the complexities of the concurrence of federal and state law, and from the fact that both the United States and the several states possess fully equipped courts systems.

Under the Constitution the United States Congress has legislative competence only in specified areas: apart from currency and coin, the levying of taxes and excises, foreign affairs, and defence, the most important are citizenship, the protection of trade and copyright, bankruptcy, maritime law, and finally the control of commerce with foreign nations and among the several states. It can be seen from this that the whole of private law and the rest of commercial law fall within the competence of the 50 individual states. Given these facts, one must ask whether one can really talk of 'American law' in the way one talks of German or English law and, if so, with what qualifications.

Regarding the division of legislative power between the United States and the member states, the Supreme Court has always been able to construe the Constitution in such a way that the development of a large and economically integrated internal market in the United States has not been seriously inhibited by legal differences. Art. I §8 of the Constitution provides that the United States has power, in addition to the powers expressly attributed to it, to enact laws 'necessary and proper' for carrying these powers into execution. As early as 1819 the Supreme Court under Chief Justice MARSHALL, himself an outstanding judicial statesman, used this clause to construct the doctrine of implied powers which gives the United States very generous room for play in its legislative activities; *McCulloch* v. *Maryland*, 4 Wheat. 316 (1819). But the principal device for extending the federal powers and thereby restricting those of the states has been the 'commerce clause', that provision of the Constitution which gives the United States power to pass laws to regulate commerce among the several states. The way the scope of this clause has been gradually extended to suit the needs of an expanding economy is one of the most fascinating chapters in the development of American constitutional law. Even today the United States has no power to pass laws regulating economic matters in 'intrastate commerce', that is, matters which occur within the boundaries of one state only, but by the decision in which the Supreme Court endorsed the New Deal legislation this principle was so emptied of content that it no longer really limits the power of the United States to pass such laws if it has any reasonable interest in doing so.

But in the central areas of private law the competence of the several states is as large as ever. This means not only that the legislatures of each of the 50 states can pass their own statutes in the area of family and succession law, contract and tort, land law, partnership, insurance, and negotiable instruments law, but also that the judges in these areas are free to develop the law of their state in different directions, as in fact they often do. Thus the

United States can be seen as a gigantic laboratory for legal policy in which any state can move forward in any direction by legislation or judicial decision and thus gain experience and reach views which enrich the debates on legal policy and may serve as an encouraging or horrifying example to other states.

Of course the egoism of individual states sometimes leads them on fairly obvious grounds to marked deviations—the extensive divorce practice of Nevada and the generous company law of Delaware are well-known examples—but there are also institutions which help the cause of legal unification or help to emphasize the similarities which already exist. Here we must mention the American *law schools*. Of course every law school is located in one state or another and law schools are largely financed by the resources of their home state unless they form part of a private university. Nevertheless most law schools would not think of training their students only in the law of New York or the law of Michigan, for example; instead, these law schools teach their students, who themselves come from all over the country, a *common American law* which admittedly does not exist as positive law anywhere. Classes and casebooks by no means ignore the interesting results which particular states may have arrived at, but they are looked at as being merely local variations of a theme which in principle is unitary and they are approached with the critical detachment of a person who knows that there are always other rules somewhere which have different formulations but reach the same results. So in the training of American lawyers the critical methods of comparative law play an important part from the very beginning; at the same time the young lawyer comes to think of American law as something which is basically unitary, though this will be counteracted by the state chauvinism which he will later meet in his professional career.

Another indication of the unitary basis of American private law, despite all the local variants, is the success with which it has for some time been being compiled in the so-called 'Restatements'. Since the increasing flood of precedents was making the law cumbrous and unmanageable it seemed sensible to record it in a clearly ordered and systematically constructed 'Restatement'; this task was entrusted to the 'American Law Institute', founded in 1923 by the American Bar Association in conjunction with judges and law teachers. The following procedure was adopted. A leading scholar is selected as 'Reporter' for each legal topic; his task is to absorb all the existing case-law, to extract general rules, and, in association with a group of advisers including experienced lawyers, judges, and professors, to formulate a text which needs the endorsement of certain committees of the American Law Institute before it is published as a 'Restatement'. The task of the reporter is to lay down the law in its *present positive form* and not to improve or modernize it. Nevertheless in cases where the rules of the various states are inconsistent they may choose the solution which seems to them to be the more progressive, even if it obtains only in a minority of states. By this means Restatements have been produced for all important areas of American private law except family law and the law of succession—for example, the general law of contract, tort, trusts, conflicts of law—and many of them have already appeared in a second edition. Restatements are rather like the Civil Law codes in their systematic structure of abstractly formulated rules, and in many cases the Continental jurist can use them as a means of easy access to the rules of American private law in the first instance. Warning should be given, however, not to use them too uncritically, for the only way to be sure whether a particular rule is in force in a particular state is by consulting the judicial decisions of that state. If the problem in question has not yet been decided or clearly decided in that state, an American judge will often have recourse to the Restatement, but will normally accord it only fractionally more weight than he would to a leading textbook, and that, in a Common Law country, is not very much.

As early as the end of the nineteenth century it was recognized in the United States that it would be very desirable to have particular topics regulated by identical statutes in all the states. On the prompting of the American Bar Association, all states eventually agreed to send three to five representatives to a national body, the *National Conference of Commissioners on Uniform State Laws*, which was given the task of drafting Uniform Acts for those areas where intra-American unification seemed especially desirable, and to propose them to the legislatures of the several states for enactment with the minimum possible amendment. This Conference met for the first time in 1892 and has since worked on many dozens of such Uniform Laws, most of them dealing with very specific and narrow questions, but sometimes also covering whole areas of law, such as the law of bills and notes. Many of the Uniform Acts so produced have been adopted by all the states, while others have had only sporadic success, but by and large the efforts of the Conference have substantially promoted legal unification in the American states, especially in the area of commercial law where the need for unitary rules is outstandingly clear.

So far, the *Uniform Commercial Code* is the most significant and successful undertaking of the Conference, in association with the American Law Institute. In 1940 the Conference determined on a fundamental revision of the existing Uniform Laws on commercial matters, of which, for example, the statute on negotiable instruments had been adopted by all states and the law of sales by most; they were then to be brought together in a Commercial Code. The work was put in charge of LLEWELLYN who left his mark on the construction, scope and methods of the Code. In 1952 a first draft was submitted for comment to hundreds of merchants, commercial agents, bankers, carriers, and warehousemen. Note was taken of their criticisms and in 1956 a final version appeared which has subsequently been adopted in all the states of the Union. Louisiana has not adopted it in its entirety, and many states found it necessary to make verbal alterations, but they do not amount to much. Thus essentially the same rules apply today in all of the United States to sale, transactions involving negotiable instruments, cheques, warehouse receipts, bills of lading, certificates of deposit, and so on, as well as to the collection of commercial paper and the very important area of credit and security, with the exception of mortgage.

Enough has been said to make it clear that there is often a confusing hodgepodge of federal law and state law. As a rule of thumb one can say that the law relating to the control of the economy is federal law, although the states often have concurrent laws or even act in place of the United States, as in the control of the insurance industry. Important areas of commercial law, especially the sale of goods and connected credit and security arrangements, are regulated by state law, but with substantially the same content in consequence of the introduction of the Uniform Commercial Code. Other areas of commercial law, such as company law (except for the federal supervision of the stock exchange and share dealings) and the law of insurance, are covered by the laws of the various states which still show marked divergencies, while the law of bankruptcy, the protection of industrial property, and maritime law fall within the exclusive competence of the United States by reason of the Constitution. In the general law of contract, in tort and land law, and in family and succession law the legal systems of the several states control; they are in general agreement in basic concepts, methods, and solutions, but often show so marked a variation on individual points that it is of the greatest importance to know which state law applies to a case which has connections with several states. Here the rules of conflicts of law, mainly unwritten, apply, being themselves part of state law and therefore capable of variation from state to state, subject to minimum standards inferred from the Constitution.

The situation in the United States is rendered even more complicated by the fact that there are complete courts systems not only in each of the several states but also in the United States. So far as the *federal courts* are concerned, by art. III §1 of the Constitution, the judicial power of the federation is vested in the Supreme Court and 'such inferior Courts as the Congress may from time to time ordain and establish'. In 1789, in one of the very first Acts passed by it, Congress exercised the power to create lower federal courts by establishing *District Courts* as federal courts of first instance and, as courts of appeal, courts which were later called *Courts of Appeals*. There are close to 100 District Courts in the United States, many states having only one while other states with large populations may be divided into two or four districts each of which has a District Court; furthermore many districts have more than one judge, so that in total there are about 650 'District Judges' who normally sit alone. For appeals from judgments of the District Courts there are 12 Courts of Appeals: the catchment area or 'circuit' of 11 of them includes several states each, and there is one for the District of Columbia

Circuit. There are about 170 judges in these Courts of Appeals who sit in benches of three. Finally, at the head of the federal courts stands the Supreme Court in Washington with nine judges.

In order to keep the Supreme Court's workload within limits, an Act of 1925 gave the judges discretion to decide which cases were important enough to justify an appeal being heard by the highest court of the land. According to the normal practice, the Supreme Court will 'grant *certiorari*' and proceed to a decision on the merits if, after a summary consideration of the case, at least four judges are in favour of so doing. If not, no reasons are given for refusal, though very occasionally one of the justices will briefly say why he would have chosen to hear the case. It does not follow from the grant of *certiorari* that there will be oral argument. The Court may decide the matter on the basis of the briefs which have been submitted; such a decision 'per curiam' is normally unanimous and contains either no reasons at all or only very brief reasons for confirming or quashing the judgment in question. In a specific group of cases the parties are entitled to a decision on the merits, for example, where the highest court of a state has held a state statute constitutional, despite attack, or a federal statute unconstitutional, or where a federal court has held a federal statute unconstitutional in a case to which the United States is a party. In these cases there must be a decision on the merits but not necessarily oral proceedings, as the Supreme Court may give a summary judgment upholding the decision in question if it is of the view that the case raises no real question of principle in federal law.

The courts systems of the different states are so diverse that one can hardly make any general statements. In rural areas trivial matters both civil and criminal are dealt with by part-time judges of the peace; they hardly ever have any legal training and the procedure they employ is a very simplified one. In the large cities the lowest courts are often the so-called 'Municipal Courts', staffed by qualified judges, which as 'Traffic Courts' concentrate on highway offences or as 'Small Claim Courts' deal with civil matters of small importance. Civil and criminal matters which are more serious first go to courts which always have a single judge, in many states called 'County Courts', in others 'District Courts', and in New York even the 'Supreme Court'; their procedure is formal and may involve a jury in specified cases. Appeals against judgements of these courts often go straight to the highest court of the state; only about 15 states with large populations have an intermediate court of appeal, thus providing three levels of court.

By far the largest number of civil suits in the United States is decided by state courts. Federal courts have jurisdiction only under specified conditions, most of which are laid down in the Constitution, for example, cases in which the United States is a party and cases where the complaint is based on a provision of federal law ('federal question jurisdiction'). The fear that the courts of a state might not afford complete justice to a party domiciled in another state explains the existence of federal jurisdiction in another class of case: the Constitution provides that the federal courts shall be competent if the parties are citizens of, that is, are domiciled in, different states ('diversity of citizenship jurisdiction'), but a federal statute imposes a further requirement, that the matter in issue must exceed $10,000 in value. A legal person counts as a citizen of the state of its incorporation, and if it has its chief place of business in some other state it counts as a citizen of that state also.

It follows from the rules of jurisdiction in 'diversity of citizenship' cases that, to take an example, a federal court sitting in California can decide a suit brought by a Texan for damages in tort against a Californian defendant. The question immediately arises whether the federal court should apply Californian or Texan tort law or whether it may not have to apply federal tort law instead. For nearly a century after the Supreme Court decision in *Swift* v. *Tyson*, 16 Pet. 1 (1842) it was established that in areas of judge-made law such as tort, the federal courts should apply not the case-law of any particular state but rules of federal law which were to be independently developed. This decision was based on the hope that in this way the decisions of the federal courts might gradually build up a 'federal common law' which might be taken over by the courts of the several states and thus form a point around which unified American law might crystallize. This hope has not borne fruit. The courts of the states were far from following decisions of the federal courts and often enough hit upon deviant rules. This gave litigants an incentive to try all kinds of devices to bring the case before the federal rather than the state courts or vice versa, depending on whether federal or state common law offered them the more favourable rule. These unfortunate effects induced the Supreme Court in *Erie Railroad Co.* v. *Tompkins*, 304 US 64 (1938) to abandon its previous holding and decide that, except in cases controlled by a federal statute, federal courts should in principle apply the written or unwritten law of the state in which it sat. This applies also to questions of conflicts of law; thus in the example with which we started this paragraph, the federal court must answer the question whether Californian or Texan tort law is to be applied in accordance with the conflict rules of California, the state in which it sits, and not by federal rules.

18

Law-Finding and Procedure in
Common Law and Civil Law

AMOS, 'The Interpretation of Statutes', 5 *Camb. LJ* 163 (1933–5).

ATIYAH/SUMMERS, *Form and Substance in Anglo-American Law, A Comparative Study of Legal Reasoning, Legal Theory, and Legal Institutions* (1987).

BENNION, *On Statute Law* (3rd edn. 1990).

BRIDGE, 'National Legal Tradition and Community Law: Legislative Drafting and Judicial Interpretation in England and the European Community', *J. Common Market Studies* 1981, 351.

CAPPELLETTI, 'The Doctrine of Stare Decisis and the Civil Law: A Fundamental Difference—Or No Difference at All?', *Festschrift Zweigert* (1981) 381.

CARDOZO, *The Nature of the Judicial Process* (1921).

COOPER, 'The Common Law and the Civil Law—A Scot's View', 63 *Harv. L. Rev.* 468 (1950).

——, 'The Civil Law and the Common Law: Some Points of Comparison', 15 *Am. J. Comp. L.* 419 (1967).

CROSS/BELL/ENGLE, *Statutory Interpretation* (2nd edn., 1987).

DAINOW (ed.), *The Role of Judicial Decisions and Doctrine in Civil Law and in Mixed Jurisdictions* (1974).

DALE, *Legislative Drafting, A New Approach* (1977).

DAWSON, *The Oracles of the Law* (1968).

DICKERSON, *The Interpretation and Application of Statutes* (1975).

ESSER, *Grundsatz und Norm in der richterlichen Fortbildung des Privatrechts* (2nd edn., 1964).

FIKENTSCHER, *Methoden des Rechts* IV (1977) 269.

——, 'Die Theorie der Fallnorm als Grundlage von Kodex- und Fallrecht (code law and case law)', *ZfRV* 1980, 161.

FRANKEL, *Partisan Justice* (1978).

FRANKFURTER, 'Some Reflections on the Reading of Statutes', 47 *Colum. L. Rev.* 527 (1947).

FRIEDMANN, 'A Re-Examination of the Relations Between English, American and Continental Jurisprudence', 20 *Can. Bar Rev.* 175 (1942).

GOODHART, 'Precedent in English and Continental Law', 50 *LQ Rev.* 40 (1934).

HERMAN, 'Quot iudices tot sententiae: A Study of the English Reaction to Continental Interpretive Techniques', 1981 *JSPTL* 165.

JACOB, *The Fabric of English Civil Justice* (Hamlyn Lectures, 1987).

JONES, 'Should Judges be Politicians?: The English Experience', 57 *Ind. LJ* 211 (1982).

KÖTZ, 'The Role of the Judge in the Court Room, The Common Law and Civil Law Compared', 1987 *S. Afr. LJ* 35.

——, 'Zur Funktionsteilung zwischen Richter und Anwalt im deutschen und englischen Zivilprozess', *Festschrift Zajtay* (1982) 277.

LAWSON, 'The Art of Drafting Statutes', *Festschrift Zweigert* (1981) 879.

LEVITSKY, 'The Europeanization of the British Legal Style', 42 *Am. J. Comp. L.* 347 (1994).

LLEWELLYN, *The Bramble Bush* (1930).

LÜCKE, 'The Common Law: Judicial Impartiality and Judge-Made Law', 98 *LQ Rev.* 29 (1982).

MARSH, *Interpretation in a National and International Context* (1974).

v. MEHREN, 'The Significance for Procedural Practice and Theory of the Concentrated Trial: Comparative Remarks', *Festschrift Coing* (1982) 361.

MUNDAY, 'The Common Lawyer's Philosophy of Legislation', *Rechtstheorie* 14 (1983) 191.

POUND, 'What Is The Common Law?', in: *The Future of the Common Law* (1937) 3.

——, *The Spirit of the Common Law* (1921).

——, 'Common Law and Legislation', 21 *Harv. L. Rev.* 383 (1908).

RABEL, 'Civil Law and Common Law', 10 *La. L. Rev.* 431 (1949), reprinted in: Rabel, *Gesammelte Aufsätze* III (ed. Leser, 1967) 312.

RADBRUCH, *Der Geist des englischen Rechts* (1947).

RADIN, 'A Short Way with Statutes', 56 *Harv. L. Rev.* 388 (1942).

RHEINSTEIN, 'The Common Law and the Civil Law: An Elementary Comparison', *Rev. jur. Univ. Puerto Rico* 22 (1952/1953) 90.

RUDDEN, 'Courts and Codes in England, France and Soviet Russia', 48 *Tul. L. Rev.* 1010 (1974).

SAUVEPLANNE, *Codified and Judge Made Law, The Role of Courts and Legislators in Civil and Common Law Systems* (1982).

SCHMITTHOFF, 'Der Zivilprozess als Schlüssel zum englischen Rechtsdenken', *JZ* 1972, 38.

——, 'Systemdenken und Fallrecht in der Entwicklung des englischen Privatrechts', *JZ* 1967, 1.

——, 'Non stamus decisis', *Festschrift Coing* (1982) 469.

STEVENS, *Law and Politics, The House of Lords as a Judicial Body* (1978).

ZANDER, *The Law-Making Process* (4th edn., 1994).

——, *A Matter of Justice, The Legal System in Ferment* (1989).

I

BEFORE embarking on a comparison of the different methods of law-finding characteristic of Common Law and Civil Law jurisdictions respectively, it is as well to remind ourselves of the great differences in political, social, and intellectual history in England and on the Continent, for they affected the whole of legal life, including the way that sources of law were dealt with. As we have seen, the Kings of England had succeeded by the early Middle Ages in concentrating the practice of law in just a few courts in London; this made it possible for a Common Law effective throughout the country to evolve from native sources. A well-organized guild of influential layers grew up around these central courts, with independence enough to select, train, and admit new members to practice and even to procure that only their own members should be appointed to the judiciary. Things were quite different in Germany, whose history in the Middle Ages is the story of the progressive enfeeblement of the Empire; this delayed the growth of central courts and administrative agencies, and prevented the rise of a 'class of Imperial jurists', which made it difficult for the indigenous law to put up much opposition to the advance of Roman law (see above Ch. 10 II). Roman law as it appeared on the scene was 'scholars' law'—professors had rediscovered it in the universities of Northern Italy, professors had refined and developed it with the methods of scholasticism and humanism, and only professors taught it—one had to go to university to learn it. Thus the law in Germany after the Reception had a rather *academic and theoretical* quality, not the *forensic and pragmatic* character it had acquired in England; it was controlled by *university teachers* rather than by *legal practitioners* and it was to be found in *textbooks* rather than in *law reports*. Here also we find the origins of the habit which still survives in Germany of treating the practice of law as a function of the state bureaucracy and the judiciary as a part of the civil service. The civilian jurists who established themselves in Germany during the Reception were mainly employed on the administrative staffs of the many territorial rulers where their dependent position as the princes' official advisers made it impossible for them to combine in guilds or professional bodies and achieve the power which an independent social group can acquire. Although in the course of the eighteenth century the practice of law became detached from the general internal government of the state, it nevertheless kept its administrative flavour, the more so as procedure of the roman-canonical cast—written, secret, and authoritarian—was replacing the old method of resolving disputes by means of lay judges and jurors. In France, too, after the Revolution had destroyed the 'noblesse de robe' of the *ancien régime*, the judges of the restored Empire, like the judges of Prussia and Austria, saw themselves as 'servants of the state', anonymous members of a Ministry of Justice which appointed, promoted, remunerated, decorated, and pensioned them off, operating a code conceived as comprehensive and conclusive, and following an extreme doctrine of the separation of powers which sought to restrict to the minimum the judges' scope for creativity and which claimed that the disputes of real life could be resolved by mere acts of subsumption.

Given that the development of political ideas and institutions in Western Europe was quite different from that in England and that in consequence the standing of the judge, the role of the advocate, the methods of legal education, and the forms of procedure all differed widely, it will come as no surprise that the techniques of discovering and applying the law, indeed the typical methods of legal thought as a whole, have developed very differently. Roscoe Pound described this difference as follows:

'Behind the characteristic doctrines and ideas and technique of the common-law lawyer there is a significant frame of mind. It is a frame of mind which habitually looks at things in the concrete, not in the abstract; which puts its faith in experience rather than in abstractions. It is a frame of mind which prefers to go forward cautiously on the basis of experience from this case or that case to the next case, as justice in each case seems to require, instead of seeking to refer everything back to supposed universals. It is a frame of mind which is not ambitious to deduce the decision for the case in hand from a proposition formulated universally . . . It is the frame of mind behind the surefooted Anglo-Saxon habit of dealing with things as they arise instead of anticipating them by abstract universal formulas' (*What is the Common Law?* (above p. 257) 18 f.).—Lord Cooper (above p. 256, p. 470 f.), an eminent Scottish judge familiar with both the Common Law and the Civil Law, expressed himself similarly: 'A civilian system differs from a common law system much as rationalism differs from empiricism or deduction from induction. The civilian naturally reasons from principles to instances, the common lawyer from instances to principles. The civilian puts his faith in syllogisms, the common lawyer in precedents; the first silently asking himself as each new problem arises, "What should we do this time?" and the second asking aloud in the same situation, "What did we do last time?" . . . The instinct of a civilian is to systematise. The working rule of the common lawyer is *solvitur ambulando*.'

But here it is as well to issue a word of warning. Undoubtedly there are differences in the style of legal thinking in the countries of the Common Law on the one hand and on the Continent of Europe on the other, but it would certainly be wrong to make out that there was an unbridgeable opposition between the former's method of inductive problem-solving and the latter's method of systematic conceptualism. Such an antithesis would emphasize the dominant trends and tendencies in the Common Law and Civil Law but, in its absolute form, it would be an increasingly inaccurate and incomplete reflection of what can actually be seen happening in these two great legal families today when lawyers set about the task of discovering the law.

II

According to a view expressed in England in 1934 by Goodhart, the critical difference between Continental and English methods of legal thinking lies in the doctrine of the *binding force of precedent* (*stare decisis*) (above p. 256, p. 42). At first sight this view seems plausible even today. The doctrine lays down that every English court is bound by all decisions handed down by courts superior to it in the hierarchy; and, until quite recently, the doctrine laid down that the superior courts, namely the Court of Appeal and the House of Lords, were bound to treat their *own* previous decisions as absolutely binding. A previous decision is 'binding' in the sense that it must be followed whether it forms part of a series of similar decisions or whether it stands quite alone, whether it was handed down the previous year or a century ago, and even if the rule it lays down now seems inappropriate because of altered social circumstances or for some other reason. It had always been recognized in England that courts which were faced with the task of discovering the law should take note of previous decisions and follow them whenever this seemed proper on the facts of the case. Indeed, given the absence of any comprehensive legislative regulation this was the only reasonable thing to do unless every individual case was to be decided *de novo* in a form of cadi-justice. But it was only in the late nineteenth century that the doctrine took the rigorous form we have sketched above—decisions binding even if the result seems repellent to the judge, superior courts bound by their own decisions; it was a product not of legislation but of judicial decision; the courts forged their own fetters.

Of course English judges have devised various ways and means which enable them to 'distinguish a precedent', that is, to avoid following a previous decision which is unsatisfactory. A previous decision is binding only where the basic reason underlying the decision, the so-called 'ratio decidendi', covers the instant dispute. But in many cases it is extremely doubtful what the 'ratio decidendi' of the previous decision is, and what is merely 'obiter dictum'. Take the case where a mother suffers a nervous shock as a result of witnessing a traffic accident in which her child is killed, and a court grants her claim for damages against the careless driver. The *ratio decidendi* of this decision will certainly cover a subsequent case in which, all the other facts being the same, a *father* witnesses the death of his child, but it is not clear that the *ratio decidendi* of the first decision would require the driver to be held liable in a later case where the child was only injured or merely endangered instead of being killed, or where the plaintiff was not a relative of the child. Before the judge can resolve these questions he must scrutinize the precedent keenly, he must examine the arguments presented by the advocates before him, but above all he must carefully sift any related decisions handed down before or after the precedent in question: this intellectual process follows certain rules of the judicial art but it is open at every step to the influence of conscious or unconscious *value-judgments*.

On this see ATIYAH/SUMMERS (above p. 256) 118 ff. The discovery of the *ratio decidendi* can be particularly difficult when the previous judge based his decision on two concurrent and equal lines of reasoning or when the precedent comes from a superior court whose judges, unanimously or by a majority, agreed on the result but differed as to the method of reaching it. Again, can a decision of a court be ignored if it is inconsistent with another decision of the same court? Can it be ignored as given *per incuriam* if it overlooked a legislative provision or if a particular legal point was not put forward by the advocates or raised by the court? English law has developed a whole series of sophisticated doctrines in reponse to these and similar questions. On this see the writings of CROSS (above p. 256). CROSS concludes that the technique of 'distinguishing a precedent' is now so lax that one must ask 'whether the spectacle of an English judge labouring under the brutal fetters of a rigid doctrine of precedent is not something which, if it exists at all, exists only in the minds of academic lawyers' (82 *LQ Rev.* 203, 214 (1966)).

The attitude of *American* courts in this matter is more flexible still. Legal publishers in the United States issue hundreds of volumes of judicial decisions every year without making any critical selection of them and the mass of material is so enormous that it is virtually impossible to expect that *all* relevant precedents be taken into account. But more than this, the political, social, and economic development of the United States has been so dramatic and the consequent alterations in the substance of the legal order so swift that the superior courts could never have adopted the view that they were absolutely bound by their *own* previous decisions. It was clear that the *Supreme Court*, dealing with constitutional matters, had to be free to depart from a previous decision ('to overrule a precedent') since otherwise the only way to overcome its obsolete decisions would have been by amending the *text* of the Constitution, an extremely complex and slow procedure requiring the ratification of three-quarters of the component states. But in the *states* as well the highest courts have shown an increasing readiness in the last few decades to ask whether the rules laid down in the case-law, even those which have repeatedly been confirmed in a series of decisions, are still in touch with the needs and interests of the times.

Such an investigation often leads to the conclusion that the old rules are no longer apt; an 'overruling decision' is rendered and a fundamental change in the case-law takes place; this can be inferred from the way courts and writers keep discussing the question what protection, if any, should be given to persons who entered into transactions in reliance on the 'old' judicial decisions. Many American courts adopt the practice of 'prospective overruling': in the judgment in which the 'new' rule is laid down for the first time they state that it is to be effective only in the future: see ATIYAH/SUMMERS (above p. 256) 146 f.; PROBST, *Die Änderung der Rechtsprechung, Eine rechtsvergleichende methodologische Untersuchung zum Phänomen der höchstrichterlichen Rechtsprechungsänderung in der Schweiz und den USA* (1993).

Even in England it seems that the doctrine of binding precedent is not accepted as wholeheartedly as it was some years ago. Indeed, the most objectionable part of the doctrine, the rule that the House of Lords was strictly bound by its own previous decisions, was abandoned in 1966. This did not, as one might have expected, occur by Act of Parliament or in the course of a judicial decision; instead the Lord Chancellor simply made a declaration ('Practice Statement') in open court in the name of all the Law Lords. It read as follows:

'Their Lordships regard the use of precedent as an indispensable foundation upon which to decide what is the law and its application to individual cases. It provides at least some degree of certainty upon which individuals can rely in the conduct of their affairs as well as a basis for orderly development of legal rules.

Their Lordships nevertheless recognise that too rigid adherence to precedent may lead to injustice in a particular case and also unduly restrict the proper development of the law. They propose, therefore, to modify their present practice and, while treating former decisions of this House as normally binding, to depart from a previous decision when it appears right to do so.

In this connection they will bear in mind the danger of disturbing retrospectively the basis on which contracts, settlements of property and fiscal arrangements have been entered into and also the special need for certainty as to the criminal law.

This announcement is not intended to affect the use of precedent elsewhere than in this House.' ([1966] 1 WLR 1234.)

By taking this step, which is primarily of psychological significance, the House of Lords has abandoned only one of the extreme outposts of the doctrine but it is probable that it will gradually lead to further restrictions on the doctrine, for in the present day it is, in its rigorous form, 'an antiquated English peculiarity', as RABEL put it (*RabelsZ* 16 (1951) 340, 344). If the view that 'too rigid adherence to precedent may . . . unduly restrict the proper development of the law' is taken seriously, it must follow that in future the *Court of Appeal* should also free itself from the binding force of its own previous judgments, a proposal for which LORD DENNING strove tirelessly, but without success.

See his dissenting opinions in *Gallie* v. *Lee* [1969] 2 Ch. 17 and *Barrington* v. *Lee* [1972] 1 QB 326. LORD DENNING's view was rejected by a unanimous House of Lords in *Davis* v. *Johnson* [1979] AC 264.

A quick look round the Continent shows that matters are not really very different there. It is true that there is never any legal rule which compels a judge to follow the decisions of a higher court, but the reality is different. In practice a judgment of the Court of Cassation or of the Bundesgerichtshof in Germany today can count on being followed by lower courts just as much as a judgment of an appeal court in England or in the United States. This is true not only when the judgment of the superior court follows a line of similar decisions; in practice even an isolated decision of the Bundesgerichtshof in Germany enjoys the greatest respect, and it is very rare and not at all typical for a judge openly to deviate from such a decision. In France the situation is much the same:

See, for example, DAVID/DE VRIES, *The French Legal System* (1958) 113 ff.: 'Despite the absence of a formal doctrine of stare decisis, there is a strong tendency on the part of the French courts, like those of other countries, to follow precedents, especially those of the higher courts . . . The Cour de Cassation can, of course, always overrule its own prior decisions. But it is equally certain that it will not do so without weighty reasons . . . The attitude of the lower courts toward decisions of the Cour de Cassation is in substance quite similar to that of the lower courts in common law jurisdictions towards decisions of superior courts. Even a single precedent established by the Cour de Cassation will usually be followed, though it cannot be cited as the only basis for the decision. Certain factors may, however, induce the lower courts to seek reasons for deciding contrary to a prior decision of the Cour de Cassation. One such factor may be the expectation that an old decision of the Cour de Cassation would not be followed by that court in the light of new conditions.' See also ANCEL, 'French Case Law', 16 *J. Comp. Leg.* I (1934), and DAVID, *Le Droit français* I (1960) 160 ff.

Accordingly it is hardly an exaggeration to say that the doctrine of *stare decisis* in the Common Law and the practice of Continental courts generally lead to the same results: 'The practical differences . . . are microscopic' (RABEL in *RabelsZ* 16 (1951) 340, 345, criticized by CAPPELLETTI (above p. 256)). In fact, when a judge can find in one or more decisions of a supreme court a rule which seems to him relevant for the decision in the case before him, he will follow those decisions and the rules they contain as much in Germany as in England or France. Of course in order to be able to *follow* a rule, the judge must first have extracted it from the case-law; and in the *method of extracting such rules* there are still very considerable differences between the Common Law and the Civil Law.

The Common Law judge's technique of approaching the case-law and extracting its rules and principles is the product of a mature and workman-like tradition of 'reasoning from case to case'. The Anglo-American judge starts his process of decision with the individual precedents which counsel for the parties before him have adduced as being most in point. In these precedents he recognizes certain 'rules', that is, solutions of particular concrete living problems. He observes how these 'rules' have been limited, extended, and refined by other 'precedents' and then, constantly keeping the practical problems in the forefront of his mind, gradually draws out of them high-level 'principles' and 'standards' which he uses to make a tentative resolution of the case before him; his solution he then tests for its appropriateness against the background of similar cases and finally arrives at the decision itself. All these steps take place in open discourse: arguments for and against are presented in speeches and rebuttals between actual or imaginary opponents. *Ambulando solvitur*.

The Anglo-American civil trial provides the ideal forum for raising problems in this discursive manner. Throughout its history it has been strongly marked by the requirements of *trial by jury*, although today it is only in the United States that the jury has any practical importance in private law. The proceedings take place in a single session, spread over several days if necessary, and all the facts, as well as questions of law, are orally presented there and then by the litigants and discussed in an open and argumentative manner, with the judge taking part. For more detail, see v below.

This inductive way of thinking, based on the particular factual problem of the case, and the intensive treatment of precedents associated with it are not to be found in Continental law, at any rate not to anything like the same extent. This is because Continental judges, in Italy and France rather more than in Germany, are still imbued with the old positivistic idea that deciding a case involves nothing more than 'applying' a particular given rule of law to the facts in issue by means of an act of categorization; indeed, they often entertain the further supposition that ideally the rules of law to be 'applied' are *statutory* texts. But in fact everyone knows that in really difficult cases the statutory text, if there is one, is too vague to provide a solution, and that the case can only be solved by engaging with the rules, principles, and maxims developed by judges in previous decisions. Nevertheless the traditional tropes are still trotted out, as can be seen in the style of judgments in France and Italy, and also in those of the supreme courts in Germany.

On this see KÜTZ, 'Über den Stil höchstrichterlicher Entscheidungen', *RabelsZ* 37 (1973) 245; GOUTAL, 'Characteristics of Judicial Style in France, Britain and the USA' (1976) 24 *Am. J. Comp. L.* 43; LAWSON, 'Comparative Judicial Style' (1977) 25 *Am. J. Comp. L.* 364; MARKESINIS, 'Conceptualism, Pragmatism and Courage, A Common Lawyer Looks at Some Judgments of the German Federal Court' (1986) 34 *Am. J. Comp. L.* 359; MARKESINIS, 'A Matter of Style' (1994) 110 *LQ Rev.* 607.

A striking piece of evidence for this is the grudging manner in which the facts of a case are treated in Continental judgments. We have already mentioned that the French Court of Cassation often does no more than make cryptic allusions to them (see above Ch. 9 I). The courts in Germany are required by §313 par. 2 ZPO to give 'only a brief statement of the essential' facts and claims based on them. Even so, when the judgment is printed in periodicals or law reports there is a characteristic tendency to curtail or even to omit it—a proceeding which the common lawyer would find unthinkable. Again, the French Court of Cassation does not even quote its *own* previous decisions, much less say why it follows one decision rather than another. Of course the judges of the Court of Cassation do in fact go through the case-law with great care, but they like to give outsiders the impression that the judgment springs from the text of the statute at a wave of the magic wand of subsumption (see the excellent treatment of this in DAWSON (above p. 256) 400 ff.). Above all, judgments of supreme courts on the Continent still sometimes reflect the traditions of the authoritarian state of a hundred years ago: judgments should primarily be impersonal acts of state which parade the majesty of the law in front of citizens in awe of authority; therefore they must not let it emerge that judges reach their decisions through a hesitant and doubtful balancing of the pros and cons of concrete solutions of the problem thrown up by the 'case', rather than by sheer intellect and cold logic.

Another indication of how underdeveloped the art of 'reasoning from case to case' remains is the uncritical use made of the 'headnotes' (*Leitsätze*) which precede published judgments all over the Continent. These headnotes present a very brief and abstract version of the essential legal proposition basic to the court decision but they omit the underlying facts or only hint at them and never give the reasoning on which the decision was founded. Common Law countries also have these 'headnotes' but they serve the judge only as a preliminary indication of the probable content of the decision which follows and never as a substitute for its investigation in detail. On the Continent, on the other hand, these headnotes, prised loose from their roots in the facts, are often treated as independent polished formulas and used in legal practice much as if they were statutory rules. In Italy, indeed, this occurrence is facilitated by the fact that most decisions of the Court of Cassation are published only in the form of headnotes (*massime*); it thus becomes practically impossible to go back to the facts of the case and discover the real scope of the headnote. In reality the principles contained in these headnotes should be treated only as working hypotheses which must be subjected to critical scrutiny in the light of later cases and the altering needs of life, for they may have to be extended or limited or refined; courts on the Continent no doubt often do this subconsciously, but they far too rarely let outsiders know, and thus be in a position to check, that they are doing so.

III

In the matter of *statutory construction* also one can observe characteristic differences between the methods of Common Law and Civil Law; they stem from the very different part played in the development of English law by statutes enacted by Parliament from that played by legislation on the Continent. Until the nineteenth century the English, again rather like the Romans, regarded legislative activity as necessary only in order to counteract some specific social or economic mischief. With their practical empiricism and habit of going step by step from case to case the English would have regarded it as dangerous and unnatural to prescribe the outcome of comparable cases in advance by making general regulations to cover the whole area of life; 'we'll cross that bridge when we come to it'. Thus English statutes were originally sporadic *ad hoc* enactments which as legal sources had much less force than the unwritten Common Law which had been developed by the judges through the centuries and which covered all areas of the law equally. The judges used to see statutes as being evil, a necessary evil, no doubt, which disturbed the lovely harmony of the Common Law and they devised rules of statutory construction which, as POLLOCK observed, obviously stemmed from the conviction that 'Parliament generally changes the law for the worse, and that the business of the judge is to keep the mischief of its interference within the narrowest possible bounds' (*Essays on*

Jurisprudence and Ethics (1882) 85). More specifically, the idea arose that every statute which deviated from the unwritten Common Law must be of an exceptional nature and therefore must be narrowly construed and applied only to the precise situations which were unquestionably covered by its terms. While it was always recognized that an enactment should be construed in the light of its purpose, it is astonishing how pedantic the courts could be in sticking to its precise wording.

In *Fisher* v. *Bell* [1961] 1 QB 394 a statute made it an offence to 'offer [a flick knife] for sale', and the accused had flick knives on display in his shop window, with a price attached. He was nevertheless acquitted on the ground that the display of goods in a shop window is not an 'offer for sale' but simply an 'invitation to buy'.—In *Bourne* v. *Norwich Crematorium Ltd.* [1967] 1 WLR 691 a tax allowance was by statute available for capital expenditure on buildings used for a trade consisting in 'the subjection of goods or materials to any process', and this allowance was claimed by a crematorium. The judge found that though the taxpayer was indeed in trade, human corpses were not 'goods' and their cremation not a 'process'. As BRIDGE observed: 'Whilst the susceptibilities of the judge were understandable and the statute clearly had not been drafted with cremation in mind, was there any real reason why those engaged in the trade of cremation should not enjoy the benefits of a statutory allowance which was enjoyed by other trades with no greater, if as great, claims on society?' (above p. 256 at p. 364).—In *Inland Revenue Com'rs* v. *Hinchy* [1960] AC 748 a person who understated his taxable income was liable to a fine of 'treble the tax which he ought to be charged'. What the statute surely meant was 'treble the tax chargeable on the income understated' rather than 'treble the tax chargeable on the whole income', but the House of Lords decided otherwise: the words were unambiguous. The result was that two taxpayers with the same taxable income would have to pay the same fine regardless of the amount of income understated. The House was unimpressed with this argument, knowing that the legislator would immediately make the necessary correction, as it did that very year (Finance Act 1960, s. 44). On this see ZANDER, *The Law Making Process* (above p. 257, at p. 105 ff.).

But the courts seem to have turned over a new leaf. They now adopt a more liberal attitude to the wording and pay more attention to the goal of the legislation:

'If one looks back to the actual decisions of [the House of Lords] on questions of statutory construction over the past 30 years one cannot fail to be struck by the evidence of a trend away from the purely literal towards the purposive construction of statutory provisions' (LORD DIPLOCK in *Carter* v. *Bradbeer* [1975] 1 WLR 1204, 1206 f.).

This development has been accelerated in recent years since it is obviously inappropriate to give a literal interpretation to the stream of British enactments which implement a European Directive or fulfil an obligation under Community Law or adopt a treaty designed to unify the law: such texts are usually drafted in the consciously open-textured continental manner, and concretization is left to the courts, which must construe them in line with their purpose of unifying the law either in Europe or worldwide.

LORD DENNING was the first to give clear expression to this view. He did it in several judgments, notably in *Buchanan & Co.* v. *Babco Forwarding and Shipping Ltd.* [1977] 1 QB 208 (CA). But see also the House of Lords in *Pickstone* v. *Freemans Plc* [1989] AC 66 and *Litster* v. *Forth Dry Dock Co.* [1990] 1 AC 546. In fact English courts and writers seem very ready to accept European developments. See, for example, BINGHAM, 'There is a World Elsewhere: The Changing Perspectives of English Law' (1992) 41 *ICLQ* 513; MARKESINIS, 'Learning from Europe and Learning in Europe' in Markesinis (ed.), *The Gradual Convergence, Foreign Ideas, Foreign Influences and English Law on the Eve of the 21st Century* (1994) 1; LEVITSKY, 'The Europeanization of the British Legal Style' (1994) 42 *Am. J. Comp. L.* 347. See also p. 19 above on the use of comparative law arguments by British courts.

For over a century it was the rule in England that in construing a statute the judge could not look at explanations given while the bill was passing through Parliament, such explanations being said to be notoriously unreliable and partial, expensive to discover, and inaccessible by the affected citizen. The House of Lords nevertheless abandoned this rule in 1993 (*Pepper* v. *Hart* [1993] AC 593). This indicates the weight now given to ascertaining the purpose of the statute:

'The days have long passed when the courts adopted a strict constructionist view of interpretation which required them to adopt the literal meaning of the language. The courts now adopt a purposive approach which seeks to give effect to the true purpose of legislation and are prepared to look at much extraneous material that bears upon the background against which the legislation was enacted. Why then cut ourselves off from the one source in which may be found an authoritative statement of the intention with which the legislation is placed before Parliament?' (LORD GRIFFITHS in *Pepper* v. *Hart* [1993] AC 593, 617.)

But if England and the Continent have become closer in past decades as regards techniques of statutory construction, there is still a vast difference in *statutory drafting*. English statutes try to be as precise as possible; they go into great detail even on trivial points and often adopt a form of expression so complex, convoluted, and pedantic that the Continental observer recoils in horror. Of course it is important that the law say exactly what it means, but exactitude has its costs, and it is equally important that the law should be clear and comprehensible, that it reveal the principle which underlies it, and that it presents in a logical order the rules it enacts. These virtues do not appeal to the English draftsmen: they put exactitude above all else.

For example, art. 6 of the European Directive on Liability for Defective Products states that one of the factors relevant to the determination of whether a product provides the safety which a person is entitled to expect is 'the presentation of the product'. In implementing the Directive the Consumer Protection Act 1987 manages to expand these five words into 45, without adding a jot of substance. In s. 3(2)(a) 'the presentation of the product' becomes 'the manner in which, and the purposes for which, the product has been marketed, its get-up, the use of any mark in relation to the product and any instructions for, or warnings with respect to, doing or refraining from doing anything with or in relation to the product.'—DALE (above p. 256) has compared the way legislation in France, Germany, and England deals with a particular point, and concludes that the laws on the Continent are considerably clearer, more comprehensible, and shorter than those in England and hardly any less easy to apply. Further details are in ZANDER, *The Law-Making Process* (above p. 257 at p. 14 ff.); BRIDGE (above p. 256); CROSS/BELL/ENGLE (above p. 256, at p. 188 ff.).

Whereas bills on the Continent are drafted in the relevant ministry, in England they are prepared by a staff of specialists, the Parliamentary draftsmen. All attempts to make them change their present practice have failed. Judges and writers have often been bitterly critical of the style of English statutes, and although this criticism was echoed by the governmental Renton Committee for the Preparation of Legislation in its 1975 Report (Cmnd. 6053), its proposals for change have so far led to nothing.

IV

The student making a comparison of the methods of legal thinking in the Common Law and the Civil Law must be constantly on his guard against one-sided views, for they are only too easily adopted by the superficial observer in this area. One can still find Anglo-American lawyers who think that in Civil Law countries the principal role of the judge is mechanically to apply statutory rules so closely interwoven that there is no room left for any vital development of the law by the judge. We have already shown in several passages how erroneous this view is. In the first place, there are large areas of law where, for various reasons, statute offers either no rules at all or only general clauses or outline provisions; here, then, is scope for judicial lawmaking. But more generally one can say that as the civil and commercial codes on the Continent grow older they lose their power and potential and that as the legislator is increasingly overtaxed by the need to make specific regulations for the novel problems of life which arise, case-law must increasingly leap into the breach; statute is thus losing the position of preeminence it once held and, as RABEL once said, 'is now no more than an expression of a global conviction' ('Die Fachgebiete des Kaiser Wilhelm-Instituts', in: Rabel, *Gesammelte Aufsätze* III (ed. Leser, 1967) 180, 201). It is true that many lawyers are not yet fully conscious of this basic change and that the processes of law, especially court decisions, still cling to traditional styles and forms. In substance, however, it is really undeniable that in Civil Law countries judges are playing a large and constantly growing part in the development of law.

As the development of uncodified law on the Continent falls increasingly to the judges, it becomes all the more important for the Civil Law to take cognisance of the techniques and methods by which judge-made law may reconcile the demand for legal certainty with the need to have rules appropriate for the changing circumstances of life. Here the accumulated experience of the Common Law should be of the greatest interest to the Continental lawyer. Anglo-American lawyers have a much more careful and precise way of delving into the distinctive facts of a case, of distinguishing these from apparently similar cases, and of delicately drawing out general rules and principles, as abstract as may be necessary but as concrete as is possible, while keeping close to the problem in hand and to its factual setting; furthermore they discuss these matters more frankly and openly than Continental lawyers who often still feel drawn to a forced 'categorization' of the facts of the case, even a rather crude and simplistic one, in order to bring the case as quickly as possible within the ambit of the closest 'leading principle' (*Leitsatz*).

If one suggests that the inductive and casuistic technique of the Common Law may be of help for the development of judge-made law on the Continent one may be charged with underrating the orderliness and rationality which come from systematic thinking and with exposing the consumer of law to a chaos of special cases. In our view this idea, though frequently expressed, is just as erroneous as the notion that the Civil Law is simply a well-organized system of exact and calculable legal concepts. The case-technique of the Anglo-American legal systems is 'not decisional pointillism, but rather the fragmentary indication of constant real principles' (ESSER (above p. 256) 284). In other words, even the Common Law technique requires the judge to look for the *general rule* behind the actual decisions in the relevant precedents, for that is the only way he can tell whether this or that decision really controls the case before him. These general rules and principles, which Common Law judges have drawn out of the mass of case material by an inductive and comparative method, give the case-law a considerable degree of inner systematic order and hence of community and predictability. It is certainly true that in a system of pure judge-made law the intrinsic forces which make for order may on occasion prove inadequate and it is undeniable that there are some areas in the Common Law where in the view of English and American specialists the case-law has reached such a state of complexity and obscurity that the intervention of the legislature is urgently required to put it in order. But observant common lawyers are increasingly aware of this danger. In American law especially there have long been attempts in various areas of the law to make a wholesale and systematic revision and reordering of the legal material.

The Restatements (see above p. 251 f.) are a good example; but the important legislative achievements of recent years, such as the Uniform Commercial Code, would have been impossible without a great deal of preliminary systematization and processing of the solutions contained in the case-law. In England also the need for systematization and rationalization of the law is increasingly recognized. Evidence for this is the establishment of the Law Commission, which is expressly given the task 'to take and keep under review all the law . . . with a view to its systematic development and reform, including in particular the codification of such law'. While it seems unlikely that the heartland of classical English law, such as the law of contract, will be codified in the foreseeable future, codification has nevertheless been much discussed of late by English writers, much of the discussion centring on Civil Law codes (see above p. 211).

But it would be a mistake, as we have already said, to suppose that the essential difference between Continental and English law is that the former is codified and the latter is not. Much more important is the following question: given that the law must be analysed and put into order, its underlying principles educed, its inconsistencies revealed, and proposals made for improvement, whose task is this and how is it to be performed? On the Continent this has been done for centuries by legal scholars. There is no such tradition in England. The first chair in English law, occupied by BLACKSTONE, was founded in Oxford in 1758, but it took another hundred years and more for legal scholars such as DICEY, ANSON, and POLLOCK to appear and write the acutely analytical works which had such an impact on English law. The law faculties themselves contributed very little to legal development or the training of lawyers for many years—as late as 1980 TWINING could say 'the British academic lawyer, unlike his continental counterpart, has tended to be a marginal man of low visibility' ('Goodbye to Lewis Elliott, The Academic Lawyer as Scholar' [1980] *JSPTL* 2)—but here, too, there has been a sea change in the last few years. England is increasingly coming to recognize what has long been accepted on the Continent, that judges and jurists both have a role to play in the development of law, and that their roles are complementary.

See BIRKS, 'Adjudication and Interpretation in the Common Law: A Century of Change' (1994) 14 *LS* 156; ATIYAH, *Pragmatism and Theory in English Law* (Hamlyn Lectures, 1987); BRIDGE, 'The Academic Lawyer: Mere Working Mason or Architect?' (1975) 91 *LQ Rev.* 488.—Evidence of this change can be seen in the fact that it is becoming common for English judges not only to consider views expressed in the literature but actually to say so, sometimes appreciatively, in their opinions. Twenty years ago this would have been unthinkable. See, for example, LORD SCARMAN in *Sidaway* v. *Governors of Bethlem Royal Hospital* [1985] AC 871, 886; LORD GOFF in *Spiliada Maritime Corp.* v. *Cansulex Ltd.* [1987] AC 460, 488 and in *Woolwich Equitable Building Soc'y* v. *IRC* [1993] AC 70, 163 f.; STEYN LJ in *White* v. *Jones* [1993] 3

All ER 481, 499 ff.—See also BIRKS *loc. cit.*; MARKESINIS, 'A Matter of Style' (1994) 110 *LQ Rev.* 607; KÖTZ, 'Scholarship and the Courts, A Comparative Survey', in CLARK (ed.), *Essays in Honor of John H. Merryman* (1990) 183.

To sum up: on the Continent the days of absolute pre-eminence of statutory law are past; contrariwise, in the Common Law there is an increasing tendency to use legislation in order to unify, rationalize, and simplify the law. On the Continent, law is increasingly being developed by the judges and consequently there is more room for an inductive method and style related to the actual problems; contrariwise, the Common Law is seeing the need to bring the rules developed by the judges into a systematic order by means of scholarly analysis and legislative action, so as to make them easier to understand and master. There are therefore grounds for believing that although the Common Law and the Civil Law started off from opposite positions, they are gradually moving closer together even in their legal methods and techniques.

V

Comparative lawyers tend to assume that in all developed legal systems in the world similar needs are met in ways that are similar, if not precisely the same. The assumption is hard to maintain when one turns to *procedural law* and compares the preparation and progress of a simple civil suit in the Common Law and the Civil Law, the way the facts are presented to the court, especially the way witnesses and experts are selected and examined, and the way the different tasks and functions are allocated to the court, the parties, and the lawyers in the different phases of the proceedings. Here the Common Law and the Civil Law have developed quite differently.

One decisive fact explains many of the peculiarities of Anglo-American procedure: it is that the procedure results from the *jury trial*. Jury trials admittedly occur only in criminal cases in England today, and then only when the crime is serious and the accused has pleaded 'not guilty', but even so, civil litigation in England is still instinct with the traditions of the jury trial. For example, all trials, civil as well as criminal, take the form of a single continuous oral hearing, lasting many hours or even days, if necessary. Since one cannot keep recalling the members of a jury, the oral hearing once started must continue without interruption. This compression of the Anglo-American trial into a single oral hearing gives rise to a whole series of further consequences, from the totality of which the Common Law trial has gained its unmistakable characteristics. (On this see also VON MEHREN (above p. 257).)

The first consequence is that enormous importance attaches to the *preparation* of the trial by the attorneys. This is not so in the Civil Law, where the division of the trial into several hearings separated by intervals means that if one party makes any surprising assertions or arguments the other party has until the next session to produce further evidence or facts in rebuttal, so that gradually, as the proceedings are resumed and with energetic assistance from the judge, the essential matters of fact get defined, what is in dispute is winnowed out from what is not, and the basis for decision is achieved step by step. But in an Anglo-American trial there is only a single hearing, so before it ever begins each party must not only have thought out his own arguments and evidence, but must also know his opponent's, because if unexpected evidence emerges one cannot simply propose an adjournment. This has two consequences: every attorney (in England, solicitor) must interview 'his' witnesses before the trial and ascertain exactly what they will say, conduct which would strike the German attorney as verging on the unprofessional in view of the risk of improper influence. Secondly, each party has the right under Anglo-American procedural law to make the other party disclose information and produce documents relevant to the forthcoming trial.

We cannot go into the details of 'discovery' here, a procedure so potent as to be capable of abuse, especially in the United States: 'a powerful litigant in a complex case may impose costly, even crushing, burdens, by demands for files, pretrial testimony of witnesses and other forms of discovery . . . A litigant may contrive to dump truckloads of files on the party demanding discovery, hoping, often not in vain, that the searcher will be so exhausted that the damaging items will be overlooked or never reached' (FRANKEL (above p. 256) 18).

When the Anglo-American trial starts, the attorneys will be carefully prepared for it, but the judge will have only the vaguest idea of what the issues and testimony may be. He is supposed to rely on the attorneys to present all the necessary facts and law by word of mouth. *How* the presentation is effected is a matter for the attorneys: they alone decide which witnesses to call, how many, and in what order; it is the attorneys also who question the witnesses, each witness after examination by 'his' side being 'handed over' for cross-examination to the other side.

The same is true of *experts*. In a medical malpractice suit, for example—or proceedings involving a question of foreign law—each party produces its own expert in court, and such experts are subject, just like any other witnesses, to examination and cross-examination by the attorneys for the two sides. This spectacle of formalized duelling between experts, with the attorneys displaying their *ad hoc* knowledge in an intrepid if amateur manner, is quite a thrill for the Continental observer, but he may be tempted to ask whether it would not be cheaper, simpler, and quicker for the *court* itself to appoint a single reputable expert whose independence and neutrality would be guaranteed by the fact that his loyalty was due to the court rather than to either of the parties.

When witnesses and experts are being questioned, the judge just listens attentively. If he speaks, it will be to rule, at the request of a party or on his own motion, on the admissibility of a question put to a witness or party, or to ensure adherence to the rules of the game in some other respect. The judge may indeed question the witness himself, but self-restraint is the rule here, as in the story of the English judge who, conscious of his tendency to ask too many questions, placed a little notice on the bench telling himself to 'Shut up!'. LORD GREENE's advice to his fellow-judges not to involve themselves in questioning witnesses is often quoted: he added that a judge who does so 'descends into the arena and is liable to have his vision clouded by the dust of the conflict' (*Yuill* v. *Yuill* [1945] P. 15, 20). A common saying is that 'The judge who opens his mouth closes his mind'. In this connection *Jones* v. *National Coal Board* [1957] 2 QB 55 is well worth reading: there the Court of Appeal remanded a case for a new trial on the sole ground that the judge at first instance had asked too many questions and made it impossible for the parties to present the evidence in the way they thought best.

The role of the Anglo-American judge may be relatively passive because knowing nothing of the case at the outset, he must learn about it as it proceeds, but the reason for giving the leading role to the parties and their lawyers has to do with certain deeply held views about the best way to get at the truth, or something akin to it, in the course of a court hearing. It is thought best to let the parties battle it out, each presenting and defending a consciously one-sided view of his own case, with the judge standing passively by, essentially seeing simply that the rules of the game are observed. '. . . truth is best discovered by powerful statements on both sides of the question', said a famous Lord Chancellor, LORD ELDON, 175 years ago (*Ex parte Lloyd*, Mont. 70, 72 n. (1822)). And a statement of LORD DENNING positively reeks of the battlefield: 'In litigation as in war. If one side makes a mistake, the other can take advantage of it. No holds are barred' (*Burmah Oil Co.* v. *Bank of England* [1979] 1 WLR 473, 484). The 'adversary procedure' which common lawyers see as the ruling principle of procedural law manifests itself in this determined if regulated confrontation between the parties to the lawsuit.

In Germany and neighbouring countries in Continental Europe procedural law is rather based on the idea that it will be easier to get at the truth if the *judge* is given a stronger role: he should be entitled, indeed bound, to question, inform, encourage, and advise the parties, lawyers, and witnesses so as to get a true and complete picture from them, as free as possible from inconsistency and ambiguity, and to counteract any mistakes due to lack of care or skill on the part of the suitors or their attorneys. It is true that the German judge cannot of his own motion call a witness simply because his evidence might cast light on the matter; it is also true that in normal civil litigation the *Verhandlungsmaxime* applies, the principle that the judge may take account only of what has been led in evidence. Even so, writers from the Common Law do not hesitate to describe the German civil trial, as compared with the Anglo-American trial, as 'inquisitorial', and the German judge as a 'paterfamilias—also endowed, to be sure, with some of the characteristics of a bureaucrat; . . . he is constantly descending to the level of the litigants as an examiner, patient or hectoring, as counselor and advisor, as insistent promoter of settlements. Withal he has not entirely lost his character as a civil servant, though of a special type, . . . in a government department' (KAPLAN, VON MEHREN, SCHAEFER, 'Phases of German Civil Procedure', 71 *Harv. L. Rev.* 1193, 1443, 1472 (1958)).

In the *United States* 'adversary procedure' is practised with particular rigour. This is largely because civil suits are still tried there by a jury in the first instance, at any rate if it is a Common Law claim as opposed to one in Equity (see above Ch. 14 III). In practice this means that almost all damages claims, such as arise from traffic accidents, are tried before a jury.

Many matters fall to the jury for decision, many more than to the lay judges occasionally used in civil and criminal cases on the Continent. For example, at the end of a hearing of, say, a claim for damages arising out of a traffic accident, the jury, in the absence of the judge, decides what *facts* have been proved. During the trial the judge will have instructed the jury on the applicable *rules of law*, but the actual application of those rules is for the jury alone. They thus decide whether on the facts as found the defendant acted 'negligently', whether the plaintiff was guilty of any 'contributory negligence', and what damages he should receive by way of compensation for pain and suffering and material harm. The right to trial by jury is constitutionally guaranteed by the Seventh Amendment, so that abolition is hardly imaginable. Indeed, there are even constitutional objections to any reduction of the number of jurymen from the traditional twelve or any qualification, in favour of a majority verdict, of the historic requirement of unanimity.

The attorney's knowledge that at the end of the day the crucial questions in the case will be decided by a group of laymen will obviously affect his tactics at the trial. First of all, he must see that the jury is composed of the 'right' persons. By law each attorney may object to a certain number of proposed jurors without giving any reason, and to an unlimited number if reason is given. In big criminal cases this 'voir-dire' examination, or selection of the jury, can last several days; hundreds of proposed jurors may be questioned by the attorneys only to be dismissed. Once a jury is impanelled, the attorney will strive to present the facts in as striking and dramatic a manner—and as favourably to his client—as possible. He will use every trick of forensic rhetoric. The questions he puts to his witnesses will often have been studiously rehearsed. Of course the attorney on the other side will be striving with equal vigour to frustrate these efforts. He will try to impugn the witnesses' credibility by putting tricky questions (for which they will have been prepared).

There is a complex set of rules, called the 'law of evidence', which determines what evidence may be given by witnesses and what questions they may be asked in examination and cross-examination. There is no counter-part for this in the Civil Law, where evidence is heard by professional judges who, in a civil suit, should get to hear *everything*; after all, they are experi-enced, even hardened, enough to make a 'free evaluation of the evidence' and separate the grain from the chaff. In a jury trial, by contrast, a 'law of evidence' is necessary to prevent laymen being led up the garden path by 'hearsay evidence', suggestive 'leading questions', and other tricks. It will be obvious that 'adversary procedure' encourages attorneys to go to the very limits of what is morally and professionally acceptable, perhaps sometimes even to overstep them, by 'preparing' their witnesses rather intensively for examination and cross-examination, and by dressing up as unalloyed truth what the attorney well knows to be a pack of lies. Scruples are easily allayed by the consideration that the other side can do likewise. Nor is the problem rendered any less acute by the prevalence of the contingent fee in the United States, for then victory or defeat in the courtroom may mean riches or ruin for the plaintiff's attorney.

If the principle of adversary procedure is sacrosanct in American writing, there has been much discussion of the question when abuse begins and how it should be met. FRANKEL mounts a spirited attack against the 'excesses, distortions and perversions' of adversary procedure (FRANKEL, above p. 256) reviewed by KÖTZ in 48 *U. Chi. L. Rev.* 478 (1981)); a contrary position is adopted by FREEDMAN, *Lawyers' Ethics in an Adversary System* (1975); and the authors exchange views in 123 *U. Pa. L. Rev.* 1031 and 1060 (1975).—Much dust has been raised by LANGBEIN's provocative article 'The German Advantage in Civil Procedure' (52) *U. Chi. Rev.* 823 (1985). Impressed by German law, he proposes that the judge should exercise more control over the pro-ceedings and have the power to collect the factual material, summon the witnesses, and select the experts. On this see STIEFEL/MAXEINER, 'Civil Justice Reform in the United States, Opportunity for Learning from "Civilized" European Procedure Instead of Continued Isolation?' (1994) 42 *Am. J. Comp. L.* 147 (with a report on the critical reaction to Langbein's article).

IV. THE NORDIC LEGAL FAMILY

19

Scandinavian Law, Past and Present

CARSTEN, 'Europäische Integration und nordische Zusammenarbeit auf dem Gebiet des Zivilrechts', *ZEuP* 1993, 335.

CHYDENIUS, 'The Swedish Lawbook of 1734: An Early German Codification', 20 *LQ Rev.* 377 (1904).

EEK, 'Évolution et structure du droit scandinave', *Rev. hell. dr. int.* 14 (1961) 33.

VON EYBEN, 'Inter-Nordic Legislative Cooperation', *Scand. Stud. L.* 6 (1962) 63.

THE FINNISH LEGAL SYSTEM (ed. Uotila, 1966).

FISCHLER/VOGEL, *Schwedisches Handels- und Wirtschaftsrecht mit Verfahrensrecht* (3rd edn., 1978).

GAMELTOFT-HANSEN/GOMARD/PHILIP (eds.), *Danish Law, A General Survey* (1982).

GINSBURG/BRUZELIUS, *Civil Procedure in Sweden* (1965).

GOMARD, 'Civil Law, Common Law and Scandinavian Law', *Scand. Stud. L.* 5 (1961) 27.

HELLNER, 'Unification of Law in Scandinavia', 16 *Am. J. Comp. L.* 88 (1968).

——, 'Rechtsvereinheitlichung im skandinavischen Rechtskreis', in: *Methoden der Rechtsvereinheitlichung* (Arbeiten zur Rechtsvergleichung vol. 69, 1974) 27.

JÄGERSKIÖLD, 'Roman Influence on Swedish Case Law in the 17th Century', *Scand. Stud. L.* 11 (1967) 175.

JØRGENSEN, 'Grundzüge der Entwicklung der skandinavischen Rechtswissenschaft', *JZ* 1970, 529.

——, 'Les Traits principaux de l'évolution des sources du droit danois', *Rev. int. dr. comp.* 23 (1971) 65.

KORKISCH, *Einführung in das Privatrecht der nordischen Länder* I (1977).

MATTEUCCI, 'The Scandinavian Legislative Co-operation as a Model for European Co-operation', in: *Liber Amicorum of Congratulations to Algot Bagge* (1956) 136.

MUNCH-PETERSEN, 'Main Features of Scandinavian Law', 43 *LQ Rev.* 366 (1927).

ORFIELD, *The Growth of Scandinavian Law* (1953).

REHFELDT, 'Rezeption in Schweden', *SavZ/Germ.* 82 (1965) 316; 85 (1968) 248.

SCHMIDT/STRÖMHOLM, *Legal Values in Modern Sweden* (1964).

STRÖHOLM (ed.), *An Introduction to Swedish Law* (2nd edn., 1988).

——, 'La Philosophie du droit scandinave', *Rev. int. dr. comp.* 32 (1980) 5.

SUNDBERG, 'Civil Law, Common Law and the Scandinavians', *Scand. Stud. L.* 13 (1969) 179.

VINDING KRUSE, *A Nordic Draft Code for Denmark, Finland, Iceland, Norway and Sweden* (1963).

I

WRITERS on comparative law often make the implicit assumption that the legal systems of the Western world belong either to the Common Law or to the Civil Law. The difficulties inherent in such an assumption are shown by asking how this scheme accommodates the legal systems of Northern Europe—Denmark, Finland, Iceland, Norway, and Sweden. It is clear that these Nordic laws cannot be allocated to the Common Law, for the only legal systems which belong to the Common Law are those which are historically traceable to medieval English law, and the history of the Nordic systems has been quite independent of English law. Furthermore, Nordic law has few, if any, of the 'stylistic' hallmarks of the Common Law, such as the typical methods of finding law, the strong emphasis on judicial decisions in important areas of private law, and the standing and career of the Anglo-American judge. More difficult is the question whether the Nordic laws can be attached to the Civil Law, that great family of legal systems such as those of Continental Europe which have been more or less imbued with Roman law and which traditionally rely on statutes or indeed comprehensive codes as the primary means of ordering their legal material. There is no denying that Roman law has played a smaller role in the legal development of the Nordic countries than in Germany, and the Nordic states have as yet no codes like the civil codes of France or Germany. Nevertheless we are of the opinion, as will be seen from what follows, that it would be right to attribute the Nordic laws to the Civil Law, even although, by reason of their close interrelationship and their common 'stylistic' hallmarks, they must undoubtedly be admitted to form a special legal family, alongside the Romanistic and German legal families.

The expressions 'Nordic' and 'Scandinavian' will here be treated as synonymous, despite the fact that neither Denmark nor Iceland forms part of Scandinavia in the geographical sense.

II

The close interrelationship of the Nordic legal systems is explained by the fact that the political and cultural ties between the Scandinavian countries have always been very close. It is true that the complete unification of the three Nordic kingdoms of Denmark, Norway and Sweden was only temporary, in the time of the Union of Kalmar (1397–1523), but the links between Sweden and Finland on the one hand, and between Denmark, Norway, and Iceland on the other, proved much more durable and lasted for centuries. In the twelfth and thirteenth centuries Finland was conquered by Sweden and then formed part of the Swedish Empire until 1809 when Sweden was forced, as a result of an unsuccessful war against Russia, to cede Finland to the

Tsars. Even so, Finland had considerable autonomy within the Russian state as an independent Grand Duchy and the Tsarist administration interfered very little with its legal system. Thus when Finland broke loose from Russia after the October Revolution and declared its independence in 1918, its legal unity with Sweden had not been greatly impaired. In *Western* Scandinavia, Denmark, Norway, and Iceland stayed under the central control of the Danish royal family for more than four centuries from the end of the fourteenth century so that Danish law was essentially in force in Norway and Iceland as well. In 1814 Denmark had to cede the territory of Norway to Sweden, but the Norwegians were able to secure a considerable degree of independence within the Swedish Empire and in 1905 peacefully obtained complete autonomy. Finally, Iceland became an independent state in 1918, though it remained under the Danish monarch until the end of the Second World War.

Historically speaking, all the Nordic laws were based on old Germanic law, though there were certain local variations in the different parts of Scandinavia. In the twelfth century these rules began to be written down in a large number of local laws and then city laws. With the increasing centralization of power the law began to be collected and unified. In the fourteenth century Sweden was able to replace the particular laws of counties and towns with a *Land Law* effective throughout the lowlands and a *City Law* valid in all towns of the Empire. By the seventeenth and eighteenth centuries progress was such that in Denmark as well as in Sweden comprehensive codes could be produced. The preparatory work was carefully done and they unified the entire private law, criminal law, and procedural law in both countries. In *Denmark* the *Danske Lov* of King CHRISTIAN V came into force in 1683; in Norwegian territory it came into force under the title *Norske Lov* in 1687. It is divided into six books; the first deals with the practice of law, the second with the church, the third with the secular classes, trade, and matrimonial law, the fourth with maritime law, the fifth with the rest of property law and the law of succession, and the final sixth book with criminal law. The Swedish code of 1734 (*Sveriges rikes lag*) is divided in a more sophisticated way. It has nine parts, of which the first five cover most of private law: these sections deal with matrimonial law, succession law, land law, building law, and the law of obligations and contract. The Swedish law-book has only 1,300 paragraphs; like the Danish law, it is drafted in a simple, clear, and homely style and prefers a wealth of casuistic detailed rules to the theoretical generalization and pedagogic conceptualism that was being currently practised on the continent by the system-builders of natural law.

This is by no means to say that Swedish and Danish law has developed in complete isolation from the law of Continental Europe. Indeed, in the seventeenth century, Sweden was in close contact with legal scholarship on the Continent. This was a consequence of the fact that at the time of the Thirty Years War Sweden had become a great power with an important role in

European politics and considerable territorial interests in the Baltic regions, territories in which the *usus modernus pandectarum* was flourishing both in legal practice and in the universities. These political and intellectual relations with central and Eastern Europe allowed continental legal thinking to make its way into Sweden. In particular, young Swedish noblemen who sought a career in the administration or in legal practice in the Swedish Empire used to obtain their legal training in the *Gemeines Recht* at the universities of Protestant Germany, and as time went by, at the universities of Uppsala and Lund as well. GUSTAVUS ADOLPHUS founded new supreme courts as part of his administrative reforms—both the Svea hofrätt in Stockholm, founded in 1614, and the Göta hofrätt in Göteborg, founded in 1634, still exist today—and it was natural that these courts, in marked contrast to England, should be staffed by learned career judges who were also familiar with Roman law. We can thus see how Roman ideas and rules came to play an important part in the supreme courts of Sweden in the seventeenth century, as JÄGERSKIÖLD (above p. 276) has shown, especially in the area of contract law, the law of real and personal security, and the law of partnerships and bankruptcy, areas where the law books of the fourteenth century were most deficient. But remarkably enough the influence of Roman law on the code of 1734 is not at all prominent, even in the part devoted to contract and commercial law. This is probably connected with the fact that under CHARLES XII Sweden had lost its position as a great European power in consequence of an unfortunate foreign policy and a series of military defeats, and suddenly found itself nearly forced out of the European continent. In consequence there was a reversion to nationalism and the draftsmen of the code of 1734 thought it advisable to link it closely in construction, style, diction, and casuistry with the traditions of the old Swedish city and land laws (see REHFELDT, above p. 276). Nevertheless the contact with Roman law was so powerful that the links with legal thought in Continental Europe were never broken and have always been much closer than in England.

Neither the Danish–Norwegian law of 1683/1687 nor the Swedish law of 1734 has been formally repealed, but of course most of their rules have been rendered obsolete by changes in circumstances or have been replaced by new statutory law.

The disturbances of the Age of Napoleon brought about great changes in the political conditions and intellectual climate of Scandinavia as elsewhere. The connections which had existed for centuries between Sweden and Finland and between Denmark and Norway were broken. The national and liberal ideas of the French Revolution found ready acceptance in Scandinavia and helped, on the one hand, to strengthen the Scandinavians' sense of cultural and linguistic separateness and, on the other hand, to vanquish what remained of absolutist government and to increase citizen participation in affairs of state. The success of the Napoleonic codification evoked proposals in Sweden that the old code of 1734 should be fundamentally reformed, and indeed in 1811 the Swedish Parliament set up a commission charged with the preparation of a new code. The draft which was produced in 1826 was heavily influenced by the French Code civil, and its family and succession law in particular departed from old Swedish law with its underlying model of patriarchally organized kin-groups. For example, under the old law unmarried women had no legal capacity, whatever their age, and they could not marry without the consent of their father or other representative of their kin-group; under the new Code women, like men, gained capacity on reaching a certain age, husband and wife were given equal rights in matrimonial property, sons and daughters were granted the same statutory right of inheritance, and many old-fashioned differences between city-dwellers and countrymen in questions of matrimonial property and succession were abolished. This draft could not be brought into force as a whole because of conservative opposition but many of its ideas were implemented in separate reforming laws. This is the way in which, starting in the middle of the nineteenth century, Denmark and Sweden have modernized their old codes, especially in family and succession law, where they brought about the legal emancipation of women usually well in advance of countries on the Continent.

Stimulated by a sense of their common historical and cultural heritage, as well as by an increase in mutual trade and the improvement of traffic, the Nordic states started to co-operate closely in the field of legislation in the last third of the nineteenth century. This was facilitated by the fact that the Scandinavian languages, except Finnish, are very closely related, so that Scandinavian lawyers can speak their own language and still understand each other quite well. In 1872 a congress of Scandinavian jurists, convened in Copenhagen with the express purpose of advancing legal unification in Scandinavia, resolved that the first and most important goal was to unify the Nordic law of negotiable instruments. This challenge was taken up by the Ministers of Justice in Sweden, Denmark, and Norway, and they carried through the preliminary work with such speed that in 1880 the unified law of negotiable instruments came into force simultaneously in all three countries. In the following years attention was still concentrated on the unification of commercial law, and before the end of the nineteenth century nearly identical laws had come into force on trade marks, commercial registers, firms, and the law of cheques. The maritime law of Scandinavia was also put on a unified statutory basis in 1891/3.

It gradually appeared that the legislation emerging from this co-operation among the Nordic states was better in *quality* as well. Since Sweden even today has only 8 million inhabitants and Denmark, Norway, and Finland between 4 and 5 million each, the experience of each country is relatively limited; only on the basis of their consolidated experience is it possible to draft good statutes. Bolder plans for unification appeared around the turn of the century. In 1899 the Danish Professor LARSEN proposed that in addition to commercial law the whole of the rest of private law should be unified, with a Scandinavian Civil Code as the eventual goal. The governments of the Nordic states were in general agreement with this proposal but the ambitious project of producing a civil code was shelved in favour of unifying specific areas of the law of property and obligations. The first fruit of these efforts was a draft statute on the sale of moveables, which came into force in Sweden in 1905, in Denmark in 1906, in Norway in 1907 and in Iceland in 1922.

In preparing the Scandinavian Sales Act the draftsmen took account of the English Sale of Goods Act, 1893 and the German BGB but they also paid much more attention than usual to the viewpoints of the commercial interests involved. This had two results: first, the Sales Act is 'a simple system of simple and clearly formulated concepts' (RABEL, *Das Recht des Warenkaufs* I (1936) 311), and secondly it answers the strict demands of mercantile practice and the need to get contracts over and done with simply and swiftly. Thus, according to the statute, a vendor is in delay if he has failed to deliver the goods to the purchaser or to the carrier at the proper time; no notice is needed to put him in delay, nor indeed need he be *responsible* for the delay in delivery. If the vendor is in delay and the delay is 'material', the purchaser, instead of demanding performance, is entitled to repudiate the contract without allowing any further time for performance; such a repudiation of the contract does not have the consequence provided by §326 BGB, that the contract is avoided *ab initio*, with the result that the purchaser has no basis for claiming damages. §24 of the Scandinavian Sales Act gives the same result as German law, but is much better formulated: the vendor of generic goods who has failed to deliver is freed from liability in damages if, and only if, the performance of the contract was rendered impossible by reason of a circumstance 'which the vendor was not bound to envisage at the time of the contract, such as the destruction of the entire class of goods or such portion of it as was to form the object of the contract, the outbreak of war, the imposition of import restrictions or similar events'. It may be added that if the goods delivered are *defective*, the Scandinavian Sales Act holds the vendor of generic goods liable for damages even in the absence of fault. All these rules are substantially incorporated in CISG (see below Ch. 36 VI).

Another important product of Nordic co-operation is the 'Law of contracts and other legal transactions in the law of property and obligations', to give it its Swedish name, which came into force in Sweden, Denmark, and Norway between 1915 and 1918 and in Finland in 1929. This Act, which has about 40 sections, does not purport to deal with all the questions covered by the BGB in its chapter 'Acts in Law' in the 'General part'; it confines itself to a few problems of proven practical importance, with rules concerning the *conclusion of contracts, agency*, and the *invalidity of legal acts*. It is very clear that the draftsmen kept an eye on the general private law doctrines of the German Pandectist School as well as the texts of the German and Swiss codes, but thanks to those twin virtues of Scandinavian jurists, namely reasonableness and realism, the Act shows no signs of that exaggerated passion for putting general rules 'right out front' which we find in the BGB (see above Ch. II II). This is already evident from the fact that the statute very sensibly purports to apply only to those legal acts which occur in the law of property and obligations, excluding family law and the law of succession; nor does the statute include any rules concerning the legal invalidity of legal acts on the ground of *minority*; those rules seemed to be functionally associated with the law of children, so they were kept for a special law dealing with the legal position of minors in all its aspects. The Contracts Law also has its own way of solving many practical problems, particularly by giving strong protection to good faith in business matters.

Thus a party who concludes a contract under the influence of mistake may in principle resile from the contract only if the other party knew or should have known of the error and therefore has no right to have his reliance on the validity of the contract protected. Offers to contract are binding, so that the offeree may count on his acceptance bringing a contract into being, provided it is communicated to the offeror within the period for which the offeror can reasonably be expected to wait. In its section on agency the Contracts Law has detailed provisions to protect those who contract in good faith with an agent whose powers have been limited or even terminated by a principal who has not made his intention sufficiently clear. This strong emphasis on the protection of commerce may be explained by the fact that in Scandinavia, as in England, commercial law has never been seen as a 'special law' for businessmen, but has always been incorporated into the general private law with a few special rules for the transactions of private citizens not in commerce. This can also be seen in §36 of the Contracts Law, a new version of which was produced in Denmark and Sweden in 1975–6. Under this provision a court may invalidate or modify a term of a contract if, given the subject-matter of the transaction and the attendant or supervening circumstances, it can be held to be 'unfair'. This applies in principle to commercial and non-commercial transactions alike, although there is an express reference to the relevance of the need to protect the consumer or other weak contracting party, and it applies to all 'unfair' terms, whether they are standard terms or individually negotiated.

In addition to the Sales Act and the Contracts Law there are several other statutes in the law of property and obligations which have come into force in Scandinavia in a unified form; one can instance the laws concerning Commission Agents. Trade Representatives, and Commercial Travellers, the Law on Instalment Sales, the Law on Insurance Contracts, and the Law on Bonds. All these laws were preceded by careful research in comparative law, scanning English as well as Continental, especially German, law for rules suited to Scandinavian conditions. Because their construction, diction, and style are almost identical with those of Continental legislation, and their basic legal concepts in harmony, the German or French lawyer finds it very much easier to cope with Scandinavian enactments than with the statutes of Anglo-American law.

With the enactments we have mentioned the Scandinavian countries have developed a substantially unified law of contract; where there are no applicable statutory provisions the device of *analogy* is very widely used by courts and writers alike. Thus in Sweden the provisions of the Sales Act regarding the delivery of defective goods have been applied by analogy to the contract of services which is not covered by the law of 1734. In the same way when judges have to decide a case involving the assignment of choses in action or the right of recourse between joint debtors, they ask whether perhaps the provisions of the Law on bonds may not be applied analogically. Again, there is no general clause in any Swedish statute which requires good faith in the performance of contracts, though specific rules to this effect can be found in the Law of Instalment Sales (1915), Law on Insurance Contracts (1927), and in the Law of Bonds (1936); in 1948 the Supreme Court of Sweden announced that contractual terms which offended against the principle of good faith were to be regarded as void in *all* contracts, even where there was no special statutory mandate. The list of such examples could easily be extended.

Scandinavian countries, with Sweden in the forefront, have been especially innovative in the field of *consumer protection*, and their ideas have often served as models elsewhere. In addition to the general clause in §36 of the Contracts Law, which has already been mentioned, Sweden has enacted special statutes which fix the terms of certain types of contract entered into by consumers. Contracts of sale are an instance: the *Consumer Sales Law* of 1973 grants inalienable rights to the consumer who buys goods for private use from a supplier, especially where the goods are defective or not delivered on time. Since 1979 all forms of credit provided to consumers fall under the *Consumer Credit Law*; where the credit is for the purchase of goods—the most important case in practice—the regulation is very detailed, and in some circumstances the consumer who has a defence against the supplier of the goods may use it against the supplier of the credit. Finally in 1981 the *Consumer Insurance Law* came into force; it gives very extensive rights to private citizens who take out property insurance against fire, accident, burglary, and other misfortunes, but not life insurance or sickness insurance. The Swedes have long realized that consumer protection can never be adequate so long as the individual consumer has to go to court to vindicate his rights in a particular case, so since 1970 they have had an Office of Consumer Protection, headed by a 'Consumer-Ombudsman'. Among its extensive powers since 1971 is the right to take a firm to a special 'Market Court' and seek an injunction against continued use of General Conditions of Business if the objectionable terms are 'unfair to the ultimate consumer with regard to the price and other circumstances'. The details may be found in BERNITZ, 'Schwedishes Verbraucherschutzrecht', *RabelsZ* 40 (1976) 593. Most other Scandinavian countries have enacted similar provisions. See also below, p. 346.

In the field of *family law* there has also been productive co-operation between the Nordic states, although here the variations from nation to nation are rather more marked than in the law of obligations. The law of marriage, the law of children, and the law of adoption are similar in principle throughout Scandinavia, and often in their details as well. It must be noticed that many questions on which reform was proposed in Continental Europe only after the Second World War were raised or even solved in Scandinavian law much earlier: one may mention the equality of husband and wife, the abandonment of the principle of fault in divorce law, the equal treatment of legitimate and illegitimate children, and the improvement in the position of the surviving spouse in succession law.

III

This survey shows how successful the Nordic countries have been in their efforts over the last hundred years to bring their legal systems closer together; indeed, the Scandinavian achievement has been put forwards as a model for co-operation in Europe as a whole (see MATTEUCCI, above p. 276). On the other hand, further progress may have become more difficult as it appears that the reformist zeal has become less pronounced in some Scandinavian countries than in others (see HELLNER, above p. 276). Also it must be remembered that the conditions for achieving the present degree of legal harmony, if not unity, were particularly propitious in the Scandinavian countries. Their historical development was very similar, their cultural links were very close, their languages were very alike, there were no serious political differences, their population and economic power was approximately equivalent, and they were all perched on the edge of Europe; all these circumstances made co-operation in good faith much easier, co-operation which for some time has extended beyond the joint preparation of draft statutes to questions of economic, social, transport and cultural policy, especially, since 1952, under the auspices of the Nordic Council. But the principal explanation for the success of this co-operation in legal matters is the fact that the law in these Nordic countries, starting from a common basis of Germanic legal ideas, has developed historically on parallel lines. Thus Roman law reached the Scandinavian countries from the South only in the seventeenth century, at a time when the traditional legal institutions had long been stabilized in provincial and city laws and were being applied in a well-constructed courts system. The influence of Roman law was therefore confined to these areas in which the rules of the medieval codes were particularly deficient: in essence contract law, the law of credit and securities, partnership and bankruptcy law. Thus the reception of Roman law in the Nordic countries took a very weak form and the links between Scandinavia and Continental legal science, although much closer than they were in England, did not lead to so extensive a 'scientification' of legal doctrine and practice as did the reception of Roman law in Germany. Furthermore, the Age of Enlightenment's idea of codification lost some of its allure in Scandinavia, as so many continental ideas seem to do when they enter the cooler climate of the North. In order to modernize their old codes the Scandinavians in the nineteenth century relied principally on a number of individual statutes indistinguishable in style and construction from similar products on the Continent. The more advanced idea of codifying the whole of private law in a comprehensive manner has not worked out in any of the Scandinavian countries; the last step in this direction, the proposal of the Danish scholar VINDING KRUSE in 1948 to draw up a draft Nordic Civil Code, has recently come to a halt. This is in line with the attitude of Nordic legal science. It has always paid attention to events on the continent and in the nineteenth century it unquestionably got its legal wares from the pandectists' shop. But the tendency to undue conceptualism and the construction of large-scale integrated theoretical systems has never really been followed in the North, thanks to the realism of the Scandinavian lawyers and their sound sense of what is useful and necessary in practice. Thus while the Scandinavian legal systems have participated in the legal development of Continental Europe they have also maintained their local characteristics, and this justifies us in allocating them to a special 'Nordic' legal group within the Civil Law.

V. LAW IN THE FAR EAST

20

Chinese Law

BODDE/MORRIS, *Law in Imperial China* (1967).

BÜNGER, *Zivil- und Handelsgesetzbuch sowie Wechsel- und Scheckgesetz von China* (1934).

CH'Ü, *Law and Society in Traditional China* (1961).

COHEN, 'Chinese Mediation on the Eve of Modernization', 54 *Calif. L. Rev.* 1201 (1966).

——/EDWARDS/CHEN, *Essays on China's Legal Tradition* (1980).

DAVID, 'Deux conceptions de l'ordre social', in: *Ius privatum gentium, Festschrift Max Rheinstein* I (1969) 53.

EPSTEIN, 'The Evolution of China's General Principles of Civil Law', 34 *Am. J. Comp. L.* 705 (1986).

GERKE, *Die Schlichtung im chinesischen Recht* (1992).

HAN PAO MA, 'Legal System of the Republic of China', *RabelsZ* 37 (1973) 101.

HZIA/SELDIN, 'Recent Legal Developments in the People's Republic of China', 28 *Harv. Int. LJ* 249 (1987).

JONES (ed.), *Basic Principles of Civil Law in China* (1989).

LUBMAN, 'Studying Contemporary Chinese Law: Limits, Possibilities and Strategy', 39 *Am. J. Comp. L.* 293 (1991).

MCALEAVY, 'Chinese Law', in: An Introduction to Legal Systems (ed. Derrett, 1968) 105.

MACNEIL, 'Contract in China: Law, Practice, and Dispute Resolution', 38 *Stan. L. Rev.* 303 (1986).

MÜNZEL, *Das Recht der Volksrepublik China* (1982).

NODA, 'The Far Eastern Conception of Law', II *Int. Enc. Comp. L.* Ch. 1 (1975).

RUETE, *Der Einfluß des abendländischen Rechtes auf die Rechtsgestaltung in Japan und China* (1940).

SENGER, 'Grundlagen und Eigenart des Rechts der Volksrepublik China', *SJZ* 1981, 1.

WEGGEL, *Chinesische Rechtsgechichte* (1980).

ZHENG, 'China's New Civil Law', 34 *Am. J. Comp. L.* 669 (1986).

I

A LEGAL system is allocated to a family or circle of legal systems on the basis of its distinctive features. One of these may be the importance it attaches to law as a means of ordering social life. This is the point on which the legal systems of the Far East differ fundamentally from the legal families dealt with so far. It is agreed in all Western systems, whether of Civil or of Common Law, that the important questions of social life should primarily be regulated by *rules of objective law* rather than simply by conventions or habits or mores. These rules of law assure to individual citizens certain claims, a certain status, and certain entitlements; statute and judicial decision specify in general terms the conditions under which all persons are to have particular *rights*, such as the right to performance of a contract or to compensation for harm, or the right to obtain a divorce or payment of maintenance money. If a person's rights are infringed, threatened, or questioned by others, he is not only *entitled* to assert and vindicate them but, as RUDOLF VON JHERING said in his book *The Struggle for Law*, may actually be *bound* to do so; the mechanism used for this purpose is court proceedings, in which a judge provided by the state resolves the dispute on the basis of objective law by issuing a conclusive and binding judgment. A glance at the legal systems of the Far East shows that this is not the only possible method: in some societies disputes are resolved by techniques other than suits at law. It is true that even in the Western world there are many conflicts which are not usually or easily resolved by judicial decision—there are examples in international law and in labour law, and even in areas where court proceedings are effective parties may well have a considerable interest in avoiding the publicity of a duel in the state courts and resolving the dispute by compromise or arbitration instead. Not only does this save a lot of money but it may help to maintain that sense of trust which commercial men may hold more important for their future relations than the vindication of their legal rights, especially under contracts of employment or licensing arrangements. Nevertheless one can hazard the view that in the Far East such informal means of dispute resolution are enormously more important, to a degree which makes the study of Far Eastern law so interesting, for it clearly demonstrates the temporary and local nature of attitudes which in the Western world can too easily be taken as axiomatic.

This may not in itself be a sufficient reason for constructing a 'Far Eastern legal family' comprising China, Japan, and other countries of South East Asia, as was done in the previous edition. For one thing, the law of the People's Republic of China and that of Japan are fundamentally different. Japan has a democratic constitution, a market economy with private ownership, and a highly developed legal system based on Western models. The People's Republic of China has certainly, in the twenty years since the 'Cultural Revolution', taken astonishing steps in the same direction and in many respects made room for entrepreneurial initiative, but it is still a socialist country in which party and state control the commanding heights of the economy. It is accordingly misleading to put them in the same legal family. It has admittedly been observed that the tradition of Confucianism in the Far East leads to a dim view of law and a characteristic tendency to resolve disputes otherwise than by recourse to the courts, but it is doubtful to what extent this tradition still obtains in the modern legal systems of China and Japan. Accordingly we take our leave of the 'Far Eastern Legal Family' without regret and present Chinese and Japanese law separately in their own right.

II

In the Chinese view, social relations are part of the natural order. This view is to be found in the doctrines of Confucianism, and it helps us to understand why in the Far East they set so little store by law and the resolution of conflicts by courts. CONFUCIUS lived from 551 to 479 BC; his importance lies not so much in the originality of his thought, which reflects the philosophical and ethical tenets of his time, as in the way he developed and refined these in discussions with his pupils which were later recorded, and especially in the way in which his admirable personal life embodied the ideals he propounded. In the following centuries his teachings were further developed, especially by the philosopher TUNG CHUNG-SHU (176–104 BC) who incorporated elements of popular beliefs into Confucianism and produced a doctrine of cosmic harmony. It is this form of Confucianism which constituted the ideology of the Chinese empire until the revolution of 1911. It starts from the proposition that man and God, Heaven and earth, all things living and inert are organic parts of a harmoniously ordered and integrated universe. The most important goal of man must therefore be to keep his thoughts, feelings, and actions in perfect accordance with cosmic harmony; in particular men must so conduct themselves as not to disturb the natural balance of their existing relations. The rules of 'proper' behaviour were called 'li' and their content characteristically depended on the social status of the person to whom they applied, his status in his family, in his clan, in the neighbourhood, in the official hierarchy, and in the state. For Confucianism, the different positions which an individual might occupy by reason of his age, sex, career, family position, employment status, and social prestige were all part of the prescribed natural order and had to be respected if one was not to disturb the balanced harmony of the world. Thus the 'li' or appropriate behaviour was carefully determined for each situation differently, according as it involved relations between superior and inferior, between older and younger, nobleman and citizen, between relatives, friends, or strangers, between father and son, older and younger brother, or husband and wife (on this see in detail CH'Ü (above p. 286) p. 226 ff.). The ideal man in the Confucian view is the person conscious of the natural order of the world who recognizes the necessity and purpose of these rules of behaviour, follows them spontaneously, and thus modestly and quietly represses his own interests in order to maintain that harmony.

It will be clear that Confucianism could have no great regard for rules of law or their enforcement by courts. Since all law tends to schematize and typify the relations of life in a simple and orderly way, it is in no position to take account of all the various imponderables inherent in the social position of the parties. Much less could Confucianism approve of establishing legal rights through court procedures. According to the ethics of Confucianism a citizen who thought that someone else had neglected the rules of 'li' in his behaviour towards him does better to seek an equitable resolution by peaceful discussion than to accentuate the existing discord by insisting on his rights or calling in a judge. The wise and virtuous man wins a gold star in the eyes of the community and of God by exercising a degree of forbearance in a conflict and by accepting the injustice he has suffered. Anyone who disturbed social tranquillity by calling in a state court and trying to put a fellow-citizen publicly in the wrong was regarded as a disruptive, boorish, and uncultivated person who lacked the cardinal virtues of modesty and readiness to compromise.

For a long time after his death in 479 BC it seemed that the doctrines of CONFUCIUS must sink in the welter of political events. For two centuries the country was incessantly riven by armed conflict between rival territorial princes and the circumstances were such that the Confucian view of law could hardly thrive. Instead, the school of the so-called 'Legists' won the upper hand; they harried the Confucians badly, and adopted the opposite stance on all important questions. CONFUCIUS and his school believed that man was intrinsically good and could be brought by education and the example of his rulers to see the need for virtuous conduct, whereas the 'Legists' held that man was basically selfish, concerned only to advance his personal interests, and therefore had to be strictly disciplined by state legislation. While CONFUCIUS taught that the differences of status in a hierarchically ordered society should be seen as an expression of the higher harmony of the world and must therefore be scrupulously observed, the 'Legists' believed that all men were equal before the law and that the proper social behaviour which could not be induced by philosophical teaching should be inculcated through severe penal sanctions imposed by every form of state coercion regardless of the person involved. Finally in 221 BC the Ts'IN dynasty emerged victorious from the wars, and China for the first time in its history found itself under unified rule; it seemed that the ideas of the 'Legists' must also be victorious, for the Ts'IN Emperors, who set up a strong centralized administration, passed draconian laws, and imposed fearful burdens on the population, also pursued the followers of CONFUCIUS and burnt their writings. But the hated Ts'IN regime lasted only a short time: fighting broke out again and in 206 BC the imperial power passed to the HAN dynasty which ruled the country for more than four centuries. Under the HAN Emperors Confucianism became the ideology of the state; its teachings were propagated throughout the land by travelling disciples and Confucianism was recognized as the spiritual and philosophical basis of the Chinese state for the next two thousand years. Readings of the classics of Confucianism played a very important role in school education and a thorough knowledge of the writings of CONFUCIUS and his pupils was called for in the state examinations which every candidate for the mandarinate and for advancement within it had to pass. Furthermore, in the course of time, the imperial magistrates, highly educated and literate men who were sent into the provinces to perform administrative duties, spread the doctrines of Confucianism throughout the entire country.

One must not infer from the triumph of Confucianism that China abandoned the use of written law or that as a result of following the unwritten rules of 'li' social life was perfectly free from disruption. Confucian thinkers had to admit that under existing conditions state laws were needed for regulating human conduct, although they had much less value and merit than the 'li'. Even before the imperial unification of China there were codes, and under the TS'IN and HAN dynasties there was an unbroken succession of them; the older codes are lost save for chapter headings or fragments, and the earliest code which has survived complete is a code of the T'ANG dynasty from about the seventh century AD. It is worth noticing that these codes deal almost exclusively with questions of criminal and administrative law, though often in a sophisticated manner; questions of family and succession law are mentioned only in connection with criminal law or administrative law, for example for taxation purposes, and the codes pay hardly any overt attention to the law of commerce and commodities. This reflects the Confucian doctrine which sees legislation as a necessary evil, only to be invoked where the state must impose a criminal sanction because the cosmic order has been very seriously disturbed, or where the organization of the state administration is in issue. Even in the criminal law one finds the unmistakable influence of Confucianism; it finds expression, for example, in the careful gradation of the penalties for homicide and assault, not only in relation to the intention of the criminal and the external circumstances of the crime, but also in relation to the social position of the criminal and his victim. Thus the severity of the sentence depended very much on whether, for example, a father had injured his son, a husband his wife, or a master his slave, and equally it made a great difference if a wife had been maltreated by her husband or vice versa; if an older brother struck a younger, no penalty was imposed at all, but if a younger brother struck his elder, he might receive thirty months of hard labour and ninety strokes of the bamboo (for details, see BODDE/MORRIS (above p. 286) 29 f.).

Given that the great bulk of the legislation in ancient China appertained to criminal and administrative law and that the practice of law was mainly the practice of *criminal law*, how were conflicts of 'private law' decided? Here, in deference to the teachings of Confucianism, there developed a wide variety of forms of conflict-resolution outside the courts. For difficulties within the family the head of the family acted as conciliator, or else more remote relatives or even outsiders who were so respected because of their extreme age or high standing in the region or on other grounds that there was no 'loss of face' to either side in accepting the compromise they proposed. The standards applied by these conciliators in seeking a compromise came from the rules of behaviour of the 'li', the practices obtaining in the area, and also their own experience and knowledge of the world. If the first proposal for compromise was not accepted by the parties, discussions continued until finally the conciliator, whose prestige enabled him to bring considerable social and moral pressure to bear, succeeded in obtaining agreement. Similar procedures applied where the parties were not related to each other but belonged to the same kin-group or lived in the same village or were members of the same mercantile guild: here the oldest of the kin-group, the local mayor, other persons of the local élite, or the seniors of the guild were invited to act as conciliators. It was always open to the parties in these cases to take their way to the state courts which were held by imperial officials in the chief city of the province or region, but it was normal for parties to try the local conciliation procedures first, as indeed they had to if they were to avoid social censure; anyone who rejected a compromise proposed by a respected conciliator and brought the case before the officials would have to bear in mind that his behaviour would be castigated by the tight community of which he was a part. Furthermore, the procedures of the state courts were extremely prolonged and expensive, and the imperial magistrates had a reputation for being preoccupied, corrupt, and lazy (on this see COHEN, above p. 286).

Thus one can see that only a very small proportion of 'private law' disputes ever came before the state courts in imperial China. This was perfectly acceptable to the Chinese emperors and their governments, for it meant that most of these disputes were 'self-regulating' within the local communities on the basis of the traditional rules of behaviour which were dependent on status, that individuals stayed rooted in their narrow social context, and that the state administration was largely relieved of the duties of judicature and legislation in the field of Civil Law. Not until the end of the nineteenth century was there a gradual change. From about 1850 China had to enter many 'unequal treaties' with England, France, Germany, Russia, and Japan; these opened up Chinese ports and trading centres, granted extraterritoriality and a degree of separate jurisdiction to foreign nationals, and involved the cession or 'lease' of territories on the edge of the Chinese Empire. In 1899 indeed, the great powers, apparently in preparation for a grand annexation of the whole of China, entered a treaty which divided up the territory among them into 'spheres of interest'. The last MANCHU Emperors had to recognize that thorough internal reforms were needed if China was to be able to withstand competition from the European powers and avoid becoming the plaything of imperialist ambition. But this realization came too late. The Chinese Empire was powerless aboard, there were riots against foreigners, there were power struggles between reformists and conservatives, and the foreign debt was growing; this led to the abdication of the MANCHU dynasty in 1911, whereupon a Constitution was hastily drawn up and the Chinese state became a republic. The republican government of the following years was admittedly only a shadow government, since most of the country was in the power of mutually hostile generals and party leaders, and there was no time to think of the central reforms which were urgently needed. A degree of stability was first achieved in 1926/1928 when the Kuomintang party and their army under CHIANG KAI SHEK, schooled on the Russian pattern, succeeded in freeing China and bringing peace to the country for a few years. This period was used to codify the whole of private law; following the example of Japan and taking advantage of the Japanese experience, the codes were principally based on German and Swiss law (on this see BÜNGER and RUETE, above p. 286). In the 1930s the country was thrown into armed unrest once again. Japan annexed Manchuria in 1931 and attacked Central China four years later; at the same time there were communist uprisings throughout the country. The communist soldiers were forced to make the famous 'Long March' back to Northern China, but then the Soviet Union started to support the Chinese communists and sought to free China from the Japanese. With this Soviet help it only took a few years for the Chinese revolutionaries under MAO TSE-TUNG to clear the troops of the National Government from mainland China and the People's Republic of China was established in 1949.

III

One of the first acts of the new government was to abrogate all the legislation of the Kuomintang period as 'reactionary' and 'Western in spirit', and for many years nothing was put in its place, apart from a law of marriage in 1950. During the liberal period in 1950s ('Let a Thousand Flowers Bloom') a start was made with a criminal code and codes of criminal and civil procedure, but this soon ground to a halt. For a time one could attribute this to a suspicion on the part of MAO and the orthodox party cadres that law was an obstacle to the spontaneity of social processes, but with the outbreak of the 'Great Proletarian Cultural Revolution' mere suspicion turned to outright enmity, and the apparatus of justice which had been created in the Soviet image broke down completely. Lawyers were in the forefront of those who were hunted down by the Revolutionary Guards, tortured, deported to work in distant fields, imprisoned or killed, especially if during the liberal period they had stressed the value of law as essential to social life and economic development, or even gone so far as to suggest it might be useful to adopt elements of foreign law. After about a decade of this, the Cultural Revolution came to an end with the death of MAO in 1976 and the arrest of the Gang of Four, and since DENG XIAOPING became the leader of the party there has been a splendid renewal of belief in the value of a sensible legal order (for the details see MÜNZEL (above p. 286, at p. 18 ff.)).

The early 1980s saw the introduction of a criminal code and a code of criminal procedure, a law on the structure of courts and finally a code of civil procedure, in force in 1982, and much amended in 1991 (see MÜNZEL in *RabelsZ* 47 (1983) 78, with a translation). Mediation and compromise, the traditional method of resolving conflicts, are still used by the state itself: countless people's arbitral committees and other similar bodies have been set up and the courts have been told that in all suitable cases they should either seek compromise themselves or remit the matter for this purpose to one of the bodies mentioned. 1981 saw a law on 'economic contracts' between the 'units' of the state or co-operative economy, a law of succession came into force in 1985, and in 1982 and 1984 the law on trade marks and patents was codified; in 1986 there was even a law on bankruptcy (see CHIANG and XIAHUA in (1987) 28 *Harv. Int. LJ* 33 and 374).

The 'Fundamentals of Private Law' which came into force on 1 January 1987 serves as a basis for these and many other laws passed in the area of private law in the 1980s; its 156 articles regulate the private law relations between citizens and equivalent legal persons.

After a few introductory provisions in Chapter 1, Chapter 2, entitled 'Citizens', deals with legal capacity, wardship, and declaration of death as well as the legal status of individuals in business either on their own or in association with others. In Chapter 3 ('Legal persons') there are general provisions on the acquisition of legal capacity as a legal person. Chapter 4 deals with acts in law, notably their invalidity or avoidability for breach of the law or being against the public interest, for essential error, deceit, duress or the exploitation of critical circumstances. It also covers agency. Chapter 5 contains provisions on the protection of public and private property, the performance of contracts, and associated security transactions such as suretyship and pledge. Liability for breach of contract and tort is covered in Chapter 8 and private international law in Chapter 9. For details see ZHENG and EPSTEIN (above p. 286); XIE HUAISHI in *Int. Enc. Comp.L.* VII ch. 6 pp. 67 ff. (1992). The law is translated by GRAY and ZHENG in (1986) 34 *Am. J. Comp. L.* 715. There is also an English translation of a Chinese textbook concerning this law in JONES (above p. 286).

In the last few years the Chinese government has seen ever more clearly that the increased productivity needed to maintain its huge and growing population can only be achieved if much of the state regulation of the economy is dismantled and initiative returned to individuals. This happened first in agriculture, with farmers being allowed to sell some of their produce on their own account, and then many wholesale and retail markets in all kinds of consumer goods opened in towns and villages. Individuals and groups were allowed to act on their own account as artisans, run shops, building, and transport enterprises, employ persons outside the family, enter leases, make loans, and sign negotiable instruments. The control of state and co-operative enterprises is gradually being loosened, and markets in capital, housing, and currency are beginning to develop. It is clear that the government is riding a tiger. In many sectors the economy is overheating; inflation, corruption, and flight from the land are all worrying, as is the ostentation with which those who were quick to profit from changing circumstances are flaunting their new-found wealth.

The amount of legislation since the 1980s, some of it based on the experience of other countries, shows that China realizes that its economic development needs a solid legal infrastructure. It is quite another question whether the regulations are affecting people's conduct and are being applied by administrative and judicial authorities in quite the manner which the Western observer takes for granted. We do not have much information on this, and it is certainly too early to come to a firm conclusion since the new laws have only been in force for a short time and it is not easy to find court decisions or administrative guidelines: very few have been published. Many observers believe that unless the *political* system is reformed, law in China will not have the value which we in the West attribute to it:

'No greater autonomy is likely to be granted to law without extensive political reform, and the events of June 1989 are only the most dramatic and tragic demonstration of the hostility of China's leaders to such reform. In the absence of fundamental political reform that would validate abandonment of the reigning ideology, Chinese law is likely to . . . remain an assortment of disparate institutions lacking some of the elements that Western ideals take as essential in a meaningful formal legal system such as hierarchy of sources of law, differentiation from other organs of state power, procedural regularity and control of discretion in decision-making, and adherence to professional values among the officials in the system' (LUBMAN (above p. 286, at p. 319).

21

Japanese Law

BAUM, 'Rechtsdenken, Rechtssystem und Rechtswirklichkeit in Japan', *RabelsZ* 59 (1995) 258.
——/DROBNIG (eds.), *Japanisches Handels- und Wirtschaftsrecht* (1994).
BEER/TOMATSU, 'A Guide to the Study of Japanese Law' (1975) 23 *Am. J. Comp. L.* 284.
BLAKEMORE, 'Post-War Developments in Japanese Law' [1947] *Wis. L. Rev.* 632.
EUBEL at al., *Das japanische Rechtssystem, Ein Grundriß mit Hinweisen und Materialien zum Studium des japanischen Rechts* (1979).
HALEY, *Authority without Power, Law and the Japanese Paradox* (1991).
HENDERSON, *Conciliation and Japanese Law, Togugawa and Modern* (2 vols. 1964).
——/HALEY, *Law and the Legal Process in Japan* (2nd edn., 2 vols. 1988).
——/TORBERT/XIE, 'Contract in the Far East—China and Japan', *Int. Enc. Comp. L.* VII ch. 6 (1992).
IGARASHI, *Einführung in das japanische Recht* (1990).
ISHIMOTO, 'L'influence du Code civil français sur le droit japonais', *Rev. int. dr. comp.* 6 (1954) 744.
KIM/LAWSON, 'The Law of the Subtle Mind: The Traditional Japanese Conception of Law', 28 *ICLQ* 491 (1978).
KITAGAWA, 'Das Methodenproblem in der Dogmatik des japanischen bürgerlichen Rechts', *AcP* 166 (1966) 330.
——, *Rezeption und Fortbildung des europäischen Zivilrechts in Japan* (1970).
Lee, 'Die Rezeption des europäischen Zivilrechts in Ostasien', *ZvglRWiss* 86 (1987) 158.
LLOMPART, 'Japanisches und europäisches Rechtsdenken', *Rechtstheorie* 16 (1985) 131.
VON MEHREN (ed.), *Law in Japan, The Legal Order in a Changing Society* (1963).
MENKHAUS (ed.), *Das Japanische im japanischen Recht* (1994).
MURAKAMI, *Einführung in die Grundlagen des japanischen Rechts* (1974).
NODA, 'The Far Eastern Conception of Law', *Int. Enc. Comp. L.* II ch. 1 (1975).
——, *Introduction to Japanese Law* (7th edn., 1987).
ODA, *Japanese Law* (1992).
OKI, 'Schlichtung als Institution des Rechts, Ein Vergleich von europäischem und japanischem Rechtsdenken', *Rechtstheorie* 16 (1985) 151.
RAHN, *Rechtsdenken und Rechtsauffassung in Japan* (1990).
RÖHL, *Fremde Einflüsse im modernen japanischen Recht* (1959).
ROKUMOTO, 'Juristen und zivilrechtliche Streitigkeiten in Japan, Die Problematik der Verkehrsunfälle', *Recht in Japan* 3 (1980) 47.
——, 'Tschotei (Schlichtung), Eine japanische Alternative zum Recht: Verfahren, Praxis und Funktionen', *Jahrbuch für Rechtssoziologie* 6 (1980) 390.

STEVENS, 'Modern Japanese Law as an Instrument of Comparison', (1971) 19 *Am. J. Comp. L.* 665.

TANAKA, *The Japanese Legal System* (1976).

I

LIKE Korea and Indo-China, *Japan* came under the influence of the highly developed Chinese civilization at an early stage. Chinese writing came to Japan in about the fifth century AD and Buddhism in the following century. In the seventh and eighth centuries the rulers of Japan were great admirers of Chinese intellect; they were familiar with Chinese literature and art, they adopted Buddhism, and they reorganized their state on the Chinese pattern by instituting a hierarchy of salaried officials and making their own position one of individual omnipotence, rather like that of the Chinese Emperors. The earliest of the Japanese statutes which have come down to us are also very like those of the Chinese T'ANG dynasty.

The Mikados were not able to maintain their unlimited governmental power against the powerful territorial rulers for long. From about the twelfth century they were emperors only in name; the Mikado was hidden away from the people in his palace and real power was exercised in his name by the Crown Field Marshal of the day, the Shogun. As the powerful families in the country waged constant war in an attempt to win the shogunate for themselves and to make it hereditary, Japan experienced hardly any extended period of internal peace until the late sixteenth century. The situation became stabilized only under the Shogunate of the TOKUGAWA family (1603–1867). At that time the country had a strongly feudal and stratified social structure: at the bottom of the social pecking-order were the craftsmen and the tradesmen, above them the farmers, who paid heavy taxes to lease their land from the feudal leaders, and above them, predominantly from the Samurai class, were the priests, doctors, and scholars, along with officials and soldiers of the princes; the Shogun was the feudal superior of all. The social philosophy best adapted to this stratified society was Confuciansim, which was dominant in the TOKUGAWA period in a variant suited to Japanese conditions. Although a comprehensive courts system developed in the course of time, disputes of 'private law' were mainly resolved, just as in China, by conciliation procedures in the relevant social groups (on this see in detail HENDERSON (above p. 295) vol. I).

It was the policy of the TOKUGAWA Shoguns to cut their Empire off as completely as possible from the outside world: no Japanese person might leave the land nor any stranger come to it. This did not apply to the Chinese, with whom trade relations continued, and the Dutch had permission, under extreme security precautions, to enter specified harbours for the purpose of trade. But gradually an interest in Western learning manifested itself. In the early eighteenth century there was a relaxation of the ban on the import of Western books, and Western technology played some part in the early development of industrialization, notably in iron production and shipbuilding. But the corresponding Western interest in trade with Japan grew very much more rapidly, and in the nineteenth century was so great that the isolation desired by the Shoguns could not be maintained for long. In 1853 the Americans gave dramatic expression to their wish for trade links by sending a fleet of warships to cruise off the Japanese coast, and this induced the Shogun to enter 'unequal treaties', first with the United States and then with England, Russia, and the Netherlands. These treaties gave foreigners the right to settle in specified cities, to indulge in trade, and to have consular representation. These policies of the Shogun evoked passionate opposition in Japan, based as much on xenophobia as on a growing desire to get rid of the Shogunate. The Emperor emerged from his retreat and placed himself at the head of the opposition; only a few years later the position of the Shogun was so weakened that in 1867 he had to withdraw and place full governmental power in the hands of the Emperor. The Emperor's advisers had meanwhile seen that the country needed to enter into close links with foreign nations and to learn from their superior technical and scientific knowledge. Even the conservative leaders soon accepted this view, and within a few decades the old feudal state had been changed into an absolute monarchy, admittedly retaining its patriarchal social structure. The army and the administration were modernized on the European model, the technology of the West was adopted, and finally, in 1889, a new Constitution was introduced, modelled on that of Prussia, which made Japan into a constitutional monarchy. All powers of decision remained with the Emperor, however; only the wealthiest citizens, about 2 per cent of the population, could vote in elections to the Lower House and only persons who were noble by birth or by imperial accolade could sit in the Upper House.

In the 'unequal treaties' Japan had had to agree that consular courts rather than the Japanese courts should have jurisdiction over foreign nationals in both private and criminal matters. In order to rid themselves of this discrimination, the Japanese were eager from the very beginning to alter their law on the European model. For this purpose they called Professor BOISSONADE from Paris and gave him the task of drafting a criminal code and a code of criminal procedure. After BOISSONADE had completed his task and seen his drafts, strongly orientated to French law, come into force in 1880, he turned to the preparation of a civil code. Concurrently Professor ROESLER, a German, was charged with drafting a commercial code. BOISSONADE's draft was largely based on the Code civil, save that family and succession law were drafted by a Japanese committee. Along with ROESLER's draft of a commercial code it was placed before the Japanese Parliament in 1890 and was due to come into force in 1893, but there was lively opposition to both drafts in Parliament. Many members objected that the draft civil code was too biased in favour of French law and should have been drawn on a broader comparative basis; others thought that the time for such codification was not yet ripe and that in any case much more attention should have been paid to traditional Japanese legal institutions. The 'codi-fication dispute' gradually broadened into a general conflict between conservatives and progressives and the end of the affair was a successful pro-posal to shelve both drafts. The preparation of the civil code was now given to a commission consisting of three Japanese professors. The draft produced by this committee in 1896/8 showed sporadic influences of French law and the Common Law here and there, but followed the two drafts of the German BGB in important points of structure and content. It was only in family law and the law of succession that the draftsmen adopted any number of Japanese institutions, notably the so-called 'family system'.

It is hard to say why the pendulum finally swung so markedly in favour of German law during the preparation of the Japanese Civil Code. One important factor was cer-tainly the fact that at the time the BGB rated as the most mature product of the Con-tinental art of legislation; another was that several technical defects had already become apparent in the Code civil. Nor did the Japanese find the heavy learning and conceptualism of the German Code at all uncongenial; rather the reverse. As time was to show, Japanese legal scholars were much drawn to systematic theorizing, and the German code went far to answer this tendency. Perhaps an additional factor was that the BGB was a product of the German Empire, whose political stance must have seemed thoroughly appealing to the extremely conservative leaders of Japan at the time.

In 1898 the Japanese Civil Code came into force and in the following year the Commercial Code; both were squarely based on their German counter-part. The organization of the courts and procedure in civil matters were also regulated by statutes on the German pattern; indeed, large parts of the Japa-nese Code of Civil Procedure of 1890 are simply literal translations of the German one. It is therefore no surprise that thereafter the principal stimulus for Japanese scholarship in private law came from Germany; it has been said that towards the end of the First World War this influence was so great 'that one could find in Japanese law a true reflection of German legal scholarship' (KITAGAWA, *AcP* 166 (1966) 330).

After the Second World War the Common Law, especially North Ameri-can law, had the strongest influence on Japanese law. American legal ideas underlie the new Japanese Constitution of 1946, which considerably strengthened the judiciary and contained a list of basic rights directly bind-ing on the courts. Criminal procedure was reformed on the American model in 1948, and even the Code of Civil Procedure was altered on some points so as to curtail the judge's power to control the proceedings and to leave more room for the initiative of the parties and their counsel. The constitutional requirement of equal treatment of man and wife necessitated a fundamental reconstruction of the family and succession law in the Civil Code and the old Japanese 'family system' had to be abandoned. In order to democratize the economy, the American occupying force insisted on the enactment of a strong 'antimonopoly law', and a new company law was enacted as well as laws on the supervision of the stock market and the issuance of shares, all based on American models. Japanese legal scholars also adopted new methods as a result of contact with Anglo-American legal thought: there is now much less of the purely dogmatic approach of the pre-war period; instead, one finds Japanese legal scholars producing many more studies of the interaction of law and society and the practical operation of individual legal institutions. Such studies have confirmed the perception that imported legal rules need to be understood and applied in a manner suited to the special conditions of the country and the values of its people. Thus in the last few years Japanese legal scholarship has increasingly emancipated itself from foreign models and become increasingly conscious of its autonomy.

Oda is accordingly in our view right to object to placing Japan along with China in a 'Far Eastern Legal Family'. He asserts 'that Japanese law is part of the Romano-germanic family of law, with some elements of American law' (above p. 296, at p. 6). On the latter point one might demur, but what it shows is that the doctrine of legal families should not be taken too seriously, for it can often lead to simplifications which do violence to the facts (see above p. 72 f.).—Basic information on the development and present state of Japanese law can be found in VON MEHREN (ed.), *Law in Japan, The Legal Order in a Changing Society* (1963), a co-operative work in which Japanese authors with American advisers report on the modern constitutional, criminal, family, and economic law. Of more recent writing one can consult especially ODA, *Japanese Law* (1992) and BAUM/DROBNIG (eds.), *Japanisches Handels- und Wirtschaftsrecht* (1994), with a bibliography by BAUM of modern writing on Japanese law in Western languages.

II

This historical sketch of Japanese law must have caused many readers to ask themselves whether the numerous statutes imported into Japanese law between 1890 and 1900 really struck root, whether they became 'living law' and were implemented in practice in the same way as in their European countries of origin. Of course, Japanese society at the end of the MEIJI period was very different from the acquisitive bourgeois society of the end of the nineteenth century for which the codes were suited. In Western Europe it was the heyday of liberalism, of the idea that the responsible individual should be in a position to determine his own fate independently of traditional social and religious authority. So, too, in the economic sphere liberalism saw individual initiative and enterprise as the motors of progress and called on the legal order to afford the individual entrepreneur the requisite room for manoeuvre by guaranteeing freedom of contract and the freedom to deal with his property more or less as he chose. Such individualism was quite foreign to Japanese society. It is true that the modernization of the state administration was precipitate, the adoption of technical knowledge and skills from abroad swift, and the reception of foreign legal institutions massive, but all this did nothing to loosen the social bonds which tradition imposed on the individual by reason of his place in the family, kin-group, and village community, on the artisan and tradesman by his membership of the guild, or on the farmer by his relationship with the landowner. It is true that within a few decades thriving industries had grown up in Japan, but they did not owe their existence to the activity and risk-taking of individual competitive entrepreneurs. On the contrary, these industries were founded by the imperial administration in order to speed up economic development and were then transferred to the feudal lords of yesteryear, rather as compensation for the loss of political influence. Industrialization changed very little in the social structure of the country to begin with: capitalist privilege took the place of feudal privilege and the patriarchal *tai-kun* was replaced by the patriarchal tycoon.

Given these circumstances it is clear that until well into the twentieth century these imported statutes had very little practical effect on Japanese legal life. Even then very few citizens made use of the legal rights that the new laws put at their disposal because in all sections of society, but especially among the farmers, the distaste for bringing one's disputes into the open before state courts was still so strong, rooted as it was in the Confucian tradition. The traditional forms of peaceful conciliation and arbitration continued to predominate and the very fact that the written law and the procedures of the state courts were so largely unused may have contributed to the extreme devotion with which Japanese legal scholars until the Second World War followed the unrewarding art of dealing in pandectist conceptualism.

One might think that at the present day the traditional tendency to resolve disputes without resort to the courts must be beginning to weaken. Indeed there is some evidence for this. At the same time, the Western observer is surprised to find how tenaciously the Japanese cling to their old practices despite all the changes in the circumstances of life. Disputes between members of a family are still predominantly resolved by internal procedures, without invoking the courts. For example, before a marriage the families of the fiancés normally commission a middleman to help with all the questions connected with the wedding, to serve as best man, and especially to intervene as arbitrator and reconciliator in any difficulties which may subsequently arise between the spouses or between them and their families. For a divorce in Japan there is no need to have court proceedings and judicial decree, except in the rare cases where the parties cannot reach agreement, even after the mediation which must precede any court proceedings. If the parties do agree, the divorce is effective as soon they communicate their agreement to the registry office. As to the *consequences* of divorce—the distribution of property, maintenance, the custody of children—agreement is reached through the offices of the middlemen mentioned above or relatives and friends of the spouses, or, if need be, in the mediation proceedings already mentioned; attorneys hardly ever figure. Disputes between neighbours or the parties to a lease are settled so far as possible by amicable arrangement. In the case of a traffic accident, the victims or their dependants, rather than go to court, often make their claims good in special mediation offices (see ODA (above p. 295) 85 f.), with the help of experienced third parties, perhaps a retired policeman, or the personnel officer in the victim's firm, or a trade union official, or a respected businessman with relevant experience (see ROKUMOTO, above p. 295). Even where difficulties arise in the performance of contracts, the courts are regarded as the last resort. This is because in deciding the case the judge cannot take account of the many imponderables which give any contract its unique flavour, such as the importance, size, age, and reputation of the business involved, the length and nature of their mutual trade relations, the actual economic situation of the parties to the contract, and much else; he must always apply abstract, impersonal, and schematic rules of law, and usually ends up by handing down a decision which does right to one party at the price of doing wrong to the other. Parties to contracts in Japan regard this as a crude, even a rude, way of proceeding. It is much better to negotiate a compromise. In so doing one should consider whether perhaps one of the parties has not done a favour to the other in the past and can therefore expect some forbearance now. In Japanese thinking a person owes a duty of gratitude to whoever renders a service or confers a benefit, and although this duty is not to be adverted to, let alone sued on, yet the other can expect it to be acted on; the rule may be unwritten but it is ethically binding. Businessmen from the West should therefore tread delicately and deal tactfully and sensitively with their Japanese partners and be quick to recognize that they keep invisible accounts. (See RAHN in BAUM/DROBNIG (above p. 295) at p. 9 ff. with further references.)

Even if it is not possible to reach agreement by negotiation or through conciliation by a third party, polarized procedure before the state judge may still be avoided. Japanese law offers the parties a special statutorily regulated arbitral procedure. On the request of a party the court may set up an arbitral committee containing two or more laymen under a judge whose chairmanship is largely nominal. This arbitral committee issues invitations to all the parties to the dispute, listens to what they have to say and tries to move them towards a friendly agreement. If this fails, a complaint can still be raised by regular procedure; and, apart from a few matters in family law, there is no need to try the arbitral procedure at all before making a claim in court. In practice, however, arbitral proceedings are very important and the regular courts themselves often adjourn a legal dispute and refer the matter to the arbitral committee.

But it would be wrong to overemphasize the Japanese preference for resolving disputes uncontentiously. Many people familiar with Japan believe it to be a myth that the Japanese are reluctant to litigate. They do not deny that there is much less resort to the courts in Japan than in West Germany or other industrialized countries of the West, but they say that this is not really due to the conditioning effect of Confucianism (*contra* NODA (above p. 295) and KAWASHIMA in VON MEHREN (above p. 295, at 43 ff.); they offer the somewhat duller explanation that the court system in Japan has long been under strain, that there are fewer judges and lawyers than elsewhere, and that a case may take many years to come to trial; that is why arbitration or other forms of dispute resolution are preferred to the courts (see ODA (above p. 295) at 86 ff., 94 ff., with statistics). They also point out that some recent lawsuits in Japan, especially in the area of environmental law and products liability, have involved thousands of plaintiffs, massive publicity, and a degree of passion and animus rarely found elsewhere.

See HALEY, 'The Myth of the Reluctant Litigant' (1978) 4 *J Japanese Stud.* 359; TANAKA, 'The Role of Law in Japanese Society: Comparisons with the West' (1985) 19 *UBCL. Rev.* 375; OKI (above p. 295); ODA (above p. 295) p. 87 f.; RAMSEYER, 'Reluctant Litigant Revisited: Rationality and Disputes in Japan' (1988) 14 *J Japanese Stud.* III.

VI. RELIGIOUS LEGAL SYSTEMS

22

Islamic Law

AFCHAR, 'The Muslim Conception of Law', II *Int. Enc. Comp. L.* Ch. 1 (1975).
AMIN, *Islamic Law in the Contemporary World* (1985).
——, *Middle East Legal Systems* (1985).
ANDERSON, *Law Reform in the Muslim World* (1976).
——, 'The Significance of Islamic Law in the Modern World', 9 *Am. J. Comp. L.* 187 (1960).
——, 'Islamic Family Law', *Int. Enc. Comp. L.* IV ch. 11 III (1969).
BADR, 'Islamic Law: Its Relation to other Legal Systems', 26 *Am. J. Comp. L.* 187 (1978).
BERGSTRÄSSER, *Grundzüge des islamischen Rechts* (ed. Schacht, 1935).
CHARLES, *Le Droit musulman* (4th edn., 1972).
CHEHATA, *Études de droit musulman* (1971).
COULSON, 'Islamic Law', *An Introduction to Legal Systems* (ed. Derrett, 1968) 54.
——, *A History of Islamic Law* (1978).
——, *Conflicts and Tensions in Islamic Jurisprudence* (1969).
FYZEE, *Outlines of Muhammadan Law* (4th edn., 1974).
——, *A Modern Approach to Islam* (1981).
HILL, 'Comparative and Historical Study of Modern Middle Eastern Law', 26 *Am. J. Comp. L.* 279 (1978).
KHOJA, *Elements of Islamic Jurisprudence* (1977).
LIEBESNY, *The Law of the Near and Middle East, Readings, Cases and Materials* (1975).
LINANT DE BELLEFONDS, *Traité de droit musulman comparé*, 3 vols. (1965–73).
RAMADAN, *Das islamische Recht, Theorie und Praxis* (1980).
SCHACHT, *The Legacy of Islam* (2nd edn., 1974).
——, *The Origins of Muhammadan Jurisprudence* (1950).
——, *An Introduction to Islamic Law* (1964).
SFEIR, 'The Saudi Approach to Law Reform', 36 *Am. J. Comp. L.* 729 (1988).
WIEDENSOHLER, 'Grundbegriffe des islamischen Rechts', *RabelsZ* 35 (1971) 632.

I

THE Shariah, as Islamic law is called in Arabic, is the complex of divinely revealed rules which the faithful Muslim must observe if he seeks to perform the duties of religion. The crucial difference between Islamic and Western law is immediately apparent from this description. The unique ground of validity of Islamic law is that it is the manifested will of the Almighty: it does not depend on the authority of any earthly law-giver. The consequences of this difference are manifold.

One of these consequences is that Islamic law is in principle *immutable*, for it is the law revealed by God. Western legal systems generally recognize that the content of law alters as it is adapted to changing needs by the legislator, the judges, and all other social forces which have a part in the creation of law, but Islam starts from the proposition that all existing law comes from ALLAH who at a certain moment in history revealed it to man through his prophet MUHAMMAD. Thus Islamic legal theory cannot accept the historical approach of studying law as a function of the changing conditions of life in a particular society. On the contrary, the law of ALLAH was given to man once and for all: society must adapt itself to the law rather than generate laws of its own as a response to the constantly changing stimulus of the problems of life. Admittedly Islamic legal theory recognizes that the divine revelation did not start out in a comprehensible and orderly form and that it needed many centuries of work by Islamic jurists to extract the full content of the recognized sources of law and fit it for practical use. But according to the orthodox Islamic view these efforts were directed not to the creation of a *new* law but to the discovery, understanding, and formulation of a law which *already exists*.

Since Islamic law reflects the will of ALLAH rather than the will of a human lawmaker, it covers *all* areas of life and not simply those which are of interest to state or society. Thus Islamic law regulates the prayers a Muslim must make, the periods of fasting he must observe, the alms he must distribute, and the pilgrimages he must undertake. The observance of these precepts may not be enforced, but even so the shariah claims to be a comprehensive ethic or doctrine of duties (*fiqh*) which controls the entire earthly existence of Muslims and shows them the way in which they must perform their religious duties in order to earn the promised reward of bliss in a better world.

With its fundamental claim to regulate the totality of human behaviour, Islamic law is followed by as many as 500 million human beings, nearly a sixth of the entire population of the world. Although Islam is the most recent of the three monotheistic world religions, its propagation was immensely wide. MUHAMMAD died in 632, and barely a century later, when the Caliphs of the Ummayyad dynasty were in power, Islam had spread in the train of the Arabian hordes across the whole northern coast of Africa and deep into Spain; in the East it crossed Persia and reached the Indus. In the fifteenth century a second wave of conquest led by the Sultans of the Ottoman dynasty overthrew the Byzantine Empire, conquered Constantinople (1453) and established the dominance of Islam in South-Eastern Europe;

Yugoslavia, Albania, and Bulgaria still have significant Muslim minorities. In *Asia*, too, Islam had great success; indeed after the Second World War the Muslims succeeded in establishing Pakistan as a state of their own; in the Republic of India about 10 per cent of the inhabitants, some 50 million people, are adherents of Islam. The non-Chinese population of Malaysia and Indonesia is predominantly Muslim. In *Africa* missionaries and tradesmen won the Nile Valley, the Sudan of today, for Islam, and it spread from there along the trade-routes of the Sahara to the West, so that not only Northern Nigeria but also most of the states in what was previously French West Africa (see above Ch. 8 V c) have populations which are mainly Muslim. On the East Coast of Africa as well Islam is fairly widespread; Somalia is almost entirely Islamic and Tanzania and Kenya have strong Islamic minorities.

II

The highest and most important source of Islamic law is the Koran, a collection, made a few years after his death, of the utterances of the prophet MUHAMMAD which are considered to be based on divine revelation. Only a few of the statements in the Koran constitute rules of law capable of direct application. It consists mainly of precepts of proper ethical behaviour too generally phrased to have the precision and point of legal rules. For example, the Koran prescribes that a Muslim must take pity on the weak and helpless, that in his business dealings he must act in good faith, that he must not bribe judges, and that he must abstain from usury and gambling, but it does not specify what legal consequences, if any, attach to a disregard of these commandments. Furthermore most of the rules of behaviour contained in the Koran concern the rituals of prayer, fasting, and pilgrimage; even where it deals with legal problems in the narrower sense, such as those of family law, it does not offer an integrated system of rules but simply gives the solution of a few individual problems with which MUHAMMAD was concerned as a judge and prophet of the law. In this role MUHAMMAD always started from the customary law prevalent among the Arab peoples; he altered or added to it only where it seemed to him inadequate or unsatisfactory, or where it ran counter to his political goal of replacing the old Arab tribalism with a community of men bound together by belief in ALLAH.

For instance, MUHAMMAD found a rule in customary Arab law that only the male relatives of a decedent might succeed him; rather than replace this rule with another rule, he modified it by recognizing that the daughters, widows, and sisters of the deceased had certain rights of succession as well as his male relatives. This represented a move away from the traditional patriarchal organization of the tribe based on the blood group towards a new model of society in which the *family* formed the basic unit in a community bound together by belief in ALLAH. In another respect also

MUHAMMAD improved the legal position of the wife. He softened the old rule that a husband could at any time unilaterally repudiate his wife without any restriction by holding that the husband could repudiate his wife only if he took equitable account of her needs and always made suitable provision for her maintenance thereafter. Whether this commandment is to be seen as a general ethical guide or as a legal duty with definite legal consequences is not a question to which the Koran offers any answer.

After the death of MUHAMMAD (632) the political leadership, which carried with it the position of supreme judge, passed to the Caliphs (literally 'representatives') of whom the first four were his disciples. In giving judgment, they and the judges they appointed mainly applied the existing customary law, having regard to any instructions the Koran might give. The greater part of the law remained 'indifferent to religion' and 'if this situation had continued there might have developed a law only sporadically influenced by the doctrines of religious duties but mainly based on practice, useful in practice, and applied in practice' (BERGSTRÄSSER, above p. 303, p. 12). The political rulers then became secularized and this provoked a reaction, especially among those who regarded themselves as guardians of the religious tradition. It was this reaction which finally brought all law into the field of the Islamic religion. After the death of the fourth Caliph, ALI, the son-in-law of MUHAMMAD, the great family of the UMMAYYADS from Mecca came to power; in the tradition of the old Arab princely leaders they saw themselves mainly as politicians and statesmen and used their seat of government in Damascus as a base from which to direct the world-wide operations of the Arabian armies.

One group of Muslims believes that the title of Imam is hereditary in the family of ALI and that only his successors can accede to the Imamate or leadership of the Islamic religious community. They therefore regard the first three Caliphs and the Ummayyads in particular as usurpers. This group is called the *Shi'a*, which means 'the party' (ALI's party). It is now split into several factions with different views about the line of ALI's succession. Their religious and legal practices differ in many respects from those of other Muslims, called the *Sunni*. About 8% of all Muslims today are Shi'a, most of whom live in Iran, Iraq, the Lebanon, and in the Southern Republics of the erstwhile Soviet Union, especially Turkmenestan, Kazakhstan, and Uzbekistan.

The Ummayyads were soon criticized for the secular style of their government. The critics were based in Medina where a group of pious scholars maintained that life in all its aspects must be subservient to the claims of religion and that all human behaviour must therefore be tested by the standard of the Islamic doctrine of duty. In examining the law in all areas to see whether it was consistent with the ethical mandates of MUHAMMAD, they had to discover what legal consequences flowed from the rules of the Koran; this was not easy since they were basically only general ethical and religious guidelines for the human behaviour which would be pleasing to the

Almighty. It soon became clear that the Koran by itself would not do, so its shortcomings in this respect were made good from the sayings and doings which tradition attributed to the prophet himself or to his immediate disciples. There is no doubt that the Sunna, as this tradition is called, is very largely unhistorical and that it was invented by Islamic scholars more or less in good faith in order to lend support to their views. Islamic scholars today see the Sunna as being 'documents not of the time to which they claim to belong, but of the successive stages of doctrinal development during the first centuries of Islam' (SCHACHT, *Origins* (above p. 303) p. 4). However this may be, Islamic theory still holds the Sunna to be the second great source of law, after the Koran. The *Abbasides* who took over the Caliphate in 750 gave strong support to the efforts of the pious legal scholars. They gave religious law greater influence in the state, recognized the authority of the leading legal scholars, and called many of them to high judicial office. Meanwhile several centres for the study of the divine revelation had grown up and were flourishing in the great Arab Empire. In addition to Medina there was the city of Kufa in Iraq where a group of important legal scholars gradually formed a school of consistent legal doctrine. The legal school of Kufa is called the *Hanafi* school, after ABU HANIFA, one of its earliest and most respected members, while the school of Medina is called the *Maliki* school, after the scholar MALIK. In the course of time serious disagreements arose between these schools of law. Individual scholars were originally allowed to make up their own mind on matters not foreclosed by the Koran and the Sunna, but the members of the different schools, which were geographically far apart, were influenced in their views by the style of life, the stage of development, and the legal practices of the surrounding population, so it was only natural that the schools should reach different views—a fact which was redeemed in Islam by reference to a saying attributed to MUHAMMAD: 'Differences of opinion in my community are a sign of the goodness of ALLAH'. Towards the end of the ninth century there arose two further law schools which are still vital: *Shafi'i*, so called after the famous scholar AS-SAFI'I, of whom we shall have to speak in a moment, and the *Hanbali* school, named after its founder IBN-HANBAL.

In the course of time these four schools of law established themselves in definite parts of the Islamic world: the Maliki in North, West and Central Africa, the Hanafi in the Near and Middle East and the Indus Valley, the Shafi'i in East Africa, Malaysia and Indonesia, and the Hanbali in Saudi Arabia. Each school of law recognized the legitimacy of the others; although the holy law is in principle unitary, the different versions are seen as divinely ordained.

Nevertheless the manifold differences of doctrine between individual scholars and schools led to some concern lest Islamic law disintegrate in a plethora of private opinions. In order to counter this risk AS-SAFI'I, a famous scholar who died in 820, produced a doctrine of the four 'roots' of Islamic law, which was to provide jurists with a fixed and common method of finding law. The first 'root' of Islamic law is naturally the *Koran*. The second 'root' is the *Sunna*, the sum total of the inspired practice of the prophet, so important for interpreting and clarifying the rules of the Koran. The third 'root' is the *igma*, the consensus reached by the entire Islamic community, laymen as well as lawyers, on any question of the doctrine of the duties of the faithful. The fourth and last 'root' is analogy (*qiyas*), that is, the application to new and similar cases of rules established by the Koran, the Sunna, or *igma*. Subsequent doctrine made only one change in this scheme, a change in the idea of *igma* which greatly increased its practical significance: a proposition was to be regarded as a rule of law if at any time the living *legal scholars* of all or even one of the schools of law agreed on it—a principle which perhaps has some historical connection with the Roman idea of *communis opinio prudentium*. It will be obvious that this classical system of the four 'roots' of Islamic law comprises very different things, namely two *sources*—the Koran and the Sunna—*a method*—the use of analogy—and a *judgement*— that of *igma*; and it will be equally clear that among these roots the agreed judgment of scholars has the critical role, for it alone can finally decide, with or without the use of analogy, what valid rule of law can be taken from the Koran or the Sunna.

III

After the classical doctrine of the 'roots' of Islamic law had been embraced by all the schools of law, the legal creativity of Islamic jurists gradually began to dry up. Whereas the earlier practice had been to resolve doubtful questions in a relatively free manner while still adhering to the spirit of the Koran and the Sunna, this was now regarded as improper, and as more and more open questions were answered by the agreement of scholars, the solutions became part of the divine law and closed to critical investigation. From about the ninth century the view prevailed that it was not open to jurists to adopt an independent opinion founded directly on the Koran or Sunna; jurists were to confine themselves to the explanation and interpretation of books of law regarded as authoritative in the individual law schools. Thus Islamic legal scholarship gradually became quite rigid and dry, a fact which may have contributed to the subsequent development of certain areas of law outside the shariah and the religious courts.

It was still implicitly recognized that the Caliph, as head of government, was entitled to refer disputes in *constitutional* and *administrative* law to special judges with an indication of the rules they were to apply; *administrative crimes* and *disputes over land* were also reserved for special courts since for political reasons the law had to be effective in these areas and the traditional courts had methods of proof by wit-

nesses and oaths which were extremely cumbrous. Thus despite its theoretical claim
to control the *totality* of human life, the practical significance of the shariah was really
limited to the area of *private law*.—The doctrinal immutability of religious law and
the actual immobility of legal scholarship led the courts to accept a large number
of *acts of evasion*. For example, loans at interest were rendered impermissible by the
prohibition of usury in the Koran, so the device of the '*double sale*' was used instead:
the borrower 'sold' some object or other to the lender, which the lender immediately
'sold back' to the borrower at a 'price' inflated by the agreed amount of interest and
payable only after the period of the loan was up. Such 'legal tricks' (*hiyal*) made it
possible for the courts to do what was required by the exigencies of practice while
adhering to the doctrine in the rules of the shariah. (For more detail, see COULSON,
History (above p. 303) 138 ff.; SCHACHT, *Introduction* (above p. 303) 78 ff.)

Until the beginning of the nineteenth century the social condition of the
peoples of the Islamic world developed very slowly and the shariah remained
quite appropriate to their needs despite its doctrinal rigidity. But from 1850
onwards it faced a decisive challenge. As the Ottoman Empire went into gradual decline there was an increase in the political influence of the great European powers in the Near East, and the leaders of the Islamic world came to
see, after contact with the outside world, that administration and law must
be completely modernized if any stand were to be made against the political
and economic competition of the European powers. Naturally, any proposals for reform in the state conflicted with the traditional Islamic doctrine
that the holy law prescribed for it was immutable and immune to legislative
intervention.

The reform legislation of the Ottoman rulers between 1840 and 1876 (see
above Ch. 8 V a) was nevertheless carried through without very great resistance from conservative circles. The adoption of the Code de commerce and
the French maritime law concerned areas in which conflict with traditional
Islamic law could rarely arise. Then the Code of Commercial Procedure gave
jurisdiction over disputes relating to property and obligations to a special
secular court. This, too, was unobjectionable, since by Islamic tradition
the state was entitled to prescribe the external conditions of life for the community of the faithful; this was the extent of its entitlement, but it included
making regulations in constitutional and administrative law and also for the
organization of the courts and their procedure. The Turkish rulers went a
step further in passing the *Majalla* (1869–76), an enactment of about 1850
articles which attempted to consolidate the Islamic law of property and obligations according to the Hanafi school. This step was as necessary as it was
novel: *necessary* because the secular courts which had just obtained jurisdiction over disputes concerning property and obligations could hardly study
the medieval law books, and *novel* in that here for the first time the rules
of the shariah were produced in the form of paragraphs in the European
style and brought into force with the authority of the state (see TEDESCHI,

'Le Centenaire de la Mejelle', *Rev. int. dr. comp.* 21 (1969) 125). None of these reforms yet involved any state interference with the heartland of the shariah, that is, the law of family and the law of succession.

In regions which were directly controlled by the colonial powers the development was different. There too it was always recognized that the rules of the shariah should be applied in disputes between Muslims. But in *British India*, for example, cases were decided by judges who were British by birth or education and in the last resort by the judges of the Privy Council in London, so in the course of time Islamic law absorbed much of the Common Law, to a degree which makes it possible even to speak of 'Anglo-Muhammadan Law'. This is because wherever the judges found the rules of the shariah to be deficient, obscure, obsolete or inconsistent with 'justice, equity and good conscience', they had recourse, often quite unconsciously, to the principles and concepts of the Common Law with which they were more familiar. It is also because of British traditions that 'Anglo-Muhammadan Law' is treated as *case-law* in India and Pakistan today and accepts the principle of binding precedent. Furthermore, a whole series of statutes which substantially codify the Common Law of property and obligations were brought into forcing starting in 1872 (see above Ch. 16 IV) so that 'Anglo-Muhammadan Law' retains its significance today only for family law and the law of succession.

As the world entered the twentieth century, government reforms began to reach even family law and the law of succession. In 1917, under one of the last Sultans, the Ottoman Law of Family Rights was enacted in which, instead of accepting all the rules of the Hanafi school which had authority in the Ottoman Empire, the legislator quite openly adopted some more progressive rules from the Hanbali and Maliki schools. Egypt and the Sudan, then an Anglo-Egyptian condominium, followed suit with similar statutes in the 1920s and 1930s, and after the Second World War laws regulating family and succession matters were enacted or proposed in nearly all Arab states. Jordan passed such a law in 1951, Syria in 1953, Tunisia in 1956, Morocco in 1958, and Iraq in 1959, and elsewhere drafting is in hand. These laws have several reforms in view: they seek to lay down conditions for the exercise of the husband's right to repudiate his wife unilaterally, to give *wives* a certain right to divorce their husband, to put limits to the way parents and guardians could arrange for the marriage of minors, and to diminish or abolish the practice of polygamy. None of the countries we have mentioned has found that these reforms required the abandonment of the shariah as the basis of family law and its replacement by something entirely new. Only Turkey found it necessary to take so drastic a step: the Swiss Civil Code which was introduced in 1926 made a radical break with traditional Islamic practices in family and succession law, and has had great difficulty in winning gradual recognition among the population at large (see above Ch. 13 III).

The decision in Islamic countries to hold fast to the shariah as the basis of family law has also had its difficulties. For orthodox Muslims Islamic law, being based on divine revelation, was in principle unalterable and could not be substantially changed by the state legislature just because some reform might be thought necessary. In order to justify the new statutory solutions in the eyes of the public and especially the faithful, it had to be shown that each of the changes was in harmony with the principles of the shariah. One transparent device was to change the substantive law by means of adopting a *procedural* rule which was within the competence of the legislator. To begin with, for example, Egypt did not explicitly forbid the marriage of minors which the Koran permitted; it was simply enacted that courts could render decisions in matrimonial affairs only if the marriage was registered, and that a marriage could only be registered if the parties to it had reached a certain age. Another principle was of more importance in practice: this was that where the views of the Islamic law schools differed the legislator had the right to prescribe by formal law which view should be applied by the judges. Even in the Majalla the legislator did not always choose the *dominant* view within the Hanafi school, but sometimes preferred the view of a *minority*. The Ottoman Law of Family Rights of 1917 went a step further, for it sometimes adopted the view dominant in other law schools. Gradually it came to suffice as justification for a statutory rule if it could be based on a view ever expressed by any author in the whole of Islamic legal history. Sometimes a provision even took its major premiss from one author, its minor premiss from another, and the conclusion from a third. A modern view which is still greatly controverted goes the full extent of saying that a jurist may reach his own conclusion in the light of contemporary requirements without regard to the classical authors of the different schools if the conclusion can be based on the Koran and the Sunna.

Until about fifteen or twenty years ago one could have supposed that sooner or later all Arab states would replace the religious courts with state courts and codify their family and inheritance law. It looked as if official registration would be needed for a marriage as well as a plighting of troth before the Imam, that polygamy would be abolished or at least restricted, and that instead of marriage being ended unilaterally by the husband, divorce would need a judicial decree based on specified grounds and be available to the wife as well. Today no one would make any such prediction. The success of the revolution in Iran under Ayatollah Khomeini triggered a powerful renaissance of religious traditions and a consequent reislamification of law. Of course conditions vary from country to country. The constitutions all provide that the Shari'a is an important, supreme or even sole source of law, but the consequences drawn from this differ a good deal. In Iran no proposed law can be valid unless approved by the 'Supreme Supervisory Council' of Islamic priests. The supreme court in Egypt has often had to decide whether or not a particular statutory provision is in conflict with the Shariah and consequently unconstitutional. In some countries the government is keen to keep the traditionalists within bounds, either out of concern for the non-Islamic minorities in their country (Lebanon, Syria) or because it sees them as an obstacle to economic development or dislikes the socialist aims of the Baath party. Given the opposition of traditional forces they are wise to think twice about law reform, especially in the field of the family.

23

Hindu Law

DERRETT, 'Hindu Law: The Dharmasastra and the Anglo-Hindu Law—Scope for Further Comparative Study', *ZvglRW* 58 (1956) 199.
——, *Introduction to Modern Hindu Law* (1963).
——, 'Hindu Law', in: *An Introduction to Legal Systems* (ed. Derrett, 1968) 80.
——, *Religion, Law and the State in India* (1968).
——/IYER, 'The Hindu Conception of Law', II *Int. Enc. Comp. L.* Ch. 1 (1975) 107.
——/SONTHEIMER/ SMITH, *Beiträge zum indischen Rechtsdenken* (1979).
DIES, 'Hindu Family Law', IV *Int. Enc. Comp. L.* ch. II IV (1981).
GALANTER, *Law and Society in Modern India* (1989).
JOLLY, *Recht und Sitte [der Hindus]* (1896); translated into English, *Hindu Law and Custom* (1928).
KANE, *History of Dharmaśāstra*, 5 vols. (1930–62).
——, *Hindu Customs and Modern Law* (1950).
LINGAT, *Les sources du droit dans le système traditional de l'Inde* (1967).
MAYNE, *Hindu Law and Usage* (11th edn., rev. Chandrasekhara Aiyar, 1951, reprinted 1953).
MULLA, *Principles of Hindu Law* (14th edn., rev. Desai, 1974).
PARAS DIVAN, *Modern Hindu Law, Codified and Uncodified* (2nd edn., 1974).
SARKAR, *Epochs in Hindu Legal History* (1958).
SEN-GUPTA, *Evolution of Ancient Indian Law* (1953).
SONTHEIMER, 'Recent Developments in Hindu Law', 13 *ICLQ* 32 (Supp. 1964).

I

HINDU law today applies to about 450 million Hindus. The vast majority, about 400 million, live in the Republic of India where they compose about 80% of the total population; most of the others live in minorities in Pakistan, Burma, Singapore, and Malaysia, and in countries on the East Coast of Africa, principally Tanzania, Uganda, and Kenya. It will be seen from this that the applicability of Hindu law does not depend on a person's being a national of a particular state or a domiciliary of a particular region: Hindu law applies regardless of nationality or domicile to all persons who are *Hindus*, that is, who accept the complex mass of religious, philosophical, and social ideas compendiously referred to as Hinduism. For practical purposes one may say that Hindu law applies to all people racially derived from the population of India except adherents of the Islamic, Christian, Jewish, or Parsee religions.

Unlike other religions Hinduism does not require its members to accept particular religious doctrines about God, and soul, the creation, redemption, and so on. It is open to every Hindu to believe in one god or another, in many or none; furthermore, Hinduism embraces a great variety of cults and rituals. Though it lacks a clearly defined theological doctrine. Hinduism does offer certain basic convictions of a religious or philosophical order which are accepted one way or another by the majority of Hindus.

In the course of time several religious creeds have developed out of this common fund of convictions, such as Buddhism or the religions of the Jains and the Sikhs; these may be regarded either as independent religions or as sects of Hinduism, but modern Indian legislation makes the rules of Hindu law apply to Buddhists and Sikhs and other devotees of these creeds.

Among the fundamental tenets of Hinduism the most important are the doctrines of the migration of souls and of *Kharma*. According to this, all the deeds, good and bad, which an individual commits on earth form the germ of his next existence, whose quality is determined by the moral balance, plus or minus, of the life just passed. If a person suffers greatly in his present life or finds himself very low in society, he is atoning for sins committed by his soul in earlier embodiments, while a person who devotes himself to the holy life and behaves with striking virtue and piety may entertain the hope that he may be born again under more propitious circumstances, perhaps as a member of a higher caste, or that his soul may even be released from the eternal circle of death and rebirth and become part of the divine nature as a higher spiritual being. This doctrine is the basis, indeed the justification, for the caste structure of Hindu society which is intrinsic to Hinduism as a religious, philosophical, and social system. A caste is a group of persons, normally in specific occupations or groups of occupation, who subscribe to a corpus of rules which regulate their behaviour towards each other and, more important, towards members of other castes. There are several thousand castes and sub-castes in the Hindu population, traditionally divided into four large groups; the *Brahmins* (originally the priests), the *Kshatriyas* (warriors), the *Vaishyas* (tradesmen), and the *Sudras* (servants and artisans). There is no way of moving from one caste to another; in particular, one cannot move upwards by dint of professional success, wealth, or political power. The castes stand in a hierarchical order, sustained by the idea that each caste has a certain 'purity' which must not be sullied by contact with certain objects, much less by contact with members of lower castes. There are therefore many rules which prohibit marriage, sexual relations, and eating with members of lower castes of lesser purity, or even being in their vicinity.

These rules of behaviour were not just mere conventions, for their infraction often had specific legal consequences recognized by the courts. Thus the Indian Courts had an intricate set of rules to determine under what circumstances a 'mixed marriage' of members of different castes was valid and what the legal position of children of such 'mixed marriages' might be, until the Hindu Marriages Validity Act, 1949 provided that 'no marriage between Hindus shall be deemed to be invalid or ever to have been invalid by reason only of the fact that the parties thereto belonged to different religions, caste, sub-castes or sects'.

In pursuance of a mandate contained in the Indian Constitution, legislation in India has now abrogated all the rules which attached a legal consequence to membership of a caste, but many Hindus still conduct themselves in accordance with the traditional rules of behaviour. It is still very rare for Hindus of different castes to marry, especially when the bride belongs to a higher caste than her groom; nor is it very common, at least among the members of the higher castes, for a widow to remarry, although in 1856 the old rule of Hindu law which rendered such a marriage invalid and the children it produced illegitimate was abolished by statute. Certainly there are signs that in many areas of life the influence of the old traditions is weakening. The whole caste system is caught up today in the process of fundamental change in a country with a modern political structure, promoted by general and equal suffrage, the gradually increasing mobility of occupation among Indians, the influence of the mass media, and the growing contact with Western culture.

II

It is often said that the Hindu legal system is the oldest in the world, but this requires some qualification. It is true that the *Veda*, that congeries of Indian religious songs, prayers, hymns, and sayings produced at various times during the second millennium BC or even earlier, contains the earliest texts in which, with some difficulty, rules for human conduct may be descried, but although the Hindus regard the Veda as a divine revelation and as the source of their religion and law, its practical influence on the spiritual life of the Hindu population has been very slight for many centuries; it cannot be said that the Veda has had much impact on the development of Hindu law, especially as it contains very little material with a specific legal content.

The oldest writings in Hindu literature any part of which can be described as 'law-books' are the *smritis*, a Sanskrit word denoting the 'remembered' wisdom of the old priests and scholars. It is extremely difficult to date them as the precise chronological ordering of particular historical events does not accord with the Hindu belief in a world process with neither beginning nor end. Consequently one must rely on conjectures that the *smritis* were produced between 800 BC and 200 AD. The oldest of them consist of aphorisms about the magic and religious rituals that should attend the important events of life. While they reflect the religious practices in early Indian history, they contain almost no rules of juristic content. Next came the so-called *dharmasutras*. These are the first law-books which lay down in detail how members of the different castes should conduct themselves towards the gods, the king, the priests, their forebears, their relatives, their neighbours, and animals, but these rules—'dharma' in Sanskrit—make no clear distinction between the mandates of religion, morals, custom, and law. The development of law took a further step forward with the *dharmasastras*: these are comprehensive collections of the rules of *dharma* in metrical form, ascribed to famous scholars. The best-known of these works in the *Manusmriti*, a collection from the second century BC, attributed to the legendary *Manu*. Here for the first time we find a relatively clear and orderly presentation of rules which today might form part of private and criminal law. The orthodox view is that all *smritis* rest on the writings of the holy Veda and it is assumed that the compilers of the *smritis* knew many texts of the holy Veda which have since disappeared. In fact, however, the *smritis* àre based on the religious practices and social customs followed by the Hindus of the time. The reason why the *smritis* differ so much from each other is that, contrary to the view of orthodox doctrine, they were written at different times by writers who attempted to account for customs which had recently arisen.

In the following period, from about 200 BC until the arrival of the British, the most important legal works were collections, extracts and commentaries which made no claim to originality but simply sought to expound the *smritis* and adapt them to practical use. Many writers sifted through the old texts, extracted the passages which seemed most topical, and presented them in a comprehensible manner. In this way the *smritis* were 'modernized' and much obsolete material gradually disappeared. Other authors wrote commentaries on the *smritis* or on subject-matters treated in them, such as the law of succession or the law of adoption. Although the *smritis* were treated as binding, since the official doctrine was that they stemmed from the Veda, the commentators had considerable scope for interpretation of the texts which were often many centuries old, ambiguous, incomplete, and inconsistent. There was a special theory and complex art of interpretation but even so the end result naturally tended to be affected by the customs and practices prevalent in the circle surrounding the authors. In view of the great variety of geographical, climatic, and racial conditions in India it is not surprising that some writers had only a local following and so, rather as happened in Islamic legal scholarship, schools of law gradually emerged in the eleventh and twelth centuries, the Dayabaga school in Bengal and the Mitakshara school, with several offshoots, in the rest of India. Furthermore Hindu law has always recognized that customs long followed in a particular region or by a particular caste, clan or family, are to be regarded as a source of law. Such customs, if known to the court or proved before it, are taken into account in interpreting the rules laid down in the *smritis* and the commentaries and are even allowed to take precedence over them.

III

The classical Hindu law of the period before British colonization rested neither on formal laws laid down by secular rulers nor yet on court decisions; essentially it rested on the works of private scholars, on the *smritis* and the commentaries and collections associated with them. Formally linked to the divine revelation of the Veda, in substance these works were comprehensive and systematic portrayals of the customary law obtaining among Hindus, though doubtless the holy Indian lawyer-priests played a large part in determining which customs deserved legal recognition. This classical Hindu law— called '*dharmasastra*' in Sanskrit, that is, the doctrine of proper behaviour— changed a great deal during the period of British rule. In the area of *property and obligations law* the traditional rules were very soon replaced by the Common Law (see above pp. 227 ff.), but things were different in the area of *family law and the law of succession*: here the principle was that 'all suits regarding inheritance, marriage, caste and other usages or institutions' were to be determined in accordance with the rules of Hindu Law. Admittedly this was not an easy principle for the British judges to apply. At the outset very few works out of the enormous legal literature had been translated from Sanskrit into English, and the judges must often have been very puzzled by them since they did not really know anything of the conditions of life among the Hindus or of their oral legal traditions. At first pandits, that is, natives learned in the *dharmasastra*, were attached to the courts, and the British judges could seek information from them on particular questions. This institution was abandoned in 1864; by then the judges had acquired some experience in dealing with Hindu law, the number of law-books in translation had increased, and, above all, there was a considerable case-law. The judges used prior decisions not only as a starting-point for argument but as binding authorities in accordance with the principle of 'stare decisis'. Although this was perfectly typical of the way English judges made law it was very far from the traditions of Hindu law which did not regard judicial decisions as binding at all; the judges not only could but should decide each case anew in relation to the relevant rules of law.

In content also, Hindu law during the period of British rule diverged considerably from the rules of *dharmasatra*. This was not so much the result of legislation, for the British used statutes only to abolish a few provisions of Hindu law which they found particularly repellent, such as the prohibition of a widow's remarriage and the rule that a Hindu forfeited all his property and rights of succession if he abandoned his religion or was excluded from his caste. It was *judicial decision* which had a much greater practical effect in modifying law, indeed, one could even say in corrupting it. The judges had at their disposition only a small part of the classical legal literature in English translation. This meant that they relied exclusively on such works, to the neglect of more recent or reliable writings. Furthermore the judges naturally found or thought they found many gaps or ambiguities in the traditional texts. Here they exercised a free judicial discretion, often with reference to 'justice, equity, and good conscience', and developed rules which, consciously or unconsciously, were influenced by the viewpoints of the Common Law or rested on 'general principles of law' which the judges found by making a comparative survey of the legal systems of the world. Thus classical Hindu jurisprudence was gradually ousted by 'Anglo-Hindu Law', as it was called; it soon stopped having direct recourse to traditional legal literature and was practised as pure case-law by the Indian courts.

During the struggle for independence a plan was mooted for complete codification of Hindu law, and soon after the achievement of independence in 1947 the Indian Government laid before Parliament the draft of a 'Hindu Code' which was to give a unified and statutory form to the whole of family law and the law of succession. The draft was strongly opposed by the archconservatives for whom any code was anathema and also by those who were unprepared to give up the special customary laws of their locality. Stormy debates in parliament and elsewhere forced the Indian government to withdraw the project. It then decided to produce separate drafts of the most important parts of Hindu law. This method succeeded. The first statute to come into force was the Hindu Marriage Act of 1955 which unified the marriage law of the Hindus and adapted it to modern thinking.

According to the traditional doctrine of the *dharmasastra*, marriage is a sacrament which inaugurates an unbreakable community between the spouses. Orthodox Hindus therefore regarded divorce as impermissible, though in many regions of India and among the lower castes custom often allowed it. Although the termination of marriage was prohibited in principle, the husband might take a second wife under certain circumstances, as when the first wife had neglected her matrimonial obligations; polygamy, however, was never much practised among the Hindus. For Hindus, marriage was primarily an affair for the *families* involved and so it was commonly arranged by the parents of the spouses, as it still often is today; according to the rules of the *dharmasastra*, the express assent of the spouses themselves was not required nor was there any minimum age for marriage. Hindu law also has a remarkable number of obstacles to marriage. We have already mentioned that marriage between members of different castes was ruled out but in addition there were detailed provisions which forbade marriage even between very distantly related parties; indeed it could be enough that the family names of the parties were similar. During the past 150 years these traditional rules have been much modified by court decision and by legislation. Admittedly the legal system does not forbid voluntary adherence to these rules and it is to be supposed that people still follow them today, especially in rural India. In this respect the Hindu Marriage Act may be in advance of social reality in curtailing the number of prohibited degrees and in abolishing the ban on marriage between members of different castes. The statute also permits divorce and forbids polygamy.

Three further statutes came into force in 1956, the Hindu Minority and Guardianship Act, the Hindu Succession Act, and the Hindu Adoptions and Maintenance Act; in consequence most of Hindu law is now codified. Indian judges and lawyers now go first to the provisions of the new statutes and to the judicial decisions which construe them. Only in the relatively unimportant areas for which there is no statutory regulation does Anglo-Hindu Law have any role to play in India. Outside India the work of codification has gone much less far and 'Anglo-Hindu Law' applies as it did before; but even there practising lawyers today look mainly to the judgments of the courts and only very rarely to the classical legal literature of the *dharmasastra*.

PART II

C. CONTRACT

VII. THE FORMATION OF CONTRACTS

24

Freedom of Contract
and its Limits

ADAMS/BROWNSWORD, 'The Ideologies of Contract Law', 7 *LS* 205 (1987).
ATIYAH, *The Rise and Fall of Freedom of Contract* (1979).
——, 'The Development of the Law of Contract' in: *An Introduction to the Law of Contract* (4th edn., 1989) Ch. 1.
BERLIOZ, *Le Contrat d'adhésion* (2nd edn., 1976).
——, 'The Protection of the Consumer in French Law', 1985 *J. Bus. L.* 342.
BORRIE/DIAMOND, *The Consumer, Society and the Law* (4th edn., 1981).
BYDLINSKI, 'Die Grundlagen des Vertragsrechts im Meinungsstreit', *Basler jur. Mitt.* 1982, 1.
CALAIS-AULOY, *Droit de la consommation* (3rd edn., 1992).
CARBONNIER, *Théorie des obligations* (1963).
——, *Droit civil, Les obligations* (13th edn., 1988).
COHEN, 'The Basis of Contract', 46 *Harv. L. Rev.* 553 (1933).
COLLINS, *The Law of Contract* (2nd edn., 1993).
CORNU, 'L'Évolution du droit des contrats en France', in: *Journées de la Société de législation comparée* 1979, 447.
DEUTCH, *Unfair Contracts, The Doctrine of Unconscionability* (1977).
EISENBERG, 'The Bargain Principle and its Limits', 95 *Colum. L. Rev.* 323 (1982).
FRIED, *Contract as Promise, A Theory of Contractual Obligations* (1981).
FRIEDMAN, *Contract Law in America* (1965).
FRIEDMANN, *Law in a Changing Society* (1959) 90 ff.
V. HIPPEL, *Verbraucherschutz* (2nd edn., 1979).
HONDIUS, *Standaardvoorwaarden* (1978).
HORWITZ, *The Transformation of American Law* (1977), Ch. 6 'The Triumph of Contract'.
JACOBS, 'The Battle of the Forms: Standard Form Contracts in Comparative Perspective', 34 *ICLQ* 297 (1985).
KESSLER, 'Contracts of Adhesion, Some Thoughts About Freedom of Contract', 43 *Colum. L. Rev.* 629 (1943).

KESSLER, 'Freiheit und Zwang im nordamerikanischen Vertragsrecht', *Festschrift für Martin Wolff* (1952) 67.

KESSLER/GILMORE/KRONMAN, 'Contract as a Principle of Order', Introduction to *Contracts, Cases and Materials* (3rd edn., 1986).

KRAMER, *Die 'Krise' des liberalen Vertragsdenkens* (1974).

——, 'Vertragsrecht im Umbau', *ÖJZ* 1980, 233.

LLEWELLYN, 'What Price Contract?, An Essay in Perspective', 40 *Yale LJ* 704 (1931).

VON MEHREN, A General View of Contract, *Int. Enc. Comp. L.* VII Ch. 1 (1982).

MERZ, *Vertrag und Vertragsschluß* (2nd edn., 1992).

MINOR, 'Consumer Protection in French Law', 33 *ICLQ* 108 (1984).

POUND, 'Promise or Bargain?', 33 *Tul. L. Rev.* 455 (1959).

L. RAISER, *Die Aufgabe des Privatrechts* (1977), containing 'Vertragsfreiheit heute', *JZ* 1958, 1, and 'Vertragsfunktion und Vertragsfreiheit',—*Hundert Jahre deutsches Rechtsleben, I Festschrift zum. 100jährigen Bestehen des Deutschen Juristentages* (1960) 101.

——, *Das Recht der Allgemeinen Geschäftsbedingungen* (1935).

RAKOFF, 'Contracts of Adhesion, An Essay in Reconstruction', 96 *Harv. L. Rev.* 1173 (1983).

TREBILCOCK, *The Limits of Freedom of Contract* (1993).

ZWEIGERT, '"Rechtsgeschäft" und "Vertrag" heute', in II *Ius Privatum Gentium, Festschrift Rheinstein* (1969) 493.

I

ANYONE looking for general statements of principle about the role of contract in society, what it consists of and what effect it has, will trawl the German Civil Code in vain. Contract law does not even have a special section to itself in the BGB. In the General Part contract is merely a subcategory of 'legal act', and even in Book Two it figures as no more than a special instance of 'obligational relationship'. Less taciturn civil codes not only have separate sections on contract (see art. 1101 ff. Code civil, art. 1 ff. OR), but sometimes even indulge in generalities about it. Thus in art. 19(1) OR we find the telling pronouncement that 'within the limits of the law the contract may have such content as the parties choose' and in art. 1134 Code civil we find the celebrated formula that 'contracts legally formed have the force of law for the parties who made them'.

Of course the fathers of the German Civil Code were perfectly well aware of the importance of contract and freedom of contract: like other nineteenth century codes, the BGB is the product of a society based on the liberalist belief that once the individual is freed from the traditional constraints and authorities of a feudal, political or religious nature, he is a reasonable person capable of determining his fate, that he must be given the freedom to shape his life responsibly; he must be put in a position to decide for himself whether or not to make a contract, to whom he will undertake a legally recognized obligation, and what its content is to be. Certainly a contract which conflicted with 'ordre public' or 'public policy' would be ineffectual, but even here the judges took it as a principle that it would not be wise

'to extend arbitrarily those rules which say that a given contract is void as being against public policy, because if there is one thing more than another which public policy requires, it is that men of full age and competent understanding shall have the utmost liberty of contracting and that their contracts, when entered into freely and voluntarily, shall be held sacred and shall be enforced by Courts of Justice'. So said SIR GEORGE JESSEL MR in *Printing and Numerical Registering Co.* v. *Sampson* (1875) LR 19 Eq. 462, 465.—Liberalism is often criticized today. It is said to be neither economically productive nor socially fair, and doubt is cast on the rules and principles it generates. We shall have more to say about this later, but let it never be forgotten that liberalism was a great emancipator which unleashed an astonishing amount of creativity. Freedom of contract has not always been accepted as a legal principle—far from it. For centuries an individual's rights and duties were determined by his birth, his family, his kin, his tribe, his status, his guild or his position as vassal to a feudal superior or as serf to a landowner. These were conditions he was born to and they lasted till his death. But the legal relationships of individuals changed as the economy became vitalized by the division of labour, and instead of being defined by their status people began to determine themselves by entering into contracts for goods, services or credit. The development is captured in SIR HENRY MAINE's famous phrase: 'the movement of the progressive societies has hitherto been a movement from Status to Contract'. (*Ancient Law* (1864) 165.)

On what grounds do legal systems today justify giving contracts binding force and enforcing them in their courts? There are many different views, but perhaps they may be reduced to two.

On one view the primary task of a legal system is to protect the freedom of the individual and safeguard his power of self-determination. Everyone should be free to act as he chooses, free from governmental or social pressures. He should be able to decide for himself what his relations with others shall be, without constraint or prescription, and he should be able to pursue his own goals as long as he does not infringe the like freedom of others. The state must therefore respect the freedom of the individual and give him space in which to construct his own lifestyle; this involves freedom of belief and opinion, freedom to own property, and freedom to choose his career. Freedom of contract as well. Whether or not to enter an exchange relationship must in principle be a matter for him to decide on, in agreement with the partner of his choice.

'The idea behind contract is that what has been agreed is binding because in making the contract the parties have agreed that it should determine their rights and liabilities.' (FLUME, *Das Rechtsgeschäft* (2nd edn, 1975) 7.)—Historically the idea of freedom of contract as a manifestation of the principle of individual autonomy is closely connected with the so-called 'will theory', according to which the true reason for recognizing and enforcing contractual obligations is that they are 'willed' by the obligor. Although the 'will theory' has now been ousted by the 'declaration theory'— you are bound not so much by what you actually meant as by what your addressee reasonably supposed you intended—this involves no conflict with the idea of autonomy: autonomy does not entitle one to disregard the proper interests of others or disavow the meaning reasonably attributed to what one says in the particular situation in which one says it.

The other view is utilitarian. To the question of how society should organize its institutions and decision-making so as to procure that people's needs are best satisfied in view of the shortage of resources in our world, utilitarians give the answer that enforcing contractual agreements can make a major contribution. This can be illustrated as follows.

A person who owns a thing worth £500 to him will normally be ready to sell it for £600, but of course he will only be able to do so if someone else values the thing at £600 and is ready to pay that much for it. The latter will be acting reasonably and in pursuance of his own advantage if he proceeds to buy the thing for £600, and if the agreement is made and executed, both parties are better off than before; both are richer, neither poorer. Multiply this operation by millions—as happens in what is called the 'market'—and you will see that by this means all participants benefit. This promotes the good of society by seeing to it that goods and services in short supply go to those who place the greatest value on them.

Before this system can operate one important precondition must be met: the law must lay down clear rules about who owns what—be it property, tangible or intangible, or any other legally protected right—so that one knows who can dispose of it and prevent others interfering with it. Sales will take place only if one party is known to be the owner of the thing and the other cannot just seize it, but must buy it.

Take the simple purchase of an armchair in a furniture shop. Behind this contract lies a host of other contracts. The trees were felled, the timber transported to the sawmill, the lumber sawn into planks, all under contract. The cabinetmaker not only bought the wood, he employed his staff, he leased his premises, and purchased the necessary machinery and varnish, all by means of contracts. He contracted with a designer for the design of the furniture and with a business agent for its distribution to the retailers. The retailers in their turn leased the shop, employed salespersons, contracted with an advertising agency for publicity, and bought the packaging material. All this took place before the armchair could finally be offered for sale to the customer. In this veritable cataract of contracts all the participants were pursuing their own interests, but the result of it is that scarce resources were put to the use that best answered the needs of individuals and so contributed to the general good.

This explains why the law allows contracts to be formed, but why does it also grant an action for performance and an action for damages for non-performance? This would not be necessary if agreed exchanges were carried out on the spot and both parties could check that the other had done what the contract called for. Though common in primitive economies, such situations are rather rare today and occur only where the goods are such that it is easy for the buyer to check them before he buys. In a developed economy contracts often involve performance in the future, and the goods supplied may have to be used for a time before one can tell whether they are satisfactory or not. Here there is always a danger that a party will pocket the other's performance and then seize the opportunity to withhold his own, especially if performance has become harder for him, or if the market has changed and he can now command a higher price. People expect the promises made to them to be fulfilled, and the law must protect their expectation and effect a fair allocation of the risks which may arise after the contract has been formed. There may, of course, be extralegal incentives to perform properly. A party who hopes to continue in business will know that opportunistic behaviour may injure his reputation as a responsible contractor, and the risk of such conduct can often be forestalled by terms in the contract or by taking a deposit or other security to be forfeited in the event of breach. But since it is often the case that the parties' reputation is not in issue and such contractual provisions are costly or impractical, the law must intervene: it must provide rules which hold the parties to their agreement, deter them from self-interested opportunism and in the interests of society as a whole promote the fulfilment of contracts for future performance.

It is true that if contractors made explicit arrangements for every imaginable contingency which might arise in the agreed exchange only one rule would be needed: *pacta sunt servanda*. But it takes a lot of negotiation to cover even the more obvious risks, and the cost can be avoided if the law itself provides rules to fill any gaps in a suitable manner. The existence of such rules (called *dispositives Recht* in Germany, *lois supplétives* in France and 'implied terms' in England) facilitates the formation of contracts and thereby increases the benefit to the parties and to society at large.

II

Freedom of contract, as we have seen, can be justified on the ground either of individual autonomy or of public benefit, but whichever basis one prefers, it is certain that contract law must have *constraints* as well; there must be rules which invalidate certain agreements, or permit their invalidation, however seriously intended or maturely considered. This is plain where the contract conflicts with public order, morality or the law itself (see ch. 28 below), but a contract may also be invalid if there is some flaw in the procedure such that the undertaking in question cannot be held to have been responsibly given: the promisor may have lacked capacity for want of the necessary power of judgement at the time of the contract (see ch. 25 below); he may have been deceived or misled by the other party or subjected to improper pressure (see below ch. 31 VI); or he may have promised only because he was labouring under a serious misapprehension (see below ch. 31 I–V).

Another kind of flaw in precontractual procedure occurs when a person is induced to enter a deal in his home or on the doorstep, in his place of work or in the street or a public conveyance, places where he has no chance of comparing prices and may, if he is unused to business, be bounced into a bad deal. That is why customers in all the member states of the European Union, unless they are acting in the course of business, are given a certain period within which to disavow such a contract without having to give any reason (Directive of 20 December 1985).

One might infer from this that the *content* of a contract does not affect its validity, unless of course it is immoral or contrary to public order, that it makes no difference whether or not the value of what is promised is fairly related to the value of what is promised in return, and that provided nothing in the way the contract was formed prevented him from reaching a well-considered and responsible decision, a person is bound to his bargain, however bad. This view would be in line with the saying in the Common Law that 'inadequacy of consideration' does not make a contract void, indeed that a promise is binding even if what is promised in return is a mere 'peppercorn'. So, too, the distinction drawn between 'procedural' and 'substantive' unfairness suggests that it is only in the former case that a contract is invalid, not because of any unfairness or inequality in its content.

On the distinction between 'procedural' and 'substantive' fairness see Leff, 'Unconscionability and the Code: The Emperor's New Clause' (1967) 115 *U. Pa. L. Rev.* 485; Farnsworth §4.28 (p. 506 ff.); von Mehren (above p. 324, at p. 64 ff.); Gordley, 'Equality in Exchange' (1981) 69 *Cal. L. Rev.* 1587, and the important articles by Atiyah, 'Contract and Fair Exchange' (1985) 35 *U. Tor. LJ* 1 =*Essays on Contract* (1988) 329 ff. and Eisenberg, 'The Bargain Principle and Its Limits' (1982) 95 *Harv. L. Rev.* 741.

The categorical distinction between 'procedural' and 'substantive' fairness, however clear in theory, is not strictly followed in practice. Commutative justice has always been seen to require a certain equivalence between performance and counterperformance, though writers have been less emphatic about this requirement at some times than at others, and courts have not always been candid in their attempts to implement it. One well-tried method of doing this is by *construing* the contract (see below ch. 30): if the terms of the agreement are unclear or incomplete, the judge is to construe the contract in line with the requirements of 'good faith' (*Treu und Glauben*, §157

BGB), 'decency' (§914 ABGB) or 'equity, common usage or the law' (art. 1135 Code civil). All of these call for a fair relationship between performance and counterperformance. The more striking the imbalance, the readier will the judge be to accept that the contract suffers from a 'procedural' flaw, that the disadvantaged party was deceived, pressured or misled. Furthermore, if the mismatch in the contract is manifestly gross, the judge will be all the readier to hold it void as immoral or incompatible with public order. CORBIN is quite right to say 'that there is sufficient flexibility in the concepts of fraud, duress, misrepresentation and undue influence . . . to enable the courts to avoid enforcement of a bargain that is shown to be unconscionable by reason of gross inadequacy of consideration accompanied by other relevant factors' (§128). Accordingly, when courts hold a contract void on one of these grounds, especially for a 'procedural' flaw, one may well suspect that what is really sticking in their throat is a breach of the principle of equivalence.

The question whether there must be a fair relationship between performance and counterperformance has been much debated in Europe for a very long time. In late Roman law if a person sold his land for less than half its true value he could avoid the sale (C.4.44.2), a rule designed to protect peasants impoverished by the emperor's brutal taxing policies against urban capitalists eager buy land at knockdown prices so as to guard their wealth against inflation. The view that all contracts must give fair value was fully accepted by lawyers in the Middle Ages: Thomas Aquinas and other fathers of the Church taught that there must be parity between the two sides of the contract: it was a sin to pay less than a just price ('iustum pretium') for what one was to get. Natural lawyers also accepted the rule that a contract was voidable for *laesio enormis*, though they attributed this to the dictates of human reason rather than Christian morality. This was picked up by the Austrian ABGB and the French Code civil, though to different extents: under §934 ABGB a party may avoid a contract in which he is promised less than half of what he is to give (*Verkürzung über die Hälfte*), while art. 1674 ff. Code civil gives the seller of land two years in which to avoid the sale if the price was less than seven-twelfths of the current value of the land. See ZIMMERMANN, *The Law of Obligations* (1990) 259 ff.; VON MEHREN (above p. 324, at 75 ff.); CARBONNIER (above p. 323) no 36 f.; MERZ (above p. 324) p. 62 ff.

More modern codes have no such rules. They were thought inappropriate in an economy dominated by liberalism: in the acquisitive bourgeois society founded on freedom of contract, trade, and competition it seemed paternalistic and prejudicial to legal security to have a rule which allowed courts to undo contracts just because they were unequal, for the individual was deemed to be smart and businesslike enough to act responsibly and look after his own interests. Right up to the last minute the draftsmen of the BGB believed that it was enough to provide that a contract was void if it was illegal or immoral (§138(1) BGB), but eventually the feeling that there is something offensive to a sense of justice in a contract which is unequal won through, and a second limb was added to §138 BGB. It contains a test combining both 'substantive' and 'procedural' unfairness: a contract is void under §138(2) BGB (as amended in 1976) if there is a 'striking disproportion' between performance and counterperformance *and* the contract was brought about by the 'exploitation of the difficulties, inexperience, lack of judgment or serious indecisiveness' of the other.

Most other European civil codes have followed suit (§879(2) no. 4 ABGB; art. 21 OR; §31 Swedish Contract Law). The Codice civile alone retains an arithmetical test of disrelation: a party who enters a disadvantageous contract in a *stato di bisogno* or out of need can avoid it only if the value of his performance is more than twice that of the counterperformance (art. 1448). By contrast, the new Dutch Civil Code does not require any mismatch between the two sides of the contract: under art. 3:44(4) NBW a contract may be avoided for 'abuse of the situation' if the creditor improperly urged the debtor to enter the contract when he knew or should have known that he was in a difficult situation, dependent, inexperienced or feckless.

There is no comparable provision in the Code civil, but the courts in France reach the same results by holding that the party overreached may avoid the contract for deceit (*dol*). A person may be guilty of *dol* if he exploits someone else's old age, serious illness, youthful inexperience or personal difficulties, even though he tells no lies and so is not guilty of deceit in the strict sense: the mere fact of taking advantage of a person's known difficulties even without contributing to them can constitute *manoeuvres dolosives*.

Nor does English law have any general principle which allows a person to back out of a manifestly prejudicial contract on the ground that advantage was taken of his inability to negotiate. It does, however, have a number of different rules, applicable in different circumstances, which enable him to escape much like his Continental counterpart. Not only may a plea of *economic duress* be available to a person pressured by circumstances into entering a disadvantageous deal (see ch. 31 V below), but very significantly a contract can be avoided for *undue influence*: if the parties are in a special relationship of trust such that the reliant party was entitled to look to the other for full information and proper advice—a relationship such as exists between child and parent, ward and guardian, patient and doctor, penitent and priest, client and legal or other professional adviser—then any contract made between them which is disadvantageous to the weaker party is presumed to be due to the 'undue influence' of the other party, to an abuse of the trust reposed in him. The presumption is capable of being rebutted, but this hardly ever happens, since almost the only way in which this can be done is by showing that the claimant had independent advice from a lawyer or other informed person.

There is some debate in England today whether rules so dispersed can be traced to a general principle. In *Lloyd's Bank* v. *Bundy* [1975] QB 326

LORD DENNING thought so. A young man who needed further credit told an officer at the bank that his father, who had a small farm, might provide security, so the officer went with the son to the farm to see him, and the father, who was given no further information about the son's financial position or any chance of obtaining independent advice, ended up by charging the farm, virtually his sole asset, as security. When the bank sought possession of the farm, the Court of Appeal rejected its claim. Two of the three judges based their decision on the rules of *undue influence* since the father had been a client of the bank for very many years and was entitled in the circumstances to expect advice and information, but LORD DENNING formulated a general principle. After relating the various ways in which the Common Law protects the weaker party from unfavourable contracts, he said:

'Gathering all together, I would suggest that through all these instances there runs a single thread. They rest on inequality of bargaining power. By virtue of it, the English law gives relief to one who, without independent advice, enters into a contract on terms which are very unfair or transfers property for a consideration which is grossly inadequate, when his bargaining power is grievously impaired by reason of his own needs or desires, or by his own ignorance or infirmity, coupled with undue influences or pressures brought to bear on him by or for the benefit of the other' (at 339).

III

The phrase 'inequality of bargaining power' raises a question much discussed by contract theorists: modern conditions being what they are, is it still right to treat contract as a central pillar of the legal system? Should it not be limited *ex lege* wherever the parties to a contract are unequal in bargaining power, where 'parity of contract' is disturbed and the weaker party needs protection? Is it not time to replace or supplement the principle of freedom of contract by a principle of 'contractual justice'?

The way contracts are made today makes the question unavoidable, for as everyone knows, their terms are very rarely negotiated in any real sense. Often this is because one party has so much more economic clout than the other that he can dictate the terms on which he will do business. In many markets, such as housing and employment, demand is so great and supply so short that the applicant has really no chance of exercising his freedom of contract and having any effect on the terms of the deal. In many other cases one party blindly accepts whatever terms are offered without any negotiations at all because he lacks business experience or bargaining skill or much interest in getting favourable terms.

All legal systems have reacted to this situation in one way or another, for everyone recognizes that devices such as competition law are needed to constrain the free play of economic forces, for otherwise economic dominance will result and be abused. Accordingly when there is no real competition and one person badly needs a resource controlled by another, the law may entitle the former and require the latter to enter into a contract for its supply, often on terms laid down by a state authority or approved by them for fairness, as in the case of provision of utilities or transport. Many other contracts, such as contracts of employment, domestic lettings, insurance contracts, and consumer credit bargains, are subject to a thicket of rules which give some protection to the weaker party. These 'regulated' contracts now seem to lead a kind of life of their own outside the pale of general contract law, thereby shrinking the area over which the flag of freedom of contract can flutter. But even the terms of 'unregulated' contracts are subject to supervision: courts in most countries now have a general power to invalidate contract terms which are 'unconscionable' or 'unfair' or which cause 'a significant imbalance between the rights and duties of the parties in a manner contrary to the dictates of good faith'. Sometimes this power can only be exercised where the term was formulated in advance by one of the parties and accepted without modification by the other, sometimes only where the party invoking the power is a 'consumer', but it is still undeniable that freedom of contract is being constrained. To what is this development due? Many observers say that it is now quite fanciful to think that the adult individual is a responsible person concerned for his advancement and capable of foreseeing and evaluating the consequences of his actions, and that the task of the law of contract today should be to ensure 'contractual justice': contract must become a device for co-operation and fairness by increasing the protection of the weaker party and obliging both parties to look out for the interests of the other.

On the pros and cons of 'contractual justice' see the authors listed above p. 323 f., and in particular KESSLER, ADAMS/BROWNSWORD, COLLINS (p. 16 ff.), RAISER, ZWEIGERT (whose views were followed in the previous edition), CARBONNIER (no. 36 f.), BYDLINSKI, MERZ (p. 59 ff.), KRAMER, and VON MEHREN, all with further details of the extensive literature.

Now it is quite true as a matter of fact that individuals often have to enter into contracts which are unfavourable, whose consequences they cannot foresee, and whose content they cannot influence. The legal system therefore cannot simply stand by and enforce every contract regardless of its content (subject only to its not being in conflict with the law or public order) just because it was formed by the normal rules of offer and acceptance. It does not follow, however, that well-meaning paternalism should become the leading principle of contract law or that it should adopt slogans as vague as 'fairness', 'social justice', and 'protection of the weaker party'. The proponents of the liberalism of which freedom of contract is a manifestation are not unaware of the changed circumstances under which contracts are now made, nor have they sought to minimize their significance or stood impotently by. They quite realize that the conditions under which freedom of contract can 'function' properly and produce its expected result in increased welfare are often, indeed increasingly often, missing. No one denies that in such cases freedom of contract must be restricted by the legislator or the courts. This must be done not only in the traditional cases when one party lacks capacity or is unable to make sensible judgments because of weakness induced by age or illness, or has been deceived or misled by the other party, or had his simplicity and gullibility exploited; it must also be done in the analogous situation where one party can dictate the terms of the contract by reason of his economic superiority. We can now see that when contracts are formed on the basis of preformulated terms of business there is often a special type of 'market failure' (see immediately below), for information is a valuable resource which is not costless to acquire. It is also perfectly justifiable in other cases to impose a duty to inform or warn or the more extensive duty to consider the interests of the other party, for the good reason—all the better for being unemotional—that the imposition of such duties contributes to a better distribution of the risks involved and thus enhances the advantages which contracts offer both to the parties and to society at large.

IV

Standard terms in contracts, or *general conditions of business* (*Allgemeine Geschäftsbedingungen*—AGB), are a byproduct of the industrial revolution of the nineteenth century. Just as the production of goods and services was standardized, so were the terms on which such goods and services were supplied. To standardize terms of contract in this way helps to rationalize big business: standard terms make it unnecessary to negotiate the provisions of each transaction separately, they may be fuller, clearer, and more suitable than the terms which would otherwise be implied by law, and finally they facilitate the conduct of transactions and the calculation of their effect. But rationalization of business is rarely the sole aim when standard terms are used. Firms also use them in order to shift to the other party as many as possible of the risks involved in the transaction. Typical clauses may exclude the firm's liability for non-performance or misperformance, or permit it to raise the price or supply substitute goods; conversely, they may prevent the *customer* from setting off debts due to him, withdrawing from the deal, or cancelling the contract, or they may impose penalties or liquidated damages in the event of delay on his part. There is general agreement nowadays that such clauses must be subject to legislative and judicial control. What is not so clear is why this is so. It cannot be the mere fact that the customer normally accepts disadvantageous terms without demur. The real

question is *why* he does so. The common view is that he does so because of
'unequal bargaining power': faced with the economic superiority of the
entrepreneur, the customer has no option but to 'submit' to his general terms
of business. Often the entrepreneur will be in a monopoly position and need
not bother to negotiate over his terms, and any competitors there may be will
often use the same terms. Again, the entrepreneur's superiority may be psychological or intellectual, so that it would appear futile for the customer to
protest in the face of so much more experience of business and familiarity
with the law. This is said to be why, as FRIEDRICH KESSLER wrote in an
influential and much-cited article in 1943

'standard contracts in particular could . . . become effective instruments in the
hands of powerful industrial and commercial overlords enabling them to impose a
new feudal order of their own making upon a vast host of vassals' (above p. 323,
at 640).

The view that general terms of business must be controlled in order to protect the weak and uninitiated against those with practised power has proved
enormously effective in discussions of legal policy. This slogan was embraced
by the modern consumer movement and since the beginning of the 1960s the
laws enacted by most European countries have been more or less based on
the view that the consumer as the 'weaker' party must be protected against
contractual terms which entrepreneurs force on him by abusing their economic superiority.

But it is very far from clear that this view goes to the heart of the matter.
Certainly there are cases in which a customer who would quite like to object
to unfavourable contract conditions refrains from doing so just because the
economic or other superiority of the entrepreneur makes negotiation seem
pointless. This is not, however, the normal case. This is shown by the fact
that preformulated contract terms are regularly accepted where there can
be no question of economic superiority, where the contractors are experienced businessmen operating in a branch of commerce where competition
is very brisk: merchants do not negotiate over the printed conditions prof-
fered by carriers, warehousemen, credit institutions, security firms or credit
information agencies. The reason the customer 'submits' to the supplier's
conditions of business in such cases is that it is not worth investing the necessary time and money in dickering over some amendment or in searching out
other suppliers whose terms might be preferable in one respect or another. A
person who parks his car in a car park or contracts for the carriage of goods
or buys a computer accepts the terms on offer without discussion, not
because they are forced on him by a 'powerful industrial or commercial overlord' but because the expense of negotiation or seeking a better alternative is
out of all proportion to the advantage to be gained thereby; and this is true
whether the customer is an individual or a business. The entrepreneur takes

advantage of this situation by using his conditions of business to shift the risks of the contract on to the customer, knowing that he will rarely object. The customer agrees to such terms, admittedly, but it does not conflict with the principle of freedom of contract to subject them to legal control, since only when both parties had a fair chance of influencing the terms of a contract does the principle require it to be respected. In these cases the customer has no such chance, not because of any superiority of the entrepreneur, whether economic or not, but because of the prohibitively high transaction costs involved.

It may be noted that whereas suppliers of goods or services often compete as regards price and quality they do not do so as regards other terms, except perhaps clauses, such as the period of guarantee of an automobile, simple enough to be understood by the customer and compared with what is offered by competitors. General conditions of business usually deal with complex matters of the allocation of risks, and normally customers cannot understand their scope, let alone compare them with others. Suppose there is a condition in the sale of a vacuum cleaner that the buyer must bear the cost of sending it back to the supplier if it proves defective and needs to be put right; why should the buyer seek to have this condition altered when only one vacuum cleaner in a hundred actually does prove defective and the cost of transport is in any case quite small?—On this see TREBILCOCK and DEWEES, 'Judicial Control of Standard Form Contracts' in BURROWS and VELJANOWSKI (eds.), *The Economic Approach to Law* (1981) 93; RAKOFF (above p. 324); SCHÄFER/OTT, *Lehrbuch der ökonomischen Analyse des Zivilrechts* (2nd edn. 1995) 420 ff.; BEHRENS, *Die ökonomischen Grundlagen des Rechts* (1986) 155 ff., 170 ff.

1. *The German Legal Family.*—For a long time it was only the courts in the Federal Republic of Germany that afforded any protection against unfair conditions of business. They first asked whether the standard terms in question had ever become part of the contract at all. This might be a matter of doubt where the terms of business were in print so small as to be barely legible, or where they were only brought to the customer's attention by an obscure reference on the back of a hat-check or by a notice displayed in the foyer of a bank. Here the judges were fairly tolerant. The Reichsgericht took the view that to contract on standard terms was hardly to make a 'genuine' contractual agreement at all, but rather, as the Court said in DR 1941, 1210, 'to submit to a legal regime already in existence'; and 'when a person voluntarily enters a legal regime it is hardly relevant what detailed knowledge of its contents he possessed'. Though the Bundesgerichtshof has not spoken in such terms, it has not hesitated to treat standard terms of business as incorporated when they are in common use and a customer who was properly alert would have known of their existence and applicability (see, for example, BGHZ 32, 216, 219). The Bundesgerichtshof has, however, held that terms cannot be regarded as validly incorporated into a contract unless they are such that 'the customer could fairly and justly suppose that they

might be included' (BGHZ 17, 1, 3): the agreement of the customer does not extend to 'unexpected' or 'unusual' clauses. But the best-tried method, used by the courts in countless cases, is that of *strict construction*. They first hold that the terms in dispute are unclear or ambiguous—and what document is not, when keenly scrutinized by a lawyer?—and then they resolve the uncertainties in favour of the customer, by invoking the rule that in case of doubt any restriction of liability is to be construed narrowly, or the rule that ambiguous clauses are to be construed *contra proferentem*, that is, against the party putting them forward.

But the real reason for the judges' going in for 'strict construction' or holding that 'surprise' clauses were not really agreed to was that they disapproved of the substance of the clause in question: they were exercising a 'covert' or 'camouflaged' control of the terms of the contract. But it is only when the courts' control becomes 'open' that the real question in these cases, namely, whether the term is acceptable in substance or not, can be properly addressed. The German courts have taken this step. At the outset the Reichsgericht would only do it where a firm was using a monopoly position to impose terms on the customer, that is, where 'firms with a virtual monopoly of an essential trade exploit the general need for their services in order to gain for themselves advantageous terms incompatible with law and in restraint of trade'. (RGZ 103, 82, 83.) But economic superiority is not the only case where freedom of contract is abused by the imposition of standard terms of business: it also occurs where the draftsman 'deploys the intellectual superiority of the legal virtuoso' and trades on the customer's indifference and inexperience, as LUDWIG RAISER pointed out in 1935 in his pathbreaking book, *The Law of Standard Terms of Business* (*Das Recht der AGB*) (at p. 284). Judgments after the Second World War took up this idea, and since the middle 1950s the Bundesgerichtshof has practised 'open control' of standard terms on a wide front. The courts quickly developed guidelines for testing the fairness of such terms, distinguishing different types of clause and different types of case. The judgments may invoke §242, the general clause of the BGB, but the invocation is mere ritual, since that paragraph simply says that contracts are to be performed in accordance with 'good faith' and therefore contains no concepts 'capable of subsumption'. What we have here is judge-made law of the purest kind, and in creating it the German courts have done a remarkable and praiseworthy job without parallel elsewhere.

In the 1970s it was generally agreed that the time had come for the legislature to act. Lawyers wanted a firm statutory basis for court decisions of such importance and increasing detail, and politicians were keen to have something to show in the way of consumer protection. A draft bill was rapidly produced. There was no doubt that it was a measure for consumer protection, for it subjected standard terms of business to control only when a non-merchant was party to the contract. This was severely criticized, especially on the cogent ground that almost all the transactions which had come before the Bundesgerichtshof had been transactions between merchants. The bill was therefore redrafted and came into force on 1 April 1977 as the Act for the Control of the Law of General Conditions of Business (AGBG). Contrary to the wish of those who felt that the matter should be dealt with in the BGB, the Act was passed as a separate statute outside the Code.

Many sections of the Act simply enact principles already laid down by the courts. These include the 'ambiguity rule' (§5), that is, the principle of 'customer-friendly' construction of ambiguous terms *contra proferentem*, the principle that an *ad hoc* agreement takes precedence over standard terms in case of conflict (§4), and the rule that 'surprise' clauses do not become part of the contract at all if they are so 'unusual that the other party could not be expected to suppose that they would be there' (§3). Nor is there anything new in §6, which says that when a standard term is invalid, the rest of the contract remains in force, the invalidated clause being replaced by the terms implied by the BGB or other legislation. The general clause in §9 gave the draftsman a good deal of trouble. Though it is longer than §242 BGB, all it does is add a few resonant but empty tropes. It says that standard terms are invalid when they 'unfairly' disadvantage the customer by modifying 'essential' rights or duties which arise from the 'nature of the contract' in such a manner 'as to imperil the achievement of the contractual purpose'.

Resort to the general clause of §9 is unnecessary if the standard terms in issue are of the kind specified in the compendious 'catalogue of terms' in §§10 and 11. Here the legislature, still guided by the valuable experience of the courts, could clarify and generalize some of the judge-made rules and include in the 'blacklist' some clauses which had not yet come before the courts.

The Act applies whenever general terms of business have been used, even if both parties are merchants. Thus it is clear that the Act is not exclusively concerned with consumer protection. It is true that by §24 of the Act transactions between merchants are exempted from certain other provisions of the Act, including §§10 and 11, with their automatic invalidation of standard terms of the specified types, but the general clause of §9 remains applicable, and, in general, when merchants use a clause which falls within one of the prohibited categories of §§10 and 11, the courts have not hesitated to invoke §9 in order to hold it invalid.

As its name suggests, the *Austrian* Konsumentenschutzgesetz applies only to 'contracts between firms and consumers'. Terms on a blacklist are invalid regardless of whether they have been 'individually negotiated' or not (§6(1)); a few terms listed in §6(2) are regarded by the legislator as less objectionable and are invalid only if they figure in standard terms of business.

Austrian law nevertheless recognizes that conditions agreed between businessmen should not be completely exempt from control, for §879(3) ABGB provides that 'a clause contained in general conditions of business or contract forms' is invalid if 'in all the circumstances of the case it is grossly disadvantageous to one of the parties'. Such clauses do not even become part of the contract if they are 'unusual', as they are when the disadvantaged party 'could not in the circumstances, especially the appearance of the document, have expected them' (§864a ABGB). No special rule was needed for unclear terms since the relevant principle of construction '*contra proferentem*' was already applicable to *all* contracts (§915 ABGB).

In *Switzerland* the only protection against unfair contract terms is given by the general law applied by the courts, and apart from the rule that a party guilty of intentional misconduct or gross negligence cannot take refuge behind a clause excluding liability (art. 100(1) OR), the protection given is almost always 'covert' or 'camouflaged'. Thus there is a rule about 'unusual' clauses, that general conditions of business which the person disadvantaged had no reason to expect are not binding. For example, the Bundesgericht has held a clause to be 'unusual' if in the case of a person unfamiliar with business it provides for jurisdiction elsewhere than at his domicile; such a clause escapes invalidity only if it is contained in 'an explicit declaration clearly separated from the other provisions of the contract, unequivocal in content and clearly expressive of the intention to found jurisdiction elsewhere' (BGE 91 I 11, 14). The 'ambiguity rule' also does yeoman service. Yet the courts which could exercise genuine control over the actual terms of contracts by reference to the standards of good morals or public order or undue restraint of freedom are very reluctant to do so (compare art. 19 f. OR, 27 par. 2 ZGB; and see, for example, BGE 109 II 213).

The Swiss Law against Unfair Competition, adopted in 1986 to deal with the problem, is not a great success. It makes it 'unfair' to use standard terms in business which 'differ significantly from the generally applicable law' or 'allocate rights and duties in a manner materially at odds with the nature of the contract', but this is so only if the terms are formulated 'in a misleading manner'; to satisfy this test, the prejudicial effect of the term must result from ambiguous, unclear or complex drafting, concealment in a long document or being located somewhere unexpected. Even if these conditions are satisfied the only conclusion is that the conduct is 'unfair', and it remains a question, much debated, whether or not the term is invalid for breach of art. 19, 20 OR. For criticism, see KRAMER in *Berner Kommentar* VI mn. 281 ff. to art. 19–20 OR; MERZ (above p. 324) p. 55 ff.

2. *The Romanistic Legal Family.*—*French* courts have also used the '*contra proferentem*' rule to give protection against unfair contract terms; they refuse to uphold clauses which are incomprehensible or printed in tiny type or brought to the customer's attention only after the conclusion of the contract (see CALAIS-AULOY (above p. 323) no. 136). Even if incorporated in the contract, exemption clauses may under certain conditions be held invalid,

and cannot be invoked by a party guilty of deceit or gross negligence (*dol ou faute lourde équivalente au dol*). One principle of great practical importance has been established by the courts, namely that a commercial seller is to be treated as if he were aware of any defects in the goods he sells. Art. 1643 Code civil then makes it impossible to invoke a contractual exemption clause, so such a clause, whether in standard terms or a specific agreement, is void unless the buyer was aware of the defect or is himself a merchant who deals in goods of that kind and therefore does not need protection (see Civ. 30 Oct. 1978, and Com. 6 Nov. 1978, JCP 1979. II. 19178, note GHES-TIN). Furthermore, exemption clauses in contracts for the carriage of goods are invalidated by art. 103 Code de Commerce.

The rules we have so far mentioned are not specifically directed towards consumer protection since they apply to exemption clauses whether they are contained in standard terms of business or result from individual negotiations. Consumer protection is, however, the aim of many recent enactments which fix the terms of certain transactions entered into by consumers in such detail as to leave no room for deviant standard terms. Notable among such contracts are residential leases, consumer credit arrangements (the rules depending on whether the credit is for goods or land), correspondence courses, 'doorstep agreements' (distinguishing sales from credit arrangements), and purchases of dwellings or buildings already built or to be built.

The French legislature has also taken action against unfair contract terms (clauses abusives) regardless of the type of contract. It is action of a very distinctive kind. The Law of 10 January 1978 (no. 78–23) empowers the government to issue decrees prohibiting specified clauses in contracts between professionals and consumers in so far as they give the professional an unfair advantage and seem to have been imposed by him on the consumer 'by an abuse of economic power' (art. 35).

The *Commission des clauses abusives* set up for this purpose produced numerous proposals for such ordinances, but with only one exception the government ignored them, and any hope that firms would voluntarily respect the Commission's proposals remained unfulfilled. In 1991, however, the Cour de Cassation held that it was open to the *courts* to hold that clauses falling within art. 35 were invalid—a bold decision consistent with the wording of the law, if not with the aims of those who drafted it. (Civ. 14 May 1991, DS 1991, 449 noted by GHESTIN; likewise Civ. 26 May 1993, JCP 1993.II.22158 noted by PAISANT; Civ. 6 Jan. 1994, JCP 1994.II.22237 noted by PAISANT.)

The special interest of the law in *Italy* is that the problem of standard terms of business has been specifically addressed by the Codice civile ever since it came into force in 1942 (arts. 1341 f., 1370). But progress has destroyed the advantage of modernity enjoyed by the Codice civile as compared with other European civil codes: the rules which seemed modern in

1942 are no longer adequate, largely because they permit only 'covert' and 'camouflaged' rather than 'open' control of standard terms. In art. 1370 we find the familiar rule of construction that in cases of doubt (so the article provides) clauses in standard terms of business or form contracts are to be construed in favour of the party on whom they are imposed. Art. 1342 provides that where there is a conflict between words added by the parties and the preformulated text, the former take precedence. The incorporation of standard terms into the contract is dealt with in art. 1341. According to para. 1 of this article it is sufficient if the customer knew of the conditions of business at the time the contract was concluded, or should, as a normally careful person, have known of them. The requirements of para. 2 are somewhat stricter: here there is a list of 'dangerous' clauses which are valid only if they are 'specifically approved in writing' by the consumer. Included here are clauses which limit the liability of the supplier, clauses which entitle him to withdraw from the contract or to withhold further performance, clauses which limit the time within which the customer must assert his rights, clauses which limit his freedom to contract with others (for example, fixing resale prices), clauses which provide for a tacit prolongation or renewal of the contract, jurisdiction clauses, and arbitration clauses.

The practical application of art. 1341 par. 2 has caused a lot of problems, not so much on the question whether a clause is 'dangerous', for here the courts have interpreted the catalogue extensively and have applied art. 1341 par. 2 to clauses not specified but similar in effect, but rather because it can be very difficult to decide when a clause has been 'specifically approved in writing' by the customer. For example, suppose that a customer is handed a complete set of the standard terms of business for signature on the dotted line: must the 'dangerous' clauses be reproduced verbatim just above the dotted line, perhaps even in bold or larger print, or is it enough if they are referred to by number only? (See Cass. 29 May 1973, no. 1610, Foro pad. 1973 I 177; Cass. 5 Nov. 1974, no. 3355, Temi 1977, 151.) This is simply to make the solution depend on the typographical skills of the draftsman, for surely no customer will be deterred from signing a clause, or spurred on to press for its modification, just because it is printed in bold type?

3. *Common Law.*—In *England* too one finds occasional cases, even as early as the nineteenth century, where the courts set limits to the validity of unfair contract terms. For example, in the so-called 'ticket cases' the courts repeatedly refused to uphold exemption clauses which had not been brought to the attention of the passenger in the proper manner, whether because they were printed on the back of the rail ticket or merely figured in the 'Conditions of Carriage' available for consultation in the railway station (for example, *Parker* v. *South Eastern Ry.* (1877) 2 CPD 416). Again, a person who hires a deck-chair on the beach cannot be expected to suppose that on the back of the ticket he receives is a clause which takes away his right to damages for personal injury caused by the deck-chair's collapse

(*Chapelton* v. *Barry UDC* [1940] 1 KB 532). A recent decision of the Court of Appeal holds that the more unexpected and prejudicial a clause is, the more clearly and emphatically it must be brought to the notice of the other party.

See *Interfoto Library Ltd.* v. *Stiletto Ltd.* [1989] 1 QB 433, where the comparative material used by BINGHAM LJ makes his opinion especially well worth reading. But is it really enough that the clause be printed in Indian ink and embellished with a scarlet arrow?

The '*contra proferentem*' rule and other artificial methods of construction were increasingly used by the courts to draw the teeth of exemption clauses, but in deference to freedom of contract they continued to hold that intrinsically such clauses were quite valid. Only after the Second World War does 'open' control of the content of such terms really start. Of particular interest here is the judge-made rule that an exemption clause was no defence to a claim based on a 'fundamental breach of contract'. The justification for this was that if a breach of contract was 'fundamental', the contract as a whole was to be regarded as at an end, with the result that the exemption clause also disappeared. Of course there were problems in distinguishing a 'fundamental' from a 'normal' breach of contract, and it was never quite clear whether the rule was simply a 'rule of construction', whereby in a case of doubt an exemption clause was to be construed as not covering a fundamental breach, or rather a 'rule of law' which invalidated an exemption clause *ipso iure* whenever there was a fundamental breach.

Finally, in 1980, in the important case of *Photo Production* v. *Securicor Transport* [1980] AC 827, the House of Lords closed the door on the doctrine of 'fundamental breach of contract'.

The plaintiff's factory was totally destroyed by a fire which was started by a night-watchman employed by the defendant security firm and which got out of control because of the inflammable material lying around. When the plaintiff claimed damages, the security firm rested its defence on a clause in the contract providing that 'under no circumstances' should it be liable for harm caused by its employees. The exemption was not to apply to harm which could have been avoided by the exercise of proper care on the part of the defendant itself, but it was agreed that the firm was not to blame as it had exercised proper care with regard to the employee in question. Nevertheless the Court of Appeal gave judgment for the plaintiff on the ground that to start a fire in an inflammable building was a 'fundamental breach' of the contract of a security firm, and that therefore the exemption clause was inapplicable. The House of Lords, however, reversed. The doctrine of 'fundamental breach' must be abandoned, and the agreement of the parties was to control, including the exemption clause which in the instant case, on its proper construction, covered the situation. In his speech LORD WILBERFORCE recognized that while the doctrine of fundamental breach had helped the courts to get round unfair exemption clauses, its application in practice had been problematical. In the meantime Parliament had enacted the Unfair Contract Terms Act 1977. This Act made it possible to nullify unfair exemption clauses, especially when they were deployed against consumers: 'After this Act, in commercial matters generally, when the parties are not of unequal bargaining power, and when the risks are normally borne by insurance, not only is the case for judicial intervention undemonstrated, but there is everything to be said, and this seems to have been Parliament's intention, for leaving the parties free to apportion the risks as they think fit and for respecting their decisions' (ibid. p. 843).

Indeed, Parliament in Britain has addressed the problem of unfair conditions of business in a whole series of statutes, such as the Consumer Credit Act 1974, which regulates credit arrangements with consumers, and, most important of all, the Unfair Contract Terms Act 1977, with its wide powers of control over clauses which purport to exclude or limit liability.

Despite its name the Act does not deal with all 'unfair contract terms', but only with those which seek to exclude or limit liability. In principle the Act applies only to 'business liability', that is, a liability which arises from some business or governmental activity, or from the possession of premises used for commercial or governmental purposes. Many provisions of the Act apply with full force only when the buyer contracted 'as a consumer', for example ss. 5–7, relating to the exclusion of the manufacturer's or seller's liability for physical or legal defects in goods. The Act is concerned mainly with contractual liability, but s. 2 applies to claims for damages in tort as well: liability in damages for *personal injury or death due to negligence* cannot be excluded or limited by any contractual clause or unilateral notice. An exemption clause which the defendant can establish to be 'reasonable' (s. 2(2), 11 (5)) may be valid in the case of *property damage* negligently caused. The test of 'reasonableness' is used in other provisions of the Act as well, in particular where the exemption clause is in a contract not made with a consumer. An exclusion of liability is 'reasonable' when it can be said that 'the term shall have been a fair and reasonable one to be included having regard to the circumstances which were, or ought reasonably to have been, known to or in the contemplation of the parties when the contract was made' (s. 11(1)). The circumstances which the judge is to take into account in determining the 'reasonableness' of an exemption are listed in 'Guidelines' in a Schedule to the Act.

The law in the *United States* is so complex that only a few basic points can be made here. Courts there, as elsewhere, will under certain circumstances deny that standard terms were incorporated in the contract, construe them *contra proferentem*, or disregard them if they conflict with a specific agreement (on this see §§203, 206, 211 Restatement of Contracts (Second), with extensive case-references). In addition, many enactments, mostly quite recent, lay down terms for certain kinds of contract typically entered into by consumers, such as sale, credit bargains, and so on. The courts do, however, have a general power of control in the principle that contractual clauses are void if they are contrary to public policy. On this basis the courts strike down clauses whereby 'common carriers' that is, carriers which offer their services to the public at large, try to immunize themselves from liability for faulty conduct, and they adopt a similar approach towards 'public utilities' such as telephone companies, radio and television stations, and health-care institutions, which in the United States are often privately run. Recently courts have held 'that a banking business is a public business, and like the common carrier, the banking institution is not allowed to exculpate itself from its own negligence' (CORBIN §1472 [Suppl. 1982]).

But the most important source of judicial control of contract terms is now to be found in §2–302 of the Uniform Commercial Code. This section permits the judge to invalidate a sales contract or individual terms in it if the contract or its terms are 'unconscionable'. This provision applies whether or not the terms in issue are standard ones, and whether or not the parties to the contract are both merchants: a sales contract made with a private individual is covered. The concept 'unconscionable' is nowhere defined. It is thus a general clause every bit as vague as §242 BGB. Being rather unfamiliar to American lawyers, it led to a flood of publications.

One particularly influential article was LEFF, 'Unconscionability in the Code, The Emperor's New Clause', 115 *U. Pa. L. Rev.* 485 (1967); see also EPSTEIN, 'Unconscionability: a Critical Reappraisal', 18 *JL & Econ.* 293 (1975); KORNHAUSER, 'Unconscionability and Standard Forms', 64 *Calif. L. Rev.* 1151 (1976); HILLMAN, 'Debunking Some Myths about Unconscionability: A New Framework for U.C.C. §2–302', 67 *Cornell L. Rev.* 1 (1981).

The courts have taken to this provision with enthusiasm, using it in preference to the traditional Common Law methods of avoiding contracts—undue influence, duress, and misrepresentation (see below Ch. 31 VI); indeed the Comments to §2–302 suggest that its principal purpose was to replace the familiar techniques of 'concealed' control of terms. The section has been applied in hundreds of decisions; so popular is it, indeed, that although strictly speaking it applies only to contracts of sale, it is commonly applied to other types of contract which fall within the Uniform Commercial Code, and even to other contracts, on the basis that it is 'merely declaratory of a general pre-existing principle' and therefore applicable throughout the whole law of contract. That is the conclusion reached by the Restatement of Contracts (Second) (1981), for §208 says:

'If a contract or term thereof is unconscionable at the time the contract is made, a court may refuse to enforce the contract, or may enforce the remainder of the contract without the unconscionable term, or may so limit the application of any unconscionable term as to avoid any unconscionable result.'

4. *European Law.*—On 5 April 1993 the EC Directive on Unfair Terms in Consumer Contracts gave member states twenty-one months in which to introduce provisions permitting the courts to hold a clause invalid 'if, contrary to the requirement of good faith, it causes a significant imbalance in

the parties' rights and obligations arising under the contract' (art. 3). The aim of the Directive being to establish a minimum level of protection in all member states, it permits states to retain or introduce provisions which give greater protection (art. 8). In consequence the law varies from state to state.

The Directive affects clauses only if they figure in contracts with consumers, a consumer being 'a natural person who is acting for purposes which are outside his trade, business or profession' (art. 2(b)). Consequently, like the French law of 10 January 1978 which gives protection only to the 'non-professionnel ou consommateur', it does not apply to contracts between businessmen. This restriction is unknown to the law in Germany, Austria, Sweden, and the Netherlands.

See §§9, 24 AGBG and §§864a, 879 (3) ABGB; §36 Swedish Contract Law. In the Netherlands the general clause in art. 6: 233a NBW cannot be prayed in aid by a business which has more than fifty employees or is required to publish annual company accounts (art. 6:235(1) NBW), but the term may still fall foul of the general principle that contractors must act consistently with 'decency and fairness' (art. 6:2 and 6:248 NBW).

To restrict the courts' power to control contract terms to cases where a consumer is affected by them is surely a mistake. Terms agreed between tradesmen should admittedly be controlled more flexibly, with more attention paid to the surrounding circumstances than in contracts with consumers, but there is no good reason for abandoning all control of clauses used by businessmen *inter se*. This is so whatever justification one adduces for controlling terms at all: if it is to protect the 'weaker' party, then one firm may be economically much inferior to another, and if it is that standard terms are accepted because transaction costs are too high (above p. 335), then surely the businessman is no more likely to waste time and money than the consumer. Furthermore the distinction between 'consumer transactions' and others is inevitably arbitrary and makes for difficulties of application, as does the distinction between consumers and other contractors ('small' businesses often being included in the former).

Thus the French courts hold that a person in business counts as a 'non-professionnel ou consommateur' when he buys goods or services in which he himself does not deal and of which he therefore understands less than his supplier. See CALAIS-AULOY (above p. 323) no. 145 and Civ. 28 Apr. 1987, D. 1988, 1, noted by DELEBECQUE (realtor purchasing an alarm system for his premises is a 'consommateur'). English courts have also held that a shipping broker or real estate agent who buys a car for the purposes of his business deals with the trade seller 'as consumer'. See *Peter Symmons & Co.* v. *Cook* [1981] New LJ 758; *R & B Customs Brokers Co.* v. *United Dominions Trust* [1988] 1 All ER 847, criticized by CHESHIRE/FIFOOT/FURMSTON 185 f. By contrast the European Court of Justice has given a narrower construction to the term 'consumer' where it appears in the Directive of 20 December 1985 on Contracts Concluded away from Business Premises: a person advertising his business for sale in a newspaper was not a 'consumer', since the test was not whether the transaction was a normal part of the business but whether it had to do with the business at all (ECJ 14 Mar. 1991 (*di Pinto*) [1991] ECR I–1189).

A contract term is only to be treated as invalid under the Directive if rather than being 'individually negotiated' it 'has been drafted in advance and the consumer has therefore not been able to influence the substance' of it (art. 3(2)). Although German law has an almost identical provision in §1 AGBG, there is no such restriction to *clauses prérédigées* in the French Law of 10 January 1978, nor in Swedish law nor to any significant extent in the law of Austria. The position of the Directive might be acceptable if there were any risk that courts equipped with the power to monitor individually negotiated terms might go in for wholesale control of the balance between the two sides of the contract, but any such fear is groundless: not only is it plain that the courts would not strike down a contract on the ground of the relative value of performance and counterperformance, but the Directive itself makes this clear (art. 4(2)), for it covers only ancillary terms. Such terms may well be 'abusive' and 'unfair' in consumer contracts even if, exceptionally, they have been individually negotiated; after all, a term which runs counter to special protective legislation such as exists for consumer contracts for credit, package holidays, sales, and distance learning is always invalid, regardless of whether it was individually negotiated or drafted in advance. But the real trouble with a rule that only preformulated terms can be scrutinized is that it makes the law uncertain, for often it is very doubtful whether or not the customer really had a chance during the negotiations to 'influence the substance' of the clause he is now impugning.

The law reports in Germany are full of cases where the dispute turned on whether on the facts the firm had 'genuinely offered room for discussion' or 'allowed the other party to modify the clause so as to protect his interests' or given him a 'real chance to influence the substance of the terms'; see BGH NJW 1988, 410.—The Bundesgerichtshof has held on several occasions that if a clause exempting the seller from liability is inserted into a contract for the sale of a new house at the suggestion of the notary, the clause is to be treated as 'individually negotiated' and the Law on General Conditions of Business does not apply; the clause does, however, remain subject to control under §242 BGB. See BGHZ 101, 350, 353 ff.

5. *Preventative Control.*—If a particular term in a contract is held invalid the party whom it would otherwise prejudice will win out over his contractor, whether as plaintiff or defendant. Satisfactory as this is, it will never by itself put an end to the use of unfair contract terms, for it often makes no sense for the affected party to invoke the rules made for his protection: it is much easier not to protest the clause, invalid though it is, and spare oneself the trouble and cost involved in digging out the relevant rules, or having a lawyer do so, negotiating with the contractor or even going to court. Firms

are well aware of this, and keep using terms known to be invalid in the hope that most customers will not object to them. If a difficult customer does come along the firm can always buy him off, accede to his wishes and continue to use the invalid clause in contracts with other customers. Even if the customer manages to get a court to hold the clause invalid, the firm can still, if it chooses, use it in contracts with other customers. For these reasons many countries have introduced systems of 'preventative control' to forestall the use of unfair clauses at the outset. The 'group action' has been much used for this purpose.

This is done in Germany (§§13 ff. AGBG), Austria (§§28 ff. Konsumentenschutzgesetz), the Netherlands (art. 6: 240 ff. NBW), and France (Laws of 5 January 1988 and 18 January 1992), see CALAIS-AULOY (above p. 323) no. 343 ff.). The EC Directive of 5 April 1993 requires member states to introduce provisions permitting 'organisations having a legitimate interest under national law in protecting consumers' to demand from courts or administrative bodies 'a decision as to whether contractual terms drawn up for general use are unfair . . .' (art. 7(2)).

Thus consumer organizations and certain others may obtain a court injunction against a firm which continues to use terms held to be unfair, and breach of the injunction can be sanctioned by a fine or in France by an *astreinte* payable to the complainant. It is true that the injunction is not binding on other firms, but it may be unwise of them to carry on using identical terms, for consumer groups see to it that the injunctions they achieve are published in the specialist and daily press and even, in Germany, entered in a publicly accessible register.

Consumer groups, however, are often strapped for funds, so it has often been proposed that the state set up administrative authorities with extensive powers to control market behaviour. Sweden was the first to take this path. Since 1971 a special authority under the 'Consumer-Ombudsman' has been tasked to see that tradesmen meet 'good commercial standards'. If it finds that a firm is marketing unreasonably dangerous goods or engaging in deceptive publicity, acting unfairly in competition or—to come to our point—using unfair contract terms, it can reason with it or the group to which it belongs and try to persuade it to mend its ways. This forms the main part of its activities, but if negotiations fail, the authority can go to the 'Market Court', set up for this very purpose, and seek an injunction.

See BERNITZ in STRÖMHOLM (ed.), *An Introduction to Swedish Law* (2nd edn. 1988) 278 ff., and for even more detail BERNITZ/DRAPER, *Consumer Protection in Sweden* (2nd edn. 1986), where all the relevant laws are given in English translation.

Great Britain also has a special authority, the Office of Fair Trading, set up by the Fair Trading Act 1973, which, *inter alia*, supervises the market behaviour of firms with regard to practices 'which may adversely affect the interests (whether they are economic interests or interests with respect to health, safety or other matters) of consumers' (s. 2)). The campaign against unfair terms of business is only one of the authority's functions. For example, it can invite the government to issue regulations to prohibit or require certain standard terms of business, and it can seek an injunction in court against a firm which is using standard terms contrary to law, be it criminal or private law. See BORRIE, *The Development of Consumer Law and Policy* (1984).

One of the great successes of the Office of Fair Trading in recent years has been to get major groups of tradesmen to draw up voluntary codes of practice to be followed by those supplying certain goods and services to consumers (for example, automobiles, furniture, package holidays). These codes of practice admittedly apply only to the members of the association in question, some of whom may even prefer to leave the association and draw up their own terms of business, but even so, the utility of the code of practice is unquestioned.

25

Contractual Capacity

HARTWIG, 'Infants' Contracts in English Law: With Commonwealth and European Comparisons', 15 *ICLQ* 780 (1966).
LAROCHE, 'La Condition juridique des malades mentaux', *Gaz. Pal.* 1968. Doctr. 12.
MONTANIER, 'Les Actes de la vie courante en matière d'incapacités', *JCP* 1982 D. 3076.
RAISON, *Le Statut des mineurs et des majeurs protégés* (4th edn., 1990).

I

ONLY if people have reached a certain minimum level of understanding and ability and are regarded by the law as having 'contractual capacity' can they bind themselves by contract. All legal systems therefore have to have rules which determine the conditions under which minors, incompetents, and those mentally deranged are to be denied such capacity. The function of these rules is basically protective: those whose mental powers are undeveloped or underdeveloped should be prevented from doing themselves an injury by their legal declarations and contracts. Obviously there must be exceptions, for to invalidate all his transactions would be an ill office to the minor one was seeking to protect, since then no one would be be ready to make a contract with him even if it were essential to his well-being or very advantageous for his estate.

The protective aim which underlies all rules relating to contractual capacity is valued so highly that it takes precedence over the needs of business. A person who deals with a minor is never safe simply because he believed the minor to have capacity, even if his belief that the minor was of age was perfectly reasonable. But all legal systems concur in answering the needs of commerce on one point: once a certain age has been reached, people are vested with contractual capacity regardless of their individual ability to look after their own affairs in a sensible way. In most countries this age is set at 18, but in Switzerland it is 20 (art. 14, Civil Code) and in Austria 19 (§21 ABGB).

While all countries fix a point at which complete contractual capacity begins, only a few lay down an age before which children have no such capacity at all—seven in Germany and Austria (§§105, 106 BGB, 865 ABGB), ten in Greece (art. 128 Civil Code). In other countries it depends on the circumstances of the individual case; they ask whether the child's capacity for judgment and comprehension is such as to enable him to understand the significance of what he was saying; if not, his declaration has no legal force.

It is mainly in the intervening period that problems arise, when the child is capable of understanding the consequences of his act but has not yet reached the age of majority. On this point all legal systems distinguish between contracts which juveniles can validly conclude on their own and other contracts which may be void *ab initio* or voidable or subject to reduction in favour of the minor.

Lunatics and incompetents raise much the same problem. People who have been interdicted on the ground of mental illness are incapable of contracting altogether, but the case of incompetents and drunkards is more delicate since it is impossible simply to annul or to uphold all their contractual declarations.

II

To go by the words of the Code civil, *French* law starts from the principle that minors' contracts are valid, since only where the law expressly invalidates a minor's obligation (as in art. 1123 Code civil) must his statutory representative contract in his place. In fact the courts start from the opposite principle that a minor's transactions are invalid, unless there is a special reason for holding otherwise.

Under the Code civil itself an adolescent may enter many of the transactions of family law without the consent of his statutory representative (marriage, marriage contracts, recognition of illegitimate children); in addition, the courts uphold 'actes conservatoires', measures taken by a minor which are necessary to ward off a danger to his property and which do not entail too great a financial burden.

Thus a minor can apply to have a mortgage registered to secure a debt owed to him, and may put the debtor in default. The textbook example of an 'acte conservatoire' is when a minor contracts with a builder to preserve his building from imminent ruin provided it is not at ruinous expense.

Under art. 389–3 and 450 Code civil a minor's contract is valid in cases where *la loi ou l'usage autorise les mineurs à agir eux-mêmes*, that is, transactions of daily life which involve no major risks for the minor and can be met within the means which are normal and appropriate to the standing and lifestyle of his family. This would include the *hire* of a motor vehicle on reasonable terms (see Civ. 4 Nov. 1970, Bull. civ. 1970.I.214), but not the *purchase* of one, even if the minor had means of his own at his disposal (Civ. 9 May 1972, Bull. civ. 1972.I.110).

All other transactions by a minor are in principle invalid. To establish this invalidity, a court action is required (*action en rescision*), but it is not enough simply to prove that the complainant was a minor at the time the contract was concluded (as in Italian law, art. 1425 Codice civile). In addition the minor must prove that the transaction would cause him an economic disadvantage (*lésion*). This extremely important limitation used to be reflected in the maxim 'Minor non restituitur tamquam minor sed tamquam laesus', and nowadays it is based on arts. 1305 ff. Code civil. The practical effect is that a minor's transactions are binding unless they are disadvantageous. Where performance and counterperformance are objectively disproportionate such a disadvantage obviously exists, and it also exists where the estate of the minor is such that it would be unreasonable to proceed with the transaction even if what he has promised is reasonable in relation to what he is to receive. Under art. 1306 Code civil, however, a minor's transaction is not rendered disadvantageous by the mere fact that an accident ('un événement casuel et imprévu') has robbed him of the benefit he was to have received. If the transaction is to the minor's benefit, the other party is bound as well: see art. 1125 Code civil.

If the contract is one which the minor's statutory representative could only conclude on his behalf by observing special forms (such as the agreement of the family council or the approval of the authorities responsible for wards) it will be absolutely void, regardless of lesion, if concluded by the minor himself. This means that some quite important transactions, such as sales of landed property, cannot be concluded by a minor even if the terms are greatly to his advantage.

A minor who attempts to rescind an unfavourable contract may be met with an *exceptio doli* if his contractor can prove that in negotiating the contract the minor used fraudulent manœuvres. A mere representation that he was of full age is not, however, enough (see also art. 1426 Codice civile), for if the rule were otherwise the adult could always protect himself against an action of rescission by asking the minor his age. The real reason for allowing the defence of fraud is that it constitutes a tort and the best way to make the minor liable is to hold him to his contract.

A special problem arises when a minor has achieved the rescission of a contract which has been carried out on both sides: can he reclaim his own performance even if he has consumed what he received? The answer is given at p. 590 below.

Mention must finally be made of *emancipation*, a striking institution of the law of minority in Romanistic systems, which only superficially resembles the emancipation of Roman law (compare arts. 476 ff. Code civil, arts. 390 ff. Codice civile).

Emancipation arises either from a formal declaration by the person with parental power over a minor at least 18 years old or by force of law when the minor marries. Its effect is to extinguish parental power and to clothe the minor with full contractual capacity.

The protection of *adults* suffering from some incapacity was reformed by the law of 3 January 1968. The previous device of taking away the capacity from the adult by judicial order (interdiction) and of charging a 'conseil judiciaire' with the task of acting on the person's behalf has been replaced by three new types of protection: protection by the court (*sauvegarde de justice*), tutorship (*tutelle*) and curatorship (*curatelle*). In the first of these cases the person's contractual capacity is in principle unrestricted, but lesionary transactions may be rescinded by the court or given only a limited effect. If a person needs constant representation in all the doings of daily life, a wardship may be set up on application or ex officio. The ward is basically incapable of contracting, but judicial decree may grant him the power to enter certain types of transaction on his own or with the support of his tutor. For a person who is capable of acting by himself but who needs protection or supervision, curatorship may be set up, even against his will. The person under care can enter quotidian transactions by himself but needs the consent of his curator for other matters.

III

Unlike Continental legal systems, the *Common Law* has no all-purpose legal representative (see below Ch. 32 III); equally, it does not have a general concept of the minor's incapacity to contract. Casuistical as always, it has been concerned to identify the types of case where a minor's contract must be invalidated for his own protection.

This is apparent in the doctrine of 'necessaries', the most interesting feature of the Anglo-American law of minority. For centuries the courts have held that despite his minority a juvenile must pay a reasonable price for 'necessaries' supplied to him. This is not a contractual liability but a liability in 'quasi-contract' which arises only when the minor receives the 'necessaries' delivered. In consequence it is not the agreed price but a reasonable sum which he must pay for the 'necessaries', though the reasonable price is usually the same as the normal commercial price.

According to the definition in the *English* Sale of Goods Act, 1979, s. 3(3), 'necessaries' are

'goods suitable to the condition in life of the minor . . . and to his actual requirements at the time of the sale and delivery'.

Thus food and clothes and medicines are classified as 'necessaries', whether they are for the minor himself or for his family. Also included are medical and similar services, education, and the hire of a car. The question ultimately turns on whether the judge in the individual case accepts that the minor really needed the objects in question and that the expenditure was reasonable in view of his income and style of life.

The *English* courts seem to have a more generous conception of 'necessaries' than the courts of the *United States*. For example, two diamond rings bought by a minister's son as engagement gifts were treated as 'necessaries' although they cost £80: *Elkington & Co.* v. *Amery*, [1936] 2 All ER 86. See also *Nash* v. *Inman*, [1908] 2 KB 1.—A great number of *American* decisions deal with the question whether *motor cars* are necessaries. Here again it is a question of fact: if the minor bought the car to drive to work in, and the distance involved and the absence of other means of transport made the purchase reasonable, he is bound to pay the normal trade price: see *Crocket Motor Co.* v. *Thomson*, 117 Ark. 495, 6 SW 2d 834 (1930); *Robertson* v. *King*, 225 Ark. 276, 280 SW 2d 402 (1955); *Braham & Co.* v. *Zittel*, 232 App. Div. 406, 250 NYS 44 (1931).—Contracts of employment, apprenticeship, and education (contracts of service) are binding if they are shown to be advantageous and useful to the minor: see *Roberts* v. *Gray*, [1913] 1 KB 520; *Doyle* v. *White City Stadium, Ltd.*, [1935] 1 KB 110. See also *Chaplin* v. *Leslie Frewin (Publishers) Ltd.*, [1966] Ch. 71 (Charlie Chaplin's 19-year old son had, for a fee, licensed a publishing house to publish his autobiography, written with the aid of a ghost-writer and sharply critical of his parents: was the contract binding?)—Yet there is no general rule that *all* economically advantageous contracts are binding on the minor. Thus contracts in a minor's trade or business may be avoided even if they are advantageous. For *England* see *Cowern* v. *Nield*, [1912] 2 KB 419; *Mercantile Union Guarantee Corp.* v. *Ball*, [1937] 2 KB 498; in the *United States* more subtle distinctions are drawn; the cases are cited in WILLISTON §242 no. 15.

All other contracts are either void *ab initio* or voidable by the minor at any time (on the distinction see TREITEL 488 ff.), so they do not bind the minor. The other party, however, is fully bound, supposing he himself has capacity.

A minor who has received anything at all under a contract which he claims not to bind him cannot reclaim any performance he himself has rendered: there must be a 'total failure of consideration'. He cannot therefore reclaim the price of a thing he has used: 'A minor cannot buy a compact disc on one Saturday and take it back the following Saturday asking for his or her money back.' (CHESHIRE/FIFOOT/ FURMSTON 439.) It is a different question whether the other party can make the minor repay any money or return any property received (or its substitute). According to s. 3(1) Minors' Contracts Act 1987, the judge can allow such a claim 'if it is just and equitable to do so', a wide discretion which allows him to weigh quite openly the need to protect the minor and the other party respectively.

If a minor deliberately deceives his contractor into believing that he was of full age or wrongfully damages property lent or hired to him under an invalid contract, can he be sued in *tort*? He is certainly not liable for claiming to be of full age (see *Leslie* v. *Sheill* [1914] 3 KB 607), but the question of damaged property is more difficult. If his conduct constitutes a breach of duty arising under the contract he is not liable in tort, but it is otherwise if his conduct goes 'outside' the contract altogether. The latter is the case when the minor contravenes a specific instruction, for example, when he jumps a horse which was hired to him only for riding, whereas if he simply rode the horse too energetically so that it was hurt, he is not liable (an unduly subtle distinction, on which see CHESHIRE/FIFOOT/FURMSTON 440 f.).

English law makes a distinction between contracts made by lunatics and those made by incompetents: if the mental affliction has been judicially ascertained, the contracts of the 'lunatic so found' are void; a 'lunatic not so found' can rescind his contracts on proof that at the time of contracting he was incapable of discernment and that the other party knew it. On the other hand, a person mentally ill is always liable to pay a reasonable sum for 'necessaries' delivered to him. In the *United States* most jurisdictions allow a person mentally ill to avoid the contract only if he is still in a position to return what he received from the other party. An exception is made if the other party knew or should have known of the affliction of his contractor or if, by reason of a judicial determination of the mental illness, the contract is void rather than voidable. Considerable differences exist between the several states on this point.

IV

In the *German* legal family a distinction is drawn between incapables and persons with limited capacity. Declarations of intention made by incapables are entirely without legal effect. Those who have limited capacity, that is, children of 7 and over in Germany and Austria and children in Switzerland who are 'capable of judgment', can indeed make declarations of will, but their contracts are 'provisionally invalid' (*schwebend unwirksam*) in the sense that the ratification of their legal representative is required to validate them. If no such ratification occurs the 'provisional invalidity' of the contract turns into permanent invalidity, equivalent to nullity.

If the parties to such an invalid contract have already performed their parts each is bound to return what he received, in accordance with the general principles of unjustified enrichment (see also art. 305(1), 411 ZGB). A minor who has received the price and spent it can defend himself on the ground that his enrichment has disappeared, on the basis of §818 par. 3 BGB (see below Ch. 39 IV 3b).

While the validity of the contract remains in doubt the other party can free himself from the contract provided he did not know of the minority (for the details see §109 BGB). In Swiss law, on the other hand, he remains bound by the contract unless he has allowed the legal representative a reasonable time to make his decision (art. 305(1), 410 ZGB).

In certain exceptional cases a minor is bound by a contract formed by his declaration of intention just like a person with unlimited capacity. This is so in German law when the contract 'procures only a legal advantage' to the minor (§107 BGB, and see also art. 19 ZGB, §865 ABGB), but the mere fact that its execution would have a beneficial effect on the minor's estate does not render a contract advantageous in this sense: the contract must not impose even the slightest obligation on the minor, however favourable the balance of advantage to him might be.

Since none of the contracts of the law of obligations, with the exception of promises of gifts to the minor, are legally advantageous in the sense of §107 BGB, this provision applies in practice only to contracts whereby the parties agree on the transfer of ownership. Thus if a minor buys a motor car without his parents' consent the contract of sale is invalid, but if it is conveyed to him, the (independent) contract of conveyance is valid under §107 BGB because the minor thereby acquires an unadulterated legal benefit. He therefore acquires ownership of the car when it is delivered to him.

The *German* BGB has a 'pocket money paragraph' which provides that a minor's contract is valid if he can perform his part of it with means provided specially or generally by his legal representative or by some third party with the representative's consent. The principal instances which fall within this provision are cases where parents have given their minor child an allowance or the means of supporting himself away from home at school or college.

Austria has a similar rule; if a minor enters a contract such as 'is normally entered by minors of his age and relates to a triviality of daily life', the contract is binding under §151 par. 3 ABGB as soon as the contractual duties affecting the minor are performed.

Those who temporarily 'lack the ability to act reasonably by reason of mental illness, intellectual debility, drunkenness or similar condition' have no legal capacity (art. 16 Swiss Civil Code, compare §§104 no. 2, 105(2) BGB, §865 ABGB). In Switzerland it is still the law that a person permanently disabled physically or mentally and unable to manage his affairs is incapacitated (*entmündigt*); this means that he no longer has legal capacity, but can at most make contracts with the agreement of his statutory representative (art. 17, 19 Swiss Civil Code). Incapacitation has now been abolished in Germany and Austria, and an 'administrator' or 'carer' (*Sachverwalter, Betreuer*) is appointed to manage the affairs of the disabled party within limits set down by the court in view of the degree of disability; outside these limits the disabled person is capable of effective legal action (see §273a ABGB, §§ 1896, 1903 BGB).

V

The three systems under review all start from the fundamental proposition that a minor, acting by himself, cannot bind himself by contract, but they differ considerably in the exceptions they make to this principle.

In the *Romanistic* systems a minor remains bound by his contracts until he brings a claim for rescission: in *French* law he must then prove that the execution of the contract would be disadvantageous to him, except in the cases—

the most important transactions—where in addition to the agreement of his legal representative the ratification of the family council or the wardship authorities is required and lacking. In practice, therefore, minors are bound by all less important transactions, provided that they are economically advantageous.

A minor is generally not bound in the *Common Law* either, but if he has had 'necessaries' supplied to him he must pay the going price; likewise if he has entered an advantageous contract of service, he must abide by it. This Common Law rule has an affinity with the *French* rule, for much the same factors are taken into account by French judges asking whether the execution of a contract would involve a 'lésion' for the minor and by English judges asking whether the objects involved were 'necessaries' or the contract of service advantageous. Thus in both legal systems a minor can by his own acts bind himself contractually or at least 'quasi-contractually', given that in the particular circumstances of the case such an obligation is reasonably in his interests.

The German legal family takes a quite different position. It is immaterial whether the court thinks a contract reasonable and advantageous to the minor, for in principle a minor's contract is valid only if his parents (or other statutory representative) have given their approval, expressly or by implication, either before the contract is made ('Einwilligung') or afterwards ('Genehmigung'). Doubtless parents will only approve of a contract if they think it to the minor's advantage, but the parents' view of the matter may well differ from that of a judge or neutral third party, and in any case youngsters have interests of their own which it may be reasonable for them to follow even if their parents disapprove. The position of the German legal family is at odds with the current trend to strengthen the youth's legal position *vis-à-vis* his parents, and it not only restricts the independence of young people more than their protection requires but also fails to respect the interests of decent third parties who confer benefits on young people under contracts on whose validity they were entitled to rely.

Only German law allows the other party to resile from a contract which the minor's legal representative has not ratified (§109 BGB). In both the Romanistic and Common Law systems the adult contractor is bound and even in Swiss law he can be freed only if the legal representative has remained silent during the period set for his decision. It is not at all clear why a person should be freed from a contract just because his declarations were made to a minor. He may, of course, want to be assured of the fate of the contract as soon as possible but it would be enough to allow him to set a reasonably short period for ratification, failing which the contract would finally become void as to both parties.

26

Offer and Acceptance

AUBERT, *Notion et rôle de l'offre et de l'acceptation dans la formation du contrat* (1970).

BRAUCHER, 'Offer and Acceptance in the Second Restatement', 74 *Yale LJ* 302 (1964).

COHEN, *Des contrats par correspondance en droit français, en droit anglais et en droit anglo-américain* (1921).

DILGER, 'Das Zustandekommen von Kaufverträgen im Außenhandel nach internationalem Einheitsrecht und nationalem Sonderrecht', *RabelsZ* 45 (1981) 169.

FARNSWORTH, 'Formation of International Sales Contracts: Three Attempts at Unification', 110 *U. Pa. L. Rev.* 305 (1961–2).

KAHN, 'Some Mysteries of Offer and Acceptance', 72 *S. Afr. LJ* 246 (1955).

KEYES, 'Consideration Reconsidered: The Problem of the Withdrawn Bid', 10 *Stan. L. Rev.* 441 (1958).

LITVINOFF, 'Offer and Acceptance in Louisiana Law: A Comparative Analysis', 28 *La. L. Rev.* 1, 153 (1969).

MACNEIL, 'Time of Acceptance: Too Many Problems for a Single Rule', 112 *U. Pa. L. Rev.* 947 (1964).

VON MEHREN, 'The Formation of Contracts', *Int. Enc. Comp. L.* VII Ch. 9 (1992).

NEUMAYER, Der Vertragsschluß nach dem Recht des internationalen Warenkaufs (Wiener Übereinkommen von 1980), *Festschrift für W. Lorenz* (1991) 747.

NUSSBAUM, 'Comparative Aspects of the Anglo-American Offer-and-Acceptance Doctrine', 36 *Colum. L. Rev.* 920 (1936).

OWSIA, 'Silence: Efficacy in Contract Formation, A Comparative Review of French and English Law', 40 *ICLQ* 784 (1991).

RODIÈRE (ed.), *La Formation du contrat* (1976).

SCHLESINGER *et al.*, *Formation of Contracts, A Study of the Common Core of Legal Systems*, 2 vols. (1968).

SCHMIDT, *Négociation et conclusion de contrats* (1982).

WINFIELD, 'Some Aspects of Offer and Acceptance', 55 *LQ. Rev.* 499 (1939).

I

ALL over the world students are taught that the way to make a contract is for one party to issue an 'offer' and the other an 'acceptance'. In many cases, however, this is not what happens. When a conveyance drafted by a notary is signed simultaneously by both parties, it is hard to say that one of them is making an offer and the other accepting it, and where parties finally reach agreement after a long period of negotiation during which each has made proposals and counterproposals to the other, 'offer' and 'acceptance' hardly fit the situation at all. In 'distance contracts', on the other hand, where the contract is made by an exchange of letters or other documents between parties some way apart, messages are indeed despatched sequentially and the question arises whether the offeror is bound by his offer or can revoke it, and if so, under what conditions and for how long. We deal with this question first.

The problem of the binding nature of an offer has produced three different solutions: the offeror is least bound in the Anglo-Saxon legal family and most strongly bound in the German systems, the Romanistic legal family adopting an intermediate position.

There exists a two-volume work which contains a comprehensive comparative treatment of all the problems connected with 'offer and acceptance'. This is *Formation of Contracts*, produced by a team of nine comparatists from all over the world under the leadership of SCHLESINGER. The general topic of 'offer and acceptance' is broken down into more than twenty complexes of problems, for each of which the contributors have produced national reports; these are then worked into general reports which show the areas of agreement and divergence. For an extensive description of this interesting method of comparative research see SCHLESINGER, 'The Common Core of Legal Systems—An Emerging Subject of Comparative Study', in: *Twentieth Century Comparative and Conflicts Law—Legal Essays in Honor of Hessel E. Yntema* (1961) 65.

II

In Anglo-American law an offer empowers its addressee to accept it and so conclude a contract; it remains capable of acceptance from the time it arrives until it lapses through the expiry of a period fixed by the offeror or determined in accordance with the circumstances. Until the offer has been accepted, however, the offeror remains free to withdraw it at any time and even if he has declared his readiness to be bound to his offer for a stated period he is legally free quite capriciously to withdraw it before that period elapses.

The reason why the Common Law will impose no obligation on the offeror is to be found in the doctrine of consideration, that is, the principle of Anglo-American contract law whereby a promise, unless contained in a special document (deed), generates a binding obligation only if the promisee has rendered or promised a counterperformance (see below Ch. 29). Offers are normally made without any counterperformance by the addressee and they are hardly ever put in a deed, so normally the offeror is not bound by his offer.

The basic rule of the Common Law can cause hardship to an offeree who has not paid the offeror not to withdraw his offer (option contract) for he may have entered engagements or incurred expenditure in reliance on the continuation of the offer which the offeror now revokes. In such cases American courts tend to hold that the offer may not be withdrawn, notwithstanding the doctrine of consideration. If a general contractor bases a tender on the price quoted by a subcontractor and his tender is accepted, the subcontractor is not entitled forthwith to withdraw his offer and so throw out all the general contractor's calculations. Where the subcontractor knew and intended that the main contractor would rely on his offer in calculating his bid the courts, with varying reasonings, hold that the offer may not be withdrawn: see *Northwestern Engineering Co.* v. *Ellermann*, 69 SD 397, 10 NW 2d 879 (1943); *Drennan* v. *Star Paving Co.*, 51 Cal. 2d 409, 333 P. 2d 757 (1958); and also 59 Colum. L. Rev. 355 (1959); but see also *James Baird Co.* v. *Gimbel Bros., Inc.*, 64 F. 2d 344 (2d Cir. 1933), noted in 20 Va. L. Rev. 214 (1933). This development in the courts has been followed by Restatement (Second) of Contracts (1981) where §87 par. 2 lays down that an offer is to be regarded as irrevocable if, as the offeror should reasonably have expected, it induces action or forbearance of a substantial character on the part of the offeree. In such a case, however, the offer is to be regarded as binding only 'to the extent necessary to avoid injustice'. The need to attribute some binding effect to offers is especially strongly felt in commerce. The Uniform Commercial Code lays down that if written offers to buy and sell commercially are stated to be binding, they may not be withdrawn during the prescribed period or, if no period is prescribed, for a reasonable period not exceeding three months (§2–205). In England the Law Revision Committee proposed in 1937 (Cmd. 5449) than 'an agreement to keep an offer open for a definite period of time or until the occurrence of some specified event shall not be unenforceable by reason of the absence of consideration' but no action has yet been taken. The whole subject is covered in SCHLESINGER/MACNEIL (above p. 356) 747 ff., 1393 ff.

In the absence of any statutory regulation the basic principle still applies that offers may be freely withdrawn at any time until they have been accepted by the offeree. But the hardship of this rule is somewhat modified by the special rule of the Common Law regarding the time when acceptance makes the contract binding. This rule goes back to the famous leading case of *Adams* v. *Lindsell*, (1818) 1 B. & Ald. 681, 106 Eng. Rep. 250, the source of the 'mailbox' theory. According to this rule it is not when the acceptance reaches the offeror that the contract is formed but at the earlier time when the offeree despatches it, that is, puts it in the mailbox or otherwise entrusts it to the Post Office. The 'mailbox' theory was originally attributed to the view that the offeror implicitly authorized the Post Office to act as his agent for the receipt of acceptances, so that the contract was formed on posting just as if the declaration of acceptance has been handed to the offeror in person. This construction is now seen to be unrealistic and unpersuasive. The real reason for the rule was the need to minimize the period during which the offeror could withdraw his offer; to put it another way, the offeree had to be relieved of the risk of the offer's being withdrawn as from the moment when he posted his acceptance rather than the later moment when it arrived.

Foreign observers may find it hard to reconcile the 'mailbox' theory with the consensual nature of contract. Even in the Common Law all other declarations (offers, withdrawal of offers, the giving of notice, and so on) must reach the addressee before they are effective, yet a *contract* can come into existence without the offeror's knowledge. A valid contract arises even if the acceptance is lost in the post, though of course the offeree must be able to prove that he really did post his acceptance.

The 'mailbox' theory is also difficult to reconcile with the fact that postal rules everywhere allow a letter to be withdrawn even in transit. This fact induced the American Court of Claims to abandon the 'mailbox' theory; see *Dick* v. *United States*, 82 F. Supp. 326 (Ct. Cl. 1949); *Rhode Island Tool Co.* v. *United States*, 128 F. Supp. 417 (Ct. Cl. 1955). Writers generally oppose it as well. See 34 *Cornell LQ* 632 (1949); 62 *Harv. L. Rev.* 1231 (1949); 59 *Yale LJ* 374 (1950); 54 *Mich. L. Rev.* 557 (1956). The traditional rule is however retained in Restatement (Second) of Contracts (1981) §63: 'An acceptance made in a manner and by a medium invited by an offer is operative . . . as soon as put out of the offeree's possession, without regard to whether it ever reaches the offeror.'

In such discussions one should always remember that the practical importance of the question whether acceptance takes effect on posting or on arrival keeps diminishing as modern techniques of data transmission enable despatch and arrival to be simultaneous, even when the parties are far apart.

III

In the *Romanistic* legal systems the binding force of offers is rather stronger. In France, after many fluctuations, the principle whereby any offer can be withdrawn until it has been accepted by the offeree has been greatly modified by the courts. If the offeror has set a given period for acceptance the offer can be withdrawn before this period has expired but the withdrawal renders the offeror liable in damages (Civ. 10 May 1968, Bull. civ. 1968. III. 162). As the courts do not require that any particular period be expressed the same is usually true of offers which contain no set period for acceptance: it is sufficient if it appears from the circumstances of the individual case or from normal trade usage that the offer was to be open for acceptance for a 'délai raisonnable'. What period for acceptance, if any, is to be regarded as implicitly agreed is decided as a matter of fact by the trial court in the light of the particular circumstances of the case (Civ. 10 May 1972, Bull. civ. 1972. III. 214). If an offer is revoked before this period elapses, the offeree, while unable to form the contract *stricto sensu* by purporting to accept, can nevertheless claim compensation for the loss which the premature revocation causes him.

Where the owner of a plot of land made an offer to sell it to an interested party and agreed that the premises might be viewed on a particular day, there was an implicit agreement that the offer would remain open until the day of viewing, and the previous withdrawal of the offer rendered the owner liable in damages; instead of money damages, there may be 'réparation en nature', which in such a case takes the form of requiring the offeror to perform the terms of the offer (see Civ. 17 Dec. 1958, D. 1959, 33; Civ. 10 May 1968, Bull. civ. 1968. III. 162).

There is some dispute about the legal basis for the offeror's liability in damages. Many writers see the offeror as being liable in tort under art. 1382 Code civil: while there may be a right to withdraw an offer its withdrawal may in certain circumstances constitute a 'faute' for which the offeror is liable (see below pp. 619 ff.). On another view, the offeror offers to enter not only the principal transaction but also a preliminary contract which binds him to keep the principal offer open for a certain time. This preliminary contract, being purely advantageous for the offeree, is concluded by tacit acceptance. If the offeror then withdraws the offer to enter the principal transaction, he is liable in damages for breach of the preliminary contract. (See GHESTIN no. 210 ff.; SCHMIDT (above p. 356) no. 223 ff.)

This was the theory used by the Court of Appeal at Colmar in a case where a subcontractor who had based his offer on an error of calculation had withdrawn it after the offeree had used it as the basis for a successful tender. The court held that an offer was binding 'dès lors qu'il résulte d'un accord exprès ou tacite, mais indiscutable, qu'elle a été formulée pour être maintenue pendant un délai déterminé', but found that in the case before it no such agreement was proved: when the offeror made his offer he did not know that the offeree was intending to use it as a basis for making a tender (Colmar, 4 Feb. 1936, DH 1936, 187).

This construction is obviously very forced: it is a sheer fiction to say that the parties have made a special preliminary contract to the effect that the offer should remain open.

It is difficult to tell from the cases what amount of damages, if any, may be ordered against an offeror who has withdrawn his offer. This is attributable in part to these theoretical differences but in part also to the fact that when it comes to determining the quantum of damages French judges have a very considerable room for discretion, not subject to the control of the Cour de Cassation. Decisions based on art. 1382 Code civil normally allow the disappointed offeree only the equivalent of the expenses he incurred in reliance on the offer's remaining open (see Bordeaux, 17 Jan. 1870, S. 1870. 2. 219); yet the offeror can also be required by way of damages to put the offeree in the position he would have enjoyed had the contract come to fruition (compare PLANIOL/RIPERT VI no. 132, and, in great detail, SCHLESINGER/ BONNASSIES (above p. 356) 769 ff.).

The Commission charged with the reform of the French Code civil proposed a rule whereby offers stated to be open for a certain period could not be withdrawn until that period elapsed unless the withdrawal reached the offeree before the offer; the same was to apply when a period during which the offer was to remain open could be inferred from the circumstances (art. II of the avant-projet of 'Sources and Formation of Obligations'). Art. 2 of the Franco-Italian Draft Law of Obligations, never enacted, was to the same effect.

The new Italian Codice civile proceeds on this modern path in arts. 1328 f. An offer cannot be withdrawn before the expiry of any specified period. If no period is specified in the offer it can be withdrawn until acceptance, but if the offeree has relied on the offer in good faith he has a claim for damages for the loss he suffered in preparing to perform.

Just as in the Common Law, the problem in the Romanistic systems can only be seen as a whole if one asks at what moment acceptance concludes the contract.

On the various doctrinal views see, for example, PLANIOL/RIPERT VI nos. 158 ff.— Of course this moment determines when an offer ceases to be revocable but it is important in practice for other reasons too: since the purchaser of specific goods becomes owner of them at the moment when the contract is concluded, he bears the risk of their accidental loss from that time (see art. 1138, 1583 Code civil); and the place where the contract is concluded may determine which court has territorial jurisdiction over any disputes which arise (see art. 420 Code de procédure civile).

The French Cour de Cassation has constantly held that the time of effective acceptance depends on the circumstances of the individual case, especially on the intention of the parties, and is therefore not a proper question for the highest court. This attitude of the Cour de Cassation is quite incomprehensible to lawyers from countries where this matter is regulated by statute. It is not very helpful to be told to interpret the will of the parties since frequently one has to determine whether the parties ever reached any agreement at all. Nevertheless the French trial courts seem to reach equitable results with the power afforded to them by the Cour de Cassation. (For details see GHESTIN no. 243 ff.)

According to art. 1326, 1335 Codice civile a contract comes into being as soon as the offeror knows of the acceptance; such knowledge is presumed as soon as the declaration of acceptance arrives at the offeror's normal address unless he can prove that his ignorance is not attributable to negligence.

IV

In Germany the offeror is 'bound' by his offer (§145 BGB) in the sense that he cannot withdraw it for the period of time he specifies or, if he specifies no period, for a reasonable time: rather than giving rise to liability in damages, a purported withdrawal simply has no legal effect at all. This is true also in

Switzerland (art. 3, 5 OR), Austria (§862 sent. 2 ABGB), Greece (art. 185 f. Civil Code), and Portugal (art. 250 Civil Code).

The offeror can prevent his offer's having binding force by using express phrases designed to have that effect ('freibleibend', 'ohne Obligo'). Normally a declaration so qualified is not an offer in the legal sense but simply an invitation to make offers: the declaration of the other party becomes the offer which in its turn requires acceptance, but in fact the German courts tend to hold that the necessary acceptance has been given if the original uncommitted proposer remains silent; good faith in the circumstances would require him to reject the offer expressly and his failure to do so counts as assent.

The BGB has no special rule for the question when *acceptance* is effective; quite rightly it sees this as simply an instance of a general problem which calls for comprehensive regulation since it affects all communicable declarations. The real problem is to divide the risks of transit fairly between the person sending the declaration and the person he sends it to. In §130 the BGB strikes a middle course between the rival theories of the old *Gemeines Recht*, traces of which may still be seen in French law. Every declaration of will, including the acceptance of an offer to contract, is effective as soon as it 'arrives', that is, as soon as it comes into the sphere of influence of the addressee. This effects a sound apportionment of the risks of transit. The person who sends off a declaration chooses the medium and route of communication and consequently must bear the attendant risks, but the risks incident to the addressee's own zone of influence must be borne by the addressee himself: if a bird-lover, to take an old school example, chooses not to empty the letter-box in his garden for fear of affrighting the tomtits within, the declaration is treated as having arrived.

V

This comparative survey has shown that the three different systems attach different legal consequences to the issuance of an offer. In the Common Law an offer has no binding force at all and is not even a ground for liability in damages. In the Romanistic legal systems the premature withdrawal of an offer leads to liability in damages, always in the case of offers with fixed periods, usually for offers without such periods attached. In German law every offer is irrevocable; a purported withdrawal has no legal effect whatever unless the offeror has excluded the binding effect of his proposal.

The critic is forced to conclude that on this point the German system is best. It is true that in practice the differences between the German system and the Common Law are slighter than might at first glance appear. Even in German law an offer may be withdrawn until it reaches the offeree, and in the Common Law an offer becomes irrevocable once the offeree has put his acceptance in the hands of the carrier. This means that in the Common Law the offeree bears the risk of revocation only for the extra period between the arrival of the offer and the despatch of the acceptance, the period during which he is considering whether to accept or not; unless the offer is stated to be open for a certain time this period is normally very short. Even so, the German system is superior. Experience shows that its results are practical and equitable; the offeree can act with assurance in the knowledge that his acceptance will bring about a contract. It also makes sense to put the risk of any changes in supplies and prices on the offeror: it is he who takes the initiative, it is he who invokes the offeree's reliance, and so it must be for him to exclude or limit the binding nature of his offer, failing which it is only fair to hold him bound.

The apostle of unification of the law on this problem would find it difficult to convert the Anglo-American lawyers. Although it may seem odd to the Continental jurist that an offeror cannot bind himself even if he wants to do so unless he goes to the unusual trouble of entering a remunerated option contract, the doctrine of consideration which is deeply rooted in their contract law is strongly opposed to the binding force of offers. Nevertheless there is a clear trend in state legislation in the United States towards making offers binding and there are also extralegal factors which limit the capricious withdrawal of offers: withdrawal may be legally permissible but it is recognized to be unfair and commercial men consequently avoid it.

The critical comparatist who approves of the German solution to the problem of the binding nature of offers will also approve of the rule of the BGB that a declaration of intention *interabsentes* becomes effective when it arrives with the addressee. The 'mailbox' theory leads to unsatisfactory results if it is taken to mean that a contract is concluded even if the acceptance is lost in the post or is withdrawn by a telegram which the offeror receives earlier than the letter. But the principal objection to the 'mailbox' theory is that it is inconsistent with all the postal regulations which allow those who send letters to recall them until they reach the addressee. The older theory on the Continent was that a declaration became effective at the moment its addressee became aware of it, but this was also unsatisfactory in that it made the issue turn on an internal event, something which a legal order should try to avoid because of difficulties of proof. German law makes the question turn on *arrival*, that is, the entry of the declaration into the addressee's zone of influence. This is not a special rule for the acceptance of contractual offers but applies to all declarations of will which need to be communicated; it not only allocates the risk of transmission as between sender and addressee in a fair manner but also makes the outcome turn on an ascertainable and provable event.

VI

Although, as we have seen, the three systems start out from different principles, the practical results are not so different. Accordingly it was possible to reach a reasonable compromise in the Vienna Convention on Contracts for the International Sale of Goods (CISG). Art. 16(1) CISG certainly starts out by stating that offers are revocable, but it makes so many exceptions to this in art. 16(2) that the result is not very different from that in Germany under §145 BGB. An offer is binding 'if it indicates, whether by stating a fixed time for acceptance or otherwise, that it is irrevocable' or 'if it was reasonable for the offeree to rely on the offer as being irrevocable and the offeree has acted in reliance on the offer'. (See further VON CAEMMERER/ SCHLECHTRIEM, *Kommentar zum Einheitlichen UN-Kaufrecht* (2nd edn., 1995) art. 16.)

In the cases where an offer may be withdrawn at all the withdrawal must, according to art. 16(1) CISG, reach the offeree before the offeree has sent off his acceptance. In allowing the recipient of a revocable offer the chance of curtailing the period of vulnerability by prompt despatch of an acceptance, the Conference took an idea from the 'mailbox' theory but it did not follow the 'mailbox' theory's rule that the mere posting of the acceptance concludes the contract: posting the acceptance puts an end to the offer's revocability but it does not conclude the contract. For the problem of the moment when contractual declarations become effective, the German rule was adopted. Art. 18(2) provides that an acceptance becomes effective when it 'reaches' the offeror, and the same is true for other communications, including the offer itself (art. 15(1)), its withdrawal (art. 15(2)), its revocation (art. 16(1)), and its rejection (art. 17). In all these cases the message 'reaches' its addressee when it is 'delivered . . . to him personally, to his place of business or mailing address or, if he does not have a place of business or mailing address, to his habitual residence' (art. 24).

On the whole it is a matter for regret that CISG did not adopt the clear German rule throughout. Although the practical differences are not great, it made for very complex drafting to start from the old-fashioned principle that offers can be withdrawn and then emptying it of substance by a series of exceptions. Still, in view of the considerable degree of legal unity which has been achieved in the area of international sales contracts, one must not complain too much of lack of juridical elegance.

27

Formal Requirements

BROOKE, *Treatise on the Office and Practice of a Notary in England* (9th edn. by CHARLES-WORTH, 1985).

BROWN, 'The Office of the Notary in France', 2 *ICLQ* 60 (1953).

COMMENT, 'The Statute of Frauds and the Business Community: A Re-Appraisal in Light of Prevailing Practices', 66 *Yale LJ* 1038 (1957).

EBEL, *Recht und Form, Vom Stilwandel im deutschen Recht* (1975).

FISCHER, 'Die Rechtsstellung des deutschen Notars im Recht der EWG', *DNotZ* 1989, 467.

FRIDMAN, 'The Necessity for Writing in Contracts within the Statute of Frauds', 35 *U. Tor. LJ* 43 (1985).

FULLER, 'Consideration and Form', 41 *Colum. L. Rev.* 799 (1941).

HÄSEMEYER, *Die gesetzliche Form der Rechtsgeschäfte* (1971).

——, 'Die Bedeutung der Form im Privatrecht', *JuS* 1980, 1.

K. HELDRICH, 'Die Form des Vertrags', *AcP* 147 (1941) 89.

V. HOFFMANN, *Das Recht des Grundstückskaufs, Eine rechtsvergleichende Untersuchung* (1982) Ch. 5.

JHERING, *Geist des römischen Rechts auf den verschiedenen Stufen seiner Entwicklung*, Pt. II(2) (4th edn., 1883) Ch. 43 ff.

KÖBL, 'Die Bedeutung der Form im heutigen Recht', *D NotZ* 1983, 207.

LLEWELLYN, 'What Price Contract?—An Essay in Perspective', 40 *Yale LJ* 704, 746 ff. (1931–2).

LORENZ, 'Das Problem der Aufrechterhaltung formnichtiger Schuldverträge', *AcP* 156 (1957) 381.

——, 'Rechtsfolgen formnichtiger Schuldverträge', *JuS* 1966, 429.

MANN, 'Die Urkunde ausländischer, insbesondere englischer Notare und der deutsche Rechtsverkehr', *NJW* 1955, 1177.

VON MEHREN, 'The French Civil Code and Contract: A Comparative Analysis of Formation and Form', 15 *La. L. Rev.* 687, 693 ff. (1955).

MEURISSE, 'Le Déclin de la preuve par écrit', *Gaz. Pal.* 1951. 2. Doctrine 50.

PERROT, Juris-Classeur civil, Artt. 1315–69 Code civil.

RABEL, 'The Statute of Frauds and Comparative Legal History', 63 *LQ Rev.* 174 (1947).

SCHLESINGER, The Notary and the Formal Contract in Civil Law, Report of the [New York] Law Revision Commission (1941), Study Relating to the Seal and to the Enforcement of Certain Written Contracts, p. 59.

I

In all modern legal systems there are some transactions which have to be in a special form if they are to receive legal recognition. Such formal requirements are, however, always exceptions to a general *principle of informality*. In many legal systems this principle is made explicit, as in art. 11 OR, which lays down that the validity of contracts depends on a particular form 'only if' the law so specifies (see also §883 ABGB). The German Civil Code, on the other hand, brief and abstract as usual rather than clear and popular, leaves it to be inferred from §125 that legal transactions are generally valid regardless of form.

The principle of informality has not always been recognized. In ancient Roman law, as in other early legal systems, legal obligations could *only* be engendered by observing special forms. The requirement of form was not a means of advancing legal goals such as certainty of proof; the form was the actual reason for the desired legal result; it was 'effective form' rather than 'protective form', to use an expression of DULCKEIT (*Festschrift Fritz Schulz* I (1951) 161). Accordingly, ancient forms combined ritual solemnity and obviousness of import; in ancient Rome spoken formulas with prescribed words had occasionally to be accompanied by stipulated gestures, such as the grasping by the purchaser in mancipatio of the person or thing sold. As Roman law developed, legal transactions which required no form became increasingly important, especially the consensual and real contracts, until in the sophisticated transactional law of the classical period they constituted the rule. At this stage formality was required for protective purposes; practically the only known form in the post-classical period was a written record of the transaction which is still the typical formal requirement today, though it has many variants, from simple writing to a document officially attested.

It is not difficult to identify the *functions* served by rules which specify formal requirements: basically they are to facilitate proof or to confirm seriousness of intention.

The former seems to be historically the older. The very title of the English Statute of Frauds, 1677—parts of it are still in force in England and most of the states of North America adopted it *in toto*—suggests why it introduced formal requirements for certain types of transaction, namely 'for the prevention of many fraudulent practices which are commonly endeavoured to be upheld by perjury and subornation of perjury', to quote the Preamble, for as long as methods of proof were cumbrous and the evidence was heard by a jury which was easily misled, there was a risk that the plaintiff would perjure himself about the making of the alleged oral contract or hire a band of witnesses to do so. The same is true of the even older French rule in art. 54 of the Ordonnance de Moulins, 1566, which prohibited oral evidence in respect of disputed contracts involving more than a hundred pounds. Today we see that formal requirements may have evidentiary functions even where the parties have no improper motives, for the required form facilitates proof not only of the *conclusion* of the contract, but also of its *content*, because a document gives rise to a presumption—rebuttable only with difficulty—that it contains a full and accurate statement of what was agreed. We can tell that the provisions we have mentioned were originally designed to strengthen the proof of the agreement because failure to observe the requisite form leads not to the substantive invalidity of the legal transaction but only to *procedural* sanctions; a contract defective in form is 'unenforceable' in Anglo-American legal systems and 'unproveable' by means of witnesses in France (art. 1341 Code civil; 'il n'est reçu aucune preuve par témoins').

The private international lawyer must not be misled by the fact that in many foreign systems a failure to observe the specified forms has only procedural sanctions. It is certainly an unwritten principle of the conflict of laws that the judge applies his own procedural law and never that of a foreign system, but it does not follow that a German judge must treat a contract to which French law applies as valid on the sole ground that the sanctions attached to the defect in form by French law, namely the exclusion of proof by witnesses, are procedural. Although it is dressed up in procedural terms, the French rule performs the substantive legal function of a formal requirement. Accordingly, the German judge should treat the contract as invalid on the ground of want of form. The Bundesgerichtshof has decided otherwise and has been criticized for it by GAMILLSCHEG (*JZ* 1955, 702). On the way American courts categorize formal requirements, see DONATH *IPrax* 1994, 333.

Rules which impose formal requirements are often concerned with *seriousness of intention*; in prescribing the conditions which the transaction must satisfy if it is to be enforced as being presumptively serious, the aim is to give persons unfamiliar with business an opportunity for thoughtful consideration and so protect them from surprise. It is true that it takes only a few seconds to draft even a contract of guarantee so that the requirement of writing does not necessarily entail a period of delay sufficient to permit reappraisal, but to insist on writing does suggest, especially to laymen, that one is leaving the area of merely social engagements and has to face the question whether one wants to enter a genuine business obligation or not.

A formal requirement is clearly directed to assuring seriousness of intention if it lays down that the transaction must be attested by an independent official with legal training such as the notary in Germany, who is bound

'to ascertain the will of the parties, explain the content of the transaction, instruct the parties about the legal consequences of the transaction, and record their statements clearly and unequivocally. In so doing he should take care that errors and doubts are avoided and that inexperienced and unknowledgeable parties are not disadvantaged' (§17 Beurkundungsgesetz).

Notaries—officials whose task is to record legal transactions—are to be found throughout Continental Europe but are quite unknown in the Anglo-American legal family, with the result that the Common Law has nothing comparable to the 'notarial document' (§128 BGB), the 'notarial act' (for example §551 ABGB), or the 'acte authentique' (art. 1312 Code civil). It is true that in England there is a respected profession of 'Public Notary', to which applicants of at least seven years professional experience may be admitted by the Court of Faculties under the supervision of the Archbishop of Canterbury (for details see BROOKE (above p. 365) p. 31 ff., MANN (above p. 365) p. 1178), but the typical task of the Public Notary is to draw up documents for use abroad by parties who need them under foreign law. The *American* 'Notary Public' has nothing in common with the Continental notary except the name. They are normally persons with little or no legal training who are empowered under the laws of the individual states to record sworn statements, to certify signatures and so on.

In private international law cases the question often arises whether the German requirement that a legal transaction be inscribed or a signature attested by a notary is satisfied if these acts are done by a foreign 'Notary'. What must be decided in each case is whether the foreign official is the equivalent of the home product, given the purpose underlying the German rule. Certainly if the rule is designed to ensure that the parties should have the advice of a legal expert before concluding the transaction, the participation of an American Notary Public, for example, would be quite inadequate (see KROPHOLLER, *Internationales Privatrecht* (2nd edn., 1994) 209 f., and BGHZ 80, 76).

II

The civil codes of the Romanistic legal family follow the French Code civil and make a basic distinction between cases where certain formalities must be observed as a precondition of the *validity* of the legal transaction and other cases in which an informal transaction, though valid, cannot be *proved* in court or can be proved only by limited means of proof. In practice the distinction between invalidity and unproveability is not very great, though if a transaction is *invalid* for want of form it must be treated by the court on its own motion as non-existent, while a transaction which is valid but simply *unproveable* may possibly be recognized by the party liable.

There are few cases in French law where the observance of a formality is a precondition of validity and in those cases the requisite formality is generally the notarial act. This class of case includes the promise of a gift (art. 931 Code civil, art. 782 Codice civile) and the marriage contract (art. 1394 Code civil, arts. 162 f. Codice civile). Holographic wills apart, simple writing is a precondition of validity in the strict sense only when prescribed by a text '*sous peine de nullité*' or necessary in view of the purpose of the requirement.

Art. 2044 par. 2 Code civil, for example, states that an agreement to compromise a dispute must be in writing, but the courts have construed this as excluding oral testimony and thereby making it more difficult to prove an oral compromise, not as making the compromise itself invalid.

Even contracts regarding land do not need to be in writing in France (art. 1534 Code civil), and though it is true that a contract made by word of mouth can only be proved by witnesses if one can proffer some document which makes the claim plausible (art. 1341 Code civil, to be discussed forthwith), a suitable document such as a letter confirming the outcome of the negotiations is often forthcoming. Even so, contracts for land are normally made before a notary, since the purchaser has to be entered as owner in the public register if he wants a title good against the world, and the registrar will insist on having a notarial document: as CARBONNIER observed, 'In practice this makes it necessary to effect sales of land by notarial act' (*Les Obligations* (15th edn., 1991) 174 f.).

Although many important transactions are valid in France without regard to form (unlike Italy, see art. 1350 Codice civile), parties in fact normally do these things in writing or by notarial document because of the practical difficulty of enforcing purely oral contracts. The difficulty arises from art. 1341 Code civil which prescribes that all transactions of more than 5,000 f. in value (50 f. until 1980) must take the form of private writing ('acte sous seing privé') or notarial document ('acte notarié'), and sanctions the non-observance of these forms by excluding the testimony of witnesses (so also art. 2721 Codice civile, where the limit of value is 5,000 lire).

The same rule is laid down by art. 1985 Code civil for powers of agency: if the value of the transaction to be concluded by the agent exceeds 5,000 f. the principal may prove the agency only by documents and not by witnesses. The Codice civile has a different rule: the power of agency must be in the form required for the contract which the agent is to conclude (art. 1392 Codice civile; the rule of §167 par. 2 BGB is different).

In principle, then, apart from everyday transactions, the conclusion of a contract must be proved by a notarial or private document. By notarial document, as has already been explained, is meant a document in which the transaction in question has been recorded, with the observance of the specified formalities, by a proper notary. It is rather more difficult to say what constitutes a private document (*acte sous seing privé, scrittura privata*). In French, unlike German, law, if the contract is commutative there must be as many originals of the contractual document as there are parties (see art. 1325 Code civil). On the other hand, difficult though this is to reconcile with art. 1325 Code civil, a letter from a purchaser accepting an oral offer of sale constitutes an *acte sous seing privé* (see Req. 6 Feb. 1928, DH 1928, 133). In the case of a unilateral undertaking to pay money, such as a guarantee, or to supply a quantity of generic goods, a document recording it will only serve as a valid *acte sous seing privé* if the sum or quantity promised is written out by the hand of the promisor in both words and figures ('en chiffres et en toutes lettres').

If an oral modification is made to an agreement recorded in writing, whether before or after the document is drawn up, it follows from art. 1341 that witnesses cannot be adduced to prove it. Nor can witnesses establish that a contract not in writing was formed by word of mouth. Both rules, however, are subject to important limitations.

The rule last mentioned does not apply in commercial transactions: thanks to art. 109 Code de commerce, such transactions may be proved against merchants by any evidence, so art. 1341 does not help a defendant for whom the alleged transaction was an act of commerce; witnesses can testify against him. Modern businessmen are often very pressed for time, and it would be inappropriate to make them resort to writing by the indirect sanction of rendering their oral agreements unenforceable.

Another very important limitation on art. 1341 Code civil is that the testimony of witnesses is admitted whenever the party wishing to introduce it can offer a 'commencement de preuve par écrit', that is, can start off his evidence with a written document. By this is meant a document emanating from the opponent which constitutes good evidence that the oral contract really was concluded between the parties (art. 1347 Code civil, art. 2724 par. 1 Codice civile). Accordingly, if there is a document signed by the opponent which for some formal reason does not satisfy the requirements of a valid *acte sous seing privé*, the testimony of witnesses may be admitted for it will normally constitute a 'commencement de preuve'. Thus a creditor claiming the repayment of a loan may call witnesses to prove the oral loan if he can put in evidence a letter from the defendant thanking him for 'the favour performed': if in all the circumstances of the case this document makes it probable that the loan was made, the plaintiff is allowed, art. 1341 notwithstanding, to use any means of proof, including proof by witnesses, to establish the fact to the satisfaction of the judge.

The notion of 'commencement de preuve' has been so widely construed by the courts that in practice the rule of art. 1341 has lost a great deal of its force. A written document in the narrow sense may not even be required: some courts have been satisfied with oral statements recorded on tape (Dijon 29 June 1955, D. 1955, 583). Under art. 1347 par. 3 Code civil, a court may find a 'commencement de preuve' if a party properly summoned fails to appear or give satisfactory answers and his conduct suggests that the contract was indeed orally concluded.

Finally, a plaintiff who has no contractual document may still call witnesses if he can show that on factual or moral grounds it was impossible for him to procure such a document (see art. 1348 Code civil). For example, in transactions between spouses, fiancés, siblings, or between parents and children, it is not exactly tactful to insist on the safeguard of a note of hand; the courts recognize the social dilemma in such cases by abandoning the requirement of written proof (for example, see Req. 2 Feb. 1920, DP 1921. 1. 40; Req. 27 June 1938, Gaz. Pal. 1938. 2. 586).

It will be seen that in practice very little survives of the impressive principle contained in art. 1341 Code civil. A judge who has heard the parties and finds the plaintiff's assertion that a contract was orally concluded prima facie credible will always discover means of allowing him to prove the matter by witnesses. This is true without qualification for commercial transactions but in other cases a judge can use documents written by the defendant or even the defendant's actual behaviour to reach the conclusion that the transaction in question was 'probable'. In the absence of such 'commencement de preuve' the court can still say that it was 'moralement impossible' for the plaintiff to obtain a proper document. But while it may be true that a well-grounded claim very seldom fails by reason of the evidentiary restriction of art. 1341 Code civil, it remains the case that this text acts as a strong inducement to have one's transactions written down, for it is always difficult to say in advance *whether* the court will, on one ground or another, let in proof by witnesses notwithstanding art. 1341, and people try to avoid this uncertainty so far as possible.

III

In the Romanistic legal family, as we have seen, provisions which lay down formal requirements are principally directed to questions of proof. Failure to observe the requisite form does not usually invalidate the transaction but just makes it harder to prove since the evidence of witnesses, regarded with disfavour because of its notorious unreliability, may be excluded. But proof by witnesses is let in if the interest in enforcing promises is backed up by even a sketchy document or other facts which suggest that the promise was really made.

In the *German* legal family matters are quite different. Certainly their provisions as to the form of transactions have some evidentiary functions, but these are subsidiary to their purpose of ensuring that the parties are serious. This is shown by the fact that in the German legal family want of form invariably makes a transaction invalid, even if it can be proved beyond a shadow of doubt that the promise was actually made or that the contracting parties actually made the agreement in question. The only explanation for attaching such a strong sanction to want of form is that the legislator was also concerned with the seriousness of the parties' intention.

Only against the background of this fundamentally different point of view do the many peculiarities of the legal rules in the German legal family become comprehensible. Thus Germany and Switzerland put in the General

Part the rule that a legal transaction not in the form legally prescribed is in principle void or invalid (§125 BGB, art. II OR). The precise formal requirements are to be found here and there throughout the civil codes wherever the legislator specifies in relation to each type of transaction whether simple writing is sufficient or whether notarial attestation is required, whether the declaration of one contractor or of both must be in the proper form, whether formal invalidity may be cured by subsequent performance, and so on. Such *ad hoc* rules are needed in the German legal family because the need for protection from surprise varies from one kind of transaction to another. Problems of proof, on the other hand, are common to all transactions, so the Romanistic legal systems can develop general clauses like art. 1341 Code civil.

Confining ourselves to the law of obligations, we can quickly indicate the kinds of transaction which require particular forms. Although *sales contracts* are valid regardless of form and regardless of the value of the object sold, Germany and Switzerland make an exception for sales of land, which must be in notarial form (§313 BGB, art. 216 OR). In Austria, by contrast, an oral contract for the sale of land is binding; a notarial document must indeed be drawn up in order to register the transfer of ownership in the land register (§432 ABGB), but the oral contract entitles the purchaser to demand the vendor's co-operation in drawing up this document, that being part of his duties.

Switzerland alone requires *assignments* of claims to be in writing (art. 165 OR). In Germany this is required only if the claim being assigned is secured by a mortgage; this is for reasons connected with the Land Register (§1154 BGB).

Contrariwise, all systems see the need for protection against surprise in *suretyship*. Thus they all require writing for the validity of a guarantee, though it is only the guarantor's promise which must be in writing since he is the only one who needs protection. In Switzerland the matter is regulated in detail by a special law of 1941: the document of guarantee must specify an upper limit in figures, written in the hand of the guarantor if he is an individual guaranteeing the claim of a private creditor, and the guarantee must be officially recorded if the limit of liability exceeds 2,000 Swiss francs (see art. 493 OR).

In German and Austrian law an *oral* guarantee is valid if it constitutes a commercial transaction from the guarantor's point of view (§350 HGB). This recalls the rule of French law that the requirements of form are generally relaxed for commercial transactions, but while the normal explanation in France is that commercial intercourse must not be hindered by undue formalities, the German provision is based on the realization that a commercial man entering commercial transactions requires no protection from surprise.

In Germany and Austria *promises of gifts* require to be notarized, as do promises of gifts of land in Switzerland, where other gifts are valid if in writing (art. 243 OR).

IV

In *Anglo-American* law, as we shall see in ch. 29 II below, an informal promise is only binding if it is given for some 'consideration' or counterperformance from the promisee. If nothing is done or promised by the promisee in return, the promise must be in a particular documentary form. Originally the document had to be given 'under seal', but the need for actual wax was dropped long ago: it was enough if the document bore the letters 'LS' (*loco sigilli*), the word 'seal', or even a red sticker put there by the promisor or his attorney. Sealing has now been abolished in England and replaced by the 'deed', a document in writing which is signed by the promisor with a declaration that it is intended as a 'deed', his signature being witnessed and the witness signing as such (Law Reform (Miscellaneous Provisions) Act 1989).

Most of the states of the United States have abolished the formality of documents under seal by legislation. This normally provides that a promise without consideration is ineffective even if it is contained in a deed. (On this, see the details in Restatement (Second) of Contracts (1981), Introductory Note to §§95 ff.)

There are very few other cases in Anglo-American law where the observance of a particular form is a precondition of validity. The normal result of failing to observe the forms legally required is to render the transaction not invalid but rather 'unenforceable', that is, incapable of forming the basis of a claim in court. The most important of these formal requirements are to be found in the Statute of Frauds, 1677, already mentioned, which requires 'a note or memorandum of the agreement in writing and signed by the party to be charged therewith' in the following cases:

1. The promise of an executor or administrator of a decedent's estate to be personally liable for the debts of the decedent;
2. A promise to answer for the debt of another;
3. A promise in relation to a forthcoming marriage;
4. A contract for the transfer of landed property or real rights therein;
5. A contract to be performed a year or more after the formation of the contract;
6. Contracts of sale where the price exceeds £10, unless the purchaser has accepted the goods or part of them, or has himself performed, by giving an earnest or paying part of the price.

In the three centuries since its enactment English lawyers and judges, both in court and extrajudicially, have criticized the Statute of Frauds as a very unhappy piece of legislation. It aimed to prevent fraudulent plaintiffs from bringing claims on non-existent contracts but its terms gave equally unscrupulous defendants the opportunity of avoiding obligations which they had in fact assumed, though only by word of mouth. Always uneasy at legislative interventions in private law, the English judges have done their best to restrict the area of application of the Statute of Frauds, helped in their tortuous construction by the remarkable opacity of the statutory text. The result was that 'by the end of the nineteenth century, practitioner and student alike had to pick their way through a tangle of case law behind which the original words of the statute were barely perceptible' (CHESHIRE/ FIFOOT/FURMSTON 202).

In England repeated efforts to abolish the Statute of Frauds were successful only in 1954: most of it was repealed by the Law Reform (Enforcement of Contracts) Act, 1954, only promises of guarantee (above no. 2) and contracts relating to land (above no. 4, now s. 2(1) Law of Property (Miscellaneous Provisions) Act 1989) remaining subject to the formal requirements.

In the United States, on the other hand, the provisions of the Statute of Frauds are still very much in force, since nearly all the states of the Union speedily enacted it, with variations in the precise wording and in the figure fixed for sales contracts (see above no. 6). American courts therefore still have the task of applying this antique enactment. CORBIN's outstanding textbook on the law of contract in the United States devotes one whole volume out of six, with more than 800 pages and a mass of cases, to expounding all the detailed application of the Statute of Frauds. Like other American writers, CORBIN would welcome the repeal or restriction of the statute in the more than fifty jurisdictions but he sees no chance of this happening: 'its repeal would deprive attorneys at law of one of their cherished defences' (CORBIN §275 (1964 supplement)).

Before the recent introduction of the Uniform Commercial Code the question whether to maintain the requirement of writing for sales contracts (above no. 6) was debated at length. In the result the old rule was adhered to, as LLEWELLYN desired (40 *Yale LJ* 704, 747 (1931)): according to §2-201 UCC, contracts for the sale of goods costing $ 500 or more are 'enforceable' only if the conclusion of the contract is evidenced by a written document, signed at least by the party whom it is sought to make liable. Various arguments have been adduced to show why it is reasonable for the United States to maintain a formal requirement for sales contracts which has been abolished in modern English legislation: it is said that claims based on doubtful oral promises are more likely to be brought in the United States than in England since the American plaintiff, unlike his English counterpart, runs no risk of paying the attorney's costs of a successful defendant, and also that in the United States contract suits are quite often tried before a jury, which is more liable to be taken in by a party's manœuvres if he is not required to produce a document (BRAUCHER, 40 *Cornell LQ* 696, 705 (1955)). These arguments are pretty unconvincing.

V

Every rule which requires contracts to be in a particular form has some legislative purpose behind it: it may be to exclude the testimony of witnesses on the ground that it is undesirable or to make a sharp demarcation between the finalized transaction and the preliminary negotiations or to give a party the opportunity for reflection or the benefit of legal advice. But once a provision requiring a certain form is enacted, it breaks away from its underlying purpose and falls to be applied even in cases where the aims of the legislator are already fully satisfied in other ways. Under the 'blinkered' provision of §766 BGB an admitted oral promise of guarantee is void even if there is no problem of proof and even if the guarantor would not have considered the matter more anxiously had it been reduced to writing. Thus provisions regarding form often cut more deeply than is required to implement the underlying policy grounds, and to apply them rigidly may lead to results so offensive to feelings of justice that legal systems must face the question whether in some circumstances they should not be ignored. For the comparative lawyer this raises the following questions: does this problem actually arise in all legal systems? What conceptual devices are used to solve them? What different solutions are reached?

The *German* lawyer is well aware of the problem for there are a great many court decisions on it. Most of these cases involve a contract for the sale of land which is not notarized and so infringes §313 BGB. The purchaser may be demanding possession from the vendor *despite* the want of form, or the vendor may be claiming to repossess from the purchaser *because of* the want of form. The courts' approach has been to ask whether in view of the dealings between the parties and all other circumstances it was 'consistent with good faith to reject contractual claims for want of form' (BGHZ 12, 6). This formula admittedly gives us little guidance, but it does show that the courts place great weight on the conduct of the parties and ask whether it would be inequitable or disloyal for a party to back out of the agreement just because it was not formalized.

It would certainly be inequitable for the seller of land to deceive the guileless buyer into supposing that the contract was valid, so as to be in a position to claim the land back if the market went up (RGZ 96, 313, 315; BGHZ 12, 6). Such cases are rare. More often both parties knew of the lack of form and did not care about it, or thought the contract valid if they thought about it at all. In such cases the plea of lack of form is particularly unmeritorious if the buyer has paid the price, taken possession of the land, and altered his position in reliance on the validity of the sale. A farmer who promised to hand over the farm to his son and then allowed him to work on it night and day for years at the cost of his career cannot then disavow his promise on the ground that it was not notarized and hand the farm over to his daughter (BGHZ 12, 286; BGHZ 2, 249). Similar decisions have been made where during abortive negotiations or after the formation of a contract invalid for want of form one party has encouraged the other to make major arrangements or has acquiesced in his doing so (BGH WM 1962, 9 and 786). Swiss courts also hold that to invoke the formal invalidity of a contract once it has been performed on both sides may constitute a 'manifest abuse of right' under art. 2(2) Civil Code (BGE 93 II 97; BGE 104 II 99; BGE 112 II 107 and 330).

In some German cases the contract has been upheld even though the buyer does not seem to have taken any detrimental action. In BGHZ 16, 334 the defendant divided an estate into plots and let them to a number of settlers, promising in writing, but without notarization, that if they performed their contractual obligations scrupulously for five years, the plots would become theirs. In 1952 one of the lessees claimed a transfer of the plot, and though there was apparently no evidence that he had made any investment in the land or lost an alternative purchase, his claim was upheld: it would be contrary to good faith for the defendant which 'with the full weight of its standing' had induced the inexperienced and innocent settlers to trust it to 'create and maintain the possibility of keeping the contract in limbo for years with freedom to fulfil it or claim that it was unenforceable at its election' (at 338).

This is the context in which English courts have developed the doctrine of 'proprietary estoppel': a landowner who has expressly or implicitly promised to transfer land or create some right in it is 'estopped' from asserting the invalidity of his promise if the promisee has made arrangements to his detriment in justified reliance on the promise.

See the details in GRAY, *Elements of Land Law* (2nd edn., 1993) 312 ff.—The promisee's reliance deserves protection only if a reasonable person in his position would have put faith in the promisor's conduct. That was not the case in *A-G of Hong Kong* v. *Humphreys Estate Ltd*. [1987] AC 114 (PC). Here two parties with extensive commercial experience had made a written 'agreement in principle' for the sale of land. The claimant immediately went into possession and reconstructed the premises to suit his needs on the perfectly reasonable assumption that the contract would be formalized. His claim was nevertheless rejected: the agreement being expressly 'subject to contract' the buyer took the risk of losing his investment if the contract were not formalized.

It was otherwise in *Pascoe* v. *Turner* [1979] 2 All ER 945. In 1972 the plaintiff told the defendant, with whom he had been living for eight years, that she could regard their home as her property. In 1976, having formed an attachment with another woman, he told the defendant to leave and sought possession of the house. The court not only dismissed his claim but required him, on the defendant's counterclaim, to make the house over to her: it was critical that he had acquiesced in her spending much of her savings on modernizing the house in reliance on his assurances.

See further *Inwards* v. *Baker* [1965] 2 QB 29; *Greasley* v. *Cooke* [1980] 1 WLR 1306; *Grant* v. *Edwards* [1986] Ch. 628; and more detail in GRAY, *Elements of Land Law* (2nd edn., 1993) 334 ff. The American case-law is summed up in §129 Restatement (Second) of Contracts (1981): 'A contract for the transfer of an interest in land may be specifically enforced notwithstanding failure to comply with the Statute of Frauds if it is established that the party seeking enforcement, in reasonable reliance on the contract and on the continuing assent of the party against whom enforcement is sought, has so changed his position that injustice can be avoided only by specific enforcement.'

Once the preconditions of proprietary estoppel are satisfied the English judge is free to decide what remedy to grant. Sometimes he orders performance, but if that would be unfair, as where the property is worth much more than what has been spent on it, he may award a sum of money instead (see GRAY ibid. at 344 ff.).

German courts in fact enjoy a somewhat similar freedom. Certainly the judge must treat the contract as valid and grant a claim for enforcement unless the promisor can fairly claim that the informality of the contract invalidates it, but if he holds the contract void he need not send the promisee away empty: he can give him a claim for unjustified enrichment, since any benefit he conferred on the promisor in reliance on the invalid contract will be without cause in law. There may also be a claim for *culpa in contrahendo*, as where an experienced contractor has given an assurance that the contract would be good when he knew or should have known that the other would naïvely arrange his affairs on the basis of that assurance, notably by forgoing the chance of doing business elsewhere (BGH NJW 1965, 812; BGH WM 1967, 798; BGH NJW 1972, 1189).

This problem is not very important in France, where oral contracts for the sale of land are perfectly valid; if the seller denies that the agreement was sufficiently definite or intended to be binding, the buyer will generally have a *commencement de preuve par écrit* and be able to rebut the denial by witnesses. It is true that art. 931 Code civil calls for a notarial act if the transfer of land is by way of *gift*, but the promisor who reneges after letting the donee stay in occupation of the land or otherwise so conducts himself as to awaken false hopes may be held liable in tort for fault under art. 1382 Code civil. It was so held by the Court of Appeal in Aix, 11 Jan. 1983, DS 1985, 169, noted by LÉGIER.

VI

This survey might lead one to conclude that there is a general move towards abolishing formal requirements. After all, the Statute of Frauds which originally applied to many kinds of transaction now covers only land contracts and promises to answer for the debts of another, while in France the courts have extended the concept of *commencement de preuve par écrit* so far that very few plausible claims now founder for want of form. It is true that in the United States the Uniform Commercial Code, so progressive in other respects, still requires writing for sales above a certain price—there may be special reasons for this (see above p. 374)—but as against that, art. 11 of CISG explicitly lays down that no form is required for international sales of goods, and that they may be proved by witnesses or in any other way.

The general position today is that, apart from transactions relating to the family or inheritance, the only contracts which have to be formalized are promises of gifts, contracts of suretyship, and land contracts. The case for the first two is obvious: the promisor is protected from thoughtlessness, feck-lessness, and precipitate generosity by having to put his promise in writing or even take a trip to the notary; the formality attests the seriousness of his intention to be bound. The case for land contracts is said to be that they gen-erally involve large sums; of course purchases of shares and such chattels as vessels or airplanes may involve equally large sums, but it is true that the purchase or sale of a house is the most important transaction ever entered into by persons of average income, and then only once or twice in a lifetime. The formal requirements may therefore be seen as a sensible consumer pro-tection device, especially as realtors are often quite aggressive salesmen. There is the further point that the formality of land transactions makes it easier to register them if required; that is why in France land transactions, though valid without any formality at all, are always executed in front of a notary.

In the last few decades, however, formal requirements have been on the increase once again, and are now required for contracts of consumer credit, leases of dwellings, package holidays, training contracts, and so on. This is because legislators see that formalities may help to protect the consumer. Indeed they have been used so widely in France that writers there have begun to speak of a *renaissance du formalisme* (see GHESTIN no. 266). These are not cases where neglect of the formalities invalidates the whole contract, for the aim is to ensure that the party needing protection is provided with certain information in writing. Well intentioned though such provisions doubtless are, they may not always be sensible. An individual in urgent need of credit will hardly ever pay any attention to, much less understand, the detailed information which the provider of credit is bound to supply, and even if he did, it is unrealistic to suppose that he would refuse to go through with the deal. Besides, the legislation often fails to specify in sufficient detail what sanctions are to apply when the duty to inform is breached, and at other times does so in a manner so complex as to make the law uncertain.

On this see the detail in GHESTIN no. 335 and STARCK/ROLAND/BOYER, *Droit Civil, Obligations, Contrat* (5th edn., 1995 no. 210): 'Il n'est pas sûr que ce fratas bureau-cratique atteindra la protection tant recherchée . . . Quel esprit morbide s'aventurera dans la lecture attentive d'une telle masse de documents. Ce qui est certain, c'est qu'un contentieux ne manquera pas de naître de cette accumulation de précisions en pratique inaccessibles.'

28

Illegality and Immorality

ABRAHAM, 'Die Doktrin der Public Policy', *AcP* 150 (1949) 385.

BONNECASE, 'La Notion juridique de bonnes mœurs; sa portée en droit civil français', *Études à la mémoire de Henri Capitant* (1939) 91.

CELLINI/WERTZ, 'Unconscionable Contract Provisions: A History of Unenforceability from Roman Law to the UCC', 42 *Tul. L. Rev.* 193 (1967).

COING, 'Allgemeine Rechtsgrundsätze in der Rechtsprechung des Reichsgerichts zum Begriff der guten Sitten', *NJW* 1948, 213.

DWYER, 'Immoral Contracts', 93 *LQ Rev.* 384 (1977).

GORDLEY, 'Equality in Exchange', 69 *Calif. L. Rev.* 1587 (1981).

KÖTZ, 'Die Ungültigkeit von Verträgen wegen Gestez- und Sittenwidrigkeit, Eine rechtsvergleichende Skizze', *RabelsZ* 58 (1994) 209.

D. LLOYD, *Public Policy, A Comparative Study in English and French Law* (1953).

MALAURIE, *L'Ordre public et le contrat, Étude de Droit civil comparé: France, Angleterre, U.R.S.S.* (1953).

MAYER-MALY, 'Renaissance der laesio enormis?', *Festschrift Larenz zum 80. Geburtstag* (1983) 395.

V. MEHREN, 'The French Doctrine of lésion in the Sale of Immovable Property', 49 *Tul. L. Rev.* 321 (1974).

K. SIMITIS, *Gute Sitten und ordre public* (1960).

SZLADITS, 'Illegality of Prohibited Contracts, Comparative Aspects', in: *Twentieth Century Comparative and Conflicts Law—Legal Essays in Honor of Hessel E. Yntema* (1961) 221.

THOMMEN, *Beitrag zur Lehre vom Begriff der guten Sitten im schweizerischen Privatrecht* (1954).

WINFIELD, 'Public Policy and the English Common Law', 42 *Harv. L. Rev.* 376 (1928).

I

DESPITE the prevalence in the Western world of the principle of freedom of contract, every legal system must reserve the right to declare a contract void if it is legally or morally offensive, 'contraire aux bonnes mœurs ou à l'ordre public' or contrary to 'public policy'. The rules which determine whether a contract is void on these grounds are all very much the same, whether they are the product of legislation or judicial decision. In all systems the principal task falls to the judge, who has to test the circumstances of the individual case in order to discover whether the contracting parties have gone beyond the bounds of the permissible. In doing so, the courts strive to reduce the vague concept of ethical behaviour or public policy to meaningful principles by carving out discrete sets of case and formulating concrete criteria of distinction, and so to minimize the irrational element necessarily contained in general clauses.

Illegality and immorality are universally seen as grounds for invalidating *contracts*, and it is in the law of contract that the question is dealt with in both Anglo-American law and the Romanistic systems. In Germany, however, it is treated as a factor which nullifies *legal acts* of all kinds, and Swiss and Italian law reach the same result in practice, for though their rules on nullity figure in the section devoted to the law of contract (see art. 19, 20 OR; art. 1343, 1346, 1418 Codice civile), they are to be applied 'to other relations of private law' (art. 7 Swiss Civil Code) or, as art. 1324 Codice civile has it, *per gli atti unilaterali tra vivi aventi contenuto patrimoniale*.

In France and Italy the question of the nullity of contracts is dealt with in terms of the doctrine of *cause* or *causa*. Under art. 1131 Code civil a contractual obligation is void if it is based on *une cause illicite*, a *cause* being *illicite* under art. 1133 when it is *prohibée par la loi* or *contraire aux bonnes moeurs ou à l'ordre public*; the same rules are to be found in the Codice civile (art. 1343, 1418). *Cause* here is taken to include not only the reason which led the party to enter the obligation, that is, his expectation of acquiring the land or its use in return for the price or rent he is to pay, but also his ulterior aim and purpose in entering the transaction, for example, to run a casino or brothel. In fact, however, in deciding whether a contract is valid or not French judges take just the same factors into account as their English or German counterparts and reach very similar conclusions, so it may well be that the whole idea of *cause* is superfluous.

The situation is further confused by the fact that in French law a contract can also be held invalid if its *content* or subject matter is unpermitted ('objet illicite': see in the same sense art. 1346 Codice civile). If a person promises to commit a crime for reward, then—according to PLANIOL/RIPERT VI no. 276—his obligation is invalid since the *objet* of the contract, the promised act, is forbidden. The object of the other party's obligation, namely to pay the reward, is by contrast intrinsically 'neutral' but his promise is equally invalid because the *cause* underlying it, here understood as the purpose of the promise, is forbidden. Distinctions such as these are quite artificial. There is really no reason to say any more than that a contract is void if its content and the surrounding circumstances, including the motives of the parties, show that its whole character offends against the standards already mentioned.

When we speak here of the nullity of contracts on the ground of illegality or immorality, we mean that such contracts give rise to no claim for performance or damages. It is a quite different question whether a party to such a contract may have to give back what he received under it. For the comparatist this latter problem falls to be categorized not as a question of contract law, where it often appears in Common Law writings, but as an instance of the great class of restitutionary problems arising when something has been transferred or done without any legal ground. For this reason the problem of reclaiming what was transferred under an illegal or immoral contract will be dealt with at a later stage (ch. 39 III below).

The question what makes a contract immoral or illegal is one which receives different answers in the various systems. The emphasis differs since ethics differ from country to country and traditional value-judgments still play a significant role. This is not the place to make a comparative study of all the cases on the question, so we will restrict ourselves. First we shall deal with contracts which offend against accepted standards of sexual morals and family life. Then we shall deal with cases where a contractual term improperly constrains a person's autonomy in the private or economic sphere. After a glance at agreements which infringe a statute we shall deal in conclusion with a few special instances.

II

Some contracts which were regarded as offensive until recently have now come to seem quite acceptable. The unbroken development of the Common Law makes such a change of attitude particularly clear and it comes as no surprise to find that the English judges are very conscious of the changing content of legal values: 'The determination of what is contrary to the so-called "policy of the law" necessarily varies from time to time. Many transactions are upheld now by our courts which a former generation would have avoided as contrary to the supposed policy of the law. The rule remains, but its application varies with the principles which for the time being guide public opinion.' (*Evanturel* v. *Evanturel*, (1874) LR 6 PC 1, 29.)

For example, claims arising from betting transactions were perfectly enforceable until the nineteenth century, even if the object of the bet, to modern sensibilities, was highly immoral. In 1771, in the case of *March* v. *Pigot*, (1771) 5 Burr. 2802, 98 Eng. Rep. 471, the parties had 'run their fathers each against the other', that is, had bet on whose father would die first, and the transaction was held valid. Gaming transactions were first rendered void by the Gaming Act, 1845.

The change is especially striking in the area of sexual morals. In the past, for example, German courts automatically struck down as immoral any contract to lease premises for use as a brothel; today such contracts are upheld in the absence of some special feature, such as a rent so high that the lessee would have to exploit the girls in order to cover his costs (BGHZ 63, 365, 367; HR NJ 1991, 266). A prostitute admittedly cannot claim the fee she was promised for her attentions, but a contract to let her have the use of premises on reasonable terms is valid even if the landlord knows what use she is going to put them to (BGH NJW 1970, 1179). Cohabitation agreements are regarded as valid today, even between parties already married to someone else, unless they are made simply to pay for sexual services or prevent the break-up of the partnership. If a promise to pay a sum of money in the event of dissolution of the living arrangement is to compensate the promisee for giving up a house or a job, it will be upheld, but not if it is to penalize the promisor for putting an end to the living arrangement, since he should be free to do so any time he wants (OLG Hamm NJW 1988, 2474).

There has also been a change of attitude towards dispositions made by a married man in favour of his mistress, such as gifts, promises of maintenance, the benefit of a life insurance policy or a legacy: they are invalid if they envisage *la formation, la continuation ou la reprise des rapports immoraux ou leur rémunération* (Civ. 2 Dec. 1981, D. 1982.I.R. 474, noted by MARTIN), but they will now be upheld if the motives are creditable, for example, if the man wants to ensure the support of the woman after a long-lasting relationship or acknowledge the care, support or nursing she has provided. (See Civ. 22 Oct. 1980, Bull. I no. 269; BGH NJW 1984, 2150; BGE 109 II 15.)

III

It would be inconsistent with the basic principles of a free legal and economic system to uphold a contract which unduly restricts an individual's personal and economic autonomy; such contracts are therefore void as being contrary to *ordre public, gute Sitten* or public order. Switzerland, indeed, has a special text for this case: under art. 27(2) of the Swiss Civil Code 'no one can dispose of his freedom or limit its exercise to a degree inconsistent with the law or ethics'.

On this see BUCHER, *Berner Kommentar* vol. i(II)(2) (1993) art. 27 ZGB mn. 92 and 162 ff.—In one English case where a borrower promised not to change his residence or place of work without the creditor's consent in writing, nor yet to take out any more loans or make any dispositions, his promise was held void (*Horwood* v. *Millar's Timber and Trading Co.* [1917] 3 KB 305). Equally void is an agreement whereby an author or songwriter grants a publisher the irrevocable right to publish his entire literary or musical output (BGHZ 22, 347; *Schroeder Music Publishing Co.* v. *Macaulay* [1974] 3 All ER 616 (CA); BGE 104 II 108).

It is quite a severe restriction on the economic freedom of the operator of a service station or inn if he agrees to take all his requirements of fuel or drinks from a particular oil company or brewery for a period of years, yet on the one hand the suppliers have an interest in the duration of such contracts since unless the customer remains bound for a long time they cannot hope to amortize or draw interest on their capital investment, and on the other it would be no kindness to petrol station operators or innkeepers to invalidate such long-term commitments, since they are normally short of capital and it would deter the oil company or brewery from providing them with the stock or funds they so badly need. The House of Lords has said that twenty-one years is too long for a service-station contract, but has upheld one for five years (*Esso Petroleum Co.* v. *Harper's Garage Ltd.* [1968] AC 269); five years is also acceptable to the Bundesgerichtshof but it would probably endorse a longer period (see BGHZ 52, 171). In Germany twenty years is the absolute limit for contracts between brewery and innkeeper; within that period the courts consider whether or not the restriction applies to the entire range of beverages, whether or not a minimum throughput is stipulated, and whether or not the brewery's investment is sizeable.

See BGH NJW 1972, 1459; BGH NJW 1979, 865; to like effect are BGE 114 II 159; OGH JBl 1992, 517.—The French courts take quite a different path. According to art. 1591 Code civil the price in a contract of sale must be *déterminé*, an idea also found in art. 1129, that the object of a contractual obligation must be a *chose déterminée*. In long-term contracts of supply such as those in question, the price is bound to change, and if one of the parties can set the new price without reference to the other, the courts regard this as inconsistent with the codal articles. Nullity therefore strikes any contract for fuel or drinks in which the supplier is to charge the current list price (Com. 25 Jan. 1982, Bull. IV no. 26; Com. 5 Oct. 1982, Bull. IV no. 298; see also GHESTIN no. 525 ff.; FRISON-ROCHE, *Rev. trim. dr. civ.* 91 (1992) 269, 288 ff.). This hardly seems the right way to approach the matter. If competition in the relevant market is vigorous there is not much risk of suppliers' inflating their list price. The real question is whether in the circumstances the customer's economic freedom is unduly constrained by being at the supplier's mercy. This is the position adopted by the Cour de Cassation in more recent decisions: see Civ. 19 Nov. 1994, JCP 1995.II.22371, noted by GHESTIN.

Another example of a contract which can unduly restrict an individual's economic autonomy is provided by an employee's covenant not to compete with his employer after leaving his employment; similar undertakings are often given by partners against the event of their leaving the partnership. Here too there is a conflict of interests which must be resolved. On the one hand the covenant is designed to prevent the employee or partner exploiting in a rival firm or in a business of his own the special knowledge he acquired in his previous engagement, such as familiarity with the clientele. On the other hand the covenant can seriously prejudice the ability of the employee or partner to profit from what is often his only capital, namely his talents and energy. All systems reach more or less the same solution, and hold the covenant valid provided it is limited in scope, time, and area and the covenantor is paid something extra for it.

Many countries have special texts which fix the acceptable limits of covenants by *employees* and *commercial agents*; see §§74 ff., 90a HGB; art. 340 ff., 418d OR; art. 1751-bis, 2125 Codice civile. Elsewhere similar rules have been laid down by the courts; see TREITEL 403 ff.; RIPERT/ROBLOT, *Traité de droit commercial* (13th edn. 1989) I, no. 476. Particularly important are cases where lawyers, accountants or engineering consultants have covenanted not to compete after leaving the partnership or firm. See *Bridge* v. *Deacons* [1984] AC 705 (PC); BGH NJW 1986, 2944; Soc. 12 June 1986, D.S. 1987 Somm. 264, noted by SERRA (lawyers); BGHZ 91, 1 and BGH NJW 1968, 1717 (accountants); Paris 7 Feb. 1980, JCP 1981.II.19669 noted by EDWARDS (engineering consultant). The same problem arises in cases when the seller of a business agrees not to compete with the buyer. See *Nordenfelt* v. *Maxim Nordenfelt* [1894] AC 535; BGH NJW 1979, 1605; Com. 19 Jan. 1981, D.S. 1982 I.R. 204 noted by SERRA.

If a covenant not to compete is drawn too widely in terms of scope, duration or area is it wholly void or may it be reduced to acceptable limits? In *Mason* v. *Provident Clothing & Supply Co.* [1913] AC 724 the defendant promised that for three years after leaving the plaintiff's employment he would not compete with him 'within 25 miles of London'. LORD MOULTON held that the area specified was too wide. The plaintiff argued that since the defendant had set up business in the very part of London in which he had been employed, the prohibition should be reduced and the injunction issued. The argument was summarily rejected:

'It would in my opinion be pessimi exempli if, when an employer had exacted a covenant deliberately framed in unreasonably wide terms, the Courts were to come to his assistance and, by applying their ingenuity and knowledge of the law, carve out of this void covenant the maximum of what he might validly have required. . . . The hardship imposed by the exaction of unreasonable covenants by employers would be greatly increased if they could continue the practice with the expectation that, having exposed the servant to the anxiety and expense of litigation, the Court would in the end enable them to obtain everything which they could have obtained by acting reasonably.' (At 754 f.) The Bundesgerichtshof has given similar reasons for reaching the same conclusion (NJW 1986, 2944).

Courts have, however, often decided otherwise. In one case before the Bundesgerichtshof a publican who for ten years had adhered to his exclusive supply contract with a brewery declined to honour it further, although it purported to bind him for twenty-four years. The court found this period excessive and void for immorality, but held the contract valid for sixteen years and made the publican pay the agreed penalty of 15 per cent of the estimated throughput of beer for each of the remaining six years (BGH NJW 1974, 2089; see also BGE 114 II 159). In England, too, courts have on occasion reduced anti-competitive clauses to an acceptable level (for example, *Goldsoll* v. *Goldman* [1915] 1 Ch. 292). So also in France: an employee who had promised not to work for a competitor in the same field during the ten years following his departure—a manifestly excessive period—nevertheless took a position with a competitor in the selfsame city on the very day he left the plaintiff's employment; he was held liable, for *une clause de non-concurrence . . . ne*

*doit être annulée que dans la mesure où elle porte atteinte à la liberté du travail
en raison de son étendue dans le temps et dans l'espace et quant à la nature de
l'activité de l'intéressé* (Soc. 21 Oct. 1960, JCP 1960.II.11886).

IV

Governments are increasingly given to promoting their economic or social
policies by means of legislation which outlaws specified conduct or makes
it illegal unless licensed by authority. Such laws always impose some penalty
or other sanction on the person who infringes them, but are often silent as to
the validity of a contract whose formation or execution involves an infringement by one or both of the parties.

A person paid to transport furniture is certainly guilty of an offence if in doing so
he unlawfully overloads his vehicle, but it is another question whether or not the contract of carriage is void: if it is, not only will the carrier be unable to claim the freight
from his customer, but the customer will equally be unable to sue him in contract for
damages should he fail to carry the furniture on time or at all, or if he negligently
damages it.

If the very act of entering the contract constitutes an offence by both parties it will normally be held void. For example, in an attempt to combat the
black market in services German law makes it an offence both for an unregistered tradesman to contract for work and for the money-conscious customer to engage him. The contract is therefore void if both parties were fully
aware of the situation and were deliberately breaking the law (BGHZ 85, 39).
Even if only one of the parties knew that the law was being broken by both
of them, the contract may be held void, as in *Re Mahmoud and Ispahani*
[1921] 2 KB 716 (CA), which concerned the sale of linseed oil at a time when
it was an offence to buy or sell it unless both parties had a licence. The buyer
had no such licence, but fraudulently told the seller that he did. Notwithstanding the seller's good faith the contract was held void and he was unable
to claim damages for non-acceptance (though he might have been able to sue
in tort for deceit or fraud).

When only one of the parties is prohibited from entering a contract its
validity may well depend on whether 'it would be contrary to the meaning
and purpose of the prohibitory enactment to tolerate and uphold the legal
situation produced by the transaction' (BGHZ 78, 263, 265). As KERR LJ
said in an English case:

'Where a statute merely prohibits one party from entering into a contract . . . it
does not follow that the contract itself is impliedly prohibited so as to render it illegal
and void. Whether or not the statute has this effect depends on considerations of public policy in the light of the mischief which the statute is designed to prevent, its language, scope and purpose, the consequences for the innocent party, and any other

relevant consideration.' (*Phoenix General Insurance Co.* v. *Administratia Asigurarilor de Stat* [1987] 2 All ER 152, 176.)

Where the statutory prohibition is directed to one of the parties in order to protect the other, the outcome is relatively clear: the contract is normally void.

See, for example, BGHZ 71, 358; BGH NJW 1979, 2092; Com. 19 Nov. 1991, noted by MESTRE in *Rev. trim. dr. civ.* 91 (1992) 381; Civ. 13 Oct. 1982, Bull. I no. 286. Even this may depend on the circumstances, however: in *Shaw* v. *Groom* [1970] 2 QB 504 (CA) a landlord was able to claim unpaid rent although he had infringed a statutory provision designed to protect the tenant by failing to provide him with a 'rent book' and other relevant information.

In a case before the Cour de Cassation a *huissier* had acted privately as a broker in breach of statute and was now claiming the agreed fee. If the aim of the law was to deter court officials from dealing on their own account, that aim would certainly be advanced by dismissing the *huissier*'s claim. As against that, the disciplinary sanctions provided by the law might be thought sufficient for the purpose, especially as they could be tailored to the gravity of the official's misconduct and strip him of his profit on the deal. If in addition one accepts that the primary purpose of the law was to maintain the *dignité professionnelle* of the *huissier* rather than to protect his client and that the latter would obtain an windfall if he did not have to pay, one can understand why the Court upheld the contract and allowed the *huissier* to claim his fee. (Civ. 15 Dec. 1961, Bull. I no. 105; Civ. 21 Oct. 1968, D.S. 1969, 81.)

See also BGHZ 78, 263 (accountant, forbidden to act as broker, could nevertheless claim the fee for so acting); Com. 11 May 1976, JCP 1976.II.18452 (unlicensed freight forwarder nevertheless obtains a lien on the consignor's goods); *St. John Shipping Co.* v. *Joseph Rank Ltd.* [1957] 1 QB 267 (shipowner may claim the freight though the captain unlawfully overloaded the vessel).

29

Indicia of Seriousness

ATIYAH, *Consideration in Contracts: A Fundamental Restatement* (1971).

BECKER, *Gegenopfer und Opferverwehrung* (1958).

BOYER, 'Promissory Estoppel: Principles from Precedents', 50 *Mich. L. Rev.* 639, 873 (1952).

——, 'Promissory Estoppel: Requirements and Limitations of the Doctrine', 98 *U. Pa. L. Rev.* 459 (1950).

CAPITANT, *De la cause des obligations* (3rd edn., 1927).

CHLOROS, 'The Doctrine of Consideration and the Reform of the Law of Contract', 17 *ICLQ* 137 (1968).

DAVID, 'Cause et Consideration', *Mélanges Maury* II (1960) III.

DAWSON, *Gifts and Promises, Continental and American Law Compared* (1980).

DENNING, 'Recent Developments in the Doctrine of Consideration', 15 *Mod. L. Rev.* I (1952).

EISENBERG, 'Donative Promises', 47 *U. Chi. L. Rev.* I (1979).

——, 'The Bargain Principle and its Limits', 95 *Calif. L. Rev.* 323 (1982).

FULLER, 'Consideration and Form', 41 *Colum. L. Rev.* 799 (1941).

GILMORE, *The Death of Contract* (1974).

GORDON, 'A Dialogue about the Doctrine of Consideration', 75 *Cornell L. Rev.* 1987 (1990).

GORLA, *Il Contratto*, Vol. I (1954) 327 ff.

HAMSON, 'The Reform of Consideration', 54 *LQ Rev.* 233 (1938).

HENDERSON, 'Promissory Estoppel and Traditional Contract Doctrine', 78 *Yale LJ* 343 (1969).

E. V. HIPPEL, *Die Kontrolle der Vertragsfreiheit nach anglo-amerikanischem Recht* (1963).

KESSLER, 'Einige Betrachtungen zur Lehre von der consideration', *Festschrift Rabel* I (1954) 251.

——, 'Der Schutz des Vertrauens bei Vertragsverhandlungen in der neueren amerikanischen Rechtsprechung', *Festschrift v. Caemmerer* (1978) 873.

KÖNDGEN, *Selbstbindung ohne Vertrag* (1981) 65 ff.

KÜHNE, 'Der Vertrauensgedanke im Schuldvertragsrecht', *RabelsZ* 36 (1972) 275.

LLEWELLYN, 'Common Law Reform of Consideration', 41 *Colum. L. Rev.* 863 (1941).

LORENZ, 'Entgeltliche und unentgeltliche Geschäfte, Eine vergleichende Betrachtung des deutschen und des anglo-amerikanischen Rechts', *Festschrift für Max Rheinstein* II (1969) 547.

LORENZEN, 'Causa and Consideration in the Law of Contracts', 28 *Yale LJ* 621 (1919).

MARKESINIS, 'Cause and Consideration: A Study in Parallel', 1978 *Camb. LJ* 53.

——, 'La Notion de consideration dans la common law', *Rev. int. dr. comp.* 35 (1983) 735.

MASON, 'The Utility of Consideration—A Comparative View', 41 *Colum. L. Rev.* 825 (1941).

VON MEHREN, 'Civil-Law Analogues to Consideration: An Exercise in Comparative Analysis', 72 *Harv. L. Rev.* 1009 (1959).

NEWMAN, 'The Doctrine of Cause or Consideration in the Civil Law', 30 *Can. Bar Rev.* 662 (1952).

PATERSON, 'An Apology for Consideration', 58 *Colum. L. Rev.* 929 (1958).

POUND, 'Promise or Bargain', 33 *Tul. L. Rev.* 455 (1959).

RHEINSTEIN, *Die Struktur des vertraglichen Schuldverhältnisses im anglo-amerikanischen Recht* (1932) 55 ff.

SEAVEY, 'Reliance on Gratuitous Promises', 64 *Harv. L. Rev.* 913 (1951).

WRIGHT, 'Ought the Doctrine of Consideration to be Abolished from the Common Law?' 49 *Harv. L. Rev.* 1225 (1936).

I

Is every bilateral agreement to be treated as a contract, or is something extra required for it to be enforceable? This is a question which all legal systems must answer. For example, promises made in a purely social or familial context are clearly not actionable. To use a standard textbook example, the guest who arrives for dinner and finds the door closed cannot go to court and claim the wasted taxi fare. If a father reneges on his promise to pay his son for mowing the lawn the boy can react by being surly, refusing to eat or getting bad marks at school, but he cannot sue for the promised sum.

It is also widely recognized that most promises which are intended to be binding are made in return for something, so when a lawyer comes across a promise for which the promisor asked for no return, not even another promise, he naturally asks himself whether such altruism can really have been sufficiently considered and seriously intended.

On the Continent the question usually arises with regard to promises of gifts—here meaning money or property or a right or at any rate an asset 'out of the promisor's estate'—and in all systems such promises have to be made in front of a notary and documented by him, lest they be prompted by unconsidered generosity, unduly spontaneous charity or thoughtlessness, or induced by empty promises or crocodile tears.

In France art. 931 Code civil provides that *tous actes portant donation entre vifs* require notarial form. Although this covers all gifts and not just promises of gifts, a *don manuel*, where the object of the gift is delivered on the spot, is regarded as valid despite its informality. This is because a person normally knows what he is about when he is actually handing over the money or property rather than just promising to do so in the future, so there is no need to require further proof of the seriousness of his intention. In most countries, accordingly, form is required only for promises of gifts (for example,

§§516, 518 BGB; art. 242 f. OR); Swiss law differs from German law, however, in that while Germany requires the form for all donative promises, Switzerland requires it only in the case where the gift promised is landed property, writing being sufficient in other cases. The Codice civile is rather stricter: informal manual gifts are effective only if they relate to moveable property of moderate value (art. 782, 783).

II

In the Common Law of England and the United States an informal promise is treated as serious only if it is made against a 'consideration', that is, some counterpart from the promisee. In the absence of such consideration a promise is unenforceable. Although no action can be brought on such a promise, the promisor who actually does what he promised and transfers the property to be given, using any appropriate form, cannot claim it back. In other words, the promise, unenforceable though it is, serves as a ground on which, if it is performed, the recipient may retain what is transferred. The same result is reached by the rather artificial provision in German law that 'the lack of form is cured by performance of the promise' (§518(2) BGB, art. 243(3) OR).

By way of exception, if a promise is made in a particular form it may be actionable despite the absence of consideration: in days gone by the promise had to be contained in a 'sealed' document, but nowadays a 'deed' consists of a document signed by the promisor or grantor and witnessed by one attesting witness (see above p. 373).

In the United States most states have abolished the formality of the declaration 'under seal', and provide either that 'sealing' does not validate a contract without consideration or that a 'seal' or even mere writing raises a rebuttable presumption that consideration was given.

Although the doctrine of consideration has become extremely complex and subtle, the basic idea is clear enough. There is consideration for a promise if the promisor makes it in order to obtain a desired counterpart. This counterpart may well be a promise—the buyer's promise to pay the price is the counterpart of the seller's promise to deliver the goods—but it may also consist of other conduct, provided that the promisor wishes it to take place and intends to reward it by doing what he promised. This is what happens when a person offers a reward for the return of his poodle. No one has agreed to look for the dog, but anyone who finds it and brings it back has done what the promisor hoped to procure by his offer. The requirement of consideration is satisfied if the promise is, so to speak, the price offered by the promisor for the desired counterpart and the promisee, by promising or acting, renders this counterpart in order to obtain the price. The following definition is offered by the Restatement (Second) of Contracts (1981) §71:

'(1) To constitute consideration, a performance or a return promise must be bargained for. (2) A performance or return promise is bargained for if it is sought by the promisor in exchange for his promise and is given by the promisee in exchange for that promise'.

If there is no consideration for a promise, it cannot be sued on. The promise may be the result of mature reflection, it may be actuated by the most praiseworthy motives, and the promisor may be morally bound to honour his word, but the Common Law requires more than this. It requires that the parties have made a 'bargain' with each other and that the promise in question be part of this 'bargain': 'An Englishman is liable, not because he has made a promise, but because he has made a bargain.' (CHESHIRE/FIFOOT/FURMSTON 28.)

One must not take the word 'bargain' too literally, for it suggests that performance and counterperformance must in some sense be more or less equivalent. This is not required by the doctrine of consideration. Consideration does not have to be 'adequate'. A promise is binding even if the counterpart is trivial or even nominal: a peppercorn will suffice. The critical point is whether there is an objective indication that the parties seriously intended to enter a binding agreement, and this is so not only when they have really made a bargain but also where they have made their transaction look like a bargain.

The requirement of consideration is also satisfied in some cases where one cannot really speak of a bargain at all. It may be enough that the promisee accepted some detriment, however trivial and economically insignificant. English judges have quite often shown a good nose for sniffing out some such detriment, as in *Ward* v. *Byham*. [1956] 2 All E.R. 318 (CA).

Mr Byham had lived in unmarried bliss with Mrs Ward for several years and a daughter was born to them. They agreed that the daughter should stay with the mother and Mr Byham promised to pay her £1 per week so that the child 'be well looked after and happy'. Mrs Ward subsequently married another man and Mr Byham stopped paying. On being sued, he argued in vain that his promise to pay was invalid for want of consideration. Two of the judges founded on the fact that the mother had promised not merely to maintain the child but also to look after it well and make it happy, LORD DENNING holding—admittedly at variance with the general view—that the mother's performance of her statutory duty was 'sufficient consideration'. See also *Williams* v. *Williams* [1956] 1 All ER 305 (CA): here consideration for a man's promise to pay maintenance to his wife—something he was not obliged to do, since she had left him for no good reason—was found in her promise to live a chaste life, not to run up debts in his name and not to sue him for maintenance.

In order to avoid the unsatisfactory results to which the doctrine of consideration can lead in certain types of case, courts in the United States have developed the device of 'promissory estoppel'. In the 'subscription cases', for example, the question is whether one can enforce a promise to subscribe to an appeal for funds for some public or charitable purpose. According to the consideration doctrine such a promise, if not under seal or in a deed, would only be actionable if the charity promised or rendered some requested counterperformance, as by assuring the subscriber that a mass would be recited for him annually or a memorial put up to him in the proposed chapel: absent any such counterperformance, the promised subscription would not be claimable, even if the promisee had embarked on the construction of the chapel or taken other steps in justifiable reliance on the promise. In other cases, too, the consideration doctrine can lead to unsatisfactory results, as in *Devecmon* v. *Shaw* 69 Md. 199, 14 A. 464 (1888):

A man promised his nephew to meet the expense of his going to Paris and immersing himself in the spirit of Europe for a year. The nephew accordingly went to Paris with his own funds and studied there for a year. On his return he sought reimbursement.

Here, too, it seems unfair that the uncle be free to back out of his promise, especially if he knew or should reasonably have realized that the nephew would rely on his promise and spend his own money on the trip to Europe. The courts in the United States therefore refuse to allow a promisor to invoke the absence of consideration if the promisee has altered his position in reliance on the validity of the promise and the promisor could have foreseen this. This is contained in the following formula in §90 Restatement (Second) of Contracts (1980):

'A promise which the promisor should reasonably expect to induce action or forbearance on the part of the promisee or a third person and which does induce such action or forbearance is binding [even in the absence of consideration] if injustice can be avoided only by enforcement of the promise. The remedy granted for breach [of such a promise] may be limited as justice requires'.

The doctrine of 'promissory estoppel', which is not yet generalized in England as it is in the United States, certainly operates as a corrective of marginal problems, but there are still many other cases in which the doctrine of consideration leads to results which the Continental jurist finds surprising or even shocking.

He feels no surprise or shock as regards promises of gifts, for other legal systems also hold quite rightly that where a person promises to effect a gratuitous transfer of money or property without getting anything in return, the promise is valid only if some form is observed, be it notarization, writing or a deed. But the consideration doctrine applies not just to promises of gifts but to *all* gratuitous promises, including those to provide a person with information, to carry or look after his property, to manage some other affair for him or to let him have the use of a house or a car. Continental systems unhesitatingly hold that such arrangements amount to valid contracts regardless of formality; indeed this is sometimes laid down in texts (for example, §§598, 662 BGB, art. 1875 f. 1986 Code civil, on loan and agency). In the Common Law, by contrast, no such promise is actionable in the absence of a formal deed. This means that while a person may be liable in tort if he damages the property he is gratuitously carrying or looking after, he is not liable in contract; the same is true of the person who gives bad advice for nothing.

The doctrine of consideration also leads to surprising results in cases where the requested counterpart is something which the promisee was already obliged to do.

When two sailors jumped ship in a Russian port and the captain was unable to find substitutes, he promised the rest of the crew a supplementary wage to get the vessel safely back to England. On arrival the captain reneged on his promise. The sailors' suit was dismissed: since they were already bound by their contract to do their best to overcome any perils of the voyage, including doing extra work due to the departure of two of their number, the captain had obtained nothing from them in return for his promise. *Stilk* v. *Myrick* (1809) 2 Camp. 317, 170 Eng. Rep. 1168.

There is nothing wrong with the actual solution if the facts were that in demanding extra payment the sailors were consciously exploiting the predicament in which the captain found himself, possibly even hinting that otherwise they might follow the example of their shipmates, but this would be because the captain's promise would be void for duress, not for want of consideration (see below Ch. 31 VII). One can see how irrelevant the consideration doctrine is here by supposing that the sailors had indeed provided some counterpart, for example, by giving up their contractual right to a teabreak or a rum ration; how could that possibly make any difference to the result? Besides, in the absence of duress, the captain's promise should surely be held valid if he made it spontaneously and with good reason, perhaps to improve the morale of his crew or stimulate them to exceptional efforts.

English decisions are beginning to reflect such ideas. In *Williams* v. *Roffey Bros.* [1991] 1 QB 1 (CA) the plaintiff contracted to fit out 27 flats but got into financial difficulties halfway through. The defendant promised him an extra £575 for each further flat completed. The plaintiff agreed and completed 8 more flats before finally abandoning the job. He claimed the bonus for the extra 8 flats and succeeded. The agreement for the bonus was not the result of any unlawful duress or deceit on the part of the plaintiff: it was a sensible proposal made by the defendant himself which took reasonable account of the interests of both parties in a properly commercial manner. The judges admittedly did obeisance to the consideration doctrine by saying that in resuming the work rather than throwing down his tools and waiting to be sued the plaintiff had suffered some kind of 'detriment', thereby providing consideration. The implausibility of this point merely shows how useless the doctrine of consideration is as a test of the validity of modifications of contractual arrangements.

In the United States it has long been accepted that a party need not show that he gave any consideration when a contract is modified in his favour before it has been fully executed. See §89 Restatement (Second) of Contracts (1981). In the case of sales this rule is actually statutory, for §2–209 UCC provides that 'an agreement modifying a contract . . . needs no consideration to be binding'. Art. 29(1) CISG is to the same effect in providing that 'A contract may be modified . . . by the mere agreement of the parties.'—A different kind of modification occurs when a creditor accepts less than his due and states that he forgoes the rest. *Foakes* v. *Beer* (1884) 9 App. Cas. 605 lays down that the creditor can still claim the balance since his promise not to sue for it is unsupported by any consideration from the debtor. This rule still obtains in the United States as well as England, but with significant restrictions. See on the one hand CORBIN §175, and on the other TREITEL: 'The law would be more consistent, as well as more satisfactory in its practical operation, if it adopted the same approach [of *Williams* v. *Roffey*] to cases of part payment of a debt. Agreements of the kind here under discussion would then be binding unless they had been made under duress.' (At p. 116.)

A promise made after the promisee has performed is also unenforceable for want of consideration: 'Past consideration is no consideration.' This is logical enough: the promise can hardly be the price of a performance already rendered, it can only be a reward for having rendered it. The rule does, however, lead to distinctions which are difficult to justify. In *Re McArdle* [1951] Ch. 669 the testator's widow was to take first under her deceased husband's will, and then the children. One of the sons, assisted by his wife, refurbished a property belonging to the estate, and his brothers and sisters promised that after the death of their mother they would pay a certain sum towards his outlay. The decision was made to turn on the question whether the promise to pay was made before or after the refurbishment was complete. More recent cases suggest that the claim would be good even in the latter case, provided that the siblings had an interest in the work being done and all parties were of the view that it should be remunerated in one way or another.

Compare *Pao On* v. *Lau Yiu Long* [1980] AC 614, 629 (PC).—A case in the United States shows how harsh the consequences of the consideration doctrine can be if the judge lacks the nerve to disregard doctrinal scruples. A saved B's life but was so severely injured in doing so that he was going to be a cripple for the rest of his days. To show his gratitude B promised to pay him $30 per month for life, but B's heirs refused to honour the promise on the ground that there was no consideration for it, the rescue having already been effected when the promise was made. The judge had to go in for rather stilted reasoning in order to give judgment for the claimant, and who can blame him? (*Webb* v. *McGowin* 27 Ala. App. 82, 168 So. 196 (1935).) See, however, *Harrington* v. *Taylor* 225 N.C. 690, 36 S.E.2d 227 (1945) where on similar facts the court said: 'However much the defendant should be impelled by common gratitude to alleviate the plaintiff's misfortune, a humanitarian act of this kind, voluntarily performed, is not such consideration as would entitle her to recover at law.' The Restatement (Second) of Contracts (1981) §86 amends this by providing that promises in respect of a benefit already received are binding, though only 'to the extent necessary to prevent injustice'.

There are yet other situations where the consideration doctrine produces disturbing results. It permits a tradesman to withdraw an offer at any time until it is accepted, even if he has unequivocally undertaken to keep it open for a given period (see above Ch. 26 II). Furthermore the doctrine of consideration is often given as the reason that a contract can vest no right of action in a third party beneficiary (see below Ch. 34 IV).

III

The core idea of the doctrine of consideration is accepted by Continental systems as regards promises of gifts in the sense mentioned above: a person who promises to make a gift of money or property is only liable if he puts his promise in the prescribed form and thereby demonstrates that he seriously intends to be bound. There are, of course, major differences between a notarial act and a deed, but the basic idea is the same.

This requirement of formality in Continental systems exists only as regards promises *à titre gratuit*, promises which are really donative. Here the courts have considerable room for play. They often deny the donative nature of a promise made for a reasonable and praiseworthy purpose where it is clear that the promisor intended to be bound and it would be unfair to allow him to wriggle out of liability by invoking the lack of form. In many French decisions a promise to subscribe for a public purpose or to pay maintenance has been held not to be a *pure libéralité*, but rather a *contrat commutatif* to which the formal requirements of art. 931 Code civil are inapplicable. In 1914, when the city of Nancy made an appeal to assist relatives of soldiers, M. Bailly promised to subscribe a million francs; later he changed his mind and said that his promise had not been notarized. He had to pay all the same: this was not a gift but a *contrat commutatif*, and the city supplied the 'counterpart' by providing matching funds, setting up a management committee, and commending M. Bailly's civic-mindedness *de la façon la plus flatteuse*.

See Nancy 17 Mar. 1920, D.P. 1920.2.65, confirmed by Civ. 5 Feb. 1923, D.P. 1923.1.20—In other cases, too, the courts have held a subscriber to his word on the ground that his purpose was not to make a gift but rather to obtain some advantage, often rather impalpable, such as an increase in social standing as a result of his ostentatious generosity. See Req. 14 Apr. 1863, D.P. 1863.1.402; Civ. 19 July 1894, D.P. 1895.1.125; Aix 30 Jan. 1882, D.P. 1883.2.245; and the excellent analysis of these cases in DAWSON (above p. 388) p. 84 ff.—So, too, the Reichsgericht upheld a written undertaking to subscribe DM 50,000 towards a crematorium, albeit with rather strained reasoning.

Courts have found various reasons to deny the donative nature of promises of money or money's worth to relatives, cohabitants, separated spouses or fiancées, cases where the beneficiary can hardly insist on having the promise notarized.

A father's promise to pay for the maintenance of an unacknowledged illegitimate child is not, according to French decisions, a gift calling for a special form but the *accomplissement d'un devoir de conscience* or the *reconnaissance d'une dette naturelle* (Civ. 14 May 1862, D.P. 1862.1.208; Civ. 8 Dec. 1959, D. 1960, 241). Likewise a man who had received most of his father's estate in his lifetime was held to his promise to give some money to his impoverished sisters who had inherited very little (Paris 25 Apr. 1932, Sem. Jur. 1932, 607). German courts decide in much the same way. A cavalry officer promised his long-term mistress, a barmaid by whom he had three children, 15,000 marks if he decided to marry a woman of his own class (RGZ 98, 176); he was held to his promise, as was the man who promised to provide the promisee with a 'dowry' if he married the promisor's pregnant mistress (RGZ 62, 273). In both cases the court first asked whether the promise was void as contrary to good morals, and rightly held that it was not; nor were the promises held to be promises of gifts. It is a gift promise only if both parties regard the transaction as pure generosity, whereas here the promises were regarded as fulfilling an obligation, admittedly not a legal obligation but nevertheless one which would be recognized as such by all right-thinking people: the promisor did not intend to make the disposition as a gift and the promisee did not intend to receive it as such (RGZ 62, 273, 277).

Swiss courts apply the same rules. See, for example, BGE 53 II 198: Herr Stähelin gave an oral undertaking to the guardianship authority that he would treat his orphaned niece as a child of his own and bring her up in his family. Later he sought to recover from the niece the expense of so doing on the ground that his promise was a gift which needed to be formalized. The Bundesgericht rejected the argument: 'It is enough that the disponent believes himself to be fulfilling a moral duty, as was certainly the case with Herr Stähelin, even if such duty is not universally recognised. In such a case it cannot be said that the disponent had a donative intention, or that his promise, though unremunerated, constitutes a gift. His agreement to look after the plaintiff without charge therefore falls within the general principle that contracts require no special form, so that the oral agreement between Stähelin and the guardianship authority was valid.' (At p. 199 f.)

Continental courts have another test to help them decide which promises are binding and which are not; they say that a promise is binding only when it was made *en vue de produire des effets juridiques*, where the promisor's intention was 'that legal validity attach to his conduct' (BGHZ 21, 102, 106). This requirement is generally satisfied when the transaction is remunerated, but may not be met when the promise is gratuitous.

The principle that a contractual obligation arises only when the parties had an 'intention to create legal relations' is also recognized in the Common Law, but there is much less need to apply it since gratuitous promises are automatically unenforceable by reason of the want of consideration (see TREITEL 149 ff.).

The leading case in Germany was decided in 1956 (BGHZ 21, 102). A carrier (A) had an urgent delivery to make but no driver available, so he asked another carrier (B) if he could supply a substitute. The driver supplied by B was inexperienced and damaged A's truck rather badly. When A sued B for damages for breach of contract, B's defence was that he was only trying to help out in a crisis and that he had acted 'out of human sympathy with no intention of assuming a legal obligation'. The defence was summarily rejected by the Bundesgerichtshof: it was certainly necessary that B had had an intention to bind himself in law, but his 'private intentions' were irrelevant; it depended on whether A 'in all the circumstances must in good faith and in the light of good commercial practice have concluded that such an intention existed' on the part of B, and that was so here since B must have realized that A was relying on the provision of a competent driver and might otherwise suffer a considerable loss.

Many French decisions also hold that no contractual obligation arises in the absence of intention to bind. When a painter claimed damages from a hotel for the loss of a portfolio he had handed to the barman for safekeeping, the Cour de Cassation dismissed the claim: the portfolio had been accepted *par pure complaisance* and there was therefore no contract of deposit (Com. 25 Sept. 1984, Bull. IV no. 242). Nor does a *contrat de dépôt ou de garde même tacite* arise when a firm *par simple tolérance* allows another to park his vehicle on the premises (Civ. 29 Mar. 1978, Bull. I no. 126), and when the manager of a Paris nightclub takes the keys of a patron's car and agrees to park it, this is a *service bénévole* and not a contract for the safekeeping of the car (Paris 14 Jan. 1988, Gaz. Pal. 1988.I.269).

IV

We have now seen that while the consent of the parties is necessary for a binding contract, it is often not sufficient. Systems differ as to what more is required and when. The Common Law's doctrine of consideration is a particularly ambitious attempt to offer a comprehensive solution, and while Continental systems tend to decide similar cases in much the same way, they have nothing directly comparable. English lawyers draw varying inferences from this. Some see the doctrine of consideration as an indispensable and characteristic feature of English contract law, the jewel in its crown. Others, noting that systems on the Continent get by quite well without it, conclude that it could be done away with in England too. Thus LORD WRIGHT, who was used to applying Scots law and, in the Privy Council, the law of South Africa, once wrote:

'In these jurisdictions consideration has no place; nor has it a place in the laws of France, Italy, Spain, Germany, Switzerland and Japan. These are all civilized countries with a highly developed system of law; how then is it possible to regard the common law rule of consideration as axiomatic or as an inevitable element in any code of law?' (At p. 1226.)

He went on to conclude as follows:

'When I review in my mind the scattered threads of argument and illustration which I have set out in this article, I cannot resist the conclusion that the doctrine is a mere incumbrance. A scientific or logical theory of contract would in my opinion take as the test of contractual intention the answer to the overriding question whether there was a deliberate and serious intention, free from illegality, immorality, mistake, fraud or duress, to make a binding contract. That must be in each case a question of fact.' (Ibid. at 1251.)

Another author concluded

'that English law would lose nothing if the doctrine of consideration were to be abolished . . . The civil law systems have been able to develop a perfectly adequate law of contract without consideration. If the idea of the harmonization of laws, therefore, is to be taken seriously the doctrine of consideration must go. In its present form it makes no contribution to English law, it is alien to the civil law and it will serve no useful purpose in an enlarged area of European law.' (CHLOROS (above p. 388) p. 164 f.)

These are strong words, but what actually irritates the English critics is not the basic idea of the doctrine of consideration but the artificial accretions it has acquired in the course of time as a result of being put to unexpected uses. One of these is its application to modifications of existing contracts and to agreements that a party may render a lesser performance than originally promised. This is the 'adjunct of the doctrine of consideration which has done most to give it a bad reputation' (PATTERSON (above p. 389) at 936). Nor is it obvious why the doctrine of consideration should prevent a third party from claiming the promised performance even when the parties have agreed for good business reasons that he may do so. Finally, the logic of the doctrine has led to the rule that a businessman who has unequivocally declared that his offer is to be binding on him for a specified period may nevertheless revoke it before that period expires, provided it has not been accepted in the meantime. There is fairly general agreement in England that these outposts of the doctrine are indefensible and that the time has come to abandon them; indeed the signal for retreat has already been given by the Law Commission as well as by courts and commentators (see TREITEL (above p. 389) at 147 f.).

As regards promises of gifts, where something is promised for nothing, something that will permanently diminish the promisor's estate and enhance that of the promisee, the matter is different. On the Continent as well as in England such promises are valid only if contained in a particular form, be it deed or notarial act. On this point all European systems are at one, and for good reason. The formal requirement provides reliable evidence that the promisor really intended to be bound by his promise. Doubtless a promise given orally or in private or business correspondence will occasionally have been maturely considered, but it would open the door to great legal uncertainty if one abandoned the formal requirements and had the judge inquire and decide on the facts of each case whether the oral or written promise rested on a 'deliberate and serious intention'.

Nevertheless there are still significant differences between the Common Law and Civil law on particular points. The Common Law doctrine of promissory estoppel enables the courts exceptionally to give effect to an informal gift promise if the promisee has justifiably relied on it to his detriment. Continental jurisdictions might find this worth considering. We have seen, too, that judges on the Continent approach the question whether a transaction was really gratuitous in rather a cavalier fashion and often hold a promise binding despite lack of form if the promisor was actuated by creditable motives. One could object that this etiolates the requirement of form and creates legal uncertainty, but this objection hardly lies in the mouth of the English jurist when one considers how astute the English judges are at snuffling out some consideration lurking in the background.

There remains the problem of promises which though unremunerated are not donative. Here there is an almost unbridgeable chasm between Common Law and Civil Law, since no English jurist could hold that there is a binding contract when one person lets another use his property for nothing or provides him with free information or manages some piece of business for him without reward. This difference would be alarming if it led to differences in result, but it is not clear that it does: Continental courts can often hold that the promisor did not really intend to assume a legal obligation, and in England some kind of consideration can commonly be conjured up. In fact the cases hardly ever involve claims for performance of the promise; they are almost all claims for damages for faulty performance, and here England can turn to the law of tort and achieve the same results as are reached on the Continent by the contractual route.

30

The Construction of Contracts

FARNSWORTH, '"Meaning" in the Law of Contracts', 76 *Yale LJ* 939 (1967).
HOLMES, 'The Theory of Legal Interpretation', 12 *Harv. L. Rev.* 417 (1899).
KÖTZ, 'Vertragsauslegung, Eine rechtsvergleichende Skizze', *Festschrift für Zeuner* (1994) 219.
LARENZ, *Die Methode der Auslegung des Rechtsgeschäfts* (1930, repr. 1966).
LEWISON, *The Interpretation of Contracts* (1989).
LÜDERITZ, *Auslegung von Rechtsgeschäften, Vergleichende Untersuchung anglo-amerikanischen und deutschen Rechts* (1966).
MARTY, 'Rôle du juge dans l'interprétation des contrats', *Travaux de l'Association Henri Capitant* V (1950) 84.
MEIER-HAYOZ, *Das Vertrauensprinzip beim Vertragsschluß* (1948).
MORRIS, 'Palm-Tree Justice in the Court of Appeal', 82 *LQ Rev.* 196 (1966).
OFTINGER, 'Einige grundsätzliche Betrachtungen über die Auslegung der Verkehrs-geschäfte', *ZSR* 58 (1939) 178.
PATTERSON, 'The Interpretation and Construction of Contracts', 64 *Colum. L. Rev.* 833 (1964).
POUND, 'The Role of Will in Law', 68 *Harv. L. Rev.* 1 (1954).
RIEG, *Le Rôle de la volonté dans l'acte juridique en droit civil français et allemand* (1961).
SWEET, 'Contract Making and Parol Evidence: Diagnosis and Treatment of a Sick Rule', 53 *Cornell LQ* 1036 (1968).
WILLIAMS, 'Language and the Law', 61 *LQ Rev.* 71, 179, 293, 384 (1945); 62 *LQ Rev.* 387 (1946).
YOUNG, 'Equivocation in the Making of Agreements', 64 *Colum. L. Rev.* 619 (1964).
YUNG, 'L'Interprétation supplétive des contrats', *ZBernJV* 97 (1961) 41.

I

LIKE the other gestures and symbols which men use to mark their entry into legal relationships words, whether written or spoken, can never fully express what was intended. Furthermore, the parties making a contract may well not have turned their minds to certain matters which later prove to be relevant. Judges are therefore constantly faced with the task of deciding the rights of parties who have expressed themselves unclearly or incompletely. This process of determining the meaning of ambiguous or incomplete expressions is called 'construction'.

Construction is called for when it is known what the parties said, wrote, or otherwise expressed, but not obvious what they meant by it. Construction may start from either of two opposed premises, neither of which is found in the pure form in practice today. On one view, it is the *intention* of the promisor which counts; this is justified by the principle of private autonomy which treats the free will of legal persons as the source and measure of legal consequences: 'Intention *per se* is really the only important and effective thing, which needs a sign by which we can recognize it only because it is an internal and invisible phenomenon' (SAVIGNY, *System des heutigen römischen Rechts* III (1840) 258).

On the other view, priority is given to the external phenomenon of *expression* on the ground that the legal order is concerned with protecting commercial intercourse: the internal will of the promisor is treated as significant only in so far as it coincides with the normal objective meaning that a reasonable man would attribute to its expression.

Roman law shows the shift in methods of construction from one of these extremes to the other. To interpret external expression strictly and literally is historically the older method. To give an example, a will in classical Roman law was invalid if the testator, in instituting his slave as heir, forgot to emancipate him. Institution of heir and emancipation of slave were seen as being quite distinct transactions and the older lawyers would have thought it improper to say that since it was common knowledge that only free persons could own property, a person who was instituting a slave must, in a case of doubt, have meant to emancipate him (Inst. 1, 6, 2; 2, 14 pr.): 'cum in verbis nulla ambiguitas est non debet admitti voluntatis quaestio' (D. 32, 25, 1). It was only JUSTINIAN who laid down in one of his constitutions (C. 6, 27, 5) that in such a case the instituted slave must be deemed to have been emancipated as well 'cum non est verisimile eum quem heredem sibi elegit, si praetermisit libertatis dationem, servum eum manere voluisse, et neminen sibi heredem fore'. Thus the development ends with a strong emphasis on the *voluntas* as against the *verba*, not only in the law of wills but also in the law of contracts: 'in conventionibus contrahentium voluntatem potius quam verba spectari placuit' (D. 50, 16, 219). For details see ZIMMERMANN, *The Law of Obligations* (1990) 622 ff.

II

The draftsmen of the European codes had widely differing views of the value of prescribing rules of construction. The *Romanistic* civil codes in particular contain a great many canons of construction (see arts. 1156 ff. Code civil, 1362 ff. Codice civile), all of very dubious merit. It is not really for the legislator to instruct the judge in what is practically reasonable or to control his application of the law by technical rules which are virtually empty of content. In any case, a judge who is construing a contract must pay such close attention to the special circumstances of the case before him that it can only make for error if he is constrained by rules enacted generally and in the abstract. It can safely be left to judges and scholars to develop proper rules of construction.

A glance at the rules of construction laid down in the French Code civil confirms this view. According to art. 1156, one should seek out the common intention of the parties rather than adhere to the meaning of their words; in case of doubt, a contract should be construed so as to have validity (art. 1157) and where one expression is ambiguous it should be given the meaning 'qui convient le plus à la matière du contrat' (art. 1158). Again, it is the contract as a whole rather than its individual provisions which indicates the right construction (art. 1161); general words should be limited to the particular contractual objects intended though, on the other hand, where only *one* situation has been mentioned one must ask whether others are not included (arts. 1163 f.). In cases of doubt, one should construe the contract against the creditor and in favour of the debtor (art. 1162) and sales contracts should be construed against the vendor (art. 1602 par. 2).

Some of these rules are simply banal, others mere rules of thumb. The failure of a judge to follow one of them is not in itself a ground for impugning his decision before an appellate court (see, for example, Com. 19.1.1981, Bull. I no. 34). Indeed one rather has the impression that the judges reach the conclusion first and then look for an appropriate rule to cite.

As between the objective and subjective approaches to interpretation, the French courts still incline to the latter, holding that, as art. 1156 Code civil says, the primary role of interpretation is to discover the *commune intention des parties*. Nonetheless, where no such common intention can be found, the judge is supposed to ascertain the 'hypothetical' intention of the parties or to adopt the interpretation which in all the circumstances, objective and subjective, must be regarded as the one the parties would reasonably have intended. While the Code civil speaks of the 'common intention' of the parties in art. 1156, it also, like §157 BGB, directs the judge to take account of objective factors, for example, to interpret unclear terms so as to bring them into line with the 'meaning of the contract' or 'usages' (art. 1158–1160), and art. 1135 further provides that a party must perform not only as expressly promised but also according to the dictates of 'equity, usage and law', depending on the type of contract. Since a judge will very rarely be able to discern any actual intention common to the parties, he has practically no option but to focus on 'objective' considerations and ask how the term in question should and would normally have been understood in that particular context by a reasonable man. He remains, of course, perfectly free to come to his conclusion on the basis of objective considerations and call it the *commune intention des parties contractantes* when he comes to write his judgment.

On the retirement of a director, Camille Blanc, a company undertook to pay him a pension and after his death to continue paying half of it to 'Mme. Camille Blanc'. Mme. Blanc died first and the widower remarried. After his death the second

Mme. Blanc demanded the continuation of the pension payments but her claim was rejected because the Court of Appeal found that 'dans l'intention des parties' only the first wife was to be entitled (Req. 31 Oct. 1934, DH 1934. 602). In the circumstances of the case this construction may be quite correct, but it is sheer fantasy to suppose that at the time the contract was concluded the parties had even considered the possibility of the aged pensioner's remarriage, let alone formed any common intention about it.

Another factor which conduces to 'objective' construction is the doctrine of *clauses claires et précises* adopted by the Cour de Cassation. Normally the construction of contracts is a question of fact which the Cour de Cassation does not review, but in the case of a *clause claire et précise* it is otherwise: it will quash a decision if the judge below, perhaps invoking a supposed common intention of the parties, has given a term some meaning other than its objective meaning. The doctrine that 'clear' terms must not be construed is perhaps odd, since terms need to be construed before they can be said to be clear, but a famous case from 1942 shows how effectively it can operate to constrain any undue tendency to 'subjective' construction.

A purchaser had agreed to buy a certain quantity of cod on the terms that the vendor should be entitled to reduce this quantity if he was so empowered by the Cod-Dealers' Association. The Association did so decide and the vendor delivered only 50% of the quantity originally agreed. The purchaser claimed damages and the Court of Appeal of Bordeaux allowed the claim. The Court of Cassation quashed this decision and remanded it to another Court of Appeal because in its view the clear text of the contract left no doubt about the vendor's right to reduce the quantity to be delivered. This second court also gave judgment for the plaintiff, apparently because in reaching their agreement the parties had implicitly assumed that the Association would permit a reduction of quantity only if the catch diminished and not, as was the case, because of a sharp increase in demand. This decision also was quashed: the term of the contract was so unambiguous that there was no room for any further inquiry into the parties' intentions. In his note on the case, Lerebours-Pigeonnière, one of the judges involved in the case, was quite specific: 'Si la clause litigieuse est claire, il n'y a pas lieu de rechercher l'intention commune des parties pour en déterminer la portée' (Civ. 14 Dec. 1942, D. 1944, 112; see also Civ. 23 April 1945, D. 1945, 261, noted Lerebours-Pigeonnière).

III

When we turn to the *German* legal family, we find that despite all the efforts to harmonize the provisions of the BGB there still remains a clear conflict between the doctrine of intention and the expression theory. On the one hand, §133 BGB, just like art. 1156 Code civil and art. 1362 Codice civile, says that the aim of construction is 'to discern the real intention'. This must mean that the crucial thing is the actual historical will of the parties. This is supported by the fact that the section on 'Ascertainment of Intention' in the Motives for the BGB rejects as 'unacceptable' the perfectly reasonable view that 'in contracts what matters is not what real intention lay behind what one contractor said but what the other contractor must in the circumstances have understood him to mean' (Motive I p. 155). On the other hand, §157 BGB applies a strongly objective standard and requires that construction be 'in accordance with good faith with reference to normal commercial usage'.

In the event it is clear that construction cannot turn on the actual historical intention of the parties except in the relatively rare case where such an intention can be ascertained. In other cases the term is given the sense that would be accorded to it by a reasonable man in the position and circumstances of the addressee. This serves to protect the justifiable reliance of the addressee, for he will count on its having its usual meaning. Although this sometimes gives a promise a meaning at variance with the secret intention of the promisor, this is quite acceptable: considering that the promise was intended to affect other people, to induce them to behave in a certain way, the promisor must accept that it will be taken to have the meaning that those people would accord to it in the circumstances and that his subjective intention will be ignored. The intention theory may have been sound enough in times gone by when contracts were made between neighbourly farmers and amicable merchants who knew each other's personal circumstances, but in the present day of impersonal mass transactions only the expression theory can provide the right solution.

Sometimes parties use words idiosyncratically. If so, systems agree that *falsa demonstratio non nocet*: it is what they both meant, not what was said, which counts. Where the parties agreed to buy and sell 'haakjöringsköd' (which properly denotes 'sharksmeat') but meant to signify 'whalemeat' the contract was for 'whalemeat' and the buyer could claim damages when sharksmeat was tendered (RGZ 99, 147). In this special case the common intention of the parties trumps the objective meaning of the words used, and rightly so, because there has been no justifiable reliance on the objective meaning of the words and it best answers the interests of the parties to construe the contract as having the meaning they intended, even if they failed to express it.

The Common Law also accepts that the contract is as the parties really agreed. If a slip is made in drafting a written document of sale so that it refers by mistake to a plot of land other than the one intended to be bought and sold, or states a rent higher than was agreed, the party adversely affected may seek 'rectification' of the text on proof that they really were agreed on something different from what the document purports to record. See TREITEL 285 ff.

'Construction of contracts' normally relates to the process of ascertaining the meaning of the words chosen by the parties, but German lawyers believe that construction is also involved when parties to a contract have omitted to specify a particular point and the problem is how to fill the resulting gap. Here the judge looks first for *dispositives Recht* (in France *règles supplétives*), statutory provisions which apply in the absence of any contrary indication to be found in the contract in issue. Although the BGB and HGB contain many such rules for the commonest and most important types of contract, quite often there is no appropriate statutory gap-filler, and so 'constructive interpretation' (*ergänzende Auslegung*) takes place. The judge must then, according to a formula much used by the courts,

'discover and attend to what the parties, instead of actually expressing, would have expressed in view of the purpose of the contract as a whole if they had indeed covered the point in their agreement and paid due attention to the requirements of good faith and good commercial practice' (BGHZ 16, 71).

In the decision from which this quotation is taken two doctors in different small towns agreed to exchange practices. One of them regretted the move and returned after nine months. The other was afraid that his new patients would go back to their previous trusted physician, and wanted to stop him resuming practice. Could he do so? Neither the contract itself nor any of the statutory default rules provided any basis for such a claim, so the Bundesgerichtshof filled the gap by 'constructive interpretation': it read into the contract a term that for a period of two to three years neither doctor was free to resume practice in the vicinity of his previous practice.

See also RGZ 131, 274; BGH NJW 1979, 1705; BGH NJW 1982, 2816.—The French courts do much the same, even if they profess to be filling the gap on the basis of the 'commune intention des parties contractantes'. In one case a radio station which had accepted and paid without demur for the manuscript of a play it had commissioned was reluctant to broadcast it. The judge was able to hold *par une interprétation rendue nécessaire par l'ambiguïté de la convention sur ce point* that the radio station was not only entitled but bound to produce and broadcast the play, and was liable in damages for its failure to do so (Civ. 2 Apr. 1974, Bull. I no. 109). The Cour de Cassation decides likewise in cases where the contract proves inoperative because a term subsequently becomes unfeasible. For example, if the 'indexation clause' agreed by the parties to a long-term contract proves unworkable because the stipulated index does not exist or is no longer published or because the clause cannot obtain the necessary official approval, the courts will substitute another clause, as close as possible to the original one, which will function and meet with official approval (Civ. 12 Feb. 1972, D. 1973, 217, noted by GHESTIN; so too BGHZ 63, 132, 136).

People may differ on the question whether such constructive interpretation is really construction or interpretation at all, or simply the judge hitting upon a rule which provides a just and appropriate solution to the dispute. It is not easy to draw the distinction. Nor is it really necessary. Certainly the judge must not reach a conclusion at variance with the terms actually agreed by the parties. Nor may he try to save a party from his nonchalance, negligence or predilection for risk-taking by inserting—at the expense of the other party—a clause which the parties would have been wise to include but did not. What the judge must do, to use the pretty formula of RIPERT/BOULAN-GER, is 'to make the contract speak' (Ripert/Boulanger, *Droit civil* II (1957) no. 4701). He must start from the terms agreed by the parties and amplify them in the light of the purpose of the contract and the interests of the parties in such a way as to resolve the point unregulated consistently with the points which have actually been covered. Judges sometimes say that it is a matter of discovering the common will of the parties, but this means what the parties as reasonable and fair-minded men would have agreed if a third party had drawn attention to the matter omitted; in this sense one can, if one wishes, speak of the 'hypothetical intention of the parties'. On the other hand, the constructive interpretation of a contract must never disturb the internal economy of the transaction, the relation of performance and counterperformance agreed by the parties, or extend the content of the contract beyond what the parties envisaged at its formation.

IV

In the *Common Law* the conflict between the theories of intention and expression has attracted much less thought and writing than on the Continent. POTHIER and SAVIGNY may have had some influence on English jurists in the nineteenth century and even today one happens upon statements that the essence of contract is a 'meeting of the minds' or 'consensus ad idem', but the courts have always clung to the position that the construction of a legal transaction is geared to the external phenomenon of expression rather than the subjective intention of the parties. This is how it is put in CHESHIRE/FIFOOT/FURMSTON at p. 28 f.:

'Agreement, however, is not a mental state but an act and, as an act, is a matter of inference from conduct. The parties are to be judged, not by what is in their minds, but by what they have said or written or done. While such must be, in some degree, the standpoint of every legal system, the common law . . . lays peculiar emphasis upon external appearance . . . The function of an English judge is not to seek and satisfy some elusive mental element but to ensure, as far as practical experience permits, that the reasonable expectations of honest men are not disappointed.'

This basic attitude of the Common Law also explains the practice of courts in England and the United States when construing a contract in writing; they try to stick to the wording of the document as long as possible and only exceptionally admit witness evidence to prove that the written agreement has been amplified or modified. 'If there be a contract which has been reduced to writing', said LORD DENMAN in *Goss* v. *Lord Nugent* (1833) 110 Eng. Rep. 713, 'verbal evidence is not allowed to be given of what passed between the parties, either before the written instrument was made, or during the time that it was in a state of preparation, so as to add to or subtract from, or in any manner to vary or qualify the written contract.'

On this see TREITEL 176ff.; CHESHIRE/FIFOOT/FURMSTON 123 ff. The law in the United States is much the same, see CORBIN §§573 ff. and Restatement (Second) of Contracts (1981) §§213 ff. Full details on all this are in LÜDERITZ III ff.

But this so-called 'parol evidence rule' is now subject to significant exceptions. For example, it does not apply when oral evidence would show that the contract was void. If the text is ambiguous, witnesses may be admitted to testify to the circumstances in which the contract was formed if this would illuminate the true meaning of the text. The rules as to rectification (above p. 404) may also be seen as an exception to the parol evidence rule. It remains true, however, that the rule can only be excluded if there is some special reason for admitting witness evidence. Parties who have put their agreement in writing must in principle be bound to what is written and nothing else; the Common Law regards the legal certainty produced by the parol evidence rule as more important than the true intention of the parties.

Continental systems pay less attention to the probative force of written agreements. It is true that in France art. 1341 Code civil lays down that where there is a written document or notarial act witnesses cannot be heard to testify to any divergent oral agreement (compare art. 2722 Codice civile), but in practice the operation of this rule is much restricted (see above p. 369 ff.). In Germany there is a presumption that the document accurately reflects the totality of the agreement, but the presumption is rebuttable, though only with difficulty.

In England, too, gaps in contracts may be made good by 'terms implied in law', rules automatically applicable to contracts of the type in question in the absence of any contraindication by the parties. Such rules are not very often of *statutory* origin, but the Sale of Goods Act 1979 and the Supply of Goods and Services Act 1982, for example, contain rules applicable to contracts of sale of goods and services which, as interpreted by the courts, are analogous in function to the dispositive law of Continental countries. In other cases the judges themselves have laid down terms to be implied into important types of contract such as sale, carriage, and insurance. For example, if a contract to build a house contains no express term regarding the quality of the house to be built, the courts hold 'that it is an implied term of the contract that the work will be done in a good and workmanlike manner, that the builder will supply good and proper material and that the house will be reasonably fit for human habitation when built or completed' (ANSON (25th edn., by GUEST, 1979) 139). Likewise a person letting a motor boat on hire will be liable in damages if he is in breach of the implied term 'that the vessel hired shall be as fit for the purpose as reasonable care and skill can make it' (*Read* v. *Dean* [1949] 1 KB 188, 193). The landlord of apartments in a fifteen-storey block is bound towards his tenants by an implied term 'to take reasonable care to maintain the common parts of the building in a state of reasonable repair', and can be held liable if in consequence of failure to make the requisite repairs the lifts and staircase lights are out of order for any considerable period (*Liverpool CC* v. *Irwin* [1977] AC 239).

'Terms implied by law' are normally drafted so generally as to be applicable to all contracts of the given type; they are not of much use when the parties have failed to address a specific point which requires a 'tailor-made' solution. In such cases the English courts ask whether the gap can be filled by a 'term implied in fact' (see TREITEL 150 ff.). This may be done if it is obvious that the proposed term would unhesitatingly have been agreed by the parties had a bystander pointed out its omission at the time the contract was being formed. It is often said that the term must be necessary 'to give the transaction such business efficacy as the parties must have intended' (*Luxor (Eastbourne) Ltd.* v. *Cooper* [1941] AC 108, 137).

See also *The Moorcock* (1889) 14 PD 64: the plaintiff paid the defendant to let him berth his vessel at the defendant's quay on the Thames where the vessel would naturally settle when the tide ebbed, but when it did so, it broke its back because the river bed at that point was uneven. The defendant was held to be in breach of a 'term implied in fact' that he should notify the plaintiff of the unevenness of the river bed if he knew of it, or of his ignorance if he did not.

V

In times gone by, the conflict between the 'intention theory' and the 'expression theory' had a role to play, perhaps more on the Continent than in England, but nowadays it hardly has any effect on the way contracts are construed. There is general agreement that a term does not necessarily have the meaning accorded to it by either of the parties at the time of the contract or afterwards. What counts is the meaning a reasonable man in the shoes of the addressee would give it in the light of its wording and all other relevant circumstances known to him. This is how the Vienna Convention formulates it in art. 8: '. . . statements made . . . by a party are to be interpreted according to his intent where the other party knew or could not have been unaware what that intent was' (art. 8(1)). If, as is the usual case, this does not fit the facts, 'statements . . . are to be interpreted according to the understanding that a reasonable person of the same kind as the other party would have had in the same circumstances' (art. 8(2)); in determining this 'due consideration is to be given to all relevant circumstances of the case including the negotiations, any practice which the parties have established between themselves, usages and any subsequent conduct of the parties' (art. 8(3)).

A similar rule is to be found in the UNIDROIT 'Principles of International Commercial Contracts'. Certainly art. 4.1(1) states that 'A contract shall be interpreted according to the common intention of the parties', but 'If such an intention cannot be established, the contract shall be interpreted according to the meaning that reasonable persons of the same kind as the parties would give to it in the same circumstances' (art. 4.1(2)). In art. 4.2 the rules are the same as in art. 8 CISG, and on the question of gap-filling art. 4.8 provides that 'Where the parties to a contract have not agreed with respect to a term which is important for a determination of their rights and duties, a term which is appropriate in the circumstances shall be supplied.'

31

Mistake, Deceit, and Duress

AMORTH, *Errore e inadempimento nel contratto* (1967).

ATIYAH/BENNION, 'Mistake in the Construction of Contracts', 24 *Mod. L. Rev.* 421 (1961).

CARTWRIGHT, *Unequal Bargaining, A Study of Vitiating Factors in the Formation of Contracts* (1991).

DAWSON, 'Economic Duress, An Essay in Perspective', 45 *Mich. L. Rev.* 253 (1947).

DREXELIUS, *Irrtum und Risiko, Rechtsvergleichende Untersuchungen und Reformvorschläge zum Recht der Irrtumsanfechtung* (1964).

EISENBERG, 'The Bargain Principle and its Limits', 95 *Colum. L. Rev.* 323 (1982).

GHESTIN, *La Notion d'erreur dans le droit positif actuel* (2nd edn., 1971).

GOODHART, 'Mistake As To Identity in the Law of Contract', 57 *LQ Rev.* 228 (1941).

GOW, 'Mistake and Error', 1 *ICLQ* 472 (1952).

HALL, 'New Developments in Mistake of Identity', 1961 *Camb. LJ* 86.

HENRICH, 'Unbewußte Irreführung', *AcP* 162 (1963) 88.

HOFF, 'Error in the Formation of Contracts in Louisiana, A Comparative Analysis', 53 *Tu. L. Rev.* 329 (1979).

KEMPERMANN, *Unlautere Ausnutzung von Vertrauensverhältnissen im englischen, französischen und deutschen Recht* (1975).

LAWSON, 'Error in substantia', 52 *LQ Rev.* 79 (1936).

LEGRAND, 'Pre-Contractual Disclosure and Information: English Law and French Law Compared', 6 *Oxf. J. Leg. Stud.* 322 (1986).

LITVINOFF, ' "Error" in the Civil Law', in: *Essays on the Civil Law of Obligations* (ed. Dainow, 1969) 222.

MALINVAUD, 'De l'erreur sur la substance', D. 1972. Chron. 215.

NEWMAN, 'Relief for Mistake in Contracting', 54 *Cornell LQ* 232 (1969).

NICHOLAS, 'The Pre-Contractual Obligation to Disclose Information', English Report in HARRIS/TALLON (eds.), *Contract Law Today, Anglo-French Comparisons* (1989) 166.

PALMER, *Mistake and Unjust Enrichment* (1962).

RODIÈRE (ed.), *Les Vices du consentement dans le contrat* (1977).

ROLLIN, 'Irrtum und Reurecht', Diss. Hamburg (1964).

VAN ROSSUM, 'Defects of Consent and Capacity in Contract Law', in HARTKAMP et al. (eds.), *Towards a European Civil Code* (1994) 135.

SCHMIDLIN, 'Das Vertrauensprinzip und die Irrtumslehre im deutschen und schweizerischen Recht', *ZSR* 89 (1970) 225.

V. SCHWIND, 'Der Irrtum im Verkehrsrecht des ABGB und BGB, Eine rechtsvergleichend-rechtspolitische Betrachtung', *Jher. Jb.* 89 (1941) 119.

SMITH, 'Error in the Scottish Law of Contract', 71 *LQ Rev.* 507 (1955).

VIVIEN, 'De l'erreur déterminante et substantielle', *Rev. trim. dr. civ.* 91 (1992) 306.

WADDAMS, 'Pre-Contractual Duties of Disclosure', in CANE/STAPLETON (eds.), *Essays for Patrick Atiyah* (1991) 237.

ZWEIGERT *et al.*, 'Der Entwurf eines einheitlichen Gesetzes über die materielle Gültigkeit internationaler Kaufverträge über bewegliche Sachen', *RabelsZ* 32 (1968) 201, 342.

I

NOT every error entitles a promisor to evade the consequences of his promise. On this all legal systems are agreed. Equally there is no doubt that in exceptional circumstances a promisor who has made a mistake may be able to shift its consequences to the other party, even at the cost of frustrating the other party's reliance on the validity of the promise. Where the dividing line is to be drawn between errors of which the law will take account and those which it will disregard is a question as old as it is controverted.

The problem is a difficult one, and there are many plausible points of view one might adopt when faced with a case of mistake. Suppose that a person has a Chinese vase which he thinks is simply a middling example of standard native ware; he sells it at a low price, delivers it to the purchaser, and then discovers that it was a priceless specimen of the Ming Dynasty. Can the vendor rescind the contract and demand the return of the vase just because he was mistaken as to its value? Does it make any difference if the vendor himself was an expert who could have found out the true value of the vase, but failed to do so, either recklessly or carelessly? What if the purchaser was aware of the true value of the vase and concealed the fact, and what if he could have discovered it? What if the parties to the contract were both experienced orientalists? Is it relevant that the purchaser, supposing the purchase valid, has restored the vase, spent a fortune in discovering its origins, gone to considerable expense to advertise it in the specialist press, or even sold and delivered it to a buyer? Suppose that the purchaser, acting in the best of good faith, had assured the vendor that it was only an average sort of vase, and the vendor sold it to him on that basis? May the purchaser keep the vase if he is ready to pay the difference in value?

Obviously there can be no simple test to tell us in which of these cases the contract can be avoided by the party in error and in which it cannot. A legal system can, however, start from either of two basic positions. One rests on the 'intention theory': if the true reason the law recognizes and enforces contractual promises is that the promisor intended to be bound, then his intention must be properly formed and not vitiated by a mistake (or deceit or duress). If it is, one speaks of a 'defect of intention' (*Willensmangel, vice de consentement*) and the party whose intention is so vitiated can claim that the contract is void.

The difficulty with this position is that it takes insufficient account of the interests of the other party. The other position protects those interests: anyone who makes a promise in business affairs must take the risk that the reasons he had for making it may not be accurate. Certainly he may inform the other party of his reasons and try to get him to agree that the contract should only be valid if they are accurate, but in the absence of such agreement, he is bound by what he says. To allow him to invoke his mistake and impugn the validity of the contract would seriously imperil the security of transactions. On this view, therefore, it is only exceptionally that a contract may be avoided for mistake, only when for some special reason the other party's reliance on its validity does not merit protection.

We are going to report on the law in various countries in order to see what standards and criteria they use in the area of mistake, and then try to compare and evaluate the results. First, however, we turn to two general problems.

The first point is that a contract can only be avoided if there is a contract to avoid. This is worth emphasizing because sometimes a mistake may prevent a contract from coming into existence. This does not often happen, since even when the offeree understands the offer in a sense different from that intended by the offeror and the parties are both mistaken as to the meaning attributed by the other to what he said, a contract nevertheless comes about. What the parties actually thought when they said what they did is immaterial, and they need not have thought the same thing or reached any true 'consensus ad idem' or 'meeting of the minds'. It is for the court to say whether the declarations of the parties were congruent in an objective sense, that is, in the view of a reasonable third party familiar with the context. When it has been ascertained in this way that a contract did come about we can ask whether it may be avoided for mistake; only when it is impossible to reach an unequivocal meaning by this process of construction, since a reasonable bystander would also find that what was said was ambiguous, can we say that there is no contract at all.

Raffles v. *Wichelhaus* (1864) 159 Eng. Rep. 375 may be an instance of such an unusual case. The plaintiff sold the defendant 125 bales of cotton 'to arrive ex *Peerless* from Bombay' and tendered cotton which arrived in Liverpool on a ship of that name in December. The defendant refused to accept it on the ground that he had supposed that the contractual cotton to was to come from a different ship of the same name which had sailed from Bombay earlier and berthed in Liverpool in October. The court held that this would be a good defence, and rightly so, if after hearing all the evidence one accepts that the reasonable bystander would have been unable to say for sure to which of the homonymous ships the agreement referred, for then there would be no contract.

The second problem is whether a buyer of goods which prove defective can avoid the sale on the ground that on entering the contract he was mistaken as to their actual quality. This is a matter of some practical importance. Normally a buyer seeks to avoid liability on the basis that the seller was in breach of contract by delivering non-conforming goods, but if he has failed to give the required notice or allowed the claim to become time-barred his claim for breach of contract is doomed, and it would be greatly to his advantage to have recourse to the rules of avoidance for mistake. Is this allowable?

Any such attempt is summarily rejected by courts in Germany (BGHZ 34, 32), the French courts vary in their response (see Civ. 11 Feb. 1981, JCP 1982. II. 19758 noted by GHESTIN; Civ. 28 June 1988, D. 1989, 450 noted by LAPOYADE DESCHAMPS), and the Swiss courts allow it readily. In a recent case the Swiss Bundesgericht (BGE 114 II 131) allowed a buyer whose claim on the contract was time-barred under art. 210 OR to found on his mistake as to the qualities of the thing since 'technical developments and the growth of mass contracts have so altered the meaning and function of the simple contract of sale that the ill-served buyer appears more than ever as the weaker party' (at p. 138). Leaving aside the point that these reasons seem ill adapted to the actual case, which concerned the purchase of an expensive painting—hardly a 'mass contract' nor yet one in which the buyer has a particular call on the sympathy of the system—there are other objections: if one thinks, as one well may, that the period within which claims for breach of warranty of quality must be made is too short, the problem should be solved at source, namely in the law of sales, and not by conscripting the rules on avoidance for mistake.—If it is an international sale to which the Vienna Convention is applicable, a buyer who, by the operation of art. 39 CISG, has lost his remedies under art. 45 ff., certainly cannot invoke national rules on avoidance for mistake, for the rules of CISG as to the rights of the buyer when defective goods have been delivered are to be seen as a *lex specialis*. See VON CAEMMERER/SCHLECHTRIEM (-HUBER) art. 45 *UN Kaufrecht* mn. 50, 54; P. HUBER, 'UN-Kaufrecht und Irrtumsanfechtung', *ZEuP* 2 (1994) 585; and the detailed treatment in FLESCH, *Mängelhaftung und Beschaffenheitsirrtum beim Kauf* (1994).

II

In *Germany* §119 BGB makes a distinction which originated with Savigny. According to him one must distinguish the stage at which a party forms his intention from the stage at which he gives it expression; a mistake at the former stage is legally insignificant since it is merely a mistake as to motive, whereas avoidance is justified if an intention unaffected by mistake is incorrectly expressed. §119(1) BGB therefore provides that a promise or other declaration may be avoided if it is one which the party 'really did not intend to make', as where he made a slip in what he said or wrote (*Erklärungsirrtum*), and §119(1) BGB proceeds to provide that even if he did intend to say or write what he did, he may avoid, provided he thought it meant something quite different from the meaning reasonably attributed to it by the other party (*Inhaltsirrtum*).

For example, if a person intended to buy ten bottles of soda water for a birthday party and by a slip of the tongue mistakenly orders a hundred bottles, he may rescind the contract, but not if he orders ten bottles because he mistakenly thinks his guests are teetotallers. The distinction is not, however, always so easy to draw: if a testator, in instituting his 'statutory heirs', has in mind those who would be statutory heirs under a statute which has been repealed, this is an *Inhaltsirrtum* under §119 par. 1 BGB (RGZ 70, 391, 394); the same is true if a guarantor mistakenly believes that the creditor's claim is a secured one (RGZ 75, 271). So also, according to STAUDINGER-DILCHER (*Bürgerliches Gesetzbuch* (12th edn., 1980) n. 20 to §119 BGB), it is an *Inhaltsirrtum* if a person buying a cellar full of wine thinks it contains 1,000 bottles when there are only 850. If so, the purchaser may rescind without any inquiry into the question whether the contract, reasonably construed, might not put the risk of any inaccuracy in the estimate of quantity on him rather than on the vendor.

However, the question whether a mistake is one which is covered by §119 par. 1 BGB or an error in motive, which is not, is not of great practical importance in Germany. This is because under §119 par. 2 BGB one may also rescind for errors of motive, provided they concern qualities of the person or the thing 'which are normally regarded as essential'. More specific meaning has been given to this general clause by the decided cases.

In the case of the Chinese vase with which we started the Reichsgericht allowed the vendor to rescind on the ground of mistake as to an essential quality (RGZ 124, 115). So, too, the buyer of land may rescind the sale if he mistakenly believed that he could prevent development on the neighbouring plot (RGZ 61, 86), as may the seller on credit for a mistake as to the buyer's creditworthiness (RGZ 66, 385). It even used to be possible to rescind an adoption, treated in Germany as a contract subject to court approval, if it transpired that at the time of adoption the child had latent vices ineradicable by education (RGZ 147, 310; 152, 228; but see now §1760 BGB).—But the concept of essential qualities includes 'only those factual and legal qualities of things which specifically characterize them, not factors which only have an indirect effect on their value' (BGHZ 16, 54, 57). Thus it is not an essential quality of a piece of land that it does not belong to the vendor (BGHZ 34, 41), nor that it is worth less than the purchaser supposed when he bought it (RG HRR 1932 no. 224, invariable holding).

What is remarkable about this rule is that it wholly ignores the question whether the promisor was at fault in being mistaken and whether the mistake was ascertainable to the other party or caused by him, even quite innocently.

The *Austrian* Civil Code offers a most original, attractive and satisfactory solution. A 'mistake in the reasons for contracting' being in principle irrelevant (§901 sent. 2 ABGB), a mistake is significant, as in the German BGB, only if it is one 'which concerns the principal object or an essential attribute of it to which the intention was principally and expressly directed' (§871 ABGB); but even if he makes a mistake of this kind the mistaken party cannot rescind his promise unless in addition he proves one of three facts: that the other party *caused* the mistake, that the mistake must have been *obvious* to the other party in all the circumstances, or finally that the mistake was *notified* to the other party in good time.

According to the cases, a mistake may be *caused* though it was induced neither deliberately nor negligently; any behaviour which causes the mistake is sufficient. Even silence can 'cause' a mistake in the sense of §871 ABGB if one party should have informed the other that the assumptions he would normally make about certain facts related to the transaction were erroneous.

Thus the Oberste Gerichtshof granted recission in a case in which the purchaser of a house erroneously believed that it was of massive construction. The court concluded that in the light of the attendant circumstances the vendor should have drawn the purchaser's attention to the fact that the house was not substantially built. Thus the vendor 'caused' the mistake and rescission was in order (OGH 20 April 1955, SZ 28 no. 103).

Rescission may also be granted for a mistake concerning 'the principal object' if it is shown that the other party *knew* of the error or *would have known* if he had exercised normal and proper care. Failing this, the mistaken party may show that he *notified* the error 'in good time', that is, brought it to the attention of the other party before the other party had acted in reliance on the mistaken promise, as by incurring expenses in performing the contract (compare OGH 31 Oct. 1951, SZ 24 no. 288). Thus a vendor in error concerning the qualities of the thing, even an 'essential' quality in the sense of §871 ABGB, loses his right to rescind as soon as the purchaser resells the object or lets it out on hire, or takes possession of the house which he bought, or rearranges his business around the purchased machinery. This rule applies unless the vendor can show that the purchaser caused his mistake or should have known of it.

Compare RUMMEL, I *Kommentar zum ABGB* (1983) §871 mn. 17. In OGH 3 March 1932, SZ 14 no. 40, a creditor who had received part payment erroneously declared that he had received payment in full. The court allowed him to rescind this declaration, even although in the circumstances of the case the mistake might well not have been known to the debtor, since 'according to the law a mistaken party is not bound to his mistaken declaration when its addressee, though entitled under the doctrine of reliance to treat it as accurate, has been informed of the error before he took any action or made any arrangements in reliance on the declaration'.

While German law gives the promisee a claim for the harm he suffered in reliance on the promise now rescinded (§122 BGB), Austrian law does not. There is a good reason for this. In Austrian law the limitations on rescission for error are such that there is no need for a claim of this sort: in the few cases where rescission is permitted, either the promisee has suffered no reliance damage worth mentioning or he deserves no protection because he himself was responsible for causing the error or not knowing of it.

Swiss law also makes the fundamental distinction between an error of motive and an error in the transaction; art. 23 OR declares that only an essential error may be taken into account, and art. 24 par. 2 OR states that an error in motive is not essential. At first sight the concept of 'essentiality' appears to be more specific than in German law since four types of essential error are listed, including errors concerning the nature of the transaction and error concerning the identity of the other party or the object of the contract, types of error which remind us of the *error in negotio, error in persona*, and *error in objecto* known to the Roman-based *Gemeines Recht*. A mistake is also relevant when a party promises much more, or qualifies his promise much less, 'than was his intention'.

An example of such an error may be found in BGE 105 II 23: a ring displayed in a jeweller's window bore a price tag of 1,380 S.fr. A customer paid this sum and took delivery of the ring. On proving that that price had been affixed by mistake and that the intended price had been 13,800 S.fr., the jeweller was allowed to rescind the sale under art 24(1) no. 3 OR, subject to paying damages under art. 26 OR because the error was due to his own negligence.

Finally an error is regarded as essential if 'it related to a particular matter which the mistaken party would, consistently with commercial good faith, regard as forming the necessary basis of the transaction' (art. 24(1) no. 4 OR). This 'error as to the basis of the transaction' is the most important of the 'essential' errors in art. 24. The legislator has left the preconditions of this type of mistake quite vague—in keeping with the style of Swiss law, which prefers to refer difficult questions to judicial discretion. It is, however, accepted that it is not a 'basic error' when a person makes a false supposition about a matter which only he would regard as important: the courts require 'a common misapprehension of both parties, whether they were conscious of it or not, regarding something which objectively was an indispensable precondition of the contract being formed'.

It was so held in BGE 113 II 25, 27; see also BGE 109 II 322; BGE 79 II 272, BGE 55 II 189.—'Common mistake' is a ground for avoidance in other legal systems also, such as the Netherlands ('if the other party suffered from the same misapprehension on making the contract as the mistaken party' (art. 6:228c NBW)), and even, quite exceptionally for that system, the Common Law (see below p. 421). Common mistake is not covered as such in the BGB, but the courts fill the gap by applying the rules of the 'collapse of the foundation of the transaction'. See, for example, BGH NJW 1976, 565 (transferor and transferee of football player both supposed he would be licensed to play); BGH NJW 1987, 98 (common belief that a third party had no right of pre-emption); BGH NJW 1990, 567 (shared mistake over the probable throughput of a bar being leased).

According to art. 26 OR the party seeking rescission of a contract for mistake must pay damages only if the mistake was due to his own negligence, and while such damages are normally limited to the other party's reliance interest the judge may award more if he thinks fit to do so. In imposing liability only where there is fault (contrast §122 BGB) Swiss law follows out the logic of *culpa in contrahendo*. But this is perhaps too lenient in view of the risks to which a perfectly innocent mistake can expose the other party.

III

When we turn to the Romanistic legal family and consider *French* law, we find that the rules in the Code civil offer the judges even less in the way of firm standards for the solution of mistake cases than German, Austrian or Swiss law: the Code civil simply says in art. 1110 that a mistake is significant when it relates to *la substance même de la chose*. The courts, however, have long since included mistakes relating to *qualités substantielles de la chose*. Thus the purchaser of a plot of land for development can avoid the purchase if it turns out to be unsuitable for building (Civ. 2 Mar. 1964, Bull. I no. 122) or to be smaller than contracted for (Civ. 15 Dec. 1981, DS 1982 I.R. 164). Likewise when the picture sold is not by the hand of the supposed painter (Civ. 20 Oct. 1970, JCP 1971.II.16916 noted by GHESTIN) or when pearls sold as natural prove to be artificial (Req. 5 Nov. 1929, S. 1930.1.180). Avoidance has been permitted to an heir who disclaimed an inheritance on the mistaken supposition that if he did so it would fall to a particular third party (Civ. 15 June 1960, JCP 1961.II.12274), and to an insured who cancelled his policy on 15 October with effect from 1 October, only to discover many months later that an insured event had occurred between these dates (Civ. 25 Feb. 1986, Bull. I no. 40). So, too, a seller can avoid the sale at a low price of a picture later found to be an Old Master.

See the various decisions in the celebrated 'Poussin affair': Civ. 13 Dec. 1983, D. 1984, 940 noted by AUBERT, and Versailles 7 Jan. 1987, JCP 1988.II.21121 noted by GHESTIN. See also Civ. 25 May 1992, JCP 1992.IV.2129: a person bought for 55,000 FF a picture 'attributed to Fragonard'; when he had it restored it turned out to be an authentic Fragonard which he sold to the Louvre for 5.15 million FF. The seller was allowed to rescind the contract for mistake, subject to a claim by the buyer for his expenses in the amount of 1.5 million FF as unjustified enrichment (!). Finally, there was the 'cantharus case' before the Hoge Raad (NJ 1960 no. 59): a metal beaker discovered in the Meuse during dredging operations turned out, after tireless research by the buyer, to be a Roman cantharus from the second century, of inestimable value. The seller's claim for rescission was rightly rejected: the public has an interest in the ascertainment of the origin of artefacts esteemed by historians, and the buyer would be deterred from spending time and energy on such research if he had to return the piece to the seller in the event his research bore fruit.

These decisions may give the impression that a contract can be avoided for any mistake whatever, provided it is not wholly trivial, but in reality French courts have found ways to restrict the right to avoid a contract for error as to qualities and so take the interests of the other party into account.

Thus a mistake is relevant only when it was the *motif principal ou déterminant* for entering the contract. A mistake constitutes the determining motive if the mistaken party would never have concluded the contract but for the mistake; it is not sufficient if he would have concluded the contract on different terms. Thus if a person undertakes a guarantee in the erroneous belief that the creditor's claim is secured and that the securities will pass to him should he pay, he cannot rescind the guarantee on the ground of this error if it appears at the trial that he had other reasons for undertaking the guarantee (Req. 16 March 1898, DP 1898. 1. 301). Naturally a person cannot point to a detail which is objectively trivial and claim that his error on that matter was the principal inducement for entering the contract. Thus while it is a relevant error to think that the picture one is buying is by Rubens, when it is not (Paris 22 Feb. D. 1950, 269), it is not a relevant error to suppose that a picture, correctly attributed to Delacroix, had hung in the painter's bedroom, even if the purchaser alleges he was induced to buy it because he thought it had. (Trib. civ. Seine 8 Dec. 1950, D. 1951, 50; similarly, Trib. paix Nantes, 23 Jan. 1947, 220, and Civ. 26 Jan. 1972, D. 1972, 517.)

French courts have also on occasion refused to allow avoidance when the claimant's mistake related only to his motive for contracting. Some scholars approve of this, notably GHESTIN (no. 401): a mistake over a 'qualité substantielle' should be relevant only if it relates to 'une qualité expressément ou tacitement convenue'. The same result emerges from the frequently used formula that erroneous suppositions or expectations justify avoidance only if they 'sont entrées dans le champ contractuel'.

The owner who insures his property against damage in the belief that the usufructuary will pay or reimburse the premiums cannot avoid the policy when this belief proves erroneous, for *les motifs vrais ou erronés qui peuvent inciter une partie à conclure une opération à titre onéreux . . . sont sans influence sur la validité de l'opération* (Civ. 3 Aug. 1942, D. A. 1943, 18). A contract for the supply of materials for an advertising campaign cannot be avoided when the campaign is a failure (Civ. 16 May 1939, S. 1939.1.260); and a bank can hold its customer to a loan agreement although the purchase of the car to be bought with the borrowed funds never came to pass (14 Dec. 1977, Bull. 1977.IV.no.293). The Cour de Cassation decided likewise in a case where the director of a company was sued on his guarantee of the company's debts, the relevant transactions having been concluded after the director had left it: even if the director supposed that his guarantee covered only debts incurred while he was in office and this was one of the 'motifs déterminants' for his giving the guarantee, these motives were irrelevant, 'n'ayant pas été introduits dans le champ contractuel' (Com. 6 Dec. 1988, D.S. 1988, 185 noted by AYNES).—The same idea crops up in German books (FLUME, *Allgemeiner Teil des Bürgerlichen Rechts, Das Rechtsgeschäft* (2nd edn. 1975) 477 f.) and in court decisions (BGHZ 16, 54, 57 f.; BGHZ 88, 240, 246).

It is also agreed—although the Code civil says nothing about it—that an error can be taken into account only if it is *excusable*. The principal instance of an inexcusable and therefore irrelevant mistake occurs when the mistaken party had the means of acquainting himself with the true state of facts before entering the contract. A person who makes an excavation pursuant to contract and quite unexpectedly hits rock cannot rescind if he had had the opportunity of investigating the ground beforehand (Paris 30 June 1866, DP 1874. 2. 182). A lessee of hunting rights who finds much less game than he expected cannot rescind the contract if a walk through the land would have disclosed the state of the game (Amiens 30 Nov. 1954, D. 1955, 420). A person who takes out an insurance policy without realizing that he already has cover for that risk cannot rescind the contract if his affairs were in evident disarray and he was a person with 'une certaine expérience des assurances' (Civ. 29 June 1959, Bull. civ. 1959. I. 267).

The rules of the *Italian* Codice civile (arts. 1427–33) are very forward-looking, having been influenced by Austrian and Swiss law as well as by the decisions of the French courts. They quite rightly abandon the notion of error in motive, and take account of mistakes only if they are essential, under art. 1429, and if the other party could have been aware of them. A mistake is essential if it concerns the nature or object of a contract; it is also essential if it concerns the identity or qualities of the contractual object or of the other party to the contract, provided that these were factors determinative of entering the contract, either objectively or in the circumstances of the case. An error of law is also essential if it was the only or principal reason for entering the contract.

In addition it must always be shown that the error would have been noticed by the other party had he exercised reasonable and proper care. If a picture bought as a real Picasso turns out to be a forgery, the purchaser can only rescind if the vendor could have known that it was a forgery; this requirement was held satisfied in a case where the vendor himself was a painter (App. Milano 5 June 1951, Foro pad. 1951. I. 874).

IV

The posture of the Common Law on the question in issue is quite distinctive. Unlike the Continental civil codes which were influenced by the intention theory, the Common Law had no general rules on avoiding contracts for mistake until well into the nineteenth century. It was true that earlier, as now, a contract could be avoided if one party during the negotiations had made an untrue statement and the other party entered the contract in reliance on that misrepresentation. But the accent is not so much on the mistake caused as on the *causing* of the mistake. Nowadays a contract may also be avoided for a mistake even if it was not caused by the other party, but this occurs only in special situations and has been so only since the second half of the nineteenth century, when judges were familiar with Roman law and were influenced by Continental doctrine, especially that of POTHIER. Finally, some modification of the strict rules of the Common Law designed to protect the security of transactions is possible under a few special rules developed by the Courts of Equity. One cannot, however, even with the best will in the world, say that these form an integrated and easily comprehensible whole.

The first striking feature of the Common Law is that it makes a special category of cases where the mistake is caused by an inaccurate statement or misrepresentation by the other party. If the misstatement was made with the deliberate intention of misleading or deceiving, it is a fraudulent misrepresentation which entitles the mistaken party to rescind the contract and claim damages. Even when the other party is in perfect good faith, that is, acted without any fraud, the mistaken party may be able to claim damages and also, if he acts quickly, rescind the contract. No damages will be awarded if the defendant can show that he had reasonable grounds for believing that what he said was true, that he was not at fault, that his misrepresentation was 'innocent' (Misrepresentation Act 1967, s. 2 (1)), but even for an innocent misrepresentation the contract may be rescinded, subject to this, that if rescission would be too severe a sanction since it would be small harm to the mistaken party to uphold the contract and a serious blow to the other to rescind it, the court can hold the mistaken party to the contract and pay him off with an award of damages, if it is of opinion that

'it would be equitable to do so, having regard to the nature of the misrepresentation and the loss that would be caused by it if the contract were upheld, as well as to the loss that rescission would cause to the other party'. On this see TREITEL 300 ff.; CHESHIRE/FIFOOT/FURMSTON 273 ff.; CARTWRIGHT 68 ff.

It is not always clear precisely what constitutes a misrepresentation. In general a misrepresentation is a false statement made before or at the time of the conclusion of the contract which caused the misrepresentee to enter the contract or contributed to his doing so. A statement as to the law or as to matters lying in the future is not taken into account, and the same is true of mere statements of opinion and of commercial puffs which no one in business could reasonably take seriously.

There may be difficult borderline cases. For example, the inaccurate statement by an auctioneer of agricultural land that it was 'very fertile and capable of development' was held to be 'a mere flourishing description by an auctioneer' (*Dimmock* v. *Hallett*, (1866) LR 2 Ch. App. 21) while the statement of a vendor of land that it was let to 'a most desirable tenant' gave rise to rescission when it was shown that at the time of the contract the tenant was already several months in arrears with the rent (*Smith* v. *Land and House Property Corp.*, (1884) 28 Ch. D. 7.—If a person inaccurately asserts that the land he is selling can graze 2,000 sheep, this will be a misrepresentation if he himself had farmed sheep there and his statement was apparently based on personal experience; otherwise it may be just sales talk not giving rise to liability (see *Bissett* v. *Wilkinson* [1927] AC 177).—Even if a misrepresentation is such as to entitle the misrepresentee to rescind, he must nevertheless stand by the contract if he waits too long (see *Leaf* v. *International Galleries* [1950] 2 KB 86), or implicitly affirms the contract in some other way.

In the Common Law 'mistake' designates only an error which is *not* due to a misrepresentation. When both parties make the same mistake (common mistake) on a critical matter the contract may be void. This is so where the person, thing or right which is the subject matter of the contract is non-existent, as where the object sold had perished before the contract was formed (*res extincta*) or belonged to the buyer already (*res sua*), or where parties made a separation or maintenance agreement on the assumption that they were married (*Galloway* v. *Galloway* (1914) 30 TLR 531), or where a life insurance policy was sold and both buyer and seller were unaware that the *cestui que vie* had already shuffled off the mortal coil (*Scott* v. *Coulson* [1903] 2 Ch. 349). There are indications in the law reports that a contract can also be void for common mistake when the mistake relates not so much to the actual object of the contract as to other matters regarded by the parties as fundamental.

See *Bell* v. *Lever Brothers Ltd.* [1932] AC 161. On the takeover of an oil company one of its managers, Bell, agreed to accept a golden handshake of £30,000. The company then discovered that he had previously been guilty of misconduct which would have justified them in dismissing him instantly without pay, and sought to be released from its agreement. Although its claim was rejected, LORD WARRINGTON asked whether there had been a 'mistake as to some facts which by the common intention of the parties, whether expressed or more generally implied, constitute the underlying assumption without which the parties would not have made the contract they did' (at 206).

Where the common mistake is not serious enough to justify avoiding a contract at law, certain rules developed by Courts of Equity may be used to complete, modify or reduce it. See, for example, *Grist* v. *Bailey* [1967] Ch. 532, where property was sold at a low price because both parties erroneously supposed that it was subject to a protected tenancy: the seller's defence of common mistake at law was rejected, but the court held that the mistake was serious enough for equity to come to his assistance and held that he need only sell at the higher price justified by the facts now known.

In cases where there is no common mistake but either the parties have mis-understood each other or only one party was in error, the sole question for the English judge is whether a contract came about at all. If so, there is in prin-ciple no possibility of avoiding the contract for mistake: the only question is whether what the parties said was congruent and unambiguous. For the few exceptions, see TREITEL 261 ff.; CHESHIRE/FIFOOT/FURMSTON 231 ff.

American law has an equally strong tendency to limit the cases where con-tracts may be avoided for error, but it does not make all the fine and some-times strained distinctions of English law. This may be because the principle of *stare decisis* is rather less strong in the United States than in England, so that unhappy precedents have a less marked effect on subsequent develop-ments, and because the much larger number of decisions on mistake in the United States makes it proportionally less likely that a subtle technicality will survive.

So far as can be seen, American courts which have to decide cases invol-ving mistake are ready to entertain all the considerations which can reason-ably be adduced in this context. The veniality of the error of the mistaken party, whether the other party should have realized it, the extent to which the other party has acted or acted reasonably in reliance on the mistaken party's promise, the possibility of resuming the status quo ante—all these circumstances play a part in proportion to their importance in cases of the type before the court.

Unfortunately there is no room here to go through the cases and show how the American courts actually take account of these various considerations, so we can only give a few instances. In *Grant Marble Co. v. Abbot*, 142 Wis. 279, 124 NW 264 (1910), the plaintiff had contracted to put marble floors in a building with six storeys, but his tender was calculated on the erroneous basis that the building had only five. After the work had been carried out, the plaintiff claimed a reasonable supplement, but his claim failed since the court held that the contract was binding notwithstanding the mistake: 'Such mistake cannot be charged to defendant, but must rest upon the party whose negligence caused it. All the facts were within reach of plaintiff and he had but to open his eyes and see them. His own architect who had full knowledge of the facts was within call and could have been consulted upon the subject if plaintiff had desired.'—See also *Leonard* v. *Howard*, 67 Ore. 203, 135 P. 549 (1913) and *Stein-meyer* v. *Schroeppel*, 226 Ill. 9, 80 NE 564 (1907).—The decision is different if the offeree purports to accept an offer which he knows to have been made in error: in such a case even a negligent offeror is not bound by the contract; see *State of Con-necticut* v. *McGraw & Co.*, 41 F. Supp. 369 (D. Conn. 1941).—The courts are especially ready to bar rescission for error if the promisee has already, in reliance on the validity of the contract, undergone a 'change of position' which makes it difficult or impos-sible to reinstate the status quo ante; on this see the cases cited in CORBIN §606. A partial explanation of this may lie in the fact that American law does not yet impose a general duty on the mistaken party to compensate the other party for his reliance damage (see PALMER (above p. 410) 58 ff.) and that therefore a court would rather leave the *mistaken party* to suffer the consequences of his error than shift the loss to the other party by giving effect to the mistake.—The rules which American courts apply when rescission is sought on the ground of mistake or misrepresentation may conveniently be approached through Restatement (Second) of Contracts (1981) §151 ff.

V

As we have seen, the various systems offer a perplexing abundance of different viewpoints on the question when a contract can or cannot be avoided for mistake. Even so, a few common principles can be discerned.

It is increasingly being recognized that a contract should not be avoided simply because one of the parties made a mistake either in forming his intention or in expressing it. Such a person would naturally like to avoid the contract, but the other party has a countervailing interest in maintaining it and having his reliance on its validity protected. Of these conflicting interests the very general tendency today is to prefer the interest in security of transactions and legal certainty, and treat avoidance for error as very much the exception. After all, in life itself one has to put up with the consequences of one's own mistakes. Why should it be any different where the mistake is made in a contract? If one accepts this natural principle it will be seen that the risk of making a mistake must rest with the party who makes it, and that the doctrine of intention, traces of which still lurk in Continental rules relating to mistake, is socially inappropriate. In other words, a mistake should have effect only if this is consistent with the contract, properly interpreted, and if in addition there are *special reasons* for not protecting the other party's reliance on its validity. This is the traditional posture of the Common Law, but it is shared also by Austria, whose §871 ABGB was formulated under the influence of the natural lawyers' predilection for protecting transactions. This position is also adopted by the more recent civil codes, notably the Codice civile and the Dutch NBW, whereas in Germany and France it has fallen to the courts to try to interpret and apply texts which are unduly lax and vague in such a way as to do justice to the idea of protecting commerce and reliance.

In many cases the very terms of the contract will show that avoidance for mistake is excluded. This is the case, for example, where the goods delivered pursuant to a sale do not match the contractual requirements as to quality, quantity or description, or indeed where no goods at all are delivered. Although the buyer could plausibly allege that he made a 'mistake' in supposing that the seller would fulfil his contract, it would be quite wrong to displace the buyer's remedies on breach by granting him an extra or alternative claim to avoid the contract for mistake. Likewise a party cannot invoke a mistake the risk of which is put on him by the contract. This is generally recognized where the contract is of an aleatory or speculative nature, but all contracts allocate risks to some extent, and any contract, if sufficiently scrutinized, will disclose whether or not particular misapprehensions or false expectations are to be borne by the party who entertained them; if so, he must bear the consequences and not seek avoidance.

If avoidance for mistake is to be exceptional, what special reasons can there be for allowing it? First, a person cannot claim that he relied on a contract if he knew or should have known that the other party was making a mistake and nevertheless failed to correct it in circumstances such that commercial decency required him to do so. So, too, if he actually caused the other party's mistake by what he said or implied and the other party reasonably relied on him in entering the contract, which he would not otherwise have done, or not on those terms. Finally, unless the contract itself puts the risk of mistake on the party now seeking avoidance, avoidance may be proper if both parties made the same mistake on a matter fundamental to the transaction.

To the same effect is the draft Law for the Unification of the Rules Relating to the Validity of International Sales of Goods (*Rev.dr.unif.* 1973 I 60 = Int. Leg. Mat. 17 (1978) 282) prepared by UNIDROIT. According to art. 6 a contract can be avoided for error only when the error is fundamental and does not relate to matters of which the risk is expressly or implicitly placed on the mistaken party. Even if these requirements are met there is a right to avoid only when in addition 'the other party has made the same mistake, or has caused the mistake, or knew or ought to have known of the mistake and it was contrary to reasonable commercial standards of fair dealing to leave the mistaken party in error'. As to this draft law see also the preliminary draft prepared by the Max Planck Institute for Foreign and International Private Law in *RabelsZ* (1968) 201 and 243.

VI

Mistake and deceit have this in common, that the deceived party enters the contract under a mistake, the difference being that in deceit this mistake is deliberately caused by the other party. One can therefore see in cases of deceit a special instance of 'caused mistake'. This is done by English law: it has a category of misrepresentation within which it distinguishes innocent or negligent misrepresentations from those where the misrepresentor was aware that what he was saying was not true. In the last case one speaks of fraudulent misrepresentation, in France and other Romanistic systems of *dol* or *dolo*, in Germany and Switzerland of *arglistige* or *absichtliche Täuschung*, in Austria of *List*, and in the Netherlands of *bedrog*.

The Romanistic systems often suggest that the deceit must be effected by specially deceptive practices. Thus art. 1116 Code civil speaks of *manoeuvres*, art. 1439 Codice civile of *raggiri*, the Spanish Civil Code of *maquinaciones insidiosas* (art. 1269). Even so, it is admitted on all hands that a simple lie can constitute deceit.

It is also accepted that avoidance is possible even if the resulting mistake is simply one of motive, or not fundamental, and would not justify avoidance in the absence of deceit.

This is explicit in art. 28 (1) OR, and true also in Austria (OGH 3 Feb. 1932, SZ 14, 18), Germany (RGZ 81, 13, 16), the Netherlands (HR 27 Jan. 1950, Ned. Jur. 1950 no. 559), France (Com. 19 Dec. 1961, D. 1962, 240), and in American decisions (see *New York Life Ins. Co.* v. *McLaughlin* 112 Vt. 402, 26 A.2d 108 (1942) and *De Joseph* v. *Zambelli* 392 Pa. 24, 139 A.2d 644 (1958).

In some Romanistic systems one finds the view that deceit entitles the deceived party to avoid only if he would not have entered the contract *at all* if properly informed, whereas if he would have contracted, but on more favourable terms, he has suffered only *dolus incidens* and can claim only damages, such as a diminution of the price.

This view stems from art. 1116 Code civil (likewise art. 1440 Codice civile, art. 1270(2) Spanish Civil Code), which permits avoidance in the case of deceit 'lorsque les manoeuvres pratiquées par l'une des parties sont telles qu'il est évident que, sans ces manoeuvres, l'autre partie n'aurait pas contracté'.—The Swiss courts have gone both ways on the question; for one view see BGE 64 II 142, for the other BGE 81 II 213. The distinction is unconvincing. After all, if the buyer has the choice between avoiding the contract and claiming a reduction in the price when the goods delivered are defective, *a fortiori* he should have a similar choice if he has been deceived about their quality.

In Anglo-American law deceit is called 'fraudulent misrepresentation' or simply 'fraud'. For this it must be shown that the representor made statements of fact (and not simply standard commercial puffs) in the knowledge, at the least, that they might well be false.

According to the leading case of *Derry* v. *Peek* (1889) 14 App. Cas. 337, 374: 'Fraud is proved when it is shown that a false representation has been made knowingly without belief in its truth, or recklessly, careless whether it be true or false.' See also Restatement (Second) of Contracts §162, and the Report of the Max Planck Institute (above p. 424) p. 110 f.

Courts everywhere are agreed on what constitutes deceit, though there are often slight variations, as in the question when mere silence regarding a relevant fact may amount to deceit so as to entitle the other party to avoid the contract.

In the view of German courts, failure to state a fact constitutes deceit only if there was a duty to declare it, and it depends on the circumstances of the individual case whether there was such a duty or not. For example, it is recognized that in negotiating a sales contract parties cannot expect to be told of the general market conditions relevant to the price; on the other hand, it has repeatedly been decided that good faith requires the disclosure of such circumstances concerning the object of the sale as are evidently material to the decision whether to enter the contract or not.

Thus if the joists or rafters of a house have been seriously affected by woodworm, the person selling it must volunteer this information (BGH NJW 1965, 34).—It has also been held deceitful for a banker to sell shares in a mining company at the normal daily price when he already knew that the mine had been flooded (see RGZ III, 235).—In the opinion of the Bundesgerichtshof the vendor of a well-maintained car is bound to volunteer the fact that the car has been involved in a collision: if he fails to do so the purchaser may avoid the contract on the ground of deceit (BGH NJW 1982, 1386).—The Court of Cassation in France has stated the following principle: 'Le dol peut être constitué par le silence d'une partie dissimulant à son cocontractant un fait qui, s'il avait été connu de lui, l'aurait empêché de contracter.' (Civ. 15 Jan. 1971, Bull. I no. 38; Civ. 2 Oct. 1974, Bull. III no. 330, and frequently thereafter). For example, a sale of land was held to be voidable for *dol par réticence* when the seller knew the buyer was planning to open a restaurant and failed to tell him that there was no connection for drinking water (Civ. 7 May 1954, Bull. III no. 186). Likewise a person who sold land to a commune was able to avoid the contract because he had not been told during the negotiations that the commune had already proceeded to alter its building plans, with consequent enhancement of the value of the land (Civ. 27 Mar. 1991, Bull. III no. 108, and on it MESTRE in *Rev. trim. dr. civ.* 91 (1992) 81). Another instance of *dol par réticence* arises when a bank fails to tell a prospective guarantor *que la situation de son débiteur est irrémédiablement compromise ou à tout le moins lourdement obérée* (Civ. 10 May 1989, Bull. I no. 187).

The Common Law is much more severe. There is admittedly a 'duty of disclosure' between insured and insurer and in certain other contracts 'uberrimae fidei', as well as where there is a particular relationship of trust between the parties, as between trustee and beneficiary, ward and pupil, parent and child, or principal and agent, but there is no general rule as to duties of disclosure in negotiations. The traditional view, dating back to the robust individualism of the nineteenth century, is that each party must obtain the necessary information for himself and cannot expect it to be supplied by the other, even when that other is aware of his ignorance and could easily put him right.

In *Smith* v. *Hughes* (1871) LR 6 QB 597 the seller well knew that the buyer was under a misapprehension about the quality of the goods being sold, but did not correct him. The court held the buyer bound: 'the question is not what a man of scrupulous morality or nice honour would do under such circumstances . . . Whatever may be the case in a court of morals there is no legal obligation on the vendor to inform the buyer that he is under a mistake, not induced by the act of the vendor' (at 603, 607). In *Banque Financière* v. *Westgate Ins. Co.* [1989] 2 All ER 952, 1010 SLADE LJ said this: 'The general principle that there is no obligation to speak within the context of negotiations for an ordinary commercial contract . . . is one of the foundations of our law of contract, and must have been the basis of many decisions over the years. There are countless cases in which one party to a contract has in the course of negotiations failed to disclose a fact known to him which the other party would have regarded as highly material, if it had been revealed. However, our law leaves that other party entirely without a remedy.'—This severe attitude of the Common Law may be appropriate for transactions between knowledgeable businessmen, but it is less sure, and sometimes questioned, that it is suited to transactions between private persons. See ATIYAH, *An Introduction to the Law of Contract* (5th edn. 1995) 268, and for comparative aspects NICHOLAS and LEGRAND (above p. 410).

Can one avoid a contract when one has been deceived not by the other party but by a *third party*? The answer everywhere is that in principle one cannot. It is true that one party has been deceived into entering the contract, but if the other was not involved in the deception, his interest in the validity of the contract is seen as superior: the party deceived remains bound by the contract and has to look for compensation to the third party who deceived him.

See §123 BGB; §875 ABGB; art. 28(2) OR; art. 3:44(5) NBW; art. 1439(2) Codice civile; art. 1116 Code civil and Civ. 26 Jan. 1977, Bull. I no. 40; Civ. 27 June 1973, D. 1973, 733 noted by MALAURIE.

This principle is restricted in two respects. First, it does not apply when the deceit is practised by the other party's representative, be he agent, assistant, proxy or confidant: if one lets someone else negotiate on one's behalf one must treat his deceit as one's own, and it is irrelevant whether one knows or should have known of the representative's deceit, or whether or not the representative has departed from his instructions. In England, too, deceit by an agent is imputed to his principal.

See, for example, BGHZ 20, 36, 39f.; BGE 63 II 77 and BGE 81 II 213, 217; OGH 28 June 1967, JBl. 1968, 365; Com. 27 Nov. 1972, Bull. IV no. 308; and BRAMWELL LJ in *Weir* v. *Bell* (1878) 3 Ex. D. 238, 245: 'Every person who authorizes another to act for him in the making of any contract, undertakes for the absence of fraud in that person in the execution of the authority given, as much as he undertakes for its absence in himself when he makes the contract.' Thus when a guarantor is sued on his guarantee by the bank he can defend on the ground that he was deceived by the debtor only if it exceptionally appears that the debtor was plainly acting at the instance of the bank as its assistant or trusted man. For such an exceptional case see OGH 29 April 1971, SZ 44 no. 59; BGH NJW 1962, 2195. A comparable case arises when a buyer who needs to finance a purchase negotiates for the loan not with the bank but with the seller whom the bank has equipped with forms and authorized to negotiate the loan; here if the buyer is deceived by the seller he can avoid the contract with the bank. See art. 11 of the EC Directive of 22 Dec. 1986 on Consumer Credit (87/102/EEC) and the relevant provisions in the consumer credit laws of the member states.

If the deceit is practised by a true 'third party' the dupe may still be able to avoid the contract if the other party knew or should in the circumstances have known of the third party's deceit.

This rule, too, is laid down in most of the laws just mentioned. In England one asks whether the other party had 'notice' or at least 'constructive notice' of the third party's deception. See *Barclays Bank Plc* v. *O'Brien* [1994] 1 AC 180: if a customer wishes to obtain credit for his own business purposes and the bank knows that he will ask his wife to go surety or to offer her interest in joint property as security, it must realize that he may downplay or conceal the risks involved or force or cajole her into assuming liability for his debts. The bank therefore has 'constructive notice' of any such deception or undue influence and the wife will have a defence against it. How can the bank protect itself? According to the House of Lords it can do so only by explaining the extent of the risk to the wife face-to-face in the absence of the husband or advising her to take independent advice. See also *CIBC Mortgages Plc* v. *Pitt* [1994] 1 AC 200.

VII

In all Continental legal systems the third 'defect of will', after mistake and deceit, is '*duress*'. Duress does not include physical compulsion, when, legally speaking, there is no declaration of will at all; duress is concerned only with psychical pressures.

Continental systems draw a sharp distinction between duress and the abuse of a predicament. No such distinction is known to Anglo-American law. This is because the Common Law, in the narrower sense, treated as 'duress' only those cases in which a person made a promise under threats of physical violence or imprisonment. The concept of 'undue influence', gradually developed by the Courts of Equity, is used for the cases which are dealt with under the concept of duress in the Continental civil codes. Comparatists who enter this area must therefore investigate the doctrine of 'undue influence' as well. Although the term is principally used in cases of abuse of positions of particular trust, such as exist between parent and child, guardian and ward, lawyer and client, doctor and patient, and confessor and penitent, cases of unfair exploitation of a person's difficulty, which are dealt with in German law as exploitation (*Wucher*) under §138 par. 2 BGB, are also dealt with in Anglo-American law as instances of 'undue influence' (see above Ch. 24 II).

A party who makes an offer of a contract may well paint a very gloomy picture of the unfortunate consequences of rejecting it. This may be a warning, but it is not duress. Duress requires a threat of evils which the threatener is in a position to engineer. Even such a threat may well be unobjectionable. A seller who tells a buyer that if he does not accept the present offer he will deliver no more goods is making a threat, but a permissible one. It would be impermissible only if there were further special circumstances, such as the seller's having so dominant a position in the market that his refusal to deliver would deprive the buyer of any chance of obtaining comparable goods. This shows that a contract can be avoided for duress only when the threat is in all the circumstances illegitimate or, as most Continental civil codes have it, 'unlawful' (*widerrechtlich*) (see §§123 BGB, 870 ABGB; art. 29(1) OR, 3:44(2) NBW). Herein lies the nub of the problem.

If what one threatens to do is contrary to law the threat is certainly illegitimate, regardless of the purpose to be achieved by it. This is the case, for example, of threats to use physical or fatal violence on the other party (*Barton* v. *Armstrong* [1976] AC 104) or take away his goods (*Maskell* v. *Horner* [1915] 3 KB 106) or have him imprisoned on a trumped-up charge. When the act threatened is not unlawful in itself the situation is more tricky, especially where the threat is to exercise a right, such as the right to bring a claim, to lay a criminal information, to protest a negotiable instrument or to terminate a contract.

Under art. 1438 Codice civile a contract can only be annulled in such cases if the threat is designed to produce an 'unjustified' or, as in art. 30(2) OR, a 'disproportionate' advantage. The Cour de Cassation requires the threatener's conduct to be 'abusive', as when the threat is to bring a claim for an ulterior purpose *en la détournant de son but* or when the threat is used to produce an advantage unconnected with or disproportionate to the other party's original obligation (Civ. 17 Jan. 1984, Bull. III no. 13). The case is particularly tricky where the threat is to prosecute the promisor's husband or other close relative. Here the Bundesgerichtshof has held the creditor's threat legitimate when the wife was in some way implicated in her husband's offence or profited from it in one way or another (BGHZ 25, 217), but in the absence of such special circumstances, the wife can avoid her promise, on the ground either of duress or of undue influence (see *Kaufman* v. *Gerson* [1904] 1 KB 591; *Mutual Finance Ltd.* v. *John Wetton & Sons* [1937] 2 KB 389).

How is one to deal with the case where a party to a contract threatens not to perform it unless it is modified in his favour? Of course the other party can resist the threat and sue for damages for breach if the threat is carried out, but to do so is often fraught with drawbacks.

When the seller of four carloads of eggs threatened his foreign buyer that unless he paid extra for the last two loads, the two loads already under way would be diverted, the buyer protested vigorously but submitted to the demand, since the alternative would have been to bring an action for damages in a foreign court: he was allowed to avoid his promise and refuse to pay the supplement demanded (BGE 32 II 641).

Decisions in England show that it can be very difficult to distinguish permissible from impermissible threats in dealings between businessmen, which can often be quite hard-nosed. Relevant considerations are whether the modification demanded is a sensible adjustment to a new situation, whether the other party protested or just gave in, whether he could reasonably be expected to stand firm and sue for damages for breach, and whether he had sufficient time for reflection on the options available. Also relevant is whether the threatened party disavowed the modification as soon as possible. In a case in 1978 a dockyard which had undertaken to build a tanker at a fixed price in dollars demanded an extra 10 per cent after the dollar fell in value; otherwise the tanker would not be delivered. The customer knew perfectly well that the demand was unjustified but submitted to it because it had already chartered the vessel to an oil company and wanted to avoid the difficulties and uncertainties of litigation. The court held that the dockyard's conduct was illegitimate and would have allowed the customer to reclaim the extra payment on the ground of *economic duress* had it not 'acquiesced' in the modification by letting eight months elapse after the crisis was brought to an end by the delivery of the tanker (*North Ocean Shipping Co.* v. *Hyundai Construction Co.* [1978] 3 All ER 1170. See also *Pao On* v. *Lau Yiu Long* [1980] AC 614 (PC); *Atlas Express Ltd.* v. *Kafco* [1989] 1 All ER 641; *Dimskal Shipping Co. S.A.* v. *International Transport Workers' Federation* [1991] 4 All ER 871). English judges may also have to ask whether the modification may not be ineffectual on the ground that there was no consideration for the disadvantaged party's agreement. See above p. 393 ff.

32

Representation

AMES, 'Undisclosed Principal—Rights and Liabilities', 18 *Yale LJ* 443 (1909).
BASEDOW, 'Das Vertretungsrecht im Spiegel konkurrierender Harmonisierungsentwürfe', *RabelsZ* 45 (1981) 196.
CAPELLE, Das Außenverhältnis bei der Vertretung fremder Interessen nach skandinavischem Recht', *Festschrift Leo Raape* (1948) 325.
FRIDMAN, *The Law of Agency* (6th edn., 1990).
GOODHART/HAMSON, 'Undisclosed Principals in Contract', 4 *Camb. LJ* 320 (1932).
HAMEL, *Le Contrat de commission* (1949).
MARKESINIS/MUNDAY, *An Outline of the Law of Agency* (3rd edn. 1992).
MÜLLER-FREIENFELS, *Die Vertretung beim Rechtsgeschäft* (1955).
——, *Stellvertretungsregelungen in Einheit und Vielfalt, Rechtsvergleichende Studien zur Stellvertretung* (1982; including reprints of most of the following articles).
——, 'Die "Anomalie" der verdeckten Stellvertretung (undisclosed agency) des englischen Rechts', *RabelsZ* 17 (1952) 578, 18 (1953) 12.
——, 'The Undisclosed Principal', 16 *Mod. L. Rev.* 299 (1953).
——, 'Comparative Aspects of Undisclosed Agency', 18 *Mod. L. Rev.* 33 (1955).
——, 'Law of Agency', 6 *Am. J. Comp. L.* 165 (1955).
——, 'Legal Relations in the Law of Agency: Power of Agency and Commercial Certainty', 13 *Am. J. Comp. L.* 193, 341 (1964).
——, 'The Law of Agency', in: *Civil Law in the Modern World* (ed. Yiannopoulos, 1965).
REYNOLDS, 'Agency: Theory and Practice', 94 *LQ Rev.* 224 (1978).
——, 'Practical Problems of the Undisclosed Principal Doctrine', 1983 *Curr. Leg. Prob.* 119.
SCHMITTHOFF, 'Agency in International Trade', *Rec. des Cours* 129 (1970–1) 107.
DE THEUX, *Le Droit de la représentation commerciale, Étude comparative et critique du statut des représentants salariés et des agents commerciaux*, 2 vols. (1975/77).

I

THE device of representation is an unavoidable necessity in any developed system which depends on the division of labour for the production and distribution of goods and services. The manufacturer delegates the purchase of raw materials to an agent, the heirs entrust the sale of the estate to an auctioneer, and the wholesaler sells his goods through trade representatives or commission agents. For any number of reasons these people, instead of acting themselves, which they may be unable or unwilling to do, use the assistance of persons who transact with third parties 'for them', 'on their account', 'as agents', or 'in their interest'. The function of these auxiliaries is always the same: they enable others to participate in commercial transactions by acting pursuant to a request, instruction or authorization from them.

This is too cursory a description of the subject matter of this chapter to satisfy the jurist: he needs rules by which to resolve the conflicts of interest involved and a conceptual structure to help him put these rules in a satisfactorily systematic order.

The concepts now found in Continental systems were first developed by the natural lawyers of the eighteenth century. Of 'agency' Roman law had no conception. Certainly the paterfamilias acquired ownership of everything any slave or member of his household obtained from a third party, but this was because in Roman society such persons were regarded as merely the extended arm of the paterfamilias, not because he had authorized them to acquire the property on his behalf. Later it was accepted that in certain situations one person might be liable for debts incurred by another, as where a person had put a vessel under the control of a captain or a business in the hands of a manager, or had equipped a son or trusted member of his household with a capital fund or *peculium* to administer. But these exceptions were narrowly circumscribed, and there was no general rule whereby the rights and duties arising from a contract made by one person could vest directly in another: 'Originally there was no direct agency at all. It is a legal miracle.'

RABEL, 'Die Stellvertretung in den hellenistischen Rechten und in Rom' (1934), reprinted in *Gesammelte Aufsätze* (Wolf ed., 1971) 492. On this and what follows see the details in ZIMMERMANN, *The Law of Obligations* (1990) 45 ff.

This 'miracle' first became possible when natural lawyers began to see that it is the autonomy of the parties on which contract law is really based, for this enabled them to view the matter from a wholly new standpoint. HUGO GROTIUS held that if a contract were made 'in the name of the person who was to have the thing' ownership would immediately vest in such person (*De iure belli ac pacis* Book 2 Ch. 11 § 18). CHRISTIAN WOLFF took an important step further and held that a contract made by a mandatary or procurator on the instruction of his principal could not only generate rights in the latter but also impose obligations and liabilities on him (*Institutiones iuris naturae et gentium* §§ 380 f.). This laid the foundation for the codes of the Enlightenment: a person conducting negotiations could generate rights and duties in a third party provided he was relevantly authorized by the latter and, as GROTIUS said, made the contract *in his name*. This rule was clearly and accurately stated by POTHIER (*Traité des obligations*, no. 74 and 75), whence it was taken over by the Code civil: art. 1984 describes mandate or agency as a transaction 'par lequel une personne donne à une autre le pouvoir de faire quelque chose pour le mandant et en son nom'.

The requirement that the agent must conclude the contract 'in the name of' his principal might lead one to infer *e contrario* that the principal acquires no rights and liabilities if the agent, though acting within the scope of his authority, does *not* act in the name of his principal, in other words does *not* make it clear that the legal consequences are to attach to him. This is indeed the conclusion drawn by Continental systems: if a person concludes a contract in his own name, it is not a case of agency, and he alone acquires the rights and is subject to the duties arising therefrom, even if he was authorized by the principal to enter the transaction, did so on the principal's behalf, was bound to account to him, and was promised a fee for his efforts.

This restriction is unknown to the Common Law. English lawyers are not familiar with the distinction drawn on the Continent between acting 'in one's own name' and acting 'in the name of another', and they cannot see why it is only in the latter case that the principal acquires rights and liabilities. For them 'agency' arises whenever a 'principal' authorizes an 'agent' to act 'on his behalf' in some way, typically by making contracts with third parties. 'Agency is a relationship which arises when one person called the principal authorizes another, called the agent, to act on his behalf, and the other agrees to do so' (TREITEL 608). It is well understood that it makes a difference whether or not the third party could tell that he was contracting with a principal—different rules are required since different interests are involved—but the Common Law prefers to emphasize the common factor in the two situations, namely that A is entering a transaction with T on behalf of and in the interest of P.

By contrast the Continental systems tend to draw a bright line between acting in the name of another and acting in one's own name, and art. 1984 Code civil says that the mandatary must act *pour le mandant et en son nom*. It may still be mandate if the mandatary acts in his own name, as *commissionnaire*, for example, but this is a *mandat sans représentation* and does not generate rights and liabilities directly in the mandator, which happens only when there is *représentation* with the agent acting in the name of his principal. The Italian Codice civile also requires that the intermediary act *in nome e nell'interesse del rappresentato* (art. 1388); where he acts in his own name, he alone is entitled and bound, and this is so, according to art. 1705, even if the third party was aware that he was acting for the account and in the interests of someone else.

Is it really justifiable to draw such a sharp distinction between acting in one's own name and acting in that of another? Even the Continental systems cannot carry it through to the end, for, as we shall see, they have to admit that even acting in one's own name has legal consequences for the person on whose behalf one is acting. But the real point is that the economic purpose of the parties is identical in the two cases. If a customer asks an art dealer to buy a certain painting for him, the customer's aim is to acquire the painting, to come up with the price, to meet the dealer's expenses, and pay him a fee. For this purpose it is quite immaterial whether in negotiating with the third party the dealer states or implies or conceals the fact that he is acting for someone else, named or unnamed. In economic reality acting in one's own name and acting in the name of another are really very much the same; this is more fully realized in the Common Law, with its wider conception of agency, than in the Continental systems.

On the other hand the Convention on Agency in the International Sale of Goods, signed in Geneva in 1983, shows that the practical importance of this difference should not be exaggerated. The Convention deals with the case where 'one person, the agent, has authority or purports to have authority on behalf of another person, the principal, to conclude a contract of sale of goods with a third party' (art. 1 (1)), and art. 1(4) makes it clear that it does not matter 'whether the agent acts in his own name or in that of the principal'. Despite this Common Law conception of agency, it was easy enough to reach agreement on the creation, the extent, and the termination of the agent's 'authority'. Much trickier was the question of the rights and duties of the principal when the agent contracted with a third party 'on his behalf' but under such circumstances that the third party had no reason to suppose that he was dealing with anyone but the agent himself. This is a matter to which we shall return. Details of the Convention can be found in BONELL, 32 *Am. J. Comp. L.* 717 (1984) (complete with text); HANISCH, *Festschrift Giger* (1989) 251; STÖCKER, *WM* 1983, 778; MOULY, *Rev. int. dr. comp.* 35 (1983) 829.

II

The doctrinal and legislative structure of the rules on representation in Continental systems is the result of a discovery made in 1847, namely the distinction between the *contract* between the principal and the agent and the *grant* of 'authority' by the principal to the agent, whereby he confers on the agent the power to represent him in making contracts with third parties. Until the nineteenth century the distinction went unnoticed, and everyone supposed that any grant of authority must come from the contract, indeed was virtually indistinguishable from it: thus §1002 ABGB starts out with a text speaking of 'of the grant of authority and other forms of managing another's affairs' (*von der Bevollmächtigung und anderen Arten der Geschäftsführung*) and of the 'contract of authorisation' (*Bevollmächtigungsvertrag*), while the French Code civil defines *mandat* as *un acte par lequel une personne donne à une autre le pouvoir de faire quelque chose pour le mandant et en son nom* (art. 1984) and includes it in the list of special types of contract.

JHERING was the first to point out that one should distinguish the contract between principal and agent—which is not necessarily one of mandate, but may be employment, partnership, and so on—from the grant of the power of representation. LABAND proceeded to regard the two as entirely independent of each other, so that the question of the duration and scope of the power (which determines whether the agent *can* act with effect, positive or negative, on the principal) must be sharply distinguished from the other question, whether there was a contract between the parties (whose content determines what the agent *shall* do). This doctrine underlies not just the BGB but all modern civil codes. It does not make much difference in practice, but it does mean that the rules on the grant, scope, duration, and revocation of powers are clearly separated from the terms of the contract between the parties, that they are dealt with in different parts of the Code, and that they receive separate treatment in textbooks and scholarly works.

See §§164 ff. BGB; art. 32 ff. OR; §§10 ff. Swedish Contract Law (adopted by other Nordic states); art. 1387 ff. Codice civile; art. 211 ff. Greek Civil Code; art. 258 ff. Portuguese Civil Code; art. 3:60 ff. NBW. See the full details in MÜLLER-FREIENFELS, *Die Vertretung beim Rechtsgeschäft* (1955) 2 ff.

Common lawyers are well aware that agency has a Janus-like quality, on one face a contractual relationship akin to that of sale or hire, on the other a grant, a bestowal of authority. It also recognizes that there may be a grant of authority even if there is no valid contract, as where consideration is lacking or the agent is a minor. This insight is not, however, reflected in the structure of the law—of course the law of agency is not codified in England, so there was no need for the conceptual clarity of good legislation—with the result, rather surprising for the Continental observer, that English textbooks on agency freely discuss such matters as the conditions under which the principal must reimburse the agent or indemnify him against third party claims, and the circumstances under which the agent is liable for breach of his fiduciary duty.

III

The comparative lawyer often discovers that an institution which he takes for granted in his own legal system almost as if it were part of the natural order of things is really no more than a contingent product of historical and sociological conditions which, much to his surprise and edification, is unknown in other systems and unregretted at that. Thus one might reasonably believe that comprehensive statutory representation was the ideal, if not the only imaginable, way of allowing incapable persons such as minors, persons under interdict, and the mentally unsound to take part in legal matters. Nevertheless, it transpires that the Common Law gets by quite nicely without having any such legal institution.

Only a few sporadic rules of statute law in England give one person power to act on behalf of another. There is no general idea that all those suffering from incapacity should have a 'statutory representative' to enable them to take part in legal life, or even that parents have a general power to represent their children in business or in the courts. The Children Act 1989 admittedly gives them 'parental responsibility', defined as 'all the rights, duties, powers, responsibilities and authority which by law a parent of a child has in relation to the child and his property' (s. 3(1)), but it fails to state *what* these rights etc. are. This must be decided from case to case, depending on whether what is involved is managing the child's property, giving consent to medical treatment or representing him in civil litigation. The validity of a minor's contract does not depend on the agreement of a 'statutory representative' but basically on whether or not the contract is for his benefit (see above p. 352 ff.). If the child owns land or intangible assets someone must have the power to manage it for him, including a power to alienate it, but this need not involve the parents; usually when a child inherits property or receives it as a gift *inter vivos* the decedent or donor vests the property in a trustee: the trustee then has the legal title and the power of management and disposition, and the child, as 'equitable owner', is entitled only to the income, depending on the terms of the settlement. If the child has to sue—as it might be, sue the trustee for failure to supply the income or other breach of trust—the parents will usually represent him, not because they are 'statutory representatives', but because the court will, if appropriate, appoint them as 'next friend' for that particular case, or as 'guardian ad litem' when the minor is being sued.

IV

We have already spoken of the fact that Continental systems distinguish the case where the intermediary contracts in his own name from the case where he does so in the name of his principal. Only the latter case, when the third party can see, or infer from the circumstances, that the contract is to be made with the principal, is regarded as one of 'representation'. If the intermediary deals in his own name, this is 'indirect' representation, a *représentation imparfaite* or *mandat sans représentation*, and only the intermediary himself becomes entitled and bound under the contract. This is so even if he was in fact acting for the account and at the risk of a principal who alone had any economic interest in the affair, exactly as happens in a case of 'true' representation.

This distinction is not drawn in the Common Law: if an agent makes a contract on behalf of his principal within the scope of his authority, it is the principal who acquires the rights and liabilities under the contract even if the agent concealed his very existence at the time of the contract and gave the impression that he himself was to be the other party.

Even common lawyers find this doctrine of the 'undisclosed principal' something of an anomaly, since it is in conflict with the general principle that contractual claims can be made only by parties to them and not by any third party, such as the undisclosed principal here. As POLLOCK said: 'The plain truth ought never to be forgotten that the whole law as to the rights and liabilities of an undisclosed principal is inconsistent with the elementary doctrines of the law of contract. The right of one person to sue another on a contract not really made with the person suing is unknown to every legal system except that of England and America.' (POLLOCK, *LQ Rev.* 3 (1887) 358, 359.) What is the true explanation of this 'anomalous' doctrine of the Common Law? Much ingenuity has been applied to the question. AMES saw the principal as being the beneficiary of a trust relationship between agent and third party, for GOODHART and HAMSON the principal takes over the contract concluded by the agent, and DIPLOCK LJ was of opinion that the rules regarding the rights and liabilities of the undisclosed principal were designed to simplify legal proceedings: 'It may be that this rule relating to "undisclosed principals", which is peculiar to English law, can be rationalised as avoiding circuity of action, for the principal could in equity compel the agent to lend his name in an action to enforce the contract against the contractor, and would at common law be liable to indemnify the agent in respect of the performance of the obligations assumed by the agent under the contract' (*Freeman & Lockyer* v. *Buckhurst Park Properties* [1964] 2 QB 480, 503).—In Germany MÜLLER-FREIENFELS, has investigated these problems comprehensively and intensively (*RabelsZ* 17 (1952) 578, 18 (1953) 12). He concludes that it is because the Common Law focuses on the persons between whom the exchange is to take place, as it does in cases of consideration, that the undisclosed principal directly acquires rights and liabilities; here these persons are the principal and the third party, the agent being simply a middleman for effecting the exchange.

The Continental lawyer will immediately ask how well the doctrine of 'undisclosed agency' serves the practical interests of principal and third party. Two problems call for special attention and will be investigated in some detail here: what protection is given to the third party who, having concluded a contract, as he thought, with the other party to the negotiations, finds himself sued for performance by a principal hitherto undisclosed? And again: how is the reverse case to be justified, that the third party contractor can demand performance not only from the middleman who contracted in his own name but also from his principal, although at the time the contract was made the contractor had no suspicion of his existence?

V

On the first question the Common Law has worked out a whole series of rules which take much of the bite out of the principle that the undisclosed principal may sue. According to MECHEM, these rules may be stated in the formula that 'The undisclosed principal may not enforce the contract where the effect is to prejudice the third party.' In other words, the principal's right to sue must not be allowed to put the third party in a worse position than he would have been in if the contract were between him and the agent only.

In *Greer* v. *Downs Supply Co.*, [1927] 2 KB 28, the defendant made a purchase from an agent only because he had a time-barred claim against the agent which he hoped to be able to set off against the price: the undisclosed principal, on whose account the agent had contracted, was not allowed to sue. The plaintiff in *Said* v. *Butt*, [1920] 3 KB 497 was minded to attend the première of a play but the management of the theatre was ill-disposed towards him and would have refused to sell him a ticket, so he had the ticket purchased by a friend. This did him no good, since the defendant, the manager of the theatre, refused to allow the plaintiff to his seat. The plaintiff sued on the ground that he was entitled as undisclosed principal to demand admission on the basis of the contract concluded by his agent. His claim was dismissed. The result can be summed up as follows: if, on a proper analysis of the situation, the third party has a justifiable interest in rendering performance only to the contractual party he knows, the undisclosed principal may not sue. As instances of cases in which the third party was found to have no such interest, and was therefore held liable to perform directly to the principal, one may cite *Kelly Asphalt Block Co.* v. *Barber Asphalt Paving Co.*, 211 NY 68, 105 NE 88 (1914); *Dyster* v. *Randall & Sons*, [1926] Ch. 932.

If a person contracts with another not knowing that the latter has a principal, he may raise against the principal who subsequently appears all the defences he could have raised against a claim by the agent. Thus the third party can defend on the ground that he has already performed to the agent, believing him to be the other party to the contract, and he can set off against the principal's claim any claim which he had against the agent at the time the contract was formed.

See *Browning* v. *Provincial Ins. Co. of Canada*, (1873) LR 5 PC 263; *Montagu* v. *Forwood*, [1893] 2 QB 350; *Cooke* v. *Eshelby*, (1887) 12 App. Cas. 271; TREITEL 630 ff. The same is true in the United States: see Restatement (Second) of Agency (1958) §§302 ff.

It will be seen that in the Common Law the practical effect of allowing the undisclosed principal to sue is generally consistent with the principle of the protection of commerce which is always used on the Continent to justify the distinction between 'real' and merely indirect representation. One might compare the balancing of interests which occurs in the German law of assignment of choses in action (see Ch. 33 II): the way the BGB protects the debtor who may have a new creditor thrust on him without his consent is very like the way the Common Law protects the third party who finds himself sued by a principal of whose existence he was unaware. Thus, for example, just as the undisclosed principal's claim may be excluded by reason of the special nature of the contractual relations between agent and third party, so in German law §399 BGB would operate to prevent the assignment; and just as the undisclosed principal may run into the defence of set-off or other matters arising from the third party's relations with the agent, so may the assignee under §406 and §407 BGB. This shows that it is not absolutely necessary to draw a strict distinction between direct and indirect representation. Indeed, the Common Law proves that one can make a fair accommodation between the undisclosed principal's interest in suing on a contract concluded on his account and the third party's right to rely on the identity of his apparent contractor, just as the interests of assignee and debtor are reconciled in Germany.

It must also be pointed out that, notwithstanding the publicity principle, Continental legal systems have ways of allowing the person indirectly represented to intervene in a contract concluded on his behalf by a middleman. Thus art. 401(1) OR lays down that rights 'which the agent acquired by acting in his own name but for the account of the principal vest in the principal as soon as the latter has himself satisfied all the obligations arising from the agency relationship'. Romanistic systems reach the same result by giving the principal an *action directe* against the third party.

See art. 1994(2) Code civil., art. 1705(2) Codice civile, and, by way of example, the following French decisions: Req. 28 Oct. 1924, DH 1924, 683; Paris 17 Oct. 1934, Gaz. Pal. 1934.2.781 (the customer whose bank entrusted the execution of his mandate to another bank may bring a direct action against the latter); Rouen, 2 Feb. 1950, Gaz. Pal. 1950.1.342 (the depositor of goods can sue the warehouseman chosen by the mandatary); Civ. 1 Dec. 1896, Gaz. Pal. 1897.1.10 (direct suit by consignor against carrier, passing over the freight forwarder). See also art. 7:412(1) NBW, whereby the principal can by written notice 'vest in himself' the agent's rights against the third party if the agent has become bankrupt or is in breach of his obligations to the principal. The Swedish Law on Commission Agents, Commercial Agents and Commercial Travellers of 18 April 1914, (adopted by Denmark and Norway) has a comparable and very finely-honed rule. Finally, see art. 13 of the Geneva Convention (above p. 434).

All systems agree that debts due from the third party vest not in the creditors of the intermediary but in the person for whose account he was acting. In English law this follows from the fact that the undisclosed principal has an action of his own against the third party, unaffected by the agent's bankruptcy; Continental systems reach the same result by treating the principal as a preferential creditor as regards debts due to the agent from the third party.

See art. 401(2) OR; art. 1707 Codice civile; art. 122 of the French Law on Insolvency of 25 Jan. 1986; also, for commission agents only, §392(2) HGB; §§57(2), 61 of the Swedish Law on Commission Agents.

VI

Although Common Law and Civil Law start out from very different positions, the results they reach are very much alike as regards the claims of the 'concealed' principal against the third party. Clear differences emerge, however, once we ask what claims the third party has against the 'concealed' principal.

In the Common Law there is no doubt about the third party's right to sue the principal, unless exceptionally it was agreed between the third party and the agent, expressly or implicitly, that only the agent should be liable. In the absence of any such agreement the third party who learns of the identity of the principal has a choice whether to sue him or the agent, and the choice continues until he obtains judgment against one of them or otherwise definitively elects which to hold liable. If the third party sues the principal for the price due under a sale effected through the agent, it is no defence for the principal to show that he has already paid the agent: if the agent fails to transmit the price to the third party, the principal is bound to pay again, this time direct to the third party. This is justified on the ground that since the principal chose the agent to represent him he must bear the risk of the agent's defalcation.

See TREITEL 634; CHESHIRE/FIFOOT/FURMSTON 490 f. Restatement (Second) of Agency (1958) §208 is to like effect.

Such a claim by the third party is unknown in Continental systems: if T contracts with A who is acting in his own name, T can sue A alone, even if he knows that A is acting, perhaps as commission agent, for the account of P, and even if he himself is liable to be sued by P as undisclosed principal.

See WAHL, *Précis de droit commercial* (1922) 464; LYON-CAEN/RENAULT, *Traité de droit commercial* (5th edn. 1923) III no. 474; RIPERT/ROBLOT, *Traité élémentaire de droit commercial* (13th edn. 1992) II no. 2658; the contrary view is held only by STARCK, *Le contrat de commission* (ed. HAMEL, 1949) 167.—The Italian Codice civile expressly provides in art. 1705(2)(2) that 'I terzi non hanno alcun rapporto col mandante'—Dutch law is different, however: see art. 7:413 NBW.

Lawyers in Common Law countries normally explain their different position by saying that because the principal sets the agent into motion by authorizing him to conclude transactions with third parties, he should also bear the risk that such third parties may be harmed in the event of the agent's insolvency.

Common lawyers may be persuaded that this makes it right to give the third party an action against the principal, but in our view an evaluation of the interests involved shows that this Anglo-Saxon attitude should not be imitated. Continental legal systems have adopted a sounder position by putting the risk of the middleman's insolvency on the third party and denying the third party any direct claim against the principal; this is in line with the reasonable view that if a person is wrong about the credit-worthiness of the person he deals with he must bear this risk himself. Why, in the case of an agency for purchase, should the third party vendor be able to claim the price from anyone but the buyer with whom he was dealing, just because it later transpires that he was buying the goods not for himself but for someone else?

Of course it is true that the principal has given the middleman his authority to conclude transactions but it does not follow, as the Common Law supposes, that he is prepared to incur liability towards all third parties with whom the middleman may contract. In any case, the third party in such cases is usually a vendor of goods who may take the usual security precautions of reserving his property rights and of taking an assignment from the middleman of the latter's indemnity claim against his principal.

On this point the Geneva Convention adopted the position of the Common Law and the law of the Netherlands: under art. 13(2)(b) the third party may bring against the principal any unsatisfied contract claims he has against the agent. This is, however, subject to any defences available to the agent against him or to the principal against the agent, so that in the result, contrary to the position in the Common Law, the principal who has paid the agent is not liable to pay again. Under art. 13(7) these rules, however, apply only in case of doubt, so not where the parties agreed that only the agent should be liable to the third party.

33

Assignment

ARNDT, *Zessionsrecht, Beiträge zum Recht der Forderungsabtretung im internationalen Verkehr* (1932).

BAILEY, Assignment of Debts in England From the Twelfth to the Twentieth Century', 47 *LQ Rev.* 516 (1931); 48 *LQ Rev.* 248, 547 (1932).

FONTAINE, 'La Transmission des obligations "de lege ferenda"', in: *La transmission des obligations (IXes Journées d'études juridiques Jean Dabin*, 1980) 611.

GHESTIN, 'La Transmission des obligations en droit français positif', in: *La Transmission des obligations (IXes Journées d'études juridiques Jean Dabin*, 1980) 3.

HUWILER, *Der Begriff der Zession in der Gesetzgebung seit dem Vernunftrecht* (1975).

JÄGGI, 'Zur "Rechtsnatur" der Zession', *SJZ* 67 (1971) 68.

KLEIN, 'Die Abtretung von Forderungen nach englischem Recht', *WM* 1978, 390.

KÖTZ, 'Rights of Third Parties: Third Party Beneficiaries and Assignment', *Int. Enc. Comp. L.* VII Ch 13 (1992) 52 ff. (The Transfer of Rights by Assignment).

LUIG, *Zur Geschichte der Zessionslehre* (1966).

——, 'Zession und Abstraktionsprinzip', in: *Wissenschaft und Kodifikation des Privatrechts im 19. Jahrhundert.* (ed. Coing and Wilhelm) II (1977) 112.

MALCOLM, 'Accounts Receivable Financing Under the Uniform Commercial Code', *RabelsZ* 30 (1966) 434.

MAIER, 'Zur Geschichte der Zession', *Festschrift Rabel* II (1954) 205.

MARSHALL, *The Assignment of Choses in Action* (1950).

MOECKE, *Kausale Zession und gutgläubiger Forderungserwerb* (1962).

MUMMENHOFF, 'Vertragliches Abtretungsverbot und Sicherungszession im deutschen, österreichischen und US-amerikanischen Recht', *JZ* 1979, 425.

NEUMAYER, 'La Transmission des obligations en droit comparé', in: *La Transmission des obligations* (IXes Journées d'études juridiques Jean Dabin, 1980) 193.

I

IN societies whose economy calls for a sophisticated system of circulating currency and credit it seems axiomatic that one should be able to transfer that form of intangible property which consists of the right to claim something from someone else. In the modern world such claims are mobile items of wealth, one of the many possible forms which 'capital' may take as a factor in production in economic life, much like goods or land, and it is therefore essential to ensure that, like other items of wealth, they should be easily transferable. In all modern legal systems there are legal forms by which this may be effected, though they differ in many respects.

But the transferability of debts and other claims was achieved only at the end of a long historical development. Like the old English Common Law, Roman law started from the position that personal rights could not be transferred at all. Along with the principle that third parties can acquire no rights by contract, this was based on the view that a claim is something highly personal which cannot be severed at will from the particular legal relationship between creditor and debtor which gave rise to it. Nevertheless in the course of time both Roman law and Common Law adopted devices which made it possible to some extent to satisfy the growing economic need to make claims transferable without the co-operation of the debtor. Thus in Roman law the creditor might authorize the 'assignee' to act as cognitor or procurator *in rem suam* in a suit against the debtor, to bring the claim in his own name and to retain any proceeds of suit. This solution had its drawbacks: the creditor could withdraw his authority before the suit was started, he could bring the claim himself, for he always remained its owner, and he could accept payment of the debt and so release the debtor. The assignee could seek to guard against these hazards by having the assignor promise by *stipulatio* that he would do nothing to frustrate the assignment. In Imperial times the purchaser of a decedent's estate was given an *actio utilis* against the debtor; this was subsequently extended to the purchaser of an individual claim and finally, under JUSTINIAN, to every assignee. The assignor retained a right of suit such as was given to the assignee, though under JUSTINIAN it was admitted that payment to the assignor by the debtor would not release the debtor if the assignee had intimated the assignment to him. On the whole matter see ZIMMERMANN, *The Law of Obligations* (1990) 58 ff.

The Common Law had the institution of 'power of attorney' which performed a function rather similar to that of '*procurare in rem suam*': here the creditor gave the 'assignee' authority to use the creditor's name to collect on the claim—called a 'chose in action' to this day—and retain the proceeds. This device also fell short of a proper assignment of a chose in action, since the creditor could at any time withdraw his authority to sue on his behalf and it normally terminated on his death. Until the end of the sixteenth century the English courts were reluctant to give any further protection to the assignee for fear that undesirable persons would take assignments of claims simply in order to bring them to court.

See WINFIELD, 35 *LQ Rev.* 143 (1919).—In the natural law codes, too, a certain odour of fraud seems to stick to assignment. For instance, they generally provide that the assignment of a disputed claim is void if the assignee is a court official, lawyer, or notary in the area of the court which would or could decide a dispute over the claim; see ALR §385 I 11, art. 1597 Code civil, and, to the same effect, art. 1261 Codice civile.—Another example is the remarkable rule of arts. 1699 ff. Code civil, modelled on the *lex Anastasiana*: If a disputed claim is transferred for a consideration, the debtor can acquit himself by giving the assignee what he paid for the debt rather than the amount of the debt itself. This rule also rests on the view that trading in disputed claims should be discouraged on the ground of the public good. Today we reject such *general* prohibitory or protective provisions, and rightly so; instead we check the particular circumstances of doubtful cases and declare an assignment void as being against public policy if it was made in pursuit of a forbidden aim; for Switzerland, see BGE 58 II 162; BGE 87 II 203; for Germany RGZ 81, 175; BGH MDR 1959, 999; BGH NJW 1974, 50; for Austria OGH JBl. 1957, 215; for England *Trendtex Trading Corp.* v. *Crédit Suisse* [1982] AC 679.

In the early seventeenth century the Equity Courts of England started to come to the aid of the assignee. The way in which they did so was typical of equity jurisprudence: they did not dispute the Common Law rule that claims were not transferable, but in practice they emptied it of content by allowing the assignee to bring a bill 'in equity' so that they could require the assignor to lend his name for the necessary action 'at law' against the debtor. This procedure was very cumbrous since it involved two trials, but it was only necessary where the right which had been assigned was a *'legal* chose in action' which had to be sued for 'at law' before the King's judges. If the claim was an *'equitable* chose in action' or claim recognized or enforced in equity, such as the claim of a beneficiary under a trust or of a legatee under a will, then the equity judges allowed the assignee to bring the claim directly in his own name.

The transfer of claims was also recognized by the *Gemeines Recht* in Germany. WINDSCHEID himself, in his *Textbook of the Pandects* in 1865, accepted that singular succession to claims 'is established as valid by customary law today' (§329 note 9). 'It is another question' admittedly 'what theoretical construction can be given to the rule established by customary law, that is, how it can be explained by established concepts.' On this point, indeed, every conceivable theory was expressed. Many authors were of the view that according to the Roman sources claims were conceptually non-transferable and that the assignee acquired at best a personal right to exercise someone else's obligation. WINDSCHEID wanted to give the assignee a claim of his own, with the qualification that the claim remained concurrently vested in the assignor until the debtor learnt of the assignment by a communication from the assignee which he called a 'denunciation' (ibid. §331). The opinion of BÄHR was that the contract of assignment made the assignee the sole creditor but that the debtor had a defence if he had paid the debt to the assignor in ignorance of the assignment (*Jher Jb.* 1 (1857) 351, 41 ff., in accordance with the Prussian General Land Law in §§376 ff. I 11. (For the full story of the development in the *Gemeines Recht* see LUIG, *Zur Geschichte der Zessionslehre* (1966).)

II

The last of these views is the one adopted into the *German* legal family by the BGB. On the conclusion of the contract of assignment the assignee takes the place of the previous creditor without any need that the debtor be informed, much less that he agree (§398 BGB). This is also the standpoint of *Austrian* and *Swiss* law (§§1392 ff. ABGB, arts. 164 ff. OR).

The *Greek* Civil Code of 1940, which so often follows the German BGB, adopts a different position. Art. 455 certainly makes the claim pass to the assignee by means of the contract of assignment without any requirement that the debtor agree, but this applies only as between assignor and assignee. As against the *debtor* and other *third parties* the assignee becomes entitled to the claim only when either he or the assignor has informed the debtor of the assignment (art. 460 Greek Civil Code). As will shortly be shown, this is also the solution of the Romanistic legal family.—The *Turkish* Civil Code, on the other hand, adopts the rule of Swiss law (art. 162).—The courts in *Austria* have special rules for assignments by way of *security*, differing from the general rules of assignment. Like the creation of a pledge (§§451 f. ABGB), an assignment by way of security requires 'titulus' and 'modus': there must therefore be not only a valid written contract of assignment but also an externally perceptible public act, either the express agreement of the third party debtor or some special entry in the books of the assignor. On this see the leading opinions of the Austrian Supreme Court in 15 Jan. 1929, SZ XI 15, and also OGH 21 Feb. 1973, JBl. 1974, 90, note BYDLINSKI.

The debtor who has a new creditor thrust upon him without his consent requires some protection. The rule therefore is that the debtor who pays the assignor is discharged, provided that he did not know of the assignment. This is the result in all the Germanic legal systems, though the formulae they use vary somewhat—'knows' of the assignment (§407 BGB), 'the transferee has been made known to him' (§1396 ABGB), or that he is not 'in good faith' in rendering performance 'to the previous creditor' (art. 167 OR): if the debtor has *any* knowledge of the assignment, whether he received it from the assignor, from the assignee, or in any other way, performance to the assignor does not release him. This is also true of other legal arrangements, such as release, stay, and set-off, which the debtor may make with the assignor in the supposition that he is still the creditor (§§407 BGB; BGE 56 II 363; OGH 27 Mar. 1979, EvBl. 1979 no. 189).

A special feature of the legal systems under consideration is the way they treat the assignment of a claim as 'abstract', that is, as a disposition independent of the contractual agreement underlying it. A claim may be transferred pursuant to a sale or a gift, in lieu of something else which was *in obligatione*, or as a security, and the systems of the German legal family make a sharp distinction between the assignment itself and the sale or gift or whatever other obligational relationship may exist between the assignor and assignee.

Not only are the two transactions distinguished, they are actually independent in law, the principle being that defects in the underlying transaction do not affect the assignment, which constitutes the performance of the transaction; thus a claim which has been transferred pursuant to a contract of sale or agreement to give security remains vested in the purchaser or the secured creditor even if the contract of sale is later rescinded for error or justifiably repudiated or if the secured claim has already been paid off.

It is clear from art. 165 OR that the *Swiss* law of assignment accepts this distinction between the obligational transaction and the performance transaction; it says that an assignment requires writing for its validity but that 'the obligation to conclude a contract of assignment may be concluded without any particular form'. Arts. 171 ff. OR specify when the assignor warrants the existence and collectibility of the claim being assigned and distinguish according to whether the assignment is 'for value' or 'gratuitous'. This is not quite logical. Strictly speaking, the assignment as such cannot be either for value or not for value, since it merely concerns property rights; only by looking at the underlying transaction can one tell whether the assignee is bound to pay for the assignment or whether it was to be a gift. No doubt the lay reader would expect to be told about the guaranteeing of claims during the discussion of their transfer, and this may justify the Swiss method of presentation, but the German legislator deals with the question in connection with the underlying transactions in pursuance of which the assignment is made: in sale (§§437 f. BGB), in gift (§523 BGB), in transfer of claim in lieu of other performance (§365 BGB).

The practical importance of the principle of abstraction in the law of assignments should not be exaggerated. If it appears from the circumstances of the individual case that the parties intended the basic transaction and the assignment to form a single transaction, the invalidity of part of the composite act may involve the nullity of the whole transaction (compare §139 BGB). The same result occurs if it can be inferred that the parties intended the assignment to be conditional on the underlying transaction's being and staying valid. See BGH NJW 1982, 275: an assignment to a bank to secure a loan which was not actually made was held void.—Indeed, the principle of abstraction, with its artificial separation of basic transaction and assignment, may not be worth retaining in this area of the law. In Switzerland the doctrine has excited a great deal of criticism; see BUCHER, *Schweizerisches Obligationenrecht, Allgemeiner Teil* (1979) 501 ff.; MOECKE (above p. 442) and JÄGGI (above p. 442). The Bundesgericht which has endorsed the principle of abstraction (BGE 67 II 123) has also expressed the view that there should be 'a renewed investigation of this basic question of the law of assignments' (BGE 84 II 355; BGE 95 II 112).

The central problem in the law of assignments is how to protect the debtor. It has already been observed that if the debtor is unaware of the assignment he will be discharged by payment to the assignor. The same idea applies if the creditor has made several successive assignments of the same claim. In such a case all Germanic systems apply the principle of priority and hold that only the first assignee acquires title. Since after the first assignment the claim no longer forms part of the property of the assignor, a subsequent assignee could only obtain title if protection were given to his honest but erroneous belief that the assignor was still a creditor. None of the legal systems here under investigation does this, nor does a subsequent assignee improve his position by being the first to inform the debtor that he has become the 'creditor'.

If an assignee is in good faith, the debtor may be barred from raising certain defences to his action. Thus if he has given the assignor a written acknowledgement of the debt and the creditor made use of this document in making the assignment, the debtor cannot raise as against the assignee the fact that the assignor had agreed that the claim should not be transferable, or that the claim was a mere sham (§405 BGB, art. 18 par. 2, 164 par. 2 OR). The same is true if a creditor makes a written assignment of a debt on an understanding with the assignee that this should merely be a simulated transaction; if the assignee then assigns the claim to a third party in good faith along with the document, the claim passes to that third party at the expense of the original creditor (RGZ 90, 273; BGE 23 I 818).—Once again Austria has an exceptional rule for assignments for security purposes: if the same claim is assigned to several assignees for security purposes, it is acquired by the assignee who first completes the required act of publicity, usually obtaining the acknowledgement of the original debtor.

The question which of several assignees becomes owner of the claim must be distinguished from the question which of them can discharge the debtor by receiving performance from him. Once again it is a matter of the debtor's knowledge of the assignment. If he pays an assignee who, having already transferred the claim, is no longer the true creditor, the debtor is discharged if at the time of payment he was unaware of the second assignment.

This is laid down in §408 BGB and art. 167 OR. If the debtor is discharged by his payment to the subsequent assignee, the latter cannot retain the payment as against the first assignee, since by accepting the payment he has extinguished the first assignee's claim against the debtor and has thus obtained at his expense a sum which he is not entitled to retain as against him. See §816(2) BGB and BGHZ 26, 185, 193; BGE 56 II 363; OGH 11 July 1985, JBl. 1986, 235, 236 f.

If the problem of protecting the debtor arises when he has transactions with a *supposed* creditor, it can also arise when there is no doubt about the assignee's entitlement, but the question is what defences the debtor can raise against his claim for payment. Since the assignment takes place without the consent of the debtor, the invariable principle is that it must not curtail the defences he can raise against the assignee. If the debtor had a good defence against the assignor on any ground, be it that the claim never arose or has ceased to exist, been stayed, or become time-barred, he may use it against the assignee (§404 BGB, art. 169 OR, §1396 ABGB). For this purpose it is immaterial that the facts giving rise to the defence took place only after the debtor had knowledge of the assignment, provided that the emergence of such a defence was inherent in the obligation before the assignment.

Thus if a contractor assigns the fee for his services and the assignee claims it from the customer, the latter may defend on the ground that the contractor was in breach of contract and had thereby caused him harm; this defence is open even if the breach occurs only after the assignment had been made and notified to the customer (RGZ 83, 279; BGH NJW 1958, 1915; BGHZ 63, 338, 347; Obergericht Zurich, *BlZüRspr*. 41 (1942) no. 65; OGH 19 Mar. 1963, 530; OGH 8 Jan. 1980, SZ 53 no. 1).

The same is true for set-off; the debtor may set off against the assignee any claim he had against the assignor at the time he learnt of the assignment. A counterclaim which falls due only after the assignment is notified can only be set off by the debtor if the claim assigned falls due even later (§406 BGB, art. 169 OR).

Finally, the debtor can oppose a suit by the assignee by showing that the assignment was invalid and that the plaintiff has consequently no title to sue. For example, he can point to the fact that the assignor lacked capacity at the time of the assignment or that the assignment is void as a simulated transaction under §117 BGB, art. 20 OR. But the principle of 'abstraction' takes effect here: the defence is good only if the assignment as such is invalid; objections based on the nullity of the *underlying transaction* are no more use to the debtor than the argument that although the assignee became entitled to the claim, the underlying transaction contained an agreement not to sue or not to sue yet.

See for example RGZ 102, 385; BGE 50 II 392; OGH 22 Dec. 1931. SZ 13 no. 271 and 4 Jan. 1934, SZ 16 no. 3.

III

The *French* Code civil deals with the assignment of debts in the law of *sales*, since the eighteenth-century jurists always saw the assignor as selling the claim assigned and the assignee as buying it (arts. 1689 ff.). Assignment is therefore not an 'abstract' transaction independent of the underlying agreement. The *Italian* Codice civile of 1942 deals with assignment in the chapter headed 'Delle obligazioni in generale' (arts. 1260 ff.), which also covers the question of the assignor's liability for the existence of the claim and the solvency of the debtor.

In the Romanistic legal systems also, an assignment transfers the debt to the assignee without any co-operation on the part of the debtor. This is explicitly stated in art. 1260 Codice civile; it has to be inferred from art. 1689 Code civil which, using the language of the law of sales, states that under an assignment 'delivery' of the claim from assignor to assignee is effected by a transfer of the document evidencing the claim. Of course the French courts recognize that a claim may be transferred even without the delivery of any relevant document, provided that the parties contractually agree thereon (Paris 12 July 1911, DP 1913. 2. 189).

This applies, however, only as between the parties to the assignment: 'entre le cédant et le cessionnaire' (art. 1689 Code civil). As against *third parties* the assignment is treated as complete only when the assignor or assignee has informed the debtor of the assignment by making the appropriate communication through the agency of a *huissier* ('signification'), or when the debtor has 'acknowledged' the assignment by judicial or notarial document ('acceptation')—(see art. 1690 Code civil). It follows that by itself the agreement to assign procures a merely relative transfer of the claim, that is, only as between assignor and assignee; this view is shared by almost all writers in France and Italy.

Italian law also requires *notificazione* to the debtor, but the courts hold that this is satisfied by any written communication from which the debtor can infer that there has been a change of creditor; see Cass. 20 Nov. 1976, no. 4372, Rep.Foro.it. s.v. *cessione dei crediti* no. 2.

Art. 1690 Code civil has several very important consequences. Unless the debtor has been informed of the assignment in the manner prescribed, or has 'acknowledged' the assignment by public document, he may discharge himself by paying the assignor, since it is the assignor who remains the creditor of the claim which has been assigned (see art. 1691 Code civil). Not only *may* the debtor pay the assignor, he *must* do so. If there has been neither 'signification' nor 'acceptation', he cannot defend on the ground that he knows in some other way that the claim being sued on has already been assigned (Civ. 20 June 1938, DP 1939.1.26; Civ. 27 Nov. 1944, D.1945, 78).

The courts have, however, qualified these rules in several respects. The assignee's statement of claim against the debtor may amount to a 'signification' provided it makes clear that the plaintiff is suing as assignee (Civ. 17 Feb. 1937, DH 1937, 221; Civ. 8 Oct. 1980, Bull. civ. I no. 249). Again, the courts do not always require that the 'acknowledgement' of art. 1690 par. 2 Code civil be contained in a public document. A private written document may suffice, or even an implicit declaration of acceptance; the result is that the assignee rates as creditor and can demand payment from the debtor (Civ. 6 Feb. 1878, DP 1878.1.275; Req. 27 Dec. 1933, DP 1934. 1. 13.; Req. 22 Dec. 1937, DH 1938, 83). In certain cases the assignee may even sue a debtor who has paid the assignor before 'signification' or 'acceptation': if at the time of payment the debtor had actual knowledge of the assignment and his behaviour constituted a fraudulent conspiracy with the assignor to the detriment of the assignee, his payment will not discharge him (Req. 17 Feb. 1874,

DP 1874. 1. 281; Paris 11 Oct. 1912, Gaz. Pal. 1913. 1. 501). On occasion the courts show a tendency to infer fraud on the part of the debtor from the mere fact of payment with knowledge of the assignment.

See Civ. 10 Jan. 1905, S. 1905. 1. 328. The trend appears to be against allowing the debtor to discharge himself by making payment to the assignor if he has even a 'connaissance de fait' of the assignment (on this see PLANIOL/RIPERT VII no. 1122). If this position were achieved, the practical result in French law would be much the same as in the German legal family, where payment to the assignor does not discharge a debtor who knows of the assignment (for example, see §407 BGB). This step has already been taken by the *Italian* legislator: according to art. 1264 Codice civile payment made by a debtor before 'notificazione' does not release him if the assignee can prove that the debtor had knowledge of the assignment. The actual legal position in France on this question is so unclear that writers advise debtors when sued by the assignor to bring in the assignee as a third party so as to avoid the risk of having to pay twice.

As we have seen, assignment is treated, in relation to third parties, as vesting the claim in the assignee only when the requirements of art. 1690 Code civil are satisfied. 'Third parties' for this purpose include not only the debtor but any creditor of the assignor as well, and also any other party to whom the assignor makes a subsequent assignment of the claim. If follows that the assignor's creditors may attach a debt even if it has already been assigned, provided that the assignment has not been notified to the debtor or that he has not 'acknowledged' it in the form required by art. 1690 Code civil. By like reasoning the debt, though assigned, still falls in the estate of a bankrupt assignor provided that the bankruptcy proceedings are opened before 'signification' or 'acceptation'; in line with this, the courts have held that notification is ineffective once bankruptcy proceedings have been opened against the estate of the assignor (Req. 6 Feb. 1934, DP 1936. 1. 39). If the creditor makes successive assignments of the same debt to two different assignees, the debt is acquired not by the one to whom it was first *assigned*, but by the one who first *notifies* the debtor (see Civ. 29 Aug. 1849, DP 1849. 1. 273; this is explicit in art. 1265 Codice civile).

These rules have also had to be modified by the courts. Applied strictly, art. 1690 Code civil leads to astonishing results where a party who knows of the assignment tries to take advantage of its invalidity on the ground that formal 'signification' or 'acceptation' have not taken place. For example, is it right that one of the assignor's creditors should be able to rely on the absence of notification when at the time of attaching the debt he knows that his debtor had long since assigned the debt to a third party? The courts have not yet evolved a clear rule on this point. The original standpoint of the Court of Cassation was that mere knowledge of the assignment was not sufficient to deprive the attaching creditor of his rights and that actual fraud must be shown (Civ. 24 Dec. 1894, DP 1895. 1. 206), but in another case it was held sufficient that there be a 'connaissance spéciale et personnelle' (Civ. 7 July 1897, DP 1898. 1. 483). A similar problem arises when the assignor has made successive assignments of the same debt. What should the decision be if the second assignee was the first to notify the debtor but knew of the first assignment at the time he did so? The lower courts have on several occasions decided in favour of the first assignee, without requiring proof of any particular fraud on the part of the second assignee (Trib. com. Seine 4 April 1892, Gaz. Pal. 1892. 1. 665; Trib. civ. Seine 5 Jan. 1905, Gaz. Trib. 1905. 2. 473 and 1 Dec. 1903, Gaz. Trib. 1904. 2. 317).

Businessman obviously have a considerable interest in having a simple procedure for the assignment of debts such that the assignee becomes owner of the debt not only against the assignor but also against the debtor and his creditors, and can make it good in bankruptcy proceedings. For example, a merchant can hardly obtain money for, or raise money on, the debts his customers still owe him if he cannot transfer them effectively as against the whole world without having to make a formal intimation to each of his customers. The relevant provisions of the Code civil, especially art. 1690, are not really practical. In practice, therefore, other legal devices have been sought and found. One method relies on the fact that the transfer of debts incorporated in a negotiable instrument; such as a bill of exchange, requires no formality: unlike the position in German law, if a creditor draws a bill on his debtor and endorses it over to a third party the underlying claim ('provision') is also transferred even if the debtor has not accepted the bill and even if the requirements of art. 1690 have not been observed (see GHESTIN (above p. 442). Furthermore, the Code civil itself contains a legal institution ('subrogation personnelle') which can be used to sidestep art. 1690: if a debt is paid off by a third party rather than by the debtor himself, the third party acquires the creditor's claim if the creditor so agrees (art. 1249, 1250 no. 1, Code civil). This is the method used in France today in the factoring business, for example: if a businessman who wishes to realize the debts owed to him by his customers declares to the factoring bank that he accepts payment by the bank as being payment by the debtor and agrees that the debts vested in him should now vest in the bank, 'subrogation' transfers the debts to the bank without the cumbrous formalities of art. 1690 (see GHESTIN (above p. 442) 36 ff., and the full details in MESTRE, *La Subrogation personnelle* (1979) 57 ff., 229 ff.). Finally the French legislature intervened. The Law to Facilitate Business Credit of 2 January 1981 (*Loi Dailly*) enables a business-man to use the debts owed to him as security for credit afforded by a bank by listing the debts in a 'bordereau' or annexure following the statutory formalities. The delivery of this 'bordereau' to the bank constitutes an assignment of the debts listed in it.

It will be seen that lawyers, courts, and legislature in France have developed many different ways of effecting assignment of debts which get round the obsolete rules contained in the Code civil. Thought is now being given to reforming the rules themselves.

On this see FONTAINE (above p. 442) 620 ff. In Belgium art. 1690 Code civil was altered by the law of 6 July 1994 so as to provide that mere agreement between assignor and assignee suffices to transfer a debt *erga omnes*, but as to the debtor only if he has knowledge of the assignment or has acknowledged it. If the same debt is assigned more than once, art. 1690(3) gives priority to the assignee who first makes the debtor aware of the assignment or procures him to acknowledge it. For details see OMMESLAGHE (above p. 442).

IV

English law, too, was very slow to accept that a debt could be informally transferred so as to enable the transferee to claim it from the debtor. The courts of equity were the first to admit this, but only when the claim assigned was one which fell within their jurisdiction as an 'equitable chose in action' such as the claim by a legatee for a testamentary bequest or one by the beneficiary for the income of a trust (see above p. 189). Debts due under contracts such as sale, services, lease, and loan were 'legal choses in action' and the assignee had to join the assignor in his lawsuit against the debtor, as co-plaintiff if he was agreeable or as co-defendant if he was not.

This inconvenience can now be avoided by 'statutory assignment', a method introduced in 1873 (now Law of Property Act 1925, s. 136): the creditor of a legal chose in action can transfer it with the effect that the transferee can claim it in his own name without any further assistance, provided that the assignment is in writing signed by the assignor and written notice has been given to the debtor. If either of these requirements is unmet, it may still be valid as an equitable assignment, for which neither writing nor notice to the debtor is necessary; it does, however, remain the case that if the chose in action is legal rather than equitable, the assignor must be involved in any suit by the assignee against the debtor.

See *Performing Right Society* v. *London Theatre of Varieties, Ltd.*, [1924] AC 1: the plaintiff, a society for the vindication of the rights of authors, claimed an injunction and damages against the defendant theatre for infringing a copyright of which the plaintiff had become owner by assignment. The House of Lords found that although there was no 'statutory assignment' since the special requirements of the Copyright Act had not been met, the transfer was nevertheless valid as an 'equitable assignment'. Even so, the plaintiff's claim failed: the copyright, being a '*legal* chose in action' could only be established in court if the plaintiff's assignor was also a party to the proceedings. After expounding these rules, VISCOUNT FINLAY said: 'We must decide according to law, however much we may regret that success in the action should depend upon a mere technicality which has no relation to the merits of the case' ([1924] AC 1, 19).

In the *United States* the requirements of modern commerce have ousted these vestiges of medieval assignment law. Founding on legislation which liberalized the law of procedure and abolished the technical distinctions between 'law' and 'equity', American courts today accept that an assignment may be valid although it is informal and although the debtor has not been notified, and allow the assignee as 'the real party in interest' to bring suit against the debtor in his own name without any participation by the assignor (see WILLISTON §430, CORBIN §856).

Since the creditor may change without the debtor's knowledge (except in the case of the English 'statutory assignment'), the debtor must be protected if he relies on the assignor's continuing to be his creditor. This protection is afforded both in England and in the United States by the rule that the debtor may use as against the assignee all the defences which at the time he learnt of the assignment he could have opposed to the assignor. Thus the debtor has a defence against the assignee if before learning of the assignment he has been allowed a period of grace or a reduction in interest or has paid the assignor. He can also raise any other defence he could raise against the assignor himself, such as that the claim never arose, that it has ceased to exist or that it is time-barred; he can also set off counterclaims he had against the assignor provided that they were acquired before he learnt of the assignment, even if they were not to fall due till later. So if a builder has assigned his right to the sum agreed in the construction contract and then breaches the contract, his employer can defend a suit by the assignee on the ground that the builder owes him damages, even if the breach did not occur till after the assignment: it is enough that the contract which generated the right assigned was capable of generating the counterclaim as well.

See *Newfoundland* v. *Newfoundland Ry. Co.* (1888) 13 App.Cas. 199, 213; *William Pickersgill & Sons* v. *London & Provincial Marine Ins. Co.* [1912] 3 KB 614; *Business Computers Ltd.* v. *Anglo-African Leasing* [1977] 2 All ER 741. See also Restatement (Second) of Contracts (1981) §§336 and 338.

Two common situations show that the validity of an assignment does not depend on the debtor's having been notified of it: one is the case where the assignor's creditor attempts to garnish or attach a debt already assigned, and the other is the case where the assignor makes successive assignments of the same debt.

In the first of these cases the Common Law holds that the creditor cannot garnish or attach a debt already assigned, regardless of the knowledge or belief of the parties (*Holt* v. *Heatherfield Trust Co.* [1942] 2 KB 1 and Restatement (Second) of Contracts (1981) §341.)

With regard to successive assignments the position adopted by the Common Law is not so uniform. *English* law gives preference to the assignee who first notifies the debtor in ignorance of the prior assignment (rule in

Dearle v. *Hall* (1828) 38 Eng. Rep. 475). In the United States the matter was hotly debated for years. Many states opted for the principle of priority of assignments and preferred the first assignee. But this principle was often qualified. For example, an assignee for consideration could keep sums paid to him by the debtor if he was unaware of the prior assignment at the time: 'Mere priority in time of assignment does not seem to be a sufficient reason for taking away from the second assignee money that he has innocently collected by the exercise of diligence and effort' (CORBIN §902). The same is true when the second assignee, without knowledge of the first, has obtained judgment against the debtor or novated it by agreement with him. This is the solution adopted by Restatement (Second) of Contracts (see §342).

Since the adoption of the Uniform Commercial Code, these rules have lost much of their practical importance in the United States. §9 UCC contains a comprehensive regulation of 'security interests' in moveables and intangibles, and since a 'security interest' is acquired when a person takes an assignment as security, be it as factor or purchaser, most assignments of any importance in modern commerce fall under it. Since the 'security interest' of an assignee is effective against third parties only if an appropriate entry has been made in a public register (§9–301 UCC), the conflict between successive assignees is resolved in favour of whichever first registered his security interest.

V

Any economy with much traffic in credit needs rules which permit the free transfer of rights to claim money: such claims should be as easily transferable as other assets, by agreement between transferor and transferee; further requirements should be imposed only where necessary.

One device which makes it easy to transfer claims has been in existence for centuries: the negotiable instrument. When a debt is incorporated in a bill of exchange or similar instrument it can be transferred simply by agreement and delivery of the document. Not all claims can be embodied in such an instrument, however, and even if they can, it may be quite impracticable now that it is a daily occurrence for whole packets of debts to be transferred to a factoring business or bank as security for a loan, since the delivery and enforcement of so many hundreds of documents would take a tremendous amount of effort, given the need to file them, mail them out, present them to the debtor on the due date, and protest them in the event of non-payment.

Apart from negotiable instruments, many systems hold that for an assignment to be effective as against the world there must, in addition to the agreement of the parties, be some more or less formal notification to the debtor. This requirement is really superfluous, for German and Common Law show that the debtor can be adequately protected even if the change of creditor takes place without his knowledge, provided he can oppose to the assignee all the defences he had against the assignor up to the time he learnt of the assignment.

French lawyers have argued that the rule of art. 1690 Code civil can be justified as providing a *système de publicité* (CARBONNIER 559; GHESTIN (above p. 442) 26 ff.): a person minded to take an assignment can always ask the debtor if he has been notified of any prior assignment, and if the answer is negative, assume that the assignor still owns the debt in question. The same argument is drummed up in support of the rule in *Dearle* v. *Hall*, but it is far from convincing. After all, there is no obligation on a debtor to give a perfect stranger prompt, full, and accurate information about prior intimations; furthermore, the parties may quite justifiably want to keep the debtor in the dark about an assignment, at least for a time, and take the risk that the debtor may discharge the debt by paying the assignor.

Dispensable though notification to the debtor seems to be, there are still good reasons for enabling people to find out with speed and assurance when and to whom an assignment has been made. If a merchant wants to assign present or future debts to his bank as security for a facility, it is in the interests not only of the bank but of legal certainty and transparency that there be some cheap and reliable method of ascertaining whether or not the customer has previously assigned the debts in question. Various methods are possible. In Austria a 'sign' (*Zeichen*) is required in addition to the agreement of the parties—notification to the debtor counts as a *Zeichen*, but so also, if the debtor is not to know of the assignment, does a written document of assignment by the assignor along with a note in his books (see §452 ABGB and OGH 21 Jan. 1975, SZ 48 no. 2)—and in France a written declaration of assignment, in the special form of a *bordereau*, is called for by the *Loi Dailly*; but if one is really serious about facilitating commerce in debts and ensuring security of transactions, one must do as is done in the Netherlands, Great Britain, and the United States, and require commercial assignments by way of security to be registered in a publicly accessible register.

In British law a 'general assignment of book debts' is effective as against creditors in the assignor's bankruptcy only if the assignment is entered in a public register: see s. 344 Insolvency Act 1986; s. 395, 396 Companies Act 1986. In the Netherlands notification to the debtor is required to make an assignment or pledge of a debt valid (art. 3:94 NBW). In the case of a pledge, however, it is possible to avoid the need for notification by registering the transaction and its date with a state authority, provided that the debt already exists or is to arise under an existing relationship with the pledgor (art. 3:239 NBW).

34

Contracts for the Benefit of
Third Parties

V. BAR, 'Contracts and Third Party Rights in German and English Law' in MAR-
KESINIS (ed.), *The Gradual Convergence: Foreign Ideas, Foreign Influences and English
Law on the Eve of the 21st Century* (1994).
BEATSON, 'Reforming the Law of Contracts for the Benefit of Third Parties, A Sec-
ond Bite at the Cherry', 1992 *Curr. Leg. Prob.* 1.
BRESCH, 'Contracts for the Benefit of Third Parties', 12 *ICLQ* 318 (1963).
V. CAEMMERER, 'Wandlungen des Deliktsrechts', *Hundert Jahre deutsches Rechtsleben,
Festschrift zum 100jährigen Bestehen des Deutschen Juristentages* II (1960) 49, 59 ff.
CORBIN, 'Contracts for the Benefit of Third Persons', 46 *LQ Rev.* 12 (1930).
DOLD, *Stipulations for a Third Party* (1948).
DOWRICK, 'A Jus Quaesitum Tertio by Way of Contract in English Law', 19 *Mod. L.
Rev.* 374 (1956).
EISENBERG, 'Third Party Beneficiaries', 92 *Colum. L. Rev.* 1358 (1992).
KÄSER, 'Der Vertrag zugunsten Dritter im englischen Recht', *RabelsZ* 21 (1956) 418.
KESSLER, 'Die soziale Funktion des Vertrages zugunsten Dritter im nordamerika-
nischen Recht', *Festschrift E. Wahl* (1973) 81.
KORTMANN/FABER, 'Contract and Third Parties', in HARTKAMP et al. (eds.), *Towards
a European Civil Code* (1994) 237.
KÖTZ, 'Third Party Beneficiaries', *Int. Enc. Comp. L.* VII Ch. 13 (1990).
LORENZ, 'Anwaltshaftung wegen Untätigkeit bei der Errichtung letztwilliger Verfü-
gungen', *JZ* 1995, 317.
——, 'Die Einbeziehung Dritter in vertragliche Schuldverhältnisse—Grenzen
zwischen vertraglicher und deliktischer Haftung', *JZ* 1960, 108.
MILLNER, 'Jus quaesitum tertio: Comparison and Synthesis', 16 *ICLQ* 446 (1967).
PACCHIONI, *I Contratti a favore di terzi* (Milan, n.d.).
PALMER, *The Paths to Privity, The History of Third Party Beneficiary Contracts in English
Law* (1992).
SIMPSON, 'Promises Without Consideration', 15 *ICLQ* 835, 848 ff. (1966).
WESENBERG, *Verträge zugunsten Dritter* (1949).
WILLIAMS, 'Contracts for the Benefit of Third Parties', 7 *Mod. L. Rev.* 123 (1944).

I

THE normal intention of persons who enter a commutative contract, such as
a contract of sale, is that the rights and obligations engendered by the contract should attach to themselves alone. The same is true even if the parties

456

provide that each of them may discharge his liability under the contract by rendering performance to someone else: if the purchaser, at the vendor's request, is to pay the price to the vendor's bank rather than to the vendor himself, or if the vendor is to deliver the goods to the purchaser's order rather than to him personally, each of them in rendering performance to a third party is performing an obligation which he owes only to his contractor and not to the third party. Quite different is the situation where the parties contract in such a manner that the third party, not himself involved in the formation of the contract, is to be entitled not only to receive the promised performance but actually to demand it in his own name: this brings us into the realm of contracts for the benefit of third parties.

It is by no means obvious that a contract should be able to create such rights in those who are not parties to it. A look at legal systems past and present shows that the concept of contracts for the benefit of third parties has been far from receiving invariable acceptance. No legal system has been able to ignore the fact that there is a great practical need to recognize contractual benefits conferred on strangers, but it is one thing to admit that occasionally the third party may be entitled to sue, and quite another to recognize the contract for the benefit of third parties as a basic institution of legal thought. The main obstacle to this is a rather dimensional and unabstract way of looking at the problem, of seeing a contract as a bond binding the parties, as a 'vinculum juris', for this makes it difficult to understand how a third party who is a stranger to the contract can take under it in the way suggested. It is not only lawyers who go in for this dimensional manner of approaching things, it is a general method by which *homo sapiens* attempts to impose order on the variety of surrounding phenomena. It is extremely useful in law since it enables one to discern and convey different types of situation, but such typology has its own dangers, since the striking pictures it develops may prove delusive in time. The picture of a contract as a necessarily bilateral 'vinculum juris' is one of these and it has led the Common Law to the dogma of 'privity of contract'.

Classical Roman lawyers granted no independent right to a third party who was a stranger to a contract: 'alteri stipulari nemo potest' (ULPIAN, D. 45, 1, 38, 17). In the post-classical law of the Empire a few exceptions were admitted, and JUSTINIAN's men increased their number. One case was where a person made a gift on the terms that the donee was to do something for a third party: in such a case the third party was given an *actio utilis* against the donee. Another instance of the recognition of contracts for the benefit of third parties lies in dispositions from one member of a family to another member or to a trustee with the direction that the transferee, possibly on the death of the transferor, transmit the property to third parties, normally descendants in need of support (on this, see WESENBERG (above p. 456) 29 ff.).

By and large the natural law codes adhered to these principles. It is true that the General Prussian Land Law laid down in §74 I 5 that 'a contract may have as its object the benefit of a third party'; but it added that 'the third party [obtains] a right from such a contract, in the formation of which he was involved neither directly nor indirectly, only if he accedes to the contract with the agreement of the principal parties' (§75). Making the third party's right depend on a formal declaration of adhesion proved unsatisfactory in practice, as emerges clearly from a passage in the famous lecture on 'The Worthlessness of Jurisprudence as a Science' [*Die Werthlosigkeit der Jurisprudenz als Wissenschaft*] delivered in 1848 by the Prussian philosopher and state attorney v. KIRCHMANN. Dealing with the farm surrender contract, used by an ageing farmer to dispose of the property on the condition that the transferee pay part of the price directly to his siblings, he says:

'People familiar with this institution had no doubt that, unless the father said otherwise, the siblings had an independent claim to the funds destined for them, even if they had not adhered to the contract. But the Land Law unfortunately overlooked this institution and its only applicable provisions were the general terms of I 5 §75 . . . When these provisions were applied to the institution in question, intolerable hardships occurred. From the very outset attempts of every kind have been made to prevent §75 having this destructive effect on the institution. Fictions, conversions, anticipated successions, and other artificial constructs of this sort were all tried out . . .' v. KIRCHMANN (id. 3rd edn., 1948) 21 f.).

In fact the Prussian courts contrived to give the siblings an independent right of suit notwithstanding the unsatisfactory terms of the Land Law: they simply held that the transferee's promise to pay his siblings must be deemed to have been accepted by the father as 'their representative'.

The plenary decision to this effect, made by the Prussian Obertribunal on 25 Aug. 1846, is very instructive (ObTr. 14, 68). The reasoning is so tortured that v. KIRCHMANN took it as further evidence for his view that most of legal science consisted of ignominious rehabilitation of moribund legislation—'so repellent a business that it is surprising so many are ready to take to it'.

Be this as it may, it is beyond question that when the legal scholars of the *Gemeines Recht* rethought the problem of the contract for the benefit of third parties, they performed a valuable service, for they produced the conceptual clarity needed for the mature solutions of the German BGB. Even the pandectists sometimes heeded the exigencies of practice. Only a few of them, such as BRINZ (*Pandektenrecht* IV (1892) 389 f.), thought that a contract for the benefit of third parties was a 'logical impossibility', a view which, when expressed by lawyers, inevitably discloses the untenability of the proposition it is adduced to support. Most of the law professors of the period saw that the new life insurance contracts or annuity contracts or the farm surrender contracts already mentioned could not be dealt with by Roman law alone. They therefore proposed a wide variety of theories, all using existing institutions, to justify giving the third party an independent claim. The device used by the Prussian Obertribunal is just one example. It was also suggested that the third party's right of suit could be based on fictional assignment, and that the third party could bring his claim as the agent of the promisee, but the view which finally won through was that the contractual will of the parties was powerful enough by itself to engender the third party's right to claim. This was the view of WINDSCHEID in particular, and he was led to this conclusion by the fact that 'in Germany . . . theory and practice have always gone beyond [the Roman principles]. This is a fact which cannot be ignored and which gives good evidence of the tendency of modern legal consciousness' (*Lehrbuch des Pandektenrechts* II (1865) §316, pp. 189 f.). It was through WINDSCHEID that the proper view of the matter entered the BGB.

II

The German BGB starts off with the proposition that one may by contract so bargain for performance to a third party that 'the third party directly acquires the right to demand performance' (§328 par. 1). The statement that the third party acquires the right 'directly' means that in order to acquire the right in his own name the third party need not make any declaration of adhesion or acceptance, or participate in any way; indeed he need not even know of the conclusion of the contract. It also follows that the right to claim to receive performance vests only in the third party; it never vests in the promisee, even for a 'legal second', although he may acquire the right to claim that performance be rendered to the third party. The third party need not, however, accept the right; he may decline it by making a declaration to this effect *vis-à-vis* the promisor (§333 BGB).

In answering the question under what circumstances a contract for the benefit of third parties is to be found, the BGB followed WINDSCHEID; if the contract contains no express provision the judge is to make an inference 'from the circumstances, especially the purpose of the contract'. The BGB facilitates the judges' task somewhat by drawing up presumptions for particular cases: in case of doubt, if the payments under life assurance contracts and annuity contracts are to be made to a third party, they are to be treated as contracts for the benefit of that third party. The same is true for farm surrender contracts and other gratuitous dispositions with provisions in favour of third parties (§330 BGB). By contrast, arrangements to pay a contractor's creditor are *not*, where any doubt arises, to be treated as contracts for the benefit of the third party: the presumption here is that the creditor, not being a party to the contract, cannot claim payment from the debtor's contractor as well as from the debtor himself (§329 BGB).

§331 deserves particular attention: if the parties have agreed that the promisor is to render performance to the third party only after the death of the promisee, the third party, in case of doubt, acquires his right only at the time of the promisee's death. In practice this means that the promisee can rescind or alter the benefit to the third party at any time during his life. There is a special rule on this in the law relating to the insurance contract [*Versicherungsvertragsgesetz*] (§§166 ff.), but more important is the general recognition in §331 BGB of the validity of contracts for the benefit of third parties which mature on the death of the promisee. Accordingly, a person who wants a particular person to have an item of property after his death may achieve his aim by making a contract whereby his contractor promises to transfer the object to the destinatee after the promisee's death. In practice, of course, this amounts to a disposition *mortis causa*, but the formal requirements regarding wills or contracts of succession can be disregarded because, as is laid down, the third party obtains his right to performance 'directly', that is, he does not acquire it through the estate of the deceased.

The courts hold that an informal agreement between a 'testator' and his bank that the bank should transfer any funds standing to his credit on his death to a third party gives that third party a right to claim those funds from the bank; they do not pass through the estate (RGZ 88, 137; BGH NJW 1975, 382; BGHZ 66, 8). Despite criticism from writers who pointed to §2301 BGB, this holding has been extended to the case where the agreement related to bonds and shares in the hands of a depositee (BGHZ 41, 95).

A contract for the benefit of third parties has also been found in cases other than the very important ones mentioned in §§329–31 BGB.

If the lessor of a private clinic provides in the lease that a named specialist should have the right to reserve beds in it, the contract may be construed under §328 BGB so as to give the specialist an independent contractual right against the lessee (BGHZ 3, 385).—The circumstances under which a person opens an account in a bank or savings bank, especially the name chosen for the account, may show that a third party should also have an immediate right to draw on the funds in the account (BGHZ 21, 148).—The dowry promised by the bride's father to his future son-in-law can be construed as a contract in favour of the daughter (RGZ 67, 204).—If a collective agreement between a trade union and an employers' federation contains a promise not to strike and the promise is broken, an individual employer may be able to claim damages in respect of the harm suffered by *himself*, since the contract made by the employers' federation is to this extent a contract in favour of the individual employers who are its members (BAG NJW 1957, 647).

Austria and *Switzerland* also recognize contracts for the benefit of third parties. Originally the ABGB, like all other natural law codes, took a contrary position, for §811 laid down that no one could accept a promise for another, and contracts for the benefit of third parties remained inadmissible until the adoption of the Third Teilnovelle to the ABGB in 1916. This amendment followed the German BGB by declaring that the entitlement of the beneficiary 'is to be judged from the agreement and the nature and the purpose of the contract'. The presumptions of §§329–31 BGB were replaced by a rather empty formula that in cases of doubt the beneficiary acquires an independent right 'if performance will principally be to his benefit'. The same presumption applies to farm surrender contracts as in Germany. The *Swiss* rule in art. 112 OR is even terser. The third party may himself demand performance of the contract 'if this accords with the intention of the contractors or if it is in line with practice'.

Contracts for the benefit of third parties can be used to fill gaps in the law of tort, as German law shows. In the leading case in 1930 a tenant contracted with the defendant firm for the repair of a gas stove which he had installed, the stove exploded through the negligence of the firm's engineer, and the tenant's cleaning woman was injured. The Reichsgericht allowed her to claim damages *in contract* on the ground that the repair contract between the firm and the tenant 'contained a contract for the benefit of the plaintiff as well' (RGZ 127, 218, 221). Nowadays this is seen not as a 'true' contract for the benefit of third parties—the cleaning woman could not sue the firm for the promised performance, that is, the proper repair of the stove—but rather as a 'contract with protective effect for third parties', since the firm's duty to take care in repairing the stove is owed to the cleaning woman also, with consequent liability to her in damages in the event of breach of this duty.

A contract has protective effect for third parties if one party is aware that they may well be endangered by faulty performance on his part and the other has a special interest in their protection. Among the many cases see RG JW 1937, 737 (contract for provision of drinking water between landlord and commune has protective effect for tenants who suffer from lead poisoning); BGHZ 33, 247 (contract for the delivery and installation of concrete slabs in a factory has protective effect for employees working there); BGH NJW 1965, 1757 (contract between club and hotel for the use of a dance hall has protective effect for a club member who slips and falls on the polished floor); BGHZ 49, 350 (lease of business premises has protective effect for a third party whose goods, left there with the tenant's consent, are damaged because of their faulty condition). So also OGH 29 April 1981, JBl. 1982, 601 (contract between landowner and landscapist had protective effect for the utility company whose high tension mast was damaged by the landscaping work). Compare also OGH 6 June 1974, SZ 47 no. 72; OGH 4 Feb. 1976, SZ 49 no. 14.

In most other European countries the plaintiff would sue in tort. This is possible in Germany, too, but unfortunately §831 BGB allows the defendant to avoid liability if he can prove that he used all due care in selecting, training, and supervising the employee who actually injured the plaintiff (see below Ch. 41 II). This *Entlastungsbeweis*, generally regarded as a legislative error, can be evaded by granting a claim in contract.

More recently courts in Germany have allowed the third party to sue in contract where the damage suffered was not personal injury or property damage but 'pure economic loss', for which he could have no claim in tort (see below Ch. 40 II). Typically a credit institution, accountant, architect or other expert is asked to provide information or state an opinion about the financial health and solvency of a firm or the value of a piece of property, and the information given is inaccurate through negligence. The party requesting the information can claim damages for breach of contract, but what of the third party who learns of the information and suffers loss through relying on it? Here, too, the German courts have accepted that the third party can be included in the protective ambit of the contract to supply the information, provided that the informant should have known that the third party would come by the information, that he would rely on it, and that he would thereby change his position adversely.

See, for example, BGH NJW 1982, 2431; BGH NJW 1984, 355; BGH NJW 1987, 1758.—In other systems the third party may be able to sue in tort here also, in France because art. 1382 calls for the reparation of all harm caused by *faute*, including mere financial harm, in England because although negligence primarily covers only personal injury and property damage, an exception is made precisely for the case where merely pecuniary loss is suffered as a result of carelessly false information. On this see below Ch. 40 III.

III

The thesis that a contract is a *vinculum juris* which creates rights and duties only for and against the parties to it is expressly stated in the *French* Code civil. Immediately afterwards, however, the legislator qualifies this by saying that the principle does not apply to contracts for the benefit of third parties. Art. 1165 Code civil provides:

'Les conventions n'ont d'effet qu'entre les parties contractantes; elles ne nuisent point au tiers, et elles ne lui profitent que dans le cas prévu par l'article 1121.'

It is only under very strict conditions that art. 1121 declares a 'stipulation au profit d'un tiers' to be admissible; this shows that while French lawyers at the end of the eighteenth century were ready to abandon the Roman principle that 'alteri stipulari nemo potest', they were still very far from accepting the modern principle that contracts for the benefit of third parties should be allowed generally. Under art. 1121 the 'stipulation au profit d'un tiers' is only valid if the person who promises to render performance to the third party simultaneously promises something to the other contractor as well, or if the contracting party makes the promisor some gift in connection with the transaction. If these requirements were taken seriously, it would mean that in order for an uncle to make a binding promise to a father to render some performance to his son, either the uncle must promise something to the father as well or receive something from the father as a gift, on condition of the performance to the son. Nowadays, however, it is established that a contract for the benefit of third parties may be perfectly valid even if these requirements are not satisfied. The performance which the promisee must make to the promisor under art. 1121 need no longer be a gift: any economic transfer will suffice, and the alternative requirement of the Code, that the promisee must at the time of the contract always stipulate for something for himself, has been understood by the courts as being satisfied if any 'profit moral' accrues to him as a result of the transaction. In the case of insurance such a 'profit moral' exists in the certainty of the insured that the insured sum will be paid to the third party on the occurrence of the insured event (Civ. 16 Jan. 1888, DP 1888, 1.77).

These decisions were adopted by the *Italian* Codice civile, whose art. 1411 states that a 'stipulazione a favore di un terzo' is valid if the promisee has an interest in the third party's being benefited. The Italian courts were prompt to state that it is sufficient if the interest is 'di natura morale' (Cass. 24 Oct. 1956, no. 3869, Giust. civ., Mass. 1956, 1318).

In practice, therefore, the limitative requirements imposed by the Code in 1804 for contracts for the benefit of third parties have been effectively struck out by the French courts: 'l'un des exemples les plus souvent cités de l'œuvre créatrice des tribunaux' (MAZEAUD/CHABAS no. 787).

Contracts for the benefit of third parties are of practical importance today in much the same areas as in Germany. *Annuities* are specially provided for in art. 1973 Code civil, which expressly grants a right to the beneficiary, as does art. 1875 Codice civile. *Life assurance contracts* were covered by the French Law of Insurance of 13 July 1930 (now *Code des assurances*) but prior to its enactment had to be treated simply as contracts for the benefit of third parties under art. 1121 Code civil; indeed the application of that article to life assurance contracts was the acid test which purified that article of its Roman dross. The French courts are also ready to recognize other arrangements as contracts for the benefit of third parties if the promisee wants to procure that a third party receive one or more payments from the promisor. Although such a disposition is normally gratuitous as between the promisee and the beneficiary, it is generally agreed that the formal requirements for donations, such as art. 931 Code civil, do not apply.

This is laid down by art. 1973 par. 2 for annuity contracts in particular, but it is also admitted generally: one of the reasons given will be familiar to German lawyers, that under a *stipulation pour autrui* the third party's rights flow not from a conveyance of property by the promisee but from the conclusion of the contract (see MAZEAUD/CHABAS no. 776 and Montpellier 22 Dec. 1932, Gaz. Pal. 1933, 421).

These contracts for the benefit of third parties are typically cases where the promisee wants to secure the support of dependants by giving them contractual claims against the promisor, but the institution is used by the French courts in many other cases as well.

For example, the purchaser of a business conducted on leased premises may acquire a contractual right to have the lease extended if the lessor had agreed with the tenant that the lease would be extended if the business were sold (Civ. 30 May 1962, Bull. civ. 1962. I. 247).—The contract between the owner of a house and a concierge may be seen as a contract for the benefit of the tenants, so that the tenants acquire their own contractual claims against the concierge if he fails to fulfil the duties he assumed in the contract (Trib. civ. Seine 4 March 1944, DA 1944 J. 84).—If the Centre National de transfusion sanguine, pursuant to a contract with a hospital to provide a blood donor if required by a patient, provides a syphilitic donor and the patient becomes worse, the patient has a contractual claim for damages against the Centre National de transfusion sanguine since the hospital's contract is for the benefit of the patient in accordance with art. 1121 Code civil (Civ. 17 Dec. 1954, Gaz. Pal. 1955. I. 54).

The Romanistic legal families have another institution, very similar in its practical effects to the contract for the benefit of third parties but entirely different from the point of view of juristic construction. This is the so-called 'action directe' ('azione diretta'). In a few specified cases the French Code civil gives a person an independent right of suit if he has a special interest in the performance of a contract concluded between two other parties. Thus art. 1994 par. 2 Code civil provides that a principal has a direct claim against the third party to whom his agent has delegated the performance of the authorized task (so art. 1705 par. 2 Codice civile; see also above Ch. 32 V). Art. 1753 Code civil further provides that if a tenant is in arrears with the rent the landlord can proceed directly against the subtenant (so art. 1595 Codice civile). Likewise the builder can bring a direct claim against the site-owner if his employer has not paid his wages nor yet received payment from the site-owner (art. 1798 Code civil; so, too, art. 1676 Codice civile). The same idea benefits the subcontractor who has done building work pursuant to a contract with the main contractor: he, too, if the main contractor becomes insolvent can sue the site-owner directly for his unpaid fee to the extent that the general contractor's claims have not been met (art. 12 Law of 31 Dec. 1975). Another instance of the *action directe* which is of great practical importance occurs in the law of insurance: if a tortfeasor is covered in respect of an accident by a policy of liability insurance, the victim can sue the insurer direct. This is now the law throughout Europe.

What these cases have in common with the *stipulation pour autrui* is that a third party who takes no part in the formation of the contract may 'force' himself as creditor on the contractual debtor and demand that performance be rendered to himself. But while under a *stipulation pour autrui* the third party's right to claim is inferred, often with the help of construction, from the will of the *parties*, in the case of the *action directe* it is the *legislator* who decides on the basis of an abstract balancing of the interests involved that the third party should have a right to intervene, regardless of whether this is in accordance with the will of the parties or not.

<h2 style="text-align:center">IV</h2>

English law has not yet been able to bring itself to adopt the contract for the benefit of third parties as a legal institution of general application. All the textbooks start their discussion of the matter with the observation of VISCOUNT HALDANE in a decision of the House of Lords:

'My Lords, in the law of England certain principles are fundamental. One is that only a person who is a party to a contract can sue on it. Our law knows nothing of a ius quaesitum tertio arising by way of contract. Such a right may be conferred by way of property, as, for example, under a trust, but it cannot be conferred on a stranger to a contract as a right to enforce the contract in personam' (*Dunlop* v. *Selfridge*, [1915] AC 847, 853).

In the middle of the eighteenth century English courts did occasionally enforce contracts for the benefit of third parties, but the leading case of *Tweddle* v. *Atkinson* (1861) 121 Eng. Rep. 762 finally set England on the path of principled refusal to accept them.

Mr Tweddle and Miss Guy were married rather young, and in order to contribute to the young couple's living expenses both fathers entered a written contract in which each bound himself to pay a named sum of money to Mr Tweddle. They further agreed 'that the said William Tweddle has full power to sue the said parties in any court of law or equity for the aforesaid sums hereby promised and specified'. The bride's father, Mr Guy, died without paying, so Mr Tweddle raised a claim against his executor, Atkinson. The claim was dismissed: the court could not bring itself to accept that the plaintiff, a third party and a stranger to the contract, had any right to sue on it.

Courts and writers in England seek to justify this rule by reference to the doctrine of 'privity of contract', regarded as a basic principle of English law. In this doctrine we meet once again the old idea of contract as a basically bilateral *vinculumjuris*. All that 'privity of contract' really means is that a contract can generate rights and obligations only for and against the parties to it. This is a very reasonable principle so far as it means that a contract may not impose burdens on third parties, since in principle no one should be lumbered with contractual obligations unless he agrees to them, but it is far from clear to the comparative lawyer why contracts in favour of third parties should offend against the doctrine of privity, especially as English law, as will be shown in a moment, has itself abandoned this principle in a whole series of cases.

The main objection to the doctrine of 'privity of contract' is simply that the law should respect the intentions of the parties. If they have agreed that a third party not involved in the conclusion of the contract should be able to claim what one of the parties has promised, their agreement should be upheld. The general requirements for any contract must of course be met, but provided there is no illegality, immorality, deceit or duress, the will of the parties should be respected and the third party permitted to sue for what was promised. To decide otherwise would be

'to make it possible for a person to snap his fingers at a bargain deliberately made, a bargain not in itself unfair, and which the person seeking to enforce it has a legitimate interest to enforce' (LORD DUNEDIN, in *Dunlop* v. *Selfridge* [1915] AC 847, 855).

This is well demonstrated by *Beswick* v. *Beswick* [1968] AC 58, where a written contract was made between a septuagenarian coal merchant in Lancashire and his nephew: the old man was to transfer his coal business to the nephew and the nephew was to pay him £6 per week for the rest of his life and then £5 per week to his widow. When the old man died, the nephew refused to pay the widow anything, and she sued him both in her own right and in her quality as administratrix of her deceased husband's estate. After divergent opinions in the courts below the case reached the House of Lords. There the widow's claim *in her own right* was rejected: she was not a party to the contract made with the nephew and therefore could acquire no rights under it. She won all the same, however, because as *administratrix* of her husband's estate she could exercise his right to claim specific performance of the nephew's promise to pay her.

The fact that the widow was the administratrix of the estate was purely adventitious and should have had no effect on the outcome; the nephew himself might have been the administrator, and then the widow would have got nothing. This is absurd.

In England itself the doctrine of privity is much criticized as 'an anachronistic shortcoming that has for many years been regarded as a reproach to English law' (LORD DIPLOCK in *Swain* v. *Law Society* [1983] 1 AC 598, 611). The doctrine has managed to survive only because Parliament and the courts have found many ways of getting round it.

For example, s. 11 of the Married Women's Property Act 1882 provides that if a person insures his life in favour of his spouse or children the beneficiary is to be regarded as the beneficiary of a trust, and therefore entitled to claim on the death of the insured. So also in motor insurance the 'permitted driver', though not a party to the insurance contract, may demand an indemnity from the insurer: *Williams* v. *Baltic Ins. Co.*, [1924] 2 KB 282, accepted the fiction that the insured becomes trustee of the claims under the insurance policy for the 'permitted driver', a solution which the legislator has since adopted in s. 148(7) of the Road Traffic Act 1988.

Apart from these instances where the *legislature* has given the third party a right to claim, English law holds in reserve other legal institutions which may under certain circumstances be used to give the desired result. The trust must be mentioned first of all. In essence, a trust arises when a person transfers an item of property to a trustee so that the latter may manage it in favour of third persons according to the instructions of the transferor. Cases like the German farm surrender contracts can thus be solved in the Common Law by saying that the transferee of the farm holds the farm as trustee and is obliged 'in equity' to make certain contributions from the farm to his relatives as beneficiaries of the trust. But even contract rights can be treated as trust property: A's rights under a contract with B may be asserted by C if the court accepts that they are held by A as trustee for C. However, in recent years English courts have been rather reluctant to use the 'trust of a promise' as an alternative to the contract for the benefit of third parties, perhaps because the trust is really an institution of property law and it might unduly weaken the principle of privity of contract if every contractual right were treated without more as the object of a fictive trust in favour of beneficiaries not parties to the contract (see TREITEL 562 ff.; CHESHIRE/FIFOOT/ FURMSTON 455 ff.).

Courts have been very ingenious in sidestepping the doctrine of privity. This is well illustrated by cases involving exemption clauses. Can a stevedore who damages cargo rely on an exemption clause contained in the contract between the owner and the carrier? Unless there is a direct contractual relationship between the owner and the stevedore the answer according to the doctrine of privity must be 'No', but the courts found it just possible to establish such a relationship by holding that in having the exemption clause inserted in the contract of carriage the carrier was acting as the 'agent' of the stevedore. See *Scruttons Ltd* v. *Midland Silicones* [1962] AC 446; *The Eurymedon* [1975] AC 154; *The New York Star* [1981] 1 WLR 138.

In the United States contracts for the benefit of third parties have been accepted since 1859, when the New York Court of Appeal decided *Lawrence* v. *Fox* 20 NY 268 (1859). Most states distinguish according to whether the transaction represents a gratuitous disposition or the payment of a debt. An instance of the first would be when a person takes out a life assurance policy and names his wife as the beneficiary: here the wife obtains a claim to payment of the insured sum without having given anything to her husband in exchange, so in American terminology she ranks as a 'donee beneficiary'. One speaks of 'creditor beneficiaries' on the other hand when a person wishes to pay off a debt and instead of paying the creditor himself he procures another person to promise him that he will make the necessary performance to the creditor. This distinction is of no significance for the critical question whether in a particular case a third party actually obtains an independent right to claim as an 'intended beneficiary', or whether he is simply an 'incidental beneficiary'. The almost unanimous view is that the answer depends on whether at the time of concluding the contract the parties intended the third party to have an independent right. If the agreement leaves the matter open, then just as in Germany it depends on the circumstances of the case, the purpose of the contract, and the intention of the promisee as known to the promisor.

For the details, see Restatement (Second) of Contracts (1981) §§302 ff., CORBIN §776, KESSLER (above p. 456), the decisions there cited, and above all EISENBERG (above p. 456).

V

Comparative lawyers sometimes say that its highly developed art of applying judicial decisions makes it easy for the Common Law to adapt itself quickly to changes in economic and social circumstances by modifying its legal principles and standards. This is contrasted with the way law develops on the Continent, where it is said to have a tendency to limp some way behind the changing world, being mainly the product of the legislator, and to be prevented from looking reality squarely in the face because its legal scholars have an undue predilection for abstract conceptualism and generalization. There may be a grain of truth in these observations, but the example of contracts for the benefit of third parties shows that they could well be stood on their heads.

It was in France that the *courts*, faced with the intractable text of art. 1121 Code civil, set themselves energetically to the task of remoulding the law and developed rules which helped them to control the new phenomenon of 'life assurance'. And it has been seen that the mature manner in which the German BGB deals with the contract for the benefit of third parties is very largely attributable to the conceptual clarity with which the *scholarship* of the *Gemeines Recht* illuminated this institution.

By contrast, English law has clung with remarkable tenacity to the principle that 'only a person who is a party to a contract can sue on it'. Whether the principle is due to the privity doctrine or the doctrine of consideration or both has been the subject of more hair-splitting discussion than one would have expected of English lawyers, and the sophisticated and artificial constructions which the courts themselves have dreamt up in their concern to keep the principle intact should evoke the admiration of Continental observers.

However, the death knell of the privity doctrine is sounding. The English Law Commission is working on a reform which would allow third parties to sue. It is true that in 1937 the Law Reform Committee had no success with its proposal 'that where a contract by its express terms purports to confer a benefit directly to a third party, the third party shall be entitled to enforce the provision in its own name' but the chances of success seem rather better today. This may be because judges have openly expressed their disdain for the doctrine and have urged the legislator to act, hinting that otherwise they could take the matter in hand themselves, or because in recent years several other jurisdictions in Common Law countries have been bold enough to abolish the doctrine, sometimes by legislation, sometimes by judicial decision.

See the decision of the High Court of Australia in *Trident General Ins. Co.* v. *McNiece Bros. Pty.* (1988) 62 ALJR 508, and on it REYNOLDS in (1989) 105 *LQ Rev.* 105.—Details on the present position as regards reform in England are given by BEATSON (above p. 456). The third party would be given a right to claim perform-ance if it was the common intention of the parties that he should have such an action, but contracts would not have what in Germany is called protective effect for third parties. This restriction is disputed in England but it is understandable in view of the fact that the third party gets better protection from the law of tort there than in Germany. On this interesting point, see BEATSON 22–26; LORENZ, 'Some Thoughts about Contract and Tort' in *Essays in Memory of Professor Lawson* (WALLINGTON and MERKIN eds., 1986) 86; LORENZ, 'Contract Beneficiaries in German Law' in *The Gradual Convergence* (MARKESINIS ed., 1994) 65; MARKESINIS, 'An Expanding Tort Law—the Price of a Rigid Contract Law', 103 *LQ Rev.* 103 (1987); MARKESINIS, *A Comparative Introduction to the German Law of Torts* (3rd edn. 1994) 50 ff.; KÖTZ, 'The Doctrine of Privity of Contract', [1990] *Tel Aviv University Studies in Law* 195.

VIII. THE PERFORMANCE OF CONTRACTS

35

Claims to Performance and Their Enforcement

BORÉ, 'La Liquidation de l'astreinte comminatoire', D. 1966 *Chron.* 159.

BURROWS, 'Specific Performance at the Crossroads', 4 *LS* 102 (1984).

DAWSON, 'Specific Performance in France and Germany', 57 *Mich. L. Rev.* 495 (1959).

DRAI, 'L'exécution des décisions judiciaires et les moyens de pression à la disposition du tribunal', *Rev. int. dr. comp.* 38 (1986) 511.

FRÉJAVILLE, 'L'Astreinte', D. 1949 *Chron.* 1.

——, 'La Valeur pratique de l'astreinte', JCP 1951. I. 910.

JEANDIDIER, 'L'Exécution forcée des obligations contractuelles' *Rev. trim. civ.* 74 (1976) 700.

JONES/GOODHART, *Specific Performance* (1986).

RABEL, *Das Recht des Warenkaufs*, vol. I (1936) 269 ff., 375 ff.

RASSAT, 'L'Astreinte définitive', JCP 1967 D. 2069.

RAYNAUD, 'La Distinction de l'astreinte et des dommages-intérêts dans la jurisprudence française récente', *Mélanges Secrétan* (1964) 249.

REMIEN, *Rechtsverwirklichung durch Zwangsgeld: Vergleich, Vereinheitlichung, Kollisionsrecht* (1992).

RHEINSTEIN, *Die Struktur des vertraglichen Schuldverhältnisses im anglo-amerikanischen Recht* (1932) 138 ff.

SAVATIER, 'L'exécution des condamnations au payement d'une astreinte', D. 1951. *Chron.* 37.

SCHOBERT, 'Die Realerfüllung, insbesondere nach anglo-amerikanischem Recht', (Diss. Berne, 1952).

SZLADITS, 'The Concept of Specific Performance in Civil Law', 4 *Am. J. Comp. L.* 208 (1955).

TREITEL, 'Specific Performance in the Sale of Goods', 1966 *J. Bus. L.* 211.

——, *Remedies for Breach of Contract, A Comparative Account* (1988), Ch. 3: Enforced Performance.

TUNC, 'Le Renouveau de l'astreinte en droit français', *Festschrift Riese* (1964) 397.

I

A PERSON who enters a contract expects the other party to do as he promised. He may be disappointed. The goods may not be delivered, the purchased premises may not be vacated, the tenant may stay on after the end of the lease, the singer may not give the covenanted recital, or the ex-employee may set himself up in competition contrary to his promise. The question then arises what forms of relief the legal system will offer the innocent contractor who has been deceived in his expectation that the contract will be performed. One point is agreed in all modern legal systems: the creditor must not simply proceed to help himself and snatch the goods from the vendor, thrust the tenant into the street, or use similar private and forcible methods to compel the other contracting party to perform his promise. The innocent party must go to court and establish the claims which accrue to him on non-performance of the contract before he takes any further steps against the debtor, and those steps too must proceed under the supervision of the state.

The contractor who has suffered a loss because he has not got what he was promised may be content with monetary compensation. This will normally be the case if something as good as what was promised can be procured elsewhere, even at a higher price, for the innocent party will be content to sue the defaulter for damages for the extra he has to pay. But what is to be done when it is difficult or even impossible to calculate the harm, or when no calculation one can do will reflect any special interest the creditor may have in having the contract performed? If a man buys a picture which has a 'sentimental value' for him, inestimable in money, perhaps because it is a portrait of a noted ancestor, is he only to claim damages if the picture is not delivered or can he ask a court to order the auctioneer to deliver the picture to him? Under what circumstances—and this is our first question—may a court, at the instance of the plaintiff, order the defendant to perform his contract *in natura*, that is, order the auctioneer to deliver the picture, the tenant to vacate the dwelling, the singer to give the concert as promised, and the employee to cease from competition?

Even if the court grants the creditor's claim for performance, he still does not have what he really wants, for many debtors do not satisfy a claim even if it has been established in court, either because they cannot do so or think they cannot, or because they do not want to. Here the state helps the creditor by set procedures for using its coercive powers to satisfy his claim against the debtor's will, unless the debtor's co-operation is required, when it will influence his will with forceful sanctions, threatened or applied.

We shall devote no further attention to the execution of money claims such as judgments for the price of goods. This is done in all countries by having state execution officials seize and sell the property of the debtor and then hand the proceeds of the sale to the creditor.

Two questions therefore remain for discussion. Under what circumstances may a contractor ask a court to issue judgment ordering the other party to perform the contract? How is such a judgment, not being simply a money judgment, actually executed?

II

In *German* law and in related systems it is axiomatic that a creditor has the right to bring a claim for performance of a contract and to obtain a judgment ordering the debtor to fulfil it. For this purpose it is immaterial whether the debtor's obligation is to deliver goods pursuant to a sale, to vacate a dwelling house, or to produce a work of art. The view that it is of the very essence of an obligation that it be actionable in this sense is so fundamental that it is not expressly stated in any legislative text, but the words of §241 of the Civil Code, that the creditor is entitled, on the grounds of the creditor–debtor relationship, 'to demand performance from the debtor', imply that actual performance may be demanded before a court and that a judgment ordering performance in kind may be issued by it.

A judgment ordering the debtor to perform his contract in kind can be issued only if performance by the debtor is still *possible*. As the Reichsgericht once said, it would be 'nonsensical to order a person to perform when it has been established that performance is objectively impossible' (RGZ 107, 15, 17). Accordingly a judgment for performance cannot be issued if, for instance, a picture has been destroyed after sale, or if a ship has been requisitioned while under charter, or if, just before the première, an opera-singer is rendered so hoarse by a bad cold that for the duration she cannot sing; in such cases the creditor can bring only a claim for damages.

This can admittedly lead to unfair results when goods are in very short supply. Suppose that a person hands a gold wrist-watch to a jeweller for repair and that the watch is stolen from the jeweller because he failed to look after it properly. A claim for money damages is not of much use in a situation such as existed shortly after the Second World War when money was virtually valueless and watches could not be bought at all but only obtained in exchange for other goods of value. The courts were able to assist here by invoking the view contained in §249 BGB, that the principal obligation of a person bound to make compensation is to 'bring about the situation which would have existed were it not for the occurrence of the circumstance which rendered him liable to make compensation'. This basic principle of 'restitution in kind' (*Naturalrestitution*), which is not of great significance in normal times, was then brought into play in cases where the defendant was responsible for his inability to hand over a specific chattel intact or at all; he was ordered to make compensation, not by the payment of money, which was then almost worthless, but by transferring to the plaintiff a different chattel of approximately the same value, either one out of his own stock or one which he had obtained in exchange for goods of his own. Thus in the case given above, the defendant jeweller was ordered to deliver a watch of equal value (AG Hamburg Süddt. JZ 1946, 180; compare also OLG Hamm MDR 1947, 100; LG Oldenburg Süddt. JZ 1946, 179). Decisions of this type ceased when the economic situation returned to normal.

When the contract fixes a time for performance and the debtor has allowed the time to elapse, another type of impossibility may arise. If the performance is such that, in itself or in the context of the contract, it can take place only within the fixed period—for example, the delivery of a wedding-cake or the participation of a singer in a Christmas concert—then, when the due date has gone by, the performance has become *impossible* and no judgment for performance can be given. But suppose a parcel of goods is to be delivered by the vendor in late October; delay does not necessarily render delivery futile, and so in November or December the purchaser can insist on a judgment for performance. In such a case the vendor may of course be in some doubt whether he is still bound to deliver or whether he must just be ready to pay damages. Doubts of this kind are undesirable, especially in commercial matters, as §376 Commercial Code shows: this provision lays down that if in a contract of sale a specific date or fixed period is set for performance and not adhered to, the innocent party can, under certain conditions, demand damages or else withdraw from the contract; if despite the delay, he wants to insist on performance in kind, he must so notify the other party as soon as the contractual date has passed; if he does not do so, his claim for performance will fail. The same result flows from §326 BGB on the expiry of the extra time allowed to dilatory contractor (compare below Ch. 36 II 2).

However, a judgment ordering the debtor to perform is not of much use to the creditor unless the legal system provides the means to make it effective. Accordingly one must turn to the question whether and how such a judgment can be enforced.

The way in which the question is dealt with in German law is quite characteristic. The Code of Civil Procedure carefully distinguishes all the various types of claim which might underlie a judgment for performance, and provides quite distinct forms of execution for each of them. Thus §§883–6 of the Code deal with the execution of judgments on claims for the delivery of property. The method provided—the only method—is for the bailiff (*Gerichtsvollzieher*) to take the chattel from the debtor or to require him to leave the premises, with the help of the police, if necessary, and then to hand over the chattel or premises to the creditor. If the claim on which the creditor has obtained judgment is that the debtor should take some positive action other than handing over the property, a distinction is made. If the act in question is one which could be equally well performed by someone else, that is, it need not be performed by the debtor personally but is, as the Code of Civil Procedure puts it, *vertretbar*, then the method of execution—the only method—is for the creditor, on the authority of the court granted at his request, to have the act performed by a third party at the expense of the debtor (*Ersatzvornahme*, §887 Code of Civil Procedure).

As examples of acts which are *vertretbar*, or capable of substitute performance, one may cite manual tasks which call for no especial talent and can therefore be carried out by third parties—the execution of building operations (LG Hagen JR 1948, 314), the installation of a lift in an apartment block (KG JW 1927, 1945), the printing of a manuscript (OLG Munich MDR 1955, 682). The making of an extract from the books of a business or the production of its accounts may also be 'vertretbar' if an expert could do it after inspecting the debtor's records (OLG Hamburg MDR 1955, 43).

If the act to which the creditor lays claim is one which can be performed only by the debtor himself, it is said to be *unvertretbar*. In such a case the method of execution provided by the Code of Civil Procedure (§888) is to threaten the unwilling debtor with a fine or imprisonment.

This is possible only when the act in question 'depends exclusively on the will of the debtor', in the words of §888 Code of Civil Procedure. It is therefore not possible where, for example, the debtor's obligation is to do something which calls for special artistic or scientific talent, for the performance of such acts does not depend exclusively on the debtor's will. However good his intentions may be, a composer cannot compose his sonata nor a law professor write his commentary without the right inspiration, mood, energy, and other preconditions of great spiritual creativity (see OLG Frankfurt OLGE 29, 251). Finally the Code of Civil Procedure lists in §888 several more specific cases where these methods of penal pressure are unavailable. Thus one may not execute a judgment obtained by one spouse requiring the other to reconstitute the conditions of married life, and one may not execute a judgment which orders the defendant to perform services under a contract of employment. The employer may certainly obtain a judgment which imposes on the employee the duty to perform his obligations under the contract of service (so, in terms, RGZ 72, 393, 394), but this judgment cannot be enforced, because the employee must at all times remain free to decide how to dispose of his labour, even if this involves a breach of contract: in such a case the employer must content himself with a claim for damages.

There is a special regulation for the case where the positive act required of the debtor by the judgment is a declaration of intention or consent (*Willenserklärung*); the effect of §894 Code of Civil Procedure is that as soon as the judgment is final the declaration is deemed to have been made.

If, instead of requiring the debtor to take positive action, the judgment orders him to *abstain* from action or to *permit* someone else to take action, §890 Code of Civil Procedure applies: should the debtor act in breach of such a duty, the court may, on the application of the creditor, imprison him or fine him, the fine going once again to the Treasury. The debtor must have notice that such sanctions are to be invoked: this notice is normally contained in the original judgment.

III

In the *Romanistic* systems also the claim for performance of a contract is generally recognized. Art 1184 par. 2 of the French Code civil provides that a party to a synallagmatic contract who has not received what he was promised is entitled to demand resolution of the contract and damages or 'to require the other to perform the agreement in so far as that is still possible' (see Civ. 6 Jan. 1932, DH 1932, 114; see also art. 1453 Codice civile). Sales contracts are covered by a special provision of the Code civil: according to art. 1610, instead of seeking resolution of the contract for non-delivery, the purchaser may demand that the vendor put him in possession of the goods. In the same way the creditor may obtain a judgment requiring the debtor to perform the promised services (Civ. 20 Jan. 1913, S. 1913. 1. 386), to provide business particulars (Civ. 7 Nov. 1923, D. 1926. 1. 171), to vacate a dwelling (Paris 28 April 1948, JCP 1948. II. 4333), or to name an arbitrator (Paris 1 March 1951, DH 1951, 1. 315).

There is, however, another provision of the French Code civil which seems in terms to prohibit any judgment which obliges a debtor to act or refrain from acting in a particular way. This is art. 1142 Code civil: 'toute obligation de faire ou de ne pas faire se résout en dommages et intérêts, en cas d'inexécution de la part du débiteur'.

The underlying idea is that, man being a free and responsible being, he should not be coerced by the state into behaving in a particular way. This is a most praiseworthy idea but it is far too vague, and its formulation in art. 1142 Code civil, as experience has shown, is much too sweeping. In consequence, the vendor's obligation to deliver the goods is treated as an 'obligation de donner' and not as an 'obligation de faire' (see art. 1101 Code civil), so that the purchaser, who becomes owner of the goods at the time of the contract, if they are specific, and at the time of the ascertainment, usually, if they are purchased by description (see art. 1138 Code civil), can make good his claim to delivery, once it is reduced to judgment, by having the *huissier* seize the goods *manu militari* from the vendor and deliver them to him ('saise-revendication' under art. 826 Code de procédure civile). The basic principle is further restricted by arts. 1143 and 1144. Under art. 1144 a court may, even before proceedings on the merits are concluded, empower the creditor to have a third party do the act promised by the debtor and charge the debtor with the cost. Of course this is done only where the personal participation of the debtor is not required, that is, in cases where the act in question is impersonal or, as §887 of the German Code of Civil Procedure has it, 'vertretbar'.

We may sum up by saying that French law generally admits the issuance of judgments for performance in kind but enforces them in a very grudging manner. Leaving aside the execution of claims for payment, only judgments for the delivery of specified goods are covered by special rules of execution: these the *huissier* may seize directly. If the judgment concerns other acts or abstentions neither the Code civil nor the Code de procédure civile prescribes any specific means of execution, although if the promised act is impersonal the creditor can ask at the trial for power under art. 1144 Code civil to do or have someone else do what the debtor should have done and to charge him for it.

This legislative coverage of compulsory execution of judgments in specie is obviously quite inadequate. In an attempt to fill the gaps, the French courts have, since the beginning of the nineteenth century, developed a special coercive technique called the 'astreinte' (for full details see REMIEN (above p. 470) 33 ff.). On issuing a judgment requiring a debtor to perform *in natura* a court may order that for every day he remains in default the debtor must pay a specified sum of money to the plaintiff as 'astreinte'. The courts have two forms of *astreinte* at their discretionary disposal. The 'astreinte provisoire' is so called because when the court later comes to finalize the amount of *astreinte* payable by the debtor it is not bound by its prior decision and may order the payment of a lesser sum than was threatened. But there is also the 'astreinte définitive', where the original judicial order is final, especially with regard to the amount to be paid per day, week, or month; later proceedings do the simple arithmetic of multiplying the sum fixed in the judgment by the number of units of time during which the debtor has remained in default contrary to the terms of the judgment. The threatened *astreinte* expires at the end of the period fixed in the judgment, but if the debtor has still not performed, the creditor can ask the court to apply a new *astreinte* for a further period.

It must not be supposed that an *astreinte* is available only where the statutory methods of execution are inapplicable or impractical. An *astreinte* may be issued to promote the delivery of a specified motor vehicle (Com. 12 Dec. 1966, Bull. civ. 1966. III. 424) or the conveyance and delivery of landed property (Req. 18 Nov. 1907, S. 1913. 1. 386), although in such cases direct execution through the *huissier* is perfectly possible. Judgments ordering a tenant to vacate a dwelling may be executed by having the *huissier* expel the tenant by force, with the assistance of other state organs if necessary, but the courts regularly apply the *astreinte* in such judgments for possession because in the post-war years when homelessness was a serious risk the state authorities used to refuse to assist in executing such judgments. The courts therefore resorted to coercion by means of the *astreinte* so as to induce the tenant to agree to quit. This device the legislator also defused by enacting in a law of 21 July 1949 that judgments for possession against tenants could carry only *astreintes provisoires* which could be finalized only after the tenant had vacated the premises and must never amount to more than the loss actually sustained by the owner.

Nor do the courts hesitate to impose *astreintes* in cases where the creditor might have used the method of 'surrogate performance' offered by art. 1144 Code civil, as where a neighbour was ordered to remove a boundary wall (Civ. 7 April 1965, Bull. civ. 1965. I. 192) or a vendor to dismantle faulty machinery he had delivered (Civ. 20 Jan. 1913, S. 1913. 1. 386). The Court of Cassation has recently held that an *astreinte* may even be attached to a money judgment, at least if the creditor has no other effective means of enforcing his claim for payment. This was the situation in Com. 17 April 1956, JCP 1956. 9330 (noted VELLIEUX). The city of Marseilles had failed to honour a judgment rendered against it in respect of compensation for expropriation; the civil judge threatened it with an *astreinte* if it persisted further in delay and was upheld by the Court of Cassation.

Such cases will not often arise, since the *saisie-exécution* of arts. 583 ff. Code de procédure civile provides the normal means of executing money judgments. Nor will a vendor often be required under pain of *astreinte* to deliver generic goods, since the purchaser can normally cover himself in the market and so has no interest in performance by the vendor personally (but see Req. 21 Dec. 1920, DP 1921. 1. 62). But the situation may be different in wartime when goods are in short supply; then the purchaser might well seek performance by the vendor *in natura*, and the latter could be ordered to deliver on pain of *astreinte* if he did not (for example, see Trib. com. Seine 16 Dec. 1919, DP 1920. 2. 34; Besançon 4 Dec. 1946, Gaz, Pal. 1947. 1. 20).

The *astreinte* really comes into its own when there is no statutory means for executing judgments, for example, where the debtor has been ordered to do something other than pay money or deliver things, such as issue a certificate of employment (Soc. 29 June 1966, Bull. civ. 1966. IV. 534), or move his business (Com. 6 Oct. 1966, Bull. civ. 1966. III. 424). The *astreinte* is also used where the plaintiff wants to prevent the defendant from doing something, the difference here being that the amount of the *astreinte* depends on how often the debtor contravened his duty to desist rather than on how long he remained in breach. Thus when a soft drink manufacturer was enjoined from using bottles so like those of the plaintiff as to constitute unfair competition, the *astreinte* was in the form that the defendant should pay 10 francs 'par infraction constatée' (Com. 31 March 1965, Bull. civ. 1965. III. 219).

Superficially it might seem that the *astreinte* is like the money penalties which may be imposed *in terrorem* under §§888 and 890 of the German Code of Civil Procedure in judgments which order the debtor to cease and desist or to co-operate in doing the requisite act. There is an important distinction, however, since the *astreintes* go into the pocket of the creditor while the monetary penalties go to the state treasury.

This significant difference becomes comprehensible if we remember that in France it was the courts which invented the *astreinte* and had to do it *extra legem*, 'en marge des textes', for they realized that in view of the inadequacy of the statutory methods of execution the only way of ensuring that judgments were satisfied was by threatening defaulting debtors with monetary penalties. Even if the idea that such payments might be made to the *state* had occurred to the French courts, they could hardly have acted on it in the absence of any statutory basis. It was much simpler to see the *astreinte* as a special form of threatening and granting *compensatory damages*, and so link it to a well-known institution of private law. This indeed was the basic point of departure for the French courts. Since the *astreinte* was a *threat* designed to induce the debtor to co-operate, it was seen that the amount he was threatened with having to pay should not be limited to the harm suffered by the creditor but should depend on the probable recalcitrance of the debtor and his capacity to perform. But when it came to quantification or 'liquidation' of the *astreinte*, the judge was to fix it solely in relation to the amount of economic harm provably suffered by the creditor through the failure to perform or delay in performing. In the nineteenth century the debtor in these cases was always threatened with the payment of 'dommages et intérêts': the word 'astreinte' entered legal language rather later.

But if at the end of the day the *astreinte* turns into an award of damages it loses all its coercive character. As French writers have often said, there is little point in a judge's threatening a debtor with a draconian *astreinte* in the event of non-performance if it is clear that he will never have to pay more than simple compensation. After many years of indecision in the courts, there are now many cases where the Court of Cassation has held that the *astreinte* has nothing to do with compensation and should normally be related in amount to the degree of the debtor's fault in not performing and to his economic circumstances. This clearly gives the institution a penal character: no longer is it a special form of damages award, but the open threat of a real private punishment.

The leading decision, noted by HOLLEAUX, is Civ. 20 Oct. 1959, D. 1959, 537. The defendant electricity company, sued by a neighbour, had been ordered 'sous astreinte' to execute certain building operations on its land. The defendant failed to do the work, and the plaintiff had the *astreinte* 'liquidated'; at the same time he asked for a new *astreinte*, and the court granted it, for a period of three months. This too failed to have any effect and again the plaintiff obtained a liquidation and yet another *astreinte*, limited as before to three months, of 10,000 francs per day. Yet again nothing happened. Only when the court fixed the amount of the *astreinte* at 900,000 francs (90 days at 10,000 francs per day) was the defendant stirred to action. He argued that on liquidation an *astreinte* must be limited to the amount of harm actually suffered. The court of appeal rejected this argument and upheld the judgment (Riom 10 Dec. 1956, S. 1957, 112), as did the Court of Cassation, which said that the *astreinte provisoire* is 'une mesure de contrainte entièrement distincte des dommages-intérêts . . . un moyen de vaincre la résistance opposée à l'exécution d'une condamnation'. It is not intended as compensation for the harm the creditor may have suffered as a result of the delay in performance but should normally be quantified 'en fonction de la gravité de la faute du débiteur récalcitrant et de ses facultés'. To the same effect see Civ. 20 Jan. 1960, JCP 1960. II. 11483; Civ. 12 July 1960, Bull. civ. 1960. I. 319; Civ. 17 March 1965, Bull. civ. 1965. I. 143.

Although the *astreinte* is an entrenched institution of French court practice, it has constantly been criticized in legal writings, and these criticisms gain in force as its coercive and penal character is increasingly admitted by the courts. Indeed, it is not at all clear why the creditor, in addition to receiving compensation for the harm he has suffered, should also obtain the amount of the *astreinte* which is designed to overcome the debtor's reluctance to honour the judgment, especially if the *astreinte* is fixed in relation to the culpability of the debtor's behaviour and to the extent of his financial resources. The hybrid nature of the *astreinte* seems to cause a certain malaise in France: when a bill to put the *astreinte* on a proper statutory footing was being discussed in 1971, it was seriously proposed—though the proposal was not adopted—that the sum payable by the debtor should go half to the state and half to the creditor. The actual law provides that the *astreinte* goes in full to the creditor, and also makes clear that the purpose of the *astreinte* is to put pressure on the debtor rather than to compensate the creditor (art. 33 ff. Law no. 91–650 of 9 July 1991, from Law of 5 July 1972).

The rules of *Dutch, Belgian,* and *Luxembourg* law, unified as from 1 Jan. 1980 by the Benelux Convention on a Uniform Law of Monetary Penalties, are given in Remien (above p. 470) 41 ff. The *astreinte* has been adopted by several other European countries, such as Greece (art. 946 f. Code of Civil Procedure), Poland (art. 1050 f. Code of Civil Procedure), and Portugal (art. 829–A Civil Code), the latter with the remarkable feature that the monetary penalty is to be split equally between the state and the creditor. The UNIDROIT Principles for International Commercial Contracts allow for the sanction of an *astreinte*, payable to the creditor, if not inconsistent with mandatory rules of the *lex fori* (art. 7.2.4).

IV

In both German and French law, as we have seen, a contractor is in principle entitled to demand that his contract be performed in specie. The standpoint of the *Common Law* is quite different: if a contractor does not do as he promised, the innocent party's only right, in general, is to bring a claim for breach of contract, a claim which is historically derived from the tort remedy of trespass and which always leads to monetary compensation or damages. The idea that the conclusion of the contract engenders an enforceable duty to perform it is a notion foreign to the Common Law; instead, it starts from the proposition expressed by O. W. Holmes (*The Common Law* (1881) 301) that 'the only universal consequence of a legally binding promise is that the law makes the promisor pay damages if the promised act does not come to pass'.

In saying that the Common Law does not render judgments obliging the debtor to perform his promise, we are referring only to the Common Law in the narrow sense, that is, to the rules of law historically developed by the royal courts. But in addition the equity of the Chancellor and later of the Court of Chancery gradually produced rules which in very hard cases mollified the rigid principle that claims for performance were inadmissible. Under these rules a plaintiff could exceptionally claim 'specific performance' if he could persuade the Equity Court that the remedies available to him 'at law', especially the action for damages for breach of contract, were inadequate. In both England and the United States today the distinction between the jurisdictions of the courts of law and of equity has largely been abolished and all courts now apply concurrently the rules developed 'at law' and 'in equity', but the idea still remains that the claim for specific performance is exceptional. Even today it is constantly emphasized that the grant of a decree of specific performance remains 'in the complete discretion' of the judge, although this discretion, as a result of much court practice, has long been exercised in accordance with fixed rules, subject to the principle of *stare decisis* as much as other areas of Anglo-American Law.

The most important requirement which a person must satisfy if he seeks a decree of specific performance is that the normal sanction of damages is 'inadequate' and that he has an interest in the performance of the contract which cannot well be translated into money terms. Where the contract is to transfer land or real rights, the creditor's interest in the land in question cannot be adequately estimated in money if there is no identical or similar plot of land in existence or for sale. The situation would of course be different if the sale were of a terraced house or a standard plot of land in a new development area. Even so the claim for performance is *always* granted in such cases, even if on the facts a claim for damages would be quite adequate. Sales of other property are treated differently. With regard to sales of securities, a distinction is made: the claim for damages is perfectly adequate as a remedy for the purchaser of treasury bonds, but if the sale concerns shares which are not to be bought in the stock-market or privately, a claim for specific performance is granted. The sale of *goods* is covered by legislation. English courts may apply s. 52 of the Sale of Goods Act 1979 at the instance of the purchaser of 'specific or ascertained goods' and issue judgment 'that the contract shall be performed specifically'. It is in the court's discretion whether to issue such a judgment or not. In the United States §2–716(1) of the Uniform Commercial Code prescribes generally that specific performance may be decreed 'where the goods are unique or in other proper circumstances', and a claim for performance is normally granted if the sale is of specific goods which are very rare or extremely valuable or of a special sentimental value to the purchaser, such as an heirloom, a triptych, a Renaissance mirror, a valuable snuff-box, or a horse already familiar to the purchaser. In sales of generic goods, on the other hand, a claim for damages is normally adequate since the purchaser can fairly easily cover himself by buying from elsewhere. The courts have sometimes granted specific performance even of sales of generic goods, especially in the United States where they are rather sceptical of the old doctrine that the claim for specific performance is exceptional. This is true, for example, of the 'requirement contract', whereby a supplier binds himself to supply a customer with raw materials or other goods as his needs arise. Here the courts decree specific performance against the supplier even if the materials could, at a pinch, be procured from elsewhere, provided that the supply would be uncertain or unreliable or would make for grave difficulties in the customer's business.

According to the official commentary to §2–716 UCC, cases of this sort present 'the typical commercial specific performance situation', but the courts in England are rather hesitant in this area and have been criticized for it by TREITEL ([1966] *J. Bus. L.* 211, 225 ff.). But note *Sky Petroleum* v. *VIP Petroleum* [1974] 1 WLR 576, where the defendant had a long-term contract to supply large quantities of petrol for the plaintiff's petrol stations. A tremendous increase in the price of oil made the defendant reluctant to perform the contract, and he ceased delivering for no sufficient reason. The plaintiff sought an injunction to prevent the defendant from withholding supplies of petrol. GOULDING J. stated that this was really a claim for specific performance since the plaintiff wanted the defendant to do something, namely to resume the contractual deliveries, rather than to desist from doing something. Although normally the non-delivery of generic goods gives rise to a claim for damages only, the judge here issued the order sought because petrol was so exceptionally scarce that the plaintiff had no other source of supply.

The inadequacy of a claim for damages is not the only relevant factor when a decree of specific performance is sought. The courts often ask whether the *execution* of a judgment for performance would involve great inconvenience. It is an argument *against* the granting of a decree of specific performance that the court might find it very difficult or time-consuming to ascertain whether it had been obeyed or that such ascertainment, in the case of long-term contracts, might be long delayed. Thus during the trial itself the court has an eye to the possibilities of prompt enforcement of the judgment, and for the same reason a claim for specific performance is denied if the debtor's obligation under the contract is so imprecise that it would be difficult to execute any judgment on the ground of 'vagueness' or 'uncertainty'.

The leading case in England is *Ryan* v. *Mutual Tontine Westminster Chambers Association*, [1893] 1 Ch. 116. In a lease to the plaintiff tenant the defendant landlord had undertaken to engage a porter to live in the basement of the dwelling and do specified tasks for the plaintiff. The plaintiff sought judgment against the defendant ordering him to perform his obligation *in natura*. The court rejected the claim on the ground that specific performance could not be decreed as the proper execution of such a long-term contract required 'constant superintendence by the Court'.—Difficulties in enforcement also provide the reason for denying specific performance of contracts for the construction of houses or the carrying out of large building operations, but the courts make exceptions where a claim for damages would not answer the plaintiff's interests, where the building operations have been sufficiently specified by plans or drawings and, where finally, at any rate in England, the defendant is in possession of the land where the building is to take place: see *Wolverhampton Corp.* v. *Emmons*, [1901] 1 KB 515; *Carpenters' Estates Ltd* v. *Davies*, [1940] Ch. 160.—Here, too, American courts grant specific performance more readily: see, for example, *Fleischer* v. *James Drug Stores*, 1 NJ 138, 62 A. 2d 383 (1948); *Gregson-Robinson Stores Inc.* v. *Iris Construction Corp.*, 8 NYS 2d 133, 168 NE 2d 377 (1960); *Roberts* v. *Brewer*, 371 SW 2d 424 (Tex. 1963).—*City Stores Co.* v. *Ammermann*, 266 F. Supp. 766 (DDC. 1967) is an excellent example of the care with which American courts weigh the plaintiff's interest in obtaining an order for specific performance as against the difficulties which a court would face in determining whether or not the defendant had conformed to the order granted. See also Restatement (Second) of Contracts (1981) § 366 and LINZER, 81 *Colum. L. Rev.* 111 (1981).

Specific performance will not be granted if the contract calls for personal services from the defendant. One reason given for this is that otherwise the defendant would be forced into a kind of involuntary servitude; another and more realistic reason is that services performed under such coercion would probably be of doubtful quality, and a third, not very convincing, reason is that it would be extremely difficult for the court to determine whether the services so performed were in accordance with the contract. In consequence, a singer cannot be ordered by judgment to give the concerts she had contracted to give. The court can however help the plaintiff in such a case by issuing a judgment forbidding the singer to appear for any of the plaintiff's competitors during the period of the contract. Such a judgment is called an 'injunction' and can only be rendered if two conditions are satisfied: first, it must clearly appear from the contract that the defendant is bound not to work for the contractor's competitors; secondly, the injunction must not debar the defendant from all activity whatsoever, since otherwise he would be indirectly forced, unemployment not being a real alternative, to perform the contract for the plaintiff.

On this see *Lumley* v. *Wagner*, (1852) 64 Eng. Rep. 1209; *Whitwood Chemical Co.* v. *Hardman*, [1891] 2 Ch. 416; *Mortimer* v. *Beckett*, [1920] 1 Ch. 571; *Warner Bros.* v. *Nelson*, [1937] 1 KB 209. For the American cases, see CORBIN §§1204 ff.

If judgment has been issued against the defendant ordering him to do or not to do a particular act, apart from the payment of money, and the defendant fails to obey the order for performance or acts in breach of the injunction the court has a whole series of different ways of enforcing the judgment. Like most of the law of procedure the relevant rules are to be found in the Rules of the Supreme Court rather than in a comprehensive code of procedure, the Rules of the Supreme Court being laid down pursuant to a legislative mandate in s. 84 ff. Supreme Court Act 1981 by a special committee, called the Rule Committee, comprising the Lord Chancellor, senior judges, and practising lawyers.

Since time immemorial English judges have exercised an inherent power to treat many kinds of behaviour as 'contempt of court' and to fine or imprison a litigant for 'contempt' if he refuses to obey a court order. Nowadays the power is recognized and regulated by the aforementioned Rules of the Supreme Court (Order 45). If the order is to deliver up a chattel or a plot of land, a 'writ of delivery' or a 'writ of possession' empowering the bailiff to take the property away from the debtor and give it to the creditor is usually issued, and failure to pay a money debt can no longer be sanctioned by imprisonment, since it was abolished by the Debtors Act 1869, but in all other cases the recalcitrant debtor can be imprisoned as well as fined, notably where he has been ordered to act or to desist from acting. The court can also issue a 'writ of sequestration' and freeze the debtor's assets 'until the defendant shall clear his contempt'. It is rather surprising that there is no clear statement anywhere of the extent and nature of the possible sanctions or even of the conditions under which an 'order of committal' may be suspended or discharged. Nor is it laid down anywhere that punishment for contempt of court should be a remedy of last resort, to be deployed only when other less drastic means of enforcement have proved unavailing. This very fact that disobedience to any court order may entail imprisonment or a fine may perhaps be one of the reasons why judges in Common Law systems are rather reluctant to order specific enforcement.

In his very thoughtful comparative study of the matter DAWSON (above p. 470) scrutinizes all the various doctrines of the Common Law which restrict claims for specific performance and concludes that the wide-ranging discretion of the Anglo-American judge is greatly to be regretted: 'Not only the initial decision whether or not to grant specific performance, and on what terms, but the choice and the severity of the sanctions imposed are all remitted to the judge's discretion. Particularly after studying the provisions of German law one is struck with our own failure to analyse and organize our system of sanctions. Instead of a carefully adjusted scale in which each mode of enforcement is assigned to its special task, we have almost no rule at all to regulate the choice or severity of sanctions' (at p. 533).

V

It is plain enough that the legal systems under consideration give very different answers to the questions posed at the beginning of this section. On the

Continent a plaintiff is in principle always entitled to a judgment requiring the defendant to perform his contract, while in the Common Law this is allowed only exceptionally. Once such a judgment is issued every legal system has its own special techniques for enforcing it; again these differ quite considerably.

While it is true that a claim for performance is the normal sanction in German and French law and that specific performance is regarded as exceptional in the Common Law, closer scrutiny reveals that the actual contrast is not quite so sharp. In Germany, on the one hand, where the claim to performance is regarded as the primary legal remedy, it does not in practice have anything like the significance originally attached to it, since whenever the failure to receive the promised performance can be made good by the payment of money commercial men prefer to claim damages rather than risk wasting time and money on a claim for performance whose execution may not produce satisfactory results. On the other hand, the traditional Common Law view, explicable only on historical grounds, that specific performance is an exceptional remedy is apparently losing some of its force. This is certainly true in the United States: according to CORBIN there is no doubt 'that the American courts have become progressively more liberal in the granting of this effective remedy and have become less astute in enforcing the requirement that the remedy in damages shall be inadequate' (§1139). In England, too, the trend is in the same direction, and TREITEL can say with justice that the distance between Common law and Civil Law

'is not as great as might appear. On the one hand, specific enforceability in civil law countries is subject to important exceptions; in particular, most of them observe the principle that obligations to render personal services cannot, in the last resort, be specifically enforced; orders for enforced performance of other obligations are sometimes more difficult to enforce than in common law countries; and, perhaps most important of all, an aggrieved contracting party will often prefer to claim compensation in money, as that is generally a quicker and to that extent a better remedy. On the other hand, some of the restrictions on specific performance are beginning to disappear in common law countries, as their historical foundations are eroded. This is not to say that there are no differences at all between civil and common law systems, but they are less considerable than the starting theories of the two approaches might suggest.' (*Remedies for Breach of Contract* (above p. 470) s. 71.)

A compromise position is adopted in the Vienna Convention on Contracts for the International Sale of Goods. On the one hand it leaves considerable scope for claims for performance: the seller can require the buyer to take delivery of the goods (art. 62 CISG) and the buyer can insist on delivery and, if the nonconformity of the goods constitutes a fundamental breach of contract, replacement by substitute goods (art. 46), even where it would be normal to enter a covering transaction and quite possible for the buyer to do so (in this last respect differing from art. 25 of its predecessor).

Art. 28, however, provides that 'a court is not bound to enter a judgment for specific performance unless the court would do so under its own law in respect of similar contracts of sale not governed by the Convention', which in practical terms means that the *English* judge faced with an international sales contract could refuse to order performance in specie whereas a *French* court seised of the same case would make that order. This provision is certainly a fly in the ointment of the Convention, but perhaps this was unavoidable.

The principle of specific enforcement is adopted by both the Principles of European Contract Law (EP) and the UNIDROIT Principles for International Commercial Contracts (UP), subject to exceptions when performance is impossible or disproportionately onerous by reason of legal or practical difficulties, when performance is of an exclusively personal character or when it would in practice be quite easy to obtain performance from some other source. See art. 4.102 EP, art. 7.2.2. UP.

So far as the *enforcement* of judgments for performance goes, French law with the *astreinte* takes a path different from both German law and the Common Law. The *astreinte* is perfectly comprehensible, indeed inevitable, if one remembers the historical and systematic development of French law and bears in mind that the provision made by the legislator in arts. 1143–4 Code civil for the enforcement of judgments requiring an act or an abstention is highly unsatisfactory. But from the independent position of a comparative lawyer the *astreinte* appears to be an institution of rather dubious value. The fact that the amount of the *astreinte* always goes into the pocket of the creditor has made it sometimes appear in the guise of damages and sometimes wear the dress of a private penalty, but for most of the history of French law it has occupied a rather uncertain and shadowy zone between the two. The closer the *astreinte* comes to a damages claim, the less practical value it has as a means of coercion; the more it takes on the colouring of a private penalty and a method of ensuring respect for the judgment of the court, as expressed in current law, the more insistent becomes the question why the creditor of a defaulting debtor in such cases should be able to claim not only compensation but an extra profit as well. It may be right from the standpoint of French law to accept that this unjustified enrichment of the creditor is a lesser evil than having no effective means of enforcing judgments at all (as TUNC says, (above p. 470) p. 404), but the comparatist will prefer a solution according to which fines are imposed only where enforcement is impossible without them, as in Germany, and the proceeds of such fines go to the treasury, as they do in the Common Law as well.

36

Breach of Contract

BORRICAND, 'La Clause résolutoire expresse dans les contrats', *Rev. trim. dr. civ.* 55 (1957) 433.

V. CAEMMERER, 'Das deutsche Schuldrecht und die Rechtsvergleichung', *NJW* 1956, 569.

——, 'Probleme des Haager einheitlichen Kaufrechts', *AcP* 178 (1978) 121.

——, 'Die wesentliche Vertragsverletzung im internationalen Einheitlichen Kaufrecht', *Festschrift Coing* II (1982) 33.

——, 'Vertragspflichten und Vertragsgültigkeit im internationalen Einheitlichen Kaufrecht', *Festschrift Beitzke* (1979) 35.

CONSTANTINESCO, *Inexécution et faute contractuelle en droit comparé* (1960).

DAWSON, 'Judicial Revision of Frustrated Contracts: The United States', 64 *BUL Rev.* 1 (1984).

DEVLIN, 'The Treatment of Breach of Contract', 1966 *Camb. LJ* 192.

ESMEIN, 'L'Obligation et la responsabilité contractuelles', *Le droit privé français au milieu du XXe siècle, Études offertes à Georges Ripert*, vol. II (1950) 101.

FARNSWORTH, 'Legal Remedies for Breach of Contract', 70 *Colum. L. Rev.* 1145 (1970).

HUBER, 'Zur Dogmatik der Vertragsverletzungen nach Einheitlichem Kaufrecht und deutschem Schuldrecht', *Festschrift v. Caemmerer* (1978) 837.

——, 'Empfiehlt sich die Einführung eines Leistungsstörungsrechts nach dem Vorbild des Einheitlichen Kaufgesetzes?', in: *Gutachten und Vorschläge zur Überarbeitung des Schuldrechts* (ed. Bundesministerium der Justiz, 1981) 647.

——, *Die Haftung des Verkäufers nach dem Kaufrechtsübereinkommen der Vereinten Nationen und nach deutschem Recht* (1991).

JØRGENSEN, 'Die skandinavische Lehre der Vertragsverletzung', *Festschrift Larenz* (1973) 549.

KÖTZ, 'Empfiehlt sich die von der Schuldrechtskommission vorgeschlagene Neuregelung des allgemeinen Leistungsstörungsrechts, der Mängelhaftung bei Kauf- und Werkvertrag und des Rechts der Verjährung?', *Verhandlungen des deutschen Juristentages* 60 (1994) K 9.

LANDFERMANN, *Die Auflösung des Vertrages nach richterlichem Ermessen als Rechtsfolge der Nichterfüllung im französischen Recht* (1968).

LAWSON, 'Fault and Contract, A Few Comparisons', 49 *Tul. L. Rev.* 295 (1975), reprinted in: *The Comparison* (Selected Essays, vol. II, 1977) 347.

NICHOLAS, 'Fault and Breach of Contract', in BEATSON/FRIEDMANN (eds.), *Good Faith and Fault in Contract Law* (1995) 337.

RABEL, *Die Unmöglichkeit der Leistung, Festschrift für Bekker* (1907) 171; reprinted in: RABEL, *Gesammelte Aufsätze*, vol. I (1965) 1.

——, 'Über Unmöglichkeit der Leistung und heutige Praxis', *RheinZ* 3 (1911) 467; reprinted in: RABEL, *Gesammelte Aufsätze*, vol. I (1965) 56.

——, 'Zur Lehre von der Unmöglichkeit der Leistung nach österreichischem Recht', *Festschrift zur Jahrhundertfeier des ABGB*, vol. II (1911) 821; reprinted in: RABEL, *Gesammelte Aufsätze*, vol. I (1965) 79.

——, *Das Recht des Warenkaufs*, vol. I (1936, reprinted 1957), vol. II (1958).

——, 'Zustandekommen und Nichterfüllung schuldrechtlicher Verträge im allgemeinen', *Deutsche Landesreferate zum internationalen Kongreß für Rechtsvergleichung im Haag* (1932) 28 ff.; reprinted in: RABEL, *Gesammelte Aufsätze*, vol. III (1967) 119 ff.

——, 'Zu den allgemeinen Bestimmungen über Nichterfüllung gegenseitiger Verträge', *Festschrift für Dolenc u.a.* (Ljubljana, 1937) 703; reprinted in: RABEL, *Gesammelte Aufsätze*, vol. III (1967) 38 ff.

REU, *Die Unmöglichkeit der Leistung im anglo-amerikanischen Recht* (1935).

RHEINSTEIN, *Die Struktur des vertraglichen Schuldverhältnisses im anglo-amerikanischen Recht* (1932).

RODIÈRE, 'Une notion menacée: La faute ordinaire dans les contrats', *Rev. trim. dr. civ.* (1954) 201.

SCHLECHTRIEM, 'Rechtsvereinheitlichung in Europa und Schuldrechtsreform in Deutschland', *ZEuP* 1993, 217.

HEINRICH STOLL, *Die Lehre von den Leistungsstörungen* (1936).

TALLON, 'L'inexécution du contrat: pour une autre présentation', *Rev. trim. dr. civ.* 93 (1994) 223.

TREITEL, *Remedies for Breach of Contract, A Comparative Account* (1988).

——, 'Remedies for Breach of Contract', *Int. Enc. Comp. L.* VII Ch. 16 (1976).

TUNC, 'Force majeure et absence de faute en matière contractuelle', *Rev. trim. dr. civ.* 43 (1945).

ZWEIGERT, 'Aspects of the German Law of Sale: Some Comparative Aspects of the Law Relating to Sale of Goods', 13 *ICLQ* (Suppl.) 1 (1964).

I

IF a vendor refuses to deliver the goods or if the owner of a dwelling declines to allow the tenant to enter on the day fixed in the lease, the buyer or tenant may want to go to court and establish a claim for performance of the contract. The question when he can do this has been dealt with in the previous chapter. But quite other questions may arise. If the goods have been destroyed or the dwelling burnt down, the only questions left for the buyer or tenant are whether this has brought the contract to an end, whether they can reclaim any advance payments they have made and whether they can sue for damages. The same questions also arise if the goods or dwelling are still intact, but the vendor or landlord are late in performing or prove that unforeseen events have made it very difficult or unduly onerous for them to perform. These questions arise also when the purchaser or tenant have been put in possession but the goods are unfit for the purpose envisaged or the house is uninhabitable because the roof leaks or the heating does not work. Finally, even if the actual contract has been performed to the letter, the vendor or landlord may be in breach of other duties which have to be performed if the transaction is to fulfil the purpose for which it was concluded. In such cases it often makes no sense to ask whether the buyer or the tenant still has a claim to performance *in natura* since it is of no practical interest. What the buyer and the tenant in such cases will normally want to know is whether they are still bound by the contract, if and how they may resile from it, and whether they may obtain damages.

The common factor in these situations is the disturbance of the smooth exchange of performances agreed on in the contract owing to the fact that one of the parties, for some reason, has failed to perform the contract altogether or fully or at the right time or place or in some other respect. We shall treat all these cases under the heading of 'breach of contract', including every case in which the performance in fact rendered falls short in some way of what was promised in the contract. In exceptional cases the contracting party will not be responsible for this shortfall, and one might object that one can hardly speak of a 'breach' of contract in such cases. Nevertheless the term 'breach of contract' is preferable to 'non-performance', since it is more flexible, it is used with this meaning in most legal systems, and it perfectly covers the normal case in which the debtor is responsible for the non-performance.

II

The *German* BGB has no unitary concept of breach of contract, and does not deal in general terms with the rights of a contractor who has not received the promised and expected performance. Instead it concentrates on the case where non-performance is due to *impossibility*, and regulates it in great detail; it also deals with the case where, for whatever reason, the promisor is *late* in performing.

1. *Impossibility*

The doctrine espoused by the BGB was elaborated in the nineteenth century by MOMMSEN and WINDSCHEID under the impression that it was Roman: a contract is invariably void if at the time the contract was formed the promised performance was objectively incapable of being rendered by anyone ('impossibilium nulla obligatio', §306 BGB; see also art. 20 OR and §878 ABGB). The Code seeks to modify this result by making the contractor who knew or should have known of the initial impossibility pay compensation to the innocent party for any harm he suffers in reliance on the validity of the contract (§307 BGB). An exception is made to the principle of §306 BGB in the case of the sale of a right: if the right does not exist, the sale contract obviously cannot be performed by anyone, but despite §306 BGB it is held valid and the vendor is liable to the purchaser for the loss of his bargain (§437 BGB).

It is now generally agreed that the policy behind the absolute rule of §306 BGB is unsound and that it should be restrictively interpreted.

If an architect promises a house-owner that the house can be reconstructed under his supervision for a certain price, the contract can be construed as meaning that the architect is to pay from his own pocket any excess over the price. Proof that no one in the world could achieve the reconstruction for the stipulated price does not make the contract void under §306 BGB (see RG SeuffA 75 no. 9).—Where a contract, properly construed, puts the risk that performance may be impossible on one of the contracting parties, the courts use the notion of 'undertaking a guarantee' (*Garantieübernahme*), hold the contract valid, and impose full liability for non-performance. The Oberlandesgericht in Hamburg had to decide a case involving a contract for the sale of 1,000 boxes of new potatoes from the Canary Islands 'aboard S.S. *Thekla Bohlen* afloat'. When the vessel arrived in Hamburg it was found that only 106 boxes had been loaded, but the court held that the vendor must pay damages for non-performance. It was certainly true that as the contract was for the whole of an identified cargo this was a sale of specific goods and that the delivery of the specified parcel of goods was impossible, since at the time of the contract not all those goods were on board. Nevertheless the vendor was liable 'because in the sale of a cargo described as "afloat" merchants take the contractual declaration of the vendor to be a warranty or the undertaking of a guarantee that the cargo has been loaded on the named vessel'. (SeuffA 65 no. 160.)

Although the idea of undertaking a guarantee enables the courts to avoid the inequitable consequences of §306 BGB, the regrettable enactment of this rule of initial impossibility has made it necessary to draw a lot of artificial distinctions. Thus as a matter of positive law 'initial impossibility' ('anfängliche Unmöglichkeit') under §306 must be distinguished from 'initial inability' ('anfängliches Unvermögen') where the promisor cannot do what was promised, but someone else could. In 'initial inability' cases most writers and the courts hold that the debtor is always liable even if not at fault. It is said that every person who enters a contract guarantees his ability to perform it, and if this ability does not then exist, for whatever reason, he must nevertheless pay the other party the benefit of the bargain. But is it not perhaps too much to apply this doctrine to *all* cases of initial inability? The real question here, as in cases of initial impossibility, is which of the contracting parties should, in the view of reasonable businessmen, bear the risk of the debtor's inability to perform. As it happens, the dominant view almost always reaches the right result, but this is only because the obstacles which prevent a party from performing are usually attributable to him, so that it is normally correct on the facts to assume that the debtor guaranteed his ability to perform.

One clear case for inclusion here is where a vendor does not own the goods at the time of the sale and is therefore in no position to transfer them to the purchaser (BGH NJW 1960, 720; WM 1972, 656). It is not quite such a clear case if the goods have just been stolen from the vendor without his knowledge before the contract is formed. The Reichsgericht treated this as a case of initial impossibility and declared the contract of sale void under §306 BGB (RGZ 105, 349). This view should be abandoned, not because performance is not 'objectively impossible' (since in theory the vendor and the thief might co-operate and transfer both ownership and possession to the purchaser) but because §306 BGB is a legislative lapse which should be narrowly construed and certainly not applied where the specific goods which have been sold are still in existence. We can treat this as a case of initial inability without having to make the vendor liable for the benefit of the bargain. The sale by a private citizen to a musician of a valuable violin which has just been stolen without the parties' knowledge may fall to be decided differently from an international sale of a cargo of coffee supposedly lying in a warehouse at Santos at the time of the contract but actually removed by thieves. In the latter case tradesmen would hold the *seller* responsible, regardless of fault, if the goods are not in the place specified by the contract, but it would be inequitable to give the purchaser a claim for the loss of his bargain in the case of the violin.

Events which render performance impossible are divided by the BGB into those which are 'initial', existing at the time of the formation of the contract, and those which are 'subsequent' and arise only later. In cases of subsequent impossibility, unlike those of initial impossibility, the question is not whether performance was objectively or just subjectively impossible; the important question is who is to blame for the obstacle to performance. If it is the debtor, he is liable to pay damages (§§280, 325 BGB); if it is the creditor who must answer for the obstacle to performance, the debtor is freed and may even be able to demand what was promised to him (§§275, 324 BGB); if neither party is responsible for the obstacle to performance, both are freed (§§275, 323 BGB, art. 119 OR). In all these cases the general rule, inferred from the principle 'pacta sunt servanda', is that the debtor who fails to perform is liable unless he proves that he was not answerable for the obstacle to performance (§282 BGB).

Each party must answer for obstacles to performance which occur because of a lack of proper care on their part or on the part of those who were helping them to perform (§§276, 278 BGB, arts. 99 and 101 OR). For example, if a picture is destroyed on being despatched by one of the gallery's employees, the purchaser may claim damages for non-performance unless the gallery proves that there was no negligence either on its own part or on the part of its assistants. If this proof is forthcoming, both parties are released; the gallery cannot claim the price and the purchaser cannot claim damages, though it is open to the purchaser to hold the gallery to the contract and claim from it any 'surrogate benefit' ('stellvertretendes commodum') such as the proceeds of an insurance policy received by the gallery in lieu of the picture (§281 BGB and BGE 43 II 234).

Instances of an impossibility for which neither party is answerable occur when a house is destroyed during the tenancy by a fire for which neither of the parties is to blame (RG JW 1905, 718), or if a bye-law prohibits dancing during the lease of a place of entertainment (RGZ 89, 203), or if an architect cannot execute the contractual works because of prohibitory building regulations (BGH LM §275 no. 7). In the last two cases one must take account of the possibility that the prohibition of dancing and building may be lifted, and ask whether in all the circumstances the parties can be expected to defer the contract until such time as that happens.

An important qualification of the general rule that a debtor is answerable only for those obstacles to performance which are attributable to his fault is contained in §279 BGB. If the contract is for things of a kind rather than for a particular thing, the vendor who cannot deliver is responsible for his inability to deliver even if he and his assistants are entirely blameless. Thus if the vendor of a quantity of cocoa of specified quality is unable to deliver on the due date because of business difficulties or a strike or because his own suppliers have failed to deliver in time, he is liable in damages for non-performance even if he is clearly not to blame for any of these obstacles. In order to exclude this strict liability, parties often include war clauses and strike clauses, or a 'subject to availability' clause ('richtige und rechtzeitige Selbstbelieferung vorbehalten'). In the absence of any such clause, a vendor is only freed from his duty to perform if the entire genus to which the object of the sale appertained has been destroyed.

It is possible, however, for the vendor to be released despite the continued existence of goods of the specified type if delivery is prevented by an embargo imposed by some foreign state (RGZ 93, 182) or by a directive that all such goods must go to a state-controlled distribution centre (RGZ 95, 20) or by requisition (RGZ 88, 287). On the other hand, a merchant who at the beginning of 1914 sold malt for delivery at the end of December 1914 or January 1915 was still held liable in damages when he could not deliver because the malt producers stopped supplies by reason of price controls introduced by the government on 19 December 1914. He should have realized that the authorities might interfere with the malt trade in this manner. 'A person who sells goods of any type in the uncertain circumstances of wartime should already have them in his possession or at his disposition so that he may use them at any time in satisfaction of his obligation. Unless he knows that thoroughly reliable suppliers have such goods and are in a position to deliver them, he relies on supplies from third parties at his own risk, and cannot defend on the ground that performance was rendered impossible by events for which he was not responsible' (RGZ 93, 17).

In practical terms, then, §279 BGB reflects the opinion of merchants that anyone who undertakes to deliver goods of a certain type or goods which he is to procure by purchase gives a guarantee of his ability to supply such goods when the time for delivery arrives.

Whether a contract is or is not for generic goods is a question of the construction of the contract. If a dairy agrees to supply a hotel with a set quantity of milk every day and the dairy's own production is adversely affected by some disturbance of its business it must procure the agreed quantity on the open market and deliver it to the hotel. On the other hand, if a farmer agrees to supply a dairy with a certain quantity of milk every day he would be partially released from his obligation if a murrain decimated his herd: it can be inferred from the nature of the transaction that the farmer only bound himself to deliver such milk as was produced on his farm ('beschränkte Gattungsschuld', see RGZ 91, 312 and BGE 57 II 110).

After the appalling inflation which followed the First World War the German courts developed a doctrine that even under §279 BGB a debtor might exceptionally be released from an obligation which it was not wholly impossible to perform if as the result of an unforeseeable collapse of the currency, a change of legislation, or a political upheaval performance would involve quite exceptional hardships which went beyond the call of duty ('überobligationsmässig'). These cases will be considered in the next chapter (Ch. 37) on the discharge of contracts by reason of subsequent events.

2. *Delay*

If the promise is capable of performance but has not been performed within the time allowed by the contract, the question arises whether the creditor can demand compensation for the damage the delay has caused him and whether he can withdraw from the contract and refuse to accept late performance.

In Germany a claim for damages for lateness in performance can only be brought if the debtor is in 'default' ('Verzug'). In order to put the debtor in default after performance has fallen due the creditor must make a protest ('Mahnung'); this starts the default running unless the debtor can prove that the lateness of performance is attributable to a circumstance for which, under rules already stated, he is not responsible (§§284 ff. BGB). In Switzerland too a protest is required to put the debtor in default, but the debtor need not be to blame and will be liable for interest even if he is not; he is not liable for other damages, however, if he can show that he is free from fault (arts. 102 ff. OR; the same is true in Austria, see OGH 29 Dec. 1954, SZ 27 no. 334).

If the contract fixes a date for performance, directly or indirectly, a protest is not necessary to put the debtor in default ('dies interpellat pro homine': §284 par. 2 BGB, art. 102 par. 2 OR); the same rule is applied by the courts if it appears on a proper construction of the contract that the time for performance is of vital importance (see BGH NJW 1959, 933).

Although putting the debtor in default gives the creditor a claim for damages for delay, it does not in principle free him from the duty to accept performance, late though it is. The creditor can only withdraw from the contract or claim damages for non-performance if he fixes a period during which the defaulting debtor must complete performance and states that he will refuse to accept after the expiry of that period (§326 BGB, §918 ABGB, art. 107 OR). Such a period may be fixed at the same time as making the protest (RGZ 93, 180), and if the period fixed is too short, a reasonable period will be substituted (RGZ 106, 90; OGH 5 Dec. 1951, SZ 24 no. 332). No such period need be fixed if the delay has robbed eventual performance of any interest the creditor had in it, as might be the case with late delivery of seasonal articles (§326 par. 2 BGB, art. 108 no. 2 OR). Neither protest nor a fixed period is required if it would serve no purpose in view of the construction of the contract or the nature of the transaction, as in the case of import sales with fixed dates for loading and delivery (RGZ 71, 308; BGH MDR 1955, 343). Finally, neither protest nor a fixed period is called for in the case of a 'Fixgeschäft', where a definite period for performance is specified and the judge can infer from the terms of the contract or the surrounding circumstances that the parties intended the transaction to 'stand or fall' depending on whether the time fixed for performance was observed or not (RGZ 108, 58). If the 'Fixgeschäft' is a commercial transaction for either party and the time for performance has gone by, the innocent party may resile forthwith or, if the other party is responsible for the delay, claim damages, but he will only have a claim for performance if he expressly demands it after the time for performance has elapsed (§376 HGB; see also art. 108 no. 3, 190 OR, and applying them, BGE 54 II 31).

It is important to note that a creditor enjoys these rights under §326 BGB only if the debtor is in default in performing a major or principal obligation ('Hauptpflicht'). Whether an obligation is such a major obligation or a minor or collateral one depends once again on the construction of the contract. In sales contracts the obligation of the vendor to deliver the goods is a principal obligation, but if the purchaser is in default in accepting the goods tendered, the vendor can only claim damages for delay: the vendor cannot withdraw from the contract after setting a time for acceptance in accordance with §326 BGB and claim damages for non-performance, unless it is a case where he has a pressing interest in prompt acceptance, as in the sale of the materials of a house being demolished or in the sale of bulky goods occupying needed space in the vendor's warehouse. Even if he has delivered the goods the vendor may still be under a principal obligation to provide the accompanying document: for example, the purchaser of a motor vehicle can exercise his rights under §326 BGB if the vendor has failed to deliver the motor licence along with the car (BGH NJW 1953, 1347; the same result was reached with different terminology in *Bentworth Finance Ltd.* v. *Lubert*, [1968] 1 QB 680).

If the debtor unequivocally evinces his intention not to perform the contract, the innocent party may immediately exercise his rights under §326 BGB even before performance has fallen due and need not make a protest or fix any period for performance (RGZ 67, 317; BGH NJW 1976, 326; art. 108 no. 1 OR). Most writers agree with the courts in explaining this by saying that the refusal to perform is a 'positive breach of contract' (*positive Forderungsverletzung*) which can give rise, as we shall see, to a claim for damages without any protest or fixing of a period for performance. As RABEL indicates (*Recht des Warenkaufs* I 382 ff.), these cases are better explained on the view that this is not a case of faulty breach of contract at all, but rather that the debtor is bound by his declaration that he will not perform and cannot complain if the other party 'takes him at his word'. On this see LESER, 'Die Erfüllungsverweigerung', *Festschrift für Max Rheinstein* II (1969) 643, with further references.

3. *Positive Breach of Contract ('Positive Forderungsverletzung')*

Under both the German BGB and the Swiss Code of Obligations, a judge who is faced with a breach of contract must put it in one of two legal categories: either it is a case of *impossibility* of performance—(the Code of Obligations speaks of 'Ausbleiben der Erfüllung')—or it is a case of *delay*. It has to be said that this dichotomy is misconceived. A debtor is of course bound to perform and he is bound to perform at the right time, but that is not the end of the matter. He may in addition have further obligations arising from the contract, failure to perform which cannot be categorized either as 'impossibility of performance' or as 'delay'; in such cases the courts have for long been holding that he is liable on the ground of 'positive breach of contract', unfortunate though the name is. If, contrary to his promise, a vendor supplies a third party with similar goods, or if a site-owner fails to give the necessary details to the building contractor, the innocent party can claim compensation for the harm caused by this breach of duty; furthermore, he can insist on performance, and if the breach of contract imperils the whole purpose of the transaction in such a way that in all the circumstances of the case the innocent party cannot be expected to continue with the contract and to perform his own obligations under it, then he is entitled, without setting any fixed period for performance, to claim damages for non-performance of the whole contract or to withdraw from the contract, as under §§325, 326 BGB.

For example, if a charterer is slow in loading the ship which the shipowner puts at his disposal in a foreign port and gives other grounds for supposing that he cannot perform the charterparty as he should, the shipowner may be entitled forthwith to abandon the contract and sail away, and claim damages for non-performance of the charter (BGHZ 11, 80).—As has already been stated, the courts hold likewise in cases of anticipatory refusal to perform (RGZ 149, 403).

The courts also use the notion of 'positive breach of contract' in cases where a reprehensible breach of contractual duties of care has caused personal injury or property damage to the other party. For example, if a guest trips and falls on the stairway of a hotel or a passenger is injured while riding in a taxi, a claim for damages for 'positive breach of contract' arises against the hotelier or the taxi-firm. So, too, where harm is caused by faulty medical treatment or where, owing to the hairdresser's negligence, a customer's hair is singed under the hair-drier (RGZ 148,148; see also BGHZ 8, 239 and 27, 236).

There is some doubt whether it is the victim in these cases who must prove that the harm was caused by the unlawful and faulty conduct of the other contracting party or whether it is the latter who must discharge the burden of proving that he used all the precautions called for in the situation. The courts ask which of the parties is responsible in the light of the contract for the area of danger in which the accident arose. This is normally the defendant, since these accidents usually occur after the victim has entered the defendant's area of responsibility by patronizing the hotel or entering the taxi or submitting to the operation. On this see HANS STOLL, 'Die Beweislastverteilung bei positiven Vertragsverletzungen', *Festschrift für Fritz von Hippel* (1967) 517.

A claim for 'positive breach of contract' is also open to the buyer of goods which prove defective. It is not at all obvious that this should be so, given that there are special rules for this case under the heading 'Guarantee against Defects' (§§459 ff. BGB). These rules provide that in principle the buyer's only remedies are to rescind the contract or claim abatement of the price (§462 BGB), and in the case of generic goods to claim replacement by goods which do conform (§480 BGB), but in the absence of fraud he has no claim for damages unless the seller expressly warranted the goods (§463 BGB). What, then, if a seller who delivers defective goods gave no such warranty but was negligent or careless? Can the buyer invoke the general law and claim damages for 'positive breach of contract'? The courts have said that he can, subject to two restrictions: first, the claim must be brought within the short time-limit laid down by §477 BGB (six months from delivery in the case of goods), and secondly, damages may be awarded only for so-called *Mangelfolgeschäden*, the consequential harm due to the defect.

For example if the seller of a cement mixer carelessly fails to notice during his pre-delivery inspection that its mixing jet is defective, the buyer may sue him for 'positive breach of contract' but has to bring suit within six months and can claim only for consequential loss. Consequential loss here does not include repair costs but would, for example, include any penalty the buyer had to pay his customer if the malfunctioning of the cement mixer delayed the completion of the house. These restrictions apply only where the fault of the seller relates to a defect in the thing, not to other breaches of contract. Thus if the cement mixer itself is perfectly satisfactory but the seller negligently fails to provide proper information about how to operate it, he will be liable for 'positive breach of contract' without any such restrictions: he will have to meet the cost of repair and remains liable to be sued for thirty years (!) under the residual rule of §195 BGB; this paragraph is applicable since the Code contains not a word about claims for 'positive breach of contract' and therefore nothing on the prescription of such claims. These distinctions are difficult to understand and apply, and they are uniformly criticized in Germany today; the general view is that the rules of the BGB for breach of contract are in urgent need of reform, and proposals to that end have already been made (see below p. 515)

III

Unlike the Germanic civil codes, those of the *Romanistic* family do have a unitary conception of 'non-performance' of bilateral contracts. If one party to a bilateral contract fails to perform his duties under it, the other is entitled to have the contract rescinded by court judgment (art. 1184 Code civil, 1453 Codice civile). In the French Code civil this rule is dressed up in old-fashioned concepts, to the effect that every bilateral contract is concluded under the implicit resolutory condition of the proper performance of the reciprocal duties, but in essence it simply means that non-performance gives the other party the right to have the contract rescinded, for which purpose he must bring a claim. (This is made clear in art. 1453 Codice civile.) Thus each party has a choice between bringing a claim for performance (dealt with in Ch. 35 above) and bringing an action to rescind the contract, which may be combined with a claim for damages. Once a claim for performance has been raised, the plaintiff may switch to a claim for rescission and damages, but not vice versa.

This rule may be found in art. 1453 par. 2 Codice civile. In France it is different: until a final judgment of rescission has been rendered, a claim for performance may be brought, even if the value of the performance has risen in the meantime; see Civ. 6 Jan. 1932, DH 1932, 114.

In a claim for rescission it must be shown that the defendant has failed to perform his contractual obligations (see art. 1184: 'ne satisfera point à son engagement'). This includes not only total non-performance because of impossibility, but also late or incomplete performance as well as breach of ancillary or collateral duties under the contract. In each case the judge decides in his discretion whether in view of the purpose of the contract the breach is serious enough to justify immediate rescission. In so doing he takes account of all the circumstances of the case, including whether and how much the defendant is to blame for the non-performance, how much harm the plaintiff has already suffered as a result of the non-performance, and whether it would be fair to hold him to the contract and restrict him to a claim for damages: 'Ce qui importe c'est que le contrat n'assure plus l'utilité économique qu'il poursuivait'.

MALAURIE/AYNÈS, *Cours de droit civil, Les obligations* (2nd edn. 1990) no. 740. For decisions, see Com. 16 June 1987, Bull. IV. no. 145; Civ. 4 Feb. 1976, Bull. I no. 53; Civ. 9 Oct. 1979, Bull. III no. 169; and LANDFERMANN (above p. 486) 35 ff., 53 ff.——The Italian Codice civile puts the same point in a different way in art. 1455 in saying that a contract is not to be rescinded 'if the non-performance by one party is immaterial in view of the interests of the other'.

This balancing act is especially necessary in cases where the contract has been performed only in part or not at the right time. If part performance is of no advantage to the plaintiff, the judge will consider rescinding the contract as a whole; otherwise he can hold the parties to the contract so far as it has been performed; as for the rest he will in a suitable case rescind the contract and give the plaintiff a claim for damages (see Civ. 5 May 1920, D. 1926. I. 37; Req. 21 Dec. 1927, DH 1928, 82; Req. 21 June 1935, Gaz. Pal. 1935. 2. 35).

French law also allows the judge to set a period in which the defendant must render the promised performance ('délai de grâce': art. 1184 par. 3 Code civil), and if he does so, he normally issues a simultaneous order that the contract be rescinded if the period of grace expires without performance (Req. 16 May 1933, Gaz. Pal. 1933. 2. 422). If performance was due on a specified date which had already passed when the claim for rescission was brought, no such period of grace can be allowed (Civ. 18 Oct. 1927, S. 1928. I. 22).

On this see LANDFERMANN (above p. 486) 52 f.——Under the Italian Codice civile it is the innocent party rather than the judge who can fix a reasonable period for performance by the other party and declare that the contract will determine forthwith if this period elapses without performance. In such a case there is no need for a court judgment which is usually a prerequisite for rescission (see art. 1454 Codice civile).

Should the defendant make a late tender of performance during the trial, the judge must determine whether to rescind the contract even so. Once again it is a matter of all the circumstances of the case, whether the court sees the debtor's original refusal to perform as simply an attempt to delay performance or whether the plaintiff has a justifiable interest in rejecting the late performance, possibly because the market situation has altered.

See Civ. 17 March 1954, Gaz. Pal. 1954. 2. 88; Civ. 30 Nov. 1949, Gaz. Pal. 1950. I. 38. The decision of the Court of Cassation of 27 Nov. 1950 (Gaz. Pal. 1951. I. 132) gives a good indication of the extent of judicial discretion in this area. The plaintiff had transferred some land to the defendant in return for the defendant's promise to clothe, feed, and care for her for the rest of her life. Irreconcilable differences arose between the parties, the defendant refused to do as promised, and the plaintiff sought rescission. Both lower courts, refusing to rescind the contract, issued a judgment of Solomon to the effect that the defendant must pay the plaintiff an annuity to the value of the promised services, so that there would be no need for personal contact between the parties. The Court of Cassation upheld this decision on the ground that the differences between the parties made it impossible for them to perform *in natura* and that the trial judge was justified in exercising his 'pouvoir souverain d'appréciation des circonstances de fait' so as to award the plaintiff a 'rente viagère compensatrice'. The courts here were really reconstructing the contract rather than rescinding it as requested, even if the terms used by the Court of Cassation suggest that it was awarding 'damages' in the form of the annuity. For further decisions of judicial 'reconstruction' of contracts after breach, see LANDFERMANN (above p. 486) 60 ff.

Judicial rescission of a contract is in principle only possible if the plaintiff has made a protest to the defendant. Such a protest must be in writing and delivered through a *huissier*. Ths rule has, however, lost almost all its importance in practice since the Court of Cassation decided that the institution of a claim for rescission may itself be seen as constituting a protest (Civ. 19 Oct. 1931, DH 1931, 537).

A rule that only courts may rescind contracts must obviously make for practical difficulties in commerce, for if it really meant that the innocent party remained fully bound by his contractual obligations until a final judgment of rescission the result would be that the vendor of goods could not resell them nor the purchaser buy in from elsewhere. The French courts have avoided this intolerable result by holding that it is not a breach of contract for the innocent party before going to court to declare the contract over by reason of the other party's non-performance, to refuse to perform his own part, and to enter covering transactions (see Paris 18 April 1912, S. 1915. 2. 66; Req. 4 Jan. 1927, S. 1927. 1. 188); this is subject to the proviso that a court would have ordered immediate rescission of the contract had it been seised of the matter, an assumption which a contractor who frees himself from a contract makes at his own risk.

The rule that only courts may rescind contracts is also weakened by the fact that unequivocal agreements to discharge the contract in certain events are effective; on this see BORRICAND (above p. 486) and LANDFERMANN (above p. 486) 73 ff.). Businessmen usually include such a clause and lawyers always do. It is often called a 'pacte commissoire', and its advantages are that the parties can specify exactly the circumstances which are to entitle the innocent party to declare the contract over; in this way one may avoid the uncertainty inherent in judicial rescission that one cannot predict whether the judge may not treat a particular breach of contract as relatively trivial and so refuse to grant rescission or grant it only after a period of grace. The parties can also agree that a contract shall only be rescinded if the innocent party makes a protest to the other or sets a period for performance, and if performance at the right time is particularly important the parties may agree that when that time has gone by the contract should be rescinded by simple declaration to that effect.

For all these reasons the principle that only a court can rescind a contract seems to be on the wane, at any rate as between businessmen: '*On peut aussi parler d'un déclin de la résolution judiciaire des contrats, ce qui approche le droit français des droits allemand et anglais*' (MALAURIE/AYNÈS, above p. 496, no. 747). In the Italian Codice civile the principle is subject to quite considerable restrictions. Parties to a contract may agree that it be determinable by simple declaration without going to court (art. 1456). Nor need the court be involved if a party has in writing set a reasonable further period for performance and this period has expired (art. 1454). Finally, if a party has promised to perform by a particular date and the observance of this limit is 'essential' for the other party in all the circumstances of the case, the expiry of that period automatically determines the contract, unless within three days the interested party informs the party in default that he insists upon performance (art. 1457).

The innocent party will often be more interested in claiming *damages* than in procuring the *rescission* of a contract which has not been performed in time. Here a distinction must be made. The innocent party can seek to hold his opponent to the contract and bring a claim for performance as well as for damages for the harm caused by the delay ('dommages-intérêts moratoires'). But if the other party will not perform or for some reason performance has lost its *utilité économique* for the claimant, he will look to a claim for damages for non-performance of the contract ('dommages-intérêts compensatoires') which normally goes hand in hand with a claim for rescission. The Code civil itself permits this cumulation of a claim for rescission and a claim for damages, for art. 1184 par. 2 provides that the creditor has the right either to demand performance of the contract or 'd'en demander la résolution avec dommages et intérêts'. The draftsmen of the German BGB ruled out such a combination of rescission and damages on the ground that one could not claim damages at the very time one was seeking to undo the contract which was its basis, and §326 BGB therefore requires the creditor to choose which of these two rights to exercise. This causes endless difficulties. French lawyers are quite aware of the formal objections to cumulating claims for resolution and damages but do not give them much weight since the practical advantages of allowing such cumulation are so great. (On this see LANDFERMANN (above p. 486) 65 ff., 91 ff.)

In principle no claim for damages, whether for delay or for non-performance, can be brought until the debtor has been put in default by a formal protest (art. 1146 Code civil, 1219 Codice civile), but as has already been stated, the courts hold that a protest is unnecessary if the terms of the contract make the consequences of delay ensue without any protest, as in the case where a particular time for performance is agreed (see Req. 16 Feb. 1921, DP 1922. 1. 102; Civ. 18 Oct. 1927, S. 1928. 1. 22) or there is a clause 'livrable de suite' (Req. 21 June 1933, DH 1933, 412). The same is true if protest would be a mere formality, as in the case where the debtor has already refused to perform (so Req. 4 Jan. 1927, S. 1927. 1. 188 and, in terms, art. 1219 no. 2 Codice civile), or is in no position to perform.

A claim for damages will only succeed if the circumstance which prevented the performance of the contract is 'imputable' to the debtor. This is expressed in art. 1147 of the French Code civil in the form that a debtor in default is freed from liability in damages only if 'l'inexécution provient d'une cause étrangère qui ne peut lui être imputée' (so also art. 1218 Codice civile); art. 1148 says the same thing in different words, by providing that an obstacle to performance serves as a defence only if it occurs 'par suite d'une force majeure ou d'un cas fortuit'. 'Force majeure' and 'cas fortuit' are synonymous, and since the courts and writers agree that they can be invoked only if the debtor is free from fault, 'absence de faute' and 'force majeure' mean very much the same thing in this connection (on this see TUNC (above p. 487)). The same principle also underlies the rule of art. 1302 Code civil that a person who is bound to deliver specific goods is freed from his obligation if the goods are destroyed without his fault ('sans la faute du débiteur'). The inference is drawn that the vendor of goods by description is only freed if they had already been properly ascertained at the time they were accidentally destroyed.

There is no space here to go into the details of the question of 'transfer of risk': if a debtor is freed from his obligation to perform by some obstacle for which he is not responsible, can he nevertheless claim what was promised to him? We can simply point to the several distinctions which are drawn in this matter in the law of sales. In most of the Romanistic legal systems the risk passes to the buyer along with ownership at the time of the formation of the contract if the goods are specific, and at the time they are ascertained if the goods are generic (art. 1138 Code civil, 1465 Codice civile; but this rule is also found in art. 185 par. 1 OR). In German, Austrian, and Scandinavian law, on the other hand, as well as under the Uniform Law of Sales, the risk passes only on delivery of the goods (§§446 BGB, 1049, 1051 ABGB, art. 17 Scandinavian Law of Sales, art. 67–9 CISG.

The critical question therefore is in what cases the courts are ready to treat an obstacle to performance as 'force majeure' or 'cas fortuit' and so to free the debtor from his obligation to pay damages. The writers say that an obstacle to performance only serves as a defence if it is an 'obstacle imprévisible et irrésistible' which renders it 'absolument impossible' for the debtor to perform (see PLANIOL/RIPERT VII no. 838). Although the courts tend to stress one of these criteria at the expense of the others, it is certain that an obstacle to performance will not serve as a defence if the debtor had even the slightest chance of avoiding it and neglected to avail himself of it. Even the very great difficulties in procuring, transporting, or delivering goods which occur in wartime do not free the vendor.

In one case a vendor who had sold 4,000 cwts. of oats from his 1914 crop had his whole crop requisitioned by the military authorities, but he had to pay damages all the same when it emerged that he had carelessly passed up an opportunity to get the goods in transit to the purchaser before the requisition (Civ. 6 May 1922, DP 1922. 1. 130; see also Req. 25 Jan. 1922, DP 1922. 1. 71).——In another case ten tons of potatoes had been sold and were requisitioned at the railway station when they were being loaded and this was held to be 'force majeure' (Civ. 19 June 1923, DP 1923. 1. 94).—The purchaser of a parcel of rice failed to open a credit making the price available to the vendor in Saigon as promised, because he did not obtain the necessary authority under the French exchange regulations which were already in force at the time of the contract; he was held liable in damages (Req. 4 Jan. 1927, S. 1927. 1. 188).—In cases where a strike prevents the production, transport, or delivery of goods, the courts are readier to find that the strike constitutes a defence the more general and unforeseeable it is proved to have been (see Civ. 2 March 1915, D. 1920. 1. 108; Civ. 20 April 1948, Gaz. Pal. 1948. 1. 285).

The rules which determine whether an obstacle to performance may constitute a defence do not apply to contracts which could never be performed at all. Here, like the German legal family, the Romanistic legal systems make a concession to the doctrine 'impossibilium nulla obligatio', and render such contracts void (art. 1346, 1418 par. 2 Codice civile). The French Code civil expressly covers the case of specific goods which are already destroyed at the time of the sale: such a contract is void (art. 1601), regardless of whether in the circumstances of the case the promisor was to bear the risk that he might not be able to perform. The Romanistic legal systems seek to qualify the harshness of this result by granting the creditor a claim for damages in delict if the debtor knew or should have known that what he promised was impossible (see Req. 11 Feb. 1878, S. 1879. 1. 196; art. 1338 Codice civile).

Despite all this it remains the principle that the seller who fails to deliver the goods or delivers them late is liable in damages unless he can prove that due performance was prevented by *force majeure* or *cas fortuit*; mere absence of fault is not a defence under art. 1147 Code civil.

However, the Code civil also suggests that the debtor's obligation as regards performance is only to show *tous les soins d'un bon père de famille* (art. 1137). For many years now the courts have found a way of resolving this apparent conflict: they apply the stricter rule of art. 1147 in cases where it emerges from the contract that the debtor has promised to procure a certain *result*—this is an *obligation de résultat*—but if it appears from what was agreed or from the thrust of the contract that the debtor was not promising a given result but only to use his best efforts in that regard, this is simply an *obligation de moyens*, and there is liability for non-performance only if the creditor can prove that the debtor did not try as hard as a reasonable man would have done in the same circumstances.

For full details see VINEY no. 519 ff.—Occasionally the courts refer to a third category: there may be an *obligation de moyens renforcée* where although the debtor's duty is only to act as a reasonable man there is a presumption that he has failed in this duty if performance is not duly forthcoming. In such a case it is the debtor who has the burden of proof, not the creditor, as it usually is where the obligation is *de moyens*.

The Code civil does not tell us when we are faced with an *obligation de résultat* as opposed to an *obligation de moyens*. The courts decide this by construing the contract, and the rules they have worked out are quite firm. For the seller to deliver the goods at the right time and place is an *obligation de résultat*; so are the obligations of the carrier to keep the goods or cargo safe and deliver them on time to the proper destination, of the builder to build as promised (art. 1792 Code civil), and of the lessor to make the thing available to the lessee at the right time. If the promised result is not achieved in these cases, the debtor can avoid liability only by proving that it was prevented by *force majeure* or *cas fortuit*.

The paradigm case of an *obligation de moyens* is the duty of the doctor to treat his patients with due care and skill, though the courts tend to find an *obligation de résultat* when harm results from a defective prosthesis or malfunctioning equipment (Civ. 29 Oct. 1985, Bull. civ. I no. 273). By contrast the lawyer's obligation in advising his client is always one *de moyens*, as is that of the person who agrees to manage a piece of business for another. Difficulties have, however, arisen where the interest involved is the personal safety of the customer.

The courts have treated as generating an *obligation de résultat* contracts involving the provision of a safe lift (Civ. 23 June 1955, D. 1955, 653), of a safe seat at an automobile race (Orléans, 19 April 1937, DH 1937, 292), of a safe autoscooter at a village fair (Civ. 30 Oct. 1968, D. 1989, 650), and contracts by a ski-lift operator to protect the user (Civ. 8 Oct. 1968, D. 1969, 157). By contrast only an *obligation de moyens* is generally generated by the hotelier's duty to provide safe rooms and stairways (Civ. 7 Feb. 1966, D. 1966, 314) and the swimming-pool operator's duty to provide safe premises (Civ. 20 Oct. 1971, Bull. I no. 227). The duty of the carrier to avoid dangers prior to embarkation and subsequent to disembarkation from the conveyance is an *obligation de moyens* (Civ. 21 July 1970, D. 1970, 767) whereas for accidents occurring *during* the voyage it is an *obligation de résultat*. On the whole question see the details in VINEY no. 550 ff.

A special regime applies to the seller who is in breach of either of the guarantees imposed by the art. 1625 Code civil, namely the guarantee against latent defects (*garantie des vices cachés*) and the guarantee against eviction by superior title (*garantie du titre*).

According to art. 1645 Code civil the seller who delivers defective goods is liable in damages only if he was aware of the defect; otherwise his only liability is to return the price and pay the *frais occasionnés par la vente*. The courts have, however, interpreted this article very widely indeed and turned the liability of the seller into one very like the general liability for breach of contract, but subject to the short prescriptive period of art. 1648. They regularly hold that the seller who is in the business of selling goods of the kind in question is to be treated as if he knew of the defects in the goods, with the effect that he is liable in damages notwithstanding any exemption clause in the contract itself. See, for example, Civ. 30 Oct. 1978 and Com. 6 Nov. 1978, JCP 1979.II.19178 noted by GHESTIN.

IV

Unlike the Continental systems the *Common Law* in principle treats every contract as containing a guarantee. If the debtor fails to do what he promised, he is liable in damages for 'breach of contract', regardless of whether or not he himself or any of his assistants or subcontractors has been at fault. This basic principle explains a great many of the numerous differences between the systems which strike anyone making a comparative study of Continental and Common Law. First, Anglo-American law has no need to separate and systematize the various causes of non-performance of a contract as German law does with its careful distinction between impossibility, delay, and positive breach of contract: it does not much matter in the Common Law whether the debtor has wholly failed to perform as promised or has performed too late or has performed unsatisfactorily in one way or another, since if the promised result has not been procured, the guarantee undertaken has not been observed and a 'breach of contract' has occurred. Furthermore, claims for damages do not depend on whether any blame for the breach attaches to the debtor or his employees. Admittedly the Common Law sometimes releases a debtor from liability when he has been prevented from performing, but this is not because he and his staff are free from blame regarding the non-performance of the contract, but rather on the ground that on a proper view of the contract he is not responsible for performance in *all* circumstances and that his guarantee does *not* cover certain obstacles to performance (on this see further below pp. 508 f.). Finally, the Common Law does not have to have any special way of dealing with defects in goods, work, or premises since for Anglo-American lawyers the breach of guarantees in contracts of sale, services, and lease are just like all other breaches of contract which themselves arise from broken guarantees: 'Claims in respect of defects are actually the paradigm of contractual liability in the Common Law as a whole' (RHEINSTEIN (above p. 487), 155). This fusion of guarantee and general liability for breach of contract explains why the vendor of defective goods is strictly liable for the harm caused to the purchaser by the defect.

The basic idea that liability for non-performance is strict is highly characteristic of the Common Law. Indeed, it is raised to the level of an axiom:

'It is axiomatic that, in relation to claims for damages for breach of contract, it is, in general, immaterial why the defendant failed to fulfil his obligation, and certainly no defence to plead that he had done his best.' (LORD EDMUND-DAVIES in *Raineri* v. *Miles* [1981] AC 1050, 1086.) 'It does not matter whether the failure to fulfil the contract by the seller is because he is indifferent or wilfully negligent or just unfortunate. It does not matter what the reason is. What matters is the fact of performance. Has he performed or not?' (SELLERS J in *Nicolene Ltd.* v. *Simmonds* [1952] 2 Lloyd's Rep., 419, 425.) Likewise LORD GREENE MR in a case involving the liability of a laundry: 'The laundry company undertakes, not to exercise due care in laundering the customer's goods, but to launder them, and if it fails to launder them it is no use saying "I did my best. I exercised due care and took reasonable precautions, and I am very sorry if as a result the linen is not properly laundered".' (*Aderslade* v. *Hendon Laundry* [1945] 1 All ER 244, 246 (CA).)

This principle is applied whenever the debtor is to provide a thing or do work with a view to its being provided. The seller who promises to deliver goods, the firm which promises to build a house or produce some other piece of tangible property, the shipowner who promises to provide a vessel, and the lessor who promises to make the dwelling available, all these must, in the absence of any contrary provision in the contract, ensure that the promised performance is duly rendered. The architect, too, guarantees that his designs and drawings are in line with the contract, whereas his obligation as regards the supervision of the construction itself is only to show care and professional skill. The guarantees of the seller of goods are laid down in the Sale of Goods Act 1979, and those who supply goods otherwise than under a contract of sale are under a similar liability (Supply of Goods and Services Act 1982). They cannot exempt themselves from such guarantees when contracting as a business with a consumer (Unfair Contract Terms Act 1977); in contracts between businessmen or between private parties any such exemption is subject to a test of reasonableness (see TREITEL 737 ff.).

It is different, however, in the case of services provided by a doctor, lawyer, accountant or other adviser.

'The law does not usually imply a warranty that [a professional man] will achieve the desired result, but only a term that he will use reasonable care and skill. The surgeon does not warrant that he will cure the patient. Nor does the solicitor warrant that he will win the case. But, when a dentist agrees to make a set of false teeth for a patient, there is an implied warranty that they will fit his gums . . . What then is the position when an architect or engineer is employed to design a house or a bridge? Is he under an implied warranty that, if the work is carried out to his design, it will be reasonably fit for the purpose? Or is he only under a duty to use reasonable care and skill? The question may require to be answered some day as a matter of law. But in the present case I do not think we need answer it. For the evidence shows that both parties were of one mind on the matter. Their common intention was that the engineer should design a warehouse which would be fit for the purpose for which it was required.' (LORD DENNING in *Greaves & Co.* v. *Baynham Meikle & Partners* [1975] 3 All ER 99, 103 f.)

The liability of the supplier of services has now been laid down by law. The Supply of Goods and Services Act 1982 provides in ss. 13–16 that the person who promises to render services by way of business is bound only 'to carry out the service with reasonable care and skill'. Of course the parties may agree on a stricter liability, and such liability may be implicit: the dentist who provides a prosthesis which does not fit cannot excuse himself on the ground that he did his best (*Samuels* v. *Davies* [1943] 1 KB 526), and two cases have generated a lively discussion of the question whether a doctor who had agreed to sterilize a patient had promised not just to do it carefully but to do it effectively so as to render the patient permanently sterile (*Thake* v. *Maurice* [1986] QB 644; *Eyre* v. *Measday* [1986] 1 All ER 488).

It is important to distinguish the question whether the innocent party has a claim for damages from the quite different question whether he can declare the contract at an end by reason of the other party's breach. If he can terminate the contract, he is no longer bound to fulfil his own promises and can claim back what he has already rendered and damages for the loss of his bargain. This can be a serious matter for the other party for it means that any investment he has made in performance will be wasted; it is true that he has broken his contract, but he would quite happily pay damages if only he could keep the contract afoot. The interest of the innocent party is quite different. Suppose that shortly after the inception of a year's charter it emerges that the charterer is in breach—not paying the hire on time, damaging the vessel, or sending it into a prohibited area; if freight rates have risen in the meantime or if the charterer is getting into financial difficulties and may not pay future instalments of the hire on time or even go bankrupt, the shipowner has a considerable interest in declaring the charterparty at an end rather than simply claiming damages for his loss (even supposing a provable loss has occurred). Plainly termination of a contract can only be justified if the breach is of an 'essential' term.

The question whether or not a promise is 'essential' in this sense is often decided by English courts in terms of 'warranty' and 'condition'. Every contractual term, express or implied, is in law a 'warranty' (express or implied). If such a term is broken, the innocent party is entitled to claim damages for breach of contract, but must continue to perform his own side of the bargain. The innocent party may only resile from the contract if the term which his opponent has broken is also a 'condition', that is, if it is especially important for the performance of the contract.

Continental lawyers find the use of the word 'condition' in this context very peculiar. 'Condition' for them signifies a future uncertain event whose occurrence or non-occurrence may trigger or suppress certain legal consequences. The word is used in this sense in the Common Law also, as in the phrases 'conditions precedent' and 'conditions subsequent', but in addition the concept of 'condition' is used in the law of contract to do what is done on the Continent by the concept of synallagma: if one party to a contract is bound to perform first or if the performance of the two parties is to take place simultaneously, common lawyers say that the duty of one contractor to perform is subject to the 'condition' that the other contracting party has already performed or is ready and willing to perform at the agreed time. Finally, English lawyers use the word 'condition' to denote an essential term of a contract whose non-performance gives the innocent party the right to declare the contract discharged and claim damages for non-performance. That is the meaning in issue here.

The Common Law view that the only terms of a contract which are 'conditions' are those which are vital for the execution of the contract is very like the position in Germany where the exercise of the rights granted by §326 BGB depends on whether the party in delay is in breach of a 'principal duty' or *Hauptpflicht* and has failed to meet a deadline which has been set, or, in the case of a positive breach of contract, 'has so imperilled the purpose of the contract that the innocent party cannot be expected to continue with it' (see above p. 493 f.; for French law see p. 496). Similar phrases can be found in English cases. Thus it has been said that a 'condition' exists if 'the consequences of the breach [are] such that it would be unfair to the injured party to leave him to the remedy in damages' (BUCKLEY LJ in *Decro-Wall International SA* v. *Practitioners in Marketing* [1971] 2 All ER 216, 232) or if the breach of contract is so serious that the innocent party would lose 'substantially the whole benefit which it was intended he should obtain from the contract'.

So said DIPLOCK LJ in the leading case of *Hong Kong Fir Shipping Co.* v. *Kawasaki Kisen Kaisha* [1962] 2 QB 26, 70. The vessel provided for the defendants at the start of a two-year time charter was unseaworthy in that the engine-room was understaffed and the staff were not trained to cope with the aged engines. On a journey from Liverpool to Osaka the ship was out of commission for five weeks because of engine failure, and after the vessel had been held up in Osaka for a further fifteen weeks the defendants threw up the charter and demanded damages, although there was no reason to believe that the ship would not be seaworthy after the repairs were finished. The shipowner argued that this withdrawal was unjustified and therefore a 'breach of contract' and claimed damages for the loss of the charter: this amounted to no less than £158,729 because freight rates had fallen greatly during the charter period and the ship could only find a substitute charter on much less favourable terms. In extended judgments the Court of Appeal held that the plaintiff had certainly broken its obligation to provide a seaworthy vessel (and thereby made itself liable to pay damages to the defendant) but that in the circumstances of the case this breach was not serious enough to justify the defendant in withdrawing from the contract. The obligation to provide a seaworthy ship was thus held not to be a 'condition' and the shipowner's claim was granted, subject to a counter-claim for damages by the charterer. See also *Bunge Corp.* v. *Tradax Export SA* [1981] 1 WLR 711 and the extensive treatment in TREITEL 670 ff.

Lawyers in England now realise that 'warranty' and 'condition' are concepts too formalistic to solve the real problem of distinguishing between essential and inessential terms of a contract. In the United States, Restatement (Second) of Contracts (1981) dispenses with these concepts on this question and grants a claim for damages for 'total breach' if the party is entitled to refuse performance of his outstanding obligations by reason of the other party's breach. This will be the case if the other party's breach constitutes a 'material failure' of performance (§§243, 237). §241 lists the circumstances which are significant in deciding whether a failure of performance is 'material' or not: whether the innocent party has received, or can still receive, essentially what was promised, whether in such circumstances damages would be an adequate remedy, and whether and to what extent the behaviour of the party in breach is consistent with 'standards of good faith and fair dealing'.

Cases where the contractor fails to perform on time constitute a special category of case, although the Common Law does not distinguish between the situation where the delay is due to impossibility and where it is not: a time fixed for performance is a term of the contract like any other and its breach gives the innocent party a claim for damages and, if the temporal provision is 'essential' to the contract, the right to resile as well. Whether the provision as to time of performance is 'essential' in this sense—English lawyers use the phrase 'of the essence of the contract'—is determined according to the circumstances of the case. The courts usually hold time to be of the essence in commercial contracts, especially contracts for the sale of goods, because it would be intolerable in a time of fluctuating prices if the parties were left in uncertainty about whether they were bound to accept a late tender or free to proceed forthwith with a covering transaction.

Examples of English cases are *Lock* v. *Bell*, [1931] 1 Ch. 35; *Harold Wood Brick Co.* v. *Ferris*, [1935] 2 KB 198, on which see TREITEL 724 ff. The same rule is laid down for the United States in Restatement (Second) of Contracts (1981) §242.

If no 'essential' time for performance is specified in the contract, the debtor must perform 'within a reasonable time'. Even here the creditor, unlike his opposite number in Germany, need not make any protest to the debtor or fix a further period for performance before withdrawing from the contract, but it is nevertheless good commercial practice to do so unless the contract contains an 'essential' time for performance. Thus GUTTERIDGE reports that

'A reputable merchant who has bought goods without specifying a time for delivery does not rush off to his solicitor with instructions for the issue of a writ if he considers that there has been unjustifiable delay. He sits down and writes a stiff letter demanding delivery by a certain date and does not embark on litigation until this demand has been ignored by the seller.' (14 *Brit. YB Int. L.* 75, 87 (1933).)

The courts approve of this practice. A party to a contract which contains no 'essential' time for performance is entitled to fix a period within which the other party must perform. If the court finds this period reasonable, its final date is treated as being 'of the essence of the contract' with the consequence that the creditor can thereafter treat the unperformed contract as discharged, and in suitable cases claim damages.

See *Stickney* v. *Keeble*, [1915] AC 386; *Rickards (Charles) Ltd.* v. *Oppenhaim*, [1950] 1 KB 616; see also the American decisions *O'Brien* v. *Bradulov*, 80 NE 2d 685 (Ohio

1948); *Sliter* v. *Creek View Cheese Factory*, 173 Wis. 137, 179 NW 745 (1920), and WILL-ISTON §852.

Cases of 'anticipatory breach' of contract are accorded special treatment in the Common Law. In principle a party can only sue for non-performance of contractual promises when the time for the performance of those promises as fixed in the contract has elapsed. But even before then, if the party clearly shows, by express declaration or deliberate behaviour, that he is not minded to perform the contract, the other party can hold him to such behaviour, treat it as a 'breach of contract', consider the contract discharged, and claim damages for non-performance. The innocent party is not bound to do this, however; he may stand by the contract, wait for the time for performance, and then claim his damages.

If a young man promises his fiancée to marry her when his father dies and he breaks the engagement without any good cause she may forthwith bring a claim for damages and need not wait for his father to die. See *Frost* v. *Knight* (1872) LR 7 Ex. III. An innocent party may, however, have an interest in holding the other party to the contract despite his refusal to perform, as in *White & Carter (Councils) Ltd.* v. *McGregor*, [1962] AC 413. If he does so, however, the innocent party bears the risk that the contract may in the meantime be avoided on some other ground, such as an exculpatory event which prevents performance. If the girl in *Frost* v. *Knight* had decided to delay bringing her claim for damages until the death of her fiancé's father, as she might have done in order to claim higher damages in view of her increased age and diminished marriageability, she would have been exposed to the risk of her fiancé's predeceasing his father and of thereby losing her claim alto-gether. A case decided under this rule is *Avery* v. *Bowden* (1855) 5 E. & B. 714, 119 Eng. Rep. 647. The charterer of a ship refused to load it, but the shipowner never-theless kept the ship at the charterer's disposal. During this period the Crimean War broke out, with the result that the charter voyage could not have been performed even if the charterer had been ready to proceed with it. This event was at the ship-owner's risk, and his claim for payment of the agreed hire was dismissed.

In the Common Law a contractor's liability in damages is not affected by the reason for his failure to perform his promise properly (see above p. 503). This was the position from which the English courts started and they were originally extremely strict in holding the debtor to the promise he had actu-ally made, though they allowed him to make express exceptions in the con-tract. Thus in the leading case of *Paradine* v. *Jane* (1647) 82 Eng. Rep. 897, a lessee tried to meet a claim for outstanding rent with the defence that during the period of the lease he had been forcibly extruded from the premises by the troops of a foreign prince. The defence was unsuccessful: 'When the party by his own contract creates a duty or charge upon himself, he is bound to make it good, notwithstanding any accident by inevitable necessity, because he might have provided against it by his contract.'

During the course of the nineteenth century the English judges invented some exceptions to qualify this principle that promises contractually given were absolutely binding. One exception covers cases where the German lawyer would speak of 'initial impossibility'. An important decision in this area is *Couturier* v. *Hastie* (1856) 5 HLC 673,10 Eng. Rep. 1065. The parties agreed to buy and sell a cargo of corn on a named vessel, not knowing that it had already been disposed of by the captain, acting as agent of necessity, because it was spoilt. The vendor's claim for the price was dismissed since the court held that the contract was based on the parties' assumption that the goods were still in existence at the time they were sold. Subsequent English decisions have treated analogous cases as instances of error and have held that a contract based on a 'common mistake' of the parties is not binding (see above p. 421). These decisions and the similar rule in art. 1601 of the French Code civil led to the adoption in the English Sale of Goods Act of the following rule

'Where there is a contract for the sale of specific goods and the goods without the knowledge of the seller have perished at the time when the contract was made, the contract is void' (s. 6). On the historical development of this rule in English law see RHEINSTEIN (above p. 487) 183 ff. The same rule is to be found in §2-613 UCC. Even so, the courts of England and the United States are always careful to check whether on a proper construction of the contract one party may not have taken the risk of the possibility of performance. See the American decisions cited in CORBIN §§1362 ff. and the Australian case of *McRae* v. *Commonwealth Disposals Commission*, (1950) 84 CLR 337.

A contractor may also be relieved from his guarantee liability in certain circumstances where obstacles to performance arise *subsequently* to the contract. The courts so hold if the performance of the contract presupposes the continued existence of a specific thing which is accidentally destroyed before the time for performance arrives. These are cases where the German lawyer would speak of 'subsequent factual impossibility' ('nachträgliche (tatsächliche) Unmöglichkeit').

The leading case is *Taylor* v. *Caldwell* (1863) 3 B. & S. 826, 122 Eng. Rep. 309. The plaintiff hired the defendant's music hall for the promotion of concerts on four future dates. Before the first of these occasions the hall was accidentally destroyed by fire, and the plaintiff claimed damages for the loss he had suffered by reason of the non-occurrence of the concerts. The claim failed, not because the owner of the hall was unable to perform the contract by reason of an event for which he was not responsible—as would have been the basis for the decision in Germany under §275 BGB—but because the contract of hire was construed to contain an 'implied condition' that

'the parties shall be excused in case . . . performance becomes impossible from the perishing of the thing without default of the contractor'.—In *Howell* v. *Coupland* (1874) LR 9 QB 462 this rule was applied to a contract of sale. The defendant sold

200 tons of potatoes to be grown on a specified field, but blight reduced his potato crop to 80 tons. The purchaser's claim for damages for the non-delivery of 120 tons was rejected. This rule has also been adopted by the Sale of Goods Act: 'Where there is an agreement to sell specific goods and subsequently the goods, without any fault on the part of the seller or buyer, perish before the risk passes to the buyer, the agreement is avoided' (s. 7).

There is a further class of case where performance is still possible but is rendered materially more difficult or actually futile by reason of unforeseen events such as a fall in the currency, a strike, or the closure of a sea route or a frontier. These cases will be dealt with in the next chapter (Ch. 37).

V

One's first impression on looking at all this material might be that the underlying doctrines are so fundamentally different that it makes no sense to compare the solutions.

Now it is certainly true that in the problems under investigation the theoretical starting-points are widely divergent and that every legal system uses technical expressions recognized nowhere else. Tell a continental lawyer that in the Common Law every contractual duty is treated as a guarantee and he will think he is entering another legal world altogether. Contrariwise, it is hard for an Englishman to credit that the delivery of non-conforming goods is anything other than a perfectly normal breach of contract. The German attempt to categorize the various types of breach and draw sharp distinctions between 'impossibility', 'delay', and 'positive breach of contract' has not been greatly esteemed elsewhere, and neither Germanic nor Anglo-American lawyers have much time for the idea in the French Code civil that it takes a judicial decree to release parties from their contractual obligations.

As against this, Treitels's brilliant contribution to the *International Encyclopedia of Comparative Law* (VII Ch. 16; published in extended form as *Remedies for Breach of Contract* (1988)) shows at many points that the different principles from which the Continental systems and the Common Law start out are subject to so many exceptions and qualifications that in practice the difference between them is nothing like as great as one might at first suppose. Differences there undeniably are, but they can be explained in part by the fact that English courts hear many more cases involving shipping law, international trade, construction contracts, and financial services than courts on the Continent; the atmosphere in such cases is naturally more bracing, so that if a choice has to be made between justice in the individual case and the security of transactions, the latter is the favoured option.

The differences are clearly not unbridgeable. This is shown by the unification of the law of international sales.

In April 1964, after decades of preliminary work in which ERNST RABEL played a leading part (see LESER's Introduction to Rabel, *Gesammelte Aufsätze* III (ed. LESER, 1967)), the Hague Conference adopted the Uniform Law for the International Sale of Goods (ULIS) and the Uniform Law on the Formation of Contracts for the International Sale of Goods (ULFIS). Italy, Germany, Belgium, Great Britain, the Netherlands, and a few other states ratified these laws, but worldwide unification was not to be expected since third-world countries and those of the then socialist bloc were barely represented at the Conference and the United States put in an appearance only at a late stage. In 1966 the United Nations Committee on International Trade Law (UNCITRAL) took up the question of the unification of sales law, and as they were able to build on the work of the Hague Conference, the business was completed relatively swiftly. Sixty-two states attended a conference convened in Vienna by the United Nations and produced a Convention on Contracts for the International Sale of Goods (CISG). By the end of 1994 this Convention, essentially a shorter and terser version of the Hague Sales Laws (now in a single text), had been ratified by about forty states, and before too long courts all over the world will be applying the same rules to international sales of goods. See VON CAEMMERER/SCHLECHTRIEM (eds.), *Kommentar zum Einheitlichen UN-Kaufrecht* (2nd edn. 1995); HONNOLD, *Uniform Law for International Sales under the* 1980 *U.N. Convention* (2nd edn. 1991); BIANCA/ BONELL (eds.), *Commentary on the International Sales Law* (1987).

The Convention is of particular interest to us because in its global treatment of breach of contract, based on intensive comparative legal studies, it 'resolves in a higher unity the peculiarities still remaining in national laws from times past, and does so without any loss and with very great gain' (RABEL in *RabelsZ* 9 (1935) 6). Even more recently uniform rules for international contracts of all types, rather than just sales, have been drawn up; they have not been enacted as positive law anywhere, so they apply only when the parties agree that they should serve as the *lex contractus.* These rules too are the result of co-operation between comparative lawyers from many different countries.

The UNIDROIT Principles of International Commercial Contracts (UP) were published in 1994 by the Rome Institute for the Unification of Private Law. See BONELL, *An International Restatement of Contract Law* (2nd edn. 1997) and the articles in 40 *Am. J. Comp. L.* 617–82 (1992), where the text of the Principles appears on pp. 703 ff.—Even more recently the European Commission of Contract Law has published its Principles of European Contract Law (EP): See LANDO/BEALE (eds.), *Principles of European Contract Law, Part I: Performance, Non-performance and Remedies* (1995). See also SCHLECHTRIEM, 'Rechtsvereinheitlichung in Europa and Schuldrechtsreform in Deutschland', *ZEuP* (1993) 217; HARTKAMP, 'The UNIDROIT Principles for International Commercial Contracts and the Principles of European Contract Law', 2 *Eur. Rev. PL* 341 (1994).

In the result there is a very fair international consensus on the rules applicable to breach of contract. After considering these rules we shall also ask

Contract

what reforms are needed if German law is to remain in touch with developments elsewhere in Europe.

VI

The German BGB was flawed at birth by its unfortunate division of breaches of contract into impossibility, in its various forms, and delay. So incomplete was this coverage that the courts had to adopt the institution of 'positive breach of contract' as a residual category for the types of breach of contract not covered. The subtle distinctions in the BGB are also inappropriate to the subject matter. No one denies that special rules are needed for the case of 'delay' since it poses a problem which does not arise in cases where performance is impossible, namely of determining how late a performance the creditor, who admittedly will have a claim for damages, must nevertheless accept. But although such special provisions are required, it is unnecessary to create a theoretically independent type of breach of contract called 'delay'. It is equally unsatisfactory that the 'doctrine of impossibility' should have led German law to produce an independent category of contracts envisaging a performance which is 'objectively impossible' which §306 BGB renders void, thereby making it necessary to distinguish initial impossibility, itself subdivided into objective impossibility and subjective inability, from subsequent impossibility. The liability of a debtor who has failed to perform his contract cannot sensibly depend on whether his inability to perform existed at the time of the contract or occurred only later, or whether, though he himself could not perform at the time of the contract, there was someone else somewhere who could. In all these cases the critical question must be the same: is the fact which prevented, delayed, or otherwise perverted the execution of the contract one of those which, given the purpose of the transaction and the views of relevant businessmen, fall within the debtor's area of risk? If this is accepted, the way is open for a unitary concept of breach of contract, matched by an equally unitary concept of the defence arising from obstacles to performance.

Such a unitary concept is by no means accepted in all Continental legal systems. In the Germanic legal family the 'fault principle' dominates: a contractor can avoid liability for breach of contract by proving that he used all the care to be expected of a reasonable person in like position. French law is somewhat stricter if the debtor is under an *obligation de résultat*, for then he must prove that non-performance was due to *force majeure* or *cas fortuit*. The Common Law is stricter still: it starts from the idea—qualified in many respects, as we have seen—that the debtor guarantees the result promised in the contract, and instead of inquiring whether the debtor can be blamed for the obstacle to performance it asks whether, on a proper construction of the contract, the obstacle falls within the guarantee. Once again we must emphasize that despite the theoretical differences, the practical results are very similar (see TREITEL, *Remedies for Breach of Contract* Ch. 2 (Fault)). Thus it has been shown that German courts can often get round the unfortunate provision of §306 BGB by finding that a contractor who has promised something 'impossible' has actually guaranteed its occurrence. Indeed, in cases of 'initial inability', the debtor is always regarded as guaranteeing his ability to perform. So far as subsequent obstacles to performance are concerned, the most important case is the delivery of *generic* goods, and both on the Continent and in the Common Law the view of commerce is that in entering the contract the debtor undertakes that whatever happens he will be in a position to produce the promised goods at the right time. Finally, if the vendor of *specific* goods later finds it impossible to deliver, the Common Law recognizes that their accidental destruction is not normally covered by the guarantee of performance (see Ch. 37 IV above).

Where different theories lead to much the same results, the comparative lawyer must choose the one which is most appropriate. Here it seems to us that the Common Law approach should be preferred. In the modern world exchange transactions are very largely standardized and they must be quickly and painlessly executed: it is truer to the reality of 'contract' as a social phenomenon if we normally treat the parties not as simply promising to do their best to produce the envisaged result but as actually guaranteeing it. It is also the better legal policy.

This is the standpoint adopted by the Vienna Convention. Under art. 30 CISG the vendor is obliged to deliver and to pass title in goods which conform to the contract, along with the accompanying documents, these obligations being specified in greater detail in art. 31–44. If the vendor delivers goods which are disconform to the contract (regardless of whether they lack a feature stipulated in the contract, a quality which was guaranteed, or a characteristic necessary for normal use, whether, indeed, they are the wrong goods altogether), if he delivers too much or too little, too early or too late, or in the wrong place, or if his performance is defective in some other respect, this is a breach of contract which entitles the purchaser to exercise the rights provided in art. 45, including the right to claim damages. It is not here relevant whether the events which prevented performance occurred before or after the contract was concluded or whether they affected everyone or just the vendor. Nor does it matter whether the non-performance or defective performance is attributable to any fault on the part of the vendor. Parties to a sale are relieved of liability for breach of contract by only one provision in CISG; art. 79 provides that a party is not answerable for non-performance of his contractual duties 'if he proves that the failure was due to an impediment beyond his control and he could not reasonably be expected to have taken the impediment into account at the time of conclusion of the contract or to have avoided or overcome it or its consequences'.

This provision is designed to offer a single test to determine when a contractor is answerable for an obstacle to performance; it depends on the *allocation of risks* explicitly agreed on by the parties or inferable from the contract properly construed. The test adopted is one which all legal systems treat as crucial, whether they say so or not, and this explains why the results of decided cases are so often alike.

The UNIDROIT Principles adopt the same position. Art. 7.1.1 UP defines non-performance as 'failure by a party to perform any of its obligations under the contract, including defective performance or late performance'. Art. 7.4.1 provides that 'any non-performance gives the aggrieved party a right to damages', and under art. 7.1.7 one can free oneself from such liability only by a defence drafted in much the same terms as art. 79 CISG. The European Principles are very similar (see art. 3.108 and 4.501 EP). Proposals for reform of the German Civil Code go in the same direction. The Commission set up by the Ministry of Justice has proposed that 'impossibility', 'delay', and 'positive breach of contract' all be replaced by a unitary notion of 'breach of duty'. Defences would still (apart from §279 BGB, above p. 491) fall under the fault principle, but a redrafted §276 BGB would make it clearer that proof of absence of fault should relieve a party in breach from liability only if 'nothing to the contrary emerges from the other terms or the nature of the contract'. This means that the court must always ask whether or not in all the circumstances the party actually gave a guarantee that the promised performance would be duly and punctually rendered. See the Final Report of the Commission for the Reform of the Law of Obligations (Federal Ministry of Justice, 1992) pp. 32 f., 121 ff.

Whether the innocent party can resile from the contract and refuse further performance by reason of the other party's breach is a different question. In *German* law the remedies of §326 BG are available to the creditor only when the debtor is in delay in performing a central obligation (*Hauptpflicht*) and has failed to perform within a given deadline; in the case of other breaches the creditor can resile and claim damages only if the conduct of the debtor is such as to make it unreasonable to expect the creditor to carry on with the contract. *French* law comes to the same result, it being the task of the judge to decide whether the *gravité* of the breach is such that he can declare the contract discharged. And the same idea underlies the *English* distinction between condition and warranty, whereby the innocent party can only declare the contract at an end when the other party has broken a promise which is 'fundamental'; otherwise he is bound to adhere to the contract and claim damages. Thus we see that despite differences in technique essentially the same criteria are applied to similar fact situations.

Accordingly the Vienna Convention grants the innocent party the right to terminate the contract when the other party's breach is 'fundamental' (art. 49(1), 51(2), 64(1) CISG). A breach of contract is 'fundamental'

'if it results in such detriment to the other party as substantially to deprive him of what he is entitled to expect under the contract, unless the party in breach did not foresee and a reasonable person of the same kind in the same circumstances would not have foreseen such a result' (art. 25). To the same effect are art. 7.3.1(2)(a) UP and art. 3.103(b) EP. Under art. 7.3.1(2)(b) UP and art. 3.103(a) EP termination of the contract is also permissible if 'strict compliance with the obligation which has not been performed is of essence under the contract', and also if the breach of contract is intentional or due to gross indifference or gives the other party reason to doubt the reliability of his contractor (art. 7.3.1(2)(c) and (d) UP and art. 3.103(c) EP). This is less likely to apply to normal sales contracts than to long-term arrangements and those calling for co-operation and mutual reliance.

It will have been seen that CISG does not deal separately with warranties of title and quality but regards them as part of the general system of breach of contract: the delivery of goods which are physically or legally defective is a breach of contract just as much as delivery which is faulty in point of time or place or in some other respect. The seller of defective goods must therefore pay damages unless he can exonerate himself under art. 79 CISG. This he will not often be able to do. If he himself manufactured the goods, he will have to prove a 'development risk', that is, show that the goods would not have been regarded as defective at all in the light of scientific knowledge and technical know-how at the time of the contract. If he only sold the goods, as importer, wholesaler or retailer, he may find it rather easier to exonerate himself, but even so it will not be enough just to prove that he never had them in his hands, that he lacked the technical knowledge to check them, and that he relied on the expertise of the person he bought them from. Of course, the seller may have stipulated for some modification of this liability.

There has been a proposal to abolish the BGB's special rules on the seller's guarantees in favour of a rule that it is a 'breach of duty' to deliver defective goods or supply defective work.

Even so the liability of the seller would not be as strict as under CISG, indeed effectively no stricter than under the present law. The seller would still be able to excuse himself by proving that he showed the care to be expected of a proper seller, as he presently can when sued for damages for 'positive breach of contract'. It is true that under present law his liability in damages is stricter when he expressly warranted that the thing had a certain quality (§463 BGB), that is, when in the light of his conduct and all other circumstances what he said would be understood as amounting to a guarantee that the goods had a particular quality (BGHZ 59, 158, 160). But even if §463 were repealed, the result would be the same under the proposed new §276 BGB.

37

The Effect of Supervening Events

Aubrey, 'Frustration of International Contracts of Sale in English and Comparative Law', 12 *ICLQ* 1165 (1963).

Berman, 'Excuse for Nonperformance in the Light of Contract Practices in International Trade', 63 *Colum. L. Rev.* 1413 (1963).

Dawson, 'Effects of Inflation on Private Contracts, Germany 1914–1924', 33 *Mich. L. Rev.* 171 (1934).

——, 'Judicial Revision of Frustrated Contracts', 1982 *Jur. Rev.* 86.

Farnsworth, 'Disputes over Omission in Contracts', 68 *Colum. L. Rev.* 860 (1968).

Gow, 'Some Observations on Frustration', 3 *ICLQ* 291 (1954).

Hay, 'Frustration and its Solution in German Law', 10 *Am. J. Comp. L.* 345 (1961).

——, 'Zum Wegfall der Geschäftsgrundlage im anglo-amerikanischen Recht', *AcP* 164 (1964) 231.

Igarashi/Rieke, 'Impossibility and Frustration in Sales Contracts', 42 *Wash. L. Rev.* 445 (1967) (Japanese law).

Kegel, 'Empfiehlt es sich, den Einfluß grundlegender Veränderungen des Wirtschaftslebens auf Verträge gesetzlich zu regeln? [with comparative reports on different systems]; *Verhandlungen des 40. Deutschen Juristentages*, vol. I (1953) 135.

——/Rupp/Zweigert, *Die Einwirkung des Krieges auf Verträge in der Rechtsprechung Deutschlands, Frankreichs, Englands und der Vereinigten Staaten von Amerika* (1941).

Larenz, *Geschäftsgrundlage und Vertragserfüllung* (3rd edn., 1963) [with comparative reports on different systems].

Lesguillons, 'Frustration, Force majeure, Imprévision, Wegfall der Geschäftsgrundlage', *DPCI* 1979, 507.

Lorenz, 'Contract Modification as a Result of Change of Circumstances' in Beatson/Friedmann (eds.), *Good Faith and Fault in Contract Law* (1995) 357.

McElroy/Williams, 'The Coronation Cases', 4 *Mod. L. Rev.* 241 (1941); 5 *Mod. L. Rev.* 1 (1942).

McKendrick, *Force Majeure and Frustration of Contract* (1991).

Philippe, *Changement de circonstances et bouleversement de l'économie contractualle* (1986).

Posner/Rosenfield, 'Impossibility and Related Doctrines in Contract Law: An Economic Analysis', 1977 *J. Leg. Stud.* 83.

Rheinstein, *Die Struktur des vertraglichen Schuldverhältnisses im anglo-amerikanischen Recht* (1932) 160 ff.

Rodhe, 'Adjustment of Contracts on Account of Changed Conditions', *Scand. Stud. L.* 3 (1959) 153.

Savatier, 'La théorie de l'imprévision dans les contrats', *Études de droit contemporain* II (1959) 1.

SCHMITTHOFF, *Frustration of International Contracts of Sale in English and Comparative Law: Report of the Proceedings of the International Association of Legal Science* (Helsinki, 1961) 127.

TRAKMAN, 'Frustrated Contracts and Legal Fictions', 46 *Mod. L. Rev.* 39 (1983).

TREITEL, *Frustration and Force Majeure* (1994).

——, *Unmöglichkeit, Impracticability und Frustration im Anglo-Amerikanischen Recht* (1991).

WALLACH, 'The Excuse Defense in the Law of Contracts, Judicial Frustration of the U. C. C. Attempt to Liberalize the Law of Commercial Impracticability', 55 *Notre Dame L.* 203 (1979).

I

A PERSON who fails to perform his contract properly is generally liable for breach of contract. If, however, he is prevented from performing by circumstances whose occurrence, according to the intention of the parties, is not at his risk, then an exception is made. In the previous chapter we tried to show that *impossibility* of a factual or legal nature may often act as an 'exculpatory obstacle to performance'. Cases of such impossibility arise if the specific object or supply of goods contracted for are destroyed without any fault on the part of the vendor or if the factory which was to produce the goods is accidentally burnt down or if a ship under short-term charter is requisitioned for a long time for naval purposes; since the actual destruction of goods, the burning of the factory, and the requisitioning of the ship are circumstances which are not, according to the general view of businessmen, at the risk of the debtor, the debtor is not liable to the creditor for nonperformance of the contract. But suppose that the unforeseen change of circumstances does not exactly render it *impossible* for the debtor to perform the contract but makes it so much more difficult or so vastly more expensive that the two sides of the contract are now quite out of proportion. What is to be done in such cases of 'distortion of parity'? And what is to be done in cases of 'frustration of purpose', when one party under the contract is to pay a sum of money and can easily do so but finds that the other party's performance has now been rendered valueless for him by subsequent events?

The distinction here drawn between circumstances which render the performance of the contract *impossible*, those which render it much *more difficult* and those which *frustrate the purpose* of the transaction, is made only so as to help classify and clarify the cases by separating them into different types. In fact, all these cases are closely interconnected, as may be seen from the following example.

Suppose that a manufacture of fertilizer makes a long-term contract to produce a special fertilizer for tobacco plants and deliver it to a dealer for export to places overseas where tobacco is grown. If the fertilizer factory is then nationalized or if the manufacture of fertilizer is forbidden or if a government decree requires all fertilizers to be delivered to a state export organisation, we have a case of *impossibility*. It would be an instance of *distortion of parity* if after the conclusion of the contract enormous import duties were imposed on the import of the raw materials required for the manufacture of the fertilizer; finally, *frustration of purpose* would occur if the importation of fertilizer was forbidden in the consumer country: it remains possible for the manufacturer to produce the fertilizer and for the dealer to accept and pay for it but it is now impossible to achieve the only purpose for which, as the manufacturer knew, the dealer entered the contract, namely to deliver the fertilizer to the consumer country. We are not concerned at the moment with the question whether or how far the nationalization of the factory, the increase of import duties, or the prohibition of importation into the consumer country may release the parties from their duties to deliver or accept the fertilizer, but it is important to realize that the critical question may be put in the same form *in all three cases*: given the express contract they have made and the typical intention of parties to such contracts, which of the parties has accepted the risk that such circumstances might arise? If it is the *manufacturer* who has accepted the risk that his factory may be nationalized or that production costs may soar, then, if either event occurs, he must still deliver the fertilizer or compensate the dealer for the damage which failure to deliver causes. If the dealer has accepted the risk that the goods may not be imported into the consumer country, then he must either take the fertilizer and tender the price or pay damages for non-acceptance. If *both* parties bear the risk of the circumstances in question, the manufacturer is released from his duty to deliver and the dealer from his obligation to accept; both lose the chance of making any profit from the execution of the contract.

II

The question whether a person may be released from his contractual obligations by supervening events has been familiar to Continental jurists for centuries. It appeared in the *clausula rebus sic stantibus*, a doctrine which, as its name suggests, made the validity of a contract depend on the continuance of the circumstances obtaining at the time of its formation. This doctrine may be traced through the Middle Ages from the Glossators right up to GROTIUS and PUFENDORF; it was accepted in the Codex Maximilianeus bavaricus civilis of 1756 and then in the Prussian General Land Law of 1794 (on the historical development, see KEGEL (above p. 516) 135 ff., and LARENZ (above p. 516) 11 ff. with further references).

The Prussian General Land Law starts out with the proposition that in general one may not refuse to perform a contract 'on the ground of altered circumstances' (§377 I 5) but proceeds to add:

'If, however, an unforeseen change of circumstances makes it impossible to achieve the aim of both parties as expressed in the contract or inferable from the nature of the transaction, then each of them may resile from the unperformed contract' (§378 I 5).
'If the alteration of circumstances frustrates the express or obvious purpose of one

party alone, that party may withdraw from the contract on condition, if the alteration is a personal matter, of fully indemnifying the other party' (§380 I 5).—There is a comparable rule in the Austrian ABGB but it is restricted to preliminary contracts, which remain binding only 'if . . . the circumstances have not so changed in the meanwhile as to frustrate the purpose expressed in the contract or inferable from the circumstances' (§936).

The scholars of the *Gemeines Recht* rejected the doctrine of the *clausula rebus sic stantibus*. Its vagueness was thought to be unconducive to legal certainty, and the fact that it had been welcomed by the natural law codes gave the adherents of the Historical School of Law an additional reason for rejecting it. Not until the middle of the nineteenth century did WINDSCHEID's 'doctrine of the contractual assumption' (*Lehre von der Voraussetzung*) make it possible once more to give proper effect to supervening events. According to WINDSCHEID, parties make contracts on the assumption 'that the intended legal consequence should only occur under certain circumstances'. Although the effects of the contract are to be dependent on the 'assumed' state of affairs, the parties' promises are not, strictly speaking, conditional, and the contract remains valid even if the assumption is falsified, but since this is not in accordance with the 'real' intention of the contractors, the contract, though valid and effective from the formal point of view, ceases to have any substantial justification. If the assumption is falsified, therefore, the contracting party may demand the rescission of the contract. In practical terms it is very much as if the contract had been concluded under a *condition* that the 'state of affairs' remain the same, so WINDSCHEID was able to call the assumption an 'inchoate condition' (*unentwickelte Bedingung*) lying midway between a mere motive and a true condition (*Lehrbuch des Pandektenrechts* (1865) §§97 ff.).

Like a few of WINDSCHEID's other ideas, the doctrine of the 'assumption' failed to gain entry into the BGB. It was severely criticized by LENEL (AcP 74 (1889) 213) who quite rightly pointed out that the 'assumption' was a kind of intermediate thing between a unilateral motive and a condition mutually agreed, and that commerce would be imperilled if it were recognized. The Commission which revised the draft BGB agreed with him and stated 'that this doctrine endangers the security of commerce'; there was also a risk 'that it might obscure the distinction between condition and motive and induce lawyers to give mistaken weight to the effect of a motive not incorporated in the contract' (Protokolle II 690 f.). Accordingly, neither the German BGB nor the Swiss codes have any general provision concerning the effect of change of circumstances in contract law.

The Swiss Code of Obligations does, however, have an isolated rule. The person who contracts to render services must do the work for the agreed price even if it proves more arduous or expensive than was foreseen. If, however, extraordinary circumstances which could not be foreseen or which were outside the assumptions made by both parties make it impossible to do the work or make it disproportionately difficult, the judge has a discretion to raise the price or rescind the contract (art. 373 part. 2 OR; see also art. 1793 Code civil).

After war broke out in 1914 the German courts were increasingly often faced with cases of supervening events, and since the legislator had left them in the lurch they had to work out equitable solutions on their own. At first they hewed to the words of the BGB and declared performance 'impossible' in the sense of §275 BGB even when it was only a case of so-called 'economic impossibility'. Two groups of decisions may be discerned. In one series of decisions the Reichsgericht saw economic impossibility in the fact that if performance was rendered after the removal of the obstacle, the delay caused by war, revolution, or transport problems, it would be *entirely different* in substance from what was originally promised in the contract.

This view was applied to contracts for the delivery of foreign raw materials which the war made it impossible or very difficult to import. In such cases the Reichsgericht released the vendor from the contract if 'delivery after the end of a prolonged war would take place in economic conditions entirely different from those prevailing in peacetime when the contracts were originally entered into' (RGZ 94, 68, 69 f.; see also RGZ 88, 71; 90, 102 and RG JW 1919, 717).

In another line of cases the Reichsgericht used to release the vendor for reasons of 'economic impossibility' if in the circumstances of the case to make him produce the goods was 'too much to ask' (*unzumutbar*).

'The chance event must not simply make it more difficult to produce the object contracted for, as by rendering it much harder to procure or more expensive to buy, but must involve such extraordinary difficulties that commercial men would say it was impossible' (RGZ 57, 116, 118 f.). Thus the vendor of salmon was freed from his obligation since the war had destroyed the German market in such foreign wares, even although the vendor had 'sporadically and exceptionally found ways and means' of obtaining some supplies previously (RG JW 1919, 499).—If goods which had been sold were requisitioned because of the war, the vendor was freed if the procurement of alternative supplies was not simply difficult and expensive but thoroughly uncertain and, if possible at all, not at a marketable price (RG WarnRspr. 1917 no. 161). On the other hand, in the case of bulk sales of generic goods with a speculative element the Reichsgericht clung stoutly to the view that the vendor remained bound by the contract notwithstanding considerable price increases, even of more than 100%, provided that there was still a market in the goods (RGZ 88, 172; 92, 322; 95, 41): 'even such an extraordinary rise in prices does not release the vendor provided that the goods are still being bought and sold in the market and are available in sufficient quantity for the performance of the contract. What the situation would be if just a few parcels of goods could be obtained only by a fantastic offer or from a single supplier need not now be decided' (RGZ 88, 172, 177).

This established rule that a vendor cannot be released by a mere increase in prices was nevertheless qualified by the Reichsgericht in several cases. If because of inflationary price increases performance of the contract on the terms originally agreed would involve the ruin of the vendor's business and bring about his immediate bankruptcy, then he may exceptionally have the 'defence of ruination' (*Einrede der Existenzvernichtung*).

See RGZ 100, 134; 101, 79.—Similar considerations can be found in the so-called 'reservoir case' decided by the Swiss Bundesgericht (BGE 45 II 386). By contract made in 1827 and renewed in 1863 the owner of a plot of land was bound to keep a reservoir on his land in good order and repair in return for a fixed 'water rate'. In 1910, as a result of changed economic conditions the cost of maintenance so greatly exceeded the water rate that the owner of land, actually a charitable institution, was faced in the long run with certain ruin. The Bundesgericht released the owner from the contract: this was permissible in an exceptional case if 'extraordinary circumstances which could not reasonably have been foreseen had the effect of rendering the debtor's obligation so onerous that to insist on it would involve his economic ruin'. But see also BGE 59 II 372, where the emphasis was laid not so much on the question of economic ruin, which unduly favours parties without resources, as on the question whether the debtor's obligations had been rendered so 'greatly, strikingly and disproportionately' more severe that the other party would be exploiting the debtor's embarrassment if he insisted on the contract. This line has been followed by the Bundesgericht in many other decisions (see BGE 62 II 45, 67 I 300, 68 II 173, criticized by MERZ, *Berner Kommentar* I (1962) art. 2 ZGB notes 230 ff.).—In NJW 1959, 2203 the German Bundesgerichtshof was faced with a case strikingly similar to the 'reservoir case'. A contract made in 1898 gave in the plaintiffs the right to mine potash on the defendant's land for an unlimited period of time on payment of an annual sum of 1,200 marks as an 'interim payment' until the right was exercised. In 1959, the year of the decision, the 'interim payment' had only one-third of its purchasing power in 1898. Nevertheless the Bundesgerichtshof held the parties to the contract: not every alteration in the relative value of performance and counterperformance justified a departure from the principle of adherence to contracts; 'on the contrary, there must be such a fundamental and crucial change in the relevant circumstances that continued adherence to the original contract would lead to an intolerable result quite incompatible with one's sense of justice'. This requirement was not fulfilled in the present case. Any other view would, according to the Bundesgerichtshof, lead to 'the general implication of an index clause into all long-term contracts' (to the same effect BGH NJW 1966, 105 and 1976, 142). The Bundesgerichtshof has exceptionally permitted the revaluation of a money claim devalued by inflation where the money was to cover the creditor's *living costs*: the employer was required to negotiate a modification of the payments due under an old-age pension if the cost of living had risen by more than 40% since the last review (BAG BB 1973, 522; and BGHZ 61, 31). The Law of 19 December 1974 for the Improvement of Old Age Pensions now enacts this principle of judge-made law (see §16, applied in BAG NJW 1976, 1861 and NJW 1977, 2370).

German legal writers soon set themselves to producing a general theory to serve as a basis for the courts' decisions on the problem of altered circumstances. The most important of these attempts was OERTMANN's doctrine of the 'basis of the transaction' (*Geschäftsgrundlage*). Like WINDSCHEID's theory, it starts from the proposition that a contract may lapse as a result of altered circumstances if the expectations, assumptions, or suppositions entertained by the parties at the time of the contract are frustrated by subsequent events. OERTMANN's theory can also be described as 'psychological' in as much as it turns on the actual state of mind of the parties at the time they concluded the contract, but he differs from WINDSCHEID in one respect: it is not enough that the assumption belied by the future course of events was privately entertained by the party now trying to resile from the contract; the assumption must either be shared by both parties or, if entertained by one party only, at least manifested by him at the conclusion of the contract and acquiesced in by the other party. An 'assumption' which satisfies these requirements OERTMANN calls the 'basis of the transaction' (*Geschäftsgrundlage*).

It will obvious that OERTMANN's doctrine is inapplicable in precisely the most important cases, where the subsequent alteration of circumstances *could* not reasonably be foreseen by the parties at the time of the contract; the parties in such a case naturally regard the continuance of the existing circumstances as self-evident and therefore do not consciously form, much less express, any assumptions about the future course of events. Nevertheless the Reichsgericht continually used the theory of the 'basis of the transaction', and the expressions they used may still be found today in the decisions of the Bundesgerichtshof. One should not pay too much heed to this, however, for cases where performance has unexpectedly been rendered much more difficult depend very much on their own particular facts, especially on the type of contract involved, which may suggest how the risk that these circumstances might occur is to be allocated between the parties. The only use of general theories like OERTMANN's is to give the courts phrases in which to dress up the really material considerations.

This is evident in the very first decision in which the Reichsgericht used the doctrine of the basis of the transaction. Property was sold which did not yet belong to the vendor but which he hoped to obtain from the then owner, a company in process of liquidation. The purchase price was in line with the market value at the time of the contract. The liquidation of the company was, however, very prolonged, and meanwhile the price of land increased many times over owing to the depreciation of the currency. In view of this the vendor asserted that he was no longer bound by the contract. The Reichsgericht agreed in principle, holding that the parties had assumed that the relationship between performance and counterperformance existing at the time of the contract would remain constant, and that this was the 'basis of the transaction' in OERTMANN's sense. But the defendant vendor could not simply resile from the contract; instead, the judge must 'adjust the price in view of the existing devaluation so as to avoid the rescission of the contract' and give the plaintiff the opportunity of buying the land at the higher price. Only if the plaintiff did not so agree could the defendant resile from the contract (RGZ 103, 328). As may be seen from the reasons given by the court, the critical factor in this decision was that it was a sale of specific property without any speculative element.

This decision already contains the seeds of the Reichsgericht's famous line of cases on revalorization. After 1923 the Reichsgericht relied on §242 BGB to make the owner of mortgaged property pay the mortgagee a supplementary sum over and above the nominal value of the mortgage so as to alleviate the very marked devaluation of paper money in Germany (RGZ 107, 78). In 1925 the legislator adopted this solution and laid down in the Law of Revalorization (*Aufwertungsgesetz*) that the owner could not only extinguish a mortgage on his property by paying a sum amounting to 25% of the value of the mortgage in gold marks, but that if the owner had already extinguished the mortgage by making payment in worthless paper money, the creditor could under certain conditions demand the reinstatement of the mortgage in the land register. This statutory resuscitation of the mortgage was very hard on the person who had sold his land 'free of mortgage' for he became liable to pay it off 'a second time', and in gold marks at that, so in another famous decision the Reichsgericht gave the vendor a 'contribution claim' against the purchaser who had to pay a subvention towards the expense of paying off the mortgage, in an amount depending on the circumstances of the case; if the purchaser refused, the vendor could rescind the contract of sale (RGZ 112, 329; see also RGZ 119, 133). The doctrine of the collapse of the basis of the transaction figures once more in the judgment, but still as a purely ornamental feature. A like decision was made in a case where the parties had fixed the purchase price in sterling on the assumption that the English pound would remain on the gold standard. When England unexpectedly abandoned the gold standard, the disadvantaged vendor was allowed to claim an increment towards the loss attributable to the devaluation (RGZ 141, 212; compare also RGZ 145, 51).

After the Second World War the courts were faced with unprecedented problems. Millions of people had to abandon their homes and their entire mode of life, domestic and business premises were very largely demolished and dismantled, and in the East expropriation added its toll. Such a catastrophe was bound to present the courts with the problem of the effect of altered circumstances on contracts.

The courts got very little help from the legislature. A law of 26 March 1952 (*Vertragshilfegesetz*) allowed the debtor under contracts antedating the day of currency reform, 21 June 1948, to seek a court judgment deferring or reducing his liability if he made a declaration of his assets; the judge was bound to grant the request 'if and in so far as due and complete performance by the debtor appears excessive on a just balance of the interests and situations of both parties'.

There were very many other cases. The courts continued to employ the doctrine of the collapse of the basis of the transaction, but stressed that in the last resort the critical thing was 'applying the standard of good faith to the circumstances of the individual case. The defence applies only . . . if and in so far as the result flowing from strict adherence to the contract would be intolerable for the debtor in view of the new situation' (OGHZ 1, 62; see also BGHZ 2, 188 and BGH LM §284 BGB no. 2). To this it has justly been objected that whether or not it would be 'intolerable' for the person disadvantaged to be kept to the contract is not the only consideration; what is essentially in issue is the division of risks typical of the type of contract in question, a question which the courts' approach tends to obscure.

We shall mention only one of these cases, the well-known 'pneumatic drill case', decided by the Bundesgerichtshof (MDR 1953, 282). The plaintiff had agreed to produce and deliver to the defendant a number of pneumatic drills of a particular model. The model was already obsolete, and the plaintiff knew that the defendant intended to send them to East Germany, that being the only place where pneumatic drills of this design could be used. After the contract had been concluded the side-effects of the Berlin Blockade made delivery of pneumatic drills to East Germany impossible. The Bundesgerichtshof quite rightly started out by saying that in contracts of sales and services the purchaser or employer must bear the risk of not being able to use the goods as originally intended, but it went on to say that 'although the blockade was in operation at the time the contract was concluded both parties shared the assumption that the delivery of pneumatic drills to East Germany would remain possible for the foreseeable future'. Thus the use which the plaintiff had in mind was 'admittedly not part of the contract, but the basis of the contract'. The defendant was therefore released from his obligation to accept and pay for the pneumatic drills, but as the contract had to be *adapted* to the new situation in the light of the demands of good faith he must pay one-quarter of the total agreed sum. This would go some way to compensate the plaintiff for its expenditures in beginning to carry out the contract.—This decision must be emphatically repudiated. A purchaser who buys goods on his own account in the hope of gaining from a resale must bear the risk of such a resale becoming impossible. This risk typically rests on him, and if he wants the vendor to share it he must so stipulate in the contract, and will doubtless find that the enhanced risk will cause the vendor to increase his price. The Swiss Bundesgericht was therefore right to decide a similar case the other way. At the end of 1939, a Swiss arms producer contracted with the French government to deliver certain weapons for the French army. He needed some special parts to fulfil the contract so on 4 June 1940 he placed an order for them with the plaintiff. Both parties knew what they were for and what the current French military situation was, but when armistice occurred between Germany and France sooner than was expected, the arms manufacturer repudiated the contract. The plaintiff claimed damages for the ensuing loss and obtained judgment from the Bundesgericht (BGE 69 II 139).

III

It has already been noted in the chapter on breach of contract (above p. 499) that the French courts are extremely chary of the defence that supervening events have rendered performance much more difficult, and treat an obstacle to performance as releasing a party only if it is an unforeseeable event, not attributable to the debtor, which renders it quite impossible to perform the contract for the duration. Transport problems, import and export restrictions, strikes, confiscations, and such matters free the debtor only if in the circumstances of the individual case they constitute 'force majeure' or 'cas fortuit'.

After the First World War the inflexibility of the courts induced French legal scholars to make all manner of attempts to render a change of circumstances legally relevant one way or another, under the comprehensive heading of 'imprévision'. Some writers sought to expand the concept of 'force majeure' so as to include mere difficulties of performance, or to reduce the liability of a person unable to perform by using art. 1150 Code civil, which makes damages payable only for *foreseeable* harm. Others pointed out that according to art. 1134 par. 3 contracts are to be performed in good faith ('de bonne foi'), while yet others tried to use the probable intention of the parties (see art. 1156 Code civil) as a ground for adapting a contract to the altered circumstances (see WAHL, note to Civ. 4 Aug. 1915, S. 1916/1917. 1. 17). On occasion the old theory of the *clausula rebus sic stantibus* was trundled out and proclaimed to be an unwritten principle of law. Lower courts in France occasionally followed these ventures, but in the cases which came to it the Court of Cassation held rigidly to its previous view. Only the Conseil d'État, the highest administrative court in France, adopted new and more flexible doctrines.

It was in a series of decisions around the middle of the nineteenth century that the views of the Court of Cassation were crystallized. The cases involved the practice of taking cover against the lottery of conscription with an insurer who promised to find a substitute if the insured were called up. On 13 April 1843 a law suddenly raised the number of conscripts from 80,000 to 140,000, and the insurance companies, arguing that this near doubling of the contingent had falsified the underlying calculations, claimed to be released from their contracts. Some of the lower courts adhered to the old principle that a contract was unaffected by difficulties and unforeseen events if its performance still remained possible and also pointed to the aleatory nature of such insurance contracts (Orléans 24 May 1854, DP 1854. 2. 132; upheld by Civ. 9 Jan. 1856, DP 1856. 1. 41). In other courts, however, there was a reaction against the rigid decisions of the Court of Cassation: it was said that the 'base essentielle' of the contract had been completely altered in an unforeseeable manner, some decisions relying on the probable will of the parties, others simply declaring that the increase in the number of conscripts constituted an instance of *force majeure* (see the decisions in DP 1854. 2. 128 ff.). Decisions which rescinded the contract of insurance were quashed by the Court of Cassation which tersely observed that this was not a case of absolute impossibility of performance (Civ. 9 Jan. 1856, DP 1856. 1. 35).

A further attempt to introduce the idea of altered circumstances into French law was made by the Court of Appeal in Aix in a judgment of 31 Dec. 1873, apparently the last such attempt before the World War. The facts were very similar to those of the Swiss 'reservoir case' (above p. 521).

In a contract dating from the sixteenth century one party had agreed for a certain sum to irrigate an orchard by means of a canal which was to be built. The agreed sum was now ridiculously small and went no way toward covering the maintenance cost of the canal. The trial court and the Court of Appeal at Aix handed down decisions referring only to 'équité' and raised the sum to a reasonable figure. The Court of Cassation quashed these decisions (Civ. 6 March 1876, DP 1876. 1. 197, where the lower court decisions may also be found), and once again encapsulated its views in the formula 'that, however equitable their decision might seem, tribunals must never use lapse of time or other circumstances in order to modify the agreements of parties and substitute new clauses for those which were freely accepted by the parties themselves'.

The Conseil d'État, by contrast, proved readier to adapt contracts to altered circumstances. Contracts for public works came first, then concessions of vital and essential undertakings, and contracts for the provision of public utilities such as gas, water, and electricity. The reason for such decisions is the public interest in the continuance of contracts which are essential to the orderly conduct of public life. This is made clearest in the decision of the Conseil d'État of 30 March 1916 (DP. 1916. 3. 25):

By contract dated 8 March 1904 the City of Bordeaux granted a company a concession for the provision of gas and electricity within the city limits for a period of thirty years. The price of gas consumed for public lighting was fixed at 8 centimes per cubic metre. After the outbreak of war the price of coal rose from roughly 28 francs to 114 francs, and the company sought to have the price of gas adapted to the altered circumstances. As no amicable settlement could be reached the parties went to the administrative courts. At first instance the company's claim was rejected but the Conseil d'État granted it. The Conseil d'État observed that coal was a necessary raw material for the production of gas and that it had risen enormously in price since the outbreak of war because the coal-producing areas of central Europe were in enemy hands and ocean transport had become extremely difficult. This had subverted the whole economic basis of the contract. The public interest in an assured and continuous supply of gas, as well as the particular circumstances of the case, called for a solution which could not be achieved simply by applying the words of the contract. If the parties were unable to reach an amicable settlement on this basis, the court must grant the utility company a claim for contribution from the consumer so as to cover some part of the loss which would otherwise be caused by the continuance of the contract (see also Conseil d'État 9 Dec. 1932, S. 1933. 3. 39 and 15 July 1949, S. 1950. 3. 61).

The civil courts were quite unmoved by such decisions of the Conseil d'État.

Apart from a few lower court decisions the view has remained intact that even catastrophic effects on contracts only justify rescission if the very strict conditions of 'force majeure' are satisfied. This is the position in France to this day.

The following cases may be consulted: Civ. 6 June 1921, D. 1921, 1. 73: Civ. 17 Nov. 1925, S. 1926. 1. 37; Civ. 15 Nov. 1933, Gaz Pal. 1934. 1. 68; Com. 18 Jan. 1950, D. 1950, 227.

This being the attitude of the civil courts in France, the legislator had to intervene after both World Wars. This very fact shows that it is wrong of he French courts to treat contracts in the private and the public sphere differently in this respect: the legislator's intervention shows that even in private law it may be against the public interest, properly understood, to require that debtors always perform their contracts according to their terms, notwithstanding a fundamental alteration in economic conditions. After the First World War a law of 21 Jan. 1918 named after Deputy FAILLIOT gave courts the power to rescind pre-war contracts for the delivery of goods and, if the case required, to grant damages

'if performance by the contractor would cause hardship or loss greatly in excess of what could reasonably be expected at the time of the contract'. A law of 22 April 1949 made similar provision for contracts concluded before the Second World War. In addition, there was comprehensive legislation for the modification of long-term leases affected by the war. Judges were even empowered under certain conditions to defer or diminish the price in sales contracts between commercial enterprises (on this see KEGEL (above p. 516) 166 ff.).

French businessmen have reacted in their own way to the restrictive attitude of the courts. They allocate the risks due to future war, strikes or currency fluctuations by express clauses in their contracts, or else have recourse to arbitration and empower the arbitrator to adapt the contract to the changed circumstances in the light of what is fair and reasonable.

Other Romanistic jurisdictions, with the exception of Belgium, have declined to follow the French example. (See KEGEL (above p. 516) 170 ff.) *Italy* calls for special mention here. The effect of subsequent changes of circumstances on contracts is covered by arts. 1467 ff. of the Codice civile of 1942. A contract which is to be performed after a long delay or in deferred or periodic instalments may be rescinded by the court on the application of a party for whom the performance of the contract would be excessively onerous ('eccessivamente onerosa') as a result of extraordinary and unforeseeable events. There are two limitations to this general principle. First, the contract will not be rescinded if the subsequent difficulty falls within the normal risks of the contract ('nell'alea normale del contratto'); secondly, the other party can resist rescission of the contract by offering to alter its terms in an equitable manner.

IV

The *English* doctrine of the effect of altered circumstances on contracts—the 'doctrine of frustration of contracts'—has two distinct historical sources. One of them has already been noted in the previous chapter, the rule in *Taylor* v. *Caldwell* (see above p. 509). This decision laid down the principle that a party was freed from his contractual obligation (and consequently from liability for damages for breach of contract) if performance of the contract required the continued existence of a particular chattel and this chattel was accidentally destroyed before the time fixed for performance. This principle was subsequently extended in several ways. It was applied in a case where a pianist was disabled through illness from appearing at a concert as promised (*Robinson* v. *Davidson* (1871) LR 6 Ex. 269), the analogy with *Taylor* v. *Caldwell* lying in the fact that by falling ill the pianist had lost a quality whose continuance until the moment of her appearance was essential to the contract. See also *Nickoll* v. *Ashton*, [1901] 2 KB 126: the vendor of a cargo of Egyptian cottonseed was to load it in Alexandria in January 1900 on SS *Orlando*, but the *Orlando* grounded in the Baltic the previous month. A majority of the judges used *Taylor* v. *Caldwell* to support their view that the contract contained an 'implied condition' to the effect that the vendor was to be freed if 'performance becomes impossible by reason of the particular specified thing—that is, the steamship "Orlando"—ceasing to exist as a cargo-carrying ship without the defendants' default'. The other judge made a more convincing analysis of the case and asked whether it was not unfair to put the risk of the timeous arrival of the *Orlando* on the purchaser alone: after all, it was the *vendor* who, with knowledge of its location, had nominated the ship and chartered it for the carriage of the goods he had sold.

Finally, the rule in *Taylor* v. *Caldwell* was applied in the famous 'coronation cases'.

In *Krell* v. *Henry* [1903] 2 KB 740, the plaintiff had a house on the route of King Edward VII's coronation procession and he hired it to the defendant for the day. The coronation procession was cancelled, and the hirer refused to pay the hire. The owner's claim was rejected: the rule in *Taylor* v. *Caldwell* was applicable not only 'where the performance of the contract becomes impossible by the cessation of the existence of the thing which is the subject-matter of the contract, but also in cases where the event which renders the contract incapable of performance is the cessation or non-existence of an express condition or state of things, going to the root of the contract, and essential to its performance'. It was true that in their letters the parties had not expressly referred to the purpose of the hiring (watching the coronation procession), but the court could look at the attendant circumstances in order to discover what the 'foundation of the contract' might be.—There was, however, another 'coronation case' in which it was held that the contract was not invalidated by the cancellation of the festivities (*Herne Bay Steamboat* v. *Hutton*, [1903] 2 KB

683). Here the defendant had hired the plaintiff's ship for the day on which King Edward VII was to review the fleet, since he wanted to watch the review and also to see the English fleet anchored at Spithead. The review was cancelled but the court held the defendant to the contract. The distinction between this case and *Krell* v. *Henry* may be that the person hiring the ship could still make the trip and show his guests the fleet, so that despite the cancellation of the naval review the contractual purpose could still be achieved in part. Furthermore, the plaintiff was in the business of letting out his ships throughout the year for all manner of purposes: he had no interest in the defendant's particular aim in engaging the ship, which therefore constituted only a unilateral motive in the defendant and not the common basis of the contract between the parties. The cases are discussed in detail in McElroy/Williams above p. 516.

The other root of the present English doctrine is a line of cases in maritime law. These are cases in which a shipowner was unable to provide the chartered ship at the right time and place because without any fault on his part the ship had been damaged or requisitioned or because the port nominated by the charterer had been closed by war. The question in these cases is whether the delay attributable to such events is such that reasonable businessmen would regard the charterparty as at an end.

See *Geipel* v. *Smith*, (1872) LR 7 QB 404; *Jackson* v. *Union Marine Ins. Co.*, (1873) LR 8 CP 572; *Dahl* v. *Nelson, Donkin & Co.*, (1881) 6 App. Cas. 38.

Since the First World War the English courts have fused these two lines of decisions into the 'doctrine of frustration of contract'. It is applied today in cases of factual or legal *impossibility*, in cases of *frustration of purpose* (as in *Krell* v. *Henry*) and finally in cases where the change of circumstances has so delayed performance or altered its nature that performance rendered thereafter would be something 'radically different' from what was envisaged by the parties at the time of the contract.

See *Davis Contractors Ltd.* v. *Fareham U. D. C.*, [1956] AC 696, 727 ff.; *F. A. Tamplin Steamship Co.* v. *Anglo-Mexican Petroleum Products Co.*, [1916] 2 AC 397.

There is some dispute in England whether the judge should decide cases of this sort by construing the contract or simply by laying down what seems to him to be reasonable and fair in the circumstances of the individual case. The first view, called the 'implied term theory', goes back to *Taylor* v. *Caldwell* and has been endorsed in a long line of later decisions. Under this theory the judge must ask what agreement reasonable parties would have reached if at the time of making the contract they had foreseen the subsequent events and made some provision for them. Thus in *Hirji Mulji* v. *Cheong Yue S. S. Co.*, [1926] AC 497, 510, Lord Sumner said: 'Frustration . . . is explained in theory as a condition or term of the contract, implied by the law ab initio, in order to supply what the parties would have inserted had the matter occurred to them, on the basis of what is fair and reasonable, having regard to the mutual interests concerned, and of the main objects of the contract'.

Other decisions speak of the 'presumed common intention of the paties'; see *Bank Line Ltd.* v. *Arthur Capel & Co.*, [1919] AC 435, 455, and the other decisions cited by McNAIR (above p. 516) 143 ff.

According to the other view, the courts have power to adapt or undo contracts on the basis of equity: 'The court imposes upon the parties the just and reasonable solution that the new situation demands'.

See CHESHIRE/FIFOOT/FURMSTON 571 ff. Among the judges who have shared this view are LORD WRIGHT (see *Denny, Mott & Dickson Ltd.* v. *Fraser*, [1944] AC 265, 274 ff.) and LORD DENNING (see *Ocean Tramp Tankers Corp.* v. *V/O Sovfracht*, [1964] 2 QB 226, 238: 'If it should happen, in the course of carrying out a contract, that a fundamentally different situation arises for which the parties made no provision—so much so that it would not be just in the new situation to hold them bound to its terms—then the contract is at an end').—Other judges prefer to use the metaphor of the collapse of the 'foundation of the contract': thus in the *Tamplin* case [1916] 2 AC 397, 406), LORD HALDANE asked whether 'the occurrence . . . may be of a character and extent so sweeping that the foundation of what the parties are deemed to have had in contemplation has disappeared, and the contract itself has vanished with that foundation'.

As English writers recognize (see TRAKMAN, above p. 517), it does not make much difference which of these views is adopted. A judge who avoids a contract on the ground of supervening events because he finds this 'just and reasonable' could and would reach the same result if he had to do so on the basis of 'construction of the contract'. In either case the critical consideration is whether the event which has brought about the change of circumstances is one of the risks which reasonable businessmen would put on the contractor seeking to avoid the contract. Two decisions on sale and charter contracts, both concerned with the effect of the closure of the Suez Canal in 1956/7, show how carefully English courts consider and evaluate all the relevant facts, regardless of the legal concepts in which they proceed to clothe the resulting decisions.

In *Tsakiroglou & Co.* v. *Noblee Thörl GmbH*, [1962] AC 93, 300 tons of Sudanese groundnuts were sold by contract dated 4 October 1956 at a price of £50 per ton c.i.f. Hamburg, and the vendor undertook to ship the goods in Port Sudan in November/December 1956. On 2 November 1956 the Suez Canal was blocked owing to the war between Israel and Egypt. Although the vendor could still have had the goods delivered to Hamburg via the Cape of Good Hope, the freight would have amounted to £15 per ton as opposed to £7 10s. by way of the Suez Canal. Accordingly the vendor refused to load the goods and declared the contract at an end. An arbitrator, appointed pursuant to contract, held that the vendor was in breach and must pay damages amounting to £5,600; this award was upheld by the courts, and by the House of Lords on final appeal. The dominant consideration was that this was a contract of sale in which it was indifferent to the purchaser by what route the vendor delivered the goods to Hamburg: the date of arrival in Hamburg, which was not fixed in the contact, was not material to him and carriage round the Cape would not have affected the condition of the goods. The doubling of the freight, on the other hand, was regarded as unimportant.

The same result was reached in the American decision of *Transatlantic Financing Corp.* v. *United States*, 363 F. 2d 312 (DC Cir. 1966), but not in *Carapanayoti & Co.* v. *E. T. Green*, [1959] 1 QB 131 where in a similar case, though more immediately in the shadow of the recent war, McNAIR J. came to the opposite conclusion.

The case of *Ocean Tramp Tankers Corp.* v. *V/O Sovfracht*, [1964] 2 QB 226, was rather more complicated. In September 1956 the defendant chartered a ship from the plaintiff for a voyage from Genoa to India via a Black Sea port at a fixed hire per month of the voyage. At the time the charter was concluded it was obvious to the parties that the Suez Canal might well be closed, but even so they included no term to cover this eventuality, meaning to 'leave it to the lawyers to sort out'. The Court of Appeal had to decide, *inter alia*, whether the charterparty was avoided by the fact that after loading in Odessa the ship could no longer proceed to India by way of the Suez Canal. In his very interesting opinion, LORD DENNING first gave the lie to the widespread belief that the 'doctrine of frustration' was applicable only if the events in question had been *unforeseen*. Then he asked whether the situation produced by the closure of the Canal entitled the defendant to throw up the charter, and held that this would only be so if the need to sail round the Cape put the defendant in a position 'fundamentally different' from that envisaged at the time of the contract. This was not the case: the voyage from Genoa to the port of discharge in India would have taken 138 days instead of 108 and would therefore have been relatively more expensive for the defendant, but the ship and its crew were such that the cargo would be perfectly safe on the voyage round the Cape. Accordingly, the increase in time and expense of the voyage did not entitle the defendant to terminate the contract. In other cases, however, first instance judges have reached a different conclusion: see *Société Franco-Tunisienne d'Armement* v. *Sidermar S.p.A.*, [1961] 2 QB 278.

In the *United States* distinctions are drawn according to whether the change in circumstances renders the performance impossible (impossibility) or very much more difficult (impracticability) or futile and pointless (frustration).

The first class of case includes not only situations in which performance is rendered absolutely impossible for the debtor—as when the concert hall which he has leased out burns down or where the specific thing he has sold is destroyed before the risk in it passes—but also situations in which the change in circumstances has rendered performance by the debtor very much more onerous or costly. In Restatement (Second) of Contracts (1981) §261 we find that the debtor is freed from his obligation to perform if after the formation of the contract his performance.

'is made impracticable without his fault by the occurrence of an event the non-occurrence of which was a basic assumption on which the contract was made'. This is very like the provision for sales contracts in §2–615 UCC, that delay in delivery or non-delivery of the goods does not constitute a breach of contract 'if performance as agreed has been made impracticable by the occurrence of a contingency the non-occurrence of which was a basic assumption on which the contract was made'.

It will be obvious that these are empty formulas without effective content; only by a close study of decided cases can one learn when a debtor will be released by a change in circumstances. It is accepted that the mere fact that performance has become more expensive does not of itself make it a case of 'impracticability'; much more important are the *facts* which have rendered performance more costly, and, further, which of the parties bore of the risk that these facts might occur. In general, changes in the price of raw materials are at the risk of the party bound to obtain them in order to perform the contract; so, too, when owing to unexpected circumstances materials cease to be available from the anticipated source of supply, but are to be had from elsewhere, though more expensively. The person who has promised to deliver goods to a particular place is not released just because unforeseen circumstances make it impossible to deliver except by a longer and more costly route, though it may be different if it is an entirely unexpected event, such as the outbreak of war, the imposition of an embargo, or a disastrous crop failure which renders performance much more difficult and expensive.

Full details are in FARNSWORTH, *Contracts* (1990) vol. ii, 533 ff., with extensive references to the decisions of state courts.

American lawyers, unlike the English, restrict the notion of 'frustration' to cases where the promised performance can still be tendered (and paid for) but has, by reason of unforeseen circumstances, become very largely worthless or pointless (see Restatement (Second) of Contracts (1981) §265). Typical cases include those in which some administrative measure, serious civil unrest, or natural events have prevented the party from using the leased property as he had planned, or from exporting the purchased goods to the intended destination.

In *Lloyd* v. *Murphy*, 25 Cal. 2d 48, 153 P. 2d 47 (1947) a person rented a property shortly before the Second World War for use as an automobile dealership. When the US government imposed strict limitations on the sale of new motor vehicles, he refused to honour the contract, but was held bound by it. The court noted that the premises lay on a main thoroughfare and could be used for other purposes, perhaps by a sub-tenant, that an experienced businessman might have foreseen such wartime restrictions, and that the sale of automobiles had not been completely banned but only curtailed. 'The doctrine of frustration has been limited to cases of extreme hardship so that businessmen, who must make their arrangements in advance, can rely with certainty on their contracts . . . The sale of automobiles was . . . merely restricted and if governmental regulation does not entirely prohibit business to be carried on in the leased premises but only limits or restricts it, thereby making it less profitable and more difficult to continue, the lease is not terminated or the lessee excused from further performance.' See also CHAPMAN, 59 *Mich. L. Rev.* 98 (1960); HAY (above p. 516); and FARNSWORTH, *Contracts* (1990) vol. ii, 564 ff.

V

Our comparative survey shows that all the legal systems under consideration have had to face the problem of contracts affected by supervening events, but have used rather different methods and formulas to solve it. The stance of French law is very distinctive, for it continues to reject the doctrine of 'imprévision', except where it would be incompatible with the immediate public interest to require the contractor to perform in the new situation and so force him out of business in the long run. This restrictive position of the French courts has compelled the legislator expressly to recognize the need to adapt or modify transactions affected by war, which is in practice the most important cause of contracts being rendered impossible or nearly impossible to perform. Businessmen have reacted to this judicial attitude by making an express allocation of risks in their contracts and by taking to arbitration, but it is hard to judge the precise extent.

The German and Anglo-American legal families, on the other hand, accept the principle that courts have power within narrow bounds to release parties from their contractual obligations, not only where the equilibrium of the transaction has been distorted but also where its purpose had been frustrated. The practical results reached by the courts are not easy to compare, partly because rather different types of case have arisen in the different countries and partly because in such cases ancillary attendant factors play an unusually important but imponderable role. Even the rule that price rises can never justify rescission of a contract is sometimes qualified: in the 'reservoir case' the Swiss Bundesgericht rescinded a 90-year-old contract because of a price rise attributable to a gradual and sustained loss of the purchasing power of currency over many decades, while the German Bundesgerichtshof held the parties to a similar contract which had run for sixty years. An important factor in the Swiss case was perhaps the fact that the party in difficulties was a charitable institution which faced liquidation if the contract were upheld without modification. In decisions regarding the revalorization of mortgages and the consequent claim for contribution, the German courts themselves have adapted contracts to a devaluation of the currency, but it must be noted that this was in a situation where, owing to a fairly sudden change in the economy, the purchasing power of the legal currency was tending towards zero at great speed.

English and American courts have not yet had to cope with such catastrophes. It is true that the First World War caused great price rises in England and the courts had to consider whether such price rises could rank as a ground of release. In a series of cases the courts held not, repeating the simple formula that 'a person was not entitled to be excused from the performance of the contract merely because it had become more costly to perform it' (*Bolckow Vaughan & Co.* v. *Compañia Minera*, (1916) 33 TLR 111) but this was surely because these price rises were simply the consequence of wartime shortages of certain raw materials rather than a symptom of a general economic collapse, as in Germany at the time. As we have seen, the German courts in similar circumstances held the parties to their contract despite price rises. It is impossible to say how English courts would react in the face of galloping inflation but one might refer to an observation of VISCOUNT SIMON in *British Movietonews Ltd.* v. *London Cinemas*, [1952] AC 166, 185 that 'a wholly abnormal rise or fall in prices, sudden depreciation of currency, an unexpected obstacle to execution' might be circumstances whose occurrence, on a proper construction of a contract, could free the parties from their obligations under it. Quite recently LORD DENNING held that a contract concluded for an unlimited period of time can be terminated if prolonged inflation, even at current levels, has seriously distorted the relation between performance and counterperformance. The defendant water company had contracted in 1929 to provide the plaintiff's hospital 'at all times hereafter' with water at a price of 2.9 p. per unit. When the price of water in the open market had risen to 45 p. per unit the water company terminated the contract and the Court of Appeal held that it was entitled to do so (*Staffordshire Area Health Auth'y* v. *South Staffordshire Waterworks*, [1978] 1 WLR 1387). The other two judges founded on the special facts of the case, but LORD DENNING stated that 'the time has come when we may have to revise our views about the principle of nominalism': seeing that the price of water had risen by a factor of twenty and would rise further, 'The situation has changed so radically since the contract was made fifty years ago that the term of the contract "at all times hereafter" ceases to bind: and it is open to the court to hold that the contract is determined by reasonable notice.' This is sharply criticized by CHESHIRE/FIFOOT/FURMSTON 578.

While the dominant German cases on the effect of altered circumstances on contracts are those which sought to deal with the 'mass calamities', to use WIEACKER's apt phrase, after the two World Wars, the English cases get their special flavour from the strong mercantile and maritime element which emerges in the judgments. Not only are cases of 'frustration of charter-parties' historically a source of the modern English doctrine but they still come before the courts in large numbers. What impresses the foreign observer is not only the careful analysis of the facts of the individual case, as one would expect of English judges practised in the art of distinguishing, but also the clear deference to the views and needs of commerce. If our very summary investigation of the question has suggested that English courts are less ready than German courts to hold that altered circumstances have brought a contract to an end, this is certainly attributable to the fact that the English courts are readier to meet the demands of international trade, for in the cases under discussion commercial men incline to keeping the contract on foot. This is shown, for example, by the fact that in the Suez Canal decisions we have mentioned, the commercial arbitrators were all in favour of maintaining the contract; such a view in relevant commercial circles is obviously adopted as law by the English courts more readily than is usual in Germany.

The general tests and standards applied in these cases by courts in different countries also differ. The German Bundesgerichtshof still uses the time-honoured language of the doctrine of the collapse of the 'foundation of the transaction', as it did in the 'pneumatic drill case', emphasizing that it is always a matter of 'evaluating the circumstances of the individual case in good faith and equity' and garnishing the dish with the assertion that release from a contract is only justifiable if there is no other way to avoid an 'intolerable result incompatible with law and justice'. The *Swiss* courts stress that when subsequent events have caused a disequilibrium between performance and counterperformance the judge may modify the contract if the creditor's insistence on his rights would constitute 'usurious exploitation' of the debtor. The *English* courts ask whether, if the debtor were required to perform in the altered circumstances, this would be something 'fundamentally different' from what was envisaged at the time of the contract.

The very vagueness of these formulas may lead the reader to conclude that any attempt to discover concrete standards of solution will be fruitless and, since in the last resort the courts are led by considerations which are hardly susceptible of rationalization, futile as well. There may be some truth in this, but a word of warning is in place. The tendency to decide these cases solely by the use of general formulas and the standards of 'Treu und Glauben', 'justice', or what is 'just and reasonable' should be resisted. The English courts may be relatively immune to the dangers inherent in such formulas, but this is less clear of the German courts. Reliance on these general formulas makes it too easy to overlook the fact that the rights of the parties must in the first instance be judged by the *contract* they have made, for it might well have contained an express allocation of the risk of the supervening events. The task for the courts is therefore to fill a gap in the contract which exists because the parties did not foresee a subsequent change of circumstances which has now occurred, or failed to make provision for it if they did foresee it. The means of filling this gap in German law is called 'ergänzende Vertragsauslegung' (suppletive construction). The aim of the exercise is not to discover the 'hypothetical intention of the parties', that is, how the parties would have dealt with the point at issue if during the contractual negotiations some third party had drawn their attention to it, nor is it to discover the 'basis of the transaction' in OERTMANN's sense, namely the actual view of the future development of events consciously entertained by one party at the time of the contract to the knowledge and with the acquiescence of the other party. The aim is to find out what the relevant commercial interests would regard as the normal and appropriate allocation of risks in contracts of the type in question (correctly so held in BGHZ 74, 370). The provision on release from liability in art. 79 CISG rests on this view, and so does the 'implied term theory' of English law which, properly understood, is sound in point of legal policy, for it constantly reminds the judge that he must not simply decide the case in accordance with what seems just and equitable to him at the time of his decision. The *contract* is the law adopted by the parties, and it is the contract which the judge must use as a starting-point for his deliberations; if it has a gap, he must fill it in accordance with the standards developed by reputable commercial men for contracts of that type. No doubt this investigation leaves the judge a great deal of room for play, but it remains true that he must take functional and equitable considerations into account only to the extent necessary for the performance of his proper task, namely the discovery of the allocation of risks typical of contracts of the same type.

D. UNJUSTIFIED ENRICHMENT

38

Unjustified Enrichment in General

BEATSON, *The Use and Abuse of Unjust Enrichment* (1991).

BIRKS, *An Introduction to the Law of Restitution* (1989).

v. CAEMMERER, 'Bereicherung und unerlaubte Handlung', *Festschrift für Ernst Rabel*, vol. I (1954) 333.

——, 'Problèmes fondamentaux de l'enrichissement sans cause', *Rev. int. dr. comp.* 18 (1966) 573.

DAVID/GUTTERIDGE, 'The Doctrine of Unjustified Enrichment', 5 *Camb. LJ* 204 (1935).

DAWSON, *Unjust Enrichment, A Comparative Analysis* (1951).

——, 'Indirect Enrichment', *Festschrift für Max Rheinstein* II (1969) 789.

DICKSON, 'The Law of Restitution in the Federal Republic of Germany', 36 *ICLQ* 751 (1987).

——, 'Unjust Enrichment Claims: A Comparative Overview', 54 *Mod. L. Rev.* 99 (1995).

DRAKIDIS, 'La "Subsidiarité", caractère spécifique et international de l'action d'enrichissement sans cause', *Rev. trim. dr. civ.* 59 (1961) 577.

ELMAN, 'Unjust Enrichment in Israel Law', 3 *Israel L. Rev.* 526 (1968).

ENGLARD, 'Restitution of Benefits Conferred without Obligation', *Int. Enc. Comp. L.* X Ch. 5 (1991).

D. FRIEDMANN, 'Some Trends in the Development of the Law of Unjust Enrichment', in *Beiträge zum deutschen und israelischen Privatrecht* (Neue Kölner rechtswissenschaftliche Abhandlungen no. 81, 1977) 155.

D. FRIEDMANN/COHEN, 'Payment of Another's Debt', *Int. Enc. Comp. L.* X Ch. 10 (1991).

——, 'Adjustment among Multiple Debtors', *Int. Enc. Comp. L.* X Ch. 11 (1991).

GALLO, 'Unjust Enrichment, A Comparative Analysis' 40 *Am. J. Comp. L.* 431 (1992).

GOFF/JONES, *The Law of Restitution* (4th edn. 1993).

GORÉ, *L'Enrichissement aux dépens d'autrui* (1949).

KELLMANN, *Grundsätze der Gewinnhaftung, Rechtsvergleichender Beitrag zum Recht der ungerechtfertigten Bereicherung* (1969).

KLIPPERT, 'The Juridical Nature of Unjust Enrichment', 30 *U. Tor. LJ* 356 (1980).

KÖNIG, *Der Bereicherungsanspruch gegen den Drittempfänger einer Vertragsleistung nach französischem Recht* (1967).

KÖTZ, *Ungerechtfertigte Bereicherung, Tatbestände und Ordnungsprobleme aus rechtsvergleichender Sicht* (1985).

——, 'Empfiehlt es sich, das Bereicherungsrecht . . . durch den Gesetzgeber neu zu ordnen?', in *Gutachten und Vorschläge zur Überarbeitung des Schuldrechts* II (Ministry of Justice ed., 1981) 1515.

KUPISCH, *Die Versionsklage, Ihre Entwicklung von der gemeinrechtlichen Theorie des 17. Jahrhunderts bis zum österreichischen ABGB* (1965).

MARTINEK, 'Der Weg des Common Law zur allgemeinen Bereicherungsklage: Ein später Sieg des Pomponius?', *RabelsZ* 47 (1983) 284.

NICHOLAS, 'Unjustified Enrichment in the Civil Law and Louisiana Law', 36 *Tul. L. Rev.* 605 (1962), 37 *Tul. L. Rev.* 49 (1962).

O'CONNELL, 'Unjust Enrichment', 5 *Am. J. Comp. L.* 1 (1956).

PALMER, *The Law of Restitution* (4 vols., 1978).

——, 'History of Restitution in Anglo-American Law', *Int. Enc. Comp. L.* X Ch. 3 (1989).

SCHLUEP, 'Über Eingriffskondiktionen', *Mélanges Paul Piotet* (1990) 173.

SWADLING, 'Restitution and Unjust Enrichment' in HARTKAMP et al. (eds.), *Towards a European Civil Code* (1994) 267.

WILBURG, *Die Lehre von der ungerechtfertigten Bereicherung nach österreichischem und deutschem Recht* (1934).

ZIMMERMANN, 'Unjustified Enrichment: The Modern Civilian Approach', 15 *Oxf. J. Leg. Stud.* 403 (1995).

I

MOST rights in all advanced systems of private law arise either from a *contract* or a *tort*. Even a layman has no difficulty in understanding the sort of situations covered by these areas of law. When one points out that there is also an important place for claims which rest neither on contract nor on tort but on 'unjustified enrichment' (*enrichissement injustifié*, *ungerechtfertigte Bereicherung*), the situation is different. The layman can make nothing of the expressions, and can hardly be blamed for it. Indeed, if the jurist asked himself why the expression 'unjustified enrichment' is so colourless, he might well find that it was because he crams under it a whole series of very disparate situations whose only common feature is a negative one, namely that they are neither contract nor tort. This is a view with which many Anglo-American lawyers would sympathize. They would unhesitatingly accept that a person who had received a payment made in error must give it back and that a person who has unwittingly used material copyrighted by another must hand over any profits even though there was no contract between the parties nor any real tort. Yet if one said that both cases rested on a unitary principle, a 'principle of unjust enrichment', they would either demur or regard the observation as mere speculation. German lawyers, for example, are readier to accept that claims for 'unjustified enrichment' have a unitary basis. This is probably attributable to an invention of the fertile jurists of ancient Rome, the 'condictio', whose significance for modern Civil Law only becomes evident if one understands how very differently the Common Law has developed in this area.

The Roman *condictio* was an *actio in personam* designed to enforce an obligation with a specific content. It was 'abstract' in the sense that the formula made no mention of the *basis* of the defendant's obligation. The *condictio* could therefore be used wherever a specific sum of money or a specific chattel had to be handed over to the plaintiff, regardless of the ground of the obligation: the creditor could use it to recover a sum of money whether he had lent it or been promised it by document or by stipulation. The Roman jurists went further, for they soon realized that the 'abstractness' of the *condictio* made it capable of use in situations where the defendant was withholding something from the plaintiff without any justification and ought to give it up. The normal case was where the plaintiff had handed over a sum of money or chattel to the defendant for some specified purpose which remained unfulfilled because of initial or subsequent impossibility. If a person handed over money to pay off a debt, to constitute a dowry, or to execute a legacy, and in reality there was no debt, the marriage did not take place or the will was invalid, the recipient could not retain what he had no title to receive (*sine causa*). In all these cases the action granted by the Roman lawyers to undo the effects of the transaction was the *condictio*.

This action did not, in classical times, rest on vague considerations of equity or as DAWSON (above p. 537, p. 59) says, 'the conscious appeal . . . to the principle of unjust enrichment and the moral ideas with which it was connected'. Admittedly the Corpus Iuris often links the *condictio* with the *jus naturae*, the *bonum et aequum*, or the *ius gentium*, especially in the famous fragment of POMPONIUS in D. 50, 17, 206: 'Iure naturae aequum est neminem cum alterius detrimento et iniuria fieri locupletiorem' (it is naturally unjust for one person to be wrongfully enriched at the expense of another), but the dominant view now has it that these are post-classical generalizations abstracted by schoolmen for pedagogical purposes. Classical Roman lawyers proceeded less on the basis of such general formulas than on a practical consideration of the individual case, and they extended the *condictio* to an increasing number of well-defined situations whose common element was not that 'the plaintiff had a special ground for claiming but that the defendant had no adequate grounds for retaining' (RABEL, *Grundzüge des römischen Privatrechts* (1955) 119). It is worth noting that although the classical *condictio* was used in many different areas it remained a single action with a unitary formula; the categorization of the *condictio* into various types is as post-classical as its affiliation to the principle of *aequitas* (on the whole matter see KASER, *Das römische Privatrecht* I (1955) §139, II (1959) §270, ZIMMERMANN, *The Law of Obligations* (1990) 838 f.).

The different types of *condictio* developed under JUSTINIAN (*condictio causa data causa non secuta, ob turpem vel iniustam causam, indebiti*, and *sine causa*; see the titles to D. 12, 4–7) still survive more or less clearly in the Continental codes and form the heart of enrichment claims. Only in one respect

has later development moved right away from Roman law: under the influence of natural lawyers who found a few handholds in the Roman sources, a
general claim for useful expenditures has been developed which entitles 'him
at whose expense something useful has been done for another' to reclaim it
in specie or its value (see ALR 13 I §§262 ff., §1041 ABGB).

This is a generalization of the Roman *actio de in rem verso*. The *actio de in rem verso*
was one of the claims, called 'actiones adjecticiae qualitatis' by the Glossators, which
could under certain circumstances be brought directly against a superior by a person
who had transacted with his slave, *filius in potestate*, or employee; it thereby served in
some measure as a substitute for the institution of direct representation otherwise
unknown in Rome. If the inferior had used any gain from his transaction with the
third party for the benefit of his master, the third party could sue the master direct
by means of the *actio de in rem verso* (see KASER, *Das römische Privatrecht* I (1955)
§§62, 141; ZIMMERMANN, *The Law of Obligations* (1990) 878 f.).

In many books on the *Gemeines Recht*, Prussian and Austrian law this general claim for the repayment of useful expenditures was treated in close
proximity with the *condictio*, and in France the lawyers adopted the *actio
de in rem verso* of the *Gemeines Recht* as the basis for a general claim for unjustified enrichment for which the Code civil itself made no provision (for the
details, see KUPISCH, above p. 538). By contrast, the German BGB did
not adopt the *actio de in rem verso*, and in the countries where it is in principle
admissible, as in Austria and France, its area of application has been
severely curtailed by judicial decision.

II

Like the *Swiss* Code of Obligations, the *German* BGB devotes a special chapter to rights arising from 'unjustified enrichment' and starts out with a comprehensive general clause.

§812 par. 1 BGB lays down that 'A person who without legal justification (*ohne
rechtlichen Grund*) obtains anything from a person at his expense, whether by transfer
or otherwise, is bound to give it up to him. This obligation also arises if the legal justification subsequently ceases to exist or if the transfer does not have the effect envisaged in the transaction.'

According to art. 62 OR, 'A person who is unjustifiably enriched at the expense of
another must return the enrichment. This obligation arises in particular if a person
has received a benefit without any valid ground or on a ground which did not come
about or subsequently ceased to exist.'

§812 BGB distinguishes according to whether the uncovenanted benefit
arises 'by transfer' or 'otherwise'. In the first group, the so-called 'Leistungskondiktionen', fall cases where the claim is brought to recover a benefit

which the plaintiff conferred on the defendant consciously and intentionally, but which he now wants back because the transfer was 'without legal justification'. The most important instance of such a transfer ('Leistung') is the payment of money or transfer of other things, but a *Leistung* may take the form of the assignment of a right, the delivery of possession, the surrender of a receipt, document of indebtedness, or negotiable instrument, or even the performance of services of one kind or another which the person receiving them would otherwise have paid for. A 'Leistung' also occurs if one person is released at the expense of another from an obligation owed to a third party. In all these cases the critical question is whether the benefit so transferred is 'without legal ground', that is, whether the recipient can point to any valid agreement or relationship with the transferor which entitles him to retain what he has received. Thus there is a 'justification' for a payment of 1,000 DM if it is made by purchaser to vendor in payment of the price or by bank to customer as a credit advance or by prospective father-in-law to son-in-law. But if the sales contract, being illegal, was void *ab initio* or if the loan was induced by fraud and the bank rescinds it or if the intended wedding never takes place, there is no longer any legal ground, if there ever was one, to justify the recipient's retention of the money.

One may find in §812 par. 1 sent. 2 BGB, art. 62 par. 2 OR and §1431 ff. ABGB the distinction between the various types of *condictio* known to Justinian, but this is of no practical importance since they are all instances of a transfer made 'sine causa'. What is worth noticing, however, is that the provisions regarding the restitution of an 'unjustified enrichment' pay no attention to the reason for the original or subsequent invalidity of the obligation. For example, it is immaterial whether the underlying obligation is illegal or immoral (see above Ch. 28), void for 'initial impossibility' (see above Ch. 36 II), or subject to rescission *ab initio* for error, duress, or deceit (see above Ch. 31); these questions all concern the validity of the contract and are therefore dealt with in the relevant section of the Code. The law of unjustified enrichment only moves in when the invalidity of the underlying transaction has been determined by reference to *other* provisions.—Nor is it a matter for the law of unjust enrichment to determine how contracts are to be unravelled which were valid to begin with but were later rescinded on the ground of a breach of contract (see above Ch. 36) or of a fundamental change of circumstances (see above Ch. 37): here it is the law of contract which controls not only the question whether the contract is rescindible but also how benefits conferred under the contract have to be given back (see §§323 ff., 346 ff. BGB, art. 109 OR, §921 ABGB), though on this matter German law calls in aid some provisions of the law of unjustified enrichment (§§323 par. 3, 327 sent. 2, 557a, 628 par. 1 sent. 3 BGB).

§814 BGB provides that a person cannot reclaim a benefit he has conferred if he knew that he was not bound to confer it. Swiss and Austrian law put the same idea more positively by prescribing that a person who has made a transfer he was not bound to make may only reclaim it if he was in 'error' about his obligation (art. 63 OR, §1431 ABGB). Of course the error in question here is quite different from the error required to justify the rescission of a contract: even a grossly negligent error, an immaterial error, or an error of law is sufficient to ground a restitutionary claim (see BGE 64 II 127; 70 II 271; BG St. Gallen SJZ 63 (1967) 110; OGH 20 June 1922, ZBl. 1922 no. 259).

This difference in the formulation of these codal provisions makes for a difference in the burden of proof: in Germany it is the *defendant* who must prove that at the time of the transfer the plaintiff knew he was not bound to make it (RGZ 133, 277), while in Switzerland and Austria it is for the *plaintiff* to establish that he made the transfer because he wrongly supposed he was bound to (see BGE 24 II 182; OGH 20 June 1894, GIU 32 no. 15158).

A claim for restitution is also excluded if the transfer satisfied a moral obligation or an obligation which was time-barred or subject to some other defence: in such cases a debtor who could not be *sued* for performance cannot reclaim if he performs *voluntarily* (§§813, 814 BGB, art. 63 OR, §1432 ABGB).

A restitutionary claim is needed to solve a special class of case which arises only in Germany; these are the cases in which, thanks to the 'principle of abstraction' (see above p. 445), a person becomes vested with ownership or some other right as the result of a conveyance or assignment based on an invalid contract. Suppose that a person sells a painting and delivers it to the purchaser and that it later appears that the contract of sale was void for want of agreement or is rescinded for error. In that case the purchaser will nevertheless have become owner of it since German law makes a clear distinction between the contract of sale and the actual conveyance. At this point §812 BGB steps in and empowers the vendor to demand the restitution of the benefit conferred, namely the ownership in the painting. In Swiss law, by contrast, a conveyance of immoveables (art. 974 par. 2 ZGB) or chattels (BGE 55 II 302) is valid only if the underlying transaction is valid, so the vendor retains his ownership of the picture and therefore has a claim based on *ownership* which, unlike the claim based on *enrichment*, will procure the retransfer of the picture even if the purchaser is bankrupt. Of course the purchaser may already have resold the painting to a third party; if so, the third party, if in good faith, will have become owner of it (art. 714, 933 ZGB) and the original vendor will have only an enrichment claim with which to sue his purchaser for what he received from the third party.

In Germany, claims for the restitution of benefits conferred by the plaintiff's own act *sine causa* lie only against the party on whom the plaintiff conferred the benefit and not against third parties indirectly benefited by the transfer. Thus if a person uses borrowed money to reconstruct his wife's house, and the loan contract is invalid, the lender cannot claim restitution from the wife, even if the borrower is insolvent. The same rule applies if a building subcontractor under contract with the builder puts bricks and mortar into the house of a third party: he can only sue the main contractor, on the contract if it is valid or in unjustified enrichment if it is not; he cannot sue the third party for any increase in the value of the house attributable to his work and materials. The German courts here speak of the need for 'directness of transfer' (*Unmittelbarkeit der Vermögensverschiebung*): the loss of the plaintiff and the benefit to the defendant must result from one and the same transaction. The purpose of this restriction is obvious. The transferor should only be able to sue the transferee with whom he had a contract and should not acquire an additional debtor just because the object transferred happens to have ended up among the assets of a third party. It is also perfectly fair that the transferor's suit, in contract or restitution, should lie only against his contractor: he made the contract in reliance on his contractor's capacity to pay, and should bear the loss himself if this reliance was misplaced and the transferee gets into financial difficulties which prevent his paying the contract price or, should the contract fail, the value of the enrichment.

In other words, German law today refuses to recognize the *actio de in rem verso* as accepted in the *Gemeines Recht* and in Prussian law (see RGZ 1, 143; 1, 159; ROHG 3, 377; the negative attitude of the German legislator may be seen in Motive II p. 872).—*Swiss* law adopts the same position. In BGE 42 II 467 a farmer was placed under interdiction and his sons took on the management of the farm. They bought two cows from the plaintiff in their own name and added them to the herd. The vendor claimed the price from the father, and the Bundesgericht rejected the claim: the defendant became owner of the cows not at the plaintiff's expense but at the expense of his sons to whom the cows belonged after they had bought them from the plaintiff in their own name.—By contrast, §1041 of the *Austrian* ABGB admits the *actio de in rem verso* in very wide terms: the owner whose property 'has been used for the benefit of another . . . without any agency' is entitled to demand its return or reimbursement from that other. Despite this, the Austrian courts have always held that the *actio de in rem verso* of §1041 ABGB is simply 'a supplementary remedy which is only to be used in the case where there is no contract or analogous relationship between the plaintiff and the third party which could be used for the decision of the case' (OGH 16 Jan. 1952, SZ 25 no. 13). Thus a building contractor retained by a tenant to improve the rented house had no claim against the landlord for payment of the amount by which his labours had improved the value of the house (OGH 7 Jan. 1930, SZ 12 no. 7; to the same effect OGH 1 June 1955, JBl. 1956, 17, with an exhaustive review of the cases and a critical note by GSCHNITZER).

It follows that a tradesman who improves or repairs an object which does not belong to his contractor cannot, if his contractor becomes insolvent, use §812 BGB to claim the value of the improvement from the *owner* of the thing. This rule is, however, qualified in cases where the tradesman is still in *possession* of the thing he has repaired: here all systems agree that the tradesman may hold on to the thing, even against its owner, until he has been paid for his work.

The method of protecting the repairman is different in the different systems: in *Germany* he is given claims for improvement under §§994 ff. BGB (see BGHZ 34, 122), in *Switzerland* he has a lien under art. 895 ZBG, and in *Austria* he is allowed to withhold the thing under §471 ABGB (see OGH 1 April 1959, ZVR 1960 no. 45).

So far we have been considering the *Leistungskondiktion*, or claim for the restitution of a benefit conferred by the plaintiff's own act, where the essential element is always a transfer, performance, or payment, that is, a benefit deliberately conferred by the plaintiff which cannot be retained because the underlying obligation was either invalid *ab initio* or has subsequently been rescinded. We must now turn to enrichments 'arising otherwise', of which the most important instance occurs when a person uses or profits from property or rights vested in another without his authorization. A defendant who was *at fault* in interfering with the rights of others will be liable to pay damages in tort, but even if his interference is perfectly innocent he is bound under §812 BGB to restore to the owner of the right the value of the use he has made of it. In such cases German lawyers speak of 'Eingriffskondiktion' (*condictio* based on interference).

For example, if a person lets his cattle graze in someone else's meadow or unwittingly consumes fuel belonging to another or utilizes a stranger's railway track (RGZ 97, 310), he must restore the value of the use which he thereby appropriated to himself, regardless of whether he was at fault in so doing. This is also the best way of solving a problem which was much discussed in Germany, where a person without any contractual relationship uses the parking place of another: a person who drives into a parking place on the highway and states that he does not intend to pay any parking fee since he thinks there is no right to charge such fees is bound, should he be wrong, to pay the value of using the parking place. The reason is not that his driving into a parking place for which fees are charged constitutes a 'de facto contract' (*faktisches Vertragsverhältnis*), though it was so held in BGHZ 21, 319, 333 ff., but because he has unjustifiably interfered with someone else's right to charge for parking.

The person who makes unauthorized use of the right of another must reimburse that person up to the value of such use even if he can show that the other would not or could not have used the right himself. The purpose of the restitutionary claim is not to compensate for a *diminution* in the assets of the plaintiff—that would be damages for loss suffered—but to transfer to the party with the better right an *accretion* to the assets of the defendant. The owner is the person with the better right, for it is to the owner alone that the legal system accords the power to use his property as he thinks fit, or to allow others to do so, for a fee, should he so choose.

Another instance of the '*condictio* based on interference' (*Eingriffskondiktion*) arises when a person sells the property of another in such circumstances that his purchaser becomes owner of it. The previous owner can require the vendor to hand over what he received from the third party purchaser, including any gain he made on the deal (BGHZ 29, 157).

See §816 par. 1 BGB. This is also the position of *Austrian* and *Swiss* law (KOZIOL/WELSER, *Grundriß des bürgerlichen Rechts* (5th edn. 1979) i, 330 and OGH 10 Nov. 1954, *SZ* 27 no. 286; VON TUHR/PETER, *Allgemeiner Teil des schweizerischen Obligationenrechts* (3rd edn. 1979) i, 495).—If the *third party* acquires the thing *gratuitously*, §816 par. 1 sent. 2 BGB exceptionally provides that the enrichment claim may be directed against him as well: whether this is true in Swiss law as well is not clear (see v. BÜREN, *Schweizerisches Obligationenrecht* (1964) 310).—There is some dispute about how to solve the case where the third party does not acquire ownership in the thing, as happens if it is stolen property (§935 BGB, art. 934 ZGB). If the third party is unknown or for some reason not practically amenable to a suit based on ownership, should the owner be able instead to make the vendor disgorge what he received from the third party? This is allowed in Germany, provided the owner ratifies the transfer of title to the third party under §185 BGB and thereby gives up his ownership. The Swiss Bundesgericht apparently decides otherwise (see BGE 71 II 90).

This *condictio* is also very important where rights other than ownership have been infringed. A person who infringes another's patent, design rights or trade mark must pay a fair and normal licence fee under §812 BGB, but need not disgorge any profits he made thereby (BGHZ 82, 299; BGHZ 99, 244). §812 BGB also applies to infringements of the right to one's *likeness* and *name*: a person who without their consent uses the picture of a famous actor or the name of well-known firm in his advertisements is liable for the sum they would normally charge for permission to use their rights for commercial purposes (BGHZ 20, 345; BGHZ 81, 75; BGH NJW 1992, 2084).

Often enough the infringer will have made a profit greatly in excess of the amount of a fair licence fee. Can the aggrieved party claim that profit? The general, though not unanimous, view is that no such claim lies under §812 BGB; however, if the infringer of a protected commercial right was at *fault*, the courts always hold him liable to disgorge his profit (see BGHZ 60, 168 and 206), a liability sometimes said to arise under §687(2) BGB, but more often attributed to a judge-made rule confirmed by *jurisprudence constante*.

III

The Civil Code in *France*, unlike those of Germany and Switzerland, has no general provision regarding the restitution of unjustified enrichment. This is because POTHIER, whose writings dominate the law of obligations in the Code civil, concentrated on the *condictio indebiti* at the expense of other forms of liability in unjust enrichment, to which he accorded no comprehensive treatment. Furthermore POTHIER gave a great deal of scope to the institution of *negotiorum gestio*, which consequently became applicable, at a pinch, in cases where a transfer had to be undone because the purpose for which it was made could not be fulfilled. Thus of the many rules related to unjustified enrichment which are strewn throughout the Code civil, the most important are those concerning the payment of a thing not due (paiement de l'indu) and *negotiorum gestio* (*gestion d'affaires*). These two institutions are brought together in the Code civil under the title 'Des Quasi-contrats' (arts. 1371 ff.).

At first the courts tried to solve enrichment cases on the basis of the Code, but since its provisions, especially those regarding *gestion d'affaires*, proved inadequate for the purpose, AUBRY and RAU proposed in their influential text-book that a *general* enrichment claim should be introduced, and eventually in 1892, in the famous *Boudier* case, the Cour de Cassation did so. Before turning to that landmark decision we shall deal briefly with the case of unjustified enrichment which is expressly regulated in arts. 1376 ff. Code civil, namely *répétition de l'indu* or the restoration of payments made pursuant to a supposed debt. The Italian Codice civile also has special rules concerning the payment of a thing not due (*pagamento dell'indebito*, arts. 2033 ff. Codice civile), although it has general provisions regarding unjustified enrichment.

In the chapter devoted to the performance of obligations, the Code civil already states that 'tout paiement suppose une dette: ce qui a été payé sans être dû, est sujet à répétition (art. 1235: 'payment presupposes a debt: what has been paid without being due may be reclaimed'). This claim for restitution is laid down in greater detail in arts. 1376 ff. Code civil as one of the claims based on quasi-contract.

The first requisite is that the recipient have been enriched by a 'payment'. This includes the payment of money, the transfer of things, and analogous transactions such as having one's account credited, but not the rendering of *services* or the provision of the use of a thing, which therefore have to be dealt with by the *general* enrichment claim.

Next, the transfer must have been made pursuant to a debt which did not exist at the time. This includes the case where a debt is owed *by a third party* and the transferor pays it in the supposition that it is owed by himself: the transferor can claim restitution from the creditor unless the latter, thinking the debt has been paid off, has destroyed the document of indebtedness (art. 1377 par. 2 Code civil) or released securities (see Civ. 27 Nov. 1912, DP 1913. 1. 96; see also art. 2036 Codice civile). However, if one pays off a time-barred debt one cannot claim back what one has paid even if one was unaware of the time bar (Req. 17 Jan. 1938, DP 1940.1.57, noted by CHE-VALLIER; Soc. 11 April 1991, Bull. V no. 192; art. 2940 Codice civile). Nor can one claim back what has been voluntarily transferred pursuant to a moral duty (art. 1235(2) Code civil; art. 2034 Codice civile).

It is enough that performance was not due, or must the plaintiff have been in error in supposing that it was? This is a much disputed question, closely connected with the question of the relevance of the plaintiff's negligence in making any such error. A bank which paid a cheque in forgetfulness of the fact that the drawer had stopped it was refused an enrichment claim against the drawer (Com. 16 July 1985, D. 1986, 373, noted by MESTRE in *Rev. trim. dr. civ.* 85 (1986) 109), whereas social insurers have often been allowed to reclaim overpayments due to their own fault in not following the relevant rules (e.g. Soc. 8 Nov. 1977, Bull. V no. 603). However, if the recipient is put in a difficulty by suddenly having to pay back all at once the various sums he has been receiving over a period, he may be able to meet the claim for repayment with a damages claim of his own under art. 1382 Code civil.

See Soc. 3 Nov. 1972, JCP 1974.II.17692, noted by GHESTIN; Soc. 21 March 1972, JCP 1973.II.17343 bis; Civ. 18 July 1979, D. 1980, 172 noted by VASSEUR; the whole subject is treated in detail by DEFRENOIS-SOULEAU, 'La répétition de l'indu', *Rev. trim. dr. civ.* 88 (1989) 243.—Italian law has one very odd rule: if a person thinks he owes money which in fact is owed by *someone else* and he pays it, he can only claim restitution if he proves not only that he made this mistake *but also* that the mistake was an excusable one to make (art. 2036 Codice civile), whereas if *no one* owed the money he thought he owed, he need not prove any mistake at all (Cass. 3 Jan. 1950, no. 8, Foro it. Mass. 1950, 4)!

It will be seen that these rules regarding the *répétition de l'indu* in French law cover most of the cases dealt with in German law by the *Leistungskondiktion*, but there remain many situations which they cannot, under present French doctrine, adequately solve. These include the claims for reimbursement for *services* rendered without legal ground, the restitution of property transferred for a purpose which fails, cases of 'interference', and, above all, those cases suited to the *actio de in rem verso* where the thing reclaimed only came into the defendant's hands through the intermediacy of a third party who received it directly from the plaintiff. Here use is made of the *general* enrichment claim as established by the Court of Cassation in the *Boudier* case (Req. 15 June 1892, DP 1892. 1. 596, S. 1893. 1. 281, noted by LABBÉ).

The facts of the case were as follows. The plaintiff Boudier had supplied fertilizer to the tenant of a farm. The fertilizer was delivered and used by the tenant, but then the lease was terminated. Landlord and tenant agreed that the unharvested (and fertilized) crop should be taken over by the landlord at a valuation made by experts and set off against the outstanding rent. When the plaintiff learnt of this agreement, he did not sue the insolvent tenant but brought an action directly against the landlord for the value of the fertilizer. The Court of Cassation allowed the claim. This is not remarkable in itself, since the same result had been reached in several previous cases with the help of the institution of *gestion d'affaires anormale*. It is the *reasoning* of the judgment which is striking, for it recognizes a general enrichment claim under the name of 'action de in rem verso', resting directly on considerations of equity and not on any codal provisions: '. . . on the third ground of appeal, that the principles of the action de in rem verso have been misapplied: given that there are no fixed conditions for the exercise of this action which derives from the principle of equity that one must not enrich oneself at the expense of another and which is not covered by any text in our laws; given that it is enough to render the claim admissible that the plaintiff allege and offer to prove that a benefit has accrued to the defendant at his expense or by his own act . . .'.

It soon became apparent that the terms of the *Boudier* decision were far too wide and that a claim for enrichment requires more than that the defendant should have received some benefit at the expense of the plaintiff. AUBRY and RAU had insisted on a further requirement, namely that the enrichment of the defendant occur 'sans cause légitime' and that in addition the plaintiff should have at his disposal no other action, contractual or delictual, for the recuperation of his loss. In the following years the Court of Cassation accepted these requirements in slightly modified form. It was then seen that the expression 'action de in rem verso' applied to only one part of the area covered by the general claim for unjustified enrichment, so nowadays writers bring it under the concept of 'enrichissement sans cause', which SALEILLES borrowed from German law.

According to the principles developed by the courts for the general enrichment claim, the first requirement today is that the plaintiff should have suffered an impoverishment ('appauvrissement') and that, in consequence, the defendant should have gained an enrichment ('enrichissement'). On this point French law makes no distinction according to whether the impoverishment/enrichment occurs as the result of a 'transfer' by the plaintiff or 'arises otherwise'. Most cases of 'Leistungskondiktionen' will fall under the rules of the Code civil regarding 'répétition de l'indu', but where this is not so, as in the case of services rendered, the action *de in rem verso* takes its place: a person who works in her fiancé's business in view of a forthcoming marriage which does not take place may claim 'une rémunération normale' for her services unless it was the intention of the parties that the services should be gratuitous (Dijon 7 Feb. 1928, Gaz. Pal. 1928. 1. 501). Cases of 'interference' are also covered: for example, if a person unaware of his relationship to a decedent is informed by a genealogist of his rights of inheritance and vindicates those rights without paying the genealogist the requested fee, the genealogist may claim the value of the information by means of the action *de in rem verso* (Poitiers 2 Dec. 1907, DP 1908. 2. 332; Riom 20 June 1950, Gaz. Pal. 1950. 2. 221). So also if a waterworks uses the plaintiff's pipes for distributing water to its consumers it must pay for this use; in its characteristic lapidary way the Court of Cassation bases this claim directly on the 'principe d'équité que nul ne peut sans juste cause s'enrichir aux dépens d'autrui' (Req. 11 Dec. 1928, DH 1929, 18). If a music publisher exercises the copyright of an opera beyond the period permitted by its contract with the composer, it must disgorge the extra profits (Civ. 6 July 1927, S. 1928. 1. 19). However, the courts seem to be unwilling to extend this idea to cases of infringement of patent rights: the Court of Appeal of Paris rejected an enrichment claim brought by the patentee on the ground that it was subsidiary to the claim for patent infringement ('contrefaçon') which was specially regulated by statute and was in the case before it already time-barred (8 March 1922, Gaz. Trib. 1922. 2. 344).

The Court of Cassation has also refused to allow the owner of stolen goods to bring an enrichment claim against a person who resold them at a profit after buying them in good faith from the thief (Civ. 11 Feb. 1931, DP 1931. 1. 129, noted by SAVA-TIER, S. 1931. 1. 273, noted by GÉGOUT; Com. 25 Nov. 1969, Bull.civ.IV no. 351). In another case, however, a trustee in bankruptcy had collected on a claim which had vested in the plaintiff before the bankruptcy, and the plaintiff was allowed to claim the amount collected as being an unjustified enrichment to the mass (Civ. 18 Jan. 1937, DH 1937, 145). It thus appears to be the law in France that if a person collects on a claim which is vested in another he must disgorge the enrichment (compare §816 par. 2 BGB), while if a person sells another's chattel he need not do so (contrast §816 par. 1 BGB and RGZ 106, 44).

A further essential ingredient of an enrichment claim is that the enrichment be 'sans cause légitime'. As in German law, this is the case when there is no valid underlying contract. The French judge does not ask whether the *plaintiff's transfer* was made pursuant to a valid contract, but only whether the *defendant's benefit was received* pursuant to such a contract. This would be a distinction without a difference if the enrichment claim only lay where the benefit comes to the defendant directly from the plaintiff, as it does in Germany owing to the principle of directness, but as the *Boudier* case itself shows, French law also allows an enrichment claim where the benefit to the defendant is merely indirect, that is, where it comes to him only after passing through the assets of a third party. In these instances of the *actio de in rem verso*, the French view is that the plaintiff's enrichment claim is excluded if the defendant received the benefit in question pursuant to either a *contract* or a *statutory duty* between himself and the third party. If there is no such contract or statutory duty between the defendant and the third party, there will be no 'cause légitime' to justify the defendant's benefit, and the defendant will have to disgorge the value of the benefit even if the plaintiff had a valid contract with the third party on which he could sue.

The Court of Cassation has affirmed these principles in many decisions, never more clearly than in Req. 22 Feb. 1939 and Civ. 28 Feb. 1939, DP 1940. 1. 5, noted by RIPERT. The plaintiff was retained by the tenant of commercial premises to do repair work on them. The tenant became insolvent, and the plaintiff brought a claim for the value of his work against the landlord-owner. In both cases the Court of Cassation decided that the claim must fail if the tenancy agreement required the tenant to return the premises *in good repair* at the end of the tenancy: it was true that the plaintiff's repair had increased the value of the lessor's premises but this benefit found 'sa juste cause' in the contract with the tenant. This is established law: see, for example, Civ. 28 May 1986, Bull.civ.III no. 83.—The outcome is different in cases where the defendant *cannot* show that he has a contract with the third party which entitles him to retain the benefit. In Req. 11 Sep. 1940, S. 1941. 1. 121, noted by Esmein, the defendant had sold land to a purchaser who then retained the plaintiff to do certain building works. After the building works had been completed the purchaser became insolvent, so the defendant rescinded the sale contract and sought to repossess the property. On this, the plaintiff, instead of suing the insolvent purchaser on the building contract, brought an *actio de in rem verso* directly against the defendant, and his action succeeded with the approval of the Court of Cassation. Here the benefit to the defendant was not justified by any 'cause légitime', since he had no contractual right against the purchaser to receive back his property improved by the building works. See also Req. 20 Dec. 1910, DP 1911. 1. 377.

These principles were only clarified in the course of the twentieth century and French writers have asked whether the decision of the Court of Cassation in the *Boudier* case itself is compatible with them. It is generally held that it is. Of course the landlord and tenant in that case had agreed that the value of the crop should be set against the outstanding rent, which makes it seem as if the landlord, sued in an *actio de in rem verso* by the supplier of the fertilizer, would have a 'cause légitime' for retaining the benefit of the crop, namely the agreement to take it over from the tenant. However, in his note on the case in S. 1893. 1. 281, Labbé observed that in valuing the crop the experts had deducted the price of the fertilizer on the ground that the landlord would make a special payment to the tenant in respect of it. If so, the enrichment of having the crop fertilized would not be justified by any 'cause légitime', that is, by any valid contract with the tenant. On these facts the plaintiff would win even today.

In addition to the requirement of 'cause légitime', the French courts have worked out a whole series of other requirements which restrict the area of application of the general enrichment claim. Scholars put these restrictions, or some of them, under the heading 'subsidiarité de l'action de in rem verso', meaning that the enrichment claim must give way if there is any other legal basis on which the plaintiff can ground his claim.

See the details in Drakidis (above p. 537).—The Italian Codice civile makes this explicit in art. 2042 which lays down that an enrichment claim may not be brought if the plaintiff has any other way of claiming compensation for his impoverishment.—As to French law, one might think that this principle of subsidiarity would defeat an enrichment claim in all the most typical cases of the *actio de in rem verso*, since where the benefit has passed to the defendant through the assets of a third party the plaintiff normally has a valid contract with that third party on which he could sue. The Court of Cassation has not accepted this implication, for it has expressly decided that the existence of such a contractual claim against a third party does not affect the 'caractére subsidiaire de l'action de in rem verso', at any rate if the contractual claim cannot be *realized* because of the insolvency of the third party, which is nearly always the case (Req. 11 Sep. 1940, S. 1941. 1. 121). The Italian courts have adopted the same position (see Cass. 26 March 1953, no. 782, Foro it. 1953 I c. 1467).

The principle of subsidiarity is of practical importance in cases where the plaintiff has a claim against the defendant on a contract or some other legal ground which is now unenforceable because of prescription or time-bar or some other reason; in such cases the plaintiff may well try to have recourse to the action *de in rem verso*, but he will try in vain. Thus if a plaintiff suing on a loan contract finds that he cannot adduce the documentary proof required by art. 1341 Code civil he is not allowed to seek recovery on the same facts on the basis of unjustified enrichment (the *Clayette* case, Civ. 12 May 1914, S. 1918. 1. 41). The same is true if, owing to a miscalculation, a builder quotes too low a price for building a house; he cannot use the *actio de in rem verso* in order to claim the shortfall, for this would be to circumvent the provisions of art. 1793 Code civil which puts the risk of such excess expenditure on the builder (Civ. 2 March 1915, DP 1920.1.102). When the Order of Jesuits was disbanded by the state, donors were given a set period in which to bring restitutionary claims against the liquidator; a donor of land who had allowed that period to expire was not allowed to bring a claim for unjustified enrichment (Civ. 22 Feb. 1922, S. 1923.1.153; compare RGZ 124, 204). To give another example, already mentioned, a patentee cannot bring an action *de in rem verso* against an infringer of his patent if the special statutory claim for infringement has prescribed (Paris 8 March 1922, Gaz. Trib. 1922. 2. 344).

IV

Not long ago it could be said that the Continental lawyer approaching the topic of enrichment in the Common Law 'might be entering another world' (previous edition p. 603). This is no longer quite true. English lawyers have stopped speaking of liability 'in quasi-contract', and since 1966, when the path-breaking work of GOFF/JONES first appeared, courts and writers have come to accept that there is a general principle of liability for 'unjust enrichment' and that the 'law of restitution' which is based on this principle is an autonomous section of the law, distinct from contract and tort. What is needed now is to concretize this principle and produce practicable rules for the benefit of lawyers, teachers, and students.

There were obstacles in the way of this development, mainly due to the fact that English law developed within its traditional forms of action, several of which were put to occasional use in situations involving what we would now classify as enrichment law. As in Rome, the first forms of action to serve restitutionary purposes in English law had the concurrent function of enforcing contracts. Just as the *condictio* was directed to procuring the transfer of a certain thing, whether the obligation to transfer it stemmed from a loan, a stipulation, or the receipt of an *indebitum*, so in England in the fourteenth and fifteenth centuries the action of debt served to recover liquidated sums of money whether owed as money borrowed, as a monetary penalty, or under a judgment, as well as in the case where the sum of money in question had been paid by the plaintiff to the defendant in performance of a contract and was now being reclaimed on a 'failure of consideration' after the collapse of the contract. The action of account also provided a method of solving unjust enrichment problems; this was primarily a means of adjusting accounts between the parties, but it could also be used by plaintiffs who had transferred something to the defendant by mistake or pursuant to a contract invalid for want of consideration. Unfortunately the actions of debt and account had an extremely cumbrous and expensive procedure, in which the defendant could even obtain judgment if he 'waged his law' by swearing with oath-helpers that he was not liable. This made the English courts in the course of the sixteenth and seventeenth centuries ready to use the more flexible action of *assumpsit* in cases previously triable by debt or account. *Assumpsit*, after emerging from the law of tort, originally lay only where one party had expressly undertaken ('assumpsit') by contract to do a particular thing; if the defendant performed badly or failed to perform altogether the plaintiff could bring the action of *assumpsit* and claim damages. Gradually this action was also allowed in cases where the defendant owed a specific sum of money which could have been claimed in an action of debt. It was enough if after the debt had arisen the debtor expressly undertook to pay it; the creditor's claim was then called 'indebitatus assumpsit'. After a path-breaking decision of 1602, *Slade's* case, it was admitted that any debt, regardless of its legal source, could be claimed by an action of *assumpsit*, even if the promise to pay had not actually been made but had to be inferred, as a mere fiction, from the circumstances. This opened the way to proving claims for unjust enrichment in the form of 'indebitatus assumpsit', but it was still based on the fiction that the debtor had 'undertaken' to pay the debt which had already arisen on some other legal ground. Consistently with the characteristic English lawyer's habit of thinking in types of case, several distinct types of case gradually separated out within the form of *indebitatus assumpsit*. The action *for money had and received* lay for the recovery of money which the plaintiff had paid to the defendant by mistake or under duress or in performance of an invalid contract. The action of *quantummeruit* or *quantumvalebat* lay when the defendant had accepted goods or services from the plaintiff without any particular price being agreed. Finally the action for *moneypaid* (laid out and expended for the use of another) lay if the plaintiff had paid money to a third party for the benefit of the defendant. 'By 1750, defendants had been forced in individual cases to give back gains on substantially all the grounds we have recognized in modern law' (DAWSON (above p. 537) 11).

No effort had yet been made in England to put these various types of case on a unitary foundation. LORD MANSFIELD was the first to make such an attempt, in the famous case of *Moses* v. *Macferlan*, (1760) 2 Burr. 1005, 97 Eng. Rep. 676.

The plaintiff had endorsed a negotiable instrument upon the defendant's agreeing in writing not to take recourse against him. The defendant proceeded to sue on the instrument and obtained judgment against the plaintiff from a court which professed itself unable to take account of the collateral agreement. The plaintiff paid off the judgement against him and raised an action for repayment before another court, the Court of King's Bench. LORD MANSFIELD granted the plaintiff's claim for money had and received, and stated the ground of the claim as follows: 'If the defendant be under an obligation, from the ties of natural justice, to refund, the law implies a debt, and gives this action, founded in the equity of the plaintiff's case, as it were upon a contract (quasi ex contractu, as the Roman law expresses it) . . . the gist of this kind of action is that the defendant, upon the circumstances of the case, is obliged by the ties of natural justice and equity to refund the money'.

This decision of LORD MANSFIELD certainly made it possible to sever the historical connection between the existing enrichment claims and the law of contract. However, the development took a different, indeed an opposite direction. Until then the supposition of the fictive contractual promise to repay had been seen as a procedural device which made it possible to use *assumpsit* to enforce enrichment claims, but from the middle of the nineteenth century the courts began to treat the fictive promise, called 'implied contract', as being the very foundation of the enrichment claim. To derive these claims from 'natural justice and equity' as LORD MANSFIELD had proposed, not only appeared to trespass over the border of equity jurisprudence in the technical sense but also ran counter to the positivism and concern with precedent typical of the English judiciary at the turn of the century.

LORD MANSFIELD's theory therefore came in for much criticism. It was described as 'vague jurisprudence which is sometimes attractively styled as "justice as between man and man"' (LORD SUMNER, in *Baylis* v. *Bishop of London* [1913] 1 Ch. 127, 140) and as 'well-meaning sloppiness of thought' (SCRUTTON LJ IN *Holt* v. *Markham*, [1923] 1 KB 504, 513). HANBURY observed that LORD MANSFIELD in *Moses* v. *Macferlan* had crossed the very narrow bridge 'which leads from the sound soil of implied contract to the shifting quicksands of natural equity' (40 *LQ Rev.* 31, 35 (1924)).—This trend reached its apogee in the House of Lords decision of *Sinclair* v. *Brougham*, [1914] AC 398. A building society had acted as a bank, *ultra vires*, that is, outside the objects of the society stipulated in its rules. When the building society went into liquidation, the depositors claimed the amount standing to their credit and, *ultra vires* contracts being void in English law at the time, did so by means of an action for money had and received. The House of Lords held that no claim for money had and received could be allowed, since such a claim was based on a promise to repay implied by the law, and in the instant case any such promise, had it been given expressly, would also have been *ultra vires* and invalid: 'The law cannot de jure impute promises to repay, whether for money had and received or otherwise, which, if made de facto, it would inexorably avoid' ([1914] AC 398, 452). A similar decision had already been made in *Cowern* v. *Nield*, [1912] 2 KB 419. In that case an infant who promised to deliver specific goods received the purchase price in advance. The purchaser rejected a part which was unsatisfactory and the infant did not deliver the remainder so the purchaser brought a claim for repayment of the price. So far as the claim was based on breach of contract it was unsuccessful, since the contract was invalid by reason of the defendant's infancy, but the claim for money had and received was equally unsuccessful, for, according to the court, this claim also arose *ex contractu* and therefore foundered on the defendant's infancy. To the same effect was *R. Leslie Ltd.* v. *Sheill*, [1914] 3 KB 607. These decisions are much criticized by English writers today, and they do indeed apply the theory that enrichment claims are based on quasi-contract with a rigour which demonstrates that even England has its own forms of *Begriffsjurisprudenz*. The true question, namely how to balance the interest of the creditor in recovering moneys unjustly withheld and the interests underlying the doctrines of *ultra vires* and infancy was not raised by the courts in either case (on this see the excellent treatment by GOFF/JONES (above p. 537) 10 f., 524 ff., 538 ff.).

Hardly anyone in England uses the term 'quasi-contract' any more in reference to a claim for unjust enrichment. 'In our view, the concept of implied contract is, in this context, a meaningless, irrelevant and misleading anachronism' (GOFF/JONES (above p. 537) 10). This view is shared by BIRKS, who concludes his portrayal of the rise and fall of quasi-contract as follows:

> 'Nowadays the most important thing to say about the relationship between restitution and quasi-contract is that the term "quasi-contract" ought to be given up altogether. It has no work to do. Quasi-contractual obligations are simply those common law obligations which arise from unjust enrichment. They are restitutionary in content, and unjust enrichment is their causative event. To persist in calling them quasi-contractual is to insist on a usage which adds no further information about them but does perpetually threaten to revive their misleading history.' (BIRKS (above p. 537) 39.)

Writers and courts today are increasingly coming to realize that the great range of restitutionary claims afforded by English case-law all rest on the principle that a benefit which the defendant has acquired at the expense of the plaintiff must be restored, so far as the defendant's retention of this benefit would rank as an 'unjust enrichment'. 'The principle of unjust enrichment', according to GOFF and JONES, 'presupposes three things. First, the defendant must have been enriched by the receipt of a *benefit*. Secondly, that benefit must have been gained at the *plaintiff's* expense. Thirdly, it would be *unjust* to allow the defendant to retain the benefit'. (Above p. 537, at 16.)

The law of restitution in the *United States* started to develop from the point reached in England under LORD MANSFIELD, but it did not follow the English attempt to make the duty of restitution rest on an 'implied contract'. As early as 1893 KEENER published a work on the law of 'Quasi-Contracts' and it was followed in 1913 by a work of the same title by WOODWARD. WOODWARD emphatically denied that 'quasi-contractual' claims rested on any 'contract implied in law'; he defined these claims as 'legal obligations arising, without reference to the assent of the obligor, from the receipt of a benefit the retention of which is unjust, and requiring the obligor to make restitution' (above p. 538, p. 4).

In 1937 a great step forward was taken by the Restatement of the Law of Restitution (hereafter called Restatement), produced by the American professors SEAVEY and SCOTT. It brought together all the rules developed by the courts for the restitution of unjustified enrichment, including for the first time the restitutionary claims developed in the Courts of Equity (on this see SEAVEY/SCOTT, 54 *LQ Rev.* 29 (1938); WINFIELD, 54 *LQ Rev.* 529 (1938), and MARTINEK (above p. 538) 294 ff.), and set out the general proposition that 'a person who has been unjustly enriched at the expense of another is required to make restitution' (§1).

On considering the most important types of case which give rise to restitutionary claims in Anglo-American law, we discover that the distinction between 'Leistungskondiktion' and 'Eingriffskondiktion' which is drawn in the German legal family is also useful for the presentation of the Common Law. Thus GOFF/JONES organize the material according to whether the defendant acquired the benefit 'from or by the act of the plaintiff'—which approximates to the 'Leistungskondiktion'—or whether he obtained it 'by his own wrongful conduct', which approximates to the 'Eingriffskondiktion'.

GOFF/JONES make a further group of the cases where the claim is for the restitution of a benefit which the defendant acquired *from a third party* ('where the defendant has acquired from a third party a benefit for which he must account to the plaintiff'). This section includes the rules which entitle a person who has paid off a debt owed by a third party to exercise all the rights against the third party which were vested in the creditor before the payment ('doctrine of subrogation'; see also Restatement §162). Thus the surety who pays off the debt may take recourse against the debtor by using the claims vested in the creditor before the payment and may exercise any securities the creditor may have had. The same is true of the insurer who has paid the insured, for he may exercise the latter's claims against the party responsible for the occurrence of the insured event. On the Continent there are special statutory rules for most of these cases, making the claims of the recipient against the third party vest in the person making the payment by means of a *cessio legis* (see §§774, 1143, 1225 BGB, 67 German Law on Insurance Contracts (VVG), art. 1251, 2029 Code civil, 36 French Law on Insurance Contracts (13 July 1930)). It is easy to forget that this statutory assignment in reality only serves to secure the plaintiff's recourse claim on paying the debt of another and that this claim is based on principles of unjust enrichment, for the idea of 'prohibition of enrichment' does not normally appear except in connection with insurance and §67 of the German VVG. In the Common Law, by contrast, the invariable justification for the doctrine of subrogation is that without it the third party would be unjustifiably enriched, and this is why the rules developed for this purpose are treated as manifestations of the principle of enrichment, not only in the Restatement but also in GOFF/JONES (on this see also v. CAEMMERER, *Festschrift Rabel*, 360 ff.).

(*a*) We now turn to the cases where the plaintiff is claiming the restitution of benefits acquired by the defendant '*from or by the act of the plaintiff* '. These are classified in the Common Law in accordance with the circumstances which render it unjustifiable for the defendant to retain the benefit he has received. One important group consists of those cases where payment was made in the erroneous supposition that there was a debt ('payment under mistake', §§6–69 Restatement). Another large group consists of transfers made under 'compulsion' or 'coercion': a person is entitled to reclaim what he has transferred under 'duress' or under circumstances which show that 'undue influence' has been brought to bear on him by the recipient, commonly by exploiting a close family relationship. Like GOFF/JONES, the Restatement finds a case of 'performance under compulsion' in the situation where one of several common debtors has paid off the creditor, under compulsion by him, as it were; his payment frees the other common debtors from their liability and he may seek payment from them under the 'doctrine of contribution'. These contribution claims are a judicial creation in the Common Law and rest directly on 'principles of justice' rather than on the *contract* which normally exists between the common debtors. Characteristically, the development in this area of English law was gradual; contribution was first recognized in cases of joint suretyship and extended only later to other forms of joint liability. Even today GOFF/JONES make a careful distinction between contribution claims lying between partners, sureties, insurers, trustees of the same property, and so on, and the special rules of contribution applicable to any of these relationships may not apply to others. Nevertheless, GOFF and JONES have been successful in their attempt to work out general principles in this area (above p. 537, p. 299 ff.; see also the Restatement §§81–5), thereby repeating the process of gradual generalization of the rules which took place in Germany in the eighteenth and nineteenth centuries and led to the unsurpassably abstract provisions on common debts contained in the BGB (§§421 ff.).

Another important group is composed of cases where the debtor has conferred a benefit in pursuance of a *contract* which was void or has been avoided for some reason such as mistake, incapacity, altered circumstances, breach of contract, or illegality or immorality. Not all these cases are yet treated by the Common Law as instances of a common type, namely the claim for restoration of benefits conferred under a defective contract. There are no general rules which apply to all such cases. What matters is the *kind of defect* which renders the contract invalid, even when it comes to undoing the effects of the invalid contract. Where the plaintiff claims from the defendant the return of some thing transferred pursuant to an invalid contract, English and American judges look to the precedents on incapacity, illegality, or whatever particular fault rendered the contract invalid, with the result that the Common Law rules regarding the restitution of benefits transferred pursuant to a defective contract differ quite widely depending on the ground of invalidity involved. This manner of proceeding has its advantages and disadvantages, as the comparative lawyer can see. On the one hand, the Common Law can regulate the effects of invalid contracts in accordance with the relevant interests, which differ depending on the type of defect. On the other hand, this adaptability is purchased at the price of a very considerable casuistical diversity which makes it bewildering to the Continental observer, since it is almost impossible to state any general rules at all.

This bewilderment stems from a fact already noted above (Ch. 38 II), namely that in the Germanic systems and, to a lesser degree, the Romanistic systems as well, the law of enrichment is not troubled with the question whether the underlying contract is valid or not (on this also v. CAEMMERER, *Festschrift Rabel* 343 ff., and DAWSON (above p. 537) 113 f.). That is a matter for the law of contract. Only when the question of the validity of the contract has been determined does the law of enrichment step in: it then asks whether any benefit has been transferred under this contract, already held invalid, and concludes that, if it has, the defendant acquired it 'without legal ground' and must therefore give it up. Of course even the Continental law of enrichment cannot be wholly indifferent to the question *for what reason* the contract was invalid. Thus in the Germanic systems there are special provisions in the law of enrichment which apply only in cases where it is *illegality* or *immorality* which renders the underlying contract invalid (see §§817, 819 par. 2 BGB, 1174 ABGB, art. 66 OR, and, in detail, below Ch. 39 III). The *reason* for the invalidity of the contract may also affect the extent of the defendant's liability in unjust enrichment: under §§818 par. 3, 819 BGB the defendant who no longer has what he received is not liable unless he *knew* at the time of receiving it that there was no ground for his doing so. In practice this means that the recipient cannot escape on the ground that his enrichment has ceased to exist if the underlying contract was tainted by his *deceit* or *duress*: conversely, a *minor* may raise this defence even if he knew of the invalidity of the contract at the time he received the benefit, since the courts, in order to protect him, do not hold this knowledge against him (on this, see also below Ch. 39 IV 3b).

(*b*) Great practical importance attaches in the Common Law to the class of case where the defendant has acquired a benefit not as the result of an act of the plaintiff but '*by his own wrongful conduct*', that is, as one would say in Germany, by making unauthorized use of a thing or right vested in another. Starting from the fact that this interference with the right of another constitutes a tort, the Common Law then allows the victim to ignore the tort claim for damages and to sue the interferer instead for the return of the economic benefits he gained from his tort; this used to be called 'waiver of tort'. For example, if a person sells or does work on a moveable which does not belong to him, he is guilty, even if he is in good faith, of the tort of conversion or trespass to chattels (see below Ch. 40 III); it is a 'trespass to land' if a person allows his cattle to graze on someone else's land or builds on it, withdraws minerals from it, or allows gases or liquids to flow over it, or in any other way disturbs another in his possession. In all these cases the victim may refrain from exercising his tort claim for damages and require the other to pay the value of the chattels he has used up or the proceeds of the sale he has made or the value of the use he has had of them.

No final answer has yet been given to the problem of the person who saves himself expense by using someone else's property without causing him any harm. He is sometimes made to pay on the facts of the case, but there is no general rule. In *Phillips* v. *Homfray* (1883) 24 Ch. D. 439 a person used roads and passages under the plaintiff's land in order to carry minerals away from his own mine. He died shortly afterwards, and under the old rule *actio personalis moritur cum persona* then in force this put paid to any claims for damages based on the tort of trespass to land, so the plaintiff sued the heirs for the value of the benefit which the decedent's estate had gained from his use of the plaintiff's roads and passages. The claim was dismissed because although the decedent had saved himself expense, he had not appropriated any property.

'He saved his estate expense, but he did not bring into it any additional property or value belonging to another person' (ibid. at 462). See also *Stoke-on-Trent CC* v. *W. & J. Wass Ltd.* [1988] 3 All ER 394: the defendant held a market in a city where he well knew the plaintiff had exclusive marketing rights, but the plaintiff could not show that this had caused it any loss. The plaintiff's claim for a reasonable licence fee was dismissed, a decision criticized by Goff/Jones (above p. 537) 717 ff.—In the United States opinions vary. With regard to the unauthorized use of *moveables*, the Restatement says in §128(1): 'A person who has tortiously used the chattel of another is under a duty of restitution to the owner for the value of the use, although the owner would not have used the chattel and although it was not harmed by the use.' A similar result was reached in *Olwell* v. *Nye & Nissen Co.* 26 Wash. 2d 282, 173 P. 2d 652 (1946), where the defendant had made unauthorized use of a machine left unused by the plaintiff in a warehouse (compare *Strand Electric and Engineering Co.* v. *Brisford Entertainments* [1952] QB 246).—The Restatement is not unequivocal concerning the unauthorized use of *land* (see §129). Several decisions have already departed from *Phillips* v. *Homfray* and have allowed the plaintiff to claim even though the value of the property was not lessened by the use and although in using it the defendant simply saved himself expenditure: see *Raven Red Ash Coal Co.* v. *Ball* 185 Va. 534, 39 SE 2d 231 (1946); *Edwards* v. *Lee's Administrator* 265 Ky. 418, 96 SW 2d 1028 (1936); *De Camp* v. *Bullard* 159 NY 450, 54 NE 26 (1899), discussed in detail by Palmer (above p. 538) §2.5 and 10.

The same rules apply where, rather than interfering with another's ownership of things, the defendant has infringed intangible rights vested in the plaintiff, such as patents, copyrights, trade marks, trade secrets, and so on. In such cases the courts allow the plaintiff to claim restitution of the profits made by the infringement.

See *Peter Pan Manufacturing Co.* v. *Corsets Silhouette Ltd.* [1964] 1 WLR 96; *Matarese* v. *Moore-McCormack Lines* 158 F. 2d 631 (2nd Cir. 1946); *Eckert* v. *Braun* 155

F. 2d 517 (7th Cir. 1946); *Reynolds* v. *Whitin Mach.Works* 167 F. 2d 78 (4th Cir. 1948).—
The courts in the United States have often had to decide whether a person whose
rights of personality have been infringed can claim the profits made by the defendant
in doing so. Here distinctions must be drawn. A claim lies for using the plaintiff's
name or likeness for commercial purposes, but not for publishing false and hurtful
facts about him or putting him in a false light. See *Hart* v. *E. P. Dutton & Co.* 197 Misc.
274, 93 N.Y.S. 2d 871 (1949) and full details in PALMER (above p. 538) §2.9 with
further references.—This raises the general question when a right carries with it an
entitlement not only to damages from the unlawful infringer but also to any profit
he made. In Germany one asks whether in granting the plaintiff a right the law also
meant to accord him an exclusive right to benefit from it, a monopoly of its value
(see, for example, ESSER/WEYERS, *Schuldrecht* II (6th edn. 1984) 399 ff.). In England
BIRKS puts the same point the other way round by asking whether the duty breached
by the defendant was imposed on him in part in order to prevent his profiting from it:
'So the question has to be asked in relation to the particular facts: Was the prevention of the enrichment which the defendant has acquired a main purpose behind
the wrong which he has committed?' ((above p. 537) 329). See also GOFF/JONES
(above. p. 537) 720 ff.

(c) The rules of Anglo-American restitution law so far portrayed are
principally the product of decisions of Common Law courts, but the *Courts
of Equity* also developed useful remedies in this field, which are incorporated
in both the Restatement and the textbook of GOFF/JONES. Apart from the
'doctrine of subrogation', which has already been mentioned, the most
important are the 'constructive trust' and the 'equitable lien'.

A trust exists when a person in whom a right is vested is bound to exercise
this right on behalf of specified beneficiaries according to rules developed by
the Courts of Equity. Normally such a trust arises as the result of a transaction between the parties and is called an 'express trust', but a 'constructive
trust' arises when the law itself treats a person as trustee of a particular
object for the benefit of another. Under both an express and a constructive
trust the beneficiaries' right to the trust property is *quasi in rem*; this right,
also developed by the Courts of Equity, enables them, *inter alia*, to claim
the object or its proceeds should the trustee go bankrupt.

While such a real right can only exist if the object in question can be identified and
distinguished from the trustee's other property, the Common Law has produced a
series of fictions in the interest of beneficiaries which permit a real claim to survive
even if trust moneys are mixed in the trustee's bank account with money of his
own, or are used by the trustee along with money of his own for the purchase of land.
In such a case an 'equitable lien' in the amount of the beneficiaries' entitlement is
imposed on the bank account or on the land, and this lien is privileged should the
trustee go bankrupt ('doctrine of tracing'; for the details see GOFF/JONES (above
p. 537) 83 ff.; *In re Tilley's Will Trusts*, [1967] Ch. 1179; Restatement §§202 ff.; KÖTZ,
Trust und Treuhand (1963) 30 ff., 77). If the trustee has conveyed the trust property
to a third party in breach of trust, this third party may be treated as constructive

trustee and made to disgorge as such unless he acquired the property as a 'bona fide purchaser for value', that is, for consideration and without knowledge that the disposition to him was in breach of trust (see KÖTZ, *Trust und Treuhand* (1963), with further references).

It is therefore very material, especially if the defendant is insolvent, to discover whether the plaintiff's restitutionary claim can be based on a constructive trust, that is, whether the defendant was a constructive trustee for the plaintiff of the property in issue. This critical question is answered differently in English and American law. In *England* the view is that a constructive trust can arise only if there is a 'fiduciary relationship', that is, a relationship of special trust and reliance; only then is there any analogy with an express trust created by legal act which would justify applying the rules of trust to the fiduciary so as to require him to give up the property belonging in equity to the other. Thus, for example, a solicitor may be constructive trustee for his client (*Re Hallett's Estate*, (1880) 13 Ch. D. 696), an executor for the next of kin (*Re Diplock*, [1948] Ch. 465), a company director for the company (*Sinclair* v. *Brougham*, [1914] AC 398), and under certain circumstances an agent for his principal (*Burdick* v. *Garrick*, (1870) LR 5 Ch. App. 233). Indeed, in one case where the plaintiff bank in New York, pursuant to instructions, had effected through an intermediary the transfer of $2 million to the defendant bank in London and then mistakenly repeated the operation a few hours later, the defendant was held to be constructive trustee of the funds mistakenly transferred; the result was that the plaintiff, as beneficiary of that trust, could claim the funds as its own in equity, if still identifiable, and thereby take priority over the defendant's general creditors (*Chase Manhattan Bank* v. *Israel-British Bank* [1981] Ch. 105).

In the *United States* it is *not* a requirement for a constructive trust that there be any special fiduciary relationship between the parties. The American courts treat the constructive trust as a legal device capable of use wherever the defendant has in his possession identifiable property which he should hand over on the ground that he would be unjustifiably enriched at the plaintiff's expense if he were allowed to keep it.

See SCOTT, 71 *LQRev.* 39 (1955) and §160 Restatement on Restitution (1938): 'Where a person holding title to property is subject to an equitable duty to convey it to another on the ground that he would be unjustly enriched if he were permitted to retain it, a constructive trust arises.' Similar phrases may be found in the cases: see *Beatty* v. *Guggenheim Exploration Co.*, 225 NY 380, 122 NE 378 (1919); *Knight Newspapers* v. *Commissioners of Internal Revenue*, 143 F. 2d 1007 (6th Cir. 1944).—In England, too, it has been proposed that instead of treating the constructive trust as a 'substantive institution' requiring a special fiduciary relationship between the parties, it should be treated, as in American law, as a 'remedial institution' to be invoked wherever the court finds that the defendant is unjustifiably withholding identifiable property from the plaintiff. In particular the proposal has been made by WATERS, *The Constructive Trust* (1964) and 'The English Constructive Trust: A Look into the Future,' 19 *Vand. L. Rev.* 1215 (1966); GOFF/JONES (above p. 537) 93 ff. agree, BIRKS (above p. 537) 375 ff. does not.

The types of case in which the American courts hold a defendant 'unjustly enriched' at the expense of the plaintiff with regard to a particular item of property are quite familiar. If the plaintiff has transferred the object to the defendant by *mistake* and the object is still ascertainable in the hands of the defendant, the defendant is treated as a constructive trustee of this property for the benefit of the plaintiff (see §163 Restatement). The same is true when the plaintiff made the transfer because he was deceived, coerced, or unduly influenced by the recipient or by a third party (see §§ 116 f. Restatement). In these cases the constructive trust is being used to undo defective dispositions of property, the same function as is performed in Romanistic systems by the 'répétition de l'indu' and in the Germanic systems by the right to reclaim the performance of a supposed obligation. The result of imposing a constructive trust, however, differs from the result on the Continent, for it accords the plaintiff a *real* claim of considerable effectiveness.

In *Re Berry*, 147 F. 208 (2d Cir. 1906) the plaintiffs had erroneously sent the defendant a cheque for $1,500 in payment of a non-existent debt. The defendant gave the cheque to his bank for collection and was credited with its value. He then became bankrupt. Withdrawals had been made from the defendant's account after it had been credited with the proceeds of the cheque, but it never fell below $1,500. The court held that the defendant and his trustee in bankruptcy held $1,500 of his bank account 'on constructive trust' for the plaintiffs, which they could claim in priority to the general creditors. For details see PALMER (above p. 538) §11.5 and GOFF/JONES (above p. 537) 131 f.

V

It has often been stated in Germany that claims for enrichment are based in the last resort on considerations of equity and justice. These claims are granted, so the argument runs, if the acquisition of benefits 'appears on some special ground to be unjustified, that is, to conflict with justice and equity' (ENNECCERUS/LEHMANN, *Recht der Schuldverhältnisse* (4th edn., 1954) §220 I), especially when, thanks to formal rules of law and the 'principle of abstraction' in particular (see above Ch. 33 II), the recipient acquires ownership in things which it would run counter to the goal of a just and equitable ordering of economic relations to allow him to retain; the law must then afford a claim for adjustment, 'in order, so far as possible, to heal the wounds which it itself inflicts' (DERNBURG, *Bürgerliches Recht* II 2 (3rd edn., 1906) 677 f.). The Reichsgericht itself once spoke of 'considerations of equity . . . which are the basis of the adjustment of benefit and detriment which the law seeks to achieve by means of the claim for enrichment' (RGZ 86, 343, 348; also BGHZ 36, 232, 235).

Today these observations should be treated with some reservation. The law of unjust enrichment is alive and well, as a comparative survey shows, in places which do not recognize the principle of the abstract nature of conveyances at all. This can be seen from the judicial decisions we have mentioned in the very common situations where the principle of abstraction has no role to play, as where enrichment claims are directed to the restitution of money paid or the value of services performed by the plaintiff *sine causa* or the profits of an unjustified interference with his rights. It is correct enough to say that the law of unjust enrichment is founded on equity and justice, but so are the law of contract and the law of tort, and to no lesser degree. Historically speaking, claims for enrichment may always have been traced to *aequitas* or the law of nature, perhaps because this was necessary at a time when these claims still had to fight for recognition alongside those resting on contract or tort. Today, however, they have an unquestioned place in all legal systems, and as compared with other areas of private law the law of unjust enrichment is neither higher nor lower in rank. As v. CAEM-MERER rightly says, 'if a person has delivered something to the wrong person or has paid his creditor twice or has made a down payment on a contract which never eventuates, his right to restitution . . . is of the same order of dignity as a claim for the repayment of a loan or on the cancellation of a contract' (*Festschrift Rabel*, 339; see also the apt observations of WILBURG (above p. 538) 18 ff.).

French writers have also attributed the *actio de in rem verso* to considerations of equity. Thus ESMEIN writes:

'The action de in rem verso has entered our law simply as a means of filling gaps which makes it possible to award an indemnity in cases where justice absolutely requires it' (S. 1941. I. 122).—DAVID said likewise: 'The doctrine has always been applied in practice with due regard to the requirements of natural justice. It is consequently impossible to state the doctrine in a form which is absolutely systematic, dominated as it is by the subjective and paramount notions of morality and fair play' (5 *Camb. LJ* 222 f. (1935)).—So also ROUAST: 'Underlying the cases concerning unjustified enrichment we find a principle of natural law, the principle of the equilibrium of performance and counterperformance' (*Rev. trim. dr. civ.* 21 (1922) 93).

This viewpoint is somewhat more plausible in French law, for it must be remembered that the general claim for enrichment is not laid down in the Code civil, and it was easy to justify its judicial creation in the *Boudier* case by the consideration that the gap in the Code civil had to be filled in accordance with the requirements of equity. As DAVID's observation shows, French writers have not been entirely successful in fixing the limits of the action *de in rem verso* with sufficient precision; until this is done, linking the claim to equity may mitigate the lack of a satisfactory systematic structure.

The striking feature of French law is its principled acceptance of the *actio de in rem verso*, which allows a claim for enrichment where the benefit was acquired by the defendant only *indirectly* from the plaintiff as a result of the plaintiff's having transferred it to a third party who then conferred it on the defendant. The Court of Cassation has certainly admitted that it went too far in giving unlimited admission to the *actio de in rem verso* in the *Boudier* case. It has therefore worked out a series of restrictive conditions which the theorists have sought to sum up in two requirements: first, the enrichment of the defendant must not be justified by an 'cause légitime', which in cases of the *actio de in rem verso* means that the benefit must not have come to the defendant as a result of any contract between him and the third party; secondly, the plaintiff must not have a claim based on any other legal ground ('principe de la subsidiarité'), which, in cases of the *actio de in rem verso*, means only that the plaintiff must not have any contractual claim against a *solvent* third party. The practical difference between German and French law in such cases may be summed up as follows: if the plaintiff confers a benefit on a third party pursuant to a valid contract and the third party transfers this benefit to the defendant, the plaintiff will never have an enrichment claim in Germany, while in France he will have one provided that the third party is insolvent and that the defendant cannot point to any valid contract with the third party which justifies his retaining the benefit as against the third party.

One must not be too quick to take issue with these decisions of the Cour de Cassation. The *actio de in rem verso* was well known to the *Gemeines Recht* and to the Prussian Land Law, and it is a tenable view that the German courts succeeded in setting proper limits to it, even if the draftsmen of the BGB found it 'an extremely confused and complicated matter' (Motive II 872) and refused to adopt it.

The restrictive conditions worked out by the Reichsgericht at that time are, not surprisingly, more or less congruent with those recognized by the Court of Cassation. Thus in RGZ 1, 143 the Reichsgericht had to deal with a case in which the father-in-law of the defendant, acting in his own name, bought machines from the plaintiff in order to instal them in the defendant's mill. Shortly after the machines had been installed, the father-in-law died without leaving any appreciable property, and the supplier sued the miller for the value of the machines. The Reichsgericht had to apply Prussian law and decided that the claim should be allowed unless the miller could show that he received the machines pursuant to a contract of sale with his father-in-law.—Now if the father-in-law, in purchasing the machines, had been acting as the miller's agent or as a *negotiorum gestor*, the supplier could have obtained a judgement against his heirs and then garnished his indemnity claim against the miller (§§670, 683, 257 BGB) and so finally have been able to bring a claim for payment against the latter. But is this not unnecessarily circuitous? Take the case that the father-in-law's estate is insolvent and in liquidation. Is it fair that his claim for indemnity from his son-in-law should be used to satisfy the other creditors of the estate when the purchase of the machines was a transaction in which the father-in-law (as was said in OGH 16 Jan. 1952, *SZ* 25 no. 13) 'had no independent economic role to play, was acting in the interest of the defendant in suit and was economically nothing more than a conduit'?

Nevertheless, there are some considerations which suggest that it was perhaps a good thing for the present German law to reject the *actio de in rem verso*. It seems a sound principle of legal policy even in the law of contract that a man should seek his reward where he has placed his trust, and that he should look to the contractor on whose capacity to pay he relied in making the contract. Furthermore, the *actio de in rem verso* can expose the defendant to an undesirable double liability, though doubtless in different amounts, first to the plaintiff in the *actio de in rem verso* and secondly to the third party. Finally, there is a risk that if a direct claim by means of the *actio de in rem verso* is allowed, defences which the third party might justifiably raise against the plaintiff may be ignored. The rejection of the *actio de in rem verso* may lead to inequitable results in a few cases where the third party acted solely in the interests of the defendant without any view to personal gain, as often happens if there is a close family relationship. The courts may sometimes be able to help by finding that the third party acted as the defendant's representative or for 'those whom it may concern', but rather than extend these institutions unduly, the courts should be prepared in exceptional cases to allow a direct claim quite openly, provided that the interests of neither the third party nor the defendant are infringed in the individual case.

As to the Common Law, we have seen that the basic function of the 'law of restitution' in the Common Law can be described in much the same terms as that of the law of enrichment on the Continent. Thus a German lawyer would accept the concept of unjustified enrichment as defined by GOFF/ JONES, who require 'first, that the defendant has been enriched by the receipt of a benefit; secondly, that he has been so enriched at the plaintiff's expense; and thirdly, that it would be unjust to allow him to retain the benefit'. And the words of art. 62 par. 1 OR that a person 'who has unjustifiably been enriched out of the assets of another' must give up the enrichment are perfectly in tune with §1 of the American Restatement which says that 'a person who has been unjustly enriched at the expense of another is required to make restitution to the other'. But we must remember, as the Restatement expressly says (Introductory Note to §1), that these propositions of Anglo-American theory are simply 'general guides for the conduct of courts'; they are 'principles', not 'rules' susceptible of direct application to the individual case. Instead they simply give the courts an idea of the direction in which they should apply and develop the specific rules worked out in the case-law. In German law it is different: when §812 BGB lays down that the defendant must have obtained 'something' 'through the act of another' 'at his expense' 'without legal ground', it is using these phrases to specify the essential ingredients of an enrichment claim which the courts apply directly to the individual case after concretizing them and equipping them with specific technical meaning. Too much should not be made of these differences. As we have seen, the Common Law, even in England in recent years, has been adopting general principles in lieu of the different forms of action which had restitutionary functions, and is now engaged in crystallizing the principles into rules adapted to the different types of case so as to meet the specific interests involved in them. Contrariwise, no German or Swiss lawyer would deny that a judge will learn very little from the abstract statutory requirements for an enrichment claim until he ascertains how other judges and writers have given them shape and content. v. CAEMMERER, who has produced a 'typology of enrichment claims', quite rightly emphasizes that 'the enrichment claim can be given form and limits . . . only with such a typology, not with general criteria' (*Festschrift Rabel*, 337). Despite the differences between the law of enrichment in Germany and the law of restitution in the Common Law, it is manifest that an approximation will take place in the theoretical treatment of these areas of law. The unduly *abstract* detail of the German code will be loosened by a typology of enrichment claims and in the Common Law general rules will be developed to give form and structure to the unduly *concrete* details of the case-law. Each system has a great deal to learn from the other.

39

Unjustified Enrichment—Specific Topics

In addition to the works cited above pp. 537–8:

AUBERT, *La Répétition des prestations illicites ou immorales en droit français, en droit suisse et dans la jurisprudence belge* (1954).

BISHOP/BEATSON, 'Mistaken Payments in the Law of Restitution', 36 *U. Tor. LJ* 149 (1986).

BIRKS, 'Konkurrierende Strategien und Interessen: Das Irrtumserforderung im Bereicherungsrecht des common law', *ZEuP* 1993, 554.

v. BÜREN, 'Bemerkungen zu Art. 66 OR', *SJZ* 58 (1962) 225.

DAWSON, 'Restitution without Enrichment', 61 *BUL Rev.* 563 (1981).

——, 'Erasable Enrichment in German Law', 61 *BUL Rev.* 271 (1981).

FLESSNER, *Wegfall der Bereicherung, Rechtsvergleichung und Kritik* (1970).

FLUME, 'Der Wegfall der Bereicherung in der Entwicklung vom römischen zum deutschen Recht', *Festschrift Niedermeyer* (1953) 160.

GRODECKI, 'In pari delicto potior est conditio defendentis', 71 *LQ Rev.* 254 (1955).

HACKBARTH, 'In pari turpitudine melior est conditio possidentis, Ein Vergleich zwischen dem anglo-amerikanischen und dem deutschen Recht', (Diss. Hamburg, 1967).

HONSELL, *Die Rückabwicklung sittenwidriger oder verbotener Geschäfte, Eine rechtsgeschichtliche und rechtsvergleichende Untersuchung zu §817 BGB* (1974).

JONES, 'Payments of Money under Mistake of Law: A Comparative View' [1993] *Camb. LJ* 225.

LAW COMMISSION (England), *Restitution of Payments Made under a Mistake of Law* (Consultation Paper no. 120, 1991).

LLOYD, *Public Policy, A Comparative Study in English and French Law* (1953) 97 ff.

NEW YORK LAW REVISION COMMISSION, Restitution of Money Paid Under Mistake of Law: Report of the Law Revision Commission of the State of New York (1942) No. 65 (B).

NIEDERLÄNDER, 'Nemo turpitudinem suam allegans auditur', *Ius et Lex, Festgabe für Gutzwiller* (1959) 621.

RIPERT, *La Règle morale dans les obligations civiles* (4th edn., 1949) 183 ff.

RITTNER, 'Rechtswissen und Rechtsirrtum im Zivilrecht', *Festschrift für Fritz von Hippel* (1967) 391.

RUMMEL, 'Kondiktion bei verbotenen und sittenwidrigen Rechtsgeschäften', *ÖJZ* 1978, 253.

RUSCH, 'Art. 66 OR im Lichte der bundesgerichtlichen Praxis', *SJZ* 47 (1951) 369.

SABBATH, 'Denial of Restitution in Unlawful Transactions—A Study in Comparative Law', 8 *ICLQ* 486, 689 (1959).

SAVEY-CASARD, *Le Refus d'action pour cause d'indignité, Étude sur la maxime Nemo auditur propriam turpitudinem allegans* (1930).

TRIMARCHI, *L'arrichimento senza causa* (1962).

v. TUHR, 'Zur Lehre von der ungerechtfertigten Bereicherung', *Festschrift für E. I. Bekker* (1907) 293.

WINFIELD, 'Mistake of Law', 59 *LQ Rev.* 327 (1943).

I

IN the previous chapter our rather compressed survey of the rules of unjustified enrichment in the German, Romanistic, and Anglo-American legal families focused more on their systematic structure than on the typical function of individual enrichment claims. It was consequently impossible to make any detailed observations of a comparative legal nature. This we shall now try to do within the limits of available space, by considering a few special topics in the law of enrichment more closely. We shall ask what happens when a plaintiff seeks restitution of a benefit he has conferred on the defendant pursuant to an illegal or immoral agreement, or for an illegal or immoral agreement, purpose (below III). We shall ask what happens when a defendant who has received an unjustified benefit seeks to raise the defence that he has lost or disposed of this benefit or otherwise altered his position in reliance on his right to keep it (below IV). But we shall start with a comparative investigation of a remarkable rule of the Common Law to the effect that restitution of money paid by mistake will be denied if the plaintiff made the payment by reason of a mistake *of law*.

II

The Common Law rule that a plaintiff cannot reclaim money he paid under a mistake of law goes back to the old English decision of *Bilbie* v. *Lumley* (1802) 2 East 469, 102 Eng. Rep. 448. Here the plaintiff was an insurer who had paid the insured sum to the defendant policy-holder and sought its repayment on the ground that the defendant had no right to the insured sum because at the time of the contract he had concealed circumstances which increased the risk. It was nevertheless clear that at the time he paid the insured sum the plaintiff knew or could have known all the facts which entitled him to withhold payment. During the course of the trial LORD ELLENBOROUGH asked the plaintiff's counsel if he could cite any precedent in which a claim for restitution of money had been allowed to a person who had paid in full knowledge of all the facts relating to his liability but in ignorance of the legal position. Although such decisions in fact existed, counsel was unable to name one. LORD ELLENBOROUGH thereupon declared that 'every man must be taken to be cognisant of the law; otherwise there is no saying to what extent the excuse of ignorance might not be carried' and dismissed the claim. Since that time it is a recognized principle of the Common Law that the restitution of money paid when not due is excluded if the defendant believed he was entitled to it and the plaintiff, though aware of all the relevant facts, believed himself bound to pay because he drew the wrong legal conclusions from them.

In the United States also the courts have by and large accepted the principle that there can be no restitution of benefits conferred under a mistake of law. The New York Law Revision Commission recommended that the distinction between mistake of law and mistake of fact be abolished (see Report 1942 no. 65 B), and this recommendation was enacted in §142 NY Civil Practice Act.—Writers also disapprove of the distinction: see, for example, PALMER (above p. 538) §§14.27 and 16.4.—§45 of the Restatement of the Law of Restitution (1937) states the principle that restitution of benefits conferred under a mistake of law is excluded, but in §§46 ff. lays down a series of exceptions so far-reaching and so well supported in the case-law that in CORBIN's view 'it would be a poor judge who cannot find sufficient authority for deciding contrary to *Bilbie* v. *Lumley*' (§617).

No comparable rule is to be found in Continental legal systems. This is obvious for *German* law since the plaintiff in an enrichment claim is not required to show that he was *in error* in conferring the benefit: a benefit may be reclaimed whenever as a matter of objective law there was no obligation to confer it, the only exceptions being if the plaintiff was positively aware that he was not bound to confer the benefit, or was so bound, but by a duty of morality or honour rather than law (§814 BGB). But even in countries such as Austria, Switzerland, and France, where the civil code expressly makes the claim for restitution dependent on the plaintiff's having been in error about his duty to perform, there is no further requirement that his error be an error *of fact* and not simply an error *of law*. Indeed, §1431 ABGB expressly allows a claim for the restitution of benefits which the plaintiff conferred 'by mistake, even a mistake of law'. After some initial doubts, resolved in BGE 40 II 249, the courts in Switzerland have adopted the same position. The same is true in France (Req. 4 Aug. 1859, DP 1859. 1. 362; Req. 21 July 1908, DP 1909. 1. 175).

If the answer given by modern German law is clear, we should not forget that until the BGB came into force courts and writers were divided on it. WINDSCHEID found in the Roman sources 'an indubitable axiom very clearly stated' that if the error were one of law the *condictio indebiti* was inadmissible unless it could exceptionally be shown that the error of law was excusable (*Lehrbuch des Pandektenrechts* (1865) §426 n. 14). In the past century researches in Roman law have benefited from the results of the critical school of interpolationists, and it now seems that in classical times an error of law only barred the *condictio* if the performance induced by the error was nevertheless required by a moral duty or by good faith. The prime example of this is the case where a testator had burdened his heir with a *fideicommissum* requiring him to transfer the estate to a subsequent heir. The *senatusconsultum Pegasianum* permitted the heir under certain conditions to retain one-quarter of the estate (the *quarta falcidia*) for himself, but if, in ignorance of the law, he failed to do so, could not reclaim as an *indebitum* the excess he had transferred. Modern scholars think that JUSTINIAN was the first to generalize the thought that an error of law was fatal (see the details in SCHWARZ, *SavZ/Rom*. 68 (1951) 266; SCHWARZ, *Die Grundlage der condictio im klassischen römischen Recht* (1952) 101 ff.)—Under the *Gemeines Recht* the dominant view was that an error of law excluded the *condictio* unless, exceptionally, it was an excusable error (an exhaustive list of views is given in SAVIGNY, *System des heutigen römischen Rechts* III (1840) 447 ff.) and this position was adopted by the courts as well (see for example Oberappellationsgericht Lübeck 29 Nov. 1856, SeuffA 13 no. 254 with further references).—By contrast, the General Land Law of Prussia had no comparable provision, and the Prussian Obertribunal allowed a *condictio* even if the plaintiff's error were one of law (29 Feb. 1840, ObTr. 6, 8) or an inexcusable error (22 Feb. 1855, ObTr. 30, 76).

This shows that English and German law take different views of the relevance of errors of law in enrichment cases, but that does not mean that similar cases will necessarily be decided differently in the courts. It could well be that English courts use the doctrine of 'mistake of law' to answer needs and interests which are equally well recognized in Germany but answered there by using other doctrinal concepts. In order to see whether this is so, we shall consider some of the types of case where the English courts reject a claim for restitution on the ground that the plaintiff's mistake was one of law.

First there are the cases where the plaintiff's view of the law *only later* proves to be incorrect, normally by reason of a supreme court decision. Taxpayers have often tried to reclaim from the treasury money paid on a construction of a taxing statute which is later shown to be erroneous. The normal reason given for rejecting such claims in England is 'mistake of law'. In *National Pari-Mutuel Ass. Ltd.* v. *The King*, (1930) 47 TLR 110, the plaintiff was a club which set up a betting office for members only and supposed that this made it liable to pay gambling taxes as a 'bookmaker' under the Finance Act, 1926. In 1929 the House of Lords held that a club which ran a betting shop for members only was not a 'bookmaker' under the Finance Act, and the club reclaimed the taxes it had paid in the intervening years. The claim was rejected because the plaintiff's error consisted of a misconstruction of a statute and was therefore a mistake of law which was fatal to the claim.

To the same effect: *Whiteley, Ltd.* v. *The King*, (1909) 101 LT 741; *Sawyer & Vincent* v. *Window Brace Ltd.*, [1943] 1 KB 32; criticized by GOFF/JONES (above p. 537) 147 f. The defendant in *Henderson* v. *Folkestone Waterworks Co.*, (1885) 1 TLR 329 was a water company entitled by private Act of Parliament to charge its consumers water rates up to a certain amount. A decision of the House of Lords in another case (*Dobbs* v. *Grand Junction Waterworks Co.*, (1883) 49 LTR 541) made it clear that the defendant, having misconstrued the statute, had charged water rates in excess of its powers. The plaintiff claimed restitution. He was unsuccessful. After suggesting that the decision of the House of Lords might have altered the law only *pro futoro*, LORD COLERIDGE held that in any case it was highly undesirable that a decision of the highest tribunal at variance with the view of the law previously entertained should set off a whole chain of restitutionary claims.—The French Cour de Cassation also regularly holds that a firm cannot reclaim social security payments just because a subsequent decision *inter alios* shows that the charges were improperly raised. The cases have so far involved firms which knew at the time of payment that the construction of the relevant rules was in doubt (see Soc. 24 May 1973, Bull. civ. 1973. V. 306; 28 Nov. 1973, Bull. civ. 1973. V. 567). In the case last cited the Cour de Cassation left open the question whether the result might not be different if the subsequent decision represented 'une évolution de la jurisprudence' rather than simply 'une interprétation nouvelle des textes en vigueur'.

The result of these cases would have been just the same in Germany but the reasoning would have been entirely different. In Germany taxes and levies are demanded of the citizen by means of a special administrative act (tax assessments and so on). Special methods are provided for questioning administrative acts and they must be exercised within certain set periods (see §§44 ff. Law on Procedure in Tax Matters (FGO), 58 ff. Law of Administrative Procedure (VwGO)). If the citizen fails to exercise his rights in the proper way and at the proper time he cannot recover what he has paid even if it later appears that it was wrongly demanded. An administrative act now immune from attack provides a legal basis which justifies the state in retaining what it received. Even if the rule authorizing the levy is later held to be unconstitutional by the Bundesverfassungsgericht, payments made cannot be reclaimed from the state on the ground of unjustified enrichment if the administrative act is no longer subject to question (expressly laid down in §79 par. 2 Law on the Federal Constitutional Court (BVerfGG)).

The New York case of *Doll* v. *Earle*, 59 NY 638 (1874) presents the problem in a different guise. Mortgagor and mortgagee could not agree whether under existing law the mortgage was to be paid off in paper money or in gold; if in gold, the mortgagor would have had to pay an extra $895. They agreed that the mortgagor would put $895 in escrow, to be returned to him or paid to the creditor depending on the law laid down by the United States Supreme Court. The Supreme Court first gave several decisions to the effect that payment should be made in gold (see *Hepburn* v. *Griswold*, 75 US 603 (1869)) and the mortgagor released the money to the mortgagee. A year later, however, the Supreme Court reversed itself (*Knox* v. *Lee*, 79 US 457 (1870)) and the mortgagor claimed the money back. His claim was rejected because it was a mistake of law which induced him to release the money.

'Every man is to be charged, at his peril, with a knowledge of the law. There is no other principle which is safe and practical in the common business of mankind. And to permit a subsequent judicial decision in any one given case, on a point of law, to open or annul everything that has been done in other cases of the like kind, for years before, under a different understanding of the law would lead to the most mischievous consequences . . .' (cited in the New York Law Revision Commission Report (1942) no. 65 (B) p. 17).—To the same effect is *Cooley* v. *Calaveras County*, 121 Cal. 482, 53 P. 1075 (1898) where the court said: 'The agreement was in exact accordance with the general understanding of the law at the time it was made. Two years afterwards the court of appeals, in another case, gave a different construction. The community would be in a miserable condition if at every change of opinion upon questions of law all their previous contracts and settlements were to be overturned. Men could never know the end of their controversies.' *Bagby* v. *Martin*, 118 Okla. 244, 247 P. 404 (1926) is to the same effect.

It will be clear that it is not the plaintiff's 'mistake of law' which is the true ground for excluding the claim for restitution in the decisions just mentioned. The claim is rejected because legal security would be gravely imperilled if transactions which were wholly executed on the basis of a particular view of the law could be reopened simply because that view of the law has been seen in the light of a later decision to be incorrect.

A similar case has been decided in Switzerland. The plaintiff had drawn a negotiable instrument which was protested for non-payment, and an endorser took recourse against him which the plaintiff satisfied in return for the protested instrument. Four years later the Bundesgericht handed down a judgment which condemned the standard practice of notaries of allowing a subordinate to make the protest at the place of payment after the notary himself had signed the document of protestation (BGE 27 II 74). After this judgment was rendered, the plaintiff discovered that the instrument he had paid off had not been validly protested, and that he had not been bound to satisfy the recourse claim against him. The Bundesgericht rejected his claim for repayment, flirting with the notion that a claim for enrichment is excluded by a mistake of law before going on to say:

'But even if one does not want to go so far as to hold that a mistake of law is insufficient in enrichment claims generally, still a mistake of the kind before us cannot ground a claim for restitution . . . not until more than eight years after the payment did the plaintiff have the idea that he might claim back what he had paid, induced so to believe through the decision of the Bundesgericht which has been cited . . . But if one allowed restitution claims in such cases because the view of the law taken by the Bundesgericht was different from that of the person making the payment, it would endanger legal security and open the door to endless lawsuits. In a case like this, at any rate, the error as to the obligation by no means satisfies the requirement of art. 72 par 1' [now art. 63 par. 1 OR] (BGE 31 II 291, 295).

The Swiss Bundesgericht here was making the same appropriate value judgments as one finds in the decisions of the Common Law courts. Admittedly it would be more candid to say that a supreme court decision which controverts a view of the law generally entertained or a practice in common use should have effect only as to the future. Such a decision often has more in common with the creation of a new legal rule or the enactment of a new statute than with the discovery and correction of a mistake long concealed (see BGH NJW 1957, 263; BVerwGE 17, 256, 260 f.). If this is so, then the reason for denying the enrichment claim in such cases cannot be that the plaintiff has conferred the benefit under a mistake of law, since in fact he made no mistake at all about his obligation, but rather simply did what, under the existing law, he was bound to do.

It is not always a subsequent judicial decision which brings to light the mistake of law pursuant to which the plaintiff conferred the benefit. It often happens that after making the payment the plaintiff realizes by himself or is told by someone else that he was in error in making it. If the plaintiff was in possession of all the relevant facts at the time he made the payment his claim for repayment will be denied for 'mistake of law', but when we look at the cases more closely we see that in many of them the denial of the claim can be based on much more cogent grounds, well known to the German lawyer.

This is well illustrated by the decision in *Derrick* v. *Williams*, [1939] 2 All ER 559. The defendant had caused fatal injuries to the plaintiff's son in a traffic accident, and the son died a few days later. The defendant denied liability but made a 'payment into court' (for the details see COHN, *JZ* 1959, 463) of some £50. The plaintiff accepted this sum and went no further with the proceedings. There was no reference in the agreement to any damages for loss of expectation of life since the Court of Appeal in *Rose* v. *Ford*, [1936] 1 KB 90 had held that no such claim descended to the victim's estate. The House of Lords reversed the Court of Appeal on this point (see *Rose* v. *Ford*, [1937] AC 826) and the plaintiff sought to continue his suit in order to obtain compensation for the items of loss not taken into account. The court held that this was inadmissible. First it stated that the plaintiff's error was a 'mistake of law' and then it founded on the argument, which we have already noted, that legal security would be imperilled if executed transactions could be reopened because the courts had changed their minds:

'It was a mistake of law, and consisted of the fact that the plaintiff was under the belief that the law as laid down by this court in *Rose* v. *Ford* was correctly laid down. In that he was wrong, and he is asking the court to say that, having acted upon the basis of a mistaken view of the law, now that the law has been enunciated by the highest tribunal, he is entitled to make another attempt. That is a thing which, it seems to me, cannot be permitted on principle. It appears to me to be completely indefensible . . . It would be an intolerable hardship on successful litigants if, in circumstances such as these, their opponents were entitled to harass them with further litigation because their view of the law had turned out to be wrong . . .' ([1939] 2 All ER 559, 565).

A judge in Germany would certainly have decided the case the same way, for the reason that in accepting the sum offered the plaintiff had concluded a *compromise* (Vergleich, §779 BGB): in cases of compromise the risk of being wrong in law is placed on the party in error.

On this see, for example, RG JW 1938, 1722.—Both in France and in Italy it is expressly laid down that compromises may not be reopened by reason of error of law (art. 2052 Code civil, art. 1969 Codice civile).

In other cases the plaintiff has, to the recipient's knowledge, been in doubt about his liability to pay, but has overcome his doubts and made the payment. In such a case the recipient should be protected in his reliance on the supposition that the payment is conclusive, and the additional ground that the person paying was labouring under a 'mistake of law' simply conceals the real reasons for denying the claim.

See *Rogers* v. *Ingham*, (1876) 3 Ch. D. 353; *Monroe National Bank* v. *Catlin*, 82 Conn. 227, 73 A. 3 (1909); *Keazer* v. *Colebrook National Bank*, 75 NH 278, 73 A. 170 (1909).

Judges in Germany are familiar with such cases as well. It is true that according to the wording of §814 BGB restitution of a benefit is only excluded if the transferor 'knew' that he was not bound to make it, but independently of §814 BGB the courts have held that the general principle of good faith in legal dealings requires restitution to be excluded even if the transferor was *merely in doubt* about his obligation, 'that is to say, when the transferor has made it clear to the recipient that he intends to make the transfer even should he not be obliged to make it, when his behaviour is such that the recipient is entitled to conclude that he will let the transfer stand whatever the true position as to the underlying obligation may turn out to be' (BGHZ 32, 273, 278; RGZ 144, 89, 91). But the same view is held in England as well. According to GOFF/JONES the claim should be dismissed not on the ground of mistake of law but because 'payments made in satisfaction of honest claims or under bona fide compromises should not be set aside merely because the prayer mistook the law,' ((above p. 537) 52, also 146 ff., and BIRKS (above p. 537) 164 ff.).

'Mistake of law' is given as the reason for denying a restitution claim in yet another class of case where the decision would be better based, as it is in Germany, on the ground that the recipient has used up the money in good faith or has otherwise made irreversible dispositions, that is, when German lawyers would use the technical term of 'disappearance of the enrichment' (*Wegfall der Bereicherung*, §818 par. 3 BGB; see the details below Ch. 39 IV).

This can be seen in an old English decision which is still used today as authority for the proposition that restitution is excluded if the mistake was one of law. In *Brisbane* v. *Dacres* (1813), 128 Eng. Rep. 641, the captain of an English warship paid the admiral, his superior officer, part of the freight he had received for the carriage of goods. This was in line with a practice recently current, but neither the captain nor the admiral knew that this practice had been brought to an end shortly before the payment was made. Nearly six years later the captain demanded the money back, without success. To a large extent the judgment was based on precedents supporting the rule that no one may reclaim money paid in full knowledge of the facts but in ignorance of the law, but SIR JAMES MANSFIELD asked the direct question whether in the circumstances it was fair and equitable to reclaim the money from the admiral. He said that it was not:

'For see how it is! If the sum be large it probably alters the habits of his life, he increases his expenses, he has spent it over and over again, perhaps he cannot repay it all or not without great distress: is he then, five years and eleven months after, to be called on to repay it?' See also *Re Hatch*, [1919] 1 Ch. 351; *Holt* v. *Markham*, [1923] 1 KB 512; and *Traweek* v. *Hagler*, 199 Ala. 664, 75 So. 152 (1917): in the last of these cases the court rejected the claim for restitution because the plaintiff had conferred the benefit under a 'mistake of law', but even if the plaintiff's mistake had been a 'mistake of fact', the judgment proceeded to say, the claim must be rejected 'where, as here, the payment has furnished the specific inducement to some affirmative action by the payee . . . whereby his situation has been unfavorably altered'.

Perhaps enough has been said to support the suggestion that the general rule of the Common Law which denies the restitution of money paid by mistake of law very often serves to answer needs and interests which are not only recognized in German law but are openly and specifically referred to in statutes and judicial decisions. But the truth of the matter is that the notion of 'mistake of law' is quite out of place in cases concerning the restitution of benefits conferred without legal ground. 'Error iuris neminem excusat' is a brocard which may in times past have been useful enough, especially in criminal law, but in modern times there are so many regulations of every kind that the citizen cannot be expected to know them, and the principle that everyone must bear the consequences of his ignorance of the law has lost much of its force even in criminal law, not to mention private law (on this see RITTNER, above p. 566). The English courts know this perfectly well. Indeed, in a few decisions they have gone in for a kind of tactical withdrawal by saying that a 'mistake of law' means only an error relating to certain fundamental legal rules, to 'the general law, the ordinary law of the country' (*Cooper* v. *Phibbs*, (1867) LR 2 HL 149). This distinction is artificial and quite impractical. Here as elsewhere it would be much better to avoid taking refuge in legal jargon and to seek to discover and to reconcile the relevant interests and needs in a perfectly open manner.

Even in England the rule that payments made under a mistake of law cannot be recovered may be on its way out. The Law Commission (above p. 566) has proposed its abolition, and the decision of the House of Lords in *Woolwich Building Society* v. *I.R.S.* [1993] AC 70 points in the same direction. The actual decision granted recovery of unjustifiable taxes paid by the plaintiff under protest (and so not under any mistake as to his liability), but it is clear, especially from the speeches of LORD GOFF and

LORD SLYNN, that the result would have been the same if the taxpayer had supposed the taxes properly levied and paid them under that misapprehension. It is true that it is tiresome for the treasury to be plagued with claims for repayment many years later, but LORD GOFF noted that it was possible to solve this problem by imposing strict time limits for such claims; he referred to the rule in Germany that the taxpayer must claim within a month of learning how to proceed (see §§355 ff. Tax Ordinance of 16 Mar. 1976, §47 Tax Courts Act of 6 Oct. 1965): 'Such draconian time limits as these may be too strong a medicine for our taste; but the example of a general right of recovery subject to strict time limits imposed as a matter of policy is instructive for us as we seek to solve the problem in the present case' (ibid. at 174). On this decision see GOFF/JONES (above p. 537) 545 ff.

III

A person who receives a benefit without having any contract or other legal title to justify his retention of it must return it to the person from whom he received it. This is the basic principle of the *Leistungskondiktion*, but if the reason for the absence of 'causa' is the illegality or immorality of the under-lying agreement the principle has to be qualified. If the plaintiff knew the transaction was illegal or immoral the legal system will have to decide whether to deny him the redress of an action for restitution. Many such cases were discussed in the Roman sources. A person could not reclaim a bribe paid to a judge or witnesses (D. 12, 5, 3) or hush-money paid to the person who caught him *inflagranti* (D. 12, 5, 4 pr.) or the price paid for immoral acts (D. 12, 5, 4, 3): 'dixi cum ob turpem causam dantis et accipientis pecunia numeretur, cessare condictionem et in delicto pari potiorem esse posses-sorem' (PAPINIAN, D. 12, 7, 5, pr.); on later developments see ZIMMERMANN, *The Law of Obligations* (1990) 863 ff.

This rule is still in force everywhere, often laid down expressly in the civil codes (see §817 sent. 2 BGB, art 66 OR, §1174 ABGB, art. 2035 Codice civile), often simply applied by the courts (as in France, not to mention the Com-mon Law countries), but its practical application has become increasingly difficult under modern conditions. In Rome during the classical period 'turpitudo' consisted of behaviour in breach of traditional ethical canons, especially of offences against the integrity of family life or the age-old conventions of proper behaviour (see KASER, *SavZ/Rom.* 60 (1940) 95), and it is still obvious that a person guilty of scandalous behaviour which contravenes these elementary rules cannot claim the assistance of the law to undo his dealings. But legal systems today increasingly invalidate transac-tions for simply running counter to the aims of social and economic policy endorsed by the state for the time being, and it may be doubtful whether it is completely fair to deny all restitutionary claims to the parties to such transactions, forbidden though they are. Even if all legal systems in principle accept the traditional rule that benefits transferred so as to procure an illegal or offensive result cannot be reclaimed, the real problem is to discover what precise form this rather amorphous principle should take in modern circumstances and how precisely the different systems apply it in different types of case. This is a question on which we can do no more than give a few pointers.

1. There are many different views about the legal policy underlying the denial of restitution claims in this area. The commonest consideration is that the state must deny its aid to a plaintiff who invokes it to help with the execution of his shady plans: 'no court will lend its aid to a man who founds his cause of action upon an immoral or illegal act' (LORD MANSFIELD in his classic opinion in *Holman* v. *Johnson*, (1775) 98 Eng. Rep. 1120). There are many variants of this view, some emphasizing the moral obliquity of the plaintiff, many laying more stress on the thought that a court would soil its hands 'by adjusting among dishonest men the results of their unholy speculations' (*Gravier* v. *Carraby*, 17 La. 118, 36 Am. Dec. 608 (1841)). Even in Germany the safeguarding of the court's dignity is often put forward as the critical consideration: restitution should be denied 'in order to protect the state from having its courts improperly invoked by deliberate criminals' (OGHZ 4, 60; so also v. CAEMMERER (above p. 537) and RAISER, JZ 1951, 719). High-minded though this position is, easy generalization should be avoided. Granted that the plaintiff consciously broke the law in entering the contract, the court should still make a careful investigation of the facts to see whether in the particular case the purpose of the law broken by the parties or some other public interest may not be better advanced by allowing rather than rejecting the claim for restitution.

Similar criticisms can also be brought to bear on another view, according to which the denial of restitution is justified by the infamy of the plaintiff: he should be 'punished', and there is no better way of deterring the public from improper transactions than by making it very clear that in such a case they will forfeit the protection of the law. Even the Reichsgericht has designated the denial of restitution 'as a punishment for the active manifestation of an evil disposition' (RGZ 105, 270, 271; see also RGZ 161, 52, 60), and the Bundesgerichtshof has stated that §817 sent. 2 BGB, which denies restitution in such cases, 'can at least be justified on the ground that the claimant should be punished by the loss of his claim for behaving contrary to law' (BGHZ 39, 87, 91). But it is odd to 'punish' people without asking whether there is any reasonable relationship between the penalty imposed and the gravity of the offence, and a 'punishment' which leads to the enrichment of the *accomplice*, by allowing him to keep the money he has received even if he is more despicable than the transferor and therefore much more 'punishable', is very peculiar indeed.

The punishment theory becomes less objectionable if *neither* of the parties gets to keep the benefit which it was forbidden to give and receive but it is transferred instead to the state or to some charity. THOMAS AQUINAS, speaking of simony (the illicit traffic in holy property), said: 'Since in this case the recipient acted improperly in accepting the benefit, he must not be allowed to keep it, but must use it for pious purposes' (Book II Part II *quaestio* 62, 5; see now Can. 729, 1435 §1 Cod. Iur. Can.).—This solution may also be found in the General Land Law of Prussia: a transferor may not reclaim what he transferred in execution of an illicit transaction, 'but the treasury has the right to take the forbidden gain from the recipient' (§§172 f. I 16). This solution is perhaps a little unrealistic since one can hardly expect plaintiffs to sue for the benefit of the treasury, but the idea keeps reappearing. Thus WIGMORE proposed that the plaintiff should be allowed to reclaim the benefit, on the condition that he pay a penalty to be fixed by the court in accordance with 'the degree of moral turpitude involved, the relative guilt of the parties and the plaintiff's motive in bringing the suit' (25 *Am. L. Rev.* 695, 712 (1891); so also WADE, 95 *U. Pa. L. Rev.* 304 f. (1947), and MERKIN, 97 *LQ Rev.* 420, 444 (1981)).

2. These attempts to find a single basic idea which explains the widespread refusal of restitutionary claims are not very satisfactory. One would do better to ask whether any concrete rules and standards are used to decide whether restitution should be granted in a particular case or not. This is an area in which the Common Law in particular has produced some interesting notions. There the courts hold that a claim for restitution should only be denied if the parties are 'in pari delicto'; if it was primarily the defendant who was guilty of the illegality or immorality, the relatively innocent plaintiff should be allowed to reclaim. This principle is used in several different type of case. For example, a plaintiff is not 'in pari delicto' with the defendant if he was induced to enter the agreement by the defendant's representation that it was lawful, nor if the defendant has exploited his difficulty, simplicity, or inexperience, and the same is true if the prohibitory law which renders the contract invalid was designed to protect a special class of persons which includes the plaintiff.

See the summary of the cases in GOFF/JONES (above p. 573) 506 ff. and PALMER (above p. 538 §8.6.—Similar considerations have often been used by the German courts as well. The general view is that §817 sent. 2 BGB only excludes a claim for restitution if the plaintiff's offence against law or morals was '*intentional*'. According to the courts, a plaintiff's behaviour is not 'intentionally immoral' if he reluctantly complied with the compelling demand of an economically stronger party or if he was in a necessitous condition (see RGZ 97, 82, 84; BGH LM §817 BGB no. 12). These are the very cases in which the Anglo-American courts would allow restitution on the ground that the plaintiff was not 'in pari delicto'.

The Common Law also allows a restitution claim to succeed if it is brought before the objectionable transaction has been completely executed. If a person makes a gambling contract forbidden by the law, he can claim back what he transferred as long as it remains uncertain whether the event on which the bet turns will occur or not; if the amount of the wager has been deposited with a third party as trustee, restitution is allowed even *after* the occurrence or non-occurrence of the critical event, provided that the trustee is still in possession of the money, for then the forbidden transaction is not yet fully executed. Behind this rule is the idea that it is good to give the plaintiff an incentive to timely regret or, as the courts say, a 'locus poenitentiae' which encourages him to abandon the objectionable transaction before it is fulfilled. Many critics admittedly think that this rule has precisely the opposite effect, for if the defendant, for one reason or another, is unwilling to execute the transaction, the plaintiff can induce him to fulfil it, objectionable though it is, by threatening that he will otherwise invoke the doctrine of 'locus poenitentiae' and claim back what he has transferred. The practical application of this doctrine has led to many borderline difficulties. In particular it is not clear how far the implementation of the forbidden transaction must have gone, nor is it clear whether the plaintiff must have been genuinely repentant or whether it is enough if the execution of the transaction was prevented or hindered by the defendant's refusal to perform or by some other cause.

See the cases in GOFF/JONES (above p. 537) 512 ff.; BIRKS (above p. 537) 424; WADE, 95 *U. Pa. L. Rev.* 282 ff. (1947); and PALMER (above p. 538) §8.7.

In another line of decisions one finds the rule that the plaintiff should be allowed to bring a claim if he can formulate it successfully without mentioning the forbidden transaction. This rule is applied in cases where pursuant to an objectionable agreement the plaintiff has pledged, leased, bailed, or made a conditional sale of his goods. In such a case the plaintiff can base his claim on his ownership or, if the defendant has already sold or altered the goods, on a tort of the 'conversion' type (see below Ch. 40 III). Here it is normally the *defendant* who raises the immorality or illegality of the contract as a defence, and the courts are tempted to think the plaintiff relatively 'innocent' and to give him judgment. There is much dispute about the propriety of applying this idea in practice, for it was quickly realized that

'permitting the plaintiff adroitly to frame his declaration so as to omit any illegal aspect and make it necessary for the defendant to call attention to the illegality involved means that the whole decision is based not upon the merits of the plaintiff's claim but upon his attorney's skill in drafting a declaration' (WADE, 95 *U. Pa. L. Rev.* 268 (1947)).—See also the decisions cited in GOFF/JONES (above p. 537) 500 f., particularly *Taylor* v. *Chester*, (1869) LR 4 QB 309 and *Bowmakers Ltd.* v. *Barnet Instruments Ltd.*, [1945] KB 65, noted by HAMSON, 10 *Camb. LJ* 249 (1948/1950).

The German courts have a doctrine analogous to this Common Law rule, that §817 sent. 2 BGB only applies to claims based on §812 and not to claims based on ownership (§985) or on tort (§§823 ff. BGB). The Bundesgerichtshof has sought to justify this rule by saying that 'when the claim can be based on §§823 or 985 ff. BGB . . . the plaintiff has on his side a right which receives stronger protection from the legal order than the right of a plaintiff with only a restitutionary claim' (BGH JZ, 1951, 716 with a critical note by RAISER). This principle is highly suspect, since it bypasses the crucial question whether the purpose of the prohibitory statute or the public interest in the repression of immoral transactions will be better advanced by allowing or by denying the claim, whatever its legal basis. v. CAEMMERER (above p. 537) and RAISER (*JZ* 1951, 716) have shown that there are certain circumstances in which §817 sent. 2 BGB must apply even to a claim based on *ownership*: according to courts and writers alike in Germany, a transfer of property pursuant to an objectionable contract is generally valid, and is only invalid if it constitutes an especially gross breach of law or morals; accordingly only in the case of the most shocking offences will the transferor remain owner of the thing he has transferred in execution of an illegal or immoral agreement; but if the principle mentioned were to be applied, this is precisely the case in which the return of the thing must always be decreed, since the plaintiff can rely on §985 BGB as well as on §812.

3. In France also there are certain circumstances in which the courts reject claims for the restitution of benefits conferred pursuant to an illegal or immoral contract. The Code civil contains no relevant provision, so the courts rely on the traditional formula 'Nemo auditur propriam turpitudinem allegans'. It is particularly difficult to discover what factors move the courts to allow or reject the claim for restitution, for the criteria mentioned in the judgments are sometimes repetitious, contradictory, and unspecific. One common view is that restitution should be denied if the agreement is immoral (*convention immorale*) but generally allowed if the agreement is simply illegal (*convention seulement illicite*). Accordingly a claim for restitution is usually granted in the case of offences against price regulations or other prohibitory laws of economic policy. Thus a person who has knowingly bought food without the requisite licence may claim back the price:

'although the courts refuse a right of suit to a person relying on a contract which is void as being immoral or contrary to good custom, this is not so if the contract is simply prohibited by statute and contrary to public order without being contrary to good customs and morals' (Aix 28 March 1945, Gaz. Pal. 1945. 2.12, noted by H. & L. MAZEAUD, *Rev. trim. dr. civ.* 44 (1946) 30).—On the other hand there was a dispute about the treatment of black market transactions; often the restitutionary claim was allowed (for example, Trib. com. Seine 23 Dec. 1948, Gaz. Pal. 1949. 1. 22), often not (for example, Trib. com. Seine 2 Nov. 1945, Gaz. Pal. 1946, 1. 21).

But if the transaction contravenes fundamental unwritten rules of behaviour, especially those of sexual morality, restitution is excluded: 'the courts of justice will not settle accounts of this nature'.

See PLANIOL/RIPERT/ESMEIN VII no. 750, and Civ. 25 Jan. 1972, D. 1972, 413; Com. 27 Apr. 1981, D. 1982, 51, noted by LE TOURNEAU. It is not surprising that the distinction between contracts which are 'immoral' and those which are 'simply forbidden' has led to the gravest borderline disputes in practice. (On this see AUBERT (above p. 566) 95 ff.) Even so, this distinction has been adopted in Italy: art. 2035 Codice civile provides that restitution is only to be denied if the transaction represents an 'offesa al buon costume' on the part of the transferor. Thus if goods are sold in defiance of a statutory prohibition, or a higher price is demanded than is allowed by law, the purchase price or the excess can be reclaimed (for example, Cass. 15 Dec. 1955 no. 3883, Giust. civ. Mass. 1955, 1457; Cass. 10 July 1958 no. 2501, Giust. civ. Mass. 1958, 889). But a person who invests in a partnership to run a forbidden gambling club cannot claim back his investment (Cass. 17 June 1950 no. 1555, Foro it. Mass. 1950, 326).

French writers have tried to explain and reconcile the decisions by saying that they allow restitution wherever this best conduces to 'ordre public'. It is true that the courts have often allowed a claim if it would be contrary to the public interest to permit the situation brought about by the objectionable transfer to continue. In such a case the plaintiff gets back what he conferred, despite his conscious participation in an illegal or immoral transaction. This may be unsatisfactory, but more important is the consideration that it would be contrary to the general interest to endorse and confirm the economic situation which the performance has brought about contrary to law.

It is for this reason that public or semi-public officials must disgorge the bribes they have accepted (see Civ. 5 Dec. 1911, S. 1913. 1. 497). If the price of a purchase is understated in a notarized land transaction, the purchaser may demand back the excess paid (Req. 24 Oct. 1928, Gaz. Pal. 1928. 2. 747; the German courts reach the same result, but only because the application of §817 sent. 2 BGB was specially excluded in such cases (see BGHZ 11, 90)). Further French decisions are cited by AUBERT (above p. 566) 108 ff.

4. The legal systems we have looked at adopt very different standpoints for the solution of the problem whether the plaintiff should or should not be allowed to reclaim what he has transferred pursuant to an illegal or immoral contract. Our discussion has been far too brief to permit a critical appraisal of the criteria employed; for that, one would require a careful comparative investigation directed to the solutions in the different types of case. Such an investigation would probably show that similar cases are decided in very much the same way, though by different methods, and that any difference in the actual results is attributable less to any difference in methods than to divergences in value judgments. The comparative lawyer is forced to the conclusion that the really interesting question here is basically whether the *purpose* of the provision which renders the contract invalid is best answered by allowing the recipient to keep what was transferred under that contract or by making him restore it to the transferor. We should consider the *purpose* of the prohibitory statute not only to discover whether a contract which conflicts with it is *invalid* or not, but also to see whether it requires the

denial of *restitution* of what has been rendered. Sometimes the disincentive desired by the legislator can only be furthered by preventing the participants from making any claim at all, even one for restitution. But not always.

In order to control the black economy Germany has a law which strikes at contracts with unregistered workmen. The Bundesgerichtshof believes that the desired deterrent effect is sufficiently procured by denying such workmen any claim for the agreed remuneration, seeing that they may be fined and made to pay back taxes, and that while the contract is void it is unnecessary to bar a restitutionary claim as well and allow the customer to keep his work for free; the customer must accordingly pay what the work is worth—always rather less than the agreed fee, in view of the fact that the customer has no action for damages for breach of contract if the work is badly done (BGHZ 111, 308, 312 f.). TREITEL is right to say that although it is the 'general rule' that what has been rendered in execution of an illegal contract cannot be reclaimed 'It would be better if the law did not adopt a "general rule" but asked in relation to each type of illegality whether it was recovery or non-recovery that was the more likely to promote the purpose of the invalidating rule.' (*Law of Contract* (8th edn., 1991) 436.)

It is much the same when the contract is void as offending against public order rather than a specific statutory prohibition. Here, too, the judge must ask whether such agreements can best be repressed by granting or denying a claim for restitution.

In *Tinsley* v. *Milligan* [1994] 1 AC 340 two women who bought a house together as joint owners registered the title in the name of the plaintiff alone so that the defendant could obtain higher social security payments by pretending to have no assets. The parties fell out and when the plaintiff sought possession of the house on the basis of her registered ownership, the defendant counterclaimed for an order that the house be sold and half of the proceeds paid to her. The counterclaim was granted both in the Court of Appeal and the House of Lords, though not without dissents. The opinion of NICHOLLS LJ comes closest to the view here put forward: 'These authorities seem to me to establish that when applying the *ex turpi causa* maxim in a case in which a defence of illegality has been raised, the court should keep in mind that the underlying principle is the so-called public conscience test. The court must weigh, or balance, the adverse consequences of granting relief against the adverse consequences of refusing relief. The ultimate decision calls for a value judgment . . . Balancing these considerations I have no doubt that, far from it being an affront to the public conscience to grant relief in this case, it would be an affront to the public conscience not to do so. Right-thinking people would not consider that condemnation of the parties' fraudulent activities ought to have the consequences of permitting the plaintiff to retain the defendant's half-share of this house. That would be to visit on the defendant a disproportionate penalty, in the circumstances as they are now.' ([1992] Ch. 310, 319, 321.) The House of Lords, however, discountenanced the 'public conscience' test and gave judgment for the defendant on other grounds. See GOFF/ JONES (above p. 537) 501 f., 519 ff.

The judge's task, then, is openly to ask the question whether in the type of case before him the public interest would be best advanced by allowing or dismissing the restitutionary claim. With characteristic deftness, the Common Law has concretized this general rule in its doctrines of 'locus poenitentiae' and 'in pari delicto'. If the public has an interest in the prevention of the execution of objectionable transactions, then in certain types of case it may well be sound to give the transferor an incentive to make prompt disclosure of the transaction by allowing him the right of restitution if he does so. Equally it is legitimate to ask whether the plaintiff belongs to the group of persons whom the statute in question was designed to protect. If so, one may allow him a restitutionary claim on the ground that he is not 'in pari delicto'. By contrast, it is quite unsound to hold that restitution must always be allowed if the plaintiff can base his claim on ownership or on tort and can thus state his claim without disclosing the objectionable transaction: this is to use formal criteria unconnected with the vital interests involved.

For the same reason one cannot accept the doctrine which keeps appearing in German decisions, that restitution must always be allowed if the recipient was not to keep the benefit for himself but only obtained it 'for temporary purposes', simply as a 'conduit'. The Bundesgerichtshof has decided that an attorney who offered to exchange German money into foreign currency in breach of exchange control regulations was bound, notwithstanding §817 sent. 2 BGBZ, to return to his client the money he received for this purpose (BGH 28, 225). This is certainly correct, not because the attorney received the money only 'for temporary purposes' and was to return it to the client after making the exchange, but because the public interest in repressing currency speculation is best served by requiring restitution of a person who used his knowledge and connections to solicit such shady dealings and who would, were he allowed to retain the money, be able in the future to offer himself with impunity for similar services. By contrast, the Bundesgerichtshof gave the right reasons for allowing the owner of premises let as a brothel to reclaim them before the expiry of the lease (BGHZ 41, 341): the court eschewed the unhappy doctrine that §817 sent. 2 BGB does not bar a claim based on ownership, and decided quite rightly that the effect of allowing the lessee to use §817 sent. 2 BGB as a defence to claim for repossession of the premises during the period of the lease would be to legalize the brothel in a manner inconsistent with the 'purpose of §138 BGB'.

IV

1. According to §818 par. 3 BGB, a person who has received a benefit without legal cause is released from the obligation to make restitution to the extent that he 'has ceased to be enriched'. Though it is questioned nowadays (see above Ch. 38 V), the underlying legislative idea is that the enrichment claim, being based simply on equity, should not cause any loss to the defendant (see Protokolle II, pp. 706 f.). For this reason, 'enrichment' in German law trad-

itionally means an economic increment, the amount by which all the advantages accruing to the recipient from the transaction which enriches him outweigh the associated disadvantages. It is inferred from this that the recipient may set off against the enrichment any disadvantages he suffered in connection with the acquisition of the benefit or which he would suffer in consequence of making restitution, up to the time when the claim for restitution was brought or he realized that he was not entitled to retain the benefit. Thus the recipient's duty is terminated or diminished if what he received is destroyed, embezzled, or confiscated (see RGZ 65, 292; 79, 285 (embezzlement); RG BankArch. 26 (1926/1927) 123 ff.; OGHZ 1, 298 (confiscation)); if he lends the money he receives to a trickster or invests it in an industrial enterprise which is dismantled after the war (see BGH JZ 1961, 699 (trickster); BGH MDR 1957, 598 (investment)); if he makes a gift of the goods he received or sells them at a loss (see RG WarnRspr. 1917 no. 140 (gift); RGZ 75, 361; RG JW 1915, 711 (sale at a loss)); if he spends money on what he received in the belief that he was entitled to keep it (RGZ 117, 112; RG WarnRspr. 1919 no. 196); if he increases his standard of living (RGZ 83, 159; 83, 161), allows claims to prescribe (RGZ 70, 350), surrenders claims (RG JW 1909, 274), or assumes obligations from which he cannot free himself without loss (RG JW 1914, 302; RG JW 1928, 2444). He may also set off the costs of acquisition and restitution (RGZ 72, 1 (brokerage charges); BGHZ 32, 240, 244; RGZ 96, 345, 347; OGHZ 4, 81, 86 f. (expense and risk of return)). In brief, the plaintiff must bear the risk of all the events which negative or neutralize the economic benefit accruing to the defendant. This is the 'weakness' of the enrichment claim which is so often referred to (as by v. TUHR (above p. 567) 305). For German lawyers, indeed, it is the characteristic feature of enrichment liability.

2. Other legal systems are not so generous towards the defendant, but the rules vary a good deal in the different countries.

(a) All Continental codes apparently grant certain privileges to the good faith recipient, but they do not all draw the dividing line between good and bad faith in the same place. Apart from the case where a claim has already been instituted, the BGB imposes the stricter liability for bad faith only where the defendant was fully aware that there was no legal justification for his receipt (§819 par. 1), and the courts do not regard mere knowledge of the facts which destroy the justification for the transfer as sufficient (see RG WarnRspr. 1918 no. 224; RG JW 1931, 529). The Austrian and Swiss codes remove the privilege if the recipient 'should have reckoned on restitution' (art. 64 OR) or 'should in the circumstances have suspected . . . that the transferor was in error' (§1437 ABGB).

(b) The extent of the liability of the bona fide recipient is often linked in the codes to the extent of liability of a good faith possessor when sued by the owner in a *vindicatio*. Thus in dealing with the liability of the recipient of a thing not due, §1437 ABGB refers to the claim of the owner against the possessor, and while arts. 1376 ff. Code civil lay down specific rules for the liability of the recipient of a thing not due, the rules themselves are very like those laid down by the other Continental codes for the relationship between owner and possessor. In Swiss law, a set-off for expenses incurred by the recipient in improving the property received is allowed in the same way as in the case of an unauthorized possessor (art. 65 OR). Frequently, the *vindicatio* itself is used, because in Swiss law, in deviation from the principle of abstraction (see above p. 542) property does not pass unless the underlying transaction is valid.

In these countries, as under §§987 ff. BGB, a person sued by the *vindicatio* has a defence if the object originally received has been lost, destroyed, or unprofitably consumed, but the only losses he gets credit for are expenditures on the very thing he received, necessary expenditures being admitted without limitation, useful expenditures only to the extent that the object is rendered more valuable at the time of restitution (§§331, 323 ABGB; art. 65 par. 1 OR: art. 1381 Code civil; PLANIOL/RIPERT/ESMEIN VII no. 746 *ad fin.*).

(c) In some Continental countries the recipient of *money* transferred without justification is treated very severely. In Roman law the payee remained absolutely liable whatever happened, being bound to repay the same sum just as if he had borrowed it (see v. TUHR (above p. 567) 297 ff.; SIBER *Römisches Recht* II (1928) 218 f.). This doctrine survived in the legal literature of Europe from the time of the Glossa Magna until the time of codification. It was followed by the Prussian General Land Law (§193 16 I), and although WINDSCHEID dissented from it, a vocal minority of the nineteenth century pandectists supported it (on the whole development from the time of the Glossa Magna, see FLUME, above p. 566).

This time-honoured rule is still adhered to in Austria, France, and Italy, not just out of loyalty to tradition but with some empirical justification. Stress is laid on the fact that the extreme fungibility of money makes it practically impossible to trace the money received through all its metamorphoses in the assets of the recipient, or on the view that since money may be used in so many different ways the recipient must be taken to have benefited from the mere fact that he once had the money to dispose of as he thought fit.

See KLANG/GSCHNITZER, *Kommentar zum ABGB* IV (2nd edn., 1951/1963) §877 n. III 2 *a* (p. 158); KLANG/WILBURG, *Kommentar zum ABGB* VI (2nd edn., 1951) §§1431 ff. n. X B 2 (p. 480); RUMMEL, *Kommentar zum ABGB* (1984) §1437 mn. 12; PLANIOL/RIPERT/ESMEIN VII no. 746; BEUDANT/LEREBOURS-PIGEONNIÈRE/RODIÈRE, *Cours de droit civil français* IX 2 (2nd edn., 1952) no. 1751; TRIMARCHI (above p. 567) 160 f.

The rule is also applied if the recipient's original duty to make restitution of a specific chattel ever takes the form of a money debt, as happens if the recipient consumes the chattel for his own purposes. In this case, further developments of the recipient's financial situation do not affect the creditor.

(d) In a recent decision the House of Lords has accepted that a claim for restitution may be refused to the extent that the good faith recipient 'has so changed his position' that it would be unfair to make him return all he had received.

In *Lipkin Gorman* v. *Karpnale Ltd.* [1991] 2 AC 548, 579 LORD GOFF said: 'We should ask ourselves: why do we feel that it would be unjust to allow restitution in cases such as these? The answer must be that, when an innocent defendant's position is so changed that he will suffer an injustice if called upon to repay or to repay in full, the injustice of requiring him so to repay outweighs the injustice of denying the plaintiff restitution.' The courts will have to work out 'on a case by case basis' under what conditions the defendant can invoke a 'change of position'. But the decision shows that the defence is available only if the recipient was in good faith, and that it is not a 'change of position' for him simply to spend the money. It is different, however, if he spends it for a purpose he would not otherwise have entertained—for example, a world cruise or a donation to charity—and if he buys and still has in his possession a thing he would not otherwise have bought, he need restore only its present value. For details see GOFF/JONES (above p. 537) 739 ff.; also MEIER *ZEuP* 1993, 365.

Prior to this decision a person sued for restitution had a defence only if he could make out an 'estoppel': a plaintiff who has asserted by speech or conduct that the money was indeed due to the defendant is 'estopped' from later saying the opposite, if on the basis of what was said the recipient had made arrangements such that it would now be unfair to require him to make restitution. The decisions suggest that the new defence of change of position will turn on the same factors which are relevant to the defence of estoppel (see GOFF/JONES (above p. 537) 746 ff.). For example, the courts are very favourable to defendants who are asked to restore excess personal income paid by mistake. The simple facts of the much-cited case of *Skyring* v. *Greenwood*, (1825) 107 Eng. Rep. 1064 were that a major of artillery had for several years been drawing too much pay because the paymaster has overlooked a Board of Ordnance directive. The judges felt able to reject the claim, on the ground that

'It is of great importance to any man that he should not be led to suppose that his annual income is greater than it really is. Every prudent man accommodates his mode of living to what he supposes to be his income. It therefore works a great prejudice to any man, if . . . he may be called upon to pay [the sums] back' (id., at 1067). The case of *Holt* v. *Markham*, [1923] 1 KB 504 was rather similar. The army paymaster omitted to take account of a relevant regulation and paid the defendant officer, who was retiring from the service, too large a gratuity. Eighteen months later, when the error was discovered, a request for repayment was made, but on an erroneous view of the facts which the defendant corrected in a long letter. Two months later the demand was renewed, this time on the right grounds. Meanwhile the defendant had invested what was left of the money and had lost it. The claim for restitution was unsuccessful. See also *Avon CC* v. *Howlett* [1983] 1 All ER 1073 (CA).

Favour is also shown to the defendant if the unjustified benefit arose between parties who were already in a duty relationship with each other. Thus in the case of *Deutsche Bank* v. *Beriro*, (1895) 73 LT 669 an importer asked his bank to collect on a negotiable instrument. The bank mistakenly reported that the instrument had been met and paid him its value. It later appeared that in fact the instrument had not been honoured, but by then the importer had irrevocably credited the amount to his foreign business partner. The judge held that the bank was 'estopped' by its behaviour from reclaiming the payment; it was also, through the oversight of one of its staff, in breach of its duties towards its principal in giving him false information regarding the collection on the instrument. This error did not affect the defendant: 'Upon what ground of law or of equity can they say that they can get rid of the consequences of their breach of duty because they had made a mistake?' (MATHEW J., 670 f.).

If there is no special duty of care between the parties the courts are less tender to the interests of the party enriched. Thus in *Weld-Blundell* v. *Synott* [1940] 2 KB 107 the first mortgagee, having foreclosed on the property, mistakenly retained too little of the proceeds for himself and sent too much to the second mortgagee. When the first mortgagee reclaimed the excess, the second mortgagee objected that the payment had made him delay taking timely action against the owner of the property on his own account. To this the judge said: 'I do not think an estoppel arises unless it can be shown that there was neglect or misconduct on the plaintiff's part in making the misrepresentation' (p. 114), and since a first mortgagee owes a second mortgagee no particular duty of care when he is calculating the distribution of the proceeds, no estoppel arose against the plaintiff.

It is not an irrevocable disposition on the faith of a mistaken payment for the recipient to use the money to buy something he would have bought anyway, even if he would have had to borrow money to buy it (*United Overseas Bank* v. *Jiwani* [1977] 1 All ER 733).

(e) American law, having accepted LORD MANSFIELD's view that the duty of restitution imposed on the party enriched rests on 'natural justice and equity' (see above Ch. 38 IV), found it easy, when weighing up the 'equities' in the individual case, to take account of the fact that no benefit remained to the defendant out of what he had acquired. In 1875 the New York Court of Appeals held that restitution should not be granted 'if payment has caused such a change in the position of the other party it would be unjust to require him to refund' (*Mayer* v. *New York*, 63 NY 455 (1875)). Nowadays the Restatement of Restitution (1937) makes 'change of circumstances' a good defence to all restitutionary claims (§142).

A 'change of circumstances' (or 'change of position') is found in those situations where German law would find that the enrichment had disappeared: destruction, loss or theft of the object received; unprofitable use or sale at a loss; expenses incurred on the property received; the assumption of legal obligations which are unavoidable or avoidable only at a loss; the surrender of rights or securities; the omission to exercise one's rights in due time; unprofitable investment of money received; gifts made out of what was received; peculation by staff. See the cases cited by PALMER (above p. 538) §16.8.

Since the defence rests on equitable considerations, the mere fact that the benefit has disappeared does not of itself extinguish the liability: the defence is successful only if the change in the situation makes it inequitable to order restitution. Here American lawyers see a problem of loss-shifting: if the situation is such that the defendant would be worse off after making restitution than he was before acquiring the benefit in the first place, then the question is whether this loss should be borne by the plaintiff by leaving his original loss uncompensated, or by the defendant by requiring him to make restitution despite the loss this will cause him. The outcome depends on a weighing of the 'equities' on both sides: the loss will be put upon the party who in view of all the facts is principally responsible. In making this judgment the behaviour and position of the parties is investigated in detail, both as of the time of the transaction which procured the transfer and later. Other circumstances also, such as the social and financial situation of the parties, may have a role to play.

The following cases illustrate the method of decision.

In *Behring* v. *Somerville*, 44 A. 641 (NJ 1899) a mortgage was assigned to B who did not know that it had already been assigned to A. B thus acquired only a secondary right, but the owner paid B the amount of the mortgage in ignorance of the first assignment, and claimed the money back when he discovered his error. Meanwhile B had surrendered the mortgage. The court rejected the claim for repayment. Both parties had made the same error, and both had the same means of checking the truth of the matter in the mortgage register. In such a case neither party had more claim to redress than the other, so they were 'to be left in the position in which they placed themselves'. In *Jefferson County Bank* v. *Hansen Lumber Co.*, 246 Ky. 384, 55 SW 2d 54 (1932) a person bought a cargo of wood under an agreement providing for payment to the defendant bank against documents. On hearing from the vendor that the goods had been shipped, the purchaser paid forthwith, without seeing the documents. In fact the goods were never shipped, and the vendor went bankrupt after the bank had remitted the purchase price to him. Nine months later the plaintiff reclaimed the purchase price from the bank, but in vain. The court stated at the outset that it was a matter for regret that in the circumstances the payment must represent a loss for one or other of the parties, but this loss must be borne by the person 'whose fault or negligence this loss is most fairly attributable to'. The court then held that since the plaintiff was entitled to withhold payment until the documents arrived, he acted with undue haste in making the payment and with undue sloth in reclaiming it. In practical terms the plaintiff was not so much asking for the restitution of an unjustified enrichment as seeking to put on the defend-ant a loss for which he himself was responsible. *Moritz* v. *Horsman*, 9 NW 2d 868 (Mich. 1943) shows that this equit-able liability may be affected not only by the conduct of the parties in the transaction which conferred the benefit but also by other circumstances. The plaintiff, an adopted child, received part of the estate of his adoptive father on the assumption that he was a statutory heir. Later it appeared that the relevant legislation gave adopted children no right to inherit. The natural children thereupon demanded back the $13,000 which the defendant had received. He still possessed $5,000 in government bonds, but he had spent $3,000 on a house and furniture, and could give no precise information about the rest. The court noted in his favour that he had only $5,000 left in his hands, that he had been out of work for some time, that his wife's illness over a year had caused him great medical expenses, and finally that all the parties had laboured under the same excusable error of law. The court then said that it would be harsh and inequitable to make the defendant liable in these circumstances for the full amount he had received. It decided that he could afford $2,500 over and above the $5,000 he still had, and should pay two-thirds of this total of $7,500, namely $5,000, which he still had in liquid form.

3. The way foreign systems set about solving these problems shows that there is nothing necessary or self-evident about the principle of liability adopted in Germany, but that despite all the differences in their theoretical starting-points, the various legal systems very often reach the same results. In the space at our disposal we can illustrate this in only two cases: (a) the erroneous overpayment of allowances, pensions, and other personal emolu-ments, and (b) the enrichment of minors.

(a) According to §818 par. 3 BGB a person who receives money paid in error ceases to be liable if he spends the money without saving himself other expense. On general principles this fact has to be proved by the recipient, but where the sum overpaid was in respect of earnings and allowances the Ger-man courts assume from experience that a recipient does not save up the increments in his earnings but uses them immediately to improve his stan-dard of living, with the result that he no longer retains the amount of the overpayment when it is reclaimed. The courts therefore allow those who receive such sums to rely on §818 par. 3 BGB on a mere showing that all the money has been used up (see RGZ 83, 159 and 161; BVerwGE 8, 261, 270; 13, 107, 110). At first this was accepted only where the money had been spent on transient items such as food and travel and so on, but more recently the courts have been ready to allow the set-off even to a recipient who still retains the equivalent of what he spent, provided that he would nevertheless suffer loss if he had to repay it, as happens in the case of furniture, whose resale produces only a fraction of its true value (BGH MDR 1959, 109).

To give further help to the recipient of extra personal income, the courts have recently been making great play with another rule which within proper limits is a well-established implication of §818 par. 3 BGB: this is the rule that a benefit is not diminished if it is used to pay off debts, since paying the creditor reduces the debt in an equal amount (see STAUDINGER/LORENZ, *Kommentar zum BGB* (12th edn., 1979) §818 n. 38). The Bundesverwaltungsgericht allows the defence of cessation of enrichment in such a case since even if he pays off some debts the official is still adjusting his standard of living to the amount he actually receives (BVerwGE 15, 15, 17 f., and see STAUDINGER/LORENZ, *Kommentar zum BGB* (12th edn. 1986) §818 mn. 38; LIEB in *Münchener Kommentar* (2nd edn. 1986) §818 mn. 83).

Such decisions rest on social considerations which arise in other countries as well. In Austria the rule that the exact amount of money received must always be repaid really ought to make such considerations inadmissible but in the case of overpayment of earnings the courts are ready to make an exception. The Oberste Gerichtsof once said in a case where the pension of a railway official had been miscalculated in his favour: 'This affects a great many people; the railways have their own office for calculating retirement pensions, for which the administration of the railways is responsible; it might even be thought that the railways were at fault in misleading people by paying them too much. It is true that retirement pensions take the form of money payments, but their purpose is to maintain the recipient. This is the purpose for which the recipient receives and uses the money, as both parties must obviously realize each time payment is made; furthermore, as has already been said, the overpayment normally causes extra expenditure. In most cases therefore a claim for repayment is grossly inequitable since the official can be in no position to keep funds on hand to meet it' (OGH 23 April 1929, SZ 11 no. 86 (p. 265)).

The same problem arises in France. The codal provisions regarding the payment of a thing not due do not permit any set-off for consequent disadvantages, but the courts allow the recipient a counterclaim for damages based on delictual liability for negligence or fault in the state administration. It is easier for French law to do this than for German law, since liability for tort in France may arise in respect of 'pure' economic loss whereas in Germany this is impossible because of the restrictive list of compensable heads of damage adopted in §823 par. 1 BGB (see below Ch. 40 II and IV). The case frequently cited as an example of a claim for repayment being met by a claim for damages is a fairly old decision by the Conseil d'État (1 July 1904, S. 1904. 3. 121). For fifteen years a pensioner received overpayments which he spent on living expenses. The Conseil d'État rejected the claim for repayment. To persist in an error for so many years must necessarily constitute a 'faute de service qui engage la responsibilité de l'État'.

See also the recent decisions (p. 547 above) which allow the recipient of undue social security payments to set off a counterclaim for damages. In other decisions the recipient of money not owed has been allowed to keep all or part of it on a showing that the mistake of the payer was due to the payer's own negligence, that he himself was in good faith in receiving the money, and that in the circumstances it would be a hardship for him to repay any part of it. See, for example, Com. 19 Nov. 1991, JCP 1993. II. 22012 noted by DONNIER.

(b) All legal systems protect *minors* in one way or another from the harm they might suffer from entering into binding contracts. For this protection to be effective, it must not only limit the contractual capacity of minors but also attach some qualification to their duty to make restitution of benefits received through the execution of contracts or otherwise.

In German law the general formula of §818 par. 3 BGB protects minors like everyone else: one is liable in restitution only up to the amount of the economic benefit still remaining in his hands. The special protection of the minor only becomes evident when one turns to the rules which determine the stricter liability of the bad faith recipient (§819 par. 1 BGB). According to the courts and writers alike, a minor's bad faith is not held against him, provided that his statutory representative was unaware of the acquisition and its want of legal justification (RG JW 1917, 465; LIEB in *Münchener Kommentar* (2nd edn. 1986) §819 mn. 7; LARENZ/CANARIS, *Lehrbuch des Schuldrechts* (13th edn. 1994) II(2) p. 312 f; a further view is that a minor is only liable if he could be held liable in delict (§§828, 829 BGB; see BGHZ 55, 128, 135 f.).

In other countries the special protection afforded to minors is more marked since the *general* rule of liability is not sufficient to protect them. For example, minors might be put at risk by the rule in Austria and France that there is absolute liability to repay money unjustifiably received, were it not that an exception is made to this rule in their interest. In both countries minors are liable only if what they received was in fact used for their benefit, a fact which must, apparently, be proved by the plaintiff.

Austria: OGH 22 Aug. 1951, SZ 24 no. 204; OGH 13 Dec. 1905, GLUNF VIII no. 3246; OGH 2 July 1913, GLUNF XVI no. 6514.—France: art. 1241, 1312 Code civil.—Italy: art. 2039 Codice civile.—But French lawyers are so attached to the rule of absolute liability for the repayment of money that it reappears even if the recipient lacks contractual capacity; he remains liable for any benefit in kind procured by the money transferred even if he does not succeed in retaining it. If he uses the money for making purchases, he remains liable for the whole sum even if what he buys is later destroyed or depreciates. It is said that the plaintiff in restitution 'n'est pas responsable de l'avenir et des causes étrangères, mais seulement de la dissipation' (PLANIOL/RIPERT/ESMEIN VI no. 323).

In English law there is no need to refer to rules about the extent of liability or the retention of the enrichment since minors are exempt *ab initio* from any duty to repay. If what the minor received or its substitute is still identifiable in his hands then equitable rules may be applied to require the minor to disgorge, as in a constructive trust (see *Stocks* v. *Wilson*, [1913] 2 KB 235; GOFF/

JONES (above p. 537) 533 ff.), but the other party cannot by rescinding acquire a purely personal money claim, for fear that this would come close to enforcing the invalid contract. 'Restitution stops where repayment begins' (ANSON/GUEST, *Principles of the English Law of Contract* (26th edn., 1984) 200). The minor therefore goes free if what he received or its substitute is not there to hand over, whether it is just lost or has been consumed by use, usefully or not. In addition, he is never under any liability consisting of an obligation to pay money, as happens if the benefit took the form of services or of money which has been mixed with his own assets.

These results are based essentially on two decisions at the beginning of the century. *Cowern* v. *Nield*, [1912] 2 KB 419 involved a prepayment which a minor received under a contract of sale which he failed to perform, and *Leslie* v. *Sheill*, [1914] 3 KB 607 involved a loan of money to an infant. In both cases it was categorically held that there was no duty to repay, partly on purely conceptual grounds (see above p. 553), but partly also because 'this would be nothing but enforcing a void contract' (LORD SUMNER, in *Leslie* v. *Sheill*, [1914] 3 KB 607, 619, criticized by GOFF/JONES (above p. 537) 530 ff.).—American law by and large follows the English pattern. The Restatement starts by saying that the defence of 'change of circumstances' is at least as available to infants as to adults (Restatement §139 Comment *d*). In fact the protection of minors goes well beyond the general defences. Most courts still apply the traditional rule that unless what he originally received or its substitute is still identifiably present in his hands, an infant party to a void contract is under no duty to make restitution to the other party. According to many decisions, the same is true if restitution in kind was impossible *ab initio* (on the whole matter see WILLISTON §238; SIMPSON, *Handbook of the Law of Contracts* (2nd edn., 1965) 228 ff.).

4. These examples show that in all legal systems liability depends on considerations appropriate to the particular type of case, and that these considerations, which are much the same everywhere, oust or temper the abstract rules of liability preformulated in general terms. Social factors are taken into account when the overpayment is of personal income, and minors who receive benefits are accorded special protection in line with the aim of the legal order as manifested in the law of contract.

The solutions in these cases seem to impose themselves automatically in the various systems, and they call for no further discussion, but several points emerge from the *general* solutions adopted by the different legal systems (see 2 above) which might be used with profit elsewhere. Even if one does not accept the theory that remedies in unjust enrichment are purely equitable (see above Ch. 38 V), it still seems a good idea, particularly prominent in American law, to make the outcome depend on the conduct and posture of both parties during and after the relevant transaction; there is also merit in the view that the party who receives the benefit is responsible for any decisions he makes in the management of his own assets, even if the doctrine it is sometimes used to justify, namely that the liability to repay is absolute, is itself too rigid.

These points are rather obscured by the accepted German law that enrichment is simply an economic imbalance. Traditionally, a decision about liability in unjustified enrichment is the result of pure mathematics in which value-judgments have little part to play (on this see DAWSON, 'Erasable Enrichment . . .' (above p. 566)), but one sees how relevant they are as soon as one puts the question asked by the American lawyer, namely, who should properly bear the *loss* resulting from the disappearance of the enrichment. On this view, the continuing liability of the defendant depends on whether the *events* which cause the loss should be *imputed* to him or to the other party.

(a) It seems right that the conduct and position of *both* parties should play a part in any such decision. A. v. TUHR complained that the rules as to liability accepted by the dominant German view took no account of the differences in the position of the parties in the various types of enrichment claim. With regard to the *Leistungskondiktion*, where the plaintiff confers the benefit on the defendant in the first instance, he was in favour of a generous relaxation of the defendant's liability; a person who wants to undo a transfer he has made because he was mistaken as to his obligations should only be allowed to rely on his error and so be 'disruptive of commerce' if, like the mistaken party under §122 BGB, he accepts the loss which restitution will cause to the other party. On the other hand, where the enrichment has come not from a giving by the plaintiff but from a taking by the defendant as, for instance, in cases covered by §816 par. 1 sent. 1 BGB, the party benefiting deserves no protection if he makes bad investments, omits to use his rights and opportunities, or enters new obligations, for harm of this sort is incurred by all those who overestimate the assets at their disposal: he should not be able to shift them to the person entitled to restitution (v. TUHR (above p. 567) 314 ff.; adumbrated by HEINRICH SIBER, *Schuldrecht* (1931) 445 f.).

But one can safely go a step further, as some other writers (especially WILBURG (above p. 538) 138 ff.; so also, with cautious agreement, RABEL in *RabelsZ* 10 (1936) 426 f.) and American lawyers do, and ask within the different types of claim which of the parties was principally responsible for the enrichment or its disappearance, as having *caused* it or been *at fault* with regard to it. If a creditor destroys a document of indebtedness after receiving payment from a third party in error, the question whether the loss attributable to the consequent difficulty of proof should be borne by the creditor or by the third party who wants to reclaim the sum may be eased by the consideration, *inter alia*, whether the creditor peremptorily and cogently demanded the sum from the third party or whether the third party, believing himself to be the debtor, spontaneously made the payment or even whether the payment was intended for someone else and was made to the creditor only through the oversight of a bank. In the latter situation one must also, in order to solve the situation satisfactorily, ask which of the parties should be responsible for the errors of the bank in question.

(b) When it comes to deciding which of the parties should bear the loss attributable to events which diminish the enrichment, it is useful to bear in mind that the recipient should be responsible for economic decisions within his own sphere. In Germany, §818 par. 3 BGB puts on the plaintiff any economic misfortunes suffered by the recipient as a result of his dealings with what he received; the plaintiff in restitution must bear the loss if the purchaser of land resells it at too low a price, if the vendor of land invests the purchase price foolishly (RGZ 75, 361; RG JW 1931, 529), if the recipient of a payment not due makes a loan of it to a third party who then goes bankrupt (RG WarnRspr. 1912 no. 360; BGHZ 26, 185, 194 ff.), or if the vendor invests the deposit received under an invalid contract in his own business which is later dismantled or destroyed by bombs (BGH MDR 1957, 598).

But it would be more realistic to hold that in general everyone should bear the normal risks of the conduct of his affairs; as RABEL once said, 'the way the recipient deals with the property he has received is . . . exclusively his own affair' (RABEL (above p. 592) 427). There is therefore a valid point in the doctrine which still obtains in many countries that the recipient of money must always pay back the same amount: money is so easily used that it is particularly easy to say that what the recipient does with it is his own responsibility.

The idea that in general a person must take responsibility for the consequences of his own 'economic conduct' (FLUME (above p. 566) 157) only loses its force in a case where the receipt of the benefit induces the recipient to be prejudicially feckless, generous, or foolhardy; such behaviour is a true type of reliance damage which should be dealt with in terms of causation and fault rather than in relation to the question within whose economic sphere the dispositions took place. Nor can the idea be applied in cases where the law makes it clear, as it does in cases of minority, that it intends so far as possible to protect special groups of people from the disadvantageous consequences of managing their affairs.

(c) The example of the liability of minors suggests a further ground for the allocation of loss which has not yet been consciously applied in the law of restitution. Even where the law of restitution is in general less favourable to the defendant than it is in Germany we have seen that the arguments of legal policy which protect minors are so powerful that their liability for the losses which would result if restitution were required is either excluded or heavily limited. In other words, the rule which decrees the invalidity of a minor's contract and permits its rescission can usefully be referred to when the question is which party should suffer losses arising from the disappearance of the benefit transferred.

In the law of tort German courts and writers are coming increasingly to accept RABEL's view that the 'purpose of the law' may be at least as important in the allocation of loss as the traditional theory of adequacy (see below p. 602). The example of the liability of minors suggests that the problem of imputing loss may be approached from this standpoint in the law of *enrichment* as well: in proper cases the extent of liability in restitution may be affected by the purpose and power of the rule which justifies the claim. This will be quite possible in cases where the underlying contract is void for breach of the law or neglect of formal requirements or some other ground of nullity where the operative policy of the law is clear. Such policy considerations may provide a valuable guide to the proper extent of restitutionary liability.

Similar considerations may be of use in certain cases where the enrichment arises as a result of the defendant's own act, provided the cases are sufficiently clearly circumscribed. For instance, there is a rule in Germany that a person who sells or consumes someone else's goods and is sued in a *condictio* by the previous owner cannot set off the price he paid the third party for them. The reason for this, *inter alia*, is that such a set-off would not have been possible in the vindication to which he would have been liable before he disposed of the goods (BGHZ 14, 7, 9 f.; v. CAEMMERER, *Festschrift Rabel* I (1954) 385 f.). This shows that ownership not only forms the basis of the *condictio* but also has the further effect of determining the extent of liability.

B. TORT

40

Tort in General

ATIYAH, 'Negligence and Economic Loss'. 83 *LQ Rev.* 248 (1967).

——/CANE, *Accidents, Compensation and the Law* (5th edn., 1993).

v. BAR/MARKESINIS, *Richterliche Rechtspolitik im Haftungsrecht* (1981).

v. CAEMMERER, 'Wandlungen des Deliktsrechts,' *Hundert Jahre deutsches Rechtsleben, Festschrift zum 100jährigen Bestehen des Deutschen Juristentages II* (1960) 49.

CATALA/WEIR, 'Delict and Torts: A Study in Parallel', 37 *Tul. L. Rev.* 573 (1963), 38 *Tul. L. Rev.* 221, 663 (1964), 39 *Tul. L. Rev.* 701 (1965).

DIAS/MARKESINIS, *The English Law of Torts, A Comparative Introduction* (1976).

FLEMING, 'Remoteness and Duty: The Control Devices in Liability for Negligence', 31 *Can. Bar Rev.* 471 (1953).

——, *The American Tort Process* (1988).

GIOVANNONI, 'Le Dommage indirect en droit suisse de la responsabilité civile, comparé aux droits allemand et français', *ZSR* 96 (1977) 31.

GREEN, 'The Duty Problem in Negligence Cases', 28 *Colum. L. Rev.* 1014 (1928), 29 *Colum. L. Rev.* 250 (1929).

GREGORY, 'Trespass to Negligence to Absolute Liability', 37 *Va. L. Rev.* 359 (1951).

HELLNER, 'Développement et rôle de la responsabilité civile délictuelle dans les pays scandinaves', *Rev. int. dr. comp.* 19 (1967) 779.

HOLMES, *The Common Law* (1881), Lecture III (Torts—Trespass and Negligence).

HONORÉ, 'Causation and Remoteness of Damage', *Int. Enc. Comp. L.* XI Ch. 2 (1972).

JAMES, 'Scope of Duty in Negligence Cases', 47 *NWUL Rev.* 778 (1953).

KESSLER, *Fahrlässigkeit im nordamerikanischen Deliktsrecht* (1932).

KRUSE, 'The Scandinavian Law of Torts', 18 *Am. J. Comp. L.* 58 (1970).

LANG, *Normzweck und Duty of Care, Eine Untersuchung über die Grenzen der Zurechnung im deutschen und anglo-amerikanischen Deliktsrecht* (1983).

LAWSON/MARKESINIS, *Tortious Liability for Unintentional Harm in the Common Law and the Civil Law*, 2 vols. (1982).

LIMPENS/KRUITHOF/MEINERTZHAGEN-LIMPENS, 'Liability for One's Own Act', *Int. Enc. Comp. L.* XI Ch. 2 (1972).

LIPSTEIN, 'Protected Interests in the Law of Torts', 1963 *Camb. LJ* 85.

MAGNUS, *Schaden und Ersatz, Eine rechtsvergleichende Untersuchung zur Ersatzfähigkeit von Einbußen* (1987).

MARKESINIS, *The German Law of Torts* (3rd edn., 1994).

——, 'The Not So Dissimilar Tort and Delict', 93 *LQ Rev.* 78 (1977).

MARKESINIS, 'La politique jurisprudentielle et la réparation du préjudice économique en Angleterre, Une approche comparative', *Rev. int. dr. comp.* 35 (1983) 31.

——, 'General Theory of Unlawful Acts', in HARTKAMP et al. (eds.), *Towards a European Civil Code* (1994) 285.

MARTY, 'L'Expérience française en matière de responsabilité civile et les enseignements du droit comparé', *Mélanges Maury* II (1961) 173.

McGREGOR,'Personal Injury and Death', *Int. Enc. Comp. L.* XI Ch. 9 (1972).

MOTULSKY, 'Die Zurechenbarkeit des Kausalzusammenhanges im französischen Schadenersatzrecht', *RabelsZ* 25 (1960) 242.

POSNER, 'A Theory of Negligence', 1 *J. Leg. Stud.* 29 (1972).

PREUSS, *Vertragsbruch als Delikt im anglo-amerikanischen Recht* (1977).

RODIÈRE/PÉDAMON (ed.), *Faute et lien de causalité, Étude comparative dans les pays du Marché commun* (1983).

SÓLYOM, *The Decline of Civil Law Liability* (1980).

STOLL, 'Consequences of Liability', *Int. Enc. Comp. L.* XI Ch. 9 (1972).

——, *Kausalzusammenhang und Normzweck im Deliktsrecht* (1968).

——, *Haftungsfolgen im bürgerlichen Recht, Eine Darstellung auf rechtsvergleichender Grundlage* (1993).

——, '"The Wagon Mound"—Eine neue Grundsatzentscheidung zum Kausalproblem im englischen Recht', *Vom deutschen zum europäischen Recht, Festschrift für Hans Dölle* I (1963) 371.

STREET, 'The Twentieth Century Development and Function of the Law of Tort in England', 14 *ICLQ* 862 (1965).

TERCIER, 'Cent ans de responsabilité civile en droit suisse', in: *Hundert Jahre Schweizerisches Obligationenrecht* (ed. Peter/Start/Tercier 1982) 203.

TUNC, 'Les Problèmes contemporains de la responsabilité civile délictuelle', *Rev. int. dr. comp.* 16 (1967) 757.

——, 'The Twentieth Century Development and Function of the Law of Torts in France', 14 *ICLQ* 1089 (1965).

——, *La responsabilité civile* (1981).

——, 'Torts, Introduction', *Int. Enc. Comp. L.* XI Ch. 1 (1972).

VINEY, La Responsabilité: conditions (Traité de droit civil (ed. Ghestin) vol. IV 1982).

——/MARKESINIS, *La réparation du dommage corporel, Essai de comparaison des droits anglais et français* (1985).

WILLIAMS, 'The Foundation of Tortious Liability', 7 *Camb. LJ* III (1939–41).

WHITE, *Tort Law in America, An Intellectual History* (1980).

WINFIELD, 'The History of Negligence in the Law of Torts', 42 *LQ Rev.* 184 (1926).

——, 'Duty in Tortious Negligence', 34 *Colum. L. Rev.* 41 (1934).

I

BOTH the law of contract and the law of tort entitle people to claim compensation for harm they have suffered. The law of contract does so only in a rather limited area, where the plaintiff has been disappointed in his justifiable expectation that the defendant would honour his promise. But citizens have many other interests and the law of tort deals with the cases where they have been infringed, where the plaintiff's health has been impaired, his reputation besmirched, his land adversely affected, his goods damaged, or where he has suffered some other economic loss. There is an enormous range of such harmful occurrences, and it is the function of the law of tort to determine when the victim ought to be able to shift on to the shoulders of another the harm to which he has been exposed.

In its early stages the law of tort normally comprises several concurrent types of liability, imposed in situations where a defined tangible interest has been invaded by specified physical conduct. Thus in Roman law the most important types of such tort liability arose from *injuria, furtum,* and the *lex Aquilia*. *Injuria* was an offence to another's person or personality; in preclassical Rome the prime instances were murder, assault, and forcible housebreaking, but *injuria* came to include all outrages against a man's honour. *Furtum* at first covered only theft proper, but it was later much extended and became a comprehensive tort to property; the scholars of the *Gemeines Recht* were following the Romans when they included embezzlement, the unjustified use of another person's property, and even the conscious acceptance of something not due and the destruction of a document of indebtedness. Most interesting of all is the development of liability under the *lex Aquilia*; as we shall see, it bears a most striking resemblance to the development of the English tort of trespass.

At the outset the *lex Aquilia* only imposed liability on those who killed someone else's slave or farm animal or damaged someone else's property by 'urere, frangere, rumpere'. The act had to be done 'injuria'; originally this required consciousness of the doing of the harm, that is, a deliberate act, but even in the pre-classical period the lawyers started to treat mere *culpa* as sufficient, and the *lex Aquilia* gradually came to embrace negligent homicide and property damage. The harm had originally to be caused by a positive act which damaged the property by direct corporeal means, but this requirement was also relaxed and in the late classical period *actiones utiles* and *actiones in factum* were granted where the harm to person or property was only an indirect consequence; for example, liability was imposed not only for setting fire to a ship but also for damaging it more cunningly by cutting the hawser (see ULPIAN, D. 9, 2, 29, 5 and on the whole matter KASER, *Das römische Privatrecht* I (1955) §§41, 118 II, 142 ff.; ZIMMERMANN, *The Law of Obligations* (1990) 975 ff.).

Roman lawyers, however, never arrived at the general principle that everyone is responsible for the harm he is to blame for causing. This principle had to wait until the seventeenth and eighteenth centuries for its promulgation by the great natural lawyers, especially GROTIUS and DOMAT. Thereafter it made its way into many of the codes of Europe.

II

The law of tort in *Germany* before the BGB came into force presented a very variegated picture. The *Gemeines Recht* was still based on the traditional types of liability inherited from Rome. Efforts had been made to adapt them to the needs of the time, and the coverage of the *lex Aquilia* in particular had been greatly extended. The requirement of damage to some physical thing was not, however, abandoned, and purely economic harm was compensable only under the *actio doli,* which required proof of deliberate wrongdoing on the part of the defendant. When it was suggested that at least *gross* negligence should generally lead to tort liability, JHERING objected:

'Just think what it would lead to if everyone could be sued in tort for gross negligence as well as fraud! Anything and everything—an unwitting utterance, carrying a tale, making a false report, giving bad advice, speaking an unconsidered judgment, recommending an undeserving serving-maid one used to employ, answering a traveller's question about the way or the time or whatever—all this, if grossly negligent, would make one liable for the harm it caused even if one was in perfect good faith; if the actio de dolo were so extended, it would become the veritable scourge of social and commercial intercourse, conversation would be gravely inhibited, and the most innocent language would become a snare' (*JherJb.* 4 (1861) 12 f.; see also Oberappellationsgericht Lübeck, 13 Oct. 1838. SeuffA 8 no. 137).

Elsewhere in Germany legislators, influenced by the idea of a purely rational law, had broken with the traditional special types of liability, and had adopted a general clause of liability in tort. We shall soon be discussing the famous example in the French Code civil which was in force in Baden and West of the Rhine. The Prussian General Land Law also laid down in §§1 ff. I 6 that 'a person who injures another intentionally or by gross negligence must pay full compensation to that other', while 'the person who injures . . . another by only moderate carelessness', need only pay for 'the palpable harm caused thereby'; according to §8 I 6 'injury' (*Beleidigung*) means the unlawful causing of harm, and 'harm' according to §1 I 6 means 'every impairment of a man's condition with regard to his body, his freedom, his honour or his wealth'. The Austrian ABGB also has a general clause: 'Everyone is entitled to demand compensation for harm from the person who causes it by his fault, whether the harm arises from breach of a contractual duty or quite apart from any contract' (§1295).

The men behind the German BGB were much tempted to follow the great model of the Code civil and to include a general clause which would impose liability in damages whenever harm was unlawfully and culpably caused. The first draftsmen believed that it would be impossible to secure sufficient protection against unlawful acts by attaching liability to particular types of tortious behaviour, since they might not cover all proper cases. After discussion a compromise solution was arrived at which avoided the casuistry of the special types of tort recognized by the *Gemeines Recht* yet stopped short of taking the crucial step to the great general clause. Such a general clause, it was felt, would simply conceal the difficulties; it would empower the judge to resolve them, and this would be inconsistent with the current German view of the judicial function. It was also feared that unless the statute laid down fixed standards the German courts might 'produce outgrowths such as one finds in many French decisions' (Protokolle II, p. 571). As a result, the BGB has no general rule covering liability for harm caused by unlawful acts. Instead, it lays down three heads of tortious liability in the two paragraphs of §823 BGB and in §826 BGB.

1. Under §823 *par.* 1 *BGB* liability for causing injury in an unlawful and culpable manner only arises if the injury affects the victim in one of the legal interests enumerated in the text; these legal interests are life, body, health, freedom, ownership and any 'other right'.

The requirement of *unlawfulness*, according to most writers, is satisfied by any invasion of one of the legal interests specified in §823 par. 1 BGB which is not justified by any of the few special privileges such as self-defence, necessity, and so on. The requirement of *culpability* or fault is satisfied if the harmful conduct is either intentional, that is, accompanied by the intention of invading the protected legal interest, or negligent. Negligence connotes a want of that degree of care which is generally regarded as necessary in society (§276 BGB); for this purpose one must consider how a conscientious and considerate man would have behaved in the same situation. If the harm was caused in the course of some specialist activity, the courts ask whether the defendant showed the degree of care to be looked for in the average member of the specialist group in question, professional or not.

In the last few years there has been some dispute among German lawyers concerning the meaning and scope of the concepts of 'unlawfulness' and 'culpability'. According to one modern view, harmful behaviour should only be qualified as 'unlawful' if it is discountenanced by law as contravening some legal prohibition or command addressed to the citizen. On this view, behaviour does not become unlawful under §823 par. 1 BGB simply because it causes an infringment of one of the legal interests there specified; it is unlawful only if the person causing the harm behaved either deliberately or without the care generally required in society. This leaves the futher question when behaviour which is unlawful in this sense is also *culpable*. Here the new doctrine simply asks whether the defendant, on the ground of his minority (§§827, 828 BGB), was unable to realize that his conduct was unlawful and that he might have to answer for the resulting damages, or whether the defendant's culpability was excluded by such individual factors as his inability to appreciate the objective circumstances which rendered the situation dangerous. There are still many points of dissension between the adherents of this new doctrine, but in fact these borderline disputes are not of much practical significance; given that a person who causes harm despite observing all the requisite precautions is not liable, it is normally quite immaterial whether his non-liability is attributed to want of *unlawfulness* or want of *culpability*.

Then it must be shown that the culpably unlawful behaviour caused harm to one of the legal interests specified in §823 par. 1 BGB. According to the terms of this section, these include, in particular, the integrity of the citizen's person and property. The right of property is infringed not only when a thing is damaged or destroyed, but also when it is taken away from the owner without his consent or he is deprived of its use or obstructed in using it. Thus it is an infringement of another's ownership to park one's car in his garage, or subject his land to undue smoke or alter the programming of his computer or disrupt his files (BGHZ 76, 216).

The plaintiff's ownership was infringed when its vessel was immobilized for eight months in a canal which the defendant had negligently blocked (BGHZ 55, 153). Indeed the Bundesgerichtshof has gone so far as to hold that the maker or seller of a thing which is defective is liable under §823(1) BGB if the defect results in the destruction of the *thing itself* (BGHZ 67, 359 and BGH NJW 1978, 2241: suit against seller; BGHZ 86, 256 and BGH NJW 1992, 1678: suit against manufacturer). This extension has been much criticized (see KÖTZ, *Deliktsrecht* (6th edn., 1994) mn 63 ff. with further references). The question has been much ventilated elsewhere, and both the House of Lords and the Supreme Court of the United States have reached the opposite conclusion (*Murphy* v. *Brentwood DC* [1990] 2 All ER 908, 921, 926 ff., 932 f.; *East River Steamship Corp.* v. *Transamerica Delaval Inc.* 106 S.Ct. 2295 (1986)). See the detailed study by BUNGERT, 'Compensating Harm to the Defective Product Itself: A Comparative Analysis of American and German Products Liability Law', 66 *Tul. L. Rev.* 1179 (1992).

§823(1) BGB also affords protection to 'other rights'. These include all the interests which the legal order protects *erga omnes*—real rights such as servitudes and rent charges, the possessory right to acquire a thing such as is enjoyed by a conditional buyer, the right to a name, patent rights, and other industrial property rights regulated in special statutes. One's estate as a whole is, however, not an 'other right' in the sense of §823 par. 1 BGB. Economic loss can be compensated under §823 par. 1 BGB only if it flows from an injury to one of the legal interests specified in that provision: a person who suffers personal injury and damage to his car in a traffic accident can claim damages for all the economic loss consequent on the personal injury, such as medical expenses, or on the property damage, such as the cost of hiring a substitute car, but if culpable behaviour causes the victim only 'pure' economic harm unconnected with any personal injury or damage to his property or the invasion of any 'other right', no claim arises under §823 par. 1 BGB.

If an excavator at work on a piece of land culpably damages a power cable with the result of cutting off the power to a factory some way away, his liability to the factory under §823 par. 1 BGB depends essentially on the nature of the harm caused by the interruption of the power supply. If all that happens is that the machines are brought to a halt and that the output is diminished the owner of the factory cannot claim damages since the carelessness of the excavator has only caused him an economic loss (see BGHZ 29, 65, and BGH NJW 1977, 2208), but if the power interruption causes the incubators in a poultry farm to cool off, the spoiling of the eggs is an injury to property and the excavator must pay not only the value of the eggs but also all other economic loss which the poultry farm suffers in consequence of their being spoilt (see BGHZ 41, 123). The Oberster Gerichtshof in Austria decides likewise (see OGH 6 Sept. 1972, *JBl* 1973, 579; 18 June 1975, *JBl* 1976, 210). The Swiss Bundesgericht, on the other hand, holds that economic harm due to the stoppage of the business is compensable, emphasizing that negligently to interrupt a power cable operated by a public utility is a punishable offence under art. 239 of the Swiss Criminal Code (BGE 101 Ib 252, 102 II 85). See also BÜRGE, *JBl* 1981, 57, and below Ch. 40 V.

The person whose unlawful and culpable behaviour infringes one of the legal interests listed in §823 par. 1 BGB must pay for all the harm which the victim suffers in consequence of the invasion. The only limit to the extent of the harm for which compensation must be paid is that there be a legally relevant causal connection between the behaviour which renders the defendant liable and the consequential harm. The Reichsgericht laid down that such a causal connection exists whenever the conduct of the defendant was such that 'it was apt to lead to the result which occurred, taking things as they normally happen and ignoring very peculiar and improbable situations which men of the world would not take into account' (the doctrine of 'adequate causal connection'; for example, see RGZ 158, 38; 170, 136). The courts of Austria and Switzerland take the same view.

This formula has been used, for example, to support a decision that the party responsible for personal injuries is also liable for their aggravation by faulty medical treatment, at any rate if the doctor's mistake was a medical error which might be expected by those in the know, and not a flagrant breach of basic and elementary rules of the art (RGZ 102, 230; RGJW 1937, 990). Similarly a defendant is liable if his victim dies in a flu epidemic which breaks out in the hospital to which he is taken (RGZ 105, 264). By contrast a defendant responsible for causing the plaintiff to lose a leg was not liable for his inability eight years later to hurry to his air-raid shelter when there was a sudden burst of artillery fire (BGH NJW 1952, 1010), although liability was imposed on a defendant responsible for an accident which caused the plaintiff to have an artificial leg when, twenty two years later, the victim, still unsteady on his feet, fell in his his room and and hurt himself again (RGZ 119, 204). Medical conditions triggered off by an accident to an unusually susceptible victim are always 'adequately' caused (RGZ 155, 37; 169, 117; but see also BGE 66 II 165, where it is said that the risk of extreme susceptibility to harm may be allocated in part to the victim under art. 43 and 44 OR).

Recent court decisions in Germany show an increasing appreciation of the fact that questions of causation in law cannot be answered by applying purely logical and abstract standards but depend essentially on a value-judgment (see BGHZ 3, 261, 267; 18, 286, 288). This is connected with the acceptance not only by many writers but also by the courts of a teleological theory propounded by RABEL, according to which one must take account of the protective function of the rule which imposes the duty to make compensation: if a person causes harm by neglecting a particular rule of conduct, he should pay for such consequences as it was the meaning and purpose of the rule of conduct infringed to guard against.

See v. CAEMMERER, *Das Problem des Kausalzusammenhangs im Privatrecht* (1956); and STOLL, *Kausalzusammenhang und Normzweck im Deliktsrecht* (1968).—The Bundesgerichtshof applied this doctrine in its decision that a person who was to blame for a traffic accident, while bound to pay the victim's medical expenses, was not bound to pay the legal expenses he incurred in retaining an attorney to defend him, and defend him successfully, in the ensuing criminal proceedings: 'the risk of being involved in criminal proceedings and incurring the expense of one's defence therein is a risk to which everyone is exposed; it does not figure among the dangers which the law seeks to guard against by bringing the integrity of health and property under the protection of §823 par. 1 BGB' (BGHZ 27, 137, 141 f.). See also BGHZ 58, 162: a person who negligently causes an accident on the Autobahn is not liable for the damage done by impatient motorists who drive over the grass verges and cycle paths in order to get past the obstruction.

2. Liability under §823 *par. 2 BGB* arises when a 'statute designed to protect another' is culpably contravened. Protective statutes in this sense include all the rules of private and public law, especially criminal law, which are substantially designed to protect an individual or a group of individuals rather than the public as a whole. Here too it is of some importance what form the harm takes, whether injury to health, damage to property, or merely economic harm, for harm is only compensable if it results from the very danger which it was the purpose of the protective statute to diminish or eliminate. If the protective statute is directed to the prevention of personal injury and property damage only, a claim for the compensation of pure economic loss based on §823 par. 2 BGB will fail.

For example, the federal railways, after being held strictly liable to the victim of an accident under the Imperial Law of Liability (*Reichshaftpflichtgesetz*), could not claim damages for its expenses from the person responsible for the accident on the ground that he was guilty of a breach of §315 Criminal Code (negligent imperilling of rail traffic) and that he was therefore liable to them under §823 par. 2 BGB. §315 Criminal Code is certainly a protective statute, but its purpose is only to afford protection against personal injury and property damage, not to safeguard the general resources of the railways (BGHZ 19, 114, 125 f.; see also BGHZ 39, 367).—But if a director of a limited company culpably fails to start liquidation proceedings when the company becomes insolvent and so commits an offence under §64 GmbHG (Companies Act), the corporate creditors who thereby suffer economic loss can claim damages from the director personally under §823 par. 2 BGB in connection with §64 GmbHG: the very purpose of §64 of the Companies Act is to guard against this type of harm suffered by creditors as a result of delay in bringing the liquidation proceedings (see BGHZ 29, 100).

3. The third head of general tort liability in the BGB is §826. A person is liable under this section if he 'intentionally causes harm to another in a manner which offends *contra bonos mores*'. The courts have used this provision to impose liability in a whole range of types of case where one party has caused harm to another by behaviour so offensive and improper as to incur strong disapprobation from the average person in the relevant section of society. It is not necessary to show that the defendant actually intended to cause the harm; it is enough if he was conscious of the possibility that harm might occur and acquiesced in its doing so. Liability is thus incurred by a person who knowingly persuades a vendor of goods already sold but not delivered to make them over to him, or by a partner who goes behind another partner's back and indulges in private transactions of a type reserved for the partnership, or by a person who markets goods which are a 'servile imitation' of another person's unprotected wares, knowing that the public may well be deceived about their provenance, or by an employer who lures away the employee of another knowing and accepting that this will cause harm, or by a person who recklessly gives false information about the creditworthiness of another party, conscious that the person seeking information could suffer harm thereby.

A person who acts *contra bonos mores* 'for purposes of competition in business' incurs liability under the general clause of §1 of the Law of Unfair competition (UWG). Many special instances of unfair competition are dealt with in detail elsewhere in this statute.

4. Not long after the BGB came into force it became clear that the three heads of tortious liability just enumerated leave considerable areas uncovered. One gap was in the protection afforded to rights of personality. Other statutes apart from the BGB admittedly have provisions which cover tortious invasions of particular aspects of one's personality, such as one's name or the right to one's picture or one's rights as artistic creator, and it was often possible to grant the victim a claim under §823 par. 2 BGB on the ground that the texts which make it an offence to insult or defame people are protective statutes. Furthermore §826 BGB could be applied if the defendant's behaviour was outrageous and it could be shown that he intended to produce the harm. But these grounds of liability sometimes proved inadequate and sometimes they forced the courts into very strained reasoning.

In 1954, therefore, the Bundesgerichtshof for the first time handed down a judgment which recognized as an 'other right' under §823 par. 1 BGB a person's right to his personality: as we shall see later (below Ch. 43), this makes it easy to deploy the law of tort against conduct injurious to the dignity of the human being such as the unauthorized publication of the details of a person's private life.

Experience has also shown that the three heads of liability in tort often do not give sufficient protection in respect of *pure economic harm* negligently caused. Modern conditions require that some economic interests be protected against merely negligent invasion, or, to put it the other way round, there are now certain situations where it seems fair to impose on the citizen special duties to take care to avoid causing mere financial injury. One legal technique to meet this new need is for the courts to recognize, as the Reichsgericht did in the first instance, a so-called 'right to an established and operative business' and rank it as an 'other right' in the sense of §823 par. 1 BGB. Whenever it is necessary on legal or practical grounds to impose liability on a person who has culpably injured interests worth protection, the defendant's behaviour has been treated as an invasion of that 'right to an established and operative business' and liability has been imposed if he was at fault. The need was first felt in cases where the defendant had caused the plaintiff to stop some productive activity by claiming that he himself had an exclusive patent, licence, or other right. If it subsequently transpired that the defendant had no such right, he was held liable for the economic loss he had thereby caused even if he had made his claim without knowledge of its baselessness, provided he had acted unreasonably after inadequate investigation (RGZ 58, 24; 94, 248; 141, 336).

Since then it has been held that there is an invasion of the 'right in an established and operative business' only when the defendant's conduct is 'business orientated' and 'directed at the business as such' rather than merely affecting 'rights or interests separable from the business' (BGHZ 29, 65). Thus a firm has no claim for its loss if it is unable to perform a contract on time because one of its essential staff is in hospital with injuries caused by the defendant's bad driving. Nor is there an invasion of the 'right in an established and operative business' when production is halted owing to an interruption of current caused by the defendant's negligence, or when the defendant carelessly lets his ship founder at the entrance to a harbour so that the plaintiff's vessel cannot get in or incurs harbour dues because it cannot get out. On the other hand, it does constitute an attack 'on the firm as such' for the defendant to publish harmful observations about it, and he may be enjoined or made liable in damages. Such cases arise if a periodical is blackguarded by a competitor as a 'religious rag' and a 'trap for fools' (BGHZ 45, 296), or when products are falsely depreciated in a consumer magazine (BGHZ 65, 325) or 'trashed' on television (BGH NJW 1987, 2746), or when a newspaper calls on the tenants of a housing association collectively to stop paying rent (BGH NJW 1985, 1620). In deciding whether there has been an invasion of the 'right to an established and operative business' in such cases, a balance must be struck between the protected business activity of the plaintiff and the equally protected freedom of expression on important economic issues, including matters of interest to consumers, which should be freely and openly discussed.

III

The *Common Law* of torts started out by having specific types of liability just like Roman law, but whereas on the Continent legal scholars ironed out the old distinctions between the several delicts to the point where a general principle of delictual liability became not only a possibility but an actuality in most legal systems, Anglo-American lawyers have largely adhered to the separate types of case and separate torts which developed under the writ system. Since the great reforms of 1875 English plaintiffs are no longer penalized for not mentioning the right tort in their statement of claim, but Anglo-American lawyers, judges and attorneys alike, still habitually and automatically tend to classify the case before them as falling within one of the traditional types of tort and to ask whether it satisfies the requirements of, say, conversion, nuisance, defamation, negligence, deceit, or the rule in *Rylands* v. *Fletcher*. Each of these separate torts is regarded as independent, each has its own constituent elements and its appropriate defences, and each protects a particular interest of the citizen against a specified form of invasion. As late as the end of the nineteenth century the question was raised in England and the United States whether in view of the number of independent causes of action in tort it made any sense at all to have a course of lectures or write a book on the 'Law of Torts'. When the first important book on the law of torts appeared in 1860, ADDISON's *Wrongs and Their Remedies, being a Treatise on the Law of Torts*, it elicited from O. W. HOLMES, who was reviewing it, the remark that 'Torts is not a proper subject for a law book' (5 *Am. L. Rev.* 340 (1871)). But only ten years later HOLMES himself wrote a masterly chapter on the law of tort in his famous book *The Common Law* and thereby did more than anyone else to disclose the common roots and lines of development in this area of law.

One of the oldest tort claims in the Common Law is trespass. The writ of trespass originally led to a penalty as well as to compensatory damages and was issued wherever a person forcibly and in breach of the peace—*vi et armis contra pacem domini regis*—invaded another's quiet possession of land or moveables (trespass to land or to chattels) or affected his physical integrity (trespass to the person). Just like the *actio legis Aquiliae*, trespass required a direct attack on the person or thing against the will of the plaintiff. If the harm to the plaintiff occurred only as the indirect result of the defendant's conduct or, even directly, from an omission to act, the trespass claim was unavailable; by contrast very little attention was paid in earlier times to the question whether the defendant's behaviour must have been deliberate or negligent. During the fourteenth century an action of trespass on the case, later called simply 'action on the case', was introduced to cover areas where trespass did not apply, where the plaintiff's injury was an indirect consequence of the defendant's conduct, positive or negative. The distinction was clearly drawn by BLACKSTONE J. in *Scott* v. *Shepherd*, (1773) 96 Eng. Rep. 525. 'If I throw a log of timber into the highway (which is an unlawful act) and another man tumbles over it and is hurt, an action on the case only lies, it being a consequential damage; but if in throwing it I hit another man, he may bring trespass because it is an immediate wrong.'.

The distinction between causing harm intentionally and negligently was not clearly made in the Common Law to begin with. In the example just given, provided that the log hit the plaintiff during its flight, the trespass claim lay whether the defendant intended to cause the harm or merely acted negligently in throwing the log into the highway. As time went on, however, the trespass claim was gradually limited to cases of intentional harm, and today intentional conduct is required for those specific torts which developed out of the writ of trespass to the person, namely *assault* (the direct threat of immediate corporeal contact), *battery* (personal injury), and *false imprisonment*. The same is true for trespass to land, the unauthorized entry on premises occupied by another.

Liability in trespass is incurred by a person who enters the land of another without his consent, whether on, above or below the surface, or causes anyone else or any thing (for example rocks, refuse, water) to do so. Liability in damages only arises if the act which constitutes or causes the invasion is intentional, though the defendant need not have known that the land in question belonged to another. If a person conducts activities on his own land which unintentionally lead to damage on a neighbouring property, the modern view is that trespass only lies if he was negligent in causing the damage. For example, if bricks fall on to the plaintiff's land or harmful vibrations are caused by the defendant's explosions, the defendant is not liable in trespass if he observed the requisite precautions, though he is generally liable regardless of fault, at least in the United States, on the principle of *Rylands* v. *Fletcher* (on this see below Ch. 42 IV). If smoke, vapours, smells, and so on unduly affect a person's land, the person causing them is liable, again regardless of fault, in the tort of *nuisance*, whose pedigree is as long as that of trespass. The distinction between liability in trespass to land, nuisance, and *Rylands* v. *Fletcher* is extremely fine and varies from jurisdiction to jurisdiction within the Common Law.

Much the same is true of the tort remedies which protect a person's *moveableproperty* against improper invasions of his rights. Here the Common Law offers three torts which partially overlap: trespass to chattels, detinue, and conversion. Conversion, the most important of these in practice, is applicable when the defendant has done something in relation to the plaintiff's moveable property which is inconsistent with the plaintiff's ownership. The thief who takes the thing away from the owner is liable in conversion, but so also is a person who consumes the goods of others or destroys or alters them or who sells or pledges them with a third party.

In certain circumstances, indeed, liability in conversion may be incurred by a defendant when the thing is taken away from him against his will by a third party. In one case the plaintiff let a motor car on hire-purchase and the hire-purchaser lent it to the defendant. The defendant used the car for smuggling and the car was confiscated by customs officers. The plaintiff withdrew from the hire-purchase transaction for non-payment of instalments, sued the defendant for conversion of the vehicle, and succeeded. It was true that the defendant had not himself disposed of the vehicle, but he had so used it that its confiscation was the 'natural and probable consequence of his acts' (*Moorgate Mercantile Co.* v. *Finch and Read*, [1962] 2 QB 701).

The sole requirement for liability in conversion is that the defendant should consciously and intentionally have dealt with the goods. The defendant need not have been at fault: he will be liable in damages even if he believed in good faith that the thing he consumed or used was his own or reasonably thought he was entitled to consume or use it. Thus the tort of conversion covers an area which in German law is uneasily divided between three fields of law: unjustified enrichment, the law relating to the relationship between owner and possessor, and the law of tort based on culpable interference with property.

So far we have been dealing mainly with torts which generally involve an intentional interference with the integrity of person and property and which normally appear in books under the heading 'Intentional Interference with Persons or Property'. But the Common Law has a number of other torts which give protection against *economic loss* intentionally caused. These torts correspond to some of the types of case in Germany where liability is imposed under §826 BGB for causing harm intentionally and immorally. A person who knowingly deceives another by means of a false statement of fact is liable for *fraud* or *deceit* and must pay for the consequent harm (*Derry* v. *Peek*, (1889) 14 App. Cas. 377). A person who knowingly induces another to break a contract with the plaintiff is liable to the plaintiff for the tort of *inducing breach of contract* (see *Lumley* v. *Gye*, (1853) 118 Eng. Rep. 749). A person is liable for *passing off*, in the absence of any special statute regarding trade-marks, design patterns, and so on, if he sells goods so like those of another manufacturer in name, construction, or packaging that consumers cannot easily distinguish their origins. If a person in bad faith makes false, but not necessarily defamatory or offensive, statements about the plaintiff which cause him harm in his trade or profession, the plaintiff may recover for this economic loss by the tort of *malicious falsehood*. If two or more people agree to restrain trade by an improper boycott or an impermissible inhibition of competition, they are liable to the injured third party in the tort of *conspiracy*. If a person threatens another with violence or other serious harm so as to cause that person to harm a third party, the third party may sue for *intimidation*, supposing he can satisfy the other requirements laid down by a series of cases.

This tort occurs most frequently in labour law, where there is an improper threat of a strike. In *Rookes* v. *Barnard*, [1964] AC 1129, the defendant trade unionists threatened their employer with a strike unless he forthwith gave notice to an employee who had just left the union after repeated disputes. The employer yielded to this threat and the employee who had lost his job brought a direct claim for intimidation against the trade unionists for compensation for the loss caused to him by his dismissal. The House of Lords allowed the claim on appeal.

Other important Common Law torts are concerned with the protection of honour, professional reputation, and privacy against attack. We shall deal with these, and also with cases of strict liability, below (see Ch. 42).

In order to complete our survey of the Anglo-American law of tort, we must now turn to the tort which is the most important in practice, namely *negligence*.

Negligence as a tort, like many other torts in the modern Common Law, developed out of the action of trespass on the case and was not recognized as an independent ground of tortious liability until the nineteenth century. The external stimulus for this development was the great growth in the use of machinery in industry and transport and the large increase in accidents which this led to. Such accidents were normally not caused intentionally, and their proliferation brought people to see that their typical feature was the reprehensible neglect of the requisite care and that *this* fact was the real ground for holding the defendant liable. This line of thought was decisively advanced by the fact that the principle of 'no liability without fault' answered the extreme liberalism of the time and served the interests of early entrepreneurial capitalism; this became the key idea of the law of tort and its appropriate legal form was the tort of negligence which now became more and more independent. Trespass itself quite soon came under the influence of the doctrine of fault for the first time. Even here the plaintiff who could not show that the invasion was intentional was gradually required to prove that the defendant had omitted to take the requisite care.

'Negligence' literally means absence of care, neglect, or inattention. The word 'negligence' is used in this general sense to describe careless conduct in all manner of different contexts throughout the law of tort, but the use of 'negligence' to denote the tort of that name must be sharply distinguished.

Here the word acquires a quite precise technical meaning as a shorthand description for the conditions under which a person can be made liable for harm he did not intend to cause. The first of these conditions is that the defendant should have been under a *duty of care* owed to the group of persons of which the victim was one. In addition the defendant must have been in *breach* of this duty of care. Finally, in order to be imputable to the defendant, the *damage* (or *injury*) for which compensation is claimed must be a reasonably relevant consequence of his careless behaviour. The three most important requirements for negligence liability are thus *duty, breach*, and *damage* (or *injury*): 'In order to support an action for damages for negligence the complainant has to show that he has been injured by the breach of a duty owed to him in the circumstances by the defendant to take reasonable care to avoid such injury' (*Donoghue* v. *Stevenson*, [1932] AC 562, 579, *per* LORD ATKIN).

We may give a simple example. If a driver runs into a pedestrian and injures him, his liability, which in the Common Law still rests on the tort of negligence rather than on any special strict statutory liability, depends first of all on whether the driver was under any *duty of care* towards the victim. In this case there is no doubt that this requirement is satisfied: every driver owes a duty to all other persons on the highway to drive his vehicle with care so as to avoid causing them personal injury. Then the victim must prove that the driver was in *breach* of his duty of care, that is, that he did not behave as a 'reasonable man of ordinary prudence' would have done in the situation to avoid the impending harm. Finally, the harm of which the victim complains must be a proper consequence of the breach of the duty of care. Such a causal connection undoubtedly exists if the car collides with the pedestrian and breaks his leg, but it is more doubtful whether the pedestrian could recover for any aggravation of his injuries through the error of a doctor or its prolongation through some additional infection contracted at the hospital or if, while he was hobbling around on crutches as a convalescent, he fell over again and broke the other leg. The question for the Common Law here is whether the careless behaviour is still to be seen as a 'proximate cause' of the harm or whether the harm for which compensation is claimed is not too distant or 'too remote' a consequence to be imputed to the defendant. One of the most disputed questions in the Anglo-American law of tort is what criterion to apply here and the Privy Council sought to give the English answer in the leading case of *Overseas Tankship (U.K.) Ltd.* v. *Morts Dock & Engineering Co. (The Wagon Mound)*, [1961] AC 388.

The defendant's tanker (*The Wagon Mound*) was being refuelled in Sydney Harbour when a large quantity of oil was spilt into the harbour by the carelessness of the defendant's employees. The oil spread over the surface of the water until it reached the plaintiff's wharf about 600 yards away. The plaintiff took advice and learnt that in normal circumstances fuel oil floating on water could not be ignited, so he continued repairing a ship tied up to his wharf. During these operations molten metal occasionally fell into the water, and two days later a couple of drops unfortunately fell on a rag or a piece of waste floating on the water and set it alight. This acted as a kind of wick in the oil and started a conflagration which caused very extensive damage to the ship and the wharf. The question was whether the defendant was responsible for this harm. Theretofore the Court of Appeal decision *In re Polemis and Furness Withy & Co.*, [1921] 3 KB 560 had been authority for the rule that a careless defendant was answerable for all 'direct' harm, even if it was not foreseeable, but in *The Wagon Mound* this rule was abandoned. It was laid down that a defendant was liable for all harm 'of such a kind as the reasonable man should have foreseen'. Here it could reasonably have been foreseen that the plaintiff's wharf might be *fouled* by the fuel oil, but not that it might be *set alight*.

In the United States there is no single approach to this question. The courts use many different phrases to describe the consequential harm for which the defendant must pay: it must be the 'direct', the 'foreseeable' or the 'natural and probable' consequence of the defendant's careless conduct. Subtle technical distinctions and general theories have not been adopted in the United States, since most people there have the sceptical view that phrases such as 'proximate cause' or 'remoteness of damage' simply conceal the fact that in determining whether a particular harmful consequence should or should not be attributed to the defendant in the case there is a constant battle between the various 'policies' of purposiveness, equity, legal certainty, and social justice. See the observation of JUDGE ANDREWS in *Palsgraf* v. *Long Island Railroad Co.*, 248 NY 339, 352, 162 NE 99, 103 (1928): 'What we do mean by the word "proximate" is that because of convenience, of public policy, of a rough sense of justice, the law arbitrarily declines to trace a series of events beyond a certain point. This is not logic. It is practical politics.'

The principle that there is liability only for 'reasonably foreseeable' consequences is not easy to reconcile with the 'thin skull rule', whereby the defendant 'must take the victim as he finds him', that is, must pay for harm due to a physical or psychical condition of the victim which is quite abnormal (and therefore perhaps not foreseeable). See *Smith* v. *Leech Brain & Co.* [1961] 3 All ER 1159; to the same effect BGHZ 20, 137 and BGH NJW 1982, 168.

Of these ingredients of liability in negligence, two are perfectly familiar to German tort lawyers, namely, failure to exercise the requisite care and adequate causal connection between the careless conduct and the harmful consequence. But the further precondition of liability for causing unintentional harm in the Common Law must be stressed: not only must the defendant have been careless but his carelessness must also be in breach of a particular duty of care owed by him to the victim. Thus until well into the twentieth century the Common Law had great difficulty in making the manufacturer of defective products liable to the consumer, since it was thought that whereas a person who manufactured or repaired goods of any kind was under a duty of care towards his purchaser or customer, he owed no such duty to any third party with whom he had no contract. Such a third party, therefore, if injured by the faulty manufacturer of the goods, could not claim damages for breach of contract, since he had none with the manufacturer, or for negligence, since he was owed no duty of care. It did not do the victim any good to prove the manufacturer had been careless if he was under no duty of care: 'A man is entitled to be as negligent as he pleases towards the whole world if he owes no duty to them' (*Le Lievre* v. *Gould*, [1893] 1 QB 491, 497, *per* LORD ESHER).

There was a gradual relaxation of the severe rule that even the proven carelessness of a manufacturer did not expose him to any tort liability towards third parties who had no contract with him. It was not applied where the defective goods were inherently dangerous (poisons, explosives, firearms), and the decision of the New York Court of Appeals in *Mac-Pherson* v. *Buick Motor Co.*, 217 NY 382, 111 NE 1050 (1916) created a further important restriction of the principle. In a judgment written by CARDOZO the court accepted that even a motor car was 'dangerous' and that the manufacturer therefore owed a duty of care not only to the person who bought it from him but also to any user of the car, with the result that he was liable in damages if the user was injured by his negligence. A step forward was taken sixteen years later by the House of Lords in the celebrated decision of *Donoghue* v. *Stevenson*, [1932] AC 562. This case held that the manufacturer owes the consumer a duty of care at least when, through the intermediacy of a dealer, he delivers to the consumer goods whose freedom from defect neither the dealer nor the consumer was in any position to ascertain. The facts of the case were as follows.

The plaintiff went into a cafe with a friend who bought her a bottle of ginger-beer. When her friend refilled her glass the remains of a decomposed snail unexpectedly floated out of the bottle. The plaintiff, shocked at the sight and at the thought that she had already drunk a whole glass of this remarkable beverage, fell victim to gastritis and sued the manufacturer of the ginger-beer. At first instance the judge decided that her statement of claim disclosed a 'good cause of action' and that she should be permitted to bring evidence that the manufacturer had been at fault. The Inner House of the Court of Session vacated this judgment and rejected the plaintiff's claim, but the House of Lords restored the decision of the trial judge by a majority of three to two.

In his speech, LORD ATKIN attempted to formulate a general definition of the relationship which must exist between two persons before the law will impose on one of them a duty of care towards the other. He said:

'The liability for negligence, whether you style it such or treat it as in other systems as a species of "culpa", is no doubt based upon a general public sentiment of moral wrongdoing for which the offender must pay. But acts or omissions which any moral code would censure cannot in a practical world be treated so as to give a right to every person injured by them to demand relief. In this way rules of law arise which limit the range of complainants and the extent of their remedy. The rule that you are to love your neighbour becomes in law, you must not injure your neighbour; and the lawyer's question, Who is my neighbour? receives a restricted reply. You must take reasonable care to avoid acts or omissions which you can reasonably foresee would be likely to injure your neighbour. Who, then, in law is my neighbour? The answer seems to be—persons who are so closely and directly affected by my act that I ought reasonably to have them in contemplation as being so affected when I am directing my mind to the acts or omissions which are called in question' ([1932] AC 562, 580; see also *Grant* v. *Australian Knitting Mills*, [1936] AC 85).

There have been further developments, at least in the United States, since *Donoghue* v. *Stevenson* and *McPherson* v. *Buick Motor Co.* Those decisions still made the outcome of a negligence suit depend on the consumer's being able to prove some want of care in the manufacturer, but nowadays the manufacturer of defective goods whose defect causes harm to the consumer may be liable even if he was not at fault at all (on this see also below Ch. 42 V).

Anglo-American judges often use the terminology of 'duty of care' in many other types of case when the policy question is whether tort liability should be imposed. Suppose that someone, not himself at physical risk, witnesses a traffic accident and suffers a nervous shock, whether because he was closely involved or because a member of his family was actually or supposedly injured. The Common Law approaches the question whether the person who caused the accident must compensate the shock victim, who may well have been some distance away from the scene, by asking whether the defendant owed him a duty of care.

See the two important decisions of the House of Lords in *McLoughlin* v. *O'Brian* [1983] AC 410 and *Alcock* v. *Chief Constable* [1992] 1 AC 310. In the latter case the police stupidly allowed far too many people into a football stadium with the result that there was a mass panic in which 95 people lost their lives and over 400 were injured. Relatives of those killed or injured saw the events on television or witnessed them in the stadium itself and suffered shock in consequence, but all their claims were dismissed: the televiewers were too far from the scene and the witnesses' relationships with the primary victims were insufficiently intimate.

The so-called 'rescue cases' are also treated in a like manner. If a person negligently causes a dangerous situation, he can be sued by one who is injured in attempting a rescue: he owes a duty of care to those of whom he should reasonably foresee that they might in the circumstances feel called upon to undertake a rescue with all the risks involved. This also applies when someone is to blame for endangering *himself*: the passenger who leaps on to a moving train at the last moment may be liable to the guard who is injured in attempting to rescue him (*Harrison* v. *British Railways Board*, [1981] 3 All ER 679).

Claims for damages for negligence are almost always brought where the plaintiff has suffered *personal injury* or *property* damage. There is no general principle in the Common Law which excludes negligence liability in cases of pure *economic* harm, but here again the duty doctrine helps the courts to prevent negligence liability going overboard. This is clearly seen in the cases where a person suffers economic harm from relying on information which his informant ought to have known was false. If the information was given pursuant to a contract for reward, the informant can be held liable for breach of contract. But in many cases no contractual claim is possible, not only where no consideration was offered or promised for the requested information (see above Ch. 29 II), but also where the information was indeed paid for, and thus provided pursuant to contract, but was passed on by the recipient to a *third party*: the 'doctrine of privity' bars any contractual claim by the third party even if he relied on the information and suffered harm in consequence (see above Ch. 34 IV). Victims are thus forced back on to the law of tort, and, since there can be no claim in deceit in the absence of an intention to deceive, to the tort of negligence, which means that the informant must be shown to have owed a duty of care to the victim who relied on the information.

For a long time the courts refused to hold that any such duty existed, even when the informant knew that the third party would incur expenditure on the faith of the accuracy of his report. This rule was applied again in *Candler* v. *Crane Christmas & Co.* [1951] 2 KB 164, but its instability is indicated by the powerful dissenting opinion of LORD DENNING (ibid. at 179 ff.). Twelve years later his opinion was endorsed by the House of Lords in *Hedley Byrne & Co.* v. *Heller & Partners*, [1964] AC 465: a person who, in a business situation, gives information, advice, or an opinion, apparently based on special skill or knowledge, incurs a duty of care towards those who, as he knows or should reasonably foresee, will take specific action in reliance on the soundness of what he said. A bank which states, contrary to the fact, that its customer is solvent is liable in damages to the inquirer if it should have realized in the circumstances that he would rely on the report and extend credit to the customer. So, too, when the informant should have realized that a *third party* would rely on the information. In *Smith* v. *Eric Bush* [1990] 1 AC 831 the plaintiff applied to a building society for a secured loan to buy a house and agreed that the society should have the property surveyed by an expert at his expense. On the expert's reporting favourably, the building society told the plaintiff that the loan would be forthcoming, and the plaintiff therefore assumed that the house was worth the price and effected the purchase. When it transpired shortly afterwards that the house was in a state of collapse the plaintiff claimed damages from the negligent surveyor and succeeded: the surveyor was familiar with mortgage practices and knew or should have known that the prospective purchaser as well as the building society would rely on the accuracy of his report and proceed with the transaction in question, here the purchase of the house. These requirements were not met in *Caparo Industries* v. *Dickman* [1990] 2 AC 605 where an accountant carelessly overstated a company's financial position when making a statutory report on it under the Companies Act 1985. The plaintiff shareholder thereupon bought further shares in the company which then went bankrupt. His claim against the accountant was dismissed on the ground that the purpose of the statutory report was to enable shareholders to control the management of the company, not to provide them (let alone anyone else) with gratuitous investment advice.

Comparable misrepresentation cases abound in the German law reports. Generally the claim against the informant is brought in contract, since the fact that the advice was free is no bar to a finding that there was a contract, provided that the information was given in a business context and the parties intended to enter legal relations (see above p. 397). A claim in contract can also be brought by a *third party* who relied on the information to his detriment. Sometimes the courts have granted the third party a claim in tort under §826 BGB: an accountant who wantonly issues a false statement as to the creditworthiness of a firm is acting *contra bonos mores* and is liable to a third party if he realized and acquiesced in the risk that the statement would be transmitted to and relied on by him (see BGH NJW 1986, 180 and NJW 1987, 1758). Most decisions, however, find a contract or contract-type relationship between the informant and the third party, and apply the rules of contractual liability. In so finding they consider the same factors as are considered by the House of Lords in deciding whether or not there is a duty of care (see BGH NJW 1982, 2431; BGH NJW 1984, 355; BGH NJW 1987, 1758; and the comparative study by Lorenz, 'Das Problem der Haftung für primäre Vermögensschäden bei der Erteilung einer unrichtigen Auskunft', *Festschrift Larenz* (1973) 575; Lorenz, 'Contracts and Third Party Rights' in Markesinis (ed.), *The Gradual Convergence* (1993) 65; Köndgen, *Selbstbindung ohne Vertrag* (1981) 352 ff.; Von Bar, 'Liability for Information and Opinions Causing Pure Economic Loss to Third Parties' in Markesinis (ed.), *The Gradual Convergence* (1993) 98; Markesinis, *The German Law of Torts* (3rd edn. 1994) 286 ff.

It is a very disputed question whether a defendant is liable for causing harm which is merely economic when he is guilty not of misrepresentation but of some other form of negligent conduct. One set of cases involves a lawyer who is retained by a client to draw up or alter a will in favour of a specified third party and negligently delays or mishandles the task with the result that the third party gets nothing on the client's death.

The House of Lords held recently, by a bare majority, that the lawyer was liable: *White* v. *Jones* [1995] 2 AC 207. The same result is reached in Australia (see *Hawkins* v. *Clayton* (1988) 62 ALJR 240) and in many states of the United States: see *Biakanja* v. *Irving* 49 Cal.2d 647, 320 P.2d 16 (1958); *Lucas* v. *Hamm* 56 Cal.2d 583, 364 P.2d 685 (1961); *Guy* v. *Leiderbach* 501 Pa. 47, 459 A.2d 744 (1983); *Ogle* v. *Fiuten* 102 Ill.2d 356, 466 N.E.2d 224 (1984); *Flaherty* v. *Weinberg* 303 Md. 116, 492 A.2d 618 (1985). In many of these American decisions the claimant is regarded as a third party beneficiary of the contract, as in Germany and the Netherlands. For a comparative view see LORENZ/MARKESINIS, 'Solicitors' Liability to Third Parties', 56 *Mod. L. Rev.* 558 (1993); MARKESINIS, *The German Law of Torts* (3rd edn., 1994) 305 ff.; LORENZ, 'Anwaltshaftung wegen Untätigkeit bei der Errichtung letztwilliger Verfügungen', *JZ* 1995, 317.

A similar problem arises in cases where the defendant is sued not by the owner of the property he has negligently damaged but by someone else who has suffered merely economic loss in consequence. Typically the defendant has damaged a power cable, a bridge or a pipeline vested in a third party and the plaintiff claims compensation because his production comes to a halt for want of power, or his trains have to take a longer alternative route, or his oil has to be transported by road (see below p. 625 f.). This raises the more general question whether it is right for tort law to distinguish between 'mere economic loss' and personal injury or damage to physical property. For a period it seemed that England was going to treat all these kinds of damage in the same way. In *Anns* v. *London Borough of Merton* [1978] AC 728 a local authority granted a permit to build a house when it should have known that the foundations were far too shallow. The plaintiff bought the house and on discovering the defect claimed damages from the local authority. Although he had suffered no personal injury or damage to other property he won his suit in negligence for the cost of repair. Thirteen years later the House of Lords made an abrupt about-turn. In *Murphy* v. *Brentwood D.C.*, on very similar facts, it overruled *Anns* and held thatwhile the local authority was under a duty of care as regards damage to person and property, this was not so as to purely economic loss ([1991] (AC 398). See the full details in VON BAR, 'Negligence, Eigentumsverletzung und reiner Vermögensschaden', *RabelsZ* 56 (1992) 410; HUTCHISON/ZIMMERMANN, 'Murphy's Law, Die Ersatzfähigkeit reiner Vermögensschäden innerhalb des "negligence"-Tatbestands nach englischem Recht', *ZvglRWiss* 94 (1995) 42, both with further references. But see also the decision of the Supreme Court of Canada in *Winnipeg Condominium Corp.* v. *Bird Construction Co.* [1995] 1 SCR 85, and HOYANO in 58 *Mod. L. Rev.* 887 (1995).

IV

Almost the whole of the *French* law of delict rests on a mere five articles in the Code civil which have remained in force virtually unchanged for 195 years. The first of these texts is the famous general clause of art. 1382, which is amplified in art. 1383. These provisions are as follows. Art. 1382: 'Every act whatever of man which causes damage to another obliges him by whose fault the damage occurred to repair it.' Art. 1383: 'Everyone is responsible not only for the damage which he has caused by his own act but also for that which he causes by his negligence or imprudence.'

These propositions are based on the idea that the whole of the law of delict can be traced to a unitary fundamental principle, an idea which first appears in the works of the great natural lawyers of the seventeenth century. Believing that a legal order could be inferred from reason alone, they were brave enough to go behind the traditional specific torts and seek out and formulate a general principle of delictual liability. As early as GROTIUS's *De jure belli ac pacis libri tres* (1625) we find the following in Book II Ch. 17:

'We have said above that there are three sources of our legal claims, pact, wrong and statute. Enough has been said about contracts. Let us come now to what is due by the law of nature in consequence of a wrong. By a wrong we here mean every fault, whether of commission or of omission, which is in conflict with what men ought to do, either from their common interest or by reason of a special quality. From such a fault, if damage has been caused, by the law of nature an obligation arises, namely, that the damage should be made good.' (tr. Kelsey.)

The formulation of the texts on delict in the code civil is mainly attributable to the great French scholar JEAN DOMAT, whose influential work *Les Loix civiles dans leur ordre naturel* (1689) made a great contribution to the intellectual basis of the Code civil with its systematic exposition of Roman law, adapted to the needs of the time and spiced with French legal ideas in the light of the new doctrines of natural law. He already employed the notion of 'faute' and erected the general principle that compensation must be made not only for harm caused intentionally but also where the actor was guilty of want of care. On this basis POTHER distinguished into 'délits' and 'quasi-délits' the conduct which involved liability in damages; the former comprised conduct marked by 'dol ou malignité', and the latter included behaviour which caused harm 'sans malignité, mais par une imprudence qui n'est pas excusable'. Following on this, the Code civil places its texts on the law of delict in a special chapter entitled 'Des délits et quasi-délits', and modern French writers likewise distinguish between 'responsabilité délictuelle' and 'responsabilité quasi-délictuelle'.

A general clause in delict appears in other great codes of the Age of Enlightenment, such as the Prussian Land Law (see above p. 598) and the Austrian ABGB of 1811 (§1295), and it has proved very successful in the twentieth century as well: the Swiss OR of 1911 (art. 41), the Greek Civil Code of 1940 (art. 914), the Italian Codice civile of 1942 (art. 2043), and the Portuguese Civil Code of 1966 (art. 483) all control delictual liability by means of a general clause. These codes, however, unlike the French Code civil, also have many special provisions to deal with important collateral questions, such as the delictual liability of minors, the relevance of the victim's fault and the compensability of moral harm.

It is clear enough that if a legislator is content with the stately enactment of texts as terse as arts. 1382 f. Code civil, the courts must perform the real task of creating comprehensive rules and standards to determine the substance and limits of a tort claim so outlined. The Code civil never explains at all what is meant by 'dommage' in art. 1382: whether moral harm is included, whether only personal injury and property damage are to be compensated or mere economic loss as well, whether ricochet victims can rely on art. 1382 Code civil, these and many other questions the legislator has left to the courts. It should therefore come as no surprise to learn that the modern French law of tort is basically pure judge-made law and that its rules have often only a very tenuous connection with the text of the Code itself. Here we can only indicate the most important lines of development taken by the courts in relation to arts. 1382 f. Code civil.

The first requirement of a successful claim for damages in delict is that the victim should have suffered harm (*dommage*). From the very beginning French lawyers have taken this to include so-called 'dommage moral', that is, non-pecuniary harm including harm to human feelings, as we shall see later when we deal with the protection of personality and privacy.

Here we may point out that the French courts have gone suprisingly far in granting a personal claim for compensation to *dependants* of a person tortiously killed, for the moral harm they suffer through 'perte d'affection'. Originally the Cour de Cassation was inclined to grant such a claim only to those who were related to the decedent by blood or marriage (see Req. 2 Feb. 1931, S. 1931. I. 123), but it has since been accepted that a foster-child (Caen 4 July 1935, DH 1935, 514) a fiancée (Crim. 5 Jan. 1956, D. 1956, 216), and even the concubine of a married man (Ch. mixte 27 Feb. 1970, D. 1970, 205; Crim. 19 June 1975, D. 1975, 679, noted by TUNC; likewise the Court of Cassation in Belgium, 15 Feb. 1990, *JT* 1990, 216) may claim compensation for their grief, provided they can prove that they were very close to the decedent and seriously affected by his death. Damages for pain and suffering are also given when severe injuries rather than death result from the accident 'car les soins et les chagrins que cause l'infirmité d'un être cher ne sont pas moins réels' (Civ. 22 Oct. 1946, JCP 1946. II. 3365). The Cour de Cassation has gone a step further: the owner of a horse killed by the defendant's fault was granted damages not only for the cost of replacing it but also for the pain and suffering 'que lui causait la perte d'un animal auquel il était attaché' (Civ. 16 Jan. 1962, D. 1962, 199). On this see MAZEAUD/TUNC nos. 320 ff. and VINEY no. 266.

In French law, unlike that of England and Germany, it is immaterial whether the harm complained of by the plaintiff is physical harm to person or property or not. Indeed the very idea of 'purely economic loss' is not to be met with in judgments or books; liability under art. 1382 Code civil attaches to a person even if his negligence affects nothing but the plaintiff's future income or business prospects.

The victim of a breach of contract might therefore wish to sue in *tort* if he could thereby evade a shorter period of prescription or sidestep a contractual exemption clause. This possibility is foreclosed: French law adopts the principle of the *non-cumul des responsabilités délictuelle et contractuelle* and will not allow a claim in tort when there are contractual relations between the parties. By contrast German and English law leave it to the plaintiff to decide whether to sue in contract or in tort; see BGHZ 9, 301; BGHZ 66, 315; *Henderson* v. *Merrett Syndicates* [1994] 3 All ER 506, 523 ff. (HL). For comparative treatment see WEIR, *Int. Enc. Comp. L.* (Torts) XI Ch. 12 s. 47 ff. and SCHLECHTRIEM, *Vertragsordnung und außervertragliche Haftung* (1972).

The fact that purely economic loss is compensable under art. 1382 Code civil gives rise to considerable borderline problems, especially in cases where death or injury to one person causes loss to another. Naturally the descendants and widow may claim damages for this loss, as may all other persons who by statute were entitled to support, but while many legal systems deny a claim to any other 'indirect victim' (see §§844 f. BGB, 1327 ABGB, art. 928 Greek Civil Code), or only grant title to sue to specified groups of persons carefully identified by statute (as in the English Fatal Accidents Act 1976, s. 1), the French courts, lacking any legislative guidance, had to feel their way from allowing a claim to the brother, the foster-mother, and the illegitimate unrecognized children to the fiancée, the *de facto* spouse, and even, though here the courts vacillated a good deal, the concubine of a lawfully married decedent, provided that they can prove that they were being maintained by the decedent until the time of his death.

See the details of the cases in VINEY nos. 271 ff., and for Italian law JAGERT, *RabelsZ* 53 (1989) 723.—Swiss law has also adopted a flexible approach here. Art. 45 par. 3 OR lays down that compensation must be paid to those whose 'provider' (*Versorger*) has been killed. 'Provider' in the sense of this text is taken to mean a person who has in fact provided support for the plaintiff or who would in the normal course of events so provide it. In consequence the Swiss courts have on several occasions given damages to the fiancée of the victim on the ground that her future right to support has been lost: see BGE 44 II 66; 57 II 53; 66 II 206; 114 II 144 (the German courts decide otherwise under §§844 f. BGB and the Austrian courts under §1327 ABGB: see KG NJW 1967, 1089 and OGH 3 Oct. 1935, SZ 17 no. 132).

The French courts have gone even further and in some decisions have even recognized the deceased's employer as a 'victime par ricochet' and allowed it to claim.

Thus a football club was able to claim damages from the person who carelessly killed one of their professional players. The court found that the club's need to pay a high transfer fee for a substitute player constituted special damage (Colmar 27 April 1955, D. 1956, 723, noted by SAVATIER; the Italian courts have come to the same conclusion: Cass. 26 Jan. 1971, n. 174, Foro it. 1971 I 342 and 1285). The Court of Appeal of Lyons granted the claim of an impresario who lost takings as a result of the death of an actor (26 Jan. 1956, D. 1958, 253) but this decision was quashed (see Civ. 14 Nov. 1958, Gaz. Pal. 1959. I. 31, noted by MAZEAUD in *Rev. trim. dr. civ.* 57 (1959) 92). MARSCHALL V. BIEBERSTEIN, *Reflexschäden und Regressrechte* (1967)

39 ff. contains an extensive discussion of the question whether and how far an employer can claim compensation for the 'ricochet damage' which he suffers as the result of the death or injury caused to his employee. There is some uncertainty in the law here. In one case the plaintiff's debtor was killed in a traffic accident for which the defendant was responsible, and the plaintiff was unable to collect his debt because the heirs refused to accept the inheritance. The case went all the way to the Cour de Cassation and the plaintiff creditor's claim was ultimately dismissed, the reason given being that the causal link between the defendant's fault and the creditor's loss was insufficiently 'direct' (Civ. 21 Feb. 1979, JCP 1979.IV.145 and see DURRY, *Rev. trim. dr. civ* 77 (1979) 612; see also Civ. 12 June 1987, JCP 1987.IV.286). But when a tram company lost income because a traffic accident temporarily blocked the tramlines, it was held that the link was sufficient. See Civ. 28 April 1965, DS 1965, 777 noted by ESMEIN.

A further requirement for liability in delict under art. 1382 Code civil is that the harm must be attributable to a 'faute', that is, culpable behaviour on the part of the defendant. The Code civil offers no definition of 'faute', but writers have produced many different theories, most of which treat 'faute' as a failure to observe a precept of behaviour which the defendant should have respected. The doctrine presented by MAZEAUD/TUNC best fits the decisions of the courts. Relying on art. 1383 Code civil it distinguishes between 'faute délictuelle' and 'faute quasi-délictuelle', the former being characterized by the defendant's intention to cause the harm, while the latter is constituted 'by criticable conduct which a responsible person similarly cir- cumstanced would not have committed' (MAZEAUD/TUNC, nos. 380 ff.). Accordingly, so far as undeliberate harm is concerned, all systems agree in testing the behaviour of the defendant against that of the 'reasonable man of ordinary prudence' or the 'homme avisé' or the conduct of a person who exercises 'the care requisite in social intercourse' (§276 BGB).

French lawyers draw no clear distinction between unlawfulness and fault. Both are contained in the concept of 'faute'. If the defendant acted in self- defence or in a state of necessity, or if there were other 'faits justificatifs', to use the expression of MAZEAUD/TUNC, nos. 488 ff., or if the court finds that the boycott or strike called by the defendant was justifiable or that the defend- ant behaved just like an 'homme avisé' in the same situation, the defendant's liability is excluded for want of 'faute'; neither the French courts nor the French writers draw any subtle doctrinal distinctions or even enter the lists on the 'concept of unlawfulness' so familiar to German controversialists.

Of particular interest are those types of case where the French courts hold that the fault of the defendant lies in an 'abus d'un droit' or abuse of a right. First there are the cases where the right was exercised with the intention of doing harm.

These are mainly cases of landowners exercising their rights in an abusive manner. For example, see the famous *Clément-Bayard* case before the Cour de Cassation, where the defendant had erected on his land an enormous wooden tower topped with metal spikes in order to prevent his neighbour from using his land as an airfield for dirigibles (Req. 3 Aug. 1915, S. 1920. I. 300). See also Civ. 20 Jan. 1964, D. 1964, 518, where the defendant maliciously and capriciously grew giant ferns to darken the plaintiff's land.

But the French courts also award damages under art. 1382 Code civil where the defendant had no intention of causing harm by the exercise of his right but simply acted without the care called for in the circumstance. Most writers, too, including MAZEAUD/TUNC, accept that a person may be liable for abuse of right even if he is guilty only of a 'faute quasi-délictuelle'. Thus the courts grant a claim for damages in delict if a contractor exercises a right under the contract in a unreasonable manner and thereby causes unintended harm. There is a well-developed line of cases in labour law which grant the employee damages for 'rupture abusive du contrat' against the employer, even if the latter did not intend to cause harm but was simply guilty of 'légèreté blâmable' (see Soc. 11 May 1964, D. 1964, 520), and the same is true if a contract of partnership or agency is prematurely determined in such a way as to prejudice the other party. But even outside contract law there are cases where liability is imposed on a person for abuse of right although he had no intention of causing harm. Thus a court may hold that it was wrong in the circumstances of the case for a party to an industrial dispute to call a strike or lock-out, or that it was improper of a tradesman to boycott or blacklist a competitor. So, too, a person may be liable if he breaks off an engagement or non-marital relationship in a brutal way, or improperly abandons precontractual negotiations, an 'abus du droit de rompre la négociation'. In German law this last situation is covered by the rules of *culpa in contrahendo*. Details of the French law can be found in VINEY nos. 197 and 475.

There is one large class of case where the doctrine of 'negligent' abuse of right gets into difficulties, and this is where procedural rights in litigation are being exercised. 'Le droit d'ester en justice'—the right to bring a claim, to make an appeal, to call witnesses, to execute judgments, and to take other steps in connection with a lawsuit—may only be exercised within certain limits and the abuse of this right leads to liability under art. 1382 Code civil. There is no difficulty in the rare case where the defendant takes procedural steps simply out of malevolence towards the other party, but if a person in good faith makes an appeal from a first instance judgment which it is grossly unreasonable of him to suppose ill-founded, what is to happen? If his appeal is dismissed is he to be liable to the other party not only for the costs of the appeal, but also for any further harm he may have suffered? Here the courts are extremely cautious and only find that a person was guilty of a 'faute' in making an appeal or raising a defence if it must have been perfectly evident to the appellant or defendant that the step he was taking was bound to be futile. On the other hand, the courts have no hesitation at all in imposing liability on a person who prematurely executes a judgment which is later quashed (see, for example, Civ. 10 Jan. 1949, S. 1950. 1. 71 and MAZEAUD/ TUNC no. 591). In all these cases the claim is based on art. 1382 Code civil, but behind the façade of this general clause the different types of case clearly have a life of their own, for a finding of 'faute' results from the application of very different factual tests, designed to produce the right results in the different types of case.

The third essential precondition of delictual liability in French private law, after 'dommage' and 'faute', is a 'lien de causalité': there must be a causal link between the faulty behaviour of the defendant and the harm suffered by the plaintiff. In the French view no such link exists if the harm is traceable to a 'cause étrangère' rather than to the defendant's conduct. *Force majeure*, defined as an irresistible and unforeseeable event outside the control of the defendant, constitutes such a 'cause étrangère', as do the fault of the victim himself and behaviour of a third party which could not normally be foreseen by the defendant. If the judge finds that the *force majeure*, the fault of the victim, or the behaviour of a third party contributed to the occurrence of the harm but was not sufficiently a 'cause étrangère' to snap the causal link, he may reduce the amount of damages by an appropriate amount. So far as remoteness of harm is concerned, the French courts take the view that harm calls for compensation only if it is a direct and immediate consequence (*une suite immédiate et directe*) of the event in question. This is inferred from art. 1151 Code civil, which by its terms applies to the law of contract.

On the whole matter see MOTULSKY (above p. 596), MAZEAUD/TUNC nos. 1417 ff., and VINEY nos. 332 ff. The French courts have not produced any fixed criteria for limiting compensable consequences: 'In France, as elsewhere, it is the good sense of the judge and not the application of a precise criterion which determines whether the occurrence of the harm was so unforeseeable or extraordinary that the defendant should not be made responsible for it' (PLANIOL/RIPERT VI no. 541).

V

The chief task of the law of delict is to select out of the enormous range of daily occasions when harm is caused those where, in accordance with the sentiment of justice and equity prevailing in the society at the time, the victim should be allowed to transfer the loss to the defendant. The legal techniques which are used for this purpose seem to vary considerably. A legal system may progressively identify particular interests as worthy of protection and give them that protection against a particular kind of behaviour by setting up a special kind of tort. Such a process of developing specific torts is historically the older method everywhere, and very clear traces of this tradition may be seen in all those legal systems, such as the Common Law, where the law of tort has not been smoothed out by thorough legislative alteration. This is in stark contrast with the solemn and formal elegance of the general clause in delict in the French Code civil, which goes back to DOMAT and POTHIER. Under the influence of natural law thinking they made extrapolations from the casuistical Roman law of delict and arrived at idealistic, if somewhat literary, formulas which were enacted into law when the enlightened zeal of the French Revolution made the time ripe. The German BGB did not follow the grand model of the Code civil but took a more cautious and intermediate position. This decision also bears the mark of its time, for in nineteenth century Germany the natural law movement had been brought to a virtual halt by the influence of SAVIGNY and his Historical School of Law. Furthermore, as is well known, it was not idealists but officials, not revolutionaries but professors, who attended the birth of the BGB.

If we leave the history and attend to the practicalities of the law of tort, we quickly see that underneath the doctrinal variations the groups and types of case which appear problematical owing to the exigencies of actual life are much the same in all the legal orders under consideration, even if they are dealt with in different portions of the legal system and even, occasionally, with divergent results. This may be demonstrated in the area of harm intentionally caused in competition and industrial disputes. Here the Common Law operates with a whole series of special torts, such as fraud, malicious falsehood, conspiracy, intimidation, and so on, while German law has only the provisions of §826 BGB and §1 UWG (Law against Unfair Competition) in addition to the general rule developed by the judges concerning the 'right to an established and operative business', and French law gets by with only a single provision, namely art. 1382 Code civil. But in Continental legal systems these general clauses only take on significance when concretized in particular types of situation which are subsumed under them. To give an example, every legal system is familiar with cases where one person induces another to break his contract with a third party. Here the Common Law has the special tort of inducing breach of contract. For the German lawyer such a case falls under the general clause of §826 BGB but when he goes to the commentaries on this section he immediately looks under the key-word 'Inducement of Breach of Contract' (*Verleitung zum Vertragsbruch*) to find a careful collection of all the judicial decisions and asks whether the case before him satisfies the conditions laid down in those decisions. French lawyers and judges operate in exactly the same way.

For example, see the collection of relevant decisions in PALANDT/THOMAS, *Bürgerliches Gesetzbuch* (53rd edn., 1994) §826 mn. 52 under the heading 'Verletzung von Vertragsrechten Dritter, insbensondere Verleitung zum Vertragsbruch' (invasion of contractual rights of third parties, including inducement of breach of contract). See also MERTENS in *Münchener Kommentar* (2nd edn., 1986) §826 BGB mn. 123 ff. under the heading 'Participation in Another's Breach of Contract'; see, too, Juris-Classeur civil, arts. 1382–3 Code civil, Responsabilité du fait personnel, La faute (Applications) nos. 47–58 with the heading 'Fault of a Third Party in Relation to a Contractor', and V. PALMER, 'A Comparative Study (from a Common Law Perspective) of the French Action for Wrongful Interference with Contract', 40 *Am. J. Comp. L.* (297 (1992). It would be easy to give further examples of different systematic treatments of the same situation. Whenever a businessman suffers loss because a trade union has called a stoppage of work, the basic question is how to accommodate the right to strike with the right to conduct one's business unhindered. Different legal methods are adopted to deal with the problem, since the French lawyer asks if there was a 'faute' in the form of an abuse of right (see MAZEAUD/TUNC no. 590) while the common lawyer inquires whether the tort of conspiracy has been committed (see, for example, *Crofter Hand Woven Harris Tweed Co. Ltd.* v. *Veitch*, [1942] AC 435), and the German lawyer asks if there has been an improper invasion of the 'right to an established and operative business' (see BAGE 15, 211, 215 f.).

Nevertheless, one must not forget the difference between the Common Law's method of having specific torts and the way in which Continental legal systems deal in particular groups of case under a general clause. The common lawyer regards the specific torts as pretty independent, only tenuously and invisibly connected with each other. In Continental law it is different, for although Continental lawyers subcategorize the cases which fall under the general clauses of §826 BGB and art. 1382 Code civil, they nevertheless realize that despite the differences between these groups of cases the imposition of liability in damages ultimately depends on the same statutory text and on the fulfilment of its requirements. This remains true even if it may be intellectually difficult to reconcile a particular type of case with the general clause, as French lawyers have found with liability for undue 'troubles de voisinage' and art. 1382 Code civil. The Common Law tends to the independence of casuistry while the Continental law tends to the coherence of a system; both methods of approach doubtless have their good and their bad points. The strength of the Common Law probably resides in the careful way it weighs and works out the specific characteristics of each individual tort and of the type of case to which it is applied; this may well conduce to more appropriate solutions but there is undoubtedly a risk that if each separate tort has its own preconditions, defences, and legal consequences, the system may become unduly complex from the technical point of view.

When we come to the important area of liability for unintentional harm, even Common Law systems virtually have a general clause in the form of the tort of negligence. All legal systems agree in principle that the defendant's liability depends first of all on whether he has fallen short of the 'care requisite in social intercourse' or has behaved otherwise than a 'reasonable man' or an 'homme avisé' would have acted in the same situation. But the satisfaction of this test does not necessarily render the defendant liable, for even if it has been established that the defendant was at fault and that the victim would not have suffered the harm but for that fault, there are still many cases in which on one ground or another the liability of the defendant is brought into question or excluded. If a restaurateur keeps rat poison in an unmarked container above the stove, this is certainly negligent in view of the risk that his patrons may be poisoned. But suppose that the rat poison *explodes* through overheating, and that the restaurateur had no idea that poison could explode at all. Should he be liable for the harm caused by the explosion? (See *Larrimore* v. *American National Insurance Co.*, 184 Okla. 614, 89 P. 2d 340 (1939)). If a person carelessly causes a traffic accident, is he also to be liable for the nervous shock sustained by someone miles away from the accident? What if a child born with serious disabilities sues the doctor for carelessly failing to diagnose the condition *in utero* and inform the mother, who would have terminated the pregnancy? What is to happen if after a traffic accident a citizen is injured during the pursuit of the escaping tortfeasor or suffers harm while attempting to look after the primary victim? What if the defendant was responsible for causing the death of a third party and the death causes harm to the plaintiff, either because the decedent would have supported him, whether bound to or not, or was under contract to do something for the plaintiff which would have saved the plaintiff expense or brought him a profit? Many more such cases could be instanced. In all of them there has undoubtedly been careless behaviour on the part of the defendant, and in all of them it can also be said that the harm for which compensation is sought would not have occurred but for that behaviour. Yet these considerations do not by themselves produce any appropriate means of limiting liability for negligence. Accordingly, all legal systems have a supply of further doctrines which permit the judge to balance the interests involved in that type of case and so to decide whether compensation should be paid or not. The comparative lawyer is not surprised to find that this same process of evaluation takes place in very different systematic contexts. Whether a defendant who is responsible for injuring a person is also liable to a third party who voluntarily undertakes to rescue the victim and is himself injured in the process is a question which in England and the United States is technically answered by asking whether the defendant owed a 'duty of care' towards the rescuer; in Germany and France, on the other hand, one asks whether there is a sufficient causal connection or 'lien de causalité' between the defendant's carelessness and the rescuer's injury.

See the 'rescue cases' cited above p. 612 and RGZ 50, 219, 223; BGHZ 56, 163; Grenoble 7 Dec. 1959, D. 1960. J. 213, and the extended treatment by RIOU, *Rev. trim. dr. civ.* 55 (1957) 221.

In Germany the question of liability for nervous shock is also treated as a problem of 'adequate causal connection', while in the Common Law it is dealt with either as a problem of 'remoteness of damage' or as a 'duty' problem. Whatever doctrine is mobilized in these cases, the crucial question remains: if a person witnesses or learns of an accident and suffers shock because of his particular sensitivity, must he bear the consequent loss himself as a misfortune built into his constitution or can he shift it to the person who caused the accident? This is a matter for evaluation and judgment involving many very different factors. The difficulties are not resolved by asking whether such damage was 'outside the probabilities of life' and consequently not 'adequately caused', or whether the shock victim was one of those to whom the person responsible for the accident owed a duty of care because such harm was 'reasonably foreseeable'. As FLEMING writes (above p. 595, p. 486), 'Recognition of a duty of care is the outcome of a value judgment that the plaintiff's interest, which has been invaded, is deemed worthy of legal protection against negligent interference by conduct of the kind alleged against the defendant.' The same is true for the doctrine of causal connection. As v. CAEMMERER has emphasized, this also involves 'a wide variety of normative problems' and in fact there is 'nothing for it but to determine the range of compensable harm by setting up a typology of critical cases and so developing the meaning of the rule which imposes liability' (v. CAEMMERER, *NJW* 1956, 569, 570).

One situation where there is a particular need to limit the liability of negligent persons is where their negligence causes merely *economic harm*. The different legal systems have very different systematic and technical devices for answering this need. As we have already seen, German law in principle denies any liability in tort for purely economic harm negligently caused, unless the defendant was in breach of a relevant protective statute or it is one of those cases in which the courts have held that the 'right to an established and operative business' has been infringed. The need to limit liability for economic loss negligently caused is answered in the Common Law by the 'duty' device once again; where the defendant's behaviour has infringed the merely 'pecuniary interests' of another the courts are very reluctant to find the duty of care which is a precondition of liability in damages for negligence.

The problem is especially clear in cases in which a builder negligently breaks a cable or pipe and interrupts the supply of electricity, water, or gas. If a third party's property is damaged or destroyed, the courts in Germany grant him a claim for the consequent economic harm (see above p. 600), since § 823 par. 1 BGB protects 'ownership' against negligent damage; but if the third party's complaint is simply that his business has been brought to a standstill so that he cannot continue production but must still pay his employees, this is 'pure economic loss' and there is no liability. §823 par. 1 BGB does not apply, even in the form of an invasion of the 'right to an established and operative business', and the defendant is not liable under §823 par. 2 BGB because he is not in breach of any protective law designed to protect people from pure economic loss (BGHZ 66, 388). English courts decide likewise, sometimes

on the ground that this is outside the scope of the builder's duty of care (as in *Weller &*
Co. v. *Foot & Mouth Disease Research Institute*, [1966] 1 QB 569), sometimes on the
ground that pure economic loss is 'too remote' and therefore not compensable
(*S.C.M. Ltd.* v. *Whittall & Son Ltd.*, [1971] 1 QB 337; *Spartan Steel & Alloys Ltd.* v. *Martin*
& Co., [1973] QB 27). But English judges naturally realize that this is a question of public
policy and that the arguments should be openly canvassed rather than hidden behind
a smokescreen of legal jargon. Thus LORD DENNING in the *Spartan Steel* case said
after reviewing the cases: 'The more I think about these cases, the more difficult I find
it to put each into its proper pigeon-hole. Sometimes I say: "There was no duty". In
others I say: "The damage was too remote". So much so that I think the time has
come to discard those tests which have proved so elusive. It seems to me better to
consider the particular relationship in hand, and see whether or not, as a matter of
policy, economic loss should be recoverable, or not' (ibid. p. 37).

If one considers which party can more easily prevent the harm or insure against loss of
production due to interference with the energy supply—the user of the energy by business interruption insurance or the building contractor by liability insurance—the position of the German and English courts is quite justifiable. Cover by business
interruption insurance is suggested by the fact that the risk in question is *invariably* covered by the manufacturer's policy, since the energy supply may be interrupted by other
events, such as act of God, and the liability of the suppliers of the energy is almost
always excluded by their general terms of business. Furthermore, policies always have
a monetary limit to their cover, and it is easier for the manufacturer than for the building
contractor to say how much harm is likely to result from business interruption and so to
fix an appropriate limit. Finally, business interruption insurance operates more
smoothly, in that the liability of the insurer does not depend on the tort liability of
the insured—often quite a complex legal question—and the manufacturer seeking compensation will be dealing with 'his own' insurer rather than with a liability insurer he has
never met before. It is true that it is the builder who can, by taking care, avoid damaging
the means of supply, so he must be given an incentive to take all appropriate precautions
by making it expensive for him if he fails to do so. People tend to say nowadays that if the
tortfeasor can insure against liability so that he does not have to put his hand in his own
pocket, the threat of liability is no deterrent, but they are wrong: careful conduct still
pays dividends, for a tortfeasor with a bad claims experience may lose his no-claims
bonus and have to pay higher premiums or meet his insurer's safety requirements. This
incentive is maintained by the rule which the German and English courts have adopted,
for the builder is held liable if any property is damaged or destroyed by his negligence.

It must be admitted that the distinction between property damage and pure economic loss may seem somewhat capricious and arbitrary, and that it may not always
be easy to draw the dividing line between them. In one famous decision the High
Court of Australia ignored it (*Caltex Oil Ltd.* v. *The Dredge 'Willemstad'*, 51 AJLR
270 (1976)). Caltex, the well-known oil company, used to deliver oil by means of a
pipeline belonging to a third party. During dredging operations the defendant negligently damaged the pipeline and Caltex had to get the oil delivered by more expensive
means. Caltex sued for the extra expense and won. Note, however, that most of the
judgments turned on the fact that Caltex was the sole user of the pipeline, as the
defendant dredger-owner could have known. See also *State of Louisiana ex rel. Guste*
v. *M/V Testbank* 752 F.2d 1019 (5 Cir. 1985): the Mississippi was closed to all river

traffic for twenty days because of a spill of chemicals in a collision for which the defendant was responsible. Claims were brought by yacht marinas, bunkering stations, restaurants, hotels, suppliers of fishing materials and so on, but by a bare majority they were all dismissed. Finally, see the decision of the Supreme Court of Canada in *Norsk Pacific Steamship Co.* v. *Canadian National Railway* [1992] 1 S.C.R. 1021: the defendant's vessel carelessly damaged a state-owned bridge which the plaintiff used for its trains under government licence. During the weeks it took to repair the bridge the plaintiff had to re-route thirty trains a day to another bridge far distant, at considerable cost. The government having excluded all liability in the event of damage to the bridge, the plaintiff claimed compensation from the owner of the vessel and the claim was allowed by a bare majority of four to three. The majority opinion is well worth reading for its frank consideration of the policy arguments on both sides and its comparative survey. See MARKESINIS 109 *LQ Rev.* 5 (1993). The literature on liability in tort for mere economic loss is enormous: see FELDTHUSEN, *Economic Negligence: The Recovery of Pure Economic Loss* (2nd edn., 1989); ATIYAH, 'Economic Loss in the United States' 5 *Oxf. J. Leg. Stud.* 485 (1985); BISHOP, 'Economic Loss in Tort', 2 *Oxf. J. Leg. Stud.* 1 (1982); RABIN, 'Tort Recovery for Negligently Inflicted Economic Loss', 37 *Stan. L. Rev.* 1513 (1985); STAPLETON, 'Duty of Care and Economic Loss: A Wider Agenda', 107 *LQ Rev.* 249 (1991); HOGG, 'Negligence and Economic Loss in England, Australia, Canada and New Zealand', 43 *ICLQ* 116 (1994).

The French Civil Code makes no distinction between 'pure economic loss' and harm, physical or non-physical, to a person's health, property, or other things to which he has a right: under arts. 1382 and 1383 whoever causes 'dommage' of any kind is bound to make compensation if the manner by which he caused it renders him liable. But, as one might expect, the courts have other devices for imposing the necessary limits on liability for pure economic loss. For harm to be compensable, it must be 'certain' (and not simply 'hypothétique' or 'éventuel'), and it must be 'une suite immédiate et directe' of the defendant's conduct. The courts have a great deal of room for play here and can invoke these formulas to reject or allow claims as they think fit. The cryptic style of judgments in the Cour de Cassation makes it very difficult to discover the true grounds on which claims for damages are accepted or rejected (see Ch. 9 I). Thus in a case where the plaintiff had suffered pure economic loss as a result of the defendant builder's negligence in interrupting the supply of energy, the Cour de Cassation allowed him to recover for it as a 'conséquence directe du fait de l'entrepreneur' (Civ. 8 May 1970, Bull. civ. 1970.II.no. 160), without making any allusion to the problems which similar cases have caused to the courts in other countries. Again the Cour de Cassation has held that when a municipal bus company lost fares because its buses were delayed owing to a traffic accident due to the defendant's fault, its loss was 'ni hypothétique ni indirect' and was consequently recoverable (Civ. 28 Apr. 1965, D. 1965, 777, noted by ESMEIN). Finally the courts can reject liability for pure economic loss by refusing to qualify the defendant's behaviour as 'faute', even if by standards normally applied the negligence would be clearly established. One can find some support for this in the cases relating to the abuse of procedural rights. A person may be very unreasonable in supposing that he has a good claim; nevertheless he may safely sue without fear that if he loses the action he may have to compensate the other party for all his loss on the ground of an 'abus du droit d'ester en justice'. German and French law may appear to have adopted fundamentally opposing starting points, since the BGB by its terms is unwilling to admit tort liability for pure economic loss whereas the Code civil does so quite readily, but in both countries the practice of the courts seems to adopt an intermediate position.

41

Liability for Others

ATIYAH, *Vicarious Liability in the Law of Torts* (1967).

BARAK, 'The Nature of Vicarious Liability in English Law', *Ann. dir. comp.* 40 (1966) 1.

BYDLINSKI, 'Zur Haftung für Verrichtungsgehilfen', *ZVR* 1980, 354.

v. CAEMMERER, 'Wandlungen des Deliktsrechts', *Hundert Jahre deutsches Rechtsleben, Festschrift zum 100jährigen Bestehen des Deutschen Juristentages* II (1960) 56 ff., 115 ff.

——, 'Reformprobleme der Haftung für Verrichtungsgehilfen' *ZfRV* 14 (1973) 241.

DOUGLAS, 'Vicarious Liability and Administration of Risk', 38 *Yale LJ* 584, 720 (1929).

JAMES, 'Vicarious Liability', 28 *Tul. L. Rev.* 161 (1954).

JOLOWICZ, 'Liability for Independent Contractors in the English Common Law—A Suggestion', 9 *Stan. L. Rev.* 690 (1957).

van MAANEN, 'Vicarious Liability in a European Civil Code', in HARTKAMP et al. (eds.), *Towards a European Civil Code* (1994) 301.

SEAVEY, 'Speculations as to "Respondeat Superior"', *Harvard Legal Essays* (1934) 433.

SEILER, 'Die deliktische Gehilfenhaftung in historischer Sicht', *JZ* 1967, 530.

SMITH, 'Frolic and Detour', 23 *Colum. L. Rev.* 444, 716 (1923).

WILLIAMS, 'Liability for Independent Contractors', 1956 *Camb. LJ* 180.

——, 'Vicarious Liability and the Master's Indemnity', 20 *Mod. L. Rev.* 220, 437 (1957).

WOELLERT, 'Die außervertragliche Gehilfenhaftung im nordischen Recht', *RabelsZ* 39 (1975) 304.

I

THE idea underlying the principle of no liability without fault, as we have seen, is that only when the defendant may be charged with careless behaviour is there sufficient reason to make him bear the loss caused to the victim. This is not to say that the careless conduct need be that of the defendant *personally*: as against the victim the defendant might be responsible for the conduct of a *third party* as well, on the ground that he has used the third party's services in some activity in the course of which the third party injured the plaintiff by malice or negligence. If a person is run over by a taxi, the principle of no liability without fault entails that the consequent loss may only be shifted to the taxi-owner if he was driving the taxi carelessly or in disregard of the rules of the road. The plaintiff's legal position should perhaps not be any different if the taxi was being driven by an employee of the taxi-owner rather than by the owner himself. Even in this case one might infer from the principle of no liability without fault that the taxi-owner should not be liable unless he personally was at fault: then instead of concentrating on whether the taxi was being driven properly and in accordance with the rules of the road one would ask whether the owner could be blamed for having a driver he should have known was incompetent or for not paying enough attention to the driver's manner of driving or perhaps for not sufficiently emphasizing the importance of obeying the rules of the road. The other view would be to make the owner liable if the *driver* had been careless, regardless of any personal fault in the owner. Whether this solution is consistent with the principle of no liability without fault is an idle question, but it may be suggested that it is, since fault, though not necessarily the personal fault of the defendant, remains a precondition of liability, unlike the cases of strict liability which will be dealt with in Chapter 42.

II

In the *Germanic* legal family, the liability of a superior for the harm caused by his staff always depends on whether any *personal* fault of his contributed to the harm. This rule is attributable to the scholars of the *Gemeines Recht* who thought that the principle of no liability without fault must apply without any qualification to vicarious liability as well, and believed Roman law to support their view. They argued that to make an entrepreneur liable for the harm caused by his workers whether he was personally at fault or not would be to impose on him a liability for mere accidents, contrary to the principle of fault which was the moral basis of the law of delict: as JHERING said, 'It is not the occurrence of harm which obliges one to make compensation, but fault. This is as simple as the chemical fact that what burns is not the light but the oxygen in the air' (*Das Schuldmoment im römischen Privatrecht* (1867) 40).

It is an invention of the pandectists that there was no liability for others in Roman law unless the superior was himself at fault. In fact the Romans never considered the problem of liability for others as a whole at all; much less did they arrive at any general solution. There were many individual types of case where they made certain superiors liable, normally without reference to their personal fault, for the consequences of the faults of their inferiors, and a different policy reason for imposing such liability underlay each type of case. Certainly the principle of the *Gemeines Recht* did not apply in the most important cases of liability for others, for most of the people whose services free Romans used were slaves and members of the family, and if any of them committed a delict, the person with power over them was unconditionally and inescapably liable, subject to this, that he could avoid his obligation to pay compensation by handing over to the victim the person who injured him (*noxae datio*).

For the development of liability for others in the *Gemeines Recht*, see SEILER (above p. 629); for Roman law see KASER, *Das römische Privatrecht* I (1955) 527 ff; ZIMMER-MANN, *The Law of Obligations* (1990) 118 ff.

The view of the *Gemeines Recht* met with some opposition in the second half of the nineteenth century. It had to be restricted in the important area of industrial accidents, and also where a business activity was so dangerous as to create a specially great risk of harm. So obvious was it that a mistake on the part of an employee might cause grave damage that it would have been very shocking if the entrepreneur had been permitted to escape liability by proving that he himself was free from fault. Accordingly, the Imperial Law of Liability of 1871 imposed strict liability on railway companies and so made it unnecessary to prove fault in either the employer or his employees (see p. 653 below), and it also laid down that owners of mines, quarries, and factories should be liable although they themselves were not at fault if their *managerial* employees caused harm to third parties in the faulty execution of their tasks. It was sought to extend vicarious liability to all business employers in respect of all employees who were at fault, and a rule to this effect was endorsed by the Eighteenth Deutsche Juristentag in 1886.

Nevertheless the draftsmen of the BGB adhered to the conservative view that the head of a business should not be liable for the harm caused by his staff unless he himself was at fault. It was admitted that the contrary opin-ions had 'an element of justification in as much as they are based on the idea that a person who enjoys the benefits of an enterprise should have to make good the harm which it causes to third parties', but it was thought that this idea could best be implemented by special legislation applying it to specified types of business and imposing at the same time an obligation to insure. Otherwise the burden would possibly be too great for 'smallholdings and many branches of industry which need protection' (MUGDAN II p. 1094). The only concession made to the opponents was that §831 enacted in favour of the victim a presumption that the employer was at fault and the onus of rebutting this presumption was placed on the defendant employer. A similar rule is to be found in Swiss law (art. 55 OR).

Austrian law differs from German and Swiss law in important respects, though the rule in §1315 ABGB is not very clear. In Austria also it is the basic principle that an employer is liable only if he himself was at fault, but, contrary to the rule in §831 BGB and art. 55 OR, it is for the victim to prove this. Only when the victim can establish that the tortfeasor was 'incompetent' (*untüchtig*) is the employer liable in the absence of personal fault. In *Switzerland* art. 55 OR is drafted very much like §831 BGB. The Swiss courts, like those in Germany, as we shall see, have contrived to make it very difficult for the employer to exculpate himself. See BGE 110 II 456 and KELLER, *Haftpflicht im Privatrecht* (5th edn. 1993) i, 155 ff.—In *Sweden* and *Finland* it used to be the law that the employer was liable only when he himself was at fault (see ANDRESEN, *RabelsZ* 27 (1962/1963) 252), but the legislature in both countries has

abolished the employer's right to exculpate himself. For the details see WOELLERT
(above p. 629).

The first precondition for the liability of a head of a business under §831
BGB for harm caused by a third party is that the third party be a person
he has 'appointed to perform a function'. In the view of the German courts
a person qualifies as a servant ('Verrichtungsgehilfe') if he is subject to the
orders of his superior and works under his supervision and control. The largest class of these are salaried and wage-earning employees. If a doctor
chooses a nurse to operate his radiological apparatus, she is his 'servant',
but if apparatus and nurse are provided by the hospital and the doctor is
not empowered to give her instructions about how to operate the apparatus,
he is not responsible for her. Independent craftsmen, carriers, and building
contractors are not 'servants' in the sense of §831 BGB unless they are dependent on those who retain them. Difficulties arise in cases where one employer
lends his employees to another on the terms that they must follow the latter's
instructions. Here again the question is whether the first employer retains
any right and duty to supervise and control the 'borrowed servants' (see
BGH VersR 1956, 322; BGE 42 II 617).

A further requirement for the liability of the superior is that the harm be
caused by the assistant 'in the exercise of the function assigned to him'. The
assistant need not have been employed to do the very act which directly
caused the harm: it is enough that his act fell within the steps normally incidental to the execution of his functions. For example, if a scaffolding erector
throws a piece of wood into the highway and injures someone, it is relevant
whether he threw it in order to deter children from endangering themselves
by playing with scaffolding materials on the sidewalk, or whether he saw an
acquaintance coming along the road and wanted to make him jump; in the
former case alone is there a sufficient internal connection between the damaging act and the duties of the workman (see BGH VersR 1955, 205). The
distinction may be difficult to draw. If an employer sends a man to do
construction work on a site some distance away, say, in the factory of a
client, and the employee causes an accident on his way there, §831 BGB only
applies if the employer specified the means of transport and the route (see
RG DR 1942, 1280, and contrast OLG Munich MDR 1959, 391). If a
truck-driver carrying goods deviates from the prescribed route and runs over
a third party, the internal connection between the accident and the course of
his employment may continue to subsist if the deviation is relatively trivial,
but not if he goes off on a trip of his own (see RG LZ 1930, 589). If the same
driver, in disregard of an express prohibition, takes a companion on the trip
and causes him an injury, his flouting his superior's instructions is so flagrant
that the accident can be treated as having occurred only 'on the occasion of'
his employment (BGH NJW 1965, 391), but it may be different if the reason

the driver contravened his instructions was to deliver the goods more swiftly (see BGH NJW 1965, 391 and NJW 1971, 31). Of course one should bear in mind that in such cases the employer is strictly liable under the Road Traffic Act (§7 par. 3 StVG) even when the requirements of §831 are not satisfied.

Once it is established that the assistant caused the harm in the 'execution of the function assigned to him', the defendant principal is liable unless he can prove that he took all the generally requisite precautions in selecting, training, and supervising the assistant, and thereby satisfy the *Entlastungsbeweis* or exculpatory proof. To go by the terms of §831 BGB, it is not actually necessary that the assistant should have been at *fault*: even where the assistant was not careless at all it would appear that his superior must bring the exculpatory proof. However, as STOLL (JZ 1958, 137) and v. CAEMMERER (above p. 633) have shown, exculpatory proof can only be required in the rare cases where the reason that the assistant was not at fault was delictual incapacity, unsuitability for the employment in question, or inadequacy of instruction or equipment, but otherwise the employer cannot be held liable under §831 BGB if the assistant has behaved with proper care. If there is an accident in a swimming pool the local authority does not need to adduce the *Entlastungsbeweis* if it is clear that the supervisor of the pool performed his duties properly (BGH NJW 1980, 392).

In the normal case where the employee was at fault or where fault on the part of the principal in the circumstances of the case cannot be ruled out in advance, the principal must seek to satisfy the requirements of the exculpatory proof under §831 BGB. The courts are extremely strict with regard to this proof, especially in the very important cases where the plaintiff has been injured by a transport employee such as a train-driver, truck-driver, tram-driver, level-crossing keeper, or station attendant. Large transport undertakings are required to supervise their drivers by having regular and secret tests in which an examiner follows behind the driver and satisfies himself as to the carefulness of the driving. In the case of young drivers and recently appointed or inexperienced truck-drivers this is of general application. One might think that the circumstances of the accident itself were the central issue, but in suits based on §831 BGB it is rather lost sight of. If a person is injured in a train crash, the claim for damages under §831 BGB depends not on the fault of the train-driver, which is normally perfectly clear, but on whether the defendant railway exercised sufficient supervision and control over the driver; the requisite degree of control and supervision depends on how well the driver passed his driving test, how much experience he had at the time of the accident, and whether he had been guilty of similar errors before, to the knowledge or constructive knowledge of his employer (see BGH VRS 16, 164). These are matters of which the plaintiff can have no cognizance before the trial and neither he nor his counsel can make any reasonable prediction about the outcome of the suit; in cases of this sort, therefore, he must either take the risk of bringing a suit in the hope that the proof turns out favourably for him or content himself with the lower sums accorded to him regardless of fault on the part of the transport undertaking or its personnel under the strict liability laid down by the Road Traffic Act or the Law of Liability.

§831 BGB is thoroughly unsound in policy and the only reason it has remained in the BGB so long is that the judges have done much to undermine its effect. Legal institutions which allow the courts to grant *contractual* claims for damages have proved especially useful although since the harm to the plaintiff is caused by breach of a general duty owed to everyone it should properly be dealt with by the law of tort (see above p. 461) and v. CAEMMERER (above p. 629) 56). If the case is moved into the law of contract and defendant is deprived of the exculpatory proof under §831 BGB and is rendered unconditionally liable to the plaintiff 'contractor' for the fault of his personnel (§278 BGB). If a car salesman omits to display a notice in the showroom warning of the freshly polished floor, a customer who slips and falls on it can always claim damages from the firm on a 'contractual' basis. If he came to discuss the details of a purchase already concluded, the contract, on the German view, would oblige the dealer not only to deliver the automobile but to see to the safety of his sales premises, and the failure to observe this duty of care, which would otherwise constitute a tort, is here concurrently a 'positive breach of contract'. The same is true if there is no contract between the parties and the customer visits the premises simply to look at the new models with a view to possible purchase. The courts give a contractual flavour to this situation by holding that as soon as negotiations start and before any contract is ever concluded there arises a mutual duty of care, breach of which makes the dealer contractually liable for 'culpa in contrahendo'. And if the customer's wife happens to accompany him and she is injured, she also has a contractual claim since it is constant German practice to extend to her the protective effects of her husband's legal relations. Accordingly, wherever an accident which should really be covered by the law of delict is sufficiently closely connected with a business matter, the party whose servant causes the harm is barred from resorting to the exculpatory proof under §831 BGB. Many people are of the view that for this purpose a mere 'social' contact is as good as a business relationship and would give a contractual claim for damages not only to injured purchasers and potential purchasers but also, for example, to a bailiff who came to the showroom not to *buy* an automobilie but to *seize* one (on this see DÖLLE; *ZgesStW* 103 (1943) 67). The English jurist POLLOCK stated that the strict liability of a master for the torts of his servants, such as exists at Common Law, was justified by the consideration that if it did not exist a 'huge expansion of implied, i.e. fictitious, contracts, to no great advantage of either law or conscience', would ensue; the development of German law has vindicated this prediction to the hilt.

See *Holmes–Pollock Letters* (ed. DEWOLFE HOWE, 1961) 234.—There are many other legal devices which render it impossible for an employer to resort to the exculpatory proof under §831 BGB and make him strictly liable for harm caused by employees at fault. They may be found in KÖTZ, *Deliktsrecht* (7th edn. 1996) mn. 289 ff., but here we may mention one of them, developed by the courts, namely the principle of the employer's duty to indemnify the employee. If an employee is charged with a 'dangerous' job and injures a third party in the course of it, he is entitled, unless he intended to cause the harm or was grossly negligent in causing it, to demand that his employer indemnify him against the damages claim brought by the third party. This is justified by the view that whereas no single error of an employee is inevitable, the chance of the occurrence of such errors has proved to be intrinsic to all human activity, and should be borne by the employer as part of the risk of the business (for example, see BAGE 5, 1). If a third party is injured by the carelessness of an employee and sues the employee and the employer in the same suit, it will do the employer no good to bring successful exculpatory proof under §831 BGB, for although the claim against him would have to be dismissed, the principle we have just mentioned requires him to indemnify the third party on behalf of his employee: §831 is effectively avoided. Obviously enough, an employer who fails to bring the exculpatory proof and is held liable to the third party personally can not bring any claim for indemnity against the employee: §840 par. 2 BGB expressly provides for such an indemnity (as does art. 55 par. 2 OR), but the courts refuse to take any notice of these provisions, so they have largely become obsolete.

In the circumstances it is not surprising that §831 BGB has been heavily criticized in the Federal Republic and the efforts to reform it have culminated in a draft statute from the Ministry of Justice. The proposed new text is as follows: 'A person who appoints another to perform a function is bound along with that other to indemnify a third party for the harm caused by an intentional or negligent tort committed by that other in the execution of his task.'

III

The French Code civil lays down in art. 1384 par. 1 that one must pay for the harm 'which is caused by the act of persons for whom one is answerable'. The subsequent paragraphs of art. 1384 list the persons for whom one is so answerable. These include the employee or *préposé*: if the employee injures a third party in the exercise of the functions assigned to him, his employer or *commettant* is bound to compensate the third party (art. 1384 par. 5).

This provision, like art. 2049 Codice civile, which is essentially the same, has always been understood to impose on the employer an unconditional liability to respond for the delicts of his employees. All that is required to render the employer liable is that the person who caused the harm be his assistant, that the assistant have caused the harm in the exercise of his functions, and that the assistant himself, he had been sued, would have been liable to the victim in tort. If these conditions are satisfied, the liability of the employer is established; he cannot escape liability by proving that he was very careful in selecting and supervising his assistant.

1. The French courts apply the same standards as the German courts in deciding whether the person who caused the harm was a 'servant' of the defendant employer in the sense of §831 BGB. For this purpose one asks whether the assistant was in a relation of dependence on the employer, that is, whether he was bound to follow the orders and instruction given to him with regard to the execution of the work assigned to him. Independent craftsmen, building contractors, forwarders, and carriers are thus generally not the *préposés* of their customers, but the doctor is the *préposé* of the hospital in which he works, even though he is not subject to its directions as regards his professional activities (Crim. 5 March 1992, JCP 1993. II. 22013 noted by CHABAS). In earlier days the courts often held that the employer must not only have the power to instruct but also the freedom to choose his assistant. Recent decisions, however, hold that a person may be an assistant under art. 1384 even if his employer is forced to employ him, provided that he must follow the instructions and orders which the employer is empowered to give: examples would be an army training officer seconded to a shooting club or a convict assigned to work in a business (see Paris 9 Dec. 1938, DH 1939, 136; Req. 21 Oct. 1942, Gaz. Pal. 1942. 2. 243).

The same test is applied in cases where an employee is 'lent' to another business for a period of time; here too the question is which of the parties in the case had the power to give the 'borrowed' servant instruction about how to do the work. On occasion the courts have tried the interesting experiment of dividing the activity of the employee into two parts, making the superiors liable respectively for the part controlled by each, and deciding to which part the harmful act appertained. If a transport firm supplies a building contractor with a truck and driver for a few days' excavations it may be relevant whether the accident is caused by bad driving or by faulty loading; the transport company would be liable for the driving and the building contractor for the loading, provided that the loading was under his control and instructions (on this see Civ. 20 July 1955, JCP 1956. II. 9052, noted by SAVATIER; Civ. 17 July 1962, Gaz. Pal. 1962. 2. 309; Com. 26 Jan. 1976, DS 1976, 449).

2. Once it is determined that the person who caused the harm was a *préposé* of the defendant employer, one asks whether he caused the harm in the execution of the tasks assigned to him. As art. 1384 par. 5 Code civil expressly says, employers are only liable for the harm which their staff cause in 'the tasks for which they are employed'. The courts frequently paraphrase this requirement in terms at least as vague as art. 1384 par. 5 itself. The phrase commonly used since 1983 is that the superior is freed from liability only *si son préposé a agi hors des fonctions auxquelles il était employé, sans autorisation et à des fins étrangères à ses attributions* (for example, in Ass.plén. 19 Aug. 1988, DS 1988, 513).

A look at the cases shows that the courts are very generous in attributing delicts to the employer. For example, a person who sends an agricultural worker to fetch a tool from a neighbour is liable if on the way the labourer is careless in filling his petrol lighter and causes a fire (Civ. 19 Dec. 1950, JCP 1951. II. 6577, noted by RODIÈRE). The same is true if a farmer sends his lad to help out a neighbour for the day: if, while riding back on an unlighted bicycle, the lad runs into a pedestrian, the farmer is liable for the harm without regard to the question, which German courts would ask, whether the farmer stipulated the route or means of transport (Soc. 7 Jan. 1965, Bull. civ. 1965. IV no. 7). If the employee is on the way between his *home* and place of work, however, the employer is not liable for any accidents he may cause (Crim. 28 Nov. 1956, JCP 1957. IV. 2). Employers are often held liable for intentional torts as well. On several occasions the courts have decided that a transport company is liable for assaults committed by its driver on other road users who objected to his mode of driving (Paris 8 July 1954, Gaz. Pal. 1954. 2. 280; Crim. 16 Feb. 1965, Gaz. Pal. 1965. 2. 24; *contra*, Montpellier 22 April 1964, JCP 1964. II. 13766, noted by MAURY). It might be possible to justify these decisions on the ground that truck-drivers whose mode of driving is questioned are not unlikely to resort to fisticuffs, and that their employers should be able to foresee it, but in other decisions this factor is lacking. Thus an employer has been held liable for a driver who spied a pheasant on the plaintiff's land, stopped the truck, shot the bird with a handy gun, and bore it off (Crim. 23 Nov. 1928, Gaz. Pal. 1928. 2. 900). The proprietor of a cinema has even been held liable for an usher who took a client who asked him for information down to the cellars and murdered her (Crim. 5 Nov. 1953, Gaz. Pal. 1953. 2. 383).

The question is much disputed, and recurrent differences of opinion between the courts of appeal and within the Cour de Cassation have had to be resolved by the *Assemblée plénière*. One case involved an employee who caused an accident while using a company car for private purposes (Ass.plén. 19 June 1977, JCP 1977. II. 18730: liability denied), another an insurance agent who deceived the customers and pocketed their money (Ass.plén. 19 May 1988, DS 1988.513, noted by LARROUMET: liability imposed). A security firm was held not liable when in order to demonstrate the shortage of fire extinguishers its employee set fire to the factory he was to guard (Ass.plén. 15 Nov. 1985, JCP 1986. II. 20568, noted by VINEY), nor was a fuel company liable when its tanker driver, on the way home to fill up his own petrol tank with his employer's petrol, saw he was being followed and dumped the petrol on the plaintiff's land in order to escape detection (Ass.plén. JCP 1983. II. 20120, noted by CHABAS).

3. Although art. 1384 par. 5 is not absolutely unambiguous, there is generally agreed to be a further requirement for the employer's liability, namely that the employee himself be guilty of a tort under art. 1382 ff. Code civil. If

the employee had no delictal capacity at the time he did the harmful act the superior is liable only if he knew or should have known of the incapacity and was himself at fault in appointing or supervising him (Civ. 15 March 1956, JCP 1956. II. 9297, noted by ESMEIN). It is for the victim to adduce such proof.

Art. 1384 par. 1 Code civil states that one must also pay for harm 'causé par le fait des personnes dont on doit répondre'. For a long time this formula was thought to be purely introductory, a preface to the following subsections of art. 1384 which render employers liable for their employees, parents for their minor children, and teachers and masters for those under their instruction. In 1991 the Cour de Cassation departed from this view (*Blieck*, Ass.plén. 29 March 1991, JCP 1991. II. 21673, noted by GHESTIN); holding that art. 1384 par. 1 creates an independent head of liability, it made an asylum pay damages for the act of an inmate who set a wood on fire, although there was no evidence of any carelessness on the part of the management or staff of the asylum. On this decision see also FERRAND, *ZEuP* 1993, 132.

If the employer is liable to the victim under art. 1384 par. 5 Code civil, the question arises whether he may claim an indemnity from the employee. It has been generally accepted in France that he can; indeed, the Cour de Cassation has so decided (Civ. 13 Nov. 1964, JCP 1965. II. 14110, noted by BIZIÈRE; Civ. 20 March 1979, D. 1980, 29, noted by LARROUMET). The Chambre Sociale of the Cour de Cassation, which deals with labour law, however, never holds the employee contractually liable except in cases of gross negligence (see, for example, Soc. 27 nov. 1958, D. 1959, 20, noted by LINDON), and it would be only logical to apply the same rule where the employer is suing on the basis of having paid the third party whom the employee was at fault in injuring (see the details in VINEY no. 811 ff.).

IV

Liability for third parties in the *Common Law* rests on much the same principles as in French law. In both systems there are essentially two conditions which must be satisfied before a defendant has to pay for the harm caused by the tort of another: the other must be the servant of the defendant, and he must have caused the harm in the course of his employment. This liability is quite independent of any fault in the master.

1. In order to decide whether the tortfeasor was a 'servant' of the defendant or an 'independent contractor', the Common Law courts ask if the defendant had sufficient power of direction and control over his activities. Whether this is so or not depends on a great variety of factors: it speaks against a person's being a servant if he has special expertise and experience or can decide how or where or when the work is to be done or if he uses his own tools or if he is paid by results rather than by time, and so on. In earlier

days the English courts adhered to the 'control test', and doubts arose whether people such as doctors or ships-captains could be classed as servants, since such experts could not be controlled in their professional spheres even by those who employed them. Today, however, it is generally recognized that the control test is of limited application to specialists and experts, and one now tends to ask whether the third party formed an integral part of the defendant's business organization.

See *Cassidy* v. *Ministry of Health*, [1951] 2 KB 343, the comment of KAHN-FREUND in 14 *Mod. L. Rev.* 504 (1951) and FLANNIGAN, 37 *U. Tor. L. J.* 25 (1987).—Cases of 'borrowed servants' also cause difficulty in the Common Law, for they raise the question which of two persons is the master. There are many reported cases in England, and in the United States they are innumerable: see ATIYAH (above p. 629) 152 ff.; SMITH, 'Scope of Business: The Borrowed Servant Problem', 38 *Mich. L. Rev.* 1222 (1940); and the interesting Comment in 76 *Yale LJ* 807 (1967), all of which have extensive references to the cases.

2. If a plaintiff has been injured by a tort committed by a servant, the liability of the defendant employer depends on whether the servant committed the tort in the course of his employment. Not very much can be gleaned from the general formulas which seek to refine on this requirement. Thus PROSSER/KEETON (p. 502) states that a servant acts 'in the course of his employment' if his acts 'are so closely connected with what the servant is employed to do, and so fairly and reasonably incidental to it, that they may be regarded as methods, even though quite improper ones, of carrying out the objectives of the employment'. See also Restatement (Second) of Agency (1958) §§228 ff.

It would be quite impossible to tackle here the immense number of relevant cases in Anglo-American law, so we shall attend only to a few topics we have referred to in our discussions of German and French law.

When an employee goes to and from his place of work, he is not in the course of his employment and his employer is not liable for accidents he causes *en route*. The situation is different if after he has finished his work an employee collects his pay on the way home and carelessly injures a fellow-employee on the employer's premises. Here the tortfeasor is still in the course of his employment and his employer is liable to damages.

See *Staton* v. *National Coal Board*, [1957] 2 All ER 667; *Bell* v. *Blackwood Morton & Sons Ltd.*, 1960 SLT 145. In such cases, since the victim is himself an employee, he has a claim to social insurance benefits, but in English law, unlike German law (§636 RVO), he also retains his more extensive rights under the general rules of tort law, subject to certain qualifications.

If an employee is directed by his employer to go and work on another site, the employer is liable if he causes a traffic accident *en route*. This is true even if the employee disregards any instructions the employer may have given on

the matter unless the employee's choice of route increased the risk of accident to an extent which the employer could not reasonably have foreseen.
If the employer tells an employee to go in a company car and leave a message
somewhere, he is liable for an accident caused *en route* even if the worker
ignores his instructions and takes his own vehicle.

See *McKean* v. *Raynor Bros. Ltd.*, [1942] 2 All ER 650; other English cases may be
found in ATIYAH (above p. 629) 225 ff., and American cases in JAMES (above p. 629)
174 f.—Similar rules are applied if at the time of the accident the employee had left
the prescribed route; on this see ATIYAH (above p. 629) 251 ff.; SMITH (above p. 629);
DOUGLAS (above p. 629), all of which contain a mass of case-law.

As in Germany, an 'inner connection' is required between the harmful act
of the servant and the task he was employed to do. This is exemplified in
cases where an employee on duty starts smoking and carelessly causes a fire.
If the job involves the carriage of inflammable materials or otherwise calls
for special care because of the intrinsic fire hazard the employer is liable,
but not if a truck driver lights a cigarette, throws the match out of the window, and thereby sets alight a pile of cuttings by the side of the highway. In
the first case it seems fair that an employer who has men perform tasks which
carry a high risk of fire should bear the inherent and foreseeable risk of fires
carelessly caused.

See *Jefferson* v. *Derbyshire Farmers Ltd.*, [1921] 2 KB 281; *Herr* v. *Simplex Box Corp.*,
330 Pa. 129, 198 A. 309 (1938); *George* v. *Bekins Van & Storage Co.*, 33 Cal. 2d 834,
205 P. 2d 1037 (1949); ATIYAH (above p. 629) 259 ff.; Restatement (Second) of Agency
(1958) §235.—What if the employer expressly prohibits certain conduct and the
employee ignores the prohibition? The courts hold that even forbidden conduct
may be 'within the course of employment' if the employee was furthering the employer's business. See *Rose* v. *Plenty* [1976] 1 All ER 97 and also BGH NJW 1971, 31.

3. A further precondition of the liability of the employer is that the
employee should have caused the harm by means of a *tort*. One constantly
speaks of the employer's 'liability for the *torts* of his servant' (see, for example, Restatement (Second) of Agency (1958) §219 and *passim*). This is
not a requirement which has attracted much attention, and it does not seem
to have led to any problems in practice.

In principle if liability is imposed on the employer as a result of the employee's
injuring a third party the employee is bound to indemnify the employer. The Common Law seems not to accept any qualification of this duty to indemnify, such as
a limitation to cases of particularly gross negligence; see the striking, not to say
shocking, decision of the House of Lords in *Lister* v. *Romford Ice & Cold Storage
Co.*, [1957] AC 555, and the comment by WILLIAMS, 20 *Mod. L. Rev.* 220, 437 (1957);
JOLOWICZ, 1957 *Camb. LJ* 21; STEFFEN, 25 *U. Chi. L. Rev.* 465 (1958); GARDINER, 22
Mod. L. Rev. 652 (1959), and ATIYAH (above p. 629) 422 ff.

4. If a third party is injured by the negligence of someone who is not a servant but an 'independent contractor', he can in principle claim damages only from the independent contractor himself, and not also from the person who paid him. This principle of the Common Law is, however, subject to important exceptions, when it is usually said that the duty of care owed to the public by the employer is 'non-delegable', that is, that it cannot be delegated to an independent contractor in such a way that the employer is freed from liability to the injured party and only the independent contractor remains liable to him. In such cases it is occasionally said that the employer owes not just the normal 'duty to take care' but the higher 'duty that care is taken', but these are empty phrases. The result is that the employer must answer for the fault of the independent contractor as he does for that of a servant (see FLEMING, *The Law of Torts* (8th edn. 1992) 388 ff.).

It is difficult to find any common thread running through the cases in which the Common Law adopts this position. Many of them smack of 'neighbour law', as German lawyers would say. *Bower* v. *Peate* (1876), 1 QBD 321 is an example. Here a builder was employed to make an excavation and the neighbouring land was damaged by the withdrawal of support. Although it was clear that the defendant landowner was not personally at fault at all and that the builder was an independent contractor, the neighbour's claim was granted. There are a great number of these cases both in England and in the United States (Restatement (Second) of Torts (1965) §422 A), and they also arise in Germany, though in a different technical guise. In Germany the question is whether the liability of the landowner for the acts of his building contractor should be judged by §831 BGB or rather, since neighbours are in a 'community relationship' analogous to contract, by §278 BGB. The Bundesgerichtshof has held that the owner is liable only under §831 BGB (BGHZ 42, 374). §831 BGB does not help the plaintiff at all, since the building contractor is normally independent and therefore not a 'functional assistant'. It would be otherwise if §278 were held applicable, since an independent contractor may very well be a 'assistant for performance' (*Erfüllungsgehilfe*) and the result would be the same as in the Common Law. The German courts try to get round their self-denying ordinance by holding the owner to extreme care in his supervision of the building contractor and in this way, if it seems desirable, they can make the owner liable, though for his *own* fault (see, for example, RGZ 132, 51, 58 f.; BGH NJW 1960, 335).

Common Law and German law reach the same result, though again with different doctrinal methods, in another group of cases as well. By granting the plaintiff a contractual claim for damages the German courts can use §278 BGB to make the defendant liable even for an independent contractor; the Common Law uses the law of tort, but exceptionally renders the defendant liable for the fault of his independent contractor. If a tenant is injured by the defective condition of premises which the landlord has promised to keep in proper condition, the landlord will be liable in damages even if he entrusted the work of maintenance and repair to independent contractors rather than to his own employees, provided that the independent contractors were at fault. The same is true if as a matter of business a person allows the public to enter or use his property. If the property is dangerous owing to the fault of an independent contractor and someone is injured in consequence, the proprietor will be liable if the victim was one of those who could be expected to enter the land or use the property for business purposes (on this see Restatement (Second) of Torts (1965) §§419–22, 425). In such cases the German courts would unhesitatingly treat the relationship of the parties as contractual or semi-contractual and hold the defendant liable under §278 for the fault of his contractor as an 'assistant for performance'.

Finally, liability for the fault of an independent contractor has been extended to cases where there is no contractual or semi-contractual or even neighbourly relationship between the parties. For example, a person who procures building operations to be done must take proper safety precautions to prevent risk to passing public traffic. This duty is also 'non-delegable'. A person subject to such a duty, very commonly a local authority, will therefore be liable if anyone on the public highway falls into an open pit or an unguarded trench or is injured by falling scaffolding owing to the fault of an independent contractor to whom he entrusted the requisite security precautions (see ATIYAH (above p. 629) 352 ff.; *Salsbury* v. *Woodland*, [1970] 1 QB 324; Restatement (Second) of Torts (1965) §§417 ff.). This overlaps with another class of case where the defendant is held liable for the fault of an independent contractor engaged on 'ultrahazardous activities' which call for special security arrangements. Here too the duty to take proper precautions is regarded as 'non-delegable'. A person who engages in building, demolition, or scaffolding operations, sprays pesticides from planes, sets up high tension electricity cables, or lays pipes close to highways will be liable for the fault of anyone to whom he entrusts these 'ultrahazardous activities' and it makes no difference that these persons are independent contactors.

See *Honeywill & Stein Ltd.* v. *Larkin Bros.* [1934] 1 KB 191, Restatement (Second) of Torts (1965) §§416, 427. In BGH JZ 1975, 733 an independent contractor retained by a company to dispose of the large quantities of dangerous materials on its premises was careless in doing so and caused harm to the plaintiff. The plaintiff's claim against the company succeeded under §823 BGB since he was able to show that in selecting the waste-disposal firm the company had failed to use the very great care required in the circumstances. It may be asked whether it would not be better in such a case to apply §831 BGB (with a *presumption* of fault in selection) or even, as in the Common Law, impose liability without any possibility of exculpation, whether for employees or independent contractors. This is apparently the present position in Dutch law (art. 6:171 NBW).

V

Our comparative survey has shown that in the Romanistic and Anglo-American legal families the rules of vicarious liability are essentially in agreement. The questions are whether the party causing the harm was the defendant's assistant, '*préposé*' or 'servant', and whether he caused the harm to the victim by means of a tort committed in connection with the functions for which he was employed or 'in the course of his employment'. If these conditions are satisfied, the liability of the superior is established even if he took all necessary care in the selection and supervision of his employees.

The new draft version of §831 BGB in Germany is in line with these rules, since it would deprive the employer of the possibility of proving that he was not personally at fault and would make his liability depend simply on the employee's having caused the harm to a third party by means of a tort. Accordingly, the enactment of the draft would achieve a large measure of legal unity in an important area of the law of tort.

But there are grounds other than those of legal unification for endorsing the proposed amendment of §831 BGB. It gives the right result. As has already been indicated, the German courts have already gone far to introduce it into the positive law, by construing situations as contractual, by making exculpatory proof extremely difficult, and by requiring the employer in many cases to indemnify his employees against tort claims by third parties, regardless of his own care in selecting and supervising them. Indeed, it is now generally admitted that the proposed version of §831 BGB provides the right solution and justifies the actual results, at least for the defendant employer who is in business and can accordingly count up the risk of harm being done by his staff and distribute to his customers the cost of insuring against it. But it has been objected that the new rule might be burdensome for *private* employers. The only significant cases in practice arise out of *traffic accidents* caused by employees. Is it really fair that a private citizen should be made liable if his chauffeur negligently causes an accident or if his housemaid goes to fetch the milk, crosses the road when the lights are red, and causes a truck to swerve into the ditch? In fact it would only be if the private employer had to pay for the resulting loss out of his own pocket that §831 BGB as proposed would lead to unsatisfactory results. But this is generally not the case so far as traffic accidents are concerned. Everyone is bound by law to take out insurance against liability for the harm caused by the person he has drive his automobile. The fear that such a person may be shortsighted enough to take out inadequate cover may be met by raising the statutory minimum. It is true that if his housemaid causes a traffic accident when cycling or on foot the employer will not be covered by the compulsory liability insurance, but here too the problems should be solved in the proper place, namely in the law of traffic accidents. One might even follow up the suggestion of

E. v. Hippel (*NJW* 1967, 1729, 1735) that traffic accident insurance covering accidents caused by pedestrians and cyclists as well should be made compulsory. It must be said, too, that both in the Common Law and in French law private employers are liable for the faults of their employees and this has caused no problems or movements for reform; the only cases which actually arise are those where the private employer is made liable for a traffic accident caused by his employees, and the same would be true in Germany.

In France and in the Common Law countries it has often been asked what the true justification for the principle of vicarious liability may be, and many different answers have been given. For example, it has been said that a legal system which affords the employer the liberty of extending the range of his activity and the amount of his profit by employing others should make him accept the increased risk that third parties may be harmed: *qui sentit commodum debet sentire et onus.* This proves too much, for the positive law does not put on the employer the risk of the harm his employees may cause *without* any fault. This objection is met by the explanation that responsibility is imposed on the employer because the employee is his *alter ego*, his 'long arm', and the legal system treats the fault of the employee in his employment as being that of the master: *qui facit per alium facit per se.* For others, the liability of the employer for the fault of his staff is justified on the ground that it gives the employer an added incentive to take precautions to avoid harm being caused to third parties and that it has the added advantage of avoiding tiresome disputes about the internal organization of his business. Another doctrine, favoured by American authors in particular, has it that the cost of accidents should be borne by the person who can most easily distribute it to the whole community by means of insurance at the smallest social cost and with the minimum waste; it is normally the employer rather than the employee, much less the victim, who is the best 'risk-absorber' and therefore he must answer for the torts of his employees. The same result is reached by another and more recently developed American theory that the principal task of the law of damages is to procure that all the costs of the production of goods and services should be reflected in their price so that people wondering whether to pay for them or not should be able to decide whether they are important and useful enough to be worth a price which includes the cost of the accidents involved in their production.

The theories adduced to justify vicarious liability in France are listed in Mazeaud/Tunc I nos. 928 ff.; Anglo-American views are collected and evaluated in Williams, 20 *Mod. L. Rev.* 220, 228 ff. (1957) and Atiyah (above p. 629) 12 ff. But see also the writings of Laski, Smith, Douglas, Seavey, and Janes (all cited above p. 629), and note the rather cool reception given by Judge Friendly to the 'economic' justification of the rule of respondeat superior (*Ira S. Bushey & Sons* v. *United States*, 398 F. 2d 167 (1968)).

No single one of these 'theories' gives a satisfactory explanation of the institution of vicarious liability since each of them emphasizes one of the underlying value-judgments at the expense of the others. Nevertheless, taken together, they indicate the policy considerations which one should bear in mind in deciding what the rules of vicarious liability should be. None of them suggests that the liability of the employer should depend on his personal fault in selecting and supervising his men: on this ground also the new version of §831 BGB is a step forward.

42

Strict Liability

ANCEL, 'La Responsabilité sans faute en droit français', *Travaux de l'Association Henri Capitant* II (1947) 249.

ATIYAH, 'No-Fault Compensation: A Question That Will Not Go Away', 54 *Tul. L. Rev.* 271 (1980).

——/CANE, *Accidents, Compensation and the Law* (5th edn. 1993).

CORNELIS, *De buitencontractuele aansprakelijkheid voor schade veroorzakt door zaken* (1982).

EHRENZWEIG, 'Assurance Oblige—A Comparative Study', 15 *L. Contemp. Probl.* 445 (1950).

——, *Negligence without Fault, Trends toward an Enterprise Liability for Insurable Loss* (1951), reprinted in 54 *Calif. L. Rev.* 1422 (1966).

ESSER, *Grundlagen und Entwicklung der Gefährdungshaftung* (1941).

——, 'Die Zweispurigkeit unseres Haftpflichtrechts', *JZ* 1953, 129.

FLEMING/HELLNER/v. HIPPEL, *Haftungsersetzung durch Versicherungsschutz* (1980).

FRIDMAN, 'The Rise and Fall of Rylands v. Fletcher', 34 *Can. Bar Rev.* 810 (1956).

FRIEDMANN, 'Social Insurance and the Principles of Tort Liability', 63 *Harv. L. Rev.* 241 (1950).

GILLIARD, 'Vers l'unification du droit de la responsabilité', *ZSR* 86 (1967) 193.

GROSSFELD, 'Haftungsverschärfung, Haftungsbeschränkung, Versicherung, Umverteilung', *Festschrift Coing* II (1982) 111.

HANNAK, *Die Verteilung der Schäden aus gefährlicher Kraft, Grundsätze einer Schadensordnung für die Gefahren der modernen Technik* (1960).

HARRIS et al., *Compensation and Support for Illness and Injury* (1984).

HELLNER, 'Tort Liability and Liability Insurance', *Scand. Stud. L.* 6 (1962) 129.

v. HIPPEL, *Schadensausgleich bei Verkehrsunfällen, Haftungsersetzung durch Versicherungsschutz, Eine rechtsvergleichende Studie* (1968).

HÜBNER, *Die Haftung des Gardien im französischen Zivilrecht* (1972).

ISON, *The Forensic Lottery, A Critique on Tort Liability as a System of a Personal Injury Compensation* (1967).

JAMES, 'Accident Liability Reconsidered: The Impact of Liability Insurance', 57 *Yale LJ* 549 (1948).

JONES, 'Strict Liability for Hazardous Enterprises', 92 *Colum. L. Rev.* 1705 (1992).

KÖTZ, *Sozialer Wandel im Unfallrecht* (1976).

MILLER, 'Compensation for Personal Injury: Social Insurance in Comparative Perspective', *Comp. L. Yb.* 4 (1980) 221.

MORRIS, 'Hazardous Enterprises and Risk Bearing Capacity', 61 *Yale LJ* 1172 (1952).

OFTINGER, 'Der soziale Gedanke im Schadenersatzrecht und in der Haftpflichtversicherung', *SJZ* 39 (1942/43) 545, 561.

OLDERT/TIDEFELT (eds.), *Compensation for Personal Injury in Sweden and Other Countries* (1988).

PRIEST, 'The Invention of Enterprise Liability: A Critical History of the Intellectual Foundations of Modern Tort Law', 14 *J. Leg. Stud.* 461 (1985).

PROSSER, 'The Principle of Rylands v. Fletcher', *Selected Essays on the Law of Torts* (1953) 135.

SAVATIER, *Comment repenser la conception française actuelle de la responsabilité civile?* (1967).

SCHILCHER, *Theorie der sozialen Schadensverteilung* (1977).

SPENCER, 'Motor-Cars and the Rule in Rylands v. Fletcher: A Chapter of Accidents in the History of Law and Motoring', 1983 *Camb. LJ* 65.

STAPLETON, *Product Liability* (1994).

STARCK, 'Les Cas de responsabilité sans faute', *Rev. trim. dr. civ.* 56 (1958) 475.

STARK, 'Probleme der Vereinheitlichung des Haftpflichtrechts', *ZSR* 86 (1967) 1.

——, 'Entschädigungsrecht am Scheideweg: Haftpflichtrecht mit Haftpflichtversicherung oder Personen- und Sachversicherung', *VersR* 1981, 1.

STONE, 'Liability for Damage Done by Things', *Int. Enc. Comp. L.* XI Ch. 5 (1983).

TERCIER, 'Quelques Considérations sur les fondements de la responsabilité civile', *ZSR* 95 (1976) 1.

TUNC, *La Responsabilité civile* (1981).

——, (ed.), *Pour une loi sur les accidents de la circulation* (1981).

——, 'Traffic Accident Compensation, Law and Proposals', *Int. Enc. Comp. L.* XI Ch. 14 (1971).

——, 'Responsabilité civile et droit des accidents', *Festschrift für W. Lorenz* (1991) 805.

VINEY, *Le Déclin de la responsabilité individuelle* (1964).

VOIRIN, 'De la responsabilité civile à la sécurité sociale pour la réparation des dommages corporels, Extension ou disparition de la branche accidents du travail', *Rev. int. dr. comp.* 31 (1979) 541.

VAN DER WALT, 'Strict Liability in the South African Law of Delict', 1 *Comp. Int. LJS Afr.* 49 (1968).

WEYERS, *Unfallschäden, Praxis und Ziele von Haftpflicht- und Vorsorgesystemen* (1972).

WILL, *Quellen erhöhter Gefahr, Rechtsvergleichende Untersuchungen zur Weiterentwicklung der deutschen Gefährdungshaftung durch richterliche Analogie oder durch gesetzliche Generalklausel* (1980).

I

IN all the legal systems considered in the previous chapter the law of tort is basically founded on the principle that the only sufficient reason for shifting a victim's loss to the person who caused it is if the latter was guilty of reprehensible or careless behaviour in causing it. This principle of no liability without fault prevailed in Germany and France apparently unchallenged until the end of the nineteenth century, as it did also in the countries of the Common Law, where its influence helped to make the tort of negligence into an independent ground of liability. As a matter of intellectual and social history, the principle of no liability without fault has its roots in the liberal individualism of a century ago: a responsible individual's freedom of movement should only be limited by the imposition of liability in damages if he culpably failed to conduct himself in accordance with the general duty to act carefully. Along with this there went, especially in England and the United States, the fear that extensive liability might inhibit nascent industries and so delay general progress. This meant that even the most serious industrial accidents had to be borne by the worker and his family unless they were attributable to the fault of the employer, but this was perfectly acceptable to the social Darwinism in English-speaking countries, indeed was actually desired as a subsidy for emerging industry.

Thus L. FRIEDMANN, *A History of American Law* (1973) 409 ff.; HORWITZ, *The Transformation of American Law 1780–1860* (1977) 67 ff.; *contra*, with good reason, SCHWARTZ, 'Tort Law and the Economy in 19th Century America: A Reinterpretation', 90 *Yale LJ* 1717 (1981).

Germany was the first country to deviate from the principle of fault, originally for the benefit of a strictly limited group of victims: in the eighteen-eighties, when capitalism still had a patriarchal streak, there was enacted under BISMARCK a system of workmen's compensation for *industrial accidents*. This removed the most acute problem concerning accidents from the law of tort and took it into the law of social insurance; private lawyers no longer had to worry about it and the rest of the law of tort could remain quietly in thrall to the traditional notion of the primacy of the fault principle, subject to the strict liability introduced for railway *accidents* by special statutes in Prussia (1838) and in the German Empire (1871). Efforts were made to introduce stricter liabilities when the BGB was being prepared but they were unavailing. The general principle that liability for harm arose only as the result of a 'fault' was thought to be intrinsically sound, as being 'the product of a high state of cultural development. It is of central importance for the delineation of the spheres of rights within which individuals can develop their individuality. In determining whether or how to act one should have to take account of the legal interests of others only if the requisite forethought suggests that they may be affected. If after careful reflection an act seems to present no danger for others one should be free to do it, and if it nevertheless causes harm to someone else's legal rights that person must put up with it just as if it were an accident' (*Motive* II p. 1074).

In modern conditions a law of damages which rested on these principles would be hard to accept. A great many factors have led industrial states in the West and in the East to limit, restrict, or evade the pure principle of fault in tort law, or even to abandon it quite openly for certain types of accident. These factors include the growing use of machines and technical devices of all kinds in industry, manufacture, and transport, the increased risk they present of causing damage to person or property so severe as to exceed the victim's capacity to bear it, the victim's consequent need for protection, the possibility of spreading the risk of loss through the community as a whole by means of insurance, and the great change in people's view of the degree of social security which a legal system should guarantee to its members. It seems obvious to us today that a person who suffers an accident at his *place of work* should obtain compensation whether his employer was at fault or not, but we should not forget that in many countries until quite recently this principle was regarded as positively revolutionary because it was irreconcilable with the principle of fault. Even in 1911 the Court of Appeals in New York declared a statute unconstitutional for making employers in certain dangerous industries strictly liable for industrial accidents. The argument that the statute simply removed the obsolete Common Law rule that a worker entering employment consciously accepted the risk of accidents met with a dry answer from JUDGE WERNER:

'It would be quite as logical and effective to argue that this legislation only reverses the laws of nature, for in everything within the sphere of human activity the risks which are inherent and unavoidable must fall upon those who are exposed to them ... The Constitution, in substance and effect, forbids that a citizen shall be penalized or subjected to liability unless he has violated some law or has been guilty of some fault.' *Ives* v. *South Buffalo Railway Co.*, 201 NY 271, 94 NE 431, 444 (1911).

Attempts to justify supposedly immutable postulates of justice by invoking the law of nature have often failed, and in this matter too the feeling gradually prevailed that it was socially unacceptable to make the worker himself bear the consequences of an accident at work. In all legal systems today the cost of industrial accidents is, by one legal mechanism or another, imposed on employers who can add it as an item of cost to the price of their products and services and so spread it throughout society: 'The cost of the product should bear the blood of the workman' (LLOYD GEORGE).

Industrial accidents are the clearest instance of open abandonment of the principle of no liability without fault but there are many rules of the law of tort which weaken the principle considerably, if more surreptitiously. It would be an error to suppose that this is an Either–Or situation, that a legal system must either accept or reject the principle of no liability without fault as a whole. What happens in practice is that liability for fault imperceptibly shades into strict liability, and it is often a meaningless question whether a particular legal system, with regard to accidents of a particular type, adopts the principle of fault or of causal liability.

As is well known, the first qualification of fault liability in its pure form arose when courts in the legal systems under discussion ceased to be satisfied with the degree of care which it was possible to expect the defendant personally to show, and look instead to the *typical* abilities of the professional or trade group to which he belonged. No one can now escape liability on the ground that he was too old or infirm or slow to avoid the harm. It is the same when courts exact a degree of care proportional to the magnitude of the risk. Thus in England and the United States a duty of 'high care', the 'highest care', or the 'utmost care' is imposed on business which deal in dangerous and potent substances (see FLEMING, *The Law of Torts* (8th edn., 1992) 490 ff.), and the same is true in Germany (see RGZ 147, 353, 356; BGH NJW 1965, 197, 199). The degree of 'care' demanded of the defendant is often so extreme as to be barely distinguishable from liability without fault. In general, whenever it seems necessary in order to achieve a socially acceptable distribution of the accident risks peculiar to modern life, the courts tend to insist on precautions which it is virtually impossible to satisfy, and they can do this because, judging a case *ex post facto*, they can always discover some precaution or other which, had the defendant adopted it in time, would have prevented the occurrence of the harm.

The results of cases of harm caused by electric power cables in the United States, where liability depends on negligence, are quite comparable with those on Germany, where the courts have at their disposal a claim based on the strict liability imposed by §2 of the Law of Liability; see, for example, *Jones* v. *Southern Utah Power Co.*, 106 Utah 482, 150 P. 2d 376 (1944); *Ottertail Power Co.* v. *Duncan*, 137 F. 2d 187 (8th Cir. 1943); *Chase* v. *Washington Power Co.*, 62 Idaho 298, 111 P. 2d 872 (1941). Even before this special statutory liability was introduced in Germany, the courts were able to assist plaintiffs by stretching the notion of fault; see RGZ 147, 353. An instructive selection of similar cases may be found in ESSER, *Grundlagen* 7 ff. and JZ 1953, 129.

One may also weaken the principle of fault by means of rules concerning the burden of proof. As a general principle it is for the victim to prove facts which show that the defendant was at fault in causing the harm, but in many cases this burden of proof has been reversed. The courts have been able to do this in Germany and France by adopting various methods of giving the victim a *contractual* claim for damages, with the benefit of the more favourable rules regarding burden of proof (see above Ch. 34 II, 36 II 3). But even within the law of tort there is a presumption that the defendant was at fault in certain types of accident; in proportion as the means of rebutting this presumption are restricted, liability for presumed fault assumes the character of strict liability. Thus, for example, the German courts have developed a principle that in a tort suit for injuries due to a defective product the plaintiff need only prove that the product was defective when it left the defendant's factory, and it is then for the manufacturer to show that neither he nor any of the employees involved in the manufacture was guilty of any want of care (BGHZ 51, 91; and see below V). Again, once it is shown that a doctor has committed a 'serious' error in treatment the burden will be on him to dispel any doubt about its causal contribution (BGH NJW 1968, 1185, and constantly thereafter). In applying art. 1384 Code civil, which we shall soon be discussing at length, the French courts speak of a 'presumption of liability', but this presumption is so difficult to rebut that it is almost identical with the special statutory torts in Germany based on strict liability ('Gefährdungshaftung'). A milder form of liability for presumed fault can be found, for example, in §§836 ff. BGB and §1319 ABGB, which require a proprietor of landed property to pay for the harm occasioned to persons or property by the collapse, in whole or in part, of a defective building or construction affixed to the land. In the Swiss OR (art. 58) liability for constructions (*Werkhaftung*) is rather stricter: 'construction' includes not only highways, squares, passageways, scaffolds, and ski-lifts but also stairlights and faulty floors, and if they are defective or badly maintained their owner can only escape liability if he proves that a third party or the victim himself was responsible or that the defect was attributable to an accident which he could not have foreseen (see BGE 63 II 95); Swiss writers describe this as a 'causal liability' (see OFTINGER, *Schweizerisches Haftpflichtrecht* I (4th edn., 1975) 26 ff.). Liability for damage done by an animal is treated as liability for presumed fault in Austria and Switzerland (see the terms of §1320 ABGB and art. 56 OR), but here too it is made so difficult to rebut the presumption that in Switzerland this liability also is described as causal liability (see OFTINGER, ibid.).

The Austrian Oberste Gerichtshof was once faced with a case in which the plaintiff motor-cyclist had collided with a dog which the defendant had taken on a country road without a lead. The defendant was held liable. 'The qualities of a dog are well-known and so the defendant ought to have realized that this dog, especially in view of its ear infection, might not notice a motor-cycle coming up behind it and might run out into the highway'. The court also dealt sharply with the point that it would not have helped to call the dog to heel. 'If the defendant had had the dog at heel, a well-timed call or whistle would have stopped it from endangering the motor-cyclist. If she did not have the dog at heel she was in no position to control it, and that is a ground of liability.' (OGH 27 Oct. 1954, SZ 27 no. 267; see also OGH 28 Sept. 1938, SZ 20 no. 198; BGE 67 II 26 and 77 II 43.)—In German law the keeper of an animal is allowed to exculpate himself if the animal is domesticated and useful, such as a guard-dog, a draught horse, or a milk cow, but the keeper of 'luxury animals' is liable for the damage they do even if he can prove that he exercised every conceivable care in looking after them (see §833 BGB).

Even where the onus of proof remains with the victim in accordance with general principle, there are many ways of making the requisite proof easier. An important instance in Germany is the 'Anscheinsbeweis' or 'prima-facie-Beweis': a victim who cannot prove facts which are direct evidence of the defendant's fault may still succeed if he proves other facts which, given one's general experience of the way things occur, justify the conclusion that the defendant failed to exercise the care called for in the circumstances. For example, if on a straight highway under normal weather conditions a motorist on the wrong side of the road collides with an oncoming car, one's immediate impression is that the motorist was not driving properly. According to the German courts this does not make for a reversal of the burden of proof; the defendant motorist need not bring positive proof that he behaved carefully but it is up to him to show that there was something untypical and extraordinary in the situation—perhaps that the stretch of road was unusually susceptible to black ice or strong side-winds—so as to suggest an alternative explanation of the accident. If the defendant fails to satisfy this requirement, as he usually does, the judge may proceed on the basis that the fault which 'normally' inheres in such a situation is proved in the case before him (invariable holding: for example, see BGHZ 8, 239).

Common Law courts do likewise with the 'doctrine of res ipsa loquitur'. The leading case is *Scott* v. *London & St. Katherine Docks Co.*, (1865) 3 H. & C. 596, 159 Eng. Rep. 665. The plaintiff was walking past a warehouse when sacks of sugar inexplicably fell on his head. The court said

> 'There must be reasonable evidence of negligence. But where the thing is shown to be under the management of the defendant or his servants, and the accident is such as in the ordinary course of things does not happen if those who have the management use proper care, it affords reasonable evidence, in the absence of explanation by the defendant, that the accident arose from want of care.'

It is not entirely agreed in England what constitutes a satisfactory 'explanation by the defendant'. Many decisions apparently require the defendant to negate possibility that the harm was caused by his fault, by proving that he was not negligent (see *Moore* v. *Fox*, [1956] 1 QB 596); other decisions apparently treat it as sufficient if the defendant shows that it is *possible* that the harm was caused without his fault (as in *The Kite*, [1933] P. 154), and this is the dominant view in the United States and in the Commonwealth countries.

In the United States there is another important factor which makes negligence liability approach a liability independent of fault, namely that tort suits are almost always tried before a jury (see Ch. 18 V). In such a suit the sole function of the judge is to control the oral proceedings, to decide how the parties may prove their allegations, and finally to lay down the rules of law for the jury to apply to the facts. The jury alone evaluates the evidence and applies the rules of law laid down by the judge to the facts; above all it decides whether the defendant was at fault or not. Only in exceptional cases can the judge require the jury to give judgment for the plaintiff or for the defendant, or vacate a verdict rendered by the jury: he may do so only if the evidence led by the parties is unquestionably inadequate to sustain the claim or ground the defence, or if the jury's verdict is in flagrant contradiction with the matters proved in evidence. It will be plain that laymen will always tend to give judgment for the plaintiff and to hold that the defendant's behaviour was negligent, especially if the defendant is a large and obviously solvent corporation or if the accident is clearly covered by the defendant's liability insurance.

II

We have seen that liability for fault may be more or less covertly made to *approximate* to strict liability: an 'objective' standard of negligence may be applied, the requisite degree of care may be raised, the burden of proof may be reversed, and doctrines such as *res ipsa loquitur* may be invoked. We must now consider the types of accident for which the legislator or the courts have *openly* broken with the principle of fault. In *German* law, apart from liability for 'luxury animals', strict liability has been introduced exclusively by the legislator in a long series of special statutes not incorporated in the BGB. The reason for this is presumably that the German legislator still regards the principle of fault as the essence of the law of delict, and considers strict liability as anomalous and exceptional, meriting the less exalted status of enactment in special detailed statutes. There is also a long tradition behind this tendency to use special statutes: in 1838 §25 of the Prussian Law of Railway Undertakings imposed strict liability on railways for all harm to persons or property occurring 'through carriage on the railway' unless the defendant could prove 'that the harm was caused by the fault of the victim or by an external and unavoidable event'. This statute was adopted in similar form by other states in Germany and in 1869 by Austria as well. 1871 saw the enactment of the Imperial Law of Liability, which is still in force today, though it has been amended frequently and is now called simply the Law of Liability. It lays down strict liability for harm to *persons* arising 'through the operation' of railways.

Harm is caused 'through the operation' of the railway if it is caused or contributed to by sudden braking, collapse of the track, sparks from the trains, signal failure, or other incidents of the technical operation of running a railway. Accidents to persons mounting or dismounting from trains or using railway stations are also included if they are due to the specific dangers of railway travel such as the height of the running-boards, the haste of passengers, or the crowd on the platform, but a person who falls on a stairway in a station simply because the steps are defective can claim damages only under §823 par. 1 BGB. The railway is not liable for accidents caused by *force majeure (höhere Gewalt)*. This is understood by the courts to mean external and elemental forces of nature or the conduct of third parties whose effects could not have been prevented even by the most extreme precautions. The railways will even be liable for flash floods, heavy snowstorms, or avalanches unless no conceivable precautions, such as a warning system or a reduction of speed, could have forestalled the accident. Nor is it a case of *force majeure* if the event which caused the harm is of such frequent occurrence that the railway should take account of it even if it can do nothing about it.

A passenger injured by sudden braking may sue the railway even if it is due to the quite unforeseeable appearance on the track of children or cattle which have broken through the protective fence. See RGZ 54, 404; BGH VersR 1955, 346.

If a victim contributes to the accident by his own fault, the courts weigh up the extent to which the dangerousness of the railway and the fault of the victim contributed to the harm and apportion the damages accordingly (see BGHZ 2, 355).

In 1943 and 1977 the Law of Liability was extended by special statutes to cover cases in which death or personal injury is caused 'by the effects of electricity, gases, vapours, or liquids' coming from 'an installation for their transmission or supply by cable, pipe, or otherwise'. Included in particular are high tension cables, gasholders, steam conduits, and waterpipes. Once again liability is in principle excluded only in cases of *force majeure*. In a case where an 11-year-old child was injured when his kite, attached by wire rather than thread, came in contact with a high tension cable the Bundesgerichtshof held the defendant liable (BGHZ 7, 338); such an accident was very unusual but it did not have that extraordinary, 'almost elemental quality' required before one could speak of *force majeure*. In such a case, however, the damages may be reduced on the ground of the plaintiff's contributory fault.

The liability of the custodian of a *motor vehicle* is less strict. It was introduced in 1908 and is now contained in the Road Traffic Act of 1952 (StVG). §7 StVG makes the custodian of a motor vehicle ('Halter'—normally, but not necessarily, the owner) liable for damage to person or property which arises 'through the operation' of the vehicle. Liability is excluded

'if the accident is caused by an unavoidable event attributable neither to a defect in the construction of the vehicle nor to a failure of any of its functional parts. In particular an event is unavoidable when it is attributable to the behaviour of the victim or of a third party not involved in the operation or of an animal, and both the custodian and the driver of the vehicle have taken all the care called for in the circumstances of the case.'

This means that even unforeseeable and unavoidable failure of the components of vehicle—such as a tyre defect, axle fracture through metal fatigue, brake failure, or the steering seizing up—makes the custodian liable, but if the accident is due to an 'external' event such as the occurrence of black ice or an animal running in front of the vehicle or faulty driving on the part of other motorists, the custodian is not liable if he can prove that both the driver and he himself observed 'all the care called for in the circumstances'. Such care is defined by the courts as 'care going beyond what is usually required, extreme and thoughtful concentration and circumspection' (BGH VersR 1962, 164; and repeatedly thereafter). In practice such proof is hardly ever forthcoming, and only in very few cases—such as when a car leaves the road because of entirely unpredictable black ice or a small child darts out on to the street from between two parked cars and is run over—has it been accepted that the accident was one which an 'ideally careful' driver could not have avoided. If any fault on the part of the victim contributed to the occurrence of the harm, damages are reduced as under the Law of Liability. Passengers in a vehicle can only sue the custodian under the Road Traffic Act if they were being carried by way of business and for reward, as in a taxi or bus; injured passengers in other cases must use the general provisions of the law of delict (§§823 ff. BGB).

The Air Traffic Law of 1922 lays down an especially strict liability for harm caused to persons and things other than those being carried in the airplane pursuant to contract. In practice this means harm caused on the surface of the earth, whether by flight noise or by crashing or crash-landing: the custodian of an airplane is liable even if he can show that the harm was caused by *force majeure* (see §§33 ff. Air Traffic Law).

A characteristic feature of all the statutes mentioned so far is that they strictly limit the amount of damages payable. Claims in respect of immaterial harm are wholly excluded, and an upper monetary limit is also fixed for the liability of the defendant. In the case of death or personal injury the custodian of a motor vehicle is liable only up to 500,000 DM, and if damages are payable in the form of an annuity, it may not exceed 30,000 DM per year. These limits are increased by statutory amendment from time to time in order to take inflation and other factors into account. If several people are injured or killed in the same accident, the applicable limits are 750,000 DM and 45,000 DM; if the total damage exceeds these limits, the victims' claims are scaled down. This is why almost all damages suits for personal injuries sustained in traffic accidents are based on §§823 ff. BGB as well as the Road Traffic Act. Indeed, only so can one obtain damages for pain and suffering. This means that even if liability under the Road Traffic Act is clear there is often a long and tiresome dispute about the proof of fault.

Since 1939 the custodian of a motor vehicle has been required by law to have insurance covering his own liability and that of the driver for the harm caused by the use of the vehicle. A licence to use the vehicle will only be issued if a certificate of insurance is produced. An analogous duty to insure is imposed on the custodian of an airplane but not on the enterprises rendered liable by the Law of Liability.

Strict liability also arises under the Atomic Energy Act of 1959. A distinction is drawn between the liability of the operator of an *installation* for the production or fission of nuclear materials and the liability of any other possessor or radioactive *materials*. The first is liable for personal injury and property damage caused by the effects of nuclear operations within the installation, even if those effects are due to *force majeure*. The possessor of radioactive materials is less strictly liable: like the custodian of a motor vehicle, he may escape liability by proving that he observed 'all the care called for in the circumstances', but this does not apply if the harm is due to a failure of safety devices, even if this could not have been known or avoided by the defendant. Here also there is a duty to take out insurance, but in view of the enormous risks appertaining to the operation of nuclear installations, further cover is mandatorily provided by the state.

Also important is the liability laid down by the Water Maintenance Act of 1957 (§22) for *pollution of water*. Water for this purpose includes all ponds, lakes, rivers, and streams as well as the water-table, and anyone who introduces into such water substances which alter its composition is liable to pay damages for the harm thereby caused to others, including pure economic loss. The same liability, with the exception of *force majeure*, attaches to the operator of an installation for the manufacture, storage, or carriage of materials: if any materials are introduced into water as defined, the operator of the installation is liable in damages. 'Installation' for the purpose of the statute includes not only storage-tanks for oil and paraffin, tanker vessels, and oil pipelines, but also the sort of petrol tankers which supply gas-stations (so BGH VersR 1967, 374). Considering that the pollution of a river or the water-table itself may cause enormous harm, especially of the pure economic variety, it is all the more surprising to find that the Water Maintenance Act diverges from the usual practice of imposing an upper monetary limit to the strict liability of the defendant. The statute does not introduce any obligation to insure, although one may be confident that practically all the operators of installations which carry a risk of water pollution will have taken out suitable insurance policies. All such policies, however, will contain an upper limit and beyond that limit the risk must be borne by the operator himself.

In 1990 a statute made those involved in genetic research strictly liable for personal injury or property damage due to organisms genetically altered.—The Law on Liability for Damages to the Environment (*Unwelthaftungsgesetz*) of the same year makes those operating certain large industrial installations liable for personal injury or property damage due to the effects of emissions. On this see HAGER NJW 1991, 134.—On the liability of the producer of defective products see below pp. 671 ff.

Given this variety in the grounds of statutory liability, it is not surprising that the German courts have always held that the imposition of strict liability is a matter for the legislature and not for the judiciary. This view may already be found in a judgment of the Reichsgericht in 1912. GRAF ZEPPELIN, whose airship had had to make a forced landing, was sued by a spectator who was struck and injured by the anchor chain when a sudden gust of wind tore the airship loose from its anchors. The question for the Reichsgericht was whether it were possible to apply by analogy the texts which laid down strict liability, such as §833 BGB, the Imperial Law of Liability, and the very recent statute which imposed liability on the custodian of a motor car. The Reichsgericht held that no such application by analogy was possible, even although the operation of an airship was an act of bravado entailing risks much less under control than those of railways or motor cars; the provisions laying down strict liability were 'by reason of their exceptional character not applicable even to the unusual circumstances of travel by airship' (RGZ 78, 171, 172). In a case in which a person was killed by a high tension cable the Reichsgericht decided likewise before the enactment of the special liability for electricity installations. It held that liability without fault could only be imposed by the legislator: 'if the legislator has not done so, it must be concluded that the legislator rejects such far-reaching liability'. Fortunately the court was able to help the widow in the case by reversing the burden of proof and by holding that the duty of care called for very remarkable precautions (see RGZ 147, 353).

In *Austria* the types of strict liability are very like those in Germany, though there is no strict liability for water pollution and there is the peculiarity that in 1959 the liabilities of the custodian of a motor vehicle and the operator of a railway were put in the same statute, with differing limits of liability. In this statute liability is generally excluded if the accident was caused by an 'unavoidable event'. 'Unavoidable event' is defined in the same way as in §7 of the German Road Traffic Act, with the difference that an event is not treated as unavoidable if it is due to an 'extraordinary operational hazard' caused by a third party. It is to be observed that unlike the Reichsgericht the Austrian Oberste Gerichtshof has felt able to go in for *analogy* and to apply the provisions of statutes imposing strict liability to other 'dangerous' undertakings. Even before the introduction of the special statutory liability for electric installations, the running of high tension cables counted as a 'dangerous undertaking' (OGH 10 Sept. 1947, SZ 21 no. 46; *contra* RGZ 147, 353). Strict liability was also imposed by analogy on a chemical factory whose emissions put paid to a circus marquee (OGH 20 Feb. 1958, SZ 31 no. 26; see also OGH 18 Mar. 1953, SZ 36 no. 75 *ad fin.*, OGH 30 Aug. 1961, SZ 34 no. 111, and OGH 9 Dec. 1987, JBl 1989, 315; see also WILL (above p. 647) 80 ff., where these cases are carefully analysed.

Although *Switzerland* also adheres to the view that strict liability can only be imposed by special statutes, it has taken a very different path from Germany and has imposed strict liability in different cases or in cases differently delineated. A comparison with German law clearly demonstrates that element of chance and caprice which is inseparable from any legislative nomination of 'dangerous' operations. Thus the Swiss Law of Railway Liability of 1905 attaches strict liability not only to the operation of railways but also to their construction. This leads to strange distinctions. If an innocent stranger is injured during quarrying operations, the general provisions of the law of tort apply unless the stone from the quarry was to be carried away by rail and used for the construction of a railway, in which case strict liability applies, as it does for the construction or repair of railway tunnels, bridges, and stations (see BGE 36 II 242). It is immaterial whether the building operations are being executed by the railway itself or by an independent contractor, but strict liability applies only in respect of personal injuries. In respect of property damage one must always prove that the railway was at fault, unless the owner of the property was himself personally injured. Thus if a person's motor vehicle is totally destroyed at a level crossing, the strictness of the railway's liability depends on whether the car-owner was bruised or not (!). Swiss law also imposes strict liability on the concessionaire of a shipping route, and it seems perfectly reasonable to treat a passenger who is hurt while embarking on a steamer on Lake Constance at least as well as a passenger who is hurt while getting on a train, which is rather less dangerous (see BGE 36 II 89). A statute of 1902 deals with liability for harm caused by the operation of low or high tension cables, but does so in a manner very different from the Imperial Law of Liability in Germany. As in Germany there is a special statute covering the liability of the custodian of motor vehicles or airplanes and the operator of nuclear installations, but in marked distinction to German law only the last two statutes, for airplanes and nuclear installations, contain any monetary limitation on the amount of compensation. The Swiss Pipeline Law of 1963 imposes strict liability on the operator of a pipeline 'for the transmission of mineral oil, natural gas or other fluid or gaseous material for combustion or fuel, as specified by the Bundesrat'; a Law of 1971 imposes liability on a person who pollutes water 'by his plant, installation, or acts or omissions'; and finally the Law on Explosives of 1977 imposes liability on the occupiers of business premises 'in which explosives or fireworks are produced, stored, or used'. On all these enactments see KELLER, *Haftpflicht im Privatrecht* (5th edn., 1993).

A glance at the patchwork of special instances of strict liability imposed by statutes in Germany, Austria, and Switzerland makes it clear that they leave uncovered many businesses, installations, and activities which pose at least as great a risk of harm. It is far from obvious why a person should be strictly liable if he decides to move earth by means of a light railway while he is liable only for negligence if he uses heavy bulldozers for the job. And why should an injured person's right to damages depend on whether the accident took place on board a steamer or a train? And if a motorized conveyance causes injury, why should liability turn on whether it is a chairlift, a motor car, a motorboat, a light railway, a hoist, a funicular, or an escalator? It may be said that the legislator can always deal with novel needs by introducing new instances of strict liability, as Switzerland did most recently in 1977 with its Law of Explosives, but even so the law will inevitably limp along behind technology; in any case, is it not perhaps unreasonable to take up the time and energy of the legislative machinery, already very stretched, on the amendment of the law on matters which, even in the context of the law of tort, are fairly interstitial?

The enactment of a general principle to amplify or replace the specific instances of the present law has often been proposed not only in Germany, but in Switzerland and Austria as well. The factual preconditions of strict liability would be stated in such a way that the courts could introduce strict liability wherever advancing technology produced a serious risk of danger. The exact wording of such a law has been a matter of debate, but the problem hardly seems insoluble. See the proposals in Kötz, 'Haftung fur besondere Gefahr, Generalklausel fur die Gefährdungshaftung', *AcP* 170 (1970) 1; v. Caemmerer, *Reform der Gefährdungshaftung* (1971); Deutsch, *Haftungsrecht* I (1976) 382 ff.; Will (above p. 647); Kötz 'Empfiehlt sich eine Vereinheitlichung und Zusammenfassung der gesetzlichen Vorschriften über die Gefährdungshaftung?' *Gutachten und Vorschläge zur Überarbeitung des Schuldrechts* (W. German Ministry of Justice, 1981) 1779, criticized by Stoll (above p. 647). There is a similar proposal in Switzerland; see Stark, 'Einige Gedanken zur Entwicklung des Haftpflichtrechts', *25 Jahre Karlsruher Forum* (Suppt. to VersR., 1983) 66, and a comparable rule in the Netherlands (art. 6:173 f. NBW). Two other reforms of strict liability in German law are urged: to abandon the monetary ceilings and to introduce damages for pain and suffering. See Kötz in the *Gutachten* mentioned above, pp. 1823 ff. Then the situation would in this respect be like that which now prevails in Switzerland as well as in all countries in which strict liability has been developed by the courts.

III

Until the end of the nineteenth century it was accepted without question by *French* courts and writers that all the delictual provisions of the Code civil rested on the principle of fault. This was clear from the very words of art. 1382 and 1383, but art. 1384 was also understood in this sense, par. 1 of which enacts that

'One is responsible not only for the damage which one causes by one's own act but also for the damage which is caused by the act of persons for whom one is answerable or of things which one has under one's control.'

So for as this provision laid down liability for *other people*, it was taken to presume some fault in the choice or supervision of one's assistants. The reference to liability for *things* was taken to be simply a preliminary indication of the liabilities imposed by art. 1385 and 1386 on the guardian of an *animal* and the owner of a *building*; according to the view then current, such persons could also exonerate themselves by proving that they were not at fault in watching over the animal or that the ruinous building was properly constructed and adequately maintained.

The growing number of industrial accidents due to the increased use of machines in industry and transport led the French Cour de Cassation in

1896 to adopt a view which had occasionally been expressed by writers and was now to become the starting-point for a revolutionary change in the law of delict. The proposition was that in ordaining liability for the things 'which one has under one's control' art. 1384 par. 1 was not simply making a preliminary announcement that arts. 1385 and 1386 were about to impose liabilities for animals and ruinous buildings, but had an independent force of its own and was applicable in all cases in which any thing under the defendant's control had caused harm in any form. At the outset, this view simply led to a reversal of the burden of proof: the victim no longer had to prove that the defendant was at fault under arts. 1382 f., but could rely on the presumption of liability enacted by art. 1384 par. 1, now that it was no longer thought to be restricted to animals and ruinous buildings. Admittedly this was not to abandon the principle of fault: the Court of Cassation on several occasions allowed the defendant to exonerate himself by proving that his control over the thing was impeccable (see, for example, Req. 30 March 1897, D. 1897. 1. 43).

In 1898 the enactment of a statute which gave workers injured in industrial accidents a claim for damages against their employer whether he was at fault or not did away with the principal reason for an extensive construction of art. 1384 par. 1, but the Court of Cassation carried it a stage further in a decision of 19 January 1914: the Court laid down that a custodian of a thing could escape liability in damages under art. 1384 par. 1 only by proving that the damaging occurrence was due (*a*) to *force majeure*, (*b*) to the fault of the victim, or (*c*) to the fault of a third party (Req. 19 Jan. 1914, S. 1914. 1. 128, and constantly thereafter).

Thenceforth it was clear that proof by the defendant custodian that he was not to blame for the occurrence of the harm was not enough to free him from liability.

These decisions regarding the liability of a custodian for harm done by the thing were affirmed and a few doubtful questions resolved by the celebrated *Jand'heur* decision of the Chambers Réunies of the Cour de Cassation. The cardinal parts of the judgment, which are still echoed by the courts today and have themselves become the object of exercises in construction, are as follows:

'The presumption of liability laid down in art. 1384 par. 1 against the person with control over an inanimate object which has caused harm to another can only be rebutted by proof of accident or *force majeure* or of some external cause not attributable to the custodian, and it is not sufficient to free the custodian from liability that he prove that he was not at fault or that the cause of the harmful event has remained unexplained.

This presumption is applicable whether the thing which caused the harm was impelled by human hand or not; nor is it necessary that the thing have any defect in its construction which made it apt to cause the harm, since art. 1384 attaches liability to the custody of the thing and not to the thing itself.' (Ch. réun. 13 Feb. 1930, S. 1930, 1. 121.)

The *Jand'heur* decision brought the French law of liability essentially to its modern position, to which we must now turn, remembering that this extensive construction of art. 1384 par. 1 has made it virtually unnecessary for French law to have special statutes to introduce strict liability for defined types of accident. The liability of railways and tramways, and of operators of installations for the production, storage, or transmission of electricity, gas, or dangerous substances are all covered by art. 1384 par. 1 and the cases which construe it.

Special strict liability statutes affect only the operator of a cable car (1941), the custodian of an airplane with regard to damage done on the surface of the earth (1955), and the operator of a nuclear installation (1965). The liability of custodians of motor vehicles was based exclusively on art. 1384 par. 1 until recently, but has now been rendered even stricter by a statute of 1985 (see below p. 665).

1. The first precondition for liability under art. 1384 is that the harm must have been caused by a *thing*. 'Thing' here includes every corporeal object. The composite form of the object is immaterial: fluids and gases are included, as are radioactive materials and electrically energized wires.

Animals and, under certain circumstances, buildings are not, however, 'things' in the sense of art. 1384 par. 1. To them the special provisions of art. 1385 and 1386 apply, which the courts construe as meaning that the custodian of an animal is liable regardless of fault, while the owner of a building is only liable if there was an objective defect in the construction or maintenance of the building (see MAZEAUD/TUNC II nos. 1054 ff., 1073).

It is irrelevant whether the thing caused the harm as a result of being impelled or not. Motor cars, trains, ships, and elevators are 'things' in the sense of art. 1384 par. 1 just as much as a board with a protruding nail (Civ. 17 Jan. 1962, D. 1962, 533) or a trapdoor on a dark stairway (Civ. 14 May 1956, JCP 1956. II. 9446). Nor is it necessary that the thing be intrinsically or potentially dangerous so as to require delicate handling or constant supervision. For a time the courts accepted this distinction as a means of limiting what might otherwise seem the boundless area of application of art. 1384 par. 1, but the *Jand'heur* decision made it clear that nothing turns on the dangerousness of the harmful object.

For the details of the development by the courts see MAZEAUD/TUNC II nos. 1209 f., 1216 ff., and VINEY nos. 631 ff.—Today a pedal cycle which collides with a pedestrian (Paris 8 March 1934, Gaz. Pal. 1934. 1. 943), a ski which comes off the skier's boot (Chambéry 15 Feb. 1944, Gaz. Pal. 1944. 1. 134), a chair that a passer-by stumbles over (Civ. 24 Feb. 1941, S. 1941. 1. 201), a basketball (Civ. 21 Feb. 1979. JCP 1979. JCP 1979. IV. 145), and a flat iron (Civ. 5 Dec. 1990, JCP 1991. IV. 43) are all agreed to be 'things' under art. 1384 par. 1 although clearly none of them is particularly dangerous.

Liability for physical harm caused by *fire* is pure fault liability, thanks to a special law of 1922, incorporated into the Code civil as art. 1384 par. 2 and 3. The victim must show that the fire was attributable to the fault of the defendant from whose premises or moveable property it arose, by proving, for example, that he stored inflammable material without adequate security precautions or that he failed to obey the instructions of the fire brigade. On this see VINEY nos. 646–8.

2. If a vehicle leaves the highway and crashes into a wall, it would be absurd to say that the wall is a 'thing' which causes harm under art. 1384 par. 1. In order to prevent its application in such cases, the French courts have laid down a further condition for liability under art. 1384 par. 1, namely that the thing should not have played a 'purely passive role' in the production of the harm but that it must have been a 'productive cause of the damage'. Thanks to this limiting criterion, art. 1384 par. 1 does not apply to cases in which one cannot speak, as art. 1384 par. 1 itself does, of the harm being caused by the 'act' of the thing, because the thing, though participating in the occurrence of the harm, was in its normal place and normal condition at the time.

Thus if there is a collision between a moving vehicle and a properly parked car, the presumption of responsibility enacted by art. 1384 par. 1 does not attach to the custodian of the car. But if the collision takes place at night and the car was inadequately lit or was parked in a place of poor visibility, even the stationary car can be seen as a 'productive cause of the harm'. If the motor vehicle was in motion at the time of the accident, this is almost always the case, but even here one can imagine exceptions: a cyclist injured in a collision with a truck cannot sue the *gardien* of the truck if at the time of the accident it was travelling at a proper speed on the correct side of the road (see, for example, Civ. 26 Oct. 1949, Gaz. Pal. 1950. 1. 79).

Art. 1384 par. 1 is not applicable if a person falls unconscious against a central heating radiator of standard temperature and burns himself on it (Civ. 19 Feb. 1941, S. 1941. 1. 49), or falls on a perfectly safe stairway (Civ. 18 July 1939, Gaz. Pal. 1940. 1. 54), or slips on a properly maintained marble floor in a hotel (Req. 28 July 1941, S. 1941. 1. 206) or stumbles over a basket of winebottles set out on the sidewalk by the vintner for normal display purposes (Paris 14 Jan. 1935, Gaz. Pal. 1935. 2. 157): the radiator, the stairway, the marble floor, and the basket of wine bottles played a 'purely passive' role in the occurrence of the harm. It is different, however, if a customer entering a restaurant in the dark falls over a chair outside it and injures himself (Civ. 24 Feb. 1941, S. 1941. 1. 201); in this case the chair can be regarded as a cause of the harm because it was in an unusual position. It must be admitted that the courts have hereby introduced the fault notion to a certain extent into liability under art. 1384 par. 1, for proof that the thing was in a normal condition at the time of the harm is often tantamount to proof that the custodian was not at fault.

3. A further requirement for liability under art. 1384 par. 1 is that the

person being sued for damages be the custodian ('gardien') of the thing which caused the harm.

According to the decision of the Chambres Réunies of the Cour de Cassation of 2 Dec. 1941 (DC 1942, J. 25) a person is 'gardien' of a thing if on the facts he has the use, management, and control of it ('usage, direction et contrôle'), that is, if he has the power of physical disposition over it. Indeed, a three-year-old child has been held to be the *gardien* of a stick which struck his playmate in the eye (Civ. 9 May 1984, D. 1984, 525 (3rd case), noted by VINEY in JCP 1985. I. 3189). Generally the owner is the *gardien*, but he may be able to show that he transferred the custody ('garde') of the thing to someone else, either pursuant to a contract of lease or services or by some purely factual act. Thus an owner who allows his employee to use a vehicle retains custody as long as the employee is using the vehicle in the scope of his employment, but if the employee takes it on an unpermitted trip, the custody of the vehicle passes from the employer (see Req. 8 Oct. 1940, Gaz. Pal. 1940. 2. 65); the owner also loses custody of a vehicle if it is stolen (Ch. réun. 2 Dec. 1941, DC 1942. J. 25) or if he takes it to a garage for repair (Civ. 8 May 1964, Gaz. Pal. 1964. 2. 362).

The French courts have difficulties with cases in which a thing causes damage during transportation. The 'liquid oxygen' case is a famous instance. Here the defendant company had filled a number of its bottles with liquid oxygen under pressure and had handed them to a carrier for delivery to a customer. When the bottles were being unloaded in the customer's factory one of them exploded and injured two workmen, who now claimed damages.

The Court of Appeal at Poitiers originally held that the carrier was the custodian of the bottles (29 Oct. 1952, JCP 1952. II. 7410), but this decision was quashed by the Court of Cassation and remained to the Court of Appeal of Angers, with an instruction to find out 'if the person to whom the custody of the thing was said to have been transferred had not only the use of the thing which caused the harm but also the power to look after it and to check all its components' (Civ. 5 Jan. 1956, D. 1957, 261). The Angers Court of Appeal again decided against the carrier (15 May 1957, JCP 1957. II. 10058) and the case came before the Court of Cassation once more, which finally declared that the defendant owner was the custodian (Civ. 10 June 1960, D. 1960, 609).

The Court of Cassation's position therefore seems to be that the owner of a bottle of gas which explodes while being carried by an independent contractor is still its 'gardien' and is liable on that basis if, as in this case, the explosion was caused not by the handling or unloading of the bottle but by an undiscovered fault in its construction. Many people think that a distinction must be drawn between control of the *handling* of the thing (*garde du comportement de la chose*) and control over the *construction* of the thing (*garde de la structure de la chose*); the first attached to the carrier, the latter to the owner of the bottle. In each case the judge must decide whether the damage was due to the handling of the thing or to a fault in its construction.

The following writers in particular have espoused this view: GOLDMAN, *Mélanges Roubier* II (1961) 51; TUNC, JCP 1957. I. 384, JCP 1960. I. 1952 and *Rev. trim. dr. civ.* 59 (1961) 125 ff., and MAZEAUD, *Rev. trim. dr. civ.* 55 (1957) 529.—ESMEIN, JCP 1960. II. 11824, also approves of the decision of the Court of Cassation on the ground, *inter alia*, that it makes good sense from the insurance point of view, since the premiums are much easier to work out if liability insurance is taken out not by the carrier but by the person who normally uses such bottles as containers for his products. The courts sometimes use the distinction between 'garde du comportement' and 'garde de la structure' in cases of products liability. A person who is injured when a bottle of mineral water explodes can use art. 1384 par. 1 against the manufacturer who bottled the water: certainly the manufacturer has relinquished possession of the bottle, but he remains its *gardien* so far as its internal structure goes, especially for faults in the material. See Poitiers, 23 Dec. 1969, Gaz. Pal. 1970. 2. 13; Civ. 12 Nov. 1975, JCP 1976. II. 18479, noted by VINEY.

4. Liability under art. 1384 par. 1 is excluded if the custodian of the thing can prove that the harm was due to *cas fortuit* or *force majeure*, these expressions being synonymous in the view of the French courts.

According to the cases, an event constitutes *cas fortuit* or *force majeure* if it is external to the thing which does the harm and is both unforeseeable and unavoidable in its consequences. (Civ. 2 July 1946, D. 1946, 392.)

One important effect of the rule that the cause must be 'external' or 'outside' the thing which does the harm is that a latent defect in the thing, such as a defect in the way it is made or the material it is made of, does not release the defendant even if it was quite impossible for him to discover and remove the defect. This rule is applied in cases in which an automobile accident is caused by something internal which the custodian could not have foreseen such as a sudden failure of brakes or steering or by the blowout of a tyre.

See for example, Paris 18 July 1930, DH 1930, 530; Req. 22 Jan. 1945, S. 1945. 1. 57; Civ. 6 March 1959, Gaz. Pal. 1959. 2. 12. Liability is also imposed if without any fault on his part a driver loses consciousness at the wheel (see Civ. 18 Dec. 1964, D. 1965, 191).

If the cause of the harm is 'external' to the thing in this sense, a further requirement is that the custodian should not have been able to foresee it even if he was exercising all the requisite care. A patch of oil on a tarred highway may count as *force majeure* if no careful and attentive driver could have seen it (Bordeaux 12 Feb. 1959, Gaz. Pal. 1959. 2. Somm. 16). Exceptionally, also, the sudden appearance of black ice has been seen as an instance of *force majeure* (Crim. 18 Dec. 1978, JCP 1980. II. 19261, noted by ALVAREZ), as has the skidding of a lorry on a pool of oily water on a wet road (Civ. 28 Nov. 1965, D. 1986, 137, noted by TUNC).

Natural events are only regarded as *force majeure* if they occur with unforeseeable suddenness and irresistible violence and the custodian in the case could not possibly or reasonably have taken the steps required to prevent the harm (see MAZEAUD/TUNC II nos. 1607 f., citing many decisions). In such a case the custodian is freed from liability entirely, but if the 'fait de la chose' contributed to the harm, courts have been known to make the *gardien* liable for an appropriate *part* of the harm only (Com. 19 June 1951, D. 1951, 717, noted by RIPERT).

It follows from the *Jand'heur* decision that liability under art. 1384 par. 1 is excluded if the cause of the harm is the *faulty conduct of the victim*, though only when the fault of the victim was so serious as to constitute, from the point of view of the *gardien*, 'force majeure', rendering the accident 'imprévisible et irrésistible'. But the courts soon held that even when the fault of the victim did not constitute 'force majeure', it might lead to a *reduction* of his claim for damages, rather than an exclusion of it. This was often criticized in the literature (above all by ANDRÉ TUNC, *La Sécurité routière* (1966)). Neverthless it was a sensation when in its *Desmares* decision in 1982 the Cour de Cassation associated itself with such criticism and suddenly held that the defence of contributory negligence was not available to the motorist.

See Civ. 21 July 1982, D. 1982, 449, conclusions by CHARBONNIER and note by LARROUMET. The decision was earth-shaking (see TUNC, *Essays in Memory of Professor Lawson* (1986) 71). Many writers saw it as an important step forward in the protection of accident victims while others regarded it as a clear instance of improper judicial legislation. Either way it gave a great impetus to the reform of traffic accident law, long demanded by ANDRÉ TUNC and others. Finally the Law 5 July 1985 (no. 85–677) came into force.

The main thrust of the enactment was to curtail the defences available in cases of traffic accidents resulting in personal injury or death. The defence of *force majeure* is totally excluded, as is the defence of contributory negligence where the victim was young (under sixteen) or old (over seventy) or seriously disabled (at least 80%). In other cases a claim can only be reduced if the fault of the victim was both a *faute inexcusable* and the *cause exclusive* of the accident. This does not apply, however, when the victim was himself driving a vehicle involved in the accident, a gap in protection which has been filled by a very popular type of insurance specifically designed for the purpose. As a result it is estimated that the fault of the driver or the victim is an issue in only 10–20% of traffic accident cases in France today.

The law applies whenever a motor vehicle is 'involved' (*impliqué*) in the accident. It need not be in motion at the time or even have its motor running; it is enough if the risks entailed in the operation of a motor vehicle contributed, however distantly, to the occurrence of the accident. Not every instance of gross negligence on the part of the victim constitutes a *faute inexcusable*, but only blatant and extreme fecklessness (see Ass.plén. 10 Nov. 1995, JCP 1996. II. 22564, noted by VINEY = ZEuP 1997, 496, noted by KÖTZ). In addition the *faute inexcusable* must be the sole cause of the accident. See Civ. 8 Nov. 1993, Bull. II. no. 316: here the plaintiff boldly climbed on to the roof of a bus stalled in traffic on New Year's Eve, and fell off when it started to move. He obtained full damages: his fault, even if inexcusable, was not the sole cause of the accident if the bus driver knew when he drove off that he had a passenger on the roof.—Meanwhile the Cour de Cassation has made it clear that in cases other than those involving traffic accidents contributory negligence is once again a (partial) defence for the *gardien*: see Civ. 6 Apr. 1987, D. 1988, 32, noted by CHABAS.

5. The Italian Codice civile, apart from imposing liability on the custodian of an animal and the owner of a building (arts. 2052 f.), makes the driver and custodian of a motor vehicle strictly liable, in a manner akin to §7 St VG: it is impossible to escape liability for harm caused by a fault in construction or maintenance but in other cases exoneration is possible if the defendant did everything possible ('tutto il possibile') to avoid the accident (see art. 2054). Furthermore, if harm is caused by a thing art. 2051 Codice civile imposes liability on the person who had control of it: this provision is the direct descendant of art. 1384 par. 1 Code civil and is construed and applied in much the same manner. The Code civile strikes out on a path of its own by imposing liability under art. 2050 on a person who conducts an activity which is *dangerous* either in itself or by reason of the materials it uses: if harm is caused in the execution of such an 'attività pericolosa' the operator is liable in damages unless he can prove that he took all the precautions which might have avoided the harm. Although this might appear to be a liability for presumed fault, the courts in fact apply the same standards to this exculpatory proof as they do in a case of liability for things. There is therefore no practical difference between liability for things under art. 2051 and liability for dangerous activities under art. 2050, but having an alternative ground of liability does allow the Italian courts to adopt a more flexible approach, for if the harm is caused by the fall of a high tension electric cable, they can say that this harm was caused by the dangerous *activity* of transmitting electricity and are not forced to say, as the French courts rather animistically do, that the harm was caused by a *thing*, namely the falling cable.

IV

1. In *English* law a person can hardly ever claim damages for personal injury or property damage without having to prove breach of a duty of care, though there are a few instances where Parliament has imposed strict liability: on the owner of an airplane for damage caused by it on the surface of the earth (Civil Aviation Act 1982), on the producer or user of atomic energy (Nuclear Installations Act 1965), and on the producer who puts defective goods into circulation (Consumer Protection Act 1987). Under certain circumstances the keeper of an animal may be liable without fault for damage done by it (Animals Act 1971).
Britain has no special law imposing strict liability on the custodian of a

motor vehicle. But while the French courts have improved the rights of the traffic victim by developing the strict liability of the *gardien* of a chattel under art. 1384 par. 1 Code civil, England still applies the general rules of negligence at Common Law. It is true that after 1930, when owners of motor vehicles were required to have liability insurance, the courts began 'in cases where the plaintiff excited their compassion . . . to twist the law of negligence to make a defendant liable for negligence when he was really not negligent at all, to make his insurers pay' (SPENCER (above p. 647) 80). So a learner driver who had just obtained a provisional licence has been held to be acting negligently in not displaying the care of an experienced driver (*Nettleship* v. *Weston*, [1971] 2 QB 691), and a truck-owner has been held liable for a defect in the brakes which no layman could ever have discovered (*Henderson* v. *Jenkins & Sons*, [1970] AC 282). Even so, cases constantly crop up such that with the best will in the world one cannot find any negligence. Many people find this unsatisfactory. LORD DENNING has written:

'In the present state of motor traffic, I am persuaded that any civilised system of law should require, as a matter of principle, that the person who uses this dangerous instrument on the roads—dealing death and destruction all around—should be liable to make compensation to anyone who is killed or injured in consequence of the use of it. There should be liability without proof of fault. To require an injured person to prove fault results in the gravest injustice to many innocent persons who have not the wherewithal to prove it' (*What Next in the Law?* (1982) 128; see also the criticisms by SPENCER (above p. 647)). The Royal [Pearson] Commission on Civil Liability and Compensation for Personal Injury agreed that reform was urgently required, but instead of simply proposing that vehicle-owners be made strictly liable in tort, it advocated the abandonment of tort law altogether and its replacement by a system of compensation run by the state (see below VI). This may be right, but it is so radical a step that it is most unlikely to be taken in England for a long time yet, so the situation where there is no liability unless there is negligence is likely to continue for some time. On this see the critical comments by SPENCER (above p. 647).

Only one case of strict liability has been developed by the English *courts*. This arises under the celebrated decision of *Rylands* v. *Fletcher* in 1868. Here the defendant was having a reservoir constructed on his land in order to power his mill. On the chosen site there were disused mine shafts, filled with earth, and they were connected with the underground mineworkings operated by the plaintiff on the neighbouring land, though the defendant had no means of knowing this. When the reservoir was filled, water flowed down the mine shafts and flooded the mine-workings next door. It could not be shown that the defendant was at fault at all, but he had to pay damages. The rule formulated by BLACKBURN J. on appeal has since become classical:

'We think that the true rule of law is, that the person who for his own purposes brings on his land and collects and keeps there anything likely to do mischief if it escapes, must keep it in at his peril, and, if he does not do so, is prima facie answerable for all the damage which is the natural consequence of its escape . . . it seems but reasonable and just that the neighbour, who has brought something on his own property (which was not naturally there), harmless to others so long as it is confined to his own property, but which he knows will be mischievous if it gets on his neighbour's, should be obliged to make good the damage which ensues if he does not succeed in confining it to his own property' (*Fletcher* v. *Rylands* (1866) LR 1 Ex. 265, 279 f.).

This decision was upheld by the House of Lords in *Rylands* v. *Fletcher* (1868), LR 3 HL 330, with the addition of the further requirement that the storage of the thing must constitute a 'non-natural user' of the land.

This precedent became the source of many different lines of cases which can only be presented in outline here.

The rule in *Rylands* v. *Fletcher* applies not only to the escape of water but also to the escape of gas or electricity stored in bulk, normally for industrial purposes, on the defendant's land, and even to the escape of water or gas from pipes in which the defendant is conveying it over the land of others. The courts have also applied *Rylands* v. *Fletcher* in cases where harm was caused by detonations in a quarry, or by the explosion of dinitrophenol in an explosives factory. The rule may also be applied to *continuing* situations, as where poisonous gases are emitted from a factory.

See, for example, *Northwestern Utilities Ltd.* v. *London Guarantee and Accident Co.*, [1936] AC 108 (fracture of subterranean gas-pipes); *Rainham Chemical Works Ltd.* v. *Belvedere Fish Guano Co.*, [1921] 2 AC 465 (explosives); *Halsey* v. *Esso Petroleum Co. Ltd.*, [1961] 2 All ER 145 (sulphurous soot).

Liability does not arise unless the bringing of the damaging thing on to the defendant's land constitutes a 'non-natural user' of the land. A claim under *Rylands* v. *Fletcher* will consequently fail if water or gas escapes from standard domestic piping or if harm is caused by defective electric wiring in a house or business premises or by a fault of a theatre's sprinkler system. An additional ground for the dismissal of a claim under *Rylands* v. *Fletcher* in such cases may be that the tenant consented to the risk of accidental defects in the utilities in the leased premises and must therefore base any claim on 'negligence'.

Another requirement for liability under *Rylands* v. *Fletcher* is that the harm must have been caused by an 'escape' of the thing: the harmful thing must have left the area under the defendant's control and have caused the harm outside it.

In *Read* v. *J. Lyons & Co.* [1947] AC 156 the plaintiff was injured by an explosion in the defendant's munitions factory while she was working there. The House of Lords dismissed her claim on the ground that the harm did not result from any 'escape' from the defendant's land but occurred entirely within his factory. The House of Lords was not impressed by the obvious objection that it could hardly make any difference whether the plaintiff was hurt just before or just after she entered the factory gates ([1947] AC 156, 177 f.).

Finally a claim lies under *Rylands* v. *Fletcher* only if the defendant could reasonably have foreseen that things which escaped from his land could cause damage of the kind actually suffered by the plaintiff: it is no defence for the defendant to show that he could not himself have prevented the escape, but he can plead that no reasonable man could have foreseen the ensuing harm.

This was the reason for the dismissal of the plaintiff's claim in *Cambridge Water Co.* v. *Eastern Counties Leather Plc* [1994] 2 AC 264. Until 1976 there were regular spillages of small quantities of perchlorethylene on the premises where the defendant degreased animal pelts prior to turning them into leather goods. The chemicals seeped some fifty metres into the earth and after being carried in the aquifer for some two kilometres polluted the well from which the plaintiff supplied drinking water. The plaintiff's claim for over £1 million was dismissed because in 1976 no one could reasonably have foreseen that any such damage could ensue from the spillage of small quantities of perchlorethylene.

In its Report the Royal [Pearson] Commission on Civil Liability and Compensation for Personal Injury (Cmnd. 7054 (1978)) recommended that new instances of strict liability be introduced by statute and imposed on railway undertakings, manufacturers of defective products, and those giving experimental treatment or drugs to 'human guinea-pigs'. In addition, strict liability should be imposed on the controllers of things or operations in two categories, those which are of an unusually hazardous nature and those which, though normally safe, are likely, if they go wrong, to cause serious and extensive harm. It would be for the relevant Minister, acting by statutory instrument, to decide which installations and activities should attract this strict liability, as the 'process of judicial legislation' would inevitably be tedious.

Although the proposals of the Pearson Commission (so called after its Chairman) fell on stony ground, they contain much of importance and interest regarding reform of the law of compensation for accidental injuries. See ALLEN/BOURN/HOLYOAK, *Accident Compensation after Pearson* (1979); FLEMING, 42 *Mod. L. Rev.* 251 (1979); MARSH, 95 *LQ Rev.* 512 (1979); KÖTZ *VersR* 1979, 585.

2. The principle underlying *Rylands* v. *Fletcher* is generally accepted in the *United States* as well: indeed, the American courts seem to be in the process of freeing it from the restrictive conditions of liability laid down in the leading decision and expanding it into a general strict liability for particularly hazardous activities. Many courts still cite *Rylands* v. *Fletcher*, but others establish an identical or similar principle without mentioning the case by name. For this purpose some of the several states have used the tort of 'nuisance', which mainly covers cases of continuing harm caused by gases, steam, smells, and so on, though it is occasionally applicable to sudden and isolated occurrences such as explosions (see PROSSER, 'Nuisance without Fault',

20 *Texas L. Rev.* 399 (1942)). Finally the courts have occasionally invoked the Restatement. §519(1) Restatement (Second) of Torts (1965) provides that 'one who carries on an abnormally dangerous activity is subject to liability for harm to the person, land, or chattels of another resulting from the activity, although he has exercised the utmost care to prevent such harm'. According to §520 whether an activity is 'abnormally dangerous' depends in part on how great the risk involved is, how serious the damage might be, whether the risk can be neutralized by the adoption of reasonable measures of prevention, and finally on whether the activity is or is not a 'matter of common usage', at any rate in the locality in question.

The cases in which American defendants have been held strictly liable are very much like those in England. They involve storing large quantities of water in tanks or reservoirs, keeping explosives or inflammable liquids in bulk, operating drilling devices in built-up areas, and using poisonous chemicals as pesticides. Strict liability is also imposed if explosions project fragments of stone on to the land of third parties or cause vibration damage to their buildings. By contrast, suppliers of gas or electricity are not normally subject to strict liability; the custodian of a motor car and the operator of a railway are also usually liable only for negligence, and this is true in most states even of the owner of an airplane which causes damage on the surface of the earth.

In deciding whether or not to impose strict liability for the harm done by an activity, business, or situation, the American courts always take account of any special circumstances in the locality which may have rendered it especially dangerous. This is the same idea as leads English courts to deny liability under *Rylands* v. *Fletcher* for 'natural' uses of land, but it seems to have particular importance in the United States because of the vast differences between different localities in terms of population and degree of industrialization. The consideration that the defendant was in an industry of special economic importance may also affect the courts, though they do not always admit it.

Thus in *Turner* v. *Big Lake Oil Co.*, 128 Tex. 115, 96 SW. 2d 222 (1936) the defendant oil company had on its land great basins for the reception of salt water from their wells. The edge of one of these basins gave way, and the escaping water caused serious harm to the plaintiffs. The defendant, who was not shown to have been guilty of any fault, was held not liable, because the court found that the rule of *Rylands* v. *Fletcher* was not applicable. One of the principal reasons given for this by the court was that in Texas, where the extraction of oil was one of the most important industries and there were thousands of oilwells, there was nothing non-natural about keeping salt water in basins, since that was an unavoidable incident of drilling for oil.— Further examples are given by PROSSER, 'The Principle of Rylands v. Fletcher' (above p. 647) 163, 170 ff., 186 ff.

Strict liability does not attach if the harm is due to an act of God or the unforeseeable intervention of a third party for whose behaviour the defendant is not answerable.

V

It emerges from our comparative survey that the tendency of the law of tort in all the legal systems investigated has been to improve the position of victims by restricting or even abandoning the principle of 'no liability without fault'. This tendency is stronger and more marked in certain types of accident than in others. Various reasons can be given: that the victims of certain types of accident deserve particular protection, that certain unusual risks are acceptable only if liability is particularly strict, that in certain types of case fault is especially difficult to prove, that the risk of certain accidents is especially easy to insure against, and that the premiums paid by the party at risk can very easily be disseminated. Industrial accidents provide the best-known example: here the long-standing practice has been not to increase liability in favour of the victim but rather to do away with it entirely and replace it with a system of social insurance. For *traffic accidents* also most countries have a specially strict liability, and many legislatures, appalled by the thalidomide tragedy, have enacted special rules for compensating those injured by *defective drugs* (see the comparative study by FLEMING, 'Drug Injury Compensation Plans', 30 *Am. J. Comp. L.* 297 (1982)). For accidents arising from the operation of a *nuclear installation* traditional rules of liability for fault have been abandoned everywhere (comparative treatment by OLLIER, XI *Int. Enc. Comp. L.* 'Torts' (1983) Ch. 5 §§214–25). But we turn now to an interesting and important type of case which attracts a particularly strict regime of liability, the case where a person suffers personal injury in consequence of a *defective product*.

What is of special importance is whether the victim has any claim *against the manufacturer*. To have such a claim is of very considerable interest to the victim, for while he may well have an action against the seller if the product was one that he had purchased, his rights will be determined by the contract of sale, and the terms of that contract may exclude or qualify any right to compensation, or subject it to a monetary limit, a short period of limitation, or a requirement of notice. Furthermore in many legal systems the liability of a seller depends on his being at fault with regard to the defect in the goods, and if the seller is merely a cog in the manufacturer's distributive system it may not be easy to establish any such fault on his part, especially as sellers often lack the technical expertise required to test the safety of complex pieces of apparatus before delivering them to the customer. But there is another reason for making the manufacturer directly liable, namely that the defect may cause harm to someone other than the purchaser, perhaps a member of his family or even a complete stranger in the vicinity. A pedestrian on the sidewalk who is injured when a car leaves the road because of a defective axle or a patron in a pub who is struck by flying glass when a defective bottle of mineral water explodes at the next table will be interested in suing the manufacturer of the car and the bottle which they have not themselves bought.

Policy reasons for imposing strict liability on the manufacturer of defective goods are not far to seek. Today as never before, thanks to the modern division of labour, people need and want to use products whose safety they themselves are in no position to check. This being so, the public must be able to rely on being able to use such products without injury to themselves or their property, all the more so as manufacturers deliberately and for commercial gain direct their advertising so as to induce consumers to count on the excellence of their wares. It is accordingly unacceptable that the consumer who without any fault on his own part is injured by a defect in the goods should be left uncompensated just because he cannot prove any lack of care on the part of the manufacturer, as normally he cannot when production is automated. But if such a victim is to have a claim for damages at all, it is only right that it should lie against the manufacturer: not only because he controls the manufacturing process and, usually, the advertisement of the product on the market, but also because he can insure against this risk most cheaply and pass on the cost to all his consumers by taking the premiums into account when he is pricing his goods.

It was the courts in the United States that led the field in developing products liability. Ever since the decision in *MacPherson* v. *Buick* (above p. 612) it has been agreed that the manufacturer of goods owes a duty of care not only to the person to whom he sells them but also to any third party injured by their use. The victim thus had a claim in negligence. But such a claim only succeeds if the victim can prove that the manufacturer was at fault, in breach of his duty of care. With the help of the courts this obstacle has been overcome. First the courts went to the law of contract and enlisted the aid of the warranty from the law of sales. Now in the Common Law a claim for breach of warranty is one of strict liability and it entitles the purchaser to full damages and not simply, as is normally the rule in German law, to a diminution or the return of the price he has paid. On the other hand, a claim for breach of warranty in principle lies only against the person with whom the injured buyer contracted, that is, the retailer, and it could be brought only by the buyer himself and not by members of his family, guests, or other persons who may be injured by the defective goods. The courts therefore sought to extend the protection of the manufacturer's contractual guarantee so as to include the final consumer, his family, and others close to him. Sometimes they spoke of 'warranties running with the goods'; sometimes they found it unduly formalistic to restrict the claim for breach of warranty to adjacent parties when there was a chain of sales, and gave the final consumer a direct claim against the manufacturer as a 'permissible short-cut' which saved time and money. Such ideas were first used in cases of bad food, then in cases of products designed for intimate bodily use such as soap, hair-dyes, clothes, cigarettes, vaccines, and so on, and finally wherever the goods would be dangerous to the user if defective, such as cars, car-tyres, domestic appliances, heating appliances, and so on. The Uniform Commercial Code has adopted this position (§2–318). But a contractual claim for breach of warranty had the further drawback that it could be affected by the terms of the contract of sale. Here too the courts used all the weapons at their command, deploying the device of restrictive construction *contra proferentem* and sometimes even holding that the exemption clause in issue was contrary to public policy and void (see *Henningsen* v. *Bloomfield Motors Inc.*, 32 NJ 358, 161 A. 2d 69 (1960)).

Contractual principles are still occasionally used in the United States, but the general view now is that when a consumer is injured by an objectively defective product, the strict liability of the manufacturer should be cut free from the law of contract and based openly on tort. It is now a '*strict liability in tort*'.

First pointers in this direction were *Escola* v. *Coca-Cola Bottling Co.*, 24 Cal. 2d 453, 150 P. 2d 436 (1944; see especially the opinion of JUDGE TRAYNOR); *Greenman* v. *Yuba Power Products Inc.*, 59 Cal. 2d 57, 377 P. 2d 897 (1963).

The breakthrough occurred in 1965 when Restatement (Second) of Torts was published, with the following §402 A:

(1) One who sells any product in a defective condition unreasonably dangerous to the user or consumer or to his property is subject to liability for physical harm thereby caused to the ultimate user or consumer, or to his property, if
  (*a*) the seller is engaged in the business of selling such a product, and
  (*b*) it is expected to and does reach the user or consumer without substantial change in the condition in which it is sold.
(2) The rule stated in Subsection (1) applies although
  (*a*) the seller has exercised all possible care in the preparation and sale of his product, and
  (*b*) the user or consumer has not bought the product from or entered into any contractual relation with the seller.

Courts in most of the states have adopted this rule in one form or another. The component elements have been more closely specified and in many respects the protection afforded to the victim has been improved. In particular it is agreed that 'innocent bystanders', that is persons who are not part of the distributive chain but who find themselves by mishap in proximity to the defective product, can base a claim on products liability. Furthermore the courts allow suits against not only the manufacturer but also wholesale and retail distributors, suppliers of defective components for incorporation into an end-product by a manufacturer, those who lease or hire out defective products (*Price* v. *Shell Oil Co.*, 2 Cal. 3d 245, 466 P. 2d 722 (1970)), and finally those who purchase the actual manufacturer's business and then engage in the manufacture of similar products (*Ray* v. *Alad Corp.*, 19 Cal. 3d 22, 560 P. 2d 3 (1977)). In exceptional cases, indeed, the plaintiff may win even although it is not established *who* produced the defective product.

The plaintiff in *Sindell* v. *Abbott Laboratories*, 26 Cal. 3d 588, 607 P. 2d 924 (1980) had suffered physical injury because her mother, while pregnant with her, had taken the drug DES which is harmful to the foetus. Claim was brought against a few of the 200-odd firms which produced DES at the time and used it in their products. The plaintiff was unable to prove which of the defendants had produced the pills her mother had taken years before, and it was quite possible that none of the defendants had made them; nevertheless the court decided in the plaintiff's favour: if, as in the case itself, the defendants between them had a 'significant' share of the market it would be presumed that the DES-drug which harmed the plaintiff was manufactured by one or other of them, and any defendant who could not rebut such a presumption—practically impossible in that case—would be liable for such percentage of the harm as represented his market share. This judgment has been much admired and heavily criticized; courts in other states have been slow to follow it and have modified it. See FLEMING, *The American Tort Process* (1988) 258 ff.; PETERSON/ZEKOLL, 'Mass Torts', 42 *Am. J. Comp. L.* (1994 supplement) 79, 88 ff.—In the Netherlands the principle of market-share liability has been adopted and indeed expanded by the Hoge Raad in a similar case: defendants are liable *jointly and severally* and any one who pays more than his market share has a claim for contribution from the others (9 Oct. 1992, Ned. Jur. 1994 no. 535). On this case see TEULINGS, 110 *LQ Rev.* 228 (1994) and ZÄTSCH, *ZVglRW* 93 (1994) 177, as well as the comparative observations in 2 *Eur. Rev. P. L.* 409 ff. (1994).

The central question in products liability cases is whether the goods were *defective* at the time the defendant put them into circulation; it is no longer relevant whether or not the defendant was guilty of any negligence. Thus the plaintiff's position is better than in a negligence case, but not so much better as one might at first suppose. Certainly the plaintiff's position is better when there is a *manufacturing defect*, where a defective example of an otherwise sound product has somehow slipped through, for liability is established simply by proof of the defect. Such cases are, however, fairly uncommon. More often the case involves a *design defect*, where the plaintiff alleges that the entire output of a particular product of the defendant's, be it a car, a lawn-mower, a heater, or whatever, has a defective design or that the entire batch of a particular drug or food product has noxious side-effects.

Is it a defect in a caterpillar tractor if the rear-view mirror is so placed in relation to the driver's seat that when he sits back there is a 'blind spot' (*Pike* v. *Frank G. Hough & Co.*,

2 Cal. 3d 465, 467 P. 2d 229 (1970))? Is it a defect in an automobile if the petrol tank is not in the best place to minimize the risk of getting damaged and letting out petrol which may catch fire? What if the petrol tank was correctly situated, but the plaintiff alleges that it should have been made of heavier metal? What if the heavier metal would have made the car more expensive, reduced its acceleration, and increased its petrol consumption? Is there a design defect in a truck if it has no grid at the rear to prevent a car sliding under it in a rear-end collision (*Mieher* v. *Brown*, 54 Ill. 2d 539, 301 NE 2d 307 (1974))? The critical question here is whether, given the state of technical knowledge at the time, some safer method of construction was possible and should have been adopted. It will be seen that many of the relevant facts and considerations are the same as in a claim based on the producer's failure to exercise reasonable care. It is undecided whether the relevant state of the art is to be judged as of the time the product was manufactured or whether the manufacturer is liable for 'development risks' as well, that is, is liable if safer methods of construction are devised after the harm has occurred. The same question arises where liability is based on a *fault of instruction*. Is the manufacturer liable if he fails to draw the customer's attention to dangers in the product which, although evident today, were quite unknown when the product was put into circulation? Only in a few cases have courts gone so far: see *Beshada* v. *Johns-Manville Products Corp.* 19 NJ 191, 447 A. 2d 539 (1982) and *Cepeda* v. *Cumberland Engineering Co.* 76 NJ 152, 386 A. 2d 816 (1978). On this see FLEMING (above p. 646) 62 ff.; HENDERSON, 'Judicial Review of Manufacturer's Conscious Design Choices: The Limits of Adjudication', 73 *Colum. L. Rev.* 1531 (1973); HENDERSON/TWERSKI, 'Doctrinal Collapse in Products Liability: The Empty Shell of Failure to Warn', 65 *NYUL Rev.* 265 (1990).

The number of 'products liability' cases decided by American courts is now stupendous, and the range of publications and multi-volume loose-leaf services on the subject testify to the enormous interest of practising lawyers in this area. What surprises the European observer is not so much the conditions of liability, which have been just as strict in many European states for some time now, but rather the procedures by which such cases are decided, the size of the awards made to successful claimants, and finally the fact that it is not uncommon for many thousands of claims to be bundled together and dealt with in a single trial.

The size of awards is explicable in part by the fact that product liability cases are heard before a jury, and it is the jury, favourably inclined to the victim in case of doubt, that decides on the amount of damages, including an extra sum by way of punitive damages if the defendant manufacturer was especially careless. Furthermore, as the jury knows, the plaintiff's attorney will keep 30–50% of any damages awarded (though he gets nothing if the plaintiff loses). Product liability cases can turn into a circus when thousands of claims are amalgamated and fought out all at once with dozens of advocates on both sides. A single court can hear numerous claims from different jurisdictions in a 'consolidated action', and in a 'class action' one or more plaintiffs represent a multitude of others similarly injured and seek a decision on a point of law or an award of damages in favour of all the victims. In view of this, a firm not yet insolvent may well go for protection against claimants under Chapter II of the Bankruptcy Act so that negotiations may lead to a settlement subject to the approval of the court; in this way the victims may obtain some satisfaction without causing the collapse of the firm. For details see FLEMING, 'Mass Torts', 42 *Am. J. Comp. L.* 507 (1994).

Special rules for the liability of the manufacturer of products have been developed by courts in Europe as well. *France* shows that to a large extent one can achieve the desirable sharpening of liability by extending claims in contract. Under art. 1645 Code civil the seller of defective goods must compensate the buyer for all harm due to the defect if he *knew* of the defect in the object sold. The French courts have repeatedly laid down 'que doit être assimilé au vendeur qui connaissait les vices de la chose celui qui par sa profession ne pouvait les ignorer' (Civ. 17 Feb. 1965, Bull. civ. 1965. III. 112). This means that anyone who has sold defective wares in the course of his business, whether as manufacturer, wholesaler, or retailer, is treated as if he had been aware of the defect. From this it follows not only that he is liable to the purchaser for all the harm resulting therefrom, but also that he is barred by art. 1643 Code civil from excluding this strict liability by any term he may put in the contract. Now this being a contractual liability, the ultimate consumer can in principle sue only the retailer from whom he bought the thing, but of course the retailer, if sued, can immediately bring an 'appel en garantie' against the wholesaler for an indemnity in respect of any liability to the consumer, for the wholesaler's liability is equally strict, and the wholesaler in his turn can sue the manufacturer on the same basis, with the result that the chain of purchasers is 'wound in' and at the end of the day the manufacturer pays and the consumer is paid without any fault being proved. 'Pour éviter cette cascade de recours' the courts have allowed the final purchaser to leapfrog over his predecessor in title, who may be insolvent or out of the jurisdiction, and sue the first seller, normally the manufacturer, directly.

In *Germany* there was a long period of doubt whether to base the manufacturer's liability on the tort provisions of the BGB or on the manufacturer's special, nearly contractual relationship with the consumer, but the Bundesgerichtshof finally decided that if the injured person is in no direct contractual relationship with the manufacturer his claim has to lie in tort. The claim must be based on §§823 ff. BGB, which means that in principle the plaintiff must prove that the defendant manufacturer was guilty of some want of care. The BGH has nevertheless made an exception to this principle in the area of products liability. The plaintiff only has to prove that the goods were in an objectively defective condition when they left the factory and that his injury was due to that defect. Once this proof has been led the liability of the manufacturer is established, unless he can prove that he and all those who were involved with the product during its manufacture took all the necessary care.

This important principle was first laid down by the Bundesgerichtshof in the so-called 'fowl-pest' decision (BGHZ 51, 91). The plaintiff was a chicken-farmer who decided to have his chickens vaccinated against fowl-pest. The veterinary surgeon used a vaccine which he had obtained from the defendant manufacturer. A few days later fowl-pest broke out in the plaintiff's farm and more than 4,000 chickens died of it. It was established that there were impurities in the vaccine because of some mistake in the manufacture and that the outbreak of fowl-pest on the plaintiff's farm was attributable to this. The Bundesgerichtshof found that this was sufficient to make the defendant liable, for once it had been shown that the vaccine had left the factory in a defective condition it was for the defendant to prove how the defect arose and that no blame attached to the firm or its staff. Such proof the defendant was unable to adduce.

This is the only means of escape for the manufacturer, a *probatio diabolica* which can hardly ever be, and never has been, successful, for there must be no gap in the manufacturer's evidence that in designing the process of manufacture, in selecting the machinery for quality control and in issuing instructions to his staff he took all the necessary and requisite precautions to be expected of a proper manufacturer of products of that kind. In addition he must prove that he was careful in choosing and supervising all the personnel who might have been at fault in causing the defect or failing to discover it (BGH NJW 1973, 1602). The same rules of proof apply in cases of *design defects* (BGHZ 67, 359, 362), and usually in cases of *inadequate instructions* (BGHZ 80,186,195 ff. and BGHZ 116,60,72 f.). No one, however, suggests that §823 BGB can render the manufacturer liable for *development risks*.

Liability for development risks does exist in one area, namely in the manufacture of medicaments, under §§84 ff. of the Medicaments Law of 1978. Under this law the manufacturer is liable if injury or death is caused by the use of a medicament 'if, by reason of the manner of its development or manufacture the medicament, being used as prescribed, has adverse effects beyond what medical science regards as acceptable'. Such liability is limited in amount and does not extend to damages for pain and suffering.

Almost every member state in the European Union has now implemented the 'Directive on the Approximation of the Laws, Regulations and Administrative Provisions of the Member States concerning Liability for Defective Products' of 25 July 1985, whereby the producer must pay for personal injury and property damage caused by a defect in a product which he has put into circulation. A product is defective 'when it does not provide the safety which a person is entitled to expect, taking all circumstances into account . . .'. The wording of the text implies that the producer may be liable although he has taken all proper care. This is true enough in the case of manufacturing defects, where a particular item in a range has a defect not found in other items in the same range, but it is not true in the case of design defects and failure to warn. After all, if the manufacturer has taken every care in the design of his product and given all reasonable warnings of any inherent dangers, his product may surely be said to provide the 'safety which a person is entitled to expect'. Furthermore, member states have exercised the option afforded to them by the Directive itself of excluding the liability of the producer if 'the state of scientific and technical knowledge at the time when he put the product into circulation was not such as to enable the existence of the defect to be discovered'. On this see STOPPA, 'The Concept of Defectiveness in the Consumer Protection Act 1987', 12 *LS* 210 (1992); PROSSER/KEETON p. 698 ff.; KÖTZ, 'Ist die Produkthaftung eine vom Verschulden unabhängige Haftung?', *Festschrift Lorenz* (1991) 109. The Directive has accordingly not made much difference to the law of product liability as developed by the courts in France, Germany, and England. Indeed it has made it more complicated, for the rules of national law remain in place despite the incorporation of the Directive, and the plaintiff often has to invoke both sets of rules, especially since certain kinds of damage are not covered by the Directive (pain and suffering, damage to commercial property, property damage below a certain threshold).

VI

Tort law turns on the concept of *liability*, on the view that a person has to pay for harm suffered by another only if for some specified reason he can be made 'liable' for that harm. Tort law specifies the reasons which justify making people liable for harm; as we know, reasons generally accepted are that he caused the harm by breach of some duty of care owed to another or that he had created a source of special risk and the harm was due to such a risk. If the victim cannot find anyone on whom to fix liability, he obtains no compensation for his harm, at any rate not through the law of tort: 'Sound policy lets losses lie where they fall except where a special reason can be shown for interference' (O. W. HOLMES, *The Common Law* 50 (1881)).

But can the law of tort, with such concepts, provide a proper solution to the problem of compensation for harm, especially for personal injury suffered in accidents? The question is being discussed all over the world. People's views of the extent to which the law must provide social security for the individual citizen have altered profoundly. As more and more people are being protected against more of the risks inherent in living, such as the economic consequences of deprivation, sickness, and unemployment, it is consistent to urge that the citizen be freed from the risks of *accident* as well, even if he cannot satisfy the traditional tests of tort law and establish a sufficiently close relationship to a 'responsible' cause of the injury. For this reason many countries have proposed, and some have enacted, schemes to replace the law of tort for certain types of accident or indeed for accidents of all kinds, so as to enable a victim to claim compensation for his personal injury regardless of any particular person's liability, or from an insurer who can spread the cost through the whole community of persons exposed to that risk. This by no means entails that the individual whom the law of tort would have held 'liable' always gets off scot-free, for he may be rendered liable to the insurer whenever indicated by considerations of accident prevention or loss distribution, for example, in cases of gross negligence. In practice the law of tort would simply be replaced for certain types or all types of accident by a system similar to that for industrial accidents, such as was introduced in Germany over a century ago and is now in force in most countries of the world.

The area of *traffic accidents* is eminently suitable for 'insurance protection rather than tort liability', because despite ubiquitous improvements in the law of tort by legislatures and courts, there are still a number of gaps in its protection of the victim.

The gap is very serious if the victim has to prove that the tortfeasor was at fault in respect of the accident, as in England (see above. p. 667). Germany has a system of strict liability: the custodian of a vehicle is liable even if the brakes unpredictably fail or a tyre suddenly blows out or the driver has a heart attack or an accident is caused by a stone thrown up by the defendant's lorry. However, if the victim wants damages for *pain and suffering* he must establish fault, and even so his claim will be reduced in amount if he was partly to blame for the accident (see above p. 655), a rule which has been criticized. In France, it is true, contributory negligence but rarely affects the victim's claim against the *gardien* of the vehicle (see above p. 665), but even here there is a lacuna in the case of a one-car accident, for example where the victim drives into a tree, whether by bad luck or bad management.

Another objection to the law of tort is that, operated as it is by courts and liability insurers, it takes more time and money than a system of accident insurance.

It has been estimated in Britain that of every £100 paid in premiums by motorists only £55 goes to victims; the rest is eaten up in court and lawyers' fees, the administration costs of insurers, and the sums paid to their agents. Under the industrial accident insurance scheme, by contrast, about £90 out of every £100 goes to victims (see the Report of the Royal [Pearson] Commission on Civil Liability and Compensation for Personal Injury (1978) (Cmnd. 7054) nos. 83, 121, 261). The difference is mainly due to the fact that every single case requires a finding on questions of fault, contributory fault, and the other components of liability at law, as well as over the extent of the victim's property damage, personal injury, and pain and suffering. These questions are often disputed, and have to be taken to court by lawyers. If an accident insurance system replaced the law of tort it would be easy to specify precise prerequisites to compensation, avoiding, in particular, the problem of establishing fault, just as is done for industrial accidents. Further savings could be made by removing property damage from the scheme, paying for personal injuries in accordance with a fixed tariff, and introducing compulsory insurance with a single insurer who need neither advertise for custom nor pay any agents.

Accident insurance has already wholly or partially replaced the law of tort as regards traffic accidents in many countries—Sweden, Norway and Finland, Israel and Poland—and in many states and provinces in Canada, Australia, and the USA.

See the detailed references given by VON HIPPEL in FLEMING/HELLNER/VON HIPPEL (above p. 646) 48; FLEMING, *The Law of Torts* (8th edn. 1992) 400 ff.—Some jurisdictions, such as Israel and Quebec, have abolished tort liability for traffic accidents altogether. Others have adopted intermediate positions. Thus in some states of the USA and some Canadian provinces accident insurance has been made mandatory, with very different minimum levels of cover; at the same time, however, tort law is preserved either in its entirety or sometimes only if the damage exceeds a certain dollar amount or is very serious in nature, such as death or permanent disability.—A system of accident insurance has long been proposed in Germany by VON HIPPEL (above p. 646) and in France by TUNC (above p. 647), the latter's proposals having been only partially implemented by the Law of 5 July 1985 (above p. 665).—In Great Britain the Pearson Commission proposed in 1968 that compensation for traffic victims should be provided by the state, much as for victims of industrial accidents, the costs to be funded from an extra tax on fuel oils. On this see FLEMING, 42 *Mod. L. Rev.* 249 (1979); MARSH, 95 *LQ Rev.* 513 (1979); KÖTZ, *VersR* 1979, 585.—Similar plans for other instances of damage to health have been proposed and sometimes implemented, for example, for damage done by *medicaments* (see FLEMING, 'Drug Injury Compensation Plans', 30 *Am. J. Comp. L.* 279 (1982)), and for harm suffered in medical treatment (see OLDERTZ, 'Security Insurance, Patient Insurance, and Pharmaceutical Insurance in Sweden', 34 *Am. J. Comp. L.* 635 (1986), and the comparative treatment in WEYERS, 'Empfiehlt es sich, im Interesse der Patienten und Ärzte ergänzende Regelungen für das ärztliche Vertrags- (Standes-) und Haftungsrecht einzuführen?', *VerhDJT* 52 (1978) A 1).

But the introduction of a system of insurance for traffic accidents does not solve the whole problem of serious and fatal accidents. After all, the needs of the victim and his family are exactly the same whether the accident occurs at work, on the way to work, on the way somewhere else, in the home, at school, or in some sporting activity. Is there any good reason for selecting certain types of accident for privileged treatment and giving them a special compensation system, especially when any distinction between 'insured' and 'uninsured' accidents is bound to lead to artificial distinctions, as the law of industrial accidents clearly shows? If this is admittedly unavoidable when certain specified types of accidents are selected for specially favourable treatment, would it not be logical, if one is to replace the law of tort by a system of insurance, to protect the citizen against *all accidents whatever*? Such systems have been discussed all over the world, and such a system was introduced in New Zealand in 1974.

The Accident Compensation Act of 1972 in New Zealand, based on the recommendations of a Government Commission chaired by Mr Justice WOODHOUSE, does away with the law of tort for all 'personal injury by accident' and confers special rights against the Accident Compensation Board, a state organ, on the victim or his dependants. To meet the expenditures of the Board, two funds were created: victims of *traffic accidents* are paid from a fund supported by taxes on owners of motor vehicles, while a different fund, fuelled by levies on employers, meets claims by employees for industrial diseases or personal injuries caused by accidents (other than traffic accidents) whether occurring at work or not. Other payments made by the Accident Compensation Board are met from general tax revenues. See PALMER, 'Accident Compensation in New Zealand: The First Two Years', 25 *Am. J. Comp. L.* 1 (1977); BROWN, 'Deterrence in Tort and No-Fault: The New Zealand Experience', 73 *Cal. L. Rev.* 976 (1985); MAHONEY, 'New Zealand's Accident Compensation Scheme: A Reassessment', 40 *Am. J. Comp. L.* 159 (1992), all with further references. Of course people have asked why the person whose health has suffered from an *accident* (or an industrial disease) should be any better off than the person who is equally disabled by a non-industrial *illness* or *congenital ailment*. Voices have been raised in favour of 'equal treatment for all victims', for the creation of a system of compensation which would in principle give the same compensation for the same injury; for example see ATIYAH/CANE (above p. 646) 397 ff.; ISON (above p. 646) 55 ff.; FLEMING/HELLNER/ VON HIPPEL (above p. 646) 59 f.

It is possible, however, to offer some arguments against replacing the law of tort by a system of accident insurance.

A system whereby all accident victims are to be treated the same can only be funded if the compensation it awards is lower than that presently afforded by the law of tort, for example, by excluding or restricting damages for pain and suffering. The money thus saved goes towards compensating those who cannot find anyone to blame for their injuries, such as those who fall in the bath or drive into a tree through not looking where they are going. But why should such persons be compensated at the expense of those who have been injured by the clear negligence of others and are now to be fobbed off with meagre social security payments? Suppose a drunk driver causes an accident by particularly reckless driving: is it really fair that he be paid as much for his own injuries as the child he has crippled? Is it fair that money should be found for him by reducing the tort claim of the crippled child?

This is not the only objection. While the aims of the law of tort may be disputed, it is agreed that deterrence is one of them: tort law provides an incentive to avoid causing accidents by threatening to make a person liable if he fails to show the prudence of the reasonable man. In the case of driving, admittedly, it is fear of injury rather than fear of liability which makes motorists take care, especially as they do not have to pay personally if they have insurance, but many other activities are dangerous to others without endangering the operator. In such cases the entrepreneur will certainly weigh up the respective risks involved in the alternative courses of action open to him. Even if he has liability insurance he will be aware that his premiums or deductible may be increased or cover withdrawn, and he will also realize that his reputation may suffer if he is careless and his products or conduct are exposed to the public eye in a trial (on this see LINDEN, 'Tort Law as Ombudsman', 51 *Can. Bar Rev.* 155 (1973)). The liability-insurance business is a competitive one, and insurers can tailor their premiums to the risks involved and so contribute to making different activities bear the cost of the harm they cause. It would not be right to exaggerate the extent to which a combination of tort liability and liability insurance can provide an incentive to safe conduct—criminal and administrative sanctions must clearly be retained—but it would be foolish to discount such deterrent effect as it can provide.

This, however, is exactly what is done by abolishing it in favour of a system of accident insurance in which the taxes or levies by which it is funded bear no relation to the amount of harm which could be avoided by contributors if they adopted sensible precautions. It is certainly not impossible to make levies proportional to the risk, but experience shows that this happens to an inadequate extent, especially if the system is run or supervised by the state. Thus the funds for victims in New Zealand and Quebec are raised by levies geared to the size of the vehicle, but not—whether for reasons of economy or political opportunism—to other relevant factors such as the age or gender of the driver, the mileage he does in his vehicle, how long he has had a driving licence, how many convictions he has for bad driving, or the frequency with which he has been involved in collisions. Such a system plainly subsidizes young males at the expense of safer drivers and conduces to the occurrence of accidents which could be prevented by exacting adequate levies from dangerous drivers and so keeping many of them off the roads.

For much more on these questions see ATIYAH/CANE (above p. 646) Ch. 25; ISON (above p. 646); ATIYAH, 'No Fault Compensation: A Question That Will Not Go Away', 54 *Tul. L. Rev.* 271 (1980); FLEMING, 'Is There a Future for Tort?', 58 *Austr. LJ* 131 (1984) = 44 *La. L. Rev.* 1193 (1984); HARRIS, 'Evaluating the Goals of Personal Injury Law; Some Empirical Evidence', in CANE/STAPLETON, *Essays for Patrick Atiyah* (1991) 289; PIERCE, 'Encouraging Safety: The Limits of Tort Law and Government Regulation', 33 *Vand. L. Rev.* 1281 (1980); SUGARMAN, 'Doing Away with Tort Law', 73 *Calif. L. Rev.* 558 (1985); TREBILCOCK, 'Incentive Issues in the Design of "No Fault" Compensation Systems', 39 *U. Tor. LJ* 19 (1989); DEWEES/DUFF/TREBILCOCK, *Exploring the Domain of Accident Law: Taking the Facts Seriously* (1996).

Even so it is fairly clear that as a system for compensating the victims of traffic accidents tort law is on the way out, and will be replaced in due course by systems of compensation where awards are made according to the nature and extent of the harm, not on how the harm occurred in the individual case or on whether it can be 'imputed' to any particular person. It must, however, be borne in mind that most accidents are due not to acts of God but to acts of man, and that the legal system cannot afford to abandon any method of affecting human conduct which could reduce the number of accidents and their severity. There is no reason to believe that criminal and administrative law will suffice on their own. Tort law may be an imperfect deterrent but it is indispensable, and anyone proposing to abolish it must consider how the deterrence it provides can be supplied, bearing in mind the relevant differences between highway and industrial accidents and between defective products and medical maltreatment.

It is uncertain what method of achieving this goal will be adopted. One way is to go for comprehensive reform, and create a system of 'people's accident insurance' on the New Zealand pattern. This way is most unlikely to be adopted in countries with traditional and complex rules of compensation. These rules may not always function in a satisfactory manner, there may be some regrettable lacunae, and they may not always be well integrated, but they often cover so much of the ground already that the need for total, radical, and immediate reform seems less urgent; furthermore, the lawyers and insurance men in these countries have a vested interest in the work and income generated by the existing system of accident compensation, so it is unrealistic to expect its conversion into a 'people's accident insurance' system overnight. In such countries, therefore, it makes more sense to go in for extending the *social security system* which is already independent of the law of tort, and on the other hand modifying the *law of tort* so as to make it function more like a system of accident insurance.

Social security systems are better developed in some countries than others, but in most industrial states in Europe today most citizens who have an accident are covered not only for medical costs, but also for loss of income, at any rate for a period. Where the accident causes permanent disability protection tends to be adequate only if the victim is an employee and the accident is an accident at work, but an accident suffered on the way to or from work is treated as an industrial accident in many countries, and some countries, such as Switzerland and the Netherlands, have gone further and include all accidents suffered by a worker, including 'accidents off work'. In Germany it has long been agreed that the same rules should in principle apply to accidents suffered by a housewife doing the housework, and only lack of funds has prevented actual implementation, but since 1971 the same protection as is given to victims of industrial accidents has been afforded to school-children and students who have an accident at, or on the way to or from, kindergarten, school, or college; indeed, the Federal Government is considering extending this protection to all accidents, and not just 'educational accidents'. All this goes to show that there is a constant increase in the number of accident victims who do not need to resort to the law of tort at all. Sweden is a leading example of a country where accidents are so fully covered and generously compensated by social insurance and supplementary systems of accident insurance that the general law of tort has become almost irrelevant. See

HELLNER, 'Compensation for Personal Injury: The Swedish Alternative', 34 *Am. J. Comp. L.* 613 (1986).

But even in the *law of tort*, as it applies to accidents, developments in the last few decades strongly suggest that one day it will really be functioning very much like a system of accident insurance. This is especially true for traffic accidents. The custodian of a motor vehicle must take out liability insurance today everywhere, and his victim is given a direct claim against the insurer, being more or less protected even if the insured has failed to pay the premium or broken a term of the policy or even if he has not insured the vehicle at all, or if the insurer is unidentifiable (as in a hit-and-run case) or insolvent. Gaps remain, but it has long been demanded that they be closed and the liability of the custodian extended.

In Germany people want damages for pain and suffering allowed and the monetary ceilings removed in cases of strict liability. Strict liability should cover passengers in the vehicle and should be excluded only in a case of true *force majeure*, not whenever there is an 'unavoidable event'. Above all the defence of contributory negligence should be excluded except where the victim was guilty of blatant negligence, as is the case in Sweden (see Ch. 6 §1 of the Law of Liability 1975) and France (Act no. 85–677 of 5 July 1985, see above p. 665). If all those proposals were implemented, the result would be very much like a system of traffic accident insurance.

43

Invasions of the Right of Personality

BADINTER, 'Le Droit au respect de la vie privée', *JCP* 1968. I. 2136.

BLOUSTEIN, 'Privacy as an Aspect of Human Dignity: An Answer to Dean Prosser', 39 *NYUL Rev.* 962 (1964).

BRITTAN, 'The Right of Privacy in England and the United States', 37 *Tul. L. Rev.* 235 (1963).

v. CAEMMERER, 'Privatrechtlicher Persönlichkeitsschutz im deutschen Recht', *Festschrift F.* v. *Hippel* (1967) 27.

COING/LAWSON/GRÖNFORS, *Das subjektive Recht und der Rechtsschutz der Persönlichkeit* (1959).

DE CUPIS, *I diritti della personalità* (2nd edn., 1982).

DWORKIN/FLEMING/HUBRECHT/STRÖMHOLM/FINŽGAR/KÜBLER, *Die Haftung der Massenmedien, insbesondere der Presse, bei Eingriffen in persönliche oder gewerbliche Rechtspositionen im englischen, amerikanischen, französischen, schwedischen, jugoslawischen und deutschen Recht* (1972).

EHLERS/BAUMANN, 'Verletzungen des Persönlichkeitsrechts in der französischen Rechtsprechung, Ein Vergleich mit dem deutschen Recht', *ZvglRW* 77 (1978) 241.

ENGEL, *La protection de la personnalité* (1985).

FLEMING, 'Libel and Constitutional Free Speech', in CANE/STAPLETON (eds.), *Essays for Patrick Atiyah* 333 (1991).

FRANK, 'Der Schutz der Persönlichkeit in der Rechtsordnung der Schweiz', *AcP* 172 (1972) 56.

GATLEY/LEWIS, *On Libel and Slander* (8th edn., 1981).

GURRY, *Breach of Confidence* (1984).

GUTTERIDGE/WALTON, 'The Comparative Law of the Right to Privacy', 47 *LQ Rev.* 203, 219 (1931).

HAUCH, 'Protecting Private Fact in France: The Warren and Brandeis Tort is Alive and Well and Flourishing in Paris', 68 *Tul. L. Rev.* 1219 (1994).

v. HIPPEL, 'Persönlichkeitsschutz und Pressefreiheit im amerikanischen und deutschen Recht', *RabelsZ* 33 (1969) 276.

KAYSER, *La protection de la vie privée* (1984).

KÖTZ, 'Der zivilrechtliche Persönlichkeitsschutz im anglo-amerikanischen Rechtskreis', in *Das Persönlichkeitsrecht im Spannungsfeld zwischen Informationsauftrag und Menschenwürde* (1989) 97.

KRAUSE, 'The Right to Privacy in Germany: Pointers for American Legislation?', 1965 *Duke LJ* 481.

LEUZE, *Die Entwicklung des Persönlichkeitsrechts im 19. Jahrhundert* (1962).

LINDON, *Les Droits de la personnalité* (1974).

LORENZ, *Privacy and the Press: The German Experience* (Butterworth Lecture, 1990).

MARKESINIS, 'Subtle Ways of Legal Borrowings, Some Comparative Reflections on the Calcutt Committee "On Privacy and Related Matters" ', *Festschrift für W. Lorenz* (1991) 717.

MAX-PLANCK-INSTITUT FÜR AUSLÄNDISCHES UND INTERNATIONALES PRIVATRECHT, *Der zivilrechtliche Persönlichkeits- und Ehrenschutz in Frankreich, der Schweiz, England und den Vereinigten Staaten von Amerika* (1960).

MORANGE, 'La protection constitutionnelle et civile de la liberté d'expression', *Rev. int. dr. comp.* 42 (1990) 1771.

PROSSER, 'Das Recht auf die Privatsphäre in Amerika', *RabelsZ* 21 (1956) 401.

——, 'Privacy', 48 *Calif. L. Rev.* 383 (1960).

REDMOND-COOPER, 'The Press and the Law of Privacy', 34 *ICLQ* 769 (1985).

RIGAUX, *La protection de la vie privée et des autres biens de la personnalité* (1990).

RUPP, 'Zur Pressefreiheit in den Vereinigten Staaten von Amerika, Anmerkungen zu einigen neueren Entscheidungen', *Festschrift Zweigert* (1981) 763.

SCHWENK, 'Das allgemeine Persönlichkeitsrecht in amerikanischer Sicht', *Rechtsvergleichung und Rechtsvereinheitlichung, Festschrift zum 50jährigen Bestehen des Instituts für ausländisches und internationales Privat- und Wirtschaftsrecht der Universität Heidelberg* (1967) 233.

SCHWERDTNER, *Das Persönlichkeitsrecht in der deutschen Zivilrechtsordnung* (1977).

SEIPP, 'English Judicial Recognition of a Right to Privacy', 3 *Oxf. J. Leg. Stud.* 325 (1983).

STOLJAR, 'A Re-Examination of Privacy', 4 *LS* 67 (1984).

HANS STOLL, 'Empfiehlt sich eine Neuregelung der Verpflichtung zum Geldersatz für immaterielle Schäden?', *Verh. DJT* 45 (1964) I/1 S. 51.

STRÖMHOLM, 'Right of Privacy and Rights of the Personality, A Comparative Survey', *Acta Instituti Upsaliensis Iurisprudentiae Comparativae*, vol. VIII (1967).

TERCIER, *Le nouveau droit de la personnalité* (1984).

——, 'Die Entwicklung des Persönlichkeitsschutzes in Kontinentaleuropa', in *Das Persönlichkeitsrecht im Spannungsfeld zwischen Informationsauftrag und Menschenwürde* (1989) 71.

WACKS, *The Protection of Privacy* (1980).

WADE, 'Defamation and the Right of Privacy' 15 *Vand. L. Rev.* 1093 (1962).

WAGNER, 'Le "Droit à l'intimité" aux États-Unis', *Rev. int. dr. comp.* 17 (1965) 365.

WARREN/BRANDEIS, 'The Right to Privacy', 4 *Harv. L. Rev.* 193 (1890).

WESTIN, *Privacy and Freedom* (1967).

WINFIELD, 'Privacy', 47 *LQ Rev.* 23 (1931).

YANG, 'Privacy: A Comparative Study of English and American Law', 15 *ICLQ* 175 (1966).

I

OUR discussion of the law of delict hitherto has mainly been concerned with rules which protect the body and health of human beings or their ownership and other economic interests. But every legal system must also decide how and how far to protect its citizens against invasions directed against their personality as such. Of course rules which provide compensation for personal injury and property damage ultimately safeguard the personality by rendering the right to life, physical integrity, and property meaningful by protecting them against attack by third parties, but private law must protect a man's personality not only where it is indirectly infringed in its physical manifestations but also where it is attacked directly by outrages against his honour, by the publication of his private affairs, by the unauthorized recording of his confidential utterances, or suchlike unpermitted trespasses into the area of his privacy. German lawyers here speak of 'invasions of the right of personality' (*Verletzungen des Persönlichkeitsrechts*).

The need for protection against invasions of the right of personality, now universally manifest, has become most strikingly evident in the course of the twentieth century. The reasons for this are not difficult to discern. While it is agreed on all hands that the press, radio, and television not only satisfy the perfectly legitimate desire to be entertained but also make a substantial contribution to informing and educating the public by means of report, commentary, and criticism and so permit the formation of public opinion in a manner essential for the functioning of a modern democratic state, it is no less indubitable that the public need for amusement and information may come into conflict with the equally deserving interests of a person who finds that his private affairs are being published, his name bandied about, and his picture broadcast, or who realizes that the incorrect or incomplete information given about him is defaming him or putting him in a false light. Modern advertising methods also endanger the right of personality for in their campaigns they notoriously tend to use the name and picture of persons known and unknown without always obtaining the necessary permission from the persons named or portrayed. Before long, also, a special need for confidentiality will arise as individuals increasingly resort to state organs for benefits and to private undertakings for services, since 'dossiers' will then be drawn up on them and as modern methods of documentation facilitate the storage and retrieval of data there will be an increasing danger that the state, the press, employers, or other interested persons may obtain such information and so be able to acquire full knowledge of every individual's life down to the last detail. Finally it should be remembered that modern technology has produced devices which offer untold possibilities of trespass into the individual's privacy, such as telephoto lenses, concealed recording machines, and tiny microphones which let one listen in to telephone conversations or even personal conversations behind four walls. All these devices are available today to government departments and private individuals alike and are constantly being improved upon (for the details see WESTIN (above p. 686)). It is not enough to mobilize the *criminal* law: private law must also contain rules which an individual may effectively use to counter such invasions of his privacy and so prevent the degradation of his personal dignity.

II

No rule in the *German* BGB protects the human personality as such against injurious invasion. It is true that §823 par. 1 BGB allows a claim for damages to be brought if one's body, health, life, or freedom are culpably affected, but this only protects the physical aspects of individual existence and does not offer any protection against invasions of one's honour or privacy. It is true that even during the nineteenth century eminent scholars asserted that the law of tort should protect 'the general human right of personality', especially the 'right to honour' and the 'right to one's private sphere'.

For example, see v. GIERKE, *Deutsches Privatrecht* I (1895) 707 and KOHLER, *ArchbürgR* 7 (1893) 94; for the history of the matter see LEUZE (above p. 685).

But the BGB contains no echo of these views, apart from providing in §12 that a person whose *name* is used by another without permission may demand the cessation of such use; this right to one's name is also treated as an 'other right' under §823 par. 1 BGB so that the person affected can also claim damages from any person who culpably uses his name for any loss he suffers. The courts were also quick to give legal protection against invasions of the '*right to one's own picture*'. In 1889 the Reichsgericht was faced with the question whether the heirs of Bismarck could insist on the destruction of flashlight photographs of Bismark's corpse taken by the defendant photographers after stealing by night into the room where he died. The Reichsgericht held that such a claim was good: the defendants had obtained these pictures by the unlawful act of trespassing on the property of others and were therefore bound to destroy the pictures under the rules of the *condictio obiniustamcausam* (RGZ 45, 170). The sense of public outrage at this incident led to the inclusion in the Law of Artistic Creations of 1907 (*Kunsturhebergesetz*) of §§22 ff. which provide that 'pictures' may only be circulated or displayed with the consent of their subject, if alive, or of his relatives. A special exception was made for figures of contemporary history, the publication of whose pictures is generally permissible without consent unless it infringes a 'justified interest' of the subject, as would be the case if he were photographed against his will in his private surroundings and there was no justifiable public interest in having such information (BGHZ 24, 200). When the statute was enacted 'picture' was understood to signify only a portrayal embodied in some physical thing but in a famous decision in 1920 the Kammergericht held that Kaiser Wilhelm II had been 'pictured' by an actor on the stage who wore a facial mask and aped his clothing, hairstyle, deportment, and accent. The Kaiser's suit for an injunction succeeded; he was certainly a figure of contemporary history, but his portrayal on the stage was 'one-sided and tendentious' (KG JW 1928, 363). Although KOHLER had emphatically insisted that everyone should be able to enjoin the 'publication of confidential letters' as a 'grave invasion of his private life', the courts were very hesitant to give any legal redress. The Reichsgericht would only afford such protection to letters which were 'an original artistic creation' so as to fall under the concept of 'literary work' in the sense of the Law of Literary Creations: NIETZSCHE's letters qualified since he showed himself to be an 'artist in correspondence' (RGZ 69, 401) but WAGNER's letters did not, as they were simply 'business letters' (RGZ 41, 43). One could hardly deny, however, that the publication of 'business letters' may also constitute an invasion of the writer's right of personality.

The courts had other means at their disposal of satisfying the need to protect the individual's personality apart from the law regarding names, the right to one's own picture, and the law of artistic and literary creations. A person whose honour or reputation was besmirched by statements about him could claim damages if he could show that the defendant was guilty of the crime of insult or slander (§§185 ff. Criminal Code), for the defendant would then be in breach of a protective statute in the sense of §823 par. 2 BGB. After much hesitation the courts also issued injunctions to prevent the future publication of such offensive statements (RGZ 156, 372). Again, §824 BGB renders a person liable in damages if he publishes facts which he knew or should have known to be untrue and which might prejudice another person's credit or cause him other harm in his trade or profession. §826 BGB is also of great importance here, since behaviour which would now constitute an invasion of the right of personality might very easily be seen as an offence *contra bonos mores*.

In RGZ 115, 416 for example, it was held to be an offence *contra bonos mores* for an information bureau to publish the details of the defendant's conviction twenty years previously: there is a general social duty not to hound a person for the whole of his life with an offence long since past; he should rather be helped to make good his lapse by creating a new life for himself and winning back his social reputation by impeccable conduct. Accordingly the most that could properly be said in the situation was that 'in his youth' the plaintiff had allowed himself to be embroiled in matters which brought him into conflict with the criminal law.

That in all these cases one and the same legal interest, namely the human personality in all its manifestations, was under different forms of attack and should be afforded protection, is a view the Reichsgericht never accepted. It resolutely declined to hold that the *general* right of personality deserved protection as much as the right to one's name or picture or artistic or literary creations.

Nor did the Reichsgericht allow its view to be affected by the fact that many years before the BGB came into force Switzerland had adopted a model rule which allowed a person who had been injured 'in his personal affairs' to enjoin the guilty party and claim damages from him if he were at fault (see art. 55 OR (1881), now art. 28 ZGB, 49 OR). The objection which the Reichsgericht raised against the proposal to recognize the general right of personality, namely that such a right is a 'concept unamenable to precise definition' (see KG JW 1928, 363) could also be levelled against the Swiss rule, but the way the Swiss courts have dealt with it shows that lawyers on the Continent too often underestimate the capacity of the courts to concretize a suggestive general clause. The Swiss Bundesgericht has gone carefully from case to case, weighing and balancing the interests on both sides, and giving protection against defamatory statements, embarrassing disclosures, invasions of family life (in particular by requiring an adulterer to pay damages: see BGE 84 II 329), and invasions of privacy. It is worth noting that art. 28 ZGB also gives protection against the 'economic side' of the right of personality, with the result that blacklists, boycotts, and other impermissible economic weapons can be dealt with under art. 28 ZGB as an invasion of the personal freedom to engage in trade or profession without interference (see, for example, BGE 82 II 292), whereas in Germany they would be dealt with under §826 BGB as an offence *contra bonos mores* (see, for example, RGZ 130, 89) or under §823 par. 1 BGB as an invasion of the 'right to an established and operative business' (see, for example, BGHZ 24, 200).

Only after the Second World War did Germany take the crucial step. The need for effective protection of human dignity and personal freedom had become abundantly manifest during the Nazi dictatorship, and the Basic Law, unlike any previous German constitution, gave these values a prominent and important position in arts. 1 and 2. In addition, technological advances had greatly increased the possibilities of unpermitted invasions of the private sphere and secret surveillance devices of all kinds had emerged from the pages of science fiction. It had also been shown that sensational press reports on the private life of individuals might constitute an invasion of their personality even if the circumstances reported were true in fact and not defamatory in effect. But in these cases no effective protection was afforded by the rules developed by the Reichsgericht. The ground was thus prepared for the path-breaking decision of the Bundesgerichtshof in 1954 in which for the first time it recognized the general right of personality as an 'other right' under §823 par. 1 BGB.

The defendant was a weekly periodical which had published an article taking exception to the foundation of a bank by Dr Schacht, an Economics Minister under Hitler. The plaintiff was retained by Dr Schacht as his attorney and in that capacity, pursuant to his client's instruction and expressly on his behalf, wrote to the defendant and demanded that certain corrections be made in the article. The defendant published this letter in its 'Readers' Letters' column with omissions which made it appear as if the plaintiff had acted spontaneously and as a private individual in making these demands in the interests of Dr Schacht. The plaintiff claimed that the defendant should be made to correct this misrepresentation by a suitable retraction, and the claim succeeded at first instance, for reasons which were in line with the decisions of the Reichsgericht: by the manner in which the defendant had published the plaintiff's letter it had brought him into disrepute and lowered him in public estimation; the defendant was therefore guilty of defamation (§187 Criminal Code) and accordingly liable under §823 par. 2 BGB. On appeal the higher court was unable to find that the publication of the letter was defamatory of the plaintiff and dismissed the claim. For the Bundesgerichtshof it was immaterial whether the defendant were guilty of a crime or not since, in reliance on arts. 1 and 2 of the Basic Law, it held that private law protected the general right of personality as such: to publish the letter in mangled form as was done here constituted an invasion of the 'private sphere of the author as protected by the right of personality' since it presented a false picture of his personality (BGHZ 13, 334).

In a quick succession of other decisions the law of tort was used to protect other manifestations of the general right of personality. The courts held it actionable to use the name of a famous artiste in an advertisement, to publish a picture under circumstances which gave the impression that the person portrayed was a murderer, and to publish a factitious interview with Princess Soraya, a well known figure of international society; making a secret recording and communicating a confidential medical certificate to a third party were also tortious, subject to the qualification that an overwhelming interest such as the discovery of a serious crime by means of the recording or medical certificate might serve as a justification. This balancing of interests is especially difficult in cases where the plaintiff claims that the picture of him published in the media is inaccurate, partial, biassed or defamatory. In such cases the defendant can invoke the constitutionally protected right of free expression of opinion (art. 5 GG), but the plaintiff too can invoke the Constitution, for in art. 1 and 2 it obliges the state to protect the dignity of the individual and the free development of his personality. In earlier days these basic rights were seen as designed to prevent invasion *by the state*, but it has long been realized that constitutional values must be observed even between individuals and that the rules of private law must be interpreted and applied so as to conform to the Constitution (BVerfGE 7, 198). Furthermore, since judicial decisions may sometimes be made the subject of a constitutional complaint (*Verfassungsbeschwerde*), the Constitutional Court may be seized of the question whether the judgment impugned has not infringed the complainant's constitutional rights by not balancing the interests involved as it should. In Germany, indeed, this has happened so often that the issue is now dominated by constitutional considerations and the solutions are much affected by the case-law of the Constitutional Court.

The first question is whether the publication in question constitutes a *statement of fact* or an *expression of opinion*. If the plaintiff can establish that a statement of fact was inaccurate he can seek an injunction and, if he can show that the journalist was in breach of his professional duty of care, damages as well; the journalist cannot rely on the constitutional right of freedom of expression for it does not protect false statements of fact. If what was said is true, the complaint is not necessarily dismissed. A balancing of interests then takes place, an inquiry about how seriously the publication invades the plaintiff's private sphere, how grave the consequences for him were, whether he himself had engaged in public controversy and perhaps raised similar complaints against others. It is also relevant whether the defendant was contributing to a debate on an issue of major public interest and advancing discussion of political, economic or social questions as opposed to promoting private concerns, or simply indulging a taste for gossip, denigration, and sensationalism. Where the publication consists of *opinion* or *value-judgments* rather than *statements of fact* (though the distinction is very hard to draw and must, in case of doubt, be found to be the former) the same balancing of interests takes place, but in practice the courts treat an expression of opinion as unlawful only when it was designed to bad-mouth the complainant out of hatred or malice and was not based on any intention to contribute to an informed debate of a controversial issue (BVerfGE 85, 1).

For example, while the public is certainly interested in knowing how easy it is for youngsters to get married abroad and many readers find a story of interest only if it deals with an 'actual incident' or particular case, this does not mean that a newspaper may publish a sensational treatment, with full names and accurate details, of how the teenage daughter of a Berlin roofer eloped with an English soldier to the 'marriage haven' of Gretna Green (BGH LM art. 5 GG no. 16). It is different if the complainant has deliberately stepped out of his private sphere in order to promote his views on how society should be run; he must accept that his conduct may be criticized by the media. A banker involved in the international arms trade cannot complain of an invasion of his personality rights if his involvement is critically ventilated and he is then cold-shouldered by his relatives, friends, and political associates, for 'In a democratic society a person who becomes active in the economic sphere exposes himself to criticism which he cannot elude by reference to his personal privacy' (BGHZ 36, 77, 80). Nor can the managing director of a firm which is a major producer of fluorohydrocarbons complain of posters put up by Greenpeace bearing his name and the name of his firm alongside the legend 'Others Talk about the Weather—We Make it Worse' (BGH NJW 1994, 124). Persons active in politics or the media get a very dusty answer from the courts: they have given their opponents the occasion to engage in personal polemics and must put up with criticism of their personal activities or political methods even if it is extremely sharp and one-sided (BGH NJW 1965, 1476; BVerfGE 12, 113, 129).

The person whose rights of personality have been infringed can seek an *injunction* (*Unterlassungsurteil*) prohibiting the defendant from repeating what he has said. In addition he can require that any remaining adverse effects of the misrepresentation be *undone* (*Beseitigung*), and obtain an order that the defendant give equal publicity to a correction. Sometimes the court permits the plaintiff to publish the judgment containing the injunction in specified newspapers at the defendant's expense (BGHZ 99, 133).

The plaintiff has a claim to *rebuttal* (*Gegendarstellung*) if any facts were published about him in a newspaper, and can demand that its next edition contain a short statement by the plaintiff of the facts as he sees them. He need not show that the facts originally published were false, and the newspaper cannot refuse to publish on the ground that what it said was true or that the rebuttal is inaccurate. For a modern rule on rebuttal see the Swiss Civil Code, art. 28 g-l.

The plaintiff may also claim *damages*, including damages for non-economic harm. It is true that §253 BGB lays down that damages in respect of such harm may not be ordained except in the cases prescribed by law, mainly for corporeal injuries. Since a decision in 1958, however, the Bundes-gerichtshof has disregarded the terms of this provision (BGHZ 26, 349 and see BVerfG NJW 1973, 1221), on the ground that the protection of the right of personality by private law would be 'patchy and inadequate' unless the defendant had to reckon on a sanction which properly reflected the serious-ness of his behaviour and its consequences (see BGHZ 35, 363). It is now standard practice for the court to award damages for moral harm if the inva-sion of the plaintiff's right of personality is 'grave'; here the motive of the defendant, the seriousness of his fault, and the mode and extent of the harm-ful invasion are relevant considerations. In so deciding, the Bundesgericht-shof has brought German law into line with Swiss law on this point: art. 49 OR allows a claim for such damages only where they are 'justified by the gravity of the invasion and it has not otherwise been remedied'.

III

In 1970 the *French* Code civil adopted a terse provision: 'Chacun a droit au respect de sa vie privée' (art. 9), but the actual effect of this enactment was slight, given that the courts had already protected the right of personality in private law by using the general clauses in arts. 1382 and 1383 Code civil, according to which everyone must pay for the harm he causes by his 'faute'. These articles of the Code civil make no overt distinction between material and moral damage. While some older authors held that damages could not be awarded for immaterial harm, and others restricted it to cases of crim-inal behaviour and yet others to particular types of immaterial harm, such restrictive views have now been abandoned; even the courts today treat both types of harm in the same way and see no need to indicate in their decisions which part of the damages awarded to the plaintiff appertains to the material and which to the moral harm.

See MAZEAUD/TUNC I nos. 301 ff. and STOLL (above p. 686) 75 ff.—The quantum of damages awarded for moral harm depends on the circumstances of the case, and may even be purely symbolic. In a case where the plaintiff's wife had committed adultery and he claimed damages for his moral harm from her and her lover, the court awarded damages of only one franc ('franc symbolique') against the wife in view of the 'extenuating circumstances', on which the court did not expatiate. (Agen 18 July 1902, DP 1903. 2. 344; see also Paris 10 July 1957, D. 1957, 622.)—Similarly the Conseil d'État awarded only one franc to a woman who had been stopped on the street by a policeman in the defendant city and asked, for no apparent reason, whether she were registered with the health police (21 Feb. 1936, Gaz. Pal. 1936. I. 605). This hesitancy on the part of the Conseil d'État may be referable to its earlier refusal to grant damages for immaterial harm at all, though more recently it has become more generous; on this see MORANGE, D. 1962. Chron. 15 and LUCE, JCP 1962. I. 1685.

It will be obvious that a legal system can adopt a very flexible approach to the problem of protecting the human personality if its law of tort applies whatever legal interests have been affected (*contra* §823 par. 1 BGB) and it can give damages quite freely for immaterial harm (*contra* §§253, 847 BGB). Accordingly, the French courts have never hesitated to characterize as 'faute' the publication of confidential letters, the dissemination of facts about a person's private life, or the unauthorized use of a person's name, and to award the plaintiff damages for the moral harm as well as the economic harm. French law has therefore not had to develop the concept of a 'general right of personality' and NERSON, one of the leading authorities in this area of law, has observed that 'no one in France today still believes in the existence, as a matter of technical law, of a general right of personality' (above p. 686, p. 84; accord AMIAUD (above p. 686, 297 f.)). French writers have simply sought to distinguish the various 'rights of personality', not without disputes whether a particular personality interest should theoretically rank as a 'right' or not, and French legal literature is replete with expressions like 'right to the confidentiality of one's correspondence', 'right to one's picture' and 'right to the privacy of one's domestic life'.

Perhaps it is because French lawyers have not had to establish the right of personality in the teeth of specific and narrow legislative texts that they include under the heading of 'protection de la personnalité' some types of case which the German lawyer would not. Decisions nullifying a testamentary condition that a legacy should determine if the legatee marries a Jew (Trib. civ. Seine 22 Jan. 1947, D. 1947, 126) or avoiding as being contrary to public policy a prohibition on competition contained in a contract of employment are justified by French writers on the ground that they vindicate the important personal freedoms to marry and choose one's place of work and so ultimately safeguard the human personality. This is also the point of view from which they observe the many judicial decisions on damages claims for breach of family duties, especially where an innocent spouse claims compensation for the moral damage caused by the other's adultery (see Crim. 17 Oct. 1956, DH 1957, 245, noted by BRETON).

The standards applied by the French courts to the 'classical' forms of the protection of the personality, such as the protection of one's picture or name, one's honour or privacy, are very like those in positive German law. *Pictures*, in general, may only be published with the agreement of the person portrayed, but the courts limit this principle, much as does §23 of the German Law of Artistic Creations, by holding that pictures of persons caught in the limelight of publicity may be published without permission. The same is true of people who appear simply as figures in a landscape or beside a monument, but even in these cases the publication should not be permitted to infringe justifiable interests of the persons portrayed. Two decisions of the Court of Appeal in Paris show how these interests are weighed up.

In Paris 24 March 1965, JCP 1965. II. 14305 the plaintiffs, a married couple, were photographed while posing for someone else in extremely scanty holiday dress in front of the Tower of Pisa, and the defendant periodical used this photograph to illustrate a satirical article on tourist attire in Italy. The court held that the defendant should have rendered the faces of the plaintiffs unrecognizable, but that by displaying themselves in such garb in front of the Tower of Pisa the plaintiffs had been at fault and had contributed to the misadventure. The Court of Appeal therefore reduced to 500 NF the damages of 2,000 NF awarded by the trial court.—In Paris 14 March 1965, JCP 1965. II. 14223, *France Dimanche*, the defendant, published a sentimental article about the family of GÉRARD PHILIPPE, the famous actor, giving details of his 9-year-old son's illness, embellished with a photograph taken by reporters who had forced their way into hospital and photographed the child in bed. PHILIPPE's family was the object of great public interest and the boy's illness had already been mentioned in the newspapers, but the trial court ordered the temporary confiscation of the article and the Court of Appeal upheld this judgment with the observation that this was an 'intolerable invasion of private life'.

When details of a person's *private life* are published, similar considerations apply.

Paris 16 March 1955, D. 1955, 295 is an interesting case on the facts. *France Dimanche* published a series of articles entitled 'My Life, by Marlene Dietrich' which purported to give the actress's reminiscences in the form of an interview, although MARLENE DIETRICH had neither given any interview nor permitted the defendant to make any such publication. The reported facts were essentially true and were probably more or less well known, but the defendant was held liable to pay 1,200,000 francs, principally because the defendant's conduct had effectively thwarted the actress's intention to write and publish her own memoirs.—Also the press did wrong to disclose that the actress Isabelle Adjani was pregnant, a fact the journalists well knew she had been at pains to conceal (Paris 27 Feb. 1981, D. 1981, 457, noted by LINDON).—The Italian cases point in the same direction; see TRIMARCHI, *RabelsZ* 25 (1960) 261.

Many French cases involve the question whether an unflattering resemblance between a person and a character in a *novel* may constitute an invasion of his personality. The author of a war story in which a French officer betrays his companion's plan of escape from a German prisoner-of-war camp must do his research thoroughly and take every care not to attribute to such a reprobate the name of any living French officer who was ever a prisoner-of-war (Paris 10 July 1957, D. 1957, 622; see also Trib. civ. Seine 24 Oct. 1936, Gaz. Pal. 1936. 2. 794). The writer of a *roman-à-clef* may also make himself liable if he gives his characters unattractive traits.

See Paris 24 April 1936, DH 1936, 319; Amiens 6 July 1932, S. 1932, 2. 233; Rennes 31 May 1951, DH 1951, 484.—The Court of Cassation in another interesting decision imposed liability on a historian of wireless telegraphy who omitted all reference to a man who, according to MARCONI himself and other leading physicists, had made a great contribution to the discovery (Civ. 27 Feb. 1951, D. 1951, 329, noted by DESBOIS; but see also Paris 23 Jan. 1965, Gaz. Pal. 1965. 1. 361).

Confidential letters have been well protected against publication by the French courts since the eighteen-eighties. Here too the principle is that the recipient of a confidential letter has no right to publish it without the consent of its writer. This used to be based on an 'implied contract' between the correspondents, but today it is recognized that the right to the confidentiality of one's letters is a right of personality.

See, for example, Trib. civ. Seine 27 Nov. 1928, DH 1928, 616. In this case some letters which ROMAIN ROLLAND had written to a well-known author had somehow come into the hands of the defendant dealer who was proposing to auction them and who had, for this purpose, published extracts from them in his catalogue. The court held that only *one* of these letters was confidential and could not be sold; the others only contained views which ROLLAND had publicly expressed in books and articles, so they could be sold, but it was wrongful to publish extracts from *any* of the letters, and the defendant had to pay damages of 2,000 francs.

The writer's consent is not required if there is a very good reason for publication, such as the disclosure of the letter in court

See the decisions cited in the Report of the Max Planck Institute.—The interest in confidentiality must yield if the publication of the letter is necessary for the conviction of a defendant in a criminal trial, but the decision of Toulouse 2 March 1933, DP 1935. 2. 55, noted by APPLETON, probably goes too far. After studying the decision of a court in a case involving his client, an attorney wrote to her saying that in his view the court had made itself into an accessory to the crime, and, with his permission, the client produced this letter in the cassation proceedings. The state prosecutor, thus alerted, brought disciplinary proceedings against the attorney and used the letter to secure his conviction.

The Court of Cassation also holds that the agreement of the parties is required for the recording and reproduction of confidential *telephone conversations*.

In one case the judicial police had authorized the defendant to install a listening device so as to catch the unknown person who was constantly bothering her with insulting telephone calls. The defendant did so and discovered that the plaintiff was the anonymous caller, but the plaintiff then turned the tables on the defendant by suing her for damages under art. 1382 Code civil for breach of the secrecy of telephone conversations. The Court of Cassation upheld the plaintiff's claim (see Civ. 18 March 1955, D. 1955, 573, noted by SAVATIER; JCP 1955. II. 8909, noted by ESMEIN).

Private law also gives protection against invasions of *honour* and *reputation* under art. 1382 Code civil, but in practice this is intimately linked with art. 29 of the Law of the Press of 29 July 1881, which makes it a crime to insult a person in public (injure) or to publish defamatory statements of fact about him (defamation). Claims for damages are normally brought in the *criminal* trial, with which the injured party associates himself as *partie civile*; if a judge, an official, or a soldier is defamed, this procedure *must* be used (art. 46). Although in general a person cannot be convicted of defamation if he can prove that what he said was true, no such proof is admissible if the dishonourable facts relate to the *private life* of the person attacked (art. 35). If the defendant cannot prove the truth of what he said, it is presumed under art. 35 bis that he was acting in bad faith; this presumption may be rebutted, not by mere proof of the defendant's good faith belief in the truth of what he said, but by the additional proof that he carefully investigated the information, that he acted with due regard for the interests involved, and that he chose the least offensive manner of publication in the circumstances.

The right of rebuttal or reply (*droit de réponse*) under art. 13 of the Law on the Press is much stronger than in German or Swiss law. It is available to anyone who has reason to feel directly or indirectly hit by a publication in the press. It is immaterial whether the publication is of fact or opinion, whether its aim is to inform or criticize, or whether it names the complainant or not. The press must print the rebuttal, unless to do so would be illegal or immoral, or infringe the interests of a third party or the honour of the journalist (Crim. 1 July 1954, D. 1954, 665), and it can be the same length as the article, save that it can never exceed 200 lines, however long the article, and may be up to 50 lines long even if the article is shorter. The preconditions for a right of reply to television programmes are rather stricter (Law no. 82–652 of 29 July 1982).

IV

The *Common Law* rules which protect the human personality are best approached by making a distinction between attacks on a person's honour and all other forms of invasion of his personality. Reflections on honour and reputation in England and the United States are mainly sanctioned by the tort of *libel* and *slander*, which together comprise *defamation*. Other invasions of personality are sanctioned in the United States as being invasions of the *right of privacy*, but the English courts have not yet recognized any such general right to the protection of one's privacy although, as will be seen shortly, they can often help in such cases by a wide application of the torts of libel and slander or by allowing a claim for breach of copyright or 'passing-off' (see above p. 607) or some other cause of action.

1. *Defamation* occurs if a person's honour, reputation, or esteem is adversely affected by someone's expressing himself to a third party in a manner calculated to bring the plaintiff into 'hatred, ridicule or contempt' or otherwise to lower him in the estimation of reasonable persons. Protection is afforded only if the plaintiff's public reputation has been affected: it is not enough, as it is in Germany, for a person's dignity or self-esteem to be wounded by objectionable remarks made *inter partes*. If the defamatory statement is made in a permanent form, especially in written or printed words or pictures or caricatures, this will be *libel*; broadcasting by radio or television is also treated as libel in England under s. 1 of the Defamation Act, 1952. It is a case of *slander* if a person's reputation is affected by oral expression, insulting mime, or derisive gesture. The practical importance of the distinction between libel and slander is that in a libel suit no special damage need be alleged or proved: the court can fix the quantum of damages in relation to the gravity of the defamation without requiring proof of any particular loss. In slander cases it is different, for the plaintiff is normally required to prove that he suffered some material loss as a result of the slander, such as a loss of promotion or custom or employment. There are certain narrow categories of case, however, where this rule does not apply: if the defendant accuses the plaintiff of a serious crime or imputes to him some loathsome disease which would exclude him from society or makes statements calculated to affect the plaintiff's trade or profession, or finally if he accuses a woman of unchastity or adultery, the slander is exceptionally said to be 'actionable per se', which means that the plaintiff need not prove any special economic harm. It need hardly be said that these rules are quite irrational. A person defamed on a postcard which only one other person ever reads can claim damages without proof of any loss, while a person slandered before an audience of 10,000 people in a manner which affects him in his private capacity and causes him no provable pecuniary or professional harm will have no claim for damages at all unless he is credited with criminality or contagion.

The explanation for these artificial distinctions, for which no one has a good word to say in the Common Law today, is to be found in English legal history. Slander, the older tort, fell within the jurisdiction of the ecclesiastical courts in the Middle Ages; the royal courts intervened only when the defamation had secular consequences in the form of some temporal loss. Defamation in print, once it was invented, should have attached itself to slander, but instead the infamous Star Chamber Court assumed jurisdiction over the press, and the special rules it developed were retained when jurisdiction in such cases passed to the regular courts.

A person may perfectly well be liable for defamation even if no blame at all attaches to his publication or transmission of the defamatory statement. If a plaintiff's reputation has objectively been affected by what a newspaper has printed about him, the newspaper will be liable in damages even if its management was unaware of the plaintiff's existence and had no intention of defaming him; indeed, the newspaper will be liable even if the publication was defamatory of the plaintiff only by reason of circumstances which the publisher did not know and could not have known.

The leading decision in England is *Hulton and Co.* v. *Jones*, [1910] AC 20. The defendant published in the *Sunday Chronicle* an article on a popular French seaside resort which made great fun of the fact that Englishmen who were perfectly decorous on their own side of the Channel immediately turned into lounge lizards and Lotharios on the other. Passing mention was made of a certain Artemus Jones, said to be a churchwarden when at home in Peckham: 'here, in the atmosphere of Dieppe, on the French side of the Channel, he is the life and soul of a gay little band that haunts the Casino and turns night into day, besides betraying a most unholy delight in the society of female butterflies'. There then emerged from the provincial backwoods of England a person who astonished the defendant by announcing himself as Artemus Jones and ready to prove that his acquaintances had identified him with the hero of the article. The defendant, though in perfect good faith, was held liable in all courts to the tune of £1,750.—See also *Cassidy* v. *Daily Mirror*, [1929] 2 KB 331. In this case the defendant newspaper published a picture of Mr Cassidy in the company of a young woman whom the caption described as his fiancée. The defendant must have supposed that this was acceptable since Cassidy himself had approved the publication of the picture and the caption, but Mrs Cassidy nevertheless sued them for damages and proved that acquaintances had inferred from the caption that she was not in fact married to Mr Cassidy.—In another case a newspaper published a true fact about the person named; another person of the same name to whom the fact as reported could be attributed was allowed to sue the newspaper regardless of whether it could have foreseen or prevented such false attribution (*Newstead* v. *London Express*, [1940] 1 KB 377).

It follows from these remarkably strict rules that the risk of paying damages attaches to everyone who says anything which might injure another's reputation even if he was not at all negligent in not realizing that it might do so. On one or two points the courts have been able to relax these rules. If a defamatory statement comes to the notice of a third party without the knowledge and consent of the defendant, he can escape liability if he shows that he was not at fault. Thus if the defendant says something defamatory in a communication to the plaintiff and a third party overhears the conversation or opens the injurious letter this would normally be a case of libel or slander, but the defendant will not be liable if he can prove that it was not careless of him not to foresee that the third party might learn what was said. The courts also allow a defendant to exculpate himself if he was involved in the publication of the defamatory statement, but only in a subsidiary capacity: a lending-library, bookshop, or news-stand, unlike the author, publisher, or printer, will not be liable if despite all care on their part they were unaware of the defamatory nature of the publications they lent or sold.

In other cases, however, it is not necessary for the defendant to have been at fault. In particular the press is liable in damages for libel even if the publisher, editor, and author could not possibly have known that the statement was false or that it might defame the plaintiff. For such cases of 'innocent defamation' an alleviation has been made by s. 4 of the Defamation Act 1952, whereby liability may be avoided if the periodical immediately publishes an apology and a correction.

What defences are open to the person who has made defamatory observations about the plaintiff? If it is a statement of fact he can avoid liability by pleading *justification* and proving that the nub of what he said was true: 'Truth is an absolute defence'. This entails that there is no liability even if the defamer was actuated by quite unmeritorious motives such as envy, hatred, revenge or sensationalism. For a long time, therefore, one could safely publish a person's criminal convictions from many years back, even if his life thereafter had been unexceptionable. The Reichsgericht had held as early as 1927 that it was immoral to publish convictions from the distant past, but it was not rendered impermissible in England until 1974, and still is so only if the defendant acted with 'malice' (Rehabilitation of Offenders Act 1974, s. 8).

Liability for defamation is also avoided if the defendant can rely on some 'privilege' attaching to the misrepresentation or critical comments. Such a privilege arises out of the interests involved, and it may be '*absolute privilege*' or '*qualified privilege*'. 'Absolute privilege' attaches to defamatory statements made by judges, jurymen, advocates, witnesses, or parties in litigation or similar proceedings, to statements made by officials in the course of their duties and by Members of Parliament in the legislative chamber. In these cases the motive behind the statement and the manner of its publication are quite irrelevant. This is not so where the privilege is only 'qualified': a person may rely on qualified privilege if he spoke in advancement of some legitimate private or public interest, but he must go on to prove that he believed in the truth of what he said, that he chose the least injurious mode of publication, and that he did not act with malice. Such *qualified privilege* is available if, for example, the defendant was laying an information with the police or writing a reference to a potential future employer. The press, on the other hand, cannot claim *qualified privilege* just because they act in the public interest.

Uttering a critical, depreciatory, polemical or hurtful opinion on facts which are true or privileged does not make one liable if the opinion counts as *fair comment*. Comment on a matter of public interest is *fair* if on the facts stated a normal decent person not actuated by malice or hatred could possibly come to the same opinion and conclusion as the defendant. There is no call for extreme forbearance and objectivity, since comment which is subjective, exaggerated, emotional or savage may still be fair, provided that the facts on which it is based are correct and that the defendant had some reason for his opinion and was not simply bad-mouthing the plaintiff out of malice and hatred.

Damages claims for defamation in England can still be heard by a *jury* of twelve. The judge instructs them as to the applicable law, but they themselves decide on the evidence whether what the defendant said was defamatory in nature, whether the truth of it has been established, and whether he acted with malice. In particular the jury fix the amount of damages payable. That is why the sums awarded are often much greater than on the Continent, even if they fall short of awards in the United States, which are sometimes astronomical. *Exemplary damages* may be awarded if the defendant published the material recklessly or with a view to increasing the circulation of his book or journal. This was why the publisher of a book which unjustly charged a naval commander with the loss of a convoy he was escorting was made to pay £40,000 (*Broome* v. *Cassell & Co.* [1972] AC 1072). In 1984, £45,000 was awarded against the *Daily Telegraph* which in an otherwise accurate report that civil servants had been making improperly large industrial grants erroneously named the plaintiff as the official responsible and said that he had been disciplined and quit the service (*Blackshaw* v. *Lord* [1984] QB 1). Awards of damages continued to increase until finally the wife of a serial killer was awarded £600,000 for an allegation that she knew of her husband's activities and had invented an alibi for him after his arrest. The Court of Appeal held the jury's award 'excessive' and urged trial judges to attempt to restrain the jury in future (*Sutcliffe* v. *Pressdram Ltd.* [1990] 2 All ER 269). But juries may well go to the other extreme. *Dering* v. *Uris* [1964] 2 QB 669 arose out of an assertion in Leon Uris's *Exodus* that in Auschwitz the plaintiff operated without anaesthetic on 17,000 detainees. After eighteen days of evidence the defendant was unable to prove that the assertions were in every respect true, so the claim was bound to succeed: the jury awarded damages of one halfpenny.

Whereas the victim on the Continent has several ways of combating defamatory publications, in England he can only sue for damages: he has no right of reply, and no right to ask a court to prevent publication of particular matters. An injunction will only be issued if it is manifest that a jury would be bound to hold the defendant liable, and will never be issued against a defendant who states that when the matter comes to trial he will rely on fair comment or seek to prove the truth of what he has said.

2. A man's personality may be impaired in other ways than by besmirching his reputation or aspersing his honour. We must now very briefly turn to the rules which have been developed in the Common Law to deal with *other*

invasions of personality, and we must start with a famous law review article published in 1890 by a well-known Boston lawyer, WARREN, in conjunction with BRANDEIS, who was later to be appointed to the United States Supreme Court (4 *Harv. L. Rev.* 193 (1890)). The authors of this, 'perhaps the most famous and certainly the most influential law review article ever written.' (HENSON (ed.), *Landmarks of Law, Highlights of Legal Opinion* (1960)) sought to prove that many precedents, apparently based on defamation, invasion of property, breach of contract, and other familiar grounds of claims were in substance sanctioning the invasion of a general right, the so-called 'right of privacy', in an individual's domestic life. The authors came to the quite novel conclusion that the positive law contained a general principle

'which may be invoked to protect the privacy of the individual from invasion either by the too enterprising press, the photographer, or the possessor of any other modern device for recording or reproducing scenes or sounds' (4 *Harv. L. Rev.* 193, 206 (1890)).

The immediate consequences of this article were meagre. A few courts seemed ready to follow the views of WARREN and BRANDEIS while others rejected them out of hand, in particular the New York Court of Appeals in a case where the picture of a pretty girl was used in a flour advertisement without her consent (*Roberson* v. *Rochester Folding Box Co.*, 171 NY 538, 64 NE 442 (1902)). This decision evoked a storm of protest in New York which promptly resulted in the enactment of a law which is still in force: §§50–1 of the New York Civil Rights Law make it actionable to use the name or picture of a person 'for advertising purposes or for the purposes of trade' without the written consent of that person. A few years later the Supreme Court of Georgia in a similar case adopted the conclusions of WARREN and BRANDEIS and supported them with cogent reasoning (*Pavesich* v. *New England Ins Co.*, 122 Ga. 190, 50 SE 68 (1905)). Since then one jurisdiction after another has recognized the 'right of privacy' as worthy of protection until today almost all of the United States accept this view.

PROSSER had sought to distinguish the extremely copious case-law into various types of case (48 *Calif. L. Rev.* 383 (1960). Within the 'law of privacy' he finds four different types of case in each of which a different interest is protected against different forms of invasion. In the first group he puts cases where there has been an unpermitted invasion of the plaintiff's private territory or a meddling in his private affairs, such as listening in to private conversations with the aid of microphones and telephone taps, surveillance of the plaintiff's dwelling, unpermitted entry into hotel rooms, and rummaging through handbags. The second group of cases deals with the unauthorized publication of facts from a person's private life which, though true in substance, are painful or embarrassing. It is clear from the decisions that the courts place a higher value on the public interest in information and entertainment than on the individual's interest in keeping his private life to himself. If the defendant publisher can show that the facts he published were true and 'newsworthy', he has won the game. Two decisions, with different outcomes, are worth mentioning; both of them deal with the question whether the press or the cinema is entitled to expose a person involuntarily to public attention many years after the public first became interested in him.

In *Melvin* v. *Reid*, 112 Cal. App. 285, 297 P. 91 (1931) the plaintiff, then a prostitute, had been the accused in a sensational murder trial. On acquittal, she gave up her unfortunate mode of life, married an excellent man, and earned the respect of her neighbours and friends who were quite ignorant of her past. Seven years after the marriage the defendant destroyed her newly won social position by producing a film about the murder trial which used the plaintiff's maiden name and gave an accurate picture of her previous mode of life. The court held that the plaintiff's claim for damages must succeed.—In *Sidis* v. *F-R Publishing Corp.*, 113 F. 2d 806 (2d Cir. 1940) the federal courts in New York came to the opposite conclusion. The plaintiff here was born with extraordinary mathematical gifts and became a famous wunderkind. At 11 he could teach experts about four-dimensional bodies and at 16 he graduated *summa cum laude* from Harvard University. He later became nauseated with mathematics and repelled by life in the limelight, so he sought to obliterate all traces of his existence and disappeared into obscurity as an accountant, collecting tram tickets in his spare time and studying a very minor tribe of Indians. More than twenty years later the defendant published an article about him, not at all unfriendly in tone, which gave a faithful portrayal of his whole life story. The plaintiff had a breakdown and died shortly thereafter. The court rejected the plaintiff's claim on the ground that in cases of this sort the legal system could only protect the average man and intervene where the normal citizen of customary phlegm would have felt himself injured by the publication and not where, as here, the plaintiff found the publication intolerable only by reason of his exceptional sensitivity and reclusiveness.—In many other cases, too, the courts have preferred free dissemination of accurate information by the media over the individual's concern to keep his private life private. Thus the United States Supreme Court has decided more than once that newspapers may publish the name of the victim of sexual abuse if they learn it from court proceedings or from the police: see *Cox Broadcasting Co.* v. *Cohn* 420 US 469 (1975) and *The Florida Star* v. *B.J.F.* 491 US 524 (1979).

PROSSER's third group of cases includes those where the defendant has placed the plaintiff in a false light in the eyes of others. If a person, without any authority, signs the plaintiff's name to a telegram to a politician lobbying him on behalf of some proposed law, or if a person illustrates an article on drugs or juvenile delinquency with a picture of someone not involved at all, or if a person ascribes to the plaintiff in a make-believe interview opinions which in fact he does not hold, he will be liable for invasion of the 'right of privacy'; such cases almost always satisfy the requirements of the tort of defamation as well, since the plaintiff's honour and reputation are usually adversely affected. Finally, in his fourth group PROSSER puts the cases in which a person uses the name or picture of the plaintiff without his consent in a written or filmed advertisement or in the name of a firm or on his goods or in a similar context.

The *English* courts have not yet accepted that the invasion of the 'right of privacy' constitutes an independent tort. In relevant cases they continue the practice observed by WARREN and BRANDEIS of using other grounds of liability, especially defamation.

The case of *Tolley* v. *J. S. Fry & Sons Ltd.*, [1930] 1 KB 467 is typical. The defendant candy manufacturer used a picture of the plaintiff, a well-known amateur golfer, in public advertisements without his consent; an accompanying lyric equated the quality of the defendant's chocolate with the excellence of the plaintiff's golf. All the courts agreed that the claim for damages could only succeed if libel were established, that is, if the plaintiff's reputation or honour had been prejudiced by the content and form of the advertisement. Since the advertisement represented the plaintiff as a golfer of great merit, it was difficult to see that his honour had been besmirched, but it was held, at least in the House of Lords ([1931] AC 333), that the public could have made the defamatory inference that the plaintiff, although an amateur, had accepted payment for his consent to the publication. That this was not the true ground for granting the plaintiff damages may be seen by asking what the result would have been had he been a professional player.—The courts also have other grounds of liability which they can use in such cases. For example, if a person who contracted to take photographs of the plaintiff disseminates them to third parties without his consent, he will be liable in damages, either because the distribution of the photographs constitutes a breach of his 'implied contract' with the plaintiff (see *Pollard* v. *Photographic Co.*, (1888) 40 Ch. D. 354) or because it constitutes an infringement of the plaintiff's copyright in the photographs (*Williams* v. *Settle*, [1960] 1 WLR 1072).—See also *Sim* v. *H.J.Heinz Co. Ltd.*, [1959] 1 WLR 313. To speak the words in one of their television advertisements the defendants retained an actor known for his ability to mimic the voice of the plaintiff, a well-known film star. The plaintiff argued that the public would suppose that he was doing the speaking in the advertisements and he sought an injunction on the basis of defamation since it would prejudice his reputation as a filmstar if he were thought to be taking part in television commercials. Subsidiarily he relied on the tort of passing-off, which applies where one person passes off his own goods as those of another (see above p. 607), and the court held that as an actor he had a commercial interest in his voice analogous to that of a tradesman in his wares.—In *Kaye* v. *Robertson* [1991] FSR 62 the plaintiff, a popular television personality, suffered serious head injuries in a car accident and was taken to hospital. A journalist suborned hospital staff and made his way, despite prominent signs forbidding entry, into the semi-comatose plaintiff's room where he took flashlight photographs. The plaintiff sought an injunction to prevent the publication of the pictures and the purported interviews. He relied on several different torts: on *defamation*, in that his reputation would suffer if it were thought that he had taken money for the publication of the pictures, on *malicious falsehood* (above p. 608), in that the defendant was consciously representing that the plaintiff had agreed to the publication and was thereby depriving him of the opportunity of charging a great deal of money for a 'first' authorized interview, and on *trespass to the person*, in that the defendant had directly infringed the plaintiff's corporeal integrity and delayed his cure by taking flash photographs of him without his consent. *Malicious falsehood* was the sole ground on which the Court of Appeal felt able to issue an injunction (above p. 700): only the misrepresentation that the plaintiff had agreed to the publication of the photographs entitled him to stop their publication. For criticism of the decision see MARKESINIS, 53 *LQ Rev.* 802 (1990) and 55 *LQ Rev.* 118 (1992); MARKESINIS (above p. 686); in rebuttal PRESCOTT, 54 *Mod. L. Rev.* (1991) 451; BEDINGFIELD, 55 *Mod. L. Rev.* 111 (1992). Much of the judgment is reproduced in WEIR, *Casebook on Torts* (8th edn., 1996) 22, and in MARKESINIS, *The German Law of Torts* (3rd edn., 1994) 435, where there is an extensive comparative discussion.

Voices have often been raised in England against this unsatisfactory state of the law, and several attempts have been made to introduce a statutory 'right of privacy'. Numerous commissions have engaged with the question, most recently the Calcutt Committee. It concluded—largely on the ground of the bitter opposition of the British press—that 'an overwhelming case for introducing a statutory tort of infringement of privacy has not so far been made out' (*Report on Privacy and Related Matters* (Cm. 1102 (1990)) p. 46); it therefore proposed that the creation of such a tort be shelved for the present and suggested instead that 'the press should be given one final chance to prove that voluntary self-regulation can be made to work'. We must wait and see.

V

Our comparative survey of the protection afforded to the right of personality by private law has been too cursory to permit of a reasoned critical appraisal, but one or two conclusions can nevertheless be drawn.

Everyone agrees that the individual should be protected against defamatory publications and also against being publicly placed in a false light or having his private affairs bruited in public for no good reason. The critical question in such cases is when this interest must yield to the other party's right to free expression of his opinion, a right so essential to the operation of a democracy that it is enshrined in many constitutions as a basic right. In both the United States and Germany this has had direct consequences for private law for, though there are significant differences, in both of them the question of protection against the media has become a matter of constitutional law. In Germany the high ranking accorded to the expression of opinion as a basic right gives rise to a presumption that those contributing to an intellectual debate on a matter of public concern may speak out without hindrance (BVerfGE 7, 198, 212, and constantly thereafter). There are, however, no specific guidelines; whether the actual or threatened harm to the plaintiff outweighs the public interest in information rather depends on the weighing of interests in the individual case. In the United States it is different. There the Supreme Court has not only educed relatively precise rules from the basic right of speech and the press in the First Amendment, but has espoused the freedom of the press more definitively than elsewhere and thus been more restrictive of the rights of the individual affected. The leading decision which redefined the relationship between protection of individual personality and the freedom of the press is *New York Times* v. *Sullivan* 376 US 254 (1964).

Disturbances over racial segregation took place at the University of Montgomery, Alabama, and a few days later the *New York Times* published a subscription advertisement which charged the police with trampling on the rights of the student protesters; it alleged that heavily armed police had surrounded the campus and closed off the refectory in order to starve the students into submission, and that they had had students sent down from the University for participating in the demonstration. The local police chief Sullivan thereupon brought an action for *defamation* against the *New York Times*, and was able to show that the advertisement was inaccurate in several respects: the police had not closed the refectory and though police forces were assembled near the University, there was no question of 'surrounding the campus'; some students had indeed been sent down, but this was because they had conducted a 'sit-in' in a restaurant in order to force the restaurateur to serve black customers, not because they had been demonstrating. The jury awarded Sullivan $500,000 by way of damages, but the Supreme Court unanimously reversed the judgment and dismissed the claim. In the view of Justice Brennan the First Amendment contained 'a profound national commitment to the principle that debate on public issues should be uninhibited, robust and wide open', a principle which would be unconstitutionally emptied of content if a defamatory observation in the press could lead to liability in damages simply because it was inaccurate. If this were the case, public criticism of officials would be suppressed, since critics would be afraid of being held liable even though they believed in the truth of what they said and indeed even though it was actually true, for they might not be able to prove it in court. 'Public officials' criticized for their conduct could sue the press in *defamation* only if in addition to proving the falsity of the facts alleged they could establish that the defendant had acted with *actual malice*, that is, was conscious of the inaccuracy of what he said or at any rate acted 'with reckless disregard of whether it was false or not'. These requirements were not satisfied in the case before them.

This relative immunity of the press has been extended by the Supreme Court to complaints of 'invasion of privacy' (*Time Inc.* v. *Hill* 385 US 374 (1967)) and to cases where the plaintiff is not an official but nevertheless a 'public figure', a person with whom the public is relatively familiar (*Curtis Publishing Co.* v. *Butts* 388 US 130 (1967)). A purely private person may sue if he can show that the journalist was in breach of his professional duty, but strict liability such as still exists in England would be unconstitutional.

See *Gertz* v. *Robert Welch Inc.* 418 US 323 (1974). Liability may be affected one way or the other depending on whether the defendant is a 'non-media defendant' or one engaged with the press, radio or television, and on whether or not the defamatory statement is to be regarded as 'speech on public issues'; see *Philadelphia Newspapers*

Inc. v. *Hepps* 475 US 767 (1986); *Dun & Bradstreet Inc.* v. *Greenmoss Builders Inc.* 472 US 749 (1985).—A person complaining of expressions of opinion as opposed to statements of fact is virtually without protection, for there is an overwhelming interest in the publication of opinions: 'Under the First Amendment there is no such thing as a false idea. However pernicious an opinion may seem, we depend for its correction not on the conscience of judges and juries, but on the competition of other ideas' (Justice Powell in *Gertz* v. *Robert Welch Inc.* p. 339 f.). This absolute protection does not attach to a statement just because the defendant dressed it up in the form of an opinion; the test is whether it contains enough matter of fact to be the subject of proof (*Milkovich* v. *Lorain Journal Co.* 497 US 1 (1990)).

But defamation is not the only wrong against which the individual needs protection. In Germany the individual has a 'right of personality' (*Persönlichkeitsrecht*), which is very generously construed and may be infringed not just by attacks on his honour and reputation but by exposing his private affairs in public for no sufficient reason. The extent of this protection may be seen from the Bundesverfassungsgericht's celebrated decision in the *Lebach* case (BVerfGE 35, 202).

In 1969 there was an attack on the military munitions depot in Lebach during which four of the soldiers on guard duty were killed. Two of the assailants were condemned to life imprisonment, the plaintiff to six years as an accessory. Shortly before he was due to be released he learned that the defendant television station had produced a documentary film on the 'Lebach Military Murders', and claimed an injunction to prevent its being broadcast. The civil courts dismissed the claim since the plaintiff's part in the affair was accurately portrayed and there was considerable public interest in learning of the background and method of the attack and the capture of the assailants. Their decisions were vacated by the Bundesverfassungsgericht. The critical fact was that the film would have a considerable impact on the public and that this would make it much more difficult for the plaintiff to reintegrate himself in society: this constituted an unlawful infringement of his right of personality.

Such a decision would be unthinkable in England or the United States, not least because an injunction, especially in interlocutory proceedings, would be seen as an intolerable piece of state censorship. Nor would a claim for damages be successful. Certainly the plaintiff in the United States could try a suit for 'invasion of privacy', but it would unquestionably fail because nothing said about him was false and furthermore the documentary film was undeniably 'newsworthy'.

In England no such claim would be possible at all, for the courts have not yet recognized any 'right of privacy'; unless the matter is defamatory, the only protection they can offer is for breach of copyright or confidence, or if the requirements of *malicious falsehood*, *trespass* or *passing off* are satisfied. Many observers regard this situation as unsatisfactory, and perhaps Parliament may one day overcome the opposition of the press and nerve themselves to introduce a 'right of privacy'.

Only in *France* has it been unproblematic for private law to afford protection to the human personality: whereas the courts in the *United States* had to follow WARREN and BRANDEIS in extending the number of traditional types of tort, and the *German* courts had to deviate from §823 par. 1 BGB, which was too narrowly drafted, and from §253 BGB, which was wholly misconceived in limiting the duty to pay damages for immaterial harm, France had no need to make comparable efforts. It is much easier for a legal system to adapt itself to rapid movements in an area of law and to afford effective and necessary protection against novel, unexpected, and sophisticated forms of invasion of the human personality if it does not have a traditional law of actions such as the Common Law has nor narrow texts like those of German tort law. It is true that the adaptability of French law is bought at the price of the boundless unspecificity of art. 1382 Code civil, which simply lays down that every 'faute' entails liability in damages. For this reason the solution of Swiss law seems the best. Art. 28 of the Swiss Civil Code and 49 of the Swiss Law of Obligations provide that a person who is injured 'in his personality' has legal protection but that monetary damages may be ordained only in cases where this is justified by 'the gravity of the injury'. These rules are as specific as is possible and as general as is necessary.

Index

709